Dear West Customer:

West Academic Publishing has changed the look of its American Casebook Series®.

In keeping with our efforts to promote sustainability, we have replaced our former covers with book covers that are more environmentally friendly. Our casebooks will now be covered in a 100% renewable natural fiber. In addition, we have migrated to an ink supplier that favors vegetable-based materials, such as soy.

Using soy inks and natural fibers to print our textbooks reduces VOC emissions. Moreover, our primary paper supplier is certified by the Forest Stewardship Council, which is testament to our commitment to conservation and responsible business management.

The new cover design has migrated from the long-standing brown cover to a contemporary charcoal fabric cover with silver-stamped lettering and black accents. Please know that inside the cover, our books continue to provide the same trusted content that you've come to expect from West.

We've retained the ample margins that you have told us you appreciate in our texts while moving to a new, larger font, improving readability. We hope that you will find these books a pleasing addition to your bookshelf.

Another visible change is that you will no longer see the brand name Thomson West on our print products. With the recent merger of Thomson and Reuters, I am pleased to announce that books published under the West Academic Publishing imprint will once again display the West brand.

It will likely be several years before all of our casebooks are published with the new cover and interior design. We ask for your patience as the new covers are rolled out on new and revised books knowing that behind both the new and old covers, you will find the finest in legal education materials for teaching and learning.

Thank you for your continued patronage of the West brand, which is both rooted in history and forward looking towards future innovations in legal education. We invite you to be a part of our next evolution.

Best regards,

Louis H. Higgins
Editor in Chief, West Academic Publishing

CASES AND MATERIALS ON
ENVIRONMENTAL LAW

Eighth Edition

■ ■ ■

By
Daniel A. Farber
Sato Sho Professor of Law
University of California, Berkeley

Jody Freeman
Professor of Law
Director of the Environmental Law Program
Harvard Law School

Ann E. Carlson
Shirley Shapiro Professor of Environmental Law
UCLA School of Law

AMERICAN CASEBOOK SERIES®

WEST®
A Thomson Reuters business

Mat #40858721

COPYRIGHT © 1981, 1985, 1991, 1995 WEST PUBLISHING CO.
© West, a Thomson business, 1999, 2003, 2006
© 2010 Thomson Reuters
    610 Opperman Drive
    St. Paul, MN 55123
    1–800–313–9378
Printed in the United States of America

ISBN: 978–0–314–90883–4

To Carl, Hallie, and Ian
Ann Carlson

To Phil Frickey
Dan Farber

PREFACE

We should begin with a few words about authorship. Ann Carlson and Dan Farber were responsible for preparing this revision. Jody Freeman did not participate in the revisions because of her current appointment as Counselor for Energy and Climate Change in the White House. However, some of the new material derives from her work on the most recently published Supplement, which appeared in print before her government appointment.

This edition marks the first time that the name of our esteemed colleague, Roger Findley, does not appear on the cover of this book. As one of the founding generation of modern environmental law, Roger played a key role in the initial edition of this casebook thirty years ago. The casebook continues to bear his imprint as well as Jody's, even though neither one took part in the latest revisions.

The 8th Edition, like its predecessors, is designed to give students an understanding of federal environmental law and policy that is both broad and thematic as well as detailed and concrete. We have made some significant changes to this edition and updated it to reflect the fast-changing pace of environmental law.

As in the Seventh Edition, our opening Perspectives on Environmental Law includes the latest scholarly analyses of the field as well as up-to-the minute details about climate change policies, particularly those emanating from the states. When students begin to study specific regulatory schemes, they will already have a rich understanding of environmental policy and a grasp of the array of regulatory instruments. We have made some minor excisions from the opening chapters in the interest of space, deleting short sections on property rights (now deferred until Chapter 4) and criminal enforcement.

As we write this preface, an extraordinary shift is taking place in the U.S. response to perhaps the most significant environmental problem of the this century, climate change. From 2001 to 2008, the federal government remained largely inactive in efforts to reduce the greenhouse gas emissions that scientists almost uniformly believe are heating the earth's temperatures. Into this policy breach stepped the states, or at least a majority of the states. Now, the federal government is finally beginning to address climate change seriously, but the situation is still fluid. The legal maneuvering surrounding these efforts is also dynamic.

At the same time, each new issue of *Science* and *Nature* seems to demonstrate that climate change is happening earlier and more rapidly than scientific models have predicted. The future of climate change is now and we are at a delicate, interesting and crucial moment in addressing the problem.

This edition reflects these developments. We have added new material on climate change to virtually every chapter of the book, covering topics including the science and economics of climate change, design of cap-and-trade systems, standing issues, potential application of current federal statutes to climate issues (NEPA, CAA, and ESA), federalism issues raised by state climate regulations, and takings problems relating to sea level rise. Because climate law is so dynamic, however, we recommend that readers consult the Berkeley/UCLA environmental law blog, Legal Planet (www.legalplanet.wordpress.com), for the latest developments.

We could not have completed this new edition without the extraordinary efforts of our research assistants and our administrative assistants Leslie Stone, and Sandra Hwang. Special thanks are due to our families for giving us support and love during the writing process. And our students, who challenge and inspire us to think about environmental issues in new and interesting ways, deserve our appreciation for spurring us to make the casebook better.

DANIEL A. FARBER
ANN E. CARLSON

September 2009

TABLE OF ACRONYMS

AB	Appellate Body
ACE	Army Corps of Engineers
ADR	Alternative Dispute Resolution
AEC	Atomic Energy Commission
AEI	American Enterprise Institute
AFL–CIO	American Federation of Labor and Congress of Industrial Organizations
AFO	Animal Feeding Operation
AID	Agency for International Development
AISA	American Iron and Steel Institute
ALJ	Administrative Law Judge
AMC	American Mining Congress
AMI	American Meat Institute
ANILCA	Alaska National Interest Lands Conservation Act
APA	Administrative Procedure Act
APHIS	Animal Plant Health and Inspection Service
API	American Petroleum Institute
AQCR	Air Quality Control Regions
ARARs	Applicable or Relevant and Appropriate Requirements
ATA	American Trucking Association
AUM	Animal Unit Month
BACT	Best Available Control Technology
BADCT	Best Available Demonstrated Control Technology
BART	Best Available Retrofit Technology
BAT	Best Achievable Technology
BATEA	Best Available Technology Economically Achievable
BCT	Best Conventional Pollutant Control Technology
BDAT	Best Demonstrated Available Technology
BLM	Bureau of Land Management
BMP	Best Management Practices
BOD	Biochemical Oxygen Demand
BOD5	Biochemical Oxygen Demand measured over a 5–day period
BODS	Biochemical Oxygen–Demanding Substances
BPCTCA	Best Practicable Control Technology Currently Available
BPJ	Best Professional Judgment
BPCT	Best Practicable Control Technology
BRD	Biological Resources Division
BTUs	British Thermal Units
BWCA	Boundary Waters Canoe Area
BWCAW	Boundary Waters Canoe Area Wilderness
CAA	Clean Air Act
CAFE	Corporate Average Fuel Economy
CAFO	Concentrated Animal Feeding Operation
CARE	Citizens Against the Refinery's Effects

CARE	Concerned Area Residents for the Environment
CASAC	Clean Air Scientific Advisory Committee
CBA	Cost–Benefit Analysis
CBD	Convention on Biological Diversity
CBI	Confidential Business Information
CEQ	Council on Environmental Quality
CERCLA	Comprehensive Environmental Response, Compensation, and Liability Act
CFR	Code of Federal Regulations
CMA	Chemical Manufacturers Association
CO	Carbon Monoxide
CO_2	Carbon Dioxide
COCC	Columbia Organic Chemical Company
COD	Chemical Oxygen Demand
COLA	Cost of Living Adjustment
COP	Conference of the Parties
CPSC	Consumer Product Safety Commission
CRJ	Commission for Racial Justice
CSD	Commission on Sustainable Development
CSMA	Chemical Specialties Manufacturers Association
CSWG	Corporate Sunshine Working Group
CV	Contingent Valuation
CWA	Clean Water Act
CZMA	Coastal Zone Management Act
D2O	Deuterium Oxide ("Heavy Water")
DAF	Dilution and Attenuation Factor
DBCP	Dibromochloropropane
DCO	Delayed Compliance Order
DDT	DichloroDiphenylTrichloroethane
DEP	Department of Environmental Protection
DES	Diethylstilbesterol
DF	Deterioration Factor
DHEC	Department of Health and Environmental Control
DMC	De Minimis Classification
DMRs	Discharge Monitoring Reports
DNA	Deoxyribonucleic Acid
DOI	Department of the Interior
DOJ	Department of Justice
DOT	Department of Transportation
DUs	Designated Uses
EA	Environmental Assessment
EC	European Community
ECJ	European Court of Justice
EDF	Environmental Defense Fund
EEC	European Economic Community
EEI	Edison Electric Institute
EGU	Electric Generating Unit
EIA	Environmental Impact Assessment
EIS	Environmental Impact Statement
ELI	Environmental Law Institute
EMSs	Environmental Management Systems
EP	Extraction Procedure

EP	Erythrocyte Protoporphyrin
EPA	Environmental Protection Agency
EPCRA	Emergency Planning and Community Right-to-Know Act
EQB	Environmental Quality Board
ESA	Endangered Species Act
ETP	Eastern Tropical Pacific
ETS	Environmental Transportation Systems
EU	European Union
EWG	The Environmental Working Group
FAA	Federal Aviation Administration
FACA	Federal Advisory Committee Act
FASB	Financial Accounting Standards Board
FBI	Federal Bureau of Investigation
FCC	Federal Communications Commission
FDA	Food and Drug Administration
FDD	Final Development Document
FDF	Fundamentally Different Factor
FEISS	Final Environmental Impact Statement Supplement
FERC	Federal Energy Regulatory Commission
FFDCA	Federal Food, Drug, and Cosmetic Act
FIFRA	Federal Insecticide, Fungicide, and Rodenticide Act
FIP	Federal Implementation Plan
FLPMA	Federal Land Policy and Management Act
FMC	Federal Maritime Commission
FOE	Friends of the Earth
FOIA	Freedom of Information Act
FONSI	Finding of No Significant Impact
FPA	Federal Power Act
FPAs	Final Project Agreements
FWPCA	Federal Water Pollution and Control Act
FWS	Fish and Wildlife Service
FY	Fiscal Year
GAAP	Generally Accepted Accounting Principles
GAO	General Accounting Office
GAP	Gap Analysis Program
GATT	General Agreement on Tariffs and Trade
GES	Global Environmental Facility
GHG	Greenhouse Gas
GIS	Geographic Information Systems
GM	General Motors
GM	Genetically Modified
GMOs	Genetically Modified Organisms
GNP	Gross National Product
GSA	General Services Administration
GWEN	Ground Wave Emergency Network
HC	Hydrocarbons
HCP	Habitat Conservation Plan
HREC	Hampton Roads Energy Company
HSWA	Hazardous and Solid Waste Amendments
HUD	Housing and Urban Development
HWIR	Hazardous Waste Identification Rule
ICC	Interstate Commerce Commission

ICR	Ignitable, Corrosive, and Reactive
ICS	Individual Control Strategies
IEPA	Illinois Environmental Protection Agency
I & M	Inspection and Maintenance
INS	Immigration and Naturalization Service
IPC	International Paper Company
IPCC	Intergovernmental Panel on Climate Change
IPM	Integrated Pest Management
IPM	Integrated Planning Model
ITC	Interagency Testing Committee
IWC	International Whaling Commission
JCAE	Joint Committee on Atomic Energy
JTU	Jackson Turbidity Unit
LAER	Lowest Achievable Emission Rate
LDRs	Land Disposal Restrictions
LEV	Low Emissions Vehicle
LIA	Lead Industry Association
LMFBR	Liquid Metal Fast Breeder Reactor
LULUs	Locally Undesirable Land Uses
LWK	Live Weight Killed
MACT	Maximum Achievable Control Technology
MCC	Metropolitan Correction Center
MCL	Maximum Contaminant Level
MCLG	Maximum Contaminant Level Goal
MGP	Manufactured Gas Plant
MMPA	Marine Mammal Protection Act
MOA	Memorandum of Agreement
MPRSA	Marine Protection, Research, and Sanctuaries Act
MSDS	Material Safety Data Sheets
MSHA	Mine Safety and Health Administration
MSW	Municipal Solid Waste
MTBE	Methyl Tertiary–Butyl Ether
NAACP	National Association for the Advancement of Colored People
NAAQS	National Ambient Air Quality Standards
NAFTA	North American Free Trade Agreement
NAS	National Academy of Sciences
NASA	National Aeronautics and Space Administration
NAZ	Nonattainment Zone
NBARs	Nonbinding Preliminary Allocations of Responsibility
NBII	National Biological Information Infrastructure
NBS	National Biological Service
NCCP	Natural Community Conservation Program
NCP	National Contingency Plan
NEPA	National Environmental Policy Act
NEPACCO	Northeastern Pharmaceutical and Chemical Company
NESHAP	National Emission Standards for Hazardous Air Pollutants
NFMA	National Forest Management Act
NGO	Nongovernmental Organization
NGPRP	Northern Great Plains Resources Program
NIEHS	National Institute of Environmental Health Sciences

NIMBY	"Not In My Back Yard"
NIPDWS	National Interim Primary Drinking Water Standards
NLEV	National Low Emission Vehicle
NO_2	Nitrogen Dioxide
NOAA	National Oceanographic and Atmospheric Agency
NODA	Notice of Data Availability
NO_x	Nitrogen Oxides
NPDES	National Pollutant Discharge Elimination System
NPL	National Priorities List
NRA	Negotiated Rulemaking Act
NRC	Nuclear Regulatory Commission
NRC	National Research Council
NRDC	Natural Resources Defense Council
NSPS	New Source Performance Standards
NSR	New Source Review
NWF	National Wildlife Federation
O_3	Ozone
OCPSF	Organic Chemicals, Plastics and Synthetic Fibers
OCS	Outer Continental Shelf
OCSLA	Outer Continental Shelf Lands Act
OMB	Office of Management and Budget
OSHA	Occupational Safety and Health Administration
OSWER	Office of Solid Waste and Emergency Response
OTAG	Ozone Transport Assessment Group
PANE	People Against Nuclear Energy
Pb	Lead
PBT	Persistent, Bioaccumulative, and Toxic
PCB	Polychlorinated Biphenyl
PEL	Permissible Exposure Limit
PG&E	Pacific Gas and Electric
PIRG	Public Interest Research Group
PM	Particulate Matter
POTWs	Publicly Owned Treatment Works
PPA	Plant Pest Act
ppm	parts per million
ppq	parts per quadrillion
ppt	parts per trillion
PRP	Potentially Responsible Party
PSD	Prevention of Significant Deterioration
PSNS	Pretreatment Standards for New Sources
PUD	Public Utility District
RACM	Reasonably Available Control Measures
RACT	Reasonably Available Control Technology
RAND	Research and Development (a think tank)
RCO	Responsible Corporate Officer
RCRA	Resource Conservation and Recovery Act
RECLAIM	Regional Clean Air Incentives Market
RFF	Resources for the Future
RPA	Renewable Resources Planning Act
RTCs	RECLAIM Trading Credits
SAB	Staff Accounting Bulletins
SAB	Scientific Advisory Board

SAP	Scientific Advisory Panel
SARA	Superfund Amendment and Reauthorization Act
SCRDI	South Carolina Recycling and Disposal, Inc.
SCS	Soil Conservation Service
SDWA	Safe Drinking Water Act
SEC	Securities and Exchange Commission
SEIS	Supplemental Environmental Impact Statement
SEPs	Supplemental Environmental Projects
SEPs	Supplemental Enforcement Plans
SIC	Standard Industrial Classification
SICEA	Steel Industry Compliance Extension Act
SIP	State Implementation Plan
SIPI	Scientists' Institute for Public Information
SIR	Supplemental Information Report
SO_2	Sulfur Dioxide
SPS	Sanitary and Phyto–Sanitary
SRF	State Revolving Fund
SWANCC	Solid Waste Agency of Northern Cook County
TC	Toxicity Characteristic
TCDD	2,3,7,8–Tetrachlorodibenzo-p-dioxin
TCLP	Toxicity Characteristic Leaching Procedure
TCP	2,4,5–Trichlorophenol
TCP	Transportation Control Plan
TMDLs	Total Maximum Daily Loads
TMI–1	Three Mile Island Unit 1 nuclear power plant
TMI–2	Three Mile Island Unit 2 nuclear power plant
TOC	Total Organic Carbon
TRI	Toxic Release Inventory
TRPA	Tahoe Regional Planning Agency
TSCA	Toxic Substances Control Act
TSD	Treatment, Storage, and Disposal
TSDFs	Treatment, Storage, and Disposal Facilities
TSS	Total Suspended Solids
TTHMs	Total Trihalomethanes
TVA	Tennessee Valley Authority
$\mu g/m3$	Micrograms per cubic meter (of air)
μg Pb/dl	Micrograms of lead per deciliter (of blood)
μg Pb/m3	Micrograms of lead per cubic meter (of air)
U.N.	United Nations
UNDP	United Nations Development Programme
UNEP	United Nations Environment Programme
UNFCCC	United Nations Framework Convention on Climate Change
USDA	United States Department of Agriculture
USEPA	United States Environmental Protection Agency
USGS	United States Geological Survey
UST	Underground Storage Tank
VCP	Voluntary Cleanup Program
VOCs	Volatile Organic Compounds
WARC	Water and Air Resources Commission
WLAs	Wasteload Allocations
WQC	Water Quality Criteria

WQSs	Water Quality Standards
WQTP	Water Quality Trading Policy
WTO	World Trade Organization
WWTP	Wastewater Treatment Plant
ZEV	Zero Emission Vehicle

Summary of Contents

TABLE OF CONTENTS

Page

TABLE OF CASES

The principal cases are in bold type. Cases cited or discussed in the text are in roman type. References are to pages. Cases cited in principal cases and within other quoted materials are not included.

CASES AND MATERIALS ON
ENVIRONMENTAL LAW
Eighth Edition

CHAPTER 1

PERSPECTIVES ON ENVIRONMENTAL LAW

■ ■ ■

It may be helpful to begin with a roadmap of the book as a whole. After this introductory chapter, the casebook proceeds as follows:

- *Tools and methods.* Chapter 2 follows the introductory perspectives of Chapter 1 with an introduction of tools and methods of environmental protection, including cost-benefit analysis, risk assessment, and tort liability.

- *A statutory case study.* Chapter 3 begins our journey into environmental regulation with a detailed study of the Endangered Species Act. The ESA illustrates many of the themes, conflicts and approaches discussed in the first two chapters.

- *The Regulatory System.* The next two chapters focus on issues of process and structure. Chapter 4 analyzes how environmental policy is made through the legislative and administrative process, and how courts interpret legislative choices while policing administrative actions. Chapter 5 considers the allocation of authority over environmental issues among various levels of government, with close attention to the constitutional issues raised by state and federal regulation. It also considers how the Taking Clause may constrain regulation of private property.

- *Pollution Regulation.* Chapter 5 is followed by two chapters focusing on pollution. Chapter 6 covers air pollution, while Chapter 7 covers water pollution. These two chapters explain the operation of two central federal statutes—the Clean Air Act and the Clean Water Act. These statutes use a variety of tools and approaches to regulate the "externalities" of productive economic activity.

- *Toxic Chemicals.* The final two chapters focus on hazardous wastes and toxic chemicals, respectively. Chapter 8 covers both RCRA and CERCLA, which together regulate the management of hazardous wastes and allocate liability for cleanups. Chapter 9 explains the regulation of toxic substances and genetically modified materials.

The journey begins with this introductory chapter. This introduction is intended to introduce you to the problem of environmental disruption and to important perspectives that shape our policy response. Section A provides an overview of the major themes and historical development of environmental law. As we shall see, environmental law is not solely the result of some logical elaboration of neutral legal principles that establish timeless solutions for static problems.

Instead, environmental law is dynamic in two important senses. First, the environment itself is dynamic. As the natural environment changes, and as new information emerges, legal solutions must adapt. Much of the material in this book, from the evolution of the constitutional doctrine of standing, to developments in takings jurisprudence, to amendments of major federal pollution statutes, provides evidence of legal adaptation.

Second, the law itself is the product of a dynamic and often deeply political interaction between legislatures, government agencies, courts, and interest groups. In a way, the legal system is its own ecosystem. Understanding how these moving parts operate together illuminates why environmental laws take the shape that they do. Moreover, the field is interdisciplinary to its core; it depends on developments in biological and health sciences as well as economics. The material in Section A explores these and other reasons why environmental law is special, and accounts for where we are in the field today.

Section B provides an introduction to a variety of perspectives on the problem of environmental disruption or harm. The materials here suggest ways of thinking about the environment that may influence our policy responses. For example, the material in the section explains how ecological concepts have helped shape our understanding of environmental problems. Some key ecological concepts include biodiversity and ecosystem services. These concepts are crucial to understanding arguments for environmental preservation.

The ecological perspective in Section B highlights the degree of interdependence between individuals whose interests may be seriously affected by each other's activities through pollution or ecosystem damage. This interdependence requires a collective response, yet such a response may be difficult to mount because of obstacles to collective action.

We explore these collective action problems in Section C. Environmental damage is often the result of a "tragedy of the commons," in which people face many incentives to exploit resources but few incentives to protect or preserve them. In the final section of Section C, we use global climate change (the greenhouse effect) as a case study of the difficulties of protecting the commons. No one owns the planetary atmosphere, or, to put it another way, everyone owns the atmosphere. This poses serious, but not necessarily insurmountable, challenges to efforts to control climate change.

A. ENVIRONMENTAL PROTECTION: AN OVERVIEW

As promised, we begin with a general overview of environmental law, focusing on some of the main themes throughout the course. We also provide a brief history of the field. Today's environmental regulations are the product of several decades of political development, rather than a deliberately designed and completely coherent system.

1. MAJOR THEMES

This book covers a wide range of environmental problems and issues—everything from automobile pollution to hazardous waste sites to biodiversity. Each of these problems has prompted a legal response, resulting in a complicated field comprised not only of common law and constitutional doctrines but also an array of federal statutes. Some of these laws are mind-boggling in their complexity. And even the relatively simple ones reveal unexpected nuances upon closer examination. All of this can be challenging to the novice. Indeed, the list of statutory acronyms alone can be intimidating to the newcomer: NEPA, CAA, RCRA, CERCLA, ESA—not to mention such lesser-known statutes as TSCA or FIFRA. (At the end of the book you will find a glossary identifying all these acronyms.) Each statute creates its own world of regulatory complexity, much like the tax code or the bankruptcy law.

To make matters even more challenging, environmental law overlaps in important ways with other areas of law, most notably constitutional law and administrative law, but also torts, criminal law, property law, and even international trade law. It is also highly interdisciplinary, with important contributions from economics as well as the sciences. All of this makes the course enormously interesting, but also difficult to distill and manage.

To help you tame this bewildering collection of statutes and legal doctrines, it is useful to focus on the perspectives and tools introduced in the first two chapters. They provide an anchor for the rest of the casebook. Fundamentally, despite all of the detail in the pages to come, we will be presented over and over again with four basic questions.

1. *Who should set environmental policy?* We will frequently ask whether an administrative agency has exceeded the bounds of its legislative authorization. Sometimes we will also ask whether the states or the federal government should have authority, or whether the courts should take an active role in setting policy.

2. *How should we make tradeoffs between environmental protection and cost?* Should we pursue environmental benefits at all costs, should we use cost-benefit analysis, or should we adopt some intermediate stance? Some crucial issues underlie these disputes,

turning on whether we should adopt a utilitarian view of environmental law or view it as protecting basic rights to environmental quality.

3. *What regulatory instruments should be used?* Conventional regulatory techniques include standards based directly on environmental goals, such as plans to achieve certain levels of air quality, and standards based on technological feasibility. Alternatives to direct government regulation include tort liability, economic incentive programs, and negotiated outcomes. Whether any particular regulatory scheme has the right mix of instruments is often debatable.

4. *How should we deal with scientific uncertainty?* The problem of scientific uncertainty crops up again and again: in determining when a possible risk must be discussed in an environmental impact statement, in analyzing whether Congress unconstitutionally delegated too much discretion to the EPA to determine the "safe" level of air quality, in regulating toxic chemicals, in attempting to preserve endangered species. These problems are compounded because many of the effects in question are long-term and cannot be reliably gauged until decades in the future. We cannot wait until we have full information to regulate because the effects will already have occurred, but we must also keep in mind that we will have better information as science progresses.

In making sense of environmental law, it may help to have a grasp of the values that underlie environmental protection and the countervailing values that may act as constraints. The following excerpt provides a good overview.

JONATHAN CANNON, ENVIRONMENTALISM AND THE SUPREME COURT: A CULTURAL ANALYSIS

33 Ecology L.Q. 363 (2006).[1]

The task here is to identify the basic set of tenets that characterize environmentalism, acknowledging from the outset that those calling themselves environmentalists hold divergent beliefs and values. In *Environmental Values in American Culture*, three anthropologists—Willett Kempton, James S. Boster, and Jennifer A. Hartley (collectively "Kempton")—distilled an interconnected set of values and beliefs identified with "American environmentalism."[2] These include beliefs that nature is a limited resource on which humans depend; that human-nature systems are interdependent, complex, and balanced; and that nature is to be valued for its own sake. In a separate study, sociologists Riley E. Dunlap and Kent D. Van Liere derived elements of an emerging "world view"—the "new

---

1. Copyright 2006 by the Regents of the University of California. Reprinted by permission.

2. Willett Kempton, James S. Boster & Jennifer A. Hartley, ENVIRONMENTAL VALUES IN AMERICAN CULTURE (1995). Kempton used "semistructured" interviews and form surveys of randomly selected "laypeople," such as workers at sawmills and dry cleaners, and "specialists" whose work or interests relate to the environment, such as Sierra Club members. Id. at 2.

environmental paradigm" (NEP). The major dimensions of their NEP—recognizing the "limits to growth," preserving the "balance of nature," and rejecting "the anthropocentric notion that nature exists solely for human use"—were very similar to Kempton's findings.[3] Recently Dunlap and Van Liere have added two additional elements to their NEP: rejection of human "exemptionalism" (that humans are not subject to natural constraints) and the potential for catastrophic environmental change or "ecocrisis."[4] The NEP strongly differentiates known environmentalists from the general public and is now the most widely used measure of environmental concern, although Dunlap has acknowledged that it "does not fully tap the richness of the construct [of environmentalism]."

In the discussion below I draw on the Kempton and Dunlap and Van Liere studies and other sources to elaborate aspects of environmentalism that have entered the Court's deliberations. I group these into three broad categories: the interdependence model, the urgency factor, and ecocentrism. These categories will serve as a useful framework when we turn to analyzing the cases.

1. *Interdependence: The Ecological Paradigm*

Environmentalists share a belief that humans and things in nature are closely interconnected and that human intervention affecting one part of a human-natural system can be expected to have deleterious effects elsewhere in the system. I will refer to this central tenet variously as the "interdependence" or "ecological" model. The interdependence model combines elements of environmentalist beliefs detected by Kempton et al. and Dunlap et al., including concepts of nature as limited and of humans as dependent upon it and also of nature as interdependent such that disturbances are likely to cause other "multiply linked chain reactions." Associated with these holistic views Kempton et al. also found beliefs that the "interdependencies are so complex that the interactions are impossible for humans to predict" and thus warrant a general "proscription against human interference with nature." The interdependence model might be confirmed or refuted in particular cases by persuasive evidence of harmful secondary effects or their absence. Without such evidence, it operates for environmentalists as a kind of presumption or default rule.

Prophets of modern environmentalism repeatedly voiced the idea of a highly interdependent human-natural system. John Muir said: "When we try to pick out anything by itself, we find it hitched to everything else in the universe." Aldo Leopold advanced the notion of a complexly interdependent "land organism" or "biotic community" which included humans as well as non-human nature. In *Silent Spring*, Rachel Carson described

---

3. Riley E. Dunlap & Kent D. Van Liere, *The New Environmental Paradigm*, 9 J. ENVTL. EDUC. 10 (Summer 1978). The authors conducted surveys from two samples of Washington state residents in the summer of 1976. One group was based on names drawn from telephone directories across the state, and the other was based on names drawn from the mailing list of a statewide environmental organization. Id. at 11.

4. Riley E. Dunlap & Kent D. Van Liere, *Measuring Endorsement of the New Ecological Paradigm: A Revised NEP Scale*, 56 J. Soc. Issues 425, 432 (2000).

diverse harms to humans and wildlife from chemical poisons as "a problem of ecology, of interrelationships, of interdependence."

The idea of interdependence occurs in images of popular discourse such as the "web of life" (interconnecting strands supporting the larger structure) and "spaceship earth" (earth as a single system with interlocking parts essential for survival of the whole). It has also made its way into public policy. It is evident, for example, in the "purpose" provisions of federal statutes such as the National Environmental Policy Act (NEPA), the Endangered Species Act, and the Clean Water Act.

Although the interdependence model embodies a belief about the way the world works, it is often associated with a collective responsibility to care for the environment. Aldo Leopold's "land ethic" extends moral consideration to an expanded "community" that includes both humans and non-human nature. Leopold believed that this "extension of ethics" would take root as society came to understand its essential dependency on an increasingly beleaguered land organism. "All ethics ... rest upon a single premise: that the individual is a member of a community of interdependent parts." In his influential account of the environmental movement, Philip Shabecoff quoted this sentence from Leopold with the comment that "[a]lmost all else in environmentalism proceeds from that premise."

2. *Urgency Factor*

A second element of environmentalism relevant to the analysis is the belief that the environment is in a serious state of decline. Kempton et al. do not separately identify this belief, but it is implicit in other elements of their environmentalism. Dunlap et al. make it explicit in their addition of "ecocrisis" to the NEP, and it is evident in numerous works in the environmentalist canon. This urgency factor may combine with the interdependence model, for which it can act as a kind of valence—spaceship earth with the rivets popping off. Or it may operate independently in areas where the interdependence model is of limited relevance, as in cases where environmental pollution poses direct health threats that do not depend on complex ecological relationships.

The urgency factor has left its mark on the law. In addition to the pesticide bans that followed Carson's book, numerous other federal regulatory measures have been prompted, or at least publicly justified, by environmental crises, such as Cleveland's Cuyahoga River catching on fire (Clean Water Act), seeping chemical wastes at Love Canal (Superfund), and the Exxon Valdez oil spill (Oil Pollution Act). Innovative or demanding provisions of these and other federal statutes are attributable to the perceived seriousness of the environmental problems they seek to remedy.

3. *Ecocentrism*

Another aspect of environmentalism that has entered the Court's deliberations is the extension of moral standing or reverence to the environmental other. In their interviews, Kempton et al. found three types of environmental values—religious, including feelings of spirituality not identified to a particular religion; anthropocentric, "concerned with only those environmental changes that affect human welfare;" and ecocentric, "which grant nature itself intrinsic rights." Environmentalism includes anthropocentric elements that emphasize non-commodity and existence values of nature and protection of environmental resources for future generations—so-called "weak anthropocentrism." But, strong forms of environmentalism are closely identified with ecocentric values and religious or spiritual regard for nature for its own sake.

NOTES

1. Cannon also identifies four elements of the "dominant culture"— "support for private property rights, support for economic growth, faith in material abundance, and support for laissez faire government—had significant negative correlation with environmental concern." 33 *Ecology L. Q.* at 372.

2. As you continue through the book, you will see large variations among judges in the extent to which they identify with environmentalist values or the dominant culture. To what extent do these value differences explain case outcomes?

3. There is no single organizing principle that "explains" all of environmental law. As we will see throughout the book, environmental law is often a messy result of complex institutional dynamics and political conflict. However, the following excerpt discusses some principles that come up fairly often. Those principles may help you make sense of some of the confusing complexity of the specific legal doctrines.

DAN TARLOCK, IS THERE A THERE THERE IN ENVIRONMENTAL LAW?[5]

19 J. LAND USE & ENVTL L. 213, 214, 248–254 (2004).

As environmental law enters its fourth decade, it is now appropriate, if not imperative, to ask the question: what have environmentalism and environmental regulation contributed to the law? Gertrude Stein, the American expatriate writer, once described Oakland, California, where she spent much of her youth before fleeing to the East Coast and Paris, as a place where "there is no there there." In addition to stigmatizing the city of my birth, her quip haunts all efforts to legitimize new, especially contested, ideas and methods in modern culture, from twelve tone music to environmental protection. In this article, I leave the question of the merits of post-modern culture to others and address only the question, does Ms. Stein's famous epigram apply to environmental law? * * *

The dynamic process-making of environmental decisions means that we can only hope to structure decisions with principles that allow us to identify decisions as legitimate efforts to advance environmental goals, but

---

5. Copyright © 2004, Journal of Land Use. Reprinted by Permission. (internal citations omitted).

do not lock us into consistent but dysfunctional decisions. I suggest the following candidate principles. They are a mix of how environmental law has evolved and how it should evolve.

A. MINIMIZE UNCERTAINTY BEFORE AND AS YOU ACT

This principle is an expansion and correction of the more familiar first principle of environmental law that activities with potentially adverse environmental impacts, however defined, should be assessed before they are undertaken. It is codified in NEPA, but over time the original purpose of assessment—real risk and environmental damage minimization—has been lost. Assessment has too often become an end in and of itself rather than a means to obtain the necessary information for long-term, informed decision-making to achieve the necessary changes in the way that resources are used and managed. The duty to minimize uncertainty is a continuing one during all phases of an activity. For example, it will often require monitoring and adaptive management for activities that will last over a long period of time.

Adaptive management was developed in the late 1970s as a criticism of static or deterministic environmental assessment. The basic argument was that "a fixed review of an independently designed policy" was inconsistent with the experience of resource managers world-wide and with what has come to be called non-equilibrium ecology. The need for rigorous but flexible procedures to make decisions under conditions of uncertainty has a long intellectual pedigree. * * * Adaptive management is designed to close the gap between the available information and the information needed to make sound environmental decisions. It posits a continuous process of acquiring and evaluating scientific information through the practice of regulatory science.

B. ENVIRONMENTAL DEGRADATION SHOULD BE A LAST RESORT AFTER ALL REASONABLE, FEASIBLE ALTERNATIVES HAVE BEEN EXHAUSTED

This principle casts another pillar of environmental law: an activity that is likely to cause the degradation of media and ecosystems environmental values should only be undertaken if there are no acceptable alternatives. A general non-degradation standard for all resources is not possible for economic and ethical reasons; human society does not, as some radical environmentalists have argued, have a duty to self-destruct. The most that we can do is to be highly skeptical of substantial departure from the baselines of environmental quality that we choose to establish. * * * My rule * * * is broader than the assertion of any duty to mitigate. It assumes that environmental values are of equal dignity to developmental ones, and thus mitigation may not always be an acceptable solution. Mitigation is generally a substitute for full compliance, and is in economic terms, a second best solution.

C. RISK CAN BE A LEGITIMATE INTERIM BASIS FOR PROHIBITION OF AN ACTIVITY

This principle attempts to strike a balance between the rejection of the due process-based common law background rule that mechanistic proof that an activity will cause demonstrable harm in the immediate future as a universal predicate for health and ecosystem protection regulation and the candidate replacement principle—the precautionary principle—endorsed in the 1992 Rio Declaration on Environment and Development. The principle that a high degree of certainty about the adverse impacts of a substance or activity is not a necessary prerequisite to limit it is well established in United States environmental law. The Constitution does not require mechanistic proof of cause in fact for pollution and toxic substance regulation because a lesser standard of proof is appropriate for public health based regulation because liability can be justified as a form of taxes imposed on those who directly profit from harmful activities and which is fairly spread over larger segments of the population.

The precautionary principle has, however, evolved, at least in the legal literature, from a limited tool to bridge the gap between current information and the societal desire to limit exposure to serious risk to a harder rule. Critics have begun to "demonize" it as incoherent and unfair compared to more rigorous decision methods such as risk analysis. The nub of the objection is the argument that once some potential, but uncertain risk of future environmental harm is established, it is legitimate to prohibit an activity that leads to "bad," "irrational" or inefficient choices.

It is essential to separate the soundness of the basic idea that society can choose to minimize risks in the face of scientific and other uncertainty from the question of implementation. The precautionary principle is firmly grounded in the scientific method. Many of the concerns can be addressed through burden of proof standards and the addition of a crucial element that is often missing in debates about the precautionary principle: a feedback loop to trigger reevaluation of the initial decision. Proponents of the precautionary principle have argued that opponents of precaution should bear the burden of rebutting the exercise of the principle, but given the risk that the precautionary principle could choke off a wide range of considerations, such as risk trade-offs, it seems more sensible to place the burden of justification on the government body that invokes it. This would ensure that alternative methods of minimizing the uncertainty, such as compensation, have been adequately explored, and that the principle is reserved for the most serious and largely irreversible risks. In addition, the idea that once the principle is invoked to minimize risk, the decision is permanent should be excised. The precautionary principle needs to be linked to the idea of adaptive management. The existence of monitoring and adaptive feedback mechanisms should be a major factor in validating the decision to limit an activity when the adverse impacts are uncertain.

D.   POLLUTERS MUST CONTINUALLY UPGRADE WASTE REDUCTION AND PROCESSING TECHNOLOGY

Environmentalism dethroned engineers from the preeminent position they enjoyed for most of the twentieth century, but much of the progress in environmental protection has come from compelling polluters to install state-of-the-art technology. Sources of media pollution should be rolled back by the installation of progressively higher standards of technology established by the government. This principle incorporates two ideas: (1) technology has a major role to play in environmental protection; and (2) the level of technology required is a moving, not fixed, target.

E. ENVIRONMENTAL DECISIONMAKING SHOULD BE INCLUSIVE RATHER THAN EXCLUSIVE WITHIN THE LIMITS OF RATIONALITY

This final principle endorses the pluralistic nature of decision-making that has emerged from the efforts to force public and private actors to consider environmental values up to a point. Environmental law helped to undermine (but not overthrow) the New Deal model of the expert managerial or regulatory agency because outsiders offered a new perspective to the experts and helped to expose many of the unstated, crucial assumptions in purported "objective" analysis. The net result has been the development of hybrid forms of shared governance which depends as much on information disclosure to alter behavior as it does on command and control regulation.

Increased lay participation in decision making to promote transparency and a broadened perspective is a laudable, democratic objective, but transparency and public participation come with costs such as delay, the introduction of extraneous issues and the rejection of science-based solutions. However, environmental policy and law must remain bonded by science. The relevant question is always: how can we bridge the gap between what we want from science and what it can supply? The goals of public participation are to legitimate the application of science to an informed lay public and to allow an avenue for relevant scientific and non-scientific perspectives. They should never be allowed to substitute deals for scientifically credible outcomes.

CONCLUSION

This summing up of environmental law may strike many as disappointing because it dismisses the possibility of powerful, general transformative nature-centered rules, emerging to tame the drive to exploit and modify all planetary life support systems. Instead, it argues that environmental law will for the foreseeable future be a messy process of adapting the contingencies and limitations of science to "wicked" problems informed by rebuttable principles. This hard road seems inevitable because of the radical nature of the objectives of environmental law. If protection is to evolve into a permanent check on the full range of resource consumption decisions, it must be grounded in the enlightenment values of knowledge and reason.

NOTE

Tarlock's guiding principles have some traction in environmental law. For example, NEPA stresses consideration of alternatives in environmental impact statements. Both NEPA and administrative law contain some mechanisms for public participation. We will give considerable attention in this chapter and the next to how environmental law handles risk and uncertainty.

However, Tarlock's principles are also open to criticism. Some critics would argue that an overarching methodology of cost-benefit analysis should take the place of these five principles. This would provide a method of dealing with risks, considering alternatives, and establishing appropriate pollution control. We will consider this alternative approach in detail in Chapter 2.

Other critics might say that Tarlock's principles are too limited. The principles focus on specific problems—alternatives to a given project, pollution control for a given industry—rather than on systemic changes that might eliminate the need for certain projects or substitute new industrial processes that produce less pollution in the first place. Tarlock's principles also could be criticized for focusing on the short-run rather than on our obligations to later generations. Yet there are serious institutional difficulties to implementing more holistic, long-term solutions. As we examine particular environmental issues, ranging from global warming to hazardous waste disposal, consider whether more systemic solutions would be feasible.

2. THE HISTORY OF ENVIRONMENTAL LAW

Today's complex regulatory process did not emerge in an instant, like Athena springing from the forehead of Zeus. Instead, it is the product of a long and sometimes conflicted evolutionary process. The following excerpt provides an overview of the history.

RICHARD J. LAZARUS, THE GREENING OF AMERICA AND THE GRAYING OF UNITED STATES ENVIRONMENTAL LAW: REFLECTIONS ON ENVIRONMENTAL LAW'S FIRST THREE DECADES IN THE UNITED STATES[6]

20 VA. ENVTL. L. REV. 75 (2001).

Those of us who have spent our professional lives as practicing lawyers, teachers, and scholars steeped in environmental law often lose sight of the discipline's relative youth. Yet, prior to 1970, environmental protection law in the United States was essentially nonexistent. Of course, there were a few, isolated states pursuing fledgling efforts, and there were common law property and tort doctrines that some of the more activist judges were willing to invoke on behalf of environmental concerns in private and public lawsuits. But there was nothing even remotely resembling a comprehensive legal regime for regulating pollution of the air, water, or land. * * *

---

6. Copyright © 2001, Virginia Environmental Law Journal. This article is reprinted with permission from the Virginia Environmental Law Journal. The text of this article may not be used or distributed in any form, including electronically, without the express written permission of the Virginia Environmental Law Journal. This article may only be copied or downloaded for personal, non-commercial use. The Virginia Environmental Law Journal retains exclusive copyright to this article, except those rights reserved by the author.

What did the first generation of laws look like? There was, at the very outset, the National Environmental Policy Act ('NEPA'), literally signed into law on the first day of the decade, January 1, 1970. NEPA requires federal agency assessment of the environmental impacts of proposed federal agency action and possible alternatives. Although NEPA's essentially procedural requirement had a massive impact on governmental decision-making, the federal legislative enactments during the early 1970s that imposed substantive requirements were even more significant.

Three of these substantive laws were the Clean Air Act of 1970, the Federal Water Pollution Control Act Amendments of 1972 (now, as further amended, referred to as the Clean Water Act), and the Endangered Species Act Amendments of 1973. These laws were dramatic, sweeping, and apparently uncompromising. Each of these laws imposed a series of specific statutory commands on polluting activities. They did not rely primarily on voluntary behavioral changes in response to mere exhortation. Nor did they turn, in the first instance, principally to financial incentives or otherwise seek to enlist market incentives to achieve their environmental protection objectives. They instead sought to identify classes and categories of polluting or environmentally destructive activities that threatened human health and the environment, and then to impose stringent standards on their performance.

The restrictions were generally not based on economic feasibility but rather on far more demanding norms. Some were based on technological standards designed not simply to replicate existing pollution control technology but rather, in effect, to force industry to develop new technology capable of substantially more reductions in existing levels of pollution. Other standards directly required that certain environmental or human health risks be eliminated regardless of either economic or technological feasibility, even if (in theory) compliance with such a standard could occur only upon shutdown of the polluting activity.

These first generation laws were also remarkably aspirational in scope and in their mandates. The standards, and corresponding deadlines for their accomplishment, were exceedingly ambitious, if not unrealistic. Indeed, as discussed below, although such ambitious laws necessarily made a strong symbolic societal statement regarding the importance of environmental protection and the need for fundamental change in humankind's relation to the natural environment, they also unwittingly triggered a pathological cycle of crisis, controversy, and public distrust, which has since hampered needed reform. * * *

It is, of course, far easier to set an ambitious goal than it is to meet one, and, almost as soon as these first generation laws were passed, it seemed as if they might well have a short half-life. Industry resisted their implementation, as did many state governments who concluded that the federal legislation improperly usurped state sovereignty.

The greatest challenge the laws faced, however, was the energy crisis of the mid–1970s. Industry promoted the notion, readily embraced by many politicians, that the energy needs of the nation were both more pressing than and inconsistent with environmental protection concerns. The country's need, for instance, to rely on abundant domestic supplies of coal, rather than petroleum imports, might require relaxing air pollution control requirements inconsistent with increased coal combustion. Likewise, the need to explore, extract, and transport domestic energy reserves of coal, petroleum, and natural gas would likely require relaxation of environmental restrictions that impeded or otherwise made such activities more costly.

The 'energy/environment' confrontation, however, ultimately fell far short of dismantling the first generation laws of the early 1970s. At the instigation of environmental citizen suits, courts insisted on strict implementation of those laws, resulting in a series of negotiated settlements between government and environmental interests, as well as judicial orders outlining schedules for agency compliance with statutory requirements. Although Congress amended the laws in certain respects, it did so without abandoning the law's basic structure and rigor. Congress extended some deadlines, fine-tuned some requirements to add incremental flexibility, and mostly relaxed standards only in terms of their application to the daily behavior of individual citizens (e.g., driving) rather than the conduct of industry.

Indeed, rather than abandon the first generation of environmental protection laws, Congress expanded upon them in the second half of the first decade. Congress enacted a new series of laws at least as ambitious and sweeping, and in some respects, even more so. These 'second generation laws' are distinguishable from the first generation largely because they tend to focus on a particular type of pollutant, rather than the identity of the particular environmental media in which pollutants are released. Hence, while the Clean Air Act, Clean Water Act, and Endangered Species Act focused on air, water, and wildlife (and habitat), the Toxic Substances Control Act ('TSCA') and Resource Conservation and Recovery Act ('RCRA') adopted in 1976, and the Comprehensive Environmental Response, Compensation, and Liability Act ('CERCLA'), each focused on that subset of more dangerous, i.e., toxic or hazardous, pollutants and substances regardless of the environmental media in which they were found.

RCRA and TSCA were both classic, prospective, and comprehensive regulatory laws. They included both health-based provisions and technology-based provisions, with some consideration of costs versus benefits. The theoretical justification for these laws was the need to supplement the media-based laws, which risked simply chasing toxic pollutants from one medium to the next, with some laws that looked at the larger, overall picture. RCRA and TSCA were meant to close the 'last remaining loophole' in environmental law.

CERCLA likewise focused on 'hazardous' substances, but was fundamentally different in its orientation than any other previous legislation. It was a retrospective liability law, not a prospective regulatory enactment. CERCLA was designed to provide for cleanup of abandoned and inactive hazardous waste sites, and to assign liability to the responsible parties for those cleanup costs. * * *

CERCLA's liability scheme was wholly unprecedented when enacted, at least in terms of U.S. law. It assigns liability for cleanup costs not just to current owners and operators of the site, but to all past and previous owners of the site at the time of waste disposal. Also included within the liability net are any persons who generated the hazardous substances that were disposed on the site, as well as parties who transported substances to the site. Moreover, because liability is strict, and almost always joint and several (because the harm is indivisible), any one of these parties may be held liable for the entire cleanup cost. * * *

Modern environmental law's second decade in the United States began as tumultuously as the first but with a very different evolutionary spin. Immediately on the heels of congressional passage of CERCLA, the most far-reaching of all the environmental statutes, President Ronald Reagan took office. He favored a substantial cutback of environmental regulation and took concerted action to accomplish that end.* * *

Surprisingly, the popular President's efforts were not only stymied but actually prompted a legislative backlash that ultimately generated even more stringent environmental protection laws. The Reagan Administration's efforts at deregulation unwittingly fueled the public's pre-existing distrust of government—the legacy of the first decade's series of failed promises—especially the public's readiness to believe that the government might be compromising public health concerns in order to bolster the corporate profits of industry. The environmental community in the United States took effective advantage of public concern—vigorously promoting public outrage—and, as a result, substantially increased both their own financial resources and membership as well as their lobbying clout before Congress.

The Reagan Administration's short-term solution was to replace its initial head of the EPA, who had sought to decrease the agency's budget, with a highly regarded individual with strong environmental credentials. The long-term impact of the Administration's effort to cut back on federal environmental protection laws, however, was precisely the opposite from the Administration's original policy objective. Congress responded to the public's disapproval of deregulatory efforts by amending the federal environmental protection laws in a manner designed both to make them stronger and to reduce executive branch discretion to diminish their effectiveness in the future.

Hence, environmental laws that in the 1970s had conferred considerable discretion on the EPA regarding how best to meet strict environmental goals now commenced to dictate to the agency not only the statutory ends, but the precise means as well. Even those statutory amendments that retained some discretion in the EPA to develop environmental protection requirements in the first instance imposed strict deadlines on their promulgation. Furthermore, in the event those deadlines were not met, the amendments mandated the automatic triggering of stringent requirements, including absolute prohibitions on specified waste disposal activities.

From 1981 through 1990, Congress substantially amended virtually all of the major environmental protection laws. Congress amended the Endangered Species Act in 1982, the Resource Conservation and Recovery Act in 1984, CERCLA in 1986, the Clean Water Act in 1987, and the Clean Air Act in 1990. These detailed, prescriptive amendments converted what had been open-ended statutes, tens of pages in length, into statutes of several hundred pages in length. Congress had, in effect, deprived the executive branch of much of the environmental policymaking authority that the latter had historically enjoyed. Although the Clean Air Act included, for the first time, a major program dependent on market incentives (tradeable emission rights to control acid deposition), the statutes generally adhered to a 'command and control' regime of strict technology and health-based standards. * * *

Environmental law's third decade momentarily began with George [H.W.] Bush, the self-declared 'environmental President,' but quickly shifted in the early 1990s to an emphasis on regulatory retrenchment. His Vice–President made environmental deregulation a major executive branch initiative, culminating in a formal moratorium on regulations, including several significant environmental protection programs.

The most remarkable challenge to federal environmental protection laws, however, came several years later in 1994, with the election of Republican majorities to both the House and Senate of Congress. The Republicans campaigned on the basis of a program they dubbed as the 'Contract With America,' the full implications of which for environmental law became apparent only in the immediate aftermath of their election. The Contract targeted federal environmental protection programs more than any other area of the law for significant curtailment.

Republican majorities in both chambers moved swiftly on several legislative fronts to convert their agenda into positive law. They proposed legislation that would have replaced environmental standards based on minimum standards of human health and technology-forcing requirements. In their place would be environmental standards based on cost/benefit analyses, comparative risk assessment, and other economic efficiency criteria. Environmentalists have long complained that such standards inevitably decrease environmental protection by discounting environmental values not susceptible to monetary valuation and environmental risks not certain to occur. * * *

Remarkably, however, practically none of these varied proposals became law (although some proposals are still pending). The reform efforts dissipated almost as quickly they formed. In a reversal of roles, while the legislative branch in 1994 sought to reform environmental law, the executive branch sought to preserve it. In the 1980s, the executive branch had sought to obtain many similar changes, only to be rebuffed by Congress, but when Congress was instigating the reforms in 1994, the executive branch maintained the opposition.

The executive branch also used the same tactics against Congress that Congress had used against it a decade beforehand. Just as Congress had effectively exploited the public's distrust of government efforts to protect the environment in the 1980s to defeat that earlier reform effort, so too the executive branch now pursued an identical strategy to block Congress. The President, Vice President, and the EPA Administrator repeatedly characterized Congress as seeking to undermine public health and environmental quality at the behest of industry profits. The American public, always ready to perceive environmental protection in such stark terms, and prone to expect such a political sell-out, responded in a manner that ultimately deprived the legislative reform effort of its political strength. Hence, the third major effort in as many decades to dismantle the demanding framework of U.S. environmental law, like the two before it, fell flat.

BARTON H. THOMPSON, JR., THE BUSH ADMINISTRATION AND ENVIRONMENTAL POLICY[7]

32 ECOLOGY L. Q. 307, 335–347 (2005).

Republican Presidents over the last forty years have often produced environmental advances, although not always out of environmental sympathies. Nudged by the prospect of a tough reelection battle with Senator George Muskie, the Nixon Administration helped usher in the era of federal environmental statutes with laws such as the National Environmental Policy Act of 1969, the Clean Air Act of 1970, and the Water Pollution Control Act of 1972. Even after Nixon won reelection in 1972, his administration supported passage of the Endangered Species Act and contemplated national land-use legislation. The Reagan Administration's fiscal conservatism led to the demise of economically unsound and environmentally detrimental water supply projects, and his State Department helped negotiate the Montreal Protocol. President George Herbert Walker Bush, claiming the mantle of the "environmental president," sought and obtained passage of the Clean Air Act Amendments of 1990, protected various areas off the coast of the United States from oil and gas development, and signed a number of important international environmental treaties. * * *

The Bush Administration has shown strong enthusiasm for positive economic incentives, particularly in protecting habitat and other environmentally sensitive land. In its first term, the administration created a number of new incentives for property owners to engage in conservation— part of what President Bush has labeled his "legacy of cooperative

---

7. Reprinted by permission.

conservation." Typical programs include the Landowner Incentive Program (which provides federal cost-sharing funds to states wishing to establish positive incentive programs for private property owners who protect and restore habitat on their land) and the Private Stewardship Grants program (which provides federal funds for local, private, and non-profit conservation benefiting species listed under the federal Endangered Species Act). Other programs help encourage wetlands restoration in Southern Oregon, the removal of invasive plants in Southeastern Florida, and mitigation measures for threatened marine species in the Kenai Fjords of Alaska.

Throughout its period in office, the Bush Administration also has supported increased funding for positive incentive programs. Despite budget cuts in a wide variety of social programs, for example, the Bush Administration currently is proposing increased funding for a wide variety of environmental incentive programs run by the Department of Agriculture, Department of the Interior, Department of Commerce, and Environmental Protection Agency. These increases would build on record budgetary outlays for a variety of environmental incentive programs in prior Bush Administration budgets. * * *

Although the Bush Administration has promoted positive incentives, it is less clear whether the administration has favored incentives programs because of their environmental benefits or because the regulated community likes them. The Bush Administration occasionally has displayed a willingness to modify incentive programs to favor politically powerful constituencies in ways that jeopardize environment benefits. One of the largest and longest standing incentive programs, for example, is the Conservation Reserve Program (CRP). Created as part of the 1985 Farm Bill, CRP pays farmers to retire marginal farm land from production and plant native grasses and other plants beneficial to wildlife on the land. With the approval of the Bush Administration, Congress in 2002 modified the program to permit farmers to engage in some light grazing and occasional haying on CRP land as part of the Farm Security and Rural Investment Act (FSRI). According to a lawsuit filed by the National Wildlife Federation against the government, the Bush Administration has used this provision to permit millions of acres of CRP land to be subjected to substantial haying and grazing—to the benefit of the landowners but the detriment of habitat value.

Another policy reform * * * is the greater use of tradable permits—or what sometimes are called "cap and trade" systems. The mechanics of such systems are now well known. The government starts by capping the amount of an activity that can occur, whether it be fishing, the discharge of pollutants, or the withdrawal of water from streams for consumption, and issuing permits for the activity in the determined amount. The government then permits individuals or entities to trade the permits. * * *

The Bush Administration has been very supportive of tradable permits. Tradable permits form a key element of the Bush Administration's Clear Skies proposal. The Clear Skies initiative would reduce current emissions of mercury, nitrogen oxides, and sulfur dioxide from power plants. Like the SO_2 tradable permit system adopted in the 1990 Clean Air Act Amendments, the Clear Skies initiative would minimize the cost of these reductions through active trading systems. As President Bush noted in announcing the initiative, "instead of the government telling utilities where and how to cut pollution, we will tell them when and how much to cut. We will give them a firm deadline and let them find the most innovative ways to meet it."

The Bush Administration also has expanded the use of tradable permits to pollution settings in which they have not been utilized in the past. Tradable permits historically have been used under the Clean Air Act to address pollutants that widely disperse and thus can be readily traded without affecting local environmental quality. As part of the Clear Skies initiative, however, the Bush Administration has proposed using tradable permits for mercury pollution, which has greater localized impacts than traditionally traded pollutants. Under the Clean Water Act, the Bush Administration also has encouraged water quality trading within a number of watersheds, including the Chesapeake Bay and the Lower Colorado River. Trading in these contexts is trickier and requires more sophisticated systems because trading from one pollution source to another can change local pollution levels, even if overall pollution loading remains the same, raising health and equity issues for those living in areas with increased pollution level* * *

Although the Bush Administration has promoted tradable permits, moreover, it is less clear whether the administration has promoted market systems merely to reduce the economic burden of environmental regulations on business or also to increase environmental protection itself. * * * Indeed, many observers have argued that the Clear Skies initiative would result in more air pollution than the Clean Air Act currently allows. Far from having to be convinced to support the Clear Skies initiative, the business community has been a strong supporter of the initiative from the outset; environmental organizations have been the skeptics.* * *

[T]he Bush Administration has provided states with more decision-making authority in a variety of contexts. Under the Endangered Species Act, for example, the Department of the Interior has promoted Candidate Conservation Agreements (CCAs) in which state and local governments, often in conjunction with private entities, enter into agreements to protect candidate species—avoiding the need to list the species. CCAs effectively give states and local governments the ability to preempt strict federal regulation by adopting protective measures of their own. In other examples of devolution, the Bush Administration has transferred title to more than ten federal reclamation projects to local users and has adopted policies providing for greater local control over national forest policy.

The Bush Administration, however, has not been consistent in its approach to federalism in the environmental area. As the above examples illustrate, the administration has promoted greater state and local involvement in areas where stakeholders have complained about federal regulation. In situations where states or local governments have tried to impose stricter regulations than the federal government, however, the Bush Administration has sometimes argued that national policies preempt the state or local efforts. In one court case, for example, the Bush Administration argued that national mining laws preempted local regulation of a proposed processing plant for federal minerals that would sit on private lands. In another example, the administration urged the United States Supreme Court to rule that national law preempts a state court from holding herbicide manufacturers liable to farmers. In one of the most important examples, the Bush Administration has sided with United States automobile manufacturers in their arguments against a California law that would require them to reduce carbon dioxide emissions from all vehicles sold in the state by the end of this decade.

The Bush Administration also has failed to support state efforts to pursue strong environmental measures and has urged Congress to preempt state and local regulations where those regulations stand in the way of national industrial policy that the administration supports. As part of its energy policy, for example, the Bush Administration has urged Congress to preempt local regulation of energy rights-of-way. According to the head of the national organization of state pollution control administrators, members of the Bush Administration "talk about states' rights, but they take away key tools states have needed to clean up the air." * * *

The Bush Administration has supported conservative environmental innovations in a number of settings. As described, the Bush Administration has created and funded a variety of new programs to provide positive incentives to property owners to protect wildlife and other environmental amenities on their land. The administration also has promoted the use of environmental markets in a variety of new contexts. Finally, the administration has devolved responsibility over a number of environmental issues to states or local decision makers. Many of these efforts are important conservative advances in environmental policy for which the Bush Administration deserves credit.

The Bush Administration's record in supporting other conservative environmental innovations, however, has been disappointing. This lackluster record may be attributable in part to the conflicts that exist among the varying strands of conservative environmental thought. Gregg Easterbrook has suggested that "environmental reform is currently impossible. Neither the left nor the right will allow it." The experiences of the Bush Administration suggest that splits within the "right," all by itself, may hinder many opportunities for environmental reform.

In examining the Bush Administration's record, however, one also notices that most of the conservative environmental reforms that the administration has pursued benefit the regulated sector. The principal reforms generally reduce the regulated community's cost of achieving various environmental goals or devolve responsibility to states in contexts where the regulated community might be more amenable to state regulation. Only a few of the reforms appear to have been adopted to provide greater protection to the environment itself. This may suggest that * * * the emphasis is on promoting economic growth, through national power where necessary. It also may suggest that politics, and the voices of corporate supporters, rather than philosophical principles, are primarily influencing the Bush Administration's decisions. The external evidence of the Bush Administration's policies are consistent with either explanation.

Whatever the reasons, the failure of the Bush Administration to more actively investigate and pursue environmental innovations * * * is a loss to the environment. Conservative presidential administrations offer an opportunity for testing new approaches that have been ignored in the past, yet hold the potential for providing increased or improved environmental protection.

Notes

1. Much of President Bush's environmental policy centered on energy issues. His energy plan came from a working group chaired by Vice President Cheney. The plan concluded that the United States would need about a third more oil by 2020. It called for building 1,000 to 2,000 additional power plants, expanding oil production on federal lands such as the Arctic National Wildlife Reserve, and streamlining the regulatory process for power plants. *See* Gary C. Bryner, *The National Energy Policy: Assessing Energy Policy Choices*, 73 U. Colo. L. Rev. 341, 345–348 (2002). The Administration also disavowed the Kyoto agreement to control greenhouse gases, which would have required limitations on American use of fossil fuels. *Id.* at 388. At the same time, President Bush's rhetoric centered on the stewardship obligations of individual landowners. *See* Jonathan Cannon & Jonathan Riehl, *Presidential Greenspeak: How Presidents Talk About the Environment and What It Means*, 23 Stan. Env. L. J. 195, 262–263 (2004).

2. One of President Bush's final acts as President was to create three separate national monuments encompassing eight patches of the Pacific and collectively covering about the same areas as Spain. This was the single largest marine preservation action in history. Earlier in the year, he had created another large protected area near the Northwestern Hawaiian Islands. See Christopher Pala, *Scientists Laud Bush's Blue Legacy But Want More*, 323 Science 192 (2009).

3. According to public choice theory, small groups with high individual stakes (like industry) should be much easier to organize than large groups with diffuse interests (like citizens or citizen groups) for several reasons, including organizing costs and "free rider" problems. The costs of organizing a small group are less, especially since the firms may already be connected through networks like trade associations. Those with small, individual stakes have little incentive to invest time and energy in learning about problems and

organizing to make changes. Finally, when a large group is involved, it is rational for each individual to sit back and let other members of the group take the initiative. This "free rider" problem is less severe for smaller groups with a higher stake in the problem. Consequently, we would expect industry to have more political clout than representatives of the public at-large. Thus, we would expect to see little—if any—legislation placing substantial economic burdens on industry to benefit the environment.

Yet, contrary to public choice theory, the reality is that a great deal of environmental regulation does exist, though the strength of industry lobbying efforts also cannot be denied. Four possible explanations have been given for the existence of major environmental statutes. First, once the public at large is informed about environmental problems, little additional investment is needed to use this information at the polls to support a candidate or referendum item. Voters can be a powerful force even if it remains true that industry has a greater incentive to engage in lobbying and public relations. Second, even if it is normally not worthwhile for citizens to go out of their way to learn about environmental problems, those problems may become highly salient during crises. This would lead us to expect a cycle of crises accompanied by public attention and new legislation, followed by quieter periods when the public's interest recedes and industry concerns receive greater government attention. Third, politicians who are eager to advance their careers may find it to their advantage to advertise their environmental commitments. These political entrepreneurs may compete to establish their environmental credentials. For instance, such a competition between President Nixon and Senator Muskie seems to have been important in the passage of the Clean Air Act. Finally, environmental organizations may play a catalyzing role, sparking public interest in environmental problems, monitoring the conduct of politicians, and providing a counterweight to industry in the legislature. For discussion of these questions, *see* Daniel A. Farber, *Politics and Procedures in Environmental Law*, 8 J.L. ECON. & ORG. 59 (1992); Cary Coglianese, *Social Movements, Law, and Society: The Institutionalization of the Environmental Movement*, 150 U. PA. L. REV. 85 (2001); Christopher H. Schroeder, *Rational Choice Versus Republican Moment—Explanations for Environmental Laws, 1969–1973*, 9 DUKE ENVTL. L. & POL'Y F. 29 (1998).

4. Although the factors discussed in the last note may explain the passage of environmental legislation in the 1970s, they apparently have not been sufficient to promote additional legislation in the more recent past. The last major environmental legislation (as of this writing) consisted of the Clean Air Act amendments passed in 1990. Since then, a legislative logjam has prevented new legislation. Increasingly acrid partisan politics may be part of the reason. For instance,

> The first example of policy considerations getting lost in the political shuffle is EPA cabinet status. . . . When the Republicans are in the White House, the Democrats oppose it; when the Democrats are in the White House, the Republicans oppose it. Neither side appears actually to care much about the merits of the issue. Both are simply determined not to allow a President of the opposite political party to get "credit" for elevating EPA to cabinet status.

Donald Elliott, *Portage Strategies for Adapting Environmental Law and Policy During a Logjam Era*, 17 NYU ENV. L.J. 24, 28–29 (2008). In Elliott's view, the "key dynamic comes down to politicians and their staffs gravitating to extreme positions to define the contrast between them in symbolic terms for an external audience that is not well-informed about the specifics of complicated issues, rather than moving to the center to achieve a compromise." Id. at 31.

3. THE IMPACT OF U.S. ENVIRONMENTAL REGULATION

The significance of U.S. environmental law is obvious if we measure it by pages of statutes, regulations, and court decisions. But, of course, that's not the point. The real question involves the impact of this legislation on improving the environment. In 2000, Resources for the Future (RFF), a respected think tank focused on the increased use of cost-benefit analysis and economic incentives, published a book surveying the impact of environmental regulation. PUBLIC POLICIES FOR ENVIRONMENTAL PROTECTION (Paul R. Portney and Robert N. Stavins, 2d ed. 2000). Given RFF's efficiency focus, its legislative appraisal is not likely to be slanted in favor of current regulations. For present purposes, we can focus on three main areas: air pollution, water pollution, and hazardous waste. (In the interest of readability, we will cite the relevant page numbers in the RFF book in parentheses.)

Air Pollution. Over roughly two decades (1979–1998), the nation's overall air quality improved substantially. Concentrations of carbon monoxide, particulates, and sulfur dioxide have been cut by about 50%. Smog and nitrogen dioxide are down 17–25%. The biggest success story is lead pollution, which was reduced by "a spectacular 96%." (p. 93). EPA estimates that the reductions in suspended particulates prevented about 180,000 premature deaths in 1990. (p. 103).

These benefits were not cheap. EPA estimates that air quality regulation cost about half a trillion dollars from 1990 to 1993. (p. 107). The Clean Air Act had major amendments in 1990. EPA estimated that the amendments would cost about $20 billion per year. (p. 109). The RFF study suggested that EPA's estimate of benefits was too optimistic, partly because of high estimates of public health impacts and partly because it placed too high a monetary value on the increased life span. Despite these errors, the actual cost-benefit ratio for at least the pre–1990 Clean Air Act was clearly positive. (p. 111).

Water Pollution. Here, the picture is less rosy. According to the RFF report, water quality has improved since 1972 but only moderately. "In terms of aggregate measures of national averages, the change has not been dramatic, but local success stories report substantial cleanup in what had been seriously polluted water bodies." (p. 189). One reason why the success has been so modest is that the Clean Water Act has effectively addressed only part of the pollution problem: discharges from industry and municipal sewage treatment. Over 80% of the suspended solids, phosphorus, and nitrogen come from nonpoint sources (mostly agricultural or urban runoff), as does over half of the "biological oxygen demand" (a measure of a pollutant's impact on the availability of oxygen for aquatic life.) (p. 179). EPA estimated the cost of compliance in 1990 at $54 billion. (p. 195).

Hazardous Waste. As of 1997, about 27 million tons of toxic waste was regulated by the federal government. (p. 219). Amendments in the mid–1980s dramatically decreased the amount of hazardous waste disposal in landfills. (p. 227). The amount of hazardous waste generated has significantly declined since the advent of federal regulation; the decrease might or might not be due in part to the increased cost of disposing of that waste. (pp. 228–29). According to RFF, the federal regulations were cost-justified (in terms of their public health benefits) for core hazardous wastes (those regulated by California even before RCRA), but not for other wastes. (p. 231).

A separate statute focuses on cleaning up existing waste sites. As of 1996, the National Priority List included almost 1,500 sites. (p. 235) About 400 sites had completed clean-ups. (p. 236). An economic study indicated that on average the clean-ups were justified by the reduction in cancer rates, but there was great variation between sites. At about 70% of the sites, the clean-up cost was too high—more than $100 million per case of cancer avoided—although some of the remaining sites obtained substantial public health benefits at very low cost. (pp. 239–240). According to estimates by RAND, another think tank, about a quarter of the total expenditures were for transaction costs such as legal fees. (p. 242).

B. THE ECOLOGICAL PERSPECTIVE

Environmental law is heavily multidisciplinary. We will frequently see the influence of economics on environmental policy. Unlike many areas of law, environmental law also relies heavily on scientific data and theories, because its subject matter is the physical world. Scientific expertise is helpful for environmental lawyers, but for those who lack such expertise, at least a basic understanding is crucial.

1. FUNDAMENTALS OF ECOLOGY AND BIODIVERSITY

In a classic book,[8] Aldo Leopold argued for recognizing a new "land ethic" governing human relations with biological communities:

> The land ethic simply enlarges the boundaries of the community to include soils, waters, plants, and animals, or collectively: the land.

> This sounds simple: do we not already sing our love for and obligation to the land of the free and the home of the brave? Yes, but

---

8. Aldo Leopold, A Sand County Almanac (1970).

just what and whom do we love? Certainly not the soil, which we are sending helter-skelter downriver. Certainly not the waters, which we assume have no function except to turn turbines, float barges, and carry off sewage. Certainly not the plants, of which we exterminate whole communities without batting an eye. Certainly not the animals, of which we have already extirpated many of the largest and most beautiful species. A land ethic of course cannot prevent the alteration, management, and use of these "resources," but it does affirm their right to continued existence, and, at least in spots, their continued existence in a natural state.

In short, a land ethic changes the role of *Homo sapiens* from conqueror of the land-community to plain member and citizen of it. It implies respect for his fellow-members, and also respect for the community as such.

Leopold based this ethic on the concept of a land pyramid:

Plants absorb energy from the sun. This energy flows through a circuit called the biota, which may be represented by a pyramid consisting of layers. The bottom layer is the soil. A plant layer rests on the soil, an insect layer on the plants, a bird and rodent layer on the insects, and so on up through various animal groups to the apex layer, which consists of the larger carnivores.

The species of a layer are alike not in where they came from, or in what they look like, but rather in what they eat. Each successive layer depends on those below it for food and often for other services, and each in turn furnishes food and services to those above. Proceeding upward, each successive layer decreases in numerical abundance. Thus, for every carnivore there are hundreds of his prey, thousands of their prey, millions of insects, uncountable plants. The pyramidal form of the system reflects this numerical progression from apex to base. Man shares an intermediate layer with the bears, raccoons, and squirrels which eat both meat and vegetables.

The lines of dependency for food and other services are called food chains. Thus soil-oak-deer-Indian is a chain that has now been largely converted to soil-corn-cow-farmer. Each species, including ourselves, is a link in many chains. The deer eats a hundred plants other than oak, and the cow a hundred plants other than corn. Both, then, are links in a hundred chains. The pyramid is a tangle of chains so complex as to seem disorderly, yet the stability of the system proves it to be a highly organized structure. Its functioning depends on the co-operation and competition of its diverse parts.

Although many environmentalists of the time conceived of a stable "balance of nature," Leopold viewed this ecological "pyramid" as dynamic rather than static:

Land, then, is not merely soil; it is a fountain of energy flowing through a circuit of soils, plants, and animals. Food chains are the living channels which conduct energy upwards; death and decay return it to the soil. The circuit is not closed; some energy is dissipated in decay, some is added by absorption from the air, some is stored in soils, peats, and long-lived forests; but it is a sustained circuit, like a slowly augmented revolving fund of life. There is always a net loss by downhill wash, but this is normally small and offset by the decay of rocks. It is deposited in the ocean and, in the course of geological time, raised to form new lands and new pyramids.

The velocity and character of the upward flow of energy depend on the complex structure of the plant and animal community, much as the upward flow of sap in a tree depends on its complex cellular organization. Without this complexity, normal circulation would presumably not occur. Structure means the characteristic numbers, as well as the characteristic kinds and functions, of the component species. This interdependence between the complex structure of the land and its smooth functioning as an energy unit is one of its basic attributes.

When a change occurs in one part of the circuit, many other parts must adjust themselves to it. Change does not necessarily obstruct or divert the flow of energy; evolution is a long series of self-induced changes, the net result of which has been to elaborate the flow mechanism and to lengthen the circuit. Evolutionary changes, however, are usually slow and local. Man's invention of tools has enabled him to make changes of unprecedented violence, rapidity, and scope.

Leopold's influence on environmental law may be rising, as one observer has noted:

[I]f legal citations are any guide, Leopold's star has never shone brighter as the new century opens. A Westlaw search covering the five-year period beginning in 1994 turned up 260 texts and periodical articles citing Leopold's work, a sharp increase from prior periods. Leopold, little interested (apparently) in law, has become one of the most cited authors in environmental law. A new emphasis on moral standards and responsibility is in the air, and the conservation community now recognizes the importance of conserving places where people live and work. A handful of states are attending finally to the problems of nonpoint source water pollution, and efforts are underway here and there to consider wildlife-habitat needs at the landscape level. And if ecosystem management is sometimes more slogan than actuality, it nonetheless reflects a yearning for integrated visions that Leopold would have endorsed.

Eric T. Freyfogle, *A Sand County Almanac at 50: Leopold in the New Century*, 30 ENVTL. L. REP. 10058, 10067 (2000).

The science of ecology has not remained static, however, since Leopold's day. In particular, concepts regarding the stability of ecosystems have become much more sophisticated, and it is no longer believed that complex systems are necessarily more stable than simple ones, at least in some respects. *See* Stuart L. Pimm, *The Balance of Nature?* ECOLOGICAL ISSUES IN THE CONSERVATION OF SPECIES AND COMMUNITIES (1991). Some recent work also questions the old concept of the local ecological community as a tightly unified entity, but continues to stress the importance of biodiversity. *See* Y. Baskin, *Ecologists Dare to Ask: How Much Does Diversity Matter?* 264 SCI. 202 (1994); M. A. Buzas and S. J. Culver, *Species Pool and Dynamics of Marine Paleocommunities*, 264 SCI. 1439 (1994).

The impact of the "New Ecology" on environmental regulation and land management was explored in a Symposium, *Beyond the Balance of Nature: Environmental Law Faces the New Ecology*, 7 DUKE ENVTL. L. & POL'Y F. 1 (1996). One writer summarizes the New Ecology as follows:

> The concept of the "Balance of Nature," so politically successful in the late 1960's and early 1970's, has been dismissed by ecological science. The "Balance of Nature" hypothesized that ecosystems would progress to a steady state, at which they could exist perpetually in "balance." Ecosystems are now seen as dynamic and stochastic rather than in equilibrium; anthropogenic actions most often are seen as inescapably intermingled with ecological systems, rather than avoidable. Unfortunately, however, many of the laws designed to regulate ecological resources were passed when the "Balance of Nature" paradigm was king and have not been redrafted to comport with advances in ecology.* * *
>
> Human actions are now seen as inextricably intertwined with the operation of ecosystems. * * * Human effects are evident in nearly every natural system. For example, even before the European colonists arrived in America, the forests of southern New England had been shaped by the burning practices of Native Americans. With universal effects such as global warming and the thinning of the ozone layer, no part of the Earth is untouched by human influence. Thus, as we now are properly identified as merely a force among ecosystems, traditional attempts to simply separate ourselves from ecosystems are no longer prudent.
>
> Ecological research has also borne out the hypothesis that ecosystems fluctuate without equilibrium and beyond the capabilities of humans to assess and control them without error. Instead of being a Kodachrome still-life, the environment is "a moving picture show" replete with random events. These random events are often just part of the system.

Timothy H. Profeta, *Managing Without A Balance: Environmental Regulation in Light of Ecological Advances*, 7 DUKE ENVTL. L. & POL'Y F. 71, 73 (1996).

The next two excerpts explore the implications of current thinking regarding biodiversity and ecological complexity.

GEORGE LEDEC AND ROBERT GOODLAND, WILDLANDS: THEIR PROTECTION AND MANAGEMENT IN ECONOMIC DEVELOPMENT[9]

5–15 (1988).

"The land is one organism," wrote the American naturalist Aldo Leopold over forty years ago. "Its parts, like our own parts, compete with each other and cooperate with each other * * *. If the biota, in the course of aeons, has built something we like but do not understand, then who but a fool would discard seemingly useless parts?" Wildlands, kept in their natural state and properly managed, provide a refuge for plant and animal species that may prove to have direct economic uses and that, more important, form part of the vast and still inadequately understood web of connections among all living things and their environment. Wildlands are also essential for the maintenance of environmental services—water control, soil conservation, and the like—most of them unpriced public goods that are indispensable for meeting human needs and supporting sustainable development.

Because wildlands make significant and even unique long-term contributions to human welfare, prudent development should minimize or mitigate damages from wildland conversion. Indeed, the timely management of strategically important wildlands often prolongs or improves the effectiveness of development projects. Conversely, the unnecessary or short-sighted destruction of wildlands can lead to unanticipated and costly consequences, such as the rapid siltation of reservoirs and waterways, the loss of topsoil and of economically important species, and even the spread of disease. By incorporating wildland management in their projects and other activities, development organizations can improve the prospects for sustainable economic development. * * *

Biological Diversity

Biological diversity usually refers to three elements: (1) the number of different ecosystems (communities of plants and animals and the environments that sustain them) and their relative frequencies in a country or in the world; (2) the number of species of animals and plants and their relative frequencies; and (3) the genetic variation within each species.

The variability we see in the life forms on Earth is primarily a result of variations in DNA (deoxyribonucleic acid), as expressed in genes—the blueprints for life. Genetic variability is greatest among species, but variability among isolated populations of a species or among individuals in a population is also important. A rare species is a genetically vulnerable species. If the number of individuals is small, the probability of advantageous genetic variations occurring is reduced, and inbreeding may perpetuate disadvantageous characteristics. Preserving biological diversity, then,

---

9. Copyright © 1988 by the International Bank for Reconstruction and Development. Reprinted by permission.

entails preserving not only species but also different populations of species and the largest feasible number of individuals within those populations.

Most of the world's wild plant and animal species depend on wildlands for their existence, as they cannot survive in areas that have been significantly modified by human beings. Moreover, most species depend on specific types of wildland habitats and have limited geographic ranges. * * * The elimination of a unique wildland habitat therefore causes the summary extinction of all the species that are completely dependent on that habitat for their survival. Appropriate wildland management is the only method of preserving large and distinct populations of most species, thereby ensuring species survival and biological diversity. Conservation measures other than wildland management (such as the establishment of plantation forests) preserve some environmental services but cannot by themselves maintain diversity.

The Modern Loss of Biological Diversity

Human activities in the last quarter of the twentieth century are reducing biological diversity at a rate that may be unprecedented in the history of life on Earth. It is impossible to assess, with our limited knowledge, the consequences of the disappearance of species for the stability of Earth's environment or the economic value lost because of extinctions. The best available estimates indicate that if current trends continue, some 15–20 percent of the estimated 10 million to 30 million species of plants and animals alive in 1980 may become extinct by 2000, and many more species could be lost in the early decades of the twenty-first century. Development activities can be modified to help reduce these disturbing trends. * * *

The most striking difference between natural and human-induced extinctions is in the rates. Over the millennia the rate of natural extinction of species has usually been slightly less than the rate of formation of new species through evolutionary processes. Human activity is greatly accelerating extinction rates; several hundred species *a day* may become extinct over the next twenty to thirty years. More species of the Earth's flora and fauna may disappear in the next several decades than were lost in the mass extinction that wiped out whole taxonomic groups of animals, including the dinosaurs, 65 million years ago.

Another difference is that whereas in the course of evolution a species that becomes extinct is often replaced by a better-adapted successor or group of successors, human-induced extinctions are evolutionary dead ends. Furthermore, although human beings are not the first species to have caused the extinction of other species, they are the first to be aware of the implications of their actions and to be capable of controlling them.

The reduction of wildland habitats to less than the critical amount necessary for the survival of a species is by far the greatest cause of modern extinctions. Although many endangered species live in temperate areas, the problem is most severe in tropical regions, where at least two-thirds of the world's species of plants and animals are found. Appropriate, low-cost wildland management can significantly reduce current extinction rates to much lower—perhaps almost "natural"—levels. * * *

The Case for Preserving Biological Diversity

There are compelling economic, scientific, aesthetic, and ethical reasons for preserving biological diversity. All of them are grounded in the view that because species extinctions are completely irreversible, preserving biological diversity keeps open important options for the future.

The *economic* justification for preserving biological diversity is that many species of wild plants and animals are undeveloped resources—that is, they have significant economic potential that is currently undiscovered, undervalued, or underutilized. Biological resources are essential to human existence, and the preservation of biological diversity is important to the maintenance and improvement of agriculture, forestry, ranching, fisheries, medicine, industry, and tourism.

The importance of genetic diversity for sustaining and increasing agricultural production is increasingly acknowledged. Without a diverse genetic base for plant breeding, the development of high-yielding crop varieties probably could not be sustained. The disappearance of many domesticated crop varieties and their wild relatives has made many of the world's productive farming areas increasingly susceptible to catastrophic attacks by pests and diseases. Despite efforts to preserve crop germplasm, many domestic varieties and wild relatives of crop plants remain threatened.

An example of the benefits of genetic diversity is a perennial wild maize (*Zea diploperennis*) which has been preserved almost accidentally. It may have seemed to be "just another weed" when it was discovered growing on a few hectares of land in Jalisco, Mexico, but it may become important for higher food production. Perennial maize could be grown in "maize orchards" that would not have to be plowed and seeded each year; the advantages for soil and energy conservation are obvious. In addition, cross-breeding with *Zea diploperennis* may significantly improve the resistance of annual varieties of maize to a number of serious diseases and insect pests. * * *

Wild plant species have even greater potential as completely new crops. Of the world's approximately 240,000 species of plants, only about 3,000 have ever been used as food, only 150 have been cultivated on any scale, and a mere 20 account for over 85 percent of present human consumption. Population growth, rising per capita consumption, and shortages of arable land may make it important in future years to cultivate new species of crops that can produce calories, protein, specific mineral nutrients, vitamins, or fibers more efficiently than many of the species currently used.

Many otherwise obscure animal species, particularly insects, should also be protected to maintain or enhance agricultural output. For example, the oil palm (*Elaeis guineensis*) is pollinated in the wild in Africa by a weevil, *Elaeidobius kamerunicus*. The oil palm was introduced in what is now Malaysia in 1917 without the weevil and required costly, inefficient, labor-intensive hand pollination. In 1980–81 the pollinator was collected from its native habitat in the forests of Cameroon and brought to Malaysia; it promptly boosted fruiting in oil palm trees by 40–60 percent. This improvement was worth approximately $57 million in foreign exchange in the first year alone. * * *

Wild plants and animals are also fundamentally important for modern medicine and offer even greater future applications. Over 40 percent of all prescriptions written in the United States contain one or more drugs that originate from wild species (fungi, bacteria, higher plants, and animals); annual sales of such drugs in this one country are over $8 billion. In many cases it is still impossible to synthesize these compounds or more costly to synthesize them than to obtain them from living sources; in any case it would not have been possible to know what compound to synthesize without first having the natural model.

Wild plant and animal species are of great and increasing importance to industry as sources of tannins, resins, gums, oils, dyes, and other commercially useful compounds. Until about 1850 even the rubber tree (*Hevea brasiliensis*) was just another Amazonian tree species of unknown economic value. The potential for new industrial products from currently unknown or poorly known plant and animal species is significant but impossible to quantify. Such products may even include hydrocarbons for an oil-short world. For example, *Copaifera langsdorfii,* a tree that grows only in northern Brazil, produces 20 liters of sap per tree every six months, and this sap, it has recently been discovered, can be used directly as a fuel in diesel engines. * * *

The *scientific* reason for species preservation is that we cannot understand the interactions of life forms and their environments unless we can observe how they function in the absence of significant human intervention. It is therefore necessary to conserve comprehensive samples of ecological systems in an undisturbed state. Moreover, each species has unique physiological, biochemical, and population characteristics, the study of which can help us to understand basic life processes. In addition to the direct economic applications of research on poorly known species, eventual economic payoffs are likely to emerge from more basic scientific research.* * *

The *aesthetic* justification is that many wild species of plants and animals are an irreplaceable source of wonder, inspiration, and joy to human beings because of their beauty, intriguing appearance, variety, or fascinating behavior. * * * Millions of people who may never actually encounter many wild species derive enrichment and vicarious satisfaction from reading and learning about them; are our descendants to be denied these pleasures?

The *ethical,* or moral, justification, espoused by a significant and growing number of people, is that human beings should not exercise their power to obliterate other species at will—even species not known to have any practical value to humankind. From this perspective nonhuman species have their own intrinsic value independent of any practical or utilitarian value they may have for human beings. This ethical viewpoint has been called the "Noah principle." A related, perhaps more traditional, view is that to eradicate other species is to deprive future generations of options and thus to fail in the duty of stewardship. For a couple of generations of human beings to eliminate unnecessarily a sizable proportion of the diversity of life on Earth can be construed as an act of considerable arrogance.

All of these considerations argue that human beings should exercise great care to avoid inadvertent extinctions. A leading biologist, Edward O. Wilson, has said:

> The worst thing that can happen—will happen—in the 1980s is not energy depletion, economic collapse, limited nuclear war, or conquest by a totalitarian government. As terrible as these catastrophes would be for us, they can be repaired within a few generations. The one process ongoing in the 1980s that will take millions of years to correct is the loss of genetic and species diversity by the destruction of natural habitats. This is the folly our descendants are least likely to forgive us.

NOTES

1. The authors sketch out four main categories to justify the preservation of biodiversity: economic, scientific, aesthetic, and ethical. Depending on what priority we give to these reasons, we might structure our efforts differently. For example, some species have more aesthetic appeal than others. Should this play a role in our preservation decisions? Moreover, some of the justifications focus more on individual species, while others focus on distinctive ecosystems, which might also influence the choice of methods for preserving biodiversity. How much of the rationale for preservation should turn on utilitarian considerations, and how much on the intrinsic value that a species might be thought to have? Suppose, for example, that it were determined that some species of whale had little potential economic value, little impact on the oceanic ecosystem (perhaps because it is quite rare to begin with), and limited aesthetic beauty. Should we preserve it anyway? In terms of priorities, should we be willing to make greater sacrifices to save such a species or a less appealing but potentially useful type of fern?

2. As we will see in Chapter 3, the Endangered Species Act is drafted in terms of preserving individual species rather than ecosystems, and gives little attention to costs. Is this legal structure consistent with the rationales for preserving biodiversity?

3. Some of the reasons for protecting an endangered species involve some immediate interaction with the species by scientists or others. Other

interests involve unknown possibilities for future economic or scientific uses, or a desire to preserve the species for the possible benefit of future generations. Yet our litigation system was originally designed to settle concrete disputes over existing harms. What kind of connection with a biodiversity issue should the law require as the basis for bringing a claim? Should anyone be allowed to sue, or only someone with a more definite short-term interest? We will consider those issues in Chapter 5.

J. B. RUHL, THINKING OF ENVIRONMENTAL LAW AS A COMPLEX ADAPTIVE SYSTEM: HOW TO CLEAN UP THE ENVIRONMENT BY MAKING A MESS OF ENVIRONMENTAL LAW[10]

34 HOUS. L. REV. 933, 954–958, 992–999 (1997).

Biological evolution is one of the most studied topics in science, and yet the amount we do not know about evolution far exceeds the amount we do know. The part we do not even begin to understand is associated with the contribution ecological forces make to evolutionary dynamics. As the eminent biologist Edward O. Wilson puts it, "[w]hat we understand best about evolution is mostly genetic, and what we understand least is mostly ecological. . . . [T]he major remaining questions of evolutionary biology are ecological rather than genetic in content."[11]

The emergence in environmental biology of the concept of ecosystems as unpredictable, dynamically changing systems has injected a heightened awareness of the role of indeterminacy and randomness into evolutionary theory.[12] The mix of species in an ecosystem depends largely on the timing of introduction and the location. But how are the assembly rules for an ecosystem determined, and how do they contribute to evolution of species across time? These are the questions of the future for evolutionary biologists.

Questions about ecosystems not only are relevant to evolutionary biologists, but also go to the heart of environmental law and policy at all levels. Here again, we find that we know less than we do not know, but we do know the following:

1. The connections between species within an ecosystem are often poorly understood, or understood too late to do any good.

2. Little is known, particularly for large carnivores, about how much habitat and how many species individuals are needed to support a species as a long-term viable population.

---

10. Copyright © 1997, Houston Law Review. Reprinted by permission.

11. Edward O. Wilson, THE DIVERSITY OF LIFE 93 (1992).

12. The past 30 years of research in biology have spawned a "new paradigm of ecology, mothballing the old notion of a 'balance of nature' and unveiling a vibrant new replacement focusing on flux." William Stolzenburg, Building a Better Refuge, NATURE CONSERVANCY, Jan.–Feb. 1996, at 18, 21. The new focus on dynamic change has led scientists to reevaluate the premises upon which many legal and policy decisions have been based, such as the size, location, and operation of wildlife refuges.

3. One of the most pernicious and least understood threats to ecosystems involves the "invasion," often unwittingly assisted by human activities, by particularly adaptable species that prey upon or outcompete the "native" species of the ecosystem.

4. Evidence of more direct adverse effects of human activities on ecosystems is abundant but difficult to understand in terms of causal effect, source of the problem, and possible solution.

5. It cannot be assumed that human influence always presents a negative for ecosystem dynamics.

6. Human efforts to conserve species may sometimes actually do more damage to ecosystems than good.

These sources of uncertainty make societal decisions all the more difficult, as we are unsure what effects our behavior will have on the environment. A growing effort to explain these properties through complexity theory and the depiction of ecosystems as complex adaptive systems promises to improve our understanding of their origins and inevitability. * * *

There has been no dominant organizing policy principle for the last two decades of environmental law. Rather, environmental policy has been decided on an ad hoc basis worked out through an ongoing struggle between two policy poles: preservationism and resourcism. Contemporary preservationism is guided by a consequentialist philosophy directed toward eliminating human interference with the environment. Resourcism might be thought of as the nihilist opposite of preservationism—eliminating environmental barriers to human pursuits. Because each principle in its polar form marginalizes either environment or humanity, neither is particularly useful in addressing environmental problems of the future, the common characteristic of which is the existence of intricate feedback cycles between the human and environmental conditions. For example, it will do little good to talk of protecting endangered species in highly-populated, poverty-stricken areas where basic daily human survival depends on extraction of water, fuelwood, and other resources from the environment. On the other hand, it will do little good in such areas to fail to address resource protection if the collapse of the resource base only worsens the human condition. By each focusing on only one side of that feedback cycle, preservationism and resourcism are fundamentally reductionist and thus doomed to miss the point more times than not.

A policy principle is needed that transcends the preservationism-resourcism dichotomy to address such complicated problems in an adaptive manner. The theme that is emerging, known as sustainable development, holds much promise in that respect. The literature attempting to define what sustainable development means and how to implement it as a coordinating policy principle is burgeoning. The prevailing definition of sustainable development at the international level comes from the 1987 Brundtland Report of the World Commission on Environment and Development: "[A] process of change in which the exploitation of resources, the direction of investments, the orientation of technological development and institutional change are all in harmony and enhance both current and future potential to meet human needs and aspirations."[13]

Further, we have learned from the President's Commission on Sustainable Development what these international ideals mean for the United States:

> A sustainable United States will have a growing economy that provides equitable opportunities for satisfying livelihoods and a safe, healthy, high quality of life for current and future generations. Our nation will protect its environment, its natural resource base, and the functions and viability of natural systems on which all life depends.[14]

It is no accident that these definitions eschew alignment with either the preservationism or resourcism orientations—terms such as sustainable growth and sustainable environment would not have transcended the debate. Sustainable development, however, implies that an economy can thrive and meet human needs without necessarily growing in the sense of increased throughput of resources. But it also implies that economic prosperity matters and that resources must be used to maintain social equity. Indeed, many diehard capitalists and environmentalists alike have begun to realize that the best business opportunity of the future is environmental sustainability and that the best environmental protection opportunity of the future is economic sustainability.

Sustainable development, the combination of economic and environmental sustainability, has always been a necessity. Usually, however, the reality of the need to practice sustainable development has only become apparent in advanced cases of localized unsustainable development. Cases of social collapse caused by unsustainable development abound in history. Today's movement to define sustainable development as an explicit policy tool is merely a reflection of the mounting reality that unsustainable development is becoming more likely in more settings, even to the point of being a global possibility. Sustainable development, in other words, must be a deliberate practice in today's world—a guiding principle for all social decisions. * * *

The emerging measure of environmental sustainability, known as biological diversity or biodiversity, has galvanized both the scientific and policy communities. The relatively new discipline of conservation biology tells us that biodiversity is the building block of conservation policy as the basic measure of ecosystem health. Regardless of whatever debate might exist over the rate of loss of biodiversity, it appears widely accepted that biodiversity provides a strong index of ecological sustainability and that we are generally experiencing more losses than gains globally. According-

---

13. World Comm'n on Env't & Dev., Our Common Future 46 (1987).

14. PRESIDENT'S COUNCIL ON SUSTAINABLE DEVELOPMENT, SUSTAINABLE AMERICA at i (1996) (quoting the Council's Vision Statement).

ly, programs such as the National Biological Information Infrastructure[15] and the Gap Analysis Program[16] are now used as means of improving environmental decision making by increasing the availability, uniformity, and scope of information regarding biodiversity. The new policy model that has emerged from the combination of those efforts is known as "ecosystem management".... [17]

In order to make information about biological diversity most useful to [ecosystem] management ..., a number of researchers have embarked on an effort to translate biological diversity information into hard data on the value of nature to the goal of sustainable development.... [They] are discovering that we can translate nature into its service values, such as the value of wild honeybee pollination to agriculture, of water filtering by wetlands, of carbon cycling by forests, and so on.

NOTE

The final paragraph of the foregoing excerpt introduces the concept of "ecosystem services." The services supplied by *soil*, for example, include: (1) buffering and moderation of the hydrological cycle, e.g., soaking up precipitation and gradually releasing it to plant roots and into underground aquifers and surface streams; (2) physical support of plants; (3) retention and delivery of nutrients to plants; (4) disposal of wastes and dead organic matter; (5) renewal of soil fertility, i.e., processing of wastes and dead organic matter by soil organisms to replenish nutrients necessary for plant production; and (6) regulation of major element cycles, e.g., of carbon, nitrogen and sulfur. Center for Resources Econs., NATURE'S SERVICES: SOCIETAL DEPENDENCE ON NATURAL ECOSYSTEMS 117 (Gretchen C. Daily ed., 1997).

2. ECOSYSTEM SERVICES

The following information, from Worldwatch Institute, STATE OF THE WORLD 1994, at 33 (1994),[18] identifies valuable services provided on a

---

15. The National Biological Information Infrastructure ("NBII") began in 1993 as a distinct bureau of the Department of the Interior known as the National Biological Survey. The program name later was changed to National Biological Service ("NBS"), and subsequent to that the program was merged into the United States Geological Survey ("USGS") as the Biological Resources Division ("BRD"). The NBII is a BRD-led initiative. The BRD was created by consolidating the biological research, inventory and monitoring, and information transfer programs of seven different Department of the Interior bureaus.

16. The Gap Analysis Program ("GAP") refers to a state-based cooperative program using Geographic Information Systems ("GIS") technology to map major indicators of biodiversity over states, along with the existing network of conservation lands. See A. Ross Kiester et al., *Conservation Prioritization Using GAP Data*, 10 CONSERV'N BIOL. 1332, 1333 (1996).

17. For excellent overviews of the ecosystem management philosophy, including its application through adaptive management techniques, *see* The Keystone Ctr., THE KEYSTONE NATIONAL POLICY DIALOGUE ON ECOSYSTEM MANAGEMENT 5–22; Steven L. Yaffee et al., ECOSYSTEM MANAGEMENT IN THE UNITED STATES 35–38 (1996); R. Edward Grumbine, *Reflections on "What is Ecosystem Management?"*, 11 CONSERV'N BIOL. 41, 41–42 (1997); R. Edward Grumbine, *What Is Ecosystem Management?*, 8 CONSERV'N BIOL. 27, 28, 31 (1994).

18. Copyright © 1994, Worldwatch Institute. Reprinted by permission of W.W. Norton & Co., Inc.

continuing basis by forest ecosystems. The material after the list explores this concept in greater depth.

Economic Services Provided by Intact Forest Ecosystems

Gene pool: Forests contain a diversity of species, habitats, and genes that is probably their most valuable asset; it is also the most difficult to measure. They provide the gene pool that can protect commercial plant strains against pests and changing conditions of climate and soil and can provide the raw material for breeding higher-yielding strains. The wild relatives of avocado, banana, cashew, cacao, cinnamon, coconut, coffee, grapefruit, lemon, paprika, oil palm, rubber, and vanilla—exports of which were worth more than $20 billion in 1991—are found in tropical forests.

Water: Forests absorb rainwater and release it gradually into streams, preventing flooding and extending water availability into dry months when it is most needed. Some 40 percent of Third World farmers depend on forested watersheds for water to irrigate crops or water livestock. In India, forests provide water regulation and flood control valued at $72 billion per year.

Watershed: Forests keep soil from eroding into rivers. Siltation of reservoirs costs the world economy about $6 billion per year in lost hydroelectricity and irrigation water.

Fisheries: Forests protect fisheries in rivers, lakes, estuaries, and coastal waters. Three fourths of fish sold in the markets of Manaus, Brazil, are nurtured in seasonally flooded *varzea* forests, where they feed on fruits and plants. The viability of 112 stocks of salmon and other fish in the Pacific Northwest depends on natural, old-growth forests; the region's salmon fishery is a $1–billion industry.

Climate: Forests stabilize climate. Tropical deforestation releases the greenhouse gases carbon dioxide, methane, and nitrous oxide, and accounts for 25 percent of the net warming effect of all greenhouse gas emissions. Replacing the carbon storage function of all tropical forests would cost an estimated $3.7 trillion—equal to the gross national product of Japan.

Recreation: Forests serve people directly for recreation. The U.S. Forest Service calculates that in eight of its nine administrative regions, the recreation, fish, wildlife, and other nonextractive benefits of national forests are more valuable than timber, grazing, mining, and other commodities.

JAMES E. SALZMAN, VALUING ECOSYSTEM SERVICES[19]

24 ECOLOGY L. Q. 887, 888–896 (1997).

* * * The primary reason that ecosystem services are taken for granted ... is that they are free. We explicitly value and place dollar

---

19. Copyright © 1997, Ecology Law Quarterly. Reprinted by permission.

figures on "ecosystem goods" such as timber and fish. Yet the services underpinning these goods generally have no market value—not because they are worthless, but rather because there is no market to capture and express their value directly.

Although awareness of ecosystem services dates back to Plato, only recently have ecologists and economists begun systematically examining the contribution of ecosystem services to social welfare. An important synthesis, entitled *Nature's Services: Societal Dependence on Natural Ecosystems*, has just been written for the general public. Edited by Stanford biologist Gretchen Daily, the book presents one of the first rigorous attempts to identify the range of ecosystem services and to value objectively the services in dollars. * * *

* * * The tough decisions revolve not around whether protecting ecosystems is a good thing but, rather, how much we should protect and at what cost. For example, how would the flood control and water purification services of a particular forest be diminished by the clearcutting or selective logging of 10%, 20% or 30% of its area? At what point does the ecosystem's net value to humans diminish, and by how much? Can the degradation of these services (in addition to ecosystem goods) be accurately measured? And, if so, how can partial loss of these services be balanced against benefits provided by development or pollution?

One might argue that ecosystem services cannot be evaluated, but this is clearly incorrect. We implicitly assess the value of these services every time we choose to protect or degrade the environment. The fundamental question is whether our implicit valuation of ecosystem services is accurate, and if not, what should be done about it. Indeed, studies such as *Nature's Services* indicate that our valuations are grossly and systematically understated.* * *

So how does one value an ecosystem? Assume our object of study is a wetland along the banks of the Potomac. The first step lies in defining the ecosystem's contribution to human well-being. An ecosystem may be characterized by its physical features (site-specific characteristics such as landscape context, vegetation type, salinity), its goods (vegetation, fish), its services (nutrient cycling, water retention) or its amenities (recreation, bird-watching). These four aspects may not be complementary. For example, one could manage a wetland for cranberry production at the expense of primary productivity and services. Furthermore, the location determines the distribution of goods and services. An ecosystem's carbon sequestration and biodiversity will be valuable even if distant from human populations, but its role in pollination and flood control likely will not. Thus two identical ecosystems may have very different values depending on their landscape context.

Economists classify these characteristics using four categories. The most obvious category includes consumable ecosystem goods such as cranberries and crabs that are exchanged in markets and easily priced (direct market uses). Activities such as hiking and fishing (direct non-market uses) as well as more intangible existence and option values (non-market, non-use) are not exchanged in markets. As a result, their values must be determined indirectly by shadow pricing techniques such as hedonic pricing, travel-cost methodologies, or contingent valuation. Ecosystem services are categorized as indirect non-market uses, for while they provide clear benefits to humans they are neither directly "consumed" nor exchanged in markets. These are also classic public goods because their use cannot be exclusively controlled.

How does one measure dollar figures for indirect non-market resources—ecosystem services—which may have the greatest value of all the economic categories? A recent investment choice made by the city of New York provides one elegant example. The watershed of the Catskills mountains provides New York City's primary source for drinking water. Water is purified as it percolates through the watershed's soil and vegetation. Recently, however, this water failed EPA standards for drinking water, due both to habitat degradation in the Catskills from development, and to increased sewage, pesticides, and fertilizers. New York faced two starkly different choices as to how to obtain large quantities of clean water. It could invest in physical capital, building a water purification plant with a capital cost of $4 billion plus operating expenses. Or, it could invest in natural capital at a much lower cost, restoring the integrity of the Catskills watershed through land acquisition and restoration. Choosing the latter option, last year New York floated an "environmental bond issue" to raise just over $660 million. The cost of restoring the ecosystem service of water purification provided a payback period of five to seven years as well as increased flood protection at no extra charge. The lesson: investments in natural capital can be more financially profitable than those in physical capital.

In many ways, the Catskills example offers an ideal measure of the worth of an ecosystem service. Replacement cost provides an effective method for valuing services because one can compare dollar investments in natural capital and physical capital to determine payback periods and overall costs. Unfortunately, ecosystem services rarely are identified so easily or valued at a local scale. Direct comparisons between manufactured services and ecosystem services break down very quickly as one moves from supplying clean water for New Yorkers to services that are not discretely purchased, such as nutrient cycling or climate regulation. Although functioning markets do not exist for these services, one could imagine calculating the value of an ecosystem service such as carbon sequestration through payments for joint implementation [e.g., under the Climate Change Convention, payments by CO_2 emitters in the U.S. to finance reforestation in Costa Rica]. Similarly, one could imagine insurance companies funding conservation of forest habitat for its flood prevention qualities. Each of these would provide a lower-bound dollar figure for services, but such market developments seem unlikely anytime soon.

Currently, there are three challenges to incorporating benefits of ecosystem services more directly into decisionmaking: identifying services on a local scale, measuring the value of these services, and projecting their future value. First, ecologists must understand the services provided by a specific ecosystem.... But in most cases, our scientific knowledge is inadequate to predict with any certainty how specific local actions affecting these factors will impact the local ecosystem services themselves. * * *

As noted above, ecosystem services rarely are exchanged in functioning markets or have readily determined replacement costs. As a result, ecologists face a second challenge in deducing the monetary value of these services from non-market valuation techniques. Contingent valuation (CV), also known as willingness-to-pay, is an important valuation method in the regulations that implement the Oil Pollution Act's provisions for natural resource damages. In the context of ecosystem services, CV suffers from a number of serious shortcomings. Most important, polling people's willingness to pay to preserve specific ecosystems assumes a knowledge of the services provided. Given the difficulties ecologists face in quantifying services provided by discrete ecosystems, it is specious to assume John and Mary Doe have an informed idea of ecosystem services, much less in a site-specific context. This information gap limits the application of CV to ecosystem services. Alternative shadow pricing techniques such as hedonic pricing and travel cost methods are equally inapt in valuing ecosystem services. The EPA is currently wrestling with this problem and has requested counsel from its Science Advisory Board. * * *

Despite these difficulties, let us assume we understand fully the ecosystem service and have determined its current value. Even then, we face a third challenge when we try to determine in dollars the *future stream* of services flowing from the current biophysical features and landscape of the ecosystem. This figure is important because the net present value of most proposed actions that will degrade an ecosystem, such as shopping mall developments, take into account future streams of income. To ensure a full accounting of costs and benefits, the future "income" flow of the ecosystem service should be factored into its current value as well, since that value may change over time due to land-use patterns, weather, pollution, etc.

NOTES

1. Does translating ecosystem services into dollar terms carry the risk of encouraging people to think of the environment as just another commodity to be exploited? What about the alternative method of contingent valuation, also described in the excerpt? On the other hand, if we don't find some way of attaching a dollar value to the environment, how do we go about deciding how much of an economic sacrifice to make in order to preserve the environment?

2. Also note the problem of computing the "present value" of environmental services by "discounting." Since the costs of resolving environmental problems are often incurred today, while important benefits may be decades or more in the future, the temporal mismatch is often a crucial problem in making policy determinations. Discounting, in effect, treats future benefits

(especially those long in the future, such as those to future generations) as being much less important than current ones. Is this ethically appropriate? If not, what is the alternative?

3. For further discussion of the ecosystem services approach, *see* the Symposium in 20 STAN. ENVTL. L.J. 309–536 (2001), and James Salzman, *Creating Markets for Ecosystem Services: Notes from the Field,* 80 N.Y.U. L. REV. 870 (2005).

4. Ruhl stresses the high level of scientific uncertainty surrounding environmental issues. How can we regulate in a sensible way when we are unsure about the causes of a problem and unclear about the appropriate cure? Would it help to use presumptions, and if so, what presumptions would be appropriate—"leave nature alone until you have enough information to know what you're doing" or "don't interfere with the free economy until you have enough information to justify regulation"? Who should have the burden of proof, regulators or industry?

5. We will return to ecological issues in Chapter 3, which covers the Endangered Species Act in detail. Many of the regulations that we will consider in this book, however, focus on protection of human health rather than of ecosystems. Thus, much of environmental law is dominated by concern over public health, which we discuss in Chapter 2.

C. THE ENVIRONMENT AS COMMONS

Because of the uncertainties associated with complex systems, responding to an environmental problem like global warming or toxic pollutants would be difficult in any event. But the difficulties are compounded by the need for collective action by multiple actors. Similarly, pollution typically comes from multiple sources and affects numerous individuals, and a solution must involve many individuals and firms. Environmental issues do not merely present scientific problems; they also present major problems of institutional design. This section considers these collective action problems and their possible solutions.

1. THE THEORY OF THE COMMONS

Many medieval and early modern villages had a "commons" where all of the peasants were entitled to graze their animals. (To this day, Boston has a "commons" that now functions as a park.) This history became the basis for an important approach to conceptualizing environmental problems. In a classic article,[20] Garrett Hardin explained what he called the tragedy of the commons:

> The tragedy of the commons develops in this way. Picture a pasture open to all. It is to be expected that each herdsman will try to keep as many cattle as possible on the commons. Such an arrangement may work reasonably satisfactorily for centuries because tribal wars,

---

20. Garrett Hardin, *The Tragedy of the Commons,* 162 SCIENCE 1243, 1244–1245 (1968).

poaching, and disease keep the numbers of both man and beast well below the carrying capacity of the land. Finally, however, comes the day of reckoning, that is, the day when the long-desired goal of social stability becomes a reality. At this point, the inherent logic of the commons remorselessly generates tragedy.

Rationally, each herdsman seeks to graze as many cattle as possible on the commons, because he gets the full benefit of selling each additional animal but suffers only a fraction of the harm to the pasture caused by the additional grazing. The result is individually rational but collectively tragic:

> Adding together the component partial utilities, the rational herdsman concludes that the only sensible course for him to pursue is to add another animal to his herd. And another; and another * * *. But this is the conclusion reached by each and every rational herdsman sharing a commons. Therein is the tragedy. Each man is locked into a system that compels him to increase his herd without limit in a world that is limited. Ruin is the destination toward which all men rush, each pursuing his own best interest in a society that believes in the freedom of the commons. Freedom in a commons brings ruin to all.

As examples, Hardin pointed to overgrazing on federally owned Western lands by ranchers and overuse of the national parks by an increasing number of tourists. He also observed that pollution is a kind of "reverse" commons issue:

> In a reverse way, the tragedy of the commons reappears in problems of pollution. Here it is not a question of taking something out of the commons, but of putting something in—sewage, or chemical, radio-active, and heat wastes into water; noxious and dangerous fumes into the air; and distracting and unpleasant advertising signs into the line of sight. The calculations of utility are much the same as before. The rational man finds that his share of the cost of the wastes he discharges into the commons is less than the cost of purifying his wastes before releasing them. Since this is true for everyone, we are locked into a system of "fouling our own nest," so long as we behave only as independent, rational, free-enterprisers.

> The tragedy of the commons as a food basket is averted by private property, or something formally like it. But the air and waters surrounding us cannot readily be fenced, and so the tragedy of the commons as a cesspool must be prevented by different means, by coercive laws or taxing devices that make it cheaper for the polluter to treat his pollutants than to discharge them untreated. We have not progressed as far with the solution of this problem as we have with the first. Indeed, our particular concept of private property, which deters us from exhausting the positive resources of the earth, favors pollution. The owner of a factory on the bank of a stream—whose property extends to the middle of the stream—often has difficulty

seeing why it is not his natural right to muddy the waters flowing past his door. The law, always behind the times, requires elaborate stitching and fitting to adapt it to this newly perceived aspect of the commons.

Fisheries are a classic commons problem. See Stephanie F. McWhinnie, *The Tragedy of the Commons in International Fisheries*, 57 J. ENV. ECON. & MANAGEMENT 321 (2009). One effort to fence the commons was the Magnuson Fishery Conservation and Management Act, enacted in 1976 and extending the territorial limits of the United States from 6 to 200 miles into the oceans. 16 U.S.C. section 1801 Rule 3.4(b). After opposing such claims by other nations for years, the United States joined the trend in 1976 because fisheries off our Atlantic and Pacific coasts had been seriously depleted by foreign trawlers.

The Magnuson Act not only established a 200–mile exclusive economic zone of the United States, but also created regional fishery councils and charged them with rebuilding depleted fish stocks. The eight regional councils were dominated by local fishing interests and authorized to allocate to boat owners transferable rights to catch specified amounts of fish. In effect, collective fishing rights were privatized and distributed as windfalls to current boat owners, rather than, for example, being auctioned off to the highest bidders with proceeds going to the federal treasury.

The intent was that the councils would limit fishing rights sufficiently so that stocks would have the opportunity to recover. In some regions, at least, it did not work out that way. Excessive numbers of rights were allocated. The result was a catastrophic decline in the numbers of salmon in the Pacific Northwest and of cod, haddock, and flounder off the New England coast. *See* Timothy Egan, *Fishing Fleet Trawling Seas That Yield Many Fewer Fish,* N.Y. TIMES, Mar. 7, 1994, at A1. Late in 1994, upon recommendation of the New England Fishery Council, the U.S. Department of Commerce issued an emergency order closing three prime Atlantic fishing grounds, encompassing about 6,600 square miles of ocean, to virtually all commercial fishing. The order also banned the use, in other New England waters, of nets with mesh sizes smaller than six inches. *See Three Depleted Fishing Grounds Ordered Closed,* L.A. TIMES, Dec. 8, 1994, at A18.

The Magnuson Act was reauthorized and amended by the 1996 Sustainable Fisheries Act, Pub. L. No. 104–297, 110 Stat. 3559 (1996). For an illuminating analysis of reasons for the failure of the 1976 Magnuson Act, and an explanation of some of the improvements and shortcomings of the 1996 Act, *see* David A. Dana, *Overcoming the Political Tragedy of the Commons: Lessons Learned from the Reauthorization of the Magnuson Act,* 24 ECOLOGY L.Q. 833 (1997). The statute gave rise to hundreds of lawsuits challenging fishing regulations for giving too little weight to economic impact. *See* Kristen M. Fletcher, *When Economics and Conservation Clash: Challenges to Economic Analysis in Fisheries Management,* 31

Envtl. L. Rep. 11,168 (2001). Despite the statute, fisheries seem increasingly imperiled.

2.   THE PRISONER'S DILEMMA

The tragedy of the commons can be considered a special case of what game theorists call a prisoner's. dilemma. This scenario gets its name from the following illustrative story.

Consider two prisoners, charged with being involved in the same crime but held in different rooms. The prosecutor gives each of them the following information: "(a) If neither of you confesses, I will charge you both with a lesser crime that I can easily prove, resulting in two-year sentences for each. (b) If you both confess, you will each get a three-year sentence. (c) If only one of you confesses, that person will get a one-year sentence and the other will get a four-year sentence." Each prisoner reasons as follows: "Either the other person will confess or not. If the other person does confess, I will get a three-year sentence if I confess but a four-year sentence if I don't. So if the other person confesses, I should do the same. If the other person doesn't confess, I will get a one-year sentence if I do confess and a two-year sentence if I don't, so the best move is to confess. Thus, no matter what the other person does, I will be better off if I confess." Following the same reasoning, the other prisoner also confesses, and they both get three-year sentences. This is the "rational" outcome. But notice that if the prisoners could somehow count on each other, neither would confess, and they would get only two-year sentences. So the individually rational set of actions leads to an inferior outcome in terms of their group welfare.

Climate change is an apt illustration of this dilemma. Consider the situation of Freedonia, a hypothetical average country. If the rest of the world fails to address the greenhouse effect, Freedonia can do little on its own, and therefore shouldn't bother. If everyone else does take action to control the greenhouse effect, Freedonia can contribute only slight additional help but will have to spend a lot of money to do so. So if everyone else "does the right thing," Freedonia should take a "free ride" on their efforts rather than wasting its own resources to minimal effect. Thus, no matter what the rest of the world does, Freedonia is better off to do nothing. Reasoning the same way, every country in the world decides to take no action.

Yet, all might be better off if they could somehow make an enforceable deal to cooperate. But such deals are difficult to negotiate and enforce on the international level, because the prisoner's dilemma takes hold again: each individual country has an incentive to sit out the negotiations and let everyone else make a deal; once a deal is made, each country has an incentive to breach the agreement and allow others to bear the costs of carrying it out.

The upshot is that, in the absence of some mechanism for making and enforcing cooperative agreements, each nation may find inaction to be the only sensible individual choice, even though everyone also knows that collective inaction will only lead to disaster. Within individual nations, the central government can lead the way out of prisoner's dilemmas by forcing a cooperative solution. (As we will see in Chapter 4, however, even a strong central government, like that in the United States, may find practical and legal obstacles to solving the prisoner's dilemma.) In the international sphere, the problem is more difficult, but as we will see in the following note, some progress has been made.

The prisoner's dilemma stands as a significant barrier to addressing the greenhouse effect, as does the remaining scientific uncertainty about the scope of the problem. What strategies could be used to overcome these barriers to agreement?

The prisoner's dilemma poses a considerable barrier to international environmental regulation. Indeed, given the formidable barriers, we do not seem to have a good explanation for why international environmental regulation has been implemented *at all*:

> [T]he standard positive political theories provide an even weaker explanation of the origin of global environmental regulation than of national environmental regulation. The beneficiaries of global environmental quality are even more diffuse and latent than their national counterparts, suggesting an even greater public choice bias against regulation at the global level. Meanwhile, civic republican discourse is even more limited at the international level because of the vastly large scale of the polity, the greater diversity of cultures involved, and the more market-like rhetoric of international treaty negotiation. The origin of environmental regulation is thus even more difficult to explain at the global level than at the national level. Moreover, the voting rule for adopting international law requires the voluntary assent of every party to be bound, rather than the majoritarian voting rule provided for national legislation in most countries. The voluntary assent voting rule makes adopting regulation a cooperation game rather than a coercive enterprise, and thus raises the hurdles to be surmounted in order to adopt broadly applicable regulation. In sum, the establishment of global environmental regulation should be (nearly) impossible—a conclusion apparently belied by reality.

Jonathan Baert Wiener, *On the Political Economy of Global Environmental Regulation*, 87 GEO. L.J. 749, 750 (1999). For this reason, Wiener concludes, "current theories are inadequate to explain the origin and content of global environmental regulation." But perhaps, as the next excerpt discusses, the tragedy of the commons is less inexorable than Hardin believed.

FRED P. BOSSELMAN, REPLAYING THE TRAGEDY OF THE COMMONS[21]

13 YALE J. ON REG. 391 (1996).

Few metaphorical creatures have had the rhetorical force of Hardin's poor peasants and their cattle. Most of the popular environmental law casebooks quote at length from Hardin's essay and, like many law teachers, I have frequently used it to introduce basic concepts of environmental law. Recently I realized with some embarrassment that I had never bothered to ask whether anyone had actually checked the health of cows that graze on common lands. I had simply assumed that the facts supported Hardin's seemingly unexceptionable thesis.

Yet Hardin's thesis has been challenged by recent studies of the management of ancient English common lands. These studies question whether the enclosure of common lands increased overall efficiency, as had long been assumed, and suggest instead that pre-enclosure management of common lands may have been much more efficient than previously believed. Model building experiments have raised similar questions about whether the medieval commons were the economic disaster postulated by Hardin's essay.

But the value of Hardin's thesis rests not in the historical accuracy of the metaphor but in the logic of his reasoning, which can be tested in its modern application. In the last decade, however, as researchers have begun to study commonly-owned property more carefully, they have found a lot of fat and happy cattle (and their symbolic equivalents) grazing on commons. Was Hardin wrong?

Rules, Games, and Common–Pool Resources (hereinafter Rules/ Games) by Elinor Ostrom and various co-authors, is a progress report on the efforts of scholars in a variety of fields to explain how the management of common lands actually works.[22] It follows Ostrom's earlier book, *Governing the Commons*,[23] and I hope that it will be followed in its turn by further and equally helpful reports on her ongoing research into common property management. * * *

The authors' overall conclusions * * * derive primarily from their analysis of the field studies rather than the game simulations. The authors conclude that certain rules seem to be essential to the optimal management of common property resources. First and foremost is the existence of strict limits on the number of persons who may use the resource. These "boundary rules" exist in all successful systems of common property management, although the rules are not always formally adopted.

---

21. Copyright Yale Law School. Reprinted with permission.

22. Elinor Ostrom et al., RULES, GAMES, AND COMMON-POOL RESOURCES (1994).

23. Elinor Ostrom, GOVERNING THE COMMONS: THE EVOLUTION OF INSTITUTIONS FOR COLLECTIVE ACTION (1990).

In a sense, therefore, Ostrom's study confirms the logic behind Hardin's theory while rejecting the appropriateness of his specific metaphor. Hardin hypothesized a commons "open to all" on which an unlimited number of English peasants could graze an unlimited number of cattle. Historically, however, such a commons never existed. Under the common law, the right to graze cattle on the common was limited to individuals who had actual grants or prescriptive servitudes, and to the residents of a locality who by custom had traditionally grazed their cattle there in the past. Furthermore, people's ability to move from one English rural community to another was also limited by both practical and legal restrictions.

Ostrom and her co-authors also emphasize that rules promoting internal communication among resource users are a key element in the development and maintenance of successful common-property management systems. Such communication makes it possible for users informally to monitor and enforce rules for the utilization of the resource. The results of the game simulations reinforce this conclusion by suggesting that communication can be far more effective than traditional game theory would predict.

More tentatively, the authors identify two characteristics of common-property resources that can be most successfully managed: (1) resources that are stationary rather than mobile; and (2) resources that can be stored, rather than having to be used at once or lost. For example, water in an underground basin is both stationary and subject to being stored, while migratory fish in an ocean are much more mobile and difficult to store. Stationary resources can more easily be limited to users within a particular geographic area, thus underscoring the importance of boundary limits noted earlier. The ability to store the resource apparently makes it easier to devise acceptable methods of allocating rights among a group of users whose access to the resource may vary over time.

Ostrom's study of common-pool resources draws on a growing body of empirical research into current conditions in countries where common lands are the norm.[24] In the 1980s, the institutions that finance development and conservation activities in third world countries began to express interest in these research results. Many of these countries had traditionally relied on common land as an important element in the local economy. Attempts by outside institutions to intervene in these countries without understanding the existing systems by which common lands were managed sometimes proved counterproductive.

In 1985, the National Research Council of the National Academies of Science and Engineering brought together a Panel on Common Property Resource Management to "assess systematically differing institutional

---

24. *See, e.g.,* Piers Blaikie & Harold Brookfield, LAND DEGRADATION AND SOCIETY (1987); Daniel W. Bromley, ECONOMIC INTERESTS AND INSTITUTIONS: THE CONCEPTUAL FOUNDATIONS OF PUBLIC POLICY (1989); COMMON PROPERTY RESOURCES: ECOLOGY AND COMMUNITY-BASED SUSTAINABLE DEVELOPMENT (Firket Berkes ed., 1989); THE QUESTION OF THE COMMONS (Bonnie J. McCay & James M. Acheson eds., 1987); Jeffrey A. McNeely, *Common Property Resource Management or Government Ownership: Improving the Conservation of Biological Resources,* 10 INT'L REL. 211 (1991).

arrangements for the effective conservation and utilization of jointly managed resources."[25] The participants looked not only at common lands but water resources and "other jointly held resources that constitute the global commons." Ostrom's work on that panel was the foundation for her continuing research.

When Ostrom began her research into common-pool resources, she found that scholars from many disciplines had been studying the management of such resources with little awareness of similar work that was taking place in other fields. In preparing her 1990 book, Ostrom looked at hundreds of such studies and formulated some tentative hypotheses for identifying successful common property management systems.

The timeliness of this research is particularly apparent as we witness the breakdown of many common resource systems. For example, the rapid and continuing decline in the world's ocean fisheries is causing violent confrontations among otherwise peaceful countries, and in places like Albania, the depletion of agricultural resources is contributing to famine and mass migration.

Legal scholars are gradually beginning to realize the valuable implications of multidisciplinary research into common property resource management. Some of the early legal research addressed the issue of common rights to land and water under the English common law and the potential application of these common law concepts to modern problems. In addition, studies like Robert Ellickson's *Order Without Law* have focused on the ways in which cohesive groups are able to manage potential property-right conflicts through the development of informal norms.[26] Like Ostrom's work, some of these studies conclude that success is achievable by a well-defined user group that anticipates its own permanence and develops good internal communication abilities. Most scholars who have analyzed these empirical studies have found no reliable correlation between any particular property rights regime and the maintenance of sustainable resources.

Outside of academia, procedural changes in legal systems parallel the research results. Proposals that stress the importance of the participation of well-defined interest groups in negotiated rulemaking involve a similar emphasis on clearly-bounded group participation. And dispute resolution mechanisms that train facilitators to encourage informal communication among potential adversaries within local communities underline the importance of communication networks in developing and implementing informal norms.

3. THE CASE OF GLOBAL CLIMATE CHANGE

Collective action problems may be particularly severe for climate change, a classic commons problem. See Daniel H. Cole, *Climate Change*

---

25. National Research Council, PROCEEDINGS OF THE CONFERENCE ON COMMON PROPERTY RESOURCE MANAGEMENT vii (1985).

26. Robert C. Ellickson, ORDER WITHOUT LAW: HOW NEIGHBORS SETTLE DISPUTES (1991).

and Collective Action, 61 Current Legal problems 229 (2008). This section provides background on the climate change issue and the current policy choices facing the United States.

In 2007, the United Nation's Intergovernmental Panel on Climate Change issued its fourth assessment on climate change and by far its least equivocal. The IPCC consists of the IPCC Plenary (often referred to as "the Panel"), and three Working Groups with clearly defined mandates.[27] The Panel has sometimes been described as a body dominated more by politics than science because it is open to national delegations from all United Nations Environment Programme (UNEP) and World Meteorological Organization (WMO) member states.[28]

The Panel elects the IPCC Chairman and members of the IPCC Bureau, who have significant authority in overseeing the assessment report process, and it decides on the scope and outline of all Reports. While lead authors and coordinating lead authors have exclusive responsibility for drafting the Reports, the IPCC process includes a review of both the first and second drafts. The first draft review is experts-only, but the review of the second draft includes both expert and governmental comments. IPCC procedures require lead authors to take "into account government and expert comments" when preparing a final draft.[29] In addition, the IPCC procedures require the national delegations from member states to provide line-by-line approval of each Assessment Report's Executive Summary and Summary for Policy Makers (SPM). IPCC procedures require consensus for *each line*.[30] As a result, the process is both deeply consensual and deeply political, leading some to be concerned that there the Report understates risks in order to garner agreement.

The result of that process is excerpted here.

INTERGOVERNMENTAL PANEL ON CLIMATE CHANGE, SYNTHESIS (FOURTH ASSESSMENT REPORT)

United Nations 2007.

Warming of the climate system is unequivocal, as is now evident from observations of increases in global average air and ocean

---

27. Intergovernmental Panel on Climate Change, *About IPCC: How the IPCC is Organized*, http://www.ipcc.ch/about/how-the-ipcc-is-organized.htm (last visited June 24, 2008).

28. *See* Bernd Siebenhüner, *The Changing Role of Nation States in International Environmental Assessments—the Case of the IPCC*, 13 Global Environmental Change 113, 118 (2003) (characterizing the Plenary in terms of "political dominance" while describing the IPCC's subject-specific Working Groups which are open to government representatives but largely dominated by scientists, in terms of a "[b]alance between science and politics.") By comparison, the authors of the Working Group reports (which go into the IPCC Assessment Reports) are exclusively derived from the scientific community, and are characterized by "[S]cientific Dominance." *Id.*

29. *See* International Panel on Climate Change, *Principles Governing IPCC Work, Appendix A: Procedures for the Preparation, Review, Acceptance, Adoption, and Publication of IPCC Reports*, amended November 6–7, 2003, 4.2.4.2, 4.2.5, *available at* http://ipcc.cac.es/pdf/ipcc-principles/ipcc-principles-appendix-a.pdf.

30. If consensus is unattainable, dissenting views are noted in the report. *See* Knut H. Alfsen and Tora Skovdin, Center for International Climate and Environmental Research Policy Note 1998:3: *The Intergovernmental Panel and Climate*, 12–13, *available at* http://www.cicero.uio.no/media/49.pdf.

temperatures, widespread melting of snow and ice and rising global average sea level.

Eleven of the last twelve years (1995–2006) rank among the twelve warmest years in the instrumental record of global surface temperature (since 1850). * * * The linear warming trend over the 50 years from 1956 to 2005 (0.13 [0.10 to 0.16]°C per decade) is nearly twice that for the 100 years from 1906 to 2005.

The temperature increase is widespread over the globe and is greater at higher northern latitudes. Average Arctic temperatures have increased at almost twice the global average rate in the past 100 years. Land regions have warmed faster than the ocean. Observations since 1961 show that the average temperature of the global ocean has increased to depths of at least 3000m and that the ocean has been taking up over 80% of the heat being added to the climate system. New analyses of balloon-borne and satellite measurements of lower- and mid-tropospheric temperature show warming rates similar to those observed in surface temperature.

* * * Observational evidence from all continents and most oceans shows that many natural systems are being affected by regional climate changes, particularly temperature increases.

There is *high confidence* that natural systems related to snow, ice and frozen ground (including permafrost) are affected. Examples are:

• enlargement and increased numbers of glacial lakes

• increasing ground instability in permafrost regions and rock avalanches in mountain regions

• changes in some Arctic and Antarctic ecosystems, including those in sea-ice biomes, and predators at high levels of the food web.

Based on growing evidence, there is *high confidence* that the following effects on hydrological systems are occurring: increased runoff and earlier spring peak discharge in many glacier- and snow-fed rivers, and warming of lakes and rivers in many regions, with effects on thermal structure and water quality. * * *

Changes in the atmospheric concentrations of GHGs and aerosols, land cover and solar radiation alter the energy balance of the climate system and are drivers of climate change. They affect the absorption, scattering and emission of radiation within the atmosphere and at the Earth's surface. The resulting positive or negative changes in energy balance due to these factors are expressed as radiative forcing, which is used to compare warming or cooling influences on global climate.

Human activities result in emissions of four long-lived GHGs: CO_2, methane (CH_4), nitrous oxide (N_2O) and halocarbons (a group of gases containing fluorine, chlorine or bromine). Atmospheric concentrations of GHGs increase when emissions are larger than removal processes.

Global atmospheric concentrations of CO_2, CH_4 and N_2O have increased markedly as a result of human activities since 1750 and now far exceed pre-industrial values determined from ice cores spanning many thousands of years. The atmospheric concentrations of CO and CH_4 in 2005 exceed by far the natural range over the last 650,000 years. Global increases in CO concentrations are due primarily to fossil fuel use, with land-use change providing another significant but smaller contribution. It is *very likely* that the observed increase in CH_4 concentration is predominantly due to agriculture and fossil fuel use. The increase in N_2O concentration is primarily due to agriculture.

The global atmospheric concentration of CO increased from a pre-industrial value of about 280ppm to 379ppm in 2005. The annual CO_2 concentration growth rate was larger during the last 10 years (1995–2005 average: 1.9ppm per year) than it has been since the beginning of continuous direct atmospheric measurements (1960–2005 average: 1.4ppm per year), although there is year-to year variability in growth rates.

The global atmospheric concentration of CH has increased from a pre-industrial value of about 715ppb to 1732ppb in the early 1990s, and was 1774ppb in 2005. Growth rates have declined since the early 1990s, consistent with total emissions (sum of anthropogenic and natural sources) being nearly constant during this period. The global atmospheric NO concentration increased from a pre-industrial value of about 270ppb to 319ppb in 2005. Many halocarbons (including hydrofluorocarbons) have increased from a near-zero pre-industrial background concentration, primarily due to human activities.

There is very high confidence that the global average net effect of human activities since 1750 has been one of warming...

The equilibrium climate sensitivity is a measure of the climate system response to sustained radiative forcing. It is defined as the equilibrium global average surface warming following a doubling of CO_2 concentration. Progress since the TAR enables an assessment that climate sensitivity is *likely* to be in the range of 2 to 4.5°C with a best estimate of about 3°C, and is *very unlikely* to be less than 1.5°C. Values substantially higher than 4.5°C cannot be excluded, but agreement of models with observations is not as good for those values.

Feedbacks can amplify or dampen the response to a given forcing. Direct emission of water vapour (a greenhouse gas) by human activities makes a negligible contribution to radiative forcing. However, as global average temperature increases, tropospheric water vapour concentrations increase and this represents a key positive feedback but not a forcing of climate change. Water vapour changes represent the largest feedback affecting equilibrium climate sensitivity and are now better understood.... Cloud feedbacks remain the largest source of uncertainty. Spatial patterns of climate response are largely controlled by climate processes and feedbacks. For example, sea-ice albedo feedbacks tend to enhance the high latitude response.

Warming reduces terrestrial and ocean uptake of atmospheric CO_2, increasing the fraction of anthropogenic emissions remaining in the atmosphere. This positive carbon cycle feedback leads to larger atmospheric CO_2 increases and greater climate change for a given emissions scenario, but the strength of this feedback effect varies markedly among models.
* * *

Continued GHG emissions at or above current rates would cause further warming and induce many changes in the global climate system during the 21st century that would very likely be larger than those observed during the 20th century.

Projected warming in the 21st century shows scenario-independent geographical patterns similar to those observed over the past several decades. Warming is expected to be greatest over land and at most high northern latitudes, and least over the Southern Ocean (near Antarctica) and northern North Atlantic, continuing recent observed trends.

Snow cover area is projected to contract. Widespread increases in thaw depth are projected over most permafrost regions. Sea ice is projected to shrink in both the Arctic and Antarctic under all SRES scenarios. In some projections, Arctic late-summer sea ice disappears almost entirely by the latter part of the 21st century.

It is *very likely* that hot extremes, heat waves and heavy precipitation events will become more frequent.

Based on a range of models, it is *likely* that future tropical cyclones (typhoons and hurricanes) will become more intense, with larger peak wind speeds and more heavy precipitation associated with ongoing increases of tropical sea-surface temperatures. There is less confidence in projections of a global decrease in numbers of tropical cyclones. The apparent increase in the proportion of very intense storms since 1970 in some regions is much larger than simulated by current models for that period.

Extra-tropical storm tracks are projected to move poleward, with consequent changes in wind, precipitation and temperature patterns, continuing the broad pattern of observed trends over the last half-century.
* * *

Warming of the climate system is unequivocal, as is now evident from observations of increases in global average air and ocean temperatures, widespread melting of snow and ice and rising global average sea level.

Many natural systems, on all continents and in some oceans, are being affected by regional climate changes. Observed changes in many physical and biological systems are consistent with warming. As a result of the uptake of anthropogenic CO_2 since 1750, the acidity of the surface ocean has increased.

Global total annual anthropogenic GHG emissions, weighted by their 100–year GWPs, have grown by 70% between 1970 and 2004. As a result of anthropogenic emissions, atmospheric concentrations of N_2O now far exceed pre-industrial values spanning many thousands of years, and those of CH_4 and CO_2 now far exceed the natural range over the last 650,000 years.

Most of the global average warming over the past 50 years is *very likely* due to anthropogenic GHG increases and it is *likely* that there is a discernible human-induced warming averaged over each continent (except Antarctica).

Anthropogenic warming over the last three decades has *likely* had a discernible influence at the global scale on observed changes in many physical and biological systems.

Climate data coverage remains limited in some regions and there is a notable lack of geographic balance in data and literature on observed changes in natural and managed systems, with marked scarcity in developing countries.

Analyzing and monitoring changes in extreme events, including drought, tropical cyclones, extreme temperatures and the frequency and intensity of precipitation, is more difficult than for climatic averages as longer data time-series of higher spatial and temporal resolutions are required.

Effects of climate changes on human and some natural systems are difficult to detect due to adaptation and non-climatic drivers.

Difficulties remain in reliably simulating and attributing observed temperature changes to natural or human causes at smaller than continental scales. At these smaller scales, factors such as land-use change and pollution also complicate the detection of anthropogenic warming influence on physical and biological systems. * * *

With current climate change mitigation policies and related sustainable development practices, global GHG emissions will continue to grow over the next few decades.

For the next two decades a warming of about 0.2°C per decade is projected for a range of SRES emissions scenarios.

Continued GHG emissions at or above current rates would cause further warming and induce many changes in the global climate system during the 21st century that would very likely be larger than those observed during the 20th century. * * *

Some systems, sectors and regions are likely to be especially affected by climate change. The systems and sectors are some ecosystems (tundra, boreal forest, mountain, mediterranean-type, mangroves, salt marshes, coral reefs and the sea-ice biome), low-lying coasts, water resources in some dry regions at mid-latitudes and in the dry tropics and in areas dependent on snow and ice melt, agriculture in low-latitude regions, and human health in areas with low adaptive capacity. The regions are the Arctic, Africa, small islands and Asian and African megadeltas. Within other regions, even those with high incomes, some people, areas and activities can be particularly at risk.

Impacts are very likely to increase due to increased frequencies and intensities of some extreme weather events. Recent events have demonstrated the vulnerability of some sectors and regions, including in developed countries, to heat waves, tropical cyclones, floods and drought, providing stronger reasons for concern. * * *

Uncertainty in the equilibrium climate sensitivity creates uncertainty in the expected warming for a given ... stabilisation scenario. Uncertainty in the carbon cycle feedback creates uncertainty in the emissions trajectory required to achieve a particular stabilisation level.

Models differ considerably in their estimates of the strength of different feedbacks in the climate system, particularly cloud feedbacks, oceanic heat uptake and carbon cycle feedbacks, although progress has been made in these areas. Also, the confidence in projections is higher for some variables (e.g. temperature) than for others (e.g. precipitation), and it is higher for larger spatial scales and longer time averaging periods.

Aerosol impacts on the magnitude of the temperature response, on clouds and on precipitation remain uncertain.

Future changes in the Greenland and Antarctic ice sheet mass, particularly due to changes in ice flow, are a major source of uncertainty that could increase sea level rise projections. The uncertainty in the penetration of the heat into the oceans also contributes to the future sea level rise uncertainty.

Large-scale ocean circulation changes beyond the 21st century cannot be reliably assessed because of uncertainties in the meltwater supply from the Greenland ice sheet and model response to the warming.

Projections of climate change and its impacts beyond about 2050 are strongly scenario-and model-dependent, and improved projections would require improved understanding of sources of uncertainty and enhancements in systematic observation networks.

Impacts research is hampered by uncertainties surrounding regional projections of climate change, particularly precipitation.

Understanding of low-probability/high-impact events and the cumulative impacts of sequences of smaller events, which is required for risk-based approaches to decision-making, is generally limited. * * *

Some planned adaptation (of human activities) is occurring now; more extensive adaptation is required to reduce vulnerability to climate change.

Unmitigated climate change would, in the long term, be *likely* to exceed the capacity of natural, managed and human systems to adapt.

A wide range of mitigation options is currently available or projected to be available by 2030 in all sectors. The economic mitigation potential, at costs that range from net negative up to US$100/ tCO_2-equivalent, is sufficient to offset the projected growth of global emissions or to reduce emissions to below current levels in 2030.

Many impacts can be reduced, delayed or avoided by mitigation. Mitigation efforts and investments over the next two to three decades will have a large impact on opportunities to achieve lower stabilisation levels. Delayed emissions reductions significantly constrain the opportunities to achieve lower stabilisation levels and increase the risk of more severe climate change impacts.

The range of stabilisation levels for GHG concentrations that have been assessed can be achieved by deployment of a portfolio of technologies that are currently available and those that are expected to be commercialised in coming decades, provided that appropriate and effective incentives are in place and barriers are removed. In addition, further RD & D would be required to improve the technical performance, reduce the costs and achieve social acceptability of new technologies. The lower the stabilisation levels, the greater the need for investment in new technologies during the next few decades.

NOTES

1. The IPCC findings rely heavily on climate modeling, so a basic understanding of modeling is helpful. A popular science writer gives a particularly clear explanation of the basics of climate modeling, discussing a particular model called GISS:

> Like all climate models, GISS's divides the world into a series of boxes. Thirty-three hundred and twelve boxes cover the earth's surface, and this pattern is repeated twenty times moving up through the atmosphere. . . . [I]n the world of the model, features such as lakes and forests and, indeed, whole mountain ranges are reduced to a limited set of properties, which are then expressed as numerical approximations. Time in this grid-world moves ahead for the most part in discrete, half-hour intervals, meaning that a new set of calculations is performed for each box for every thirty minutes that is supposed to have elapsed in actuality. Depending on what part of the globe a box represents, these calculations may involve dozens of different algorithms, so a model run [may involve] more than a quadrillion separate operations. A single run of the GISS model, done on a supercomputer, usually takes about a month.[31]

The model calculates changes in each block based on fundamental laws and on "parameterizations." These parameterizations approximate complex physical processes with simpler equations that capture the physical results but without all the details of the process.

Climate modeling has developed quickly over the past few decades.[32] The publications on climate research have doubled approximately every eleven

---

31. Elizabeth Kolbert, FIELD NOTES FROM A CATASTROPHE: MAN, NATURE, AND CLIMATE CHANGE 99–101 (2006).

32. A detailed discussion can be found in Herve Le Treut *et al.*, *Historical Overview of Climate Change Science*, in CLIMATE CHANGE 2007: THE PHYSICAL SCIENCE BASIS: WORKING GROUP I CONTRIBUTION TO THE FOURTH ASSESSMENT REPORT OF THE INTERGOVERNMENTAL PANEL ON CLIMATE CHANGE 93 (Susan Solomon *et al.* eds., 2007).

years since the middle of the last century.[33] Supercomputer speed has increased by a million-fold in the past three decades.[34] There has been a shift from traditional supercomputers (in which all processors use the same memory space) to massively parallel machines in which each processor has its own memory.[35] As everyone knows, chip speeds have also grown exponentially. These technological advances allow models to be more fine-grained (smaller cells providing more detail on processes) and enable the incorporation of ocean currents and other factors too complex for the early models.[36] Faster computer speeds also allowed ensemble runs in which model parameters are varied in order to study their effect on climate.[37]

Today, Atmospheric–Ocean General Circulation Models (AOGCMs) are able to include consideration of aerosols (such as sulfur dioxide plumes caused by industrial sources), river and estuary water mixing (affecting ocean salinity), sea ice, and terrestrial processes.[38] Instead of using rough approximations (like average levels of cloudiness in a given locale), models are increasingly able to "represent such processes as cloud particles and raindrop formation" to "predict the distributions of liquid and ice clouds."[39] Models also increasingly incorporate the terrestrial biosphere, including vegetation and soil carbon cycles.[40] Many factors turn out to be relevant: snow-vegetations interactions, evaporation from forest canopies, and soil moisture. Vegetation and land use may be held fixed in some models, however, rather than responding to climate change.

Because of improvements in modeling and data, the 2007 Report was able to eliminate some concerns that had previously been raised about climate change. In particular, four key issues were resolved. First, could evidence of warming be skewed because previously rural measurement sites have been swept into urban areas, which are warmer than their surroundings? The answer is no. While the urban heat-island effect, caused by the tendency of urban concrete and asphalt to absorb heat, is real, it is "a negligible influence" on overall temperature. Second, do satellite measurements show that the world is not really warming (unlike the ground level measurements)? Again, the answer is no. The previous discrepancy between earth-based and satellite-based temperature measurements has been resolved by improved satellite measurements, which are more in line with the earth-based results. Third, could warming be due to natural forces? Again, no. While natural forces such as volcanos and variations in solar intensity can influence climate and have done so in the past, these natural variations cannot produce the currently observed patterns of climate change. And fourth, is it plausible to

---

33. *Id.* at 98.

34. *Id.* at 112.

35. Kendal McGuffie & Ann Henderson–Sellers, A CLIMATE MODELLING PRIMER 177 (3d ed. 2005).

36. *Id.* at 113.

37. *Id.* at 48.

38. David A. Randall et al., *Climate Models and Their Evaluation,* in CLIMATE CHANGE 2007: THE PHYSICAL SCIENCE BASIS, WORKING GROUP I CONTRIBUTION TO THE FOURTH ASSESSMENT REPORT OF THE INTERGOVERNMENTAL PANEL ON CLIMATE CHANGE, 589, 592 (Susan Solomon *et al.* eds., 2007).

39. *Id.* at 602.

40. *Id.* at 604.

think that small changes in the gas composition of the atmosphere could cause significant climate change? Yes, the evidence does show that the climate system is sufficiently sensitive to atmospheric composition to produce the observed climate change, as shown by the response to other disturbances such as the Mount Pinatubo eruption of 1990. Resolving these issues eliminates some of the residual uncertainty that had still clouded discussions of climate change, leaving little room for doubt that human-caused climate change is real and serious.

2. Models differ significantly in their predictions. Disagreement about climate sensitivity is one indication of model differences. Climate sensitivity means the equilibrium average temperature change resulting from a doubling of carbon dioxide concentrations—thus, climate sensitivity indicates what the temperature will be in the very long run, after transitional effects have damped down. It is "largely determined by internal feedback processes that amplify or dampen the influence of radiative forcing on climate."[41] As it turns out, the biggest source of differences between models relates to cloud formation and effects on heat radiation. Clouds reflect light back into space, but also trap heat emitted from below; the balance between these processes is complex.[42] How should policy makers treat differences in predictions among models? Should they credit the most pessimistic predictions and act accordingly?

3. Given that the models are necessarily imperfect, what reasons do we have for crediting their results? Perhaps the most basic reason is that the cores of the models are based on well-understood laws of physics relating to fluid behavior, thermodynamics, radiation absorption, and other processes.

In addition, models have undergone three important "reality checks." First, some models have been successfully tested for short-term and season weather forecasting, with good results. This provides some grounds for confidence that major weather factors have not been omitted.[43]

Second, models have been tested at the component level. Standardized tests are applied to the components through organized activities, such as regularly held Workshops on Partial Differential Equations on the Sphere. The physical parameters in the models are tested through case studies, run by programs specializing in cloud systems, atmospheric radiation, and other topics.[44]

Third, models are tested against past and present climate. They have been extensively used to simulate Twentieth Century climate changes. The results are encouraging:

---

41. Randall *et al.*, *supra* note 38, at 629.

42. *Id.* at 633–635. The IPCC's summary on clouds is as follows:

Despite some advances in the understanding of the physical processes that control the cloud response to climate change and in the evaluation of some components of cloud feedbacks in current models, it is not yet possible to assess which of the model estimates of cloud feedback is the most reliable. However, progress has been made in the identification of the cloud types, the dynamical regimes and the regions of the globe responsible for the large spread of cloud feedback estimates among current models.

Id. at 638.

43. *Id.* at 593.

44. *Id.*

Models show significant and increasing skill in representing many important mean climate features, such as the large-scale distributions of atmospheric temperature, precipitation, radiation and wind, and of oceanic temperatures, currents and sea ice cover. Models can also simulate essential aspects of many of the patterns of climate variability observed across a range of time scales. Examples include the advance and retreat of the major monsoon systems, the seasonal shifts of temperatures, storm tracks and rain belts, and the hemispheric-scale seesawing of extratropical surface pressures (the Northern and Southern "annular modes.")[45]

For example, there has been "steady progress" in simulating and predicting El Niño events.[46] Models have also been successful in simulating global statistics of extreme events, especially heat and cold waves.[47] It is difficult to check models against pre-industrial history because the weather data from those periods is spotty and its interpretation is controversial.[48] In addition, we do not have completely firm evidence about the past magnitude of other climate drivers such as solar and volcanic activity.[49]

4. Although it is possible that the IPCC analysis overstates the likely warming effect,[50] it is at least equally possible that the Report understates it. The high-end risks relating to climate change, while not considered to be likely, would impose extraordinary costs. See Melinda Kimble and Letha Tawney, THE ENVIRONMENTAL FORUM, May/June 2009 at 24. Indeed, understatement is the more likely scenario for a number of reasons. First, the models omit some important variables. It is still uncertain how much warming will occur, and at what rate, partly because factors that could amplify the effects of rising CO2 concentrations in the atmosphere, like water vapor, are difficult to measure or model.[51] In addition, there remains the possibility of "tipping points" or "threshold effects" that could dramatically increase the concentration of GHGs in the atmosphere, and result in "abrupt and irreversible change in the climate system."[52] These include the potential for a rapid collapse of ice sheets in Greenland or the Antarctic. These possibilities are not factored into the conclusions in the IPCC Report. Second, the empirical record to date shows that every surprise about climate change has been in the "wrong" direction. For example, arctic sea ice is retreating at a significantly faster rate than predicted by the best computer models, including all eighteen models used by the IPCC in preparing the FAR.[53] Indeed, it now appears that

---

45. *Id.* at 600. "Skill" is an indication of a model's ability to predict patterns of events rather than averages.

46. *Id.* at 623.

47. *Id.* at 627.

48. Myles Allen et al., *Scientific Challenges in the Attribution of Harm to Human Influence on Climate*, 155 U. PA. L. REV. 1353, 1364 (2007).

49. *Id.* at 1366.

50. *See e.g.,* David Henderson, *Governments and Climate Change Issues, The Case for Rethinking,* 8 (2) WORLD ECONOMICS 183, (April–June 2007) arguing that that the IPCC process is run by "true believers," has made numerous mistakes, especially in its treatment of economics, and is insufficiently transparent.

51. *Id.* at 173.

52. Daniel P. Schrag, *Confronting the Climate–Energy Connection,* ELEMENTS Vol. 3, 171–8, at 174 (June 2007).

53. *See* Julienne Stroeve *et al., Arctic Sea Ice Decline: Faster Than Forecast?* 34 GEOPHYSICAL RESEARCH LETTERS L09501 (2007), available at: http://www.agu.org/pubs/crossref/2007/2007GL

the arctic will be seasonally free of sea ice thirty years ahead of expectations.[54] The arctic permafrost too appears to be melting faster than scientists had predicted, and because the permafrost contains both carbon dioxide and methane, its melting can have very serious amplifying effects on warming.[55] The best models also appear to have understated the rate at which the world's largest glaciers will melt. The Bering Glacier, North America's biggest, is melting at twice the rate scientists previously thought.[56]

5. The IPCC shared the 2007 Nobel Peace Prize with Al Gore for their work on climate change. Yet the IPCC has come in for some criticism. There have been numerous allegations of political influence over the process, from charges that members have been voted out of the Panel for being overly aggressive in advocating policy responses,[57] to claims that parts of the Report offensive to some high oil producing and energy consuming states have been softened or deleted.[58] Governments with an interest in delaying progress on climate change have been known to aggressively challenge conclusions in assessment reports during the line-by-line approval process, leading to allegations that the results are "conservative."[59] Quite apart from any political pressure, scientists may also tend toward conservative estimates as a matter of disciplinary training and shared norms. In light of such concerns, it may be appropriate for policymakers to treat the IPCC projections as conservative, and to approach climate change policy with a measure of risk aversion.

6. Critics alleged that the Bush Administration has suppressed scientific information about the dangers of global warming, *see, e.g.,* United States House of Representatives Committee on Oversight and Government Reform, *Political Interference with Climate Change Science Under the Bush Administration,* (Dec. 2007). In June, 2008, as the result of a lawsuit, *Center for*

029703.shtml. The study was conducted by scientists at the National Snow and Ice Data Center and the National Center for Atmospheric Research.

54. Press Release: *Models Underestimate Loss of Arctic Sea Ice,* April 30 2007, available at: http://nsidc.org/news/press/20070430_StroeveGRL.html.

55. The Arctic contains more carbon dioxide than the entire atmosphere holds today, and thawing permafrost can release methane, which is approximately 23 times more potent than carbon dioxide as a greenhouse gas.

56. Doug O'Hara, *Bering Glacier Melts Faster,* FAR NORTH SCIENCE, June 4, 2007, available at: http://www.farnorthscience.com/2007/06/04/climate-news/bering-glacier-melts-faster/.

57. In 2002, IPCC Chairman Dr. Robert Watson was voted out of his position by the IPCC Plenary. Watson, an aggressive advocate for political responses to global warming, was replaced by Dr. Rajendra Pachauri, perceived as more industry-friendly. This change was initiated by the U.S. and was followed by allegations that the U.S. acted in response to a memo from ExxonMobil to the White House seeking to blackball Watson. *See* Al Gore, *Op–Ed,* NEW YORK TIMES, Apr. 21, 2002, Section 4, at 13.

58. Following the release of the Fourth Assessment Report in 2007, David Wasdell, who served as "an accredit reviewer of the report" viewed preliminary drafts of the report and asserted that: " 'reference to possible acceleration of climate change [was] consistently removed' from the report. This happened both in the treatment of positive feedbacks from global warming in the future and in its discussion of recent observations of collapsing ice sheets and an accelerating rise in sea levels." Fred Pearce, *Climate report 'was watered down',* NEW SCIENTIST, Mar. 10, 2007, at 10.

59. "For example, after objections by Saudi Arabia and China, the report dropped a sentence stating that the impact of human activity on the earth's heat budget exceeds that of the sun by fivefold. 'The difference is really a factor of 10,' says lead author Piers Forster of the University of Leeds in England. . . ." David Biello, *Consensus Document may Underestimate the Climate Change Problem,* SCIENTIFIC AM., Apr. 2007.

Biological Diversity v. Brennan, 571 F.Supp.2d 1105 (N.D. Cal. 2007), the U.S. Climate Change Science Program released an extensive report on climate change that largely affirms the IPCC report. *See* U.S. Climate Change Science Program, *Weather and Climate Extremes in an Changing Climate*, SYNTHESIS AND ASSESSMENT PRODUCT 3.3 (June 2008) at 81 ("Changes in some weather and climate extremes are attributable to human-induced emissions of greenhouse gases").

The next excerpt discusses the international response to climate change.

DAVID M. DRIESEN, SUSTAINABLE DEVELOPMENT AND MARKET LIBERALISM'S SHOTGUN WEDDING: EMISSIONS TRADING UNDER THE KYOTO PROTOCOL

83 IND. L.J. 21 (2008).**60**

The international community responded to the mounting scientific evidence that human activities seriously disrupt the global climate by enacting the United Nations Framework Convention on Climate Change ("Framework Convention") in 1992. The Framework Convention reflects both international support for the sustainable development ideal and market liberalism's ascendancy.

The Framework Convention proclaims that "[t]he Parties ... should ... promote sustainable development" and "protect the climate system for the benefit of future generations." This proclamation is consistent with the intergenerational concerns at the heart of sustainable development. The general goal more concretely expresses sustainable development's possible meaning in this context by declaring an "ultimate objective" of stabilizing "greenhouse gas concentrations in the atmosphere at a level that would prevent dangerous anthropogenic interference with the climate system."

The Framework Convention simultaneously embraces market liberalism by stating that "policies and measures to deal with climate change should be cost-effective so as to ensure global benefits at the lowest possible cost." Employing the language of neoliberal CBA proponents, this clause refers to measures reducing greenhouse gas emissions not as avoiding harm, but as ensuring "benefits." At the same time, this language suggests the need for emissions trading by establishing cost-effectiveness as a major objective of the climate change regime. This language did not enter the agreement by accident. The United States, a leading bastion of market liberalism, resisted mandatory emission reduction targets, partially because it considered their achievement too costly. United States negotiators also argued that liberal international emissions trading should become part of the agreement. This position created a tension between the United States and countries more interested in binding limits and skeptical of emissions trading. This tension led to a clause establishing an "aim of returning individually or jointly to ... 1990" developed

---

60. Copyright 2008 by Indiana Law Journal. Reprinted by permission.

country greenhouse gas emission levels. This language established an emission reduction goal in lieu of an emission reduction requirement. And the reference to joint achievement of the stabilization "aim" suggests using international emissions trading to achieve this goal.

The United States continued its emissions trading advocacy and its opposition to binding emission reduction targets during the meetings that produced the Kyoto Protocol. This placed the United States in tension with the European Union (EU), which supported strict targets and less use of trading. Then Vice President Al Gore helped break an impasse that threatened to scuttle a Kyoto agreement by signaling the United States' willingness to accept modest binding emission reduction targets in exchange for a liberal international emissions trading regime. The resulting Kyoto Protocol generally obligates advanced, industrialized countries to deliver emission reductions representing a five percent cut below their joint 1990 emission levels, but it allows them to substitute carbon credits generated abroad for some of these cuts.

The Kyoto Protocol provides for no fewer than three international emission trading programs, usually referred to as the Kyoto "flexibility mechanisms," as a means of achieving the reduction targets for individual countries. Article 16 authorizes trades of national allowances among the developed countries that assumed reduction obligations under the Kyoto Protocol. Article 6, the joint implementation provision, authorizes project-based trades among developed countries or among private parties within developed countries. Article 12 establishes a Clean Development Mechanism (CDM) that authorizes developed countries, or private companies within developed countries, to purchase credits from projects in developing countries, even though developing countries have assumed no emission reduction obligations under the Kyoto Protocol. The CDM's purpose is to assist developing countries in "achieving sustainable development."

In order to meet CDM's sustainable development goals, the parties to the Kyoto Protocol established a process for public participation and collective decision making in choosing CDM projects. This process requires Designated Operational Entities (often a private consulting firm paid for by project developers) to comment on proposed projects, estimate emission reductions, and validate the subsequent emissions. A Designated National Authority within the country hosting the project reviews the project for compatibility with sustainable development goals. An international Executive Board reviews credit estimation techniques and exercises oversight.

NOTES

1. A follow-up conference in Bali created a roadmap for the next round of international negotiations:

> At Bali, U.S. negotiators rejected proposals by the European Union and others to agree to seek agreement on measures requiring industrialized countries to cut emissions by 2020 to levels 25 to 40 percent below 1990

levels. U.S. negotiators maintained that it was inappropriate to set such targets at the outset of negotiations, that the proposed targets were unrealistic and unattainable, and that any outcome also must include meaningful participation by rapidly industrializing countries like Brazil, China, and India.

The U.S. delegation ultimately agreed to adoption by consensus of a framework for future negotiations that calls for both the industrialized world and emerging industrial powers to commit to take quantifiable, verifiable measures to reduce future emissions. The final compromise package also included provisions calling for developed countries to facilitate access to clean energy technology, to provide increased financial aid to developing countries in adapting to climate change, and to provide incentives and assistance to developing countries that preserve their tropical forests.

Note, *U.S. Positions In International Climate Change Negotiations*, 102 Am. J. Int'l L. 164 (2008).

A further conference took place in December 2008 in Poznan, Poland. The conference also took a small step forward in two areas. The Adaptation Fund Board was established after a dispute about how to constitute its membership, although efforts to agree on a proposal to increase available funding for adaptation projects failed. The meeting also produced a tentative decision to include Reducing Emissions from Deforestation and Degradation (REDD) as a key part of the Copenhagen emissions reduction agreement. The Copenhagen conference is scheduled for December 2009.

2. Although the U.S. government took little action in response to climate change prior to 2009, state governments have been much more active. Some of the major initiatives include the widespread use of renewable portfolio standards for electrical utilities, California's effort to impose greenhouse gas limitations on automobile emissions, state and regional cap-and-trade systems, local "green" building codes, and subsidies for clean energy technologies. See John C. Dernbach and Seema Kakade, *Climate Change Law: An Introduction*, 29 Energy L.J. 1, 15–19 (2008).

Prominent state climate regulators may have engaged in ambitious regulatory efforts at least in part because the federal government—through the Clean Air Act—has boosted their regulatory capacity and expertise. California's greenhouse gas regulations for automobiles, for example, came about as the result of California's long-standing experience regulating conventional pollutants under special CAA regulatory authority. The Regional Greenhouse Gas Initiative (RGGI) is modeled after nearly identical legislation that is the product of the federally created Ozone Transport Commission under the CAA. See Ann E. Carlson, Iterative Federalism and Climate Change, available at http://www.law.ucla.edu/home/index.asp?page=456.

3. What effect does state regulation have on the prospects of federal regulation, in terms of both its timing and its form? DeShazo and Freeman have argued that state activity can be an important catalyst of a federal policy response not by setting an example or "shaming" the federal government, but by making all the relevant interest groups unhappy. In their account, state measures have stimulated *both* pro-regulatory and anti-regulatory forces to

appeal to the federal government for relief. States have hit a "regulatory sweet spot," they argue, by doing two things simultaneously: creating a patchwork of inconsistent and costly regulation that drives industry to seek federal uniformity through preemption, and adopting fairly weak and necessarily limited measures, which ultimately drive environmentalists to Congress as well. See J.R. DeShazo and Jody Freeman, *Timing and Form of Federal Regulation: The Case of Climate Change*, 155 U. PENN. L. REV. 1499 (2007).

4. Along with mitigation (reducing GHG emissions) and adaptation (adopting strategies to adjust to some inevitable amount of warming), scientists and policymakers are increasingly discussing the possibility of "geo-engineering" the climate, which refers to strategies by which the effects of warming might be prevented or counteracted through manipulation of the earth's environment. These strategies include injecting sulfates aerosols into the stratosphere (much as volcanoes do) to reflect radiation; placing a solar deflector in space; and increasing Earth's surface reflectivity by, for example, placing reflectors in the oceans to alter its albedo. Though geo-engineering can sound like science fiction, it is not. The U.S. military has long pursued a program of research into "weather control" (with limited success). Many serious scientists think geo-engineering is promising and at least worth some investment in research. Geo-engineering raises difficult ethical, technological, economic and legal issues. Some commentators object to even discussing geo-engineering out of concern that it will detract from efforts to cut emissions, and give people false hopes about a "magic bullet" solution to climate change. Others believe that pursuing basic research into geo-engineering is the only responsible course given that it is unrealistic that governments will make the necessary dramatic cuts to avoid many serious effects of warming. After all, they point out, we are already geo-engineering the earth's environment by emitting such high volumes of greenhouse gases. *See* Paul Crutzen, *Albedo Enhancement by Stratospheric Sulfur Injections: A Contribution to Resolve a Policy Dilemma?* 77 CLIMACTIC CHANGE 211 (2006); for a series of commentaries on Crutzen's article, see 77 CLIMACTIC CHANGE (2006). In the absence of an international consensus, geoengineering efforts might give rise to substantial strife. If such an effort produced unintended side-effects, would the firms or nations involved be subject to liability? Note that, even if successful in controlling global temperatures, geoengineering would not address acidification of the ocean.

CHAPTER 2

APPROACHES TO ENVIRONMENTAL PROTECTION

■ ■ ■

In Chapter 1, we explored several general perspectives on environmental protection. Much of this book consists of detailed examinations of particular regulatory schemes. This leaves something of a gap between the very general and the very specific in environmental law. That gap is bridged by mechanism design, which involves key choices between various techniques for setting and implementing environmental standards. This chapter will survey the basic tools and methods of environmental protection, which are used in some form or another in all areas of environmental law. We will examine a series of basic techniques of environmental protection: risk prevention, cost-benefit analysis, market incentives, civil liability, and collaborative governance.

We will begin by examining three different methods for regulating environmental hazards. The first approach asks whether significant risks exist and seeks to engage in the maximum feasible reduction of such risks. The second uses economics to gauge the appropriate level and methods of risk reduction. The third focuses on how risks are distributed and seeks to remedy inequities. Having considered these three approaches to regulation, we will consider proposals for less conventional approaches for environmental protection.

A. PUBLIC HEALTH AND RISK–BASED APPROACHES TO REGULATION

Environmental law is partly about preserving nature and partly about protecting human health from pollution and other hazards. Cancer risks have received particular attention in this regard. We will examine some of the techniques for determining the extent of these hazards and for then determining how much priority they should receive. Neither determination is as straightforward as one might expect. Instead, they involve difficult scientific and normative judgments.

1. RISK ASSESSMENT

Public health concerns in environmental law have focused on potential environmental sources of cancer. At present, there are two major methods for estimating cancer risks. The first is based on epidemiology—that is, statistical studies of human populations. These studies are easiest to perform when identifiable occupational groups are exposed to high levels of some substance. The basic idea is simply to compare cancer rates in the occupational group with those in the general population. But in practice, this is much harder than it sounds. Cancer latency periods are measured in decades, making it necessary to identify whom was exposed to what levels several decades earlier. People move in and out of particular occupations, making it difficult to track the exposed group in occupational studies. Moreover, members of specific occupational groups usually differ from the general population in other ways such as dietary habits, smoking, or alcohol use, and statistical controls are necessary to eliminate these confounding factors. (For instance, if members of the occupational group tend to be heavy smokers, they will have an elevated lung cancer rate regardless of any occupational exposures.) Finally, it is necessary to extrapolate from the high levels of past occupational exposures to what are typically much lower levels of exposure that concern current regulators. This requires an estimate of the "dose-response curve," which is often controversial.

Instead of using an occupational group, epidemiologists can also study how disease levels vary with risk exposure among the general population. This avoids the need to assume a specific dose-response curve, but the problems of estimating exposure and eliminating confounding factors still remain. Because effects in the general population are typically much smaller, they are statistically much harder to distinguish from random variations in the background rate or from the effects of confounding factors.

The other major method for estimating cancer risks involves animal studies. Because these are controlled experiments, confounding factors can be eliminated. But other problems then arise. Small groups of laboratory animals must be used because of the expenses of the experiments. Hence, only very large effects can be detected. An experiment with thirty lab rats cannot detect a one in a thousand risk to the rats, let alone the even lower risks levels that are often of regulatory concern. Rather, the rate must be in the neighborhood of one in thirty, and even then could be missed by chance in some experiments. The only way to obtain these high rates is to use high doses, but then it is necessary to use a dose-response curve to estimate the effects of much lower human exposures. Moreover, mammals vary in their susceptibility to carcinogens: a substance that causes cancer in rats might not do so in humans, and vice versa.

There are many uncertainties in risk assessment. EPA's method of handling these uncertainties has been the subject of considerable controversy. EPA's current approach to dealing with uncertainty and extrapolating from incomplete data is explained in the following excerpt.

ENVIRONMENTAL PROTECTION AGENCY, GUIDELINES FOR CARCINOGEN RISK ASSESSMENT AND SUPPLEMENTAL GUIDANCE FOR ASSESSING SUSCEPTIBILITY FROM EARLY–LIFE EXPOSURE TO CARCINOGENS

70 Federal Register 17766 (2005).

1.3. KEY FEATURES OF THE CANCER GUIDELINES

1.3.1. Critical Analysis of Available Information as the Starting Point for Evaluation

* * * Use of health protective risk assessment procedures as described in these cancer guidelines means that estimates, while uncertain, are more likely to overstate than understate hazard and/or risk. * * *

In the absence of sufficient data or understanding to develop of a robust, biologically based model, an appropriate policy choice is to have a single preferred curve-fitting model for each type of data set. Many different curve-fitting models have been developed, and those that fit the observed data reasonably well may lead to several-fold differences in estimated risk at the lower end of the observed range. In addition, goodness-of-fit to the experimental observations is not by itself an effective means of discriminating among models that adequately fit the data. To provide some measure of consistency across different carcinogen assessments, EPA uses a standard curve-fitting procedure for tumor incidence data. Assessments that include a different approach should provide an adequate justification and compare their results with those from the standard procedure. Application of models to data should be conducted in an open and transparent manner.

1.3.2. Mode of Action

The use of mode of action in the assessment of potential carcinogens is a main focus of these cancer guidelines. This area of emphasis arose because of the significant scientific advances that have developed concerning the causes of cancer induction. Elucidation of a mode of action for a particular cancer response in animals or humans is a data-rich determination. Significant information should be developed to ensure that a scientifically justifiable mode of action underlies the process leading to cancer at a given site. In the absence of sufficiently, scientifically justifiable mode of action information, EPA generally takes public health—protective, default positions regarding the interpretation of toxicologic and epidemiologic data: Animal tumor findings are judged to be relevant to humans, and cancer risks are assumed to conform with low dose linearity.

Understanding of mode of action can be a key to identifying processes that may cause chemical exposures to differentially affect a particular population segment or lifestage. Some modes of action are anticipated to be mutagenic and are assessed with a linear approach. This is the mode of action of radiation and several other agents that are known carcinogens. Other modes of action may be modeled with either linear or nonlinear approaches after a rigorous analysis of available data under the guidance provided in the framework for mode of action analysis.

1.3.3. Weight of Evidence Narrative

The cancer guidelines emphasize the importance of weighing all of the evidence in reaching conclusions about the human carcinogenic potential of agents. This is accomplished in a single integrative step after assessing all of the individual lines of evidence, which is in contrast to the step-wise approach in the 1986 cancer guidelines. Evidence considered includes tumor findings, or lack thereof, in humans and laboratory animals; an agent's chemical and physical properties; its structure-activity relationships (SARs) as compared with other carcinogenic agents; and studies addressing potential carcinogenic processes and mode(s) of action, either *in vivo* or *in vitro*. Data from epidemiologic studies are generally preferred for characterizing human cancer hazard and risk. However, all of the information discussed above could provide valuable insights into the possible mode(s) of action and likelihood of human cancer hazard and risk. The cancer guidelines recognize the growing sophistication of research methods, particularly in their ability to reveal the modes of action of carcinogenic agents at cellular and subcellular levels as well as toxicokinetic processes. Weighing of the evidence includes addressing not only the likelihood of human carcinogenic effects of the agent but also the conditions under which such effects may be expressed, to the extent that these are revealed in the toxicological and other biologically important features of the agent. * * *

1.3.4. Dose-response Assessment

Dose-response assessment evaluates potential risks to humans at particular exposure levels. The approach to dose-response assessment for a particular agent is based on the conclusion reached as to its potential mode(s) of action for each tumor type. Because an agent may induce multiple tumor types, the dose-response assessment includes an analysis of all tumor types, followed by an overall synthesis that includes a characterization of the risk estimates across tumor types, the strength of the mode of action information of each tumor type, and the anticipated relevance of each tumor type to humans, including susceptible populations and lifestages (e.g., childhood).

Dose-response assessment for each tumor type is performed in two steps: assessment of observed data to derive a point of departure (POD), followed by extrapolation to lower exposures to the extent that is necessary. Data from epidemiologic studies, of sufficient quality, are generally preferred for estimating risks. When animal studies are the basis of the analysis, the estimation of a human-equivalent dose should utilize toxicokinetic data to inform cross—species dose scaling if appropriate and if adequate data are available. Otherwise, default procedures should be applied. For oral dose, based on current science, an appropriate default option is to scale daily applied doses experienced for a lifetime in proportion to body weight raised to the 3/4 power. * * *

The POD for extrapolating the relationship to environmental exposure levels of interest, when the latter are outside the range of observed data, is generally the lower 95% confidence limit on the lowest dose level that can be supported for modeling by the data. SAB (1997) [eds: SAB is EPA's Science Advisory Board] suggested that, "it may be appropriate to emphasize lower statistical bounds in screening analyses and in activities designed to develop an appropriate human exposure value, since such activities require accounting for various types of uncertainties and a lower bound on the central estimate is a scientifically-based approach accounting for the uncertainty in the true value of the ED10 [or central estimate]." However, the consensus of the SAB (1997) was that, "both point estimates and statistical bounds can be useful in different circumstances, and recommended that the Agency routinely calculate and present the point estimate of the ED10 [or central estimate] and the corresponding upper and lower 95% statistical bounds." For example, it may be appropriate to emphasize the central estimate in activities that involve formal uncertainty analysis that are required by OMB Circular A–4 (OMB, 2003) as well as ranking agents as to their carcinogenic hazard. Thus, risk assessors should calculate, to the extent practicable, and present the central estimate and the corresponding upper and lower statistical bounds (such as confidence limits) to inform decisionmakers.

The second step of dose-response assessment is extrapolation to lower dose levels, if needed. This extrapolation is based on extension of a biologically based model if supported by substantial data. Otherwise, default approaches can be applied that are consistent with current understanding of mode(s) of action of the agent, including approaches that assume linearity or nonlinearity of the dose-response relationship, or both. A default approach for linearity extends a straight line from the POD to zero dose/zero response. The linear approach is used when: (1) there is an absence of sufficient information on modes of action or (2) the mode of action information indicates that the dose response curve at low dose is or is expected to be linear. Where alternative approaches have significant biological support, and no scientific consensus favors a single approach, an assessment may present results using alternative approaches. A nonlinear approach can be used to develop a reference dose or a reference concentration. * * *

1.3.6. Evaluating Risks from Childhood Exposures

NRC [the National Research Council] (1994) recommended that "EPA should assess risks to infants and children whenever it appears that their risks might be greater than those of adults." Executive Order 13045 (1997) requires that "each Federal Agency shall make it a high priority to identify and assess environmental health and safety risks that may disproportionately affect children, and shall ensure that their policies, programs, and standards address disproportionate risks that result from environmental health risks or safety risks." In assessing risks to children, EPA considers both effects manifest during childhood and early-life exposures that can contribute to effects at any time later in life.

These cancer guidelines view childhood as a sequence of lifestages rather than viewing children as a subpopulation, the distinction being that a subpopulation refers to a portion of the population, whereas a lifestage is inclusive of the entire population. Exposures that are of concern extend from conception through adolescence and also include pre-conception exposures of both parents. These cancer guidelines use the term "childhood" in this more inclusive sense.

Rarely are there studies that directly evaluate risks following early-life exposure. Epidemiologic studies of early-life exposure to environmental agents are seldom available. Standard animal bioassays generally begin dosing after the animals are several weeks old, when many organ systems are mature. This could lead to an understatement of risk, because an accepted concept in the science of carcinogenesis is that young animals are usually more susceptible to the carcinogenic activity of a chemical than are mature animals (McConnell, 1992). * * *

The risk attributable to early-life exposure often appears modest compared with the risk from lifetime exposure, but it can be about 10–fold higher than the risk from an exposure of similar duration occurring later in life. Further research is warranted to investigate the extent to which these findings apply to specific agents, chemical classes, and modes of action or in general. * * *

NOTES

1. Controversy continues over the dose-response curve. Some evidence suggests a "u-shaped curve," in which very small doses even have a beneficial health effect. This effect, known as hormesis, might sometimes support relaxation of risk regulations, but may also support more stringent regulation because of the possibility of obtaining health benefits by mandating "sub-threshold" doses. See Frank B. Cross, *Incorporating Hormesis in Risk Regulation*, 30 ENVTL. L. REP. 10778 (2000). Other studies suggest that one-time exposures to some chemicals may cause cancer, even at doses too small to create other toxic effects. *See* Edward J. Calabrese & Robyn Blain, *A Single Exposure to Many Carcinogens Can Cause Cancer*, 28 ENVTL. L. REP.. 10254 (1998). OMB attempted in January 2006 to create technical guidelines for risk assessments, but the proposal was sharply criticized by the National Academies' National Research Council. See Daniel Charles, *Panel Pans Proposed Change in U.S. Risk Assessment*, 315 SCIENCE 316 (2007). Some of the practical difficulties in public health studies are explored in Carole Bass, *Solving a Massive Worker Health Puzzle*, SCIENTIFIC AMERICAN, March 2008, at 86.

2. Attention has also increasingly focused on non-carcinogenic effects, particularly of steroids. Recent studies indicate that estrogenic chemicals can cause biological effects at doses previously considered safe. *See* Jocelyn Kaiser, *Panel Cautiously Confirms Low–Dose Effects*, 290 Sci. 695 (2000).

3. Risk assessment involves difficult scientific judgments, given the often-inconclusive nature of the data. One approach to improved decision making has been to mandate peer review of EPA's scientific findings:

> In recent years, lawmakers of all sorts have become interested in scientific peer review, and have the hope that scrutiny by independent experts can improve the quality of their own decision-making. As the phrase implies, peer review refers to the process of having work scrutinized by fellow experts, and it has long served as a quality control mechanism for the scientific community. Traditionally relegated to research funding and publication decisions, peer review recently has become of interest to regulatory agencies making decisions in the face of scientific uncertainty as well as to judges struggling to make sense of conflicting claims by expert witnesses. Although noteworthy, these applications remain fairly *ad hoc* to date.

> Peer review, in its broadest sense, represents the scientific community's effort to police itself and to assure a certain minimum level of quality so that scientists and others can rely on the results of reported scientific research. Peer review contributes to the advancement of science not merely through the screening of scientific work (its quality control function), but also by helping proponents of new hypotheses to improve their research and interpretations and by engaging others in a dialogue about important new discoveries. * * * As legal institutions often must do, peer review operates under constraints of limited time and information. Over the long haul, science may approach a gradual maturation of consensus, but the scientific community's various peer review techniques do not purport to anoint particular results as finally settling contested questions.

Lars Noah, *Peer Review and Regulatory Reform*, 30 Envtl. L. Rep. 10606 (2000). However, peer review may not be able to help with another problem, which is that scientists may be asked to address issues that are as much normative as scientific. This issue is discussed in the next excerpt.

WENDY E. WAGNER, CONGRESS, SCIENCE, AND ENVIRONMENTAL POLICY[1]
1999 U. Ill. L. Rev. 181 (1999).

Resolution of environmental problems requires a mix of science and values, and both provide their share of policymaking aggravations Values obviously play an important role in framing environmental policy options. Indeed, environmental controversies are often portrayed as battles between starkly divided proeconomy and proenvironment forces. How these issues are addressed in environmental legislation depends, to a great extent, on the political philosophies of legislators.

---

1. Copyright © 1999 University of Illinois. Reprinted with permission.

Science also plays an important role in the development of environmental legislation. General cause-and-effect relationships between various pollutants and human health are discovered and elucidated by scientific methods. In general, however, the contributions that science makes to environmental policymaking are much more limited than what one might want or expect. For example, although science is certainly helpful in narrowing and guiding the search for safe pollutant levels, a number of scientific uncertainties prevent science from arriving at definitive quantitative standards that ensure a cancer risk of only one in one million to the average exposed human.* * *

After recognizing that there will be limits to how scientific knowledge can be used to address most environmental questions, it is then important to understand the nature of these limits and why they occur. There are three different types of scientific uncertainty, although the boundaries between them are not always easily delineated. First, scientific uncertainties exist because scientists simply have not gotten around to researching the question, even though research is quite possible and likely to be undertaken in the near future. Indeed, scientists may be in the process of investigating the question at the time the policymakers' need for the information arises. Because this category of uncertainties is remediable, it is not included within the set of deeply entrenched knowledge gaps that are the focus of this study.

Second, gaps in knowledge may exist because scientists have no financial or professional incentives to research the question. For example, manufacturers of products that could cause cancer or other latent harms may be penalized by regulators and consumers if they test their products and find them dangerous. Until policymakers intervene to correct these entrenched knowledge gaps, they will remain unresolved.

Third, although scientists might be eager to research a question, they may be precluded from doing so because of ethical prohibitions, resource constraints, or limits in the capabilities of experimentation. Scientists are prevented from running controlled experiments on the effects of carcinogens on humans, for example, because of prevailing ethical norms. Although scientists familiar with the relevant positive scientific knowledge may offer important insights regarding the choices that are most plausible to fill the knowledge gaps, their educated guesses still remain unverifiable hypotheses.

Understanding how scientific uncertainty affects policymaking is complicated because knowledge gaps may arise at a number of points in the policymaking process. A series of scientific findings and nonscientific assumptions must be linked together to answer a larger policy question. Even more inconveniently, the gaps in knowledge are not clumped at the beginning or end of the inquiry, but tend to weave in and out, or zigzag, with sub-questions that science can answer. As a result, it is difficult to summarize the varied scientific uncertainties that arise in a policymaking exercise as simply the error around a mean.

One example of this zigzag occurs when policymakers ask scientists to determine when one in one million persons exposed to a substance will develop cancer. Largely because ethical prohibitions preclude experimentation on humans, scientists must look to animals and other organisms for insights into possible health effects. But existing scientific knowledge cannot provide definitive (experiment-based) guidance on: which species of rodent to select (point A); whether to count all tumors that form (benign and malignant) or only those that are malignant (point B); how to extrapolate from high dose studies (necessary for practical reasons) to possible low dose effects (point D); and how to extrapolate from animal to human (point E). Resolving these sub-questions requires value judgments that zigzag with the positive information that scientific experimentation is able to provide, such as how many tumors (malignant or total) occur in a given species of mice exposed to high concentrations of a suspected toxin (point C); and the average amount of water consumed daily by a normal adult (point F). Each environmental problem will be characterized by its own unique zigzag pattern of positive scientific knowledge and knowledge gaps, and, as this example illustrates, mapping the zigzag for any particular problem requires assistance from scientific experts. * * *

Resolving the mixed science policy questions that lie at the core of environmental disputes requires sophisticated legislative techniques. Members of Congress must identify the different types of knowledge gaps that arise in understanding environmental problems and then build legislation around these gaps. Perhaps predictably, however, legislators rarely do this. In a number of major environmental laws, Congress frames the legislative resolution of these multidisciplinary problems as essentially science puzzles. Rather than address the inevitable and often momentous policy choices that are left in the wake of incomplete science, Congress regularly produces mandates that misconstrue environmental problems as scientific ones. In the development of environmental laws, then, rather than perverting good science in the name of politics, Congress seems to do exactly the reverse and perverts politics in the name of good science.

NOTES

1. In theory, science and values can be separated. An agency can first estimate the quantitative extent of a risk ("science"), and then make a separate determination of how significant that level of risk may be ("values"). In practice, however, this may be more difficult. Estimating the risks may involve a number of judgment calls or the use of presumptions, and these may well be affected by normative considerations.

2. Congress sometimes calls for use of the "best" available science. Does "best" means "most reliable" or "most advanced"? How should EPA determine whether to incorporate the latest research into its methodology, given that cutting-edge work has not been refined or confirmed to the same extent as conventional methodologies? How should a court review such a determination by EPA? These questions may soon become pressing in light of the recent scientific advances discussed in the following article.

DAN TARLOCK, GENETIC SUSCEPTIBILITY AND ENVIRONMENTAL RISK ASSESSMENT: AN EMERGING LINK[2]

30 ENVTL. L. REP. 10277 (2000).

Toxic pollution and hazardous substance regulation is not yet based on advances in our understanding of the relationship between human genetics and exposure to a potentially dangerous substance, but this could change in the future. Put differently, pollution regulation is not based on individual susceptibility to risk; it is based on group susceptibility. We do not base environmental and occupational health regulation on the possibility that substantial variability in risk exists among individuals within the protected class. We do base some standards on worst-case scenarios; for example, many risk assessments are based on worst-case individual susceptibility. This practice, however, is different from explicitly assuming that each member of a protected class has a different cellular response to exposure or ingestion. The reason is that society normally assumes that all exposures are involuntary, but this is not always the case. Air pollutants are the clearest example of involuntary exposure, but even in this case, those at risk could move to less polluted areas.

Regulators have either had to assume that all persons subject to a specific exposure pathway are equally vulnerable to the same health risk or that exposure levels have been calculated for identifiable sub-populations for whom sufficient information exists that suggests that they are subject to higher exposure risks. These at-risk groups might include children, asthmatics, pregnant women, and members of particular ethnic groups. Our assumption that pollution and workplace regulation should be based on statistically observed population susceptibilities rather than the potentially more accurate individual genetic susceptibility to exposure to dangerous substances is at variance with advances in genetic research. For example, exposure to environmental agents at various stages of a child's life from gestation to young adulthood can cause severe damage to developing systems. Our understanding of the relationship between exposure to a toxic and harmful substance and the clinical appearance of cancer is still incomplete, but we now recognize that genetic sensitivity or susceptibility may kick in at any stage of carcinogenesis and may play a large role in explaining what risks actually materialize in specific individuals or sub-groups in the form of illness. The actual risk to which an individual is subject is ultimately a function of an individual response to a given dose of a hazardous substance, and this response is a function of individual genetic susceptibility. As a leading environmental geneticist has said, "Each person basically has his own fingerprint of drug-metabolizing enzymes and receptors, so we all handle drugs [and chemicals] differently."[3]

---

2. Copyright 2000. Environmental Law Reporter. Reprinted by permission.

3. *Environmental Institute Lays Plans for Gene Hunt*, 278 SCI. 569 (1997).

These advances in genetic research may now be applied to bear on environmental and workplace safety policy through the National Institute of Environmental Health Sciences' (NIEHS) Environmental Genome Project. The Environmental Genome Project builds on the Human Genome Project. The goal of the new project is to attempt to identify the genes that determine individual susceptibility to environmentally induced diseases. One plan is to select a group of candidate genes "on the basis of their hypothesized ability to influence vulnerability to noxious environmental agents." There are over 200 genes known to control susceptibility to environmental diseases. Having identified a number of potentially important genes, subsequent functional and epidemiological studies could then be used to infer individual associations between those genes and environmental response, and these links can be made at relatively low cost. Many differences among individuals exist that affect a person's sensitivity to or ability to resist environmentally induced diseases. Preexisting inherited genetic mutations can increase a person's risk of contracting cancer. The genes that we inherit affect the balance of enzymes that can either detoxify or enhance the toxicity of chemicals, causing different sensitivities to an exposure. Substantial differences exist among individuals with respect to the ability of their cells to repair deoxyribonucleic acid (DNA) damage caused by environmental exposure. Biological markers may improve the science of risk and open up new risk prevention strategies. This latter possibility has potentially profound implications for regulation designed to minimize public health risks. These risks include the presumed cellular responses to the effects of genotoxins, but there are many other potential uses of genetic information. When the information is combined with external factors such as occupational exposure or lifestyle, scientists can give more informed answers to questions such as why do some smokers get cancer and others do not, why certain groups have higher incidents of cancer after exposure to a toxicant and others do not, and why certain women are more prone to breast cancer. * * *

There are many possible outcomes of the Human and Environmental Genome Projects that could influence future risk assessment and management. It is possible that the projects will not produce sufficient information about individual genetic variability to warrant a change from the existing risk reduction strategy. Three other outcomes seem more likely. First, the study could produce information to identify new at-risk classes. This would support the growing environmental justice movement and provide more credible scientific support for existing regulations or more stringent regulations. One strand of the movement posits that existing environmental regulations under-protect minority populations; for example, minority groups who consume higher levels of contaminated fish. The Presidential/Congressional Commission on Risk Assessment and Risk Management assumed that standards would only go up not down.[4] Second, the strategy could both identify those individuals who are susceptible to

---

4. Presidential/Congressional Commission on Risk Assessment and Risk Management, *Final Report, Risk Assessment and Risk Management in Regulatory Decision–Making* 65, 71 (1997).

adverse consequences from exposure and could identify individual mitigation strategies. This is more likely in the workplace, but one cannot exclude the use of genetic information to alter human behavior to lessen the risks of pollutant and toxic substance exposure. Identified "at-risk" individuals can be medically monitored and subjected to preventive strategies, including, perhaps, prophylactic surgery to remove susceptible tissues. To date, medical monitoring has been a victim's remedy in toxic tort and Superfund suits. Sometimes it is the primary remedy, and in other cases, it is a consolation prize for the general denial of recovery for the tort of increased cancer risk. However, genetic information would be welcomed by those who argue that current regulations over-protect and are economically inefficient. Third, the research could undermine the scientific basis of existing health-based regulation by demonstrating that assumed dose-response curves are grossly inaccurate. * * *

As this project moves forward, the environmental community must monitor it closely. The precautionary principle is ultimately based on advances in science and implicit in it is the idea that new information can confirm or modify the need for initial conservative standards. The best interim policy guidelines to follow are: (1) that no existing standard should be changed without extensive peer review of the science, opportunity for public comment (including lay comment), and full compliance with the notice-and-comment procedures of the Administrative Procedure Act (APA) because of the present difficulties of establishing clear associations between genetic variants and environmental exposures; (2) if research is used to lower standards for any currently protected group, the regulatory agency must fully comply with the APA, include a monitoring and mid-course correction process in any regulation, as was attempted with the 1992 Clean Water Act, and provide a credible, peer-reviewed, scientific justification for the new standard; and (3) the incorporation of possible genetic information scenarios in the EPA's comparative risk evaluations should be done with full disclosure of the uncertainties surrounding the use of this information.

NOTES

1. The potential link between genomics and risk assessment has already been the subject of considerable discussion, with varying degrees of optimism about the potential for genomics to promote rapid improvements in risk assessment. *See* Jamie Grodsky, *Genetics and Environmental Law, Redefining Public Health,* 93 Cal. L. Rev., 171 (2005); Gary Marchant: *Genomics and Toxic Substances: Part I—Toxiogenomics,* 33 ENVTL. L. REP. 10071 (Jan. 2003); *Genomics and Toxic Substances: Part II—Genetic Susceptibility to Environmental Agents,* 33 ENVTL. L. REP. 10641 (Sept. 2003); Council on Biological Markers of the National Research Council, *Biological Markers in Environmental Health Research,* 74 ENVTL. HEALTH PERSPS. 3 (1987).

2. Genomics may cause increased emphasis on the disparate effects of pollutants on different individuals. This may create some difficult questions of

equity. As Tarlock explains, it may also shift some of the burden of avoiding environmental risks onto the susceptible individuals.

3.   The preceding materials discuss the problem of quantifying the degree of risk to the public health. But once these risks have been quantified, we still must set priorities in addressing these risks. What determines the urgency of a risk? The projected death rate, the number of years of life that people will lose, or additional qualitative factors? The next two excerpts consider this issue.

2.   SETTING PRIORITIES FOR ADDRESSING RISKS

CLAYTON P. GILLETTE & JAMES E. KRIER, RISK, COURTS, AND AGENCIES[5]

138 U. PA. L. REV. 1027, 1027–1029, 1039, 1071–1073, 1076–1079 (1990).

* * * What does "risk" *mean?* To anticipate our argument, suppose that the concept signifies different things to different people—more particularly, one thing to agency experts and another to the lay public. Suppose, in addition, that while each of these meanings is sensible, the expert definition implies levels of public risk that are, by the lay definition, almost invariably too high. It then follows that a selfless agency, determined and free (because of expansive deference) to assess and manage public risk in accord with its own conception, will end up regulating less than called for from the public's point of view. The resulting contest is, at bottom, one of competing rationalities, and its resolution is a matter of ethics and politics, not technical expertise. Nothing in the training, credentials, or legitimacy of risk assessors or bureaucrats qualifies them to settle the issue. Hence deference to agencies would grant them ground they have no right to claim. Deference would beg a central question in the control of public risk. * * *

* * * Risk, we suggested, can be seen as the function of expected mortality or morbidity, or what we shall here refer to as expected annual fatalities or "body counts," and in these terms many public risk technologies might indeed seem to be relatively safe. Those who favor modern technological developments do so in part precisely because they, like most experts, gauge risk in just this way. They may disagree about details, such as whether one looks at total expected deaths, deaths per person or per hour of exposure, or loss of life expectancy due to exposure, but generally speaking "experts appear to see riskiness as synonymous with expected annual mortality [and morbidity]."[6] So, for example, when technical experts are asked to rank the risks of various activities and technologies, "their responses correlate highly with technical estimates of annual fatali-

---

5.   Copyright © 1990, University of Pennsylvania Law Review. Reprinted by permission.

6.   Slovic, *"Perception of Risk,"* 236 SCI. 280, 283 (1983) (citation omitted); *see also* Slovic, Fischhoff & Lichtenstein, *Facts and Fears: Understanding Perceived Risk, in* SOCIETAL RISK ASSESSMENT: HOW SAFE IS SAFE ENOUGH? 181, 191–92 (R. Schwing & W. Albers, Jr. eds. 1980) (experts view risk as synonymous with technical fatality estimates).

ties."[7] When experts write about relative risk, they implicitly or explicitly use body counts as the relevant measure. And, in a way seemingly consistent with the logic of their method, they insist that a death is a death is a death—1,000 lives lost in a single anticipated annual catastrophe, or through many accidents expected every year, or lost ten-fold but only once every decade on average, or lost in a single community or across the country, are all the same to them.

In the view of experts, then, risk is a one-dimensional phenomenon. * * *

For the lay person, risk is n-dimensional, as William Lowrance suggested in an early study. He observed that a variety of considerations in addition to expected fatalities and injuries affect people's judgments about risk: involuntary exposure, delayed effects, scientific uncertainty about the hazard in question, "dreaded" versus common hazards (for example, the threat of death from invisible radiation as opposed to an auto accident), irreversible consequences, and others. Since the time of Lowrance's work, any number of studies have found "that many attributes other than death rates determine judgments of riskiness" by lay people, whose "model of what constitutes risk appears to be much richer than that held by most technical experts." Thus the public is known to be concerned about risks that have catastrophic potential, that are unfamiliar, uncontrollable, or involuntary, that threaten future generations, that would concentrate fatalities in time or space, that are distinctively threatening as opposed to widespread and shared by the general population, that are manmade as opposed to natural. * * *

Return, then, to the public's rich image of risk, and reflect for a moment on its many dimensions. People have a lower tolerance for involuntary than for voluntary exposure.[8] Even on its surface, the concern here is easily understood, and closely related to the dimensions of uncontrollability and uncertainty. Voluntary exposure presupposes knowledge. Knowledge coupled with freedom of action facilitates individual choice and efforts to control events bearing on the choice. To be forced to face a risk, on the other hand, or to be ignorant of it, or to sense that no one is really in command of it, leaves one's well-being in the hands of others, or of no one. Either alternative is obviously inferior, under most circumstances, to being in charge.

Upon deeper examination, this sense of voluntariness might trivialize the true concern. Suppose my situation (say I am an unskilled worker) "forces" me to "choose" a risky occupation, in exchange for some wage premium. Is my exposure to the risk "voluntary"? Suppose, more general-

---

7. Slovic, Fischhoff & Lichtenstein, *Regulation of Risk: A Psychological Perspective, in* REGULATORY POLICY AND THE SOCIAL SCIENCES 241, 263 (R. Noll ed., 1985) [hereinafter Slovic, Fischhoff & Lichtenstein, *Regulation of Risk*]; *see also id.* at 266 (Fig. 4) (showing that experts' risk judgments are closely associated with annual fatality rates) * * *

8. There is some indication that the voluntary-involuntary distinction actually serves as a proxy for other concerns, such as catastrophic potential, dread, uncontrollability, and like factors * * *.

ly, that I rightly see life as full of difficult choices. Is it sensible to say that, given my power to choose—given that any choice is "voluntary"—I should accept without complaint whatever consequences follow? The answer might be yes if the world were organized in a way consistent with ideal values and principles, but it is not. Behind the notion of voluntariness, then, there may lurk more fundamental concerns about autonomy and equality and power among individuals in the society, for it is the preexistence of these that lets free choice be morally interesting. People perhaps are saying that some risks seem consistent with such ideals and others not, and registering the view by showing a greater acceptance of risks that they regard as "voluntary" in fundamentally important ways, as opposed to "chosen" in some narrower sense.

The foregoing account enlightens us about other popular dimensions of risk, such as the enhanced dislike of delayed (latent) effects, and of irreversible ones. Latency frustrates knowledge, and irreversibility frustrates control. They make it more difficult for us to govern our own circumstances—and also to govern our governors. How do we hold accountable officials whose mistakes or misdeeds manifest themselves only decades after a term of office? And how do we correct for what they have done, if what they have done is uncorrectable? Latency and irreversibility practically deny us the fruits of trial-and-error, perhaps the best means yet devised by which to resolve uncertainty.

What of the special dislike of manmade as opposed to natural hazards? Once again, a story grows out of what has been said thus far: Humans might treat each other with motives that Nature could never have, and this matters. Mark Sagoff develops this theme in the course of considering why the government should regulate artificial risks more strictly than natural ones, even if they are "no more dangerous" (obviously, in the sense of body counting). First, people are responsible for artificial risks, but not for natural ones, and the government's job is to regulate what people do. Second, only manmade risks can, in any meaningful sense, threaten autonomy, an additional reason to be especially wary of them. Third, the harms we suffer because of the acts of others carry special injury; we mourn the deaths from a natural flood but resent, deeply, the ones from a broken dam. We "are concerned not simply with safety but with responsibility and guilt as well."

These same concerns arise in the case of those manmade risks we and others classify as "public": risks generated by highly centralized high technologies. This is especially so because public risks entail so much uncertainty (given their complexity), imply such considerable power, and are capable of such calamitous effects. The last consideration, in particular, implicates the public's aversion to the possibility of disastrous consequences and brings us to the cluster of factors that enter into what is termed "dread." Dread correlates significantly with some aspects of risk that we have already discussed, such as involuntariness and uncontrollability, but also with such others as inequitable distributions, threats to future generations, and catastrophic potential—each of which speaks almost for itself.

The idea of inequitable distributions, for example, reflects the view that just as a right thinking society should concern itself with the distribution of wealth, so too should it do so with the distribution of risk. For example, risks that might result in death or disease are often considered worth taking because they confer significant benefits not otherwise available. This risk burden may be regarded as equitably distributed only if it is borne by those who simultaneously enjoy the benefits. Burdens imposed on others, or diverted to future generations, generate worries about exploitation. Alternatively, risks concentrated in time and space might be regarded as inequitable or otherwise unacceptable because concentration can result in losses that are avoided by broader distributions. This suggests, then, a link between inequitable distributions and catastrophic potential. Concentrated risks can threaten whole communities, and the loss of a community is the loss of a valued thing distinct and apart from the disaggregated bodies of a community's citizens.

NOTES

1. Cognitive psychologists have developed a descriptive theory of how people make decisions under conditions of risk and uncertainty. A dominant theme in the theory is that most people do not evaluate risky circumstances in the manner assumed by conventional decision theory: specifically, they do not seek to maximize the expected value of some function when selecting among actions with uncertain outcome. This cognitive theory has implications for regulatory policies designed to control risk to life, health, and the environment. For further discussion, *see* Roger G. Noll & James E. Krier, *Some Implications of Cognitive Psychology for Risk Regulation*, 19 J. LEGAL STUD. 747 (1990).

2. For more discussion of how and why experts and lay persons assess environmental risks differently, *see* Dan M. Kahan, *Two Conceptions of Emotion in Risk Regulation,* 156 U. PA. L. REV. 741 (2008); HOWARD MARGOLIS, DEALING WITH RISK: WHY THE PUBLIC AND THE EXPERTS DISAGREE ON ENVIRONMENTAL ISSUES (1996); Cass R. Sunstein, *The Laws of Fear*, 115 HARV. L. REV. 1119 (2002); Howard Margolis, *A New Account of Expert/Lay Conflicts of Risk Intuition*, 8 DUKE ENVTL L. & POL'Y F. 115 (1997).[9]

3. An additional question is what aspect of a risk is most salient? Is a risk that affects children more important than one affecting the elderly, even if the death rates are the same?

---

9. A striking example of the divergence between popular and expert assessment of risk involves impacts by extraterrestrial objects. While the chance of a major impact is very small in any one time period (only about four every million years), the possible harm is truly catastrophic (including up to one billion deaths. Yet we spend only $3 million annually on efforts to detect possible impacts. Because no harmful impact has taken place in the relatively brief period of written history, most people do not take the risk seriously. *See* Michael B. Gerrard, *Risk of Hazardous Waste Sites Versus Asteroid and Comet Impacts: Accounting for the Discrepancies in U.S. Research Allocation*, 29 RISK ANALYSIS 895 (2000).

CASS R. SUNSTEIN, WHICH RISKS FIRST?[10]

1997 THE U. CHI. LEGAL F. 101, 103–105, 112–114 (1997).

Environmental protection has many purposes in addition to the protection of human life, including prevention of adverse health effects short of mortality, aesthetic goals, recreational goals, and prevention of deaths and adverse health effects in animals and plants. These purposes should also be taken into account in deciding which risks are most serious.* * *

* * * Some people think that the government should try to maximize the number of total lives saved.[11] If one program would save one hundred lives, and another eighty, the government should (other things being equal) begin with the first program. But other people, referring to pervasive differences between lay and expert evaluations of risk, reject this idea. They say that lay people have more complex, "richer" judgments about which risks are worst and that these judgments should govern regulatory policy. On this view, there is a danger that expert judgments will hide controversial ideas about rationality behind a technocratic smokescreen.

* * * I reject both of these views. A basic assumption is that the American constitutional order is a republic, or a deliberative democracy, in which public representatives are not supposed merely to register existing judgments but "to refine and enlarge the public view."[12] If the issue of risk regulation is seen in these terms, representatives should attend to reflective citizen judgments, but they should not treat those judgments uncritically or accept them regardless of the reasons offered on their behalf.* * * And if we examine the reasons that underlie risk-related judgments, we will conclude that it would be obtuse to say that government should attempt to maximize the number of lives saved, no matter the source and nature of relevant risks. Lives are not fungible with lives; it matters a great deal for what purpose and in what context lives are being put in danger. But it would also be odd to rely entirely on lay judgments, which are frequently based on confusion, ignorance, and selective attention. When those judgments are based on misunderstandings of the facts, they should play no role in policy.

I contend that government should attempt a three-step inquiry. First it should try to estimate *decently-livable life-years saved*, rather than total lives saved. Thus the first step in its analysis should be to see how much aggregate extension of decently-livable years can be brought about by different regulatory initiatives. The second step should incorporate lay judgments to the extent that these are based on reasonable judgments of

---

10. Copyright © 1997, the University of Chicago. Reprinted by permission of the University of Chicago Legal Forum.

11. This is the tendency in STEPHEN BREYER, BREAKING THE VICIOUS CIRCLE: TOWARD EFFECTIVE RISK REGULATION (Harvard 1993).

12. Federalist 10 (Madison), in Max Beloff, ed., THE FEDERALIST 45 (Basil Blackwell 2d ed. 1987).

value rather than factual error or selective attention. In this way, regulators should ask if regulatory priorities should be shifted from the aggregate measure by exploring whether there are important qualities in the context that call for a shift. The key questions here are:

—Is the risk inequitably distributed?

—Is it especially dreaded?

—Is it run involuntarily?

—How easily can it be controlled by those exposed?

Answers to these questions may call for an adjustment of the first-stage judgment. As we will see, however, the second two questions raise complex issues, for risks are not "voluntary or not" or "uncontrollable or not," but instead come with small or high costs of avoidance. The ordinary criterion of decently-livable life-years should be adjusted upward when the costs of risk avoidance are especially high, and adjusted downward when the costs of risk avoidance are especially low. The third step consists of an incorporation of effects short of mortality, including (but not limited to) morbidity, adverse effects on aesthetics and recreation, and mortality effects for plants and animals. * * *

There is considerable crudeness * * * in the idea of "lives saved" as the regulatory maximand. Of course no program "saves lives"; at best it extends them. Compare two regulations. The first extends the lives of one hundred elderly people, but in doing so, it gives them five additional years, accompanied by considerable pain and distress. The second extends the lives of eighty children, and in doing so, it gives each of them a statistical likelihood of fifty or more years of life. The second policy seems preferable to the first along two important dimensions. *First*: Lives are certainly not fungible, but where regulatory resources are limited and where choices have to be made, it makes sense (other things being equal and as an administrable start) to save as many years as possible. Other things being equal, many years should be chosen over few. *Second*: If government has a choice between preserving lives in a way that ensures decently-livable years and preserving lives in a way that ensures a barely functional and extremely painful continued existence, it should choose the former. To someone who has a choice between death and five years of constant and considerable pain, the latter will probably seem a lot better; but for government regulators, it is preferable to provide five good years rather than five difficult ones if there is a choice. We might conclude, then, that government agencies should shift their attention from "lives saved" to "decently-livable life-years saved." * * *

An especially controversial issue lurks in the background: it is possible that some lives might be considered not decently-livable because of unjust or highly disadvantageous social conditions. Desperately poor people, for example, may lack decent life prospects already, and a small incremental reduction in their health may seem to push them below the relevant "floor." For purposes of regulatory policy, this ought not to be counted. If it did count, regulatory policy would be devoted to the protection of those already well-off and to the neglect of those in desperate conditions; thus one social injustice would be compounded by another. The question is whether the saved years meet a decent floor, and it should be stipulated that this criterion is met by lives filled with extreme difficulty because of social and economic deprivation alone.

NOTES

1. Sunstein's proposal has some interesting normative implications. Consider a situation where the government has the choice between saving the lives of one infant (with a life expectancy of eighty years) and seventy elderly people (each with a life expectancy of a year). Under Sunstein's analysis, the seventy elderly people count for less than the one infant. Is this tilt against saving the lives of the elderly normatively appealing as a governmental policy? Isn't it age discrimination? On the other hand, isn't Sunstein correct that weighing a risk to an infant and an eighty-year-old equally violates common cultural norms?

2. Sunstein's hope that regulators can be insulated from public "irrationality" does not seem to be supported by the empirical evidence. In a study of Superfund (the federal program for cleaning up hazardous waste sites), two economists concluded that, besides the economically rational factors of expected cancer cases versus clean-up costs, regulatory action "is influenced by many additional factors relating both to risk perceptions and the political nature of the community bearing the risks." *See* W. Kip Viscusi & James T.Hamilton, *Are Risk Regulators Rational? Evidence from Hazardous Waste Cleanup Decisions*, 89 AM. ECON. REV. 1012 (1999).

3. So far, we have looked at the theory of risk assessment, but what of the actual practice? In the cases below, courts attempt to grapple with the complexities of risk assessment.

RESERVE MINING CO. v. ENVIRONMENTAL PROTECTION AGENCY

United States Court of Appeals, Eighth Circuit, 1975.
514 F.2d 492.

BRIGHT, CIRCUIT JUDGE.

[Reserve Mining disposed of great quantities of mining byproducts by discharging them into Lake Superior. These materials contained asbestos, which is known to be a cause of cancer when inhaled. The district court enjoined further discharges, which meant the closing of the facility. On appeal, the Eighth Circuit began by considering two issues: "first, whether the ingestion of fibers, as compared with their inhalation, poses any danger whatsoever; and second, should ingestion pose a danger, whether the exposure resulting from Reserve's discharge may be said to present a legally cognizable risk to health."]

1.   Ingestion of Fibers as a Danger to Health

All epidemiological studies which associate asbestos fibers with harm to health are based upon inhalation of these fibers by humans. Thus, although medical opinion agrees that fibers entering the respiratory tract can interact with body tissues and produce disease, it is unknown whether the same can be said of fibers entering the digestive tract. If asbestos fibers do not interact with digestive tissue, they are presumably eliminated as waste without harmful effect upon the body.

The evidence bearing upon possible harm from ingestion of fibers falls into three areas: first, the court-sponsored tissue study, designed to measure whether asbestos fibers are present in the tissues of long-time Duluth residents; second, animal experiments designed to measure whether, as a biological phenomenon, fibers can penetrate the gastrointestinal mucosa and thus interact with body tissues; third, the increased incidence of gastrointestinal cancer among workers occupationally exposed to asbestos, and the hypothesis that this increase may be due to the ingestion of fibers initially inhaled.

a.   The Tissue Study

Recognizing the complete lack of any direct evidence (epidemiological or otherwise) on the issue of whether the ingestion of fibers poses a risk, the trial court directed that a tissue study be conducted to determine whether the tissues of long-time Duluth residents contain any residue of asbestos-like fibers.

The study sought to analyze by electron microscope the tissues of recently deceased Duluth residents who had ingested Duluth water for at least 15 years; that is, approximately since the beginning of Reserve's operations. As a "control" check on results, tissue samples were obtained from the deceased residents of Houston, Texas, where the water is free of asbestos fibers. Although this study was necessarily expedited, plaintiffs' principal medical witness, Dr. Selikoff, testified to the sound design of the study and expressed his belief that it would yield significant information.

One of the court-appointed experts, Dr. Frederick Pooley, in explaining the results of the study, stated that he found that the tissues of the Duluth residents were virtually free of any fibers which could be attributed to the Reserve discharge. Dr. Brown said of this study:

> It is my conclusion, from the tissue study, that residents of Duluth have not been found to have asbestiform fibers in their tissues when compared with Houston. * * *

* * * [P]laintiffs argued, and the district court agreed, that because the specimens of tissue represented only a microscopically minute body area, the actual presence of fibers may have been overlooked.

We note that this limitation had not seemed dispositive prior to the study when Dr. Selikoff commented:

I would think we should find some fibers there. We're looking for needles in a haystack, but that's all right, we should find needles in the haystack with all the difficulties of the study, the technical difficulties, if we examine sufficiently large numbers of samples in some instances we should find some fibers there.

The district court decided, and we agree, that the study cannot be deemed conclusive in exonerating the ingestion of fibers in Lake Superior water as a hazard. The negative results must, however, be given some weight in assessing the probabilities of harm from Reserve's discharge into water. The results also weigh heavily in indicating that no emergency or imminent hazard to health exists. Thus, while this study crucially bears on the determination of whether it is necessary to close Reserve down immediately, the negative results do not dispose of the broader issue of whether the ingestion of fibers poses some danger to public health justifying abatement on less immediate terms.

b. Animal Studies and Penetration of the Gastrointestinal Mucosa

At a somewhat more theoretical level, the determination of whether ingested fibers can penetrate the gastrointestinal mucosa bears on the issue of harm through ingestion. If penetration is biologically impossible, then presumably the interaction of the fibers with body tissues will not occur.

This medical issue has been investigated through experiments with animals which, unfortunately, have produced conflicting results. For example, Reserve witness Dr. Davis reported on his experiment in feeding crocidolite and chrysotile asbestos to rats for varying periods of up to six months. He killed the rats at the end of the period and examined their gastrointestinal tissues for evidence of fibers. At the time of trial, light and electron microscopy has so far revealed no evidence of fibers in the tissues.

Plaintiffs, however, cited contrary studies. Research by George Westlake, in which rats were fed a diet including chrysotile fibers, indicated that fibers had traveled through the colon wall and accumulated in the area of the mesothelium. Pontrefact, who injected chrysotile fibers into the stomachs of rats, found that fibers had dispersed throughout the body tissues.

On this conflicting scientific evidence, Dr. Brown testified that the Westlake and Pontrefact studies provide some support for the hypothesis that asbestos fibers can penetrate the gastrointestinal mucosa.[13]

---

13. We note from the record that while attempts to induce tumors in experimental animals through the inhalation of fibers have succeeded, attempts to induce tumors by ingestion have generally failed. Reserve witness Dr. Smith ventured the opinion, based on such studies, that there is no proof that the ingestion of fibers causes cancer in man. The failure to induce animal tumors by ingestion cannot be dispositive on the issue of whether the ingestion of fibers poses a risk to humans. This is because, as a general matter, animal cancer susceptibility is not directly equivalent to human experience, and, more particularly, because the studies so far undertaken may be criticized for various shortcomings in experimental design. Thus, one of Reserve's own

c. Excess Gastrointestinal Cancer Among the Occupationally Exposed

The affirmative evidence supporting the proposition that the ingestion of fibers poses a danger to health focuses on the increased rate of gastrointestinal cancer among workers occupationally exposed to asbestos dust. Plaintiffs' experts attribute this excess incidence of gastrointestinal cancer to a theory that the asbestos workers first inhaled the asbestos dust and thereafter coughed up and swallowed the asbestos particles.

The attribution of health harm from ingestion rests upon a theoretical basis. As Dr. Selikoff explained, there are several possible explanations for the increased evidence of gastrointestinal cancer, some of which do not involve ingestion. Moreover, as noted previously, the excess rates of gastrointestinal cancer are generally "modest" and substantially lower than the excess rates of mesothelioma and lung cancer associated with inhalation of asbestos dust. Also, the experts advised that an analysis of a small exposed population may produce statistically "unstable" results.

The existence of an excess rate of gastrointestinal cancer among asbestos workers is a matter of concern. The theory that excess cancers may be attributed to the ingestion of asbestos fibers rests on a tenable medical hypothesis. Indeed, Dr. Selikoff testified that ingestion is the "probable" route accounting for the excess in gastrointestinal cancer. The occupational studies support the proposition that the ingestion of asbestos fibers can result in harm to health.

2. Level of Exposure Via Ingestion

The second primary uncertainty with respect to ingestion involves the attempt to assess whether the level of exposure from drinking water is hazardous. Of course, this inquiry is handicapped by the great variation in fiber counts, and Dr. Brown's admonition that only a qualitative, and not a quantitative, statement can be made about the presence of fibers.

In spite of these difficulties, the district court found that the level of exposure resulting from the drinking of Duluth water was "comparable" to that found to cause gastrointestinal cancer in asbestos workers. The court drew this finding from an elaborate calculation by Dr. Nicholson in which he attempted to make a statistical comparison between the fibers probably ingested by an asbestos worker subject to an excess risk of gastrointestinal cancer with the probable number of amphibole fibers ingested by a Duluth resident over a period of 18 years. * * * As is evident, this calculation is beset by several uncertainties. * * * Reserve witness Dr. Gross performed a calculation similar to Dr. Nicholson's, but using somewhat different assumptions, and concluded that Duluth water would have to contain several hundred million fibers/liter and be ingested for 60 years before an exposure comparable with occupational levels would be reached.

---

witnesses, Dr. Wright, testified that at least one of the studies may be criticized for using too few animals over too brief an experimental time.

The comparison has other weaknesses, for without regard to the comparability of the gross exposure levels, the dynamics of the exposure process are markedly different. The vagaries attendant to the use of assumptions rather than facts result in comparisons which are of dubious accuracy. Thus, Dr. Brown testified that, if Nicholson's calculations were correct, he would conclude only that the risk was non-negligible.

The Nicholson comparison, although evidentially weak, must be considered with other evidence. The record does show that the ingestion of asbestos fibers poses some risk to health, but to an undetermined degree. Given these circumstances, Dr. Brown testified that the possibility of a future excess incidence of cancer attributable to the discharge cannot be ignored:[14]

> * * * I would say that it is conceivable that gastrointestinal cancers can develop from the ingestion of asbestos, and what I don't know, Your Honor, is just how low that level of ingestion must be before the likelihood of GI cancer becomes so remote as to be, for all intents and purposes, ignored as a real live possibility. * * *

c. Conclusion

The preceding extensive discussion of the evidence demonstrates that the medical and scientific conclusions here in dispute clearly lie "on the frontiers of scientific knowledge."

The trial court, not having any proof of actual harm, was faced with a consideration of (1) the probabilities of any health harm and (2) the consequences, if any, should the harm actually occur. * * *

In assessing probabilities in this case, it cannot be said that the probability of harm is more likely than not. Moreover, the level of probability does not readily convert into a prediction of consequences. On this record it cannot be forecast that the rates of cancer will increase from drinking Lake Superior water or breathing Silver Bay air. The best that can be said is that the existence of this asbestos contaminant in air and water gives rise to a reasonable medical concern for the public health. The public's exposure to asbestos fibers in air and water creates some health risk. Such a contaminant should be removed.

The district court found that Reserve's discharge into Lake Superior violated sections 1160(c)(5) and (g)(1) of the Federal Water Pollution Control Act (FWPCA). These two provisions authorize an action by the United States to secure abatement of water discharges in interstate waters where the discharges violate state water quality standards and "endanger * * * the health or welfare of persons." § 1160(g)(1).

---

14. Since Lake Superior affords water supplies to an estimated 200,000 people of Duluth and other North Shore Minnesota municipalities, as well as Superior, Wisconsin, we think it is essential that the facts regarding the present disease effects of the discharge be accurately stated. As our review below demonstrates, we conclude that there is no evidence on a scientific or medical basis showing that Duluth residents experience an excess rate of cancer attributable to Reserve's discharge.

In the context of this environmental legislation, we believe that Congress used the term "endangering" in a precautionary or preventive sense, and, therefore, evidence of potential harm as well as actual harm comes within the purview of that term. We are fortified in this view by the flexible provisions for injunctive relief which permit a court "to enter such judgment and orders enforcing such judgment as the public interest and the equities of the case may require." 33 U.S.C. § 1160(c)(5). * * *

Concededly, the trial court considered many appropriate factors in arriving at a remedy, such as a) the nature of the anticipated harm, b) the burden on Reserve and its employees from the issuance of the injunction, c) the financial ability of Reserve to convert to other methods of waste disposal, and d) a margin of safety for the public.

An additional crucial element necessary for a proper assessment of the health hazard rests upon a proper analysis of the probabilities of harm.

With respect to the water, these probabilities must be deemed low for they do not rest on a history of past health harm attributable to ingestion but on a medical theory implicating the ingestion of asbestos fibers as a causative factor in increasing the rates of gastrointestinal cancer among asbestos workers. With respect to air, the assessment of the risk of harm rests on a higher degree of proof, a correlation between inhalation of asbestos dust and subsequent illness. But here, too, the hazard cannot be measured in terms of predictability, but the assessment must be made without direct proof. But, the hazard in both the air and water can be measured in only the most general terms as a concern for the public health resting upon a reasonable medical theory. Serious consequences could result if the hypothesis on which it is based should ultimately prove true.

A court is not powerless to act in these circumstances. But an immediate injunction cannot be justified in striking a balance between unpredictable health effects and the clearly predictable social and economic consequences that would follow the plant closing.

In addition to the health risk posed by Reserve's discharges, the district court premised its immediate termination of the discharges upon Reserve's persistent refusal to implement a reasonable alternative plan for on-land disposal of tailings.

During these appeal proceedings, Reserve has indicated its willingness to deposit its tailings on land and to properly filter its air emissions. At oral argument, Reserve advised us of a willingness to spend 243 million dollars in plant alteration and construction to halt its pollution of air and water. Reserve's offer to continue operations and proceed to construction of land disposal facilities for its tailings, if permitted to do so by the State of Minnesota, when viewed in conjunction with the uncertain quality of the health risk created by Reserve's discharges, weighs heavily against a ruling which closes Reserve's plant immediately.

Indeed, the intervening union argues, with some persuasiveness, that ill health effects resulting from the prolonged unemployment of the head of the family on a closing of the Reserve facility may be more certain than the harm from drinking Lake Superior water or breathing Silver Bay air.

Furthermore, Congress has generally geared its national environmental policy to allowing polluting industries a reasonable period of time to make adjustments in their efforts to conform to federal standards.

We believe that on this record the district court abused its discretion by immediately closing this major industrial plant. In this case, the risk of harm to the public is potential, not imminent or certain, and Reserve says it earnestly seeks a practical way to abate the pollution. A remedy should be fashioned which will serve the ultimate public weal by insuring clean air, clean water, and continued jobs in an industry vital to the nation's welfare. * * *

Reserve shall be given a reasonable time to stop discharging its wastes into Lake Superior. A reasonable time includes the time necessary for Minnesota to act on Reserve's present application to dispose of its tailings at Milepost 7 (Lax Lake site), or to come to agreement on some other site acceptable to both Reserve and the state. Assuming agreement and designation of an appropriate land disposal site, Reserve is entitled to a reasonable turn-around time to construct the necessary facilities and accomplish a changeover in the means of disposing of its taconite wastes.

NOTES

1. On the basis of the evidence discussed in the opinion, would a court be justified in finding by the preponderance of the evidence that waterborne asbestos fibers cause cancer? If not, how can the court justify forcing Reserve to spend $243 million to end the problem?

2. Consider the aftermath of the case:

Reserve's dumping in Lake Superior ended on March 16, 1980—five years (almost to the day) after the Eighth Circuit's en banc opinion, ... and *eleven and a half years* after the Stoddard Report recommended disposal at essentially the same location. Intransigence, in the end, bought Reserve eleven years of continued pollution and continued profits.

The epilogue is cruelly ironic. Over the years, from the original permit hearings to Milepost 7, Reserve had maintained that an end to dumping in the lake would be an end to its operations. In fact, Reserve profitably shifted to on-land disposal in 1980—only to shut down two years later in the general economic downturn of 1982. [Ultimately, the plant] was sold in bankruptcy to Cyprus Mineral Company in 1989, which reopened the facility at half capacity as Northshore Mining Company. Northshore is now a wholly owned subsidiary of Cleveland–Cliffs, coincidentally one of the original owners of Reserve.

John S. Applegate, *The Story of Reserve Mining: Managing Scientific Uncertainty in Environmental Regulation*, in RICHARD J. LAZARUS & OLIVER A. HOUCK, ENVIRONMENTAL LAW STORIES 70 (2005).

3. The *Reserve* decision received strong support from the D.C. Circuit's opinion in *Ethyl Corp. v. EPA*, 541 F.2d 1 (D.C. Cir. 1976) (en banc). That case involved section 211(c)(1)(A) of the Clean Air Act, authorizing EPA to regulate gasoline additives whose emission products "will endanger the public health or welfare." Acting pursuant to this power, EPA determined that lead additives in gasoline presented "a significant risk of harm" to the public health and issued orders limiting the use of such additives. In upholding the EPA, the court stressed that risk management involves policy judgments rather than simply factual determinations. Thus, the court accorded substantial deference to the EPA's conclusion. As the court explained:

> Questions involving the environment are particularly prone to uncertainty. Technological man has altered his world in ways never before experienced or anticipated. The health effects of such alterations are often unknown, sometimes unknowable. While a concerned Congress has passed legislation providing for protection of the public health against gross environmental modifications, the regulators entrusted with the enforcement of such laws have not thereby been endowed with a prescience that removes all doubt from their decision making. Rather, speculation, conflicts, and theoretical extrapolation typify their every action. How else can they act, given a mandate to protect the public health but only a slight or nonexistent data base upon which to draw?

Thus, the court concluded that a rigorous, step-by-step proof of cause and effect should not be demanded where a statute is precautionary in nature, the evidence is on the frontiers of scientific knowledge, and regulations are designed to protect the public health. Instead, EPA may apply its expertise to draw conclusions from "suspected, but not completely substantiated" relationships between facts, from trends among facts, from theoretical projections, and so forth.

This approach was followed in numerous lower court opinions. For example, in *Lead Industries Association, Inc. v. EPA,* 647 F.2d 1130 (D.C.Cir. 1980), the D.C. Circuit upheld a primary air quality standard for lead that incorporated an "adequate margin of safety." In setting the margin of safety, EPA had given no consideration to feasibility or cost. Moreover, the evidence of harm was unclear. Nevertheless, the court held that feasibility and cost were irrelevant and that EPA had acted properly in setting the margin of safety. The court explained that use of a margin of safety is an important method of protecting against effects that have not yet been uncovered by research and effects whose medical significance is a matter of disagreement. As the court also explained, "Congress has recently acknowledged that more often than not the 'margins of safety' that are incorporated into air quality standards turn out to be very modest or nonexistent, as new information reveals adverse health effects at pollution levels once thought to be harmless." The court also reiterated the need for deference to EPA's expert judgments on these issues. Finally, the court held that the margin of safety requirement could be fulfilled by making conservative decisions at various points in the regulatory process, rather than by determining a safe level and adding a percentage to that as the "margin of safety."

In general, these lower court decisions demonstrated a high degree of deference to EPA's expert judgment. The lower courts, by and large, gave little weight to questions of cost and feasibility when dealing with toxic chemicals. Finally, these courts recognized that administrative action was justified without a showing that harmful effects were more likely than not. Instead, these courts concluded that regulatory intervention was justified whenever a reasonable likelihood of danger could be found.

4.   The Supreme Court did not have occasion to consider the issue of risk management until 1980. It then decided two cases in as many years. Before proceeding to consider these cases, it should be noted that they arise in a somewhat different context from most environmental issues. Both of the Supreme Court cases involve protection of workers by the Occupational Safety and Health Administration (OSHA).

OSHA is primarily concerned with quite different problems of worker protection, such as safety equipment. The only statutory provision dealing expressly with toxic chemicals is section 6(b)(5) of the OSH Act, 29 U.S.C. section 655(d)(5). This provision requires the agency to set a standard for any toxic material "which most adequately assures, to the extent feasible, that no employee will suffer material impairment of health or functional capacity." Another section of the Act, section 3(8), 29 U.S.C. section 652(8), is also relevant. This section simply defines an occupational safety and health standard as a regulation setting any one of a variety of requirements "reasonably necessary or appropriate to provide safe or healthful places of employment."

INDUSTRIAL UNION DEPARTMENT, AFL–CIO v. AMERICAN PETROLEUM INSTITUTE

Supreme Court of the United States, 1980.
448 U.S. 607, 100 S.Ct. 2844, 65 L.Ed.2d 1010.

JUSTICE STEVENS announced the judgment of the Court and delivered an opinion in which THE CHIEF JUSTICE and JUSTICE STEWART join and in Parts I, II, III–A–C and E of which JUSTICE POWELL joins.

I.

[In sections I and II of the opinion, Justice Stevens set out the background of the case. The case involved an OSHA regulation governing exposure to benzene. The Secretary of Labor had found that benzene was a carcinogen and that no known safe level existed. Hence, he lowered the permissible exposure level for workers from 10 ppm (parts per million) to 1 ppm, which he considered the lowest feasible level. OSHA (the Occupational Safety and Health Administration, within the Department of Labor) estimated the total costs of compliance as including $266 million in capital investments, $200 million in first-year start-up costs, and $34 million in annual costs. About 35,000 employees would benefit from the regulation. There were two arguably relevant statutory provisions. section 3(8) of the Act, 29 U.S.C. section 652(8), defined an occupational safety and health standard as a standard setting any one of a variety of requirements "reasonably necessary or appropriate to provide safe or healthful employment or places of employment." § 6(b)(5) of the Act, 29 U.S.C. § 655(b)(5), required the Secretary to set a standard for any toxic materials "which most adequately assures, to the extent feasible, that no employee will suffer material impairment of health or functional capacity."]

III.

A.

[This section sets out the statutes and the contentions of the parties. Essentially, industry argued that § 3(8) required a cost-benefit analysis, while the Secretary argued that he was "required to impose standards that either guarantee workplaces that are free from any risk of material health impairment, however small, or that come as close as possible to doing so without ruining entire industries."]

If the purpose of the statute were to eliminate completely and with absolute certainty any risk of serious harm, we would agree that it would be proper for the Secretary to interpret §§ 3(8) and 6(b)(5) in this fashion. But we think it is clear that the statute was not designed to require employers to provide absolutely risk-free workplaces whenever it is technologically feasible to do so, so long as the cost is not great enough to destroy an entire industry. Rather, both the language and structure of the Act, as well as its legislative history, indicate that it was intended to require the elimination, as far as feasible, of significant risks of harm.

B.

By empowering the Secretary to promulgate standards that are "reasonably necessary or appropriate to provide safe or healthful employment and places of employment," the Act implies that, before promulgating any standard, the Secretary must make a finding that the workplaces in question are not safe. But "safe" is not the equivalent of "risk-free." There are many activities that we engage in every day—such as driving a car or even breathing city air—that entail some risk of accident or material health impairment; nevertheless, few people would consider these activities "unsafe." Similarly, a workplace can hardly be considered "unsafe" unless it threatens the workers with a significant risk of harm.

Therefore, before he can promulgate *any* permanent health or safety standard, the Secretary is required to make a threshold finding that a place of employment is unsafe—in the sense that significant risks are present and can be eliminated or lessened by a change in practices. This requirement applies to permanent standards promulgated pursuant to § 6(b)(5), as well as to other types of permanent standards. For there is no reason why § 3(8)'s definition of a standard should not be deemed incorporated by reference into § 6(b)(5). The standards promulgated pursuant to § 6(b)(5) are just one species of the genus of standards governed by the basic requirement. That section repeatedly uses the term "standard" without suggesting any exception from, or qualification of the general definition; on the contrary, it directs the Secretary to select "*the standard*"—that is to say, one of various possible alternatives that satisfy the basic definition in § 3(8)—that is most protective. Moreover, requiring the Secretary to make a threshold finding of significant risk is consistent with the scope of the regulatory power granted to him by § 6(b)(5), which empowers the Secretary to promulgate standards, not for chemical and physical agents generally, but for "*toxic* chemicals" and "*harmful* physical agents." * * *

In the absence of a clear mandate in the Act, it is unreasonable to assume that Congress intended to give the Secretary the unprecedented power over American industry that would result from the Government's view of §§ 3(8) and 6(b)(5), coupled with OSHA's cancer policy. Expert testimony that a substance is probably a human carcinogen—either because it has caused cancer in animals or because individuals have contracted cancer following extremely high exposures—would justify the conclusion that the substance poses some risk of serious harm no matter how minute the exposure and no matter how many experts testified that they regarded the risk as insignificant. That conclusion would in turn justify pervasive regulation limited only by the constraint of feasibility. In light of the fact that there are literally thousands of substances used in the workplace that have been identified as carcinogens or suspect carcinogens, the Government's theory would give OSHA power to impose enormous costs that might produce little, if any, discernible benefit.

If the Government was correct in arguing that neither § 3(8) nor § 6(b)(5) requires that the risk from a toxic substance be quantified sufficiently to enable the Secretary to characterize it as significant in an understandable way, the statute would make such a "sweeping delegation of legislative power" that it might be unconstitutional under the Court's reasoning in *Schechter Poultry Corp. v. United States,* 295 U.S. 495, 539, 55 S. Ct. 837, 847, 79 L. Ed. 1570, and *Panama Refining Co. v. Ryan,* 293 U.S. 388, 55 S. Ct. 241, 79 L. Ed. 446. A construction of the statute that avoids this kind of open-ended grant should certainly be favored.

C.

[In this section of the opinion, Justice Stevens argues that this construction of the statute is supported by the legislative history.]

D.

Given the conclusion that the Act empowers the Secretary to promulgate health and safety standards only where a significant risk of harm exists, the critical issue becomes how to define and allocate the burden of proving the significance of the risk in a case such as this, where scientific knowledge is imperfect and the precise quantification of risks is therefore impossible. The Agency's position is that there is substantial evidence in the record to support its conclusion that there is no absolutely safe level for a carcinogen and that, therefore, the burden is properly on industry to prove, apparently beyond a shadow of a doubt, that there is a safe level for benzene exposure. The Agency argues that, because of the uncertainties in this area, any other approach would render it helpless, forcing it to wait for the leukemia deaths that it believes are likely to occur before taking any regulatory action.

We disagree. As we read the statute, the burden was on the Agency to show, on the basis of substantial evidence, that it is at least more likely than not that long-term exposure to 10 ppm of benzene presents a significant risk of material health impairment. Ordinarily, it is the proponent of a rule or order who has the burden of proof in administrative proceedings. *See* 5 U.S.C. § 556(d). In some cases involving toxic substances, Congress has shifted the burden of proving that a particular substance is safe onto the party opposing the proposed rule.[15] The fact that Congress did not follow this course in enacting OSHA indicates that it intended the Agency to bear the normal burden of establishing the need for a proposed standard.

In this case OSHA did not even attempt to carry its burden of proof. The closest it came to making a finding that benzene presented a significant risk of harm in the workplace was its statement that the benefits to be derived from lowering the permissible exposure level from 10 to 1 ppm were "likely" to be "appreciable." The Court of Appeals held that this finding was not supported by substantial evidence. Of greater importance, even if it were supported by substantial evidence, such a finding would not be sufficient to satisfy the Agency's obligations under the Act.

The inadequacy of the Agency's findings can perhaps be illustrated best by its rejection of industry testimony that a dose-response curve can be formulated on the basis of current epidemiological evidence and that, even under the most conservative extrapolation theory, current exposure levels would cause at most two deaths out of a population of about 30,000 workers every six years. In rejecting this testimony, OSHA made the following statement:

> In the face of the record evidence of numerous actual deaths attributable to benzene-induced leukemia and other fatal blood diseases, OSHA is unwilling to rely on the hypothesis that at most two cancers every six years would be prevented by the proposed standard. By way of example, the Infante study disclosed seven excess leukemia deaths in a population of about 600 people over a 25–year period. While the Infante study involved higher exposures than those currently encountered, the incidence rates found by Infante, together with the numerous other cases reported in the literature of benzene leukemia and other fatal blood diseases, makes it difficult for OSHA to rely on the [witness'] hypothesis to assure that statutorily mandated protection

---

15.   *See Envtl. Defense Fund v. EPA*, 548 F.2d 998, 1004, 1012–1018 (1976), *cert. denied*, 431 U.S. 925, 97 S.Ct. 2199, 53 L.Ed.2d 239, where the court rejected the argument that the EPA has the burden of proving that a pesticide is unsafe in order to suspend its registration under the Federal Insecticide, Fungicide and Rodenticide Act. The court noted that Congress had deliberately shifted the ordinary burden of proof under the APA, requiring manufacturers to establish the continued safety of their products.

for employees. In any event, due to the fact that there is no safe level of exposure to benzene and that it is impossible to precisely quantify the anticipated benefits, OSHA must select the level of exposure which is most protective of exposed employees.

There are three possible interpretations of OSHA's stated reason for rejecting the witness' testimony: (1) OSHA considered it probable that a greater number of lives would be saved by lowering the standard from 10 ppm; (2) OSHA thought that saving two lives every six years in a work force of 30,000 persons is a significant savings that makes it reasonable and appropriate to adopt a new standard; or (3) even if the small number is not significant and even if the savings may be even smaller, the Agency nevertheless believed it had a statutory duty to select the level of exposure that is most protective of the exposed employees if it is economically and technologically feasible to do so. Even if the Secretary did not intend to rely entirely on this third theory, his construction of the statute would make it proper for him to do so. Moreover, he made no express findings of fact that would support his 1 ppm standard on any less drastic theory. Under these circumstances, we can hardly agree with the Government that OSHA discharged its duty under the Act.

Contrary to the Government's contentions, imposing a burden on the Agency of demonstrating a significant risk of harm will not strip it of its ability to regulate carcinogens, nor will it require the Agency to wait for deaths to occur before taking any action. First, the requirement that a "significant" risk be identified is not a mathematical straitjacket. It is the Agency's responsibility to determine, in the first instance, what it considers to be a "significant" risk. Some risks are plainly acceptable and others are plainly unacceptable. If, for example, the odds are one in a billion that a person will die from cancer by taking a drink of chlorinated water, the risk clearly could not be considered significant. On the other hand, if the odds are one in a thousand that regular inhalation of gasoline vapors that are two percent benzene will be fatal, a reasonable person might well consider the risk significant and take appropriate steps to decrease or eliminate it. Although the Agency has no duty to calculate the exact probability of harm, it does have an obligation to find that a significant risk is present before it can characterize a place of employment as "unsafe."[16]

Second, OSHA is not required to support its finding that a significant risk exists with anything approaching scientific certainty. Although the Agency's findings must be supported by substantial evidence, 29 U.S.C.

---

16. In his dissenting opinion, Mr. Justice Marshall states that "when the question involves determination of the acceptable level of risk, the ultimate decision must necessarily be based on considerations of policy as well as empirically verifiable facts. Factual determinations can at most define the risk in some statistical way; the judgment whether that risk is tolerable cannot be based solely on a resolution of the facts." We agree. Thus, while the Agency must support its finding that a certain level of risk exists by substantial evidence, we recognize that its determination that a particular level of risk is "significant" will be based largely on policy considerations. At this point we have no need to reach the issue of what level of scrutiny a reviewing court should apply to the latter type of determination.

§ 655(f), § 6(b)(5) specifically allows the Secretary to regulate on the basis of the "best available evidence." As several courts of appeals have held, this provision requires a reviewing court to give OSHA some leeway where its findings must be made on the frontiers of scientific knowledge. Thus, so long as they are supported by a body of reputable scientific thought, the Agency is free to use conservative assumptions in interpreting the data with respect to carcinogens, risking error on the side of over-protection rather than under-protection.[17]

Finally, the record in this case and OSHA's own rulings on other carcinogens indicate that there are a number of ways in which the Agency can make a rational judgment about the relative significance of the risks associated with exposure to a particular carcinogen.[18] * * *

E.

Because our review of this case has involved a more detailed examination of the record than is customary, it must be emphasized that we have neither made any factual determinations of our own, nor have we rejected any factual findings made by the Secretary. We express no opinion on what factual findings this record might support, either on the basis of empirical evidence or on the basis of expert testimony; nor do we express any opinion on the more difficult question of what factual determinations would warrant a conclusion that significant risks are present which make promulgation of a new standard reasonably necessary or appropriate. The standard must, of course, be supported by the findings actually made by the Secretary, not merely by findings that we believe he might have made.

In this case the record makes it perfectly clear that the Secretary relied squarely on a special policy for carcinogens that imposed the burden on industry of proving the existence of a safe level of exposure, thereby avoiding the Secretary's threshold responsibility of establishing the need for more stringent standards. In so interpreting his statutory authority, the Secretary exceeded his power.

IV.

[In this part of the opinion, the court remanded a standard governing skin contact with benzene, for similar reasons.]

---

17. Mr. Justice Marshall states that, under our approach, the agency must either wait for deaths to occur or must "deceive the public" by making a basically meaningless determination of significance based on totally inadequate evidence. Mr. Justice Marshall's view, however, rests on the erroneous premise that the only reason OSHA did not attempt to quantify benefits in this case was because it could not do so in any reasonable manner. As the discussion of the Agency's rejection of an industry attempt at formulating a dose-response curve demonstrates, however, the Agency's rejection of methods such as dose-response curves was based at least in part on its view that nothing less than absolute safety would suffice.

18. For example, in the coke oven emissions standard, OSHA had calculated that 21,000 exposed coke oven workers had an annual excess mortality of over 200 and that the proposed standard might well eliminate the risk entirely.In other proceedings, the Agency has had a good deal of data from animal experiments on which it could base a conclusion on the significance of the risk. For example, the record on the vinyl chloride standard indicated that a significant number of animals had developed tumors of the liver, lung and skin when they were exposed to 50 ppm of vinyl chloride over a period of 11 months. One hundred out of 200 animals died during that period.

The judgment of the Court of Appeals remanding the petition for review to the Secretary for further proceedings is affirmed.

It is so ordered.

CHIEF JUSTICE BURGER, concurring.

This case presses upon the Court difficult unanswered questions on the frontiers of science and medicine. The statute and the legislative history give ambiguous signals as to how the Secretary is directed to operate in this area. The opinion by Mr. Justice Stevens takes on a difficult task to decode the message of the statute as to guidelines for administrative action.

To comply with statutory requirements, the Secretary must bear the burden of "finding" that a proposed health and safety standard is "reasonably necessary or appropriate to provide safe or healthful employment and places of employment." This policy judgment entails the subsidiary finding that the pre-existing standard presents a "significant risk" of material health impairment for a worker who spends his entire employment life in a working environment where exposure remains at maximum permissible levels. The Secretary's factual finding of "risk" must be "quantified sufficiently to enable the Secretary to characterize it as significant in an understandable way." Precisely what this means is difficult to say. But because these mandated findings were not made by the Secretary, I agree that the 1 ppm benzene standard must be invalidated. However, I would stress the differing functions of the courts and the administrative agency with respect to such health and safety regulation.

The Congress is the ultimate regulator and the narrow function of the courts is to discern the meaning of the statute and the implementing regulations with the objective of ensuring that in promulgating health and safety standards the Secretary "has given reasoned consideration to each of the pertinent factors" and has complied with statutory commands. Our holding that the Secretary must retrace his steps with greater care and consideration is not to be taken in derogation of the scope of legitimate agency discretion. When the facts and arguments have been presented and duly considered, the Secretary must make a policy judgment as to whether a specific risk of health impairment is significant in terms of the policy objectives of the statute. When he acts in this capacity, pursuant to the legislative authority delegated by Congress, he exercises the prerogatives of the legislature—to focus on only one aspect of a larger problem, or to promulgate regulations that, to some, may appear as imprudent policy or inefficient allocation of resources. The judicial function does not extend to substantive revision of regulatory policy. That function lies elsewhere—in Congressional and Executive oversight or amendatory legislation; although to be sure the boundaries are often ill defined and indistinct.

Nevertheless, when discharging his duties under the statute, the Secretary is well admonished to remember that a heavy responsibility burdens his authority. Inherent in this statutory scheme is authority to refrain from regulation of insignificant or de minimis risks. * * * When the administrative record reveals only scant or minimal risk of material health impairment, responsible administration calls for avoidance of extravagant, comprehensive regulation. Perfect safety is a chimera; regulation must not strangle human activity in the search for the impossible.

JUSTICE POWELL, concurring in part and in the judgment.

I join Parts I, II, III A–C, and III–E of the plurality opinion.[19] The Occupational Safety and Health Agency relied in large part on its "carcinogen policy"—which had not been adopted formally—in promulgating the benzene exposure and dermal contact regulation at issue in this case. For the reasons stated by the plurality, I agree that §§ 6(b)(5) and 3(8) must be read together. They require OSHA to make a threshold finding that proposed occupational health standards are reasonably necessary to provide safe workplaces. When OSHA acts to reduce existing national consensus standards, therefore, it must find that (i) currently permissible exposure levels create a significant risk of material health impairment; and (ii) a reduction of those levels would significantly reduce the hazard.

Although I would not rule out the possibility that the necessary findings could rest in part on generic policies properly adopted by OSHA, see Thomas O. McGarity, Substantive and Procedural Discretion in Administrative Resolution of Science Policy Questions: Regulating Carcinogens in EPA and OSHA, 67 Geo. L. J. 729, 754–759 (1979), no properly supported agency policies are before us in this case.[20] I therefore agree with the plurality that the regulation is invalid to the extent it rests upon the assumption that exposure to known carcinogens always should be reduced to a level proven to be safe or, if no such level is found, to the lowest level that the affected industry can achieve with available technology.

[Justice Powell concluded that the agency had failed to carry its burden and also had failed to give adequate consideration to cost.]

JUSTICE REHNQUIST, concurring in the judgment.

In considering these alternative interpretations, my colleagues manifest a good deal of uncertainty, and ultimately divide over whether the Secretary produced sufficient evidence that the proposed standard for benzene will result in any appreciable benefits at all. This uncertainty, I would suggest, is eminently justified, since I believe that this case presents the Court with what has to be one of the most difficult issues that could

---

19. These portions of the plurality opinion primarily address OSHA's special carcinogen policy, rather than OSHA's argument that it also made evidentiary findings. I do not necessarily agree with every observation in the plurality opinion concerning the presence or absence of such findings. I also express no view on the question whether a different interpretation of the statute would violate the nondelegation doctrine of Schechter Poultry Corp. v. United States, 295 U.S. 495 (1935), and Panama Refining Co. v. Ryan, 293 U.S. 388 (1935).

20. OSHA has adopted a formal policy for regulating carcinogens effective April 12, 1980. 45 Fed. Reg. 5002 (Jan. 22, 1980). But no such policy was in effect when the agency promulgated its benzene regulation. Moreover, neither the factual determinations nor the administrative judgments upon which the policy rests are supported adequately on this record alone. Accordingly, we have no occasion to consider the extent to which valid agency policies may supply a basis for a finding that health risks exist in particular cases.

confront a decision-maker: whether the statistical possibility of future deaths should ever be disregarded in light of the economic costs of preventing those deaths. I would also suggest that the widely varying positions advanced in the briefs of the parties and in the opinions of Mr. Justice Stevens, The Chief Justice, Mr. Justice Powell, and Mr. Justice Marshall demonstrate, perhaps better than any other fact, that Congress, the governmental body best suited and most obligated to make the choice confronting us in this case, has improperly delegated that choice to the Secretary of Labor and, derivatively, to this Court. * * *

If we are ever to reshoulder the burden of ensuring that Congress itself makes the critical policy decisions, this is surely the case in which to do it. It is difficult to imagine a more obvious example of Congress simply avoiding a choice which was both fundamental for purposes of the statute and yet politically so divisive that the necessary decision or compromise was difficult, if not impossible, to hammer out in the legislative forge. Far from detracting from the substantive authority of Congress, a declaration that the first sentence of § 6(b)(5) of the OSHA constitutes an invalid delegation to the Secretary of Labor would preserve the authority of Congress. If Congress wishes to legislate in an area which it has not previously sought to enter, it will in today's political world undoubtedly run into opposition no matter how the legislation is formulated. But that is the very essence of legislative authority under our system. It is the hard choices, and not the filling in of the blanks, which must be made by the elected representatives of the people. When fundamental policy decisions underlying important legislation about to be enacted are to be made, the buck stops with Congress and the President insofar as he exercises his constitutional role in the legislative process.

I would invalidate the first sentence of § 6(b)(5) of the Occupational Safety and Health Act of 1970 as it applies to any toxic substance or harmful physical agent for which a safe level, that is a level at which "no employee will suffer material impairment of health or functional capacity even if such employee has regular exposure to [that hazard] for the period of his working life[,]" is, according to the Secretary, unknown or otherwise "infeasible." Absent further congressional action, the Secretary would then have to choose, when acting pursuant to § 6(b)(5), between setting a safe standard or setting no standard at all.[21] Accordingly, for the reasons stated above, I concur in the judgment of the Court affirming the judgment of the Court of Appeals.

JUSTICE MARSHALL, with whom JUSTICE BRENNAN, JUSTICE WHITE, and JUSTICE BLACKMUN join, dissenting.

In cases of statutory construction, this Court's authority is limited. If the statutory language and legislative intent are plain, the judicial inquiry is at an end. Under our jurisprudence, it is presumed that ill-considered or

---

21. This ruling would not have any effect upon standards governing toxic substances or harmful physical agents for which safe levels are feasible, upon extant standards promulgated as "national consensus standards" under § 6(a), nor upon the Secretary's authority to promulgate "emergency temporary standards" under § 6(c).

unwise legislation will be corrected through the democratic process; a court is not permitted to distort a statute's meaning in order to make it conform with the Justices' own views of sound social policy. *See TVA v. Hill* [*page* 192 infra].

Today's decision flagrantly disregards these restrictions on judicial authority. The plurality ignores the plain meaning of the Occupational Safety and Health Act of 1970 in order to bring the authority of the Secretary of Labor in line with the plurality's own views of proper regulatory policy. The unfortunate consequence is that the Federal Government's efforts to protect American workers from cancer and other crippling diseases may be substantially impaired.

The first sentence of § 6(b)(5) of the Act provides:

"The Secretary, in promulgating standards dealing with toxic materials or harmful physical agents under this subsection, shall set the standard which most adequately assures, to the extent feasible, on the basis of the best available evidence, that no employee will suffer material impairment of health or functional capacity even if such employee has regular exposure to the hazard dealt with by such standard for the period of his working life."

In this case the Secretary of Labor found, on the basis of substantial evidence, that (1) exposure to benzene creates a risk of cancer, chromosomal damage, and a variety of nonmalignant but potentially fatal blood disorders, even at the level of 1 ppm; (2) no safe level of exposure has been shown; (3) benefits in the form of saved lives would be derived from the permanent standard; (4) the number of lives that would be saved could turn out to be either substantial or relatively small; (5) under the present state of scientific knowledge, it is impossible to calculate even in a rough way the number of lives that would be saved, at least without making assumptions that would appear absurd to much of the medical community; and (6) the standard would not materially harm the financial condition of the covered industries. The Court does not set aside any of these findings. Thus, it could not be plainer that the Secretary's decision was fully in accord with his statutory mandate "most adequately [to] assure[ ] * * * that no employee will suffer material impairment of health or functional capacity."

The plurality's conclusion to the contrary is based on its interpretation of [section 3(8)], which defines an occupational safety and health standard as one "which requires conditions * * * reasonably necessary or appropriate to provide safe or healthful employment." According to the plurality, a standard is not "reasonably necessary or appropriate" unless the Secretary is able to show that it is "at least more likely than not" that the risk he seeks to regulate is a "significant" one. Nothing in the statute's language or legislative history, however, indicates that the "reasonably necessary or appropriate" language should be given this meaning. Indeed, both demonstrate that the plurality's standard bears no connection with the acts or intentions of Congress and is based only on the plurality's solicitude for the welfare of regulated industries. And the plurality uses this standard to evaluate not the agency's decision in this case, but a strawman of its own creation. * * *

The plurality's discussion of the record in this case is both extraordinarily arrogant and extraordinarily unfair. It is arrogant because the plurality presumes to make its own factual findings with respect to a variety of disputed issues relating to carcinogen regulation. It should not be necessary to remind the Members of this Court that they were not appointed to undertake independent review of adequately supported scientific findings made by a technically expert agency. And the plurality's discussion is unfair because its characterization of the Secretary's report bears practically no resemblance to what the Secretary actually did in this case. Contrary to the plurality's suggestion, the Secretary did not rely blindly on some draconian carcinogen "policy." If he had, it would have been sufficient for him to have observed that benzene is a carcinogen, a proposition that respondents do not dispute. Instead, the Secretary gathered over 50 volumes of exhibits and testimony and offered a detailed and evenhanded discussion of the relationship between exposure to benzene at all recorded exposure levels and chromosomal damage, aplastic anemia, and leukemia. In that discussion he evaluated, and took seriously, respondents' evidence of a safe exposure level. * * *

In recent years there has been increasing recognition that the products of technological development may have harmful effects whose incidence and severity cannot be predicted with certainty. The responsibility to regulate such products has fallen to administrative agencies. Their task is not an enviable one. Frequently no clear causal link can be established between the regulated substance and the harm to be averted. Risks of harm are often uncertain, but inaction has considerable costs of its own. The agency must decide whether to take regulatory action against possibly substantial risks or to wait until more definitive information becomes available—a judgment which by its very nature cannot be based solely on determinations of fact.

Those delegations, in turn, have been made on the understanding that judicial review would be available to ensure that the agency's determinations are supported by substantial evidence and that its actions do not exceed the limits set by Congress. In the Occupational Safety and Health Act, Congress expressed confidence that the courts would carry out this important responsibility. But in this case the plurality has far exceeded its authority. The plurality's "threshold finding" requirement is nowhere to be found in the Act and is antithetical to its basic purposes. "The fundamental policy questions appropriately resolved in Congress * * * are *not* subject to re-examination in the federal courts under the guise of judicial review of agency action." *Vermont Yankee Nuclear Power Corp. v. NRDC*, [page 443, *infra*]. Surely this is no less true of the decision to ensure safety for the American worker than the decision to proceed with nuclear power.

Because the approach taken by the plurality is so plainly irreconcilable with the Court's proper institutional role, I am certain that it will not stand the test of time. In all likelihood, today's decision will come to be regarded as an extreme reaction to a regulatory scheme that, as the Members of the plurality perceived it, imposed an unduly harsh burden on regulated industries. But as the Constitution "does not enact Mr. Herbert Spencer's Social Statics," *Lochner v. New York,* 198 U.S. 45, 75, 25 S. Ct. 539, 546, 49 L. Ed. 937 (1905) (Holmes, J., dissenting), so the responsibility to scrutinize federal administrative action does not authorize this Court to strike its own balance between the costs and benefits of occupational safety standards. I am confident that the approach taken by the plurality today, like that in *Lochner* itself, will eventually be abandoned, and that the representative branches of government will once again be allowed to determine the level of safety and health protection to be accorded to the American worker.

NOTES

1.   According to the plurality, a one in a thousand risk "might well" be significant. As applied to the general population, such a risk level would mean approximately 300,000 deaths. How many *additional* deaths would be required before the plurality would find a risk *clearly* significant?

2.   Much of the disagreement in *Industrial Union Department* seemed to stem from varying concepts of risk. The plurality seemed to identify risk with the actual mortality rate caused by existing conditions. The plurality apparently would require the Secretary to find that it is more likely than not that the mortality rate would be "significant." In other words, the Secretary sets a threshold and acts only if the mortality rate exceeds that threshold. Justice Marshall, on the other hand, believes the Secretary should act if there is a substantial likelihood, even though less than 50%, that the mortality rate caused by existing conditions is significant.

3.   The disagreement between Stevens and Marshall can also be viewed as a dispute over burden of proof. Justice Stevens would require the Secretary to establish that present levels are unsafe. On the other hand, Justice Marshall, in effect, would recognize a presumption of danger at present levels once a chemical is shown to be toxic at higher levels. Under the Marshall approach, the Secretary must set a level of exposure at which he can make an affirmative finding of safety. As a result, in the "grey area" where the evidence is too unclear to permit the Secretary to reach a definite conclusion about risk or safety, Marshall would allow regulation but Stevens apparently would not. For a critique of the plurality's treatment of this issue, *see* Howard A. Latin, *The "Significance" of Toxic Health Risks: An Essay on Legal Decisionmaking Under Uncertainty,* 10 ECOLOGY L.Q. 339, 339–56, 381–86, 394 (1982).

4.   The further history of the benzene standard is instructive. Under pressure from a public interest group, OSHA returned to the benzene issue in 1983. It made a protracted but ultimately unsuccessful attempt to use a negotiated rulemaking to set a new standard. One complication was industry's

fear that, by determining that benzene exposure presented a "significant risk" under the Supreme Court's standards, any new rule would encourage tort litigation against the industry. Moreover, the Reagan White House allegedly intervened to assure industry that it would have veto power over any new standard. When the negotiations broke down, the steelworker's union went to court again to force OSHA to begin a new rulemaking. OSHA finally issued the new standard in 1987. The new standard, 1 ppm, was the same as the one that the Supreme Court had remanded. OSHA's documentation of its risk determination was more complete, however. OSHA estimated that reducing the standard from 10 ppm to 1 ppm would result in somewhere between 40 and 140 fewer leukemia deaths among lifelong workers in the affected industries. The agency was able to rely on three major new studies that had not been available at the time of its original rulemaking. *See* Charles Caldart, *Negotiation as a Means of Developing and Implementing Environmental and Occupational Health and Safety Policy*, 23 Harv. Envtl. L. Rev. 141, 165–68 (1999). However, recent studies suggest that even exposures below 1 ppm may have adverse health effects. *See Factory Study Shows Low Levels of Benzene Reduce Blood Cell Counts,* 306 Sci. 1665 (2004).

5. Once the Secretary finds a significant risk level, what level of protection against the risk is required? Consider the following case.

AMERICAN TEXTILE MANUFACTURERS INSTITUTE, INC. v. DONOVAN

Supreme Court of the United States, 1981.
452 U.S. 490, 101 S.Ct. 2478, 69 L.Ed.2d 185.

[This case involved a disease called byssinosis, more commonly known as "brown lung" disease. The disease is primarily caused by the inhalation of cotton dust, a byproduct of textile manufacturing. One study showed that over 25% of the sample of cotton workers suffered at least some form of the disease, while 35,000 workers suffer from the most disabling form. In a footnote early in the opinion, the Court considered whether OSHA had complied with *Industrial Union Department* in promulgating a standard to govern cotton dust:

> OSHA amended its Cancer Policy to "carry out the Court's interpretation of the Occupational Safety and Health Act of 1970 that consideration must be given to the significance of the risk in the issuance of a carcinogen standard and that OSHA must consider all relevant evidence in making these determinations." 46 Fed. Reg. 4889, col. 3 (1981). Previously, although lacking such evidence as dose response data, the Secretary presumed that no safe exposure level existed for carcinogenic substances. Following this Court's decision, OSHA deleted those provisions of the Cancer Policy which required the "automatic setting of the lowest feasible level" without regard to determinations of risk significance.

> In distinct contrast with its Cancer Policy, OSHA expressly found that "exposure to cotton dust presents a significant health hazard to employees," and that "cotton dust produced significant health effects

at low levels of exposure." In addition, the agency noted that "grade ½ byssinosis and associated pulmonary function decrements are significant health effects in themselves and should be prevented in so far as possible." In making its assessment of significant risk, OSHA relied on dose response curve data (the Merchant Study) showing that 25% of employees suffered at least Grade 1/2 byssinosis at a 500 ug/m3 PEL, and that 12.7% of all employees would suffer byssinosis at the 200 ug/m 3PEL standard. Examining the Merchant Study in light of other studies in the record, the agency found that "the Merchant Study provides a reliable assessment of health risk to cotton textile workers from cotton dust." OSHA concluded that the "prevalence of byssinosis should be significantly reduced" by the 200 ug/m 3PEL. * * * It is difficult to imagine what else the agency could do to comply with this Court's decision in *Industrial Union Department v. American Petroleum Institute.*

452 U.S. at 505–06 n.25, 101 S. Ct. at 2488–89 n.25. Having addressed this preliminary issue, the Court then turned to the primary issue in the case.]

JUSTICE BRENNAN delivered the opinion of the Court.

The principal question presented in this case is whether the Occupational Safety and Health Act requires the Secretary, in promulgating a standard pursuant to § 6(b)(5) of the Act, to determine that the costs of the standard bear a reasonable relationship to its benefits. Relying on §§ 6(b)(5) and 3(8) of the Act, petitioners urge not only that OSHA must show that a standard addresses a significant risk of material health impairment, but also that OSHA must demonstrate that the reduction in risk of material health impairment is significant in light of the costs of attaining that reduction. Respondents on the other hand contend that the Act requires OSHA to promulgate standards that eliminate or reduce such risks "to the extent such protection is technologically and economically feasible." * * *

The starting point of our analysis is the language of the statute itself. § 6(b)(5) of the Act provides:

The Secretary, in promulgating standards dealing with toxic materials or harmful physical agents under this subsection, shall set the standard which most adequately assures, *to the extent feasible,* on the basis of the best available evidence, that no employee will suffer material impairment of health or functional capacity even if such employee has regular exposure to the hazard dealt with by such standard for the period of his working life.

Although their interpretations differ, all parties agree that the phrase "to the extent feasible" contains the critical language in § 6(b)(5) for purposes of this case.

The plain meaning of the word "feasible" supports respondents' interpretation of the statute. According to Webster's Third New International Dictionary of the English Language, "feasible" means "capable of being done, executed, or effected." Accord, The Oxford English Dictionary 116 (1933) ("Capable of being done, accomplished or carried out"); Funk & Wagnalls New "Standard" Dictionary of the English Language 903 (1957) ("That may be done, performed or effected"). Thus, § 6(b)(5) directs the Secretary to issue the standard that "most adequately assures * * * that no employee will suffer material impairment of health," limited only by the extent to which this is "capable of being done." In effect then, as the Court of Appeals held, Congress itself defined the basic relationship between costs and benefits, by placing the "benefit" of worker health above all other considerations save those making attainment of this "benefit" unachievable. Any standard based on a balancing of costs and benefits by the Secretary that strikes a different balance than that struck by Congress would be inconsistent with the command set forth in § 6(b)(5). Thus, cost-benefit analysis by OSHA is not required by the statute because feasibility analysis is.[22] * * *

Even though the plain language of § 6(b)(5) supports this construction, we must still decide whether § 3(8), the general definition of an occupational safety and health standard, either alone or in tandem with § 6(b)(5), incorporates a cost-benefit requirement for standards dealing with toxic materials or harmful physical agents. § 3(8) of the Act provides:

> The term "occupational safety and health standard" means a standard which requires conditions, or the adoption or use of one or more practices, means, methods, operations, or processes, *reasonably necessary or appropriate* to provide safe or healthful employment and places of employment.

Taken alone, the phrase "reasonably necessary or appropriate" might be construed to contemplate some balancing of the costs and benefits of a standard. Petitioners urge that, so construed, § 3(8) engrafts a cost-benefit analysis requirement on the issuance of § 6(b)(5) standards, even if § 6(b)(5) itself does not authorize such analysis. We need not decide whether § 3(8), standing alone, would contemplate some form of cost-benefit analysis. For even if it does, Congress specifically chose in § 6(b)(5) to impose separate and additional requirements for issuance of a subcategory of occupational safety and health standards dealing with toxic materials and harmful physical agents; it required that those standards be issued to prevent material impairment of health *to the extent feasible.* Congress could reasonably have concluded that *health* standards should be

---

22. In this case we are faced with the issue whether the Act requires OSHA to balance costs and benefits in promulgating a *single* toxic material and harmful physical agent standard under § 6(b)(5). Petitioners argue that without cost-benefit balancing, the issuance of a single standard might result in a "serious misallocation of the finite resources that are available for the protection of worker safety and health," given the other health hazards in the workplace. This argument is more properly addressed to other provisions of the Act which may authorize OSHA to explore costs and benefits before deciding between issuance of several standards regulating different varieties of health and safety hazards, e.g., § 6(g) of the Act, 29 U.S.C. § 655(g); *see Industrial Union Department v. American Petroleum Institute, supra,* 448 U.S., at 644, 100 S.Ct., at 2865; see also Case Comment, 60 B.U.L.R. 115, 122, n. 52, or for promulgating other types of standards not issued under § 6(b)(5). We express no view on these questions.

subject to different criteria than *safety* standards because of the special problems presented in regulating them.

Agreement with petitioners' argument that § 3(8) imposes an additional and overriding requirement of cost-benefit analysis on the issuance of § 6(b)(5) standards would eviscerate the "to the extent feasible" requirement. Standards would inevitably be set at the level indicated by cost-benefit analysis, and not at the level specified by § 6(b)(5). For example, if cost-benefit analysis indicated a protective standard of 1000 ug/m 3PEL, while feasibility analysis indicated a 500 ug/m3 PEL, the agency would be forced by the cost-benefit requirement to choose the less stringent point. We cannot believe that Congress intended the general terms of § 3(8) to countermand the specific feasibility requirement of § 6(b)(5). Adoption of petitioners' interpretation would effectively write § 6(b)(5) out of the Act. We decline to render Congress' decision to include a feasibility requirement nugatory, thereby offending the well-settled rule that all parts of a statute, if possible, are to be given effect. Congress did not contemplate any further balancing by the agency for toxic material and harmful physical agents standards, and we should not "impute to Congress a purpose to paralyze with one hand what it sought to promote with the other."

[In the remaining portions of the opinion, the Court concluded that: (1) its construction of the statute was supported by the legislative history, and (2) the agency's finding that its cotton dust standard was feasible was supported by substantial evidence. Justice Stewart dissented from the substantial evidence holding. Justice Rehnquist, in an opinion joined by Chief Justice Burger, reiterated his view that the "feasibility" standard is no standard at all, and hence is unconstitutional.]

Notes

1. The upshot of the Court's two OSHA opinions is that risk and cost are separated: the agency first decides if there is currently a "significant risk," and then it regulates to decrease the extent feasible. From an economist's point of view, this leads to odd results, since a minor risk might be worth regulating if eliminating the risk is cheap enough, whereas a major risk might not be worth regulating if the solution would be disproportionately expensive (even though not enough to bankrupt the industry). The result of the Court's decisions is that the final level of environmental quality depends on the current level of risk rather than achieving the risk level with the best tradeoff between costs and benefits.

But if we think in terms of incentives for regulators and industry, perhaps something can be said for the Court's approach: it screens minor risks out of the regulatory process entirely, thereby saving administrative resources and limiting the possibility of an industry being targeted for purely political reasons, and it also gives industry an incentive to reduce risks voluntarily below the "significant" level so as to avoid more onerous regulations later. By using separate qualitative standards to assess risk and cost, rather than demanding calculation of a precise ratio, the Court's approach might be more responsive to the uncertainties surrounding risk regulation. Of course, even if the Court's approach does make at least some small sense as a matter of policy, is there any reason to think that this approach is what Congress had in mind? Reread the statutory language.

2. The *Benzene/Cotton Dust* approach was reaffirmed in *American Trucking Association* Chapter 6, page 623, *infra*. The Court held that the Clean Air Act's standard of "requisite to protect public health" was sufficiently clear to be a valid delegation of authority and that it precluded cost-benefit analysis. For some thoughts about the decision's implications, *see* Cass R. Sunstein, *Regulating Risks After* ATA, 2001 Sup. Ct. Rev. 1 (2001). On the other hand, in *Entergy Corp. v. Riverkeeper*, page 746, *infra,* the Supreme Court seemed willing to stretch statutory language in order to allow a form of cost-benefit analysis (determining whether costs were disproportionate to benefits).

3.   Consider this critique of the feasibility approach:

> If a standard with exceedingly high costs (or that would cause severe economic disruption) would also save thousands of lives, then society almost certainly would be better off even if the costs might seem unacceptably high. For example, government regulations eliminating lead from gasoline resulted in hundreds of millions of dollars in annual costs and appeared to threaten not only layoffs in the industrial firms that produced lead additives but also gasoline shortages during the transition to unleaded fuels. Nevertheless, these regulations also resulted in dramatic health benefits that substantially dwarfed the costs. If regulatory agencies had adhered to an approach that avoided all regulations that imposed costs exceeding a specified level or threatened economic dislocation, without any concern for the level of corresponding benefits, they may well have delayed or avoided phasing out lead additives in gasoline.

Cary Coglianese & Gary E. Marchant, *Shifting Sands: The Limits of Science in Setting Risk Standards,* 152 U. PA. L. REV. 1255, 1336 (2004). In addition, the authors observe, the feasibility approach allows agencies to "affirm standards that impose significant costs without proportional health protection benefits." They recommend cost-benefit analysis as a solution to these problems. In light of this critique, consider the following defense of the feasibility approach.

DAVID M. DRIESEN, DISTRIBUTING THE COSTS OF ENVIRONMENTAL, HEALTH, AND SAFETY PROTECTION: THE FEASIBILITY PRINCIPLE, COST–BENEFIT ANALYSIS, AND REGULATORY REFORM[23]

32 BOSTON COLLEGE ENVIRONMENTAL AFFAIRS LAW REVIEW 1, 35–42 (2005).

[W]hen economic losses become concentrated in ways that devastate individuals, they can have drastic effects, even if the total amount of cost

---

is low. Conversely, widely distributed costs can have minor effects, even if total aggregate costs are high. This "concentration" principle suggests that the distribution of costs can tell us a lot about their significance.

Reliance upon the feasibility principle tends to produce high employment. As a general rule, environmental regulations not closing plants may increase employment. Regulations often force companies to hire more workers or pay contractors to install and operate pollution controls or to redesign processes to prevent pollution. Indeed, more stringent and costly regulation may force more pollution control-related hiring than less stringent and costly regulation, as long as the regulation does not make plants unprofitable and lead to shutdowns.

Increased expenditures (short of those causing shutdowns) may maximize net employment, even after considering the possible negative impacts of taking resources away from something else to pay for pollution control. Pollution control hiring may redistribute money from managers, stockholders, or customers to employees. If employees earn less than managers and stockholders and losses to customers are widely distributed, this redistribution may significantly improve the lives of unemployed people who gain the new pollution-related jobs without significant harm to others.

Often, costs imposed on companies become distributed so widely that they have little real impact on human lives. Profitable industries can absorb some costs without any major impact on consumers or workers. Costs distributed widely might properly be characterized as de minimis even when they seem quite large. One hundred million dollars a year, for example, may seem like a lot of money to an individual. But that cost distributed among one hundred million people equals just a dollar a year. A regulation costing one hundred million dollars a year may distribute that cost among hundreds or thousands of regulated firms. And each of these firms may spread these costs over its entire customer base through modest price increases. One hundred million dollars sounds like a high number, because most of us think in terms of individual incomes and not industry cash flows. But such a small amount of money may have impacts so trivial as to merit little consideration.

Furthermore, firms can creatively compensate for or avoid costs. Indeed, when environmental regulation has been demanding, firms have often engaged in innovative changes to avoid the cost of regulation. This conforms to the induced innovation hypothesis that economists use to model innovation, which posits that firms will tend to innovate to avoid using scarce and expensive production factors. For years, many industries considered ozone depleting substances essential to their businesses and paid large amounts of money to obtain them. Many of these companies switched to soap and water, saving lots of money, when phase-outs began to raise the price and threaten the future availability of these chemicals. High costs for polluting industries can sometimes improve the business prospects of cleaner competitors, rather than lead to any net losses at all.

And emissions trading, even if it does not encourage major innovation as many have argued, makes possible a lot of tweaking to avoid costs. Cost avoidance behavior further reduces the impact of costs upon people's lives.

By contrast, regulations that force a plant owner to shut down decrease employment, at least in the short run. This can concentrate severe economic losses on small numbers of workers who can ill afford them. This sort of loss can have a devastating impact on workers' lives, leading to depression, a terrible feeling of loss, and an inability to cope economically, especially if unemployment or very severe underemployment proves permanent.

Regulations shutting down plants may not decrease net employment. If demand remains constant, employment may shift to less polluting enterprises producing equivalent goods or services. Nevertheless, such regulations can impose significant hardships upon the individual workers who lose their jobs. Environmental regulations, which have historically included a combination of health-based standards and technology-based regulation, have produced a small net increase in employment. The feasibility principle may help account for this positive record.

While firms often can systematically distribute regulatory costs widely or avoid them altogether, harms from pollution often devastate randomly selected individuals. Cancer, for example, can lead to a long, slow, painful death for some unfortunates. Birth defects can ruin the lives of children born with them and afflict their parents with enormous burdens. Asthma can make its victims gasp for air, send asthmatics to hospital emergency rooms in summer, and force children from the playground on hot days. As these examples demonstrate, we should think of most pollution control programs as efforts to ameliorate concentrated harms.

Furthermore, while imposition of regulatory costs tends to spawn cost avoidance behavior, some of which can be very socially productive, pollution can impose burdens that one cannot easily escape. Since people must breathe, they cannot escape air pollution. Of course, relatively wealthy individuals can choose among the cleanest areas and escape some of the worst effects of pollution. But others have fewer options.

Many pollution sources concentrate their impacts upon particular regions or communities, often communities of color. Concentrations of facilities can exacerbate pollution's tendency to single out individuals for devastating consequences by making those consequences much more likely in communities of color (which may also experience disproportionate poverty).

At the same time, the feasibility principle limits the discretion of agencies to forego environmental improvements that do not concentrate costs in ways that lead to plant shutdowns, which may involve massive job losses. It should make some decisions relatively easy. This relative ease matters a lot, because major environmental problems typically stem from many sources of individually minor pollution that add up to a significant problem. Most environmental statutes regulate large numbers of facilities in a wide variety of industries for this reason. If every regulation led to a protracted general debate, standard setting would grind to a halt and pollution would increase markedly.

This relative ease also helps regulators keep up with the economic dynamics of pollution increases. Pollution tends to increase with rising consumption and population, so that a regulatory system always has to run just to keep in place. The clearest example of this involves automobile pollution. In spite of requirements to drastically reduce the tailpipe emissions of cars, car emissions have only modestly declined. Increased driving has wiped out much of the improvement. This is not an indictment of technology-based regulation. It does show, however, that pollution control regulators have a lot of work to do just to stay in place, especially since regulators are reluctant to regulate consumer behavior (such as driving habits). For the most part, government does not regulate consumption or population increases, so the regulatory system must make up for pollution increases due to those factors just to avoid slipping backwards. This dynamic further supports the need to avoid making each regulation into an occasion for protracted analysis and litigation.

Ease of regulation also matters because of the extraordinary ability of special interests to resist regulation. Any company converting natural resources to products for human consumption can extract profits from the entire society to finance resistance to environmental regulation. The regulated company can then hire a battalion of lawyers and other experts to fend off regulation. This has predictable consequences. Regulated firms provide the overwhelming majority of significant written comments in rulemaking, meet with regulators incessantly, ask the elected beneficiaries of their campaign contributions to hound EPA when it seeks to regulate them, litigate often, and frequently resist enforcement. Environmental regulation always takes place on an uneven playing field, in spite of strong efforts by a handful of environmental organizations to counterbalance regulated firms' influence. This does not mean that the environment always loses. But it does mean that regulated firms seize nearly every opportunity for obstruction available to them, so that ease of regulation matters to its success.

The feasibility constraint focuses analytical attention on costs likely to be significant, in the sense of having a distribution likely to have a serious impact on people's lives. It avoids lavishing administrative resources on calibrating responses to what one might call de minimis costs.

The feasibility principle offers an appropriate response to problems characterized by de minimis cost and concentrated harms. It calls for stringent regulation. On the other hand, it constrains regulation when the costs concentrate in ways likely to produce greater than de minimis impacts. * * *

NOTES

1.   The feasibility approach seeks to minimize plant closings, a goal that Driesen defends. An economist might respond that it is better in the long run to select efficient regulations that will help the economy as a whole grow, and use unemployment benefits and retraining to cushion the blow to workers if plants are forced to close. Which approach is more promising in terms of public policy and of political feasibility?

2.   The other part of Driesen's argument is that the significant risk/feasibility approach provides a streamlined administrative process, helping to counter the resource advantage enjoyed by regulated firms in the rulemaking process. This is a difficult argument to appraise in the abstract. You should keep it in mind when you get to the detailed chapters on pollution regulation later in this book.

3.   "Best Available Technology" is a widespread approach to regulation. The core of the *Benzene/Cotton Dust* approach is to identify significant risks and then regulate at the greatest feasible level. Many pollution statutes use a related approach. Commonly, either Congress or the agency identifies a particular form of pollution as posing a significant risk to the environment or to human health. The agency is charged with identifying the best available technology (BAT) for dealing with the risk. BAT comes in various flavors, each with its own acronym, that vary primarily in how heavily cost is weighted in the equation. In the OSHA setting, essentially BAT is set at the most stringent level that will not cause widespread plant-closings. Others varieties of BAT allow consideration of whether costs would be completely disproportionate to benefits or stress moving the whole industry to the form of pollution control currently used by the best firms. All forms of BAT can be considered as different interpretations of what is truly "feasible" under the circumstances. You will learn much more about these varying BAT requirements and their implementation in the chapters on air and water pollution.

BAT schemes typically have two additional features. The first is a deadline or series of deadlines for phasing in the new technology. Often, firms are given several years before heightened control requirements are applied to existing plants. The second is a separate BAT standard for new plants. The idea is that it is cheaper to build in new technology from the start rather than retrofitting existing plans, so more pollution control is feasible. Also, projected new plants do not raise the same politically sensitive issue of plant closings, making the government more willing to impose stricter requirements. The downside of the separate standard for new plants is that it creates an incentive to keep old plants in operation so as to avoid the stricter standard. To avoid this strategy, BAT rules typically impose "new plant" standards on existing plants that are substantially modified, but this in turn creates incentives for owners to keep their modifications just below the trigger point. Because of these strategic incentives, enforcement of new plant standards is difficult, and critics argue that the standards actually end up increasing pollution by preventing the installation of improved equipment that might trigger new source review.

B. ECONOMIC APPROACHES

The economic perspective on environmental regulation has become increasingly influential, though it remains controversial. We will begin by examining cost-benefit analysis, an important alternative to the significant risk/feasibility approach for setting the level of environmental protection. We will then consider some tools that economists advocate using, as an alternative to BAT, in reaching environmental goals.

1. COST–BENEFIT ANALYSIS

One of the major impacts of economic analysis has been the growing use of cost-benefit analysis (CBA). The first part of this Note explains some of the methods used to conduct a cost-benefit analysis. The second part of the Note discusses how CBA has become a part of the regulatory process.

a. CBA in the Administrative Process

You may or may not find cost-benefit analysis an appealing technique, but there can be little question about its practical significance. Shortly after taking office President Reagan signed Executive Order 12,291, 46 Fed. Reg. 13,193 (1981), aimed at improving the efficiency of informal rulemaking by executive agencies. Section 2 directed that "major" regulations not be promulgated unless, "taking into account affected industries [and] the condition of the national economy," the potential benefits to society outweigh potential costs, and net benefits are at a maximum. Review of agency cost-benefit analyses was conducted by the Office of Management and Budget. In 1993, President Clinton issued an executive order maintaining the basic approach but attempting to streamline the process of OMB review. The rule was intended to reduce the number of regulations sent to OMB for approval and to make OMB's review more flexible. *See* Ellen Siegler, *Executive Order 12866: An Analysis of the New Executive Order on Regulatory Planning and Review*, 24 Envtl. L. Rep. 10070 (1994).

The George W. Bush Administration pursued cost-benefit analysis with particular fervor:

> [T]he battle continued to rage when President George W. Bush appointed John D. Graham, a strong proponent of cost-benefit analysis from the Harvard Center for Risk Analysis, to head the Office of Information and Regulatory Affairs (OIRA) in the Office of Management and Budget. This nomination was strongly supported by regulated industries and equally strongly opposed by public interest groups. From that position, to which he was confirmed in late 2001, Graham has overseen the centralized review process for health and safety regulations. To the chagrin of public interest groups and the joy of industry-funded think tanks, OIRA greatly stemmed the flow of

health, safety and environmental regulation during the Bush Administration. Although EPA promulgated several important regulations, most of which were required by statute, OSHA did not promulgate a single significant health standard during the entire four years.

Thomas O. McGarity, *The Story of the Benzene Case: Judicially Imposed Regulatory Reform Through Risk Assessment, in* RICHARD J. LAZARUS & OLIVER A. HOUCK, ENVIRONMENTAL LAW STORIES 169 (2005). Upon taking office, President Obama rescinded President Bush's executive orders on cost-benefit analysis, pending issuance of a new executive order of his own.

Although the National Environmental Policy Act (NEPA) does not require the use of cost-benefit analysis, it may affect the use and presentation of that analysis. The CEQ regulations provide:

> If a cost-benefit analysis relevant to the choice among environmentally different alternatives is being considered for the proposed action, it shall be incorporated by reference or appended to the statement as an aid in evaluating the environmental consequences. To assess the adequacy of compliance with § 102(2)(B) of the Act the statement shall, when a cost-benefit analysis is prepared, discuss the relationship between the analysis and any analyses of unquantified environmental impacts, values, and amenities. For purposes of complying with the Act, the weighing of the merits and drawbacks of the various alternatives need not be displayed in a monetary cost-benefit analysis and should not be when there are important qualitative considerations. In any event, an environmental impact statement should at least indicate those considerations, including factors not related to environmental quality, which are likely to be relevant and important to a decision. 40 C.F.R. § 1502.23 (2004).

b. How CBA Works

Whether you feel favorable or hostile toward environmental economics, a basic understanding of cost-benefit analysis is important for any environmental lawyer. An examination of the details would obviously be well beyond the scope of this chapter, but the following brief notes will at least introduce you to some of the basic concepts. The "cost" side of CBA is relatively straightforward, since it normally involves immediate economic impacts that (at least in theory) are readily determined. But the "benefit" side can be more complex. In this note, we consider two difficulties on the benefit side of the analysis: the difficulty of determining monetary measures for environmental benefits and the fact that these benefits often accrue far in the future. For a vigorous critique of the way cost-benefit analysis treats environmental and health benefits, *see* Frank Ackerman & Lisa Heinzerling, *Pricing the Priceless: Cost–Benefit Analysis of Environmental Protection*, 150 U. PA. L. REV. 1553 (2002).

c. Valuation Problems

Let's suppose we wanted to do a cost-benefit analysis for a method of ending some form of water pollution. On the benefit side of the equation, we would need to assign values, based on willingness to pay, for the elimination of this source of pollution. Some of these values would be relatively easy to determine, given the necessary scientific information—for example, loss in profits to fishing boats caused by pollution. (At least, the calculations would be straightforward in theory, although in litigation expert witnesses may differ sharply with each other about these lost profit issues.)

Some other kinds of benefits are fairly easy to assess, at least in principle, because we can look at the choices people actually make in order to figure out their preferences. Examples of these measurable benefits include the recreational benefits enjoyed by tourists. Those recreational benefits can be indirectly measured through the amount of travel time they're willing to invest traveling to sites; and the quality-of-life benefits to local residents, which can be indirectly measured through the effect of site access on house prices. For a discussion of some of these methods, *see* David Pearce & R. Kerry Turner, ECONOMICS OF NATURAL RESOURCES AND THE ENVIRONMENT 140–148 (1990).

Although we may start to feel some qualms at this point, we can even put dollar amounts on the health effects of asbestos (provided, of course, that we can figure out just what those health effects may be). Without worrying right now about the technicalities, we could assign monetary values to different levels of risk by looking at how much consumers are willing to pay for safer products, or how much income workers are willing to give up for safer jobs, or at how much travel time people are willing to sacrifice for the safety benefits of driving more slowly. All of these would be different ways of determining the market value of safety.

If people demand $1,000 in return for being exposed to a one in a thousand risk of death, it's conventional to say that the "value of life" is $1 million. This is a bit misleading, since they probably wouldn't be willing to commit suicide for that amount of money! To express this distinction, economists often speak of the value of a statistical (as opposed to individual) life. To assign a value of $1 million per statistical life is the same as saying that people would demand $1 in return for running a one-in-a-million chance of death.

Controversy continues over the correct way to value life. Some suggest that instead of using a single uniform figure, the government should assign a higher value for some risks such as cancer, but that a lower value should often be used for risks that disproportionately affect the poor. *See* Cass R. Sunstein, *Valuing Life: A Plea for Disaggregation,* 54 DUKE L.J. 385 (2004). But see Laura J. Lowenstein & Richard L. Revesz, *Anti–Regulation Under the Guise of Rational Regulation: The Bush Administration's Approaches to Valuing Human Lives in Environmental Cost–Benefit Analyses,* 34 ENVTL. L. REP. 10954 (2004).

There are additional difficulties associated with measuring the value of some other environmental benefits: so-called option and existence values. An example of option value might be posed by someone who has no particular plans to see Lake Tahoe, but who would be willing to pay something in order to keep open the option of seeing the lake again if he or she chooses to do so. Existence values are even more ethereal—for example, the amount of money a person would be willing to pay to save rain forests, although her allergies make it extremely unlikely that she would ever go there. The benefits we discussed previously involved "use values" which actually flow from some direct physical interaction with a natural resource like Lake Tahoe. In contrast, non-use values don't involve any observable current conduct. For introductions to these concepts, *see* Christopher D. Stone, *What to do About Biodiversity: Property Rights, Public Goods, and the Earth's Biological Riches*, 68 S. CAL. L. REV. 577, 580–88 (1995).

Some economists advocate the use of "contingent valuation" studies to measure how much people are willing to pay for non-use values. Contingent valuation is essentially a survey technique. People are given information about an environmental issue and then asked if they would be willing to pay a certain amount to solve the problem. There is a great deal of dispute about whether contingent valuation, even if done carefully, provides a genuine measure of preferences. See CASS R. SUNSTEIN, FREE MARKETS AND SOCIAL JUSTICE 142–43 (1997). But advocates of contingent valuation argue that the critics have exaggerated the problems, that many problems can be limited through careful survey design, and that contingent valuation can be validated against other measures of environmental benefits.

d. Discounting Future Benefits

Often, the costs and benefits of a regulatory measure occur at different times. When the costs accrue today but the benefits are in the future, we need some method of taking the time factor into account. Global warming or endangered species provide obvious examples because the effects of our policy choices are multi-generational. Long-term delayed harms are ubiquitous, however, in environmental law. As Lisa Heinzerling points out:

> Radioactive substances are perhaps the most dramatic example of such a long-lived threat. [I]n planning for the disposal of the most radioactive of our radioactive wastes, EPA has dictated that the disposal site must be one that will remain undisturbed for at least 10,000 years.

> Other persistent contaminants include [PCBs, DDT], chlordane, dieldrin, and dioxin. These can persist in the environment, and in human tissue for many years.... While the precise definition of "persistence" remains largely political and practical rather than scientific, it nonetheless remains true that today's use and disposal of radioactive substances, chlorinated organic compounds, and heavy metals will

continue to pose threats to human health for many decades, in some cases centuries, to come.

Lisa Heinzerling, *The Temporal Dimension in Environmental Law*, 31 ENVTL. L. REP. 11,055, 11,067 (2001). For this reason, discounting plays a key part in the economic analysis of environmental regulation.

The basic idea of discounting is not simple. If $1 invested at compound interest today will produce $2 in five years, we "discount" the $2 at the same interest rate, concluding that the "present value" of $2 receivable in five years is $1 today. Making this adjustment allows us to compare different investments whose payoffs have varying time profiles. To take a simple example, suppose we are comparing two different contracts. If one contract pays $1.50 today, we know that it is a better deal than another which pays $2 in five years, because we can take the $1.50, invest it, and have more than $2 in five years. The shorthand way of saying this is that present value of the first contract is $1.50, while the present value of the other is only $1.

Discounting is closely related to compound interest. Compound interest can have remarkable effects over long periods of time, which is why it is easy for total payments over the life of a mortgage to far exceed the amount of the principal. Because exponential discounting is essentially the reverse of compounding, we might call it an application of "compound *dis*interest"—the longer the period of time, the less interested we are in the same cost or benefit. Like looking into the wrong end of a telescope, discounting makes distant objects look smaller. This can have important policy implications because the costs and benefits of environmental regulation are often distributed differently over time: the major costs are frequently incurred immediately, thereby receiving their full monetary value in the analysis, while the concrete benefits of regulation spread out into the future and are therefore subject to discounting. For example, because cancer has a long latency period, OMB's choice of discount rates had dramatic implications for regulatory policy.

Over long time periods, the results of changes in discount rates are enormous, as Cass Sunstein explains, "[i]f a human life is valued at $8 million, and if an agency chooses a 10% discount rate, a life saved 100 years from now is worth only $581." Cass R. Sunstein, *Cost–Benefit Default Principles*, 99 MICH. L. REV. 1651, 1711 (2001). Thus, what seems at first blush to be a niggling technical issue turns out to have a grave significance in evaluating long-term regulatory decisions. Discounting is particularly controversial in the multigenerational context. For a review of the debate, *see* Daniel A. Farber, *From Here to Eternity*, 2003 U. ILL. L. REV. 289 (2003).

CBA has been quite controversial, especially as applied to health and safety regulations. The following two excerpts provide contrasting perspectives.

STEVE P. CALANDRILLO, RESPONSIBLE REGULATION: A SENSIBLE COST–BENEFIT, RISK VERSUS RISK APPROACH TO FEDERAL HEALTH AND SAFETY REGULATION[24]

81 B. U. L. Rev. 957 (2001).

Federal health and safety regulations have saved or improved the lives of thousands of Americans, but protecting our citizens from risk entails significant costs. In a world of limited resources, we must spend our regulatory dollars responsibly in order to do the most we can with the money we have. Given the infeasibility of creating a risk-free society, this paper argues that a sensible cost-benefit, risk versus risk approach be taken in the design of U.S. regulatory oversight policy. The goal should always be to further the best interests of the nation, rather than to satisfy the narrow agenda of powerful industry or political forces. This entails designing safety regulations efficiently to maximize society's welfare, choosing the point where their marginal benefits equal their marginal costs—rather than simply asking whether total benefits exceed total costs in the aggregate. Federal regulatory oversight policy should also ask that proposed regulations compare the risks they reduce to the new risks they unintentionally create (substitution risks). Additionally, our citizens should be educated regarding systematic risk misperceptions, and regulatory agencies should make their risk assessments objectively. Moreover, most-likely scenarios must be addressed by responsible regulatory solutions, rather than the current practice of focusing on worst-case estimates. Finally, agencies should publish and justify their regulatory triggers and perform ex-post evaluations of their programs in an attempt to continuously improve the quality of regulatory design.

Efforts by the executive branch, from Presidents Ford, Carter, Reagan and Clinton, have attempted to inject similar common sense into the regulatory oversight process. Unfortunately, the congressional mandates given to government agencies are often silent on the subject of cost-benefit analysis, and recent Supreme Court cases have held that regulatory agencies are not obligated to even consider the costs of their proposals. I will explore several legislative reform bills that are aimed at overriding congressional mandates, but to date, none have been successful.

Finally, this paper will address certain common criticisms to which a marginal cost benefit, risk-risk approach to responsible regulatory reform would be subject. Most notably, the measurement of costs and benefits is not an exact science, and using "willingness to pay" as a marker of individual and social utility has its limitations. Regulatory reform also faces challenges on moral grounds, as scholars openly decry the explicit tradeoff between human lives and financial resources. While these criticisms contain merit, this paper concludes that to ignore a sensible cost-benefit analysis of federal safety regulations is to divert resources from

---

24. Copyright © 2001, *Boston University Law Review*. Reprinted with permission.

their most beneficial uses and to settle for second best. In a world of scarcity, we must make regulatory tradeoffs as efficiently as possible in order to do the greatest good for the greatest number, and to save the most lives we can. It would be unethical to do anything less. * * *

"We live in a world of limited resources." "We can't place a dollar value on protecting human life or preserving our environment." Neither statement taken independently strikes the reader as particularly controversial—they both seem perfectly reasonable. Yet there is an inherent and unmistakable tension between the two, for no society has unlimited resources to devote to the protection of human health and the creation of a risk-free world. The questions become: Is it possible to balance the common sense concept of scarce public resources with our deep moral aversion to placing a dollar value on saving human lives? And, more importantly, how do we do it?

We would like to be able to protect every citizen from every harm in our society, but most understand this is neither possible nor financially feasible. Federal environmental and safety regulations aimed at preventing harm have yielded tremendous benefits, but they carry staggering costs—on the order of half a trillion dollars annually! However, despite this reality, there is a startling disconnect between common sense notions of maximizing the effect of scarce resources and of actually putting that notion into practice in carrying out U.S. regulatory programs. Hypothetically, would it be worth tens of millions of dollars to save one person's life if President Bush were to tighten arsenic standards in drinking water to the level proposed by President Clinton in his last days in office? Or would that same money be better spent if it could save thousands of lives by providing subsidized food and prenatal care to low-income mothers and free vaccinations to their babies? If we allocated all our resources to preventing accidental deaths in one area, we would have nothing left over to spend to prevent cancer or to provide food, housing or medical care.

To a large degree, the problem is one of public perception. No politician wants to admit that "we can't save that elderly person's life or institute a proposed environmental protection program, because it will simply cost us too much money to do so." Yet, this cost-benefit rationale is inherent in countless personal decisions made every day, from what career to pursue to what city in which to reside. Similarly, in the regulatory arena, fiscal balancing of the costs against the benefits should play a role in responsible decisionmaking. The tradeoff between costs and results is always present, but we are sometimes gripped by a fear that prevents us from acknowledging it openly. This reluctance limits us as a society because it diverts resources from where they are most needed. Even worse, this diversion is not based on a well-articulated reason, but rather on a fear of the repercussions experienced by those who voice such opinions. For instance, can you imagine a Presidential candidate who said on election-day eve, "I want to do the greatest good for the greatest number, and that means I choose not to help you." Not likely.

This paper proposes that given the reality of limited public resources, America must efficiently reformulate its environmental and health regulatory policies in order to save and improve the most lives possible given the accompanying costs. This is not always going to be politically correct. It entails making tough choices and preferencing certain programs and policies over others, which necessarily implies that some causes will be sacrificed for the greater good. But I urge that given our reality, society must consider carefully how best to structure federal regulatory oversight policy—not how to make it perfect. Perfection is dangerous precisely because it cannot ever be achieved. This paper therefore concentrates on how to efficiently formulate government regulations under the constraint of limited resources, in the hope that such an approach will maximize the overall benefits to our society. * * *

[T]his paper outlines an alternative regulatory approach for America, proposing a sensible cost-benefit, risk versus risk approach to easing the tension between scarce public resources and the deontological value of protecting human lives. In analyzing this tradeoff, we as a caring, thoughtful society should require a cost-benefit analysis of all potential government regulation whether it is aimed at making our environment, air, water, food, or workplace safer. I take this cost-benefit notion one step further than most commentators by suggesting that not only should overall costs and benefits of potential programs be evaluated, but that government agencies must act to set the appropriate regulation at the level where marginal benefits equal marginal costs. Setting our regulatory triggers at this point will have a far greater impact on improving overall social welfare than an absolute cost-benefit comparison would. Most everyone in society should favor a form of regulation that maximizes the benefits minus the costs, and not one that merely asks whether the benefits exceed the costs in the aggregate. * * *

While the achievements made possible by executive oversight have been notable, the success of regulatory reform proposals may also implicitly depend upon rewriting the existing legislative mandates given to government agencies by Congress. Often, the relevant statutory authority governing the mission of U.S. regulatory agencies is oblivious to marginal cost-benefit assessments, or it may even prohibit such comparisons outright. For instance, the Occupational Safety and Health Administration ("OSHA") is charged with assuring "so far as possible [that] every working man and woman in the Nation [have] safe and healthful working conditions." This mandate ignores the fact that nothing can ever be made 100% safe, and that extreme safety precautions necessarily entail extreme costs. Instead, the congressional mandates given to federal regulatory bodies should require, or at a minimum, permit cost-benefit and risk-risk tradeoffs to be made. Such an approach will empower courts to enforce common sense notions about how to best allocate scarce public resources in order to benefit a greater number of our citizens than we do today. Modifying legislative mandates will also force regulatory decisionmakers to be accountable for the policy choices they make. * * *

Moreover, some have raised serious moral criticisms, openly deriding cost-benefit analysis as incurably insensitive to the intrinsic value of life.* * * This moral resistance also surfaces in the rhetoric of our politicians and in the language of our existing federal regulatory legislation. Our policies often eschew cost-benefit analysis as irresponsible and insensitive to the ultimate goal at hand, and instead opt for a world that should be made as safe as possible—whatever the costs may be.

I am the first to agree that there are serious problems that would make any marginal cost-benefit standard subject to potential manipulation and abuse. But that does not mean we should not try to improve upon what we currently have. The difficulty of measuring these values does not undermine the principle that responsible regulatory programs should focus their efforts where they can save the most lives given limited resources. We as a country would be foolhardy to choose to ignore cost, benefit and risk tradeoffs merely because of the difficulty in their assessment, because we would then be consciously deciding to do something less than the best we can. Thus, despite the valid concerns raised by critics, we must strive to conquer these problems if our ultimate goal is the betterment of society and the maximization of scarce resources.

Finally, we should bear in mind in conducting the foregoing regulatory oversight analysis that it is a matter of common sense that people weigh costs and benefits in making life decisions all the time. American businesses make cost-benefit and cost-effectiveness calculations daily. While individuals are understandably upset by public health and safety decisions that explicitly trade off lives for dollars, no one really wants to spend everything on safety. Policymakers should similarly be able to balance costs, benefits and risks openly in America's regulatory oversight policy. The choice is not between helping all of our citizens or helping none. Given limited resources, the government can only help some. This paper is therefore intended to provoke thought about how responsible, efficient regulatory policy can maximize the number and the value included within that "some."

NOTES

1.   As we saw in the last section, estimating risk levels can be a difficult and uncertain exercise. How much of a problem is this for cost-benefit analysis? At what point do the uncertainties of cost-benefit analysis overwhelm its possible advantages?

2.   For recent defenses of cost-benefit analysis, see John D. Graham, *Saving Lives Through Administrative Law and Economics*, 157 U. PA. L. REV. 395 (2008); W. Kip Viscusi, *Monetizing the Benefits of Risk and Environmental Regulation*, 33 FORDHAM URBAN L.J. 1003 (2006).

3.   Quite apart from any practical problems with implementing cost-benefit analysis, some authors raise ethical objections to its use in risk management. These objections are the subject of the next article.

FRANK ACKERMAN AND LISA HEINZERLING, PRICING THE PRICELESS: COST–BENEFIT ANALYSIS OF ENVIRONMENTAL PROTECTION[25]

150 U. PA. L. REV. 1553 (2002).

Many analytical approaches to setting environmental standards require some consideration of costs and benefits. Even technology-based regulation, maligned by cost-benefit enthusiasts as the worst form of regulatory excess, typically entails consideration of economic costs. Cost-benefit analysis differs, however, from other analytical approaches in the following respect: it demands that the advantages and disadvantages of a regulatory policy be reduced, as far as possible, to numbers, and then further reduced to dollars and cents. In this feature of cost-benefit analysis lies its doom. Indeed, looking closely at the products of this pricing scheme makes it seem not only a little cold, but a little crazy as well.

Consider the following examples, which we are not making up. They are not the work of a lunatic fringe, but, on the contrary, they reflect the work products of some of the most influential and reputable of today's cost-benefit practitioners. We are not sure whether to laugh or cry; we find it impossible to treat these studies as serious contributions to a rational discussion.

Several years ago, states were in the middle of their litigation against tobacco companies, seeking to recoup the medical expenditures they had incurred as a result of smoking. At that time, W. Kip Viscusi—a professor of law and economics at Harvard and the primary source of the current $6.3 million estimate for the value of a statistical life—undertook research concluding that states, in fact, saved money as the result of smoking by their citizens.[26] Why? Because they died early! They thus saved their states the trouble and expense of providing nursing home care and other services associated with an aging population.

Viscusi didn't stop there. So great, under Viscusi's assumptions, were the financial benefits to the states of their citizens' premature deaths that, he suggested, 'cigarette smoking should be subsidized rather than taxed.'

Amazingly, this cynical conclusion has not been swept into the dustbin where it belongs, but instead recently has been revived: the tobacco company Philip Morris commissioned the well-known consulting group Arthur D. Little to examine the financial benefits to the Czech Republic of smoking among Czech citizens. Arthur D. Little International, Inc., found that smoking was a financial boon for the government—partly because, again, it caused citizens to die earlier and thus reduced government

---

25. Copyright © 2002, University of Pennsylvania. Reprinted with permission.

26. W. Kip Viscusi, *Cigarette Taxation and the Social Consequences of Smoking* 47 (Nat'l Bureau of Econ. Research, Working Paper No. 4891, 1994), *available at* http://papers.nber.org/papers/w4891.pdf.

expenditure on pensions, housing, and health care. This conclusion relies, so far as we can determine, on perfectly conventional cost-benefit analysis.

There is more. In recent years, much has been learned about the special risks children face due to pesticides in their food, contaminants in their drinking water, ozone in the air, and so on. Because cost-benefit analysis has become much more prominent at the same time, there is now a budding industry in valuing children's health. Its products are often bizarre.

Take the problem of lead poisoning in children. One of the most serious and disturbing effects of lead contamination is the neurological damage it can cause in young children, including permanently diminished mental ability. Putting a dollar value on the (avoidable, environmentally caused) retardation of children is a daunting task, but economic analysts have not been deterred.

Randall Lutter, a frequent regulatory critic and a scholar at the AEI–Brookings Joint Center for Regulatory Studies, argues that the way to value the damage lead causes in children is to look at the amount parents of affected children spend on chelation therapy, a chemical treatment that is supposed to cause excretion of lead from the body.[27] Parental spending on chelation supports an estimated valuation of as low as $1100 per IQ point lost due to lead poisoning. Previous economic analyses by the EPA, based on the children's loss of expected future earnings, have estimated the value to be much higher—up to $9000 per IQ point. Based on his lower figure, Lutter claims to have discovered that too much effort is going into controlling lead: 'Hazard standards that protect children far more than their parents think is appropriate may make little sense'; thus, '[t]he agencies should consider relaxing their lead standards.'

In fact, Lutter presents no evidence about what parents think, only about what they spend on one rare variety of private medical treatment (which, as it turns out, has not been proven medically effective for chronic, low-level lead poisoning). Why should environmental standards be based on what individuals are now spending on desperate personal efforts to overcome social problems? * * *

Cost-benefit analysis sets out to do for government what the market does for business: add up the benefits of a public policy and compare them to the costs. The two sides of the ledger raise very different issues.

The first step in a cost-benefit analysis is to calculate the costs of a public policy. For example, the government may require a certain kind of pollution control equipment, for which businesses must pay. Even if a regulation is less detailed and only sets a ceiling on emissions, it results in costs that can be at least roughly estimated through research into available technologies and business strategies for compliance.

---

27. Randall Lutter, *Valuing Children's Health: A Reassessment of the Benefits of Lower Lead Levels* 3 (AEI–Brookings Joint Ctr. for Regulatory Studies, Working Paper No. 00–02, 2000), *available at* **http://www.reg-markets.org/publications/index.php?menuid=3**.

The costs of protecting human health and the environment through the use of pollution control devices and other approaches are, by their very nature, measured in dollars. Thus, at least in theory, the cost side of cost-benefit analysis is relatively straightforward. In practice, as we shall see, it is not quite that simple.

The consideration of the costs of environmental protection is not unique to cost-benefit analysis. Development of environmental regulations has almost always involved consideration of economic costs, with or without formal cost-benefit techniques. What is unique to cost-benefit analysis, and far more problematic, is the other side of the balance, the monetary valuation of the benefits of life, health, and nature itself. * * *

What can it mean to say that saving one life is worth $6.3 million? Human life is the ultimate example of a value that is not a commodity and does not have a price. You cannot buy the right to kill someone for $6.3 million, nor for any other price. Most systems of ethical and religious belief maintain that every life is sacred. If analysts calculated the value of life itself by asking people what it is worth to them (the most common method of valuation of other environmental benefits), the answer would be infinite. * * *

The standard response is that a value like $6.3 million is not actually a price on an individual's life or death. Rather, it is a way of expressing the value of small risks of death; for example, it is one million times the value of a one in a million risk. If people are willing to pay $6.30 to avoid a one in a million increase in the risk of death, then the 'value of a statistical life' is $6.3 million.

Unfortunately, this explanation fails to resolve the dilemma. It is true that risk (or 'statistical life') and life itself are distinct concepts. In practice, however, analysts often ignore the distinction between valuing risk and valuing life. Many regulations reduce risk for a large number of people and avoid actual death for a much smaller number. A complete cost-benefit analysis should, therefore, include valuation of both of these benefits. However, the standard practice is to calculate a value only for 'statistical' life and to ignore life itself.

The confusion between the valuation of risk and the valuation of life itself is embedded in current regulatory practice in another way as well. The Office of Management and Budget, which reviews cost-benefit analyses prepared by federal agencies pursuant to executive order, instructs agencies to discount the benefits of life-saving regulations from the moment of avoided death, rather than from the time when the risk of death is reduced. This approach to discounting is plainly inconsistent with the claim that cost-benefit analysis seeks to evaluate risk. When a life-threatening disease, such as cancer, has a long latency period, many years may pass between the time when a risk is imposed and the time of death. If monetary valuations of statistical life represented risk, instead of life, then the value of statistical life would be discounted from the date of a change in risk (typically, when a new regulation is enforced) rather than from the much later date of avoided actual death.

In acknowledging the monetary value of reducing risk, economic analysts have contributed to our growing awareness that life-threatening risk itself—and not just the end result of such risk, death—is an injury. But they have blurred the line between risks and actual deaths, by calculating the value of reduced risk while pretending that they have produced a valuation of life itself. The paradox of monetizing the infinite or immeasurable value of human life has not been resolved; it only has been glossed over. * * *

Finally, the economic valuation called for by cost-benefit analysis is fundamentally flawed because it demands an enormous volume of consistently updated information, which is beyond the practical capacity of our society to generate.

All attempts at valuation of the environment begin with a problem: the goal is to assign monetary prices to things that have no prices because they are not for sale. One of the great strengths of the market is that it provides so much information about real prices. For any commodity that actually is bought and sold, prices are communicated automatically, almost costlessly, and with constant updates as needed. To create artificial prices for environmental values, economists have to find some way to mimic the operation of the market. Unfortunately, the process is far from automatic, certainly not costless, and has to be repeated every time an updated price is needed. * * *

For the reasons we have discussed, there is nothing objective about the basic premises of cost-benefit analysis. Treating individuals solely as consumers, rather than as citizens with a sense of moral responsibility to the larger society, represents a distinct and highly contestable world view. Likewise, the use of discounting reflects judgments about the nature of environmental risks and citizens' responsibilities toward future generations that are, at a minimum, debatable. Because value-laden premises permeate cost-benefit analysis, the claim that cost-benefit analysis offers an 'objective' way to make government decisions is simply bogus.

Furthermore, as we have seen, cost-benefit analysis relies on a byzantine array of approximations, simplifications, and counterfactual hypotheses. Thus, the actual use of cost-benefit analysis inevitably involves countless judgment calls. People with strong, and clashing, partisan positions naturally will advocate that discretion in the application of this methodology be exercised in favor of their positions, further undermining the claim that cost-benefit analysis is objective.

Perhaps the best way to illustrate how little economic analysis has to contribute, objectively, to the fundamental question of how clean and safe we want our environment to be is to refer again to the controversy over cost-benefit analysis of the EPA's regulation of arsenic in drinking water. As Cass Sunstein has recently argued, the available information on the benefits of arsenic reduction supports estimates of net benefits from regulation ranging from less than zero up to $560 million or more.[28] The number of deaths avoided annually by regulation is, according to Sunstein, between zero and 112. A procedure that allows such an enormous range of different evaluations of a single rule is certainly not the objective, transparent decision rule that its advocates have advertised.

These uncertainties arise from the limited knowledge of the epidemiology and toxicology of exposure to arsenic as well as the controversial series of assumptions required for valuation and discounting of costs and (particularly) benefits. As Sunstein explains, a number of different positions, including most of those heard in the recent controversy over arsenic regulation, could be supported by one or another reading of the evidence.[29]

Some analysts might respond that this enormous range of outcomes is not possible if the proper economic assumptions are used—if, for example, human lives are valued at $6 million apiece and discounted at a five percent yearly rate (or, depending on the analyst, other favorite numbers). But these assumptions beg fundamental questions about ethics and equity, and one cannot decide whether to embrace them without thinking through the whole range of moral issues they raise. Yet once one has thought through these issues, there is no need then to collapse the complex moral inquiry into a series of numbers. Pricing the priceless merely translates our inquiry into a different, and foreign, language—one with a painfully impoverished vocabulary.

For many of the same reasons, cost-benefit analysis also generally fails to achieve the goal of transparency. Cost-benefit analysis is a complex, resource-intensive, and expert-driven process. It requires a great deal of time and effort to attempt to unpack even the simplest cost-benefit analysis. Few community groups, for example, have access to the kind of scientific and technical expertise that would allow them to evaluate whether, intentionally or unintentionally, the authors of a cost-benefit analysis have unfairly slighted the interests of the community or some of its members. Few members of the public can participate meaningfully in the debates about the use of particular regression analyses or discount rates which are central to the cost-benefit method.

The translation of lives, health, and nature into dollars also renders decision making about the underlying social values less rather than more transparent. As we have discussed, all of the various steps required to reduce a human life to a dollar value are open to debate and subject to uncertainty. However, the specific dollar values kicked out by cost-benefit analysis tend to obscure these underlying issues rather than encourage full public debate about them.

---

28. Cass R. Sunstein, *The Arithmetic of Arsenic,* 90 GEO. L.J. 2255 (2002).

29. Given this enormous range of uncertainty, it is hard to understand Sunstein's belief (expressed in the same article) that cost-benefit analysis is still useful for screening regulatory options. This could be true only if a significant number of serious proposals had costs that were many orders of magnitude greater than their benefits. As we have discussed, this is a widely held, but empirically false, view of environmental regulation.

NOTES

1.   One question raised by Ackerman and Heinzerling is whether market valuations should be the basis for government policy. Arguably, the government's determination of the public interest might be based on different criteria than those that individuals use to make private choices. Is it rational for people to use different values as voters than as workers or consumers? Is it paternalistic for the government to impose trade-offs (for example, more workplace safety but lower wages) that people would not voluntarily accept in the market?

2.   Is it morally offensive to put a dollar value on life? After all, we do make trade-offs between safety and cost all the time. Isn't cost-benefit analysis just a more systematic way of thinking about these trade-offs? Or does the use of cost-benefit analysis depersonalize our approach to these problems?

3.   The following excerpt considers how cost-benefit analysis functions in the context of climate change policy.

DANIEL H. COLE, THE STERN REVIEW AND ITS CRITICS: IMPLICATIONS FOR THE THEORY AND PRACTICE OF BENEFIT–COST ANALYSIS

48 NAT. RESOURCES J. 53 (2008).[30]

In 2003, the United Kingdom's Chancellor of the Exchequer, Gordon Brown, appointed Nicholas Stern, an Oxford economist and former World Bank chief economist and senior vice president, as second permanent secretary at Her Majesty's (HM) Treasury. Two years later, Chancellor Brown asked Secretary Stern to head up an official governmental review of the economics of climate change. The UK Treasury published the Stern Review on the Economics of Climate Change on October 30, 2006.[31] It was not the first benefit-cost analysis (BCA) on climate change ever,[32] but it was the first such analysis to be issued with the imprimatur of a major government. Consequently, the Stern Review had unusually high political salience and potential to influence policy.

Unsurprisingly, politicians and NGOs that favor rapid and strong action to mitigate greenhouse gas emissions greeted the nearly 600–page Stern Review with uncritical adulation, while climate-change skeptics summarily bashed it. More serious academic critiques of the Review were not long in coming. Several well-respected economists have argued that the Review's assumptions, arguments, and recommendations are seriously flawed, even biased,[33] while others have read the Review more generously.

---

30.   Copyright 2008 by Daniel H. Cole. Reprinted with permission of Natural Resources Journal, University of New Mexico School of Law.

31.   Nicholas Stern, THE ECONOMICS OF CLIMATE CHANGE: THE STERN REVIEW (2007).

32.   See, e.g., William R. Cline, THE ECONOMICS OF GLOBAL WARMING (1992); Robert O. Mendelsohn et al., *Country–Specific Market Impacts of Climate Change*, 45 CLIMATIC CHANGE 553 (2000); William D. Nordhaus & Joseph G. Boyer, WARMING THE WORLD: ECONOMIC MODELS OF GLOBAL WARMING (2000).

33.   See, e.g., William D. Nordhaus, *A Review of the Stern Review on the Economics of Climate Change*, 45 J. ECON. LITERATURE 686 (2007); Partha Dasgupta, *Commentary: The Stern Review's*

In perhaps the most nuanced and interesting of all the reviews, Martin Weitzman deftly criticizes the Stern Review's assumptions and analysis, but goes on to suggest why, ultimately, the Review's conclusions might be sound.[34] Weitzman's analysis, in particular, has important implications for the practice of BCA as it applies to policies like climate change, which involve long time horizons, potentially catastrophic levels of harm, and very high levels of uncertainty.

One purpose of this article is to critically assess the Stern Review and its various reviews. Another is to explain that the disagreements over the quality of the Stern Review (among serious scholars without ostensible political or ideological agendas) largely reflect disagreements about how BCAs generally should—and should not—be done. To that end, the article focuses on the Stern Review's BCA from a process-oriented perspective and asks what producers and consumers of benefit-cost analyses can learn from the Stern Review and its critics about the theory and practice of benefit-cost analysis. The lessons are several, including many negative lessons about how benefit-cost analyses should not be done. Less obvious, but just as important, are one or two positive lessons from the Stern Review. The lessons, both positive and negative, relate to the selection of parameter values, including discount rates, and methods of estimating damages.

* * *

In deriving its damage figures, the Stern Review employs standard economic assumptions from welfare economics theory, including the assumption of diminishing marginal utility of income in evaluating risks and future welfare. But then Stern deliberately courts controversy by choosing a very low pure rate of time preference (utility discount rate) of 0.1 percent per year. * * *

Based on its preferred parameter values, the Stern Review's analysis shows that under BAU (uncontrolled GHG emissions indefinitely into the future) the risks of climate change between 2100 and 2200 will be equivalent to about five percent of the gross global product each year, and possibly as high as 20 percent, "forever." As noted earlier, estimated damages would be only one one-hundredth as large with different parameter values yielding $r = 6$ percent. [r is the discount rate, which includes the time preference and other factors.] This is not to say, however, that the Stern Review's parameter values were "wrong" or that its damage estimate is "too high." As the article later discusses, such conclusions involve ethical value judgments, which are inherently contestable. * * *

Next, the Stern Review authors assess the economics of mitigation/stabilization. In accordance with IPCC TAR and more recent data,

---

Economics of Climate Change, 199 NAT'L INST. ECON. Rev. 4 (2006); * * * Richard S.J. Tol, *The Stern Review of the Economics of Climate Change: A Comment*, 17 ENERGY & ENV'T 977 (2006) * * *.

34. *Martin Weitzman, A Review of the Stern Review on the Economics of Climate Change,* 45 J. ECON. LITERATURE 703, 717 (2007).

they find that stabilizing GHG concentrations at levels that would avoid very costly climate changes will require "deep emissions cuts of at least 25 percent by 2050," implying a nominal decline of 30 to 35 $GtCO_2$. To achieve that goal, emissions would peak during the next 10 to 20 years and then decline by between one percent and three percent per year. Stern Review estimates that cutting emissions 25 percent by 2050 would cost approximately one percent of annual global GDP (about $1 trillion in 2050), plus or minus three percent, and would stabilize concentration levels at between 500 to 550 ppm of carbon dioxide equivalent (CO_{2eq}). At concentration levels in that range, the most harmful effects of climate change would be averted. Stern calculates that by investing one percent of annual global GDP starting now and continuing potentially forever, the world could avert costs to annual global GDP of ten percent "forever." In the "worst case," climate change mitigation would yield net costs amounting to 3.4 percent of annual global GDP. In the "best case," climate change mitigation would add 3.9 percent net to annual global GDP. * * *

Compared to other studies, the Stern Review's discount rate is indeed very low, and its estimate of damages correspondingly high. Tol analyzed 28 published studies that provided 103 total estimates of the marginal damage costs of carbon dioxide emissions. The utility discount rates in those 28 studies generally ranged between one and three percent (with some cases of hyperbolic discounting). Tol's comparison found that the utility discount rate/pure rate of time preference starkly influences both the central estimate and the uncertainty:

> If we use a pure rate of time preference of 3 percent-corresponding to a social rate of discount of 4–5 percent, close to what most western governments use for most long-term investments—the combined mean estimate is $16/tC (ton of carbon), not exceeding $62/tC with a probability of 95 percent. Lower social rates of discount lead to higher estimates but particularly to greater uncertainty, but even for a 1 percent pure rate of time preference the combined mean is $51/tC. Even lower discount rates may be morally preferable, but are clearly out of line with common practice.

That last sentence is intriguing. If lower discount rates are "morally preferable" but "out of line with common practice," as Tol suggests they might be, which should be adjusted, the "morally preferable" discount rate or the "common practice"? As we shall see later, Weitzman presents a strong ethical argument that the discount rate should be made to comport to convention. But Weitzman also notes that structural uncertainties in climate change damage estimates might justify the selection of a very low discount rate (although he would prefer to deal with such structural uncertainties via the damage function, rather than the discount rate).

The Stern Review's estimate of $85/$tCO_{2eq}$ under BAU [business as usual] exceeded by more than a factor of five Tol's combined mean estimate from 28 previous studies. No wonder the Stern Review calls for quicker and steeper reductions in GHG emissions than any previous BCA. This is not to say, however, that the Stern Review's cost-estimate is necessarily wrong. Tol concedes that

> [t]he current generation of aggregate estimates may understate the true cost of climate change because they tend to ignore extreme weather events; exclude low probability/high consequence scenarios, such as a shut-down of the thermohaline circulation [basically the Gulf Stream] or a collapse of the West–Antarctic ice sheet; underestimate the compounding effect of multiple stresses; and ignore the costs of transition and learning.

Each of the factors missing from the earlier generation of aggregate estimates is present and accounted for in the Stern Review. That must justify a higher cost-estimate. How much higher? Tol does not tell us, but concludes that the Stern Review "overestimates the impacts of climate change, and therefore the benefits of emission reduction."

But why did the Stern Review authors choose such a low utility discount rate in the first place? Was their intent simply to manipulate cost estimates so as to justify more rapid and extreme measures to control GHG emissions? The Stern Review is replete with expressions of concern that earlier studies had underestimated the costs of climate change, but the authors do not attempt to justify the choice of a low discount rate based on that concern alone. Rather, they follow the lead of several other prominent economists such as Frank Ramsey, Amartya Sen, and Robert Solow in presenting affirmative and legitimate ethical reasons against anything higher than a minimal discount rate for estimating the costs of climate change. Ramsey famously argued that discounting is "ethically indefensible and arises merely from the weakness of the imagination." The late David Pearce argued that discounting is a "brute fact" because people are observed to discount for time and space in making individual investment/consumption decisions. But just because people are observed to do it does not make it right. Ramsey's point is that both the decision to discount and the choice of a social discount rate are not just matters of positive economics but normative ethics. Stern agrees with Ramsey that people should not discount for time and space. Indeed, the only reason the Stern Review uses a 0.1 percent pure rate of time preference, rather than a zero rate, is the risk of human extinction during the course of the current century.

The bottom-line question for present purposes is whether the Stern Review's pure rate of time preference is so low as to violate some presumed "best practice" standard. As a matter of theory and practice, this is a difficult question to answer. The choice of a social discount rate is inherently subjective and as Portney and Weyant have observed, "Those looking for guidance on the choice of discount rate could find justification [in the literature] for a rate at or near zero, as high as 20 percent, and any and all values in between." Thus, the Stern Review's choice of a discount rate close to zero does not seem invalid per se. That it deviates from the literature does not make it wrong, only deviant. We might conclude that deviance from an accepted norm would violate a duty of BCA producers not to impose their own values paternalistically on society. But it is not at all clear that such a norm (yet) exists. * * *

Although Weitzman strongly criticizes the Stern Review for its assumptions and analytical weaknesses, he is not as quick as other reviewers to denounce its conclusions or policy recommendations. To the contrary, he suggests that the Stern Review's value of r "may end up being more right than wrong when full accounting is made for the uncertainty of the discount rate itself, which arguably is the most important uncertainty of all in the economics of climate change" Why?

> The very same force of compound interest that makes costs and benefits a century from now seem relatively insignificant, and that additionally creates the "majority tilt" of a pain-postponing climate policy ramp of emissions reductions starting from a low gradual base [as in Nordhaus's model], also forces us to recognize the logic that over such long periods we should be using interest rates at the lower end of the spectrum of possible values.

Specifically, Weitzman suggests that uncertainty over which discount rates to use for the costs and benefits of climate change a century from now might reduce the value of r from six percent to as low as two percent, which is not far above the Stern Review's value of r. * * *

The "moral" drawn by Weitzman "is that the nature of the impacts of climate change determine[s] whether we should end up closer to using the risk-free rate or the economy-wide return on capital." But "trying to forecast costs and benefits of climate change scenarios a hundred years or so from now is more the art of inspired guesstimating by analogy than a science (imagine forecasting today's world a century ago)." Is Weitzman suggesting that "state of the art" economic analysis is not yet up to the task of dealing with a problem as potentially large and long-term as climate change? The last three sections of Weitzman's review of the Stern Review suggest that the answer to this question is a qualified yes.

The problem, in a nutshell, is the wide range of possible temperature increases under the IPCC's most current climate change models, including a five-percent possibility that temperature increases will equal or exceed 6 C° and a two-percent probability of increases equal to or greater than 8 C° within the next 100 to 200 years. Weitzman notes that "any honest economic modeler would have to admit" to complete uncertainty about the social, economic, and environmental effects of such a temperature increase because "such high temperatures have not existed for some tens of millions of years." * * * We don't even know how much we don't know about the probabilities. The structural uncertainties, Weitzman notes, are highly likely to matter more than the risk for "whomever wants to model optimal-expected-utility growth under endogenous greenhouse warming." * * *

Beyond the social discount rate and the factors that comprise it, concern about structural uncertainties might have broader implications about whether standard BCA remains the proper tool for making policy decisions concerning climate change. Structural uncertainties might, instead, favor the use of a "Safe Minimum Standards" (SMS) approach to regulatory decision making. SMS applies a relatively hard precautionary principle—harder, perhaps, than Weitzman's "generalized precautionary principle"—by establishing a floor "below which the flow of key ecosystem services should not be permitted to fall." The floor could be set to avoid the very kinds of potential discontinuities that complicate efforts to model climate change using traditional BCA. But just where should the floor be set? It would seem that the same structural uncertainties that vex conventional BCA would also create problems for SMS. The only difference is that SMS utilizes a hard precautionary principle according to which uncertainty would automatically support greater efforts at mitigation and stabilization. In other words, it builds in a higher level of risk aversion. Naturally, economists who prefer not to presume a high level of risk aversion would oppose the hard precautionary principle of SMS and would prefer BCA, either with or without Weitzman's presumably softer "generalized precautionary principle." Obviously, much work remains to be done to determine the best means of factoring risk aversion—in particular aversion to potentially catastrophic harms—into economic analyses. * * *

Economic analyses of problems and policies at the frontiers of scientific knowledge are bound to be controversial and error prone, especially where time horizons are long and uncertainty looms large. In some cases, they amount to little more than shots in the dark. This is not an argument against making the effort to economically analyze complex problems like climate change. For such problems all of our approaches to decisionmaking are likely to be controversial and error-prone, and there is little reason to suppose that any other approach would provide policy makers with better quality information than multiple BCAs. Nevertheless, given the special analytical—particularly measurement—problems of long-term, highly complex problems like climate change, authors of BCAs should be especially cautious about the conclusions they draw and the recommendations they make. Nearly all reviewers agree that the Stern group pretended to greater confidence in their comparatively radical conclusions and recommendations than the facts and analysis warranted. While the Stern Review contained several warnings about the problems associated with forecasting the costs and benefits of climate change and mitigation, it did not heed its own warnings when presenting its conclusions and recommendations unconditionally.

* * * Given the inherently subjective elements of BCA—from the valuations of nonmarket goods (including human lives) to the choice of value parameters (including discount rates)—and given the influence of those subjective elements on outcomes, each and every BCA inevitably is informed by the ethical, political, and/or ideological predilections of its

author(s). The range of subjective choice may (or may not) be bounded by the observed behavior of market actors, but the choices remain inevitably subjective. A chief virtue of BCA as a decision tool is that it makes those predilections transparent (at least compared to other decision tools) because, according to "best practices," authors are supposed to make their assumptions-including choices of parameter values-explicit.

The authors of the Stern Review did not fully meet the standard of transparency. To their credit, they specified parameter values, including the utility discount rate. Even if they chose a rate based on paternalistic ethics that ignored observed economic behavior, at least they were explicit about it and provided reasoned arguments to support it. They were not explicit, however, about their valuations of nonmarket goods, including human lives. Those valuations, just like the discount rate, are subjective and therefore subject to manipulation for political purposes. For that reason, BCA authors must state and support them explicitly.

Because of the potential for subjective elements including parameter values and valuations of nonmarket goods to affect the outcome of BCAs, the Stern Review certainly should have included a sensitivity analysis. Sensitivity analyses are helpful in demonstrating the relative robustness of outcomes across alternative valuations. The failure of the Stern Review authors to include one in their original BCA was a significant omission, to say the least. In response to their critics, they eventually did prepare what Weitzman has called "a halfhearted sensitivity analysis postscript." Stern's sensitivity analysis purported to demonstrate the robustness of the Review's conclusions but succeeded only in demonstrating their high sensitivity to the choice of parameter values (something that critiques of the Stern Review already had demonstrated). Arguably, Arrow provides a more convincing argument for the robustness of the Stern Review's conclusions than the Review's own sensitivity analysis.* * *

Anyone interested in BCA as a discipline should read both the Stern Review and its serious academic critics because they raise serious issues about the practice and practicability of BCA for long-run problems and policies with potentially severe consequences under high levels of Knightian uncertainty. Stern takes a strong position that such uncertainty is not an excuse for inaction, especially where the stakes are enormous, as is arguably the case with climate change. Whatever its analytical flaws, Stern is surely right about that most important point, as Weitzman notes.

NOTES ON COST-BENEFIT ANALYSIS AND CLIMATE CHANGE

1. There are now about a dozen models that couple climate change predictions to economic analysis. These models differ in a number of dimensions: whether they focus on the energy sector or rely on a broad macroeconomic analysis, the degree to which they analyze localized versus average global impacts, and their treatment of uncertainty. Models also differed in their assessments of the costs of complying with the Kyoto Protocol, with the range running from negligible losses to at least one to two percent of GDP

annually.[35] The models differed in terms of three critical assumptions about the timing of abatement efforts, the types of policy instruments used, and the likelihood of technological innovation.[36] Other relevant factors include the willingness of economic actors to substitute away from high carbon technologies and trends in energy efficiency.[37] On the energy technology dimensions, see Scott Barrett, *The Coming Global Climate–Technology Revolution*, 23 J. ECON. PERSP. 53 (Spring 2009).

2. There are similar difficulties in modeling the costs of mitigating and adapting to climate change. Most of the model results are in the range of two to five percent of GDP in 2050, but the range is from a four percent *gain* in GDP due to reduced use of carbon to a fifteen percent *loss* of GDP.[38] A meta-analysis shows that key factors in explaining these differences are whether revenue from carbon taxes is recycled, what kinds of technological changes are assumed, whether shifts in energy sources have non-climate benefits, and whether the model includes international carbon trading.[39] Many of the individual elements of the economic impact analysis are hotly disputed. For instance, economists hotly dispute the net effect of climate change on agriculture, with some finding an overall positive effect on U.S. agriculture (but with very large regional variations),[40] while others find substantial negative effects.[41] See Richard S.J. Tol, *The Economic Effects of Climate Changes*, 23 J. ECON. PERSP. 29 (29 (Spring 2009); Daniel A. Farber, *Modeling Climate Change and Its Impacts: Law, Policy, and Science*, 86 TEX. L. REV. 1655 (2008).

3. The conventional account of the U.S. national interest regarding climate change may be incomplete. Our critique of the climate change winner perspective focuses, by contrast, on its curiously "isolationist" approach—its failure to consider, at least in any serious way, the possibility that many of the costs and burdens that other countries are likely to experience as a result of climate change will, to varying extents, spill over to the U.S. This could occur in the form of national security threats, which climate change will exacerbate in various regions of the world; economic spillovers, such as higher oil and other resource and commodity prices, supply shocks, demand shocks and disruption to financial markets; as well as spillovers that result from the spread of infectious disease and significant migration. A number of studies have now determined that climate change is likely to be a "threat multiplier" in precisely this way. For further discussion of these issues, see Jody Freeman and Andrew Guzman, *Seawalls Are Not Enough: Climate Change "Spill-*

---

35. Jason F. Shogren & Michael A. Toman, *How Much Climate Change is Too Much?*, in CLIMATE CHANGE ECONOMICS AND POLICY: AN RFF ANTHOLOGY 35, 42 (Michael A. Toman ed., 2001).

36. *Id.*

37. *Id.* at 43.

38. NICHOLAS STERN, THE ECONOMICS OF CLIMATE CHANGE: THE STERN REVIEW 269 (2007).

39. *Id.* at 271.

40. *See* Olivier Deschenes & Michael Greenstone, *The Economic Impacts of Climate Change: Evidence from Agricultural Output and Random Fluctuations in Weather*, 97 AM. ECON. REV. 354 (2007) (but note that this study excludes possible impacts of increased in extreme events such as storms and droughts).

41. Wolfram Schlenker, W. Michael Hanemann, & Anthony C. Fisher, *The Impact of Global Warming on U.S. Agriculture: An Econometric Analysis of Optimal Growing Conditions*, 88 REV. ECON. & STAT. 113 (2006).

overs" and The U.S. National Interest, draft available at http://www.law. harvard.edu/faculty/freeman/.

2. MARKET–BASED INSTRUMENTS

Cost-benefit analysis provides a standard for assessing regulatory outcomes. But economists also have ideas about how to attain these outcomes most efficiently. Those methods can be used whether pollution levels are set based on cost-benefit analysis, the significant risk test, or some other method.

BYRON SWIFT, U.S. EMISSIONS TRADING: MYTHS, REALITIES, AND OPPORTUNITIES[42]

20 Nat. Resources & Envt. 3 (2005).

The major U.S. cap-and-trade programs reduce SO_2 and NO_x emissions from power plants. These programs were implemented in part as a response to the failure of traditional health-based rate standards set under Title I of the Clean Air Act (CAA) to achieve significant pollutant reductions from the utility sector. National SO_2 emissions only declined from 17 million tons to 16 million tons between 1970 and 1990, and NO_x emissions only declined from 7 million tons to 6 million tons from 1980 to 1998. Although the rate standards then in place helped prevent growth in emissions during this period of economic expansion, the need for further overall reductions in tons emitted to address the regional impacts of these pollutants (acid rain and urban ozone) led to the imposition of cap-and-trade programs to guarantee major reductions.

Congress passed the Acid Rain Program in 1990 to reduce the SO_2 emissions of electric utilities, then responsible for 70 percent of national emissions. Phase I began in 1995 and Phase II in 2000, which requires all 3,497 affected electricity-generating units to collectively reduce their emissions to the final cap amount of 8.95 million tons, or roughly half their 1980 baseline emissions. The NO_x cap-and-trade program for power plants began in 1999 with a program carried out for nine northeastern states to achieve a 54 percent reduction from 1990 baseline NO_x emissions. The EPA SIP Call regulation basically expanded this program to cover nineteen eastern states in 2004, and requires a total 65 percent reduction.

Both cap-and-trade programs have stringent emissions monitoring rules that require continuous emissions monitors and impose high penalties that are automatically assessed if a source does not have enough allowances to cover its emissions at year-end. This system has led to virtually 100 percent compliance in both programs, significantly higher than in most other regulatory programs. The salient elements of cap-and-trade programs, with particular attention to the largest program, the national Acid Rain Program for SO_2, are discussed below. Where possible,

---

42. Copyright © 2005 by the American Bar Association. Reprinted with permission.

these will be compared with the alternative results under traditional rate standards.

Cap-and-trade programs work by reducing on a national or regional basis the emissions from a category of emission sources, primarily power plants to date, and then prohibiting increases above this collective reduced level, capping emissions. Possibly the primary environmental benefit of these programs has been their guarantee of major reductions in pollutant emissions, as they permanently cap emissions at well below baseline levels. The Acid Rain Program cuts SO_2 emissions in half, and the NO_x program achieves a 65 percent reduction. Greater reductions are also possible: a 90 percent reduction in NO_x is achieved by a local cap-and-trade program in the Houston–Galveston area, and bills in Congress would use cap-and-trade programs to achieve a further 75 percent reduction in national SO_2 and NO_x emissions.

The permanence of the reductions when caps are used is in line with the needs of the environment, which requires that ambient pollution levels not increase over time. This is a much better environmental result than is typical under rate-based standards, which allow emissions to grow over time as more plants are built or as output increases. The permanent cap also implements essentially a zero new source standard, again a better result than can be obtained under rate standards.

By using a standard expressed in amounts (tons) of pollution instead of emission rates, cap-and-trade programs create a fundamentally better performance standard and regulatory result, both environmentally and economically, than traditional rate-based standards. Along with the permanence of the reduction, this is probably the most important, although little-discussed, reason to implement cap-and-trade programs. * * *

A significant advantage of cap-and-trade systems is that they impose a uniform standard that does not vary with a plant's age or technology, unlike rate standards that are highly technology-specific. This creates a number of commonsense results by linking cost to environmental performance. Under uniform standards such as a cap, businesses seek to reduce pollution wherever it is economical to do so. However, rate standards have left unregulated sources of pollution like small cyclone boilers that emit over 1,000 ppm NO_x, while forcing clean new sources to install expensive technologies to reduce NO_x from 9 ppm to 3 ppm. Absurd results like this are commonplace under differentiated rate standards, but do not occur under uniform standards such as cap-and-trade programs.

Another major benefit is the ease of stepped reductions. Cap-and-trade programs allow all regulated sources to be included in a stepped reduction in the standards, even if such reductions are imposed every few years. However, it would be unfair to impose serially reducing rate standards on a source, as each step would require a new investment in abatement technology. Therefore, when rate standards are used, all previously regulated sources tend to be grandfathered whenever there is a stepped reduction (such as in the Phase II NO_x rates established under Title IV), a much worse result for the environment.

Finally, uniform standards such as cap-and-trade programs also completely avoid the pitfalls of New Source Review (NSR), which can have the effect of imposing added burdens on clean new plants while grandfathering older polluting plants. To achieve the benefits of using a uniform standard, technology-based requirements such as NSR rate standards must be removed once sources are covered under a stringent emissions cap.

Another major difference between rate standards and cap-and-trade systems is the compliance and enforcement system. Rate systems require a complex permitting system that requires government review and approval of each technology choice by the source. This is expensive, takes time (months or years for major sources), discourages innovation, and creates conflict between regulator and regulated. Cap-and-trade programs have a far simpler enforcement system. There are strict monitoring protocols, such as using continuous emissions monitoring devices, coupled with high financial penalties and the loss of allowances if sources exceed their allowed emissions. This has led to virtually 100 percent compliance in all years of the NO_x and SO_2 programs, higher than other clean air programs, with any exceedances leading to swift and automatic penalties, and applied with virtually no enforcement effort.

Note that this enforcement system has two features that promote innovation. First, there is no government review of technology choice, such as reasonably or best available control technologies (RACT or BACT), that exists under rate standards, freeing sources to experiment with technology choice. Second, risk-taking is encouraged. If an innovative technology fails to perform as planned, the source can simply buy allowances to make up the needed reductions instead of facing civil or criminal penalties for the failure that would apply under a rate-based system. Both of these features encourage greater risk-taking.

Cap-and-trade programs have also achieved very significant economic results in reducing the cost of compliance: the national Acid Rain Program is now expected to cost between $1.3 to $1.5 billion while providing health benefits of over $70 billion. This cost is several times below predictions, * * * and significantly below what it would have cost to achieve equivalent reduction through the use of various forms of rate standards.

The key element that drives these cost reductions is the greater flexibility in technology choice allowed under cap-and-trade programs. Rate standards [standards based on emission rates] are far more rigid, in many cases dictating technology choices by their specifications. * * *

The history of NO_x regulation of power plants leads to a similar conclusion. Rate regulations have led principally to the installation of identified control technologies. Weak rate regulations under Title IV led to the installation of low-NO_x burners and overfire air, whereas stringent ones such as BACT have led principally to Selective Catalytic Reduction technology. The NO_x cap-and-trade programs, however, allowed firms to use a far broader set of technologies and methods to reduce emissions, including boiler optimization, fuel switching or repowering, the use of low-NO_x coals, load shifting, Selective Non-catalytic Reduction, gas reburn, and many others.

This flexibility was exemplified in the first year of the NO_x cap-and-trade program in 1999, when 126 of the 142 affected coal-fired units achieved up to 30 percent NO_x reductions through operational changes alone, and without significant capital costs. Firms were able to "look everywhere" for reductions, and not just install a new round of available control technologies, which is the result with rate standards. As a consequence, compliance costs were greatly reduced, to $500 to $1,000 per ton, well below estimates.

The greater technology choice under cap-and-trade programs has environmental as well as economic implications. Unlike rate standards, cap-and-trade programs allow compliance through lowering the use of dirty technologies, and shifting generation to cleaner base technologies. These incentives are essential if we are to move toward sustainable development.

Two factors inherent in cap-and-trade programs promote innovation. First, the breadth of technology choice broadens the opportunity for unexpected innovation. In Phase I of the SO_2 cap-and-trade program, this led to unexpected innovation in fuel blending that allowed far greater use of low-sulfur coal for compliance, dramatically reducing the cost of compliance. It also created competition for scrubbing, driving innovation and major cost reductions. Scrubber technologies had experienced relatively little innovation in the decade prior to the Acid Rain Program, when they enjoyed a monopoly position, but capital cost of scrubbing declined from an average of $265 to around $100 per kilowatt once scrubbers were exposed to competition from low-sulfur coal under the cap-and-trade program.

Second, trading programs drive businesses to continuously seek environmental quality improvements because emissions are capped and the opportunity exists to profit through trading. This opens the door to innovation in management practices and leads to the kind of learning-by-using and learning-by-doing that underlies much innovation. Finally, as noted above, compliance systems under cap-and-trade programs are more friendly to innovation.

Cap-and-trade programs allow the integration of economic and environmental variables to a far greater extent than traditional rate standards. The effect of trading in establishing a market price for a ton of reductions helps integrate environmental and economic decision-making within a firm. One example of this integration in the SO_2 program is that allowance prices are fully integrated into the price of coal depending on its sulfur content. A second example is that allowance prices are regularly updated in the dispatch models that dictate which plants will operate at any time within a utility system. Both of these create efficiency in merging the environmental quality demanded by society with industry decision-making.

This integration also breaks down the "green wall" that typically keeps the environmental compliance unit within a firm walled off from the rest of the company. The only task under rate standards is to keep the control devices operating properly to ensure the lack of enforcement problems; there are few other incentives. However, the need to reduce pollution to stay under the cap combined with the opportunity to benefit from trading introduces new drivers to reduce pollution, and leads to the same concern for continuous quality improvement in the environmental sector as in the firm's normal business operations.

Transaction and administrative costs are far lower in cap-and-trade programs than in traditional rate-based standards. Instead of lengthy permitting proceedings, transactions in the Acid Rain Program take place in less than twenty-four hours, allowing firms to rapidly shift strategies and experiment with new ideas. The economic costs of transactions have dropped markedly: emissions brokers charged $3 to $10 per allowance to carry out trades at the beginning of the Acid Rain Program in 1995, whereas brokers now charge less than 20 cents per allowance traded, and many utilities are trading themselves.

Governmental administration costs are lower for cap-and-trade because the role of the government regulator is transformed from that of evaluating and approving technologies to one of monitoring emissions and enforcing compliance. Eliminating the former vastly simplifies permitting policies and also reduces government costs. In Phase I of the Acid Rain Program, only 150 people were needed to operate the program, out of the approximately 15,000 people working on air pollution control.

Some writers have been concerned that trading programs may shift the locus of emissions, potentially causing areas of higher localized pollution levels or hot spots. However, an assessment of the actual performance of trading programs shows that the choice of regulatory method has little to no environmental impact on hot spots. In fact, because trading programs promote reductions at the largest plants, they outperform rate standards and tend to reduce instead of create hot spots.

A regional analysis shows that neither major SO_2 or NO_x cap-and-trade program has resulted in regional shifts of emissions. The hot spot issue was an early concern in the Acid Rain Program, as it was feared that trading might exacerbate the high emissions levels in the Midwest. In fact, the opposite happened, and in both Phases I and II a greater proportion of reductions were made in the Midwest than in other major regions * * *

Similarly, the NO_x trading programs show that emissions reductions were consistent, even at the state level. In 2003, all states with significant emissions achieved a similar reduction from baseline emissions levels. EPA, NO_x Budget Trading Program (SIP Call) 2003 Progress Report (2003). In the earlier OTC NO_x cap-and-trade program that lasted from

1999 to 2002, there was only a slight 3 percent shift in emissions from north to south, and all states continuously involved in the program achieved similar results in the amount of reductions achieved and the effect of trading.

A more striking finding is made when the data is examined at the plant level. Both cap-and-trade and credit-based trading programs have resulted in disproportionately high emissions reductions at the largest plants. This is because the economics of installing capital equipment to reduce emissions provides the greatest financial rewards when installed at the largest sources, leading to disproportionate emissions reductions at these most polluting sources. Therefore, in the Acid Rain Program Phase II, the quartile of plants with the largest emissions reduced emissions by 73 percent, the next largest by 48 percent, the next by 41 percent, and the smallest quartile by 10 percent. Similarly, for the NO_x state credit trading programs discussed below, more than 90 percent of credits were generated at the very largest sources in most states. This attribute of trading programs would be expected to have a significant effect in reducing hot spots by reducing emissions at the most polluting plants. * * *

There are, however, two types of standards that still make sense once a national cap-and-trade program is implemented. First, from its earliest years, the CAA has imposed primary and secondary emissions rate standards for NO_x and SO_2 to protect human health and welfare in the vicinity of plants. These, however, are relatively weak standards and were inadequate to control the regional effects of these pollutants, which led to the cap-and-trade programs.

Second, a more significant justification exists for local standards whenever greater reductions are necessary. If a national cap-and-trade program reduces NO_x emissions by 65 percent, but a metropolitan area requires a 90 percent reduction, a more stringent local standard is called for. These local standards can be implemented by a cap-and-trade program, as used in Houston to reduce local NO_x emissions by 90 percent, or can be achieved less elegantly through the existing CAA emissions offset rules for nonattainment areas. * * *

Emissions credit trading programs are far less comprehensive regulatory programs than cap-and-trade programs and only add a trading element to existing regulatory programs. They have primarily economic benefits by providing greater flexibility to sources in order to lower compliance costs and, therefore, have none of the systematic benefits of cap-and-trade programs.

Credit trading programs are "open-market" trading systems in which sources carry out specific projects that create emissions reductions and obtain regulatory approval to trade the tons of reductions in the form of emission credits. They have been established for criteria pollutants since the CAA Amendments of 1977 and are part of a suite of EPA market-incentive policies, including bubbles, netting, and offsets, which attempt to reduce the costs of compliance without sacrificing air quality.

More recently, discrete emission reductions credit trading programs have been adopted in six states. A review of these programs from 1995 to 2000 showed that many more credits have been generated (156,666) than used (21,918). Two reasons for the lack of use are the legal uncertainties regarding the use of credits under existing CAA standards and the transaction costs for creating credits.

Overall, the review found three problem areas with credit trading. The first, integrity, is an inherent problem with credit trading because one can never be sure that the pollution reduction action generating the credits would not have been undertaken anyway. If credit is given for these reductions, pollution levels are increased, leading to a lack of integrity of the program. Second, measurement protocols are not standardized due to the variety of projects, and regulators often end up accepting the source's proposed methodology. Finally, transaction costs are high and so discourage trading. The study found the average emissions credit project costs $20,000 and requires several regulatory approvals.

None of these problems exist with cap-and-trade programs, which have 100 percent integrity due to the emissions cap, strict measurement protocols, and very low transaction costs.

Although credit trading programs are very much the weak sister of cap-and-trade programs, they can be made to work better. States like Massachusetts have tried to address the first and second problems by limiting the life of credit-generating projects to a few years and discounting the number of credits given if estimation protocols are used.

A more successful credit trading program is the CAA emissions offset program, which requires every new or expanding source in a nonattainment area to offset its emissions. It achieves greater integrity than most programs due to the strict regulatory framework for nonattainment areas, thereby assuring that every large source in the area is permitted and its emissions levels controlled. This framework in effect creates a semi-capped environment for the area, which in turn lends greater integrity to the credit trading program.

Overall, although their rationale is to reduce costs, credit trading programs have generally failed to generate considerable trades or economic benefits. Reviews have tended to blame their shortcomings on high transaction costs, the uncertainty and risk in obtaining the needed government approvals, the lack of clear legal authority and clearly specified objectives, and the timing of the credit trading programs. Another reason is that most CAA standards are not designed with the use of tradable credits in mind, which tends to limit the use and effectiveness of credit trading programs. Finally, these programs have led to uncertain environmental impacts, creating criticism by environmental advocates.

NOTE

Consider the following, somewhat contrasting, appraisal of possible difficulties with cap-and-trade systems:

[B]oth market and prescriptive approaches share some of the same weaknesses. For example, just as prescriptive regulation runs into obstacles in the implementation and enforcement stage, so do market mechanisms. Indeed, the challenge of designing market mechanisms can be just as great, and in some instances greater, than the challenge facing regulators who must establish and implement prescriptive standards. Some of these design problems can be acute. Markets can be too narrowly or too broadly drawn. Political considerations may dominate the initial allocation of entitlements in market trading schemes, which, though often necessary to generate political support for the adoption of the regulatory program, can undermine their purported efficiency.

Trading schemes can falter because of difficulties in both valuing environmental commodities and ensuring that trades involve commensurate goods. For this reason, it may be especially challenging to devise market approaches to natural resource management as compared to pollution control, because natural resources like ecosystems perform functions that may be enormously difficult to value and to trade. They raise problems of incommensurability and non-fungibility that may not arise in the context or air or water quality regulation. Markets can also create "hotspots" of concentrated pollution, which can disproportionately affect sub-populations, leading to claims of distributional inequity. Conceivably market tools can be modified to address some of these problems, but in some instances prescriptive regulation may still be necessary because market mechanisms are too risky or unworkable.

JODY FREEMAN & CHARLES KOLSTAD, MOVING TO MARKETS IN ENVIRONMENTAL REGULATION, LESSONS FROM TWENTY YEARS OF EXPERIENCE (Oxford University Press 2006). For a discussion of cap-and-trade and carbon tax options in the climate context, see Gilbert E. Metcalf, *Market-based Policy Options to Control U.S. Greenhouse Gas Emissions,* 23 J. ECON. PERSP. 5 (Spring 2009).

The problem of distributional inequities such as hotspots is discussed in depth in the next section. Some environmentalists also object to market mechanisms on principle, because they treat environmental protection as simply a cost of doing business and in effect "sell" an entitlement to pollute the environment. Other environmentalists, however, view them as a welcome way in which to reach environmental goals more cheaply.

Market mechanisms are central to discussions of climate mitigation. The Regional Greenhouse Gas Initiative (RGGI) is the most notable of the existing regional plans. RGGI is currently supported by the governors or legislators of Connecticut, Delaware, Maine, Maryland, New Hampshire, New Jersey, New York, and Vermont.[43] RGGI is aimed at creating a multistate trading system, capping emissions at current levels until 2015 and then achieving a ten

---

43. See *Regional Greenhouse Gas Initiative: An Initiative of the Northeast & Mid–Atlantic States of the U.S.,* http://www.rggi.org (last visited July 9, 2008) for more detail.

percent reduction by 2019. The most ambitious state trading system will be established under California's A.B. 32. A.B. 32 requires California to reduce emissions to the 1990 level by 2020. This law generated world-wide attention, including a statement by the British Prime Minister that its signing represented a "historic day for the rest of the world as well." The Prime Minister and the Governor of California also entered an agreement to share best practices on market-based systems and to cooperate to investigate new technologies; similar agreements now exist between California and states and provinces in Australia and Canada. Although A.B. 32 does not mandate the use of cap-and-trade, the state's Air Resources Board, which is charged with implementing the bill, is recommending the adoption of such a program. *See* California Air Resources Board (CARB), CLIMATE CHANGE DRAFT SCOPING PLAN: A FRAMEWORK FOR CHANGE (June 2008), http://www.arb.ca.gov/cc/scopingplan/document/draftscopingplan.htm.

It seems increasingly likely that federal climate legislation will be forthcoming. The following excerpt discusses the available options and their desirability.

VICTOR B. FLATT, TAKING THE LEGISLATIVE TEMPERATURE: WHICH FEDERAL CLIMATE CHANGE LEGISLATIVE PROPOSAL IS "BEST"?
102 NW. U. L. REV. COLLOQUY 123 (2007).**44**

It may seem difficult to propose a framework to judge the effectiveness of climate change proposals when there is no agreement on the standards with which we judge legislation generally. Our legislative process is not transparent, which increases the likelihood of rent seeking and renders it difficult to hold the normative discussions necessary to inform the public so that it can demand the particular kinds of consideration it desires. Political power-games add another dimension that makes the discussion even more complex.

I will not attempt to devise a comprehensive framework with which to analyze the desirability of all legislation. But with respect to climate change, there are certain policy choices that must be debated. An analysis of these policy choices and their importance creates a common framework for discussion. We may not all agree that rising temperatures in Alaska are bad, but knowing the outcome of a particular policy choice provides a basis for understanding the popular will and opinion regarding the choice. Therefore, this Colloquy Essay specifies: 1) the most important policy choices at stake in climate change legislation, 2) why they are important, 3) the best resolution of these issues, and 4) how the current legislative proposals deal with them.

Legislation is a dynamic and iterative process. The legislative proposals analyzed in this Essay may be dropped or changed and other legislation may be proposed before comprehensive climate change legislation is passed. Indeed, this Essay and the comments that follow will hopefully provide impetus for changing legislative proposals in response to a consid-

---

eration of issues herein. Nevertheless, the scientific underpinnings of climate change, including the range of remaining uncertainties, are well enough understood that the analytical principles associated with climate change issues will not change in the immediate future. Therefore, the analysis of the policy choices herein should inform any forthcoming climate change legislation and also serve as a resource for examining inevitable shortcomings and possible amendments in climate change legislation of the future. * * *

While each of the proposed statutes reference the importance of avoiding climate change harm, these percentage reductions are not defined with respect to what variables could affect such a choice, such as what community is considered, the allocation of costs and benefits, and the expectations of other reductions or future technological changes or solutions. From the press releases of the legislative sponsors, it appears that all believe that their reductions are just enough to avoid the worst harm, while inflicting minimal damage on the economy. Though these "Goldilocks" targets all claim to be "just right," they lack valid supporting studies that prove these targets accomplish the climate change mitigation that the legislative sponsors claim. Even the scientists themselves may not be sure of the probability of temperature rise associated with certain reductions or the distribution and effects of that rise, but failure to be more specific leaves the focus on direct economic impacts to the detriment of the other concerns.

Moreover, detailing what sectors the percentage reductions cover may be critical; lack of reductions in certain areas will reduce the supposed overall reduction and thus the possibility of avoiding the worst climate change harms. Thus, bills that target a 50% reduction in CO_2 from 1990 levels by mid-century, which are qualified by exceptions, such as the Lieberman–McCain proposal, may be less "costly" to the economy in one sense. However, the costs associated with too many exceptions means that such a bill may in fact be more costly to our society and economy in the long run * * *

A tax system can control pollution by setting a tax on emissions (such as for CO_2) at a high enough level to discourage such emissions. For instance, one could presumably set a tax on CO_2 emissions (or energy production associated with CO_2 emissions) that would discourage emissions enough to reach a CO_2 reduction target. Cap-and-trade systems adopt the target first and then allocate the overall amount allowed by the target to parties in the market to use, sell, or buy (trade) as they please. Cap-and-trade can be an efficient pollution reduction mechanism because the trading allows the private sector to control emissions at the lowest possible cost (to the private sector) and also encourages innovation. * * *

There are several good critiques of market-based systems to control pollution and comparisons of market based regimes, command and control regimes, and other regimes. The primary critiques of market-based systems are that they may create hot-spots of pollution which hurt specific groups, usually the poor or politically powerless; that they are not fair because they do not necessarily penalize a polluter with the money to purchase pollution rights; that they send the wrong moral signals; and that they are difficult to enforce.

Of these criticisms, three do not appear to be of much concern when addressing the regulation of CO_2 specifically. Because CO_2's harm is worldwide and dispersed, there are no "hotspots" for concern. Moreover, concerns over moral signals seem lessened with CO_2 as compared to almost any other pollutant because CO_2 historically has not been seen as a "bad" thing, so producers are not said to have historically engaged in a bad behavior. Fairness is not as large a concern since all high-energy sector use usually has direct benefit to the general public.

The enforcement issue, however, could be more important than the others for the regulation of CO_2. One of the unique features of the cap-and-trade market in SO_2, is that only large coal-fired power plants are involved in the market. These are relatively limited in number, and already regulated. Therefore, the enforcement and administration costs as well as the possibility of costs from regulatory failure are relatively low for the benefit that can be derived from the system. CO_2 regulation would be a different animal altogether. First, CO_2 and other greenhouse gases are not limited to coal-fired power plants, though they are a major source. Mobile sources play a large role, and if a system were to include offsets (see discussion, infra), the entities that must be monitored and regulated mushroom exponentially. * * *

Even if CO_2 met all of the criteria necessary for the efficient use of cap and trade, some kinds of command and control, particularly those that mandate the adoption of some market standard in certain sectors, can overcome commons problems and "split actor" problems and bring reductions at lower cost because of the ease of enforcement. For instance, the EU consideration on the ban of incandescent light bulb sales seems a very cost-effective way to increase energy efficiency and thereby reduce the production of CO_2. Thus, efficient reduction of climate-changing emissions might be accompanied by command and control systems, at least in some arenas, such as automobile design.

In addition, a major nationwide survey demonstrated that a majority of the American public would actually prefer a command and control system rather than a market system to control climate change. The fact that this has not had a major impact on the legislative proposals to date suggests either that the parties proposing the laws have a better sense of what regulation will be effective, or those who propose the laws realize that market systems may not be as fair and effective but may benefit a particular favored industry or constituency—or some combination of the two. * * *

The enforcement problems inherent to a cap-and-trade system should spur a closer look at the legislative proposals that embrace taxation of CO_2 content. Such taxes are easier to enforce than cap and trade because they are picked up at product and service origination and added to final prices. Economists generally favor a tax because it internalizes any efficiencies of a trading system (if the price of producing carbon is not recouped in one sector, it will cease production) without having to monitor a complicated trading system.

The main objection to a tax system seems to be the belief that the American public abhors any "tax" and will punish any legislator who proposes or votes for one, even if the tax is incorporated into final prices. Representative Dingell has recently challenged this assumption, and I leave it to political scientists to further analyze this question and educate the public. There is also some concern that the appropriate level of "tax" will not be selected to reach the intended reduction target, a problem that one need not worry about in cap-and-trade. This is considered an economic science problem, but a general aversion to taxes may mean that this "target" gets set by other considerations than the most efficient production of CO_2. * * *

If a cap-and-trade system is chosen, legislators must choose how to best distribute the initial allocations that will be subject to trade. Allocations for the right to emit carbon dioxide and equivalent greenhouse gases will be very valuable. There is already much jockeying for this windfall. Whether allocations are auctioned or given away will have little effect on the ultimate economic efficiency of the policy, since trade will efficiently allocate the allotments. But, this decision will have a large effect on the United States treasury, consumer prices, and distribution of costs.

If a cap-and-trade system is ultimately chosen, it is imperative that CO_2 allocations be auctioned or sold, rather than given away. Current industrial infrastructure has developed under a different legal regime, meaning that additional costs will fall heavily on sectors that rely largely on coal-fired power or utilize other fossil fuel generation, but the additional costs are not so large that they will completely disrupt an industry sector. Electricity costs will rise in the South and Midwest, which depend heavily on coal-fired power, but according to auction advocates, it should not increase more than 15%. Some of the money raised through an auction could be set aside to help low income persons who are hit especially hard by a price increase in electricity or other staples of survival (shelter, food, and clothing), meeting the legislative goals of equity.

If the right to emit CO_2 is auctioned off, it will generate money for the U.S .Treasury which could be used for spurring low carbon technology or other purposes. However, this means that the cost of producing energy (at least for those whose energy production emits large amounts of CO_2) would rise. That likely will cost consumers more.

Like a tax system, a cap-and-trade system that features allocation auctions sends a better market signal and encourages all users to efficiently price the externalities of CO_2. It imposes the price hike more specifically on the industries that produce the CO_2, which should send an economic signal to produce less of it. An auction also avoids the need to decide whether to allocate credits based on CO_2 production or based on energy output.

If CO_2 credits are not sold or auctioned, legislators must decide whether to allocate the credits based on energy output or historic CO_2 output. Between the two, allocation based on energy output is preferable since it more accurately prices the externalities of CO_2 producing activities and would tilt energy usage towards renewables and efficiency. An allocation based on energy output would reward those who produce non-CO_2 based power production but still cost consumers of CO_2 intensive energy more, even without money going to the U.S. Treasury. An allocation based on historic CO_2 production, on the other hand, means that CO_2 intensive energy producers will still be able to produce energy for the same cost structure as they have always done, which means that at least theoretically prices would not disproportionately rise in the CO_2 intensive areas. However, since CO_2 would still be rationed, the price of energy would still eventually go up overall. It just wouldn't rise as much in the CO_2 intensive areas and wouldn't affect the bottom line as much as those who sell CO_2 intensive products (such as coal-fired electricity).

As expected, the electric utilities that already consider themselves energy efficient, or those that produce power without fossil fuels, would prefer either a carbon tax or an allocation based on energy production. Doing this imposes the cost of reducing CO_2 on the largest producers of CO_2 and puts the producers (and, by extension, the consumers) of non-CO_2 generating energy or more efficiently produced energy at an advantage. Those that have high CO_2 production, such as coal-fired power plants, would prefer that allocations be distributed based on historic CO_2 production. These producers cite the historic precedent with SO_2 and the costs that would fall on the consumer if allocations are not "given" to coal producers.

Determining how to award allocations also implicates the difficulties of ascertaining information about CO_2 production and energy production and setting a time baseline for making the allocations. The time period the allocations are based on influences how we deal with prior CO_2 cutbacks. For instance, credits awarded based on CO_2 production in a time past (like 1997) would temper the unfairness to producers who made voluntary reductions since that time—this would award them allocations that they can then sell. This would also penalize producers who have created new CO_2 sources for the sole purpose of capturing possible cap-and-trade allocation benefits. * * *

It is surprising that whether allocation should be based on energy output or historic CO_2 output has not received more attention. In many of the bills, it is difficult to determine which method is being used (some use terms such as "heat output" rather than CO_2 or energy output), and the legislative press reports do not focus on this distinction. Even major environmental organizations have been more likely to focus on the "safety valve" issue as the environmental bugaboo rather than the impact that allocation of credits based on historic CO_2 emissions might have on encouraging clean energy. However, since this decision alone is worth billions of dollars to certain segments of the economy and since the initial distribution will have a large impact on how quickly consumers and industry turn to energy with lower CO_2 production, this is a very important point. Part of the tendency to award based on historic CO_2 production may be a hold over from the use of the SO2 system as a model or a holdover from what was at one time believed to be politically feasible. Closer examination of the costs and benefits of the different allocation systems may push the American public towards a different conclusion. * **

Any cap-and-trade system for CO_2 must also address the question of offsets. An offset is anything that will actually reduce CO_2 production (or sometimes future CO_2 production) at one location, which can then be credited against CO_2 production at another location. For instance, if a party has 100 credits which allow the production of 100 tons of CO_2, but wishes to emit 110 tons, instead of buying 10 more credits under the cap-and-trade system, that person might "offset" the extra ten tons of CO_2 by eliminating ten tons of CO_2 production elsewhere. This could be done through retiring a source, creating a physical system to absorb CO_2, or (more controversially) avoiding an increase in future CO_2 production by providing alternate methods of energy that do not produce CO_2. This is essentially a "purchase" of offsets that takes place outside a cap-and-trade system.

Offsets are very complex, but would add greatly to the efficiency of a system, allowing for faster and cheaper reductions. They are also a mechanism for transferring some of the benefits of compliance to developing countries. The main concern with offsets is which ones should be allowed. Presumably, we wish offsets to actually do what they are intended to do. This means that any offsets will require proper measurement systems, verification systems, scientific consensus and consideration of possible unintended consequences. With respect to verification, the current state of the CO_2 trading system in the EU is under critical evaluation. The EU has recently discovered that its initial CO_2 allocations and some offsets were improperly reported by the CO_2 producers, which inflated the number of credits in the system. Because the EU did not have any mechanism in place to verify what sources were actually producing, the system was improperly designed.

Some proposals for carbon offsets may be scientifically suspect. Biological carbon sinks, which—theoretically, at least—absorb CO_2, are under increased scientific scrutiny and criticism because some, such as tree planting in the far northern hemisphere, may contribute to warming rather than offsetting it. Others, such as a plan to seed the ocean with iron filings near the Galapagos Islands to spur plankton, have been blasted as not being based on sound science, harmful, and motivated by nothing but profit. Lastly, offsets purchased in developing countries under the Kyoto Protocol's Clean Development Mechanism ("CDM") are not required to be sustainable or environmentally beneficial, and may only enrich the traders themselves.

Moreover, verifying trades and offsets can be a daunting problem. It is difficult to track small sources, such as the CO2 from the 300 million automobiles in the United States, meaning that mobile source usage intensity will not be a reliable offset. Offsets in foreign countries present particular difficulties. The Kyoto Protocol's CDM program which allows the purchase of offsets in foreign countries, has been roundly criticized for the questionable validity of the offsets purchased. Creating an independent international agency to vet international offsets, perhaps in conjunction with the EU, may help ease international offset enforcement. With respect to both international and domestic offsets, choosing limited, but heavily vetted offset possibilities, while having a mechanism to approve new offsets that "are in the public interest" is appropriate. This legislative choice will drive lobbying and rent seeking for pet projects, but this may be the best alternative. * * *

Climate change legislation is complex; we cannot get by on vague calls for CO2 reduction. The devil is in the details and the intent behind those details. While the current legislative proposals address some of the issues associated with climate change legislation, none do so completely; and without examining all of the issues together, incorrect choices will be made. Armed with a checklist of issues, we can weigh the benefits and harms of current proposals and better tailor them to avoid climate change harms in a fair and efficient manner. We may not all agree on necessary reduction levels, acceptable harms, or what is fair or efficient, but a focus on the issues in this essay will make such discussions and decisions more transparent.

NOTE

At this writing (summer 2009), the front-runner in Congress is the Waxman–Markey bill. Under the bill, beginning in 2012, all electricity generators would be required to have allowances for all GHG emissions from their sites, with the exception of emissions from the combustion of liquid fuels, coke, and renewable biomass. Also beginning in 2012, any facility or entity that produces or imports petroleum- or coal-based liquids, petroleum coke, or natural gas liquids would be required to submit allowances for the GHG emissions that would result from the combustion of those fuels, if combustion of the fuel resulted in the emission of more than 25,000 mtCO2e per year. Similarly, all facilities or entities that produce or import GHGs for direct use would be required to submit allowances for the emissions that would result when those gases were released into the atmosphere. Emissions from sites that geologically sequester CO2 also would be covered beginning in 2012. Many industrial facilities would be covered beginning in 2014, and natural gas distributors beginnings in 2016.

Limited borrowing of allowances (that is, the use in one year of an allowance that has been established for use in a future year) also would be permitted.

The program would allocate to covered entities 4,627 million mtCO2e allowances in 2012, about 97 percent of the amount of such emissions by covered entities in 2005 (meaning a return from 2011 to 2005 emissions). The number of allowances would increase to as high as 5,482 million mtCO2e in 2016 to account for certain covered entities that would not begin compliance until that time, and then decline by 100 million to 150 million mtCO2e per year—falling to 1,035 million mtCO2e in 2050, about 14 percent of projected emissions from covered entities in the absence of regulation of such emissions. A separate program covers certain other greenhouse gases.

C. EQUITY-BASED APPROACHES

Risk-based approaches and economic approaches have one thing in common: they are both primarily interested in the cumulative degree of harm rather than on how the harm is distributed. Environmental justice focuses on the distributional issue.

1. EVIDENCE OF UNEQUAL RISK LEVELS

RICHARD J. LAZARUS, PURSUING 'ENVIRONMENTAL JUSTICE': THE DISTRIBUTIONAL EFFECTS OF ENVIRONMENTAL PROTECTION[45]

87 Nw. U. L. Rev. 787, 792–96, 808, 812 (1993).

Environmental protection confers benefits and imposes burdens in several ways. To the extent that the recipients of related benefits and burdens are identical, no problem of discrimination is presented (there may, of course, be other problems with the tradeoff). But identical recipients are rarely, if ever, the result. Hardly any laws provide Pareto optimality in the classic sense of making everyone better off and no one worse off. Virtually all laws have distributional consequences, including those laws designed to further a particular conception of the public interest. Problems of discrimination, therefore, may arise in the disparities between the distribution of benefits and their related burdens.[46]

The benefits of environmental protection are obvious and significant. A reduction in pollution decreases the public health risks associated with exposure to pollution. It also enhances public welfare by allowing greater opportunity for enjoyment of the amenities associated with a cleaner natural environment. Many would also contend that environmental protection furthers the human spirit by restoring balance between humankind and the natural environment. More pragmatically, environmental

---

45. Copyright © 1993 by Northwestern University, School of Law. Reprinted with permission.

46. Of course, the perception among developing nations of just such a disparity is what prompted many of them, during the recent United Nations Conference on the Environment and Development held in Rio De Janeiro, to demand monies from wealthier nations. The justification for these payments was to compensate the developing nations for the costs associated with their taking action (for example, greater protection of tropical rain forests) that would provide environmental benefits to the entire world, including industrialized nations.

protection laws are the source of new jobs in pollution control industries. EPA recently estimated, for instance, that the recently amended Clean Air Act would result in the creation of 30,000 to 45,000 full-time equivalent positions during 1996–2000.

The burdens of environmental protection range from the obvious to the more subtle. They include the economic costs borne by both the producer and the consumer of goods and services that become more expensive as a result of environmental legislation. For consumers, product and service prices may increase; some may become unavailable because the costs of environmental compliance renders their production unprofitable; while other goods and services may be specifically banned because of their adverse impact on the natural environment. For those persons who produce goods and services made more costly by environmental laws, personal income may decrease, employment opportunities may be reduced or displaced, and certain employment opportunities may be eliminated altogether. Finally, environmental protection requires governmental expenditures, the source of which varies from general personal and corporate income taxes to special environmental taxes. These expenditures necessarily decrease public monies available for other social welfare programs.

The burdens of environmental protection, however, also include the redistribution of the risks that invariably occur with pollution control techniques that treat pollution following its production. For instance, air pollution scrubbers and municipal wastewater treatment facilities reduce air and water pollution, but only by creating a sludge that, when disposed, will likely impose risks on a segment of the population different than the segment which would have been exposed to the initial pollution in the air or water. Additionally, the incineration of hazardous wastes stored in drums and tanks converts a land disposal problem into an air pollution issue (leaving, of course, a sludge residue that presents a different land disposal problem), and thereby may change the identity of those in the general population exposed to the resulting pollution. Just transporting solid and hazardous wastes from one geographic area to another for treatment or storage results in a major redistribution of the risks associated with environmental protection. Indeed, such transportation, and the resulting shift of environmental risks, has been the recent subject of massive litigation, as various jurisdictions have sought to export their wastes or prevent the importation of waste from elsewhere.

Nor does the purported prevention of pollution, as opposed to its treatment, necessarily eliminate the distributional issue. "Pollution prevention" frequently depends upon production processes that reduce one kind of pollution by increasing another. For example, water pollution may increase as air pollution is decreased, or a decrease in the mining of one kind of natural resource may be limited or completely offset by the increase in mining of another. Such shifts in the type of pollution or activity allowed will almost invariably shift those risks arising with the "new" pollution or activity to different persons. Hence, pollution may decrease for society as a whole, yet simultaneously increase for certain subpopulations.

Racial minorities could therefore be disproportionately disadvantaged by environmental laws in a number of ways. For example, with regard to the benefits of environmental protection, the natural environments that are selected for protection may be less accessible, or otherwise less important, to minorities. This may be the result of priorities expressly established by statute, or by agency regulations or enforcement agenda.

Inequities in the ultimate distribution of environmental protection benefits may also result, paradoxically, from environmental improvement itself. A cleaner physical environment may increase property values to such an extent that members of a racial minority with fewer economic resources can no longer afford to live in that community. Indeed, the exclusionary impact of environmental protection can be more than just an incidental effect; it can be the raison d'etre, with environmental quality acting as a socially acceptable facade for attitudes that cannot be broadcast.

Minorities may at the same time incur a share of the burdens of environmental protection that are disproportionate to those benefits that they receive. Higher product and service prices may be regressive, as may some taxes depending on their form. Although whites are poorer in greater absolute numbers than nonwhites, the latter group is disproportionately poorer in terms of population percentages. Minorities may also more likely be the victims of reduced or eliminated job opportunities. Similarly, they may be less likely to enjoy the economic, educational, or personal positions necessary to exploit the new job opportunities that environmental protection creates. Finally, minorities may receive an unfair share of the environmental risks that are redistributed by environmental protection. Elimination of the risks in one location may result in the creation or increase of risks in another location where the exposure to minorities is greater. * * *

* * * Minority interests have traditionally had little voice in the various points of influence that strike the distributional balances necessary to get environmental protection laws enacted, regulations promulgated, and enforcement actions initiated. The interest groups historically active in the environmental protection area include a variety of mainstream environmental organizations representing a spectrum of interests (conservation, recreation, hunting, wildlife protection, resource protection, human health), as well as a variety of commercial and industrial concerns. Until very recently, if at all, the implications for racial minorities of environmental protection laws have not been a focal point of concern for any of these organizations.

OMAR SALEEM, OVERCOMING ENVIRONMENTAL DISCRIMINATION: THE NEED FOR A DISPARATE IMPACT TEST AND IMPROVED NOTICE REQUIREMENTS IN FACILITY SITING DECISIONS[47]

19 COLUMB. JO. OF ENVTL. L. 211, 213–19 (1994).

In 1982, a predominately African–American community in Warren County, North Carolina, became the proposed site for a polychlorinated biphenyl (PCB) disposal facility. The decision to site the facility in Warren County ushered forth the first national African–American protest against hazardous waste siting practices. The local community, along with civil rights leaders, protested the siting of the facility. Despite efforts by the National Association for the Advancement of Colored People (NAACP) to secure a preliminary injunction to prohibit the siting of the facility—on the ground of racial discrimination—the facility was approved. The protest, however, led to a statewide review of hazardous waste siting procedures. North Carolina then passed a law barring additional sites in Warren County.

GAO Report

In response to the siting of the proposed facility in Warren County, Congressman Walter E. Fauntroy asked the Government Accounting Office (GAO) to determine the correlation between the location of hazardous waste landfills and the racial and economic status of the surrounding communities.[48] The GAO did so and found in pertinent part:

> There are four off-site hazardous waste landfills in [EPA] Region IV's eight States. Blacks make up the majority of the population in three of the four communities where the landfills are located. At least 26 percent of the population in all four communities have income below the poverty level and most of this population is Black.

An unrelated 1983 study presented similar data on the siting of solid waste facilities in Houston, Texas. The findings revealed solid waste facilities tended to be located in predominantly African–American neighborhoods.[49] Four years after the GAO report, the United Church of Christ Commission for Racial Justice (CRJ) published the report on toxic wastes and race in the United States.[50] The CRJ report, similar to the GAO report, examined the correlation between the location of hazardous waste

---

47. Copyright © 1994 by the Columbia Journal of Environmental Law. Reprinted with permission.

48. U.S. General Accounting Office, *Siting of Hazardous Waste Landfills and Their Correlation With Racial and Economic Status of Surrounding Communities*, GAO/RCED–83–168 (June 1, 1983).

49. Robert D. Bullard, *Solid Waste and the Black Houston Community*, 53 SOC. INQUIRY 273 (1983).

50. United Church of Christ Commission for Racial Justice, Toxic Wastes and Race in the United States: A National Report on the Racial and Socio–Economic Characteristics of Communities With Hazardous Waste Sites (1987).

landfills and the racial and economic status of surrounding communities. While the GAO report examined only the southeastern United States, the CRJ report examined the entire nation. The CRJ report concluded: "Race proved to be the most significant among variables tested in association with the location of commercial hazardous waste facilities. This represented a consistent national pattern." * * *

The GAO and CRJ reports nurtured a burgeoning movement that has been examining the functional relationship between race, poverty, and environmental hazards. The movement is called the "environmental justice movement." The term denotes an effort to broaden the goals of environmental protection to include providing a clean and safe environment where racial minorities and low-income people live and work. The movement seeks to identify and address "environmental racism" which has been defined to include "any policy, practice, or directive that differentially affects or disadvantages (whether intended or unintended) individuals, groups, or communities based on race or color [as well as] exclusionary and restrictive practices that limit participation by people of color in decision-making boards, commissions, and regulating bodies."[51]

EPA Actions and Reports

As part of their efforts, members of the environmental justice movement met with William K. Reilly, the U.S. Environmental Protection Agency [EPA] Administrator, in September 1990.[52] * * * As a result of this meeting the EPA subsequently formed the "Environmental Equity Workgroup" to "assess the evidence that racial minority and low-income communities bear a higher environmental burden than the general population, and consider what EPA might do about any identified disparities." The Workgroup consisted of senior-level officials from EPA regional offices and EPA headquarters. * * *

Although the GAO and CRJ reports were focal points, the movement is not limited to the siting of hazardous waste facilities. Other areas of concern include proposals to site incinerators, landfills, and nuclear waste facilities on Indian lands; farmworkers' exposure to pesticides; discharges from chemical plants; air pollution problems in minority communities; lead poisoning; workplace conditions; the exportation of hazardous waste to developing countries; placement of homes for the homeless; and international trade. * * *

In mid-1992 the EPA released its finding, which stated:

1. There are clear differences between racial groups in terms of disease and death rates. There are also limited data to explain the environmental contribution to these differences * * *. The notable exception is lead poisoning.

---

51. Robert Bullard, *The Threat of Environmental Racism*, 7 NAT. RESOURCES & ENV'T 23 (1993).

52. U.S. EPA, ENVIRONMENTAL EQUITY-REDUCING RISK FOR ALL COMMUNITIES 2 (June 1992).

2. Racial minority and low-income populations experience higher than average exposures to selected air pollutants, hazardous waste facilities, contaminated fish, and agricultural pesticides in the work-place. Exposure does not always result in an immediate or acute health effect. High exposures, and the possibility of chronic effects, are nevertheless a clear cause for health concerns.

3. Environmental and health data are not routinely collected and analyzed by income and race. Nor are data routinely collected on health risks posed by multiple industrial facilities, cumulative and synergistic effects, or multiple and different pathways of exposure * * *. However, risk assessment and risk management procedures can be improved to better take into account equity considerations.

4. Great opportunities exist for EPA and other government agencies to improve communication about environmental problems with members of low-income and racial minority groups * * *.

5. Since they have broad contact with affected communities, EPA's program and regional offices are well suited to address equity concerns * * *.

6. Native Americans are a unique racial group that has a special relationship with the federal government and distinct environmental problems.[53]

National Law Journal Findings

Beside government agencies, others were sparked into action by the efforts and advocacy of the environmental justice movement. For example, the *National Law Journal* examined the correlation between race and income and the EPA's enforcement of environmental laws. The resulting report revealed that not only are a disproportionate number of hazardous waste facilities located in low-income racial minority communities, but in addition, the EPA discriminates against minority communities in enforcing all federal environmental laws.[54] According to the *National Law Journal* report: 1) Penalties under hazardous waste laws at sites having the greatest proportion of white residents are 500% higher than penalties at sites with the greatest minority population, averaging $335,566 for white areas compared to $55,318 for minority areas. 2) The disparity under the toxic waste laws occurs by race alone, not income. 3) For all the federal environmental laws aimed at protecting citizens from air, water, and waste pollution, penalties in white communities are 46% higher than in minority communities. 4) Under the giant Superfund cleanup program, abandoned hazardous waste sites in minority areas take 20% longer to be placed on the national priority list than those in white areas. 5) In more than half of the ten autonomous regions that administer EPA programs around the country, action on cleanup at superfund sites begins 12% to

---

53. *Id.*

54. Marianne Lavelle & Marcia Loyle, *Unequal Protection–The Racial Divide in Environmental Law*, NAT'L L.J., Sept. 21, 1992, at S1–S12.

42% later at minority sites than at white sites. 6) At sites in minority communities, the EPA chooses "containment," the capping or walling off of a hazardous waste dump site, 7% more frequently than the cleanup method preferred under the law permanent "treatment"—to eliminate the waste or rid it of toxins. At sites in white neighborhoods, the EPA orders treatment 22% more often than containment.

NOTES

1. Another study was reported in Vicki Been & Francis Gupta, *Coming to the Nuisance or Going to the Barrios? A Longitudinal Analysis of Environmental Justice Claims*, 24 ECOLOGY L.Q. 1 (1997). This study looked at the demographics of the 544 communities which in 1994 hosted active commercial hazardous waste treatment, storage, and disposal facilities (TSDFs). The authors looked first at the demographics of the communities at the time of the census taken immediately before they became hosts, then examined the demographic changes in each subsequent decade through the 1990 census. The authors summarized their findings as follows:

> [W]e found no substantial evidence that the facilities that began operating between 1970 and 1990 were sited in areas that were disproportionately African American. Nor did we find any evidence that these facilities were sited in areas with high concentrations of the poor; indeed, the evidence indicates that poverty is negatively correlated with sitings. We did find evidence that the facilities were sited in areas that were disproportionately Hispanic at the time of the siting. The analysis produced little evidence that the siting of a facility was followed by substantial changes in a neighborhood's socioeconomic status or racial or ethnic composition. Finally, the analysis shows that the areas surrounding TSDFs currently are disproportionately populated by African Americans and Hispanics. *Id*. at 9.

2. In another study, Thomas Lambert & Christopher Boerner, *Environmental Inequity: Economic Causes, Economic Solutions*, 14 YALE J. ON REG. 195 (1997), the authors analyzed demographic characteristics around three types of industrial facilities and waste sites in and around St. Louis, Missouri: TSDFs, permitted solid waste landfills and incinerators, and inactive hazardous waste (CERCLA) sites. There were 167 facilities and sites in all. The authors found "no significant difference in poverty rates and percentages of minority residents between census tracts with active facilities (TSDFs, landfills, and incinerators) and those tracts without such facilities. Including inactive CERCLA waste sites in the data set, however, uncovered weak evidence that the percentages of poor and minority residents living near industrial and waste sites are significantly higher than the corresponding percentages living in tracts without facilities." The authors believed that they had "empirical support for the theory that housing values are closely related to existing environmental inequities, raising the possibility that siting decisions caused an influx of minority and poor residents, as opposed to the contrary causation assumptions made by environmental discrimination theorists." *Id*. at 203–204. As a solution to falling real estate values around facilities, the authors propose providing compensation to those who live near

locally undesirable facilities so that, on balance, the surrounding property is not rendered less desirable. Possible forms of compensation include: (1) direct payments to affected landowners, (2) host fees which are paid into a community's general revenue fund to be used to finance a variety of public projects or to lower property taxes, (3) grants for improving local healthcare delivery and education, and (4) the provision of parks and other recreational amenities. *Id.* at 214.

3. Another study, using more sophisticated statistical methods, considered both the effect of site location on housing values and the relationship between neighborhood composition and risk. It reached the following conclusions:

> [The statistical model] indicates that the price-risk tradeoff is higher for households in high-educated and high-income neighborhoods, and lower for households in neighborhoods with a high proportion of non-whites. * * * These results suggest that the welfare effects of risk reduction vary by neighborhood demographics, and a regulatory strategy based strictly on efficiency grounds would target these neighborhoods, increasing the concentration of environmental risk in low-educated, low-income, and high-nonwhite neighborhoods. * * *

> By estimating the neighborhood characteristics that affect the level of risk exposure, I find that the level of risk is not a function of the income and education levels of the neighborhoods. Additionally, the level of risk is lower for neighborhoods with a large proportion of nonwhites. This could suggest that nonwhites have not been exposed to higher Superfund risks, or it could suggest that risk reduction efforts have been responsive to concerns of environmental racism. * * * Finally, this paper offers evidence that pollution is more likely in neighborhoods with a low propensity for collective action.

Ted Gayer, *Neighborhood Demographics and the Distribution of Hazardous Waste Risks: An Instrumental Variables Estimation*, 17 J. REG. ECON. 131, 152–53 (2000).

4. Suppose that low-income and minority communities are exposed to higher levels of toxics, but that the cause is not bias or discrimination in the location of facilities. Should this unequal distribution of risks still be a concern? Or should we view the distribution as irrelevant, since someone else would be suffering the risks anyway? *See* Alice Kaswan, *Distributive Justice and the Environment*, 81 N.C. L. REV. 1031 (2003) (arguing that risk distribution should still be a concern).

2. THE LEGAL IMPLEMENTATION OF ENVIRONMENTAL EQUITY

In 1994, President Clinton signed Executive Order 12,898, Federal Actions to Address Environmental Justice in Minority Populations and Low–Income Populations, 59 FED. REG. 7629 (Feb. 16, 1994). The order provided that each federal agency "shall make achieving environmental justice part of its mission by identifying and addressing, as appropriate, disproportionately high and adverse human health or environmental effects of its programs, policies, and activities on minority populations and low-income populations in the United States and its territories and possessions." The Administrator of the EPA was directed to convene an interagency Federal Working Group on Environmental Justice, to assist each agency to develop an agency-wide environmental justice strategy. The Bush Administration left this order in effect but interpreted narrowly.

In 1995, EPA issued its environmental justice strategy, based on the principle that communities affected by decisions with environmental impacts should be actively involved in the decision-making process. The strategy calls for EPA to increase coordination with affected communities, state, tribal, and local governments, business, and nongovernmental organizations. To develop local knowledge bases necessary for effective participation in complex decision making, EPA would promote technical assistance programs and grants for minority and low-income areas. The Agency also would focus enforcement activities on minority and low-income areas suffering disproportionate environmental and health impacts. *See* Terry Schnell & Kathleen Davis, *The Increased Significance of Environmental Justice in Facility Siting, Permitting*, 29 ENVTL. L. REP. 528, 529 (1998).

Pursuant to Executive Order 12,898 and Title VI of the Civil Rights Act of 1964, as amended, 42 U.S.C. §§ 2000d to 2000d–7, which prohibits discrimination under any program receiving federal financial assistance, EPA has begun to include environmental justice as a factor in its review of state permits under federally delegated programs pursuant to the Clean Air and Clean Water Acts and the Resource Conservation and Recovery Act. For further information about EPA's response to the executive order, *see* Denis Binder et al., *A Survey of Federal Agency Responses to President Clinton's Executive Order No. 12898 on Environmental Justice*, 31 ENVTL. L. REP. 11,133 (2001).

Environmental justice advocates saw Title VI of the 1964 Civil Rights Act as one of their most promising weapons. Title VI prohibits discrimination by recipients of federal funds, and the regulations under Title VI cover not only intentional discrimination but also actions having a disparate impact on minority groups. *See* Bradford C. Mank, *Is There a Private Cause of Action Under EPA's Title VI Regulations?: The Need to Empower Environmental Justice Plaintiffs*, 24 COLUM. J. ENVTL. L. 1 (1999). But the viability of private actions to enforce the Title VI regulations is doubtful. In *Alexander v. Sandoval*, 532 U.S. 275 (2001), the Court held that the Title VI regulations do not create a private cause of action. In dissent, however, Justice Stevens suggested that the decision had limited practical effect:

[T]o the extent that the majority denies relief to the respondents merely because they neglected to mention 42 U.S.C. § 1983 in framing their Title VI claim, this case is something of a sport. Litigants who in the future wish to enforce the Title VI regulations against state actors in all likelihood must only reference § 1983 to obtain relief.

Id. at 1527. Soon afterwards, a federal appeals court rejected this theory. *See South Camden Citizens in Action v. New Jersey Dep't of Envtl. Prot.*, 274 F.3d 771 (3d Cir. 2001)*; see also Save Our Valley v. Sound Transit*, 335 F.3d 932 (9th Cir. 2003). This makes evidence of intentional discrimination critical. *See* Browne C. Lewis, *Changing the Bathwater and Keeping the Baby: Exploring New Ways of Evaluating Intent in Environmental Discrimination Cases*, 50 ST. LOUIS U.L.J. 469 (2006) (discussing the intent test and alternatives).

A related question involves the extent to which EPA has authority under various environmental statutes to consider environmental justice issues. For a discussion of the issue by two scholars advocating a broad interpretation of EPA's authority, *see* Richard J. Lazarus & Stephanie Tai, *Integrating Environmental Justice Into EPA Permitting Authority*, 26 ECOLOGY L.Q. 617 (1999). In any event, EPA so far has not pursued EJ issues with much enthusiasm. According to a 2003 survey, of the 139 Title VI complaints received by EPA since 1993, seventy-five were rejected without investigation; twenty-six were accepted for investigation, but in none was timely evidence of discrimination found. The remaining thirty were still pending. Michael B. Gerrard, *EPA Dismissal of Civil Rights Complaints*, NY L.J., Nov. 28, 2003, at 3.

Another thrust of advocates of environmental justice is to provide opportunities for disadvantaged groups to participate in decision making in a meaningful way. Some possible approaches are discussed in Alejandro Esteban Camacho, *Mastering the Missing Voices: A Collaborative Model for Fostering Equality, Community Involvement and Adaptive Planning in Land Use Decisions*, 24 STAN. ENV. L.J. 3 (2005); Sheila Foster, *Environmental Justice in an Era of Devolved Collaboration*, 26 HARV. ENV. L. REV. 459 (2002). Consider this problem again when we discuss collaborative governance in the final section of the chapter.

3. GLOBAL EQUITY ISSUES AND CLIMATE CHANGE

Environmental justice is also relevant to climate change. Because, historically, the heaviest emissions have come from industrialized countries like the United States, while the heaviest impacts fall on poorer countries, claims for "climate justice" have already emerged. The following excerpt presents a critical appraisal of those claims.

ERIC POSNER AND CASS SUNSTEIN, CLIMATE JUSTICE
96 GEO. L.J. 1565 (2008).[55]

Let us assume, most starkly, that the United States would lose, on net, from a climate change agreement that is optimal from the standpoint

assume US would suffer net loss

---

55. Copyright 2008 by Eric Posner and Cass Sunstein. Reprinted by permission.

of the world taken as a whole. As a matter of actual practice, the standard resolution of the problem is clear: The world should enter into the optimal agreement, and the United States should be given side-payments in return for its participation. The reason for this approach is straightforward. On conventional assumptions, the optimal agreement should be assessed by reference to the overall benefits and costs of the relevant commitments for the world. To the extent that the United States is a net loser, the world should act so as to induce it to participate in an agreement that would promote the welfare of the world's citizens, taken as a whole. With side-payments to the United States, of the kind that have elsewhere induced reluctant nations to join environmental treaties, an international agreement could be designed so as to make all nations better off and no nation worse off. Call this a form of international Paretianism. [Editor's note: a Pareto improvement is one that makes everyone involved better off than they would be otherwise.] Who could oppose an agreement based on international Paretianism?

Our puzzle is that almost everyone does so. No one is suggesting that the world should offer side-payments to the United States. Indeed, the United States is not even arguing for side-payments, perhaps on the ground that the argument would be regarded as preposterous. One reason involves distributive justice. The United States is the richest nation in the world, and many people would find it odd to suggest that the world's richest nation should receive compensation for helping to solve a problem faced by the world as a whole, and above all by poor nations. On this view, wealthy nations should be expected to contribute a great deal to solving the climate change problem; side-payments would be perverse. If ideas of distributive justice are at work, it might be far more plausible to suggest that nations should pay China for agreeing to participate in a climate change agreement. And indeed, developing nations, including China, were given financial assistance as an inducement to reduce their emissions of ozone-depleting chemicals. Some people think that a climate change agreement should build on this precedent, and indeed the "Bali Roadmap" seems to do so, by suggesting financial assistance to developing nations. No one thinks that assistance to the United States, or to other wealthy countries, is in order.

But claims about distributive justice are only part of the story here. Corrective justice matters as well. The basic thought is that the largest emitters, above all the United States, have imposed serious risks on other nations. Surely it cannot be right for nations to request payments in return for ceasing to harm others. On the conventional view, wrongdoers should pay for the damage that they have caused and should be asked to stop. They should not be compensated for taking corrective action.

We shall raise serious questions about both accounts here. Rejecting international Paretianism, we agree that in many domains, resources should be redistributed from rich nations and rich people to poor nations and poor people. Such redistribution might well increase aggregate social welfare, since a dollar is worth more to a poor person than to a wealthy one; prominent nonwelfarist arguments also favor such redistribution. But significant greenhouse gas reductions are a crude and somewhat puzzling way of attempting to achieve redistributive goals. The arc of human history suggests that in the future, people are likely to be much wealthier than people are now. Why should wealthy countries give money to future poor people, rather than to current poor people? In any case, nations are not people; they are collections of people. Redistribution from wealthy countries to poor countries is hardly the same as redistribution from wealthy people to poor people. For one thing, many poor people in some countries will benefit from global warming, to the extent that agricultural productivity will increase and to the extent that they will suffer less from extremes of cold. For another thing, poor people in wealthy countries may well pay a large part of the bill for emissions reductions; a stiff tax on carbon emissions would come down especially hard on the poor.

The upshot is that if wealthy people in wealthy nations want to help poor people in poor nations, emissions reductions are unlikely to be the best means by which they might to do so. Our puzzle, then, is why distributive justice is taken to require wealthy nations to help poor ones in the context of climate change, when wealthy nations are not being asked to help poor ones in areas in which the argument for help is significantly stronger.

We also accept, for purposes of argument, the view that when people in one nation wrongfully harm people in another nation, the wrongdoers have a moral obligation to provide a remedy to the victims. It might seem to follow that the largest emitters, and above all the United States, have a special obligation to remedy the harms they have helped cause and certainly should not be given side-payments. But the application of standard principles of corrective justice to problems of climate change runs into serious objections. As we shall show, corrective justice arguments in the domain of climate change raise many of the same problems that beset such arguments in the context of reparations more generally. Nations are not individuals: they do not have mental states and cannot, except metaphorically, act. Blame must ordinarily be apportioned to individuals, and it is hard to blame all greenhouse gas-emitters for wrongful behavior, especially those from the past who are partly responsible for the current stock of greenhouse gases in the atmosphere.

Our principal submissions are that the distributive justice argument must be separated from the corrective justice argument, and that once the two arguments are separated, both of them face serious difficulties. If the United States wants to assist poor nations, reductions in greenhouse gas emissions are unlikely to be the best way for it to accomplish that goal. It is true that many people in poor nations are at risk because of the actions of many people in the United States, but the idea of corrective justice does not easily justify any kind of transfer from contemporary Americans to people now or eventually living in (for example) India and Africa.

* * *

The current stock of greenhouse gases in the atmosphere is a result of the behavior of people living in the past. Much of it is due to the behavior of people who are dead. The basic problem for corrective justice is that dead wrongdoers cannot be punished or held responsible for their behavior, or forced to compensate those they have harmed. At first glance, holding Americans today responsible for the activities of their ancestors is not fair or reasonable on corrective justice grounds, because current Americans are not the relevant wrongdoers; they are not responsible for the harm.

Indeed, many Americans today do not support the current American energy policy and already make some sacrifices to reduce the greenhouse gas emissions that result from their behavior. They avoid driving, they turn down the heat in their homes, and they support electoral candidates who advocate greener policies. Holding these people responsible for the wrongful activities of people who lived in the past seems perverse. An approach that emphasized corrective justice would attempt to be more finely tuned, focusing on particular actors, rather than Americans as a class, which would appear to violate deeply held moral objections to collective responsibility. The task would be to distinguish between the contributions of those who are living and those who are dead.

The most natural and best response to this point is to insist that all or most Americans today benefit from the greenhouse gas emitting activities of Americans living in the past, and therefore it would not be wrong to require Americans today to pay for abatement measures. This argument is familiar from debates about slave reparations, where it is argued that Americans today have benefited from the toil of slaves 150 years ago. To the extent that members of current generations have gained from past wrongdoing, it may well make sense to ask them to make compensation to those harmed as a result. On one view, compensation can work to restore the status quo ante, that is, to put members of different groups, and citizens of different nations, in the position that they would have occupied if the wrongdoing had not occurred.

In the context of climate, however, this argument runs into serious problems. The most obvious difficulty is empirical. It is true that many Americans benefit from past greenhouse-gas-emissions, but how many benefit, and how much do they benefit? Many Americans today are, of course, immigrants or children of immigrants, and so not the descendants of greenhouse-gas-emitting Americans of the past. Such people may nonetheless gain from past emissions, because they enjoy the kind of technological advance and material wealth that those emissions made possible. But have they actually benefited, and to what degree? Further, not all Americans inherit the wealth of their ancestors, and even those who do would not necessarily have inherited less if their ancestors' generations had not engaged in the greenhouse-gas-emitting activities. The idea of corrective justice, building on the tort analogy, does not seem to fit the climate change situation.

Suppose that these various obstacles could be overcome and that we could trace, with sufficient accuracy, the extent to which current Americans have benefited from past emissions. As long as the costs are being toted up, the benefits should be as well, and used to offset the requirements of corrective justice. We have noted that climate change is itself anticipated to produce benefits for many nations, both by increasing agricultural productivity and by reducing extremes of cold. And if past generations of Americans have imposed costs on the rest of the world, they have also conferred substantial benefits. American industrial activity has produced products that were consumed in foreign countries, for example, and has driven technological advances from which citizens in other countries have gained. Many of these benefits are positive externalities, for which Americans have not been fully compensated. To be sure, many citizens in, say, India have not much benefited from those advances, just as many citizens of the United States have not much benefited from them. But what would the world, or India, look like if the United States had engaged in 10% of its level of greenhouse gas emissions, or 20%, or 40%? For purposes of corrective justice, a proper accounting would seem to be necessary, and it presents formidable empirical and conceptual problems.

In the context of slave reparations, the analogous points have led to interminable debates, again empirical and conceptual, about historical causation and difficult counterfactuals. But-for causation arguments, used in standard legal analysis and conventional for purposes of conventional justice, present serious and perhaps insuperable problems when applied historically. We can meaningfully ask whether an accident would have occurred if the driver had operated the vehicle more carefully, but conceptual and empirical questions make it difficult to answer the question whether and to what extent white Americans today would have been worse off if there had been no slavery—and difficult too to ask whether Indians would be better off today if Americans of prior generations had not emitted greenhouse gases. What kind of a question is that? In this hypothetical world of limited industrialization in the United States, India would be an entirely different country, and the rest of the world would be unrecognizably different as well.

Proponents of slave reparations have sometimes appealed to principles of corporate liability. Corporations can be immortal, and many corporations today benefited from the slave economy in the nineteenth century. Corporations are collectivities, not individuals, yet they can be held liable for their actions, which means that shareholders today are "punished" (in the sense of losing share value) as a result of actions taken by managers and employees long before the shareholders obtained their ownership interest. If innocent shareholders can be made to pay for the wrongdoing of employees who are long gone, why can't citizens be made to pay for the wrongful actions of citizens who lived in the past?

The best answer is that corporate liability is most easily justified on grounds other than corrective justice. Shareholder liability can be defended on the basis of consent or (in our view most plausibly) on the welfarist ground that corporate liability deters employees from engaging in wrongdoing on behalf of the corporate entity. A factor that distinguishes corporate liability is that purchasing shares is a voluntary activity and one does so with the knowledge that the share price will decline if a past legal violation comes to light, and this is reflected in the share price at the time of purchase. (One also benefits if an unknown past action enhances the value of the company.) But because the corporate form itself is a fiction, and the shareholders today are different from the wrongdoers yesterday, corporate liability cannot be grounded in corrective justice. Thus, it provides no analogy on behalf of corrective justice for the climate change debate. * * *

Many people do seem to be reducing their emissions on the basis of an assessment of roughly this kind. Those concerned about climate change rarely believe that they should altogether stop engaging in activities that produce greenhouse gases (a difficult task!); instead, they think that they should cut back on activities that generate unreasonable emissions of greenhouse gases in light of whatever benefits they produce. Some people go farther and purchase carbon offsets, but this type of activity seems, at present, supererogatory, whereas a case could be made today that a reasonable reduction of greenhouse gas emitting activities is morally required—that it represents an emerging community standard or norm.

Even if this is so, there is a problem with this argument, which is that the calculation given above assumes that everyone around the world, or at least hundreds of millions of people, are also cutting back on greenhouse-gas-producing activities. If many or most people fail to pay a carbon tax or (as we argue) fail to act as if they pay it by cutting back on less important activities that produce greenhouse gases, then the contribution of Americans who do this is quite small. And if this is the case, it cannot be considered negligent for Americans to fail to reduce their greenhouse-gas-emitting activities. Put differently, it is not negligent to fail to contribute to a public good if not enough others are doing similarly, so that the public good would not be created even if one did contribute. This is a "moral collective action problem," and however it should be assessed in moral terms, the failure to act when other people are not acting, so that positive action would generate no benefit, does not seem to constitute negligence.

NOTES

1. How much of the responsibility for climate changes rests on past generations? The following table gives U.S. emissions by decade:[56]

---

56. These figures were derived from Gregg Marland *et al.*, carbon dioxide info. analysis ctr., global co2 emissions from fossil-fuel burning, cement manufacture, and gas flaring: 1751–2004 (2007), http://cdiac.ornl.gov/ftp/trends/emissions/usa.dat by adding the annual data for total CO2 emissions.

U.S. CO2 Emissions by Decade

Decades	Total Fossil Fuel CO2 Emissions Per Decade (in thousand metric tons)
1800–09	897
1810–19	1,625
1820–29	3,190
1830–39	10,695
1840–49	30,040
1850–59	93,002
1860–69	169,487
1870–79	364,865
1880–89	748,407
1890–99	1,307,514
1900–09	2,553,862
1910–19	3,928,812
1920–29	4,669,836
1930–39	4,141,926
1940–49	6,117,256
1950–59	7,327,215
1960–69	9,344,693
1970–79	12,282,447
1980–89	12,325,868
1990–99	14,306,218
2000–2004	8,127,919

The pattern, obviously, is a sharp upward movement in the amount of emissions. Emissions growth reversed itself only during the Great Depression (though only slightly even then) and slowed only in the 1980s (perhaps due to the energy crisis and recession triggered by OPEC oil price increases.) With the exception of those two decades, emissions have grown substantially in every decade in U.S. history. The degree of increase can be seen by comparing the total amount of emissions in U.S. history (about 80 billion tons) with the emissions from 2000–2004—which shows that about ten percent of all the CO2 the U.S. has ever produced came from the first term of George W. Bush's presidency.

It is also useful to consider current contributions to climate change, both on an absolute and per capita basis. In 2007 China surpassed the United States as the world's largest contributor of carbon dioxide, the most prevalent greenhouse gas.[57] Yet on a per capita basis the U.S. produces more than five times as much carbon dioxide as China.[58] Moreover, as of 2005, 34 percent of Chinese emissions could be attributed to its manufacturing of goods for export, and between 7 and 14 percent of its emissions to the manufacture of goods for export to the U.S. market.[59]

---

57. *See* John Vidal & David Adam, *China Overtakes US as World's Biggest CO2 Emitter*, THE GUARDIAN, June 20, 2007, Top Stories Section, at 1.

58. Steven Kull & Doug Miller, *Let the People Lead in Addressing Problems of Climate Change*, DAILY NEWS, June 3, 2008, at 4A.

59. Bin Shui and Robert C. Harriss, *The Role of CO2 Embodiment in US–China Trade,* 34 ENERGY POL'Y 4063 (2006).

Note that this discussion focuses on CO2 from industrial sources. Attribution of responsibility is more complex, and the U.S. role looks smaller if other greenhouse gases and non-industrial sources of CO2 such as deforestation are included. See David A. Weisbach, *Responsibility for Climate Change by the Numbers*, available at www.ssrn.com/abstract=1324857 (Jan. 2009).

2.   One fundamental question is whether controlling greenhouse gases should be a considered a "redistributive mechanism," as Posner and Sunstein call it. It can only be considered *re*distributive if unrestricted emission—and therefore, unlimited climate change—is considered to be the baseline. Compared to this baseline of unrestricted emissions, restricting emissions makes poor countries better off and costs rich countries money, so it can be considered a redistribution of wealth. If, instead, we consider the baseline to be a world in which climate is stable, then the shoe is on the other foot. Starting with that baseline, we would say that the U.S. and other wealthy emitters are redistributing income to themselves at the expense of poor countries by their on-going damage to the planetary climate system. If we start with this baseline, reducing emissions is not a redistribution of income; it merely leaves the distribution of income where it would be in the baseline state. The question, in other words, is whether we should think of pollution as a right—so that limitations on polluters are seen a redistribution of wealth to their victims—or whether we should view freedom from pollution as a right, which would imply that the polluters are unjustly prospering at the expense of others.

3.   Posner and Sunstein begin their article by expressing puzzlement by the lack of support for side-payments from impacted countries such as India to the United States as part of an international climate agreement. Do they make a persuasive argument for such side-payments? One might imagine such side payments, for example, in the form of "debt for carbon swaps," in which China would forgive U.S. debt in return for greater reductions in U.S. emissions. Does this seem like a plausible proposal?

D.   USING THE TORT SYSTEM TO ADDRESS ENVIRONMENTAL ISSUES

Some economic incentives, such as cap-and-trade programs, are relatively novel. Other economic incentives are much older. The common law of torts provides one such system—firms whose conduct causes injury may have to pay damages. In this section, we consider the common law of torts and related compensation schemes as tools for achieving environmental protection. At the same time, unlike regulation, compensation schemes also attempt to remedy the harm to victims, which may make them more attractive from the perspective of environmental justice than conventional forms of regulation.

ALBERT C. LIN, BEYOND TORT: COMPENSATING VICTIMS OF ENVIRONMENTAL TOXIC INJURY[60]

78 S. CAL. L. REV. 1439, 1445–52 (2005).

The paradigmatic traditional tort case involves a single identifiable plaintiff, a single identifiable defendant, and a readily determinable cause of the tortious event. For example, a pedestrian struck by a car can identify the driver of the car and the driver's negligence as the cause of the pedestrian's resulting injuries. Although the parties may dispute the driver's negligence or the harm suffered by the plaintiff, the judicial process is well equipped to determine such issues. Our judicial system is similarly able to handle classic strict liability claims, such as a dynamite explosion, a sudden flood from a reservoir, or even a catastrophic Bhopal-type accident. In such cases, cause and effect are readily identifiable. An environmental tort plaintiff, however, often faces far more formidable problems of proof. As an initial matter, courts generally apply a negligence standard rather than a strict liability standard to ordinary economic activities. Only where a polluter is engaged in abnormally dangerous activities do courts apply a strict liability standard. Furthermore, environmental tort plaintiffs must overcome the high hurdles of causation and latency of harm.

1. Latency of Harm

Latency of harm complicates proving causation with any environmental disease that takes time to develop. For example, consider an individual who is diagnosed with cancer many years after an exposure to carcinogenic pollutants released from an industrial facility. Over the course of a lifetime, this individual has been exposed to numerous carcinogens through various pathways, including air, water, and food supply. In contrast to the paradigmatic tort plaintiff described above, this plaintiff's injury is latent, appearing some time after exposure. The length of the latency period may vary among individuals. Thus, even when a population is exposed simultaneously to a pollutant, incidences of disease occur over a period of time that can span several decades.

This latency and lack of simultaneity make evidence more difficult to gather. For example, victims may not have been aware of their first exposure to a toxic substance. Therefore, years later, they will likely be unable to prove the fact, timing, or extent of exposure. Exposure often occurs at low levels over extended periods of time. The passage of time not only complicates proof, but also increases the risk that a defendant will no longer be financially viable, assuming that the defendant can even be identified. Compounding plaintiffs' difficulties, statutes of limitations may bar suit, although some jurisdictions have rules tolling the statutory period until the time when the injury is discovered.

---

60. Copyright © 2005, University of Southern California. Reprinted with permission.

2.　Causation

An even greater barrier faced by plaintiffs is causation. Toxic tort plaintiffs typically must establish two types of causation. First, a plaintiff must prove general causation—that a substance is capable of causing the injury at issue. Second, a plaintiff must prove specific causation—that exposure to the substance in fact caused that plaintiff's injury. The scientific uncertainty that surrounds causation can make these burdens insurmountable.

A few diseases, such as asbestosis, are so-called "signature diseases"—diseases that are extremely rare in the general population, but far more prevalent in persons exposed to a particular substance. These illnesses can be traced to exposure to a specific substance. Illnesses involving environmental toxic exposure, however, often can result from multiple causes. For example, an individual instance of lung cancer might be attributed to exposure to tobacco smoke, exposure to pollutants from a nearby factory, or exposure to pollutants from traffic on a local highway. Separating the roles of the potential causal agents, which may interact in complex ways, is often problematic, if not impossible. Unlike our automobile accident example, there is usually no obvious evidence that a particular agent caused the plaintiff's harm in environmental tort cases.

a.　General Causation

Much of the difficulty with environmental tort litigation is due to an insufficient scientific understanding of general causation. Essentially, the question is whether a certain chemical has the ability to cause a particular illness and, if so, to what extent. Reliable information regarding carcinogenic and other health effects is available for relatively few substances. For many substances, health effects are unknown. Molecular assays and animal bioassays provide some information on mutagenicity or carcinogenicity. Scientists, however, caution that this information cannot always be extrapolated in a reliable manner to estimate human cancer risks.

Courts tend to view epidemiological studies, which apply statistical techniques to explain variations in disease rates of human populations, as the most persuasive and acceptable type of general causation evidence in toxic tort cases. Yet the very use of such studies creates difficulties. * * * Detailed epidemiological data is available only for relatively few toxic substances. Furthermore, where such data is available, there may be uncertainty regarding the magnitude of the risk involved.

b.　Specific Causation

Specific causation is also frequently uncertain with environmental toxic injuries. Epidemiological studies may establish that a substance can cause the type of harm suffered by a plaintiff, satisfying general causation. But a plaintiff must still demonstrate that the particular harm was in fact the result of exposure to a given substance. Epidemiological studies, however, can only attribute a proportion of the incidence of disease in a population to any particular source. They are not designed to prove specific causation. Specific causation requires a plaintiff to prove by a preponderance of the evidence that the defendant caused that particular plaintiff's harm. Many courts interpret the preponderance standard to require a relative risk ratio of 2.0 or greater—for example, a defendant's conduct more than doubled the plaintiff's risk of injury. This doubled-risk requirement, however, conflates two distinct burdens: the plaintiff's substantive burden of proof and the standard of persuasion applicable to that burden. Thus, if an epidemiological study indicates that exposure to a particular substance increases the incidence of a disease among those exposed by only forty percent, then a court will probably find that the plaintiff has failed to meet the burden of proving specific causation unless more direct evidence is offered.

Indeed, some courts demand particularistic proof of a causal connection—probabilistic proof is insufficient on its own. In such cases, it is insufficient even to prove that exposure to a substance more than doubled a plaintiff's risk of injury. In addition, if a particular disease-causing substance was generated by more than one source, a plaintiff may also have to demonstrate which of multiple potential defendants produced the substance responsible for the injury. But if a plaintiff is able to identify two or more tortfeasors who collectively released sufficient pollutants to cause the harm, courts may be willing to attach liability to each one. Courts may treat each as a causal agent under a "substantial factor" test, under a theory of joint and several liability, or under a theory of market share liability.

Resolution of all of these issues requires costly expert testimony. Here, environmental tort plaintiffs face another hurdle—the fairly rigorous standard for expert testimony mandated by *Daubert v. Merrell Dow Pharmaceuticals*.[61] In *Daubert*, the Supreme Court interpreted the Federal Rules of Evidence to require that the trial judge serve as a gatekeeper for scientific testimony. The Court identified several factors for trial courts to consider in determining the admissibility of scientific testimony. The *Daubert* standard has proven to be too strict for many toxic tort plaintiffs to meet—courts often find the proposed experts' testimony to be too unreliable to be admissible in light of scientific uncertainty and incomplete scientific knowledge.

NOTES

1. Professor Lin recommends replacing the tort system with an administrative system:

From an institutional analysis perspective, administrative systems have certain characteristics that make them a superior alternative for address-

---

61. *Daubert v. Merrell Dow Pharm., Inc.*, 509 U.S. 579 (1993). *Daubert* was itself a toxic tort case. On remand from the Supreme Court, the Ninth Circuit held that the plaintiffs' scientific evidence, which consisted of a reanalysis of epidemiological evidence, lab studies on animal tissues, and chemical structure analysis, was insufficiently reliable to be admitted under the Federal Rules of Evidence. *See also Daubert v. Merrell Dow Pharm., Inc.*, 43 F.3d 1311 (9th Cir. 1995).

ing the environmental toxic injury problem. Administrative systems typically employ specialized or expert decisionmakers who can conduct their own studies and consider a broad range of information. Administrative systems can also provide more continuous oversight and distribute compensation more fairly among a class of victims. In addition, administrative systems are, in theory, more politically accountable than the judicial system. This is not to suggest that setting compensation should be politicized; rather, the scientific uncertainty inherent in environmental toxic injuries necessitates making policy decisions. In an administrative system, that inescapably political judgment is subject to indirect democratic control.

2. For a recent application of *Daubert* in the context of radiation effects, see *In re Hanford Nuclear Reservation Litigation*, 534 F.3d 986 (9th Cir. 2008). On the use of *Daubert* when expert opinion is based on computer modeling, see Note, *Remedying* Daubert's *Inadequacy in Evaluating the Scientific Models Used in Environmental–Tort Litigation*, 86 Tex. L. Rev. 1281 (2008).

3. Another problem in toxic tort litigation is establishing a link between a specific defendant and the release of the substance. For example, many hazardous waste generators may have shipped similar materials to the site in question. It may be quite difficult to establish whose containers leaked or in what quantities. A similar issue can arise in products liability cases.

In *Sindell v. Abbott Laboratories,*[62] the plaintiff's mother was administered the drug diethylstilbesterol (DES) during pregnancy. Although DES was routinely given to prevent miscarriage, it is now known to cause a rare form of cancer in some daughters of women who took the drug. After developing such cancer, the plaintiff sued eleven of the more than 200 manufacturers of DES. Although the plaintiff was unable to identify the manufacturer of the particular DES which her mother took, the court held that she had stated a cause of action against manufacturers of the drug using an identical formula. Resting this holding on a broad social policy, the court noted that the defendants were "better able to bear the cost of injury resulting from the manufacture of a defective product." The *Sindell* court then adopted a novel theory of liability by making each defendant liable for a share of the plaintiff's damages, based on its share of the DES market.

4. As proportional liability illustrates, problems of proof are derived from substantive compensation rules. For example, negligence may be quite difficult to prove, but tort law may or may not make fault a necessary element of the plaintiff's case. Thus, strict liability can ease the plaintiff's burden of proving liability. Similarly, it may be very hard to prove after the fact that a specific plaintiff's injury was caused by the defendant. Tort law might avoid such problems of proof by providing more limited compensation to everyone who is wrongfully exposed to the risk of injury from toxic chemicals, whether or not the risk materializes. The following two cases consider these issues, starting with the question of liability.

---

62. 26 Cal.3d 588, 607 P.2d 924, 163 Cal.Rptr. 132, *cert. denied,* 449 U.S. 912 (1980).

STATE v. VENTRON CORP.

Supreme Court of New Jersey, 1983.
94 N.J. 473, 468 A.2d 150.

POLLOCK, J.

This appeal concerns the responsibility of various corporations for the cost of the cleanup and removal of mercury pollution seeping from a forty-acre tract of land into Berry's Creek, a tidal estuary of the Hackensack River that flows through the Meadowlands. The plaintiff is the State of New Jersey, Department of Environmental Protection (DEP); the primary defendants are Velsicol Chemical Corporation (Velsicol), its former subsidiary, Wood Ridge Chemical Corporation (Wood Ridge), and Ventron Corporation (Ventron), into which Wood Ridge was merged. Other defendants are F.W. Berk and Company, Inc. (Berk), which no longer exists, United States Life Insurance Company, which was dismissed by the lower courts in an unappealed judgment, and Robert M. and Rita W. Wolf (the Wolfs), who purchased part of the polluted property from Ventron.

Beneath its surface, the tract is saturated by an estimated 268 tons of toxic waste, primarily mercury. For a stretch of several thousand feet, the concentration of mercury in Berry's Creek is the highest found in fresh water sediments in the world. The waters of the creek are contaminated by the compound methyl mercury, which continues to be released as the mercury interacts with other elements. Due to depleted oxygen levels, fish no longer inhabit Berry's Creek, but are present only when swept in by the tide and, thus, irreversibly toxified.

The contamination at Berry's Creek results from mercury processing operations carried on at the site for almost fifty years. * * *

After a fifty-five-day trial, the trial court determined that Berk and Wood Ridge were jointly liable for the cleanup and removal of the mercury; that Velsicol and Ventron were severally liable for half of the costs; that the Wolfs were not liable * * *.

The Appellate Division substantially affirmed the judgment, but modified it in several respects, including the imposition of joint and several liability on Ventron and Velsicol for all costs incurred in the cleanup and removal of the mercury pollution in Berry's Creek. * * *

I

From 1929 to 1960, first as lessee and then as owner of the entire forty-acre tract, Berk operated a mercury processing plant, dumping untreated waste material and allowing mercury-laden effluent to drain on the tract. Berk continued uninterrupted operations until 1960, at which time it sold its assets to Wood Ridge and ceased its corporate existence.

In 1960, Velsicol formed Wood Ridge as a wholly-owned subsidiary for the sole purpose of purchasing Berk's assets and operating the mercury processing plant. In 1967, Wood Ridge subdivided the tract and declared a thirty-three-acre land dividend to Velsicol, which continued to permit Wood Ridge to dump material on the thirty-three acres. As a Velsicol subsidiary, Wood Ridge continued to operate the processing plant on the 7.1–acre tract from 1960 to 1968, when Velsicol sold Wood Ridge to Ventron.

Although Velsicol created Wood Ridge as a separate corporate entity, the trial court found that Velsicol treated it not as an independent subsidiary, but as a division. * * * Without spelling out all the details, we find that the record amply supports the conclusion of the trial court that "Velsicol personnel, directors, and officers were constantly involved in the day-to-day operations of the business of [Wood Ridge]."

In 1968, Velsicol sold 100% of the Wood Ridge stock to Ventron, which began to consider a course of treatment for plant wastes. * * *

Starting in the mid–1960's, DEP began testing effluent on the tract, but did not take any action against Wood Ridge. The trial court found, in fact, that the defendants were not liable under intentional tort or negligence theories.

Nonetheless, in 1970, the contamination at Berry's Creek came to the attention of the United States Environmental Protection Agency (EPA), which conducted a test of Wood Ridge's waste water. The tests indicated that the effluent carried two to four pounds of mercury into Berry's Creek each day. Later that year, Wood Ridge installed a waste treatment system that abated, but did not altogether halt, the flow of mercury into the creek. The operations of the plant continued until 1974, at which time Wood Ridge merged into Ventron. Consistent with *N.J.S.A.* 14A:10–6(e), the certificate of ownership and merger provided that Ventron would assume the liabilities and obligations of Wood Ridge. Ventron terminated the plant operations and sold the movable operating assets to Troy Chemical Company, not a party to these proceedings.

On February 5, 1974, Wood Ridge granted to Robert Wolf, a commercial real estate developer, an operation to purchase the 7.1–acre tract on which the plant was located, and on May 20, 1974, Ventron conveyed the tract to the Wolfs. The Wolfs planned to demolish the plant and construct a warehousing facility. In the course of the demolition, mercury-contaminated water was used to wet down the structures and allowed to run into the creek. The problem came to the attention of DEP, which ordered a halt to the demolition, pending adequate removal or containment of the contamination. DEP proposed a containment plan, but the Wolfs implemented another plan and proceeded with their project. DEP then instituted this action. * * *

II

Twenty-one years ago, * * * this Court adopted the proposition that "an ultrahazardous activity which introduces an unusual danger into the community ... should pay its own way in the event it actually causes damage to others." *Berg v. Reaction Motors Div., Thiokol Chem. Corp.*, 37 *N.J.* 396, 410, 181 *A.2d* 487 (1962). * * *

In imposing liability on a landowner for an ultrahazardous activity, *Berg* adopted the test of the *Restatement of the Law of Torts* (1938). See id., §§ 519–20. Since *Berg,* the Restatement (Second) of the Law of Torts (1977) has replaced the "ultrahazardous" standard with one predicated on whether the activity is "abnormally dangerous." Imposition of liability on a landowner for "abnormally dangerous" activities incorporates, in effect, the *Rylands* test. RESTATEMENT (SECOND) § 520, comments (d) & (e). * * *

[T]he RESTATEMENT (SECOND) OF TORTS reformulated the standard of landowner liability, substituting "abnormally dangerous" for "ultrahazardous" and providing a list of elements to consider in applying the new standard. *Id.,* §§ 519–20. As noted, this standard incorporates the theory developed in *Rylands v. Fletcher.* Under the *Restatement* analysis, whether an activity is abnormally dangerous is to be determined on a case-by-case basis, taking all relevant circumstances into consideration. As set forth in the *Restatement*:

In determining whether an activity is abnormally dangerous, the following factors are to be considered:

(a) existence of a high degree of risk of some harm to the person, land or chattels of others;

(b) likelihood that the harm that results from it will be great;

(c) inability to eliminate the risk by the exercise of reasonable care;

(d) extent to which the activity is not a matter of common usage;

(e) inappropriateness of the activity to the place where it is carried on; and

(f) extent to which its value to the community is outweighed by its dangerous attributes.

RESTATEMENT (SECOND) OF TORTS § 520 (1977). * * *

We approve the trial court's finding that Berk, Wood Ridge, Velsicol, and Ventron are liable under common-law principles for the abatement of the resulting nuisance and damage. The courts below found that the Wolfs are not liable for the costs of cleanup and containment. DEP did not petition for certification on that issue, and we do not consider it on this appeal. Berk and Wood Ridge, not Mr. and Mrs. Wolf, polluted the environment. During their ownership, the Wolfs have not continued to dump mercury and they have been responsible for only a minimal aggravation of the underlying hazardous condition.

NOTE

TENTATIVE DRAFT NO. 1, RESTATEMENT (THIRD) OF TORTS: LIABILITY FOR PHYSICAL HARM (BASIC PRINCIPLES) (Mar. 28, 2001), Chapter IV, section 20, "Abnormally Dangerous Activities," provides:

(a) A defendant who carries on an abnormally dangerous activity is subject to strict liability for physical harm resulting from the activity.

(b) An activity is abnormally dangerous if:

(1) the activity creates a foreseeable and highly significant risk of physical harm even when reasonable care is exercised by all actors; and

(2) the activity is not a matter of common usage.

Comment *g* to section 20 states that a risk of physical harm can be "highly significant" for either or both of two reasons: because the *likelihood* of harm is unusually high, even though the severity of expected harm is no more than ordinary; or because the *severity* of the harm could be enormous, although the likelihood of a harm-causing incident is low.

AYERS v. TOWNSHIP OF JACKSON

Supreme Court of New Jersey, 1987.
106 N.J. 557, 525 A.2d 287.

STEIN, JUSTICE.

In this case we consider the application of the New Jersey Tort Claims Act [which limits the kinds of damages recoverable against public entities], N.J.S.A. 59:1–1 to 12–3, to the claims asserted by 339 residents of Jackson Township against that municipality.

The litigation involves claims for damages sustained because plaintiffs' well water was contaminated by toxic pollutants leaching into the Cohansey Aquifer from a landfill established and operated by Jackson Township. After an extensive trial, the jury found that the township had created a "nuisance" and a "dangerous condition" by virtue of its operation of the landfill, that its conduct was "palpably unreasonable,"—a prerequisite to recovery under *N.J.S.A.* 59:4–2—and that it was the proximate cause of the contamination of plaintiffs' water supply. The jury verdict resulted in an aggregate judgment of $15,854,392.78 [including $2,056,480 for emotional distress, $5,396,940 for deterioration of quality of life, and $8,204,500 for costs of future medical surveillance. The excerpts below focus on damages for increased risk exposure and medical surveillance]. * * *

In our view, an enhanced risk of disease caused by significant exposure to toxic chemicals is clearly an "injury" under the Act. In this case, neither the trial court nor the Appellate Division challenged the contention that the enhanced risk of disease was a tortiously-inflicted injury, but both concluded that the proof quantifying the likelihood of disease was insufficient to submit the issue to the jury. * * *

Among the recent toxic tort cases rejecting liability for damages based on enhanced risk is *Anderson v. W.R. Grace & Co.,* 628 *F.Supp.* 1219 (D. Mass.1986). That case involved defendants' alleged chemical contamination of the groundwater in areas of Woburn, Massachusetts. Plaintiffs alleged that two wells supplying water to the City of Woburn drew upon the contaminated water, and that exposure to the contaminated water caused five deaths and severe personal injuries among plaintiffs. Among the claims for personal injuries dismissed before trial were plaintiff's claims for damages based on enhanced risk. Relying on the Massachusetts rule regarding prospective damages, the *Anderson* court reasoned that "recovery depends on establishing a 'reasonable probability' that the harm will occur." However, the *Anderson* court held that the plaintiffs failed to satisfy this threshold standard. They had not quantified their alleged enhanced risk: "Nothing in the present record indicates the magnitude of the increased risk or the diseases which plaintiffs may suffer." * * *

Other courts have acknowledged the propriety of the enhanced risk cause of action, but have emphasized the requirement that proof of future injury be reasonably certain. * * *

Additionally, several courts have permitted recovery for increased risk of disease, but only where the plaintiff exhibited some present manifestation of disease. * * *

Our disposition of this difficult and important issue requires that we choose between two alternatives, each having a potential for imposing unfair and undesirable consequences on the affected interests. A holding that recognizes a cause of action for unquantified enhanced risk claims exposes the tort system, and the public it serves, to the task of litigating vast numbers of claims for compensation based on threats of injuries that may never occur. * * *

Our dissenting colleague, arguing in favor of recognizing a cause of action based on an unquantified claim of enhanced risk, points out that "courts have not allowed the difficulty of quantifying injury to prevent them from offering compensation for assault, trespass, emotional distress, invasion of privacy or damage to reputation." Although lawsuits grounded in one or more of these causes of action may involve claims for damages that are difficult to quantify, such damages are awarded on the basis of events that have occurred and can be proved at the time of trial. In contrast, the compensability of the enhanced risk claim depends upon the likelihood of an event that has not yet occurred and may never occur—the contracting of one or more diseases the risk of which has been enhanced by defendant's conduct. It is the highly contingent and speculative quality of an unquantified claim based on enhanced risk that renders it novel and difficult to manage and resolve. * * *

In * * * our view, the speculative nature of an unquantified enhanced risk claim, the difficulties inherent in adjudicating such claims, and the policies underlying the Tort Claims Act argue persuasively against the recognition of this cause of action. Accordingly, we decline to recognize plaintiffs' cause of action for the *unquantified* enhanced risk of disease, and affirm the judgment of the Appellate Division dismissing such claims. We need not and do not decide whether a claim based on enhanced risk of disease that is supported by testimony demonstrating that the onset of the disease is reasonably probable could be maintained under the Tort Claims Act.

The claim for medical surveillance expenses stands on a different footing from the claim based on enhanced risk. It seeks to recover the cost of periodic medical examinations intended to monitor plaintiffs' health and facilitate early diagnosis and treatment of disease caused by plaintiffs' exposure to toxic chemicals. At trial, competent medical testimony was offered to prove that a program of regular medical testing and evaluation was reasonably necessary and consistent with contemporary scientific principles applied by physicians experienced in the diagnosis and treatment of chemically-induced injuries.

The Appellate Division's rejection of the medical surveillance claim is rooted in the premise that even if medical experts testify convincingly that medical surveillance is necessary, the claim for compensation for these costs must fall, as a matter of law, if the risk of injury is not quantified, or, if quantified, is not reasonably probable. This analysis assumes that the reasonableness of medical intervention, and, therefore, its compensability, depends solely on the sufficiency of proof that the occurrence of the disease is probable. We think this formulation unduly impedes the ability of courts to recognize that medical science may necessarily and properly intervene where there is a significant but unquantified risk of serious disease. * * *

Compensation for reasonable and necessary medical expenses is consistent with well-accepted legal principles. It is also consistent with the important public health interest in fostering access to medical testing for individuals whose exposure to toxic chemicals creates an enhanced risk of disease. The value of early diagnosis and treatment for cancer patients is well-documented. * * *

Although some individuals exposed to hazardous chemicals may seek regular medical surveillance whether or not the cost is reimbursed, the lack of reimbursement will undoubtedly deter others from doing so. An application of tort law that allows post-injury, pre-symptom recovery in toxic tort litigation for reasonable medical surveillance costs is manifestly consistent with the public interest in early detection and treatment of disease. * * *

Accordingly, we hold that the cost of medical surveillance is a compensable item of damages where the proofs demonstrate, through reliable expert testimony predicated upon the significance and extent of exposure to chemicals, the toxicity of the chemicals, the seriousness of the diseases for which individuals are at risk, the relative increase in the chance of onset of disease in those exposed, and the value of early diagnosis, that such surveillance to monitor the effect of exposure to toxic chemicals is reasonable and necessary. * * *

We find that the proofs in this case were sufficient to support the trial court's decision to submit the medical surveillance issue to the jury, and were sufficient to support the jury's verdict.

The medical surveillance issue was tried as if it were a conventional claim for compensatory damages susceptible to a jury verdict in a lump sum. The jury was so instructed by the trial court, and neither plaintiffs' nor defendant's request to charge on this issue sought a different instruction. * * *

The indeterminate nature of damage claims in toxic-tort litigation suggests that the use of court-supervised funds to pay medical-surveillance claims as they accrue, rather than lump-sum verdicts, may provide a more efficient mechanism for compensating plaintiffs. A funded settlement was used in the Agent Orange litigation. *In re "Agent Orange" Prod. Liab. Litig.,* 611 F.Supp. 1396, 1399 (E.D.N.Y. 1985), aff'd, 818 F.2d 194 (2d Cir. 1987). The use of insurance to fund future medical claims is frequently recommended by commentators. * * *

In our view, the use of a court-supervised fund to administer medical-surveillance payments in mass exposure cases, particularly for claims under the Tort Claims Act, is a highly appropriate exercise of the Court's equitable powers. * * *

Although there may be administrative and procedural questions in the establishment and operation of such a fund, we encourage its use by trial courts in managing mass-exposure cases. In litigation involving public-entity defendants, we conclude that the use of a fund to administer medical-surveillance payments should be the general rule, in the absence of factors that render it impractical or inappropriate. This will insure that in future mass-exposure litigation against public entities, medical-surveillance damages will be paid only to compensate for medical examinations and tests actually administered, and will encourage plaintiffs to safeguard their health by not allowing them the option of spending the money for other purposes. The fund mechanism will also foster the legislative objective of limiting the liability of public entities and facilitating the deduction from damage awards of collateral-source benefits.

However, we decline to upset the jury verdict awarding medical-surveillance damages in this case. Such a result would be unfair to these plaintiffs, since the medical-surveillance issue was tried conventionally, and neither party requested the trial court to withhold from the jury the power to return a lump-sum verdict for each plaintiff in order that relief by way of a fund could be provided. * * *

NOTES

1. The *Ayers* case distinguishes four kinds of claims related to potential future harms:

> (a) Plaintiff has an *existing physical injury* that may worsen or develop into a more serious illness;

> (b) Plaintiff has no existing injury or disease but, because of exposure to toxic substances, is at an *increased risk* of developing a particular disease, such as cancer, in the future;

(c) Plaintiff, because of her susceptibility to the disease, suffers present *emotional distress*, usually fear or anxiety, which may or may not be accompanied by physical manifestations;

(d) Plaintiff, again because of the enhanced risk of future serious illness, incurs or should incur present and future medical expenses for *surveillance* of the possible development of the disease.

The prevailing rule for cases in at least the first three categories is that increased risk of developing a future disease, such as cancer, as a consequence of exposure to toxic chemicals is not compensable unless plaintiff can establish that the probability of the future disease is greater than 50%. *See* Lisa Heinzerling & Cameron Hoffman, *Tortious Toxics*, 26 WM. & MARY L. REV. 67, 73 (2001). The fourth category is discussed below.

2. *In re Paoli R.R. Yard PCB Litigation,* 916 F.2d 829 (3d Cir. 1990), held that a medical monitoring claimant must show (1) that she was significantly exposed to a proven hazardous substance through the negligent actions of defendant, (2) that as a proximate result of exposure she suffers an increased risk of contracting a serious latent disease, (3) that the increased risk makes medical examinations reasonably necessary, and (4) that monitoring and testing procedures exist which make early detection and treatment of the disease possible and beneficial.

In most medical monitoring cases plaintiffs have sought or courts have awarded a traditional common-law lump sum of monetary damages. In a few toxic exposure cases, however, litigants have pursued or courts have expressed their preference for periodic payment of future medical surveillance expenses out of a court-supervised trust fund or similar mechanism. *See* Amy B. Blumenberg, *Medical Monitoring Funds: The Periodic Payment of Future Medical Surveillance Expenses in Toxic Exposure Litigation*, 43 HASTINGS L.J. 661 (1992).

3. The Supreme Court dealt with medical surveillance liability a decade ago in *Metro–North Commuter R.R. Co. v. Buckley*,[63] a case arising under the Federal Employers' Liability Act ("FELA").[64] The plaintiff had been exposed to asbestos as a pipe fitter while working for the railroad. After he learned that he faced an increase risk of cancer, he sought to recover damages for the resulting emotional distress and a lump-sum recovery for future medical check-ups. The Court noted a number of general concerns about allowing recovery for medical monitoring not connected with any existing injury, including the potentially wide scope of liability, the lower priority of claimants with monitoring costs versus those with already realized injury, the difficulty of identifying what extra monitoring is warranted by an exposure, and the possibility that monitoring expenses would be covered by health insurance or some other source. The Court's observations suggest some unease with medical monitoring damages in general.

Ultimately, however, the Court's holding was narrow and rejected only what it considered to be a very broad rule of recovery of lump-sum damages:

---

63. 521 U.S. 424 (1997).

64. Employers' Liability Acts (Federal Employers' Liability Act) (FELA), 45 U.S.C. § 51–60 (2007).

We have not tried to balance these, or other, competing considerations here. We point them out to help explain why we consider the limitations and cautions to be important—and integral—parts of the state-court decisions that permit asymptomatic plaintiffs a separate tort claim for medical monitoring costs. That being so, we do not find sufficient support in the common law for the unqualified rule of lump-sum damages recovery that is, at least arguably, before us here. And given the mix of competing general policy considerations, plaintiff's policy-based arguments do not convince us that the FELA contains a tort liability rule of that unqualified kind.

This limited conclusion disposes of the matter before us. We need not, and do not, express any view here about the extent to which the FELA might, or might not, accommodate medical cost recovery rules more finely tailored than the rule we have considered.[65]

Some state courts have interpreted this limited holding as a broad rejection of medical monitoring expenses.[66]

In another setback for this theory of recovery, the court held in *In re Hanford Nuclear Reservation Litigation*, 534 F.3d 986 (9th Cir. 2008), that medical monitoring liability for radiation risks was precluded by a federal statute, the Price–Anderson Act.

4. What about tort liability and climate change? The U.S. and other industrialized countries are responsible for a disproportionate share of emissions, many of them after 1990 when the international community had already acknowledged the reality of climate change and its causes. Should failure to reduce emissions (at least after 1990) be considered negligence (a failure to exercise due care)? Should there be strict liability in tort? What issues do you foresee in any such tort litigation? Even if tort lawsuits seem inappropriate, would some other compensation mechanism make sense?

Besides the possibility of liability for failure to mitigate, there are also possible sources of liability in the use of new mitigation technologies. See, e.g., Alexandra B. Klass and Elizabeth J. Wilson, *Climate Change and Carbon Sequestration: Assessing Liability Regime for Long–Term Storage of Carbon*, 58 EMORY L.J. 103 (2008).

---

65. *Metro–North Commuter R.R. Co.*, 521 U.S. at 444. The Court's lack of sympathy to tort plaintiffs is fairly palpable here—not the willingness to dispose of the case on a ground that the court says is only "arguably present" in the case before it. In addition, as the dissent pointed out, the majority's discussion is extremely muddled:

It is not apparent why (or even whether) the Court reverses the Second Circuit's determination on Buckley's second claim. The Court of Appeals held that a medical monitoring claim is solidly grounded, and this Court does not hold otherwise. Hypothesizing that Buckley demands lump-sum damages and nothing else, the Court ruminates on the appropriate remedy without answering the anterior question: Does the plaintiff have a claim for relief? Buckley has shown that Metro–North negligently exposed him to "extremely high levels of asbestos," 79 F.3d, at 1341, and that this exposure warrants "medical monitoring in order to detect and treat [asbestos-related] diseases as they may arise." Id., at 1346. Buckley's expert medical witness estimated the annual costs of proper monitoring at $950. We do not know from the Court's opinion what more a plaintiff must show to qualify for relief.

Id. at 448 (Ginsburg, J., dissenting in part and concurring in the judgment).

66. *See* Jamie A. Grodsky, *Genomics and Toxic Torts: Dismantling the Risk–Injury Divide*, 59 STAN. L. REV. 1671, 1712 (2007).

E. NEW DIRECTIONS IN ENVIRONMENTAL PROTECTION

The approaches we have considered in this chapter are diverse, ranging from risk-based or BAT regulation to market mechanisms to criminal and civil liability. Still, they share a common structure. Regulation under each of them proceeds from the top down: the government creates a regulation, cap-and-trade scheme, or liability rule; then it is up to firms to comply. In other words, there is a purely hierarchical relationship between government and regulated firms, with public interest groups sitting on the sidelines as vocal spectators. A number of efforts have been made to move away from this hierarchical and often adversarial relationship in the direction of greater collaboration between government, environmental groups, and regulated businesses. These efforts are discussed in this section. Sometimes the result may appear to involve "contract" as much as "regulation."

JODY FREEMAN, THE CONTRACTING STATE[67]
28 FLA. ST. U. L. REV. 155 (2000).

To date, there is no formal contractual mechanism for either establishing or implementing regulatory standards. Indeed, the notion of private contract is anathema to public regulation. And yet, to a significant extent, negotiation and exchange pervade the regulatory process. This observation is at once banal and too frequently overlooked. It is banal in the sense that it was precisely the pervasiveness of secret, informal bargains that vindicated capture theory and prompted the procedural administrative law reforms of the 1960s. These judicially imposed reforms opened the administrative process to public scrutiny and both balanced and structured private influence, developments that Richard Stewart captured so effectively in his interest representation model of administrative law.

At the same time, the full impact of negotiation and exchange has been overlooked to the extent that it pervades implementation and enforcement as well as rulemaking. Even in a command-and-control system, the regulatory process is deeply, if informally, contractual. For example, regulated entities negotiate the terms of their permits and litigants frequently settle conflicts through negotiated consent decrees. That is, the procedural reforms Professor Stewart identified were designed to structure only part of the "regime of exchange" that constitutes the regulatory process.

In fact, the conceptual distinction between contract and regulation may not be as clear as we think. Regulation does not conform to an idealized hierarchical model of government power, in which agencies

---

67. Copyright © 2000, Florida State University Law Review. Reprinted with permission.

directly deliver services or unilaterally impose rules on regulated entities under threat of sanction. Instead, the regulatory process can be understood as a set of residual choices that must be made by regulated entities, together with government and other interested parties, after some of the choices have been ruled out. This understanding focuses attention on the space left for working out the content of the regulation and its implementation, rather than on the initial move by the state to shrink that space. At virtually every step in the regulatory process—standard setting, implementation, and enforcement—the state forecloses some options and conditions others. * * *

* * * Contractual regulatory instruments consist of a handful of loosely defined innovations, distinguishable from conventional approaches because they feature negotiation, bargain, and/or consensus among stakeholders, and because they usually manifest themselves in written agreements. This includes not only regulatory negotiation, but also examples like EPA's Project XL and a host of other implementation and enforcement strategies that run the gamut from standard setting to implementation and enforcement, most of which have developed in environmental or health and safety regulation. For example, Caldart and Ashford recently identified a number of OSHA and EPA efforts to informally negotiate implementation and compliance with regulated entities.[68] Congress has explicitly authorized some of these initiatives, while others are instances of agency enforcement discretion, as when an agency agrees not to enforce formal legal requirements in exchange for a regulated entity's agreement to perform obligations not required by formal law. Although these agreements are not enforceable, David Dana argues that they exemplify a "contractarian" approach to regulation.

Regulatory negotiation—a formal consensus-based stakeholder process for developing regulations—is probably the most frequently cited example of a contract-like instrument In passing the Negotiated Rulemaking Act (NRA), Congress authorized agencies to use this nontraditional method of rule development (reg-neg) when agencies believe it to be in "the public interest" after considering a number of factors, including whether the agency can convene a balanced negotiating committee capable of representing the interests that will be significantly affected by the rule. Reg-neg was originally intended to achieve a number of goals, including improved rule quality and greater legitimacy for the resulting rules. Early proponents also expected that it would reduce litigation and conserve resources by bringing parties likely to challenge the rule or obstruct its implementation directly into the development process. Its innovation was to bring principles of alternative dispute resolution to rulemaking—in the form of direct negotiations among the affected parties—in order to ameliorate the adversarialism that had come to characterize the conventional approach.

---

68. *See* Charles C. Caldart & Nicholas A. Ashford, *Negotiation as a Means of Developing and Implementing Environmental and Occupational Health and Safety Policy*, 23 HARV. ENVTL. L. REV. 141, 180–93 (1999).

Because negotiated rules must still go through the notice-and-comment process and because the convening agency is not bound to promulgate the consensus rule, reg-neg falls well short of embodying a formal contract. Still, reg-neg is a meaningful example of a contract-like mechanism. Participants in a reg-neg clearly form alliances, stake out positions, and bargain. Typically, they sign an agreement not to legally challenge any rule produced by a consensus of which they are a part. Although these agreements are unlikely to be legally enforceable, there may be a price for noncompliance, particularly for repeat players who face informal sanctions and reputational costs. At a minimum, the parties in a reg-neg clearly take their participation seriously (devoting significant time and resources to it) and they expect their consensus to form the basis of the final rule.

Beyond the rule-writing process, the implementation stage of regulation has produced a number of contract-like innovations. For example, the EPA has adopted a quasi-contractual approach to implementing environmental regulations in its Project XL initiative, the national pilot program designed to test methods of achieving superior and more cost-effective environmental protection through project agreements with individual facilities or industry sectors. Through XL, the agency exercises its enforcement discretion to go one step beyond the informal negotiation that already occurs in the traditional permitting process, by granting regulatory flexibility to applicants in exchange for commitments to achieve better environmental performance than might otherwise be achieved through compliance with applicable regulations. The idea is to allow firms to devise innovative compliance strategies that result in a net environmental benefit in exchange for relief from rigid regulations.

In a typical XL project, the EPA might grant a single, streamlined permit that authorizes cross-pollutant and cross-media trades that might not otherwise be allowed by regulations. XL allows the agency to grant preapproval of process changes or emissions increases that would normally trigger a lengthy separate approval process. While these initiatives do not produce legally enforceable contracts, they culminate in detailed, written documents known as final project agreements (FPAs). XL thus has some contractual features: the parties bargain, they produce written agreements, and they undertake mutual commitments. The terms and conditions of the FPAs are then incorporated into permits, which are legally enforceable. * * *

A contractual approach is currently built into the agency enforcement process as well, in the form of "supplemental enforcement plans" (SEPs) by which agencies waive monetary penalties in exchange for remedial measures to which the regulated entity may not otherwise submit. Proponents of this enforcement innovation argue that SEPs are more problem oriented than conventional penalty assessment; they claim that SEPs provide both short-and long-term benefits by enabling firms to identify opportunities for technological change that might have additional beneficial environmental effects beyond the immediate lawsuit.

For the most part, however, environmental contracting is in an early developmental phase. To take effect, most such agreements still require independent agency action such as rule promulgation or permit issuance, and most purport to be independently unenforceable. Still, both Congress and individual agencies appear willing to experiment with regulatory contracts, and a handful of scholars find them promising enough to pursue as an alternative approach. For example, Don Elliott has proposed that "command and covenant" might replace command-and-control regulation.[69] Based on an XL-like approach, this model would rely on a government-established minimum standard of performance, while allowing regulated entities to essentially contract around regulatory inefficiencies by devising implementation strategies. Dan Farber recently described efforts such as reg-neg and Project XL as illustrations of a bilateral bargaining model of regulation, and he suggested that it seems the "most promising" way to conceptualize regulation.[70]

Moreover, although a contractual regulatory model is new to the United States, enforceable contracts are an increasingly common feature of environmental regulation in the European Union. In Belgium, the Netherlands, France, and Germany, a variety of contractual instruments have emerged, including "agreements" or "covenants" between governments and industrial polluters, as well as agreements between polluters and local communities Some of these instruments are considered "voluntary" and unenforceable but nonetheless replace procedural requirements and regulatory commitments; others have the status of legally enforceable contracts. * * *

One need not look to Europe, however, for examples of hybrid instruments that combine regulation and contract. Local land use regulation presents a precedent for the theory and practice of regulatory contracting. Through contract zoning and development agreements, local government bodies routinely bargain with private developers and residents and reach legally enforceable agreements that contain, among other things, regulatory freezes and exactions. This form of government action is neither regulatory in a traditional sense nor conventionally contractual: it depends on a convergence of regulatory and contract power.

CHRISTOPHER H. SCHROEDER, THIRD WAY ENVIRONMENTALISM[71]

48 U. KAN. L. REV. 801 (2000).

Proposition 65 is a state-level program that has also had significant effects on reducing exposure at the source. Enacted by referendum in

---

69. E. Donald Elliott, *Toward Ecological Law and Policy*, in Thinking Ecologically: The Next Generation of Environmental Policy 171, 183 (Marian Chertow and Daniel Esty eds., 1997).

70. Daniel A. Farber, *Triangulating the Future of Reinvention: Three Emerging Models of Environmental Protection*, 2000 U. ILL. L. REV. 61, 76–77. Farber proposes a "bilateral bargaining" model and compares it to alternatives, including a "governance" model, which is multilateral and eco-system-based. * * *

71. Copyright © 2000, Kansas Law Review. Reprinted by permission.

California in 1986, Proposition 65 also mandates disclosure of information from firms or other entities, in this case not the quantity of releases, but rather the fact that the firm is exposing individuals to risk. If a product contains substances calculated to produce risks of cancer or reproductive toxicity over certain thresholds, producers must notify people of that fact. Proposition 65 thus puts manufacturers of products to the choice of providing a clear and reasonable notice of hazard at the point of sale, or else changing their manufacturing process so as to eliminate the risk. If the manufacturer chooses the disclosure option, customers concerned about their health might well choose to buy other products. Knowing this, a number of manufacturers have changed their production procedures in ways that eliminate the risk. * * *

Like market-creation measures, information-disclosure measures take advantage of self-interested behavior on the part of individuals and firms. In this way, they "get the incentives right," aligning incentives for private behavior with the collective goal of reducing toxic emissions. One difference between the two measures is that information-disclosure programs do not establish a cap on emissions; they simply let the incentives produce individual behavior that is consistent with a general pollution reduction objective. For this reason, it remains possible that policymakers would revisit the level of relevant exposures after the information disclosure was in place, determine that the amount of reductions was unsatisfactory, and resort to additional control measures.

Neither market-creation devices nor information-disclosure devices will invariably prove attractive substitutes or complements to prescriptive regulation. They have, however, moved from devices of primarily academic interest, peripheral to actual policy implementation, to accepted components of the overall regulatory tool kit for environmental problem solving.

One of the more intriguing questions about policy change is why certain policy approaches move from the classroom to the statute books or the Code of Federal Regulations when they do. With respect to incentive-based instruments, I believe that five factors have contributed to these recent developments. First, the prescriptive strategies that have been the backbone of federal environmental regulation since 1970 are approaching the point of accomplishing as much as they feasibly can. Automobile emissions provide an excellent illustration. Through the application of increasingly stringent emission controls, we have reduced individual automobile emissions by approximately 90% of their pre–1970 levels. As a result, total annual emissions nationwide of the principal automobile-related criteria pollutants, carbon monoxide, hydrocarbons and nitrogen dioxide, have appreciably declined. However, during the period, 1977–1998, gross domestic product rose by 64%, and vehicle miles traveled rose by 160%. Because we have come close to the limits of what is technologically and economically feasible with existing technology, continued growth in vehicle miles traveled will soon begin to completely offset technological improvements. For instance, the EPA projects that total hydrocarbon emissions produced by mobile sources will start to rise again in 2005.

The automobile case typifies a general problem: if further progress is to be made in pollution reduction, we need to explore alternative strategies that may enable us to avoid the problem of diminishing returns on existing approaches.

Among the available alternatives, pollution prevention techniques hold out some hope for further progress at a reasonable cost. Pollution prevention poses difficulties for traditional command-and-control regulation, however, because government regulation runs into considerable resistance whenever it begins to intrude into decisions inside an industry's production processes. The Environmental Era has, in many circumstances, legitimated government's regulation of what industries dump into the public commons, but so far, direct intervention into the production processes of American industry by government has seldom even been attempted. In contrast to end-of-the-pipe controls, direct government intrusion into the "very processes of production themselves" has had very little political support in domestic politics.

The reasons for this selective endorsement of government environmental regulation relate to a second development in American society that has been occurring alongside the environmental movement. During the same period in time in which the major federal environmental statutes have been enacted and amended, American hostility toward government, and American distrust of government, has never been more pronounced. That distrust manifests itself in a variety of ways, including the readiness of the American electorate to believe that government bureaucracy is cumbersome, slow, and often verging on incompetence. Government is often derided as incapable of understanding how any industry functions and, as a consequence, likely to regulate industry in ways that are oppressive and counter-productive. This sentiment dramatically ascended to the national stage when President Reagan remarked in his first inaugural address that "government is not the solution to our problem." Major elements of the criticism have now been embraced by both political parties. President Clinton signaled this convergence when he announced that "the era of big government is over" in his 1996 State of the Union address.

Compared to prescriptive command-and-control regulation, third way measures reduce the role of government. Under market-creation strategies, for example, government sets the standards and then lets the ingenuity of American industry locate the best techniques for achieving them. This both reduces the role of government in the problem solving process, which the public likes, and also may make the heavy hand of government less noticeable, which beleaguered bureaucrats like. The resulting division of labor also arguably plays to the strength of each sector—government figures out the level of protection appropriate to protect public health, discharging the more public-oriented aspect of the regulatory function, and then industry finds the best technical means to meet those standards, discharging the more private aspects of that function. So, the second reason that third way measures may be emerging is that they allocate responsibilities in ways that coincide with our attributions of competence to the various sectors of our society.

Third, these third way measures enable us to continue to believe in American exceptionalism. Within the environmental arena, American exceptionalism holds that America can solve its environmental problems through technological advance. When the Environmental Era began, such technological optimism was at a zenith. In 1968, the country had succeeded in placing a man on the moon, closing the gap between the United States' space program and that of the Soviet Union in a remarkably short period of time after President Kennedy had made this a national objective. The sentiment that, if we can put a man on the moon, we can solve the pollution problem rang through the debates on national environmental legislation.

The space program provided more than a rhetorical argument for bold action; its approach to problem solving was mimicked in our early pollution statutes. While the space program drew on the capacities of private industry, the actions of industry were carefully specified and overseen by NASA. Translating this public-private arrangement into environmental affairs produced the kind of prescriptive regulation that typified the early period: government was to study engineering capabilities, health data, and other relevant information, decide in fine detail the best action to take, and industry was to comply. Beyond the NASA example, this approach to industry resonated with a fairly widespread suspicion that industry could not be trusted to perform according to collective mandates without it. * * * In this environment, command-and-control seemed consistent with the American expectation that we can solve any problem once we focus our attention on it.

By the end of the century, social attitudes toward corporate power had shifted and have become now considerably more accepting of that power. The presence of international competition and the swift rise of the computer industries and e-commerce have convinced many that competition and the dynamics of markets themselves discipline corporate excesses. Firms also argue that they need flexibility to meet competition and thereby to generate the new jobs upon which the country must rely for future prosperity. In this new environment, American technological optimism has remained but has shifted from valorizing government to valorizing private industry. Now it is popular to believe that American industry, once unfettered so that it can experiment and create new solutions, will use its ingenuity to produce significant amounts of environmental improvement at acceptable costs. Both market-creation devices and information-disclosure devices rely upon a confidence that they will lead to cost-effective pollution reduction because we believe that getting the incentives right will produce such change. If it turns out that industry lacks the capacity to respond to those incentives in ways that are both environmentally meaningful and economically viable, third way measures will come under pressure. At present, though, many people seem content to believe that third way measures are, in fact, approaches that will make the environment/economic growth clash into the "false choice" that President Clinton insists it is.

Fourth, third way measures benefit from the suffusion of environmental values throughout the society. For some time, a number of early ardent environmentalists conceived of environmentalism as a vanguard movement, devoted to strenuous criticism of current ideologies but remaining a minor voice on the large political scene. * * * It is fair to say that in recent years this authoritarian element in environmentalism has been receding. In its place, environmental scholars are propounding theories of environmental politics that seek to reconcile environmentalism and democracy, some even arguing that meaningful democratic participation is essential to achieving environmental goals This happier union of environmentalism and democracy comes more easily now that environmental values are widely shared within American society. The American public has strongly supported environmental measures for better than three decades and that record of endurance makes environmentalism stand apart from the normal pattern of issues that push onto the public agenda, have their moment in the sun, and then recede from view.

The third way measures that rely upon consumer or citizen response draw upon this same base of support. Thus information-disclosure measures can be supported by environmentalists with some confidence that citizens in fact will react to the knowledge that is being disseminated. TRI disclosures, Proposition 65, the dolphin-free-tuna boycott movement, the interest in eco-labeling, and the recently initiated push to have grocery stores disclose whether they are selling genetically modified food stuffs all trade on the confidence that consumers care enough about the health and environmental effects of their purchases to base consumption decisions on that concern—at least when reasonably comparable alternative products are available. So long as that is the case, information-disclosure techniques will have some efficacy.

Fifth, incentive-based instruments have increasing influence because they have developed a track record. The success of TRI, Proposition 65, the acid rain program and other market-creation devices lends some credence to the claim that they are indeed "ideas that actually work." Early successes induce policymakers to consider new applications. Tradeable permits have become an integral part of the Kyoto Accords on greenhouse gases, for instance.

The regulatory instruments that the Clinton Administration has emphasized under its reinventing environmental protection umbrella, which extend beyond market-creation and information-disclosure devices have thus far been promoted in a political environment that has largely permitted the suppression of ideological debate, thus reflecting the way in which President Clinton and Vice President Gore have advocated them. Eschewing ideological battles, and embracing only the view that we need to do more, the Administration pursues solutions that seek to gain further progress by blunting the major deregulatory argument against big government while building on broad popular agreement with that view.

The tactical nature of these third way measures constitutes both their strength and their potential weakness. Avoiding ideological debate enables people of differing ideological commitments to come together around practical measures that make progress, that move in a direction congenial to each of their differing ideologies without being explicitly derived from any of them. So long as targets of opportunity exist for such tactics, they can be applauded as "ideas that actually work," and it becomes a point of merely academic interest whether they are globally nonideological in nature, or simply locally nonideological.

Their political weaknesses are that they are dependent upon external circumstances being such that these targets do exist, and that they are completely unequipped to resolve significant disputes between environmental improvement and economic growth, say, when and if those disputes can no longer be avoided. Indeed, most ecologists will continue to dissent from these tactics precisely because they believe that a commitment to non-human-centered environmental principles compels action much bolder and much more discontinuous with existing practices than the third way measures described here. It may be that the ideological dimension of the third way debate will have to be engaged, but in the meantime it makes good sense to explore and capture the gains that can be made through third way environmental solutions.

NOTES

1. There is now a voluminous body of scholarship about various efforts at "reinvention." A thorough review of reinvention efforts can be found in Richard B. Stewart, *A New Generation of Environmental Regulation?*, 29 CAP. U. L. REV. 21 (2001), and in the commentaries about Stewart's article by Daniel Esty, David Spence, Rena Steinzor, and E. Donald Elliott in the same volume. For an overview of the debate, *see* Jody Freeman and Daniel A. Farber, *Modular Environmental Regulation*, 54 DUKE L.J. 795, 822–35 (2005). An extensive discussion of TRI and its broader implications can be found in Bradley C. Karkkainen, *Information as Environmental Regulation: TRI and Performance Benchmarking, Precursors to a New Paradigm*, 89 GEO. L.J. 257 (2001).

2. Critics of reinvention argue that the current regulatory system has had notable successes and that reinvention may simply open the door to evasive tactics by industry. *See* Rena I. Steinzor, *Reinventing Environmental Regulation: The Dangerous Journey From Command to Self–Control*, 22 HARV. ENVTL. L. REV. 103 (1998). On the other hand, there have been some success stories, such as a four-year collaboration between FedEx and Environmental Defense that resulted in a hybrid low-emissions diesel delivery truck. *See Case Studies Suggest Corporate–Environmental Group Partnerships Can Work*, 28 INT. ENV. REP. 235 (Apr. 6, 2005).

3. As the following excerpt explains, such efforts to reinvent government have not been limited to environmental law. These efforts involve not only a

shift toward collaboration but also a more dynamic approach to solving problems.

BRADLEY C. KARKKAINEN, "NEW GOVERNANCE" IN LEGAL THOUGHT AND IN THE WORLD: SOME SPLITTING AS AN ANTIDOTE TO OVERZEALOUS LUMPING[72]

89 MINN. L. REV. 471, 473–79 (2004).

[T]he older, command-style regulatory model grew to dominance in the United States in the New Deal era, but arguably it found its fullest expression a bit later, in the Great Society of the 1960s and the consumer protection and "environmental decade" of the 1970s. Unquestionably, it also has rough counterparts in other legal and political cultures in Europe and elsewhere. The old regulatory model was hierarchical, state-centric, bureaucratic, top-down and expert-driven. The old model attempted to microengineer solutions to societal problems through a series of fragmentary, piecemeal, and highly prescriptive regulatory interventions, and it tended to produce an impossibly complex and tangled web of rigid, uniform one-size-fits-all rules that in truth did not quite fit anyone.

In contrast, the New Governance model (at least according to its proponents) breaks with fixity, state-centrism, hierarchy, excessive reliance on bureaucratic expertise, and intrusive prescription. It aspires instead to be more open-textured, participatory, bottom-up, consensus-oriented, contextual, flexible, integrative, and pragmatic. On some variants, it also aspires to be adaptive, claiming both the capacity and the necessity to continuously generate new learning and to adjust in response to new information and changing conditions, systematically employing information feedback loops, benchmarking, rolling standards of best practice, and principles of continuous improvement. New Governance scholars claim to have discerned the emergence of at least a nascent form of this New Governance model in disparate areas of public policy. In the United States, New Governance scholars have written on developments in, inter alia, environmental protection, public school reform, "problem-solving courts," health care reform, workplace gender discrimination, equal protection generally, labor rights, community policing, community economic development, and public law litigation. In the European context, discussions of New Governance tend to focus on the European Union's Open Method of Coordination and other "soft law" approaches to policy development and coordination on a European Union-wide basis, although the emergence of New Governance methods within European Union member states is also noted.

Despite a profusion of literature and the ambitious claims of its authors, however, these developments—both the collective body of New Governance scholarship and the underlying social and political developments upon which that scholarship is predicated—have been widely un-

---

72. Copyright 2005, Minnesota Law Review. Reprinted with permission.

derappreciated in the legal academic literature at large. There may be several reasons for this.

First, by all accounts the actual transition of New Governance approaches to public problem solving thus far has been spotty. Innovations occur here and there, discernible within a number of disparate policy domains but dominant in few, and the outcomes of these scattered policy experiments remain ambiguous and contested. Even the most successful experiments have yet to be replicated widely, leaving them vulnerable to the skeptics' charge that their success depends upon factors unique to their own time, place, and fortuitous circumstances. Consequently, within any given field of inquiry, New Governance approaches may appear to some to be aberrational, idiosyncratic, or unproven, and the anecdotes and case studies heralding these developments unconvincing, except to the choir of the already converted.

Some fault may also lie in the narrow, subject-specific orientation of some New Governance scholars themselves, who may neglect to link observed innovations in their own fields to broader trends in patterns of social organization elsewhere, and who may not always be attentive to where their own work fits into the broader sweep of emerging New Governance scholarship. Additionally, some New Governance scholars may be more keenly attuned to the differences that separate their own work from that of others working in the same genre than to the commonalities that link them, even if at some level they recognize a distant kinship. Some, perhaps, may be more interested in winning debating points on the fine-grained particulars than in persuading a broader audience of the merits of the general approach.

Finally, in its sheer novelty, the recent profusion of New Governance scholarship has not yet settled upon a common nomenclature, leaving even the most dedicated reader with the daunting task of sorting through and translating a bewildering babel of unfamiliar, competing, and possibly incompatible terminology, which may or may not describe similar phenomena in different terms, or different phenomena in similar terms. In this area of scholarship, as in many others, contestation over naming rights appears to be half the battle, but as a byproduct it tends to generate opacity and outright confusion.

Taken as a whole, however—and setting aside for the moment both the underlying merits of New Governance approaches to public problem solving and the important conceptual differences that separate competing intellectual camps within this larger body of thought—the burgeoning New Governance literature surely represents a major trend, and arguably an important emerging intellectual movement in legal, public policy, and social science scholarship. It is high time that the participants, as well as the broader intellectual community, acknowledged as much.

NOTES

1. What role would lawyers play in the New Governance? In environmental law today, lawyers often play an adversarial role, initiating or defending compliance actions, or drafting or challenging regulations. Under the new governance model, such activities would no doubt continue, but lawyers would spend much more time doing transactional work—helping to negotiate standards or create management structures. Of course, many such activities already take place today, though we tend not to think of them as fundamental to the role of the environmental lawyer.

2. It remains to be seen whether reinvention will be a success, and if so, whether it will result in a fundamental shift in governance of the sort discussed by Karkkainen, or instead will be a supplement to more conventional forms of regulation. See David J. Sousa and Christopher McGrory Klyza, *New Direction in Environmental Policy Making: An Emerging Collaborative Regime or Reinventing Interest Group Liberalism?* 47 NAT. RES. J. 377 (2007). The study of the Endangered Species Act in the next chapter will provide you an opportunity to assess the pros and cons of efforts to transform conventional regulation.

3. Both conventional regulation and "reinvention" focus on behavior by business firms. An area of increasing interest concerns environmentally harmful behavior by individuals and possible ways of changing consumer conduct to reduce environmental impacts. For a survey, see Special Symposium Issue, 35 ENV. L. REP. 10721–10799 (2005).

CHAPTER 3

ENDANGERED SPECIES

■ ■ ■

A. INTRODUCTION TO THE ENDANGERED SPECIES ACT

The ESA seeks to protect species at risk of extinction. To do this, Congress crafted some rather powerful prohibitions and requirements. The statute provides for the listing of species as either "threatened" or "endangered," and once listed, the species are entitled to a variety of protections. These include a prohibition on any federal agency action likely to jeopardize their continued existence (so the ESA can block large infrastructure projects like dams and highways that are built, funded or sponsored by federal agencies), and an obligation to conserve the species and provide for their recovery. In addition, the Act prohibits anyone from "taking" listed endangered species, whether on public or private land. Because of these outright prohibitions and requirements, and their potential impact on private land, the ESA is very controversial. As you will see when you encounter the Clean Air Act, Clean Water Act, and hazardous waste laws in later chapters, the ESA is by comparison relatively simple and straightforward. Unlike the pollution laws, it is relatively free of technical jargon and detailed prescriptive standards. But it is far from mild-mannered.

Though it protects only individual species, the ESA might be viewed as a means of preserving habitat, or more broadly, biodiversity. The excerpt by Ledec and Goodland in Chapter 1 introduced you to arguments about why protecting individual species is so important to biodiversity. The excerpt below elaborates on those themes but stresses the instrumental value of species to humans.

JOHN KUNICH, PRESERVING THE WOMB OF THE UNKNOWN SPECIES WITH HOTSPOTS LEGISLATION[1]
52 HASTINGS L. J. 1149, 1162–69 (2001).

* * * If the ESA or other pieces of legislation are to be given a chance of making a difference, people will need to understand the benefits they

can expect to derive from the bargain. The reasons for humans to attempt to prevent the extinction of other creatures can be bundled into four main groups: (1) present practical value; (2) potential future practical value; (3) intangible value; and (4) moral duty. * * *

First, many species of plants and animals currently provide *Homo sapiens* with a variety of tangible, practical benefits of real value to people. A host of domesticated animals and crop plants are obvious examples, directly supplying nutrients for the human diet. * * * In addition to food, plants and animals are the producers of essentials such as cotton, wool, silk, leather, wood, paper, dyes, and their ancillary commodities. However, only twenty species provide ninety percent of the global food supply today, and three species (corn, wheat, and rice) contribute more than half of the total. Countless other species, currently known or unknown, could perhaps "be bred or provide genes to increase production in deserts, saline flats and other marginal habitats" to feed the world's expanding population in the future.

Plants are the source of many medicinal drugs, and about half of all prescription drugs in the United States come from wild organisms, of a total value estimated to exceed $14 billion per year. Our antibiotics, anticancer agents, pain killers, and blood thinners have been derived thus far from only a few hundred species, leaving the biochemistry and genetic components of millions of other species unexplored and untapped as a potentially colossal reservoir of new medicines and healing agents. * * *

The role of animals in medical and other scientific research has been of inestimable worth, and largely the contribution of otherwise insignificant or despised creatures such as the common mouse, rat, and fruit fly. Less obvious but still practical benefits come from creatures that facilitate the production of other plants or animals which in turn are consumed or otherwise used. This includes a vast array of insects, which pollinate many flowering plants, including fruit-bearing varieties, and which are the primary food source for many birds; it also includes annelids (earthworms) and other burrowing organisms which similarly play an unobtrusive yet vital role in aerating soil, making it suitable for producing plant life.

* * * In addition to all of the human-centered practical reasons for preserving species as individual species, there are tangible synergistic benefits produced by species interactions on an ecosystem level. The concept of "ecosystem services" is fairly new, but several enormously significant examples have been identified. These include the decomposition and detoxification of organic matter and other wastes, which is mostly performed by the smallest, least charismatic organisms in any ecosystem. * * * Other examples are generation and renewal of soil, mitigation of floods, purification of air and water, and partial stabilization of climate. * * *

Among the most fundamental of ecosystem services is the photosynthetic process of most plants, which not only fixes, or converts, solar energy into usable nutrients, but also converts carbon dioxide into oxygen, literally the life-breath of our species. And the exquisitely intricate natural system of checks and balances by which various species keep one another's populations—including those of pest and disease-causing organisms—within manageable limits is far more effective and safe than any pesticide program.

Most previously-identified species that provide obvious, practical benefits to humans are not in danger of extinction. In fact, many are actively safeguarded, raised, cultivated, and otherwise managed to maximize their productivity. There have been some cases of over-harvesting of such species, but for the most part this type of species is safe, due to our own self-interest. Of course, this presupposes that humans have (1) discovered the species and (2) learned of the benefits the species has to offer. In the case of the myriad unidentified species inhabiting the world's hotspots, neither of these presuppositions obtains.

The species that are less ostentatious about their value to people, moreover, may be even less fortunate. In some cases, for example, it is not even known which species of insects pollinate which useful plants, or which species are depended on by birds, fish, and other creatures for their sustenance, so humans may destroy or allow the destruction of these insects without realizing the consequences.

A second basic reason for humans to preserve species is that they may have future practical value to people. New uses are continually being discovered for living things, often transforming apparently inconsequential species into valuable assets. By definition, of course, it is impossible to know which or how many species fall into this category at any point in time. * * *

Each living species can be viewed as the end product of countless years of research and development, the culmination of eons of experimentation in nature's laboratory. * * * [W]ith the advent of genetic engineering, wherein it is increasingly possible to transfer genetic material from one taxonomic group to another (even across the kingdom barrier) to confer previously lacking biological traits, each species is potentially a significant genetic resource. * * *

It is possible, and even probable, that some currently "insignificant" species could take on a crucial role in the ecosystems of the future. Wild relatives of current crop species can be an invaluable source of genetic diversity in the event the monoculture cultivated plants fall prey to disease or other environmental conditions. And if environmental conditions change, through global warming, increased pollution, or other habitat alterations, some other species may possess traits that will prove preadapted to these new circumstances. Some species that occupy key positions in today's ecosystems may be unable to adapt, and unless other species are available to fill their niche, the ecosystems may suffer catastrophic degradation. The redundancy provided for by millions of years of natural selection cannot be fully understood and appreciated unless and until it is needed. It is not necessarily the large, obvious life forms that play these pivotal roles; in fact, the "lower" levels of the food web are the foundation upon which all other components of each ecosystem depend. * * *

* * * [S]ome species may be valuable precisely because they are endangered or threatened. A particularly vulnerable species within a given habitat may someday provide an early warning signal that there are problems that may eventually affect far more species. This has been termed the "canary in the mine" syndrome. * * *

A third main reason to preserve species is their intangible value. Although less practical, and less susceptible to being reduced to monetary worth, there is real wealth in living things. Many people find great beauty in nature, and nowhere else is the maxim more true that beauty is in the eye of the beholder. * * *

Other life forms also have intangible value as educational tools and entertainment sources. The persistent popularity of zoos, circuses, and televised nature programs is evidence of the deep-seated fascination other species hold for their human admirers. * * *

Finally, fourth, and least pragmatic, is the moral duty not to exterminate our fellow passengers on this planet. With its origins at least as ancient as the biblical injunction to "replenish" the earth as its caretakers, this moral duty has strong precedential support. Although most people accept the propriety of human use of other species for food, clothing, and other purposes, they likely would draw the line at exploiting these species into extinction.

* * * Additionally, people may want to preserve other species as a living legacy for their children and grandchildren, feeling it is wrong to deprive their posterity of a heritage their own ancestors had passed down for their enjoyment. * * *

The first ESA case to reach the Supreme Court, and the most famous, is excerpted below. It illustrates the potential power of the Act.

TENNESSEE VALLEY AUTHORITY v. HILL

Supreme Court of the United States, 1978.
437 U.S. 153, 98 S.Ct. 2279, 57 L.Ed.2d 117.

MR. CHIEF JUSTICE BURGER delivered the opinion of the Court.

I.

* * * [T]he Tennessee Valley Authority, a wholly owned public corporation of the United States, began constructing the Tellico Dam and Reservoir Project in 1967, shortly after Congress appropriated initial funds for its development. Tellico is a multipurpose regional development project designed principally to stimulate shoreline development, generate

sufficient electric current to heat 20,000 homes, and provide flatwater recreation and flood control, as well as improve economic conditions* * **. When fully operational, the dam would impound water covering some 16,500 acres—much of which represents valuable and productive farmland—thereby converting the river's shallow, fast-flowing waters into a deep reservoir over 30 miles in length.

The Tellico Dam has never opened, however, despite the fact that construction has been virtually completed and the dam is essentially ready for operation. Although Congress has appropriated monies for Tellico every year since 1967, progress was delayed, and ultimately stopped, by a tangle of lawsuits and administrative proceedings. After unsuccessfully urging TVA to consider alternatives to damming the Little Tennessee, local citizens and national conservation groups brought suit in the District Court, claiming that the project did not conform to the requirements of the National Environmental Policy Act of 1969 (NEPA)* * *. After finding TVA to be in violation of NEPA, the District Court enjoined the dam's completion pending the filing of an appropriate environmental impact statement. * * * The injunction remained in effect until late 1973, when the District Court concluded that TVA's final environmental impact statement for Tellico was in compliance with the law. * * *

A few months prior to the District Court's decision dissolving the NEPA injunction, a discovery was made in the waters of the Little Tennessee which would profoundly affect the Tellico Project. Exploring the area around Coytee Springs, which is about seven miles from the mouth of the river, a University of Tennessee ichthyologist, Dr. David A. Etnier, found a previously unknown species of perch, the snail darter, or *Percina (Imostoma) tanasi.* This three-inch, tannish-colored fish, whose numbers are estimated to be in the range of 10,000 to 15,000, would soon engage the attention of environmentalists, the TVA, the Department of the Interior, the Congress of the United States, and ultimately the federal courts, as a new and additional basis to halt construction of the dam. * * *

The moving force behind the snail darter's sudden fame came some four months after its discovery, when the Congress passed the Endangered Species Act of 1973 (Act), 87 Stat. 884, 16 U.S.C. § 1531 et seq. (1976 ed.). This legislation, among other things, authorizes the Secretary of the Interior to declare species of animal life "endangered" and to identify the "critical habitat" of these creatures. When a species or its habitat is so listed, the following portion of the Act—relevant here—becomes effective:

> "The Secretary [of the Interior] shall review other programs administered by him and utilize such programs in furtherance of the purposes of this chapter. All other Federal departments and agencies shall, in consultation with and with the assistance of the Secretary, utilize their authorities in furtherance of the purposes of this chapter by carrying out programs for the conservation of endangered species and threatened species listed pursuant to section 1533 of this title and *by*

taking such action necessary to insure that actions authorized, funded, or carried out by them do not jeopardize the continued existence of such endangered species and threatened species or result in the destruction or modification of habitat of such species which is determined by the Secretary, after consultation as appropriate with the affected States, to be critical." 16 U.S.C. § 1536 (1976 ed.) (emphasis added). * * *

In January 1975, the respondents in this case and others petitioned the Secretary of the Interior to list the snail darter as an endangered species. After receiving comments from various interested parties, including TVA and the State of Tennessee, the Secretary formally listed the snail darter as an endangered species on October 8, 1975. * * * In so acting, it was noted that "the snail darter is a living entity which is genetically distinct and reproductively isolated from other fishes." 40 Fed. Reg. 47505. More important for the purposes of this case, the Secretary determined that the snail darter apparently lives only in that portion of the Little Tennessee River which would be completely inundated by the reservoir created as a consequence of the Tellico Dam's completion. * * *

Subsequent to this determination, the Secretary declared the area of the Little Tennessee which would be affected by the Tellico Dam to be the "critical habitat" of the snail darter. * * * Using these determinations as a predicate, and notwithstanding the near completion of the dam, the Secretary declared that pursuant to § 7 of the Act, "all Federal agencies must take such action as is necessary to insure that actions authorized, funded, or carried out by them do not result in the destruction or modification of this critical habitat area." * * * This notice, of course, was pointedly directed at TVA and clearly aimed at halting completion or operation of the dam. * * *

Meanwhile, Congress had also become involved in the fate of the snail darter. Appearing before a Subcommittee of the House Committee on Appropriations in April 1975–some seven months before the snail darter was listed as endangered—TVA representatives described the discovery of the fish and the relevance of the Endangered Species Act to the Tellico Project. * * * At that time TVA presented a position which it would advance in successive forums thereafter, namely, that the Act did not prohibit the completion of a project authorized, funded, and substantially constructed before the Act was passed. TVA also described its efforts to transplant the snail darter, but contended that the dam should be finished regardless of the experiment's success. Thereafter, the House Committee on Appropriations, in its June 20, 1975, Report, stated the following in the course of recommending that an additional $29 million be appropriated for Tellico:

"The Committee directs that the project, for which an environmental impact statement has been completed and provided the Committee, should be completed as promptly as possible.…" H.R. Rep. No. 94–319, page 76 (1975). (Emphasis added.)

Congress then approved the TVA general budget, which contained funds for continued construction of the Tellico Project. In December 1975, one month after the snail darter was declared an endangered species, the President signed the bill into law. * * *

* * * The District Court found that closure of the dam and the consequent impoundment of the reservoir would "result in the adverse modification, if not complete destruction, of the snail darter's critical habitat," making it "highly probable" that "the continued existence of the snail darter" would be "[jeopardized]." * * * Despite these findings, the District Court declined to embrace the plaintiffs' position on the merits: that once a federal project was shown to jeopardize an endangered species, a court of equity is compelled to issue an injunction restraining violation of the Endangered Species Act. * * *

To accept the plaintiffs' position, the District Court argued, would inexorably lead to what it characterized as the absurd result of requiring "a court to halt impoundment of water behind a fully completed dam if an endangered species were discovered in the river on the day before such impoundment was scheduled to take place. We cannot conceive that Congress intended such a result." * * *

[I]n the Court of Appeals, respondents argued that the District Court had abused its discretion by not issuing an injunction in the face of "a blatant statutory violation." * * * The Court of Appeals agreed, and on January 31, 1977, it reversed, remanding "with instructions that a permanent injunction issue halting all activities incident to the Tellico Project which may destroy or modify the critical habitat of the snail darter." * * * The Court of Appeals directed that the injunction "remain in effect until Congress, by appropriate legislation, exempts Tellico from compliance with the Act or the snail darter has been deleted from the list of endangered species or its critical habitat materially redefined." * * *

Following the issuance of the permanent injunction, members of TVA's Board of Directors appeared before Subcommittees of the House and Senate Appropriations Committees to testify in support of continued appropriations for Tellico. The Subcommittees were apprised of all aspects of Tellico's status, including the Court of Appeals' decision. TVA reported that the dam stood "ready for the gates to be closed and the reservoir filled," * * * and requested funds for completion of certain ancillary parts of the project, such as public use areas, roads, and bridges. As to the snail darter itself, TVA commented optimistically on its transplantation efforts, expressing the opinion that the relocated fish were "doing well and [had] reproduced." * * *

Both Appropriations Committees subsequently recommended the full amount requested for completion of the Tellico Project. In its June 2, 1977, Report, the House Appropriations Committee stated:

"It is *the Committee's view* that the Endangered Species Act was not intended to halt projects such as these in their advanced stage of completion, and [the Committee] strongly recommends that these projects not be stopped because of misuse of the Act." H.R. Rep. No. 95–379, page 104. (Emphasis added.)

As a solution to the problem, the House Committee advised that TVA should cooperate with the Department of the Interior "to relocate the endangered species to another suitable habitat so as to permit the project to proceed as rapidly as possible." * * * Toward this end, the Committee recommended a special appropriation of $2 million to facilitate relocation of the snail darter and other endangered species which threatened to delay or stop TVA projects. Much the same occurred on the Senate side, with its Appropriations Committee recommending both the amount requested to complete Tellico and the special appropriation for transplantation of endangered species. Reporting to the Senate on these measures, the Appropriations Committee took a particularly strong stand on the snail darter issue:

> "This *committee has not viewed* the Endangered Species Act as preventing the completion and use of these projects which were well under way at the time the affected species were listed as endangered. If the act has such an effect, which is contrary to *the Committee's understanding* of the intent of Congress in enacting the Endangered Species Act, funds should be appropriated to allow these projects to be completed and their benefits realized in the public interest, the Endangered Species Act notwithstanding." S. Rep. No. 95–301, page 99 (1977). (Emphasis added.)

TVA's budget, including funds for completion of Tellico and relocation of the snail darter, passed both Houses of Congress and was signed into law on August 7, 1977. * * *

We granted certiorari, 434 U.S. 954 (1977), to review the judgment of the Court of Appeals.

II.

We begin with the premise that operation of the Tellico Dam will either eradicate the known population of snail darters or destroy their critical habitat. Petitioner does not now seriously dispute this fact. In any event, under § 4(a)(1) of the Act, 87 Stat. 886, 16 U.S.C. § 1533(a)(1) (1976 ed.), the Secretary of the Interior is vested with exclusive authority to determine whether a species such as the snail darter is "endangered" or "threatened" and to ascertain the factors which have led to such a precarious existence. By § 4(d) Congress has authorized—indeed commanded—the Secretary to "issue such regulations as he deems necessary and advisable to provide for the conservation of such species." 16 U.S.C. § 1533(d) (1976 ed.). As we have seen, the Secretary promulgated regulations which declared the snail darter an endangered species whose critical habitat would be destroyed by creation of the Tellico Reservoir. Doubtless petitioner would prefer not to have these regulations on the books, but there is no suggestion that the Secretary exceeded his authority or abused his discretion in issuing the regulations. Indeed, no judicial review of the

Secretary's determinations has ever been sought and hence the validity of his actions are not open to review in this Court. * * *

Starting from the above premise, two questions are presented: (a) would TVA be in violation of the Act if it completed and operated the Tellico Dam as planned? (b) if TVA's actions would offend the Act, is an injunction the appropriate remedy for the violation? For the reasons stated hereinafter, we hold that both questions must be answered in the affirmative.

A

It may seem curious to some that the survival of a relatively small number of three-inch fish among all the countless millions of species extant would require the permanent halting of a virtually completed dam for which Congress has expended more than $100 million. The paradox is not minimized by the fact that Congress continued to appropriate large sums of public money for the project, even after congressional Appropriations Committees were apprised of its apparent impact upon the survival of the snail darter. We conclude, however, that the explicit provisions of the Endangered Species Act require precisely that result.

One would be hard pressed to find a statutory provision whose terms were any plainer than those in § 7 of the Endangered Species Act. Its very words affirmatively command all federal agencies "to insure that actions authorized, funded, or carried out by them do not jeopardize the continued existence" of an endangered species or "result in the destruction or modification of habitat of such species...." 16 U.S.C. § 1536 (1976 ed.). (Emphasis added.) This language admits of no exception. Nonetheless, petitioner urges, as do the dissenters, that the Act cannot reasonably be interpreted as applying to a federal project which was well under way when Congress passed the Endangered Species Act of 1973. To sustain that position, however, we would be forced to ignore the ordinary meaning of plain language. It has not been shown, for example, how TVA can close the gates of the Tellico Dam without "carrying out" an action that has been "authorized" and "funded" by a federal agency. Nor can we understand how such action will "insure" that the snail darter's habitat is not disrupted.[2] Accepting the Secretary's determinations, as we must, it is

---

2. In dissent, MR. JUSTICE POWELL argues that the meaning of "actions" in § 7 is "far from 'plain,'" and that "it seems evident that the 'actions' referred to are not all actions that an agency can ever take, but rather actions that the agency is *deciding whether* to authorize, to fund, or to carry out." * * * Aside from this bare assertion, however, no explanation is given to support the proffered interpretation. This recalls Lewis Carroll's classic advice on the construction of language:

" 'When *I* use a word,' Humpty Dumpty said, in rather a scornful tone, 'it means just what *I* choose it to mean—neither more nor less.' " Through the Looking Glass, in The Complete Works of Lewis Carroll 196 (1939).

Aside from being unexplicated, the dissent's reading of § 7 is flawed on several counts. First, under its view, the words "or carry out" in § 7 would be superfluous since all prospective actions of an agency remain to be "authorized" or "funded." Second, the dissent's position logically means that an agency would be obligated to comply with § 7 only when a project is in the planning stage. But if Congress had meant to so limit the Act, it surely would have used words to that effect, as it did in the National Environmental Policy Act, 42 U.S.C. §§ 4332(2)(A), (C).

clear that TVA's proposed operation of the dam will have precisely the opposite effect, namely the eradication of an endangered species.

Concededly, this view of the Act will produce results requiring the sacrifice of the anticipated benefits of the project and of many millions of dollars in public funds. But examination of the language, history, and structure of the legislation under review here indicates beyond doubt that Congress intended endangered species to be afforded the highest of priorities. * * *

When Congress passed the Act in 1973, it was not legislating on a clean slate. The first major congressional concern for the preservation of the endangered species had come with passage of the Endangered Species Act of 1966 * * *. In that legislation Congress gave the Secretary power to identify "the names of the species of native fish and wildlife found to be threatened with extinction," * * * as well as authorization to purchase land for the conservation, protection, restoration, and propagation of "selected species" of "native fish and wildlife" threatened with extinction. * * * Declaring the preservation of endangered species a national policy, the 1966 Act directed all federal agencies both to protect these species and *"insofar as is practicable and consistent with [their] primary purposes,"* * * * "preserve the habitats of such threatened species on lands under their jurisdiction." * * * The 1966 statute was not a sweeping prohibition on the taking of endangered species, however, except on federal lands, * * * and even in those federal areas the Secretary was authorized to allow the hunting and fishing of endangered species. * * *

In 1969 Congress enacted the Endangered Species Conservation Act, * * * which continued the provisions of the 1966 Act while at the same time broadening federal involvement in the preservation of endangered species. Under the 1969 legislation, the Secretary was empowered to list species "threatened with worldwide extinction," * * * in addition, the importation of any species so recognized into the United States was prohibited. * * * An indirect approach to the taking of endangered species was also adopted in the Conservation Act by way of a ban on the transportation and sale of wildlife taken in violation of any federal, state, or foreign law. * * *

Despite the fact that the 1966 and 1969 legislation represented "the most comprehensive of its type to be enacted by any nation" up to that time, Congress was soon persuaded that a more expansive approach was needed if the newly declared national policy of preserving endangered species was to be realized. By 1973, when Congress held hearings on what would later become the Endangered Species Act of 1973, it was informed that species were still being lost at the rate of about one per year, * * * and "the pace of disappearance of species" appeared to be "accelerating." * * * Moreover, Congress was also told that the primary cause of this trend was something other than the normal process of natural selection:

> "[Man] and his technology has *[sic]* continued at an ever-increasing rate to disrupt the natural ecosystem. This has resulted in a dramatic

rise in the number and severity of the threats faced by the world's wildlife. The truth in this is apparent when one realizes that half of the recorded extinctions of mammals over the past 2,000 years have occurred in the most recent 50–year period." * * *

That Congress did not view these developments lightly was stressed by one commentator:

"The dominant theme pervading all congressional discussion of the proposed [Endangered Species Act of 1973] was the overriding need *to devote whatever effort and resources were necessary* to avoid further diminution of national and worldwide wildlife resources. Much of the testimony at the hearings and much debate was devoted to the biological problem of extinction. Senators and Congressmen uniformly deplored the irreplaceable loss to aesthetics, science, ecology, and the national heritage should more species disappear." * * *

The legislative proceedings in 1973 are, in fact, replete with expressions of concern over the risk that might lie in the loss of *any* endangered species. Typifying these sentiments is the Report of the House Committee on Merchant Marine and Fisheries on H.R. 37, a bill which contained the essential features of the subsequently enacted Act of 1973; in explaining the need for the legislation, the Report stated:

"As we homogenize the habitats in which these plants and animals evolved, and as we increase the pressure for products that they are in a position to supply (usually unwillingly) we threaten their—and our own—genetic heritage.

"The value of this genetic heritage is, quite literally, incalculable.
* * *

"Who knows, or can say, what potential cures for cancer or other scourges, present or future, may lie locked up in the structures of plants which may yet be undiscovered, much less analyzed? ... Sheer self-interest impels us to be cautious.* * * "

As the examples cited here demonstrate, Congress was concerned about the *unknown* uses that endangered species might have and about the *unforeseeable* place such creatures may have in the chain of life on this planet. * * *

In shaping legislation to deal with the problem thus presented, Congress started from the finding that "[the] two major causes of extinction are hunting and destruction of natural habitat." * * * Of these twin threats, Congress was informed that the greatest was destruction of natural habitats * * *. Virtually every bill introduced in Congress during the 1973 session responded to this concern by incorporating language similar, if not identical, to that found in the present § 7 of the Act. * * *

As it was finally passed, the Endangered Species Act of 1973 represented the most comprehensive legislation for the preservation of endangered species ever enacted by any nation. Its stated purposes were "to provide a means whereby the ecosystems upon which endangered species and threatened species depend may be conserved," and "to provide a program for the conservation of such ... species...." 16 U.S.C. § 1531(b) (1976 ed.). In furtherance of these goals, Congress expressly stated in § 2(c) that "all Federal departments and agencies *shall* seek *to conserve endangered species* and threatened species...." 16 U.S.C. § 1531(c) (1976 ed.). (Emphasis added.) Lest there be any ambiguity as to the meaning of this statutory directive, the Act specifically defined "conserve" as meaning "to use and the use of *all methods and procedures which are necessary* to bring *any endangered species* or threatened species to the point at which the measures provided pursuant to this chapter are no longer necessary." § 1532(2). (Emphasis added.) Aside from § 7, other provisions indicated the seriousness with which Congress viewed this issue: Virtually all dealings with endangered species, including taking, possession, transportation, and sale, were prohibited, 16 U.S.C. § 1538 (1976 ed.), except in extremely narrow circumstances, *see* § 1539(b). The Secretary was also given extensive power to develop regulations and programs for the preservation of endangered and threatened species. § 1533(d). Citizen involvement was encouraged by the Act, with provisions allowing interested persons to petition the Secretary to list a species as endangered or threatened, § 1533(c)(2), * * * and bring civil suits in United States district courts to force compliance with any provision of the Act, §§ 1540(c) and (g). * * *

Section 7 of the Act, which of course is relied upon by respondents in this case, provides a particularly good gauge of congressional intent. As we have seen, this provision had its genesis in the Endangered Species Act of 1966, but that legislation qualified the obligation of federal agencies by stating that they should seek to preserve endangered species only "*insofar as is practicable and consistent with [their] primary purposes....*" Likewise, every bill introduced in 1973 contained a qualification similar to that found in the earlier statutes. * * *

What is very significant in this sequence is that the final version of the 1973 Act carefully omitted all of the reservations described above. * * * [I]ndeed all phrases which might have qualified an agency's responsibilities had been omitted from the [House version of the] bill. * * *

* * * The Conference Report, H.R. Conf. Rep. No. 93–740 (1973), basically adopted the Senate bill, S. 1983; but the conferees rejected the Senate version of § 7 and adopted the stringent, mandatory language in H.R. 37. While the Conference Report made no specific reference to this choice of provisions, the House manager of the bill, Representative Dingell, provided an interpretation of what the Conference bill would require, making it clear that the mandatory provisions of § 7 were not casually or inadvertently included:

> "[Section 7] substantially [amplifies] the obligation of [federal agencies] to take steps within their power to carry out the purposes of this act. * * *

"The purposes of the bill included the conservation of the species and of the ecosystems upon which they depend, and *every agency of government is committed* to see that those purposes are carried out.... [The] agencies of Government can no longer plead that they can do nothing about it. *They can, and they must. The law is clear.*" 119 Cong. Rec. 42913 (1973). (Emphasis added.)

It is against this legislative background that we must measure TVA's claim that the Act was not intended to stop operation of a project which, like Tellico Dam, was near completion when an endangered species was discovered in its path. While there is no discussion in the legislative history of precisely this problem, the totality of congressional action makes it abundantly clear that the result we reach today is wholly in accord with both the words of the statute and the intent of Congress. The plain intent of Congress in enacting this statute was to halt and reverse the trend toward species extinction, whatever the cost. This is reflected not only in the stated policies of the Act, but in literally every section of the statute. All persons, including federal agencies, are specifically instructed not to "take" endangered species, meaning that no one is "to harass, harm, pursue, hunt, shoot, wound, kill, trap, capture, or collect" such life forms. * * * Agencies in particular are directed * * * to "use ... *all methods* and procedures which are necessary" to preserve endangered species. * * * In addition, the legislative history undergirding § 7 reveals an explicit congressional decision to require agencies to afford first priority to the declared national policy of saving endangered species. The pointed omission of the type of qualifying language previously included in endangered species legislation reveals a conscious decision by Congress to give endangered species priority over the "primary missions" of federal agencies. * * *

[I]t is clear Congress foresaw that § 7 would, on occasion, require agencies to alter ongoing projects in order to fulfill the goals of the Act. Congressman Dingell's discussion of Air Force practice bombing, for instance, obviously pinpoints a particular activity—intimately related to the national defense—which a major federal department would be obliged to alter in deference to the strictures of § 7. * * *

One might dispute the applicability of these examples to the Tellico Dam by saying that in this case the burden on the public through the loss of millions of unrecoverable dollars would greatly outweigh the loss of the snail darter. But neither the Endangered Species Act nor Art. III of the Constitution provides federal courts with authority to make such fine utilitarian calculations. On the contrary, the plain language of the Act, buttressed by its legislative history, shows clearly that Congress viewed the value of endangered species as "incalculable." Quite obviously, it would be difficult for a court to balance the loss of a sum certain—even $100 million—against a congressionally declared "incalculable" value, even assuming we had the power to engage in such a weighing process, which we emphatically do not. * * *

In passing the Endangered Species Act of 1973, Congress was also aware of certain instances in which exceptions to the statute's broad sweep would be necessary. Thus, § 10, 16 U.S.C. § 1539 (1976 ed.), creates a number of limited "hardship exemptions," none of which would even remotely apply to the Tellico Project. In fact, there are no exemptions in the Endangered Species Act for federal agencies, meaning that under the maxim *expressio unius est exclusio alterius*, we must presume that these were the only "hardship cases" Congress intended to exempt. * * *

Notwithstanding Congress' expression of intent in 1973, we are urged to find that the continuing appropriations for Tellico Dam constitute an implied repeal of the 1973 Act, at least insofar as it applies to the Tellico Project. In support of this view, TVA points to the statements found in various House and Senate Appropriations Committees' Reports* * *. Since we are unwilling to assume that these latter Committee statements constituted advice to ignore the provisions of a duly enacted law, we assume that these Committees believed that the Act simply was not applicable in this situation. But even under this interpretation of the Committees' actions, we are unable to conclude that the Act has been in any respect amended or repealed.

There is nothing in the appropriations measures, as passed, which states that the Tellico Project was to be completed irrespective of the requirements of the Endangered Species Act. These appropriations, in fact, represented relatively minor components of the lump-sum amounts for the *entire* TVA budget. To find a repeal of the Endangered Species Act under these circumstances would surely do violence to the " 'cardinal rule ... that repeals by implication are not favored.' " *Morton v. Mancari*, 417 U.S. 535, 549 (1974)* * *. In practical terms, this "cardinal rule" means that "[in] the absence of some affirmative showing of an intention to repeal, the only permissible justification for a repeal by implication is when the earlier and later statutes are irreconcilable." *Mancari, supra*, at 550.

The doctrine disfavoring repeals by implication "applies with full vigor when ... the subsequent legislation is an *appropriations* measure." * * * This is perhaps an understatement since it would be more accurate to say that the policy applies with even *greater* force when the claimed repeal rests solely on an Appropriations Act. We recognize that both substantive enactments and appropriations measures are "Acts of Congress," but the latter have the limited and specific purpose of providing funds for authorized programs. When voting on appropriations measures, legislators are entitled to operate under the assumption that the funds will be devoted to purposes which are lawful and not for any purpose forbidden. Without such an assurance, every appropriations measure would be pregnant with prospects of altering substantive legislation, repealing by implication any prior statute which might prohibit the expenditure. Not only would this lead to the absurd result of requiring Members to review exhaustively the background of every authorization before voting on an appropriation, but it would flout the very rules the Congress carefully adopted to avoid this need. * * * Thus, to sustain petitioner's position, we would be obliged to assume that Congress meant to repeal *pro tanto* § 7 of the Act by means of a procedure expressly prohibited under the rules of Congress.

Perhaps mindful of the fact that it is "swimming upstream" against a strong current of well-established precedent, TVA argues for an exception to the rule against implied repealers in a circumstance where, as here, Appropriations Committees have expressly stated their "understanding" that the earlier legislation would not prohibit the proposed expenditure. We cannot accept such a proposition. Expressions of committees dealing with requests for appropriations cannot be equated with statutes enacted by Congress, particularly not in the circumstances presented by this case. First, the Appropriations Committees had no jurisdiction over the subject of endangered species, much less did they conduct the type of extensive hearings which preceded passage of the earlier Endangered Species Acts, especially the 1973 Act. * * *

Second, there is no indication that Congress as a whole was aware of TVA's position, although the Appropriations Committees apparently agreed with petitioner's views. Only recently, in *SEC* v. *Sloan*, 436 U.S. 103 (1978), we declined to presume general congressional acquiescence in a 34–year–old practice of the Securities and Exchange Commission, despite the fact that the Senate Committee *having jurisdiction over the Commission's activities* had long expressed approval of the practice. * * *

B

Having determined that there is an irreconcilable conflict between operation of the Tellico Dam and the explicit provisions of § 7 of the Endangered Species Act, we must now consider what remedy, if any, is appropriate. It is correct, of course, that a federal judge sitting as a chancellor is not mechanically obligated to grant an injunction for every violation of law. * * *

But these principles take a court only so far. Our system of government is, after all, a tripartite one, with each branch having certain defined functions delegated to it by the Constitution. While "[it] is emphatically the province and duty of the judicial department to say what the law is," *Marbury v. Madison*, 1 Cranch 137, 177 (1803), it is equally—and emphatically—the exclusive province of the Congress not only to formulate legislative policies and mandate programs and projects, but also to establish their relative priority for the Nation. Once Congress, exercising its delegated powers, has decided the order of priorities in a given area, it is for the Executive to administer the laws and for the courts to enforce them when enforcement is sought.

Here we are urged to view the Endangered Species Act "reasonably," and hence shape a remedy "that accords with some modicum of common sense and the public weal." * * * But is that our function? We have no expert knowledge on the subject of endangered species, much less do we have a mandate from the people to strike a balance of equities on the side of the Tellico Dam. Congress has spoken in the plainest of words, making it abundantly clear that the balance has been struck in favor of affording endangered species the highest of priorities, thereby adopting a policy which it described as "institutionalized caution."

Our individual appraisal of the wisdom or unwisdom of a particular course consciously selected by the Congress is to be put aside in the process of interpreting a statute. Once the meaning of an enactment is discerned and its constitutionality determined, the judicial process comes to an end. We do not sit as a committee of review, nor are we vested with the power of veto. The lines ascribed to Sir Thomas More by Robert Bolt are not without relevance here:

> "The law, Roper, the law. I know what's legal, not what's right. And I'll stick to what's legal.... I'm *not* God. The currents and eddies of right and wrong, which you find such plain-sailing, I can't navigate, I'm no voyager. But in the thickets of the law, oh there I'm a forester.... What would you do? Cut a great road through the law to get after the Devil? ... And when the last law was down, and the Devil turned round on you—where would you hide, Roper, the laws all being flat? ... This country's planted thick with laws from coast to coast—Man's laws, not God's—and if you cut them down ... d'you really think you could stand upright in the winds that would below then? ... Yes, I'd give the Devil benefit of law, for my own safety's sake."

We agree with the Court of Appeals that in our constitutional system the commitment to the separation of powers is too fundamental for us to pre-empt congressional action by judicially decreeing what accords with "common sense and the public weal." Our Constitution vests such responsibilities in the political branches.

Affirmed.

MR. JUSTICE POWELL, with whom MR. JUSTICE BLACKMUN joins, dissenting.

The Court today holds that § 7 of the Endangered Species Act requires a federal court, for the purpose of protecting an endangered species or its habitat, to enjoin permanently the operation of any federal project, whether completed or substantially completed. This decision casts a long shadow over the operation of even the most important projects, serving vital needs of society and national defense, whenever it is determined that continued operation would threaten extinction of an endangered species or its habitat. This result is said to be required by the "plain intent of Congress" as well as by the language of the statute.

In my view § 7 cannot reasonably be interpreted as applying to a project that is completed or substantially completed when its threat to an endangered species is discovered. Nor can I believe that Congress could have intended this Act to produce the "absurd result"—in the words of the District Court—of this case. If it were clear from the language of the Act and its legislative history that Congress intended to authorize this result, this Court would be compelled to enforce it. It is not our province to rectify policy or political judgments by the Legislative Branch, however egregiously they may disserve the public interest. But where the statutory language and legislative history, as in this case, need not be construed to reach such a result, I view it as the duty of this Court to adopt a permissible construction that accords with some modicum of common sense and the public weal. * * *

Today the Court, like the Court of Appeals below, adopts a reading of § 7 of the Act that gives it a retroactive effect and disregards 12 years of consistently expressed congressional intent to complete the Tellico Project. With all due respect, I view this result as an extreme example of a literalist construction, not required by the language of the Act and adopted without regard to its manifest purpose. Moreover, it ignores established canons of statutory construction. * * *

The critical word in § 7 is "actions" and its meaning is far from "plain." It is part of the phrase: "actions authorized, funded or carried out." In terms of planning and executing various activities, it seems evident that the "actions" referred to are not all actions that an agency can ever take, but rather actions that the agency is *deciding whether* to authorize, to fund, or to carry out. In short, these words reasonably may be read as applying only to *prospective actions* * * *. The Court concedes that as of this time and for the purpose of deciding this case, the Tellico Dam Project is "completed" or "virtually completed and the dam is essentially ready for operation * * *." Thus, under a prospective reading of § 7, the action already had been "carried out" in terms of any remaining reasonable decisionmaking power. * * *

* * * [U]nder § 7 of the Endangered Species Act, at some stage of a federal project, and certainly where a project has been completed, the agency no longer has a reasonable choice simply to abandon it. When that point is reached, as it was in this case, the presumption against retrospective interpretation is at its strongest. The Court today gives no weight to that presumption. * * *

If the relevant Committees that considered the Act, and the Members of Congress who voted on it, had been aware that the Act could be used to terminate major federal projects authorized years earlier and nearly completed, * * * we can be certain that there would have been hearings, testimony, and debate * * *. The absence of any such consideration by the Committees or in the floor debates indicates quite clearly that no one participating in the legislative process considered these consequences as within the intendment of the Act. * * *

* * * [T]his view of legislative intent at the time of enactment is abundantly confirmed by the subsequent congressional actions and expressions. * * *

I have little doubt that Congress will amend the Endangered Species Act to prevent the grave consequences made possible by today's decision. Few, if any, Members of that body will wish to defend an interpretation of the Act that requires the waste of at least $53 million, * * * and denies the people of the Tennessee Valley area the benefits of the reservoir that Congress intended to confer. There will be little sentiment to leave this dam standing before an empty reservoir, serving no purpose other than a conversation piece for incredulous tourists.

But more far reaching than the adverse effect on the people of this economically depressed area is the continuing threat to the operation of every federal project, no matter how important to the Nation. If Congress acts expeditiously, as may be anticipated, the Court's decision probably will have no lasting adverse consequences. But I had not thought it to be the province of this Court to force Congress into otherwise unnecessary action by interpreting a statute to produce a result no one intended.

MR. JUSTICE REHNQUIST, dissenting.

In the light of my Brother Powell's dissenting opinion, I am far less convinced than is the Court that the Endangered Species Act of 1973 * * * was intended to prohibit the completion of the Tellico Dam. But the very difficulty and doubtfulness of the correct answer to this legal question convinces me that the Act did *not* prohibit the District Court from refusing, in the exercise of its traditional equitable powers, to enjoin petitioner from completing the Dam. § 11(g)(1) of the Act * * * merely provides that "any person may commence a civil suit on his own behalf ... to enjoin any person, including the United States and any other governmental instrumentality or agency ..., who is alleged to be in violation of any provision of this chapter." * * *

* * * I choose to adhere to *Hecht Co.*'s teaching:

"A grant of *jurisdiction* to issue compliance orders hardly suggests an absolute duty to do so under any and all circumstances. We cannot but think that if Congress had intended to make such a drastic departure from the traditions of equity practice, an unequivocal statement of its purpose would have been made." * * *

* * * Here the District Court recognized that Congress, when it enacted the Endangered Species Act, made the preservation of the habitat of the snail darter an important public concern. But it concluded that this interest on one side of the balance was more than outweighed by other equally significant factors. These factors, further elaborated in the dissent of my Brother Powell, satisfy me that the District Court's refusal to issue an injunction was not an abuse of its discretion. I therefore dissent from the Court's opinion holding otherwise.

NOTES

1. In response to *TVA v. Hill,* Congress amended the Endangered Species Act by creating a special Endangered Species Committee, consisting of

several cabinet level officers and other high-ranking officials. The Committee may grant an exemption to § 7's "no jeopardy" prohibition if it determines (by a vote of at least 5 to 2) that there are no reasonable alternatives to the agency action, that the benefits clearly outweigh those of compliance with the Act, and that the action is in the public interest and of at least regional significance. The Committee must also consider mitigation efforts. (These provisions are found in Endangered Species Amendment of 1978, § 7(e), (h), 16 U.S.C. § 1536(e), (h).) The Committee unanimously denied an exemption for Tellico Dam, on the ground that reasonable alternatives to completion of the dam were available with acceptable cost-benefit ratios. The Committee also found that, despite the $100 million already invested in the dam, the benefits of completing the dam did not clearly outweigh the benefits of the alternatives. Essentially, the dam might easily fail to produce as much economic benefit as the farms it would flood. Congress then passed a bill mandating completion of the dam. Does this further history show that the Supreme Court's decision was an exercise in futility, or does it show on the contrary that the Court was right to "remand" the problem to Congress? Should the Court have given a more "reasonable" interpretation to the ESA? Or would that have been inconsistent with the legislative mandate? *See* Daniel A. Farber, *Statutory Interpretation and Legislative Supremacy*, 78 GEO. L.J. 281, 294–298 (1989). For a retrospective view on *TVA v. Hill, see* Zygmunt J.B. Plater, *In the Wake of the Snail Darter*, 19 U. MICH. J.L. REFORM 805 (1986).

2. As the first Endangered Species Act case before the Supreme Court, *TVA v. Hill* is (and was) viewed to be about as bad a set of facts as environmental plaintiffs could have hoped for. The species in question was a small, neutral-colored fish whose existence was completely unknown before the project began, and the project itself was a nearly completed dam with, purportedly, important economic and political benefits. Though the litigation later uncovered the fact that the dam was a "pork barrel" project the benefits of which were suspect at best, this was not widely known at the outset. You may wonder how a dam could ever be approved in the first place if even the relatively small marginal cost of completion was not clearly outweighed by the benefits. For a study of the pathology of government cost-benefit analyses for dams during this period, *see* Roger W. Findley, *The Planning of a Corps of Engineers Reservoir Project: Law, Economics and Politics*, 3 ECOLOGY L.Q. 1 (1973). Pragmatically speaking, it seemed clear that the case should fail. It was remarkable, then, that the Supreme Court ruled the way it did, adhering faithfully to the stringency of the law and setting aside the pragmatic aspects of the case as irrelevant. Imagine instead that the species in question was charismatic megafauna or that the project was much smaller. Would the outcome have been different? As controversial?

B. LISTING: SECTION 4

1. LISTING ENDANGERED AND THREATENED SPECIES

The first step in the statutory scheme of the Endangered Species Act is the listing of endangered or threatened species. Under § 4 of the Act, the Secretary of the Interior (in the case of land-based and freshwater species) or the Secretary of Commerce (in the case of marine species) shall:

> determine whether any species is an endangered species or a threatened species because of any of the following factors:
>
> > (A) the present or threatened destruction, modification, or curtailment of its habitat or range;
> >
> > (B) overutilization for commercial, recreational, scientific, or educational purposes;
> >
> > (C) disease or predation;
> >
> > (D) the inadequacy of existing regulatory mechanisms; or
> >
> > (E) other natural or manmade factors affecting its continued existence.

16 U.S.C. § 1533(a) (2000).

The Act defines an "endangered species" as "any species which is in danger of extinction throughout all or a significant portion of its range...." 16 U.S.C. § 1532(6) (2000). A "threatened species," on the other hand, is "any species which is likely to become an endangered species within the foreseeable future throughout all or a significant portion of its range." 16 U.S.C. § 1532(20).

In the listing of a species, the Secretary may not consider economic impacts. Rather, the Secretary must make the determination "solely on the basis of the best scientific and commercial data available to him." 16 U.S.C. § 1533(b)(1)(A). *See New Mexico Cattle Growers Ass'n v. United States Fish & Wildlife Serv.*, 248 F.3d 1277 (10th Cir. 2001) (holding that Service may not consider economic impacts in listing decision). *See also Center for Biological Diversity v. Badgley*, 335 F.3d 1097 (9th Cir. 2003) (holding decision not to list was based only on best available scientific and commercial data and therefore was not arbitrary or capricious).

In the designation of critical habitat, however, discussed *infra*, which is made at the same time as the listing of the species, the Secretary may consider other factors, including "the economic impact, the impact on national security, and any other relevant impact." 16 U.S.C. § 1533(b)(2).

The saga of the spotted owl nicely illustrates the workings of the listing process. It began in the late 1980s, when environmental groups petitioned for the listing of the owl, a bird whose habitat was (and is) the remaining stands of old-growth forest native to the Pacific Northwest. Because of continued and increasing logging of old-growth forests, the owl's habitat had been diminished greatly. Although biologists and environmentalists agreed that the species should be listed at the very least as threatened, the Fish and Wildlife Service under the Reagan Administration claimed that a listing was not warranted. Environmental groups consequently brought suit to compel the listing.

NORTHERN SPOTTED OWL v. HODEL

United States District Court for the Western District of Washington, 1988.
716 F.Supp. 479.

THOMAS S. ZILLY, UNITED STATES DISTRICT JUDGE.

A number of environmental organizations bring this action against the United States Fish & Wildlife Service ("Service") and others, alleging that the Service's decision not to list the northern spotted owl as endangered or threatened under the Endangered Species Act of 1973, as amended, 16 U.S.C. § 1531 et seq. ("ESA" or "the Act"), was arbitrary and capricious or contrary to law.

Since the 1970s the northern spotted owl has received much scientific attention, beginning with comprehensive studies of its natural history by Dr. Eric Forsman, whose most significant discovery was the close association between spotted owls and old-growth forests. This discovery raised concerns because the majority of remaining old-growth owl habitat is on public land available for harvest.

In January 1987, plaintiff Greenworld, pursuant to Sec. 4(b)(3) of the ESA, 16 U.S.C. § 1533(b)(3), petitioned the Service to list the northern spotted owl as endangered. In August 1987, 29 conservation organizations filed a second petition to list the owl as endangered both in the Olympic Peninsula in Washington and in the Oregon Coast Range, and as threatened throughout the rest of its range.

The ESA directs the Secretary of the Interior to determine whether any species have become endangered or threatened[3] due to habitat destruction, overutilization, disease or predation, or other natural or manmade factors. 16 U.S.C. § 1533(a)(1). The Act was amended in 1982 to ensure that the decision whether to list a species as endangered or threatened was based solely on an evaluation of the biological risks faced by the species, to the exclusion of all other factors. *See* Conf. Report 97–835, 97th Cong. 2d Sess. (Sept. 17, 1982) at 19, reprinted in 1982 U.S. Code Cong. & Admin. News 2860.

The Service's role in deciding whether to list the northern spotted owl as endangered or threatened is to assess the technical and scientific data in the administrative record against the relevant listing criteria in

---

3. The ESA defines an "endangered species" as "any species which is in danger of extinction throughout all or a significant portion of its range...." 16 U.S.C. § 1532(6). A "threatened species" is "any species which is likely to become an endangered species within the foreseeable future throughout all or a significant portion of its range." 16 U.S.C. § 1532(20).

§ 4(a)(1) and then to exercise its own expert discretion in reaching its decision. *Cayman Turtle Farm, Ltd. v. Andrus*, 478 F.Supp. 125, 131 (D.C. Cir. 1979).

In July 1987, the Service announced that it would initiate a status review of the spotted owl and requested public comment. 52 Fed. Reg. 34396 (Sept. 11, 1987). The Service assembled a group of Service biologists, including Dr. Mark Shaffer, its staff expert on population viability, to conduct the review. The Service charged Dr. Shaffer with analyzing current scientific information on the owl. Dr. Shaffer concluded that:

> the most reasonable interpretation of current data and knowledge indicate continued old growth harvesting is likely to lead to the extinction of the subspecies in the foreseeable future which argues strongly for listing the subspecies as threatened or endangered at this time.

M. Shaffer, letter of November 11, 1987, to Jay Gore, U.S. Fish and Wildlife Service, Region 1, Endangered Species, attached to Final Assessment of Population Viability Projections for the Northern Spotted Owl [Administrative Record at III.A.1].

The Service invited a peer review of Dr. Shaffer's analysis by a number of U.S. experts on population viability, all of whom agreed with Dr. Shaffer's prognosis for the owl, although each had some criticisms of his work.

The Service's decision is contained in its 1987 Status Review of the owl ("Status Review") [Administrative Record at II.C] and summarized in its Finding on Greenworld's petition ("Finding") [Administrative Record at I.D.1]. The Status Review was completed on December 14, 1987, and on December 17 the Service announced that listing the owl as endangered under the Act was not warranted at that time. 52 Fed. Reg. 48552, 48554 (Dec. 23, 1987). This suit followed. Both sides now move for summary judgment on the administrative record before the Court.* * *

The Status Review and the Finding to the listing petition offer little insight into how the Service found that the owl currently has a viable population. Although the Status Review cites extensive empirical data and lists various conclusions, it fails to provide any analysis. The Service asserts that it is entitled to make its own decision, yet it provides no explanation for its findings. An agency must set forth clearly the grounds on which it acted. *Atchison T. & S.F. Ry. v. Wichita Bd. of Trade*, 412 U.S. 800, 807, 37 L. Ed. 2d 350, 93 S. Ct. 2367 (1973). Judicial deference to agency expertise is proper, but the Court will not do so blindly. The Court finds that the Service has not set forth the grounds for its decision against listing the owl.

The Service's documents also lack any expert analysis supporting its conclusion. Rather, the expert opinion is entirely to the contrary. The only reference in the Status Review to an actual opinion that the owl does not face a significant likelihood of extinction is a mischaracterization of a conclusion of Dr. Mark Boyce:

> Boyce (1987) in his analysis of the draft preferred alternative concluded that there is a low probability that the spotted owls will go extinct. He does point out that population fragmentation appears to impose the greatest risks to extinction.

Status Review at 24 * * *. Dr. Boyce responded to the Service:

> I did not conclude that the Spotted Owl enjoys a low probability of extinction, and I would be very disappointed if efforts to preserve the Spotted Owl were in any way thwarted by a misinterpretation of something I wrote.

M. Boyce, letter of February 18, 1988, to Rolf Wallenstrom, U.S. Fish and Wildlife Service, Region 1, exhibit 7 to Complaint. * * *

Numerous other experts on population viability contributed to or reviewed drafts of the Status Review, or otherwise assessed spotted owl viability. Some were employed by the Service; others were independent. None concluded that the northern spotted owl is not at risk of extinction.* * *

The Service invited a peer review of Dr. Shaffer's analysis. Drs. Michael Soule, Bruce Wilcox, and Daniel Goodman, three leading U.S. experts on population viability, reviewed and agreed completely with Dr. Shaffer's prognosis for the owl.

For example, Dr. Soule, the acknowledged founder of the discipline of "conservation biology" (the study of species extinction), concluded:

> I completely concur with your conclusions, and the methods by which you reached them. The more one hears about *Strix occidentalis caurina*, the more concern one feels. Problems with the data base and in the models notwithstanding, and politics notwithstanding, I just can't see how a responsible biologist could reach any other conclusion than yours.

M. Soule, letter of November 1, 1987, to Dr. Mark Shaffer [Administrative Record at III.B.4].

The Court will reject conclusory assertions of agency "expertise" where the agency spurns unrebutted expert opinions without itself offering a credible alternative explanation. *See, e.g., American Tunaboat Ass'n v. Baldrige*, 738 F.2d 1013, 1016 (9th Cir. 1984). Here, the Service disregarded all the expert opinion on population viability, including that of its own expert, that the owl is facing extinction, and instead merely asserted its expertise in support of its conclusions. The Service has failed to provide its own or other expert analysis supporting its conclusions. Such analysis is necessary to establish a rational connection between the evidence presented and the Service's decision. Accordingly, the United States Fish and Wildlife Service's decision not to list at this time the northern spotted owl as endangered or threatened under the Endangered Species Act was arbitrary and capricious and contrary to law.

The Court further finds that it is not possible from the record to determine that the Service considered the related issue of whether the northern spotted owl is a threatened species. This failure of the Service to review and make an express finding on the issue of threatened status is also arbitrary and capricious and contrary to law.

In deference to the Service's expertise and its role under the Endangered Species Act, the Court remands this matter to the Service, which has 90 days from the date of this order to provide an analysis for its decision that listing the northern spotted owl as threatened or endangered is not currently warranted. Further, the Service is ordered to supplement its Status Review and petition Finding consistent with this Court's ruling.

It is so ordered.

NOTES

1.   In the aftermath of the *Northern Spotted Owl* decision, the Fish and Wildlife Service was forced to return to its status review of the owl. In 1989, the Service proposed that the owl be listed as a threatened species throughout all its range in the Pacific Northwest and British Columbia. *See* Proposed Threatened Status for the Northern Spotted Owl, 54 Fed. Reg. 26,666 (June 23, 1989). In the same notice, the Service declined, however, to designate critical habitat for the owl, as it found the habitat to be "not presently determinable." *Id.* at 26,675. Consequently, as will be excerpted and discussed in more depth *infra*, the Service had set itself up for the next round of litigation.

2.   Throughout the statutory text of the ESA, the relevant agency actor is typically the "Secretary." Within ESA cases, however, the courts typically refer to the U.S. Fish and Wildlife Service or the NOAA Fisheries Service (previously titled "the National Marine Fisheries Service" (NMFS)). In short form, the courts often will refer to these two agencies as the "Services." This can be confusing, but some brief history is helpful.

At the time of the Act's passage in 1973, the "Secretary" referred to the Secretary of Interior, whose department housed the U.S. Fish and Wildlife Service (FWS), and the Secretary of Commerce, whose department housed the National Marine Fisheries Service. As noted above, FWS is responsible for land-based and freshwater species, while NOAA Fisheries is responsible for all marine species and anadromous fish, which spend their lives in both fresh and saltwater. The reason for the divide between the two agencies is that, in 1970, President Nixon proposed a reorganization plan, under which the jurisdiction over marine fisheries would be transferred from the Department of Interior to the Department of Commerce. The two wildlife agencies under the departments often must work closely together, but the technical and legal divide still exists. For example, the agencies operate under different sets of regulations, and the agencies must be listed as individual parties where suit is brought against both.

For the purposes of this chapter, the terms "Secretary" or "Service" should be understood as referring to the respective wildlife agency being discussed.

3. As noted in the statutory text, *supra*, the Secretary must consider five factors under § 4(a)(1) in determining whether to list a species. If the Secretary determines that one or more of the five factors demonstrates that a species is endangered or threatened, she must list the species as such. In *Defenders of Wildlife v. Norton*, 258 F.3d 1136 (9th Cir. 2001), the Court overturned the Secretary's decision not to list the flat-tailed horned lizard, as the Secretary had failed to consider properly all five of the factors in determining whether the lizard was threatened or endangered. The Secretary earlier had recommended the lizard for listing but later withdrew the recommendation on the basis of new factors, including a newly devised conservation agreement and that, in spite of ongoing threats on private land, the lizard still had "large blocks of habitat with few anticipated impacts . . . on public lands throughout the range of th[e] species." Looking to the definition of endangered under § 3(6), "in danger of extinction throughout . . . a significant portion of its range," the court held that the Secretary, by excluding consideration of the private lands, failed properly to address this danger of extinction.

4. What is the "best available science" mandate that the statute references, *supra*? According to Holly Doremus, there is little to guide us on this point in the ESA itself, its legislative history, or the Services' regulations. The Services have, however, issued two policy statements that give more substance to the mandate.

> One deals with the use of information. It requires evaluation by biologists of all information used in listing, recovery planning, preparation of biological opinions, and issuance of permits, and documentation of that evaluation. It also directs agency biologists to prefer primary sources when possible and to affirmatively seek and impartially evaluate data contrary to the agency's official position or proposed actions.

> The second policy statement calls for the wildlife agencies to seek peer review of listing proposals by three independent specialists and to actively solicit peer review of draft recovery plans. In both cases, the final document must summarize the opinions of the reviewers, and the full opinions must be included in the administrative record. * * * In individual listing decisions, FWS has recognized that expert judgment plays a legitimate role in the analysis of data, and that internal technical review of the sort typical of many government reports carries indicia of reliability.

Holly Doremus, Symposium Article, *The Purposes, Effects, and Future of the Endangered Species Act's Best Available Science Mandate*, 34 ENVTL. L. 397, 408–09 (2004). Doremus speculates that the "best available science" mandate serves any or all of four purposes: (1) the promotion of more accurate decision making; (2) increasing public trust and political credibility; (3) affecting judicial review, either by invoking special deference or, alternatively, by inviting more stringent review by giving the courts another standard to enforce; and (4) altering the decision-making process substantively one way or another. *Id.* at 418.

5. There are suspicions, however, that the listing process is driven in part by politics and not just scientific data. Indeed, there is some empirical evidence to this effect. Consider the following excerpt, which summarizes an empirical study of the listing process, showing congressional influence over it.

> Our data show that a member's "institutional identities"—party affiliation, committee jurisdiction, and chamber—determine the relative influence of that member with regard to the implementation of the ESA. Moreover, once these institutional identities are aggregated, their cumulative impact strongly influences both whether a subspecies will be listed and the amount of funding allocated for its recovery. Generally, we find that statutory criteria weakly affect listing and funding decisions, and that institutional identity and the influence derived therefrom have a significant effect.

> Note that these aggregated institutional identities, which amount to political considerations—the number of representatives per species on the committee, the location of the committee in House or Senate, and the party affiliation of committee members—have nothing to do with the subspecies' endangerment ranking or its genetic uniqueness, which are the statutory criteria most relevant to whether subspecies should be listed. We also find that different committees may affect different aspects of FWS decisionmaking. Members on the Appropriations Committee affect FWS spending decisions more than do oversight committee members. Conversely, oversight members affect the FWS species listing decisions far more than do members on the Appropriations Committee. Our results are striking because given the clear choices made in the statute, political considerations should not matter at all. And yet they do: Extinction may turn on the preferences of members of oversight committees, not on the criteria established by law.

> To make this more concrete, imagine for a moment that you are an endangered species. The best case scenario for your survival and recovery would be for your geographic range to map onto states with exclusively Democratic representation; for all of your elected members of Congress— especially your Senators—to sit on committees with oversight and appropriations authority over the implementation of the ESA; and for you to be a mammal (or at least not a mollusk, arachnid, or reptile). As it turns out, who you are matters, but who you know—who represents you on what committees—might matter more. J.R. DeShazo & Jody Freeman, *The Congressional Competition to Control Delegated Power.* 81 TEX. L. REV. 1443, 1468 (2003).

How could you remedy this situation? Is there anything wrong with a current Congress directing an agency to follow its wishes? After all, the members of Congress on oversight committees are elected and accountable.

6. Under § 3(16) of the ESA, a species, for the purposes of listing decisions, is defined as "includ[ing] any subspecies of fish or wildlife or plants, and any distinct population segment of any species of vertebrate fish or

wildlife which interbreeds when mature." 16 U.S.C. § 1532(16). Congress did not define this last term, "distinct population segment" (DPS), and accordingly, the definition and application of the DPS requirement has been a frequent subject in the litigation of listing decisions by the Services. In *Trout Unlimited v. Lohn*, 559 F.3d 946 (9th Cir. 2009), the court upheld a regulation requiring hatchery fish to be considered as part of the same evolutionarily significant unit (ESU), but making the endangered or threatened status of the fish turn on the viability of a natural, self-sustaining population, with the hatchery fish considered in terms of their possible positive or negative impacts on that goal. The court said that the debate about whether to include the hatchery fish in the ESU was "a good faith disagreement that is supported by science on both sides . . . In such situations we stay our hand." The court did agree, however, that "the ESA's primary goal is to preserve the ability of natural populations to survive in the wild."

7.   Listed species may be in one of two categories: endangered or threatened. What is the difference? Statutorily, the main difference between these categories is that the § 9 prohibition on take, discussed *infra*, applies only to endangered species. That is, per the terms of the statute, there is no prohibition against taking threatened species. The proviso to this comes in the text of § 4(d), which provides: "The Secretary may by regulation prohibit with respect to any threatened species any act prohibited under § 9(a)(1), in the case of fish or wildlife, or § 9(a)(2), in the case of plants, with respect to endangered species." 16 U.S.C.§ 1533(d) (2000).

Based on this authority, FWS has implemented a regulation that treats threatened species with the full force of § 9 unless otherwise noted. *See* 50 C.F.R.§ 17.31 (2005). NOAA Fisheries, on the other hand, prefers to adopt a species-by-species approach in applying § 9 prohibitions to threatened species under its jurisdiction. To date, NOAA Fisheries has applied § 9 prohibitions to four main classes of threatened species: the Guadalupe fur seal, the Steller sea lion, anadromous fish, and sea turtles. *See* 50 C.F.R. pt. 223 (2005); *see also* Robert L. Fischman and Jaelith Hall–Rivera, *A Lesson for Conservation from Pollution Control Law: Cooperative Federalism for Recovery Under the Endangered Species Act*, 27 COLUM. J. ENVTL. L. 45, 63–64 (2002) (discussing the § 9 take prohibition and its application to threatened species).

8.   In 2005, the Center for Biological Diversity petitioned the Department of the Interior to list the polar bear as a threatened species on the grounds that global warming was melting its sea ice habitat. After a lengthy evaluation period and litigation to force the listing, the Department issued a final rule listing the bear as threatened. Secretary of the Interior Dirk Kempthorne issued the ruling in May, 2008 by explaining that he was compelled to do so by "the legal standards under the ESA." Concurrently, however, the Department of the Interior proposed a special rule "that is tailored to the conservation needs of the polar bear." In announcing the listing, Secretary Kempthorne explained both his finding that the polar bear is threatened and why a special rule, Interim Rule 4(d), is necessary.

U.S. DEPARTMENT OF THE INTERIOR, SECRETARY KEMPTHORNE ANNOUNCES DECISION TO PROTECT POLAR BEARS UNDER THE ENDANGERED SPECIES ACT

http://ww.doi.gov/issues/polar_bears.html (2008).

Today I am listing the polar bear as a "threatened" species under the Endangered Species Act.

I believe this decision is most consistent with the record and legal standards of the Endangered Species Act—perhaps the least flexible law Congress has ever enacted.

I am also announcing that this listing decision will be accompanied by administrative guidance and a rule that defines the scope of impact my decision will have, in order to protect the polar bear while preventing unintended harm to the society and economy of the United States. * * *

* * * sea ice is receding in the arctic. Last year, arctic sea ice fell to the lowest level ever recorded by satellite, 39% lower than the long-term average from 1979 to 2000.

I asked the U.S. Geological Survey to project future sea ice and its relationship to polar bears. They produced a peer-reviewed analysis of computer models. All ten computer models projected declines in September sea ice, averaging 30% by the middle of this century.

My hope is that the projections from these models are wrong, and that sea ice does not further recede. But the best science available to me currently says that is not likely to happen in the next 45 years.

Although the population of bears has grown from a low of about 12,000 in the late 1960's to approximately 25,000 today, our scientists advise me that computer modeling projects a significant population decline by the year 2050. This, in my judgment, makes the polar bear a threatened species—one likely to become in danger of extinction in the foreseeable future.

I have accepted the science presented to me by the Fish and Wildlife Service and the U.S. Geological Survey. I have also accepted these professionals' best scientific and legal judgments that the loss of sea ice, <u>not</u> oil and gas development or subsistence activities, are the reason the polar bear is threatened.

Polar bears are already protected under the Marine Mammal Protection Act, which has more stringent protections for polar bears than the Endangered Species Act does. The oil and gas industry has been operating in the Arctic for decades in compliance with these stricter protections. The Fish and Wildlife Service says that no polar bears have been killed due to encounters associated with oil and gas operations.

The most significant part of today's decision is what President Bush observed about climate change policy last month. President Bush noted that "The Clean Air Act, the Endangered Species Act and the National Environmental Policy Act were never meant to regulate global climate change."

The President is right. Listing the polar bear as threatened can reduce avoidable losses of polar bears. But it should not open the door to use the ESA to regulate greenhouse gas emissions from automobiles, power plants, and other sources. That would be a wholly inappropriate use of the Endangered Species Act. ESA is not the right tool to set U.S. climate policy.

The Endangered Species Act neither allows nor requires the Fish and Wildlife Service to make such interventions. The Service must articulate a causal connection between the effects of any action and loss of a polar bear. As the U.S. Geological Survey has advised me, the best scientific data available do not demonstrate significant impacts on individual polar bears from specific power plants, resource projects, government permits, or other indirect effects of activities in the lower 48 states that are potentially reviewable under the "consultation" requirements of the ESA.

The President is right when he says: "There is a right way and wrong way to approach reducing greenhouse gas emissions. The American people deserve an honest assessment of the costs, benefits and feasibility of any proposed solution. Discussions with such far-reaching impact should not be left to unelected regulators and judges but should be debated openly and made by the elected representatives of the people they affect."

This Administration has taken real action to deal with the challenges of climate change. The Administration and the private sector plan to dedicate nearly a billion dollars to clean coal research and development. Our incentives for power production from wind and solar energy have helped to more than quadruple its use. We have worked with Congress to make available more than $40 billion in loan guarantees to support investments that will avoid, reduce, or sequester greenhouse gas emissions or air pollutants.

To make sure that the Endangered Species Act is not misused to regulate global climate change, I will take the following specific actions:

First, to provide clarity and certainty to those regulated under the Endangered Species Act, the Fish and Wildlife Service will propose what is known as a 4(d) rule that states that if an activity is permissible under the stricter standards imposed by the Marine Mammal Protection Act, it is also permissible under the Endangered Species Act with respect to the polar bear. This rule, effective immediately, will ensure the protection of the bear while allowing us to continue to develop our natural resources in the arctic region in an environmentally sound way.

Second, Director Hall will issue guidance to Fish and Wildlife Service staff that the best scientific data available today cannot make a causal connection between harm to listed species or their habitats and green-

Specific?

house gas emissions from a specific facility, or resource development project, or government action.

Third, the Department will issue a Solicitor's Opinion further clarifying these points.

Fourth, the ESA regulatory language needs to be clarified. We will propose common sense modifications to the existing regulation to provide greater certainty that this listing will not set backdoor climate policy outside our normal system of political accountability.

I sought to reform the Endangered Species Act with Senators Harry Reid and Max Baucus and the late John Chaffee when I served in the United States Senate. I had lived with the consequences of ESA decisions as Governor of Idaho. As Secretary I have now experienced the reality that the current ESA is among the most inflexible laws Congress has passed. It prevents me, as Secretary, from taking into account economic conditions and adverse consequences in making listing decisions.

In many ways, the polar bear poses a unique conservation challenge. With most threatened and endangered species, we can identify a localized threat that we can seek to address. The threat to the polar bear, however, comes from global influences and their effect on sea ice.

While the legal standards under the ESA compel me to list the polar bear as threatened, I want to make clear that this listing will not stop global climate change or prevent any sea ice from melting. Any real solution requires action by all major economies for it to be effective. That's why I'm taking administrative and regulatory action to make certain the ESA isn't abused to make global warming policies.

NOTES

1. Although given the opportunity to do so by Congress under the Omnibus Appropriations Act of 2009, the Obama Administration declined to withdraw the interim rule. Secretary of Interior Salazar said, "We must do all we can to help the polar bear recovery * * * However, the Endangered Species Act is not the proper mechanism for controlling our nation's carbon emissions." At the same time, however, Salazar did disapprove another last minute regulation by the Bush Administration that had redefined the consultation requirement under § 7 more generally, narrowing the actions that were considered proximate causes of jeopardy.

2. If § 7 of the ESA were applied to the polar bear, would any federal action be exempt from consideration as a source of jeopardy? Could there be a minimum threshold of greenhouse gas emissions before ESA consultation is required? Consider the excerpt below.

J.B. RUHL, CLIMATE CHANGE AND THE ENDANGERED SPECIES ACT: BUILDING BRIDGES TO THE NO–ANALOG FUTURE

88 B.U.L. Rev. 1 (2008).**4**

Like most other existing regulatory statutes, the ESA was not enacted with global climate change in mind, and the ESA alone will not arrest the causes or effects of our planet's no-analog future. But for the foreseeable future, until Congress or the states adopt statutes responding directly and comprehensively to climate change, the ESA is the nation's principal species conservation program. Even if the ESA cannot reverse climate change, pressure will be brought to bear on the FWS, just as it was on the EPA, to use its regulatory powers to "whittle away" at the problem.* * *

[The regulatory] authority [of the ESA] is only useful in circumstances where intervention is feasible and effective. For example, habitat loss, the leading cause of species decline, is often the result of easily identifiable human-induced factors susceptible to discrete and effective regulation. By contrast, invasive species, the runner-up in causes of species decline, typically present exceedingly complex causes and solutions, meaning there usually is no identifiable regulatory target.

In this respect, climate change presents a complicated scenario. To be sure, there is an easily identifiable regulatory target: greenhouse gas emissions. Leaving until later the question of how much discretion the ESA affords the FWS to regulate greenhouse gas emissions, there are obvious practical obstacles to this approach. First, regulating emissions in the United States alone is highly unlikely to sufficiently reduce global emission levels. Second, even if regulatory measures are implemented worldwide to curtail emissions, the political reality is that the measures will impose phased-in reductions taking several decades to return to benchmark emission levels designed to stabilize or reduce greenhouse gas concentrations in the troposphere. Third, and most significantly, even if benchmark levels are attained in the near future, the physical dynamics of greenhouse gas effects on climate are such that climate change will continue on its present trajectory for a significant time period.* * *

[W]hat matters for most regulatory agencies is not how well we predict global trends such as surface temperature and sea levels, but what happens at the sub-global regional and local levels at which agencies act. * * * Yet even rather fundamental secondary effects questions, such as where it will rain more and less and how fast the ice will melt, remain open to wide variation in available models.

[F]or the FWS it often will be the case that what matters for a particular species is primarily a function of local ecological conditions and their effects on the species. The FWS, in other words, has to find models that predict the effects of global climate warming on a wide range of physical and biological cycles, "downscale" those effects to local ecological

---

4. Copyright © 2008 by Boston University Law Review. Reprinted by permission.

conditions, and then evaluate the effects of those local changes on the species of concern. Such specific downscaling efforts encounter the same nonlinear feedback properties that make climate change effects difficult to model and predict at mean global levels, but they operate with even more volatility at regional and local levels. Fundamentally, * * * the FWS has no models of this sort at its disposal because nobody has the experience or knowledge upon which to base them. Ultimately, they may simply be beyond our capacity. * * *

This is the no-analog future of the ESA. Some effects will be more predictable than others, such as that warmer waters will exceed the temperature limits of some fish species. But many effects will be difficult to predict, such as the cascade effects the loss of a top-level predator fish causes in its ecosystem. Where and when these effects will occur, their magnitude and duration, and the other effects they will set in motion are questions the FWS has only begun to confront.* * *

The effects of climate change * * * are unambiguously within the ambit of the listing criteria, leaving no room for the FWS to argue that it may leave climate change out of the listing calculus. Hence, like the EPA under the Clean Air Act, the FWS seems stuck with the challenge of identifying which species are endangered or threatened partly or primarily because of climate change. * * *

Although § 4 leaves no room for debate over whether the agency must integrate climate change effects in the listing decision, the statute provides considerable flexibility for how the agency does so. For example, a species is endangered if it is "in danger of extinction throughout all or a significant portion of its range" and is threatened if it "is likely to become an endangered species within the foreseeable future throughout all or a significant portion of its range." These are not precise concepts * * * the FWS may not be so hemmed in after all. Given the extent of agency expertise that must necessarily go into making such judgments, and given the uncertainty associated with downscaling global climate change effects to local species-specific ecological contexts, the FWS likely has considerable play in terms of matching different climate change threat scenarios with the ESA's endangered, threatened, not-threatened matrix. Indeed, the agency thus far has weaved between these terms and used its agency expertise and administrative discretion to find climate change a factor in some cases and not in others. * * *

Prosecuting a climate change case would be no mean feat either, given the generic effects of greenhouse gas emissions and the imprecision of downscaling models. Consider, for example, a scenario in which the pika is listed as endangered due to climate change. Who is taking the pika? Are greenhouse gas emissions from, say, a coal-fired power plant in Florida taking the pika? The plaintiff in such a case would have to show that the power plant emissions are the actual as well as proximate, foreseeable cause of the primary and secondary ecological effects which are in turn the actual as well as proximate, foreseeable cause of the pika's demise.

Proving that would prove too much, however, as it would necessarily follow that *all* sources of greenhouse gases are taking the pika. This is an inherent feature of the take prohibition that makes it inapposite when take of a species occurs through large-scale, dispersed causal agents, such as water consumption and pollution—if *anyone* is taking the species, *everyone* is taking the species. Although nothing in the ESA prevents the FWS from attempting to prosecute such a case, it would be a daunting prosecutorial undertaking as well as likely political suicide. * * *

The take prohibition would prove more adept at enforcing discrete, identifiable actions that make it less likely a climate-threatened species will survive through the climate change transition. In particular, climate change is likely to present collisions between many species, climate-threatened or not, and human adaptations such as relocated agricultural and urban land uses, technological structures designed to impede sea level rise and floods, and new and intensified water diversions to sustain parched urban centers. Enforcement of the take prohibition in such settings, where proximate cause may be less difficult to establish, could help ensure that human adaptation measures do not disregard the interests of imperiled species. In this sense, § 9 would be used no differently from the way it is already used—climate change effects would simply be a reason to use it more vigilantly.* * *

[handwritten margin note: Could consider effect of human adaptation to climate ∆]

The FWS has issued no official guidance on climate change with respect to the § 7 jeopardy consultation program, but it takes no stretch of imagination to fit climate change into this framework. Consider a project being carried out, funded, or authorized by a federal agency, the construction of which will remove habitat of a listed species and the operation of which will emit greenhouse gases. The removal of habitat and emission of greenhouse gases are clearly direct effects of the action added to the environmental baseline, both of which could have indirect effects that adversely affect the species. At some later time, the habitat removal could adversely affect the reproduction, numbers, or distribution of that species. Greenhouse gas emissions contribute to tropospheric warming, and the secondary effects of such warming could also, at some later time, adversely affect the species. Moreover, other state and private activities emitting greenhouse gases may also contribute to cumulative climate change effects that adversely affect the species. In short, greenhouse gas emissions and their climate change consequences both appear to be wrapped tightly into the framework for consultations under 7(a)(2).

To be sure, as with the listing decision, the FWS consultation decision depends on a three-part causal chain: greenhouse gas emissions cause tropospheric warming, which in turn causes secondary climate change effects, which in turn cause ecological changes that adversely affect the species. Although determining whether these downscale effects actually occur may be difficult to say in particular scenarios, the point is that they could occur. Unless the FWS intends on ruling out that possibility entirely—a difficult proposition after *Massachusetts v. EPA*—it stands to reason that consultations under § 7(a)(2) should consider the possible direct, indirect, and cumulative effects of greenhouse gas emissions and climate change.* * *

[T]he problem with fitting climate change into the consultation framework is that it exhibits more certainty at macro levels than at micro levels. Consider, for example, the proposed coal-fired power plant in Florida and its effects on the pika in the Sierra Nevada Mountains. It would seem quite a stretch to conclude that the power plant emissions will jeopardize the pika. Yet, at a macro level the analysis is rather straight forward: the power plant emits greenhouse gases (a direct effect of the action), greenhouse gases are reasonably certain to warm the troposphere (an indirect effect of the action), a warming troposphere is reasonably certain to adversely alter ecological conditions for the pika, and it is reasonably expected that such ecological changes will bring an end to the pika. At the micro level, however, it becomes difficult to link the *individual* plant's emissions as the jeopardizing agent for the pika, given that *all* greenhouse gas emissions worldwide are subject to the same macro analysis. Other than quantity of emissions, the FWS would have no reasoned basis for distinguishing between the power plant in Florida, a farm in Kansas, or an elementary school in Oregon. * * * Given these attributes of greenhouse gas emission effects on climate, it is difficult to conceive of how the agency would go about aggressively regulating greenhouse gas emissions through the jeopardy consultation program. The FWS does not have the pollution control expertise of the EPA, nor does any provision of the ESA explicitly provide authority to engage in emissions regulation. Given that all emission sources contribute to warming effects, the threat of jeopardy findings would have to be applied universally to all sources. * * * But is the FWS equipped to assume the role of nationwide regulator of farms, industrial facilities, auto emissions, and everything else? In short, the idea that *all* emission sources present jeopardy conditions to each and every climate-threatened species would prove too much, and likely render the ESA and the FWS political targets in the first degree.* * *

The ESA will be best served if the FWS adopts a cautious optimism that recognizes the limits of the ESA but keeps the statute relevant.... The job of the ESA is to help as many species as is reasonably possible get [to a point where the global community has achieved a stable climate outcome] with us—to serve as their bridge across the climate change transition into the no-analog future. Ironically, to do this will take some humility and restraint. Going for the jugular by regulating greenhouse gas emissions is *not* where the ESA can be of most help to imperiled species. There is little to be gained for the FWS or for climate-threatened species by having the agency go down this road. * * * Rather, the FWS can provide expert assistance to the agencies more appropriately charged with regulating greenhouse gas emissions, such as the EPA, by advising them about the effects of climate change on species.

As for its direct role in addressing climate change, the FWS can employ the ESA most effectively by identifying species threatened by climate change, identifying which of those can be helped through the ESA's habitat-based programs, and devising a management plan—one that uses regulatory action as well as recovery planning—to build each such species its bridge. Indeed, this strategy allows the FWS to dispense with the distinction between human-induced and natural climate variation. Climate change is climate change—it does not matter to the species what is causing it. What does matter to them is whether and in what shape they survive it.

___

2.   CRITICAL HABITAT

What happens after a listing? The listing of a species can be understood as the "trigger" of the Endangered Species Act. That is, once the Services list a species as endangered or threatened, the rest of the statutory requirements, prohibitions, and protections apply. Without a listing, a jeopardy determination cannot be made and the prohibition against take does not exist. Accordingly, for both those supporting the protection of endangered species and those for whom endangered species protection would be problematic, the § 4 determination is crucial.

As noted *supra*, the Secretary must, subject to important conditions, determine a species' critical habitat at the time of its listing. 16 U.S.C. § 1533(a)(3)(A). The Act defines "critical habitat" as:

> the specific areas *within* the geographical area occupied by the species, at the time it is listed * * * on which are found those physical or biological features (I) essential to the conservation of the species and (II) which may require special management considerations or protection; and

> specific areas *outside* the geographical area occupied by the species at the time it is listed * * * upon a determination by the Secretary that such areas are essential for the conservation of the species.

16 U.S.C. § 1532(5)(A) (2000) (emphasis added).

Except in circumstances determined by the Secretary, "critical habitat shall not include the entire geographical area which can be occupied by the threatened or endangered species." 16 U.S.C. § 1532(5)(C).

Unlike the listing process, the critical habitat determination may involve considerations of "the economic impact, the impact on national security, and any other relevant impact." Indeed, the Secretary may choose not to designate an area as critical habitat:

> if he determines that the benefits of such exclusion outweigh the benefits of specifying such area as part of the critical habitat, unless he determines, based on the best scientific and commercial data available, that the failure to designate such area as critical habitat will result in the extinction of the species concerned.

16 U.S.C. § 1533(b)(2).

The next major event in the case of the Northern Spotted Owl was the Service's decision not to designate critical habitat at the time of the listing of the owl. Environmental groups challenged this decision, just as they had challenged the service's failure to list the owl. The opinion that follows is a good illustration of the considerations that must go into the decision whether or not to designate critical habitat.

NORTHERN SPOTTED OWL v. LUJAN

United States District Court for the Western District of Washington, 1991.
758 F.Supp. 621.

THOMAS S. ZILLY, UNITED STATES DISTRICT JUDGE.

On June 23, 1989, the Service proposed to list the northern spotted owl as a "threatened" species under the Endangered Species Act. *See* 54 Fed. Reg. 26,666 (1989). On June 26, 1990, the Service published its final rule confirming that listing decision. *See* 55 Fed. Reg. 26,114 (1990). In both the proposed and final listing rules, the Service expressly deferred designation of critical habitat for the spotted owl on grounds that it was not "determinable." * * *

Plaintiffs move this Court to order the federal defendants to designate "critical habitat" for the northern spotted owl. As defined under the ESA, "critical habitat" refers to geographic areas which are essential to the conservation of the spotted owl and which may require special management considerations or protection. 16 U.S.C. § 1532(5)(A)(i). Thus, even though more extensive habitat may be essential to maintain the species over the long term, critical habitat only includes the minimum amount of habitat needed to avoid short-term jeopardy or habitat in need of immediate intervention. Habitat not currently occupied by the spotted owl may be designated as critical only upon a determination by the Secretary of the Interior that such areas are essential to ensure the conservation of the species. 16 U.S.C. § 1532(5)(A)(ii). The Secretary must consult with other federal agencies to ensure that governmental actions do not "result in the destruction or adverse modification" of land designated as critical habitat. 16 U.S.C. § 1536(a)(2).

The initial determination of what areas constitute critical habitat is to be made on the basis of "the best scientific data available." 16 U.S.C. § 1533(b)(2). This requires identifying geographic areas containing the physical and biological features considered to be essential to the conservation of the species. *See* 50 C.F.R. § 424.12(b) (listing criteria for designating critical habitat). In addition, Congress directed the Secretary of the Interior to consider the probable economic or other impacts on human activities resulting from the critical habitat designation. The Secretary is expressly authorized to exclude any area from critical habitat if he determines that the benefits of such exclusion outweigh the conservation benefits, unless to do so would result in the extinction of the species. 16 U.S.C. § 1533(b)(2).

* * * The ESA requires the Secretary, "to the maximum extent prudent and determinable," to designate critical habitat *concurrently* with his decision to list a species as endangered or threatened. 16 U.S.C. § 1533(a)(3). When critical habitat is not determinable at the time of the final listing rule, the Secretary is authorized up to twelve additional months to complete the designation. 16 U.S.C. § 1533(b)(6)(C). The governing administrative regulations specify that the Secretary must state his reasons for not designating critical habitat in the proposed and final listing rules. 50 C.F.R. § 424.12(a).

* * * Plaintiffs charge that the Secretary has violated the Endangered Species Act and the Administrative Procedure Act by failing to designate critical habitat concurrently with the listing of the northern spotted owl. * * *

The language employed in § 4(a)(3) and its place in the overall statutory scheme evidence a clear design by Congress that designation of critical habitat coincide with the species listing determination. The linkage of these issues was not the product of chance; rather, it reflects the studied and deliberate judgment of Congress that destruction of habitat was the most significant cause of species endangerment. * * *

As originally enacted, the ESA admitted no exceptions to the requirement that the critical habitat designation occur concurrently with the listing determination. * * *

By its 1978 amendments, Congress expressly linked the timing of the critical habitat designation to the decision to list the species. A single exception to this duty was recognized when the habitat designation was not "prudent." * * *

* * * Under current regulations, a critical habitat designation is not "prudent" only if it is not in the best interest of the species.[5] * * *

In 1982, Congress expressed frustration at the slow pace of implementing the Endangered Species Act. Particular concern focused on the Secretary's critical habitat responsibilities as a source of delay. * * *

The solution adopted by Congress permits the Secretary to defer the habitat designation upon finding that critical habitat is not "determinable" at the time the Secretary proposes to list the species under the ESA or at the time of his final listing decision. 16 U.S.C. § 1533(b)(6)(C). In no event may the Secretary delay the designation of critical habitat for more than twelve months after publication of the final listing rule. * * * The authoring committee of the 1982 amendments, the House Committee on Merchant Marine and Fisheries, expressly emphasized the narrow nature of this exception:

---

5. The regulations of the Fish and Wildlife Service define only two situations when designation of critical habitat is not "prudent" within the meaning of 16 U.S.C. § 1533(a)(3):

(i) The species is threatened by taking or other human activity, and identification of critical habitat can be expected to increase the degree of such threat to the species, or

(ii) Such designation of critical habitat would not be beneficial to the species. 50 C.F.R. § 424.12(a)(1).

* * * The Committee feels strongly, however, that, where the biology relating to the status of the species is clear, it should not be denied the protection of the Act because of the inability of the Secretary to complete the work necessary to designate critical habitat.... *The Committee expects the agencies to make the strongest attempt possible to determine critical habitat within the time period designated for listing* * * *.

* * * The conference report to the 1982 amendments further emphasizes that designation is to occur at *the earliest possible time*, not to exceed twelve months after publication of the final listing rule. * * *

The conference report also states that the Secretary must "justify listing a species without designating critical habitat" to support it. * * *

This legislative history leaves little room for doubt regarding the intent of Congress: The designation of critical habitat is to coincide with the final listing decision absent extraordinary circumstances. * * *

This Court rejects as incongruous the federal defendants' argument that § 4(b)(6)(C) authorizes an automatic extension of time merely upon a finding that critical habitat is not presently "determinable," even where no effort has been made to secure the information necessary to make the designation. To relieve the Secretary of any affirmative information gathering responsibilities would effectively nullify Congress' charge that the species listing and habitat designation occur concurrently, "to the maximum extent ... determinable." 16 U.S.C. § 1533(a)(3). * * *

* * * The federal defendants fail to direct this Court to any portion of the administrative record which adequately explains or justifies the decision not to designate critical habitat for the northern spotted owl. Nowhere in the proposed or final rules did the Service state what efforts had been made to determine critical habitat. Nowhere did the Service specify what additional biological or economic information was necessary to complete the designation. Nowhere did the Service explain why critical habitat was not determinable. * * *

Indeed, the Service candidly acknowledged in its June 1989 proposed rule that it had not conducted the analyses required by § 4(b)(2). *See* 54 Fed. Reg. at 26,675. This Court interprets the Service's statement one year later that it "*will* evaluate the economic and other relevant impacts," absent any evidence of having done so, as tacitly reaffirming that the studies still had not been performed. * * *

More is required under the ESA and the Service's own regulations than the mere conclusion that more work needs to be done. * * * It cannot be established upon the record presented that the Service "considered the relevant factors" or that it "articulated a rational connection between the facts found and the choice made." * * * Accordingly, this Court must find the Service abused its discretion when it declined to designate critical habitat for the northern spotted owl. * * *

This Court is mindful of the prodigious resources dedicated by the Service to the spotted owl. The listing process required a truly remarkable effort by the Service given the volume of comments received and the complexity of the issues raised. The inter-agency consultations have consumed additional manpower and financial resources. * * *

In any event, such efforts, which the Court assumes have been on-going since prior to June 1989, do not relieve the Service of its statutory obligation to designate critical habitat concurrently with the species listing, or to provide a rational and articulated basis for concluding that critical habitat is not determinable. * * *

Common sense dictates that the spotted owl would be poorly served by a hastily crafted or uninformed habitat plan. Congress expressly provided for periodic revisions to critical habitat plans to avoid this result. *See* 16 U.S.C. § 1533(a)(3)(B). Accordingly, the Service is ordered to submit to the Court by March 15, 1991 a written plan for completing its review of critical habitat for the northern spotted owl. The Service is further ordered to publish its proposed critical habitat plan no later than forty-five days thereafter. The final rule is to be published at the earliest possible time under the appropriate circumstances. * * *

NOTES

1. Following Judge Zilly's order to list critical habitat by April 30, 1991, the Fish and Wildlife Service surprised everyone when it designated 11.6 million acres of habitat on May 6, 1991. The designation included "6.5 million acres of [Forest Service] land, 1.4 acres of [Bureau of Land Management] land, 0.7 million acres of state and tribal lands, and 3 million acres of private land." *See* Steven Lewis Yaffee, THE WISDOM OF THE SPOTTED OWL: POLICY LESSONS FOR A NEW CENTURY 132 (1994).

Two weeks after this contentious designation, Judge William Dwyer of the U.S. District Court for the Western District of Washington added to the controversy by permanently enjoining Forest Service timber sales in spotted owl habitat until the Forest Service completed a new spotted owl management plan and environmental analysis. *Id.* at 133; *see also Seattle Audubon Soc. v. Evans*, 771 F.Supp. 1081 (W.D. Wash. 1991).

2. The combination of these two related controversies led the Bush Administration to invoke the Endangered Species Committee provision of the Act. *See* 16 U.S.C. § 1536(e). As noted *supra,* the ESC was added to the Act in the 1978 in response to the Tellico Dam controversy, as a last resort to offer exemptions to those projects that could not comply with the terms of the Act. Because the Committee can officially sanction the demise of an endangered species, it has been colloquially termed the "God Squad." The God Squad is comprised of the Secretary of Agriculture, the Secretary of the Army, the Chairman of the Council of Economic Advisors, the Administrator of the Environmental Protection Agency, the Secretary of the Interior, the Administrator of the National Oceanic and Atmospheric Administration, and "one

individual from each affected State" appointed by the President. 16 U.S.C. § 1536(e)(3).

An agency filing an ESC exemption application must satisfy several requirements under § 7(h):

(1) The Committee shall make a final determination whether or not to grant an exemption within 30 days after receiving the report of the Secretary pursuant to subsection (g)(5). The Committee shall grant an exemption from the requirements of subsection (a)(2) for an agency action if, by a vote of not less than five of its members voting in person—

(A) it determines on the record, based on the report of the Secretary, the record of the hearing held under subsection (g)(4) and on such other testimony or evidence as it may receive, that—

(i) there are no reasonable and prudent alternatives to the agency action;

(ii) the benefits of such action clearly outweigh the benefits of alternative courses of action consistent with conserving the species or its critical habitat, and such action is in the public interest;

(iii) the action is of regional or national significance; and

(iv) neither the Federal agency concerned nor the exemption applicant made any irreversible or irretrievable commitment of resources prohibited by subsection (d); and

(B) it establishes such reasonable mitigation and enhancement measures, including, but not limited to, live propagation, transplantation, and habitat acquisition and improvement, as are necessary and appropriate to minimize the adverse effects of the agency action upon the endangered species, threatened species, or critical habitat concerned.

Any final determination by the Committee under this subsection shall be considered final agency action for purposes of [the Administrative Procedure Act].

16 U.S.C. § 1536(h)(1)(A).

Believing that its Northwest timber sales met these guidelines, the Bush Administration applied for an exemption from the Committee. This was, in fact, the first and only time the ESC has granted an exemption.

However, the saga did not end there. Throughout the Committee's deliberations, there were allegations of political interference by the White House. When the Committee finally handed down its decision to grant an exemption on May 14, 1992, environmental plaintiffs immediately filed suit in federal court. In *Portland Audubon Society v. Endangered Species Committee*, 984 F.2d 1534 (9th Cir. 1993), plaintiffs alleged that "improper ex parte contacts between the White House and members of the Committee tainted the decision-making process." The Ninth Circuit remanded the matter to the Committee for further proceedings, holding that the Committee was subject to the provisions of the Administrative Procedure Act and that, should the plaintiffs' allegations be true, the Committee would be in violation of the

APA. For this reason, the court remanded for an evidentiary hearing by an administrative law judge.

In response to the ongoing litigation, as well as public demand for change in the management of Northwest forests, newly elected President Clinton convened a Forest Conference in 1993 and created a Forest Ecosystem Management Assessment Team (FEMAT) to study and develop a new, ecology-based management plan for the forests of the Northwest. In 1994, FEMAT's work resulted in the Northwest Forest Plan, which was the first ecosystem management plan for public lands. The Plan covered 24 million acres of public land in northern California, Oregon, and Washington, and had several conservation-based components. Among these were the creation of forest reserves, in which logging and roadbuilding were limited; the Aquatic Conservation Strategy, which protected salmon and other species in rivers and streams; and the Survey and Manage program, which required pre-logging inspections for lesser-known old-growth species on lands outside of the designated reserves. In *Seattle Audubon Soc'y v. Moseley*, 80 F.3d 1401 (9th Cir. 1996), the Ninth Circuit upheld the Plan and its accompanying EIS.

Beginning in 2002, the George W. Bush administration made attempts to roll back the protections under the Plan in several different ways: (1) lowering restrictions under the Aquatic Conservation Strategy; (2) initiating review of the ESA status of the spotted owl and marbled murrelet; (3) reverting to optional protections under Survey and Manage; and (4) settling a decade-old lawsuit with industry to reinterpret protections of the Bureau of Land Management's O & C lands.

3.   Is the consultation requirement in § 7 for a threat to "existence" of a species the same as for the "destruction or adverse modification" of critical habitat? In *Sierra Club v. United States Fish & Wildlife Serv.*, 245 F.3d 434 (5th Cir. 2001), the U.S. Fish and Wildlife Service the National Marine Fisheries Service had listed the Gulf sturgeon, but chose not to designate critical habitat for the fish, concluding that it was not prudent to do so, as the designation would not provide any additional benefit for the sturgeon beyond the basic consultation requirement. Environmental plaintiffs sued, challenging the decision and the regulation on which the Services based the decision. The problem, as plaintiffs saw it—and as the Fifth Circuit agreed—was that the regulation conflicted with the requirements of the ESA. The ESA requires consultation when a federal action will either jeopardize the existence of a listed species *or* will result in the "destruction or adverse modification" of the species' critical habitat. The court noted that these consultation standards were different, since critical habitat is meant to provide for the recovery—and not just the survival—of a species. In the Services' regulations, however, "destruction or adverse modification" was defined as "a direct or indirect alteration that appreciably diminishes the value of critical habitat for *both the survival and recovery of a listed species.*" *Id.* at 439. Accordingly, the Services had set the consultation bar for critical habitat higher than what the ESA required.

The Ninth Circuit followed this decision on "the recovery goal of critical habitat." In *Gifford Pinchot Task Force v. United States Fish & Wildlife*

Serv., 378 F.3d 1059 (9th Cir. 2004), the court held the same regulation to be impermissible under the ESA, noting:

> [T]he ESA was enacted not merely to forestall the extinction of species (i.e., promote a species survival), but to allow a species to recover to the point where it may be delisted. *See* 16 U.S.C. § 1532(3) (defining conservation as all methods that can be employed to "bring any endangered species or threatened species to the point at which the measures provided pursuant to this [Act] are no longer necessary") * * *. * * * By these definitions, it is clear that Congress intended that conservation and survival be two different (though complementary) goals of the ESA. * * * Clearly, then, the purpose of establishing "critical habitat" is for the government to carve out territory that is not only necessary for the species' survival but also essential for the species' recovery.

> Congress, by its own language, viewed conservation and survival as distinct, though complementary, goals, and the requirement to preserve critical habitat is designed to promote both conservation and survival. Congress said that "destruction or adverse modification" could occur when sufficient critical habitat is lost so as to threaten a species' recovery even if there remains sufficient critical habitat for the species' survival.

Id. at 1070. *See also New Mexico Cattle Growers v. United States Fish & Wildlife Serv.*, 248 F.3d 1277 (10th Cir. 2001).

4. As noted above, one of the findings the Services can make in deciding not to list critical habitat is that the designation would not be "prudent." This springs from the requirement under § 4 of the ESA that the listing of a species must be accompanied by a designation of critical habitat "to the maximum extent prudent...." *See* 16 U.S.C. § 1533(a)(3) (2000). What is prudence? In *Natural Resources Defense Council v. United States Dep't of Interior*, 113 F.3d 1121 (9th Cir. 1997), plaintiffs challenged the U.S. Fish and Wildlife Service's failure to list critical habitat for the coastal California gnatcatcher, a songbird unique to southern California. Though the ESA does not define prudence, the Service had based its findings on its own regulatory definition of what is *not* prudent: (i) The species is threatened by taking or other human activity, and identification of critical habitat can be expected to increase the degree of such threat to the species, or (ii) Such designation of critical habitat would not be beneficial to the species. *Id.* at 1125.

Based on this regulation, the Service claimed that the designation would not be prudent because (1) it would harm the species, since hostile landowners had a history of identifying and destroying gnatcatcher habitat; and (2) the designation would not appreciably benefit species, since most of the birds were located on private land, outside the ambit of § 7. The court rejected both of these bases, holding that the first violated the ESA requirement that the Service weigh the benefits against the risks of designation. In this case, the Service had performed no such weighing. As to the second basis, the court held that the Service impermissibly broadened the narrow statutory exception for imprudent designations by construing "no benefit" as no benefit to *most of* the species. This cut against the clear congressional intent that an imprudence designation should occur only *"in rare circumstances."* *Id.* at 1126.

Thus, even though most of the species' habitat was on private land, this fell far short of showing that the designation would have *no* benefit.

C. CONSULTATION: SECTION 7

Section 7(a)(2) of the Act provides that:

[e]ach Federal agency shall, in consultation with and with the assistance of the Secretary, insure that any action authorized, funded, or carried out by such agency (hereinafter in this section referred to as an "agency action") is not likely to jeopardize the continued existence of any endangered species or threatened species or result in the destruction or adverse modification of habitat of such species which is determined by the Secretary, after consultation as appropriate with affected States, to be critical, unless such agency has been granted an exemption for such action by the Committee pursuant to subsection (h) of this section. In fulfilling the requirements of this paragraph each agency shall use the best scientific and commercial data available.

16 U.S.C. § 1536(a)(2).

Accordingly, § 7(a)(2) is known as the "consultation" requirement of the ESA. The *TVA* case excerpted earlier showed the power of § 7. The next case explains the mechanics of the § 7 consultation process.

THOMAS v. PETERSON

United States Court of Appeals for the Ninth Circuit, 1985.
753 F.2d 754.

SNEED, CIRCUIT JUDGE

Plaintiffs sought to enjoin construction of a timber road in a former National Forest roadless area. The District Court granted summary judgment in favor of defendant R. Max Peterson, Chief of the Forest Service, and plaintiffs appealed. We affirm in part, reverse in part, and remand for further proceedings consistent with this opinion.

We conclude that: * * * The Endangered Species Act (ESA) requires the Forest Service to prepare a biological assessment to determine whether the road and the timber sales that the road is designed to facilitate are likely to affect the endangered Rocky Mountain Gray Wolf, and construction of the road should be enjoined pending compliance with the ESA. * * *

The Endangered Species Act Claim

The plaintiffs' third claim concerns the Forest Service's alleged failure to comply with the Endangered Species Act (ESA) in considering the effects of the road and timber sales on the endangered Rocky Mountain Gray Wolf.

The ESA contains both substantive and procedural provisions. Substantively, the Act prohibits the taking or importation of endangered species, *see* 16 U.S.C. § 1538, and requires federal agencies to ensure that their actions are not "likely to jeopardize the continued existence of any endangered species or threatened species or result in the destruction or adverse modification" of critical habitat of such species, *see* 16 U.S.C. § 1536(a)(2).

The Act prescribes a three-step process to ensure compliance with its substantive provisions by federal agencies. Each of the first two steps serves a screening function to determine if the successive steps are required. The steps are:

> (1) An agency proposing to take an action must inquire of the Fish & Wildlife Service (FWS) whether any threatened or endangered species "may be present" in the area of the proposed action. *See* 16 U.S.C. § 1536(c)(1).

> (2) If the answer is affirmative, the agency must prepare a "biological assessment" to determine whether such species "is likely to be affected" by the action. *Id.* The biological assessment may be part of an environmental impact statement or environmental assessment. *Id.*

> (3) If the assessment determines that a threatened or endangered species "is likely to be affected," the agency must formally consult with the FWS. *Id.* § 1536(a)(2). The formal consultation results in a "biological opinion" issued by the FWS. See *id.* § 1536(b). If the biological opinion concludes that the proposed action would jeopardize the species or destroy or adversely modify critical habitat, *see id.* § 1536(a)(2), then the action may not go forward unless the FWS can suggest an alternative that avoids such jeopardization, destruction, or adverse modification. *Id.* § 1536(b)(3)(A). If the opinion concludes that the action will not violate the Act, the FWS may still require measures to minimize its impact. *Id.* § 1536(b)(4)(ii)–(iii).

Plaintiffs first allege that, with respect to the Jersey Jack road, the Forest Service did not undertake step (1), a formal request to the FWS. The district court found that to be the case, but concluded that the procedural violation was insignificant because the Forest Service was already aware that wolves may be present in the area. The court therefore refused to enjoin the construction of the road. Plaintiffs insist, based on *TVA v. Hill*, 437 U.S. 153 (1978), that an injunction is mandatory once any ESA violation is found. Defendants respond, citing *Village of False Pass v. Clark*, 733 F.2d 605 (9th Cir. 1984), that *TVA* applies only to substantive violations of the ESA, and that a court has discretion to deny an injunction when it finds a procedural violation to be *de minimis*.

We need not reach this issue. The Forest Service's failure goes beyond the technical violation cited by the district court, and is not *de minimis*.

Once an agency is aware that an endangered species may be present in the area of its proposed action, the ESA requires it to prepare a biological assessment to determine whether the proposed action "is likely to affect" the species and therefore requires formal consultation with the FWS. *See supra.* The Forest Service did not prepare such an assessment prior to its decision to build the Jersey Jack road. Without a biological assessment, it cannot be determined whether the proposed project will result in a violation of the ESA's substantive provisions. A failure to prepare a biological assessment for a project in an area in which it has been determined that an endangered species may be present cannot be considered a *de minimis* violation of the ESA.

The district court found that the Forest Service had "undertaken sufficient study and action to further the purposes of the ESA." * * * Its finding was based on affidavits submitted by the Forest Service for the litigation. * * * These do not constitute a substitute for the preparation of the biological assessment required by the ESA.

Given a substantial procedural violation of the ESA in connection with a federal project, the remedy must be an injunction of the project pending compliance with the ESA. The procedural requirements of the ESA are analogous to those of NEPA: under NEPA, agencies are required to evaluate the environmental impact of federal projects "significantly affecting the quality of the human environment," 42 U.S.C. § 4332(2)(C); under the ESA, agencies are required to assess the effect on endangered species of projects in areas where such species may be present. 16 U.S.C. § 1536(c). A failure to prepare a biological assessment is comparable to a failure to prepare an environmental impact statement.

Our cases repeatedly have held that, absent " 'unusual circumstances,' an injunction is the appropriate remedy for a violation of NEPA's procedural requirements." * * * We see no reason that the same principle should not apply to procedural violations of the ESA.

The Forest Service argues that the procedural requirements of the ESA should be enforced less stringently than those of NEPA because, unlike NEPA, the ESA also contains substantive provisions. We acknowledge that the ESA's substantive provisions distinguish it from NEPA, but the distinction acts the other way. If anything, the strict substantive provisions of the ESA justify *more* stringent enforcement of its procedural requirements, because the procedural requirements are designed to ensure compliance with the substantive provisions. The ESA's procedural requirements call for a systematic determination of the effects of a federal project on endangered species. If a project is allowed to proceed without substantial compliance with those procedural requirements, there can be no assurance that a violation of the ESA's substantive provisions will not result. The latter, of course, impermissible. *See TVA v. Hill,* 437 U.S. 153.

The district court, citing *Palila v. Hawaii Dept. of Land and Natural Resources,* 639 F.2d 495 (9th Cir. 1981), held that "[a] party asserting a violation of the Endangered Species Act has the burden of showing the proposed action would have some prohibited effect on an endangered species or its critical habitat," and found that the plaintiffs in this case had not met that burden. * * * This is a misapplication of *Palila*. That case concerned the ESA's prohibition of the "taking" of an endangered species, 16 U.S.C. § 1538(a)(1)(B), not the ESA's procedural requirements. Quite naturally, the court in *Palila* found that a plaintiff, in order to establish a violation of the "taking" provision, must show that such a "taking" has occurred. *See* 639 F.2d at 497. The holding does not apply to violations of the ESA's procedural requirements. A plaintifs' burden in establishing a procedural violation is to show that the circumstances triggering the procedural requirement exist, and that the required procedures have not been followed. The plaintiffs in this case have clearly met that burden.

The Forest Service would require the district court, absent proof by the plaintiffs to the contrary, to make a finding that the Jersey Jack road is not likely to effect the Rocky Mountain Gray Wolf, and that therefore any failure to comply with ESA procedures is harmless. This is not a finding appropriate to the district court at the present time. Congress has assigned to the agencies and to the Fish & Wildlife Service the responsibility for evaluation of the impact of agency actions on endangered species, and has prescribed procedures for such evaluation. Only by following the procedures can proper evaluations be made. It is not the responsibility of the plaintiffs to prove, nor the function of the courts to judge, the effect of a proposed action on an endangered species when proper procedures have not been followed. *Cf. City of Davis v. Coleman*, 521 F.2d 661, 671 (9th Cir. 1975) (under NEPA, agency, not plaintiff, is responsible for investigating the environmental effects of a proposed action).

We therefore hold that the district court erred in declining to enjoin construction of the Jersey Jack road pending compliance with the ESA.

NOTES

1. What are the contents of a biological opinion? In discussing standing and jurisdictional issues under the ESA, Justice Scalia provides a concise synopsis in *Bennett v. Spear* (described in more detail in Chapter 5, *infra*).

If an agency determines that action it proposes to take may adversely affect a listed species, it must engage in formal consultation with the Fish and Wildlife Service, as delegate of the Secretary, ibid.; 50 CFR § 402.14 (1995), after which the Service must provide the agency with a written statement (the Biological Opinion) explaining how the proposed action will affect the species or its habitat, 16 U.S.C. § 1536(b)(3)(A). If the Service concludes that the proposed action will "jeopardize the continued existence of any [listed] species or result in the destruction or adverse modification of [critical habitat]," § 1536(a)(2), the Biological Opinion must outline any "reasonable and prudent alternatives" that the Service believes will avoid that consequence, § 1536(b)(3)(A). Additionally, if the Biological Opinion concludes that the agency action will not result in jeopardy or adverse habitat modification, or if it offers reasonable and prudent alternatives to avoid that consequence, the Service must provide the agency with a written statement (known as the "Incidental Take Statement") specifying the "impact of such incidental taking on the species," any "reasonable and prudent measures that the [Service] considers necessary or appropriate to minimize such impact," and setting forth "the terms and conditions . . . that must be complied with by the Federal agency . . . to implement [those measures]." § 1536(b)(4). 520 U.S. 154, 158 (1997).

2. Aside from the core requirement of the consultation provision, two main qualifiers to note are that the requirement only applies to *actions* by *federal agencies*. While the definition of federal agencies is narrow and for the most part obvious, what defines an action is broader. As § 7(a)(2) itself states, the consultation requirement applies to "any action *authorized, funded, or carried out*" by a federal agency. 16 U.S.C. § 1536(a)(2) (emphasis added). Repeated litigation over the scope of this requirement has revealed a broad definition of federal actions.

In *Conner v. Burford*, 848 F.2d 1441, 1457–58 (9th Cir. 1988), the court held that, in preparing a biological opinion before the issuance of oil and gas leases, the agency action must be defined to encompass not only the leasing decision itself but also all post-leasing activities and their impacts. In *Tinoqui–Chalola Council of Kitanemuk & Yowlumne Tejon Indians v. United States Department of Energy*, 232 F.3d 1300 (9th Cir. 2000), the court held that the negotiation and execution of contracts constitutes an agency action. In *Turtle Island Restoration Network v. National Marine Fisheries Service*, 340 F.3d 969 (9th Cir. 2003), the court held that NMFS' issuance of fishing permits to boats clearly constituted agency action under the ESA.

On the other hand, in *Sierra Club v. Babbitt*, 65 F.3d 1502 (9th Cir. 1995), the court held that § 7 consultation does not apply to agreements finalized before the passage of the ESA over which the agency currently lacks discretion. In that case, the Bureau of Land Management (whose land is often "checkerboarded" with private land for complex historical reasons) entered into a reciprocal right-of-way agreement in 1962 with a logging company that owned adjacent lands. The agreement granted the company the right to construct logging roads over BLM land to access its private property. The agreement gave BLM the right to refuse construction of such roads, but only for three limited reasons. Pursuant to this agreement, the company submitted a road construction proposal in 1990, and environmental plaintiffs sued BLM on the basis that its approval of the proposal amounted to federal action under § 7 of the ESA. The court disagreed, however, for two reasons. First, the agreement occurred prior to the enactment of the ESA; and, second, the BLM lacked any discretion to take action pursuant to endangered species.

National Ass'n of Home Builders v. Defenders of Wildlife, 551 U.S. 644 (2007) presented a difficult question of statutory construction involving § 7 and § 402(b) of the Clean Water Act. Section 402(b) sets forth nine statutory criteria a state must meet in order to receive permitting power under the CWA; so long as a state meets those criteria, the EPA must transfer the authority. Section 7, of course, creates a mandatory duty on the part of federal agencies to insure that federal action is not likely to jeopardize endangered or threatened species. The question raised in *National Home-*

builders was whether the EPA, in evaluating the State of Arizona's application for permitting authority, had to insure under § 7 of the ESA that the transfer would not jeopardize the continued existence of endangered or threatened species or whether it simply had to find that Arizona met the nine CWA statutory criteria. The Court, in a 5–4 decision, held that as long as the nine statutory criteria are met, the EPA must transfer permitting authority. Since the EPA does not have discretion to deny permitting authority so long as the CWA statutory criteria are met, § 7 does not apply.

3.   Section 7 applies with as much force to the "destruction or adverse modification" of critical habitat as it does to actions that may jeopardize the species. 16 U.S.C. § 1536(a)(2); *see also Gifford Pinchot Task Force v. United States Fish & Wildlife Serv.*, 378 F.3d 1059 (9th Cir. 2004) (remanding Service's biological opinions to lower court on the basis that "agency's finding that loss of critical habitat was not an 'adverse modification' because of the existence of suitable external habitat is arbitrary and capricious and is contrary to law.").

4.   As with NEPA, the scope of analysis under § 7 is important, and a faulty or insufficient scope can result in the overturning of the biological opinion. In *Pacific Coast Federation of Fishermen's Association v. National Marine Fisheries Service*, 71 F.Supp.2d 1063 (W.D. Wash. 1999), the court overturned NMFS's biological opinion with regard to several fish species. The Service improperly employed a long-term, watershed approach in making jeopardy determinations and failed to require the action agencies to adequately incorporate watershed analysis into their biological opinions. *See also Conner v. Burford*, *supra*, regarding the incorporation of post-leasing activities into the scope of the biological opinion.

5.   What happens after a jeopardy determination? The overwhelming majority of consultations under § 7(a)(2) result in a finding of 'no jeopardy' and, accordingly, only a minimal adjustment to the original plan of the federal action, such as scaling back a proposed timber cut, excluding particularly vital pieces of habitat from a plan, or adjusting the location or flow of a dam. In the small number of cases for which the determination is jeopardy or an injunction issues because of a failure of consultation, the on-the-ground results can be monumental. For example, in the aftermath of the listing of the Northern Spotted Owl, the designation of critical habitat, and President Clinton's Northwest Forest Plan, all noted *supra*, and the listing of other species such as the Marbled Murrelet, there has been a significant reduction in the annual timber cut in the Pacific Northwest.

The ESA can also have a dramatic effect on water supply and allocation, a matter of great political salience in the west where water supply remains a subject of intense conflict. Because of the ESA, water supply for irrigation or domestic consumption may need to be reduced—even during peak growing season—to leave sufficient in-stream flows for the survival and reproduction of endangered species. For example, in *National Wildlife Federation v. National Marine Fisheries Service*, 2005 WL 1398223 (D. Or. 2005), environmental plaintiffs won a preliminary injunction against the National Marine Fisheries Service (NMFS) due to the insufficiency of NMFS' biological opinions addressing the impact of the continuing operation of dams on salmon in the Columbia and Snake Rivers. Under the injunction, Judge Redden ordered the action agencies (the U.S. Army Corps of Engineers and the Bureau of Reclamation) to:

> (1) Provide spill from June 20, 2005, through August 31, 2005, of all water in excess of that required for station service, on a 24–hour basis, at the Lower Granite, Little Goose, Lower Monumental, and Ice Harbor Dams on the lower Snake River; and

> (2) Provide spill from July 1, 2005, through August 31, 2005, of all flows above 50,000 cfs, on 24–hour basis, at the McNary Dam on the Columbia River. *Id.* at *17.

The "spill" referred to in the injunction is the release of water through the spill gates of the dams rather than the hydroelectric turbines. Such spill would allow for the safe and easier passage of juvenile salmon in their downstream journey. Judge Redden found such spill to be necessary in order "to avoid irreparable harm to juvenile fall chinook" salmon.

Though the agencies alleged that such spill would account for millions of dollars in lost revenue and electricity (indeed, among the appellants was the Bonneville Power Administration Customer Group), the Ninth Circuit affirmed the injunction. *National Wildlife Fed'n v. National Marine Fisheries Serv.*, 422 F.3d 782 (9th Cir. 2005).

D.   THE TAKE PROHIBITION: SECTION 9

Section 9 of the ESA, arguably the most controversial aspect of the statute, establishes the broad prohibition against "taking" endangered species. The text of the prohibition is brief, stating simply:

> with respect to any endangered species of fish or wildlife listed pursuant to section 4 of this Act it is unlawful for any person subject to the jurisdiction of the United States to—* * *

> (B) take any such species within the United States or the territorial sea of the United States;

> (C) take any such species upon the high seas * * *.

16 U.S.C. § 1538(a)(1) (2000).

Unlike § 7, which applies only to federal agencies, § 9 applies to "any person subject to the jurisdiction of the United States." Also unlike § 7, the take prohibition only applies to endangered species (though the current regulations of the Fish and Wildlife Service apply the prohibition to both threatened and endangered species).

To understand the take prohibition, it is necessary to consult § 3, the definitions section of the Act. Under § 3(19), "take" is defined as meaning "to harass, harm, pursue, hunt, shoot, wound, kill, trap, capture, or collect, or to attempt to engage in any such conduct." 16 U.S.C. § 1532(19) (2000). During the 1980s, a series of ESA cases were litigated in the U.S. District Court for the District of Hawaii and the Ninth Circuit concerning the Palila, an endangered bird native to Hawaii. To date, they remain the only line of cases in which a party was held liable under § 9 for failing to prevent a non-native species from destroying the habitat of an endangered species. In *Palila v. Hawaii Department of Land and Natural Resources*, 639 F.2d 495 (9th Cir. 1981) (*Palila I*) the Ninth Circuit addressed the question of whether the Hawaii Department of Land and Natural Resources could be held liable for failure to remove feral, non-native goats and sheep from the Palila's critical habitat. The Department had maintained a herd of the goats and sheep on the slopes of Mauna Kea, within the Palila's critical habitat, for the purposes of sport hunting. As the goats and sheep grazed on the slopes, the forest receded, thereby reducing the Palila's habitat. Though the Department fenced off about 25% of the forest, it chose not to remove the goats and sheep. In holding that this failure to remove the goats and sheep was a violation of § 9, the court noted that the regulatory definition of "harm" as "activity that results in significant environmental modification or degradation of the endangered animal's habitat." *Id.* at 497 (citing 50 C.F.R. § 17.3(c) (1981)). Since the goats and sheep were harming the Palila under this definition, and since the eradication of the goats and sheep was necessary to prevent this harm, the court held the Department to have violated § 9.

In the aftermath of *Palila I*, the Secretary of the Interior changed the definition of harm under 50 C.F.R. § 17.3. The new definition included the requirement that harm include significant habitat modification or degradation where it actually kills or injures wildlife by significantly impairing essential behavioral patterns, including breeding, feeding or sheltering." *See* Endangered and Threatened Wildlife and Plants; Final Redefinition of "Harm," 46 Fed. Reg. 54,748, 54,750 (Nov. 4, 1981) (later codified at 50 C.F.R. § 17.3). While the definition still allowed for harm via habitat modification or degradation, it added the seemingly more stringent requirement that such modification or degradation must actually kill or injure wildlife. In *Palila v. Hawaii Department of Land and Natural Resources*, 649 F.Supp. 1070 (D. Haw. 1986) (*Palila II*), the District Court for the District of Hawaii revisited the Palila controversy on the basis of defendants' argument that, under the new regulation, plaintiffs must show actual injury or death. The court refused to accept the narrow definition of harm under this argument. Instead, the court stated:

> A finding of "harm" does not require death to individual members of the species; nor does it require a finding that habitat degradation is presently driving the species further toward extinction. Habitat destruction that prevents the recovery of the species by affecting essential behavioral patterns causes actual injury to the species and effects a taking under § 9 of the Act.

Id. at 1075. Subsequently, the Ninth Circuit affirmed this holding. *Palila v. Hawaii Department of Land and Natural Resources*, 852 F.2d 1106 (9th Cir. 1988) (affirming district court and ordering removal of sheep). The litigation over the new regulation culminated in the Supreme Court decision excerpted below.

In the case below, the Supreme Court considered whether the regulatory definition was a lawful interpretation of the Act.

BABBITT v. SWEET HOME CHAPTER OF COMMUNITIES FOR A GREAT OREGON

Supreme Court of the United States, 1995.
515 U.S. 687, 115 S.Ct. 2407, 132 L.Ed.2d 597.

[The plaintiffs were small landowners, logging companies, and families dependent on the logging industry in the Pacific Northwest and in the Southeast. They brought this action to challenge the Secretary of the Interior's regulation defining the term "take" under § 9 of the ESA. Section 9 makes it unlawful for any person to take endangered species, and defines "take" to mean "harass, harm, pursue," "wound," or "kill." The regulation further defines "harm" to include "significant habitat modification or degradation where it actually kills or injures wildlife." The plaintiffs alleged that application of the "harm" regulation to the red-cockaded woodpecker, an endangered species, and the northern spotted owl, a threatened species, covered by § 9 through regulation, had injured them economically. In an *en banc* opinion, the D.C. Circuit held that the word "harm" was limited to the direct application of force, partly because of its concern regarding the implications of the regulation in terms of the resulting extinction of "property rights."]

JUSTICE STEVENS delivered the opinion of the Court.

Because this case was decided on motions for summary judgment, we may appropriately make certain factual assumptions in order to frame the legal issue. First, we assume respondents have no desire to harm either the red-cockaded woodpecker or the spotted owl; they merely wish to continue logging activities that would be entirely proper if not prohibited by the ESA. On the other hand, we must assume arguendo that those activities will have the effect, even though unintended, of detrimentally changing the natural habitat of both listed species and that, as a consequence, members of those species will be killed or injured. Under respondents' view of the law, the Secretary's only means of forestalling that grave result—even when the actor knows it is certain to occur[6]—is to use his § 5 authority to purchase the lands on which the survival of the species depends. The Secretary, on the other hand, submits that the § 9 prohibition on takings, which Congress defined to include "harm," places on respondents a duty to avoid harm that habitat alteration will cause the birds unless respondents first obtain a permit pursuant to § 10.

---

6. As discussed above, the Secretary's definition of "harm" is limited to "act[s] which actually kil[l] or injur[e] wildlife." * * * We do not agree with the dissent that the regulation covers results that are not "even foreseeable * * * no matter how long the chain of causality between modification and injury." Respondents have suggested no reason why either the "knowingly violates" or the "otherwise violates" provision of the statute—or the "harm" regulation itself—should not be read to incorporate ordinary requirements of proximate causation and foreseeability.

The text of the Act provides three reasons for concluding that the Secretary's interpretation is reasonable. First, an ordinary understanding of the word "harm" supports it. The dictionary definition of the verb form of "harm" is "to cause hurt or damage to: injure." In the context of the ESA, that definition naturally encompasses habitat modification that results in actual injury or death to members of an endangered or threatened species.

def of (harm)

Respondents argue that the Secretary should have limited the purview of "harm" to direct applications of force against protected species, but the dictionary definition does not include the word "directly" or suggest in any way that only direct or willful action that leads to injury constitutes "harm." Moreover, unless the statutory term "harm" encompasses indirect as well as direct injuries, the word has no meaning that does not duplicate the meaning of other words that § 3 uses to define "take." A reluctance to treat statutory terms as surplusage supports the reasonableness of the Secretary's interpretation.

harm may be indirect

Second, the broad purpose of the ESA supports the Secretary's decision to extend protection against activities that cause the precise harms Congress enacted the statute to avoid. In *TVA v. Hill* [page 192, *supra*], we described the Act as "the most comprehensive legislation for the preservation of endangered species ever enacted by any nation." Whereas predecessor statutes enacted in 1966 and 1969 had not contained any sweeping prohibition against the taking of endangered species except on federal lands, the 1973 Act applied to all land in the United States and to the Nation's territorial seas. As stated in § 2 of the Act, among its central purposes is "to provide a means whereby the ecosystems upon which endangered species and threatened species depend may be conserved * * *."

In *Hill*, we construed § 7 as precluding the completion of the Tellico Dam because of its predicted impact on the survival of the snail darter. Both our holding and the language in our opinion stressed the importance of the statutory policy. "The plain intent of Congress in enacting this statute," we recognized, "was to halt and reverse the trend toward species extinction, whatever the cost. This is reflected not only in the stated policies of the Act, but in literally every section of the statute." Although the § 9 "take" prohibition was not at issue in *Hill*, we took note of that prohibition, placing particular emphasis on the Secretary's inclusion of habitat modification in his definition of "harm." In light of that provision for habitat protection, we could "not understand how TVA intends to operate Tellico Dam without 'harming' the snail darter." Congress' intent to provide comprehensive protection for endangered and threatened species supports the permissibility of the Secretary's "harm" regulation.

Respondents advance strong arguments that activities that cause minimal or unforeseeable harm will not violate the Act as construed in the "harm" regulation. Respondents, however, present a facial challenge to the regulation. Thus, they ask us to invalidate the Secretary's understanding of "harm" in every circumstance, even when an actor knows that an activity, such as draining a pond, would actually result in the extinction of a listed species by destroying its habitat. Given Congress' clear expression of the ESA's broad purpose to protect endangered and threatened wildlife, the Secretary's definition of "harm" is reasonable.[7]

Third, the fact that Congress in 1982 authorized the Secretary to issue permits for takings that § 9(a)(1)(B) would otherwise prohibit, "if such taking is incidental to, and not the purpose of, the carrying out of an otherwise lawful activity," 16 U.S.C. § 1539(a)(1)(B), strongly suggests that Congress understood § 9(a)(1)(B) to prohibit indirect as well as deliberate takings. The permit process requires the applicant to prepare a "conservation plan" that specifies how he intends to "minimize and mitigate" the "impact" of his activity on endangered and threatened species, 16 U.S.C. § 1539(a)(2)(A), making clear that Congress had in mind foreseeable rather than merely accidental effects on listed species. No one could seriously request an "incidental" take permit to avert § 9 liability for direct, deliberate action against a member of an endangered or threatened species, but respondents would read "harm" so narrowly that the permit procedure would have little more than that absurd purpose. "When Congress acts to amend a statute, we presume it intends its amendment to have real and substantial effect." Congress' addition of the § 10 permit provision supports the Secretary's conclusion that activities not intended to harm an endangered species, such as habitat modification, may constitute unlawful takings under the ESA unless the Secretary permits them.

We need not decide whether the statutory definition of "take" compels the Secretary's interpretation of "harm," because our conclusions that Congress did not unambiguously manifest its intent to adopt respondents' view and that the Secretary's interpretation is reasonable suffice to decide this case. The latitude the ESA gives the Secretary in enforcing the statute, together with the degree of regulatory expertise necessary to its enforcement, establishes that we owe some degree of deference to the Secretary's reasonable interpretation. * * *

When it enacted the ESA, Congress delegated broad administrative and interpretive power to the Secretary. The task of defining and listing endangered and threatened species requires an expertise and attention to detail that exceeds the normal province of Congress. Fashioning appropriate standards for issuing permits under § 10 for takings that would

---

7. The dissent incorrectly asserts that the Secretary's regulation (1) "dispenses with the foreseeability of harm" and (2) "fail[s] to require injury to particular animals." As to the first assertion, the regulation merely implements the statute, and it is therefore subject to the statute's "knowingly violates" language, *see* 16 U.S.C. §§ 1540(a)(1), (b)(1), and ordinary requirements of proximate causation and foreseeability. Nothing in the regulation purports to weaken those requirements. To the contrary, the word "actually" in the regulation should be construed to limit the liability about which the dissent appears most concerned, liability under the statute's "otherwise violates" provision. The Secretary did not need to include "actually" to connote "but for" causation, which the other words in the definition obviously require. As to the dissent's second assertion, every term in the regulation's definition of "harm" is subservient to the phrase "an act which actually kills or injures wildlife."

otherwise violate § 9 necessarily requires the exercise of broad discretion. The proper interpretation of a term such as "harm" involves a complex policy choice. When Congress has entrusted the Secretary with broad discretion, we are especially reluctant to substitute our views of wise policy for his. In this case, that reluctance accords with our conclusion, based on the text, structure, and legislative history of the ESA, that the Secretary reasonably construed the intent of Congress when he defined "harm" to include "significant habitat modification or degradation that actually kills or injures wildlife."

In the elaboration and enforcement of the ESA, the Secretary and all persons who must comply with the law will confront difficult questions of proximity and degree; for, as all recognize, the Act encompasses a vast range of economic and social enterprises and endeavors. These questions must be addressed in the usual course of the law, through case-by-case resolution and adjudication.

JUSTICE O'CONNOR, concurring.

My agreement with the Court is founded on two understandings. First, the challenged regulation is limited to significant habitat modification that causes actual, as opposed to hypothetical or speculative, death or injury to identifiable protected animals. Second, even setting aside difficult questions of scienter, the regulation's application is limited by ordinary principles of proximate causation, which introduce notions of foreseeability. These limitations, in my view, call into question *Palila v. Hawaii Dept. of Land and Natural Resources*, 852 F.2d 1106 (C.A.9 1988) (*Palila II*), and with it, many of the applications derided by the dissent. Because there is no need to strike a regulation on a facial challenge out of concern that it is susceptible of erroneous application, however, and because there are many habitat-related circumstances in which the regulation might validly apply, I join the opinion of the Court.

In my view, the regulation is limited by its terms to actions that actually kill or injure individual animals. Justice Scalia disagrees, arguing that the harm regulation "encompasses injury inflicted, not only upon individual animals, but upon populations of the protected species." At one level, I could not reasonably quarrel with this observation; death to an individual animal always reduces the size of the population in which it lives, and in that sense, "injures" that population. But by its insight, the dissent means something else. Building upon the regulation's use of the word "breeding," Justice Scalia suggests that the regulation facially bars significant habitat modification that actually kills or injures hypothetical animals (or, perhaps more aptly, causes potential additions to the population not to come into being). Because "[i]mpairment of breeding does not 'injure' living creatures," Justice Scalia reasons, the regulation must contemplate application to "a population of animals which would otherwise have maintained or increased its numbers."

I disagree. As an initial matter, I do not find it as easy as Justice Scalia does to dismiss the notion that significant impairment of breeding injures living creatures. To raze the last remaining ground on which the piping plover currently breeds, thereby making it impossible for any piping plovers to reproduce, would obviously injure the population (causing the species' extinction in a generation). But by completely preventing breeding, it would also injure the individual living bird, in the same way that sterilizing the creature injures the individual living bird. To "injure" is, among other things, "to impair." One need not subscribe to theories of "psychic harm," to recognize that to make it impossible for an animal to reproduce is to impair its most essential physical functions and to render that animal, and its genetic material, biologically obsolete. This, in my view, is actual injury.

In any event, even if impairing an animal's ability to breed were not, in and of itself, an injury to that animal, interference with breeding can cause an animal to suffer other, perhaps more obvious, kinds of injury. The regulation has clear application, for example, to significant habitat modification that kills or physically injures animals which, because they are in a vulnerable breeding state, do not or cannot flee or defend themselves, or to environmental pollutants that cause an animal to suffer physical complications during gestation. Breeding, feeding, and sheltering are what animals do. If significant habitat modification, by interfering with these essential behaviors, actually kills or injures an animal protected by the Act, it causes "harm" within the meaning of the regulation. In contrast to Justice Scalia, I do not read the regulation's "breeding" reference to vitiate or somehow to qualify the clear actual death or injury requirement, or to suggest that the regulation contemplates extension to nonexistent animals.

JUSTICE SCALIA, with whom THE CHIEF JUSTICE and JUSTICE THOMAS join, dissenting.

I think it unmistakably clear that the legislation at issue here (1) forbade the hunting and killing of endangered animals, and (2) provided federal lands and federal funds for the acquisition of private lands, to preserve the habitat of endangered animals. The Court's holding that the hunting and killing prohibition incidentally preserves habitat on private lands imposes unfairness to the point of financial ruin—not just upon the rich, but upon the simplest farmer who finds his land conscripted to national zoological use. I respectfully dissent. * * *

The regulation has three features which, for reasons I shall discuss at length below, do not comport with the statute. First, it interprets the statute to prohibit habitat modification that is no more than the cause-in-fact of death or injury to wildlife. Any "significant habitat modification" that in fact produces that result by "impairing essential behavioral patterns" is made unlawful, regardless of whether that result is intended or even foreseeable, and no matter how long the chain of causality between modification and injury. See, e.g., *Palila v. Hawaii Dept. of Land and Natural Resources (Palila II)*, 852 F.2d 1106, 1108–1109 (C.A.9 1988) (sheep grazing constituted "taking" of palila birds, since although sheep do not destroy full-grown mamane trees, they do destroy mamane seed-lings, which will not grow to full-grown trees, on which the palila feeds and nests).

Second, the regulation does not require an "act": the Secretary's officially stated position is that an omission will do. The previous version of the regulation made this explicit. * * * When the regulation was modified in 1981 the phrase "or omission" was taken out, but only because (as the final publication of the rule advised) "the [Fish and Wildlife] Service feels that 'act' is inclusive of either commissions or omissions which would be prohibited by § [1538(a)(1)(B)]." In its brief here the Government agrees that the regulation covers omissions (although it argues that "[a]n 'omission' constitutes an 'act' * * * only if there is a legal duty to act").

The third and most important unlawful feature of the regulation is that it encompasses injury inflicted, not only upon individual animals, but upon populations of the protected species. "Injury" in the regulation includes "significantly impairing essential behavioral patterns, including breeding." Impairment of breeding does not "injure" living creatures; it prevents them from propagating, thus "injuring" a population of animals which would otherwise have maintained or increased its numbers. What the face of the regulation shows, the Secretary's official pronouncements confirm. The Final Redefinition of "Harm" accompanying publication of the regulation said that "harm" is not limited to "direct physical injury to an individual member of the wildlife species," and refers to "injury to a population."

None of these three features of the regulation can be found in the statutory provisions supposed to authorize it. The term "harm" in § 1532(19) has no legal force of its own. An indictment or civil complaint that charged the defendant with "harming" an animal protected under the Act would be dismissed as defective, for the only operative term in the statute is to "take." If "take" were not elsewhere defined in the Act, none could dispute what it means, for the term is as old as the law itself. To "take," when applied to wild animals, means to reduce those animals, by killing or capturing, to human control. See, e.g., 11 *Oxford English Dictionary* (1933) ("Take . . . To catch, capture (a wild beast, bird, fish, etc.)"); *Webster's New International Dictionary of the English Language* (2d ed. 1949) (take defined as "to catch or capture by trapping, snaring, etc., or as prey"); *Geer v. Connecticut*, 161 U.S. 519, 523, 16 S.Ct. 600, 602, 40 L.Ed. 793 (1896) ("[A]ll the animals which can be taken upon the earth, in the sea, or in the air, that is to say, wild animals, belong to those who take them") (quoting the Digest of Justinian); 2 W. Blackstone, *Commentaries* 411 (1766) ("Every man . . . has an equal right of pursuing and taking to his own use all such creatures as are ferae naturae"). This is just the sense in which "take" is used elsewhere in federal legislation and treaty. And that meaning fits neatly with the rest of § 1538(a)(1), which makes it unlawful not only to take protected species, but also to import or export them; to possess, sell, deliver, carry, transport, or ship any taken species; and to transport, sell, or offer to sell them in interstate or foreign commerce. The taking prohibition, in other words, is only part of the regulatory plan of § 1538(a)(1), which covers all the stages of the process by which protected wildlife is reduced to man's dominion and made the object of profit. It is obvious that "take" in this sense—a term of art deeply embedded in the statutory and common law concerning wildlife—describes a class of acts (not omissions) done directly and intentionally (not indirectly and by accident) to particular animals (not populations of animals).

The Act's definition of "take" does expand the word slightly (and not unusually), so as to make clear that it includes not just a completed taking, but the process of taking, and all of the acts that are customarily identified with or accompany that process ("to harass, harm, pursue, hunt, shoot, wound, kill, trap, capture, or collect"); and so as to include attempts. § 1532(19). The tempting fallacy—which the Court commits with abandon—is to assume that once defined, "take" loses any significance, and it is only the definition that matters. The Court treats the statute as though Congress had directly enacted the § 1532(19) definition as a self-executing prohibition, and had not enacted § 1538(a)(1)(B) at all. But § 1538(a)(1)(B) is there, and if the terms contained in the definitional section are susceptible of two readings, one of which comports with the standard meaning of "take" as used in application to wildlife, and one of which does not, an agency regulation that adopts the latter reading is necessarily unreasonable, for it reads the defined term "take"—the only operative term—out of the statute altogether. * * *

The Endangered Species Act is a carefully considered piece of legislation that forbids all persons to hunt or harm endangered animals, but places upon the public at large, rather than upon fortuitously accountable individual landowners, the cost of preserving the habitat of endangered species. There is neither textual support for, nor even evidence of congressional consideration of, the radically different disposition contained in the regulation that the Court sustains. For these reasons, I respectfully dissent.

NOTES

1. Justice Scalia is the primary proponent of "textualism" in statutory interpretation. How persuasive is his argument that the ESA unambiguously precludes the agency's interpretation? The centerpiece of the dissent is his assertion that the word "take", as applied to wildlife, is "as old as the law itself," and means "to reduce those animals, by killing or capturing, to human control." How likely is it that a reasonable member of Congress would have had in mind the meaning of the term "take" in game law? After all, the statute is not an amendment to other game or fishing laws, but instead is an aggressive addition to the corpus of federal environmental law, where the historic meaning of the word "take" might not immediately spring to mind. Moreover, while Justice Scalia is only willing to concede that the statutory

definition of a taking "does expand the word slightly," surely a member of Congress who wanted to know what the word meant would have been more likely to look at the plain language of the definition section of the bill than to consult a treatise on game law.

Wouldn't it be peculiar to say that Mrs. O'Leary's cow didn't "harm" the people of Chicago when she kicked over the lantern that started the Chicago fire. (After all, she "only" modified their habitat!) Similarly, as a matter of ordinary English usage, doesn't someone who destroys the nesting grounds used by an endangered species or eliminates their food supply thereby harm them? Is Justice Scalia's interpretation really driven by the demands of the statutory text, or is he more motivated by his concern that the agency's interpretation "imposes unfairness to the point of financial ruin not just upon the rich, but upon the simplest farmer who finds his land conscripted to national zoological use"?

2. How much does *Sweet Home* narrow the regulatory definition through concepts such as proximate cause? For instance, if logging removes forest cover that helps protect an endangered bird from raptors, is the logging a proximate cause of harm? *See* Steven P. Quarles et al., Sweet Home *and the Narrowing of Wildlife 'Take' Under Section 9 of the Endangered Species Act,* 26 ENVTL. L. REP. 10,003, 10,012 (1996) (arguing against liability). The *Sweet Home* criteria may pose significant practical problems for developers:

> Questions of proximate cause and foreseeability are usually debatable. This uncertainty becomes more acute as the scale of activity and potential number of species members affected become smaller in scope. While we may know enough to conclude with reasonable certainty that a species as a whole is endangered, the localized effects of habitat loss on identifiable members of the species can be difficult to pinpoint. Even where a species' behavior characteristics and the habitat associated with them are well-defined, the effect of disturbance in or near areas of the habitat can be uncertain in terms of both predictability in advance and causal determination in retrospect.... Failure to investigate the potential effects of a project leaves the project fully exposed to subsequent liability should a take occur, with little basis for arguing unforeseeability given the absence of any effort to foresee. [But even] with intensive on-site studies it is usually difficult, if not impossible, to conclusively rule out all the possibilities.

J.B. Ruhl, *How to Kill Endangered Species, Legally: the Nuts and Bolts of Endangered Species Act 'HCP' Permits for Real Estate Development,* 5 ENVTL. LAW. 345, 361 (1999).

3. Should a property owner be deprived of the right to modify the habitat of an endangered species without compensation? Consider whether this would be a taking under current Supreme Court doctrine. *See Good v. United States,* 39 Fed. Cl. 81 (1997) (no taking unless all economic value is destroyed). *See also* Robert Meltz, *Where the Wild Things Are: The Endangered Species Act and Private Property,* 24 ENVTL. L. 369 (1994). On the other hand, if no compensation is offered, doesn't that give landowners an incentive to develop land quickly, eliminating possible endangered species, before legal restrictions can be imposed? *See* David A. Dana, *Natural Preservation and the*

Race to Develop, 143 U. PA. L. REV. 655 (1995). For a policy argument in favor of building compensation payments into habitat conservation plans, see Barton H. Thompson, *The Endangered Species Act: A Case Study in Takings and Incentives*, 49 STAN. L. REV. 305 (1997). One possibility is a scheme in which land is assigned values based on its significance for conservation purposes; property owners wishing to develop land must acquire units from other landowners. *Id.* at 342. (Compare the marketable permit schemes discussed in Chapter 6.) For a detailed analysis of the economic issues, *see* Robert Innes, et al., *Takings, Compensation and Endangered Species Protection on Private Lands*, 12 J. ECON. PERSP. 35 (Summer 1998).

4.   Under § 11(b) of the ESA, criminal liability is attached to "knowing" violations of § 9. *See* 16 U.S.C. § 1538(b). Such a knowing violation was the subject of *United States v. McKittrick*, 142 F.3d 1170 (9th Cir. 1998), in which the respondent was charged with knowingly taking an endangered gray wolf in violation of § 9(a)(1)(G) of the Act and regulations promulgated under that section. The court of appeals affirmed the conviction over respondent's allegation that he "did not realize what he was shooting," holding that "McKittrick need not have known he was shooting a wolf to 'knowingly violate[ ]' the regulations protecting the experimental population." 142 F.3d at 1173, 1177. As Congress had reduced in § 11 "the standard for criminal violations from 'willfully' to 'knowingly,'" the section "requires only that McKittrick knew he was shooting an animal, and that the animal turned out to be a protected gray wolf." *Id.* at 1177 (internal citations omitted). Is this standard for criminal liability defensible in this context?

5.   Is § 9 constitutional? In *Gibbs v. Babbitt*, 214 F.3d 483 (4th Cir. 2000) (Wilkinson, J.), the court rebuffed a constitutional challenge to a regulation under the ESA which prohibited the taking of red wolves on private lands. Yet there remain questions about how to categorize the underlying "regulated activity" in these cases for Commerce Clause purposes. In *GDF Realty Investments, Ltd. v. Norton*, 169 F.Supp.2d 648 (W.D. Tex. 2001), landowner plaintiffs alleged that § 9, as applied to habitat modifications on their properties, overstepped Congress' Commerce Clause authority. The case involved six species of listed invertebrates that resided entirely in underground caves ("Cave Species"). The court held that the activity regulated by § 9 in this case was the commercial development, which easily could be categorized as "activities that substantially affect interstate commerce." On appeal, the Fifth Circuit affirmed but rejected the lower court's rationale that commercial development was the regulated activity. Looking to the Supreme Court's recent decisions in *United States v. Morrison*, 529 U.S. 598 (2000) and *United States v. Lopez*, 514 U.S. 549 (1995), the court stated that, in performing an analysis of constitutionality under the Commerce Clause, a court must look to the conduct regulated by Congress (here, the taking of Cave Species) rather than the broader conduct implicated by the regulation (commercial development). Nevertheless, the court found that the aggregation of Cave Species takes together with the takes of all endangered species did implicate interstate commerce. *GDF Realty Investments, Ltd. v. Norton*, 326 F.3d 622 (5th Cir. 2003). *See also Rancho Viejo, LLC v. Norton*, 323 F.3d 1062 (D.C. Cir. 2003) (affirming dismissal of plaintiffs' Commerce Clause challenge to § 9); *cf. Rancho Viejo, LLC v. Norton*, 334 F.3d 1158 (D.C. Cir. 2003) (Roberts, J.,

dissenting) (noting the limiting necessity of looking only to the regulated activity and not beyond it). For more on the Commerce Clause analysis relevant to the ESA *see* Chapter 4, *infra*.

E. INCIDENTAL TAKE STATEMENTS

The § 7 consultation process often concludes with the issuance of an incidental take statement (ITS), which allows for the otherwise prohibited taking of listed species, so long as the taking is incidental to the agency action and within the terms of the ITS.

The governing provision for the issuance of incidental take statements is § 7(b)(4) of the Act. If, after § 7 consultation, the Secretary concludes:

(A) the agency action will not violate [Section 7(a)(2)], or offers reasonable and prudent alternatives which the Secretary believes would not violate such subsection;

(B) the taking of an endangered species or a threatened species incidental to the agency action will not violate such subsection; * * *

the Secretary shall provide the Federal agency and the applicant concerned, if any, with a written statement that—

(i) specifies the impact of such incidental taking on the species,

(ii) specifies those reasonable and prudent measures that the Secretary considers necessary or appropriate to minimize such impact, * * * [and]

(iv) sets forth the terms and conditions (including, but not limited to, reporting requirements) that must be complied with by the Federal agency or applicant (if any), or both, to implement the measures specified under clauses (ii) and (iii).

16 U.S.C. § 1536(b)(4) (2000).

This "written statement" has become known as an incidental take statement because it authorizes taking incidental to the permitted activity. Typically, the issuance of a biological opinion is accompanied by such an incidental take statement. A recent illustrative case concerning when an incidental take statement should be issued and what it must contain appears below.

ARIZONA CATTLE GROWERS' ASS'N v. UNITED STATES FISH AND WILDLIFE SERVICE

United States Court of Appeals for the Ninth Circuit, 2001.
273 F.3d 1229.

WARDLAW, CIRCUIT JUDGE:

[The Fish and Wildlife Service had consulted with the Bureau of Land Management over the issuance of several grazing permits on BLM lands. Though the Service concluded that none of the permits would jeopardize the continued existence of listed species, it still chose to issue incidental take statements for all of the permits. Arizona Cattle Grower's Association challenged the issuance of the ITSs as arbitrary and capricious. The district court agreed with plaintiffs on all but one of the permits, whose issuance it held was not arbitrary and capricious. The Ninth Circuit affirmed.]

V. Determining When the Fish and Wildlife Service Must Issue an Incidental Take Statement* * *

The Fish and Wildlife Service argues that the plain language of the statute and implementing regulations "expressly direct" it to issue an Incidental Take Statement in every case. * * *

* * * It is a "fundamental canon of statutory construction that the words of a statute must be read in their context and with a view to their place in the overall statutory scheme." Davis v. Mich. Dep't of Treasury, 489 U.S. 803, 809 * * * (1989). * * *

When read in context, it is clear that the issuance of the Incidental Take Statement is subject to the finding of the factors enumerated in the ESA. The statute explicitly provides that the written statement is subject to the consultation and the Secretary's conclusions. A contrary interpretation would render meaningless the clause stating that the Incidental Take Statement will specify "the impact of such incidental taking." 16 U.S.C. § 1536(b)(4)(C)(i) * * *. We therefore agree with ACGA that the plain language of the ESA does not dictate that the Fish and Wildlife Service must issue an Incidental Take Statement irrespective of whether any incidental takings will occur. * * *

The plain language of the implementing regulations also supports ACGA's argument. One regulation specifically instructs the Fish and Wildlife Service that its "responsibilities during formal consultation are . . . to formulate a statement concerning incidental take, if such take may occur." 50 C.F.R. § 402.14(g)(7) * * *. Moreover, the same regulation also instructs:

> (1) In those cases where the Service concludes that an action (or the implementation of any reasonable and prudent alternatives) and the resultant incidental take of listed species will not violate section 7(a)(2), . . . the Service will provide with the biological opinion a statement concerning incidental take that:
>
> > (i) Specifies the impact, i.e., the amount or extent, of such incidental taking on the species;

50 C.F.R. § 402.14(i)(1) (2001). Thus, consistent with the language of the statute, the regulations only require the issuance of an Incidental Take Statement when the "resultant incidental take of listed species will not violate section 7(a)(2)." Id. * * *.

Likewise, the legislative history supports this interpretation of the statute. If the sole purpose of the Incidental Take Statement is to provide shelter from § 9 penalties, as previously noted, it would be nonsensical to require the issuance of a Incidental Take Statement when no takings cognizable under Section 9 are to occur. * * *

* * * Accordingly, we hold that absent rare circumstances such as those involving migratory species, it is arbitrary and capricious to issue an Incidental Take Statement when the Fish and Wildlife Service has no rational basis to conclude that a take will occur incident to the otherwise lawful activity.

VI. Review of the Incidental Take Statements under the Arbitrary and Capricious Standard Pursuant to the APA

Because we reject the Fish and Wildlife Service's interpretation of the ESA and hold that it is not required to provide an Incidental Take Statement whenever it issues a Biological Opinion, we must now examine each Incidental Take Statement at issue under § 706. [Addressing each of the Incidental Take Statements issued by the Service, the court affirmed the district court's finding that the Service had not shown the existence of endangered species in any of the areas. Accordingly, the court affirmed the invalidation of the Incidental Take Statements.]

2. *The Anticipated Take Provisions*

[The court next approached the incidental take statements—for the "Cow Flat Allotment"—that the district court had not set aside, addressing the question as to whether the Service had acted arbitrarily and capriciously in failing to specify a certain number amount of anticipated take in the statements. In lieu of such number amounts, the Service had used language requiring certain conditions on land use.]

In general, Incidental Take Statements set forth a "trigger" that, when reached, results in an unacceptable level of incidental take, invalidating the safe harbor provision, and requiring the parties to reinitiate consultation. Ideally, this "trigger" should be a specific number. *See, e.g.,* Mausolf v. Babbitt, 125 F.3d 661 (8th Cir. 1997) (snowmobiling activity may take no more than two wolves); Fund for Animals v. Rice, 85 F.3d 535 (11th Cir. 1996) (municipal landfill may take fifty-two snakes during construction and an additional two snakes per year thereafter); Mt. Graham Red Squirrel v. Madigan, 954 F.2d 1441 (9th Cir. 1992) (telescope construction may take six red squirrels per year); Ctr. for Marine Conservation v. Brown, 917 F.Supp. 1128 (S.D. Tex. 1996) (shrimping operation may take four hawksbill turtles, four leatherback turtles, ten Kemp's ridley turtles, ten green turtles, or 370 loggerhead turtles). Here, however, the "trigger" took the form of several conditions. We must therefore determine whether the linking of the level of permissible take to the conditions set forth in the various Incidental Take Statements was arbitrary and capricious.

ACGA argues that the Incidental Take Statements fail to specify the amount or extent of authorized take with the required degree of exactness. Specifically, ACGA objected to the first condition:

The service concludes that incidental take of loach minnow from the proposed action will be considered to be exceeded if any of the following conditions are met:

[Condition 1] Ecological conditions do not improve under the proposed livestock management. Improving conditions can be defined through improvements in watershed, soil condition, trend and condition of rangelands (e.g., vegetative litter, plant vigor, and native species diversity), riparian conditions (e.g., vegetative and geomorphologic: bank, terrace, and flood plain conditions), and streamchannel conditions (e.g., channel profile, embeddedness, water temperature, and base flow) within the natural capabilities of the landscape in all pastures on the allotment within the Blue River watershed.

We have never held that a numerical limit is required. Indeed, we have upheld Incidental Take Statements that used a combination of numbers and estimates. * * *

Moreover, while Congress indicated its preference for a numerical value, it anticipated situations in which impact could not be contemplated in terms of a precise number. * * * In the absence of a specific numerical value, however, the Fish and Wildlife Service must establish that no such numerical value could be practically obtained.

We agree with the ACGA II court's conclusion that, "the use of ecological conditions as a surrogate for defining the amount or extent of incidental take is reasonable so long as these conditions are linked to the take of the protected species." * * * By "causal link" we do not mean that the Fish and Wildlife Service must demonstrate a specific number of takings; only that it must establish a link between the activity and the taking of species before setting forth specific conditions.

ACGA argues that it is entitled to more certainty than "vague and undetectable criteria such as changes in a 22,000 acre allotment's 'ecological condition.'" In response, the Fish and Wildlife Service argues that "the [Incidental Take Statement] provides for those studies necessary to provide the quantification of impacts which the Cattle Growers claim is lacking."

We disagree with the government's position. The Incidental Take Statements at issue here do not sufficiently discuss the causal connection between Condition 1 and the taking of the species at issue. Based on the Incidental Take Statement, if "ecological conditions do not improve," takings will occur. This vague analysis, however, cannot be what Congress contemplated when it anticipated that surrogate indices might be used in place of specific numbers. Moreover, whether there has been compliance with this vague directive is within the unfettered discretion of the Fish and Wildlife Service, leaving no method by which the applicant or the action agency can gauge their performance. * * *

Based upon the lack of an articulated, rational connection between Condition 1 and the taking of species, as well as the vagueness of the condition itself, we hold that its implementation was arbitrary and capricious. The terms of an Incidental Take Statement do not operate in a vacuum. To the contrary, they are integral parts of the statutory scheme, determining, among other things, when consultation must be reinitiated. Thus, even though the Fish and Wildlife Service was not arbitrary and capricious in issuing Incidental Take Statements for the Cow Flat Allotment, its failure to properly specify the amount of anticipated take and to provide a clear standard for determining when the authorized level of take has been exceeded is arbitrary and capricious. * * *

NOTE

Justice Scalia discusses the impact of a BO and ITS in *Bennett v. Spear*:

A Biological Opinion of the sort rendered here alters the legal regime to which the action agency is subject. When it "offers reasonable and prudent alternatives" to the proposed action, a Biological Opinion must include a so-called "Incidental Take Statement"—a written statement specifying, among other things, those "measures that the [Service] considers necessary or appropriate to minimize [the action's impact on the affected species]" and the "terms and conditions * * * that must be complied with by the Federal agency ... to implement [such] measures." 16 U.S.C. § 1536(b)(4). Any taking that is in compliance with these terms and conditions "shall not be considered to be a prohibited taking of the species concerned." § 1536(*o*)(2). Thus, the Biological Opinion's Incidental Take Statement constitutes a permit authorizing the action agency to "take" the endangered or threatened species so long as it respects the Service's "terms and conditions." The action agency is technically free to disregard the Biological Opinion and proceed with its proposed action, but it does so at its own peril (and that of its employees), for "any person" who knowingly "takes" an endangered or threatened species is subject to substantial civil and criminal penalties, including imprisonment. *See* § s 1540(a) and (b) (authorizing civil fines of up to $25,000 per violation and criminal penalties of up to $50,000 and imprisonment for one year); *see also Babbitt* v. *Sweet Home Chapter, Communities for Great Ore.*, 515 U.S. 687 (1995) (upholding interpretation of the term "take" to include significant habitat degradation).

The Service itself is, to put it mildly, keenly aware of the virtually determinative effect of its biological opinions. 520 U.S. 154, 169–70 (1997).

F.   RECOVERY OF LISTED SPECIES: SECTION 4(f)

Section 4(f) of the ESA governs recovery planning for threatened and endangered species. The pertinent text provides:

(1) The Secretary shall develop and implement plans (hereinafter in this subsection referred to as "recovery plans") for the conservation

and survival of endangered species and threatened species listed pursuant to this section, unless he finds that such a plan will not promote the conservation of the species. The Secretary, in developing and implementing recovery plans, shall, to the maximum extent practicable—* * *

   (B) incorporate in each plan—

      (i) a description of such site-specific management actions as may be necessary to achieve the plan's goal for the conservation and survival of the species;

      (ii) objective, measurable criteria which, when met, would result in a determination, in accordance with the provisions of this section, that the species be removed from the list; and

      (iii) estimates of the time required and the cost to carry out those measures needed to achieve the plan's goal and to achieve intermediate steps toward that goal.

16 U.S.C. § 1533(f) (2000). The excerpt below uses an appealing metaphor to help explain the role of recovery planning compared to the other provisions of the ESA.

FEDERICO CHEEVER, THE ROAD TO RECOVERY: A NEW WAY OF THINKING ABOUT THE ENDANGERED SPECIES ACT[8]

23 ECOLOGY L.Q. 1, 23–27 (1996).

The Wranglers and the Herd

A homey metaphor may assist in comprehending the relationship between designated species and the provisions of the Endangered Species Act designed to protect them. One may conceive of the population of administratively listed species as a herd of sick and injured animals (each animal representing an entire species) crossing the apocalyptic landscape created by human destruction of the natural environment and subject to threats by a variety of human predators. This herd of beasts moving across the landscape is under the protection of an eccentric set of "wranglers" representing the protections created by the provisions of the Endangered Species Act.

The wrangler who represents the § 4 listing process gathers new animals into the herd when they are sufficiently sick or injured to require protection. As she does, she brands each either "endangered" or "threatened." Ideally, her only concern is whether the animals she encounters meet the scientific criteria required for each brand. However, she has more work than she can reasonably handle, and has identified many animals apparently deserving the protection of the herd which she has not yet been able to brand. Once an animal is branded and placed in the herd, it is no longer the concern of the § 4 wrangler.

---

8. Copyright 1996. Reprinted by permission.

The wrangler who represents § 7 protects the entire herd—both threatened and endangered species. However, he only protects them from a specific type of threat—actions authorized, funded, or carried out by federal agencies—and he only protects them if the injury they suffer is potentially life-threatening, that is, likely to jeopardize the continued existence of the entire species. A non-federal actor might annihilate the herd and it would be of no concern to our § 7 wrangler. Federal actors or federally authorized actors may injure the herd members, prevent their return to health or harass them, and so long as the action does not significantly increase the chance of extinction it too would be of no concern to our § 7 wrangler.

The wrangler who represents § 9 will only protect some members of the herd, endangered species of fish and wildlife (threatened species of fish and wildlife may be protected by regulation and generally are), but will protect them against all threats, federally authorized or not, and protect them against all sorts of injury, whether it will jeopardize the continued existence of the species or not. Although potentially the most energetic of the wranglers, she has often been ignored until recently.

The § 7 wrangler is relatively incorruptible. He will discharge his duty to prevent jeopardy from federal actions unless expressly told not to do so by his superiors on the "God Committee." This is a rare occurrence indeed.

The § 9 wrangler is more open to persuasion, and may agree to stop protecting her charges against a certain threat if the predator in question obtains leave under one of two exemption processes created by the Endangered Species Act—§ 7(b)(4), under which a federal actor or federally authorized actor may obtain an exemption from the takings prohibition, or § 10(a), under which any actor may get an exemption from the taking prohibition. However, the § 9 wrangler's flexibility goes only so far. She will not allow you to get her into trouble with the § 7 wrangler by jeopardizing the continued existence of any species. Her caution is sufficiently great to lead her to reject exemptions from the taking prohibition by federal or non-federal actors. These three wranglers and their herd move across the landscape. As more species on or near the brink of extinction appear, they are branded "endangered" or "threatened" and added to the herd. The herd gets larger. As time goes by, a few branded animals die despite the wranglers' best efforts (no one is perfect), and a few recover from their wounds and injuries without assistance, but most continue on in the herd.

The Role of Recovery Planning: The Fourth Wrangler

Section 4(f) of the Endangered Species Act requires USFWS or NMFS to "develop and implement" documents called "recovery plans" for "the conservation and survival of endangered species and threatened species" unless the agency finds that "such a plan will not promote the conservation of the species." To the "maximum extent practicable" each plan should include "a description of such site—specific management actions as may be necessary to achieve the plan's goal," "objective measurable criteria which, when met, would result in a determination ... that the species be removed from the list," and "estimates of the time required and the cost to carry out those measures needed to achieve the plan's goal."

The recovery planning section can be thought of as a fourth wrangler, charged with nursing the members of the herd back to health, thereby reducing the size of the herd and rendering protected species less susceptible to threats beyond the control of the section 7 and 9 wranglers. Indeed, all the wranglers, sitting around their evening fire, would agree that their ultimate goal is to nurse all the members of the herd back to health. For this reason, they might recognize that the recovery wrangler has a special status and should coordinate the actions of the company when disputes arise among them or when the extent of their specific duties is ambiguous.

Recovery planning could give the agencies charged with administering the Endangered Species Act more flexible authority to take actions to enhance the prospects of protected species without dealing with the immediate, inflexible, and sometimes politically charged threat from a planned project or program that may violate § 7 or 9. These benefits might also extend to other federal agencies with activities affected by species protection. As one commentator, discussing agency behavior under the Endangered Species Act, noted:

> Federal agencies ought to recognize that their interests lie in participating in [recovery] plan development. If the plans are binding, the agencies need to ensure that their discretion is explicitly preserved in the plan ... If the plans are not binding, agencies should still find participation on recovery teams worthwhile to shape conservation activities that will occur on their geographic or functional turf. [Citation omitted.]

However, to date, this fourth member of the company has had little or no power to assist the herd or boss the other wranglers. Although the Endangered Species Act states that recovery or conservation of protected species and the ecosystems on which they depend is the central purpose of the Act, and USFWS informs us that "recovery planning under § 4(f) of the Act is the 'umbrella' that eventually guides all [Endangered Species Act] activities and promotes a species' conservation and eventual delisting," the recovery planning section and the concept of recovery it embodies have played an insignificant role in the legal protection of endangered and threatened species. The same agency that declares recovery planning the umbrella that eventually guides all activities also tells us that recovery plans are "guidance documents" and not "decision-making" documents. Although recovery plans are required by law to identify specific recovery actions and a specific time frame for implementing them, the agencies and courts agree that these "implementation schedules" are unenforceable. In 1993, researchers at the University of Idaho announced findings indicating that recovery plans for many species prescribed "management for extinction" rather than management for recovery by setting recovery goals so low that they could not significantly increase the chance of species survival. Not surprisingly, the size of the metaphorical herd continues to grow, and the health of its members does not often improve.

NOTES

1.   Recovery planning does not occupy a prominent role in the day-to-day implementation of the ESA and, consequently, it is not well understood. There has been relatively little litigation over recovery planning. Most decisions reviewing recovery plans concluded that they are highly discretionary and for guidance purposes only.

In *United States v. McKittrick*, 142 F.3d 1170 (9th Cir. 1998), defendant McKittrick was convicted of killing a gray wolf that was a member of an experimental population released in Yellowstone National Park. McKittrick challenged the conviction on several grounds, including that FWS's regulations establishing the experimental population were invalid under § 4(f), since the Secretary did not adopt a recovery plan giving priority to those species "most likely to benefit from such plans." *Id.* at 1176 (quoting 16 U.S.C. § 1533(f)). That is, since gray wolves were plentiful in Canada and Alaska, McKittrick alleged the reintroduction efforts to be a poor allocation of resources. The court disagreed, holding that the "Secretary has broad discretion to determine what methods to use in species conservation, * * * adoption of recovery plans is discretionary, * * * and the presence of healthy wolf populations in Canada and Alaska does not, in any event, make the recovery of U.S. populations any less crucial." *Id.*

Similarly, in *Fund for Animals v. Rice*, 85 F.3d 535 (11th Cir. 1996), the court rejected environmental plaintiffs' position that FWS was bound by a recovery plan not to make a "no jeopardy" finding. Plaintiffs had claimed that a recovery plan that the Service had developed in 1987 for the Florida Panther required that it preserve the species' habitat. Accordingly, by the Service's finding of "no jeopardy," which allowed for the construction of a landfill, the Service failed to implement the plan. The court strongly disagreed on several grounds, including that "the practical effect of the Plaintiffs' position would be to elevate the 1987 Recovery Plan into a document with the force of law." *Id.* at 547. Instead, the court noted, § 4(f) makes it clear that recovery plans are "for guidance purposes only," and that, with respect to recovery plans, the Act "breathes discretion at every pore." *Id.* (internal citations omitted). In *National Wildlife Federation v. Norton*, 386 F.Supp.2d 553, 568 (D. Vt. 2005), the court held that it would not overturn "the Secretary's decision to proceed with three recovery plans for the gray wolf rather than one comprehensive national plan," in spite of plaintiffs' allegation that the Secretary had violated § 4(f) in her failure to issue such a national recovery plan for the wolf.

2.   Though courts have held the force of recovery plans to be discretionary, they have been more demanding with respect to the actual content of the plans. As noted by Fischman and Hall–Rivera, *supra*, courts have required the Services to prepare adequate plans with objective and measurable criteria. In *Defenders of Wildlife v. Babbitt*, 130 F.Supp.2d 121 (D.D.C. 2001), defendant

FWS had downlisted the pronghorned antelope from endangered to threatened "without explaining the reasoning behind that determination or outlining where the record supports that determination." *Id.* at 133. The court found this to be inadequate, and held that the Service must either incorporate delisting criteria into its recovery plan or "provide an adequate explanation as to why the delisting criteria cannot practicably be incorporated at this time." *Id.* at 134. Similarly, in *Fund for Animals v. Babbitt*, 903 F.Supp. 96 (D.D.C. 1995), *amended by* 967 F.Supp. 6 (D.D.C. 1997), also addressing a downlisting, the court remanded a recovery plan in part because FWS had failed to include in the plan "objective, measurable criteria which, when met, would result in a determination, in accordance with the provisions of this section, that the species be removed from the list," as required by section 4(f)(1)(B)(ii) of the Act. What difference does it make if courts require "adequate plans" if they view them as discretionary and for guidance purposes only? Does the failure to enforce recovery plans undermine the other provisions of the ESA?

G. HABITAT CONSERVATION PLANS: SECTION 10

Under § 10 of the ESA, the Secretary may issue permits to private parties authorizing an otherwise prohibited taking, so long as the taking is "incidental to, and the not the purpose of, the carrying out of an otherwise lawful activity." 16 U.S.C. § 1539(a)(1)(B) (2000). In order to be eligible for such a permit, the applicant must submit a conservation plan specifying:

(i) the impact which will likely result from such taking;

(ii) what steps the applicant will take to minimize and mitigate such impacts, and the funding that will be available to implement such steps;

(iii) what alternative actions to such taking the applicant considered and the reasons why such alternatives are not being utilized; and

(iv) such other measures that the Secretary may require as being necessary or appropriate for purposes of the plan.

16 U.S.C. § 1539(a)(2)(A).

After the applicant submits the conservation plan, the Secretary must make certain findings before the issuance of the permit. These findings are that:

(i) the taking will be incidental;

(ii) the applicant will, to the maximum extent practicable, minimize and mitigate the impacts of such taking;

(iii) the applicant will ensure that adequate funding for the plan will be provided;

(iv) the taking will not appreciably reduce the likelihood of the survival and recovery of the species in the wild; and

(v) the measures, if any, required under subparagraph (A)(iv) will be met.

16 U.S.C. § 1539(a)(2)(B).

In practice, HCPs have become a mechanism for softening the impact of the otherwise stringent "take" prohibition. As a result, HCPs have much in common with Incidental Take Statements, discussed *supra*. Indeed, HCPs and ITSs are very similar in their description and requirements, but—to put the distinction simply—HCPs are for private parties and ITSs are for agencies. A review of the history of HCPs demonstrates these similarities.

The HCP provision was introduced into the scheme of the ESA in the 1982 amendments. Per the amendments, private parties may apply for an "incidental take permit" under § 10 of the Act. The permits are issued by Secretary upon approval of a "conservation plan" submitted by the private applicant under § 10(a)(2)(A). Once the Secretary approves the plan, the applicant is given limited immunity to § 9 "take" liability. As long as the applicant acts in accordance with the approved conservation plan (or, as we now know it, a Habitat Conservation Plan) and so long as the applicant satisfies the Secretary's findings noted *supra*, any incidental takings will not be subject to § 9 liability.

The use of HCPs was broadened during the Clinton administration with the development of the "No Surprises" policy. *See* Habitat Conservation Plans ("No Surprises") Rule, 63 Fed. Reg. 8,859 (1998). The "No Surprises" Policy is essentially a guarantee to applicants that they will be obligated only to perform the mitigation required by the HCP and will not bear the burden or risk of misinformation or change. That is, if it becomes apparent after the issuance of an HCP that a listed species or its habitat is present on the permittee's land, or that the needs of the species are greater than initially thought, and this information was not known either to the government or the permittee, the permittee will not be "surprised" by additional liability beyond the terms of the HCP. Is the No Surprises policy the right balance of risks? Is it appropriate under the goals of the ESA? Is it necessary to provide HCP applicants with some degree of certainty?

Since their introduction, HCPs have been controversial, with supporters praising them as a desirable alternative to litigation—indeed as an instrument that can be *more* protective of species in some instances than the Act would otherwise be—and detractors claiming that they amount to the legalized killing of endangered species. The excerpt below captures the arguments for and against HCPs.

SHI–LING HSU, THE POTENTIAL AND PITFALLS OF HABITAT CONSERVATION PLANNING UNDER THE ENDANGERED SPECIES ACT[9]

29 Envtl. L. Rep. 10592 (1999).

The HCP concept stemmed from an early ESA conflict involving the rare mission blue butterfly's only habitat, which is located in the San Bruno hills south of San Francisco. Potential ESA restrictions had jeopardized plans to develop private property within the butterfly's habitat, and local environmental groups had threatened to use the ESA's citizen suit provision to derail development plans. After seeking out local environmental groups and local governments interested in the development plans, the developer initiated and obtained a negotiated agreement regarding habitat preservation for the mission blue butterfly. The FWS, which also participated in the negotiations, gave the agreement its blessing and sought to amend the ESA to legitimize these types of negotiated solutions. The mission blue butterfly plan thus became the first HCP formally recognized under the ESA with the passage of 1982 amendments to the ESA.

The duration of HCPs have varied. Individual landowners desiring to construct a single-family home on their lot are often issued permits lasting five years, which is sufficient time for them to construct their house. Logging companies, on the other hand, that plan their harvests over long periods of time sometimes have HCPs lasting 100 years. HCPs drew only modest interest in their earlier years, but experienced a dramatic upsurge in interest in 1994. From 1982 to 1989, only three HCPs were approved and only three incidental take permits were issued. From 1990 to 1993, 22 HCPs were approved, but from 1994 to 1997, the number of HCPs skyrocketed to 193. As of January 31, 1998, the FWS had approved 230 HCPs. The upsurge in interest in HCPs has strained the FWS' resources, but citing a desire to engage in long-term, comprehensive, ecosystem-level planning, the FWS has embraced the HCP process. Affected landowners have also expressed enthusiasm for the HCP process, especially the increased regulatory certainty associated with HCPs. * * *

The FWS manifested its commitment to HCPs not only by processing significantly more HCPs than they ever had in the past, but also by further sweetening the deal for landowners. In August 1994, the FWS introduced the "No Surprises" policy. Under the No Surprises policy, the FWS may grant an assurance that if a permittee fully complies with the terms of an HCP that adequately covers a species, the FWS will not require the permittee to undertake any further mitigation measures deemed necessary in the future. Further mitigation measures may be deemed necessary in the future if it is determined that a species' habitat needs are greater than previously thought, if previously absent listed species migrate onto the landowner's property, or if species not currently listed become listed and trigger a series of habitat protection regulations.

---

9. Copyright 1999. Reprinted by permission.

A landowner with an HCP but without a No Surprises assurance may face additional regulations under those circumstances. A No Surprises assurance guarantees that the landowner's liability to undertake mitigation measures is limited to those set forth in the HCP. A No Surprises assurance will typically require the landowner to undertake additional mitigation measures in the short term, but landowners have not been hesitant to seize a guarantee that barring the occurrence of extraordinary circumstances, the HCP represents an exhaustive list of obligations with respect to the species covered by the HCP.

One question, however, remains. Have HCPs been an effective tool for addressing these problems?

The criticisms of the HCP process are many. The most fundamental criticism is that HCPs allow the FWS to cede too much in the way of concessions to developers and loggers. The FWS has not used HCPs to aid in the recovery of listed species and has apparently settled for the more modest goal of only making sure that HCPs do not appreciably reduce the likelihood of survival and recovery of the species in the wild. In general, the FWS is criticized for implementing HCPs too generously by conceding to landowners far more than necessary in order to obtain their assent to an HCP. The evidence to support this assertion can be found in HCPs that seem to allow landowners to develop or log their property in substantially the same manner that they would in the absence of any ESA restrictions. * * *

It is premature to conclude, however, that this is simply a matter of the FWS giving away the store. Given the resources it has to work with, the FWS may simply be making the best of a bad situation. The FWS has shown more vigor in negotiations involving land that is more ecologically valuable. In cases where the quality of the habitat is poor, the FWS will strike a more generous bargain with the landowner than it will when the habitat is of high quality. For example, the FWS has been more willing to permit development in the portions of Alabama beach mouse habitat that has been heavily developed than in those portions where the habitat is rich and important. * * *

A second fundamental criticism of the HCP process pertains to the very long-term commitments that are being made by the FWS. While it is true that logging companies in particular need to plan for time horizons on the order of 100 years, it is also true that much can happen in 100 years. Wetlands were not even considered ecologically valuable until several decades ago. What might the FWS be agreeing to give away that will be deemed highly valuable 50 years from now? This is an especially compelling question in forest HCPs, where the complexity of the ecosystem interactions are still only beginning to be understood. Thus, there is a good reason that forest HCPs are the only class of HCPs for which "No Surprises" assurances are not automatically attached to the HCP as a matter of FWS policy.

A third criticism of HCPs is that it has curbed citizen participation in the ESA. Citizen participation has been perhaps most beneficial in the case of the ESA because many listings of endangered or threatened species have been made pursuant to citizen petitions. Professor Holly Doremus * * * points out three ways in which citizens are effectively shut out of the HCP process: (1) the early negotiations of HCPs take place between the FWS and the landowner, with no public input; (2) too little information is provided to the public too late in the process; and (3) citizen suits are effectively undermined by the issuance of an incidental take permit that eliminates the possibility that a landowner is operating in violation of the ESA. * * *

A final criticism of HCPs is that the precedent set by the HCP process poses some gaming problems for federal regulators in general. The success regulated parties have had in forcing the FWS to the bargaining table by threatening to sue or lobby for legislative reform and by shooting, shoveling, and shutting up invites further intimidation. While we may hope that our regulatory agencies can persist in representing broader interests, in many cases they will not. Moreover, the mere threat of litigation or legislative attack, even if unmeritorious, imposes costs upon agencies that must evaluate the seriousness of each attack. The resources required to put out such fires would almost certainly be better spent carrying out its regulatory duties.

Not all the news is bad for HCPs. The HCP program has also attracted many advocates, the most prominent of which is Secretary of the Interior Bruce Babbitt. Secretary Babbitt has long sought to avoid the logjam created by the litigation and political conflict over logging in the Pacific Northwest habitat of the northern spotted owl, which he characterized as a "national train wreck." HCPs represented such an opportunity. They are a mechanism for the FWS and landowners to avoid litigation and its attendant costs, both in terms of resources spent and the uncertainty introduced into the regulatory process. Litigation is particularly ominous if, as is often the case in the ESA, the only possible outcomes for a parcel of private property are: (1) the FWS regulates the property, and (2) the FWS doesn't regulate the property. The most efficient outcome is likely to be one in which there is some development or logging and some preservation because it is a rare case where complete development or logging or complete preservation are the most desirable outcomes from a societal standpoint. Thus, HCPs allow the FWS and landowners to escape from a binary world where either the FWS or the landowner is a winner, and the other is a loser.

HCPs also offer the opportunity to perform planning on a regional or ecosystem level. California's Natural Community Conservation Program (NCCP), which is also meant to facilitate planning on a regional level, offered the Secretary a model that could be coopted into the HCP mechanism. Indeed, the pilot NCCP programs in the San Diego area and in Orange County, California, are hailed as examples of how comprehensive planning can be done at the regional level and with the input of developers, environmental organizations, community groups, and local, state, and federal government. Ideally, planning on a regional or ecosystem level for multiple affected species and with multiple stakeholders participating in the process allows for broader and more comprehensive ecological considerations and helps to avoid litigation, providing more certainty for all parties. A broader planning scale also allows for the identification of the best areas for development and the best areas for conservation. In addition, such comprehensive plans, if done well, can effectively delegate significant authority to local governments to carry out some of the more ministerial aspects of habitat management. The city of Austin, Texas, and the county of Travis, Texas,—where Austin is located—are authorized to issue permits for development in certain areas of golden-cheeked warbler habitat, provided that certain mitigation measures are agreed to by the landowners, many of whom are individuals seeking to construct single-family homes on a single lot. The city of Austin and Travis County must also contribute to the acquisition of some prime golden-cheeked warbler habitat in an area known as the Balcones Canyonlands. Multiple species and regional HCPs are also being developed in Las Vegas, Nevada; St. George, Utah; and Western Riverside County, California.

Perhaps the most compelling argument in favor of HCPs is that they allow the FWS to make the best of a bad situation. Apart from the unfortunate need to mollify its political enemies, the FWS must solve its "shoot, shovel, and shut up" problem. There are two aspects to the problem: one regarding illegal behavior and one regarding legal behavior, but both can be addressed by HCPs. With respect to the problem of deterring the illegal killing of species, HCPs serve as a means of ameliorating the FWS' enforcement problem. If the FWS cannot compel lawful observance of the ESA, perhaps it can induce landowners to agree to it. This seems an unfortunate necessary evil, but given the resources of the FWS, it may be necessary.

NOTES

1. HCPs vary greatly. The large majority are under 500 acres, and about an eighth are under one acre. But about 5% are over 100,000 acres, and a small minority are over a million acres. *See* 65 Fed. Reg. 35,248 (July 1, 2000). Does it matter whether these agreements cover a lot of territory, or whether they last five or fifty years?

2. Clearly, there are two very different perspectives on HCPs. Either they are a creative way to find win-win solutions and advance eco-system planning, or they are regrettable means to rescue an imperiled statute. Which seems more accurate? Would we be better off with full enforcement of the "take" prohibition, or do we need some entirely new approach to protecting biodiversity? As Alejandro Comacho points out, we would be in a better position to answer these questions if agencies had treated HCPs like an experiment, with systematic monitoring of the program's success. Alejandro

E. Camocho, *Can Regulation Evolve? Lessons From a Study in Maladaptive Management*, 55 UCLA L. Rev. 293 (2007).

3. HCPs resemble wetlands mitigation banking, in that they are an effort to prevent head-on collisions between land developers and environmental goals. They also share this characteristic with offset requirements under the Clean Air Act. Does this suggest something about future trends in environmental regulation? Recall the discussion of regulatory contracts in Chapter 2. Based on HCPs and experiences with similar mechanisms, should we consider this trend an encouraging sign of regulatory creativity or a discouraging sign of lack of commitment? Should we make more extensive use of market-techniques in HCPs themselves? For a suggestion to that effect, see Jonathan Remy Nash, *Trading Species: A New Direction for Habitat Conservation Programs*, 31 Colum. J. Envt. L. 1 (2007).

4. The question of public participation in HCPs and more generally in regulatory contracts is a difficult one. On the one hand, without broad public participation, negotiations are likely to proceed much more smoothly. On the other hand, excluding the public sacrifices important democratic values of transparency and accountability. How we can best accommodate these conflicting values? Could we amend the HCP process to make it more "democratic"?

H.   IMPLEMENTATION: CRITIQUES AND THE FUTURE OF THE ACT

1.   CRITIQUES

The Endangered Species Act has attracted a great deal of criticism since its inception. Not a political cycle goes by without threats to repeal or substantially amend the Act. Property rights advocates take aim at the law with zeal while environmentalists defend it with equal tenacity. Clearly, whether it is viewed more narrowly, as a statute designed to protect species, or more broadly, as a law aimed at preserving habitat and, ultimately biodiversity, the ESA is far from perfect. Some of the critiques focus on its initial design, while others focus on implementation and effectiveness. Still others reflect more ideological concerns. The excerpt below describes the dominant criticisms of the Act.

ERIC BIBER, THE APPLICATION OF THE ENDANGERED SPECIES ACT TO THE PROTECTION OF FRESHWATER MUSSELS: A CASE STUDY[10]

32 Envtl. L. 91, 140–47 (2002).

Various explanations have been proposed for the lack of recovery success under the ESA. First, critics argue that the ESA, by attempting to conserve all species, effectively conserves none, because it spreads re-

---

10. Copyright 2002. Reprinted by permission.

sources too thinly among too many listed species, resulting in underprotection for all, instead of fully recovering some species and allowing others to go extinct. What system of "triage" or prioritization should actually be used by the Act to determine which species to protect and which to allow to disappear, however, is less clear. Some critics argue that only charismatic, popular species deserve protection; others call for focusing on species that are most likely to benefit from recovery efforts (maximal marginal recovery benefits from dollars spent); still others argue for focusing on species that are crucial to ecosystem functioning and survival; and others argue that priority should be given to species that have the most genetic information or taxonomic uniqueness, or that would protect entire ecosystems.

Second, the critics argue that the Act is counterproductive, at least when it comes to private lands. Because the Act is solely mandatory and prohibitive, at the very least it creates a disincentive for landowners to take proactive measures to conserve listed species. Increasing the numbers of listed species will result in the risk that landowners will face increased restrictions on their property through the § 9 take prohibition. At the worst, the punitive nature of the ESA toward private landowners engenders hostility and fear, which results in efforts by landowners to illegally and surreptitiously eliminate listed species from their property before the Service can enforce the law against them ("shoot, shovel, and shut up"), and a lack of cooperation (or outright anger) by landowners against the biologists seeking to recover the listed species. The horror stories and perceived threats against private property rights and extractive industries that the ESA has created has also contributed to the political opposition to the ESA. This critique of the ESA has produced a wave of suggestions for developing positive incentives for landowners under the ESA, including the use of tax credits and direct payments, the implementation of HCPs (with guarantees that agreements between the landowner and the government will not be overturned without payment ("No surprises")), and the "safe harbor" program, in which landowners are promised no additional land-use restrictions in return for proactively managing their property to encourage endangered species. Some of these suggestions have prompted actual administrative changes to the ESA's implementation.

A substantial number of the threats facing endangered species, however, are beyond the power of the ESA to address through its prohibitions on private actions. Some threats, particularly exotic species, are difficult or impossible for humans to correct. The task of controlling a species such as the zebra mussel, which is prolific in reproduction (producing millions or billions of offspring), and spreads by water currents and attachments to boats, seems impossible. Even where the threats may be feasibly dealt with, in many cases they will not be addressed by ESA regulation because the ESA does not (and probably could not) mandate positive actions by private or public actors. Thus, the ESA cannot eliminate the dams that currently have destroyed the vast majority of mussel habitat along the Tennessee and Cumberland Rivers in Kentucky and Tennessee, formerly the best and most diverse mussel communities in North America. Similarly, for the control of exotic species, or the maintenance of natural disturbance patterns (such as fire) that are needed to maintain suitable habitats for certain species, even if such actions are achievable by humans, they often would require positive, proactive management by private and public landowners. Critics of the law argue that the punitive nature of the ESA, and its incentive structure, give rise to the inevitable result that no economically rational landowner will ever undertake such actions.

Another major criticism of the Act has been that it is too oriented on individual species and, as a result, inefficiently wastes time, money, and resources on attempting to save particular species as they become endangered, rather than attempting to protect entire functioning ecosystems and environments. By more proactively and holistically dealing with conservation threats, it is argued, the Act would more efficiently use its resources, saving whole communities of species from extinction rather than dealing with individual species one at a time. As one commentator argued, ecosystems all over the nation are quickly shrinking, but nothing is being done about them until they shrink far enough that a particular species in that ecosystem is listed under the Act: "the Endangered Species Act is treating the symptom and not the disease." [citation omitted.] Thus, there has been an avalanche of proposals to convert (or supplement) the ESA into an Endangered Ecosystems Act, which focuses on preserving whole ecosystems instead of individual species. The result, it is argued, would be more efficient, effective, and thoughtful conservation. To protect endangered species, we either must attempt to re-create or revive ecosystems ourselves, an enormously expensive proposition, or protect the ecosystems in the first place. Why not use ecosystem protection as the focus of the Act to begin with?

A fourth criticism of the effectiveness of the ESA is that conservation efforts under the Act often occur far too late. Indeed, one study found that the median population for a species of vertebrate animals at the time of listing was 1075 individuals, and for plants at the time of listing it was 120 individuals. Thus, by the time a species has been listed under the Act, its population is so low that recovery efforts may be unable to succeed, or will take extraordinary amounts of time and money to succeed. As a result, the ESA makes recovery and conservation efforts harder than they otherwise might be by delaying intervention until the threshold of "endangered" or "threatened" status has been reached. At that point, options have been foreclosed (by changes in land-use decisions, or falling population levels for the species) and expensive rescue efforts are the only possible solutions. Even if the populations of such species can be kept from falling any further, the encroachment of human development activities and the elimination of suitable habitat may mean that increasing the numbers or range of a species is impossible (at least given current economic and political constraints).

Finally, some commentators and environmental groups have argued that the Service's implementation of the law has been too weak, and that by changing key definitions of terms the Service has removed the effectiveness of some important legal tools within the ESA. For example, many environmentalists argue that critical habitat designation could be an extremely effective tool in the enforcement of the Act. They argue that the ban on alteration or degradation of critical habitat would provide significantly greater protection to endangered species habitat from federal actions than the current § 9 take prohibition on the damage to habitat, which requires a showing of harm to individual listed animals. Environmentalists also argue that, in terms of judicial enforcement of the ESA through citizen suits against the federal government, the designation of critical habitat may be crucial to success for a lawsuit. However, the Service's current interpretation of critical habitat means that, in many cases, the adverse modification standard under § 7 is redundant with the jeopardy standard because adverse modification is defined as habitat modification that would result in jeopardy to the species. Under that interpretation, the value of designating critical habitat for mussel species might be negligible. The Service has used this narrow definition of critical habitat to argue that designating critical habitat would not be "prudent" for the vast majority of species because critical habitat would not add any protection for those species through § 7. Environmentalists respond that this construction of the Act is illegal, and that the problem with critical habitat rests in the Service's definition of adverse modification of critical habitat as requiring a showing of harm both to survival and to recovery of the species. Arguably, a broader definition of adverse modification that included recovery would provide a much tougher critical habitat requirement under the ESA. A broader definition would have the potential to restrict far more federal actions, or to force the modification of those actions to provide much greater protection for listed species.

The fight over critical habitat designation is part of a larger critique of the ESA by a few commentators, who argue that (at least under current interpretation of the ESA by the Service) the ESA effectively manages species to avoid extinction rather than to promote recovery. Thus, all of the legal tools in § 7 (the jeopardy standard and the adverse modification standard, as applied through the consultation process) only prevent federal action that leads to jeopardy, not federal action that retards recovery (at least as currently interpreted by the Service). Similarly, the application of the § 9 take standards to the HCP process by the Service have allowed permits to be granted for projects as long as they do not jeopardize the survival of the species, rather than to require permitted projects to provide a net recovery benefit for the species. Thus, all of the pressure for recovering listed species is placed on an overburdened, underfunded recovery program rather than being built into the regulatory programs of sections 7 and 9.

2. THE FUTURE OF THE ENDANGERED SPECIES ACT

The Endangered Species Act is now over thirty years old, and it has survived remarkably well. In spite of Justice Powell's certainty in his *TVA v. Hill* concurrence that Congress would amend the Act to address its outrageous and unforeseen outcomes, there have been no substantial rollbacks of the Act's core provisions. Even through the "Wise Use" movement and several presidential administrations unfriendly to environmental regulation, the Act has survived. The excerpt below puts the ESA in historical context and discusses its evolution.

JOSEPH SAX, ENVIRONMENTAL LAW AT THE TURN OF THE CENTURY: A REPORTORIAL FRAGMENT OF CONTEMPORARY HISTORY[11]

88 CAL. L. REV. 2375 (2000).

[C]urrent environmental goals, though they have very broad public support, simultaneously generate a great deal of public uncertainty and unease. Oft repeated in the popular press, and usually formulated by self-interested sources, the familiar questions are nonetheless revealing of a widespread bafflement about where we are, and should be, going: Ought we really try to save every species? Does not all human activity (farming, housing, manufacturing) necessarily diminish biodiversity? Where does the restoration agenda end: Should a place such as the Columbia River basin be restored to its pre-European-settlement condition in order to bring back the salmon?

One of the fascinating things about the way American law and policy-making functions is that it seems quite unresponsive to these, or similarly probing, questions. Instead, it appears content to acknowledge that loss of biodiversity is a serious problem, that it has been undervalued, and that we need somehow to shift our priorities, without knowing (or trying to determine in advance) exactly where these efforts will, or should, end up. The process of change seems to be driven by what might be called the dynamics of possibility—political, economic, and legal—rather than by theory or by response to any coherent legislative mandate. * * *

Although the Endangered Species Act (ESA) had been in place since 1973, it was not until the 1990s that its full potential came to the fore. As increasing numbers of species began to be listed as threatened or endangered in response to litigation by environmental plaintiffs, the scope of the Act was recognized: in particular, its applicability to habitat on private land and its prohibition of any "take," even of a single exemplar, of a listed species without an approved conservation plan. It became increasingly clear that a crisis of enforcement was in the offing. Water users from rivers with listed species and property owners who found themselves with

---

11. Copyright 2000. Reprinted by permission.

listed species on their land often encountered frustration. The Fish and Wildlife Service, which administers the Act for most species, was not well organized to operate a permit-granting enterprise. The available permitting device for private activities, the Habitat Conservation Plan (HCP), pursuant to § 10 of the ESA was cumbersome and had been very little used. It had not been conceived as an expeditious device, suitable to relatively small enterprises or individuals. People who made inquiries about their obligations often found there was no way to get a simple yes or no, even when the answer could have been quite straightforward. An atmosphere of anxiety built up. Farmers began to fear they could not continue to cultivate existing farmland, and landowners worried that their land would become unsalable because of doubt whether it could be built on or even whether improvement work could be done on existing structures. Irrigators were afraid their water supply would be cut off whenever there was a dry year.

The press and property-rights advocates picked up on these anxieties, and political pressures built for legislative revision of the Act, with provisions that would have greatly weakened it. Though much of the anti-ESA publicity overstated or even misstated the reality, it called to public attention not only a genuine failure of effective administration, but also that the ESA had an extraordinary potential to constrain economic activity and that it lacked the discretion or economic practicability tests that characterized most regulatory laws. All these tensions were dramatically sharpened following the congressional elections in November 1994, when the Republicans took over both houses of Congress with an agenda that included a strong property-rights element, heavily focused on the ESA and the wetlands regulation provisions of the Clean Water Act. Congressional concern about the ESA was by no means limited to one party in the Congress, and the strategy I am about to describe was developed in the spring of 1994, well before the election.

From the perspective of the Department of the Interior, a new approach was critical to avoid a weakened reauthorization of the ESA. To prevent that result, a two-part strategy was adopted: first, to see that no ESA legislation emerged from the Congress. That was done largely by offering no Administration bill at all, while working with entities such as the Western Governors Association to hammer out a series of mutually acceptable provisions. While no one ever openly said so, it would be reasonable to conclude that the exercise was largely designed to preempt other legislative drafting efforts, in the expectation that the outcome would be sufficiently bland that it would please neither ESA supporters nor skeptics. That, in any event, was the eventual outcome. * * *

The second part of the strategy, congruent with the no-legislation effort, was both bolder and more interesting. Its goal was to demonstrate that the ESA, as it stood, was both workable (did not have to be revised) and working (was being effectively enforced and was accomplishing species protection). The essential idea was to bring the largely moribund Habitat Conservation Plan program to life, that is, to bring about negotiated solutions to sensitive ESA problems. In that way, legislative pressures for weakening the Act would be abated, litigation challenging it would be avoided, and the regulated parties would in effect be recruited as partners in asserting the Administration's "message": The Act is working, and we are engaged in a common effort with the private sector to make it work.

Nowhere was this more important than in the mountain West, much of it deeply committed to its history of resource exploitation, strongly aligned with mining, grazing, and irrigation interests, and home to a number of the most conservative members of Congress. The essential question was how to bring about acceptable results without either creating resistance that would produce undesired legislative pressures, or litigation that would both delay progress and potentially undermine the legal foundations of the ESA. * * *

One factor that impedes making a transition from one set of societal priorities to another is the embodiment of settled expectations in law, in particular in various versions of property and related rights. While such rights are always malleable to some degree in a dynamic social system, they inevitably shape the process of transition from one set of values to another. The interplay of forces that occurs when a rooted economic system encounters new environmental claims provides an instructive instance of the way this process unfolds. Change occurs against the background of claims of legal right.

[Several detailed case studies] illustrate how biodiversity values are being integrated into established resource economies. Essentially the idea is (1) to try to bring users together for a negotiated solution, sometimes described as the partnership approach; (2) to do so on a biologically rational scale (by region or watershed); (3) to employ multi-species plans to try to get ahead of the sort of repeated crises that arise out of a sequence of isolated ESA consultations; (4) to build enough achievement into such a program that there is a cushion against future projects or activities, so that there is not a risk of a shutdown every time someone wants to do something; (5) to craft a road map so that everyone will know what sort of measures will be considered first if reinitiation of consultation is required (that is, in effect to anticipate future reasonable and prudent alternatives); (6) in line with the effort to create a cushion, to strive for recovery as the essence of a program, as opposed to simply avoiding jeopardy; and (7) to look for creative solutions that avoid the most intractable prospects (for example, trapping cowbirds that were preying on a listed species at a reservoir, thus increasing the surviving number of nesting pairs, as an alternative to drawing down the reservoir's water supply, cutting down quantities available for use in order to provide additional habitat).

[T]hese efforts are by no means easy to implement, even under the pressures that the ESA can bring to bear. But when one considers how extraordinary it is to transition at all from the established developmental eco-economy into an economy that seriously values biodiversity, the fact that any real headway can be made seems almost miraculous. Of course, as the preceding case instances reveal, we are progressing in the disorderly, untheoretic, pragmatic way that is characteristically American. Only time will tell how extensively, and how successfully, the efforts described here will be carried out. But if the notion of a worthy experiment means anything, surely this is it.

NOTES

1. Prior to the change in party control of Congress in 2006, there were ongoing attempts in Congress to amend key provisions of the Act. The most prominent of these changes is Rep. Richard Pombo's Threatened and Endangered Species Recovery Act, which passed the House of Representatives. Such proposals are perennial, so there will likely be similar bills in the future. Below is an excerpt of an article which addressed the provisions of Rep. Pombo's proposal:

> The Threatened and Endangered Species Recovery Act of 2005 (TESRA, HR 3824), sponsored by Rep. Richard Pombo, R–CA, has passed the House, posing one of the most far-reaching reversals of environmental policy in history. Pombo, a former rancher, has made property rights and opposition to ESA the lodestar of his political career. Under his bill, the process of listing a species under ESA would become more difficult, saddling such efforts with new economic analysis requirements. But the bill's core provision eliminates the current system of designating "critical habitat," territory deemed critical to species' survival. Such designation can open the door to significant land-use restrictions. But the designation of critical habitat is obviously a crucial prerequisite to the survival and eventual recovery of endangered species. The bill would create "recovery teams" that prepare "recovery plans" based on "the best available scientific data." The teams could delineate lands that would help a species survive. Federal agencies would be less obligated to take a species' needs into account in making land-use decisions. The legislation also has provisions for the reimbursement of property owners whose land values are reduced by the law and financial incentives for those who work for species conservation, which several Democrats derided as federal payments for obeying the law. Pombo argued that under current law, federal wildlife management agencies had little incentive to negotiate. "With this bill, there is a cost," he said. "So the incentive is there not just for the property owner but for the Fish and Wildlife Service to work out a deal."

October Federal Update: Appropriations, U.S. FED. NEWS, October 5, 2005.

2. These direct threats to the statute have abated with Democratic control of Congress. It remains to be seen, however, whether improvements in U.S. biodiversity policy will obtain legislative attention. Consider the options discussed in the following section.

3. ALTERNATIVE APPROACHES TO PROTECTING BIODIVERSITY

One of the criticisms of the ESA is that it protects only individual species that are on the verge of extinction, rather than prompting earlier intervention at the ecosystem level. The articles excerpted below go beyond an evaluation of the ESA and examine our efforts to protect biodiversity more generally. In the first excerpt, Professor Ruhl considers some alternatives to our current regulatory approach. In the second article, Professor Doremus suggests that biodiversity protection will require a more dramatic change in our relationship to nature.

J.B. RUHL, BIODIVERSITY CONSERVATION AND THE EVER–EXPANDING WEB OF FEDERAL LAWS REGULATING NONFEDERAL LANDS: TIME FOR SOMETHING COMPLETELY DIFFERENT?[12]

66 U. COLO. L. REV. 555, 632, 634, 642–44, 646–57 (1995).

* * * Federal regulation of nonfederal land use decisions has generally followed three models with respect to relations between federal, state, and local jurisdictions—coercion, coordination, and cooperation. * * *

1. Coercion Model—Cannons Aimed at Anthills

Statutes fitting the Coercion model, such as the ESA * * * start from the premise that a specified activity or condition is flatly prohibited. * * *

The central advantage the Coercion model offers to biodiversity conservation * * * is its potent ability to translate specified uniform federal goals into desired behavior responses by the regulated community. The Coercion model is fast, easy, and cheap in that respect. It is fast in the sense that the structure for compliance can be established within the framework of the legislation itself; no third party contribution is needed. The Coercion model is easy in the sense that the desired response by the regulated community can be shaped with a great degree of precision through the coercive qualities of the prohibition and permitting elements. And the Coercion approach is cheap because, other than the cost of administration and enforcement necessary to support the coercive framework, the desired behavior response comes at no cost to the federal government.

Those strengths, however, are the source of the Coercion model's ultimate downfall. Fearing the potential for runaway administrative policies when agencies are armed with too much coercive power, Congress tightly controls both the scope of the prohibitory element of the Coercion model statutes and the criteria for administration. * * *

2. Coordination Model—Popguns Aimed at Elephants

Whereas the Coercion model relies on extensive power directed in a narrow zone of focus, Coordination model statutes rely on diffused regula-

---

12. Copyright 1995. Reprinted by permission.

tory burdens aimed at a wide target. The basic structure of these statutes begins with a broad statement of federal goals and policies geared towards coordinating "federal action." The Coordination model statutes then inject a procedural review step into the decision-making process of the covered federal actions to ensure the decisions are made with at least some level of coordination around the goals and policies expressed in the statute. * * *

* * * Coordination model statutes seldom have a substantive dimension in the sense of requiring or influencing a particular outcome in the underlying decision-making process. Given the wide jurisdiction of the statutes (usually all federal actions are covered) Congress may be leery of providing real power over decision-making outcomes. Hence, although the procedural requirement can act as a sword against administrative action, as it has quite effectively under NEPA, in the final analysis the Coordination model seldom achieves the broadly stated goals and policies of the statute. * * *

3. Cooperation Model—Choosing the Right–Sized Gun for Each Target

The Cooperation model offers some measure of balance between Coercion and Coordination model statutes, holding traits of each. The essence of the Cooperation model is the expression of strong federal goals and policies in the context of a flexible partnership between federal, state, and local interests in seeing to it that the federal policies are implemented in the form of substantive legal requirements. Cooperation model statutes often hold out some form of regulatory carrot or stick, or blend of both, as an incentive for the partners to act together within the framework of the federal goals and policies, but substantive review criteria and outcomes generally are not prescribed. Rather, it is left to the cooperative process to formulate a regulatory response directed at the particular state or local planning area.

The Cooperation model statutes thus are expensive to operate. They involve substantial transactions costs and time as the cooperating partners force consensus over the final substantive shape of the regulatory policy. But the final result offers promise of achieving the substantive outcome with greater impact than the Coordination model offers, and with greater consensus than the Coercion model offers. * * *

III. A SURVEY OF RECENT AND CURRENT PROPOSALS FOR ENHANCING BIODIVERSITY CONSERVATION * * *

1. The EPA as Biodiversity Czar * * *

[This] proposal, if as comprehensively implemented as EPA appears to be headed, would fall none short of elevating EPA to the position of biodiversity czar among federal agencies and converting its various pollution control programs into biodiversity conservation programs. The fallacies of that approach are numerous. First, although some of the pollution control statutes, particularly the CWA, contain a significant element of habitat protection as a goal, none is principally directed at that purpose. Squeezing the round peg of biodiversity conservation into the square hole of pollution control programs both dilutes the basic regulatory purpose of the statutes and creates a tenuous biodiversity conservation authority. * * * Even putting those considerations aside, however, it is difficult to imagine an effective biodiversity conservation program emerging from policies scattered under yet additional statutory programs. * * *

2. A Federal Ecosystems Protection Act

[An] "Ecosystems Protection Act" modeled on the ESA, but with an expanded focus, would dramatically improve biodiversity protection. [Legislation could] authorize a comprehensive inventory of all ecosystems in the United States and [ecosystems can be categorized according to their need for protection]. In essence, this ecosystem designation process is a parallel to the ESA species listing process. * * *

* * * [F]or Congress to attempt to enact anything like th[is] program * * * would invite a full scale political rumble, because [the] proposal amplifies rather than suppresses the fundamental shortcomings of the Coercion model. The Ecosystem Protection Act would depend on *federal* designation of ecosystems, *federal* permitting of ecosystem development, and *federal* determination of mitigation, and, to boot, would not supplant or replace the existing web of *federal* regulations that already have become the focal point of the nonfederal regulated community's scourge. It is hardly likely that the regulated community's strong sentiments would be reversed by adding a new, omnipotent regulatory regime to the picture. * * *

3. A Federal Land Use Act

The boldest Coercion model biodiversity conservation proposal to surface to date is premised on the goal that "duplicative layers of state and federal regulation, which hinder rational, long-term land use planning, be eliminated or consolidated." In other words, this proposal would completely displace the state and local component of land use control with a supreme Federal Land Use Act. * * * The shell for the proposed Federal Land Use Act would be NEPA's environmental impact review procedure, administered by the Department of Interior rather than CEQ and the EPA; however, from there NEPA and the Federal Land Use Act would bear little resemblance. The Federal Land Use Act would, in all measures, exemplify the Coercion model.

The proposed Federal Land Use Act would create a comprehensive environmental review and permitting program for *all* land development projects, not just those within NEPA's scope of actions federally carried out, funded, or authorized. Unlike NEPA, the Federal Land Use Act would have a powerful substantive application to all such projects. * * *

* * * The new law thus would have the virtue, not shared by the proposed Ecosystem Protection Act, of supplanting all other state and federal land use regulation statutes and providing a uniform federal program in their place. However, the proposal also would supplant all state and local autonomy and the flexibility to adapt the regulatory program to localized and specialized biodiversity issues.

To an extent, moreover, the patchwork qualities of the existing network of environmental laws is not entirely irrational or inefficient. There is an advantage to charging statutes and agencies with a narrowly focused mission in order to maximize the program's effectiveness and the agency's expertise. It is questionable whether the DOI, despite its experience under the ESA and other land use statutes, could establish authoritative expertise in all aspects of land use planning or could fashion a land use review procedure for the entire nation that effectively accommodates all the variations and nuances experienced in different locations and different ecosystem types. * * *

* * * [Other proposals include] federal tax credits for habitat improvement and ESA compliance measures and federal tax penalties for habitat conversion, a system of tradable development credits awarded to landowners who preserve habitat, and a system of tiered development impact fees designed to promote development in less environmentally sensitive areas. All of the proposals either rely on the existing Coercive model regulatory structure within which to build the incentives, or replace the regulatory structure with a financial program that duplicates the coercive effect of the regulatory scheme. * * *

* * * One must question whether society genuinely is willing to pay private landowners for what *society* values about their land to that degree. Although there is an impressive history of public willingness to acquire private land for public use in large blocs devoted, in some cases, to habitat conservation, the scale of land preservation and conservation required to accomplish a meaningful biodiversity policy for nonfederal lands may be orders of magnitude larger than what has ever been contemplated in the past. * * *

The concept of economic incentives, however, should not be abandoned. Indeed, there is strong evidence from a recent report by the Northern Forest Lands Council that our present estate and transfer tax structure is perversely inconsistent with biodiversity conservation and that, at the very least, reform is necessary in that and other financially related respects to weed out those counterproductive elements. The broader question is whether economic incentives can be blended with a regulatory approach that results in enhanced compliance without enhanced resentment. * * *

HOLLY DOREMUS, BIODIVERSITY AND THE CHALLENGE OF SAVING THE ORDINARY[12]

38 IDAHO L. REV. 325, 326–27, 329–37, 339–40, 346–53 (2002).

Both scientists and policymakers today tout the goal of protecting biodiversity, understood to encompass the range of biotic resources. Ecologists and conservation biologists wholeheartedly endorse biodiversity protection. It is enshrined as a goal for the Forest Service, through the National Forest Management Act and that Act's implementing regulations. Other federal agencies, although lacking statutory mandates to conserve biodiversity, have nevertheless enthusiastically adopted that goal. The Fish and Wildlife Service, for example, has instituted an "ecosystem approach" to maximize biodiversity conservation under the ESA, and the Council on Environmental Quality has issued guidelines for using the National Environmental Policy Act to conserve biodiversity. The protection of biodiversity has even been enshrined as a goal of international law, through the adoption of the Convention on Biological Diversity. * * *

Unfortunately, our dominant strategy for achieving that goal remains one developed in another era for different purposes. As we did in the earliest days of conscious nature protection, we continue to concentrate on setting aside special places and protecting dwindling special resources against exhaustion. Given today's conditions, that strategy is not likely to achieve our current goal of protecting a wide range of biotic resources over a long period of time. If we are to succeed in protecting biodiversity, we must find ways to focus the law and the public on ordinary nature rather than merely the obviously special or unique aspects of nature. * * *

A. Conventional Criticisms of Current Strategies for Biodiversity Protection

* * * We have not yet acknowledged, however, that the root problem is our focus on the special. Instead, critics have focused on the way we identify the special elements of nature on which our strategies concentrate. Two frequently repeated criticisms of the ESA illustrate this point. The first is that biodiversity protection could be accomplished more efficiently and effectively if we emphasized the protection of ecosystems, biodiversity hot spots, or more carefully selected focal species. The second is that we delay taking protective action until it is nearly, and perhaps entirely, too late.

* * * Protection of individual endangered species through the ESA is not effectively protecting the range of biodiversity. At first, this may seem surprising. The ESA, which is framed as a safety net for all plant and wildlife species, should in theory be capable of protecting biodiversity

---

12. Copyright 2002. Reprinted by permission.

which, after all, equates at least roughly to the sum of all species. Indeed, the ESA should be a very sensible mechanism for biodiversity protection, covering all plant and animal species but concentrating our efforts on those in most dire need of our immediate attention. In reality, however, as the critics point out, only the most extraordinarily special species, and only those special in a very particular way, are actually helped by the ESA. Only those species with significant public appeal or tenacious human advocates are able to run the gauntlet of the ESA's listing process. Of those species that do make it to listing, a handful of the most charismatic, not necessarily the most threatened or ecologically critical, receive the bulk of the resources put into species recovery.

By interpreting specialness differently, perhaps we could use individual species more effectively as surrogates for biodiversity. It has been suggested that by setting our species protection priorities carefully, concentrating on indicator, keystone, and umbrella species, we might wind up protecting far more than the relatively small number of species that become listed. Indicator species are supposed to reflect the health of the larger ecosystem, so that by ensuring their health we ensure that of the ecosystem. Keystone species are thought to be especially important contributors to community structure, so saving them should keep the community intact. Umbrella species are those that require extremely large ranges; their protection, it is hoped, will guarantee that of many smaller-range species. Alternatively, critics suggest that we should shift our focus to protecting key ecosystems, or "hotspots"—locations that harbor unusually high levels of biodiversity. * * *

[However,] it may not be possible to use special locations or species as effective surrogates for larger systems. Ecologists have found it difficult to define the keystone concept or identify species that fit it, and umbrella species now appear far less useful than we once thought. * * *

* * * For species to be chosen on the basis of their ability to stand in for biodiversity protection, we would need to convince the public that biodiversity itself is special.

That is difficult to do because biodiversity is so abstract, and so ordinary. Human beings simply are not wired to care about, or even to notice, the ordinary. We cannot attend to everything that competes for our attention. We have therefore developed a variety of filtering mechanisms to help us focus effectively on some things by more or less shutting out others. * * * It is therefore much easier to convince people to take action to save whales, wolves, or other specific, eye and imagination-catching creatures, than it is to persuade them that they must act to save nature as a whole, or biodiversity, which is nearly the same thing.

* * * Another filter we typically rely on is ordinariness in the sense of being common or abundant. "Special" equates strongly with limited or rare. It will always be an uphill battle to convince the public that species or ecosystems are special before they become severely reduced.* * *

The law's resistance to change is even more pronounced when regulation is sought in an area where unrestricted individual choice has been (or is perceived to have been) the norm. * * * Landowners assume that they are or should be free to use their land in virtually any way they please, so long as other people are not directly injured by that use. Because that assumption is widespread and politically powerful, the effort to impose the kinds of regulatory controls on land use that are essential to biodiversity protection faces particularly formidable institutional barriers. That kind of change to the legal status quo must be supported by an appealing focal point, something special enough to rally the needed political support.

The law also needs focal points for effective implementation. By concentrating on the special, the ESA provides the necessary focus, protecting "species" that are "threatened" or "endangered." Although the boundaries of those statutory terms are necessarily fuzzy, we can define them with enough specificity to allow regulators, the regulated, and advocates on both sides to understand in general terms what is included and what is not. The agency knows roughly the breadth and limits of its authority, citizen suits can force it to act if it obviously shirks its duties, and the regulated community has some assurance that it will not be subjected to arbitrary regulation. * * *

* * * Although the law needs focal points, those focal points need not be the places or things we are protecting. We have experience with other focal points in environmental regulation; NEPA, which provides some protection to the ordinary aspects of nature by choosing as its focal point particular actions, is one example. * * *

Our portfolio of biodiversity protection should include regulation that proscribes, limits, or establishes prerequisites to those activities that predictably pose a threat to biodiversity. * * * Regulating all of those activities seems like a tall order, but in fact many of them already are subject to some kind of federal, state, or local regulation. The trick with respect to those activities is to ensure that biodiversity considerations are adequately factored into existing regulatory schemes. That is a political problem, not an institutional one. * * *

We can also, if we care enough, limit many of the currently unregulated activities that threaten biodiversity. Many of them may not be suitable for regulation at the federal level. * * * But state and local governments can identify and regulate earth-moving activities that, in their particular context, pose serious threats to biodiversity. * * *

Broad geographic regions can also provide useful focal points for the law. Again we have some experience with this sort of strategy; the Coastal Zone Management Act has successfully encouraged coastal states to adopt broad coastal planning through the provision of federal funds and the promise of greater control over federal actions in the coastal zone. * * *

Local land use regulation, which has developed institutions for long-range area-wide planning applicable to a wide range of activities, has an important role to play in our biodiversity protection efforts * * *. However, because of the need for coordination and a broader vision, balkanized local regulation is not likely to be effective. Multi-jurisdictional regional plans are needed. Habitat conservation plans (HCPs) under the Endangered Species Act, which are evolving in many areas into something akin to a collaborative local/federal land use planning process, can sometimes fulfill that role. HCPs crossing county boundaries, however, have proven difficult to hold together, and most still tend to focus on a small number of listed species. * * *

If we are to save the full tapestry [of biodiversity], we must turn from appeals to material self-interest to emotional connections. * * *

We must not only nurture love of nature, we must do so at a local level. I mean that in two senses. First, we will need to ensure that people in communities across the landscape feel emotionally connected to nature. Many of the actions that threaten biodiversity are local, and many of the decisions about nature protection must inevitably be made at the local level. If those decisions are to protect biodiversity, concern for nature must be planted and nurtured, not just in a few places, but across the country.

Second, people must care about local nature. A general, broadbrush love of nature can inspire us to save striking locations and charismatic species. But to save biodiversity, to keep the tapestry whole, we must protect many far less distinctive places and creatures. To motivate that, we must inspire people to appreciate the value of the species that are ordinary to their location but that, taken together, make their location distinctive. * * *

NOTES

1. Both Professors Ruhl and Doremus refer to the possibility of a stronger federal role in biodiversity-related regulation. What are the potential obstacles to such an approach? What level of government is best situated to protect biodiversity, which requires regulating land use?

2. A different approach is suggested in Katrina Miriam Wyman, *Rethinking the ESA to Reflect Human Dominion Over Nature*, 17 NYU ENVT. L.J. 490 (2008). She argues that "[e]ven if the FWS was able to list all of the thousands of unlisted species currently at-risk, the listing process could collapse in the future under the weight of the pressures to add species that climate change may generate." She argues that the FWS should continue to list species as today, but that the actual effort to preserve species be based on the most cost-effective ways to protect the species, with the goal of "making it unlikely that the species would become extinct over three human generations, or reducing the risk of extinction to a certain percentage of a 100–year time period." Do you agree with her view that "we would do better at protecting species generally by reducing the momentousness of the listing decision and, after listing, crafting legally tailored protections that could actually be enforced"?

CHAPTER 4

ENVIRONMENTAL PROTECTION
AND THE CONSTITUTION

■ ■ ■

Environmental protection is complicated by the division of the world into political subunits. Environmental problems themselves recognize no such boundaries. As we saw in Chapter I, where the units of government are nation states, existing institutions for environmental cooperation are primitive. But the same is not true today within the U.S., which has adopted an elaborate system of "cooperative federalism" to divide responsibility for much environmental regulation between the federal government and the 50 states. Much of this chapter will be devoted to considering the extent to which the constitutional federalism restrictions limit regulation.

We will begin our exploration of federalism by examining the policy debate over centralization versus federalism in environmental regulation. We will then consider a key mechanism created by the U.S. Constitution in response to the difficulty of obtaining cooperation between states: empowering the federal government to take action on a national basis. Next, we will consider the possibility that state environmental regulations may be unconstitutional because of their effect on interstate commerce. As we will see, state environmental regulations are increasingly challenged as violations of the Supreme Court's "dormant commerce clause" doctrine. We also explore the analogous problem at the international level, where trade agreements may impose similar restraints on environmental regulation by individual nations.

Another significant constitutional restriction on environmental protection relates to private property. Efforts to regulate land use in order to protect biodiversity or other environmental values may be challenged as "takings" of private property. Under some circumstances, the government may need to provide compensation if it wishes to prohibit environmentally harmful land uses.

A. UNIFORMITY VERSUS DIVERSITY IN ENVIRONMENTAL REGULATION

Most of this chapter focuses on the legal rules governing centralization and decentralization of environmental regulations—constitutional limits on federal regulation, commerce clause restraints on state regulation, and WTO limits on national regulation. In the midst of these quarrels over regulatory authority, it is easy to lose track of an equally important question: As a matter of policy, how much centralization is wise?

RICHARD L. REVESZ, THE RACE TO THE BOTTOM AND FEDERAL ENVIRONMENTAL REGULATION: A RESPONSE TO CRITICS

82 MINN. L. REV. 535 (1997).

My starting point is a rebuttable presumption in favor of decentralization. This presumption rests on three independent grounds. First, our country is large and diverse; it is therefore likely that different regions have different preferences for environmental protection. Environmental protection addresses an important resource-allocation question: as a society we can generally purchase additional environmental protection at some price, paid in the currency of jobs, wages, shareholders' profits, tax revenues, and economic growth. Given the existence of the states as plausible regulatory units, the tradeoffs reflecting the preferences of citizens of different regions should not be wholly disregarded in the regulatory process, absent strong reasons for doing so. * * *

Second, the benefits of environmental protection also vary throughout the country. For example, a stringent ambient standard may benefit many people in densely populated areas but only a few elsewhere. Similarly, a particular level of exposure to a contaminant may be more detrimental if it is combined with exposure to other contaminants with which it has synergistic effects.

Third, the costs of meeting a given standard also differ across geographic regions. For example, a source may have a large detrimental impact on ambient air quality if it is directly upwind from a mountain or other topographical barrier. Similarly, a water polluter will have a far larger impact on water quality standards if it disposes its effluents in relatively small bodies of water. Climate might also play a role: certain emission or effluent standards may be easier (and cheaper) to meet in warmer weather.* * *

This presumption for decentralization should be overcome, however, if there is a systemic evil in letting states decide the level of environmental protection that will apply within their jurisdictions. In my work, I have explored in detail the two most prominent justifications for vesting responsibility over environmental regulation at the federal level: that inter-state competition over environmental standards would result in a "race to the bottom," and that federal regulation is necessary to prevent interstate externalities.

The race-to-the-bottom rationale posits that states will try to induce geographically mobile firms to locate within their jurisdictions, in order to benefit from additional jobs and tax revenues, by offering them suboptimally lax environmental standards. The problem of interstate externalities arises because a state that sends pollution to another state obtains the labor and fiscal benefits of the economic activity that generates the pollution but does not suffer the full costs of the activity. Under these conditions, economic theory maintains that an undesirably large amount of pollution will cross state lines. * * *

My argument attacking the race-to-the-bottom justification proceeds in four steps. I start by pointing out that when states compete for industry through environmental standards, they are competing for the sale of a good: the right to locate within their jurisdictions. If competition for the sale of most goods is generally good, why should competition for the sale of this good be clearly bad? I show, moreover, why possible distinctions between a state as seller of location rights and sellers of traditional consumer products do not provide support for race-to-the-bottom claims.

Second, I analyze the leading economic model of the effects of inter-state competition on the choice of environmental standards, which shows that interjurisdictional competition leads to the maximization of social welfare, rather than to a race to the bottom. In this model, Wallace Oates and Robert Schwab posit jurisdictions that compete for mobile capital through the choice of taxes and environmental standards. A higher capital stock benefits residents in the form of higher wages, but hurts them as a result of the foregone tax revenues and lower environmental quality needed to attract the capital.

Each jurisdiction makes two policy decisions: it sets a tax rate on capital and establishes an environmental standard. Professors Oates and Schwab show that competitive jurisdictions will set a net tax rate on capital of zero (the rate that exactly covers the cost of public services provided to the capital, such as police and fire protection). In turn, competitive jurisdictions will set an environmental standard that is defined by equating the willingness to pay for an additional unit of environmental quality with the corresponding change in wages. Professors Oates and Schwab show that these choices of tax rates and environmental standards are socially optimal.

Third, I acknowledge that, in particular instances, game-theoretic interactions among the states could lead to underregulation absent federal intervention. In such cases, federal minimum standards would be desirable. But it is equally plausible that in other instances the reverse would be true: that game-theoretic interactions among the states would lead to overregulation absent federal intervention. * * *

Fourth, I argue that even if states systematically enacted suboptimally lax environmental standards, federal environmental regulation would not necessarily improve the situation. If states cannot compete over environmental regulation because it has been federalized, they will compete along other regulatory dimensions, leading to suboptimally lax standards in other areas, or along the fiscal dimension, leading to the underprovision of public goods. Thus, the reduction in social welfare implicit in race-to-the-bottom arguments would not be eliminated merely by federalizing environmental regulation: the federalization of all regulatory and fiscal decisions would be necessary to solve the problem.

With respect to the interstate externality justification for federal environmental regulation, four features of my argument are worth emphasizing. First, the presence of interstate externalities provides a compelling argument for federal regulation under conditions in which ... bargaining is unlikely to occur. Particularly with respect to air pollution, transaction costs are likely to be sufficiently high to prevent the formation of interstate compacts. It is difficult for such compacts to emerge in the absence of a clearly defined baseline concerning when upwind states have the right to send pollution downwind and in the absence of generally accepted mathematical models for translating a source's emissions into a quantity of ambient air quality degradation at all the places at which the emissions affect ambient air quality. Moreover, for different pollution sources, the range of affected states will vary; this shifting membership among the participants at the bargaining table makes it less likely that the emergence of conditions favoring cooperation will occur.

Second, the fact that interstate externalities provide a compelling justification for intervention does not mean that all federal environmental regulation can be justified on these grounds. For environmental problems such as the control of drinking water quality, there are virtually no interstate pollution externalities; the effects are almost exclusively local. Even with respect to problems for which there are interstate externalities, such as air pollution, the rationale calls only for a response specific to the problem. This may include a limit on the amount of pollution that can cross state lines, rather than across-the-board federal regulation.

Third, the environmental statutes have been an ineffective response to the problem of interstate externalities. For example, the core of the Clean Air Act—the statute designed to deal with the pollution that gives rise to the most serious problems of interstate externalities—consists of a series of federally prescribed ambient standards and emission standards. The federal emission standards do not effectively combat the problem of interstate externalities because they do not regulate the number of sources within a state or the location of the sources. Similarly, the various federal ambient air quality standards are not well-targeted to address the problem of interstate externalities. They are overinclusive because they require a state to restrict pollution that has only in-state consequences. But they are also underinclusive because a state could meet the applicable ambient standards but nonetheless export a great deal of pollution to downwind states (through tall stacks or a location near the interstate border). In fact, a state might meet its ambient standards precisely because it exports a large proportion of its pollution.

Fourth, in some ways the federal environmental statutes have exacerbated, rather than ameliorated, the problem of interstate externalities. Again, in the context of the Clean Air Act, the federal ambient standards give states an incentive to encourage sources within their jurisdiction to use taller stacks. In this way, states can externalize not only the health and environmental effects of the pollution but also the regulatory costs of complying with the federal ambient standards. Thus, not surprisingly, the use of tall stacks expanded considerably after the passage of the Clean Air Act in 1970. In 1970, only two stacks in the United States were higher than 500 feet. By 1985, more than 180 stacks were higher than 500 feet and twenty-three were higher than 1000 feet. While this method of externalizing pollution is now less of a problem as a result of stack height regulations that followed the 1977 amendments to the Clean Air Act, tall stacks remain a means by which excessive pollution can be sent to downwind states.

NOTES

1. As the subtitle of this excerpt indicates, Revesz's critique of existing federal regulation has itself come in for a great deal of criticism.[1] Are you persuaded by Revesz's claim that state governments will not unduly lower their standards to attract industry? Given the nature of environmental problems, is it possible to draw a clear line between local environmental problems and spillover effects?

2. If Revesz is right, should courts attempt to tilt the balance toward decentralization? Should they require a showing that federal regulation is tailored to spillover effects, to maintaining minimum national health standards, or to filling some other identifiable shortcoming in state regulation? Should they have a strong presumption that differences in state regulations are justified, even when such differences may cause some adverse economic effects? Or should the proper balance between federal and state regulation be left to the national political process to decide?

3. In a later article, Dean Revesz argues against another justification for federal regulation, the idea that state governments are more prone to capture by industry groups. *See* Richard L. Revesz, *Federalism and Environment Regulation: A Public Choice Analysis*, 115 HARV. L. REV. 553 (2001). Besides contesting the theoretical validity of this idea, Revesz argues that state

---

1. *See, e.g.*, Kirsten H. Engel, *State Environmental Standard–Setting: Is There a 'Race' and is It 'to the Bottom'?*, 48 Hastings L.J. 271 (1997); Daniel C. Esty, *Revitalizing Environmental Federalism*, 95 Mich. L. Rev. 570 (1996); Joshua Sarnoff, *The Continuing Imperative (But Only from a National Perspective) for Federal Environmental Regulation*, 7 Duke Envtl. L. & Pol'y F. 225 (1997); Peter P. Swire, *The Race to Laxity and the Race to Undesirability: Explaining Failures in Competition Among Jurisdictions in Environmental Law*, 14 Yale J. on Reg. 67 (1996). *See also* Kirsten H. Engel & Scott R. Saleska, *'Facts Are Stubborn Things': An Empirical Reality Check in the Theoretical Debate Over the Race–To–The–Bottom in State Environmental Standard–Setting*, 8 Cornell J.L. & Pub. Pol'y 55 (1998).

governments were doing a reasonably good job of regulating before the federal government entered the picture. He also suggests that they continue to be sources for innovative environmental measures today. William Buzbee argues, however, that the state-federal dichotomy Revesz sets up fails to take into account the specific context of individual state and/or federal policies. *See* William W. Buzbee, *Contextual Environmental Federalism*, 14 N.Y.U. ENVTL L. J. 108 (2005). If Revesz is correct in his criticisms of federal regulation, how do we account for its popularity? The following excerpt considers one possible answer and its implications for regulatory reform.

RICHARD B. STEWART, ENVIRONMENTAL QUALITY AS A NATIONAL GOOD IN A FEDERAL STATE

1997 U. CHI. L. F. 199 (1997).

The problem exists of how to explain the dominance of federal environmental regulation in the face of public choice skepticism about the political efficacy of diffuse interests and the failure to develop a convincing welfare economic justification for the scope and scale of current federal programs.

I think we must simply conclude, as a matter of fact, that many Americans regard environmental quality as an important national good that transcends individual or local interest. This regard is the result of historical, cultural, and political contingencies that have yet to be fully or satisfactorily explained. The settlement and pioneer experiences; certain strands in American religious experience and sensibility; the acquisition and retention of the public lands, including many of exceptional scenic grandeur; and growing ambivalence towards technology and established economic and governmental institutions, along with other factors, all seem to have played a role in the emerging recognition of environmental quality and natural resource preservation as a national good.

Rather than attempting here to explain how Americans have come to regard environmental quality as a national good, I will simply posit it as fact that is reflected in various ways, including the following:

*Overwhelming support in public opinion polls for strong environmental measures.

*Widespread, sustained, effective political support for establishing, maintaining, implementing and enforcing far-reaching federal environmental regulatory programs.

*High levels of membership in and financial contributions to national environmental groups.

*Evidence of significant individual and constituent concern with and support for federal resource management and regulatory programs to secure environmental quality or preserve natural resources in other parts of the nation.

These manifestations are most powerful in the case of the Endangered Species Act, wilderness legislation, and other federal regulatory measures designed to protect natural resources of special rarity, beauty, or other significance. But public opinion and political support for other far-reaching forms of federal environmental regulation, including air and water pollution control and toxic waste regulation and cleanup suggest that these aspects of environmental quality are also regarded as part of the national good. This regard is probably to a considerable extent symbolic, but that in no way diminishes its political and social significance. To the extent that environmental protection is a symbolic good, public support for regulatory measures need not be based solely on environmental problems faced by individuals within their own locality, and can more readily be regarded as part of the national good.

If environmental quality is viewed as a national good, the benefits of environmental protection measures to deal with local pollution, toxic wastes, or habitat alteration are no longer individual and local but national and collective, undercutting the usual assumptions of the welfare economic/optimal environmental jurisdictional analysis, which generally defines environmental quality in terms of factors experienced directly by individuals (such as levels of pollution), making environmental policy a function of aggregate individual preferences, costs, and benefits. This analysis is methodologically "bottom up." It presumes that decentralized regulation is preferable because of variations in individual preferences and local circumstances. Centralized regulation is justified only if there are severe "decentralization failures" due to causes such as the "race to the bottom" or systematic state underprovision because of political distortions. To the extent, however, that environmental quality is regulated as a national good, a presumption in favor of a "top down" approach is logical: environmental programs should presumptively be federal unless "centralization failure" dictates decentralization.* * *

To say, however, that Americans regard and demand environmental quality as a national good is only a starting point for further analysis. Environmental quality is a highly complex and variable good that comes in many shapes and sizes. Scientific and technical complexity and uncertainty abound. Many different types of government measures can be deployed to promote environmental protection. The appropriate means for securing environmental quality is often complex and obscure. The media and political and policy entrepreneurs, including environmental groups and industrial, labor, and other organized commercial interests, play a key role in mobilizing and shaping public concern for environmental protection, defining the "problem," setting priorities, and advancing solutions.

The existing system of centralized federal command-and-control regulation and liability that has emerged out of this untidy tug and pull of factors and interests displays many grievous flaws. These include excessive rigidity and cost, barriers to innovation, lack of democratic political accountability, skewed priorities, excessive delay and transaction costs, and excessive legalization. Given the status of environmental quality as a national good, however, the appropriate response is not wholesale federal deregulation and devolution of regulatory responsibilities to lower levels of government. Advocates of dismantling the existing federal environmental regulatory system, including policy scholars and the more aggressive of House Republicans, have wholly failed to persuade. Accordingly, the question is how to advance the national commitment to environmental quality through new forms and structures that respond to the need for intelligent priority setting, avoid economic waste, reduce the dysfunctions of over-centralized regulation, and provide appropriate flexibility to deal with variations in local circumstances and accommodate values of local decisionmaking, which remain important. In short, the aim is not to dismantle but to reconstitute national environmental law and policy.

Some aspects of the centralization failures of our federal environmental regulatory system have been moderated by giving state regulators a substantial role in the implementation and enforcement of federal law. This development assumed increasing importance in the 1980s, once the basic apparatus of federal statutes and regulations had been established and attention shifted to implementation and enforcement. This arrangement avoids the need to create a more massive, duplicative federal administrative apparatus, takes advantage of state regulators' familiarity with local circumstances, and affords a degree of flexibility in adjusting regulatory requirements to those circumstances. Further, states generally enjoy the latitude to adopt measures more stringent than those required by federal law, and many have done so. These arrangements are not inconsistent with the status of environmental quality as a national good. The states no less than the federal government can be instruments for realizing national goals. Opinion polls indicate that the public wants both the federal and the state governments to play a substantial role in environmental protection, according a clear preference to neither. The public, consistent with Madison's view of the states and the federal government as competitors in promoting the public good, seems to favor this redundancy as providing greater assurance of effective environmental protection.

NOTES

1.   Unlike the European Union, the federal government does not have any explicit assignment of responsibility for environmental matters. If Stewart is right that Americans regard environmental quality as a national good, should this affect judicial interpretation of the commerce clause and other constitutional texts? Or should the Constitution be interpreted purely on the basis of the original understanding rather than the values of Americans today?

2.   Although their general approaches to environmental law are in many respects similar, Revesz and Stewart reach their shared conclusions from opposite directions. Revesz views environmental problems as presumptively local concerns, whereas Stewart views them as presumptively national concerns. Which presumption is more appealing?

B. THE SCOPE OF FEDERAL POWER

The federal government was formed to deal with problems that could not be solved without centralized intervention. Under the Articles of Confederation, federal action could only be taken with unanimous agreement of all states, which severely hindered the government's role. This made the states the equivalent of nations that can only cooperate based on unanimous consent; we saw in Chapter 1 that this creates serious difficulties. Thus, the Constitution is a solution to what economists call a collective action problem.

One of the basic assumptions of American constitutional law is that the federal government is a government of limited, delegated powers. Its authority was defined by the issues that at the time seemed to require a collective response. It does not always have the power even today to take whatever action it deems in the public interest. Instead, the federal government has a collection of specific powers: the power to regulate interstate commerce, the power to tax and spend, the power to enter treaties, etc. In this section, we will explore the scope of these federal powers and the extent to which they are limited by "states' rights." We begin with a case on the treaty power.

MISSOURI v. HOLLAND

Supreme Court of the United States, 1920.
252 U.S. 416, 40 S.Ct. 382, 64 L.Ed. 641.

Mr. Justice Holmes delivered the opinion of the Court.

This is a bill in equity brought by the State of Missouri to prevent a game warden of the United States from attempting to enforce the Migratory Bird Treaty Act of July 3, 1918, and the regulations made by the Secretary of Agriculture in pursuance of the same. The ground of the bill is that the statute is an unconstitutional interference with the rights reserved to the States by the Tenth Amendment, and that the acts of the defendant done and threatened under that authority invade the sovereign right of the State and contravene its will manifested in statutes. * * *

On December 8, 1916, a treaty between the United States and Great Britain was proclaimed by the President. It recited that many species of birds in their annual migrations traversed certain parts of the United States and of Canada, that they were of great value as a source of food and in destroying insects injurious to vegetation, but were in danger of extermination through lack of adequate protection. It therefore provided for specified close seasons and protection in other forms, and agreed that the two powers would take or propose to their law-making bodies the necessary measures for carrying the treaty out. The above mentioned Act of July 3, 1918, entitled an act to give effect to the convention, prohibited the killing, capturing or selling of any of the migratory birds included in the terms of the treaty except as permitted by regulations compatible with those terms, to be made by the Secretary of Agriculture. Regulations were proclaimed on July 31, and October 25, 1918. It is unnecessary to go into any details, because, as we have said, the question raised is the general one whether the treaty and statute are void as an interference with the rights reserved to the States.

To answer this question it is not enough to refer to the Tenth Amendment, reserving the powers not delegated to the United States, because by Article II, § 2, the power to make treaties is delegated expressly, and by Article VI treaties made under the authority of the United States, along with the Constitution and laws of the United States made in pursuance thereof, are declared the supreme law of the land. If the treaty is valid there can be no dispute about the validity of the statute under Article I, § 8, as a necessary and proper means to execute the powers of the Government. The language of the Constitution as to the supremacy of treaties being general, the question before us is narrowed to an inquiry into the ground upon which the present supposed exception is placed.* * *

* * * [W]hen we are dealing with words that also are a constituent act, like the Constitution of the United States, we must realize that they have called into life a being the development of which could not have been foreseen completely by the most gifted of its begetters. It was enough for them to realize or to hope that they had created an organism; it has taken a century and has cost their successors much sweat and blood to prove that they created a nation. The case before us must be considered in the light of our whole experience and not merely in that of what was said a hundred years ago. The treaty in question does not contravene any prohibitory words to be found in the Constitution. The only question is whether it is forbidden by some invisible radiation from the general terms of the Tenth Amendment. We must consider what this country has become in deciding what that Amendment has reserved.

The State as we have intimated founds its claim of exclusive authority upon an assertion of title to migratory birds, an assertion that is embodied in statute. No doubt it is true that as between a State and its inhabitants the State may regulate the killing and sale of such birds, but it does not follow that its authority is exclusive of paramount powers. To put the claim of the State upon title is to lean upon a slender reed. Wild birds are not in the possession of anyone; and possession is the beginning of ownership. The whole foundation of the State's rights is the presence within their jurisdiction of birds that yesterday had not arrived, tomorrow may be in another State and in a week a thousand miles away. If we are to be accurate we cannot put the case of the State upon higher ground than that the treaty deals with creatures that for the moment are within the state borders, that it must be carried out by officers of the United States within the same territory, and that but for the treaty the State would be free to regulate this subject itself.

As most of the laws of the United States are carried out within the States and as many of them deal with matters which in the silence of such laws the State might regulate, such general grounds are not enough to support Missouri's claim. Valid treaties of course "are as binding within the territorial limits of the States as they are elsewhere throughout the dominion of the United States." No doubt the great body of private relations usually fall within the control of the State, but a treaty may override its power. * * *

Here a national interest of very nearly the first magnitude is involved. It can be protected only by national action in concert with that of another power. The subject-matter is only transitorily within the State and has no permanent habitat therein. But for the treaty and the statute there soon might be no birds for any powers to deal with. We see nothing in the Constitution that compels the Government to sit by while a food supply is cut off and the protectors of our forests and our crops are destroyed. It is not sufficient to rely upon the States. The reliance is vain, and were it otherwise, the question is whether the United States is forbidden to act. We are of the opinion that the treaty and statute must be upheld.

NOTES

1.   The Tenth Amendment states:

The powers not delegated to the United States by the Constitution, nor prohibited by it to the States, are reserved to the States respectively, or to the people.

Is this anything more than a "truism," that "all is retained which has not been surrendered," as the Court said in *United States v. Darby*, 312 U.S. 100, 124 (1941)? Does Justice Holmes give it any more meaning than this?

2.   Does federalism place any limit on the treaty power? As part of an air pollution treaty with Canada, could the federal government require officials in the State of Washington to engage in an extensive program of automobile inspections?

3.   The most important congressional power is the power to regulate interstate commerce, as the next case illustrates. As we will see, the issue remains controversial even today.

HODEL v. INDIANA

Supreme Court of the United States, 1981.
452 U.S. 314, 101 S.Ct. 2376, 69 L.Ed.2d 40.

JUSTICE MARSHALL delivered the opinion of the Court.

[In the Surface Mining Control and Reclamation Act of 1977, 30 U.S.C.A. §§ 1201–1328, Congress adopted a program of nationwide environmental standards for stripmining, with enforcement primarily in the hands of the states if they elect to exercise the authority. Generally, no person may conduct surface coal mining without a permit issued under a state or federal program. The Act specifies environmental protection performance standards which every permit must require. The coal mining operation must "restore the land affected to a condition capable of supporting the uses which it was capable of supporting prior to any mining, or higher or better uses of which there is reasonable likelihood," and use the best technology currently available to minimize environmental impacts. The statute also contains special provisions strictly regulating mining on "prime farmland." The issue before the Court in the following case was whether the surface mining statute exceeded the federal government's constitutional powers.]

The District Court gave two rationales for its decision on the Commerce Clause issue. The court first held that the six "prime farmland" provisions are beyond congressional power to regulate interstate commerce because they are "directed at facets of surface coal mining which have no substantial and adverse effect on interstate commerce." The court reached this conclusion by examining statistics in the *Report of the Interagency Task Force on the Issue of a Moratorium or a Ban on Mining in Prime Agricultural Lands (Interagency Report)* (1977). These statistics compared the prime farmland acreage being disturbed annually by surface mining to the total prime farmland acreage in the United States. The *Interagency Report* stated that approximately 21,800 acres of prime farmland were being disturbed annually and that this acreage amounted to .006% of the total prime farmland acreage in the Nation. This statistic and others derived from it, together with similar comparisons for Indiana, persuaded the court that surface coal mining on prime farmland has "an infinitesimal effect or trivial impact on interstate commerce."

With respect to the other 15 substantive provisions which apply to surface mining generally, the District Court reasoned that the only possible adverse effects on interstate commerce justifying congressional action are air and water pollution and determined that these effects are adequately addressed by other provisions of the Act. The court therefore concluded that these 15 provisions as well as the six prime farmland provisions "are not directed at the alleviation of water or air pollution, to the extent that there are any such effects, and are not means reasonably and plainly adapted to the legitimate end of removing any substantial and adverse effect on interstate commerce." We find both of the District Court's rationales untenable.

It is established beyond peradventure that "legislative Acts adjusting the burdens and benefits of economic life come to the Court with a presumption of constitutionality * * *." A court may invalidate legislation enacted under the Commerce Clause only if it is clear that there is no rational basis for a congressional finding that the regulated activity affects interstate commerce, or that there is no reasonable connection between the regulatory means selected and the asserted ends. * * *

In our view, Congress was entitled to find that the protection of prime farmland is a federal interest that may be addressed through Commerce

Clause legislation. The *Interagency Report* provides no basis for the District Court's contrary view. That report dealt only with the question whether a complete moratorium or ban on surface coal mining on prime farmland was advisable as a matter of policy. The report neither purported to examine the full impact of surface mining on interstate commerce in agricultural commodities, nor concluded that the impact is too negligible to warrant federal regulation. More important, the court below incorrectly assumed that the relevant inquiry under the rational basis test is the volume of commerce actually affected by the regulated activity. * * *

We also conclude that the court below erred in holding that the prime farmland and 15 other substantive provisions challenged by appellees are not reasonably related to the legitimate goal of protecting interstate commerce from adverse effects attributable to surface coal mining. The court incorrectly assumed that the Act's goals are limited to preventing air and water pollution. * * *

Congress adopted the Surface Mining Act in order to ensure that production of coal for interstate commerce would not be at the expense of agriculture, the environment, or public health and safety, injury to any of which interests would have deleterious effects on interstate commerce. * * * The statutory provisions invalidated by the District Court advance these legitimate goals and we conclude that Congress acted reasonably in adopting the regulatory scheme contained in the Act.

The District Court also held that the 21 substantive statutory provisions discussed above violate the Tenth Amendment because they constitute "displacement or regulation of the management structure and operation of the traditional governmental function of the States in the area of land use control and planning * * *."

* * * [T]he sections of the Act under attack in this case regulate only the activities of surface mine operators who are private individuals and businesses, and the District Court's conclusion that the Act directly regulates the States as States is untenable. * * *

NOTES

1. The Court applied a rational basis test to assess the validity of the statute. As a practical matter, does this test impose any significant constraints on Congress?

2. It may be helpful to consider how the theories discussed in Section A apply in a specific case such as *Hodel*. On which of the following theories, if any, is federal regulation to protect prime farmland from strip mining justified: interstate environmental effects of strip mining such as water pollution, the economic impact of such strip mining on agricultural production, the potential for a "race to the bottom" among state regulators of strip mining, or the greater expertise available to federal regulatory agencies than to state governments? On the other hand, are there reasons why, at least as a policy matter, we might prefer to leave the matter to state governments? (For

instance, are people in different states likely to have conflicting views about the importance of preserving prime farmland? Is it better for land use regulation to take place at a level of government more accessible to ordinary people?)

1. THE REVIVAL OF LIMITS ON THE COMMERCE CLAUSE

As *Hodel* illustrates, Congress has not been shy about exercising the commerce power. Between 1965 and 1980, Richard Stewart reports, "Congress adopted sweeping new environmental, health, safety, and antidiscrimination regulatory statutes. There are at present over sixty major federal programs regulating business and non-profit organizations." Richard B. Stewart, *Madison's Nightmare*, 57 U. CHI. L. REV. 335, 339 (1990). In particular, Congress took the lead on environmental issues. *See* William W. Buzbee, *Brownfields, Environmental Federalism, and Institutional Determinism*, 21 WM. & MARY L. REV. 1 (1997) (discussing federal government's "first mover" status).

By the later 1980s, however, some conservative theorists were beginning to lay the groundwork for a retreat from this expansive view of federal power. The Commerce Clause debate seemed entirely "academic" until the Supreme Court unexpectedly put its weight behind the effort to limit federal legislative power in *United States v. Lopez*, 514 U.S. 549 (1995). Chief Justice Rehnquist's opinion invalidated a federal ban on possession of firearms in the vicinity of schools (a subject on which the need for federal regulation does seem less than obvious). At the outset, Rehnquist invoked Madison's characterization of federal powers as "few and defined" while state powers are "numerous and indefinite." *Id*. at 549. Admittedly, he added, the scope of federal power had greatly increased in the post-New Deal era, partly because of the "great changes" in the economy and partly because of a desire to eliminate "artificial" restraints on federal power. *Id*. at 554. Rehnquist concluded, however, that the school gun law did not fall squarely within the post-New Deal judicial holdings, and he declined to further expand the scope of the commerce power.

The Court's most recent pronouncement on the scope of federal power narrows the scope of *Lopez*. In *Gonzales v. Raich,* 545 U.S. 1 (2005), the Court upheld the application of the federal Controlled Substances Act to cultivators of medical marijuana who cultivated the marijuana for home use consistent with a doctor's prescription under California's Compassionate Use Act. In so ruling, the Court made clear that "[w]e need not determine whether respondents' activities, taken in the aggregate, substantially affect interstate commerce in fact, but only whether a 'rational basis' exists for so concluding." *Id*. at 125 S.Ct. 2197. Justice Stevens wrote the opinion of the Court, with Justices O'Connor, Rehnquist and

Thomas dissenting. Notably, Justice Scalia concurred with the majority opinion.

Congress has used the commerce power as the basis for regulating air and water pollution, hazardous waste disposal, and a host of other environmental problems. For the present, at least, the bulk of federal environmental statutes resting on the commerce power still seems safe from constitutional attack. *See United States v. Olin Corp.*, 107 F.3d 1506 (11th Cir. 1997) (upholding application of CERCLA without proof that any off-site damage had occurred). But *Lopez* does seem to leave open the possibility of attacking some particular federal environmental regulations, though *Raich* will make such attacks more difficult. Nevertheless, courts will still be asked to consider whether environmental laws that govern noncommercial activity in a traditional area of state concern and lack any evident interstate impact are constitutional.

One possible area of concern involves federal regulation of isolated wetlands. Such concerns are heightened by the following opinion.

SOLID WASTE AGENCY OF NORTHERN COOK COUNTY [SWANCC] v. UNITED STATES ARMY CORPS OF ENGINEERS

Supreme Court of the United States, 2001.
531 U.S. 159, 121 S.Ct. 675, 148 L.Ed.2d 576.

[page 805 of this Casebook]

NOTES

1.   The majority opinion articulates an important rule of statutory interpretation in federalism cases: "Where an administrative interpretation of a statute invokes the outer limits of Congress' power, we expect a clear indication that Congress intended that result." This rule is "strongest where the administrative interpretation alters the federal-state framework by permitting federal encroachment upon a traditional state power." This canon may be relevant to other areas of environmental law, such as interpretation of the Endangered Species Act or the Clean Water Act, where federalism claims may be raised.

2.   More recently, Supreme Court ruled on a case involving the statutory definition of navigable waters under the CWA as applied to wetlands, as well as Commerce Clause challenges to the application of the CWA to non-adjacent wetlands. *Rapanos v. United States*, [casebook p. 811]. The Court rejected the government's broad definition of wetlands, but without discussing the constitutional issue.

3.   What about the Endangered Species Act? Does Congress have the power to protect a species that exists only in a single state? Consider the following case.

ALABAMA–TOMBIGBEE RIVERS COALITION
v. KEMPTHORNE

U.S. Court of Appeals for the Eleventh Circuit, 2007.
477 F.3d 1250.

CARNES, CIRCUIT JUDGE: Two fish, or not two fish? That is the question. More specifically, are the Alabama sturgeon and the shovelnose sturgeon separate species? The answer lies primarily in the field of taxonomy, which one observer has noted "is described sometimes as a science and sometimes as an art, but really it's a battleground." The battle over the Alabama sturgeon has been more like the Thirty Years War. A scientist first classified this small freshwater fish found in the Mobile River Basin of Alabama as endangered in 1976. Three decades and three trips to this Court later the fight over whether the Alabama sturgeon is an endangered species continues. On one side are various business interests, including the Alabama–Tombigbee Rivers Coalition, and on the other are the Fish and Wildlife Service and several federal officials involved with it. * * *

The Coalition's third contention is that the Final Rule should be vacated because Congress has exceeded the power granted to it under the Commerce Clause by authorizing protection of the Alabama sturgeon, which the Coalition characterizes as an intrastate, noncommercial species. In the Coalition's view, protecting the Alabama sturgeon is not one of the three categories of activities Congress may regulate using its Commerce Clause powers. [Lopez] As the Supreme Court has recently summarized the law in this area, there are three permissible exercises of congressional authority over commerce: "First, Congress can regulate the channels of interstate commerce. Second, Congress has authority to regulate and protect the instrumentalities of interstate commerce, and persons or things in interstate commerce. Third, Congress has the power to regulate activities that substantially affect interstate commerce." *Gonzales v. Raich,* 545 U.S. 1, 17, 125 S.Ct. 2195, 2205, 162 L.Ed.2d 1 (2005) (citations omitted). The parties agree that the third category or power, regulating activities that substantially affect interstate commerce, is the one at issue here.

The Service counters that three circuits, in four published opinions issued since *Lopez,* have already upheld the constitutionality of Congress authorizing the Fish and Wildlife Service to list a purely intrastate species as endangered under the Endangered Species Act. *See GDF Realty Invs. v. Norton,* 326 F.3d 622 (5th Cir.2003); *Rancho Viejo, LLC v. Norton,* 323 F.3d 1062 (D.C.Cir.2003); *Gibbs v. Babbitt,* 214 F.3d 483 (4th Cir.2000); *Nat'l Ass'n of Home Builders v. Babbitt,* 130 F.3d 1041, 1052–54 (D.C.Cir. 1997). No circuit has held to the contrary. Meanwhile the Supreme Court has had the Endangered Species Act before it several times but has never questioned its constitutionality. Not only that, but last year in *Raich* the Supreme Court cited the prohibition on "takes" of eagles in the Bald and Golden Eagle Protection Act, which is a close cousin to the Endangered

Species Act's "take" provision, as an example of "a rational (and commonly utilized) means of regulating commerce."

The Coalition characterizes its claim as an as-applied challenge to the Final Rule, and its briefs are carefully tailored to the argument that federal protection of the Alabama sturgeon, which is one homely looking fish to be found only with the greatest effort in one river system in one state, does not concern commerce or economic activity. Nonetheless, the necessary first step in addressing its challenge is an examination of the total economic impact of the Endangered Species Act itself. In *Lopez,* the Supreme Court held that aggregation of economic effects is permissible where the federal action in question is "an essential part of a larger regulation of economic activity, in which the regulatory scheme could be undercut unless the intrastate activity were regulated."

In *Raich,* the Court upheld the application of provisions in the Controlled Substances Act criminalizing the manufacture, distribution, and possession of marijuana to intrastate growers and users of marijuana for medicinal purposes. In doing so, the Court explained the statement it had made in *Lopez* regarding the regulation of intrastate activity as part of a larger regulation of economic activity: "Our case law firmly establishes Congress' power to regulate purely local activities that are part of an economic 'class of activities' that have a substantial effect on interstate commerce." The courts "have never required Congress to legislate with scientific exactitude. When Congress decides that the 'total incidence' of a practice poses a threat to a national market, it may regulate the entire class."

This principle poses a problem for the Coalition's as-applied challenge, because "when 'a general regulatory statute bears a substantial relation to commerce, the *de minimis* character of individual instances arising under that statute is of no consequence.' " *Id.* If the process of listing endangered species is "an essential part of a larger regulation of economic activity," then whether that process "ensnares some purely intrastate activity is of no moment." *Id.* at 24. When Congress can and has regulated a class of activities, we "have no power to excise, as trivial, individual instances of the class." [*Raich*]

We agree with the three circuits that have concluded the Endangered Species Act is a general regulatory statute bearing a substantial relation to commerce. The Coalition does not argue to the contrary, nor could it do so persuasively. The Act prohibits all interstate and foreign commerce in endangered species. Although the true size of an illegal market is difficult to gauge, the United Nations Environment Programme estimates the illegal component of the worldwide trade in wildlife generates $5 billion to $8 billion in proceeds annually. Other reports state that the trade in wildlife products comprises the world's second largest black market, trailing only trade in illegal narcotics. The United States is not a bit player in this market. The Service conservatively estimates that Americans pay $200 million annually for illegally caught domestic animals and $1 billion for those illegally caught in other countries.

The commercial impact of the Endangered Species Act is even greater than those large numbers suggest, because the economic value of endangered species extends far beyond their sale price. The House Report accompanying the Endangered Species Act explains that as human development pushes species towards extinction, "we threaten their—and our own—genetic heritage. The value of this genetic heritage is, quite literally, incalculable." Biodiversity's value is not ethereal; its preservation produces economic gain in even the most narrow sense. For example, species diversity is essential to medicine. Half of the most commonly prescribed medicines are derived from plant and animal species. Nine of the ten most commonly used prescription drugs in the United States are derived from natural plant products.

Genetic diversity is also important to improving agriculture and aquaculture. As the D.C. Circuit explained in *NAHB*, "the genetic material of wild species of plants and animals is inbred into domestic crops and animals to improve their commercial value and productivity." Of the explosive growth in this nation's farm production since the 1930s, genetic diversity is responsible "for at least one-half of the doubling in yields of rice, soybeans, wheat, and sugarcane, and a three-fold increase in corn and potatoes." The growing use of genetic modification in aquaculture, meanwhile, may prove essential to meeting the rising world demand for fish and fishmeal.

A species' simple presence in its natural habitat may stimulate commerce by encouraging fishing, hunting, and tourism. A Fish and Wildlife Service report found that in 2001 recreational anglers spent $35.6 billion, recreational hunters spent $20.6 billion, and wildlife watchers spent $38.4 billion. The report estimated direct expenditures only, and the total commercial impact of each activity may be greater still. A 1996 estimate found that recreational anglers alone had "a nationwide economic impact of about $108.4 billion, support[ed] 1.2 million jobs, and add[ed] $5.5 billion to Federal and State tax revenues." All of the industries we have mentioned—pharmaceuticals, agriculture, fishing, hunting, and wildlife tourism—fundamentally depend on a diverse stock of wildlife, and the Endangered Species Act is designed to safeguard that stock.

Just as it is apparent that the "comprehensive scheme" of species protection contained in the Endangered Species Act has a substantial effect on interstate commerce, it is clear that the listing process is "an essential part" of that "larger regulation of economic activity." [*Raich*] The decision to list a species as endangered or threatened is a necessary precondition to the protections afforded species under the Act. There would be no point to the Act if no species could be listed as endangered or threatened.

The Coalition does seek a more narrow remedy than a declaration that Congress' delegation of listing authority to the Service is unconstitutional. It wants us to treat the Alabama sturgeon, a purely intrastate species, separately from all species that have demonstrated commercial value. Congress could have excluded all intrastate species from the scope of the Endangered Species Act, but it chose not to do so. This court has "no power to excise, as trivial, individual instances of the class." The only remaining question before us "is whether Congress' contrary policy judgment, i.e., its decision to include this narrower 'class of activities' within the larger regulatory scheme, was constitutionally deficient." That depends on whether Congress could have rationally concluded that the regulation of intrastate species was an essential part of the larger regulatory scheme.

There are several reasons for Congress' decision to regulate all endangered species, instead of only interstate ones. For one thing, Congress was concerned with "the unknown uses that endangered species might have." The extinction of species poses the risk that humanity may lose forever the opportunity to learn some of nature's secrets. Deforestation drove the rosy periwinkle, a delicate pink flower native to Madagascar, nearly to extinction before scientists discovered that it contained two substances now used to treat childhood leukemia and Hodgkin's lymphoma. Inside fragile living things, in little flowers or even in ugly fish, may hidden treasures lie. Because Congress could not anticipate which species might have undiscovered scientific and economic value, it made sense to protect all those species that are endangered. Because a species' scientific or other commercial value is not dependent on whether its habitat straddles a state line, Congress had good reason to include all species within the protection of the Act. It did not behave irrationally by taking the broader approach.

Congress also recognized "the unforeseeable place such creatures may have in the chain of life on this planet." As biologist Edward O. Wilson explained: "Every species is part of an ecosystem, an expert specialist of its kind, tested relentlessly as it spreads its influence through the food web. To remove it is to entrain changes in other species, raising the populations of some, reducing or even extinguishing others, risking a downward spiral of the larger assemblage." An insect with no apparent commercial value may be the favorite meal of a spider whose venom will soon emerge as a powerful and profitable anesthetic agent. That spider may in turn be the dietary staple of a brightly colored bird that people, who are notoriously biased against creepy crawlers and in favor of winsome winged wonders, will travel to see as tourists. Faced with the prospect that the loss of any one species could trigger the decline of an entire ecosystem, destroying a trove of natural and commercial treasures, it was rational for Congress to choose to protect them all.

Congress also reasoned that protection of an endangered species could "permit the regeneration of that species to a level where controlled exploitation of that species can be resumed. In such a case businessmen may profit from the trading and marketing of that species for an indefinite number of years, where otherwise it would have been completely eliminated from commercial channels. The Alabama sturgeon is potentially an example of that congressional hope. It was once harvested commercially, and over harvesting was one of the factors in the species' decline. The protection the Endangered Species Act affords may one day allow the replenishment of its numbers and eventual, controlled commercial exploitation of the fish. Indeed, this possibility underscores the fundamental irony in the Coalition's position. Under the Coalition's theory, Congress is free to protect a commercially thriving species that exists in abundance across the United States because it has economic worth, but once economic exploitation has driven that species so close to the brink of extinction that it desperately needs the government's protection, Congress is powerless to act. * * *

This case, like *Raich,* also turns on whether Congress had a rational basis for believing that regulation of an intrastate activity was an essential part of a larger regulation of economic activity. Unlike the statute involved in *Raich,* Congress did not rely on commodity pricing in justifying the Endangered Species Act. Instead, it made a determination that the most effective way to safeguard the commercial benefits of biodiversity was to protect all endangered species, regardless of their geographic range. That rational decision was within Congress' authority to make.

NOTES

1. Suppose Congress had passed a special law to protect the sturgeon (as it did for the bald eagle), rather than a broader protection of all endangered species. Would such a law pass constitutional muster?

2. Putting aside constitutional issues, as a matter of policy, should protection of endangered species be a federal or state responsibility? Why?

3. Could Congress use the *Raich* theory to support regulation of all wetlands, whether or not they are connected in any way with navigable streams?

2. STATE SOVEREIGNTY AND ENVIRONMENTAL LAW

For many years, the Tenth Amendment was considered to be nothing more than a reminder that the states retained whatever powers that had not been given to the federal government. In 1976, however, the Court resurrected the Amendment in *National League of Cities v. Usery,* 426 U.S. 833 (1976), striking down a law that extended the federal minimum wage to cover state employees.

Justice Blackmun had been the swing vote in *National League of Cities.* In *Garcia v. San Antonio Metropolitan Transit Authority,* 469 U.S. 528 (1985), he changed his mind, and became the decisive vote to overrule *National League of Cities.* Like the earlier case, *Garcia* involved the federal minimum wage law, this time as applied to public transit workers.

Despairing of the effort to distinguish integral state functions from other state activities, the Court held that the political process is the primary shield of the states against Congress. At least in the absence of a clear breakdown in the political process, courts should not intervene. The dissenters in *Garcia* predicted a rapid demise for that case, but since then the Court (perhaps somewhat surprisingly) has given no signal of interest in overruling *Garcia*.

The following case focuses on the narrower problem posed by statutes that target *only* state governments. It may represent the first step toward resurrecting *National League of Cities*.

NEW YORK v. UNITED STATES

Supreme Court of the United States, 1992.
505 U.S. 144, 112 S.Ct. 2408, 120 L.Ed.2d 120.

JUSTICE O'CONNOR delivered the opinion of the Court.

[This case involves three provisions of the Low–Level Radioactive Waste Policy Amendments Act of 1985. Since 1979, only three disposal sites for low-level waste have been in operation. The statute is designed to create incentives for states to take responsibility for the waste they produce. Based largely upon a proposal of the National Governors' Association, the 1985 statute was a compromise between sited and unsited states (those containing or not containing disposal sites). The sited states agreed to accept waste for another seven years, and the unsited states agreed to handle their own waste by 1992. The statute provides several incentives to encourage states to tackle this problem. First, the sited states are authorized to charge gradually increasing fees for waste from unsited states. Second, states that miss certain deadlines may be charged higher surcharges and, eventually, may be denied access to disposal facilities altogether. Third, the so-called "take title" provision tells states that eventually they will literally own the problem themselves if they don't cooperate.

[New York joined no regional compact. It complied with the initial requirements of the statute by enacting legislation providing for the siting of a facility in the state. Residents of the two counties containing potential sites opposed the state's choice of location—a classic example of the NIMBY ("Not In My Back Yard") syndrome. Fearing that it could not comply with the statutory deadlines, New York and these two counties brought suit, contending that the statute is inconsistent with the Tenth Amendment and with the guarantee of a republican form of government in Article IV.]

Most of our recent cases interpreting the Tenth Amendment have concerned the authority of Congress to subject state governments to generally applicable laws. The Court's jurisprudence in this area has traveled an unsteady path. [Citing *National League of Cities* and *Garcia*.] This case presents no occasion to apply or revisit the holdings of any of these cases, as this is not a case in which Congress has subjected a State to the same legislation applicable to private parties.

This case instead concerns the circumstances under which Congress may use the States as implements of regulation; that is, whether Congress may direct or otherwise motivate the States to regulate in a particular field or a particular way. * * *

* * * While Congress has substantial powers to govern the Nation directly, including in areas of intimate concern to the States, the Constitution has never been understood to confer upon Congress the ability to require the States to govern according to Congress' instructions. The Court has been explicit about this distinction. "Both the States and the United States existed before the Constitution. The people, through that instrument, established a more perfect union by substituting a national government, acting, with ample power, *directly upon the citizens,* instead of the Confederate government, which acted with powers, greatly restricted, only upon the States."

This is not to say that Congress lacks the ability to encourage a State to regulate in a particular way, or that Congress may not hold out incentives to the States as a method of influencing a State's policy choices. Our cases have identified a variety of methods, short of outright coercion, by which Congress may urge a State to adopt a legislative program consistent with federal interests. Two of these methods are of particular relevance here.

First, under Congress' spending power, "Congress may attach conditions on the receipt of federal funds." Such conditions must (among other requirements) bear some relationship to the purpose of the federal spending; otherwise, of course, the spending power could render academic the Constitution's other grants and limits of federal authority. Where the recipient of federal funds is a State, as is not unusual today, the conditions attached to the funds by Congress may influence a State's legislative choices. * * *

Second, where Congress has the authority to regulate private activity under the Commerce Clause, we have recognized Congress' power to offer States the choice of regulating that activity according to federal standards or having state law pre-empted by federal regulation. This arrangement, which has been termed "a program of cooperative federalism," is replicated in numerous federal statutory schemes. * * *

By either of these two methods, as by any other permissible method of encouraging a State to conform to federal policy choices, the residents of the State retain the ultimate decision as to whether or not the State will comply. If a State's citizens view federal policy as sufficiently contrary to local interests, they may elect to decline a federal grant. If state residents would prefer their government to devote its attention and resources to problems other than those deemed important by Congress, they may choose to have the Federal Government rather than the State bear the expense of a federally mandated regulatory program, and they may continue to supplement that program to the extent state law is not preempted. Where Congress encourages state regulation rather than compelling it, state governments remain responsive to the local electorate's preferences; state officials remain accountable to the people.

By contrast, where the Federal Government compels States to regulate, the accountability of both state and federal officials is diminished. If the citizens of New York, for example, do not consider that making provision for the disposal of radioactive waste is in their best interest, they may elect state officials who share their view. That view can always be preempted under the Supremacy Clause if it is contrary to the national view, but in such a case it is the Federal Government that makes the decision in full view of the public, and it will be federal officials that suffer the consequences if the decision turns out to be detrimental or unpopular. But where the Federal Government directs the States to regulate, it may be state officials who will bear the brunt of public disapproval, while the federal officials who devised the regulatory program may remain insulated from the electoral ramifications of their decision. Accountability is thus diminished when, due to federal coercion, elected state officials cannot regulate in accordance with the views of the local electorate in matters not pre-empted by federal regulation.

[The Court upheld the Act's provision authorizing sited states to impose a surcharge on waste received from other states. These charges are intended to provide financial incentives for states to cooperate with the waste disposal scheme. The Court called this provision "an unexceptional exercise of Congress' power to authorize the states to burden interstate commerce." The Court upheld the provision under which the federal government collects a portion of this surcharge and places it into an escrow account, calling it "no more than a federal tax on interstate commerce." Also held valid was the provision under which states reaching a series of milestones in combating radioactive waste receive portions of these federally collected funds, which was considered an appropriate "conditional exercise of Congress' authority under the Spending Clause." The Court also upheld a provision authorizing states and regional compacts with disposal sites to increase the costs of access to those sites, and deny access altogether, to waste generated in states that do not meet federal guidelines. This was viewed as a "conditional exercise of Congress' commerce power." The Court then turned to the remaining provision, requiring states to take title to the waste if they fail to meet the 1996 deadline.]

The take title provision is of a different character. [It] offers States, as an alternative to regulating pursuant to Congress' direction, the option of taking title to and possession of the low level radioactive waste generated within their borders and becoming liable for all damages waste generators suffer as a result of the States' failure to do so promptly. In this provision, Congress has crossed the line distinguishing encouragement from coercion.

The take title provision appears to be unique. No other federal statute has been cited which offers a state government no option other than that of implementing legislation enacted by Congress. Whether one views the take title provision as lying outside Congress' enumerated powers, or as infringing upon the core of state sovereignty reserved by the Tenth Amendment, the provision is inconsistent with the federal structure of our Government established by the Constitution.

JUSTICE WHITE, with whom JUSTICE BLACKMUN and JUSTICE STEVENS join, concurring in part and dissenting in part.

Curiously absent from the Court's analysis is any effort to place the take title provision within the overall context of the legislation. * * * Congress could have pre-empted the field by directly regulating the disposal of this waste pursuant to its powers under the Commerce and Spending Clauses, but instead it *unanimously* assented to the States' request for congressional ratification of agreements to which they had acceded. * * * [T]he States wished to take the lead in achieving a solution to this problem and agreed among themselves to the various incentives and penalties implemented by Congress to insure adherence to the various deadlines and goals. The chief executives of the States proposed this approach, and I am unmoved by the Court's vehemence in taking away Congress' authority to sanction a recalcitrant unsited State now that New York has reaped the benefits of the sited States' concessions.

Ultimately, I suppose, the entire structure of our federal constitutional government can be traced to an interest in establishing checks and balances to prevent the exercise of tyranny against individuals. But these fears seem extremely far distant to me in a situation such as this. We face a crisis of national proportions in the disposal of low-level radioactive waste, and Congress has acceded to the wishes of the States by permitting local decisionmaking rather than imposing a solution from Washington. New York itself participated and supported passage of this legislation at both the gubernatorial and federal representative levels, and then enacted state laws specifically to comply with the deadlines and timetables agreed upon by the States in the 1985 Act. For me, the Court's civics lecture has a decidedly hollow ring at a time when action, rather than rhetoric, is needed to solve a national problem. * * *

NOTES

1. *New York* seems to create something of a dilemma. On the one hand, individual states are clearly subject to a NIMBY problem. *See* Hamilton, *Political and Social Costs: Estimating the Impact of Collective Action on Hazardous Waste Facilities*, 24 RAND J. ECON. 101 (1993). They wish to have the benefits of using low-level radioactive materials for medical and other purposes, but would prefer to have the burden (political and otherwise) of disposing of the waste fall elsewhere. This is a classic collective action problem of the kind that motivated the formation of the national government.

One solution would be for each state to establish a quarantine, so that states would not be able to export their waste problems to each other. As we will see in the next section, however, this solution probably violates the dormant commerce clause. This leaves the states in what game theorists call a prisoner's dilemma; every state needs a place to dispose of the waste, but it is rational for each state to impose a ban on such sites, fearing that it will be flooded with waste from other states. *See* Paul E. McGreal, *The Flawed Economics of the Dormant Commerce Clause*, 39 WM. & MARY L. REV. 1191 (1998).

Another method of solving this problem would be for the states to agree to behave responsibly in establishing disposal sites, rather than trying to free ride on each other. Obviously, there is an incentive for states to default on such an agreement. In order to avoid default, the states requested that Congress make the agreement legally binding on them. But the Court says that this violates federalism. Is there any way to resolve this dilemma of federalism? What would Justice O'Connor suggest?

Query: Suppose that the states had embodied their agreement in an interstate compact, which would have required congressional approval to be enforceable. Would using this mechanism have avoided the *New York* holding? Could Congress simply replace its direct mandate with draconian funding cut-offs? Is some other mechanism available? Or is this dilemma simply an inescapable price of our federalist constitutional scheme?

2. In *Board of Natural Resources v. Brown,* 992 F.2d 937 (9th Cir. 1993), the state of Washington challenged portions of the 1990 Forest Resources Conservation and Shortage Relief Act, 16 U.S.C.A. sections 620–620(j), which restricted the export of unprocessed timber from federal and state public lands in western states. The purpose of the restrictions was to preserve jobs at domestic sawmills in the face of reduced cutting in old-growth forests, due in part to efforts to protect the habitat of the Western Spotted Owl, an endangered species. The statute provided that "[e]ach state shall determine the species, grade, and geographic origin of unprocessed timber to be prohibited from export * * * and shall administer such prohibitions consistent with the intent of sections 620 to 620(j)," and that "the Governor * * * shall * * * issue regulations to carry out the purposes" of the Act. The court held that these provisions violate the Tenth Amendment as interpreted in *New York.*

Note that *Brown* expanded *New York* from a protection of the state legislature to a protection of state administrative officials. Although there is some reason to question whether this expansion is consistent with the original understanding of the Constitution (*see* Saikrishna Bangalore Prakash, *Field Office Federalism*, 79 VA. L. REV. 1957 (1993)), the Supreme Court ultimately ruled that Congress has no more power to commandeer state administrators than state legislators. *See* Printz v. United States, 521 U.S. 898 (1997) (striking down portions of a federal gun control statute on this basis). Note, however, that while *New York* prohibits direct commandeering, it does allow Congress to use a battery of incentives to obtain state cooperation. As we will see in the next two chapters, the Clean Air Act and the Clean Water Act rely heavily on state agencies to implement the federal programs, providing various incentives for states to participate.

3. The problem of federal power discussed in this section has an analogue in the European Union. Unlike our constitution, however, the Maas-

tricht treaty contains an explicit grant of power over environmental matters. This environmental authority is created by Article 130. The EU can also use its other regulatory powers, such as the general power to eliminate barriers to a unified economy, as a basis for environmental protection. (There are, however, some subtle differences in the legislative procedures involved with these various powers and in their preemptive effects on member states.) Should specific environmental regulatory authority be added to the U.S. Constitution or state constitutions?

C. COMMERCE CLAUSE RESTRICTIONS ON STATE POWER

In a unified national economy, the existence of a multitude of differing state pollution laws can impede the free flow of commerce. Yet the states have often taken the lead in the environmental area because of pressing local problems. This section deals with the need to accommodate these conflicting interests, which takes place under the auspices of the commerce clause.

The dormant commerce clause, like the grants of federal regulatory power discussed in the previous section, can be considered the solution to a collective action problem. Because out-of-state residents are not represented in the state legislature, the state may attempt to export the costs of regulation, while retaining the benefits. While the strategy makes sense for each state individually, it may leave the states worse off collectively. The federal courts step in to prevent this regulatory equivalent of the NIMBY syndrome.

The Commerce Clause, on its face, is a grant of power to Congress, not a restriction on state legislation. Yet, beginning with the period of the Marshall Court, the Supreme Court has always construed the Commerce Clause as preventing certain kinds of state regulation even when Congress has not spoken. Despite some indications to the contrary in the earliest cases, however, the states are not completely disabled from regulating interstate commerce. For instance, in *Huron Portland Cement Co. v. Detroit*, 362 U.S. 440 (1960), the Court upheld the application of an anti-smoke ordinance to ships that were temporarily docked in Detroit while engaged in transporting cement on the Great Lakes. Finding the ordinance to be "a regulation of general application," which did not discriminate against interstate commerce, the Court found no evidence that the regulation placed an "impermissible burden" on interstate commerce. *Huron Portland Cement* illustrates one aspect of commerce clause doctrine, the undue burden test, which applies to *nondiscriminatory* state regulations. In applying this test, the Court will uphold a statute which effectuates a valid local purpose "unless the burden imposed on [interstate] commerce is clearly excessive in relation to the putative local benefits." *Pike v. Bruce Church, Inc.*, 397 U.S. 137, 142 (1970).

The next case involves the application of the *Pike* balancing test to environmental regulations. We will then turn to some categories of cases where different tests apply.

MINNESOTA v. CLOVER LEAF CREAMERY CO.

Supreme Court of the United States, 1981.
449 U.S. 456, 101 S.Ct. 715, 66 L.Ed.2d 659.

Justice Brennan delivered the opinion of the Court.

In 1977, the Minnesota Legislature enacted a statute banning the retail sale of milk in plastic nonreturnable, nonrefillable containers, but permitting such sale in other nonreturnable, nonrefillable containers, such as paperboard milk cartons. Respondents contend that the statute violates the Equal Protection and Commerce Clauses of the Constitution.* * *

Since the statute does not discriminate between interstate and intrastate commerce, the controlling question is whether the incidental burden imposed on interstate commerce by the Minnesota Act is "clearly excessive in relation to the putative local benefits." We conclude that it is not.

The burden imposed on interstate commerce by the statute is relatively minor. Milk products may continue to move freely across the Minnesota border, and since most dairies package their products in more than one type of containers, the inconvenience of having to conform to different packaging requirements in Minnesota and the surrounding States should be slight. Within Minnesota, business will presumably shift from manufacturers of plastic nonreturnable containers to producers of paperboard cartons, refillable bottles, and plastic pouches, but there is no reason to suspect that the gainers will be Minnesota firms, or the losers out-of-state firms. Indeed, two of the three dairies, the sole milk retailer, and the sole milk container producer challenging the statute in this litigation are Minnesota firms.

Pulpwood producers are the only Minnesota industry likely to benefit significantly from the Act at the expense of out-of-state firms. Respondents point out that plastic resin, the raw material used for making plastic nonreturnable milk jugs, is produced entirely by non-Minnesota firms, while pulpwood, used for making paperboard, is a major Minnesota product. Nevertheless, it is clear that respondents exaggerate the degree of burden on out-of-state interests, both because plastics will continue to be used in the production of plastic pouches, plastic returnable bottles, and paperboard itself, and because out-of-state pulpwood producers will presumably absorb some of the business generated by the Act.

Even granting that the out-of-state plastics industry is burdened relatively more heavily than the Minnesota pulpwood industry, we find that this burden is not "clearly excessive" in light of the substantial state interest in promoting conservation of energy and other natural resources and easing solid waste disposal problems, which we have already reviewed in the context of equal protection analysis. We find these local benefits ample to support Minnesota's decision under the Commerce Clause. Moreover, we find that no approach with "a lesser impact on interstate activities," is available. Respondents have suggested several alternative statutory schemes, but these alternatives are either more burdensome on commerce than the Act (as, for example, banning all nonreturnables) or less likely to be effective (as, for example, providing incentives for recycling).

In *Exxon Corp. v. Governor of Maryland*, 437 U.S. 117, 98 S. Ct. 2207, 57 L. Ed. 2d 91 (1978), we upheld a Maryland statute barring producers and refiners of petroleum products—all of which were out-of-state businesses—from retailing gasoline in the State. We stressed that the Commerce Clause "protects the interstate market, not particular interstate firms, from prohibitive or burdensome regulations." A nondiscriminatory regulation serving substantial state purposes is not invalid simply because it causes some business to shift from a predominantly out-of-state industry to a predominantly in-state industry. Only if the burden on interstate commerce clearly outweighs the State's legitimate purposes does such a regulation violate the Commerce Clause.

The judgment of the Minnesota Supreme Court is reversed.

NOTES

1. To what extent should a court probe behind the face of a statute to determine whether legislators' true motives were protectionist? What kind of fact-finding procedures would be appropriate in such an inquiry?

2. Interestingly enough, the Minnesota statute was repealed after the Court's decision upholding it. Why do you think the state repealed the plastic container ban?

3. The *Pike* test calls for a determination of whether the burden on commerce is clearly excessive compared to the environmental benefits. Isn't that a classic example of a legislative determination? Should courts be second-guessing legislatures in this way?

4. The preceding case illustrates the use of the *Pike* balancing test. As the next three cases show, however, the Supreme Court has not always found balancing to be appropriate in commerce clause cases.

HUGHES v. ALEXANDRIA SCRAP CORP.

Supreme Court of the United States, 1976.
426 U.S. 794, 96 S.Ct. 2488, 49 L.Ed.2d 220.

JUSTICE POWELL delivered the opinion of the Court.

[Maryland enacted a bounty system for old, abandoned cars ("hulks"). Prior to 1974, no title certificate was needed by the scrap processor in order to claim the bounty. After 1974, Maryland processors needed only to submit an indemnity agreement in which suppliers certify their own rights to the hulks. Out-of-state processors had to submit a title certificate or police certificate for each car. The appellee, a Virginia processor, challenged the amended statute as a violation of the Commerce Clause.]

The District Court accepted appellee's analysis, and concluded that the 1974 amendment failed the *Pike* test. First, the court found that the amendment did impose "substantial burdens upon the free flow of inter-state commerce." Moreover, it considered the disadvantage suffered by out-of-state processors to be particularly suspect under previous decisions of this Court, noting that to avoid the disadvantage those processors would have to build new plants inside Maryland to carry on a business which, prior to the amendment, they had pursued efficiently outside the State. Maryland's principal argument in support of the amendment was that, by making it difficult for out-of-state processors to claim bounties on hulks delivered by unlicensed suppliers, the amendment tends to reduce the amount of state funds paid for destruction of Maryland-titled hulks abandoned in the States where those processors are located instead of in Maryland. The District Court acknowledged the validity of this interest, but considered the means employed inappropriate under *Pike* because the same interest could have been furthered, with less impact upon interstate commerce, by amending the statute to condition the bounty upon a hulk's abandonment in Maryland instead of its previous titling there.

This line of reasoning is not without force if its basic premise is accepted. That premise is that every action by a State that has the effect of reducing in some manner the flow of goods in interstate commerce is potentially an impermissible burden. But we are not persuaded that Maryland's action in amending its statute was the kind of action with which the Commerce Clause is concerned.

The situation presented by this statute and the 1974 amendment is quite unlike that found in the cases upon which appellee relies.* * *

The common thread of all these cases is that the State interfered with the natural functioning of the interstate market either through prohibi-tion or through burdensome regulation. By contrast, Maryland has not sought to prohibit the flow of hulks, or to regulate the conditions under which it may occur. Instead, it has entered into the market itself to bid up their price. There has been an impact upon the interstate flow of hulks only because, since the 1974 amendment, Maryland effectively has made it more lucrative for unlicensed suppliers to dispose of their hulks in Maryland rather than take them outside the State.* * *

We do not believe the Commerce Clause was intended to require independent justification for such action. Maryland entered the market for the purpose, agreed by all to be commendable as well as legitimate, of protecting the State's environment. As the means of furthering this purpose, it elected the payment of state funds—in the form of bounties—to encourage the removal of automobile hulks from Maryland streets and junkyards. It is true that the state money initially was made available to licensed out-of-state processors as well as those located within Maryland, and not until the 1974 amendment was the financial benefit channeled, in practical effect, to domestic processors. But this chronology does not distinguish the case, for Commerce Clause purposes, from one in which a State offered bounties only to domestic processors from the start. Regard-less of when the State's largesse is first confined to domestic processors, the effect upon the flow of hulks resting within the State is the same: they will tend to be processed inside the State rather than flowing to foreign processors. But no trade barrier of the type forbidden by the Commerce Clause, and involved in previous cases, impedes their movement out of State. They remain within Maryland in response to market forces, including that exerted by money from the State. Nothing in the purposes animating the Commerce Clause prohibits a State, in the absence of congressional action, from participating in the market and exercising the right to favor its own citizens over others.

JUSTICE STEVENS, concurring.

The dissent creates the impression that the Court's opinion, which I join without reservation, represents a significant retreat from its settled practice in adjudicating claims that a state program places an unconstitutional burden on interstate commerce. This is not the fact. There is no prior decision of this Court even addressing the critical Commerce Clause issue presented by this case.

It is important to differentiate between commerce which flourishes in a free market and commerce which owes its existence to a state subsidy program. Our cases finding that a state regulation constitutes an impermissible burden on interstate commerce all dealt with restrictions that adversely affected the operation of a free market. This case is unique because the commerce which Maryland has "burdened" is commerce which would not exist if Maryland had not decided to subsidize a portion of the automobile scrap-processing business.

By artificially enhancing the value of certain abandoned hulks, Maryland created a market that did not previously exist. The program which Maryland initiated in 1969 included subsidies for scrapping plants located in Virginia and Pennsylvania as well as for plants located in Maryland. Those subsidies stimulated the movement of abandoned hulks from Maryland to out-of-state scrapping plants and thereby gave rise to the interstate commerce which is at stake in this litigation.

That commerce, which is now said to be burdened, would never have existed if in the first instance Maryland had decided to confine its subsidy to operators of Maryland plants. A failure to create that commerce would have been unobjectionable because the Commerce Clause surely does not impose on the States any obligation to subsidize out-of-state business. Nor, in my judgment, does that Clause inhibit a State's power to experiment with different methods of encouraging local industry. Whether the encouragement takes the form of a cash subsidy, a tax credit, or a special privilege intended to attract investment capital, it should not be characterized as a "burden" on commerce. * * *

NOTES

1. Suppose a state paid a bounty to utilities that purchased power from in-state renewable sources? Would such a bounty scheme be constitutional

after *Hughes?* Would it matter if the state used a tax deduction instead of a bounty to achieve the same result? How about an increased tax on users of power generated out-of-state? Is there any constitutional limit on state economic incentives after *Hughes?*

2. *Hughes* was decided the same day as *National League of Cities,* discussed on page 298–299, *supra.* Both cases hold that certain state activities have unusual status under the commerce clause. *Hughes* arguably holds that a state's regulatory programs are subject to judicial scrutiny under the commerce clause, but that its proprietary activities are immune from judicial control. *National League of Cities* reached just the opposite conclusion about congressional power: state proprietary activities are subject to federal control, nonproprietary activities are not.

CITY OF PHILADELPHIA v. NEW JERSEY

Supreme Court of the United States, 1978.
437 U.S. 617, 98 S.Ct. 2531, 57 L.Ed.2d 475.

JUSTICE STEWART delivered the opinion of the Court.

[A New Jersey statute, chapter 363, prohibited the import of most waste originating out of the State. After a remand on a preemption issue, the case returned to the Supreme Court. The Court agreed with the lower court that the New Jersey statute was not preempted. It disagreed, however, on the commerce clause issue].

The opinions of the Court through the years have reflected an alertness to the evils of "economic isolation" and protectionism, while at the same time recognizing that incidental burdens on interstate commerce may be unavoidable when a State legislates to safeguard the health and safety of its people. Thus, where simple economic protectionism is effected by state legislation, a virtually *per se* rule of invalidity has been erected. The clearest example of such legislation is a law that overtly blocks the flow of interstate commerce at a State's borders. But where other legislative objectives are credibly advanced and there is no patent discrimination against interstate trade, the Court has adopted a much more flexible approach * * *. The crucial inquiry, therefore, must be directed to determining whether ch. 363 is basically a protectionist measure, or whether it can fairly be viewed as a law directed to legitimate local concerns, with effects upon interstate commerce that are only incidental.

* * * The state court * * * found that New Jersey's existing landfill sites will be exhausted within a few years; that to go on using these sites or to develop new ones will take a heavy environmental toll, both from pollution and from loss of scarce open lands; that new techniques to divert waste from landfills to other methods of disposal and resource recovery processes are under development, but that these changes will require time; and finally, that "the extension of the lifespan of existing landfills, resulting from the exclusion of out-of-state waste, may be of crucial importance in preventing further virgin wetlands or other undeveloped

lands from being devoted to landfill purposes.'' [The appellants argued, on the other hand, that the statute's real purpose was economic.]

This dispute about ultimate legislative purpose need not be resolved, because its resolution would not be relevant to the constitutional issue to be decided in this case. Contrary to the evident assumption of the state court and the parties, the evil of protectionism can reside in legislative means as well as legislative ends. Thus, it does not matter whether the ultimate aim of ch. 363 is to reduce the waste disposal costs of New Jersey residents or to save remaining open lands from pollution, for we assume New Jersey has every right to protect its residents' pocketbooks as well as their environment. And it may be assumed as well that New Jersey may pursue those ends by slowing the flow of *all* waste into the State's remaining landfills, even though interstate commerce may incidentally be affected. But whatever New Jersey's ultimate purpose, it may not be accomplished by discriminating against articles of commerce coming from outside the State unless there is some reason, apart from their origin, to treat them differently. Both on its face and in its plain effect, ch. 363 violates this principle of nondiscrimination. * * *

The New Jersey law at issue in this case falls squarely within the area that the Commerce Clause puts off-limits to state regulation. On its face, it imposes on out-of-state commercial interests the full burden of conserving the State's remaining landfill space. It is true that in our previous cases the scarce natural resource was itself the article of commerce, whereas here the scarce resource and the article of commerce are distinct. But that difference is without consequence. In both instances, the State has overtly moved to slow or freeze the flow of commerce for protectionist reasons. It does not matter that the State has shut the article of commerce inside the State in one case and outside the State in the other. What is crucial is the attempt by one State to isolate itself from a problem common to many by erecting a barrier against the movement of interstate trade.

The appellees argue that not all laws which facially discriminate against out-of-state commerce are forbidden protectionist regulations. In particular, they point to quarantine laws, which this Court has repeatedly upheld even though they appear to single out interstate commerce for special treatment. * * *

It is true that certain quarantine laws have not been considered forbidden protectionist measures, even though they were directed against out-of-state commerce. But those quarantine laws banned the importation of articles such as diseased livestock that required destruction as soon as possible because their very movement risked contagion and other evils. Those laws thus did not discriminate against interstate commerce as such, but simply prevented traffic in noxious articles, whatever their origin.

The New Jersey statute is not such a quarantine law. There has been no claim here that the very movement of waste into or through New Jersey endangers health, or that waste must be disposed of as soon and as close to its point of generation as possible. The harms caused by waste are said to arise after its disposal in landfill sites, and at that point, as New Jersey concedes, there is no basis to distinguish out-of-state waste from domestic waste. If one is inherently harmful, so is the other. Yet New Jersey has banned the former while leaving its landfill sites open to the latter. The New Jersey law blocks the importation of waste in an obvious effort to saddle those outside the State with the entire burden of slowing the flow of refuse into New Jersey's remaining landfill sites. That legislative effort is clearly impermissible under the Commerce Clause of the Constitution.

Today, cities in Pennsylvania and New York find it expedient or necessary to send their waste into New Jersey for disposal, and New Jersey claims the right to close its borders to such traffic. Tomorrow, cities in New Jersey may find it expedient or necessary to send their waste into Pennsylvania or New York for disposal, and those States might then claim the right to close their borders. The Commerce Clause will protect New Jersey in the future, just as it protects her neighbors now, from efforts by one State to isolate itself in the stream of interstate commerce from a problem shared by all.

JUSTICE REHNQUIST, with whom THE CHIEF JUSTICE (BURGER) joins, dissenting.

A growing problem in our Nation is the sanitary treatment and disposal of solid waste. For many years, solid waste was incinerated. Because of the significant environmental problems attendant to incineration, however, this method of solid waste disposal has declined in use in many localities, including New Jersey. "Sanitary" landfills have replaced incineration as the principal method of disposing of solid waste. In Chapter 363 of the Laws of 1973, the State of New Jersey legislatively recognized the unfortunate fact that landfills also present extremely serious health and safety problems. First, in New Jersey, "virtually all sanitary landfills can be expected to produce leachate, a noxious and highly polluted liquid which is seldom visible and frequently pollutes * * * ground and surface waters." The natural decomposition process which occurs in landfills also produces large quantities of methane and thereby presents a significant explosion hazard. Landfills can also generate "health hazards caused by rodents, fires, and scavenger birds" and, "needless to say, do not help New Jersey's aesthetic appearance nor New Jersey's noise or water or air pollution problems."

The health and safety hazards associated with landfills presents appellees with a currently unsolvable dilemma. Other, hopefully safer, methods of disposing of solid wastes are still in the development stage and cannot presently be used. But appellees obviously cannot completely stop the tide of solid waste that its citizens will produce in the interim. For the moment, therefore, appellees must continue to use sanitary landfills to dispose of New Jersey's own solid waste despite the critical environmental problems thereby created.

The question presented in this case is whether New Jersey must also continue to receive and dispose of solid waste from neighboring States, even though these will inexorably increase the health problems discussed above. The Court answers this question in the affirmative. New Jersey must either prohibit *all* landfill operations, leaving itself to cast about for a presently nonexistent solution to the serious problem of disposing of the waste generated within its own borders, or it must accept waste from every portion of the United States, thereby multiplying the health and safety problems which would result if it dealt only with such wastes generated within the State. Because past precedents [the quarantine cases] establish that the Commerce Clause does not present appellees with such a Hobson's choice, I dissent.

NOTES

1.   Would it matter if all available landfill areas were owned by the state? Suppose the state refused to accept waste from out-of-state. Would the market participant exception apply? In this connection, consider *Reeves, Inc. v. Stake,* 447 U.S. 429 (1980), in which a closely divided Court held that South Dakota could refuse to sell cement from a state-owned factory to out-of-state buyers during a shortage. On the other hand, the Court has also held that a state's theoretical title in wild animals does not justify discrimination against out-of-state businesses. *Hughes v. Oklahoma,* 441 U.S. 322 (1979); *see also, South–Central Timber Dev. v. Wunnicke,* 467 U.S. 82 (1984) (striking down an Alaska law requiring that timber taken from state lands be processed in Alaska before shipment elsewhere); *GSW, Inc. v. Long County,* 999 F.2d 1508 (11th Cir. 1993) (finding that county cannot require company, which it earlier hired to build and operate a landfill, to reject waste originating more than 150 miles away). *Hughes v. Oklahoma* also holds that the definition of "commerce" is "the same when relied on to strike down or restrict legislation as when relied on to support some exertion of federal control or regulation." Does this mean that the state program at issue in *Hughes v. Alexandria Scrap Corp.* is immune from congressional regulation?

2.   The Supreme Court strongly reaffirmed the *City of Philadelphia* rule in *Fort Gratiot Sanitary Landfill, Inc. v. Michigan Department of Natural Resources,* 504 U.S. 353 (1992). *Fort Gratiot* involved regulations prohibiting landfills from accepting waste from outside a county unless authorized by the county's solid waste management plan. The Court considered the restriction on out-of-county waste to be equivalent to a restriction on out-of-state waste. Because the state regulations "discriminate against interstate commerce, the State bears the burden of proving that they further health and safety concerns that cannot be adequately served by nondiscriminatory alternatives." The state was unable to carry that burden of proof. In a companion case, *Chemical Waste Management, Inc. v. Hunt,* 504 U.S. 334 (1992), the Court struck down an Alabama statute that imposed an additional fee on all out-of-state hazardous waste disposed of within the state. The Court found no basis for the state's exemption of in-state waste from this charge.

3. In *Philadelphia* and its progeny, the state was attempting to control the import of waste. In the following case, in contrast, the state had imposed an export ban.

C & A CARBONE, INC. v. TOWN OF CLARKSTOWN, N.Y.

Supreme Court of the United States, 1994.
511 U.S. 383, 114 S.Ct. 1677, 128 L.Ed.2d 399.

JUSTICE KENNEDY delivered the opinion of the Court.

We consider a so-called flow control ordinance, which requires all solid waste to be processed at a designated transfer station before leaving the municipality. The avowed purpose of the ordinance is to retain the processing fees charged at the transfer station to amortize the cost of the facility. Because it attains this goal by depriving competitors, including out-of-state firms, of access to a local market, we hold that the flow control ordinance violates the Commerce Clause.

The town of Clarkstown, New York, lies in the lower Hudson River valley, just upstream from the Tappan Zee Bridge and by highway minutes from New Jersey. Within the town limits are the village of Nyack and the hamlet of West Nyack. In August 1989, Clarkstown entered into a consent decree with the New York State Department of Environmental Conservation. The town agreed to close its landfill located on Route 303 in West Nyack and build a new solid waste transfer station on the same site. The station would receive bulk solid waste and separate recyclable from nonrecyclable items. Recyclable waste would be baled for shipment to a recycling facility; nonrecyclable waste, to a suitable landfill or incinerator.

The cost of building the transfer station was estimated at $1.4 million. A local private contractor agreed to construct the facility and operate it for five years, after which the town would buy it for one dollar. During those five years, the town guaranteed a minimum waste flow of 120,000 tons per year, for which the contractor could charge the hauler a so-called tipping fee of $81 per ton. If the station received less than 120,000 tons in a year, the town promised to make up the tipping fee deficit. The object of this arrangement was to amortize the cost of the transfer station: The town would finance its new facility with the income generated by the tipping fees.

The problem, of course, was how to meet the yearly guarantee. This difficulty was compounded by the fact that the tipping fee of $81 per ton exceeded the disposal cost of unsorted solid waste on the private market. The solution the town adopted was the flow control ordinance here in question, Local Laws 1990, No. 9 of the Town of Clarkstown. The ordinance requires all nonhazardous solid waste within the town to be deposited at the Route 303 transfer station.* * *

The central rationale for the rule against discrimination is to prohibit state or municipal laws whose object is local economic protectionism, laws that would excite those jealousies and retaliatory measures the Constitution was designed to prevent. We have interpreted the Commerce Clause to invalidate local laws that impose commercial barriers or discriminate against an article of commerce by reason of its origin or destination out of State.

Clarkstown protests that its ordinance does not discriminate because it does not differentiate solid waste on the basis of its geographic origin. All solid waste, regardless of origin, must be processed at the designated transfer station before it leaves the town. Unlike the statute in Philadelphia, says the town, the ordinance erects no barrier to the import or export of any solid waste but requires only that the waste be channeled through the designated facility.

Our initial discussion of the effects of the ordinance on interstate commerce goes far toward refuting the town's contention that there is no discrimination in its regulatory scheme. The town's own arguments go the rest of the way. As the town itself points out, what makes garbage a profitable business is not its own worth but the fact that its possessor must pay to get rid of it. In other words, the article of commerce is not so much the solid waste itself, but rather the service of processing and disposing of it.

With respect to this stream of commerce, the flow control ordinance discriminates, for it allows only the favored operator to process waste that is within the limits of the town. The ordinance is no less discriminatory because in-state or in-town processors are also covered by the prohibition. In *Dean Milk Co. v. Madison,* 340 U.S. 349, 71 S.Ct. 295, 95 L.Ed. 329 (1951), we struck down a city ordinance that required all milk sold in the city to be pasteurized within five miles of the city lines. We found it "immaterial that Wisconsin milk from outside the Madison area is subjected to the same proscription as that moving in interstate commerce."

In this light, the flow control ordinance is just one more instance of local processing requirements that we long have held invalid. The essential vice in laws of this sort is that they bar the import of the processing service. Out-of-state meat inspectors, or shrimp hullers, or milk pasteurizers, are deprived of access to local demand for their services. Put another way, the offending local laws hoard a local resource—be it meat, shrimp, or milk—for the benefit of local businesses that treat it.

The flow control ordinance has the same design and effect. It hoards solid waste, and the demand to get rid of it, for the benefit of the preferred processing facility. The only conceivable distinction from the cases cited above is that the flow control ordinance favors a single local proprietor. But this difference just makes the protectionist effect of the ordinance more acute. In *Dean Milk,* the local processing requirement at least permitted pasteurizers within five miles of the city to compete. An out-of-state pasteurizer who wanted access to that market might have built a pasteurizing facility within the radius. The flow control ordinance at issue here squelches competition in the waste-processing service altogether, leaving no room for investment from outside.

Discrimination against interstate commerce in favor of local business or investment is per se invalid, save in a narrow class of cases in which the municipality can demonstrate, under rigorous scrutiny, that it has no other means to advance a legitimate local interest. A number of amici contend that the flow control ordinance fits into this narrow class. They suggest that as landfill space diminishes and environmental cleanup costs escalate, measures like flow control become necessary to ensure the safe handling and proper treatment of solid waste.

The teaching of our cases is that these arguments must be rejected absent the clearest showing that the unobstructed flow of interstate commerce itself is unable to solve the local problem. The Commerce Clause presumes a national market free from local legislation that discriminates in favor of local interests. Here Clarkstown has any number of nondiscriminatory alternatives for addressing the health and environmental problems alleged to justify the ordinance in question. The most obvious would be uniform safety regulations enacted without the object to discriminate. These regulations would ensure that competitors like Carbone do not underprice the market by cutting corners on environmental safety.

Nor may Clarkstown justify the flow control ordinance as a way to steer solid waste away from out-of-town disposal sites that it might deem harmful to the environment. To do so would extend the town's police power beyond its jurisdictional bounds. States and localities may not attach restrictions to exports or imports in order to control commerce in other states.

The flow control ordinance does serve a central purpose that a nonprotectionist regulation would not: It ensures that the town-sponsored facility will be profitable, so that the local contractor can build it and Clarkstown can buy it back at nominal cost in five years. In other words, as the most candid of amici and even Clarkstown admit, the flow control ordinance is a financing measure. By itself, of course, revenue generation is not a local interest that can justify discrimination against interstate commerce. Otherwise States could impose discriminatory taxes against solid waste originating outside the State.

Clarkstown maintains that special financing is necessary to ensure the long-term survival of the designated facility. If so, the town may subsidize the facility through general taxes or municipal bonds. But having elected to use the open market to earn revenues for its project, the town may not employ discriminatory regulation to give that project an advantage over rival businesses from out of State.

Though the Clarkstown ordinance may not in explicit terms seek to regulate interstate commerce, it does so nonetheless by its practical effect and design. In this respect the ordinance is not far different from the state law this Court found invalid in *Buck v. Kuykendall,* 267 U.S. 307, 45 S. Ct. 324, 69 L. Ed. 623 (1925). That statute prohibited common carriers from using state highways over certain routes without a certificate of public convenience. Writing for the Court, Justice Brandeis said of the law: "Its primary purpose is not regulation with a view to safety or to conservation of the highways, but the prohibition of competition. It determines not the manner of use, but the persons by whom the highways may be used. It prohibits such use to some persons while permitting it to others for the same purpose and in the same manner."

State and local governments may not use their regulatory power to favor local enterprise by prohibiting patronage of out-of-state competitors or their facilities. We reverse the judgment and remand the case for proceedings not inconsistent with this decision.

JUSTICE O'CONNOR, concurring in the judgment.

In my view, the majority fails to come to terms with a significant distinction between the laws in the local processing cases discussed above and Local Law 9. Unlike the regulations we have previously struck down, Local Law 9 does not give more favorable treatment to local interests as a group as compared to out-of-state or out-of-town economic interests. Rather, the garbage sorting monopoly is achieved at the expense of all competitors, be they local or nonlocal. That the ordinance does not discriminate on the basis of geographic origin is vividly illustrated by the identity of the plaintiff in this very action: petitioner is a local recycler, physically located in Clarkstown, that desires to process waste itself, and thus bypass the town's designated transfer facility. Because in-town processors—like petitioner—and out-of-town processors are treated equally, I cannot agree that Local Law 9 "discriminates" against interstate commerce. Rather, Local Law 9 "discriminates" evenhandedly against all potential participants in the waste processing business, while benefiting only the chosen operator of the transfer facility.* * *

That the ordinance does not discriminate against interstate commerce does not, however, end the Commerce Clause inquiry. Even a nondiscriminatory regulation may nonetheless impose an excessive burden on interstate trade when considered in relation to the local benefits conferred. Indeed, we have long recognized that "a burden imposed by a State upon interstate commerce is not to be sustained simply because the statute imposing it applies alike to ... the people of the State enacting such statute." Moreover, "the extent of the burden that will be tolerated will of course depend on the nature of the local interest involved, and on whether it could be promoted as well with a lesser impact on interstate activities." Judged against these standards, Local Law 9 fails.

The local interest in proper disposal of waste is obviously significant. But this interest could be achieved by simply requiring that all waste disposed of in the town be properly processed somewhere. For example, the town could ensure proper processing by setting specific standards with which all town processors must comply.

In fact, however, the town's purpose is narrower than merely ensuring proper disposal. Local Law 9 is intended to ensure the financial viability of the transfer facility. I agree with the majority that this purpose can be achieved by other means that would have a less dramatic impact on the flow of goods. For example, the town could finance the project by imposing taxes, by issuing municipal bonds, or even by lowering its price for processing to a level competitive with other waste processing facilities. But by requiring that all waste be processed at the town's facility, the ordinance "squelches competition in the waste-processing service altogether, leaving no room for investment from outside."

JUSTICE SOUTER, with whom THE CHIEF JUSTICE and JUSTICE BLACKMUN join, dissenting.

The majority may invoke "well-settled principles of our Commerce Clause jurisprudence," but it does so to strike down an ordinance unlike anything this Court has ever invalidated. Previous cases have held that the "negative" or "dormant" aspect of the Commerce Clause renders state or local legislation unconstitutional when it discriminates against out-of-state or out-of-town businesses such as those that pasteurize milk, hull shrimp, or mill lumber, and the majority relies on these cases because of what they have in common with this one: out-of-state processors are excluded from the local market (here, from the market for trash processing services). What the majority ignores, however, are the differences between our local processing cases and this one: the exclusion worked by Clarkstown's Local Law 9 bestows no benefit on a class of local private actors, but instead directly aids the government in satisfying a traditional governmental responsibility. The law does not differentiate between all local and all out-of-town providers of a service, but instead between the one entity responsible for ensuring that the job gets done and all other enterprises, regardless of their location. The ordinance thus falls outside that class of tariff or protectionist measures that the Commerce Clause has traditionally been thought to bar States from enacting against each other, and when the majority subsumes the ordinance within the class of laws this Court has struck down as facially discriminatory (and so avails itself of our "virtually per se rule" against such statutes, *see Philadelphia v. New Jersey*, page 309 *supra*, the majority is in fact greatly extending the Clause's dormant reach.* * *

[F]low control offers an additional benefit that could not be gained by financing through a subsidy derived from general tax revenues, in spreading the cost of the facility among all Clarkstown residents who generate trash. The ordinance does, of course, protect taxpayers, including those who already support the transfer station by patronizing it, from ending up with the tab for making provision for large-volume trash producers like Carbone, who would rely on the municipal facility when that was advantageous but opt out whenever the transfer station's price rose above the market price. In proportioning each resident's burden to the amount of trash generated, the ordinance has the added virtue of providing a direct and measurable deterrent to the generation of unnecessary waste in the first place. And in any event it is far from clear that the alternative to flow control (i.e., subsidies from general tax revenues or municipal bonds) would be less disruptive of interstate commerce than flow control, since a subsidized competitor can effectively squelch competition by underbidding it.

NOTES

1.   As this case illustrates, the Supreme Court's three-part scheme for the dormant commerce clause is less tidy than it seems. *See* Daniel A. Farber & Robert E. Hudec, *Free Trade and the Regulatory State: A GATT's–Eye View of the Dormant Commerce Clause*, 47 VAND. L. REV. 1401 (1994). In *Carbone,* the Court divided 5–4 over whether to apply the *Philadelphia v. New Jersey* test or the *Pike* test—and the four favoring the *Pike* test could not agree on the test's result. Should the Court attempt to reformulate its approach? For instance, should it look only for evidence of protectionist intent?

2.   Note the majority's statement that Clarkstown does not have jurisdiction to steer waste away from out-of-town disposal sites that have inferior environmental standards. We will consider later whether the United States as a nation can legitimately take action to protect the environment outside its boundaries. *Carbone,* by analogy, suggests that the answer is "no."

3.   *Carbone* gave rise to a rash of litigation in the lower courts because of the widespread use of flow control ordinances by municipalities. In the meantime, local governments struggled to find ways to meet their goals without violating the Commerce Clause. These efforts met with success in the following case.

UNITED HAULERS ASS'N, INC. v. ONEIDA–HERKIMER SOLID WASTE MANAGEMENT AUTHORITY

Supreme Court of the United States, 2007.
550 U.S. 330, 127 S.Ct. 1786, 167 L.Ed.2d 655.

CHIEF JUSTICE ROBERTS delivered the opinion of the Court.

"Flow control" ordinances require trash haulers to deliver solid waste to a particular waste processing facility. In *Carbone* [casebook p. 313], this Court struck down under the Commerce Clause a flow control ordinance that forced haulers to deliver waste to a particular *private* processing facility. In this case, we face flow control ordinances quite similar to the one invalidated in *Carbone.* The only salient difference is that the laws at issue here require haulers to bring waste to facilities owned and operated by a state-created public benefit corporation. We find this difference constitutionally significant. Disposing of trash has been a traditional government activity for years, and laws that favor the government in such areas—but treat every private business, whether in-state or out-of-state, exactly the same—do not discriminate against interstate commerce for purposes of the Commerce Clause. Applying the Commerce Clause test reserved for regulations that do not discriminate against interstate commerce, we uphold these ordinances because any incidental burden they may have on interstate commerce does not outweigh the benefits they confer on the citizens of Oneida and Herkimer Counties.* * *

The *Carbone* majority viewed Clarkstown's flow control ordinance as "just one more instance of local processing requirements that we long have held invalid." It then cited six local processing cases, every one of which involved discrimination in favor of *private* enterprise. The Court's own description of the cases acknowledges that the "offending local laws hoard a local resource—be it meat, shrimp, or milk-for the benefit of *local businesses* that treat it." If the Court were extending this line of local processing cases to cover discrimination in favor of local government, one would expect it to have said so.

The *Carbone* majority stated that "[t]he *only conceivable distinction*" between the laws in the local processing cases and Clarkstown's flow control ordinance was that Clarkstown's ordinance favored a single local business, rather than a group of them. If the Court thought Clarkstown's processing facility was public, that additional distinction was not merely "conceivable"—it was conceived, and discussed at length, by three Justices in dissent. *Carbone* cannot be regarded as having decided the public-private question.

The flow control ordinances in this case benefit a clearly public facility, while treating all private companies exactly the same. Because the question is now squarely presented on the facts of the case before us, we decide that such flow control ordinances do not discriminate against interstate commerce for purposes of the dormant Commerce Clause.

Compelling reasons justify treating these laws differently from laws favoring particular private businesses over their competitors. "Conceptually, of course, any notion of discrimination assumes a comparison of substantially similar entities." But States and municipalities are not private businesses—far from it. Unlike private enterprise, government is vested with the responsibility of protecting the health, safety, and welfare of its citizens.

Given these differences, it does not make sense to regard laws favoring local government and laws favoring private industry with equal skepticism. As our local processing cases demonstrate, when a law favors in-state business over out-of-state competition, rigorous scrutiny is appropriate because the law is often the product of "simple economic protectionism. Laws favoring local government, by contrast, may be directed toward any number of legitimate goals unrelated to protectionism. Here the flow control ordinances enable the Counties to pursue particular policies with respect to the handling and treatment of waste generated in the Counties, while allocating the costs of those policies on citizens and businesses according to the volume of waste they generate.

The contrary approach of treating public and private entities the same under the dormant Commerce Clause would lead to unprecedented and unbounded interference by the courts with state and local government. The dormant Commerce Clause is not a roving license for federal courts to decide what activities are appropriate for state and local government to undertake, and what activities must be the province of private market competition. In this case, the citizens of Oneida and Herkimer Counties have chosen the government to provide waste management services, with a limited role for the private sector in arranging for transport of waste from the curb to the public facilities. The citizens could have left the entire matter for the private sector, in which case any regulation they undertook could not discriminate against interstate commerce. But it was also open to them to vest responsibility for the matter with their government, and to adopt flow control ordinances to support the government effort. It is not the office of the Commerce Clause to control the decision of the voters on whether government or the private sector should provide waste management services. "The Commerce Clause significantly limits the ability of States and localities to regulate or otherwise burden the flow of interstate commerce, but it does not elevate free trade above all other values."

We should be particularly hesitant to interfere with the Counties' efforts under the guise of the Commerce Clause because "[w]aste disposal is both typically and traditionally a local government function." Congress itself has recognized local government's vital role in waste management, making clear that "collection and disposal of solid wastes should continue to be primarily the function of State, regional, and local agencies." Resource Conservation and Recovery Act of 1976, 42 U.S.C. § 6901(a)(4). The policy of the State of New York favors "displac[ing] competition with regulation or monopoly control" in this area. We may or may not agree with that approach, but nothing in the Commerce Clause vests the responsibility for that policy judgment with the Federal Judiciary.

Finally, it bears mentioning that the most palpable harm imposed by the ordinances—more expensive trash removal—is likely to fall upon the very people who voted for the laws. Our dormant Commerce Clause cases often find discrimination when a State shifts the costs of regulation to other States, because when "the burden of state regulation falls on interests outside the state, it is unlikely to be alleviated by the operation of those political restraints normally exerted when interests within the state are affected." Here, the citizens and businesses of the Counties bear the costs of the ordinances. There is no reason to step in and hand local businesses a victory they could not obtain through the political process.

[The preceding portions of the opinion represent the "opinion of the Court," but Justice Scalia did not join the remaining portions, which apply the *Pike* test, making it only a plurality view.]

We hold that the Counties' flow control ordinances, which treat in-state private business interests exactly the same as out-of-state ones, do not "discriminate against interstate commerce" for purposes of the dormant Commerce Clause.

The Counties' flow control ordinances are properly analyzed under the [*Pike*] test, which is reserved for laws "directed to legitimate local concerns, with effects upon interstate commerce that are only incidental." Under the *Pike* test, we will uphold a nondiscriminatory statute like this one "unless the burden imposed on [interstate] commerce is clearly excessive in relation to the putative local benefits."

After years of discovery, both the Magistrate Judge and the District Court could not detect *any* disparate impact on out-of-state as opposed to in-state businesses. The Second Circuit alluded to, but did not endorse, a "rather abstract harm" that may exist because "the Counties' flow control ordinances have removed the waste generated in Oneida and Herkimer Counties from the national marketplace for waste processing services." We find it unnecessary to decide whether the ordinances impose any incidental burden on interstate commerce because any arguable burden does not exceed the public benefits of the ordinances.

The ordinances give the Counties a convenient and effective way to finance their integrated package of waste-disposal services. While "revenue generation is not a local interest that can justify *discrimination* against interstate commerce," we think it is a cognizable benefit for purposes of the *Pike* test.

At the same time, the ordinances are more than financing tools. They increase recycling in at least two ways, conferring significant health and environmental benefits upon the citizens of the Counties. First, they create enhanced incentives for recycling and proper disposal of other kinds of waste. Solid waste disposal is expensive in Oneida–Herkimer, but the Counties accept recyclables and many forms of hazardous waste for free, effectively encouraging their citizens to sort their own trash. Second, by requiring all waste to be deposited at Authority facilities, the Counties have markedly increased their ability to enforce recycling laws. If the haulers could take waste to any disposal site, achieving an equal level of enforcement would be much more costly, if not impossible. For these reasons, any arguable burden the ordinances impose on interstate commerce does not exceed their public benefits. * * * The Counties' ordinances are exercises of the police power in an effort to address waste disposal, a typical and traditional concern of local government. The haulers nevertheless ask us to hold that laws favoring public entities while treating all private businesses the same are subject to an almost *per se* rule of invalidity, because of asserted discrimination. In the alternative, they maintain that the Counties' laws cannot survive the more permissive *Pike* test, because of asserted burdens on commerce. There is a common thread to these arguments: They are invitations to rigorously scrutinize economic legislation passed under the auspices of the police power. There was a time when this Court presumed to make such binding judgments for society, under the guise of interpreting the Due Process Clause. We should not seek to reclaim that ground for judicial supremacy under the banner of the dormant Commerce Clause.

JUSTICE SCALIA, concurring in part.

I write separately to reaffirm my view that "the so-called 'negative' Commerce Clause is an unjustified judicial invention, not to be expanded beyond its existing domain." "The historical record provides no grounds for reading the Commerce Clause to be other than what it says—an authorization for Congress to regulate commerce."

I have been willing to enforce on *stare decisis* grounds a "negative" self-executing Commerce Clause in two situations: "(1) against a state law that facially discriminates against interstate commerce, and (2) against a state law that is indistinguishable from a type of law previously held unconstitutional by the Court." As today's opinion makes clear, the flow-control law at issue in this case meets neither condition. It benefits a *public entity* performing a traditional local-government function and treats *all private entities* precisely the same way. "Disparate treatment constitutes discrimination only if the objects of the disparate treatment are, for the relevant purposes, similarly situated." None of this Court's cases concludes that public entities and private entities are similarly situated for Commerce Clause purposes. To hold that they are "would broaden the negative Commerce Clause beyond its existing scope, and intrude on a regulatory sphere traditionally occupied by . . . the States."

I am unable to join [the section of the opinion] in which the plurality performs so-called "*Pike* balancing." Generally speaking, the balancing of various values is left to Congress—which is precisely what the Commerce Clause (the *real* Commerce Clause) envisions.

JUSTICE THOMAS, concurring in the judgment.

I concur in the judgment. Although I joined [*Carbone*], I no longer believe it was correctly decided. The negative Commerce Clause has no basis in the Constitution and has proved unworkable in practice. As the debate between the majority and dissent shows, application of the negative Commerce Clause turns solely on policy considerations, not on the Constitution. Because this Court has no policy role in regulating interstate commerce, I would discard the Court's negative Commerce Clause jurisprudence.* * *

Many of the * * * cases (and today's majority and dissent) rest on the erroneous assumption that the Court must choose between economic protectionism and the free market. But the Constitution vests that fundamentally legislative choice in Congress. To the extent that Congress does not exercise its authority to make that choice, the Constitution does not limit the States' power to regulate commerce. In the face of congressional silence, the States are free to set the balance between protectionism and the free market. Instead of accepting this constitutional reality, the Court's negative Commerce Clause jurisprudence gives nine Justices of this Court the power to decide the appropriate balance.

JUSTICE ALITO, joined by JUSTICE STEVENS and JUSTICE KENNEDY, dissenting.

This case cannot be meaningfully distinguished from *Carbone*. As the Court itself acknowledges, "[t]he only salient difference" between the cases is that the ordinance invalidated in *Carbone* discriminated in favor of a privately owned facility, whereas the laws at issue here discriminate in favor of "facilities owned and operated by a state-created public benefit corporation." The Court relies on the distinction between public and private ownership to uphold the flow-control laws, even though a straightforward application of *Carbone* would lead to the opposite result. The public-private distinction drawn by the Court is both illusory and without precedent.

The fact that the flow control laws at issue discriminate in favor of a government-owned enterprise does not meaningfully distinguish this case from *Carbone*. The preferred facility in *Carbone* was, to be sure, nominally owned by a private contractor who had built the facility on the town's behalf, but it would be misleading to describe the facility as private. In exchange for the contractor's promise to build the facility for the town free of charge and then to sell it to the town five years later for $1, the town guaranteed that, during the first five years of the facility's existence, the contractor would receive "a minimum waste flow of 120,000 tons per year" and that the contractor could charge an above-market tipping fee. If the facility "received less than 120,000 tons in a year, the town [would] make up the tipping fee deficit." To prevent residents, businesses, and trash haulers from taking their waste elsewhere in pursuit of lower tipping fees (leaving the town responsible for covering any shortfall in the contractor's guaranteed revenue stream), the town enacted an ordinance "requir[ing] all nonhazardous solid waste within the town to be deposited at" the preferred facility. * * *

The only real difference between the facility at issue in *Carbone* and its counterpart in this case is that title to the former had not yet formally passed to the municipality. The Court exalts form over substance in adopting a test that turns on this technical distinction, particularly since, barring any obstacle presented by state law, the transaction in *Carbone* could have been restructured to provide for the passage of title at the beginning, rather than the end, of the 5–year period.* * *

In any event, we have never treated discriminatory legislation with greater deference simply because the entity favored by that legislation was a government-owned enterprise. In suggesting otherwise, the Court relies unduly on *Carbone's* passing observation that " 'offending local laws hoard a local resource—be it meat, shrimp, or milk-for the benefit of *local businesses.*' " *Carbone's* use of the word "businesses," the Court insists, somehow reveals that *Carbone* was not "extending" our dormant Commerce Clause jurisprudence "to cover discrimination in favor of local government."

But no "exten[sion]" was required. The Court has long subjected discriminatory legislation to strict scrutiny, and has never, until today, recognized an exception for discrimination in favor of a state-owned entity. * * *

The fallacy in the Court's approach can be illustrated by comparing a law that discriminates in favor of an in-state facility, owned by a corporation whose shares are publicly held, and a law discriminating in favor of an otherwise identical facility that is owned by the State or municipality.

Those who are favored and disfavored by these two laws are essentially the same with one major exception: The law favoring the corporate facility presumably benefits the corporation's shareholders, most of whom are probably not local residents, whereas the law favoring the government-owned facility presumably benefits the people of the enacting State or municipality. I cannot understand why only the former law, and not the latter, should be regarded as a tool of economic protectionism. Nor do I think it is realistic or consistent with our precedents to condemn some discriminatory laws as protectionist while upholding other, equally discriminatory laws as lawful measures designed to serve legitimate local interests unrelated to protectionism.

For these reasons, I cannot accept the proposition that laws discriminating in favor of state-owned enterprises are so unlikely to be the product of economic protectionism that they should be exempt from the usual dormant Commerce Clause standards.

NOTES

1.   Is government ownership of the facility a persuasive basis for distinguishing *Carbone*? Certainly, from the point of view of a municipality wishing to implement flow control, *United Haulers* allows it to achieve much the same end without much hindrance from the Dormant Commerce Clause. Is this a distinction without a real difference, or does public ownership create a greater degree of legitimacy for a local monopoly?

2.   Justice Scalia views the dormant commerce clause doctrine as illegitimate but is willing to retain certain aspects as a matter of stare decisis; Justice Thomas would toss the whole thing out. Are they right about the illegitimacy of the doctrine? And if so, is Scalia or Thomas right about the stare decisis issue? Or are they both wrong—that is, should the *Pike* test be retained as a matter of stare decisis?

3.   Consider the impact of the dormant commerce clause on state climate change efforts. For instance, suppose that a state wants to ensure that electricity is produced from renewable sources, in a state where a significant amount of electricity used locally is actually generated out-of-state. What issues do you see under the dormant commerce clause? How would you advise the state to structure its program to limits its legal risks?

D.   FEDERAL PREEMPTION
OF STATE STATUTES

The preceding material dealt with the validity of state regulation in the absence of federal regulation. Here we are concerned with the validity of state regulations in areas where Congress has acted. It is clear, of course, that in cases of direct conflict, the state statute must give way. The Supremacy Clause of the Constitution provides:

This Constitution, and the Laws of the United States which shall be made in Pursuance thereof; and all Treaties made, or which shall be made, under the authority of the United States, shall be the Supreme Law of the Land; and the Judges in every State shall be bound thereby, any Thing in the Constitution or Laws of any State to the Contrary notwithstanding.

The presence of a conflict between federal and state law, however, is often less than obvious.

The Supreme Court has set forth various factors that are to be considered in preemption cases. First, the federal regulatory scheme may be so pervasive and detailed as to suggest that Congress left no room for the state to supplement it. Or the statute enacted by Congress may involve a field in which the federal interest is so dominant that enforcement of state laws is precluded. Other aspects of the regulatory scheme imposed by Congress may also support the inference that Congress has completely foreclosed state legislation in a particular area. Even where Congress has not completely foreclosed state regulation, a state statute is void to the extent that it actually conflicts with a valid federal statute. Such a conflict can be found where compliance with both the federal and state regulations is impossible, or more often, where the state law interferes with the accomplishment of the full objectives of Congress.

These factors are obviously rather vague and difficult to apply. The Supreme Court has done little to create any more rigorous framework for analysis. Therefore, the only way to get some degree of understanding of the field is to examine particular cases in order to see what kinds of situations have been found appropriate for application of the preemption doctrine.

Interstate transportation frequently raises preemption questions. Many of the same arguments supporting federal power under the commerce clause also suggest that state regulation is inappropriate in this area. Such state regulation might well be struck down under the commerce clause even if Congress had not spoken, but where Congress has addressed a regulatory problem, the argument against state regulation is even stronger. For instance, the Supreme Court held in *City of Burbank v. Lockheed Air Terminal Inc.,* 411 U.S. 624 (1973), that a local municipality may not impose a night curfew on commercial jet flights at a privately owned airport. The *Burbank* Court concluded that the widespread imposition of such local restrictions would interfere with flight scheduling and navigational patterns nationwide, thus hindering federal management of the national air traffic network. (The *Burbank* Court did not impose similar restrictions on the rights of a municipality which owns a local airport. The lower courts have generally held that regulations by a municipal owner are not necessarily forbidden by *Burbank,* but are subject to a requirement of reasonableness.)

Another important preemption issue involves nuclear energy. In a 1971 case, *Northern States Power Co. v. Minnesota,* 447 F.2d 1143 (8th Cir. 1971), *aff'd,* 405 U.S. 1035 (1972), the Court held that the state lacked the authority to impose conditions on nuclear waste releases stricter than those imposed by the Atomic Energy Commission. In contrast, the Supreme Court upheld a California nuclear moratorium in a later decision, *Pacific Gas & Electric Co. v. State Energy Resources Conservation & Development Commission,* 461 U.S. 190 (1983). In an opinion by Justice White, the Court upheld a California statute prohibiting nuclear plant operation until the federal government approved a permanent method of waste disposal. The Court found that the state statute was aimed not at radiation hazards but instead at economic problems posed by the failure of the federal government to approve a permanent method of waste disposal. The Court concluded that Congress had not intended to promote nuclear power at all costs, but rather had decided to leave the choice as to the necessity or economic benefits of a nuclear plant to the state through its utility regulatory powers. Thus, it appears that if the state casts its legislation in the form of utility regulation, it may indirectly accomplish what federal law would not allow it to do directly—that is, impose its own views as to the safety of nuclear reactors under various circumstances. So long as it can reasonably be argued that a possible safety risk would have repercussions on the economic desirability of nuclear energy, the Supreme Court would apparently allow the state to regulate.

A year after the *PG & E* case, the Court again displayed a permissive attitude toward state laws dealing with the nuclear industry. In *Silkwood v. Kerr–McGee Corp.,* 464 U.S. 238 (1984), the Court upheld an award of punitive damages against a utility for an employee's radiation injuries. As the dissent pointed out, the jury was told it could impose punitive damages even if the defendant had complied with all federal regulations. Thus, the state was allowed to hold the defendant to higher standards of conduct in the handling of radioactive materials than those imposed by the federal government.

More recently, courts have addressed preemption arguments under both the Clean Air Act (CAA) and the Comprehensive Environmental Response, Compensation and Liability Act (CERCLA). The majority of the CERCLA cases involve litigation between two or more potentially responsible parties about whether various state law claims and affirmative defenses are preempted by federal law. *See, e.g., New York v. Moulds Holding Corp.,* 196 F.Supp.2d 210 (N.D.N.Y. 2002) (holding state law claim of restitution and indemnification precluded by CERCLA); *O'Connor v. Boeing N. Am., Inc.,* 311 F.3d 1139 (9th Cir. 2002) (refusing to dismiss CERCLA claim on state statute of limitations grounds).

The most significant CAA preemption cases involve the regulation of mobile source emissions. As explained in more detail on page 634, *supra,* Congress has preempted all states from regulating emissions from motor vehicle tailpipes under § 209 of the CAA with the exception of California. California may promulgate its own standards provided those standards are at least as protective of public health as the federal standards. Other states may opt into the California standards under § 177 as long as the standards are identical to California's. Many northeastern states have opted into the California standards, including standards California developed to require auto manufacturers to produce so-called zero and low emissions vehicles (ZEVs and LEVs).

California's ZEV and LEV regulations were struck down in *Central Valley Chrysler–Plymouth v. California Air Resources Board*, No. CV–F–02–5017, 2002 WL 34499459 (2002), on the grounds that the regulations were preempted by the federal Energy Policy and Conservation Act. The case settled on appeal, though not before the Bush Administration filed an amicus brief arguing that California's regulations were preempted. Massachusetts and New York lost preemption challenges brought by auto manufacturers against regulations that opted into California's ZEV regulations on the grounds that California's regulations were contained in voluntary memoranda of agreements with the auto manufacturers, not in traditional regulations. *Association of Int'l Auto. Mfrs. v. Commissioner, Mass. Dept. of Envtl. Prot.*, 208 F.3d 1 (1st Cir. 2000); *American Auto. Mfrs. Ass'n v. Cahill*, 152 F.3d 196 (2nd Cir. 1998).

Most recently, the Supreme Court decided a preemption case involving mobile source emissions regulations promulgated by the South Coast Air Quality Management District (SCAQMD), the agency responsible for regulating the most polluted air district in the country, southern California.

ENGINE MANUFACTURERS ASS'N AND WESTERN STATES PETROLEUM ASS'N v. SOUTH COAST AIR QUALITY MANAGEMENT DISTRICT

Supreme Court of the United States, 2004.
541 U.S. 246, 124 S.Ct. 1756, 158 L.E.2d 529.

JUSTICE SCALIA delivered the opinion of the Court

[Although California has special status to issue its own mobile source emissions regulations, the SCAQMD does not. Instead, the local district is subject to the mobile source preemption provision of the CAA. At issue in the Supreme Court case were District "fleet rules" that required certain operators of vehicle fleets—street sweepers; fleets comprised of passenger cars, light and medium duty trucks; public transit vehicles and buses; solid waste collection vehicles; airport transport services; and heavy duty on-road vehicles—to purchase alternative fuel vehicles and low or zero emissions vehicles already approved by California's Air Resources Board (the state agency that generally sets policy on mobile source emissions) and already commercially available. The fleet rules were challenged on preemption grounds.] * * *

In August 2000, petitioner Engine Manufacturers Association sued the District and its officials, * * * claiming that the Fleet Rules are preempted by § 209 of the CAA, which prohibits the adoption or attempted enforcement of any state or local "standard relating to the control of emissions from new motor vehicles or new motor vehicle engines." 42 U.S.C. § 7543(a). The District Court granted summary judgment to respondents, upholding the Rules in their entirety. It held that the Rules were not "standard[s]" under § 209(a) because they regulate only the purchase of vehicles that are otherwise certified for sale in California. * * *

The Ninth Circuit affirmed the reasoning of the District Court.* * *

Section 209(a) of the CAA states:

> "No State or any political subdivision thereof shall adopt or attempt to enforce any standard relating to the control of emissions from new motor vehicles or new motor vehicle engines subject to this part. No State shall require certification, inspection, or any other approval relating to the control of emissions * * * as condition precedent to the initial retail sale, titling (if any), or registration of such motor vehicle, motor vehicle engine, or equipment."

42 U.S.C. § 7543(a).

The District Court's determination that this express pre-emption provision did not invalidate the Fleet Rules hinged on its interpretation of the word "standard" to include only regulations that compel manufacturers to meet specified emission limits. This interpretation of "standard" in turn caused the court to draw a distinction between purchase restrictions (not pre-empted) and sale restrictions (pre-empted). Neither the manufacturer-specific interpretation of "standard" nor the resulting distinction between purchase and sale restrictions finds support in the text of § 209(a) or the structure of the CAA.

"Statutory construction must begin with the language employed by Congress and the assumption that the ordinary meaning of that language accurately expresses the legislative purpose." (Citation omitted.) Today, as in 1967 when § 209(a) became law, "standard" is defined as that which "is established by authority, custom, or general consent, as a model or example; criterion; test." Webster's Second New International Dictionary 2455 (1945). The criteria referred to in § 209(a) relate to the emission characteristics of a vehicle or engine. To meet them the vehicle or engine must not emit more than a certain amount of a given pollutant, must be equipped with a certain type of pollution-control device, or must have some other design feature related to the control of emissions. This interpretation is consistent with the use of "standard" throughout Title II of the CAA (which governs emissions from moving sources) to denote requirements such as numerical emission levels with which vehicles or engines must comply, e.g., 42 U.S.C. § 7521(a)(1)(B)(ii), or emission-control technology with which they must be equipped, e.g., § 7521(a)(6).

Respondents, like the courts below, engraft onto this meaning of "standard" a limiting component, defining it as only "[a] *production* mandat[e] that require [s] *manufacturers* to ensure that the vehicles they produce have particular emissions characteristics, whether individually or in the aggregate." Brief for Respondent South Coast Air Quality Management District 13 (emphases added). This confuses standards with the means of enforcing standards. Manufacturers (or purchasers) can be made responsible for ensuring that vehicles *comply* with emission standards, but the standards themselves are separate from those enforcement techniques. While standards target vehicles or engines, standard-enforcement efforts that are proscribed by § 209 can be directed to manufacturers or purchasers.

The distinction between "standards," on the one hand, and methods of standard enforcement, on the other, is borne out in the provisions immediately following § 202. These separate provisions enforce the emission criteria—*i.e.,* the § 202 standards. Section 203 prohibits manufacturers from selling any new motor vehicle that is not covered by a "certificate of conformity." 42 U.S.C. § 7522(a). Section 206 enables manufacturers to obtain such a certificate by demonstrating to the EPA that their vehicles or engines conform to the § 202 standards. § 7525. Sections 204 and 205 subject manufacturers, dealers, and others who violate the CAA to fines imposed in civil or administrative enforcement actions. §§ 7523–7524. By defining "standard" as a "production mandate directed toward manufacturers," respondents lump together § 202 and these other distinct statutory provisions, acknowledging a standard to be such only when it is combined with a mandate that prevents manufacturers from selling noncomplying vehicles.

That a standard is a standard even when not enforced through manufacturer-directed regulation can be seen in Congress's use of the term in another portion of the CAA. As the District Court recognized, CAA § 246 (in conjunction with its accompanying provisions) requires state-adopted and federally approved "restrictions on the purchase of fleet vehicles *to meet clean-air standards*." (emphasis added); * * * Clearly, Congress contemplated the enforcement of emission standards through purchase requirements.

Respondents contend that their qualified meaning of "standard" is necessary to prevent § 209(a) from pre-empting "far too much" by "encompass [ing] a broad range of state-level clean-air initiatives" such as voluntary incentive programs. * * * But it is hard to see why limitation to mandates on manufacturers is necessary for this purpose; limitation to mandates on manufacturers and purchasers, or to mandates on *anyone,* would have the same salvific effect. We need not resolve application of § 209(a) to voluntary incentive programs in this case, since all the Fleet Rules are mandates.

In addition to having no basis in the text of the statute, treating sales restrictions and purchase restrictions differently for pre-emption purposes would make no sense. The manufacturer's right to sell federally approved vehicles is meaningless in the absence of a purchaser's right to buy them. It is true that the Fleet Rules at issue here cover only certain purchasers and certain federally certified vehicles, and thus do not eliminate all demand for covered vehicles. But if one State or political subdivision may enact such rules, then so may any other; and the end result would undo Congress's carefully calibrated regulatory scheme.

A command, accompanied by sanctions, that certain purchasers may buy only vehicles with particular emission characteristics is as much an "attempt to enforce" a "standard" as a command, accompanied by sanctions, that a certain percentage of a manufacturer's sales volume must consist of such vehicles. We decline to read into § 209(a) a purchase/sale distinction that is not to be found in the text of § 209(a) or the structure of the CAA. * * *

The judgment is vacated, and the case is remanded for further proceedings consistent with this opinion.

remand

NOTES

1. Should it matter that the SCAQMD is located in California, a state that possesses special authority to regulate mobile source emissions under the CAA? Why do you think the state's Air Resources Board has not passed a fleet rule applicable to SCAQMD?

2. The SCAQMD fleet rules were applicable only to the extent that low emissions vehicles were commercially available. Can you construct an argument about why this "commercially available" qualification should help insulate the fleet rules from legal attack? Put a different way, why would Congress prohibit the states from enacting separate motor vehicle emission standards? Are the fleet rules consistent or inconsistent with congressional intent?

3. According to studies by the SCAQMD, mobile source emissions are the leading contributor to air toxics and air pollution by a large measure. Seventy-one percent of all toxic air contaminants, according to the district, come from diesel particulate. Another 20 percent of toxic air contaminants come from non-diesel mobile sources. *See* SCAQMD, MULTIPLE AIR TOXICS EXPOSURE STUDY IN THE SOUTH COAST AIR BASIN (2000), at ES–3, *available at* http://aqmd.gov/matesiidf/es.pdf. The fleet rules represented a significant part of the District's strategy to reduce mobile source pollution. On remand, SCAQMD reinstated those portions of the fleet rules that apply to state and local public agencies and private fleets under contract to those agencies, based on a federal district court opinion that such rules are not preempted. SCAQMD, AQMD *Reinstates Major Portions of its Clean Fleet Rules* (2005), *available at* http://aqmd.gov/news1/2005/FleetRuleAdvisoryPR.html.

4. Every preemption case in a sense is unique. Apart from some vague and usually unhelpful maxims, little can be said about this area of law that is of much help in deciding individual cases. The question before the court in each case is whether Congress in passing a particular statute would have been willing to allow the state to impose certain kinds of regulations in the same area. This is essentially an issue of statutory construction. It can only be resolved by close attention to the language of the federal statute, to its legislative history, and to its purposes. Thus, the best advice in analyzing preemption problems is to carefully consider the legislative materials and the

extent to which the state statute would have a practical effect on the implementation of the federal statute.

5.   What legal standard should apply if a federal administrative agency implementing a statute issues a regulation that preempts state law? Should the standard differ from the standard applied to statutory preemption claims?

NOTE ON STATE REGULATION OF GREENHOUSE GASES

As noted in Chapter 1, global warming is an example of a classic commons problem, one requiring an international response. In addition to (or in lieu of) an international agreement, one might expect a coherent federal response to emerge, in the form of a statute. Yet over the past several years an interesting phenomenon has occurred: many states have moved independently to address the problem. Since 2001, when the United States announced its intention to withdraw from the Kyoto Protocol, almost half the states have adopted measures to reduce their emissions of greenhouse gases (GHG) (of which carbon dioxide is the most prevalent). The measures range from the establishment of registries to track emissions by source to the enactment of renewable energy portfolio standards for utilities. Two of the most ambitious and interesting efforts include California's adoption of greenhouse gas emissions standards for mobile sources and a proposed cap and trade program known as the Regional Greenhouse Gas Initiative (RGGI) adopted by a consortium of northeastern states to limit GHG emissions from power plants.

The enactment of climate change initiatives to solve a global commons problem presents something of a puzzle. Why would States, who presumably have little incentive to reduce GHG emissions, nevertheless enact measures to do so? Possible explanations include concerns over potential localized effects of global warning (loss of snow pack, flooding, coastal erosion, increased air pollution); predicted cost savings from enacting measures to require energy efficiency; political and public concern over the lack of U.S. leadership on the issue; and political advantages for demonstrating environmental leadership. *See* Kirsten H. Engel, *Mitigating Global Climate Change in the Unites States: A Regional Approach*, 14 N.Y.U. ENVTL. L.J. 55–63 (2006).

The leadership exhibited by California and RGGI states may also be the product of unusual forms of federalism under the Clean Air Act. Under California's special CAA status to regulate mobile source emissions, the state is using its "superregulator" status to issue its greenhouse gas regulations, known by the name of the bill that enacted them, AB 1493. Professor Carlson argues that this special status has created a regulatory dynamic that has led California to enact more environmentally stringent regulations than the state would have adopted in the absence of the CAA provision granting California its special role. *See* Ann E. Carlson, *Federalism, Preemption, and Greenhouse Gas Emissions*, 37 U.C. DAVIS L. REV. 281 (2003)

AB 1493 faced legal challenges by auto manufacturers and by the Bush administration on the grounds that the regulations are preempted by the Energy Policy Conservation Act ("EPCA"), the CAA, and the foreign affairs clause of the U.S. Constitution. See id. The EPCA preemption argument is that California's regulations impermissibly (though indirectly) set fuel economy standards and are therefore preempted by EPCA's provision preempting state regulation of fuel economy. Finally, the manufacturers argued that California's regulations interfere with the President's power to conduct foreign affairs by impinging upon his authority to negotiate greenhouse gas emissions reductions with other countries. If the regulations were upheld, ten states indicated their intent to follow California's lead, including Oregon and Washington. The districts courts sided with California, but the cases were settled as part of an agreement over the adoption of federal restrictions on greenhouse emissions.

RGGI, while not the direct product of federal authority under the Clean Air Act, involves many of the states included in the Ozone Transport Commission (OTC), established by the 1990 Amendments to the CAA. As explained in Chapter 6 at page 642, *infra* in 1999, the OTC adopted a successful cap and trade program to reduce ground level ozone. The states cooperated with each other in establishing the program, with EPA playing an important monitoring and coordinating role. The RGGI cap and trade program is based on the OTC experience and is designed to cap CO_2 emissions. Two of the OTC states, Massachusetts and Rhode Island, have dropped out of the RGGI and Pennsylvania is serving only as an observer. For more information about RGGI, see http://www.rggi.org.

What role should states play in the climate arena if and when the federal government adopts a national cap-and-trade scheme? For exploration of this issue, see Symposium, Federalism and Climate Change: The Role of the States in a Future Federal Regime, 50 Ariz. 673–938 (2008). For discussion of preemption and dormant commerce clause issues, see Daniel Farber, *Climate Change, Federalism, and the Constitution*, 50 ARIZ. L. REV. 879 (2008); Lisa Heinzerling, *Climate, Preemption, and the Executive Branches*, 50 ARIZ. L. REV. 925 (2008); William Andreen, *Federal Climate Change Legislation and the Constitution*, 3 ENV. & ENERGY L. & POLICY JOURNAL 261 (2008).

E. ENVIRONMENTAL REGULATION AND INTERNATIONAL TRADE: THE CASE OF GATT AND DOMESTIC ENVIRONMENTAL LAW

The primary subject of the preceding section was how to reconcile state environmental regulation and an open national economy. This issue is not unique to the United States. For example, the European Court of Justice [ECJ] has evolved its own set of doctrines analogous to the dormant commerce clause. Based on Articles 30 and 36 of the EEC Treaty, the ECJ has struck down regulations of member nations that act as trade barriers. The best-known case is *Commission v. Kingdom of Denmark,* 1988 WL 765475, Case 302/86, 1988 E.C.R. 4607, which is better known as the "Danish beer case." Denmark had imposed rigorous requirements that beverage containers be not only recyclable but actually reused. The ECJ applied a balancing test akin to *Pike* to uphold much of the measure, while invalidating provisions that were unnecessarily burdensome for foreign manufacturers. The ECJ has also sometimes reached results interestingly different from U.S. law. For instance, it has allowed member states to ban the import of solid waste, on the theory that waste disposal is a responsibility of the member generating the waste. For discussions of this case and other aspects of European Union law, *see* Rod Hunter & Koen Muylle, *European Community Environmental Law: Institutions, Law Making, and Free Trade*, 28 ENVTL. L. REP. 10,477 (1998); Richard B. Stewart, *International Trade and Environment: Lessons from the Federal Experience*, 49 WASH. & LEE L. REV. 1329, 1339 (1992); Ray V. Hartwell & Lucas Bergkamp, *Environmental Trade Barriers and International Competitiveness*, 24 ENVTL. L. REP. 10109 (1994).

For most American lawyers, let alone environmentalists and politicians, EU law is still an obscure subject. Other tensions between trade and the environment have become front-page news. Such conflicts featured heavily in the debate over the North American Free Trade Agreement [NAFTA], which became an issue in the 1992 Presidential elections. Similarly, the Uruguay Round amendments to GATT were vocally opposed by some environmentalists. More recently, efforts to expand free trade have sparked major protests in Seattle and elsewhere. Trade liberalization inevitably raises questions about environmental regulations. Because different countries, even more than different American states, have widely varying approaches to environmental regulation, tensions of various kinds are bound to arise.

So far, the tensions seem to fall into two major categories. First, as under the dormant commerce clause, there are situations in which stringent domestic regulations are attacked as trade barriers. The next Note will discuss the complicated international trade provisions applying to this situation. Second, there are situations in which a nation adopts trade measures, not as part of domestic regulations, but because of concerns about environmental degradation abroad. For example, the U.S. once imposed trade sanctions on Taiwan for refusing to halt the sale of tiger bones and rhinoceros horns. Thomas L. Friedman, *U.S. Puts Sanctions on Taiwan*, N.Y. TIMES, Apr. 12, 1994, at D6. Often, the reason for the trade measure is that the processes used to produce the goods, rather than the goods themselves, are environmentally questionable.

Because our focus in this book is domestic environmental law, we cannot explore the complex (not to mention spirited) debate in detail. We will, however, try to present those themes of trade law that most affect domestic regulation.

Unlike the constraints imposed on state government under the dormant commerce clause, the GATT restrictions imposed on member governments rest on an explicit mandate. GATT is a formal international agreement containing explicit prohibitions of certain kinds of protectionist trade barriers. The basic structure of the GATT agreement begins with "tariff bindings" setting a maximum rate for tariffs on an item-by-item basis. Then, to protect against other measures that would subvert the commercial opportunity created by tariff bindings, the GATT agreement adds a rather detailed code of rules prohibiting most other forms of trade barriers.[2] Similar provisions are contained in NAFTA, which applies to trade among the United States, Canada, and Mexico.

The threat of interference with strict regulations has been accentuated by recent changes in GATT. The two changes raising the most concern are the new code on the Application of Sanitary and Phytosanitary Measures,[3] and the new and expanded rule on trade-restricting technical measures in the Standards Code.[4] Both texts were adopted in the Uruguay Round negotiations. Both make explicit that differentially burdensome regulations that deviate from internationally accepted standards may be subject to legal challenge. The result has been to heighten environmentalist concerns.

The application of GATT rules ultimately raises the same type of legal issues confronted by U.S. courts in dormant commerce clause cases. Like U.S. law, GATT allows consideration of the strength of a regulation's benefits. GATT's prohibitions are qualified by GATT Article XX, which authorizes exceptions whenever trade barriers are found to be required by other widely-accepted government regulatory objectives such as health, safety or law-enforcement.[5] Application of Article XX requires GATT

---

2. The main provisions are the prohibition of non-tariff restrictions under GATT Article XI:1 and the prohibition of discriminatory internal taxes and regulations under the so-called "national treatment" rule of GATT Article III. The text of Article XI:1, which is subject to numerous exceptions, provides quite simply and broadly,

1. No prohibitions or restrictions other than duties, taxes or other charges, whether made effective through quotas, import or export licenses or other measures, shall be instituted or maintained by any contracting party on the importation of any product from the territory of any other contracting party or on the exportation or sale for export of any product destined for the territory of any other contracting party.

The two key provisions of the national treatment rule of GATT Article III are paragraphs 2 and 4:

2. The products of the territory of any contracting party imported into the territory of any other contracting party shall not be subject, directly or indirectly, to internal taxes or other internal charges of any kind in excess of those applied, directly or indirectly, to like domestic products. Moreover, no contracting party shall otherwise apply internal taxes or other internal charges in a manner contrary to the principles set forth in paragraph 1 [i.e., internal measures should not "afford protection to domestic production."]

4. The products of the territory of any contracting party imported into the territory of any other contracting party shall be accorded treatment no less favourable than that accorded to like products of national origin in respect of all laws, regulations and requirements affecting their internal sale, offering for sale, purchase, transportation, distribution or use. * * *

3. GATT, DRAFT FINAL ACT EMBODYING THE RESULTS OF THE URUGUAY ROUND OF MULTILATERAL TRADE NEGOTIATIONS, MTN.TNC/W/FA, at L.35–L.52 (Dec. 20, 1991), (hereinafter GATT Doc.).

4. In particular, a new Article 2.2, contained in GATT Doc., *supra* note 3, at pages G.2 and G.3.

5. Article XX reads as follows:

Subject to the requirement that such measures are not applied in a manner which would constitute a means of arbitrary or unjustifiable discrimination between countries where the same conditions prevail, or a disguised restriction on international trade, nothing in this Agreement shall be construed to prevent the adoption or enforcement by any contracting party of measures:

(a) necessary to protect public morals;

(b) necessary to protect human, animal or plant life or health;* * *

tribunals to analyze the extent to which claimed regulatory objectives are served by a particular trade-restricting measure.

GATT law imposes the greatest restraints on trade-restricting measures that explicitly discriminate between domestic and foreign goods. Under GATT, such discriminatory measures are *prima facie* outlawed by Article III. However, Article XX permits even explicitly discriminatory measures when such discrimination is necessary to legitimate regulatory objectives. Like U.S. doctrine, the GATT law also deals with facially neutral measures that may have a trade-restricting effect. For example, a different tax or regulatory burden may be placed on products with certain characteristics; it "just happens" that all or most foreign products fall into the disadvantaged category. An example might be emission controls that impose less burdensome requirements for large-bore engines used in domestic automobiles than for small-bore engines normally used in foreign autos.

Recent decisions focus on the general anti-protectionism language of Articles III and XX. Article III:1 states that taxes and regulations "should not be applied to imported or domestic products so as to afford protection to domestic production." The "chapeau" to Article XX states that taxes and regulations must not be applied "in a manner which would constitute a means of arbitrary or unjustifiable discrimination between countries where the same conditions prevail" or be "a disguised restriction on international trade."

Recent decisions call for a "totality of the circumstances" analysis in applying such language. In one noteworthy decision, the WTO Appellate Body upheld a French ban on chrysotile asbestos imports. The Appellate Body held that, because of its health risks, chrysotile asbestos was not a "like product" to other products designed for the same uses. The Appellate Body rejected the argument that less restrictive regulations of asbestos use could have eliminated the health risk. *See WTO Appellate Body Upholds French Ban on Asbestos Imports*, 18 INT'L TRADE REP. DECISIONS (BNA) 426 (2001).

Both the Standards Code and the SPS Agreement explicitly adopt balancing tests. Article 2.2 of the Standards Code provides as follows:

> Members shall ensure that technical regulations are not prepared, adopted or applied with a view to or with the effect of creating unnecessary obstacles to international trade. For this purpose, technical regulations shall not be more trade-restrictive than necessary to fulfil a legitimate objective, taking account of the risks non-fulfillment would create. Such legitimate objectives are, *inter alia,* national security requirements; the prevention of deceptive practices; protection of human health or safety, animal or plant life or health, or the environment. In assessing such risks, relevant elements of consider-

---

(f) imposed for the protection of national treasures of artistic, historic or archaeological value;

(g) relating to the conservation of exhaustible natural resources if such measures are made effective in conjunction with restrictions on domestic production or consumption;* * *

ation are, *inter alia,* available scientific and technical information, related processing technology or intended end use of products.

This text clearly calls for an analysis and evaluation of the regulatory purpose of the measure.

The SPS Agreement contains a rather lengthy and convoluted set of legal standards, but the basic provisions are similar to those of the Standards Code. Paragraphs 6 and 7 of the Agreement provide:

> 6. Members shall ensure that any sanitary or phytosanitary measure is applied only to the extent necessary to protect human, animal or plant life or health, is based on scientific principles and is not maintained without sufficient scientific evidence [with some exceptions].

> 7. * * * Sanitary and phytosanitary measures shall not be applied in a manner which would constitute a disguised restriction on international trade.

The concept of "disguised restriction" has been interpreted to refer to cases where a claimed regulatory purpose is found to be of so little importance, or so little served, that it can be called a disguise.[6]

The SPS Agreement and the Standards Code are like the *Pike* test under the dormant commerce clause: they allow a balancing of trade effects and regulatory benefits. But the basic GATT agreement is more awkwardly drafted: first trade effects are considered under Article III, then regulatory benefits are considered under Article XX, but the two are never compared with each other. For the past few years, GATT tribunals have engaged in complicated maneuvers in an attempt to avoid this dilemma.

Obviously, trade law is at least as complex as U.S. doctrines protecting free trade. Indeed, because it is based on a rather complicated set of legal codes, it may be even less understandable to outsiders than the common law doctrines developed by the Supreme Court. It is also at a much earlier stage of its development. GATT is less than a third as old as the dormant commerce clause. Despite these differences, however, GATT tribunals do seem to be wrestling with the same basic difficulty as the U.S. courts. On the one hand, they have a mandate to protect free trade, a goal that could be rapidly undermined unless protectionist regulations are kept under control. Moreover, their professional training and experience emphasize free trade as a value. On the other hand, neither GATT tribunals nor the U.S. courts have any authority to decide broad issues of public policy at the expense of other organs of government. Moreover, the judges themselves, like other citizens, are likely to be concerned about maintaining the effectiveness of environmental regulation.

---

6. This interpretation was first adopted by a dispute settlement panel convened under the U.S.–Canada Free Trade Agreement. *In the Matter of Canada's Landing Requirement for Pacific Coast Salmon and Herring,* 12 Int'l Trade Rep. Decisions (BNA) 1026, ¶ 7.11 and n.20 (1991).

Much of the preceding discussion has been most directly relevant to the situation in which domestic regulations are attacked as trade barriers. The use of trade sanctions to deal with extraterritorial environmental problems is even more controversial. This topic is the primary focus of the following excerpts.

STEVE CHARNOVITZ, THE ENVIRONMENT vs. TRADE RULES: DEFOGGING THE DEBATE[7]

23 ENVTL. L. 475 (1993).

[O]ne front of GATT activity was the conciliation panel for the United States–Mexico dispute regarding dolphins and tuna. This dispute concerned an import provision of the U.S. Marine Mammal Protection Act (MMPA). The MMPA bans the importation of fish caught using techniques which result in an incidental kill of ocean mammals in excess of U.S. practices. In 1990, following a court order, the National Oceanic and Atmospheric Administration (NOAA) imposed a ban on imports of yellowfin tuna and tuna products caught by Mexican vessels using purse seine nets in the Eastern Tropical Pacific (ETP). In response, Mexico lodged a complaint at the GATT, and in August 1991, a GATT panel ruled against the United States.

The panel reached three main conclusions. First, the U.S. import prohibition on tuna could not be considered an internal regulation under GATT Article III because it was concerned with the process of tuna harvesting rather than tuna as a product.[8] Second, the MMPA violated GATT Article XI as an import prohibition other than a duty, tax, or other charge.[9] Third, the MMPA did not qualify for the Article XX(b) or (g) exceptions because these exceptions do not have "extrajurisdictional" application.[10] Article XX(b) provides an exception for measures designed for protection of human, animal, or plant life or health. Article XX(g) provides an exception for measures taken to preserve exhaustible natural resources if taken in conjunction with domestic restrictions. In other words, the exceptions could only be invoked by a country to protect living organisms or natural resources within that country's borders.

At first, word of the panel's decision merely disappointed advocates of marine mammal conservation. But after the report was leaked and studied, it sent shock waves through the international environmental community. In addition to ruling that the MMPA violated international trade rules, the GATT panel implicitly dropped a wide net over decades of environmental treaties and laws protecting everything from deep sea whales to stratospheric ozone. Indeed, the panel seemed to go out of its

---

7. Copyright © 1993 by Steven Charnovitz. Reprinted by permission.

8. Tuna–Dolphin Report, *supra* note 11, paras. 5.8–5.16. Article III permits certain types of laws, regulations, and requirements affecting products "as such," but not ones affecting process, according to the panel deciding the Tuna–Dolphin case.

9. *Id*. para. 5.18.

10. *Id*. paras. 5.24–5.34.

way to validate the popular caricature of the GATT as an inflexible, myopic, moss-grown institution inherently indifferent, if not downright antagonistic, toward ecological protection.[11] There was also bitterness about the way in which the GATT operated. How could a secretive panel presume the right to issue such a sweeping ruling without any consultation with environmental institutions?[12] The fact that the panel had refused to hear the dolphin conservation experts who had come to Geneva for the oral arguments served to heighten the widespread view among environmentalists that the GATT was a hostile institution.[13]

The most straightforward course for the United States in this situation would have been to defend the validity of import prohibitions at the GATT Council, and to attack the panel's report for its weak evidence and reasoning. The United States also could have attempted to rally other countries to its side, particularly those with strong environmental records. But the Bush administration chose an entirely different course. Taking advantage of Mexico's eagerness for a trade agreement with the United States, the administration prevailed upon the Salinas Government not to seek adoption of the report by the GATT Council. Belatedly recognizing that allowing its fishing fleets to slaughter about sixty dolphins a day was not the best way to garner support from American environmentalists, the Mexican government took out full page ads in six major newspapers trumpeting new conservation measures and announcing postponement of the GATT case "as a further demonstration of our good faith effort to develop better protection for the dolphin."

By gaining an agreement with Mexico to delay the report's consideration, the administration headed off a domestic political backlash against both Mexico and the GATT. The administration also avoided putting itself in the position where it had to block adoption of the report by the GATT Council, a step which might have made it more difficult to conclude the Uruguay Round. As a result, the Tuna–Dolphin Report was left in limbo. It seems doubtful that the Tuna–Dolphin Report will ever gain official GATT approval. In the meantime, the U.S. ban on Mexican tuna remains in effect.

In October 1992, Congress amended the MMPA so that an import ban on any country can be halted if that country agrees to implement a global

---

11. It remains unclear why the panel issued such a far-reaching decision rather than ruling against the U.S. law on more narrow grounds. Perhaps the panel may have been influenced by the unusually large number of contracting parties who appeared before it to argue against the United States. Eight nations or instrumentalities spoke against the MMPA and three offered neutral statements. No party sided with the United States. *See* Tuna–Dolphin Report, *supra* note 11, paras. 4.7–4.30.

12. GATT panels do occasionally consult with intergovernmental organizations as provided for in Article XXIII:2. No rule bars consultation with outside groups.

13. Had the panel listened to the marine mammal experts, it might have learned about the long history of U.S. government efforts to negotiate agreements to protect dolphins, as mandated by U.S. law in 1972. Instead, in apparent ignorance of this information, the panel suggests the option of "international cooperative arrangements which would seem to be desirable in view of the fact that dolphins roam the waters of many states and the high seas." Tuna–Dolphin Report, *supra* note 11, para. 5.28.

moratorium by March 1994, to reduce dolphin mortality each year until then, and to require observers. But if the country fails to meet these commitments, the ban on tuna would be reinstated. If this ban is not successful within sixty days, then the U.S. government will impose a trade sanction by excluding forty percent of the normal level of fish and fish product imports from that country. The MMPA amendments also ban the sale or shipment in the United States of tuna that is not dolphin-safe beginning in June 1994.

NOTES

1. In a sequel to the decision discussed above, another GATT panel ruled on a different aspect of the U.S. tuna restrictions in June 1994. The decision primarily involved secondary restrictions on imports from countries buying tuna from Mexico. The panel rejected the extraterritoriality rationale of the first Tuna/Dolphin decision. It concluded that the Article XX defenses include actions taken to protect the environment outside of one's own borders. GATT panels are not subject to any strict rule of precedent, and the panel did not feel obligated to follow *Tuna/Dolphin I*. Nevertheless, the panel concluded that the U.S. tuna restriction was a GATT violation anyway. Although GATT allows trade measures to be used to regulate commercial activities taking place abroad, it does not allow trade sanctions to be used to coerce regulatory action by other governments. The U.S. was not willing to import "dolphin safe" tuna on a case by case basis. Instead, it was demanding that the Mexican government adopt protective regulations for dolphins. According to the panel, this was impermissible.

2. The WTO more recently decided another similar case, this time involving restrictions on shrimp imports. U.S. law requires shrimp trawlers to use "turtle exclusion devices" to prevent incidental killing of endangered sea turtles by shrimping vessels. Shrimp cannot be exported without a certification that the exporting country has a comparable regulatory program. A GATT panel held the U.S. ban illegal, on the ground that unilateral actions by individual member states would threaten to unravel the entire trade agreement, and thus violated the prohibition on "inappropriate" trade measures in the introductory section of Article XX (the "chapeau"). The Appellate Body invalidated the U.S. measure on narrower grounds relating to allegedly unfair methods of implementation. The implications of this decision are discussed in the following article.

ROBERT HOWSE, THE APPELLATE BODY RULINGS IN THE SHRIMP/TURTLE CASE: A NEW LEGAL BASELINE FOR THE TRADE AND ENVIRONMENT DEBATE

27 COLUM. J. TRANSNAT'L L. LAW 491 (2002).

In the Shrimp/Turtle case,[14] the Appellate Body (AB) repudiated the Tuna/Dolphin panel's approach to trade measures to protect the global

---

14. WTO Appellate Body Report on U.S.–Import Prohibition of Certain Shrimp and Shrimp Products, WT/DS58/AB/R (October 12, 1998) [hereinafter Shrimp/Turtle], available at http://www. wto.org/english/tratop_e/dispu_e/cases_e/ds58_e.htm.

environment. The AB ruled that there is no per se rule of impermissibility in the text of Article XX. Rather, the article imposes two requirements on trade measures that condition market access on other countries' policies. First, such measures must fit within one of Article XX's specific exceptions. Second, such measures must be applied in a manner consistent with Article XX's chapeau (preamble). That is, their application must neither give rise to unjustified or arbitrary discrimination between countries where the same conditions prevail, nor create a disguised restriction on international trade.

In Shrimp/Turtle, the AB held that the U.S. measure—which prohibited imports of shrimp from any country that did not have a turtle-conservation program comparable to that of the United States—fit the Article XX(g) exception for conservation of exhaustible natural resources. However, the AB also found that the U.S. measures had been applied in a way that violated the chapeau: by treating certain Asian countries differently than its trading partners in the western hemisphere, the U.S. had engaged in unjustified and arbitrary discrimination.

The AB report's subtle language and the fact that the ruling went against the United States' application of its environmental scheme blunted the impact the decision could have had. At first, few people fully appreciate that the AB was fundamentally changing the Tuna/Dolphin approach on the consistency of environmental trade measures with the multilateral legal framework for liberalized trade. Indeed, some environmentalists feared (and some free-trade advocates hoped) that the AB had made the standard for application of environmental trade measures so high that the net effect of its decision on the status quo as represented by the Tuna/Dolphin rulings would be minimal.

In 2001 (3 years after its Shrimp/Turtle ruling), the AB clarified and elaborated on its original holding. One of the Shrimp/Turtle complainants, Malaysia, had challenged the corrective measures the United States had taken in response to the AB decision. This second AB panel held that the United States had brought its turtle-friendly trade measures into compliance with Article XX, and it underscored those aspects of its original ruling that constituted a fundamental departure from the Tuna/Dolphin approach.[15] * * *

One of the issues that the AB raised but did not decide was whether Article XX(g) requires a territorial nexus between the exhaustible resource and the WTO Member seeking to justify its measure. Merely noting that all of the endangered species of turtles could be observed at one time or another in U.S. waters, the AB stated that were a nexus required, it existed under these facts. The AB's failure to resolve the question of whether Article XX(g) has jurisdictional or territorial limits must be understood in light of the section's condition that unilateral trade meas-

---

15. Report of the Appellate Body, U.S.–Import Prohibitions of Certain Shrimp & Shrimp Products; Recourse to Article 21.5 of the DSU by Malaysia, WT/DS58/AB/RW (Oct. 22, 2001) [hereinafter Shrimp/Turtle 21.5 Report], available at http://www.wto.org/english/tratop_e/dispu_e/cases_e/ds58_e.htm.

ures be taken in conjunction with restrictions on domestic resource production or consumption. By virtue of this condition, Article XX(g) already requires a link between environmental trade measures and domestic regulation dealing with the same conservation problem. Were a WTO Member to target its conservation concerns solely at the policies of other countries, without putting its own house in order, then it would not be able to meet this condition of XX(g). The question, then, of whether there is an implicit territorial or jurisdictional limitation in XX(g) may therefore be largely moot, since Article XX(g) by its explicit language only applies to environmental trade measures that are coupled with domestic environmental regulation.

Once it has been established that the state taking the environmental trade measures is equivalent to restrictions on its own producers and/or consumers, why should it be necessary to identify whether the species being protected is itself sometimes to be found within the state's territory? The purpose of a territorial nexus is to prevent a state that lacks legitimate concern from using a global environmental problem as a pretext for protectionist interventionism. Therefore, it should be sufficient, as required by the text of Article XX(g), that the U.S. measure was even-handed, imposing a conservation burden on its own producers and consumers, and not merely attempting to externalize the costs of environmental protection to the producers of other countries.

The overall boldness with which the AB rejected the bright line rule against unilateral environmental trade measures seems to suggest that the AB simply gives short shrift to concerns that such measures are susceptible to protectionist abuse or that they tend to impose on other countries policy solutions that are ill-adapted to the particular conditions in those countries.

But a careful reading of the AB's application of the chapeau undermines this interpretation. According to the AB, the chapeau's safeguards limit the damage that unilateralism can do to non-discriminatory, rules-based trade. As the AB emphasizes, the conditions in the chapeau control the abuse of rights and they regulate the overall balance of rights and obligations struck by Art. XX. However, interpreting the chapeau so as to vitiate the meaning of the rights contained in the operative paragraphs of Art. XX would be inappropriate. Just as a bright-line rule against unilateral environmental measures would make Article XX inutile, so too would an excessively strict interpretation of the chapeau's conditions. Such an interpretation would make it impossible, in practice, for unilateral measures to survive judicial scrutiny.* * *

An even more serious misreading of the AB's invocation of international environmental law with respect to the duty of cooperation is that the AB held that global environmental trade measures may only be taken, if at all, pursuant to an already negotiated multilateral framework. In other words, a Member not only has a duty to negotiate but to actually succeed in achieving a multilateral framework under which trade measures are permissible (or required), before taking such measures. This reading simply ignores the exact wording of the international environmental instruments cited by the Appellate Body. These instruments require cooperation and the avoidance of unilateralism "as far as possible." This wording clearly anticipates that there will be situations where it will not be possible to avoid unilateralism. If it were not the case, then the language "as far as possible" would be utterly inutile. One of the cornerstones of the AB's approach to WTO interpretation, established in the earlier Japan Alcohol and Reformulated Gasoline cases is that interpretations of treaty provisions should be avoided that render other treaty provisions useless or meaningless.

In the [second] Shrimp/Turtle Report, the AB puts to rest any misunderstanding concerning the need to conclude a multilateral environmental agreement:

> Requiring that a multilateral agreement be concluded by the United States in order to avoid 'arbitrary or unjustifiable discrimination' in applying its measure would mean that any country party to the negotiations with the United States, whether a WTO Member or not, would have, in effect, a veto over whether the United States could fulfill its WTO obligations. Such a requirement would not be reasonable.

There is nothing in the wording of the chapeau (or any other part of Article XX) to suggest that a nation must first secure agreement by WTO Members or any other nation before exercising its rights under Article XX(g). By contrast, where the drafters wanted to make the exercise of some kind of exception to GATT disciplines contingent on agreement or collective action among Members or states generally, they did so explicitly. For example, Article XXI(c) provides an exception where Members are taking action "in pursuance of . . . obligations under the United Nations Charter for the maintenance of international peace and security." * * *

Having swept away almost all the pillars of the GATT anti-environmentalist edifice, it is not surprising that the AB would be criticized for illegitimate judicial activism. A fairly representative criticism is that of Jagdish Baghwati of Columbia University:

> I have some sympathy for [the] view that the dispute settlement panels and the appellate court must defer somewhat more to the political process instead of making law in controversial matters. I was astounded that the appellate court, in effect, reversed long-standing jurisprudence on process and production methods in the Shrimp/Turtle case. I have little doubt that the jurists were reflecting the political pressures brought by the rich-country environmental NGOs and essentially made law that affected the developing countries adversely.[16]

---

16. Jagdish Bhagwati, *After Seattle: Free Trade and the WTO*, in EFFICIENCY, EQUITY, AND LEGITIMACY: THE MULTILATERAL TRADING SYSTEM AT THE MILLENNIUM 60–61 (Roger B. Porter et al. eds., 2001). *See also* CLAUDE E. BARFIELD, FREE TRADE, SOVEREIGNTY, DEMOCRACY: THE FUTURE OF THE WORLD TRADE ORGANIZATION, at Ch. 4 (2001).

The only "jurisprudence" clearly establishing the principles to which Bhagwati is referring consists in the two unadopted Tuna/Dolphin panel reports ["unadopted" means that the opinions were not formally ratified by the GATT membership]. Although unadopted, these reports embody a perspective almost universally held by the trade-insider network. Was it "activist" of the Appellate Body not to defer to that insider perspective, but instead to go back to the treaty texts themselves and to sources of interpretation authorized by the Vienna Convention on the Law of Treaties?* * *

It is well established public international law that some provisions of treaties are to be interpreted in an evolutionary fashion. By reverting to the preamble of the WTO Agreement to establish that exhaustible natural resources is an evolutionary term, the Appellate Body merely followed Vienna Convention Article 31, which specifically mentions the "preamble" as part of the "context" which is fundamental to the interpretation of treaty text. However, the "preamble" in question was one that was written nearly 40 years after the original GATT text. The AB was implicitly accepting the notion that there is a new framework for the interpretation of GATT—that the creation of the WTO represented a foundational moment, one that in this case placed the relevant provisions of GATT within a broader universe of international law and policy relevant to environment and development, as well as general public international law.

Of course, the insider network, generally speaking, had boasted of the creation of the WTO as a new founding for the multilateral trading system, including the placement of the system on a more unambiguous, or unquestionable, foundation of international legality. They do not like to reap what they have sown.

NOTES

1. Should measures like the shrimp and tuna restrictions be seen as simple refusals to consume goods that are considered morally tainted by the importing country? Or should they be considered efforts at coercion of other governments? And is coercion in this context justified or merely cultural imperialism? Consider, for example, the trade sanctions against Taiwan for allowing sale of products derived from endangered species. Eco-globalism or neo-imperialism? For further discussion, *see* Daniel A. Farber, *Stretching the Margins: The Geographic Nexus in Environmental Law*, 48 STAN. L. REV. 1247 (1996); Howard F. Chang, *An Economic Analysis of Trade Measures to Protect the Global Environment*, 83 GEO. L.J. 2131 (1995).

2. Another issue involving trade versus the environment relates to what some have called "environmental dumping." The question is whether firms which are allowed to pollute are thereby being given an unfair cost-advantage. A countervailing tariff might be used to cancel this advantage. For a critical discussion, *see* Richard B. Stewart, *Environmental Regulation and International Competitiveness*, 102 YALE L.J. 2039 (1993). *See also* DANIEL C. ESTY,

GREENING THE GATT: TRADE, ENVIRONMENT, AND THE FUTURE (1994). Is allowing a firm to pollute freely the equivalent of a subsidy? If so, a countervailing duty might be consistent with the GATT treatment of subsidies.

3.　Clearly, conflicts over trade and the environment are likely to continue. For further discussion of WTO/environmental issues, *see* Steve Charnovitz, *The WTO's Environmental Progress*, 10 J. of Int'l Econ. L.685 (2007); David M. Driesen, *What is Free Trade?: The Real Issue Lurking Behind the Trade and Environment Debate*, 41 VA. J. INT'L L. 279 (2001); John O. McGinnis & Mark L. Movsesian, *The World Trade Constitution*, 114 HARV. L. REV. 511 (2000).

F.　PRIVATE PROPERTY, THE ENVIRONMENT, AND THE CONSTITUTION

Environmental law challenges borders in the form of national or state jurisdiction. It also can challenge borders in terms of the ownership of a parcel, imposing restrictions on the owner's use of land because of potential environmental effects on others. In this section, we consider the interaction between traditional concepts of owner autonomy and newer ideas of ecological interdependence, as seen through the lense of legal doctrine.

1.　THE TAKINGS CLAUSE

Like federalism, the takings clause (found in the 5th Amendment to the U.S. Constitution but long held to apply against the states via the due process clause of the 14th Amendment) presents a limitation on governmental power to regulate. Modern takings doctrine originated in *Pennsylvania Coal Co. v. Mahon*, 260 U.S. 393 (1922). This case involved a Pennsylvania statute making it unlawful for coal companies to cause the collapse or subsidence of any public building, any street, or any private residence. The Mahons were bound by a covenant to allow a coal company, which had sold to the Mahons or their predecessor only the surface rights to their lot, to remove all the coal without liability. The effect of the statute was to annul this covenant. Pennsylvania law recognized three separate property rights: the right to use the surface, the ownership of the subsurface minerals, and the right to have the surface supported by the subsurface earth. The coal company claimed that the statute operated as a taking of both the second and third rights, which belonged to them under their deed with the Mahons. In perhaps the most important single decision under the takings clause, Justice Holmes held that the statute was indeed a taking. The heart of the opinion is to be found in the following famous passage:

> Government hardly could go on if to some extent values incident to property could not be diminished without paying for every such change in the general law. As long recognized, some values are

enjoyed under an implied limitation and must yield to the police power. But obviously the implied limitation must have its limits, or the contract and due process clauses are gone. One fact for consideration in determining such limits is the extent of the diminution. When it reaches a certain magnitude, in most if not in all cases there must be an exercise of eminent domain and compensation to sustain the act. So the question depends upon the particular facts. The greatest weight is given to the judgment of the legislature, but it always is open to interested parties to contend that the legislature has gone beyond its constitutional power.

In applying this test, the Court stressed that the statute made coal mining in certain areas impractical and thus had "very nearly the same effect for constitutional purposes as appropriating or destroying it." The Court concluded that so long as "private persons or communities have seen fit to take the risk of acquiring only surface rights, we cannot see that the fact that the risk has become a danger warrants the giving to them greater rights than they bought." Justice Brandeis filed a strong dissent.

Trying to decide when a regulation has "gone too far" has been extremely difficult. *Penn Central Transportation Co. v. New York*, 438 U.S. 104 (1978), has probably been the Court's most significant effort at synthesis. *Penn Central* involved a New York historic preservation ordinance. Under the ordinance a special commission was empowered to designate buildings as landmarks, subject to administrative and judicial review. After designation, the exterior of a building had to be kept in good repair and exterior alterations had to be approved by the Commission. Development rights lost because of the landmark designation could be transferred to nearby plots of land, thereby allowing additional development on that land beyond the normal restrictions of the zoning and building codes. Penn Central owned Grand Central Terminal, a designated landmark. A plan by Penn Central to build a multistory office building perched above the terminal was rejected by the Commission. Penn Central then brought suit claiming that its property had been taken without compensation. It conceded, however, that the transferable development rights had some value and that the terminal was still capable of earning a reasonable return on its initial investment.

The Court began by reviewing the factors that had shaped prior decisions. The Court admitted that it had been unable to develop any "set formula" for determining when compensation was required. Instead, it referred to the prior cases as involving "essentially ad hoc, factual inquiries." The Court did point, however, to several relevant factors. The most important were (1) whether the regulation had "interfered with distinct investment backed expectations," and (2) whether the government had physically invaded the property or instead had simply enacted "some public program adjusting the benefits and burdens of economic life to promote the common good." In reviewing the specific regulation before it, the Court concluded that the purposes of the ordinance were permissible because the ordinance was "expected to produce a widespread public benefit and applicable to all similarly situated property." The Court then held that the regulation passed the *Pennsylvania Coal* test because it did not deprive the company of all use of the property, but instead allowed continuation of a past use, and more importantly, permitted the company to obtain a "reasonable return" on its investment.

Since *Penn Central*, takings doctrine has burgeoned. Because space limitations preclude a review of all of the significant decisions, we will devote our attention to those with the greatest environmental significance. There have been three major areas of doctrinal development, one of which will be our focus. But the other two deserve at least a brief description.

First, the procedural rules governing takings claims have become increasingly complex. In *First English Evangelical Lutheran Church v. Los Angeles County*, 482 U.S. 304 (1987), the Court held that the government must pay damages for the temporary restriction on property use caused by an unconstitutional regulation prior to the time the regulation is struck down. Another key procedural rule is that a claim which has been brought too early will be dismissed as unripe. There must be a definitive government denial of development rights before a federal action can be brought. But just what constitutes such a definitive government action remains somewhat unclear. *See* Suitum v. Tahoe Reg'l Planning Agency, 520 U.S. 725 (1997). Additional procedural wrinkles were introduced by *City of Monterey v. Del Monte Dunes at Monterey, Ltd.*, 526 U.S. 687 (1999), which held that some aspects of the taking question must go to the jury.

Second, the Court has elaborated on the "physical occupation" branch of the takings doctrine. It seems clear that a public access easement on otherwise private property qualifies as a physical occupation. But such an easement may be a legitimate condition of a permit where it mitigates a project's impact. In two major decisions, the Court has articulated the necessary relationship between the project and the access condition. In *Nollan v. California Coastal Commission*, 483 U.S. 825 (1987), owners of beach property were required to dedicate an easement from the street to the beach, as a condition for a permit to demolish an existing house and build a new one. The Court held that this was a taking because of the absence of any "nexus" between the access condition and the construction project, which did not meaningfully impede existing public access to the beach. The Court took *Nollan* one step further in *Dolan v. City of Tigard*, 512 U.S. 374 (1994), by requiring the city to "make some sort of individualized determination" of "rough proportionality" between the permit condition and the impact of the project.

The third area of doctrinal development has involved restrictions on development. It is the subject of the next two cases.

LUCAS v. SOUTH CAROLINA COASTAL COUNCIL

Supreme Court of the United States, 1992.
505 U.S. 1003, 112 S.Ct. 2886, 120 L.Ed.2d 798.

Justice Scalia delivered the opinion of the Court.

In 1986, petitioner David H. Lucas paid $975,000 for two residential lots on the Isle of Palms in Charleston County, South Carolina, on which he intended to build single family homes. In 1988, however, the South Carolina Legislature enacted the Beachfront Management Act, which had the direct effect of barring petitioner from erecting any permanent habitable structures on his two parcels. A state trial court found that this prohibition rendered Lucas's parcels "valueless." This case requires us to decide whether the Act's dramatic effect on the economic value of Lucas's lots accomplished a taking of private property under the Fifth and Fourteenth Amendments requiring the payment of "just compensation."
* * *

[O]ur decision in *Mahon* offered little insight into when, and under what circumstances, a given regulation would be seen as going "too far" for purposes of the Fifth Amendment. In 70-odd years of succeeding "regulatory takings" jurisprudence, we have generally eschewed any " 'set formula' " for determining how far is too far, preferring to "engag[e] in * * * essentially ad hoc, factual inquiries," [quoting *Penn Central*]. We have, however, described at least two discrete categories of regulatory action as compensable without case-specific inquiry into the public interest advanced in support of the restraint. The first encompasses regulations that compel the property owner to suffer a physical "invasion" of his property. * * *

The second situation in which we have found categorical treatment appropriate is where regulation denies all economically beneficial or productive use of land. As we have said on numerous occasions, the Fifth Amendment is violated when land-use regulation "does not substantially advance legitimate state interests *or denies an owner economically viable use of his land.*"[17]

---

17. Regrettably, the rhetorical force of our "deprivation of all economically feasible use" rule is greater than its precision, since the rule does not make clear the "property interest" against which the loss of value is to be measured. When, for example, a regulation requires a developer to leave 90% of a rural tract in its natural state, it is unclear whether we would analyze the situation as one in which the owner has been deprived of all economically beneficial use of the burdened portion of the tract, or as one in which the owner has suffered a mere diminution in value of the tract as a whole. (For an extreme—and, we think, unsupportable—view of the relevant calculus, see *Penn Central Transportation Co. v. New York City,* 42 N.Y.2d 324, 333–334, 397 N.Y.S.2d 914, 920, 366 N.E.2d 1271, 1276–1277 (1977), aff'd, 438 U.S. 104, 98 S.Ct. 2646, 57 L.Ed.2d 631 (1978), where the state court examined the diminution in a particular parcel's value produced by a municipal ordinance in light of total value of the taking claimant's other holdings in the vicinity.) Unsurprisingly, this uncertainty regarding the composition of the denominator in our "deprivation" fraction has produced inconsistent pronouncements by the Court. The answer to this difficult question may lie in how the owner's reasonable expectations have been shaped by the State's law of property—*i.e.,* whether and to what degree the State's law has accorded legal recognition and protection to the particular interest in land with respect to which the takings claimant alleges a diminution in (or elimination of) value. In any event, we avoid this difficulty in

We have never set forth the justification for this rule. Perhaps it is simply, as Justice Brennan suggested, that total deprivation of beneficial use is, from the landowner's point of view, the equivalent of a physical appropriation. * * * Surely, at least, in the extraordinary circumstance when *no* productive or economically beneficial use of land is permitted, it is less realistic to indulge our usual assumption that the legislature is simply "adjusting the benefits and burdens of economic life," [*Penn Central*], in a manner that secures an "average reciprocity of advantage" to everyone concerned. And the *functional* basis for permitting the government, by regulation, to affect property values without compensation—that "Government hardly could go on if to some extent values incident to property could not be diminished without paying for every such change in the general law"—does not apply to the relatively rare situations where the government has deprived a landowner of all economically beneficial uses.

On the other side of the balance, affirmatively supporting a compensation requirement, is the fact that regulations that leave the owner of land without economically beneficial or productive options for its use— typically, as here, by requiring land to be left substantially in its natural state—carry with them a heightened risk that private property is being pressed into some form of public service under the guise of mitigating serious public harm. See, *e.g., Annicelli v. South Kingstown,* 463 A.2d 133, 140–141 (R.I.1983) (prohibition on construction adjacent to beach justified on twin grounds of safety and "conservation of open space"); *Morris County Land Improvement Co. v. Parsippany–Troy Hills Township,* 40 N.J. 539, 552–553, 193 A.2d 232, 240 (1963) (prohibition on filling marshlands imposed in order to preserve region as water detention basin and create wildlife refuge). As Justice Brennan explained: "From the government's point of view, the benefits flowing to the public from preservation of open space through regulation may be equally great as from creating a wildlife refuge through formal condemnation or increasing electricity production through a dam project that floods private property." The many statutes on the books, both state and federal, that provide for the use of eminent domain to impose servitudes on private scenic lands preventing developmental uses, or to acquire such lands altogether, suggest the practical equivalence in this setting of negative regulation and appropriation.

We think, in short, that there are good reasons for our frequently expressed belief that when the owner of real property has been called upon to sacrifice *all* economically beneficial uses in the name of the common good, that is, to leave his property economically idle, he has suffered a taking.* * *

the present case, since the "interest in land" that Lucas has pleaded (a fee simple interest) is an estate with a rich tradition of protection at common law, and since the South Carolina Court of Common Pleas found that the Beachfront Management Act left each of Lucas's beachfront lots without economic value.

It is correct that many of our prior opinions have suggested that "harmful or noxious uses" of property may be proscribed by government regulation without the requirement of compensation. For a number of reasons, however, we think the South Carolina Supreme Court was too quick to conclude that that principle decides the present case. The "harmful or noxious uses" principle was the Court's early attempt to describe in theoretical terms why government may, consistent with the Takings Clause, affect property values by regulation without incurring an obligation to compensate—a reality we nowadays acknowledge explicitly with respect to the full scope of the State's police power. * * *

The transition from our early focus on control of "noxious" uses to our contemporary understanding of the broad realm within which government may regulate without compensation was an easy one, since the distinction between "harm-preventing" and "benefit-conferring" regulation is often in the eye of the beholder. It is quite possible, for example, to describe in *either* fashion the ecological, economic, and aesthetic concerns that inspired the South Carolina legislature in the present case. One could say that imposing a servitude on Lucas's land is necessary in order to prevent his use of it from "harming" South Carolina's ecological resources; or, instead, in order to achieve the "benefits" of an ecological preserve. Whether one or the other of the competing characterizations will come to one's lips in a particular case depends primarily upon one's evaluation of the worth of competing uses of real estate. * * *

Where the State seeks to sustain regulation that deprives land of all economically beneficial use, we think it may resist compensation only if the logically antecedent inquiry into the nature of the owner's estate shows that the proscribed use interests were not part of his title to begin with.[18] This accords, we think, with our "takings" jurisprudence, which has traditionally been guided by the understandings of our citizens regarding the content of, and the State's power over, the "bundle of rights" that they acquire when they obtain title to property. It seems to us that the property owner necessarily expects the uses of his property to be restricted, from time to time, by various measures newly enacted by the State in legitimate exercise of its police powers; "[a]s long recognized, some values are enjoyed under an implied limitation and must yield to the police power." [*Mahon.*] And in the case of personal property, by reason of the State's traditionally high degree of control over commercial dealings, he

---

18. Drawing on our First Amendment jurisprudence, Justice Stevens would "loo[k] to the *generality* of a regulation of property" to determine whether compensation is owing. The Beachfront Management Act is general, in his view, because it "regulates the use of the coastline of the entire state." There may be some validity to the principle Justice Stevens proposes, but it does not properly apply to the present case. The equivalent of a law of general application that inhibits the practice of religion without being aimed at religion, is a law that destroys the value of land without being aimed at land. Perhaps such a law—the generally applicable criminal prohibition on the manufacturing of alcoholic beverages challenged in *Mugler* [*v. Kansas,* 123 U.S. 623, 8 S.Ct. 273, 31 L.Ed. 205 (1887)] (1887), comes to mind—cannot constitute a compensable taking. But a regulation *specifically directed to land use* no more acquires immunity by plundering landowners generally than does a law specifically directed at religious practice acquire immunity by prohibiting all religions. Justice Stevens' approach renders the Takings Clause little more than a particularized restatement of the Equal Protection Clause.

ought to be aware of the possibility that new regulation might even render his property economically worthless (at least if the property's only economically productive use is sale or manufacture for sale). In the case of land, however, we think the notion pressed by the Council that title is somehow held subject to the "implied limitation" that the State may subsequently eliminate all economically valuable use is inconsistent with the historical compact recorded in the Takings Clause that has become part of our constitutional culture.* * *

It seems unlikely that common-law principles would have prevented the erection of any habitable or productive improvements on petitioner's land; they rarely support prohibition of the "essential use" of land. The question, however, is one of state law to be dealt with on remand. We emphasize that to win its case South Carolina must do more than proffer the legislature's declaration that the uses Lucas desires are inconsistent with the public interest, or the conclusory assertion that they violate a common-law maxim such as *sic utere tuo ut alienum non laedas.* As we have said, a "State, by *ipse dixit,* may not transform private property into public property without compensation * * *." Instead, as it would be required to do if it sought to restrain Lucas in a common-law action for public nuisance, South Carolina must identify background principles of nuisance and property law that prohibit the uses he now intends in the circumstances in which the property is presently found. Only on this showing can the State fairly claim that, in proscribing all such beneficial uses, the Beachfront Management Act is taking nothing.[19]

JUSTICE KENNEDY, concurring in the judgment.

In my view, reasonable expectations must be understood in light of the whole of our legal tradition. The common law of nuisance is too narrow a confine for the exercise of regulatory power in a complex and interdependent society. The State should not be prevented from enacting new regulatory initiatives in response to changing conditions, and courts must consider all reasonable expectations whatever their source. The Takings Clause does not require a static body of state property law; it protects private expectations to ensure private investment. I agree with the Court that nuisance prevention accords with the most common expectations of property owners who face regulation, but I do not believe this can be the sole source of state authority to impose severe restrictions. Coastal property may present such unique concerns for a fragile land system that the State can go further in regulating its development and use than the common law of nuisance might otherwise permit.

The Supreme Court of South Carolina erred, in my view, by reciting the general purposes for which the state regulations were enacted without a determination that they were in accord with the owner's reasonable expectations and therefore sufficient to support a severe restriction on

---

19. * * * We stress that an affirmative decree eliminating all economically beneficial uses may be defended only if an *objectively reasonable application* of relevant precedents would exclude those beneficial uses in the circumstances in which the land is presently found.

specific parcels of property. The promotion of tourism, for instance, ought not to suffice to deprive specific property of all value without a corresponding duty to compensate. Furthermore, the means as well as the ends of regulation must accord with the owner's reasonable expectations. Here, the State did not act until after the property had been zoned for individual lot development and most other parcels had been improved, throwing the whole burden of the regulation on the remaining lots. This too must be measured in the balance.

JUSTICE BLACKMUN, dissenting.

[T]he Court justifies its new rule that the legislature may not deprive a property owner of the only economically valuable use of his land, even if the legislature finds it to be a harmful use, because such action is not part of the "long recognized" "understandings of our citizens." These "understandings" permit such regulation only if the use is a nuisance under the common law. Any other course is "inconsistent with the historical compact recorded in the Takings Clause." It is not clear from the Court's opinion where our "historical compact" or "citizens' understanding" comes from, but it does not appear to be history.

The principle that the State should compensate individuals for property taken for public use was not widely established in America at the time of the Revolution. * * *

Even into the 19th century, state governments often felt free to take property for roads and other public projects without paying compensation to the owners. As one court declared in 1802, citizens "were bound to contribute as much of [land], as by the laws of the country, were deemed necessary for the public convenience." * * *

In short, I find no clear and accepted "historical compact" or "understanding of our citizens" justifying the Court's new taking doctrine. Instead, the Court seems to treat history as a grab-bag of principles, to be adopted where they support the Court's theory, and ignored where they do not. If the Court decided that the early common law provides the background principles for interpreting the Taking Clause, then regulation, as opposed to physical confiscation, would not be compensable. If the Court decided that the law of a later period provides the background principles, then regulation might be compensable, but the Court would have to confront the fact that legislatures regularly determined which uses were prohibited, independent of the common law, and independent of whether the uses were lawful when the owner purchased. What makes the Court's analysis unworkable is its attempt to package the law of two incompatible eras and peddle it as historical fact.

JUSTICE STEVENS, dissenting.

In considering Lucas' claim, the generality of the Beachfront Management Act is significant. The Act does not target particular landowners, but rather regulates the use of the coastline of the entire State. Indeed, South Carolina's Act is best understood as part of a national effort to protect the coastline, one initiated by the Federal Coastal Zone Management Act of 1972. * * * Moreover, the Act did not single out owners of undeveloped land. The Act also prohibited owners of developed land from rebuilding if their structures were destroyed, and what is equally significant, from repairing erosion control devices, such as seawalls. In addition, in some situations, owners of developed land were required to "renouris[h] the beach * * * on a yearly basis with an amount * * * of sand * * * not * * * less than one and one-half times the yearly volume of sand lost due to erosion." In short, the South Carolina Act imposed substantial burdens on owners of developed and undeveloped land alike. This generality indicates that the Act is not an effort to expropriate owners of undeveloped land.

Admittedly, the economic impact of this regulation is dramatic and petitioner's investment-backed expectations are substantial. Yet, if anything, the costs to and expectations of the owners of developed land are even greater: I doubt, however, that the cost to owners of developed land of renourishing the beach and allowing their seawalls to deteriorate effects a taking. The costs imposed on the owners of undeveloped land, such as petitioner, differ from these costs only in degree, not in kind.

NOTES

1. After Hurricane Hugo, so many structures were damaged in the area of the Isle of Palms that the state relented on its ban on rebuilding existing houses. After further negotiations, South Carolina eventually bought the lots for over $1.5 million. The area has been flooded many times since the Supreme Court's ruling, and the inhabitants have constructed walls of two-ton and three-ton sandbags. Carol M. Rose, *The Story of Lucas: Environmental Land Use Regulation Between Developers and the Deep Blue Sea*, in RICHARD J. LAZARUS & OLIVER A. HOUCK, ENVIRONMENTAL LAW STORIES 268–69 (2005).

2. One noteworthy aspect of *Lucas* is Justice Scalia's use of a narrowly construed "nuisance exception," at least in total takings cases. Justice Scalia's use of nuisance law has attracted attention from commentators, who have suggested that nuisance law has been far more fluid and adaptable than Scalia suggests. We will return later to the question of *Lucas*'s "categorical exemptions" from takings analysis.

3. It seems to be very difficult to win a *Penn Central* claim, whereas successfully characterizing a claim as involving a "total taking" guarantees victory. Thus, it is critical to determine the boundary between *Penn Central* and *Lucas*. The following case is part of the on-going effort to determine the parameters of the *Lucas* doctrine.

TAHOE–SIERRA PRESERVATION COUNCIL, INC.
v. TAHOE REGIONAL PLANNING AGENCY

Supreme Court of the United States, 2002.
535 U.S. 302, 122 S.Ct. 1465, 152 L.Ed.2d 517.

JUSTICE STEVENS delivered the opinion of the Court.

[Lake Tahoe was described by the Court (quoting President Clinton) as a "national treasure that must be protected and preserved." The Court also quoted Mark Twain's description of the clarity of its waters as "not *merely* transparent, but dazzlingly, brilliantly so." But the clarity of the lake is threatened by algae, which in turn are fed by runoff. Development, particularly on steep ground, increases runoff because of the heavy water flow from paved areas. The Tahoe Regional Planning Agency (TRPA) was established by an interstate compact with the goal of preserving the lake. Because of the complexity of the planning process, a moratorium was imposed for thirty-two months on all development in the area. TRPA's proposed new plan was challenged in court by the state of California, and development was prohibited for roughly three additional years under an injunction. The dissenters viewed the entire construction freeze to be relevant. However, the majority considered only the initial moratorium. The plaintiff claimed that the moratorium was a taking. The District Court agreed, applying the *Lucas* theory, but the Court of Appeals held that the *Penn Central* test applied instead.]

Certainly, our holding that the permanent "obliteration of the value" of a fee simple estate constitutes a categorical taking does not answer the question whether a regulation prohibiting any economic use of land for a 32–month period has the same legal effect. Petitioners seek to bring this case under the rule announced in *Lucas* by arguing that we can effectively sever a 32–month segment from the remainder of each landowner's fee simple estate, and then ask whether that segment has been taken in its entirety by the moratoria. Of course, defining the property interest taken in terms of the very regulation being challenged is circular. With property so divided, every delay would become a total ban; the moratorium and the normal permit process alike would constitute categorical takings. Petitioners' "conceptual severance" argument is unavailing because it ignores *Penn Central's* admonition that in regulatory takings cases we must focus on "the parcel as a whole." We have consistently rejected such an approach to the "denominator" question. Thus, the District Court erred when it disaggregated petitioners' property into temporal segments corresponding to the regulations at issue and then analyzed whether petitioners were deprived of all economically viable use during each period. The starting point for the court's analysis should have been to ask whether there was a total taking of the entire parcel; if not, then *Penn Central* was the proper framework.

An interest in real property is defined by the metes and bounds that describe its geographic dimensions and the term of years that describes the temporal aspect of the owner's interest. Both dimensions must be considered if the interest is to be viewed in its entirety. Hence, a permanent deprivation of the owner's use of the entire area is a taking of "the parcel as a whole," whereas a temporary restriction that merely causes a diminution in value is not. Logically, a fee simple estate cannot be rendered valueless by a temporary prohibition on economic use, because the property will recover value as soon as the prohibition is lifted.

Neither *Lucas* * * * nor any of our other regulatory takings cases compels us to accept petitioners' categorical submission. In fact, these cases make clear that the categorical rule in *Lucas* was carved out for the "extraordinary case" in which a regulation permanently deprives property of all value; the default rule remains that, in the regulatory taking context, we require a more fact specific inquiry. Nevertheless, we will consider whether the interest in protecting individual property owners from bearing public burdens "which, in all fairness and justice, should be borne by the public as a whole," justifies creating a new rule for these circumstances.

[The] ultimate constitutional question is whether the concepts of "fairness and justice" that underlie the Takings Clause will be better served by . . . categorical rules or by a *Penn Central* inquiry into all of the relevant circumstances in particular cases. From that perspective, the extreme categorical rule that any deprivation of all economic use, no matter how brief, constitutes a compensable taking surely cannot be sustained. Petitioners' broad submission would apply to numerous "normal delays in obtaining building permits, changes in zoning ordinances, variances, and the like," as well as to orders temporarily prohibiting access to crime scenes, businesses that violate health codes, fire-damaged buildings, or other areas that we cannot now foresee. Such a rule would undoubtedly require changes in numerous practices that have long been considered permissible exercises of the police power. As Justice Holmes warned in *Mahon,* "[g]overnment hardly could go on if to some extent values incident to property could not be diminished without paying for every such change in the general law." A rule that required compensation for every delay in the use of property would render routine government processes prohibitively expensive or encourage hasty decisionmaking. Such an important change in the law should be the product of legislative rulemaking rather than adjudication.* * *

The interest in facilitating informed decisionmaking by regulatory agencies counsels against adopting a *per se* rule that would impose such severe costs on their deliberations. Otherwise, the financial constraints of compensating property owners during a moratorium may force officials to rush through the planning process or to abandon the practice altogether. To the extent that communities are forced to abandon using moratoria, landowners will have incentives to develop their property quickly before a comprehensive plan can be enacted, thereby fostering inefficient and ill-conceived growth. A finding in the 1980 Compact itself, which presumably was endorsed by all three legislative bodies that participated in its enactment, attests to the importance of that concern.* * *

It may well be true that any moratorium that lasts for more than one year should be viewed with special skepticism. But given the fact that the District Court found that the 32 months required by TRPA to formulate the 1984 Regional Plan was not unreasonable, we could not possibly conclude that every delay of over one year is constitutionally unacceptable. Formulating a general rule of this kind is a suitable task for state legislatures. In our view, the duration of the restriction is one of the important factors that a court must consider in the appraisal of a regulatory takings claim, but with respect to that factor as with respect to other factors, the "temptation to adopt what amount to *per se* rules in either direction must be resisted." There may be moratoria that last longer than one year which interfere with reasonable investment-backed expectations, but as the District Court's opinion illustrates, petitioners' proposed rule is simply "too blunt an instrument," for identifying those cases. We conclude, therefore, that the interest in "fairness and justice" will be best served by relying on the familiar *Penn Central* approach when deciding cases like this, rather than by attempting to craft a new categorical rule.

CHIEF JUSTICE REHNQUIST, with whom JUSTICE SCALIA and JUSTICE THOMAS join, dissenting.

For over half a decade petitioners were prohibited from building homes, or any other structures, on their land. Because the Takings Clause requires the government to pay compensation when it deprives owners of all economically viable use of their land, and because a ban on all development lasting almost six years does not resemble any traditional land-use planning device, I dissent.* * *

The Court worries that applying *Lucas* here compels finding that an array of traditional, short-term, land-use planning devices are takings. But since the beginning of our regulatory takings jurisprudence, we have recognized that property rights "are enjoyed under an implied limitation." Thus, in *Lucas,* after holding that the regulation prohibiting all economically beneficial use of the coastal land came within our categorical takings rule, we nonetheless inquired into whether such a result "inhere[d] in the title itself, in the restrictions that background principles of the State's law of property and nuisance already place upon land ownership." Because the regulation at issue in *Lucas* purported to be permanent, or at least long term, we concluded that the only implied limitation of state property law that could achieve a similar long-term deprivation of all economic use would be something "achieved in the courts—by adjacent landowners (or other uniquely affected persons) under the State's law of private nuisance, or by the State under its complementary power to abate nuisances that affect the public generally, or otherwise." * * *

But a moratorium prohibiting all economic use for a period of six years is not one of the longstanding, implied limitations of state property law. Moratoria are "interim controls on the use of land that seek to maintain the status quo with respect to land development in an area by either 'freezing' existing land uses or by allowing the issuance of building permits for only certain land uses that would not be inconsistent with a contemplated zoning plan or zoning change." Typical moratoria thus prohibit only certain categories of development, such as fast-food, or adult businesses, or all commercial development. Such moratoria do not implicate *Lucas* because they do not deprive landowners of all economically beneficial use of their land. As for moratoria that prohibit all development, these do not have the lineage of permit and zoning requirements and thus it is less certain that property is acquired under the "implied limitation" of a moratorium prohibiting all development. Moreover, unlike a permit system in which it is expected that a project will be approved so long as certain conditions are satisfied, a moratorium that prohibits all uses is by definition contemplating a new land-use plan that would prohibit all uses.

NOTES

1. *Lucas* applies only when virtually all of the utility of property has been destroyed. This makes it critical to define the "denominator"—the total property interest considered relevant to the claim. For example, a setback requirement could be considered a complete taking of the strip where construction is forbidden, or it could be considered a restriction on only a minor percentage of the full parcel. Similarly, a five-day freeze on development could be considered a total taking of a five-day interest in the property, or a negligible intrusion on the fee simple as a whole. In *Lake Tahoe*, the Court defines the denominator (the total property interest) quite broadly, rather than separating the various "sticks" in the bundle of property rights.

In a brief separate dissent, Justice Thomas (joined by Justice Scalia) disavowed the Court's focus on the "parcel as a whole," calling that approach "questionable." Justice Thomas observed that if the agency had enacted a permanent ban on development, there would have been a taking under *Lucas* even if the ban had been repealed thirty-two months later. The repeal would only be relevant to the amount of compensation. Is Justice Thomas right that the two situations are indistinguishable?

2. The setback issue is something of a challenge for the dissenters in *Lake Tahoe*. Setback requirements are ubiquitous, partly for aesthetic reasons but also because of concerns about fire. To require cities to condemn all of the strips of land in question would be absurd, but at first blush, that seems to be required by the dissent's rejection of the "total parcel" approach. Similarly, it would seem that even a one-day delay in granting a permit would seem to be a total taking of that one-day slice of development rights. The dissent avoids this result by a broad interpretation of the idea of background expectations, rendering setbacks, brief permit delays, and possibly even limited moratoria acceptable as implicit conditions on property ownership. Is this a more satisfactory approach than the "total parcel" rule? How different are these

"background expectations" from the "investment-backed expectations" that provide the underpinnings of *Penn Central*?

3. In the takings area, as in other fields of constitutional law, Justice Scalia has pushed for the use of hard-edged rules as opposed to more flexible standards. At present, it appears that in the area of takings at least, this effort has stalled. The "physical occupation" test has been limited to regulations granting the general public access to property otherwise dedicated to private use. The "total taking" test has been limited by the "parcel as a whole" rule. Even the supporters of *Lucas* seem to be willing to graft a fairly amorphous concept of background expectations onto the rule. Rather than a flat rule on retroactivity of one kind or another—either making it completely decisive or completely irrelevant that the regulation was adopted before the current owner acquired title—we now have a balancing test. In short, Justice Brennan's *Penn Central* approach has seemingly been established as the general rule with only a few narrow exceptions. Balancing, it would appear, is triumphant. Is such balancing a return to substantive due process, allowing the Court to make its own determination of the reasonableness of a government regulation? Or does it reflect a desirable openness to regulatory context?

4. In *Lingle v. Chevron USA, Inc.*, 544 U.S. 528 (2005), the Court described *Lucas* as establishing a narrow exception from *Penn Central*:

> Our precedents stake out two categories of regulatory action that generally will be deemed *per se* takings for Fifth Amendment purposes. First, where government requires an owner to suffer a permanent physical invasion of her property—however minor—it must provide just compensation. A second categorical rule applies to regulations that completely deprive an owner of "*all* economically beneficial us[e]" of her property. [citing *Lucas*] We held in *Lucas* that the government must pay just compensation for such "total regulatory takings," except to the extent that "background principles of nuisance and property law" independently restrict the owner's intended use of the property.

> Outside these two relatively narrow categories [and the category of easements required in compensation for grants of permits], regulatory takings challenges are governed by the standards set forth in [*Penn Central*.]

5. So far, we have been considering the private owner's property interest in land. But under certain circumstances, the public may have a well-defined property interest in private land (a background principle of state law in terms of *Lucas*). We consider such property interests in the next subsection.

2. THE PUBLIC TRUST DOCTRINE

In *Lucas*, Justice Scalia pointed to nuisance law as a categorical exemption from takings claims. This subsection focuses on another doctrine that limits the rights of property owners.

ILLINOIS CENTRAL RAILROAD CO. v. ILLINOIS

Supreme Court of the United States, 1892.
146 U.S. 387, 13 S.Ct. 110, 36 L.Ed. 1018.

JUSTICE FIELD delivered the opinion of the court.

[In 1869 the Illinois legislature granted title to certain submerged lands under Lake Michigan to the Illinois Central Railroad. When the bill was introduced, it had conveyed these lands to the City of Chicago, but somehow before final passage the grantee had been changed to the railroad. In 1873, the State repealed the 1869 Act making the grant. Illinois sued to quiet title.]

The question, therefore, to be considered is whether the legislature was competent to thus deprive the State of its ownership of the submerged lands in the harbor of Chicago, and of the consequent control of its waters; or, in other words, whether the railroad corporation can hold the lands and control the waters by the grant, against any future exercise of power over them by the State.

That the State holds the title to the lands under the navigable waters of Lake Michigan, within its limits, in the same manner that the State holds title to soils under tide water, by the common law, we have already shown, and that title necessarily carries with it control over the waters above them whenever the lands are subjected to use. But it is a title different in character from that which the State holds in lands intended for sale. It is different from the title which the United States holds in the public lands which are open to preemption and sale. It is a title held in trust for the people of the State that they may enjoy the navigation of the waters, carry on commerce over them, and have liberty of fishing therein freed from the obstruction or interference of private parties. The interest of the people in the navigation of the waters and in commerce over them may be improved in many instances by the erection of wharves, docks and piers therein, for which purpose the State may grant parcels of the submerged lands; and, so long as their disposition is made for such purpose, no valid objections can be made to the grants. * * * The trust devolving upon the State for the public, and which can only be discharged by the management and control of property in which the public has an interest, cannot be relinquished by a transfer of the property. The control of the State for the purposes of the trust can never be lost, except as to such parcels as are used in promoting the interests of the public therein, or can be disposed of without any substantial impairment of the public interest in the lands and waters remaining. * * * A grant of all the lands under the navigable waters of a State has never been adjudged to be within the legislative power; and any attempted grant of the kind would be held, if not absolutely void on its face, as subject to revocation. The State can no more abdicate its trust over property in which the whole people are interested, like navigable waters and soils under them, so as to leave them entirely under the use and control of private parties, except in the instance of parcels mentioned for the improvement of the navigation and use of the waters, or when parcels can be disposed of without impairment of the public interest in what remains, than it can abdicate its police powers in the administration of government and the preservation of the peace. In the administration of government the use of such powers may for a limited period be delegated to a municipality or other body, but there always remains with the State the right to revoke those powers and exercise them in a more direct manner, and one more conformable to its wishes. So with trusts connected with public property, or property of a special character, like lands under navigable waters, they cannot be placed entirely beyond the direction and control of the State.

The harbor of Chicago is of immense value to the people of the State of Illinois in the facilities it affords to its vast and constantly increasing commerce; and the idea that its legislature can deprive the State of control over its bed and waters and place the same in the hands of a private corporation created for a different purpose, one limited to transportation of passengers and freight between distant points and the city, is a proposition that cannot be defended.

* * * It is hardly conceivable that the legislature can divest the State of the control and management of this harbor and vest it absolutely in a private corporation.

* * * The position advanced by the railroad company in support of its claim to the ownership of the submerged lands and the right to the erection of wharves, piers and docks at its pleasure, or for its business in the harbor of Chicago, would place every harbor in the country at the mercy of a majority of the legislature of the State in which the harbor is situated.

NOTES

1. *Illinois Central* holds that certain lands are held by the state in trust for the people, and that legislative actions are void (or at least voidable) if a court finds they violate the trust. With reference to the federal government, the Supreme Court has adopted only half of this doctrine:

"All the public lands of the nation are held in trust for the people of the whole country." *United States v. Trinidad Coal & Coking Co.*, 137 U.S. 160, 11 S.Ct. 57, 34 L.Ed. 640 (1890). And it is not for the courts to say how that trust shall be administered. That is for Congress to determine. The courts cannot compel it to set aside the lands for settlement, or to suffer them to be used for agricultural or grazing purposes, nor interfere when, in the exercise of its discretion, Congress establishes a forest reserve for what it decides to be national and public purposes. In the same way and in the exercise of the same trust it may disestablish a reserve, and devote the property to some other national and public purpose. These are rights incident to proprietorship, to say nothing of the power of the United States as a sovereign over the property belonging to it.

Light v. United States, 220 U.S. 523, 537 (1911). (Note that Article IV, section 3 of the Constitution is a grant of plenary power to Congress to dispose of public lands.) *Light* implies that congressional actions that arguably violate the public trust are nevertheless immune from judicial scrutiny.

2. For a critique of *Illinois Central, see* Eric Pearson, Illinois Central *and the Public Trust Doctrine in State Law,* 15 VA. ENVTL. L. REV. 713 (1996). Pearson argues that the Court underestimated the amount of sovereign control which the state would retain even if title to the lake bed had actually passed to the railroad. He also argues that the state law was actually intended merely to authorize the railroad to operate a wharf, rather than permanently transferring title to property. For an exhaustive review of the history, *see* Joseph D. Kearney & Thomas W. Merrill, *The Origins of the American Public Trust Doctrine: What Really Happened in Illinois Central,* 71 U. CHI. L. REV. 799 (2004) (concluding that the railroad had legitimate reasons for seeking the legislation but probably used bribery to win).

MARKS v. WHITNEY

Supreme Court of California, In Bank, 1971.
6 Cal.3d 251, 98 Cal.Rptr. 790, 491 P.2d 374.

McComb, Justice.

This is a quiet title action to settle a boundary line dispute caused by overlapping and defective surveys and to enjoin defendants (herein "Whitney") from asserting any claim or right in or to the property of plaintiff Marks. The unique feature here is that a part of Marks' property is tidelands acquired under an 1874 patent issued pursuant to the Act of March 28, 1868; a small portion of these tidelands adjoins almost the entire shoreline of Whitney's upland property. Marks asserted complete ownership of the tidelands and the right to fill and develop them. Whitney opposed on the ground that this would cut off his rights as a littoral owner and as a member of the public in these tidelands and the navigable waters covering them. He requested a declaration in the decree that Marks' title was burdened with a public trust easement; also that it was burdened with certain prescriptive rights claimed by Whitney.* * *

Appearing as *amici curiae* on the appeal are: the Attorney General, on behalf of the State Lands Commission, the Bay Area Conservation and Development Commission (BCDC) and as chief law enforcement officer of the state;[20] Sierra Club; and Westbay Community Associates.

---

20. California holds the state-wide public easement in tidelands and owns the submerged lands abutting the tidelands. The Legislature has vested in the State Lands Commission "All jurisdiction and authority remaining in the State as to tidelands and submerged lands as to which grants have been or may be made" and has given the commission exclusive administration and control of such lands. (Pub.Resources Code, section 6301.) BCDC is charged with specific duties concerning dredging and filling in San Francisco Bay (Gov.Code, sections 66600–66610). The Attorney General is presently involved in litigation involving lands in San Francisco Bay which were patented under the Act of March 23, 1868 and other statutes. The Attorney General asks this court to declare the existence of the public easement and to recognize the right of Whitney as a member of the public and as a littoral owner to have the existence of the easement in these tidelands declared in this action.

Questions: First. *Are these tidelands subject to the public trust; if so, should the judgment so declare?*

Yes. Regardless of the issue of Whitney's standing to raise this issue the court may take judicial notice of public trust burdens in quieting title to tidelands. This matter is of great public importance, particularly in view of population pressures, demands for recreational property, and the increasing development of seashore and waterfront property. A present declaration that the title of Marks in these tidelands is burdened with a public easement may avoid needless future litigation.

[The court then traced the development of the public trust doctrine in California].

The public uses to which tidelands are subject are sufficiently flexible to encompass changing public needs. In administering the trust the state is not burdened with an outmoded classification favoring one mode of utilization over another. There is a growing public recognition that one of the most important public uses of the tidelands—a use encompassed within the tidelands trust—is the preservation of those lands in their natural state, so that they may serve as ecological units for scientific study, as open space, and as environments which provide food and habitat for birds and marine life, and which favorably affect the scenery and climate of the area. It is not necessary to here define precisely all the public uses which encumber tidelands.* * *

* * * It is within the province of the trier of fact to determine whether any particular use made or asserted by Whitney in or over these tidelands would constitute an infringement either upon the *jus privatum* of Marks or upon the *jus publicum* of the people. It is also within the province of the trier of fact to determine whether any particular use to which Marks wishes to devote his tidelands constitutes an unlawful infringement upon the *jus publicum* therein. It is a political question, within the wisdom and power of the Legislature, acting within the scope of its duties as trustee, to determine whether public trust uses should be modified or extinguished and to take the necessary steps to free them from such burden. In the absence of state or federal action the court may not bar members of the public from lawfully asserting or exercising public trust rights on this privately owned tidelands.

There is absolutely no merit in Marks' contention that as the owner of the *jus privatum* under this patent he may fill and develop his property, whether for navigational purposes or not; nor in his contention that his past and present plan for development of these tidelands as a marina have caused the extinguishment of the public easement. Reclamation with or without prior authorization from the state does not *ipso facto* terminate the public trust nor render the issue moot.* * *

Second: *Does Whitney have "standing" to request the court to recognize and declare the public trust easement on Marks' tidelands?*

Yes. The relief sought by Marks resulted in taking away from Whitney rights to which he is entitled as a member of the general public. It is immaterial that Marks asserted he was not seeking to enjoin the public. The decree as rendered does enjoin a member of the public.

Members of the public have been permitted *to bring* an action to enforce a public right to use a beach access route; *to bring* an action to quiet title to private and public easements in a public beach; and *to bring* an action to restrain improper filling of a bay and secure a general declaration of the rights of the people to the waterways and wildlife areas of the bay. Members of the public have been allowed *to defend* a quiet title action by asserting the right to use a public right of way through private property. They have been allowed to assert the public trust easement for hunting, fishing and navigation in privately owned tidelands *as a defense* in an action to enjoin such use, and to navigate on shallow navigable waters in small boats.

Whitney had standing to raise this issue. The court could have raised this issue on its own.

NOTES

1. What does the California Supreme Court mean when it says that the trial court could have raised this issue "on its own"? To what extent should judges act as "private attorneys general" and take an active role in litigation?

2. The court says that the "trier of fact" should determine whether some particular proposed use conflicts with the public trust. Should this "trier of fact" be a judge or jury, or should it be an administrative agency such as the California Coastal Commission? Not all courts have taken such a dynamic view of the public trust. *See Bott v. Natural Res. Comm'n,* 327 N.W.2d 838 (1982) (public trust does not protect access to recreational waters).

3. A later California Supreme Court case considered the problem of legislative termination of the trust. Overruling two prior decisions, the court held that an 1870 act conveying title to submerged and tidal lands did not extinguish the public trust over those lands. *City of Berkeley v. Superior Ct.,* 606 P.2d 362 (Cal.1980). The court's holding was based on a strong presumption against termination of the trust. The court held, however, that its decision would not apply retroactively to individuals who had already reclaimed their land.

4. What waters are within the scope of the public trust? In *Phillips Petroleum Co. v. Mississippi,* 484 U.S. 469 (1988), the Court ruled that the public trust extended to all tidal waters, not just navigable waters. The Court rejected the argument that this ruling would upset "settled expectations":

> We have recognized the importance of honoring reasonable expectations in property interests. But such expectations can only be of consequence where they are "reasonable" ones. Here, Mississippi appears to have consistently held that the public trust in lands under water includes "title to all the land under tidewater." Although the Mississippi Supreme Court acknowledged that this case may be the first where it faced the question

of the public trust interest in non-navigable tidelands, the clear and unequivocal statements in its earlier opinions should have been ample indication of the State's claim to tidelands. Moreover, cases which have discussed the State's public trust interest in these lands have described uses of them not related to navigability, such as bathing, swimming, recreation, fishing, and mineral development. These statements, too, should have made clear that the State's claims were not limited to lands under navigable waterways. Any contrary expectations cannot be considered reasonable.

The Court observed that even in states where tidelands are privately held, public rights to use tidelands for fishing, hunting, and swimming have long been recognized, and might be undermined by limiting the public trust to navigable waters.

5.   One of the most important modern applications of the public trust doctrine is *National Audubon Society v. Superior Court,* 658 P.2d 709 (1983). At issue was the diversion by the City of Los Angeles of the streams feeding Mono Lake, which threatened to dry up the lake entirely. Under California water law, Los Angeles was entitled to the water as the first appropriator. The California Supreme Court held, however, that this system of prior appropriation must be reconciled with public trust doctrine, and mandated reconsideration of the water allocation in light of its detrimental environmental effects.

For further developments under California water law, *see* Gregory S. Weber, *Articulating the Public Trust: Text, Near–Text, and Context,* 27 ARIZ. ST. L.J. 1155 (1995):

While the [California Water Resources Control] Board has sketched a virtually boundless reach for the trust [in terms of scope of application and potential remedies], it simultaneously has limited the doctrine's application pragmatically. Most prominently, the Board has demonstrated an unwillingness to kowtow to the mere invocation of the trust. Rather, the Board has demonstrated that not all trust-protected resources are equal. Thus, it has prioritized the protection to be given among trust resources in a given ecosystem. * * * In addition, the Board has placed specific evidentiary burdens on persons who would invoke the trust-doctrine. At the very least, such a party bears an initial burden of coming forward with specific evidence to demonstrate harm to trust uses and to sketch a less-harmful alternative accommodation of trust and consumptive uses. * * *

In addition to these practical limitations, the Board has made some accommodations with the needs to divert for consumptive uses. For example, while the Board has not attempted a full accounting of costs and benefits of various trust balances, it has acknowledged that it is inappropriate to dedicate huge amounts of water for little environmental gain. Conversely, if only small amounts of water are needed to bring relatively large environmental gains, the Board likely will require dedication of such flows. Indeed, the Board has been careful not to force dedications of even small flows if such are unlikely to bring much ecological benefit. * * * Finally, the Board has recognized that the quality of water available to a diverter is as legitimate a concern as the quantity available.

Id. at 1229–31.

6. What is the effect of the public trust doctrine on takings claims under *Lucas* or the *Penn Central* test? The next excerpt argues that *Lucas* has had an unexpected effect on taking law by creating the concept of categorical exemptions such as public trust.

MICHAEL C. BLUMM AND LUCAS RITCHIE, *LUCAS'S* UNLIKELY LEGACY: THE RISE OF BACKGROUND PRINCIPLES AS CATEGORICAL TAKINGS DEFENSES[21]

29 Harv. Envtl. L. Rev. 321, 321–366 (2005).

The Supreme Court's decision in *Lucas v. South Carolina Coastal Council* is one of the most celebrated cases of the Rehnquist Court's property jurisprudence. Justice Scalia's opinion for a 6–3 Court declared that a regulation depriving a landowner of all economic value was a categorical constitutional taking of private property for public use requiring government compensation regardless of the public purpose served by the regulation. This new categorical rule was welcomed by private property advocates but denounced by defenders of government regulations.

But now, over a dozen years later, the legacy of the *Lucas* decision seems neither as revolutionary as its advocates hoped, nor as dire as its detractors feared. In fact, the *Lucas* legacy represents one of the starkest recent examples of the law of unintended consequences. For rather than heralding in a new era of landowner compensation or government deregulation, *Lucas* instead spawned a surprising rise of categorical defenses to takings claims in which governments can defeat compensation suits without case-specific inquiries into the economic effects and public purposes of regulations. *Lucas* accomplished this by establishing the prerequisite that a claimant must first demonstrate that its property interest was unrestrained by prior restrictions. The decision suggested that those restrictions had to be imposed by common law courts interpreting state nuisance and property law, but *Lucas* has not been interpreted by either the lower courts or the Supreme Court so narrowly.

Adding to the unanticipated consequences of the *Lucas* opinion was the fact that the categorical takings rule concerning economic wipeouts it established turned out to apply only to a very narrow class of takings cases, while the categorical defenses authorized by the decision are quite expansive in scope. In effect, the *Lucas* decision fundamentally revised all takings analysis by making the nature of the landowner's property rights a threshold issue in every takings case. Thus, although *Lucas* has proved to revolutionize takings jurisprudence, it did so in ways that hardly were anticipated, and which have proved to be much more protective of government defendants than anyone imagined at the time of the decision.* * *

---

21. © 2005, Harvard Environmental Law Review. Reprinted by permission.

In 2002, the Ninth Circuit decided, in *Esplanade Properties, LLC v. City of Seattle*,[22] that a Washington landowner had no compensable interest in a proposal to construct structures in the navigable tidelands of Elliot Bay, an area regularly used by the public for various recreational activities, because the purpose "was inconsistent with the public trust that [the state] is obligated to protect."[23] Similarly, the Wisconsin Supreme Court recently upheld the denial of a state fill permit to complete the last phase of a marina on the bed and in the waters of Lake Superior, concluding that the public trust doctrine prevented the fill.[24] The developers were left with riparian rights of use and access only, which are "qualified, subordinate, and subject to the paramount interest of the state and the paramount rights of the public in navigable waters."[25] And in *Wilson v. Massachusetts*,[26] Massachusetts Court of Appeals ruled that the claimants' coastal landholdings were "impressed with a public trust," leaving them only limited rights to their beachfront property.[27] * * *

Closely related to the public trust doctrine are state common law natural use restrictions. The "natural use" doctrine maintains that landowners have no inherent property right to transform lands from their existing state. The leading case justifying application of natural use limits as part of the background principles of property law is *Just v. Marinette County*.[28] In *Just*, the Wisconsin Supreme Court rejected a takings challenge to the denial of a county permit required to fill a wetland, stating:

> An owner of land has no absolute and unlimited right to change the essential natural character of his land so as to use it for a purpose for which it was unsuited in its natural state and which injures the rights of others. * * * It seems to us that filling a swamp not otherwise commercially usable is not in and of itself an existing use, which is prevented, but rather is the preparation for some future use which is not indigenous to a swamp.[29]

Once mislabeled as a "phantom doctrine," *Just*'s natural use rationale was reaffirmed and expanded in scope by the Wisconsin Supreme Court fifteen years later in a case involving county-imposed wetland conservancy restrictions that precluded the claimant from developing ninety percent of its land.[30] The court ruled that the natural use principle applies regardless of "whether the regulated land is a wetland within a shoreland area, or land within a primary environmental corridor, or an isolated swamp."[31]

---

22. 307 F.3d 978 (9th Cir. 2002).

23. *Id.* at 987.

24. *See* R.W. Docks & Slips v. Wisconsin, 628 N.W.2d 781 (Wis. 2001).

25. *Id.* at 788.

26. 583 N.E.2d 894 (Mass. App. Ct. 1992), *aff'd*, 597 N.E.2d 43 (Mass. 1992).

27. Id. at 901.

28. 201 N.W.2d at 768–70.

29. 201 N.W.2d at 768–70.

30. See M & I Marshall & Isley Bank v. Town of Somers, 414 N.W.2d 824, 825 (Wis. 1987).

31. *Id.* at 830. The court elaborated:

Other state courts have explicitly relied on *Just* to clarify that compensation is not due for restrictions placed on land that, in its natural and existing condition, is unsuitable for development. Jurisdictions approving the *Just* rationale include Florida, New Hampshire, South Dakota, South Carolina, Georgia, and New Jersey.

The natural use doctrine, at least as it concerns wetlands, seems to be well supported by English common law. * * * In fact, England's common law consistently upheld natural use-like limitations by promoting the "continuation of existing patterns of wetland ownership and use." Because American courts frequently look to English common law as authority for their decisions, government defendants may rely on relevant English common law analogues when making natural use arguments in state courts.* * *

At least two post-*Lucas* courts have endorsed state ownership of wildlife as a defense to takings challenges. In *New York v. Sour Mountain Realty, Inc.*,[32] New York's intermediate appellate court addressed a takings claim based on a county court injunction seeking removal of a landowner's fence, which precluded threatened snakes from important forage habitat. The court affirmed the injunction and denied claimant's takings challenge, determining that:

> The State, through the exercise of its police power, is safeguarding the welfare of an indigenous species that has been found to be threatened with extinction. . . . The State's interest in protecting its wild animals is a venerable principle that can properly serve as a legitimate basis for the exercise of its police power.[33]

The California Court of Appeals has also employed wildlife protections as a background principle to reject a takings challenge concerning the denial of a timber harvest permit in order to prevent threats to endangered species, including the marbled murrelet.[34] Importantly, the Court of Appeals observed that "wildlife regulation of some sort has been historically a part of the preexisting law of property."[35]

These courts' observations that state wildlife protection can be a background principle of property law appear to be a reasonable application of *Lucas*. The full extent of the usefulness of this doctrine, however, will be determined as more courts encounter the issue.* * *

[A] parcel of land which consists of continuing wetland which is partly within and partly outside a shoreland area should be treated as if the entire wetland was located within a shoreland area. There would be little value to the wetland within the shoreland if the part of the wetland outside the shoreland area was allowed to be altered. Id. at 831.

32. 714 N.Y.S.2d 78 (2000).

33. *Id.* at 84.

34. *See Sierra Club v. Dep't of Forestry & Fire Prot.*, 26 Cal. Rptr. 2d 338, 347 (Cal. Ct. App. 1993). The California Supreme Court denied review of this case without opinion on March 18, 1994, thereby upholding the appellate court's decision. However, in denying review, the Supreme Court also determined, pursuant to California Court Rules 976, 977, and 979, that the lower court decision would not be officially published (even though it was previously published). Consequently, the *Sierra Club* decision cannot be cited in documents submitted to California courts.

35. *Id.*

All of these observations lead to the conclusion that the background principles defense authorized in *Lucas* is alive and well and will continue to function as a useful tool for government defendants to defeat takings claims. Although the Supreme Court has not endorsed all of the many categorical defenses ushered in by the background principles inquiry, its ability to constrict background principles grounded in state law is quite limited, and the Court has explicitly approved federal defenses grounded on both common law and statutes.

NOTES

1.   Some historical support for a wildlife exception can be found in John F. Hart, *Fish, Dams, and James Madison: Eighteenth–Century Species Protection and the Original Understanding of the Takings Clause,* 63 MD. L. REV. 287 (2004) (discussing "fish passage" laws that seriously restricted water mills). Hart also provides an interesting discussion of Madison's views:

> James Madison raised the prospect of mankind's "extirpating every useless production of nature." He felt it was:
>
> > Not probable that nature, after covering the earth with so great a variety of animal & vegetable inhabitants, and establishing among them so systematic a proportion, could permit one favorite offspring, by destroying every other, to render vain all her wise arrangements and contrivances.
> >
> > Destruction "not only of individuals, but of entire species," Madison insisted, was "forbidden ... by the principles and laws which operate in various department's of her [that is, nature's] economy."

Id. at 291.

2.   Takings law is, of course, an interesting and significant part of constitutional doctrine in its own right. But it also provides a gauge of how our society draws the line between legitimate individual interests and the needs of others. *Lucas* provides some protection for core property interests. At the same time, the concept of category exemptions recognizes areas of overriding public interest. In the intermediate zone, the *Penn Central* test calls for a more individualized determination of legitimate investment-backed expectations, one that is sensitive to the reasonable foreseeability of future regulation when investments are made. No doubt, over coming decades, we will see shifts in these zones along with society's understanding of the legitimate limits of regulations.

3.   As with most areas of environmental law, climate change raises novel questions relating to the takings clause, as discussed in the following excerpt.

MEG CALDWELL AND CRAIG HOLT SEGALL, NO DAY AT THE BEACH: SEA LEVEL RISE, ECOSYSTEM LOSS, AND PUBLIC ACCESS ALONG THE CALIFORNIA COAST

34 ECOLOGY L.Q. 533 (2007).36

The sea is rising. All along the hundreds of miles of the California coast, global warming will cause higher water, more powerful storms, and increased coastal erosion. The California Coastal Commission and its predecessor regional commissions have worked to protect the state's coastal resources since the Commission's creation by voter initiative in 1972 and formalization in the California Coastal Act of 1976. Climate change-induced sea level rise presents the Commission—and all those who use and value the state's coastal resources—with a stark new set of challenges.

As sea level rises, pressure to armor the coast will grow. The bluffs and cliffs of the California coast may appear stable, but they are, in many places, riven with faults, joints, and fractures, and are often composed of unstable rock. Battering winter storms and high tides have and will continue to cause bluff collapse and the loss of structures built upon bluffs. Property owners, if allowed to do so, will attempt to forestall the inevitable with seawalls, rock revetments, and other barriers to the sea. But these walls, though temporarily freezing the coast in place, will have significant social and ecological costs. Beaches below the walls may be eroded away, or the thin ribbon of sand remaining will be blocked from the public by massive shoreline protection structures. Where estuarine marshes, which provide significant nursery habitat for many marine species, are threatened by sea level rise, coastal armoring will prevent marsh migration, leading to the eventual loss of ecosystem function. All along the coast, the dire effects of climate change may be amplified by the effects of shoreline armoring. * * *

How would rolling easements work in practice in California? Consider the scenario of a housing development slated to be built just above the beach. Below the low terrace where the housing is planned is a small strip of beach. As the sea rises and El Niño storms hammer the beach, the shoreline begins to erode towards the uplands. Without a rolling easement in place, the property owners would likely seek to erect some form of armoring, such as a seawall, revetment, or gunnite application to a bluff or cliff—perhaps covering the remaining beach with rock and concrete and certainly preventing the natural migration and survival of the beach. Similar scenarios apply to structures built slightly inland on marshlands and estuaries; there, storm waves will not often threaten but gradual sea level rise will cause the salt marsh to gradually migrate towards the buildings. If the buildings sit behind a bulkhead, the marsh will ultimately be unable to migrate and will drown beneath the rising waters. In the alternate case, where the state holds a rolling easement, the property owners do not own the right to prevent the shore from moving. Instead, they may use their property as normal until the sea reaches it. At this critical point, they must either move their structures or cede them to the ocean or advancing marshlands. Erosion will likely occur relatively slowly, over several decades. Thus this eventual end date will likely not appreciably reduce property values. It will, however, ensure that the coast will remain public and healthy at the reasonable cost of discouraging unwise overdevelopment of areas vulnerable to near-term erosion.

This general easement model does not rely upon any particular legal device: rather, it describes the ecological effects of allowing the shore to move rather than impeding that movement with an armoring device. The appropriate legal device to reach this ecological and social goal will vary, as discussed above, based upon the age of the structure in question and the potential ecological and social costs associated with allowing versus preventing armoring. Below, we discuss the array of tools that the Commission and the state can rely upon to allow the shoreline to migrate when appropriate. These tools are underlain by the central concept of the public trust doctrine, which both motivates and requires the state to protect its coastal resources that are under attack from the combined effect of sea level rise and development that impedes the natural and expected shore migration process. * * *

Could California impose a blanket rolling easement along its coastline without running into takings prohibitions and without being stymied by political opposition? The answer is probably yes, as a constitutional matter, but with serious practical caveats. Few judges, if any, will initially be comfortable with allowing structures built under one understanding of the law to yield to the sea, even if the public trust doctrine would appear to require this result. Because takings lawsuits are most likely if political processes break down, implementing easements in a savvy way is vital. Developing a mixed strategy, including the purchase of rolling easements from existing landowners in appropriate circumstances, will reduce political pressure and is the more equitable course. The cost of rolling easements for existing structures in sensitive areas has the potential to be relatively low if they are implemented within the context of a larger policy. As part of a general strategy * * * to deflect development away from highly sensitive areas, the imposition of rolling easements in undeveloped areas and requirements to mitigate permitted armoring can provide the lynch pin for sea level rise management.

James G. Titus of the EPA provides valuable analysis of the takings problems at issue.[37] Under the Supreme Court's decision in *Lucas v. South Carolina Coastal Council*, a taking will occur if a regulation "denies all economically beneficial or productive use of land." Even then, regulations that actualize title restrictions arising from "background principles of the State's law of property and nuisance" do not effect a taking. Under

---

37. [James G. Titus, *Rising Seas, Coastal Erosion, and the Takings Clause: How to Save Wetlands and Beaches Without Hurting Property Owners*, 57 Md. L. Rev. 1279, 1313 (1998).]

both prongs of analysis, rolling easements—even if imposed by the state without compensation—would probably not be a taking. As Titus argues, the common law of erosion and the public trust jointly act to "diminish the rights of coastal lowland owners, compared with the rights of noncoastal dryland owners." The public trust doctrine is a background principle of the common law and so would obviate a *Lucas* taking as applied in this case. The easement, simply put, has always been there: it is not an imposition on the property owner but part of the nature of his or her property. This is precisely the reasoning of a U.S. District Court in Texas, upholding that state's rolling easement policy in *Severance v. Patterson*.[38] As Judge Hoyt wrote in that recent decision, issued in May 2007, "the public's rolling beach easement was established long before" the property owner took possession. The extent of the easement depends on the behavior of the ocean, not the caprice of government: "The natural movement of the beach's boundaries may result in a temporary (or long-term) expansion of the physical area covered by the easement, but it may also result in a contraction of the covered area. This natural movement does not work a constitutional wrong."

But even if a case did not involve this background principle, a state's direct imposition of a rolling easement would likely not cause the total loss of economically beneficial uses of land required for a *Lucas* taking. This is because rolling easements impose a future loss that will not occur for decades. Discounted for present value, a rolling easement will not significantly diminish property values. The change in value would be truly minimal for undeveloped land and would likely still be minor for most developed land, except those properties in almost immediate danger of loss.

NOTES

1.   Under the "background principles" approach, would the constitutionality of rolling easements depend on the specific state's previous case law regarding coastal property rights? Could Congress create a uniform federal rule?

2.   The Supreme Court granted cert. in *Stop the Beach Renourishment, Inc. v. Florida Department of Environmental Protection*, No. 08–1151. In that case, the Florida Supreme Court rejected shoreline property owners' takings challenge to a state law authorizing the state to nourish beachfront areas with sand, and to assert public ownership of the created land area. The Florida court concluded that the law did not constitute a compensable taking, because it did not fundamentally interfere with the shoreline owners' common law rights to use and obtain access to the ocean. The grant of cert. may mean a renewed interest by the Justices in takings law, after a hiatus of several years. It remains to be seen what implications the Court's opinion will have for the "rolling easement" theory propounded by Caldwell and Segall.

---

38.   *Severance v. Patterson*, No. H–06–2467, 2007 WL 1296218 (S.D. Tex. May 2, 2007).

CHAPTER 5

JUDICIAL REVIEW AND ADMINISTRATIVE PROCESS

∎ ∎ ∎

A. UNDERSTANDING THE ADMINISTRATIVE STATE

In this chapter, we will be concerned primarily with the role of the courts in reviewing environmental actions by administrative agencies. Because environmental statutes are implemented by administrative agencies, environmental regulation is inseparable from administrative law. As a collection of legal doctrines governing administrative agencies, traditional administrative law is concerned with *constraining* agency action to ensure that agencies act within the bounds of their statutory mandates. The questions that arise in administrative law include: Is it constitutional for Congress to delegate this power to the agency? Does the statute authorize the agency to do what it did? Did the agency follow the appropriate procedures? Does the agency's decision—its actual policy choice—have enough factual support? One might approach nearly every environmental case with these questions in mind.

As you will see throughout the casebook, environmental litigation arising under federal environmental statutes often takes the form of challenges by a regulated firm, industry associations, environmental groups, or states, arguing that a federal agency has erred in executing the power delegated to it by Congress. The alleged agency errors can be procedural or substantive, as suggested above. To understand how such challenges work, and to grasp the importance of them to the development of environmental law, it is helpful to be familiar with the institutional context in which environmental law and policy are produced.

When Congress passes statutes, it typically enunciates general goals and then delegates the task of implementing those goals to administrative agencies. Delegation makes sense for a variety of reasons. Most notably, Congress could not possibly make every detailed decision regarding the implementation of every regulatory statute itself. Managing such detailed decision-making would consume considerable time and resources, and members of Congress have other priorities to attend to (including policy-making tasks and constituency casework, but also including fundraising in order to pursue re-election). Institutional competence is another justification for delegating the details of implementation to an administrative agency. These agencies are staffed with experts, whereas Congress is full of generalist lawmakers, who are in most cases relatively untrained and inexperienced in more than one or two regulatory areas. On this reasoning, an agency like the EPA, which was specifically created for the purpose of administering environmental statutes, and which is staffed by trained scientists, economists and lawyers, is best situated to translate legislative policy choices into operational rules.

Though agencies are technically empowered merely to "implement" legislative policy, all but the most committed formalists would agree that agencies to some extent "make law". Agency rules, once promulgated, have the force of law. Many agencies are authorized to issue administrative enforcement orders and to assess significant monetary penalties against violators of statutory or regulatory requirements, which are enforceable in civil court. Agencies also make policy through the resolution of specific matters in formal, trial-like administrative adjudications presided over by administrative law judges (ALJs). (While these judges are not Article III judges with lifetime tenure, they share many of the same powers, including the authority to issue binding orders.) Agencies also have other, less formal methods to affect the behavior of private actors. Agencies may, for instance, issue interpretations of their own regulations through guidance documents, opinion letters and the like, which in practice guide the conduct of regulated entities. In other words, agency action has real consequences for the regulated community.

The concern is that agency staff are not directly accountable to the electorate. Top-level officials of Executive agencies are political appointees who serve at the pleasure of the President. The bulk of the agency is made up of "career staff" protected by civil service rules and likely to outlast presidential administrations as they come and go. When Congress delegates substantial decision-making power to administrative agencies, agencies may use that power in ways that Congress did not desire, because the staff or the political appointees have their own vision of public policy. Thus, delegated power creates what economists call "slack" that agencies can exploit. Slack arises in any relationship where a principal delegates power to an agent. As a consequence, the principal is burdened with the requirement of monitoring the agent to ensure it exercises its power consistently with the principal's preferences. Complicating the picture further, in this case the "principal" is not the current Congress but the Congress that passed the statute, whereas the actual oversight of the agency belongs to the current Congress and President.

How can the public discipline these agencies if it is unable to turn agency staff out of office? This is where judicial review comes in. Courts play a role in ensuring that agency action remains within lawful bounds. The purpose of judicial review is to ensure that administrative agencies, like the EPA and the DOI, comply with their statutory mandates, and do not abuse the discretion conferred upon them by the politically accountable legislative branch. In performing this role, courts must, of course, interpret the relevant statutes to discern legislative intent. Thus, statutory interpretation, with all its attendant complexity, plays a major role in environmental law, as it does in administrative law generally. This affords courts considerable power to affect agency behavior and determine policy outcomes.

As we shall see at numerous points throughout this casebook, the process of statutory construction is hardly a straightforward one. The student who has not previously studied the interpretation of federal statutes might benefit from the overview provided in, Philip P. Frickey, Elizabeth Garrett, and William N. Eskridge, Jr., LEGISLATION AND STATUTORY INTERPRETATION (2nd ed. 2006). For more specific discussions of statutory interpretation in the context of environmental law, *see* Symposium, *Statutory Interpretation and Environmental Law*, 5 N.Y.U. ENVTL. L.J. 292 (1996); Bradford Mank, *Is a Textualist Approach to Statutory Interpretation Pro–Environmentalist?: Why Pragmatic Agency Decisionmaking Is Better than Judicial Literalism*, 53 WASH. & LEE L. REV. 1231 (1996). One important point of contention has been whether courts should consider the legislative history of the statute (committee reports, hearings, and floor debate).

Historically, legal debates about statutory interpretation have centered on the goals judges should pursue when interpreting statutes (e.g., discerning legislative intent or interpreting statutes "dynamically" in light of context) and the tools they ought to use in attaining those goals (e.g., legislative history, canons of construction, dictionaries). Different judges pursue different goals and use different tools when construing statutes. Making matters more complicated, sometimes the same judge will resort to different methodologies in different cases.

Courts frequently defer to the construction of the statute adopted by the agency that administers the statute. In cases involving environmental statutes, courts may defer because of the technical nature of the statutes and the complexity of the subjects they regulate. Courts may take the view that expert agencies are better positioned to make technical policy decisions regarding the implementation of these laws or that Congress has delegated this authority to agencies. However, courts do not always defer, especially in cases involving politically contentious and economically costly policy decisions, or where the agency appears to be interpreting the outer limits of its own legal authority. In all cases, the final decision on statutory construction is made by the court after an independent consideration of the statute's meaning.

Reviewing courts are not the only institution playing an oversight role over agencies. Federal agencies must answer to congressional committees (in both the House and Senate) charged with overseeing their fidelity to legislative mandates. These committees can make life miserable for agency staff by, for example, ordering audits by the Government Accountability Office, requiring staff to appear at hearings on Capitol Hill, and cutting agency funding through the appropriations process. Agencies generally pay very close attention to the preferences of their oversight committees because of the powerful role of committees in the legislative process; in a very real way, agency budgets, and the scope of discretion agencies are given to make policy, depend on keeping these legislators happy. A Congress that is displeased with an agency might go so far as to amend the governing environmental statute in ways that narrow the agency's discretionary authority, or make other programmatic or procedural changes that agency staff would prefer to avoid.

In addition to judicial and congressional oversight, the President also oversees the performance of his executive agencies. Political appointees are expected to implement legislation consistent with the President's policy preferences. While agencies must comply with their legislative mandates and may not ignore or act contrary to them at the behest of the President, there is often substantial enough room to maneuver within broad legislative language to enable agencies to implement the law according to the President's priorities. To do this, an agency might simply shift discretionary funding to one program from another, exercise its enforcement discretion to focus on some compliance problems and not others, interpret vague statutory language in a new way, or merely exercise discretion to adopt a new policy regarding an existing problem. Without violating any statutory mandate, in other words, an agency can change course very significantly at the behest of a new administration.

Federal agencies must, therefore, answer to Congress, the Executive and the judiciary. Moreover, when Congress and the White House are engaged in a power struggle, it can create perilous conditions for agency staff. For example, when the Reagan administration sought to curtail dramatically the EPA's enforcement capacity in the 1980s under Administrator Anne Gorsuch, the Democratic Congress at the time countered by writing increasingly specific action-forcing environmental legislation. Agencies can thus find themselves caught in the cross-fire when the executive and legislative branches are controlled by opposing parties. In addition to dealing with the three branches, agencies must respond to interest group pressure and media attention. This is the complex institutional environment in which agencies like the EPA find themselves, and in which environmental law is made.

To appreciate fully the context in which environmental law takes shape, moreover, one must recognize that environmental statutes have a life cycle, beginning with the legislative process (when the bill is shaped by various committees and then enacted into law), through delegation of authority to an agency, agency implementation, legal challenge, judicial review, remand, and so on. At various points, Congress might amend the statute, which will require the agency to adjust accordingly. A new administration might sweep into office, bringing new priorities with it. Courts might begin to review agency action with greater or lesser scrutiny, requiring the agency to build better records supporting their decisions, or freeing the agency to exercise greater discretion. In the background, congressional appropriations for particular agencies, and specific programs, waxes and wanes. The policy environment is dynamic and continuous.

The implementation of statutes is itself far more complicated than is reflected in most appellate cases. For example, the first step in environmental law implementation typically requires the EPA to write a regulation setting a standard. But this is just the beginning of the implementation process. The standard must be further elaborated or explained in guidance documents and interpretive rulings. Applying general rules and fluid concepts to regulated industries and individual actors is an uncertain business. Nevertheless despite the uncertainty, people go on working out resolutions to problems, interpreting regulations, settling lawsuits, etc. Often, it is hard to know what the law is—or at least there is a healthy debate about it. Environmental law implementation necessarily takes place in a context of uncertainty and often involves substantial compromise. Indeed, a great deal of day-to-day environmental law is interpreted and applied in relatively low visibility settings: when the agency inspector visits a firm and chooses whether to write up regulatory violations; when a lawyer representing a client phones a state agency official seeking an interpretation of an ambiguous agency rule for which no guidance has been issued; when citizen suits challenging agency action result in settlements that, while never producing a published legal opinion, effectively change the agency's approach on the ground. The law thus takes shape in the interplay of parties and government officials making daily decisions, many of which occur out of the public eye. As a result, law is more fluid than we might be led to believe when we focus almost exclusively on the pronouncements of appellate judges. And the line between law-making (a job for the legislature) and law implementation (a job for the agency) is less clear in practice than it is in theory.

Although courts are thus only part of the dynamic institutional setting in which environmental law is made, they nevertheless play a crucial role in overseeing the implementation of environmental statutes. Yet, in order to enlist courts in overseeing agency decisions, litigants must first satisfy the test for gaining access to judicial review, known as "standing." Meeting this test is crucial for environmental litigants who seek access to courts to vindicate what are sometimes non-economic and indirect interests in environmental values which, contrary to the interests of many plaintiffs in other settings, are shared by many people. Over time, the judiciary has adopted relatively liberalized standing principles, which has enabled environmental groups and private citizens to access the courts more easily. Congress has also helped these plaintiffs satisfy standing requirements by inserting citizen-suit provisions into many environmental statutes. As a result, citizen suits have served as a vital mechanism for enforcing environmental law, against both recalcitrant polluters and reluctant or careless agencies. The cases below trace the history of standing law, and illustrate how it has expanded and contracted over time.

B. STANDING

In suits challenging actions by government agencies, often the first issue raised is whether the plaintiff has the right to file the suit at all. Determining whether the particular party before the court may bring the claim is called the question of "standing." It is quite possible to imagine a system in which any individual could bring suit to halt any government action that violated the law. American law, however, has not evolved along this line. Instead, a plaintiff must have some specific connection with the controversy. In environmental cases, plaintiffs are frequently not themselves the object of the agency's regulatory efforts. Instead, they wish to complain because the outcome of the agency's decision-making process adversely affects the environment in which everyone has an interest. Citizen suits are thought to vindicate the public interest in lawful government action, rather than vindicating a private interest unique to the litigant. Still, courts have traditionally resisted the notion that anyone, no matter how remote from the challenged action, has standing to bring a claim. Standing doctrine stems in part from the constitutional requirement in Article III that federal courts hear only "cases or controversies," and in part from prudential principles developed by courts to restrict access to judicial review.

1. INJURY–IN–FACT

Courts have interpreted the Article III limitation on standing as requiring litigants to be situated specially in order to file a claim. Traditionally, private suits against government were limited to vindicating "legal rights," meaning that the litigant had to allege injury to a "legally protected interest" granted by statute or the common law. The litigant could not, under this test, seek to vindicate an undifferentiated interest in seeing that government agencies enforce environmental laws generally. The purpose of standing law is to ensure that courts are not flooded with suits brought by people who are in fact not harmed by agency action, and to ensure that the litigants before the court are those best able to vigorously present the case. In practice, however, the restrictive "legal interest" test was criticized as keeping many meritorious claims from going forward, and it gradually eroded. Although the Sierra Club lost the case below, this landmark case represents a step toward more liberal standing law. The Court makes clear that non-economic, environmental injuries, when properly pleaded, can satisfy the injury-in-fact test.

SIERRA CLUB v. MORTON

Supreme Court of the United States, 1972.
405 U.S. 727, 92 S.Ct. 1361, 31 L.Ed.2d 636.

[The Forest Service approved a plan by Walt Disney Enterprises, Inc., to build a $35 million resort in the Mineral King Valley, "an area of great natural beauty nestled in the Sierra Nevada Mountains." Construction of the huge resort-complex was opposed by the Sierra Club on the ground that the Forest Service had violated several federal statutes. The Sierra Club filed suit to enjoin approval of the Disney plan. It sued as a membership corporation with "a special interest in the conservation and the sound maintenance of the national parks, game refuges and forests of the country." As the Court noted, there was "no allegation in the complaint that members of the Sierra Club would be affected by the actions of [the respondents] other than the fact that the actions are personally displeasing or distasteful to them." The lower court had concluded: "We do not believe such club concern without a showing of more direct interest can constitute standing in the legal sense sufficient to challenge the exercise of responsibilities on behalf of all the citizens by two cabinet level officials of the government acting under congressional and constitutional authority."]

JUSTICE STEWART delivered the opinion of the Court.

The first question presented is whether the Sierra Club has alleged facts that entitle it to obtain judicial review of the challenged action. Whether a party has a sufficient stake in an otherwise justiciable controversy to obtain judicial resolution of that controversy is what has traditionally been referred to as the question of standing to sue. Where the party does not rely on any specific statute authorizing invocation of the judicial process, the question of standing depends upon whether the party has alleged such a "personal stake in the outcome of the controversy," as to ensure that "the dispute sought to be adjudicated will be presented in an adversary context and in a form historically viewed as capable of judicial resolution." Where, however, Congress has authorized public officials to perform certain functions according to law, and has provided by statute for judicial review of those actions under certain circumstances, the inquiry as to standing must begin with a determination of whether the statute in question authorizes review at the behest of the plaintiff.[1]

The Sierra Club relies upon § 10 of the Administrative Procedure Act (APA) which provides:

A person suffering legal wrong because of agency action, or adversely affected or aggrieved by agency action within the meaning of a relevant statute, is entitled to judicial review thereof.

Early decisions under this statute interpreted the language as adopting the various formulations of "legal interest" and "legal wrong" then prevailing as constitutional requirements of standing. But, in *Association of Data Processing Service Organizations, Inc. v. Camp,* 397 U.S. 150, 90 S.Ct. 827, 25 L.Ed.2d 184, and *Barlow v. Collins,* 397 U.S. 159, 90 S.Ct. 832, 25 L.Ed.2d 192, decided the same day, we held more broadly that persons had standing to obtain judicial review of federal agency action

---

1. Congress may not confer jurisdiction on Art. III federal courts to render advisory opinions, or to entertain "friendly" suits, because suits of this character are inconsistent with the judicial function under Art. III. But where a dispute is otherwise justiciable, the question whether the litigant is a "proper party to request an adjudication of a particular issue," is one within the power of Congress to determine.

under § 10 of the APA where they had alleged that the challenged action had caused them "injury in fact," and where the alleged injury was to an interest "arguably within the zone of interests to be protected or regulated" by the statutes that the agencies were claimed to have violated.[2]

In *Data Processing,* the injury claimed by the petitioners consisted of harm to their competitive position in the computer-servicing market through a ruling by the Comptroller of the Currency that national banks might perform data-processing services for their customers. In *Barlow,* the petitioners were tenant farmers who claimed that certain regulations of the Secretary of Agriculture adversely affected their economic position vis-a-vis their landlords. These palpable economic injuries have long been recognized as sufficient to lay the basis for standing, with or without a specific statutory provision for judicial review. Thus, neither *Data Processing* nor *Barlow* addressed itself to the question, which has arisen with increasing frequency in federal courts in recent years, as to what must be alleged by persons who claim injury of a noneconomic nature to interests that are widely shared. That question is presented in this case.

The injury alleged by the Sierra Club will be incurred entirely by reason of the change in the uses to which Mineral King will be put, and the attendant change in the aesthetics and ecology of the area. Thus, in referring to the road to be built through Sequoia National Park, the complaint alleged that the development "would destroy or otherwise adversely affect the scenery, natural and historic objects and wildlife of the park and would impair the enjoyment of the park for future generations." We do not question that this type of harm may amount to an "injury in fact" sufficient to lay the basis for standing under § 10 of the APA. Aesthetic and environmental well-being, like economic well-being, are important ingredients of the quality of life in our society, and the fact that particular environmental interests are shared by the many rather than the few does not make them less deserving of legal protection through the judicial process. But the "injury in fact" test requires more than an injury to a cognizable interest. It requires that the party seeking review be himself among the injured.

The impact of the proposed changes in the environment of Mineral King will not fall indiscriminately upon every citizen. The alleged injury will be felt directly only by those who use Mineral King and Sequoia National Park, and for whom the aesthetic and recreational values of the area will be lessened by the highway and ski resort. The Sierra Club failed to allege that it or its members would be affected in any of their activities or pastimes by the Disney development. Nowhere in the pleadings or affidavits did the Club state that its members use Mineral King for any purpose, much less that they use it in any way that would be significantly affected by the proposed actions of the respondents.[3]

---

2.   In deciding this case we do not reach any questions concerning the meaning of the "zone of interests" test or its possible application to the facts here presented.

3.   * * * In an amici curiae brief filed in this Court by the Wilderness Society and others, it is asserted that the Sierra Club has conducted regular camping trips into the Mineral King area,

The Club apparently regarded any allegations of individualized injury as superfluous, on the theory that this was a "public" action involving questions as to the use of natural resources, and that the Club's long-standing concern with and expertise in such matters were sufficient to give it standing as a "representative of the public." This theory reflects a misunderstanding of our cases involving so-called "public actions" in the area of administrative law. * * *

The trend of cases arising under the APA and other statutes authorizing judicial review of federal agency action has been toward recognizing that injuries other than economic harm are sufficient to bring a person within the meaning of the statutory language, and toward discarding the notion that an injury that is widely shared is *ipso facto* not an injury sufficient to provide the basis for judicial review. We noted this development with approval in *Data Processing,* in saying that the interest alleged to have been injured "may reflect 'aesthetic, conversational, and recreational' as well as economic values." But broadening the categories of injury that may be alleged in support of standing is a different matter from abandoning the requirement that the party seeking review must himself have suffered an injury.

Some courts have indicated a willingness to take this latter step by conferring standing upon organizations that have demonstrated "an organizational interest in the problem" of environmental or consumer protection. It is clear that an organization whose members are injured may represent those members in a proceeding for judicial review. But a mere "interest in a problem," no matter how longstanding the interest and no matter how qualified the organization is in evaluating the problem, is not sufficient by itself to render the organization "adversely affected" or "aggrieved" within the meaning of the APA. The Sierra Club is a large and long-established organization, with a historic commitment to the cause of protecting our Nation's natural heritage from man's depredations. But if a "special interest" in this subject were enough to entitle the Sierra Club to commence this litigation, there would appear to be no objective basis upon which to disallow a suit by any other bona fide "special interest" organization however small or short-lived. And if any group with a bona fide "special interest" could initiate such litigation, it is difficult to perceive why any individual citizen with the same bona fide special interest would not also be entitled to do so.

The requirement that a party seeking review must allege facts showing that he is himself adversely affected does not insulate executive action from judicial review, nor does it prevent any public interests from being protected through the judicial process.[4] It does serve as at least a rough

---

and that various members of the Club have used and continue to use the area for recreational purposes. These allegations were not contained in the pleadings, nor were they brought to the attention of the Court of Appeals. Moreover, the Sierra Club in its reply brief specifically declines to rely on its individualized interest, as a basis for standing.

Our decision does not, of course, bar the Sierra Club from seeking in the District Court to amend its complaint by a motion under Rule 15, Federal Rules of Civil Procedure.

4. In its reply brief, after noting the fact that it might have chosen to assert individualized injury to itself or to its members as a basis for standing, the Sierra Club states:

attempt to put the decision as to whether review will be sought in the hands of those who have a direct stake in the outcome. That goal would be undermined were we to construe the APA to authorize judicial review at the behest of organizations or individuals who seek to do no more than vindicate their own value preferences through the judicial process. The principle that the Sierra Club would have us establish in this case would do just that.

JUSTICE DOUGLAS, dissenting.

The critical question of "standing" would be simplified and also put neatly in focus if we fashioned a federal rule that allowed environmental issues to be litigated before federal agencies or federal courts in the name of the inanimate object about to be despoiled, defaced, or invaded by roads and bulldozers and where injury is the subject of public outrage. Contemporary public concern for protecting nature's ecological equilibrium should lead to the conferral of standing upon environmental objects to sue for their own preservation. *See* [Christopher D.] Stone, *Should Trees Have Standing? Toward Legal Rights for Natural Objects*, 45 S. CAL. L. REV. 450 (1972). This suit would therefore be more properly labeled as *Mineral King v. Morton*.

Inanimate objects are sometimes parties in litigation. A ship has a legal personality, a fiction found useful for maritime purposes. The corporation sole—a creature of ecclesiastical law—is an acceptable adversary and large fortunes ride on its cases. The ordinary corporation is a "person" for purposes of the adjudicatory processes, whether it represents proprietary, spiritual, aesthetic, or charitable causes.

So it should be as respects valleys, alpine meadows, rivers, lakes, estuaries, beaches, ridges, groves of trees, swampland, or even air that feels the destructive pressures of modern technology and modern life. The river, for example, is the living symbol of all the life it sustains or nourishes—fish, aquatic insects, water ouzels, otter, fisher, deer, elk, bear, and all other animals, including man, who are dependent on it or who enjoy it for its sight, its sound, or its life. The river as plaintiff speaks for the ecological unit of life that is part of it. Those people who have a meaningful relation to that body of water—whether it be a fisherman, a canoeist, a zoologist, or a logger—must be able to speak for the values which the river represents and which are threatened with destruction.
* * *

Mineral King is doubtless like other wonders of the Sierra Nevada such as Tuolumne Meadows and the John Muir Trail. Those who hike it,

---

The Government seeks to create a 'heads I win, tails you lose' situation in which either the courthouse door is barred for lack of assertion of a private, unique injury or a preliminary injunction is denied on the ground that the litigant has advanced private injury which does not warrant an injunction adverse to a competing public interest. Counsel have shaped their case to avoid this trap.

The short answer to this contention is that the "trap" does not exist. The test of injury in fact goes only to the question of standing to obtain judicial review. Once this standing is established, the party may assert the interests of the general public in support of his claims for equitable relief.

fish it, hunt it, camp in it, frequent it, or visit it merely to sit in solitude and wonderment are legitimate spokesmen for it, whether they may be a few or many. Those who have that intimate relation with the inanimate object about to be injured, polluted, or otherwise despoiled are its legitimate spokesmen.

JUSTICE BLACKMUN, dissenting.

* * * I would permit an imaginative expansion of our traditional concepts of standing in order to enable an organization such as the Sierra Club, possessed, as it is, of pertinent, bona fide, and well-recognized attributes and purposes in the area of the environment, to litigate environmental issues. This incursion upon tradition need not be very extensive. Certainly, it should be no cause for alarm. It is no more progressive than was the decision in *Data Processing* itself. It need only recognize the interest of one who has a provable, sincere, dedicated, and established status. We need not fear that Pandora's box will be opened or that there will be no limit to the number of those who desire to participate in environmental litigation. The courts will exercise appropriate restraints just as they have exercised them in the past. Who would have suspected 20 years ago that the concepts of standing enunciated in *Data Processing* and *Barlow* would be the measure for today?

NOTES

1. The trend toward liberalizing standing law is a key component in what Professor Richard Stewart has called the "interest representation" theory of administrative law, in which agencies are seen not as detached from politics, but as sites of interest-group conflict. *See* Richard B. Stewart, *The Reformation of American Administrative Law*, 88 HARV. L. REV. 1669 (1975). According to this theory, courts ensure that agencies are accountable by requiring them to conduct a "surrogate political process," made possible by broad participation rights for interest groups and liberal access to judicial review. *Id.* at 1760–62. Wouldn't it be better, however, to insulate agencies from the pressures of interest groups in order to let agencies exercise their expertise? Why expose agencies to the costs and delays associated with public participation in the rulemaking process, and then to the costs and delays associated with litigation? Are there better ways to make agencies accountable?

2. The case below represents what many regard as the high water mark of liberal standing principles.

UNITED STATES v. STUDENTS CHALLENGING REGULATORY AGENCY PROCEDURES (SCRAP I)

Supreme Court of the United States, 1973.
412 U.S. 669, 93 S.Ct. 2405, 37 L.Ed.2d 254.

JUSTICE STEWART delivered the opinion of the Court.

[The plaintiffs filed suit to challenge the Interstate Commerce Commission's refusal to suspend a railroad rate increase. The railroads were seeking an across-the-board increase to augment revenue. The plaintiffs contended that the increase would discourage recycling of various goods by magnifying existing distortions in the rate structure.]

The appellants challenge the appellees' standing to sue, arguing that the allegations in the pleadings as to standing were vague, unsubstantiated, and insufficient under our recent decision in *Sierra Club v. Morton*; the appellees respond that unlike the petitioner in *Sierra Club*, their pleadings sufficiently alleged that they were "adversely affected" or "aggrieved" within the meaning of § 10 of the administrative procedure act (APA). They point specifically to the allegations that their members used the forests, streams, mountains, and other resources in the Washington metropolitan area for camping, hiking, fishing, and sightseeing, and that this use was disturbed by the adverse environmental impact caused by the nonuse of recyclable goods brought about by a rate increase on those commodities. The district court found these allegations sufficient to withstand a motion to dismiss. We agree. * * *

Unlike the specific and geographically limited federal action of which the petitioner complained in *Sierra Club,* the challenged agency action in this case is applicable to substantially all of the Nation's railroads, and thus allegedly has an adverse environmental impact on all the natural resources of the country. Rather than a limited group of persons who used a picturesque valley in California, all persons who utilize the scenic resources of the country, and indeed all who breathe its air, could claim harm similar to that alleged by the environmental groups here. But we have already made it clear that standing is not to be denied simply because many people suffer the same injury. Indeed some of the cases on which we relied in *Sierra Club* demonstrated the patent fact that persons across the Nation could be adversely affected by major governmental actions. * * * To deny standing to persons who are in fact injured simply because many others are also injured, would mean that the most injurious and widespread Government actions could be questioned by nobody. We cannot accept that conclusion.

But the injury alleged here is also very different from that at issue in *Sierra Club* because here the alleged injury to the environment is far less direct and perceptible. The petitioner there complained about the construction of a specific project that would directly affect the Mineral King Valley. Here, the Court was asked to follow a far more attenuated line of causation to the eventual injury of which the appellees complained—a general rate increase would allegedly cause increased use of non-recyclable commodities as compared to recyclable goods, thus resulting in the need to use more natural resources to produce such goods, some of which resources might be taken from the Washington area, and resulting in more refuse that might be discarded in national parks in the Washington area. The railroads protest that the appellees could never prove that a general increase in rates would have this effect, and they contend that these allegations were a ploy to avoid the need to show some injury in fact.

Of course, pleadings must be something more than an ingenious academic exercise in the conceivable. A plaintiff must allege that he has been or will in fact be perceptibly harmed by the challenged agency action, not that he can imagine circumstances in which he could be affected by the agency's action. And it is equally clear that the allegations must be true and capable of proof at trial. But we deal here simply with the pleadings in which the appellees alleged a specific and perceptible harm that distinguished them from other citizens who had not used the natural resources that were claimed to be affected.[5] If, as the railroads now assert, these allegations were in fact untrue, then the appellants should have moved for summary judgment on the standing issue and demonstrated to the District Court that the allegations were sham and raised no genuine issue of fact. We cannot say on these pleadings that the appellees could not prove their allegations which, if proved, would place them squarely among those persons injured in fact by the Commission's action, and entitled under the clear import of *Sierra Club* to seek review. The District Court was correct in denying the appellants' motion to dismiss the complaint for failure to allege sufficient standing to bring this lawsuit.

NOTES

1. One commentator has suggested that the *SCRAP* Court should have focused more carefully on the nature of the statutory claim before it:

> The issue in *SCRAP* was whether under NEPA an EIS had to be prepared before the rate increase could be implemented. The standing question was whether plaintiffs were entitled to insist that NEPA be followed. * * * A perfectly plausible—and I believe the best—reading of NEPA is that anyone who can make a colorable claim that the proposed actions may possibly affect her should have standing, even if the effect is remote or speculative and even if the person's sense of what constitutes injury is somewhat idiosyncratic. This should be so because of the nature of the remedy plaintiff is seeking. She wishes to compel an investigation and the preparation of a report that spells out in detail what she has claimed will be the likely environmental consequences of the proposed federal action. To require a greater showing by plaintiff of actual effect would be to require, as a condition of bringing suit, that plaintiff show much of what she claims should be investigated.

---

5. The Government urges us to limit standing to those who have been "significantly" affected by agency action. But, even if we could begin to define what such a test would mean, we think it fundamentally misconceived. "Injury in fact" reflects the statutory requirement that a person be "adversely affected" or "aggrieved," and it serves to distinguish a person with a direct stake in the outcome of a litigation—even though small—from a person with a mere interest in the problem. We have allowed important interests to be vindicated by plaintiffs with no more at stake in the outcome of an action than a fraction of a vote, a $5 fine and costs, and a $1.50 poll tax.

* * * While these cases were not dealing specifically with § 10 of the APA, we see no reason to adopt a more restrictive interpretation of "adversely affected" or "aggrieved." As Professor Davis has put it: "The basic idea that comes out in numerous cases is that an identifiable trifle is enough for standing to fight out a question of principle; the trifle is the basis for standing and the principle supplies the motivation." Kenneth C. Davis, *Standing: Taxpayers and Others*, 35 U. CHI. L. REV. 601, 613 (1968).

William A. Fletcher, *The Structure of Standing*, 98 YALE L. J. 221, 259 (1988). The Supreme Court, however, later referred to *SCRAP* as "[p]robably the most attenuated injury" conferring standing, and added that the *SCRAP* decision "surely went to the very outer limit of the law." Whitmore v. Arkansas, 495 U.S. 149, 159 (1990). But the dissent in *Massachusetts v. EPA*, casebook p. 403, nearly twenty years after *Whitmore*, accuses the Court of resurrecting *SCRAP*.

2. Beginning in 1970 with the Clean Air Act, Congress included citizen suit provisions in most of the major environmental statutes in order to allow ordinary citizens to bring suits to enforce these laws. *See, e.g.*, section 304 of the Clean Air Act, section 505 of the Clean Water Act, section 18 of the Toxic Substances Control Act (TSCA), section 7002 of the Resource Conservation and Recovery Act (RCRA), section 326 of the Emergency Planning and Community Right–To–Know Act, section 11(g) of the Endangered Species Act, and section 310 of CERCLA. An exception is the Federal Insecticide, Fungicide, and Rodenticide Act (FIFRA), which does not authorize citizen suits.

The citizen suit provisions of the environmental laws generally authorize "any person" to commence an action against "any person" alleged to be in violation of the laws. They require plaintiffs to give notice, usually 60 days, to the alleged violator and to federal and state authorities prior to filing suit. (However, the Clean Water Act allows suits alleging violation of New Source Performance Standards or toxic effluent standards to be brought immediately after notice, as does RCRA for violations of subtitle C.) Most of the statutes specify that if federal or state authorities are diligently prosecuting compliance actions, citizen suits are barred, though citizens are authorized to intervene in federal enforcement actions.

Among the persons against whom citizen suits may be brought are federal officials who fail to perform mandatory regulatory duties. For example, the Clean Water Act authorizes citizen suits against the EPA "where there is alleged a failure of the Administrator to perform any act or duty * * * which is not discretionary." This type of provision, found in most of the statutes that establish regulatory programs, has been important in ensuring that the EPA issues regulations to implement the statutes.

Citizen suits have made it much easier for environmental organizations to play a key role in enforcing the nation's environmental laws. In the 1980s, when there was significant decline in federal enforcement of the environmental laws under the Reagan administration, more citizen suits were brought (especially by several national environmental organizations) to fill the void. These focused particularly on enforcement of the Clean Water Act because it was easy for plaintiffs to prove violations. Point-source dischargers were required to file discharge-monitoring reports, which were available to the public and could serve as prima facie evidence of noncompliance with permits. In addition, remedies available in Clean Water Act suits included not only injunctions against further violations but also the assessment of civil penalties payable to the government.

However, citizen suit provisions still required the plaintiffs to demonstrate standing. In the 1990s, the Supreme Court began to restrict standing law considerably. The case below represents the Court's move toward a narrower interpretation of what is necessary to demonstrate injury in fact.

LUJAN v. DEFENDERS OF WILDLIFE

Supreme Court of the United States, 1992.
504 U.S. 555, 112 S.Ct. 2130, 119 L.Ed.2d 351.

JUSTICE SCALIA delivered the opinion of the Court with respect to Parts I, II, III–A, and IV, and an opinion with respect to Part III–B in which THE CHIEF JUSTICE, JUSTICE WHITE, and JUSTICE THOMAS join.

[As discussed in Chapter 3, the Endangered Species Act seeks to protect plant and animal species against human threats to their continuing existence. Endangered or threatened species are identified by a list compiled by the Secretary of the Interior. Section 7(a)(2) of the Act provides that each federal agency must, in consultation with the Secretary of Interior, ensure that "any action authorized, funded, or carried out by such agency * * * is not likely to jeopardize the continued existence of any endangered species or threatened species or result in the destruction or adverse modification of the habitat of such species." By regulation, the Secretary determined that § 7 applies only to species and habitats within the United States or on the High Seas. Thus, the Director of USAID was not obligated to consult with the Secretary of Interior over whether the proposed overseas projects, to be funded partly by USAID, would be likely to jeopardize listed species. The statute authorizes "citizen suits" to challenge violations of the Act. The plaintiffs obtained an injunction requiring the Secretary to promulgate a revised regulation applying § 7 extraterritorially.]

II

While the Constitution of the United States divides all power conferred upon the Federal Government into "legislative Powers," Art. I, § 1, "[t]he executive Power," Art. II, § 1, and "[t]he judicial Power," Art. III, § 1, it does not attempt to define those terms. To be sure, it limits the jurisdiction of federal courts to "Cases" and "Controversies," but an executive inquiry can bear the name "case" (the Hoffa case) and a legislative dispute can bear the name "controversy" (the Smoot–Hawley controversy). Obviously, then, the Constitution's central mechanism of separation of powers depends largely upon common understanding of what activities are appropriate to legislatures, to executives, and to courts. In The Federalist No. 48, Madison expressed the view that "[i]t is not infrequently a question of real nicety in legislative bodies whether the operation of a particular measure will, or will not, extend beyond the legislative sphere," whereas "the executive power [is] restrained within a narrower compass and * * * more simple in its nature," and "the judiciary [is] described by landmarks still less uncertain." One of those landmarks, setting apart the "Cases" and "Controversies" that are of the justiciable sort referred to in Article III "serv[ing] to identify those disputes which are appropriately resolved through the judicial process"—

is the doctrine of standing. Though some of its elements express merely prudential considerations that are part of judicial self-government, the core component of standing is an essential and unchanging part of the case-or-controversy requirement of Article III.

Over the years, our cases have established that the irreducible constitutional minimum of standing contains three elements: First, the plaintiff must have suffered an "injury in fact"—an invasion of a legally-protected interest which is (a) concrete and particularized, and (b) "actual or imminent, not 'conjectural' or 'hypothetical.'" Second, there must be a causal connection between the injury and the conduct complained of—the injury has to be "fairly * * * trace[able] to the challenged action of the defendant, and not * * * th[e] result [of] the independent action of some third party not before the court." Third, it must be "likely," as opposed to merely "speculative," that the injury will be "redressed by a favorable decision."

III

holding

We think the Court of Appeals failed to apply the foregoing principles in denying the Secretary's motion for summary judgment. Respondents had not made the requisite demonstration of (at least) injury and redressability.

A

Respondents' claim to injury is that the lack of consultation with respect to certain funded activities abroad "increase[s] the rate of extinction of endangered and threatened species." * * * To survive the Secretary's summary judgment motion, respondents had to submit affidavits or other evidence showing, through specific facts, not only that listed species were in fact being threatened by funded activities abroad, but also that one or more of respondents' members would thereby be "directly" affected apart from their " 'special interest' in th[e] subject."

[The affidavits] alleged that two members, Kelly and Skilbred, had visited two project areas in the past and intended to return in the future to observe endangered species.

no evid of injury

[The affidavits] plainly contain no facts * * * showing how damage to the species will produce "imminent" injury to Mss. Kelly and Skilbred. That the women "had visited" the areas of the projects before the projects commenced proves nothing. As we have said in a related context, "[p]ast exposure to illegal conduct does not in itself show a present case or controversy regarding injunctive relief * * * if unaccompanied by any continuing, present adverse effects." And the affiants' profession of an "inten[t]" to return to the places they had visited before—where they will presumably, this time, be deprived of the opportunity to observe animals of the endangered species—is simply not enough. * * *

Besides relying upon the Kelly and Skilbred affidavits, respondents propose a series of novel standing theories. The first, inelegantly styled "ecosystem nexus," proposes that any person who uses *any part* of a "contiguous ecosystem" adversely affected by a funded activity has standing even if the activity is located a great distance away. This approach, as the Court of Appeals correctly observed, is inconsistent with our opinion in *National Wildlife Federation,* which held that a plaintiff claiming injury from environmental damage must use the area affected by the challenged activity and not an area roughly "in the vicinity" of it. It makes no difference that the general-purpose section of the ESA states that the Act was intended in part "to provide a means whereby the ecosystems upon which endangered species and threatened species depend may be conserved." To say that the Act protects ecosystems is not to say that the Act creates (if it were possible) rights of action in persons who have not been injured in fact, that is, persons who use portions of an ecosystem not perceptibly affected by the unlawful action in question.

Respondents' other theories are called, alas, the "animal nexus" approach, whereby anyone who has an interest in studying or seeing the endangered animals anywhere on the globe has standing; and the "vocational nexus" approach, under which anyone with a professional interest in such animals can sue. Under these theories, anyone who goes to see Asian elephants in the Bronx Zoo, and anyone who is a keeper of Asian elephants in the Bronx Zoo, has standing to sue because the Director of AID did not consult with the Secretary regarding the AID-funded project in Sri Lanka. This is beyond all reason. Standing is not "an ingenious academic exercise in the conceivable," but as we have said, requires, at the summary judgment stage, a factual showing of perceptible harm. It is clear that the person who observes or works with a particular animal threatened by a federal decision is facing perceptible harm, since the very subject of his interest will no longer exist. It is even plausible—though it goes to the outermost limit of plausibility—to think that a person who observes or works with animals of a particular species in the very area of the world where that species is threatened by a federal decision is facing such harm, since some animals that might have been the subject of his interest will no longer exist. It goes beyond the limit, however, and into pure speculation and fantasy, to say that anyone who observes or works with an endangered species, anywhere in the world, is appreciably harmed by a single project affecting some portion of that species with which he has no more specific connection.

B

The most obvious problem in the present case is redressability. Since the agencies funding the projects were not parties to the case, the District Court could accord relief only against the Secretary: He could be ordered to revise his regulation to require consultation for foreign projects. But this would not remedy respondents' alleged injury unless the funding agencies were bound by the Secretary's regulation, which is very much an open question. [Although the Secretary of Interior thought his regulation binding upon other federal agencies, the Solicitor General opined that it was not, and the other agencies agreed with him. Since these other agencies were not parties to the lawsuit, no relief could be entered against them, according to Justice Scalia.]

IV

The Court of Appeals found that respondents had standing for an additional reason: because they had suffered a "procedural injury." The so-called "citizen-suit" provision of the ESA provides, in pertinent part, that "any person may commence a civil suit on his own behalf (A) to enjoin any person, including the United States and any other governmental instrumentality or agency * * * who is alleged to be in violation of any provision of this chapter." The court held that, because § 7(a)(2) requires interagency consultation, the citizen-suit provision creates a "procedural righ[t]" to consultation in all "persons"—so that *anyone* can file suit in federal court to challenge the Secretary's (or presumably any other official's) failure to follow the assertedly correct consultative procedure, notwithstanding their inability to allege any discrete injury flowing from that failure. To understand the remarkable nature of this holding one must be clear about what it does *not* rest upon: This is not a case where plaintiffs are seeking to enforce a procedural requirement the disregard of which could impair a separate concrete interest of theirs (*e.g.,* the procedural requirement for a hearing prior to denial of their license application, or the procedural requirement for an environmental impact statement before a federal facility is constructed next door to them). Nor is it simply a case where concrete injury has been suffered by many persons, as in mass fraud or mass tort situations. Nor, finally, is it the unusual case in which Congress has created a concrete private interest in the outcome of a suit against a private party for the government's benefit, by providing a cash bounty for the victorious plaintiff. Rather, the court held that the injury-in-fact requirement had been satisfied by congressional conferral upon *all* persons of an abstract, self-contained, noninstrumental "right" to have the Executive observe the procedures required by law. We reject this view.

* * * "The province of the court," as Chief Justice Marshall said in *Marbury v. Madison,* "is, solely, to decide on the rights of individuals." Vindicating the *public* interest (including the public interest in government observance of the Constitution and laws) is the function of Congress and the Chief Executive. The question presented here is whether the public interest in proper administration of the laws (specifically, in agencies' observance of a particular, statutorily prescribed procedure) can be converted into an individual right by a statute that denominates it as such, and that permits all citizens (or, for that matter, a subclass of citizens who suffer no distinctive concrete harm) to sue. If the concrete injury requirement has the separation-of-powers significance we have always said, the answer must be obvious: To permit Congress to convert the undifferentiated public interest in executive officers' compliance with the law into an "individual right" vindicable in the courts is to permit

Congress to transfer from the President to the courts the Chief Executive's most important constitutional duty, to "take Care that the Laws be faithfully executed," Art. II, § 3. It would enable the courts, with the permission of Congress, "to assume a position of authority over the governmental acts of another and co-equal department," and to become " 'virtually continuing monitors of the wisdom and soundness of Executive action.' " We have always rejected that vision of our role. * * *

JUSTICE BLACKMUN, with whom JUSTICE O'CONNOR joins, dissenting.

I part company with the Court in this case in two respects. First, I believe that respondents have raised genuine issues of fact—sufficient to survive summary judgment—both as to injury and as to redressability. Second, I question the Court's breadth of language in rejecting standing for "procedural" injuries. I fear the Court seeks to impose fresh limitations on the constitutional authority of Congress to allow citizen suits in the federal courts for injuries deemed "procedural" in nature. I dissent. * * *

I think a reasonable finder of fact could conclude from the information in the affidavits and deposition testimony that either Kelly or Skilbred will soon return to the project sites, thereby satisfying the "actual or imminent" injury standard. The Court dismisses Kelly's and Skilbred's general statements that they intended to revisit the project sites as "simply not enough." But those statements did not stand alone. A reasonable finder of fact could conclude, based not only upon their statements of intent to return, but upon their past visits to the project sites, as well as their professional backgrounds, that it was likely that Kelly and Skilbred would make a return trip to the project areas. Contrary to the Court's contention that Kelly's and Skilbred's past visits "prove nothing," the fact of their past visits could demonstrate to a reasonable factfinder that Kelly and Skilbred have the requisite resources and personal interest in the preservation of the species endangered by the Aswan and Mahaweli projects to make good on their intention to return again. * * * Similarly, Kelly's and Skilbred's professional backgrounds in wildlife preservation, also make it likely—at least far more likely than for the average citizen—that they would choose to visit these areas of the world where species are vanishing.

By requiring a "description of concrete plans" or "specification of *when* the some day [for a return visit] will be," the Court, in my view, demands what is likely an empty formality. No substantial barriers prevent Kelly or Skilbred from simply purchasing plane tickets to return to the Aswan and Mahaweli projects. This case differs from other cases in which the imminence of harm turned largely on the affirmative actions of third parties beyond a plaintiff's control. * * *

I fear the Court's demand for detailed descriptions of future conduct will do little to weed out those who are genuinely harmed from those who are not. More likely, it will resurrect a code-pleading formalism in federal court summary judgment practice, as federal courts, newly doubting their jurisdiction, will demand more and more particularized showings of future harm. * * *

I have difficulty imagining this Court applying its rigid principles of geographic formalism anywhere outside the context of environmental claims. As I understand it, environmental plaintiffs are under no special constitutional standing disabilities. Like other plaintiffs, they need show only that the action they challenge has injured them, without necessarily showing they happened to be physically near the location of the alleged wrong. * * *

A plurality of the Court suggests that respondents have not demonstrated redressability: a likelihood that a court ruling in their favor would remedy their injury. * * * The plurality identifies two obstacles. The first is that the "action agencies" (*e. g.*, AID) cannot be required to undertake consultation with petitioner Secretary, because they are not directly bound as parties to the suit and are otherwise not indirectly bound by being subject to petitioner Secretary's regulation. Petitioner, however, officially and publicly has taken the position that his regulations regarding consultation under § 7 of the Act are binding on action agencies. And he has previously taken the same position in this very litigation, having stated in his answer to the complaint that petitioner "admits the Fish and Wildlife Service (FWS) was designated the lead agency for the formulation of regulations concerning section 7 of the [Endangered Species Act]." I cannot agree with the plurality that the Secretary (or the Solicitor General) is now free, for the convenience of this appeal, to disavow his prior public and litigation positions. More generally, I cannot agree that the Government is free to play "Three–Card Monte" with its description of agencies' authority to defeat standing against the agency given the lead in administering a statutory scheme.

* * * I am not as willing as the plurality is to assume that agencies at least will not try to follow the law. Moreover, I wonder if the plurality has not overlooked the extensive involvement from the inception of this litigation by the Department of State and AID. Under principles of collateral estoppel, these agencies are precluded from subsequently relitigating the issues decided in this suit. * * *

The second redressability obstacle relied on by the plurality is that "the [action] agencies generally supply only a fraction of the funding for a foreign project." What this Court might "generally" take to be true does not eliminate the existence of a genuine issue of fact to withstand summary judgment. Even if the action agencies supply only a fraction of the funding for a particular foreign project, it remains at least a question for the finder of fact whether threatened withdrawal of that fraction would affect foreign government conduct sufficiently to avoid harm to listed species.

The plurality states that "AID, for example, has provided less than 10% of the funding for the Mahaweli project." The plurality neglects to mention that this "fraction" amounts to $170 million, not so paltry a sum for a country of only 16 million people with a gross national product of less than $6 billion in 1986 when respondents filed the complaint in this action. * * *

* * * As an initial matter, the relevant inquiry is not, as the plurality suggests, what will happen if AID or other agencies stop funding projects, but what will happen if AID or other agencies comply with the consultation requirement for projects abroad. Respondents filed suit to require consultation, not a termination of funding. Respondents have raised at least a genuine issue of fact that the projects harm endangered species and that the actions of AID and other United States agencies can mitigate that harm. * * *

II

The Court concludes that any "procedural injury" suffered by respondents is insufficient to confer standing. It rejects the view that the "injury-in-fact requirement [is] satisfied by congressional conferral upon *all* persons of an abstract, self-contained, noninstrumental 'right' to have the Executive observe the procedures required by law." Whatever the Court might mean with that very broad language, it cannot be saying that "procedural injuries" *as a class* are necessarily insufficient for purposes of Article III standing.

Most governmental conduct can be classified as "procedural." Many injuries caused by governmental conduct, therefore, are categorizable at some level of generality as "procedural" injuries. Yet, these injuries are not categorically beyond the pale of redress by the federal courts. When the Government, for example, "procedurally" issues a pollution permit, those affected by the permittee's pollutants are not without standing to sue. Only later cases will tell just what the Court means by its intimation that "procedural" injuries are not constitutionally cognizable injuries. In the meantime, I have the greatest of sympathy for the courts across the country that will struggle to understand the Court's standardless exposition of this concept today.

The Court expresses concern that allowing judicial enforcement of "agencies' observance of a particular, statutorily prescribed procedure" would "transfer from the President to the courts the Chief Executive's most important constitutional duty, to 'take Care that the Laws be faithfully executed,' Art. II, § 3." In fact, the principal effect of foreclosing judicial enforcement of such procedures is to transfer power into the hands of the Executive at the expense—not of the courts—but of Congress, from which that power originates and emanates.

Under the Court's anachronistically formal view of the separation of powers, Congress legislates pure, substantive mandates and has no business structuring the procedural manner in which the Executive implements these mandates. To be sure, in the ordinary course, Congress does legislate in black-and-white terms of affirmative commands or negative prohibitions on the conduct of officers of the Executive Branch. In complex regulatory areas, however, Congress often legislates, as it were, in procedural shades of gray. That is, it sets forth substantive policy goals and provides for their attainment by requiring Executive Branch officials to follow certain procedures, for example, in the form of reporting, consultation, and certification requirements. * * *

The consultation requirement of § 7 of the Endangered Species Act is [an] action-forcing statute. Consultation is designed as an integral check on federal agency action, ensuring that such action does not go forward without full consideration of its effects on listed species. Once consultation is initiated, the Secretary is under a duty to provide to the action agency "a written statement setting forth the Secretary's opinion, and a summary of the information on which the opinion is based, detailing how the agency action affects the species or its critical habitat." 16 U. S. C. § 1536(b)(3)(A). The Secretary is also obligated to suggest "reasonable and prudent alternatives" to prevent jeopardy to listed species. *Ibid.* The action agency must undertake as well its own "biological assessment for the purpose of identifying any endangered species or threatened species" likely to be affected by agency action. § 1536(c)(1). After the initiation of consultation, the action agency "shall not make any irreversible or irretrievable commitment of resources" which would foreclose the "formulation or implementation of any reasonable and prudent alternative measures" to avoid jeopardizing listed species. § 1536(d). These action-forcing procedures are "designed to protect some threatened concrete interest," of persons who observe and work with endangered or threatened species. That is why I am mystified by the Court's unsupported conclusion that "this is not a case where plaintiffs are seeking to enforce a procedural requirement the disregard of which could impair a separate concrete interest of theirs."

* * * The Court never has questioned Congress' authority to impose such procedural constraints on Executive power. Just as Congress does not violate separation of powers by structuring the procedural manner in which the Executive shall carry out the laws, surely the federal courts do not violate separation of powers when, at the very instruction and command of Congress, they enforce these procedures.

To prevent Congress from conferring standing for "procedural injuries" is another way of saying that Congress may not delegate to the courts authority deemed "executive" in nature. * * * Here Congress seeks not to delegate "executive" power but only to strengthen the procedures it has legislatively mandated. * * *

It is to be hoped that over time the Court will acknowledge that some classes of procedural duties are so enmeshed with the prevention of a substantive, concrete harm that an individual plaintiff may be able to demonstrate a sufficient likelihood of injury just through the breach of that procedural duty. For example, in the context of the NEPA requirement of environmental-impact statements, this Court has acknowledged "it is now well settled that NEPA itself does not mandate particular

results [and] simply prescribes the necessary process," but *"these procedures are almost certain to affect the agency's substantive decision."
Robertson v. Methow Valley Citizens Council*, 490 U.S. at 350 (emphasis
added). * * * This acknowledgment of an inextricable link between procedural and substantive harm does not reflect improper appellate factfind-
ing. It reflects nothing more than the proper deference owed to the
judgment of a coordinate branch—Congress—that certain procedures are
directly tied to protection against a substantive harm.

Notes

1. Can plaintiffs satisfy the majority in *Defenders* with careful drafting
of the affidavits? *See* James McElfish, *Drafting Standing Affidavits After
Defenders: In the Court's Own Words*, 23 Envtl. L. Rep. (Envtl. L. Inst.) 10026
(1993). In retrospect, *Defenders* may be seen as a very early stage of a general
move toward requiring more factual specificity in complaints.

2. Environmental organizations frequently use member plaintiffs strategically to file lawsuits, without carefully developing evidence about how those
plaintiffs actually use the resource in question. Stricter standards for alleging
injury may have a salutary effect on the ability of environmental organizations to convince the court that the agency action complained of causes real
harm to real people. *See* Ann E. Carlson, *Standing for the Environment*, 45
UCLA L. Rev. 931 (1998). For an illustration of why plaintiffs must take care
in establishing standing, *see* Sierra Club v. EPA, 292 F.3d 895, 902 (D.C. Cir.
2002), where a Sierra Club complaint disputing an EPA waste management
regulation was dismissed when the Sierra Club failed to establish injury
adequately, with the Court particularly (and disapprovingly) noting that the
only member affidavit attesting to actual contamination from a particular
plant was recycled from another, unrelated case, and had to do with an
entirely different contaminant.

3. Satisfying the "fairly traceable" requirement may be more difficult
when the causation is behavioral rather than physical. In *Florida Audubon
Society v. Bentsen*, 94 F.3d 658 (D.C. Cir. 1996) (en banc), the plaintiffs
claimed that an environmental impact statement was required on the effects
of a tax credit for a fuel additive. The plaintiffs alleged that the tax credit
would increase corn and sugar production, resulting in increased agricultural
cultivation and accompanying environmental harms in regions that border
wildlife areas used by the plaintiffs. The court found this line of reasoning far
too speculative.

4. In *Defenders*, a plurality would have denied standing because the
plaintiff's injury was not redressable. The issue of redressability sometimes
overlaps with concerns about mootness in cases involving statutory violations
that appear, at the time of the court hearing, to be "wholly past." In
Gwaltney of Smithfield, Ltd. v. Chesapeake Bay Foundation, 484 U.S. 49
(1987), in which plaintiffs brought a citizen suit under the Clean Water Act
alleging that the defendant "has violated * * * [and] will continue to violate
its NPDES permit." Plaintiffs sought declaratory and injunctive relief, imposition of civil penalties, and attorneys' fees and costs. Defendant moved for

dismissal for lack of subject-matter jurisdiction because its last recorded permit violation occurred several weeks before plaintiffs filed their complaint. The Supreme Court concluded that section 505 did not permit citizen suits for wholly past violations, and remanded the case for the trial court to decide whether plaintiffs' complaint contained a good faith allegation of an ongoing violation by defendant. The Court indicated that plaintiffs would have to offer evidence in the trial court to support their allegation, at which point the defendant would have an opportunity to demonstrate that the allegations were a sham and raised no genuine issue of fact.

Steel Co.

The issue of redressability arose more centrally in *Steel Co. v. Citizens for a Better Environment*, 523 U.S. 83 (1998), in which an environmental group brought suit against a steel manufacturer under the Emergency Planning and Community Right-to-Know Act (EPCRA) for failing to file timely reports about toxic chemicals. By the time the suit was filed, however, the company had brought all of its reports up to date. The complaint requested a declaratory judgment, authorization to inspect the company's facilities and records, copies of the company's future compliance reports, civil penalties to be paid to the government, reimbursement of litigation costs and attorneys' fees, and a blanket plea for any other appropriate relief. The Court denied standing because none of the requested remedies would redress the plaintiff's injury. Writing for the majority, Justice Scalia noted that civil penalties authorized by the statute were payable to the U.S. Treasury, not to the plaintiff:

> In requesting them, therefore, respondent seeks not remediation of its own injury—reimbursement for the costs it incurred as a result of the late filing—but vindication of the rule of law—the "undifferentiated public interest" in faithful execution of EPCRA. This does not suffice. * * * [A]lthough a suitor may derive great comfort and joy from the fact that the United States Treasury is not cheated, that a wrongdoer gets his just deserts, or that the nation's laws are faithfully enforced, that psychic satisfaction is not an acceptable Article III remedy because it does not redress a cognizable Article III injury. Relief that does not remedy the injury suffered cannot bootstrap a plaintiff into federal court; that is the very essence of the redressability requirement. *Id.* at 106–07.

In *Steel Co.*, the Supreme Court denied standing for civil penalties to assess wholly past violations (noncompliance that has abated by the time of the suit). However, in a later pronouncement on redressability, excerpted below, the Court held that civil penalties for *ongoing* violations provide sufficient deterrence to support redressability. The case also clarifies the relationship between the doctrines of mootness and standing.

FRIENDS OF THE EARTH, INC. v. LAIDLAW ENVIRONMENTAL SERVICES (TOC), INC.

Supreme Court of the United States, 2000.
528 U.S. 167, 120 S.Ct. 693, 145 L.Ed.2d 610.

[The plaintiffs sued defendant Laidlaw for repeatedly exceeding the effluent limits set by its National Pollutant Discharge Elimination System (NPDES) permit, granted under the Clean Water Act (CWA), for a wastewater treatment plant at its hazardous waste incinerator near Roe-buck, South Carolina. Laidlaw had repeatedly dumped excessive levels of mercury into the Tyger River in violation of the permit. The District Court held that Friends of the Earth (FOE) had standing, noting that Laidlaw had continued to violate its permit after FOE filed suit. The Court assessed $405,800 in civil penalties against the company, but denied injunctive relief because Laidlaw had since come into "substantial compliance" with its permit requirements. On appeal, the Fourth Circuit assumed that FOE had standing, but held that the case had become moot under the *Steel Co.* decision, and that civil penalties payable to the government, the only remedy available, would not redress any injury plaintiff had suffered.]

JUSTICE GINSBURG delivered the opinion of the Court.

The Constitution's case-or-controversy limitation on federal judicial authority, Art. III, § 2, underpins both our standing and our mootness jurisprudence, but the two inquiries differ in respects critical to the proper resolution of this case, so we address them separately. Because the Court of Appeals was persuaded that the case had become moot and so held, it simply assumed without deciding that FOE had initial standing. But because we hold that the Court of Appeals erred in declaring the case moot, we have an obligation to assure ourselves that FOE had Article III standing at the outset of the litigation. We therefore address the question of standing before turning to mootness.

[The Court reviewed Article III's standing requirements that a plaintiff must show (1) it has suffered an "injury in fact" that is (a) concrete and particularized and (b) actual or imminent, not conjectural or hypothetical; (2) the injury is fairly traceable to the challenged action of the defendant; and (3) it is likely, as opposed to merely speculative, that the injury will be redressed by a favorable decision.]* * *

Laidlaw contends first that FOE lacked standing from the outset even to seek injunctive relief, because the plaintiff organizations failed to show that any of their members had sustained or faced the threat of any "injury in fact" from Laidlaw's activities. In support of this contention Laidlaw points to the District Court's finding, made in the course of setting the penalty amount, that there had been "no demonstrated proof of harm to the environment" from Laidlaw's mercury discharge violations.

The relevant showing for purposes of Article III standing, however, is not injury to the environment but injury to the plaintiff. To insist upon the former rather than the latter as part of the standing inquiry (as the dissent in essence does) is to raise the standing hurdle higher than the necessary showing for success on the merits in an action alleging noncompliance with an NPDES permit. Focusing properly on injury to the plaintiff, the District Court found that FOE had demonstrated sufficient injury to establish standing. * * *

* * * We have held that environmental plaintiffs adequately allege injury in fact when they aver that they use the affected area and are

persons "for whom the aesthetic and recreational values of the area will be lessened" by the challenged activity. *Sierra Club v. Morton,* [*supra,* page 376]. * * * [T]he affidavits and testimony presented by FOE in this case assert that Laidlaw's discharges, and the affiant members' reasonable concerns about the effects of those discharges, directly affected those affiants' recreational, aesthetic, and economic interests. These submissions present dispositively more than the mere "general averments" and "conclusory allegations" found inadequate in *National Wildlife Federation.* Nor can the affiants' conditional statements—that they would use the nearby North Tyger River for recreation if Laidlaw were not discharging pollutants into it—be equated with the speculative " 'some day' intentions" to visit endangered species halfway around the world that we held insufficient to show injury in fact. *Defenders of Wildlife* [*supra,* page 385].

[I]t is undisputed that Laidlaw's unlawful conduct—discharging pollutants in excess of permit limits—was occurring at the time the complaint was filed. * * * [T]he only "subjective" issue here is "[t]he reasonableness of [the] fear" that led the affiants to respond to that concededly ongoing conduct by refraining from use of the North Tyger River and surrounding areas. Unlike the dissent, we see nothing "improbable" about the proposition that a company's continuous and pervasive illegal discharges of pollutants into a river would cause nearby residents to curtail their recreational use of that waterway and would subject them to other economic and aesthetic harms. The proposition is entirely reasonable, the District Court found it was true in this case, and that is enough for injury in fact.

Laidlaw argues next that even if FOE had standing to seek injunctive relief, it lacked standing to seek civil penalties. Here the asserted defect is not injury but redressability. Civil penalties offer no redress to private plaintiffs, Laidlaw argues, because they are paid to the government, and therefore a citizen plaintiff can never have standing to seek them.

Laidlaw is right to insist that a plaintiff must demonstrate standing separately for each form of relief sought. But it is wrong to maintain that citizen plaintiffs facing ongoing violations never have standing to seek civil penalties.

We have recognized on numerous occasions that "all civil penalties have some deterrent effect." More specifically, Congress has found that civil penalties in Clean Water Act cases do more than promote immediate compliance by limiting the defendant's economic incentive to delay its attainment of permit limits; they also deter future violations. This congressional determination warrants judicial attention and respect. "The legislative history of the Act reveals that Congress wanted the district court to consider the need for retribution and deterrence, in addition to restitution, when it imposed civil penalties.... [The district court may] seek to deter future violations by basing the penalty on its economic impact."

It can scarcely be doubted that, for a plaintiff who is injured or faces the threat of future injury due to illegal conduct ongoing at the time of suit, a sanction that effectively abates that conduct and prevents its recurrence provides a form of redress. Civil penalties can fit that description. To the extent that they encourage defendants to discontinue current violations and deter them from committing future ones, they afford redress to citizen plaintiffs who are injured or threatened with injury as a consequence of ongoing unlawful conduct.

The dissent argues that it is the *availability* rather than the *imposition* of civil penalties that deters any particular polluter from continuing to pollute. This argument misses the mark in two ways. First, it overlooks the interdependence of the availability and the imposition; a threat has no deterrent value unless it is credible that it will be carried out. Second, it is reasonable for Congress to conclude that an actual award of civil penalties does in fact bring with it a significant quantum of deterrence over and above what is achieved by the mere prospect of such penalties. A would-be polluter may or may not be dissuaded by the existence of a remedy on the books, but a defendant once hit in its pocketbook will surely think twice before polluting again.

We recognize that there may be a point at which the deterrent effect of a claim for civil penalties becomes so insubstantial or so remote that it cannot support citizen standing. The fact that this vanishing point is not easy to ascertain does not detract from the deterrent power of such penalties in the ordinary case. * * *

In this case we need not explore the outer limits of the principle that civil penalties provide sufficient deterrence to support redressability. Here, the civil penalties sought by FOE carried with them a deterrent effect that made it likely, as opposed to merely speculative, that the penalties would redress FOE's injuries by abating current violations and preventing future ones—as the District Court reasonably found when it assessed a penalty of $405,800.

Laidlaw contends that the reasoning of our decision in *Steel Co.* directs the conclusion that citizen plaintiffs have no standing to seek civil penalties under the Act. We disagree. *Steel Co.* established that citizen suitors lack standing to seek civil penalties for violations that have abated by the time of suit. We specifically noted in that case that there was no allegation in the complaint of any continuing or imminent violation, and that no basis for such an allegation appeared to exist. In short, *Steel Co.* held that private plaintiffs, unlike the Federal Government, may not sue to assess penalties for wholly past violations, but our decision in that case did not reach the issue of standing to seek penalties for violations that are ongoing at the time of the complaint and that could continue into the future if undeterred. * * *

Satisfied that FOE had standing under Article III to bring this action, we turn to the question of mootness.

The only conceivable basis for a finding of mootness in this case is Laidlaw's voluntary conduct—either its achievement by August 1992 of substantial compliance with its NPDES permit or its more recent shutdown of the Roebuck facility. It is well settled that "a defendant's voluntary cessation of a challenged practice does not deprive a federal court of its power to determine the legality of the practice." "[I]f it did, the courts would be compelled to leave '[t]he defendant . . . free to return to his old ways.'" In accordance with this principle, the standard we have announced for determining whether a case has been mooted by the defendant's voluntary conduct is stringent: "A case might become moot if subsequent events made it absolutely clear that the allegedly wrongful behavior could not reasonably be expected to recur." The "heavy burden of persua[ding]" the court that the challenged conduct cannot reasonably be expected to start up again lies with the party asserting mootness.

* * * In relying on *Steel Co.,* the Court of Appeals confused mootness with standing. The confusion is understandable, given this Court's repeated statements that the doctrine of mootness can be described as "the doctrine of standing set in a time frame: The requisite personal interest that must exist at the commencement of the litigation (standing) must continue throughout its existence (mootness)."

Careful reflection on the long-recognized exceptions to mootness, however, reveals that the description of mootness as "standing set in a time frame" is not comprehensive. As just noted, a defendant claiming that its voluntary compliance moots a case bears the formidable burden of showing that it is absolutely clear the allegedly wrongful behavior could not reasonably be expected to recur. By contrast, in a lawsuit brought to force compliance, it is the plaintiff's burden to establish standing by demonstrating that, if unchecked by the litigation, the defendant's allegedly wrongful behavior will likely occur or continue, and that the "threatened injury [is] certainly impending." * * *

Furthermore, if mootness were simply "standing set in a time frame," the exception to mootness that arises when the defendant's allegedly unlawful activity is "capable of repetition, yet evading review" could not exist. * * * Standing admits of no similar exception; if a plaintiff lacks standing at the time the action commences, the fact that the dispute is capable of repetition yet evading review will not entitle the complainant to a federal judicial forum* * *

Standing doctrine functions to ensure, among other things, that the scarce resources of the federal courts are devoted to those disputes in which the parties have a concrete stake. In contrast, by the time mootness is an issue, the case has been brought and litigated, often (as here) for years. * * *

Laidlaw also asserts, in a supplemental suggestion of mootness, that the closure of its Roebuck facility, which took place after the Court of Appeals issued its decision, mooted the case. The facility closure, like Laidlaw's earlier achievement of substantial compliance with its permit requirements, might moot the case, but—we once more reiterate—only if one or the other of these events made it absolutely clear that Laidlaw's permit violations could not reasonably be expected to recur. The effect of both Laidlaw's compliance and the facility closure on the prospect of future violations is a disputed factual matter. FOE points out, for example—and Laidlaw does not appear to contest—that Laidlaw retains its NPDES permit. These issues have not been aired in the lower courts; they remain open for consideration on remand.

JUSTICE SCALIA, with whom JUSTICE THOMAS joins, dissenting.

* * * The plaintiffs in this case fell far short of carrying their burden of demonstrating injury in fact. The Court cites affiants' testimony asserting that their enjoyment of the North Tyger River has been diminished due to "concern" that the water was polluted, and that they "believed" that Laidlaw's mercury exceedances had reduced the value of their homes. These averments alone cannot carry the plaintiffs' burden of demonstrating that they have suffered a "concrete and particularized" injury, *Lujan*. General allegations of injury may suffice at the pleading stage, but at summary judgment plaintiffs must set forth "specific facts" to support their claims. And where, as here, the case has proceeded to judgment, those specific facts must be "supported adequately by the evidence adduced at trial." In this case, the affidavits themselves are woefully short on "specific facts," and the vague allegations of injury they do make are undermined by the evidence adduced at trial.

Typically, an environmental plaintiff claiming injury due to discharges in violation of the Clean Water Act argues that the discharges harm the environment, and that the harm to the environment injures him. This route to injury is barred in the present case, however, since the District Court concluded after considering all the evidence that there had been "no demonstrated proof of harm to the environment," that the "permit violations at issue in this citizen suit did not result in any health risk or environmental harm," that "[a]ll available data ... fail to show that Laidlaw's *actual* discharges have resulted in harm to the North Tyger River," and that "the overall quality of the river exceeds levels necessary to support ... recreation in and on the water."

The Court finds these conclusions unproblematic for standing, because "[t]he relevant showing for purposes of Article III standing ... is not injury to the environment but injury to the plaintiff." This statement is correct, as far as it goes. We have certainly held that a demonstration of harm to the environment is not *enough* to satisfy the injury-in-fact requirement unless the plaintiff can demonstrate how he personally was harmed. In the normal course, however, a lack of demonstrable harm to the environment will translate, as it plainly does here, into a lack of demonstrable harm to citizen plaintiffs. While it is perhaps possible that a plaintiff could be harmed even though the environment was not, such a plaintiff would have the burden of articulating and demonstrating the nature of that injury. Ongoing "concerns" about the environment are not enough, for "[i]t is the *reality* of the threat of repeated injury that is relevant to the standing inquiry, not the plaintiff's subjective apprehensions." At the very least, in the present case, one would expect to see evidence supporting the affidavits' bald assertions regarding decreasing recreational usage and declining home values, as well as evidence for the improbable proposition that Laidlaw's violations, even though harmless to the environment, are somehow responsible for these effects. Plaintiffs here have made no attempt at such a showing, but rely entirely upon unsupported and unexplained affidavit allegations of "concern." * * *

The Court is correct that the District Court explicitly found standing—albeit "by the very slimmest of margins," and as "an awfully close call." That cautious finding, however, was made in 1993, long before the court's 1997 conclusion that Laidlaw's discharges did not harm the environment. As we have previously recognized, an initial conclusion that plaintiffs have standing is subject to reexamination, particularly if later evidence proves inconsistent with that conclusion. Laidlaw challenged the existence of injury in fact on appeal to the Fourth Circuit, but that court did not reach the question. Thus no lower court has reviewed the injury-in-fact issue in light of the extensive studies that led the District Court to conclude that the environment was not harmed by Laidlaw's discharges.

Inexplicably, the Court is untroubled by this, but proceeds to find injury in fact in the most casual fashion, as though it is merely confirming a careful analysis made below. Although we have previously refused to find standing based on the "conclusory allegations of an affidavit," *Lujan v. National Wildlife Federation*, the Court is content to do just that today. By accepting plaintiffs' vague, contradictory, and unsubstantiated allegations of "concern" about the environment as adequate to prove injury in fact, and accepting them even in the face of a finding that the environment was not demonstrably harmed, the Court makes the injury-in-fact requirement a sham. If there are permit violations, and a member of a plaintiff environmental organization lives near the offending plant, it would be difficult not to satisfy today's lenient standard.

The Court's treatment of the redressability requirement—which would have been unnecessary if it resolved the injury-in-fact question correctly—is equally cavalier. As discussed above, petitioners allege ongoing injury consisting of diminished enjoyment of the affected waterways and decreased property values. They allege that these injuries are caused by Laidlaw's continuing permit violations. But the remedy petitioners seek is neither recompense for their injuries nor an injunction against future violations. Instead, the remedy is a statutorily specified "penalty" for past violations, payable entirely to the United States Treasury. Only last Term, we held that such penalties do not redress any injury a citizen plaintiff has suffered from past violations. *Steel Co. v. Citizens for a Better Environment,* [*supra,* page 394]. The Court nonetheless finds the redressability requirement satisfied here, distinguishing *Steel Co.* on the ground that in this case the petitioners allege ongoing violations; payment of the penalties, it says, will remedy petitioners' injury by deterring future violations by Laidlaw. It holds that a penalty payable to the public "remedies" a threatened private harm, and suffices to sustain a private suit.

That holding has no precedent in our jurisprudence, and takes this Court beyond the "cases and controversies" that Article III of the Constitution has entrusted to its resolution. Even if it were appropriate, moreover, to allow Article III's remediation requirement to be satisfied by the indirect private consequences of a public penalty, those consequences are entirely too speculative in the present case. The new standing law that the Court makes—like all expansions of standing beyond the traditional constitutional limits—has grave implications for democratic governance. * * *

The Court's opinion reads as though the only purpose and effect of the redressability requirement is to assure that the plaintiff receive *some* of the benefit of the relief that a court orders. That is not so. * * * [T]he traditional business of Anglo–American courts is relief specifically tailored to the plaintiff's injury, and not *any* sort of relief that has some incidental benefit to the plaintiff. Just as a "generalized grievance" that affects the entire citizenry cannot satisfy the injury-in-fact requirement even though it aggrieves the plaintiff along with everyone else, so also a generalized remedy that deters all future unlawful activity against all persons cannot satisfy the remediation requirement, even though it deters (among other things) repetition of this particular unlawful activity against these particular plaintiffs.

* * * [B]y giving an individual plaintiff the power to invoke a public remedy, Congress has done precisely what we have said it cannot do: convert an "undifferentiated public interest" into an "individual right" vindicable in the courts. * * * A claim of particularized future injury has today been made the vehicle for pursuing generalized penalties for past violations, and a threshold showing of injury-in-fact has become a lever that will move the world.

As I have just discussed, it is my view that a plaintiff's desire to benefit from the deterrent effect of a public penalty for past conduct can never suffice to establish a case or controversy of the sort known to our law. Such deterrent effect is, so to speak, "speculative as a matter of law." Even if that were not so, however, the deterrent effect in the present case would surely be speculative as a matter of fact.

* * * [T]he Court recognizes that not *all* deterrent effects of *all* civil penalties will meet this standard—though it declines to "explore the outer limits" of adequate deterrence. It concludes, however, that in the present case "the civil penalties sought by FOE carried with them a deterrent effect" that satisfied the "likely [rather than] speculative" standard. There is little in the Court's opinion to explain why it believes this is so. * * *

In sum, if this case is, as the Court suggests, within the central core of "deterrence" standing, it is impossible to imagine what the "outer limits" could possibly be. The Court's expressed reluctance to define those "outer limits" serves only to disguise the fact that it has promulgated a revolutionary new doctrine of standing that will permit the entire body of public civil penalties to be handed over to enforcement by private interests. * * *

By permitting citizens to pursue civil penalties payable to the Federal Treasury, the Act does not provide a mechanism for individual relief in any traditional sense, but turns over to private citizens the function of enforcing the law. A Clean Water Act plaintiff pursuing civil penalties acts as a self-appointed mini-EPA. Where, as is often the case, the plaintiff is a national association, it has significant discretion in choosing enforcement targets. Once the association is aware of a reported violation, it need not look long for an injured member, at least under the theory of injury the Court applies today. And once the target is chosen, the suit goes forward without meaningful public control. The availability of civil penalties vastly disproportionate to the individual injury gives citizen plaintiffs massive bargaining power—which is often used to achieve settlements requiring the defendant to support environmental projects of the plaintiffs' choosing. Thus is a public fine diverted to a private interest. * * *

[The dissent expresses puzzlement at why the Court engages in a discussion of the differences between mootness and standing, since Laidlaw's claimed compliance is "squarely within the bounds of our 'voluntary cessation' doctrine which is the basis for remand."]

By uncritically accepting vague claims of injury, the Court has turned the Article III requirement of injury-in-fact into a "mere pleading requirement," and by approving the novel theory that public penalties can redress anticipated private wrongs, it has come close to "mak[ing] the redressability requirement vanish." The undesirable and unconstitutional consequence of today's decision is to place the immense power of suing to enforce the public laws in private hands. I respectfully dissent.

NOTES

1. Does the dissent have a point that empowering private parties to enforce public laws is risky? Might self-appointed private attorneys general, with their own agendas, derail the enforcement agenda of public agencies? Some of the separate opinions in *Laidlaw* raise the constitutional question whether citizen suits intrude upon the President's authority under Article II to "take care that the laws be faithfully executed." *See* 528 U.S. at 197 (Kennedy, J., concurring); *id.* at 209 (Scalia, J., dissenting). A related issue is whether plaintiffs are performing an executive function and are therefore governed by the Appointments Clause. Or are citizen suits necessary and desirable because public agencies often fall short? Does it affect your view that in *Laidlaw*, to preclude the citizen suit, the company arranged to have itself sued by the state environmental agency? This is what happened: The CWA bars citizen suits if the EPA or a state agency has already commenced and is "diligently prosecuting" an enforcement action. Laidlaw's attorney drafted

the state's complaint and paid the filing fee. Laidlaw then settled with the state agency for $100,000 in civil penalties and a promise to make "every effort" to comply in the future. It then continued to violate the effluent limits in its permit, and FOE sued. In finding that FOE had standing, the District Court held that the state enforcement action had not been "diligently prosecuted." Since standing rules require an injury-in-fact to the plaintiff, and remedies (including civil penalties) must be designed to remedy that injury, citizen suits may be more analogous to private nuisance actions than to governmental law enforcement. *See* Robin Kundis Craig, *Will Separation of Powers Challenges 'Take Care' of Environmental Citizen Suits? Article II, Injury-in-Fact, Private 'Enforcers,' and Lessons From* Qui Tam *Litigation*, 72 U. COLO. L. REV. 93 (2001).

2. After *Laidlaw*, citizens must be able to allege and ultimately prove that the defendant was in violation of the relevant statute or permit on the date the complaint was filed. In addition, at least until the time of judgment, there must be some possibility of future violations. Did *Laidlaw* represent a retreat from the Supreme Court's alleged "erosion" of standing doctrine in recent years, or is it simply a limited brake on Justice Scalia's far-reaching approach to redressability, articulated in *Steel Co.*, which would preclude private parties from vindicating the "undifferentiated public interest" in the rule of law? *See* Michael J. Wray, *Still Standing? Citizen Suits, Justice Scalia's New Theory of Standing and the Decision in* Steel Company v. Citizens for a Better Environment, 8 S.C. ENVTL. L.J. 207 (2000). *See also* San Francisco BayKeeper v. Tosco Corp., 309 F.3d 1153 (9th Cir. 2002) (allowing a suit to continue against Tosco for illegal chemical discharges into San Francisco Bay, even after Tosco sold the plant at issue, citing the important general deterrent functions of the Clean Water Act).

3. In finding standing, the Court in *Laidlaw* relied on affidavits filed by members of the plaintiff organization. For instance, one member said he lived a half-mile from the river and would like to use it (and its surroundings) for recreational purposes, as he had when he was younger. But when he occasionally drove across a bridge over the river, it looked and smelled polluted, and as a result he did not make use of the river "because of his concerns about Laidlaw's discharges." 528 U.S. at 182. Other affidavits were similar. *See id.* at 183.

In his dissent, Justice Scalia was incredulous that these allegations would suffice as a basis for standing, particularly given the absence of careful consideration of the injury issue by the lower courts. Justice Scalia's view was not unreasonable, given the relevant precedents (including several he himself had written). But the Court carefully distinguished prior cases on their facts. *Id.* at 183. This in itself reflects a noteworthy change in emphasis, from a rule-based approach to a more common law, case-by-case approach to standing. Second, the Court re-fashioned the notion of injury.

MASSACHUSETTS v. EPA

Supreme Court of the United States, 2007.
549 U.S. 497, 127 S.Ct. 1438, 167 L.Ed.2d 248.

[States, local governments, and environmental organizations petitioned for review of EPA's denial of their petition, which had asked EPA to begin a rulemaking to regulate greenhouse gas emissions from motor vehicles under the Clean Air Act. A divided panel of the D.C. Circuit ruled in favor of the EPA, in part on the basis of questions about the petitioners' standing.]

JUSTICE STEVENS delivered the opinion of the Court.

A well-documented rise in global temperatures has coincided with a significant increase in the concentration of carbon dioxide in the atmosphere. Respected scientists believe the two trends are related. For when carbon dioxide is released into the atmosphere, it acts like the ceiling of a greenhouse, trapping solar energy and retarding the escape of reflected heat. It is therefore a species—the most important species—of a "greenhouse gas."

Calling global warming "the most pressing environmental challenge of our time," a group of States, local governments, and private organizations, alleged in a petition for certiorari that the Environmental Protection Agency (EPA) has abdicated its responsibility under the Clean Air Act to regulate the emissions of four greenhouse gases, including carbon dioxide. Specifically, petitioners asked us to answer two questions concerning the meaning of § 202(a)(1) of the Act: whether EPA has the statutory authority to regulate greenhouse gas emissions from new motor vehicles; and if so, whether its stated reasons for refusing to do so are consistent with the statute. * * *

Article III of the Constitution limits federal-court jurisdiction to "Cases" and "Controversies." Those two words confine "the business of federal courts to questions presented in an adversary context and in a form historically viewed as capable of resolution through the judicial process." It is therefore familiar learning that no justiciable "controversy" exists when parties seek adjudication of a political question, when they ask for an advisory opinion, or when the question sought to be adjudicated has been mooted by subsequent developments. This case suffers from none of these defects.

The parties' dispute turns on the proper construction of a congressional statute, a question eminently suitable to resolution in federal court. Congress has moreover authorized this type of challenge to EPA action. That authorization is of critical importance to the standing inquiry: "Congress has the power to define injuries and articulate chains of causation that will give rise to a case or controversy where none existed before." "In exercising this power, however, Congress must at the very least identify the injury it seeks to vindicate and relate the injury to the class of persons entitled to bring suit." We will not, therefore, "entertain citizen suits to vindicate the public's nonconcrete interest in the proper administration of the laws." [The three preceding sentences are quotations from Justice Kennedy's *Lujan* concurrence.]

EPA maintains that because greenhouse gas emissions inflict widespread harm, the doctrine of standing presents an insuperable jurisdictional obstacle. We do not agree. At bottom, "the gist of the question of standing" is whether petitioners have "such a personal stake in the outcome of the controversy as to assure that concrete adverseness which sharpens the presentation of issues upon which the court so largely depends for illumination." As Justice Kennedy explained in his *Lujan* concurrence:

While it does not matter how many persons have been injured by the challenged action, the party bringing suit must show that the action injures him in a concrete and personal way. This requirement is not just an empty formality. It preserves the vitality of the adversarial process by assuring both that the parties before the court have an actual, as opposed to professed, stake in the outcome, and that the legal questions presented . . . will be resolved, not in the rarified atmosphere of a debating society, but in a concrete factual context conducive to a realistic appreciation of the consequences of judicial action."

To ensure the proper adversarial presentation, *Lujan* holds that a litigant must demonstrate that it has suffered a concrete and particularized injury that is either actual or imminent, that the injury is fairly traceable to the defendant, and that it is likely that a favorable decision will redress that injury. However, a litigant to whom Congress has "accorded a procedural right to protect his concrete interests,"—here, the right to challenge agency action unlawfully withheld—"can assert that right without meeting all the normal standards for redressability and immediacy." When a litigant is vested with a procedural right, that litigant has standing if there is some possibility that the requested relief will prompt the injury-causing party to reconsider the decision that allegedly harmed the litigant.

Only one of the petitioners needs to have standing to permit us to consider the petition for review. We stress here, as did Judge Tatel below, the special position and interest of Massachusetts. It is of considerable relevance that the party seeking review here is a sovereign State and not, as it was in *Lujan,* a private individual. * * *

When a State enters the Union, it surrenders certain sovereign prerogatives. Massachusetts cannot invade Rhode Island to force reductions in greenhouse gas emissions, it cannot negotiate an emissions treaty with China or India, and in some circumstances the exercise of its police powers to reduce in-state motor-vehicle emissions might well be preempted.

These sovereign prerogatives are now lodged in the Federal Government, and Congress has ordered EPA to protect Massachusetts (among others) by prescribing standards applicable to the "emission of any air pollutant from any class or classes of new motor vehicle engines, which in [the Administrator's] judgment cause, or contribute to, air pollution which may reasonably be anticipated to endanger public health or welfare." Congress has moreover recognized a concomitant procedural right to challenge the rejection of its rulemaking petition as arbitrary and capricious. Given that procedural right and Massachusetts' stake in protecting its quasi-sovereign interests, the Commonwealth is entitled to special solicitude in our standing analysis.

holding

With that in mind, it is clear that petitioners' submissions as they pertain to Massachusetts have satisfied the most demanding standards of the adversarial process. EPA's steadfast refusal to regulate greenhouse gas emissions presents a risk of harm to Massachusetts that is both "actual" and "imminent." There is, moreover, a "substantial likelihood that the judicial relief requested" will prompt EPA to take steps to reduce that risk.

THE INJURY

The harms associated with climate change are serious and well recognized. Indeed, the NRC Report itself—which EPA regards as an "objective and independent assessment of the relevant science,"—identifies a number of environmental changes that have already inflicted significant harms, including "the global retreat of mountain glaciers, reduction in snow-cover extent, the earlier spring melting of rivers and lakes, [and] the accelerated rate of rise of sea levels during the 20th century relative to the past few thousand years...."

Petitioners allege that this only hints at the environmental damage yet to come. According to the [declaration filed by] climate scientist Michael MacCracken, "qualified scientific experts involved in climate change research" have reached a "strong consensus" that global warming threatens (among other things) a precipitate rise in sea levels by the end of the century, "severe and irreversible changes to natural ecosystems," a "significant reduction in water storage in winter snowpack in mountainous regions with direct and important economic consequences," and an increase in the spread of disease. He also observes that rising ocean temperatures may contribute to the ferocity of hurricanes.

That these climate-change risks are "widely shared" does not minimize Massachusetts' interest in the outcome of this litigation. According to petitioners' unchallenged affidavits, global sea levels rose somewhere between 10 and 20 centimeters over the 20th century as a result of global warming. These rising seas have already begun to swallow Massachusetts' coastal land. Because the Commonwealth "owns a substantial portion of the state's coastal property," it has alleged a particularized injury in its capacity as a landowner. The severity of that injury will only increase over the course of the next century: If sea levels continue to rise as predicted, one Massachusetts official believes that a significant fraction of coastal property will be "either permanently lost through inundation or temporarily lost through periodic storm surge and flooding events." Remediation costs alone, petitioners allege, could run well into the hundreds of millions of dollars.

CAUSATION

EPA does not dispute the existence of a causal connection between man-made greenhouse gas emissions and global warming. At a minimum, therefore, EPA's refusal to regulate such emissions "contributes" to Massachusetts' injuries.

EPA nevertheless maintains that its decision not to regulate greenhouse gas emissions from new motor vehicles contributes so insignificantly to petitioners' injuries that the agency cannot be haled into federal court to answer for them. For the same reason, EPA does not believe that any realistic possibility exists that the relief petitioners seek would mitigate global climate change and remedy their injuries. That is especially so because predicted increases in greenhouse gas emissions from developing nations, particularly China and India, are likely to offset any marginal domestic decrease.

But EPA overstates its case. Its argument rests on the erroneous assumption that a small incremental step, because it is incremental, can never be attacked in a federal judicial forum. Yet accepting that premise would doom most challenges to regulatory action. Agencies, like legislatures, do not generally resolve massive problems in one fell regulatory swoop. They instead whittle away at them over time, refining their preferred approach as circumstances change and as they develop a more-nuanced understanding of how best to proceed. That a first step might be tentative does not by itself support the notion that federal courts lack jurisdiction to determine whether that step conforms to law.

And reducing domestic automobile emissions is hardly a tentative step. Even leaving aside the other greenhouse gases, the United States transportation sector emits an enormous quantity of carbon dioxide into the atmosphere—according to the MacCracken affidavit, more than 1.7 billion metric tons in 1999 alone. That accounts for more than 6% of worldwide carbon dioxide emissions. To put this in perspective: Considering just emissions from the transportation sector, which represent less than one-third of this country's total carbon dioxide emissions, the United States would still rank as the third-largest emitter of carbon dioxide in the world, outpaced only by the European Union and China. Judged by any standard, U.S. motor-vehicle emissions make a meaningful contribution to greenhouse gas concentrations and hence, according to petitioners, to global warming.

THE REMEDY

While it may be true that regulating motor-vehicle emissions will not by itself *reverse* global warming, it by no means follows that we lack jurisdiction to decide whether EPA has a duty to take steps to *slow* or *reduce* it. Because of the enormity of the potential consequences associated with man-made climate change, the fact that the effectiveness of a remedy might be delayed during the (relatively short) time it takes for a new motor-vehicle fleet to replace an older one is essentially irrelevant. Nor is it dispositive that developing countries such as China and India are poised to increase greenhouse gas emissions substantially over the next century: A reduction in domestic emissions would slow the pace of global emissions increases, no matter what happens elsewhere.

We moreover attach considerable significance to EPA's "agree[ment] with the President that 'we must address the issue of global climate change,'" and to EPA's ardent support for various voluntary emission-reduction programs. As Judge Tatel observed in dissent below, "EPA would presumably not bother with such efforts if it thought emissions reductions would have no discernable impact on future global warming."

In sum—at least according to petitioners' uncontested affidavits—the rise in sea levels associated with global warming has already harmed and will continue to harm Massachusetts. The risk of catastrophic harm, though remote, is nevertheless real. That risk would be reduced to some extent if petitioners received the relief they seek. We therefore hold that petitioners have standing to challenge the EPA's denial of their rulemaking petition.

CHIEF JUSTICE ROBERTS, with whom JUSTICE SCALIA, JUSTICE THOMAS, and JUSTICE ALITO join, dissenting.

Global warming may be a "crisis," even "the most pressing environmental problem of our time." Pet. for Cert. 26, 22. Indeed, it may ultimately affect nearly everyone on the planet in some potentially adverse way, and it may be that governments have done too little to address it. It is not a problem, however, that has escaped the attention of policymakers in the Executive and Legislative Branches of our Government, who continue to consider regulatory, legislative, and treaty-based means of addressing global climate change.

Apparently dissatisfied with the pace of progress on this issue in the elected branches, petitioners have come to the courts claiming broad-ranging injury, and attempting to tie that injury to the Government's alleged failure to comply with a rather narrow statutory provision. I would reject these challenges as nonjusticiable. Such a conclusion involves no judgment on whether global warming exists, what causes it, or the extent of the problem. Nor does it render petitioners without recourse. This Court's standing jurisprudence simply recognizes that redress of grievances of the sort at issue here "is the function of Congress and the Chief Executive," not the federal courts. [Quoting *Lujan*] I would vacate the judgment below and remand for dismissal of the petitions for review. * * *

Before determining whether petitioners can meet [the normal test for standing] the Court changes the rules. It asserts that "States are not normal litigants for the purposes of invoking federal jurisdiction," and that given "Massachusetts' stake in protecting its quasi-sovereign interests, the Commonwealth is entitled to *special solicitude* in our standing analysis."

Relaxing Article III standing requirements because asserted injuries are pressed by a State, however, has no basis in our jurisprudence, and support for any such "special solicitude" is conspicuously absent from the Court's opinion. The general judicial review provision cited by the Court, affords States no special rights or status. The Court states that "Congress has ordered EPA to protect Massachusetts (among others)" through the statutory provision at issue, and that "Congress has ... recognized a concomitant procedural right to challenge the rejection of its rulemaking petition as arbitrary and capricious." The reader might think from this unfortunate phrasing that Congress said something about the rights of States in this particular provision of the statute. Congress knows how to do that when it wants to, but it has done nothing of the sort here. Under the law on which petitioners rely, Congress treated public and private litigants exactly the same.

Nor does the case law cited by the Court provide any support for the notion that Article III somehow implicitly treats public and private litigants differently. * * *

It is not at all clear how the Court's "special solicitude" for Massachusetts plays out in the standing analysis, except as an implicit concession that petitioners cannot establish standing on traditional terms. But the status of Massachusetts as a State cannot compensate for petitioners' failure to demonstrate injury in fact, causation, and redressability.

When the Court actually applies the three-part test, it focuses, as did the dissent below on the State's asserted loss of coastal land as the injury in fact. If petitioners rely on loss of land as the Article III injury, however, they must ground the rest of the standing analysis in that specific injury. * * * Without "particularized injury, there can be no confidence of 'a real need to exercise the power of judicial review' or that relief can be framed 'no broader than required by the precise facts to which the court's ruling would be applied.' "

The very concept of global warming seems inconsistent with this particularization requirement. Global warming is a phenomenon "harmful to humanity at large," and the redress petitioners seek is focused no more on them than on the public generally—it is literally to change the atmosphere around the world.

If petitioners' particularized injury is loss of coastal land, it is also that injury that must be "actual or imminent, not conjectural or hypothetical," "real and immediate," and "certainly impending."

As to "actual" injury, the Court observes that "global sea levels rose somewhere between 10 and 20 centimeters over the 20th century as a result of global warming" and that "[t]hese rising seas have already begun to swallow Massachusetts' coastal land." But none of petitioners' declarations supports that connection. [A]side from a single conclusory statement, there is nothing in petitioners' 43 standing declarations and accompanying exhibits to support an inference of actual loss of Massachusetts coastal land from 20th century global sea level increases. It is pure conjecture.

The Court's attempts to identify "imminent" or "certainly impending" loss of Massachusetts coastal land fares no better. One of petitioners' declarants predicts global warming will cause sea level to rise by 20 to 70 centimeters *by the year 2100*. [A]ccepting a century-long time horizon and a series of compounded estimates renders requirements of imminence and immediacy utterly toothless. * * *

Petitioners view the relationship between their injuries and EPA's failure to promulgate new motor vehicle greenhouse gas emission standards as simple and direct: Domestic motor vehicles emit carbon dioxide and other greenhouse gases. Worldwide emissions of greenhouse gases contribute to global warming and therefore also to petitioners' alleged injuries. Without the new vehicle standards, greenhouse gas emissions-and therefore global warming and its attendant harms-have been higher than they otherwise would have been; once EPA changes course, the trend will be reversed.

The Court ignores the complexities of global warming, and does so by now disregarding the "particularized" injury it relied on in step one, and using the dire nature of global warming itself as a bootstrap for finding causation and redressability. First, it is important to recognize the extent of the emissions at issue here. Because local greenhouse gas emissions disperse throughout the atmosphere and remain there for anywhere from 50 to 200 years, it is global emissions data that are relevant. According to one of petitioners' declarations, domestic motor vehicles contribute about 6 percent of global carbon dioxide emissions and 4 percent of global greenhouse gas emissions. The amount of global emissions at issue here is smaller still; [the applicable section] of the Clean Air Act covers only *new* motor vehicles and *new* motor vehicle engines, so petitioners' desired emission standards might reduce only a fraction of 4 percent of global emissions.

This gets us only to the relevant greenhouse gas emissions; linking them to global warming and ultimately to petitioners' alleged injuries next requires consideration of further complexities. As EPA explained in its denial of petitioners' request for rulemaking, "predicting future climate change necessarily involves a complex web of economic and physical factors * * *." Petitioners are never able to trace their alleged injuries back through this complex web to the fractional amount of global emissions that might have been limited with EPA standards. In light of the bit-part domestic new motor vehicle greenhouse gas emissions have played in what petitioners describe as a 150–year global phenomenon, and the myriad additional factors bearing on petitioners' alleged injury—the loss of Massachusetts coastal land-the connection is far too speculative to establish causation.

Redressability is even more problematic. To the tenuous link between petitioners' alleged injury and the indeterminate fractional domestic emissions at issue here, add the fact that petitioners cannot meaningfully predict what will come of the 80 percent of global greenhouse gas emissions that originate outside the United States. As the Court acknowledges, "developing countries such as China and India are poised to increase greenhouse gas emissions substantially over the next century," so the domestic emissions at issue here may become an increasingly marginal portion of global emissions, and any decreases produced by petitioners' desired standards are likely to be overwhelmed many times over by emissions increases elsewhere in the world. * * *

The Court reasons that] *any* decrease in domestic emissions will "slow the pace of global emissions increases, no matter what happens elsewhere." Every little bit helps, so Massachusetts can sue over any little bit.

The Court's sleight-of-hand is in failing to link up the different elements of the three-part standing test. What must be *likely* to be redressed is the particular injury in fact. The injury the Court looks to is the asserted loss of land. The Court contends that regulating domestic motor vehicle emissions will reduce carbon dioxide in the atmosphere, *and therefore* redress Massachusetts's injury.

But even if regulation *does* reduce emissions—to some indeterminate degree, given events elsewhere in the world—the Court never explains why that makes it *likely* that the injury in fact—the loss of land—will be redressed. Schoolchildren know that a kingdom might be lost "all for the want of a horseshoe nail," but "likely" redressability is a different matter. The realities make it pure conjecture to suppose that EPA regulation of new automobile emissions will *likely* prevent the loss of Massachusetts coastal land. * * *

When dealing with legal doctrine phrased in terms of what is "fairly" traceable or "likely" to be redressed, it is perhaps not surprising that the matter is subject to some debate. But in considering how loosely or rigorously to define those adverbs, it is vital to keep in mind the purpose of the inquiry. The limitation of the judicial power to cases and controversies "is crucial in maintaining the tripartite allocation of power set forth in the Constitution." In my view, the Court today—addressing Article III's "core component of standing," * * * fails to take this limitation seriously.

NOTES

1. The *MA v. EPA* majority purports to distinguish *Lujan*, but the Court clearly bases its ruling much more on the Kennedy concurrence than on the Scalia opinion. Is Justice Scalia's plurality opinion in *Lujan* still good law after *EPA v. MA*?

2. Justice Stevens makes much of the sovereign status of the state and its implication for the state's claim of standing. The result may be to empower the states to challenge federal actions that would otherwise be immune from suit by private parties. Is this a healthy reinforcement of the states' role in the federalist system, or is it an invitation to litigate questions that are essentially political disagreements rather than live controversies? Putting that question aside, to what extent is the state's sovereign status determinative of the outcome? Connecticut v. American Elec. Power Co., ___ F.3d ___, 2009

WL 2996729 (2d Cir. 2009), extended climate standing to include private land trusts as well as States.

3. Justice Stevens seems to have done a remarkable job of corralling Justice Kennedy's vote—note how frequently he refers to Justice Kennedy's *Lujan* performance as the gold standard in standing doctrine. As in so many other contexts, Justice Kennedy's swing vote was crucial here, a fact that was not lost on Justice Stevens. It was Justice Kennedy who, at oral argument, asked (and then supplied) petitioners with the key case that that the majority opinion cites to support the "special solicitude" rationale for granting states standing—*Georgia v. Tennessee Copper*. Is "special solicitude" an opportunistic invention justified only by the effort to win Justice Kennedy's vote? Or is it a fair reading of the caselaw?

4. Is the Chief Justice right, in his dissent, when he says that the "very concept of global warming" seems inconsistent with the particularization requirement in Article III because global warming is a phenomenon "harmful to humanity at large"? If this is the case, should the federal courts never hear challenges to agency decisions that have an impact on "humanity at large?" Would some groups be more negatively affected by this restrictive approach to standing than others? Suppose that Congress passes a regulatory scheme governing climate change. In the Chief Justice's view, would judicial review of the implementing regulations be limited to cases brought by industry, or is there some way that environmentalists could also obtain standing?

How would you respond to the Chief Justice's concerns about the imminence and certainty of climate harm? Should standing law require such imminence or reflect a more precautionary approach? See Jonathan Remy Nash, *Standing and the Precautionary Principle*, 108 COLUM. L. REV. 494 (2008).

5. Consider the following alternative standing argument that might have been made in *Massachusetts v. EPA*. Implementing regulation of CO_2 would almost certainly require improvements in fuel economy. By reducing the amount of gasoline burned, such restrictions would reduce the emissions of conventional pollutants from automobiles, thus assisting in the attainment of air quality standards designed to protect human health. This would be a relatively short-term, concrete impact that would have improved the health of residents in urban areas. Can you make an argument for why this would satisfy *Lujan*? (Consider *National Resources Defense Council v. EPA*, 464 F.3d 1 (D. C. Cir. 2006), holding that a lifetime risk of about one in 200,000 of developing a nonfatal skin cancer constituted injury in fact.) Assuming that this would have been a sound argument for standing, can you see why the plaintiffs might have chosen not to take this route?

6. Standing doctrine could be greatly simplified by adopting a place-based approach to standing. Under this approach, a plaintiff would have standing to contest environmental violations involving a specific geographic area, provided that the plaintiff has an appropriate personal connection to the area. *Massachusetts v. EPA* would be an easy case under this approach, because the state would clearly have the requisite connection with its own territory, given that sea level rise and other effects of climate change threatened the state's territory. For further discussion of this approach, see Daniel A. Farber, *A Place–Based Approach to Standing*, 55 UCLA L. REV. 1505 (2008). Would this approach be too great a modification of current doctrine to be plausible? Or, on the contrary, should a more radical approach be taken, perhaps by disconnecting standing from Article III entirely?

7. On the question of whether *MA v. EPA* is a "straightforward administrative law case," as the Chief Justice suggests, see Jody Freeman and Adrian Vermeule, MA v. EPA: *From Politics to Expertise*, 2007 S. Ct. Rev. 51 (2008). The authors argue that the decision has significant implications for administrative law, primarily because it makes agency refusals to make threshold findings that would trigger regulation ("decisions not to decide") reviewable on the same terms as affirmative decisions to regulate. The result is that a category of agency decisionmaking that once enjoyed all the benefits of "inaction" is treated as if it were "action" and subjected to review. In this sense, the authors claim, the case is not *SCRAP*, for a new generation (as the Chief Justice noted in his dissent when decrying the grant of standing and referring to SCRAP as the highwater mark of liberal standing cases); it is instead, *State Farm* for a new generation—*State Farm* being the case in which the Court first decided that even *de*-regulatory decisions by agencies attract "hard look" arbitrary and capricious review, just like affirmative regulatory decisions. *Id.* at 98. This has potentially important implications for environmental law, since many suits involve plaintiff challenges to government failures to act, and these suits have historically been unsuccessful. *See e.g.* Norton v. Southern Utah Wilderness Alliance, 542 U.S. 55 (2004). *See also,* Lisa Bressman, Judicial Review of Agency Inaction: An Arbitrariness Approach, 79 NYU L. Rev. 1657 (2004) (arguing for revision of the Court's nonreviewability doctrine for inaction cases).

SUMMERS v. EARTH ISLAND INSTITUTE

Supreme Court of the United States, 2009.
555 U.S. ___, 129 S.Ct. 1142, 173 L.Ed.2d 1.

[After the U.S. Forest Service approved the Burnt Ridge Project, a salvage sale of timber on 238 acres of fire-damaged federal land, several environmentalist organizations filed suit to enjoin the Service from applying its regulations exempting such small sales from the notice, comment, and appeal process it uses for more significant land management decisions. The District Court granted a preliminary injunction against the sale, and the parties then settled their dispute as to Burnt Ridge. Nevertheless, the Ninth Circuit held that the dispute about the regulations was still alive because the regulations applied to many other sites. It then held the regulations unlawful.]

JUSTICE SCALIA delivered the opinion of the Court.

The regulations under challenge here neither require nor forbid any action on the part of respondents. The standards and procedures that they prescribe for Forest Service appeals govern only the conduct of Forest Service officials engaged in project planning. "[W]hen the plaintiff is not himself the object of the government action or inaction he challenges, standing is not precluded, but it is ordinarily 'substantially more difficult' to establish." *Defenders of Wildlife*. Here, respondents can demonstrate standing only if application of the regulations by the Government will affect *them* in the manner described above. * * *

Respondents have identified no other application of the invalidated regulations that threatens imminent and concrete harm to the interests of their members. The only other affidavit relied on was that of Jim Bensman. He asserted, first, that he had suffered injury in the past from development on Forest Service land. That does not suffice for several reasons: because it was not tied to application of the challenged regulations, because it does not identify any particular site, and because it relates to past injury rather than imminent future injury that is sought to be enjoined.

Bensman's affidavit further asserts that he has visited many National Forests and plans to visit several unnamed National Forests in the future. Respondents describe this as a mere failure to "provide the name of each timber sale that affected [Bensman's] interests." It is much more (or much less) than that. It is a failure to allege that *any* particular timber sale or other project claimed to be unlawfully subject to the regulations will impede a specific and concrete plan of Bensman's to enjoy the National Forests. The National Forests occupy more than 190 million acres, an area larger than Texas. There may be a chance, but is hardly a likelihood, that Bensman's wanderings will bring him to a parcel about to be affected by a project unlawfully subject to the regulations. Indeed, without further specification it is impossible to tell *which* projects are (in respondents' view) unlawfully subject to the regulations. * * * Here we are asked to assume not only that Bensman will stumble across a project tract unlawfully subject to the regulations, but also that the tract is about to be developed by the Forest Service in a way that harms his recreational interests, and that he would have commented on the project but for the regulation. Accepting an intention to visit the National Forests as adequate to confer standing to challenge any Government action affecting any portion of those forests would be tantamount to eliminating the requirement of concrete, particularized injury in fact.

The Bensman affidavit does refer specifically to a series of projects in the Allegheny National Forest that are subject to the challenged regulations. It does not assert, however, any firm intention to visit their locations, saying only that Bensman " 'want[s] to' " go there. This vague desire to return is insufficient to satisfy the requirement of imminent injury: "Such 'some day' intentions—without any description of concrete plans, or indeed any specification of *when* the some day will be—do not support a finding of the 'actual or imminent' injury that our cases require." *Defenders of Wildlife.*

Respondents argue that they have standing to bring their challenge because they have suffered procedural injury, namely that they have been denied the ability to file comments on some Forest Service actions and will continue to be so denied. But deprivation of a procedural right without some concrete interest that is affected by the deprivation—a procedural right *in vacuo*—is insufficient to create Article III standing. Only a "person who has been accorded a procedural right to protect *his concrete interests* can assert that right without meeting all the normal standards for redressability and immediacy." Respondents alleged such injury in their challenge to the Burnt Ridge Project, claiming that but for the allegedly unlawful abridged procedures they would have been able to oppose the project that threatened to impinge on their concrete plans to observe nature in that specific area. But Burnt Ridge is now off the table.

It makes no difference that the procedural right has been accorded by Congress. That can loosen the strictures of the redressability prong of our standing inquiry—so that standing existed with regard to the Burnt Ridge Project, for example, despite the possibility that Earth Island's allegedly guaranteed right to comment would not be successful in persuading the Forest Service to avoid impairment of Earth Island's concrete interests. Unlike redressability, however, the requirement of injury in fact is a hard floor of Article III jurisdiction that cannot be removed by statute. * * *

The dissent proposes a hitherto unheard-of test for organizational standing: whether, accepting the organization's self-description of the activities of its members, there is a statistical probability that some of those members are threatened with concrete injury. Since, for example, the Sierra Club asserts in its pleadings that it has more than " '700,000 members nationwide, including thousands of members in California' " who " 'use and enjoy the Sequoia National Forest,' it is probable (according to the dissent) that some (unidentified) members have planned to visit some (unidentified) small parcels affected by the Forest Service's procedures and will suffer (unidentified) concrete harm as a result. This novel approach to the law of organizational standing would make a mockery of our prior cases, which have required plaintiff-organizations to make specific allegations establishing that at least one identified member had suffered or would suffer harm. * * *

JUSTICE KENNEDY, concurring.

I join in full the opinion of the Court. As the opinion explains, "deprivation of a procedural right without some concrete interest that is affected by the deprivation—a procedural right *in vacuo*—is insufficient to create Article III standing." The procedural injury must "impair a separate concrete interest."

This case would present different considerations if Congress had sought to provide redress for a concrete injury "giv[ing] rise to a case or controversy where none existed before." [citing his concurrence in *Defenders*.] Nothing in the statute at issue here, however, indicates Congress intended to identify or confer some interest separate and apart from a procedural right.

JUSTICE BREYER, with whom JUSTICE STEVENS, JUSTICE SOUTER, and JUSTICE GINSBURG join, dissenting.

The Court holds that the Sierra Club and its members (along with other environmental organizations) do not suffer any "concrete injury" when the Forest Service sells timber for logging on "many thousands" of small (250–acre or less) woodland parcels without following legally required procedures—procedures which, if followed, could lead the Service to cancel or to modify the sales. Nothing in the record or the law justifies this counterintuitive conclusion. * * *

How can the majority credibly claim that salvage-timber sales, and similar projects, are unlikely to harm the asserted interests of the members of these environmental groups? The majority apparently does so in part by arguing that the Forest Service actions are not "imminent"—a requirement more appropriately considered in the context of ripeness or the necessity of injunctive relief. I concede that the Court has sometimes used the word "imminent" in the context of constitutional standing. But it has done so primarily to emphasize that the harm in question—the harm that was not "imminent"—was merely "conjectural" or "hypothetical" or otherwise speculative. Where the Court has directly focused upon the matter, *i.e.*, where, as here, a plaintiff has *already* been subject to the injury it wishes to challenge, the Court has asked whether there is a *realistic likelihood* that the challenged future conduct will, in fact, recur and harm the plaintiff. * * *

How could the Court impose a stricter criterion? Would courts deny *standing* to a holder of a future interest in property who complains that a life tenant's waste of the land will almost inevitably hurt the value of his interest—though he will have no personal interest for several years into the future? Would courts deny *standing* to a landowner who complains that a neighbor's upstream dam constitutes a nuisance—even if the harm to his downstream property (while bound to occur) will not occur for several years? Would courts deny *standing* to an injured person seeking a protection order from future realistic (but nongeographically specific) threats of further attacks?

To the contrary, a threat of future harm may be realistic even where the plaintiff cannot specify precise times, dates, and GPS coordinates. Thus, we recently held that Massachusetts has *standing* to complain of a procedural failing, namely, EPA's failure properly to determine whether to restrict carbon dioxide emissions, even though that failing would create Massachusetts-based harm which (though likely to occur) might not occur for several decades.

The Forest Service admits that it intends to conduct thousands of further salvage-timber sales and other projects exempted under the challenged regulations "in the reasonably near future." How then can the Court deny that the plaintiffs have shown a "realistic" threat that the Forest Service will continue to authorize (without the procedures claimed necessary) salvage-timber sales, and other Forest Service projects, that adversely affect the recreational, aesthetic, and environmental interests of the plaintiffs' members?

Consider: Respondents allege, and the Government has conceded, that the Forest Service took wrongful actions (such as selling salvage timber) "thousands" of times in the two years prior to suit. The Complaint alleges, and no one denies, that the organizations, the Sierra Club for example, have hundreds of thousands of members who use forests regularly across the Nation for recreational, scientific, aesthetic, and environmental purposes. The Complaint further alleges, and no one denies, that these organizations (and their members), believing that actions such as salvage-timber sales harm those interests, regularly oppose salvage-timber sales (and similar actions) in proceedings before the agency. And the Complaint alleges, and no one denies, that the organizations intend to continue to express their opposition to such actions in those proceedings in the future.

Consider further: The affidavit of a member of Sequoia ForestKeeper, Ara Marderosian, attached to the Complaint, specifies that Marderosian had visited the Burnt Ridge Project site in the past and intended to return. The majority concedes that this is sufficient to show that Marderosian had standing to challenge the Burnt Ridge Project. The majority must therefore agree that "at least one identified member ha[s] suffered ... harm." Why then does it find insufficient the affidavit, also attached to the Complaint, of Jim Bensman, a member of Heartwood, Inc.? That affidavit states, among other things, that Bensman has visited 70 National Forests, that he has visited some of those forests "hundreds of times," that he has often visited the Allegheny National Forest in the past, that he has "probably commented on a thousand" Forest Service projects including salvage-timber sale proposals, that he intends to continue to comment on similar Forest Service proposals, and that the Forest Service plans in the future to conduct salvage-timber sales on 20 parcels in the Allegheny National Forest—one of the forests he has visited in the past.

The Bensman affidavit does not say *which particular* sites will be affected by future Forest Service projects, but the Service itself has conceded that it will conduct thousands of exempted projects in the future. Why is more specificity needed to show a "realistic" threat that a project will impact land Bensman uses? To know, virtually for certain, that snow will fall in New England this winter is not to know the name of each particular town where it is bound to arrive. The law of standing does not require the latter kind of specificity. How could it? * * *

I recognize that the Government raises other claims and bases upon which to deny standing or to hold that the case is not ripe for adjudication. I believe that these arguments are without merit. But because the majority does not discuss them here, I shall not do so either.

With respect, I dissent.

NOTES

1. The key to environmental standing seems to be proof that a particular person would be at a particular affected place. The debate between the majority and the dissent is largely about how specific this allegation needs to be. But why is physical presence so critical to the existence of a "live dispute"? Given that the real disputes in these cases are between organizations and agencies rather than the individuals who end up being selected as

plaintiffs, should it really matter whether the organization can come up with a detailed allegation about continued physical use of an area by one of its members?

2. Justice Kennedy seems to agree that a procedural injury is not enough by itself to create standing but he contends that Congress can specifically identify nonconventional types of injury. Environmental economists speak about "option values" associated with natural areas—the that people might be willing to pay in the future to visit a place even though they have no specific plans to do so. Such option values are frequently used in cost-benefit analysis of projects or regulations. Under Kennedy's approach, could Congress specifically designate loss of option value as a cognizable injury? Would that create standing under Kennedy's approach?

3. How much specificity is required? Suppose that the government banned logging on small tracts. To have standing, would a logging company have to identify the specific tracts that it would otherwise have liked to log and show that it would have at least had a good chance of winning the bids for the specific tracts? Or would it be enough to show that it had logged many such tracts in the past and planned to continue to do so in the future? If the latter showing would be enough, why isn't the company required to meet the same standard of specificity as an environmental organization?

Note on the Zone of Interests Requirement

The so-called "zone of interests" test is also known as the statutory (as opposed to Article III) test for standing. We can imagine a plaintiff who has demonstrated injury-in-fact, when the injury is both clearly caused by the defendant's illegal conduct and redressable by the court—yet the injury might be only coincidentally related to the reasons why the conduct is illegal. For instance, suppose the suit in *Sierra Club v. Morton* had been brought by a nearby ski resort, which wanted to keep Mineral King from being developed because the new resort would reduce its business. While satisfying the requirements of the injury-in-fact test (dollars out of pocket), causation (easily proved with expert witnesses), and redressability (no new resort, no competitive injury), there still seems to be something fishy about this lawsuit. After all, the environmental statutes aren't designed to protect competitors; they're designed to protect the environment. Is such a "coincidental" connection between the plaintiff's harm and a law designed for entirely different purposes enough to create standing? The doctrinal question in such cases is whether the litigant is "arguably within the zone of interests" meant to be protected by the statute. Answering this question typically involves an inquiry into legislative intent.

In *Bennett v. Spear*, 520 U.S. 154, 117 S.Ct. 1154, 137 L.Ed.2d 281 (1997), the Court clarified the scope of this requirement. The Bureau of Reclamation informed the Fish and Wildlife Service that the operation of the Klamath Irrigation Project might harm two endangered species of fish (Lost River and shortnose suckers). The Service issued a Biological Opinion agreeing with the concern and recommending that the Bureau maintain minimum water levels in reservoirs. The Bureau then agreed to do so. The plaintiffs were irrigation districts and ranchers who claimed that the Biological Opinion violated various provisions of the ESA and the Administrative Procedure Act. The Ninth Circuit held that they lacked standing because their economic interests did not lie within the "zone of interests" protected by the ESA. There's a certain common sense appeal to this holding, because the plaintiffs were seeking to frustrate rather than advance the main purpose of the statute, protection of endangered species.

In an opinion by Justice Scalia, the Court held that the zone of interests test did not apply to the citizen suit provisions of the ESA, which extended standing to the constitutional limit. Some of the plaintiff's claims, however, could only be brought under the APA and therefore were subject to this requirement. The Court concluded, however, that the requirement was satisfied because the plaintiffs were within the zone of interests of the specific provision that they invoked, which was intended to prevent against overzealous action by administrators in protecting endangered species at the expense of land owners:

> Whether a plaintiff's interest is "arguably * * * protected * * * by the statute" within the meaning of the zone-of-interests test is to be determined not by reference to the overall purpose of the Act in question (here, species preservation), but by reference to the particular provision of law upon which the plaintiff relies. * * *

> In the claims that we have found not to be covered by the ESA's citizen-suit provision, petitioners allege a violation of § 7 of the ESA, which requires, inter alia, that each agency "use the best scientific and commercial data available." Petitioners contend that the available scientific and commercial data show that the continued operation of the Klamath Project will not have a detrimental impact on the endangered suckers, that the imposition of minimum lake levels is not necessary to protect the fish, and that by issuing a Biological Opinion which makes unsubstantiated findings to the contrary the defendants have acted arbitrarily and in violation of § 1536(a)(2). The obvious purpose of the requirement that each agency "use the best scientific and commercial data available" is to ensure that the ESA not be implemented haphazardly, on the basis of speculation or surmise. While this no doubt serves to advance the ESA's overall goal of species preservation, we think it readily apparent that another objective (if not indeed the primary one) is to avoid needless economic dislocation produced by agency officials zealously but unintelligently pursuing their environmental objectives. That economic consequences are an explicit concern of the Act is evidenced by § 1536(h), which provides exemption from § 1536(a)(2)'s no-jeopardy mandate where there are no reasonable and prudent alternatives to the agency action and the benefits of the agency action clearly outweigh the benefits of any alternatives. We believe the "best scientific and commercial data" provision is similarly intended, at least in part, to prevent uneconomic (because erroneous) jeopardy determinations. Petitioners' claim that they are victims of such a mistake is plainly within the zone of interests that the provision protects. * * *

Bennett makes it clear that the "zone-of-interests" test is not part of Article III standing. Instead, it is either a prudential requirement imposed by the courts or a consequence of specific statutory language, such as that used in the APA. It seems that Congress can essentially "negate" the zone-of-interests test by clearly specifying in the legislation the parties that are entitled to file suit.

Bennett also addressed a question relating to Article III standing: the government's claim that the plaintiff's injury (the ultimate water allocation by one agency) was not "fairly traceable" to the contested government action (issuance of the Biological Opinion by another agency). The Court found that as a practical matter the Biological Opinion would have a major, probably decisive influence, on the ultimate decision. In the course of this discussion, however, the Court only added to the confusion about the requirements of standing to challenge "procedural" decisions, such as an EIS or a Biological Opinion. Under the Court's later opinion in *Summers*, should the farmers have had to show that the water delivered to a particular plot was immediately threatened by the Biological Opinion?

NOTE ON THE COMPLEXITY OF STANDING DOCTRINE

A closing thought: The Court's struggles with standing stem from the fact that the traditional function of lawsuits—that of vindicating private rights—is really not central to the modern function of judicial review of agency decisions, which operates more to uphold the public interest than to protect private rights. This mismatch between current function and traditional model clearly creates some intellectual tensions, which Justice Scalia seeks to resolve by endorsing the traditional model and branding the current function as illegitimate. Yet, unless the traditional model is applied very restrictively indeed, overturning *Sierra Club* and related cases, it may be impossible for the Court to return judicial review to its older function. See David Driesen, *Standing for Nothing: The Paradox of Demanding Concrete Context for Formalist Adjudication*, 89 CORNELL L. REV. 808 (2004), (questioning whether standing is too focused on the issue of concreteness, when plaintiffs' injuries do not actually provide much guidance in what are often actually reviews of wide-ranging policy issues).

Retired Judge Patricia Wald of the D.C. Circuit has questioned whether the increasingly baroque law of standing has become dysfunctional. In *Humane Soc. of United States v. Babbitt*, 46 F.3d 93 (D.C. Cir. 1995), for example, the court rejected an effort by the Humane Society to prevent the transfer of Lota, an Asian elephant, from the Milwaukee Zoo. The transfer allegedly violated the Endangered Species Act. The court held that no one had standing to raise the question—not zoo visitors who claimed emotional harm, not visitors who wanted to learn about endangered elephants (there were others at the zoo), not those who wanted to see Lota in a conservation setting (too imprecisely defined). And besides, the court said, the government certificate only covered the transfer to the ultimate destination (an exhibition farm) rather than the departure from the Milwaukee Zoo (though it seems unlikely that the elephant would have left the zoo without any permission for a final destination). Hence, the Court said, the elephant's departure from the zoo was not "fairly traceable" to the government certificate for the transfer to the farm. Judge Wald is skeptical of the usefulness of this analysis:

I ask you: Is this work for sophisticated adult jurists? There was a real dispute here, whether Lota's transfer to the animal exhibition in Illinois was in violation of the Endangered Species Act; and who was more qualified to raise it than those whose concern about animal welfare had caused them to join a professional organization dedicated to that cause, including members who had personally viewed and visited Lota, and yes, by golly, missed her and worried about her survival in her new environment? The descent in Talmudic refinements about whether one must be a student of the animal in that particular environment to bring suit, and whether the disputed permit covered the transport away from the zoo as well as to the animal exhibition would strike an ordinary person as the essence of caprice. More than most subjects of lawsuits, the use of our natural resources is a communitarian matter. Why then must a genuine dispute over an acknowledged injury to the environment stemming from a violation of law be judgeable only when one individual can show a minutely particularized use of the resource that is threatened, down to the last square inch of hiked soil, or the date of the next planned visit to the zoo? I believe it is truly time to reconceptualize environmental standing. Whether our substantive environmental law changes or remains the same, surely the incorporation into our law of more realistic notions of which affected persons or communities have the right to protest environmental violations is subject to rethinking. But in the meantime, as practical men and women of the law, I can only tell you to consult your zoology manual for details of the specialty fields of your putative plaintiffs and have them make their appointments well ahead of time at the local zoo. "Gotcha" is still the name of the standing game.

Patricia Wald, *Environmental Postcards from the Edge: The Year That Was and the Year That Might Be*, 26 ENVTL. L. REP. 10182 (1996).

A case illustrating some of Judge Wald's concern about the standing inquiry is *ASPCA v. Ringling Bros. & Barnum & Bailey Circus*, 317 F.3d 334 (D.C. Cir. 2003). This presented somewhat similar circumstances to the *Humane Society* case, with a former animal handler at the circus challenging Ringling's alleged mistreatment of its elephants. The Court found that he had standing, although not based on his status as a former employee; the judges felt that his status as a current and future audience member with a "personal attachment" to the animals (he had established an emotional rapport with the elephants and went back to see them after his employment) was enough to satisfy injury-in-fact, since he might observe evidence of the abuse of the elephants. Although unlike *Humane Society* in that standing was granted, this is still an instance of what is ostensibly an important matter of environmental concern, the treatment of animals, being premised on harm to people rather than on harm to the environment itself. The different outcome in *ASPCA* may indicate that *Humane Society* is something of an aberration, and that instances of the ridiculous in standing jurisprudence are fairly uncommon. But for an example of a standing inquiry with a similar flavor, *see* Cetacean Community v. Bush, 386 F.3d 1169 (9th Cir. 2004), discussing whether all cetaceans (dolphins, whales, and porpoises) in the world should be granted standing in the person of a single attorney in order to challenge a Navy use of sonar which might harm those species.

Is it time for the Court to rethink standing doctrine before it becomes even more complex?

2. CITIZEN SUITS

While citizen suits are an important litigation tool, there remains controversy over whether they promote compliance with the law or hinder the ability of government officials to find the best balance between enforcement and flexibility. One commentary has reviewed the evidence supporting both these viewpoints:

MARK SEIDENFELD AND JANNA SATZ NUGENT, "THE FRIENDSHIP OF THE PEOPLE": CITIZEN PARTICIPATION IN ENVIRONMENTAL ENFORCEMENT[6]

73 GEORGE WASHINGTON LAW REVIEW 269, 284–88, 301–02 (2005).

Citizen suits have contributed to the EPA's ultimate goal of increasing compliance in the regulated community and, in many ways, have acted as sustenance to a starving agency. Plagued with the difficult task of detection, a lack of resources, and political constraints, the EPA has, to some extent, welcomed citizen suits to alleviate the tension created by demand for enforcement that outstrips the agency's supply.

Although statutes authorizing private suits to prevent environmental harm predate public enforcement of environmental laws, the Clean Air Act incorporated the first modern civil suit provision in 1970. Since then, almost all major environmental statutes have included citizen suit provisions that closely model those in the Clean Air Act. In essence, Congress has created a cause of action for private citizens to enforce federal environmental regulations by allowing plaintiffs to seek injunctions against ongoing violations and, in some instances, penalties that are paid to the government.

Citizen suit provisions contain notice requirements that were designed to protect the government's position as primary enforcer. First, at least sixty days prior to initiating a citizen suit, a person must notify the EPA, the violator, and under some statutes, the state where the violation occurred. This built-in "grace period" gives the EPA approximately two months to analyze the complaint and to decide whether to take over enforcement. If the government can show that it is already "diligently prosecuting" the alleged violation, the citizen suit is barred, although citizen groups may then intervene in the government's suit. The EPA cannot stop a citizen suit merely by commencing an administrative enforcement proceeding, although the EPA can bar such a suit by commencing an administrative proceeding prior to notice of the citizen suit or if a citizen group fails to file suit within 120 days of the notice. Finally, once the citizen suit has commenced, a settlement agreement or consent

---

order may not be entered until the DOJ and EPA receive a forty-five day notice. In theory, these notification requirements keep the crown on the sovereign enforcer: the EPA's diligent prosecution bars a citizen suit, and even its failure to prosecute does not forfeit its right to block a settlement negotiated by the private parties.

But reality often diverges from theory. The balance between public and private enforcement shifted in 1982 with the emergence of national and regional environmental groups that were well-funded and staffed. Public interest groups studied Discharge Monitoring Reports, which the Clean Water Act requires regulated entities to file, and initiated a plethora of citizen suits under that Act. A year later, private enforcement exceeded federal enforcement efforts, and has been the driving force of environmental litigation ever since. In some years, private enforcement has almost equaled overall government enforcement. * * *

Today, national and regional environmental groups like the Sierra Club, NRDC, and the Atlantic States Legal Foundation are responsible for filing a substantial number of citizen suits. As plaintiffs, the groups seek settlement agreements that provide compliance orders, SEPs [supplemental environmental projects], monetary penalties, and of course, attorneys' fees. This emphasis on financial reward has drawn criticism from those who see cost calculations as a sign of insincerity. At least one observer has noted that although groups may portray themselves as ardent defenders of the environment, they generally choose to prosecute when a company reports numerous violations to the EPA, thereby decreasing discovery costs and increasing the potential for large penalties. Supporters of interest groups' reliance on economic "rewards" insist that having violators pay such rewards offsets a corporation's calculated choice to violate environmental regulations. Moreover, even if the monetary rewards are aimed at self-preservation of the interest groups' business of private enforcement, long-term funding may greatly benefit the environment.

The propensity of the group to reach a reasonable settlement with the alleged violator varies, depending on the nature of the group bringing suit. When the plaintiff is a mass membership group, it might prefer the notoriety that comes from pressing for a big penalty to the certainty of a moderate settlement. When the plaintiff is a group dominated by a central staff, however, it may be more interested in obtaining attorneys' fees and payments to third-party groups controlled by the same staff than in either making a name for itself or improving the environment. It is even possible for a national interest group to derive publicity from having prevented the continuation of an ongoing violation while reaping the direct monetary payment of costs and fees.

In fact, there is reason to believe that defendant corporations sometimes prefer negotiating with citizen enforcers rather than with the EPA and DOJ officials. In 1984, the Environmental Law Institute ("ELI") studied the negotiation processes leading to settlement of four citizen suits and concluded that interest groups frequently lack the leverage of government enforcers and therefore often settle for amounts below the average consent decree filed by the government. Although researchers also determined that there is no "typical" citizen suit settlement process, they did find common characteristics among the suits. For example, over half of the cases are initiated by national environmental organizations acting under the Clean Water Act, and many result in a "relatively fast (and fair) settlement for the large corporation" found in violation of its permit. * * *

Although legislators authorizing the citizen suit provision under the 1970 Clean Air Act believed they were merely extending an established history of private compensation and qui tam actions, controversy has surrounded the power delegated to private citizens acting under environmental citizen suit provisions. Regulated entities cringe at the prospect of dual enforcement and worry that private enforcers will interfere with established relationships and understandings. For example, one of the major impediments to the efforts of states and EPA to induce companies to implement self-audit programs is the fear on the part of the companies that some overly zealous interest group will use the information they provide to sue them. Other members of the regulatory community share "widespread skepticism about both the motivations of private enforcers and their legitimacy as surrogates for government." Critics fear that private enforcers will replace the government's "leniency error," its failure to pursue actions that would produce public benefits, with the "zealousness error," which is created when pursuit of individual benefits imposes public costs. Even the federal courts have expressed concern that enforcement of the law is the proper province of the executive branch and not the citizenry generally.

But citizen suits are not necessarily maniacal exercises of power. Indeed, one of the benefits produced by citizen suits, namely, increased competition for enforcement, has far surpassed the effects originally envisioned. At the federal level, "the growth of private enforcement is acting as a competitive spur to government enforcers, prodding them to improve their management tools for measuring, securing, and overseeing compliance." Additionally, competition from private enforcers may have been the impetus for the EPA's innovative settlements and its reconciliation of policies and practices.

Citizen suits can also reinforce democratic values in our system of environmental regulation. Giving citizens a voice at the enforcement stage of the regulatory process can play an important role in keeping regulators publicly accountable. Although the Administrative Procedure Act affords citizens the opportunity to affect the content of regulation, the actual impact of regulation on the behavior of polluters depends on how those regulations are applied. An agency could alter the meaning of a regulation simply by construing it in a manner contrary to the understanding of the citizens who may have been involved in and even supported its promulgation, and "many interpretive issues arise only at the enforcement stage of a statute's implementation." Without the private right to file suit, agencies could simply elide the interpretive issue by refusing to attempt to enforce the regulation in a context that would raise the issue.

NOTE

While Seidenfeld and Nugent explain the ways in which citizen suits can be misused, another scholar has highlighted the problems with government enforcement, especially by state officials, who are often responsible for enforcement of federal statutes such as the Clean Air Act and Clean Water Act. This article argues that citizen suits have been successful in fulfilling their purpose: to prevent government officials from sliding into lax enforcement practices.

DAVID R. HODAS, ENFORCEMENT OF ENVIRONMENTAL LAW IN A TRIANGULAR FEDERAL SYSTEM: CAN THREE NOT BE A CROWD WHEN ENFORCEMENT AUTHORITY IS SHARED BY THE UNITED STATES, THE STATES, AND THEIR CITIZENS?[7]

54 MARYLAND LAW REVIEW 1552, 1619–23, 1651–54 (1995).

Amazingly, as of 1993, citizen suit judicial enforcement nearly equaled all CWA judicial enforcement efforts brought throughout the nation by all the states and the federal government combined. Because of the realities of enforcement at the federal level, EPA and DOJ have become openly supportive of citizen suits, which significantly augment federal government enforcement efforts. * * *

One of the important lessons citizen suits have taught is that "private industry, left to its own initiative, will procrastinate indefinitely, even at the expense of the environment, [and] the government agencies empowered with protecting the environment are far from diligent in that regard." Only from the impetus of citizen suits do government agencies take meaningful enforcement action.

Unfortunately, when the government takes an enforcement action, it does not mean necessarily that CWA violations actually end. Typical federal and state enforcement consists of administratively issued consent orders comprised of extended compliance schedules and de minimis civil penalties, under which pollution can remain unabated for years. * * *

Most troubling is that the compliance orders, which enable violators to delay compliance and to avoid civil penalties for present and past violations, are often prompted by the state's and polluter's desire to preempt citizen suits after the polluter receives a 60–day letter. Many states routinely preempt citizen suits by entering into mild enforcement consent orders after the citizen group sends 60–day notices to a violator who had not been previously subject to state enforcement attention.

---

7. Copyright 1995. Reprinted by permission.

Because states know that EPA resources are so thin that EPA will not overfile or interfere, they can easily keep enforcement lax while simultaneously preempting citizen suits, particularly in light of several recent court decisions hostile to citizen enforcement. * * *

[S]ome commentators worry that citizen suits, which enforce formally established, legally binding permit terms, may discourage innovation by interfering with nonpublic, informal understandings between EPA and the regulated community. As a result, they speculate that a mechanism under which industry may be willing to try new pollution control technology may be lost. * * *

Other critics complain that CWA citizen suits brought by the "environmentalist enforcement cartel" are economically inefficient. This "over-enforcement" then begets pollution control expenditures whose costs exceed the marginal benefits to society from the reduced pollution, and thus diminishes the power of governmental discretion to achieve economic efficiency by selectively not enforcing CWA violations. * * *

[C]itizen suits account for most of the important CWA enforcement court decisions, almost all of which have made CWA enforcement easier. For instance, citizen suits have established that DMRs containing permit violations are a sufficient basis for obtaining summary judgment against the polluter. Citizen suits have also limited some defenses that polluters can assert, and have led courts to reject other defenses as a matter of law.

Citizen suits are valuable for many other reasons. First, a citizen suit in federal court exposes the violator to the risk of substantially greater civil penalties than tend to be at stake in state courts or agencies or in EPA administrative actions. Citizen suits also expose violators to the equitable power of federal courts to order expensive abatement. As a result, polluters seem to be more fearful of citizen enforcement than state enforcement, and are thus more willing to settle the citizen suits than state judicial actions. * * *

Third, citizen suits are not subject to the individual reluctance some regulators bring to the enforcement arena. Because government engineers tend to move on to industry positions during their careers, disincentives may exist for a state engineer to antagonize local industry or to earn a reputation for being unreasonable by refusing to tolerate small deviations from permit limitations. On a deeper level, government and industry engineers often share similar professional outlooks, which can blur the line separating the two sides and result in a mindset that perceives certain violations as too insignificant to enforce. * * *

Fifth, for similar political reasons, citizen groups are more willing and better able to enforce the CWA against municipalities and state facilities than is the state. As a result of vigorously prosecuted citizen suits, state agencies now can improve compliance from municipalities by threatening to turn cases over to citizen groups if the municipality does not bring its POTW into compliance. When states and citizens understand and respect each other's strengths and weaknesses and use their respective strengths in support of the others' weaknesses, the impact of the enforcement program can be greater than the sum of its parts. * * *

Sixth, without citizen suits, regulators would pursue few, if any, actions against non-major polluters, those discharging less than 1,000,000 gallons per day. * * *

Seventh, citizens are better able than state inspectors to discover unpermitted discharges. Sneak pipe discharging and intermittent dumping, often called "midnight dumping," take place at odd hours in hidden locations. Catching a polluter in the act may require days of continuous observation, which state inspectors, who are already overburdened and who usually work only normal business hours, cannot maintain. But regional citizen groups with dedicated memberships can and do maintain the intensive, prolonged surveillance necessary to catch these polluters.

NOTES

1. The debate over the merits and purposes of citizen suits continues to surface in standing opinions, and in cases like *Defenders* and *Steel Co.* at least some citizen suits in recent years have come out on the losing end. In part IV of the plurality opinion in *Defenders*, Justice Scalia said that the injury-in-fact requirement could not be satisfied by congressional conferral upon *all* persons of "an abstract, self-contained, noninstrumental 'right' to have the Executive observe the procedures required by law." However, Justices Kennedy and Souter joined part IV subject to the "observation" that "Congress has the power to define injuries and articulate chains of causation that will give rise to a case or controversy where none existed before." In *Federal Election Commission v. Akins*, 524 U.S. 11 (1998), the Court firmly rejected Justice Scalia's view that widely shared harms do not qualify as injury in fact.

2. A few studies have looked beyond the theoretical arguments for and against citizen suits to examine the on-the-ground reality of how citizen suits are used. In 1984, the Environmental Protection Agency commissioned the Environmental Law Institute to analyze the use of citizen suits under the Clean Air Act, Clean Water Act, Resource Conservation and Recovery Act, Toxic Substances Control Act, Safe Drinking Water Act, and Noise Control Act. ENVIRONMENTAL LAW INSTITUTE, CITIZEN SUITS: AN ANALYSIS OF CITIZEN ENFORCEMENT ACTIONS UNDER EPA–ADMINISTERED STATUTES (1984). This report presented a picture of early citizen suits as brought primarily under the Clean Water Act, often by large regional or national environmental organizations such as the Conservation Law Foundation of New England, the Sierra Club, and the Natural Resources Defense Council, and against large private defendants (in contrast to suits against public entities to force them to perform mandated statutory duties). Citizen suits were also being employed more often than either the EPA or the ELI had predicted, and the report hypothesized that this was due to perceived laxity of government enforcement efforts. It also recognized that the prevalence of CWA suits was due to the unique availability of reliable information about pollution discharges under that statute's reporting requirements. *See generally id.*

A private, more limited study updated the ELI report, looking at citizen suits from 1995 to 2000, using Freedom of Information Act requests to gather information from the Department of Justice. Kristi M. Smith, *Who's Suing Whom?: A Comparison of Government and Citizen Suit Environmental Enforcement Actions Brought Under EPA–Administered Statutes, 1995–2000*, 29 COLUM. J. ENVTL. L. 359 (2004). This review found a significant change in the use of citizen suits, with large environmental organizations playing a far less prominent role, and more suits (about a third of the total in this time span) against public defendants. Individuals and organizations operating within a single state or smaller area brought the majority of suits within this period. Actions under the CWA were still the most common, although the study showed the number of CAA and RCRA suits increasing over the five years in question. *See id.* at 362, 382–92.

3. As indicated at the beginning of this section, environmental statutes usually require that notice of intention to sue be given to the EPA, to the state in which the violation occurred, and to the alleged violator, at least 60 days prior to the filing of a citizen suit. In *Hallstrom v. Tillamook County,* 493 U.S. 20 (1989), the Supreme Court held that such notice requirements must be strictly interpreted and applied by the courts. *Hallstrom* presented the issue whether full compliance with the notice requirement in section 7002 of RCRA was a mandatory precondition to suit, or whether a failure to comply fully could be disregarded by the trial court at its discretion. Eight federal courts of appeals had divided evenly on this question. Four had interpreted notice provisions as "procedural" requirements that left trial courts flexibility to stay an action or allow it to proceed even though plaintiff had failed to comply with the 60–day requirement. The other four appellate courts took the position that plaintiff's failure to comply with the notice requirement deprived the trial court of jurisdiction to hear the case.

In *Hallstrom,* plaintiffs were concerned that leachate from the defendant county's landfill was causing chemical and bacterial pollution of plaintiffs' soil and groundwater. Plaintiffs gave the defendant proper notice of their intent to sue but did not give notice to the federal EPA or to the state environmental agency until after the suit was filed. The federal district court found that the purpose of the notice requirement was to give the public agencies the opportunity to take over the enforcement of the statute from the private plaintiffs. Since neither the EPA nor the state agency showed any interest in taking action against the county, the court found that dismissing the action and forcing plaintiffs to refile would only waste judicial resources. After a trial on the merits, the district court found that defendant had violated RCRA. The county was given two years to take the necessary steps to contain the leachate. Plaintiffs appealed the denial of immediate injunctive relief, and the county cross-appealed from denial of its motion for summary judgment because of plaintiffs' failure to comply with the notice requirement. The Ninth Circuit held in favor of the county, rejecting the view that the notice requirement was procedural and therefore subject to waiver or equitable modification. The Supreme Court affirmed.

4. What constitutes diligent prosecution sufficient to bar a citizen suit? In *Washington Public Interest Research Group v. Pendleton Woolen Mills,* 11 F.3d 883 (9th Cir. 1993), the EPA had issued a compliance order in 1988,

stating that defendant was in violation of its NPDES permit. The order required Pendleton to prepare a report describing the causes of the violations and identifying the actions necessary to bring it into compliance. The order further required Pendleton to make those physical improvements identified as necessary. An amended compliance order included a threat of a sanction of $25,000 per day if Pendleton violated its terms. In 1990, WashPIRG notified EPA and Pendleton of its intent to bring suit against Pendleton for alleged permit violations. More than 60 days thereafter, WashPIRG filed a complaint seeking (1) a declaration establishing Pendleton's violations, (2) an injunction ordering Pendleton into compliance, and (3) civil penalties for Pendleton's violations from 1985 to the present. The district court entered summary judgment in favor of Pendleton, holding that the existence of EPA's action against Pendleton barred WashPIRG's citizen suit. The court of appeals reversed, holding that section 309(g)(6) of the Clean Water Act precludes citizen suits seeking civil penalties *only* if the EPA is diligently pursuing an administrative penalty action, and that the administrative compliance order which EPA had issued to Pendleton did not seek monetary penalties.

On the other hand, *Arkansas Wildlife Federation v. ICI Americas, Inc.*, 29 F.3d 376 (8th Cir. 1994), held that a citizen suit was jurisdictionally barred under the Clean Water Act because the state pollution control agency was diligently prosecuting, against the same defendant, an action under the state pollution control act. The bar to the citizen suit applied to *all* of ICI's past CWA violations, even though the original consent administrative order, which called for ICI to pay a civil penalty and to comply with applicable effluent limitations, did not cover all of ICI's violations. The consent order later was amended to incorporate all of ICI's past violations, but not until after AWF already had given proper notice of its intent to initiate a citizen suit and had filed a complaint alleging ICI's ongoing violation of the Act and seeking civil penalties and declaratory and injunctive relief. The basis for the court's action was section 309(g)(6)(A)(ii) of the Clean Water Act, which precludes "a civil penalty action" for a violation "with respect to which a State has commenced and is diligently prosecuting an action under a State law comparable to this subsection." The court found that Arkansas had commenced a comparable action when it issued the original consent administrative order, prior to AWF's notice of intent to sue.

5. Harmonizing citizen suits and governmental enforcement actions continues to prove troublesome. For a proposal to regularize the relationship between the two, *see* Jeffrey G. Miller, *Theme and Variations in Statutory Preclusions Against Successive Environmental Enforcement Actions by EPA and Citizens, Part One: Statutory Bars in Citizen Suit Provisions*, 28 HARV. ENVTL. L. REV. 401 (2004) (arguing for a narrow interpretation of the prosecution bar, applying it only when the state-undertaken enforcement will actually lead to compliance by regulated entity). Another coordination problem exists when the federal EPA "overfiles"—that is, files a federal enforcement action even though the state has already begun or completed its own enforcement effort. For a thorough summary of the rulings on this issue, *see* Jerry Organ, *Environmental Federalism Part II: The Impact of* Harmon, Smithfield, *and*

CLEAN *on Overfiling Under RCRA, the CWA, and the CAA,* 30 Envtl. L. Rep. 10732 (2000).

6. As noted, much of the most important environmental litigation is brought by public interest groups. Their ability to bring these suits is dependent on their access to funding. One of the most important sources of funding for these groups is the award of attorneys' fees authorized by many environmental statutes. The availability of fee awards and their size have been the subject of much litigation, both in the environmental area and elsewhere. Two basic rules are that (a) fees are available only to "prevailing parties," and (b) the fee usually is calculated by multiplying a reasonable hourly rate times the number of hours reasonably invested in the suit.

In *Alyeska Pipeline Service Co. v. Wilderness Society,* 421 U.S. 240 (1975), there was no applicable statute authorizing an award of attorneys' fees to the plaintiff organizations, which had sued to prevent the Secretary of the Interior from issuing permits for construction of the trans-Alaska oil pipeline. Plaintiffs prevailed, and the court of appeals awarded them attorneys' fees based upon the court's equitable powers and the theory that plaintiffs were entitled to fees because they were performing the services of a "private attorney general." The Supreme Court reversed, saying that in the United States a prevailing litigant is ordinarily not entitled to collect a reasonable attorneys' fee from the loser, and that exceptions to this "American Rule" are to be established by Congress and not by the courts.

In *Ruckelshaus v. Sierra Club,* 463 U.S. 680 (1983), the issue was whether it was "appropriate," within the meaning of section 307(f) of the Clean Air Act, to award attorneys' fees to a party that had achieved no success on the merits of its claim. Section 307(f) provided, "In any judicial proceeding under this section, the court may award costs of litigation (including reasonable attorney and expert witness fees) whenever it determines that such an award is appropriate." The Supreme Court held that consistent with the "American Rule," it was "appropriate" for lower courts to award attorneys' fees under this section only to a "prevailing litigant." Four Justices dissented, arguing that section 307(f) deliberately contained language differing from the "prevailing party" standard expressly adopted in the attorney fee provisions of many other federal statutes because Congress intended, as was shown by the legislative history, to give the courts of appeals discretionary authority to award fees and costs to a broader category of parties. The dissenters stressed that the Sierra Club was the only party to brief and advocate opposition to the core concept of the EPA regulation in question, "an issue conceded by EPA to be critically important." For a critique of *Ruckelshaus,* see Daniel A. Farber, *Statutory Interpretation and Legislative Supremacy,* 78 GEO. L.J. 281, 301–02 (1989).

Until eight years ago, a plaintiff could recover fees, even without a formal victory in court, if the lawsuit was the catalyst in forcing the defendant to comply. The Supreme Court rejected the catalyst theory in *Buckhannon Board & Care Home, Inc. v. West Virginia Department of Health,* 532 U.S. 598 (2001). In a 5–4 decision, the majority (per Chief Justice Rehnquist) held that under statutes awarding fees to "prevailing parties," the plaintiff must be awarded some relief by the court in order to qualify for fees. Thus, if the defendant surrenders after the litigation begins and renders the case moot, no relief is available. Fortunately for plaintiffs, *Laidlaw* makes it difficult for defendants to make a citizen suit moot.

7. Some commentators urge that citizens may take on more of a role outside the traditional citizen-suit mechanism of suing violators of statutes, especially in increasing their enforcement and monitoring role to include private settlements. *See, e.g.* Thomas Stowe Mullikin & Nancy S. Smith, *Community Participation in Environmental Protection*, 21 UCLA J. ENVTL. L. & POL'Y 75 (2002/2003) (proposing "collaborative compacts" between community and industry as an alternative to citizen suits and Title VI environmental justice actions); Edward Lloyd, *Supplemental Environmental Projects Have Been Effectively Used in Citizen Suits to Deter Future Violations as Well as to Achieve Significant Additional Environmental Benefits*, 10 WIDENER L. REV. 413 (2004) (proposing supplemental environmental projects (SEPs) in settlement of citizen suits to allow some benefit to the community as well as or instead of punishment of the violator); Jessica E. Jay, *Third–Party Enforcement of Conservation Easements*, 29 VT. L. REV. 757 (2005) (discussing third-party enforcement of conservation easements). This type of citizen participation has been especially prominent in habitat conservation plans, which are agreements negotiated between developers and the Department of the Interior under section 11 of the Endangered Species Act, to allow more flexibility than the ESA usually allows for land with endangered species to be developed while still protecting the species. *See* Jody Freeman, *The Private Role in Public Governance*, 75 N.Y.U. L. REV. 543, 659 (2000) (citing Lee P. Breckenridge, *Nonprofit Environmental Organizations and the Restructuring of Institutions for Ecosystem Management*, 25 ECOLOGY L.Q. 692 (1999)). HCP's are discussed in Chapter 3, supra.

C. LEGAL BASES FOR CHALLENGING AGENCY ACTION

1. CONSTITUTIONAL CHALLENGES

Once plaintiffs overcome the obstacles to court access, what claims may they bring? As an initial matter, plaintiffs may allege that a statute violates the non-delegation doctrine—the constitutional principle that forbids Congress from delegating legislative power to agencies. The Supreme Court has only rarely invalidated legislation on these grounds. Prior to *American Trucking* (excerpted below) there had been murmurs from individual Justices on the Court signaling the doctrine's potential revival. *See, e.g.*, Industrial Union Dep't, AFL–CIO v. American Petroleum Inst., 448 U.S. 607 (1980) (Rehnquist, J., concurring in plurality's rejection of OSHA's benzene standard but urging rejection on non-delegation grounds). *American Trucking* seems to lay that possibility to rest, however.

WHITMAN v. AMERICAN TRUCKING ASSOCIATIONS, INC.

Supreme Court of the United States, 2001.
531 U.S. 457, 121 S.Ct. 903, 149 L.Ed.2d 1.

[Section 109(a) of the Clean Air Act requires the EPA Administrator to promulgate National Ambient Air Quality Standards (NAAQS) for each pollutant for which the agency has issued air quality criteria under § 108. Such standards and criteria are to be reviewed every five years. In 1997, when the EPA revised its standards for particulate matter (soot) and ozone (smog), a coalition of industry and states sued the agency for failing to use cost-benefit analysis in setting the new standards. In addition to holding that the EPA may not consider implementation costs in setting standards for NAAQS, the District of Columbia Circuit Court of Appeals found that CAA § 109(b)(1) unconstitutionally delegated legislative power to the EPA Administrator because the EPA's interpretation of the statute offered no "intelligible principle" to limit agency discretion. However, rather than declaring the statute itself unconstitutional as a violation of the non-delegation doctrine, the Circuit Court remanded the issue and invited the EPA to adopt a more restrictive construction of the statute. The Supreme Court granted *certiorari* on petitions from both sides of the litigation.]

JUSTICE SCALIA delivered the opinion of the Court.

Section 109(b)(1) of the CAA instructs the EPA to set "ambient air quality standards the attainment and maintenance of which in the judgment of the Administrator, based on [the] criteria [documents of § 108] and allowing an adequate margin of safety, are requisite to protect the public health." The Court of Appeals held that this section as interpreted by the Administrator did not provide an "intelligible principle" to guide the EPA's exercise of authority in setting NAAQS. "[The] EPA," it said, "lack[ed] any determinate criteria for drawing lines. It has failed to state intelligibly how much is too much." The court hence found that the EPA's interpretation (but not the statute itself) violated the non-delegation doctrine. We disagree.

In a delegation challenge, the constitutional question is whether the statute has delegated legislative power to the agency. Article I, § 1, of the Constitution vests "[a]ll legislative Powers herein granted ... in a Congress of the United States." This text permits no delegation of those powers, and so we repeatedly have said that when Congress confers decisionmaking authority upon agencies *Congress* must "lay down by legislative act an intelligible principle to which the person or body authorized to [act] is directed to conform." We have never suggested that an agency can cure an unlawful delegation of legislative power by adopting in its discretion a limiting construction of the statute. * * * The idea that an agency can cure an unconstitutionally standardless delegation of power by declining to exercise some of that power seems to us internally contradictory. The very choice of which portion of the power to exercise—that is to say, the prescription of the standard that Congress had omitted—would *itself* be an exercise of the forbidden legislative authority. Whether the statute delegates legislative power is a question for the courts, and an agency's voluntary self-denial has no bearing upon the answer.

We agree with the Solicitor General that the text of § 109(b)(1) of the CAA at a minimum requires that "[f]or a discrete set of pollutants and based on published air quality criteria that reflect the latest scientific knowledge, [the] EPA must establish uniform national standards at a level that is requisite to protect public health from the adverse effects of the pollutant in the ambient air." Requisite, in turn, "mean[s] sufficient, but not more than necessary." * * *

The scope of discretion § 109(b)(1) allows is in fact well within the outer limits of our non-delegation precedents. In the history of the Court we have found the requisite "intelligible principle" lacking in only two statutes, one of which provided literally no guidance for the exercise of discretion, and the other of which conferred authority to regulate the entire economy on the basis of no more precise a standard than stimulating the economy by assuring "fair competition." * * * And we have found an "intelligible principle" in various statutes authorizing regulation in the "public interest." In short, we have "almost never felt qualified to second-guess Congress regarding the permissible degree of policy judgment that can be left to those executing or applying the law."

It is true enough that the degree of agency discretion that is acceptable varies according to the scope of the power congressionally conferred. * * * [Congress] must provide substantial guidance on setting air standards that affect the entire national economy. But even in sweeping regulatory schemes we have never demanded, as the Court of Appeals did here, that statutes provide a "determinate criterion" for saying "how much [of the regulated harm] is too much." * * * It is therefore not conclusive for delegation purposes that, as respondents argue, ozone and particulate matter are "non-threshold" pollutants that inflict a continuum of adverse health effects at any airborne concentration greater than zero, and hence require the EPA to make judgments of degree. "[A] certain degree of discretion, and thus of lawmaking, inheres in most executive or judicial action." Section 109(b)(1) of the CAA, which to repeat we interpret as requiring the EPA to set air quality standards at the level that is "requisite"—that is, not lower or higher than is necessary—to protect the public health with an adequate margin of safety, fits comfortably within the scope of discretion permitted by our precedent.

We therefore reverse the judgment of the Court of Appeals remanding for reinterpretation that would avoid a supposed delegation of legislative power. It will remain for the Court of Appeals—on the remand that we direct for other reasons—to dispose of any other preserved challenge to the NAAQS under the judicial-review provisions contained in 42 U.S.C. § 7607(d)(9).

NOTES

1. The D.C. Circuit opinion in *American Trucking* attracted significant criticism. *See, e.g.*, Richard Pierce, *The Inherent Limits on Judicial Control of Agency Discretion: The D.C. Circuit and the Non–Delegation Doctrine*, 52 ADMIN. L. REV. 63 (2000); Cass R. Sunstein, *Is the Clean Air Act Unconstitutional?* 98 MICH. L. REV. 303 (1999). The D.C. Circuit had adopted a novel view of the non-delegation doctrine, essentially arguing that a delegation that would otherwise be unconstitutional could be saved by the agency's construction of the statutory grant. The court wrote: "Where (as here) statutory language and an existing agency interpretation involve an unconstitutional delegation of power, but an interpretation without the constitutional weakness is or may be available, our response is not to strike down the statute but to give the agency an opportunity to extract a determinate standard on its own." American Trucking Ass'ns v. EPA, 175 F.3d 1027, 1038 (D.C. Cir. 1999). Doesn't it make sense to allow the agency to salvage an unconstitutional statute by restricting its own authority? On the one hand, this would accomplish the goal of ensuring that agencies do not exercise unconstrained discretionary power, which is one of the purposes of the non-delegation doctrine. See Lisa Schultz Bressman, *Disciplining Delegation After* Whitman v. American Trucking Ass'ns, 87 CORNELL L. REV. 452 (2002). On the other hand, perhaps this would do little to ensure that Congress makes the crucial policy decisions itself, another purpose of the doctrine. Indeed, allowing agencies to "save" overly broad delegations might encourage Congress to be careless in drafting statutes.

2. The scholarly literature on the non-delegation doctrine is voluminous. *See, e.g.*, DAVID SCHOENBROD, POWER WITHOUT RESPONSIBILITY: HOW CONGRESS ABUSES THE PEOPLE THROUGH DELEGATION (1993) (arguing that delegation weakens democracy and urging federal courts to resurrect the non-delegation doctrine); THEODORE J. LOWI, THE END OF LIBERALISM 93 (2d ed. 1979) (arguing that broad delegations are "policy without law"). *But cf.* Richard J. Pierce, Jr., *Political Accountability and Delegated Power: A Response to Professor Lowi*, 36 AM. U. L. REV. 391, 392 (1987) (arguing that judicial enforcement of the non-delegation doctrine would be a "terrible" response to broad delegations); Jerry L. Mashaw, *Prodelegation: Why Administrators Should Make Political Decisions*, 1 J.L. ECON. & ORG. 81, 83 (1985) (arguing that broad delegations increase administrative responsiveness); Thomas W. Merrill, *Rethinking Article I, Section I: From Nondelegation to Exclusive Delegation*, 104 COLUM. L. REV. 2097 (2004) (arguing that agencies should be allowed some legislative power, as long such authority stems exclusively from explicit statutory delegations by Congress, in order to take advantage of agencies' superior institutional capacity to make certain decisions).

2. ADMINISTRATIVE LAW CHALLENGES

Because non-delegation challenges are futile, the more common challenge to agency action attacks the procedural regularity and/or substantive lawfulness of an agency's decision. Litigants wishing to challenge agency decisions typically make at least two different arguments: First, that the agency missed or mishandled one of the procedural steps it is obligated to take under the applicable environmental statute or under the Administrative Procedure Act (APA) (which is the federal law generally applicable to all federal agency action). Second, that the agency made a substantive error, meaning that, although it observed all of the required procedures, the actual decision it made on the merits was unlawful. If a plaintiff prevails using either of these arguments, the court will invalidate the agency action. Sometimes, then, important victories turn on what might seem like rather technical claims that an agency mishandled a procedure, or that it missed a step in its reasoning.

If Congress wishes to provide for a different standard of review for a particular agency action, it can do so in the specific governing legislation. This would essentially trump the APA, which operates as a default. Indeed, it is important to remember that the legislation under which the agency derives its authority for the disputed action (for our purposes this would be a specific environmental law) is the first place to look to determine both which procedures the agency is obligated to follow, and what standard of review applies. Where that statute is silent, however, one must consult the APA.

At least in theory, however, courts pay different degrees of deference to different kinds of agency decisions. These degrees of deference are expressed as different "standards of review". The question of which of these standards ought to apply in any given instance of judicial review of agency action is called the "scope of review" issue. For example, courts generally review agency decisions of fact or policy using the "arbitrary or capricious" standard of review, whereas they review formal (trial type) adjudicative decisions using a "substantial evidence" standard of review because this is what the APA requires. Traditionally, courts have been least deferential to agency interpretations of law. While in theory these standards of review are different—scrutinizing an agency's rationale for arbitrariness is seemingly more deferential than demanding the agency provide "substantial evidence" based on the hearing record—in practice, they can conflate into the same thing. This is a secret that administrative law professors reveal only toward the end of the semester, but it behooves us, in an environmental law course, to reveal it early. Indeed, critics of these different standards of review have argued that they devolve into a general and rather unprincipled test of "reasonableness" which allows courts to defer or not defer as they wish. Others claim that the difference is meaningful.

The scope-of-review issue cannot be fully understood without a grasp of the basics of administrative procedure, however. Indeed, effective environmental lawyers are necessarily very adept at administrative law. For our purposes, there are three important categories of administrative actions, all governed by the APA. The first category consists of "formal" adjudications. This type of procedure applies whenever the specific statute governing the agency action (e.g., the Endangered Species Act section 7(h) exemption provision) requires an issue to be "determined on the record after opportunity for an agency hearing." 5 U.S.C. § 554. The procedures required for a formal adjudication are essentially similar to those of a judicial trial. Administrative law judges preside over these quasi-trials and have considerable discretionary authority over the proceedings. In reviewing the agency's ruling following a formal adjudication, courts must uphold the action unless it is unsupported by "substantial evidence" or violates substantive limits on the agency's powers. This standard of review applies by virtue of the APA, which specifies a list of standards of review, if rather obliquely, in 5 U.S.C. § 706(2)(A)–(E).

The second category of administrative action that is important for our purposes is informal rulemaking. Agencies like the EPA translate their legislative mandates into more specific requirements by promulgating regulations, which are also called "legislative rules," and which have the force and effect of legislation itself. Section 553 of the APA requires agencies to go through a notice-and-comment process when promulgating rules:

1.　The first step of informal rulemaking is publication of a notice in the Federal Register describing the proposed rule.

2.　The agency must then provide for an "opportunity to comment," during which interested parties have at least 30 days to respond to the proposed rule.

3.　Then, the agency must issue, in conjunction with its promulgation of the rule, a "concise general statement" of the rule's basis and purpose.

In practice, this simple-sounding procedure has become a highly contested, time-consuming and costly process. In a typical rulemaking involving a major environmental rule with significant implications, a variety of interested parties on all sides of the issue will participate in the comment process by submitting voluminous materials to the agency, which the agency then considers as it deliberates over the rule. The agency must usually comply with other analytic requirements imposed by other statutes or Executive Orders, such as cost-benefit analysis. The agency then develops an extremely detailed defense of its ultimate policy choice (which it publishes in the federal register as a rule), often carefully responding to objections from the comments and building its case with scientific data, all in order to withstand judicial review. The APA fails to specify clearly the scope of review for agency rules, but by default, "arbitrary or capricious" review applies. § 706 (2)(A). There is also another kind of rulemaking procedure known as "formal rulemaking" which is akin to formal adjudication, but has virtually no practical importance.

The final category of agency action, and in a way the most important, is informal adjudication. Informal adjudications include the vast number of government actions that require neither a formal trial-type hearing (producing an order binding the instant parties) nor an informal notice-and-comment process (producing a rule affecting future conduct of all regulated parties). Informal adjudications encompass, therefore, all the every-day discretionary decisions an agency makes, including allocations of discretionary funds and approvals of projects. Many important environmental decisions fall into this category, including many funding decisions, project approvals, and enforcement choices. The APA has little to say about the procedures to be used in these cases, and § 706 of the APA does not specify a standard of review for them. However, as we shall see in the case below, over time, courts have come to review these informal adjudications using the "arbitrary or capricious" standard. Thus, at a minimum, most agency decisions of any importance in environmental law will be subject to the arbitrary and capricious standard of review.

CITIZENS TO PRESERVE OVERTON PARK, INC. v. VOLPE

Supreme Court of the United States, 1971.
401 U.S. 402, 91 S.Ct. 814, 28 L.Ed.2d 136.

Opinion of the Court by JUSTICE MARSHALL, announced by JUSTICE STEWART.

The growing public concern about the quality of our natural environment has prompted Congress in recent years to enact legislation designed to curb the accelerating destruction of our country's natural beauty. We are concerned in this case with § 4(f) of the Department of Transportation Act of 1966, as amended, and § 18(a) of the Federal–Aid Highway Act of 1968, 82 Stat. 823, 23 U.S.C.A. § 138 (hereafter § 138). These statutes prohibit the Secretary of Transportation from authorizing the use of federal funds to finance the construction of highways through public parks if a "feasible and prudent" alternative route exists. If no such route is available, the statutes allow him to approve construction through parks only if there has been "all possible planning to minimize harm" to the park. [The plaintiffs contended that the Secretary violated these restrictions in approving the construction of an interstate highway through Overton Park, a 342–acre park in Memphis.]

A threshold question—whether petitioners are entitled to any judicial review—is easily answered. Section 701 of the Administrative Procedure Act, 5 U.S.C.A. § 701, provides that the action of "each authority of the Government of the United States," which includes the Department of Transportation, is subject to judicial review except where there is a statutory prohibition on review or where "agency action is committed to agency discretion by law." In this case there is no indication that Congress sought to prohibit judicial review and there is most certainly no "showing of 'clear and convincing evidence' of a * * * legislative intent" to restrict access to judicial review. * * *

Similarly, the Secretary's decision here does not fall within the exception for action "committed to agency discretion." This is a very narrow exception. The legislative history of the Administrative Procedure Act indicates that it is applicable in those rare instances where "statutes are drawn in such broad terms that in a given case there is no law to apply."

Section 4(f) of the Department of Transportation Act and § 138 of the Federal–Aid Highway Act are clear and specific directives. Both the Department of Transportation Act and the Federal–Aid Highway Act provide that the Secretary "shall not approve any program or project" that requires the use of any public parkland "unless (1) there is no feasible and prudent alternative to the use of such land, and (2) such program includes all possible planning to minimize harm to such park * * *." This language is a plain and explicit bar to the use of federal funds for construction of highways through parks—only the most unusual situations are exempted.

Despite the clarity of the statutory language, respondents argue that the Secretary has wide discretion. They recognize that the requirement that there be no "feasible" alternative route admits of little administrative discretion. For this exemption to apply the Secretary must find that as a matter of sound engineering it would not be feasible to build the highway along any other route. Respondents argue, however, that the requirement that there be no other "prudent" route requires the Secretary to engage in a wide-ranging balancing of competing interests. They contend that the Secretary should weigh the detriment resulting from the destruction of parkland against the cost of other routes, safety considerations, and other factors, and determine on the basis of the importance that he attaches to these other factors whether, on balance, alternative feasible routes would be "prudent."

But no such wide-ranging endeavor was intended. It is obvious that in most cases considerations of cost, directness of route, and community disruption will indicate that parkland should be used for highway construction whenever possible. * * * Thus, if Congress intended these factors to be on an equal footing with preservation of parkland there would have been no need for the statutes.

Congress clearly did not intend that cost and disruption of the community were to be ignored by the Secretary. But the very existence of the statutes indicates that protection of parkland was to be given paramount importance. The few green havens that are public parks were not to be lost unless there were truly unusual factors present in a particular case or the cost or community disruption resulting from alternative routes reached extraordinary magnitudes. If the statutes are to have any meaning, the Secretary cannot approve the destruction of parkland unless he finds that alternative routes present unique problems.

Plainly, there is "law to apply" and thus the exemption for action "committed to agency discretion" is inapplicable. * * *

But the existence of judicial review is only the start: the standard for review must also be determined. For that we must look to § 706 of the Administrative Procedure Act, 5 U.S.C.A. § 706, which provides that a "reviewing court shall * * * hold unlawful and set aside agency action, findings, and conclusions found" not to meet six separate standards. In all cases agency action must be set aside if the action was "arbitrary, capricious, an abuse of discretion, or otherwise not in accordance with law" or if the action failed to meet statutory, procedural, or constitutional requirements. In certain narrow, specifically limited situations, the agency action is to be set aside if the action was not supported by "substantial evidence." And in other equally narrow circumstances the reviewing court is to engage in a *de novo* review of the action and set it aside if it was "unwarranted by the facts." * * *

[The Court rejected the plaintiff's arguments that either the "substantial evidence" test or the *"de novo* review" requirement applied.]

Even though there is no *de novo* review in this case and the Secretary's approval of the route of I–40 does not have ultimately to meet the substantial evidence test, the generally applicable standards of § 706 require the reviewing court to engage in a substantial inquiry. Certainly, the Secretary's decision is entitled to a presumption of regularity. * * * But that presumption is not to shield his action from a thorough, probing, in-depth review.

The court is first required to decide whether the Secretary acted within the scope of his authority. * * * This determination naturally begins with a delineation of the scope of the Secretary's authority and discretion. As has been shown, Congress has specified only a small range of choices that the Secretary can make. Also involved in this initial inquiry is a determination of whether on the facts the Secretary's decision can reasonably be said to be within that range. The reviewing court must consider whether the Secretary properly construed his authority to approve the use of parkland as limited to situations where there are no feasible alternative routes or where feasible alternative routes involve uniquely difficult problems. And the reviewing court must be able to find that the Secretary could have reasonably believed that in this case there are no feasible alternatives or that alternatives do involve unique problems.

Scrutiny of the facts does not end, however, with the determination that the Secretary has acted within the scope of his statutory authority. Section 706(2)(A) requires a finding that the actual choice made was not "arbitrary, capricious, an abuse of discretion, or otherwise not in accordance with law." To make this finding the Court must consider whether the decision was based on a consideration of the relevant factors and whether there has been a clear error of judgment.

* * * Although this inquiry into the facts is to be searching and careful, the ultimate standard of review is a narrow one. The court is not empowered to substitute its judgment for that of the agency.

* * * The lower courts based their review on the litigation affidavits that were presented. These affidavits were merely *"post hoc"* rationalizations * * * which have traditionally been found to be an inadequate basis for review. * * * And they clearly do not constitute the "whole record"

compiled by the agency: the basis for review required by § 706 of the Administrative Procedure Act. * * *

Thus it is necessary to remand this case to the District Court for plenary review of the Secretary's decision. That review is to be based on the full administrative record that was before the Secretary at the time he made his decision. But since the bare record may not disclose the factors that were considered or the Secretary's construction of the evidence it may be necessary for the District Court to require some explanation in order to determine if the Secretary acted within the scope of his authority and if the Secretary's action was justifiable under the applicable standard.

The court may require the administrative officials who participated in the decision to give testimony explaining their action. Of course, such inquiry into the mental processes of administrative decisionmakers is usually to be avoided. *United States v. Morgan,* 313 U.S. 409, 422, 61 S.Ct. 999, 85 L.Ed. 1429 (1941). And where there are administrative findings that were made at the same time as the decision, as was the case in *Morgan,* there must be a strong showing of bad faith or improper behavior before such inquiry may be made. But here there are no such formal findings and it may be that the only way there can be effective judicial review is by examining the decisionmakers themselves. * * *

The District Court is not, however, required to make such an inquiry. It may be that the Secretary can prepare formal findings including the information required by DOT Order 5610.1 that will provide an adequate explanation for his action. Such an explanation will, to some extent, be a *"post hoc* rationalization" and thus must be viewed critically. If the District Court decides that additional explanation is necessary, that court should consider which method will prove the most expeditious so that full review may be had as soon as possible.

NOTES

1. The Secretary ultimately decided to disapprove the highway, a decision that was upheld on appeal. *See* Citizens to Preserve Overton Park, Inc. v. Brinegar, 494 F.2d 1212 (6th Cir. 1974). For a critique of the outcome in *Overton Park,* see Peter L. Strauss, *Considering Political Alternatives to "Hard Look" Review,* 1989 DUKE L.J. 538, 544–47. Professor Strauss later wrote a detailed history of section 4(f) of the Transportation Act and the events leading up to *Overton Park.* He concluded that the Court misinterpreted the statute:

> Political controls, so far as one can tell, were the only controls Congress had considered; and in the instance, they were working well. A fuller appreciation for the Overton Park controversy, whether viewed from Washington, D.C., or Memphis, Tennessee, shows wide and effective engagement of a variety of political actors in the controversy. The effect of the Court's action * * * was to empower one of those actors to an extent that had not been contemplated. * * *

Peter L. Strauss, *Revisiting Overton Park: Political and Judicial Controls Over Administrative Actions Affecting the Community*, 39 UCLA L. REV. 1251 (1992). Professor Strauss suggested that the Court interfered in a functioning political process, just one that resulted in a loss for the citizen group. But should courts leave these decisions to the political process? Is there any reason to believe that environmental interests will be as powerful and well-resourced as other interests?

2. *Overton Park* is one of the Supreme Court's clearest explanations of the different standards of review in the APA. As Justice Marshall points out, under the APA § 702, there is a category of agency action that is "committed to agency discretion". But what does this mean? If a matter is literally committed to agency discretion such that Congress has provided no standards by which it might be reviewed by a Court, wouldn't the legislation also lack an "intelligible principle" sufficient to satisfy the non-delegation doctrine? This is just one category of action that is, in theory, unreviewable. Enforcement discretion appears to be another. In *Heckler v. Chaney*, 470 U.S. 821 (1985), the Court held that an agency's decision to eschew enforcement action is unreviewable. The Court generally considers enforcement decisions unsuitable for judicial review, likening them to "prosecutorial" discretion and being loath to interfere with agency judgments. *See also* Arnow v. United States Nuclear Regulatory Comm'n, 868 F.2d 223 (7th Cir. 1989) (applying *Chaney* to an NRC enforcement decision). For a critique of *Chaney, see* Cass R. Sunstein, *Reviewing Agency Inaction After* Heckler v. Chaney, 52 U. CHI. L. REV. 653 (1985). The obstacles to enlisting courts in overseeing agency enforcement decisions, or in prodding reluctant agencies to take action where they have chosen not to, is of major significance to environmental plaintiffs. Yet the Court draws a rather bright line between "action" *versus* "inaction" and "discretionary" *versus* "non-discretionary" decisions for purposes of judicial review. The most recent word from the Supreme Court on this subject came in *Norton v. Southern Utah Wilderness Alliance*, 542 U.S. 55 (2004). The Court held that it could not review the Bureau of Land Management's refusal to regulate increased off-road vehicle use in an area under consideration for designation as wilderness even though a statute required the agency to manage such land so as not to compromise its wilderness character. The Court ruled that the land use plan in which the BLM promised to monitor vehicle use did not bind it to restrict use of the vehicles, and thus review of the BLM's implementation of the plan would allow a broad attack on policy rather than a challenge of a specific failure of an agency to perform a discrete and required action. For an argument that the judiciary should review agency enforcement actions, including agency inaction, *see* Lisa Schultz Bressman, *Judicial Review of Agency Inaction: An Arbitrariness Approach*, 79 N.Y.U. L. REV. 1657 (2004) (proposing that suits against agencies be allowed in such situations as long as the plaintiff is contesting arbitrary agency action or inaction and not just expressing a generalized grievance about an executive decision).

3. Note that there are two review "moments" in the *Overton Park* case: First, the court scrutinized the statutory grant of authority, deferring not at all to the agency's view of what was required. Second, the court reviewed the agency's application of its discretion and found it arbitrary or capricious.

4. The *Overton Park* approach to reviewing informal adjudication by an agency (in this case the Secretary's approval) was strongly reconfirmed in *Motor Vehicle Manufacturers Ass'n v. State Farm Mutual Automobile Insurance Co.*, 463 U.S. 29 (1983), in which the Court applied the "arbitrary or capricious" test to overturn an administrative decision to rescind a legislative rule. As background, the National Highway Traffic Safety Administration in 1981 rescinded a 1977 decision requiring all new cars produced after September 1982 to be equipped with passive restraints (such as automatic seatbelts). After a detailed examination of the rulemaking record, the Court found the rescission to be arbitrary or capricious. The Court found that the agency failed to consider the possibility of modifying rather than rescinding the regulation and had been too quick to dismiss the safety benefits of automatic seatbelts. The agency had also failed to consider an obvious alternative: requiring air bags.

Thus, after *Overton Park* and *State Farm* it became clear that even when using the deferential-sounding standard of review like "arbitrary or capricious," courts would be inclined to engage in close scrutiny of agency action, demanding that agencies take a "hard look" at the data, arguments and alternatives before making a policy decision. And this standard of review would apply to reviewing informal adjudications (as in *Overton Park*) as well as informal rulemaking (as in *State Farm*). Many environmental decisions involve this standard of review. *State Farm* remains the Supreme Court's clearest statement of what constitutes "arbitrary or capricious review," and it is routinely cited in environmental cases.

5. A major scholarly debate surrounds the kind of "hard look" review endorsed by *Overton Park* and *State Farm*. The following statement is typical of the view of the critics:

> The predictable result of stringent "hard look" judicial review of complex rulemaking is ossification. Because the agencies perceive that the reviewing courts are inconsistent in the degree to which they are deferential, they are constrained to prepare for the worst-case scenario on judicial review. This can be extremely resource-intensive and time-consuming. Moreover, since the criteria for substantive judicial review are the same for repealing old rules as for promulgating new rules, the agencies are equally chary of revisiting old rules, even in the name of flexibility.

Thomas O. McGarity, *Some Thoughts on "Deossifying" the Rulemaking Process*, 41 DUKE L.J. 1385, 1419–20 (1992). In response to the critics of "hard look" review, Mark Seidenfeld contends that his "experience as an agency lawyer leads me to believe that, without some external constraint on agency decisionmaking processes, staff members are apt to take shortcuts to avoid extra work, to yield to short-run political pressures that take time and energy to counter, or to alter a decision to make it easier to defend to their superiors." Mark Seidenfeld, *Demystifying Deossification: Rethinking Recent Proposals to Modify Judicial Review of Notice and Comment Rulemaking*, 75 TEX. L. REV. 483, 564 (1997). McGarity counters that judicial discretion is "in fact so wide that a single unsympathetic or confused reviewing court can bring about a dramatic shift in focus or even the complete destruction of an entire regulatory program." *Id.* at 541.

6. In the early 1970s, a number of appellate courts appeared to find the APA's dichotomy between formal adjudication (with all its attendant "trial-type" procedural protections) and informal rulemaking (with only a guarantee of notice and comment) too confining. In several cases involving the review of agency rulemaking, courts seemed to require agencies to adopt procedures going beyond the basic statutory requirements in section 553 of the APA, thereby making the relatively low intensity process of informal rulemaking look more like the procedure-laden process of formal adjudication. *See, e.g.,* Mobil Oil Corp. v. Federal Power Comm'n, 483 F.2d 1238, 1257 (D.C.Cir. 1973); Appalachian Power Co. v. EPA, 477 F.2d 495 (4th Cir. 1973). The primary reason for these "hybrid rulemaking" cases was an apparent belief that the basic APA procedures failed in complex cases to provide fairness to the parties and to compel reasoned decision-making by the agencies.

7. The hybrid rulemaking issue finally reached the Supreme Court in the following case, which grew out of the long-standing controversy over nuclear waste disposal. Critics of atomic energy argued that nuclear energy plants should not be built until the disposal problem was solved. The Atomic Energy Commission consistently rejected this and other concerns about the safety of nuclear power. The issue before the Court was whether the agency had employed the proper procedures to consider this issue. If waste disposal had been considered during the proceeding to license a specific plant, a full trial-type hearing would have been required because the APA requires formal adjudication for licensing. By shifting consideration of the issue to a rulemaking process, could the agency escape all but the minimal "notice and comment" requirements?

VERMONT YANKEE NUCLEAR POWER CORP. v. NATURAL RESOURCES DEFENSE COUNCIL, INC.

Supreme Court of the United States, 1978.
435 U.S. 519, 98 S.Ct. 1197, 55 L.Ed.2d 460.

JUSTICE REHNQUIST delivered the opinion of the Court.

In December 1967, after the mandatory adjudicatory hearing and necessary review, the Commission granted petitioner Vermont Yankee a permit to build a nuclear power plant in Vernon, Vt. Thereafter, Vermont Yankee applied for an operating license. Respondent Natural Resources Defense Council (NRDC) objected to the granting of a license, however, and therefore a hearing on the application commenced on August 10, 1971. Excluded from consideration at the hearings, over NRDC's objection, was the issue of the environmental effects of operations to reprocess fuel or dispose of wastes resulting from the reprocessing operations.[8] This ruling was affirmed by the Appeal Board in June 1972.

---

8. The nuclear fission which takes place in light water nuclear reactors apparently converts its principal fuel, uranium, into plutonium, which is itself highly radioactive but can be used as reactor fuel if separated from the remaining uranium and radioactive waste products. Fuel reprocessing refers to the process necessary to recapture usable plutonium. Waste disposal, at the present stage of technological development, refers to the storage of the highly and very long-lived radioactive waste products until they detoxify sufficiently that they no longer present an

In November 1972, however, the Commission, making specific reference to the Appeal Board's decision with respect to the Vermont Yankee license, instituted rulemaking proceedings "that would specifically deal with the question of consideration of environmental effects associated with the uranium fuel cycle in the individual cost-benefit analyses for light water cooled nuclear power reactors." * * *

Much of the controversy in this case revolves around the procedures used in the rulemaking hearing which commenced in February 1973. In a supplemental notice of hearing the Commission indicated that while discovery or cross-examination would not be utilized, the Environmental Survey would be available to the public before the hearing along with the extensive background documents cited therein. All participants would be given a reasonable opportunity to present their position and could be represented by counsel if they so desired. Written and, time permitting, oral statements would be received and incorporated into the record. All persons giving oral statements would be subject to questioning by the Commission. At the conclusion of the hearing, a transcript would be made available to the public and the record would remain open for 30 days to allow the filing of supplemental written statements. More than 40 individuals and organizations representing a wide variety of interests submitted written comments. On January 17, 1973, the Hearing Board held a planning session to schedule the appearance of witnesses and to discuss methods for compiling a record. The hearing was held on February 1 and 2, with participation from a number of groups, including the Commission's staff, the United States Environmental Protection Agency, a manufacturer of reactor equipment, a trade association from the nuclear industry, a group of electric utility companies, and a group called Consolidated National Intervenors who represented 79 groups and individuals including respondent NRDC.

After the hearing, the Commission's staff filed a supplemental document for the purpose of clarifying and revising the Environmental Survey. Then, the Hearing Board forwarded its report to the Commission without rendering any decision.

[The Commission approved the procedures used, issued a final rule concluding that "the environmental effects of the uranium fuel cycle have been shown to be relatively insignificant," and issued the license requested by Vermont Yankee].

Respondents appealed from both the Commission's adoption of the rule and its decision to grant Vermont Yankee's license to the Court of Appeals for the District of Columbia Circuit. * * *

* * * [B]efore determining whether the Court of Appeals reached a permissible result, we must determine exactly what result it did reach, and in this case that is no mean feat. Vermont Yankee argues that the court invalidated the rule because of the inadequacy of the procedures

---

environmental hazard. There are presently no physical or chemical steps which render this waste less toxic, other than simply the passage of time.

employed in the proceedings. Respondent NRDC, on the other hand, labeling petitioner's view of the decision a "straw man," argues to this Court that the court merely held that the record was inadequate to enable the reviewing court to determine whether the agency had fulfilled its statutory obligation. But we unfortunately have not found the parties' characterization of the opinion to be entirely reliable; it appears here, as in *Orloff v. Willoughby,* 345 U.S. 83, 87 (1953), that "in this Court the parties changed positions as nimbly as if dancing a quadrille."

[The Court concluded, however, that the court of appeals had invalidated the Atomic Energy's decision on procedural grounds, because the agency failed to allow cross-examination of the fairly conclusory evidence presented by the key expert witness on whom it relied].

In prior opinions we have intimated that even in a rulemaking proceeding when an agency is making a "quasi-judicial" determination by which a very small number of persons are "exceptionally affected, in each case upon individual grounds," in some circumstances additional procedures may be required in order to afford the aggrieved individuals due process. *United States v. Florida East Coast R. Co.,* 410 U.S. at 242–245, 93 S.Ct. at 819–821, quoting from *Bi–Metallic Investment Co. v. State Board of Equalization,* 239 U.S. 441 (1915). It might also be true, although we do not think the issue is presented in this case and accordingly do not decide it, that a totally unjustified departure from well settled agency procedures of long standing might require judicial correction.

But this much is absolutely clear. Absent constitutional constraints or extremely compelling circumstances "the administrative agencies 'should be free to fashion their own rules of procedure and to pursue methods of inquiry capable of permitting them to discharge their multitudinous duties.' " *Federal Communications Comm'n v. Schreiber,* 381 U.S. at 290, 85 S.Ct. at 1467. Indeed, our cases could hardly be more explicit in this regard. The Court has, as we noted in *FCC v. Schreiber,* upheld this principle in a variety of applications, including that case where the District Court, instead of inquiring into the validity of the FCC's exercise of its rulemaking authority, devised procedures to be followed by the agency on the basis of its conception of how the public and private interest involved could best be served. Examining § 4(j) of the Communications Act, the Court unanimously held that the Court of Appeals erred in upholding that action. And the basic reason for this decision was the Court of Appeals' serious departure from the very basic tenet of administrative law that agencies should be free to fashion their own rules of procedure. * * *

Respondent NRDC argues that § 553 of the Administrative Procedure Act merely establishes lower procedural bounds and that a court may routinely require more than the minimum when an agency's proposed rule addresses complex or technical factual issues or "issues of great public import." We have, however, previously shown that our decisions reject this view. We also think the legislative history, even the part which it cites, does not bear out its contention. The Senate Report explains what eventually became § 533(c) thusly:

> "This subsection states * * * the minimum requirements of public rule making procedure short of statutory hearing. Under it agencies might in addition confer with industry advisory committees, consult organizations, hold informal 'hearings,' and the like. Considerations of practicality, necessity, and public interest * * * will naturally govern the agency's determination of the extent to which public proceedings should go. Matters of great import, or those where the public submission of facts will be either useful to the agency or a protection to the public, should naturally be accorded more elaborate public procedures."

The House Report is in complete accord. * * *

There are compelling reasons for construing § 553 in this manner. In the first place, if courts continually review agency proceedings to determine whether the agency employed procedures which were, in the Court's opinion, perfectly tailored to reach what the court perceives to be the "best" or "correct" result, judicial review would be totally unpredictable. And the agencies, operating under this vague injunction to employ the "best" procedures and facing the threat of reversal if they did not, would undoubtedly adopt full adjudicatory procedures in every instance. Not only would this totally disrupt the statutory scheme, through which Congress enacted "a formula upon which opposing social and political forces have come to rest," but all the inherent advantages of informal rulemaking would be totally lost.

Secondly, it is obvious that the court in this case reviewed the agency's choice of procedures on the basis of the record actually produced at the hearing, and not on the basis of the information available to the agency when it made the decision to structure the proceedings in a certain way. This sort of Monday morning quarterbacking not only encourages but almost compels the agency to conduct all rule-making proceedings with the full panoply of procedural devices normally associated only with adjudicatory hearings.

Finally, and perhaps most importantly, this sort of review fundamentally misconceives the nature of the standard for judicial review of an agency rule. The court below uncritically assumed that additional procedures will automatically result in a more adequate record because it will give interested parties more of an opportunity to participate and contribute to the proceedings. But informal rulemaking need not be based solely on the transcript of a hearing held before an agency. Indeed, the agency need not even hold a formal hearing. *See* 5 U.S.C.A. § 553(c). Thus, the adequacy of the "record" in this type of proceeding is not correlated directly to the type of procedural devices employed, but rather turns on whether the agency has followed the statutory mandate of the Administrative Procedure Act or other relevant statutes. If the agency is compelled to support the rule which it ultimately adopts with the type of record produced only after a full adjudicatory hearing, it simply will have no choice but to conduct a full adjudication prior to promulgating every rule. In sum, this sort of unwarranted judicial examination of perceived procedural shortcomings of a rulemaking proceeding can do nothing but seriously interfere with that process prescribed by Congress.

Respondent NRDC also argues that the fact that the Commission's inquiry was undertaken in the context of NEPA somehow permits a court to require procedures beyond those specified in § 553 when investigating factual issues through rulemaking. The Court of Appeals was apparently also of this view, indicating that agencies may be required to "develop new procedures to accomplish the innovative task of implementing NEPA through rulemaking." But we search in vain for something in NEPA which would mandate such a result. We have before observed that "NEPA does not repeal by implication any other statute." In fact, just two Terms ago, we emphasized that the only procedural requirements imposed by NEPA are those stated in the plain language of the Act. *Kleppe v. Sierra Club,* [*infra,* page 483]. Thus, it is clear NEPA cannot serve as the basis for a substantial revision of the carefully constructed procedural specifications of the APA.

In short, nothing in the APA, NEPA, the circumstances of this case, the nature of the issues being considered, past agency practice, or the statutory mandate under which the Commission operates permitted the court to review and overturn the rulemaking proceeding on the basis of the procedural devices employed (or not employed) by the Commission so long as the Commission employed at least the statutory *minima,* a matter about which there is no doubt in this case.

NOTES

1. *Vermont Yankee* thus appeared to close the door on judicial augmentation of the APA-required procedures. Yet despite *Vermont Yankee,* additional procedural restrictions have in effect been imposed on agencies through a liberal construction of the specific APA provisions themselves. Further, a reviewing court may remand a matter to an agency because the agency's record is not sufficiently developed to enable the court to perform "whole record" review, as required by section 706. Indeed, on one reading, this is all the D.C. Circuit in *Vermont Yankee* was doing. (At one point in the decision, the D.C. Circuit emphasized that it was not prescribing procedures for the agency to follow.) Is remanding a decision to an agency on the basis of "whole record" review any different, in practice, from adding procedures to the section 553 minimum, as prohibited by *Vermont Yankee?*

2. Disputes about the environmental effects of fuel reprocessing was excluded from the individual plant licensing (adjudicatory) proceeding and treated as a "generic" issue to be handled through rulemaking. This treatment of the issue effectively denied the NRDC the advantages of cross-examination, discovery, and other procedures available in an adjudicatory proceeding under section 554 of the Administrative Procedure Act. Courts

usually defer to agency decisions of this sort—to essentially "hive off" some aspect of an adjudicatory proceeding into a rulemaking. As we will see later, the rulemaking itself had problems. For the next installment in the *Vermont Yankee* litigation, *see Baltimore Gas & Electric Co. v. NRDC,* page 551, *infra.*

3.   Some political scientists argue that administrative procedures serve a political function by empowering interest groups to play an oversight role as agencies implement legislation. According to a school of thought known as "public choice theory," Congress can "stack the deck" by enfranchising those interest groups that benefited from the legislation to participate in agency decision making, replicating at the implementation phase the same political environment that gave rise to the initial legislative deal. Mathew D. McCubbins et al., *Structure and Process, Politics and Policy: Administrative Arrangements and the Political Control of Agencies,* 75 VA. L. REV. 431 (1989). From a public choice perspective, the role of courts is to enforce the original "deal" struck in the legislation. In the public choice view, administrative procedure is understood as the product of strategic behavior. Congress uses both procedure and structure to control and constrain agencies and to deliver benefits to favored interest groups. Jonathan R. Macey, *Organizational Design and the Political Control of Administrative Agencies,* 8 J.L. ECON. & ORG. 93 (1992) (arguing that Congress can exert control by defining the agency's mission, establishing internal organizational structure, and choosing to make the agency independent or executive). *But cf.* Jerry L. Mashaw, *Explaining Administrative Process: Normative, Positive, and Critical Stories of Legal Development,* 6 J.L. ECON. & ORG. 267 (1990) (arguing that procedural controls enfranchise not only favored interest groups but even disfavored ones); *see also* Jonathan R. Macey, *Separated Powers and Positive Political Economy: The Tug of War Over Administrative Agencies,* 80 GEO. L.J. 671 (1992) (arguing, in contrast to McCubbins, et al, that Congress uses procedure to enfranchise the legislative *losers*); David B. Spence, *Administrative Law and Agency Policymaking: Rethinking the Positive Theory of Political Control,* 14 YALE J. ON REG. 407 (1997).

4.   There may be a point of diminishing returns in imposing procedural requirements, where the effect of adding them is to divert the agency from engaging in explicit rulemaking at all. In order to avoid the burden of heavy procedural demands, an agency may make rules through informal policy pronouncements such as guidance documents, or it may use case-by-case adjudication or even settlements to alter rules. Richard Lazarus reports:

> Another adverse effect of excessive oversight of EPA is that it has caused the agency to go "underground" in its lawmaking. To avoid overseers, EPA has increasingly resorted to less formal means of announcing agency policy determinations. Instead of promulgating rules pursuant to the Administrative Procedure Act, EPA now frequently issues guidance memoranda and directives. Also, many important agency rulings are not reflected in generic rulemaking, but in individual permit decisions. OMB oversight is thereby avoided, and judicial review of agency action is limited.

Richard Lazarus, *The Tragedy of Distrust in the Implementation of Federal Environmental Law,* 54 L. & CONTEMP. PROBS. 311, 356 (Autumn, 1991). There is widespread suspicion that these informal mechanisms of policy making have been on the rise in recent years, though almost no empirical evidence to prove it. One unfortunate effect of this development, if it is occurring with greater frequency, is that it diminishes the public accountability of the agency, because it becomes increasingly difficult for outsiders to appraise the agency's activities. Additionally, regulated industries may also prefer "aboveground" regulation in order to avoid the uncertainties of informal adjudication. *See* James W. Conrad, Jr., *Draft Guidance on the Appropriate Use of Rules Versus Guidance*, 32 Envtl. L. Rep. (Envtl. L. Inst.) 10721 (2002).

Alternatively, an agency may regulate on the "back end," using tools such as variances and deadline extensions to make rules more flexible. Sidney A. Shapiro & Robert L. Glicksman, *The APA and the Back–End of Regulation: Procedures for Informal Adjudication,* 56 Admin. L. Rev. 1159 (2004) (supporting such methods if their use is constrained by Congressionally-outlined standards). If, as in California, the legislature seeks to cut off these informal methods as well, the result, at least in the states, may be to stymie needed regulations or to encourage agencies to ignore or evade the procedural requirements. *See* Michael Asimow, *California's Underground Regulations,* 44 Admin. L. Rev. 43 (1992).

5. An alternative approach to traditional rulemaking is to continue issuing regulations, but to do so only after reaching a consensus among all interested parties about the content of the regulations. This approach has become known as regulatory negotiation, or "reg-neg". In 1990, Congress provided explicit statutory authority for reg-neg in the Negotiated Rulemaking Act of 1990, 5 U.S.C. sections 561–570 (1994 & Supp. IV 1998). Several agencies, including the EPA, have used the process with success. The Act requires that negotiated rules still go through notice and comment prior to promulgation, but the hope is that most of the important objections will have been ventilated in the negotiation. Similarly, judicial invalidation should be less of a risk with negotiated rules because everyone who might be likely to attack the regulation in court has already "signed on" in advance. The academic debate over reg-neg has been fierce despite its relatively infrequent use. For an empirically based argument that reg-neg leads to greater learning, higher quality rules and higher satisfaction with negotiated rules than with conventional rules, without leading to agency capture by regulated interests, *see* Jody Freeman & Laura I. Langbein, *Regulatory Negotiation and the Legitimacy Benefit*, 9 N.Y.U. Envtl. L.J. 60 (2000). For the contrary argument that reg-neg does not deliver on its promise to save time and cut litigation rates, *see* Cary Coglianese, *Assessing Consensus: The Promise and Performance of Negotiated Rulemaking*, 46 Duke L.J. 1255 (1997).

———————

So far, we have considered how courts review agency determinations of factual and policy matters. However, what is the standard of review for an agency's interpretations of law? Traditionally, courts have paid little, if any, deference to an agency's construction of its governing statute (recall how, in *Overton Park*, the Supreme Court paid no heed to the Secretary of Transportation's position, adopted in the litigation, that the governing statute gave him broad discretion). Statutory interpretation is, after all, thought to be the special province of courts. Agencies can claim no special institutional competence in this regard. This view traditionally led courts to adopt a multi-factored test for determining whether agency interpretations of law were entitled to deference (including a host of considerations, such as, whether the interpretation was contained in a "legislative rule" or an "interpretive rule;" whether the matter fell within the agency's area of expertise; whether the interpretation was supported by reasoned analysis, etc.) This issue of what degree of judicial deference to pay to agency interpretations of law is critical to environmental law because so many cases involve challenges to agency interpretations of the meaning of an environmental statute. In the landmark case excerpted below, the Supreme Court announced a new deferential approach to agency interpretations of law. As with *Overton Park* and *Vermont Yankee*, this administrative law decision comes in an environmental case.

CHEVRON U.S.A. INC. v. NATURAL RESOURCES DEFENSE COUNCIL

Supreme Court of the United States, 1984.
467 U.S. 837, 104 S.Ct. 2778, 81 L.Ed.2d 694.

JUSTICE STEVENS delivered the opinion of the Court.

The question presented by this case is whether EPA's decision to allow States to treat all of the pollution-emitting devices within the same industrial grouping as though they were encased within a single "bubble" is based on a reasonable construction of the statutory term "stationary source." [The court of appeals had held the use of bubbles impermissible for nonattainment areas even though it found no explicit statutory language or legislative history on point.]

When a court reviews an agency's construction of the statute which it administers, it is confronted with two questions. First, always, is the question whether Congress has directly spoken to the precise question at issue. If the intent of Congress is clear, that is the end of the matter; for the court, as well as the agency, must give effect to the unambiguously expressed intent of Congress. If, however, the court determines Congress has not directly addressed the precise question at issue, the court does not simply impose its own construction on the statute, as would be necessary in the absence of an administrative interpretation. Rather, if the statute is silent or ambiguous with respect to the specific issue, the question for the court is whether the agency's answer is based on a permissible construction of the statute.

In light of these well-settled principles it is clear that the Court of Appeals misconceived the nature of its role in reviewing the regulations at issue. Once it determined, after its own examination of the legislation, that Congress did not actually have an intent regarding the applicability of the bubble concept to the permit program, the question before it was not whether in its view the concept is "inappropriate" in the general context of a program designed to improve air quality, but whether the Administrator's view that it is appropriate in the context of this particular program is a reasonable one. Based on the examination of the legislation and its history which follows, we agree with the Court of Appeals that Congress did not have a specific intention on the applicability of the bubble concept in these cases, and conclude that the EPA's use of that concept here is a reasonable policy choice for the agency to make. * * *

The Clean Air Act Amendments of 1977 are a lengthy, detailed, technical, complex, and comprehensive response to a major social issue. A small portion of the statute expressly deals with nonattainment areas. The focal point of this controversy is one phrase in that portion of the Amendments. * * *

The 1977 Amendments contain no specific reference to the "bubble concept." Nor do they contain a specific definition of the term "stationary source," though they did not disturb the definition of "stationary source" contained in § 111(a)(3), applicable by the terms of the Act to [all new sources in the New Source Performance Standards program]. Section 302(j), however, defines the term "major stationary source" as follows:

> Except as otherwise expressly provided the terms "major stationary source" and "major emitting facility" mean any stationary facility or source of air pollutants which directly emits, or has the potential to emit, one hundred tons per year or more of any air pollutant (including any major emitting facility or source of fugitive emissions of any such pollutant, as determined by rule by the Administrator).

Statutory Language

The definition of the term stationary source in § 111(a)(3) refers to "any building, structure, facility, or installation" which emits air pollution. This definition is applicable only to the NSPS program by the express terms of the statute; the text of the statute does not make this definition applicable to the permit program [for nonattainment areas]. Petitioners therefore maintain that there is no statutory language even relevant to ascertaining the meaning of stationary source in the permit program aside from § 302(j), which defines the term major stationary source. We disagree with petitioners on this point.

The definition in § 302(j) tells us what the word "major" means—a source must emit at least 100 tons of pollution to qualify—but it sheds virtually no light on the meaning of the term "stationary source." It does equate a source with a facility—a "major emitting facility" and a "major stationary source" are synonymous under § 302(j). The ordinary meaning of the term facility is some collection of integrated elements which has been designed and constructed to achieve some purpose. Moreover, it is certainly no affront to common English usage to take a reference to a major facility or a major source to connote an entire plant as opposed to its constituent parts. Basically, however, the language of § 302(j) simply does not compel any given interpretation of the term source.

Respondents recognize that, and hence point to § 111(a)(3). Although the definition in that section is not literally applicable to the permit program, it sheds as much light on the meaning of the word source as anything in the statute. As respondents point out, use of the words "building, structure, facility, or installation," as the definition of source, could be read to impose the permit conditions on an individual building that is a part of a plant. A "word may have a character of its own not to be submerged by its association." On the other hand, the meaning of a word must be ascertained in the context of achieving particular objectives, and the words associated with it may indicate that the true meaning of the series is to convey a common idea. The language may reasonably be interpreted to impose the requirement on any discrete, but integrated, operation which pollutes. This gives meaning to all of the terms—a single building, not part of a larger operation, would be covered if it emits more than 100 tons of pollution, as would any facility, structure, or installation. Indeed, the language itself implies a bubble concept of sorts: each enumerated item would seem to be treated as if it were encased in a bubble. While respondents insist that each of these terms must be given a discrete meaning, they also argue that § 111(a)(3) defines "source" as that term is used in § 302(j). The latter section, however, equates a source with a facility, whereas the former defines source as a facility, among other items.

We are not persuaded that parsing of general terms in the text of the statute will reveal an actual intent of Congress. We know full well that this language is not dispositive; the terms are overlapping and the language is not precisely directed to the question of the applicability of a given term in the context of a larger operation. To the extent any congressional "intent" can be discerned from this language, it would appear that the listing of overlapping, illustrative terms was intended to enlarge, rather than to confine, the scope of the agency's power to regulate particular sources in order to effectuate the policies of the Act.

Legislative History

In addition, respondents argue that the legislative history and policies of the Act foreclose the plantwide definition, and that the EPA's interpretation is not entitled to deference because it represents a sharp break with prior interpretations of the Act.

Based on our examination of the legislative history, we agree with the Court of Appeals that it is unilluminating. * * *. We find that the legislative history as a whole is silent on the precise issue before us. It is, however, consistent with the view that the EPA should have broad discretion in implementing the policies of the 1977 Amendments.

More importantly, that history plainly identifies the policy concerns that motivated the enactment; the plantwide definition is fully consistent with one of those concerns—the allowance of reasonable economic growth—and, whether or not we believe it most effectively implements the other, we must recognize that the EPA has advanced a reasonable explanation for its conclusion that the regulations serve the environmental objectives as well. Indeed, its reasoning is supported by the public record developed in the rulemaking process, as well as by certain private studies.

Our review of the EPA's varying interpretations of the word "source"—both before and after the 1977 Amendments—convince us that the agency primarily responsible for administering this important legislation has consistently interpreted it flexibly—not in a sterile textual vacuum, but in the context of implementing policy decisions in a technical and complex arena. The fact that the agency has from time to time changed its interpretation of the term source does not, as respondents argue, lead us to conclude that no deference should be accorded the agency's interpretation of the statute. An initial agency interpretation is not instantly carved in stone. On the contrary, the agency, to engage in informed rulemaking, must consider varying interpretations and the wisdom of its policy on a continuing basis. Moreover, the fact that the agency has adopted different definitions in different contexts adds force to the argument that the definition itself is flexible, particularly since Congress has never indicated any disapproval of a flexible reading of the statute.

Significantly, it was not the agency in 1980, but rather the Court of Appeals that read the statute inflexibly to command a plantwide definition for programs designed to maintain clean air and to forbid such a definition for programs designed to improve air quality. The distinction the court drew may well be a sensible one, but our labored review of the problem has surely disclosed that it is not a distinction that Congress ever articulated itself, or one that the EPA found in the statute before the courts began to review the legislative work product. We conclude that it was the Court of Appeals, rather than Congress or any of the decisionmakers who are authorized by Congress to administer this legislation, that was primarily responsible for the 1980 position taken by the agency.

Policy

The arguments over policy that are advanced in the parties' briefs create the impression that respondents are now waging in a judicial forum a specific policy battle which they ultimately lost in the agency and in the 32 jurisdictions opting for the bubble concept, but one which was never waged in the Congress. Such policy arguments are more properly addressed to legislators or administrators, not to judges.

In this case, the Administrator's interpretation represents a reasonable accommodation of manifestly competing interests and is entitled to deference: the regulatory scheme is technical and complex, the agency considered the matter in a detailed and reasoned fashion, and the decision involves reconciling conflicting policies. Congress intended to accommodate both interests, but did not do so itself on the level of specificity presented by this case. Perhaps that body consciously desired the Administrator to strike the balance at this level, thinking that those with great expertise and charged with responsibility for administering the provision would be in a better position to do so; perhaps it simply did not consider the question at this level; and perhaps Congress was unable to forge a coalition on either side of the question, and those on each side decided to take their chances with the scheme devised by the agency. For judicial purposes, it matters not which of these things occurred.

Judges are not experts in the field, and are not part of either political branch of the Government. Courts must, in some cases, reconcile competing political interests, but not on the basis of the judges' personal policy preferences. In contrast, an agency to which Congress has delegated policymaking responsibilities may, within the limits of that delegation, properly rely upon the incumbent administration's views of wise policy to inform its judgments. While agencies are not directly accountable to the people, the Chief Executive is, and it is entirely appropriate for this political branch of the Government to make such policy choices—resolving the competing interests which Congress itself either inadvertently did not resolve, or intentionally left to be resolved by the agency charged with the administration of the statute in light of everyday realities.

When a challenge to an agency construction of a statutory provision, fairly conceptualized, really centers on the wisdom of the agency's policy, rather than whether it is a reasonable choice within a gap left open by Congress, the challenge must fail. In such a case, federal judges—who have no constituency—have a duty to respect legitimate policy choices made by those who do.

NOTES

1. Is "*Chevron* deference" desirable? Apparently, it makes no difference to the Court whether Congress explicitly delegates interpretive power to an agency, simply fails to address it, or shunts it to the agency because members of Congress can't agree. Should the reason for the statutory ambiguity matter to the reviewing court? Is there any reason to believe that Congress prefers to have ambiguities resolved by administrators (potentially from the opposing political party) rather than courts?

2. While deferential on its face, the *Chevron* test has proved sufficiently malleable to enable reviewing courts to preserve their traditional authority over determining statutory meaning. *See, e.g.*, FDA v. Brown & Williamson Tobacco Corp., 529 U.S. 120 (2000) (striking down at step one the FDA's assertion of regulatory authority over tobacco products as "drug delivery devices" within the meaning of the Food, Drug and Cosmetic Act). If the Court proceeds to step two, however, the "permissibility" inquiry is similar to arbitrary or capricious review: if the agency's interpretation is reasonable, it will typically be upheld. *See* INS v. Aguirre–Aguirre, 526 U.S. 415 (1999) (overruling the Court of Appeals for not accepting, at step two, the United States Board of Immigration Appeals' definition of "serious nonpolitical crime").

3. Does *Chevron* mean that once an agency has interpreted a statute it must stick with that interpretation for all purposes? Under a new Executive

administration, could the EPA decide that bubbles should not be permitted under the Clean Air Act and bar the states from using them? Could the EPA adopt a different construction of "stationary source" for a different program under the Act? *See* ASARCO v. EPA, 578 F.2d 319 (D.C. Cir. 1978) (holding bubble incompatible with section 111 mandate to "enhance" air quality) and Alabama Power Co. v. Costle, 636 F.2d 323 (D.C. Cir. 1979) (holding bubble permissible in areas where goal is to "prevent significant deterioration" of air quality), both cases decided prior to *Chevron. See also* Cass Sunstein, *Avoiding Absurdity? A New Canon in Regulatory Law,* 32 Envtl. L. Rep. 11126 (2002) (arguing that agencies should be allowed to interpret statutes to avoid absurdity using their technical expertise, thus permitting the "updating" of statutes to deal with situations the legislature could not or did not foresee). For a history of the *Chevron* litigation and an analysis of its implications for environmental law, *see* Jody Freeman, *The Story of* Chevron: *Environmental Law and Administrative Discretion, in* ENVIRONMENTAL LAW STORIES 171 (Richard J. Lazarus & Oliver A. Houck, eds. 2005).

4.   The reach of *Chevron* was circumscribed in 2001 when the Supreme Court decided *United States v. Mead Corp.,* 533 U.S. 218 (2001). This opinion, on the validity of a Customs Service classification of day planners as "bound diaries" in deciding the correct tariff to be applied, held that *Chevron* deference should apply only where "Congress delegated authority to the agency generally to make rules carrying the force of law, and that the agency interpretation claiming deference was promulgated in the exercise of that authority." *Id*. at 226–27. In *Mead,* the Court decided that the procedures Congress set out for the Customs Service to make such rulings did not indicate any intention to grant the agency rulemaking authority, and thus the Customs ruling deserved less deference than it would be accorded under *Chevron. Id*. at 231–32. *Mead* moved from *Chevron*'s seemingly clear-cut two-step rule towards a more case-by-case approach. It invites courts to apply *Chevron* more narrowly and resurrects the never-resolved debate over how much deference agencies should receive. *See* Cass R. Sunstein, *Chevron Step Zero,* 92 VA. L. REV. 187 (2006) (arguing that *Chevron* should be applied more broadly than it was even before *Mead,* to allow decisions to be made by institutions more expert and more politically accountable than the courts). A further wrinkle was added in *Coeur Alaska, Inc. v. Southeast Alaska Conservation Council,* 129 S.Ct. 2458 (2009), in which the Court found that both the statute and regulations were ambiguous, but ended up deferring to an intra-agency memorandum as a reasonable interpretation of the agency's regulations.

The implications of the *Chevron–Mead* line of cases are obviously very significant for environmental law. Note, however, that one's views on degrees of deference are likely to be independent of one's substantive views on environmental issues, and likely have more to do with feelings about institutional expertise and legitimacy. Generally speaking, it is hard to claim that more or less deference is better or worse for environmental plaintiffs—what is clear is that more deference is better for administrators.

D. THE NATIONAL ENVIRONMENTAL POLICY ACT

Observing the procedural requirements of the APA is intended to improve agency decision-making by making decisions both more rational and open to public scrutiny. There are, in addition to the APA, a number of other laws that seek to improve agency decision making. One of the earliest is the National Environmental Policy Act, signed in 1970 by Richard Nixon and frequently cited as a landmark environmental law. Yet NEPA is not a regulatory statute like the Clean Air Act or the Clean Water Act. It is not aimed at individuals or firms but instead at federal government agencies. To be sure, NEPA contains bold language. For example, the statute declares it to be the policy of the federal government to "use all practicable means and measures * * * to create the conditions under which man and nature can exist in productive harmony." § 101(a). The Act also states that "each person should enjoy a healthful environment." § 101(c). But its most important provision is a seemingly mild-mannered requirement that federal agencies file environmental impact statements (EISs) for major federal actions significantly affecting the human environment. This "impact" requirement would transform agency decision making, and provide a wedge issue for environmental plaintiffs seeking to challenge agency action.

Specifically, § 102(2)(C) requires all agencies of the federal government to:

(C) include in every recommendation or report on proposals for legislation and other major Federal actions significantly affecting the quality of the human environment, a detailed statement by the responsible official on—

(i) the environmental impact of the proposed action,

(ii) any adverse environmental effects which cannot be avoided should the proposal be implemented,

(iii) alternatives to the proposed action,

(iv) the relationship between local short-term uses of man's environment and the maintenance and enhancement of long-term productivity, and

(v) any irreversible and irretrievable commitments of resources which would be involved in the proposed action should it be implemented.

Compared to the other federal environmental statutes, NEPA seems fairly innocuous. It contains no action-forcing mechanisms beyond the simple EIS filing requirement and no citizen-suit provision (litigants have relied on the APA to meet standing requirements). Nonetheless, soon after NEPA was passed the nascent environmental movement began to use it as a tool to challenge projects proposed, funded and/or approved by federal agencies, and the federal courts embraced NEPA as an important vehicle for advancing environmental values that—some judges felt—had been under-represented in the political process.

The key provisions of the statute are well-summarized below in Judge Skelly Wright's opinion in *Calvert Cliffs' Coordinating Committee* v. *United States AEC,* 449 F.2d 1109 (D.C. Cir. 1971), one of the earliest major cases involving NEPA. Although the specific holdings of the case have been largely superseded by later developments, the opinion provides a flavor of how appellate courts approached NEPA in the early years. It also illustrates how federal agencies resisted complying with the statute. In *Calvert Cliffs* the Court invalidated an Atomic Energy Commission regulation that permitted the EIS merely to "accompany" an application for a license before the agency, rather than be part of the material considered in deciding whether or not to license a nuclear facility. The Court declared emphatically that this *pro forma* nod to NEPA was insufficient:

> The relevant portion of NEPA is Title I, consisting of five sections. Section 101 sets forth the Act's basic substantive policy: that the federal government "use all practicable means and measures" to protect environmental values. Congress did not establish environmental protection as an exclusive goal; rather, it desired a reordering of priorities, so that environmental costs and benefits will assume their proper place along with other considerations. In Section 101(b), imposing an explicit duty on federal officials, the Act provides that "it is the continuing responsibility of the Federal Government to use all practicable means, consistent with other essential considerations of national policy," to avoid environmental degradation, preserve "historic, cultural, and natural" resources, and promote "the widest range of beneficial uses of the environment without * * * undesirable and unintended consequences."

> Thus the general substantive policy of the Act is a flexible one. It leaves room for a responsible exercise of discretion and may not require particular substantive results in particular problematic instances. However, the Act also contains very important "procedural" provisions—provisions which are designed to see that all federal agencies do in fact exercise the substantive discretion given them. These provisions are not highly flexible. Indeed, they establish a strict standard of compliance.

> NEPA, first of all, makes environmental protection a part of the mandate of every federal agency and department. The Atomic Energy Commission, for example, had continually asserted, prior to NEPA, that it had no statutory authority to concern itself with the adverse environmental effects of its actions. Now, however, its hands are no longer tied. It is not only permitted, but compelled, to take environmental values into account. Perhaps the greatest importance of NEPA is to require the Atomic Energy Commission and other agencies to

consider environmental issues just as they consider other matters within their mandates. This compulsion is most plainly stated in § 102. There, "Congress authorizes and directs that, to the fullest extent possible: (1) the policies, regulations, and public laws of the United States shall be interpreted and administered in accordance with the policies set forth in this Act * * *." Congress also "authorizes and directs" that "(2) all agencies of the Federal Government shall" follow certain rigorous procedures in considering environmental values. Senator Jackson, NEPA's principal sponsor, stated that "[n]o agency will [now] be able to maintain that it has no mandate or no requirement to consider the environmental consequences of its actions." He characterized the requirements of § 102 as "action-forcing" and stated that "[o]therwise, these lofty declarations [in § 101] are nothing more than that."

The sort of consideration of environmental values which NEPA compels is clarified in § 102(2)(A) and (B). In general, all agencies must use a "systematic, interdisciplinary approach" to environmental planning and evaluation "in decisionmaking which may have an impact on man's environment." In order to include all possible environmental factors in the decisional equation, agencies must "identify and develop methods and procedures * * * which will insure that presently unquantified environmental amenities and values may be given appropriate consideration in decisionmaking along with economic and technical considerations." "Environmental amenities" will often be in conflict with "economic and technical considerations." To "consider" the former "along with" the latter must involve a balancing process. In some instances environmental costs may outweigh economic and technical benefits and in other instances they may not. But NEPA mandates a rather finely tuned and "systematic" balancing analysis in each instance.

After explaining how NEPA supplements the statutory mandates of non-environmental agencies, the court went on to explain the role of the environmental impact statement:

To ensure that the balancing analysis is carried out and given full effect, § 102(2)(C) requires that responsible officials of all agencies prepare a "detailed statement" covering the impact of particular actions on the environment, the environmental costs which might be avoided, and alternative measures which might alter the cost-benefit equation. The apparent purpose of the "detailed statement" is to aid in the agencies' own decision-making process and to advise other interested agencies and the public of the environmental consequences of planned federal action. Beyond the "detailed statement," Section 102(2)(D) requires all agencies specifically to "study, develop, and describe appropriate alternatives to recommended courses of action in any proposal which involves unresolved conflicts concerning alternative uses of available resources." This requirement, like the "detailed statement" requirement, seeks to ensure that each agency decisionmaker has before him and takes into proper account all possible approaches to a particular project (including total abandonment of the project) which would alter the environmental impact and the cost-benefit balance. Only in that fashion is it likely that the most intelligent, optimally beneficial decision will ultimately be made. Moreover, by compelling a formal "detailed statement" and a description of alternatives, NEPA provides evidence that the mandated decision-making process has in fact taken place and, most importantly, allows those removed from the initial process to evaluate and balance the factors on their own.

Of course, all of these § 102 duties are qualified by the phrase "to the fullest extent possible." We must stress as forcefully as possible that this language does not provide an escape hatch for footdragging agencies; it does not make NEPA's procedural requirements somehow "discretionary." Congress did not intend the Act to be such a paper tiger. Indeed, the requirement of environmental consideration "to the fullest extent possible" sets a high standard for the agencies, a standard which must be rigorously enforced by the reviewing courts. * * *

Thus the § 102 duties are not inherently flexible. They must be complied with to the fullest extent, unless there is a clear conflict of *statutory* authority. Considerations of administrative difficulty, delay or economic cost will not suffice to strip the section of its fundamental importance.

rigid requirmts under nepa sec. 102

We conclude, then, that § 102 of NEPA mandates a particular sort of careful and informed decision-making process and creates judicially enforceable duties. The reviewing courts probably cannot reverse a substantive decision on its merits, under Section 101, unless it be shown that the actual balance of costs and benefits that was struck was arbitrary or clearly gave insufficient weight to environmental values. But if the decision was reached procedurally without individualized consideration and balancing of environmental factors— conducted fully and in good faith—it is the responsibility of the courts to reverse. * * *

Title II of NEPA establishes the Council on Environmental Quality (CEQ) in the Executive Office of the President, which Congress has charged chiefly with information gathering and disseminating responsibilities. The CEQ advises the President in preparation of annual environmental reports, gathers and publishes information on environmental trends, and reviews federal government programs to ensure that they are contributing to the achievement of NEPA's policy goals. § 204. In addition, the CEQ is tasked, by Executive Order, with issuing regulations to assist with the implementation of NEPA. *See* Executive Order No. 11514 (1970) *as amended by* Executive Order No.11991 (1977).

The CEQ regulations, codified at 40 C.F.R. §§ 1500–1508, now contain detailed procedural requirements governing the entire EIS process, which are binding on all federal executive agencies. *See* 40 C.F.R. § 1500.3. Courts have held that CEQ regulations are entitled to "substantial deference." *See* Andrus v. Sierra Club, 442 U.S. 347 (1979). Many agencies have supplemented the CEQ regulations with EIS regulations of their own. The regulations have proved helpful to courts in interpreting NEPA's provisions and have provided guidance to agencies on how to perform their NEPA obligations.

The process normally begins with an "environmental assessment" (EA), 40 C.F.R. §§ 1501.3–1501.4, which is to be prepared under procedures the agencies are required to develop themselves. § 1507.3. The environmental assessment is to be "a concise public document" that "[b]riefly provide[s] sufficient evidence and analysis" for deciding whether to produce an EIS, and that also considers alternatives to the proposed action, as required by § 102(2)(E) of NEPA. 40 C.F.R. § 1508.9. If the agency decides not to prepare an EIS, it must make a "finding of no significant impact" (FONSI) available to the public. 40 C.F.R. § 1501.4(e)(1). This finding is subject to judicial review using the "arbitrary or capricious" standard. Courts have consistently held that a FONSI may be based on the impact as lessened by mitigation measures, subject to certain limitations. *See, e.g.*, Cabinet Mountains Wilderness v. Peterson, 685 F.2d 678, 682 (D.C. Cir. 1982). Another situation in which agencies need not do an EIS, or even an EA, is if the activity in question merits a "categorical exclusion," a statutory exception for activities that have been previously determined neither individually nor cumulatively to have a significant effect on the human environment. 40 C.F.R. § 1508.4. *See also* Kevin H. Moriarty, Note, *Circumventing the National Environmental Policy Act: Agency Abuse of the Categorical Exclusion,* 79 N.Y.U. L. REV. 2312 (2004) for more on the categorical exclusion process.

The first step in preparing an EIS is called "scoping." Scoping is intended: (a) to obtain early participation by other agencies and the public in planning the EIS, (b) to determine the scope of the EIS, and (c) to determine the significant issues to be discussed in the EIS. 40 C.F.R. § 1501.7(a).

The actual preparation of the EIS itself involves a draft EIS, a comment period, and a final EIS. 40 C.F.R. §§ 1503.1, 1503.4. Agencies with jurisdiction or special expertise relating to the project are required to comment. 40 C.F.R. § 1503.2. Major interagency disagreements are to be referred to CEQ, which can then take a variety of actions, including publication of recommendations or referral to the President. 40 C.F.R. §§ 1504.1, 1504.3(f). When an agency reaches a final decision on the project, it must prepare a "record of decision" summarizing its actions, and explaining why it rejected environmentally preferable alternatives and mitigation measures. 40 C.F.R. § 1503.3. *See* DANIEL MANDELKER, NEPA LAW AND LITIGATION (2d ed. 1994), for a comprehensive description of the EIS process.

The early decisions under NEPA were strongly influenced by judges such as Skelly Wright, who used the statute to advance environmental values and, some would say, to slow the federal government's push for atomic energy—in this regard, consider again *Vermont Yankee* and the Supreme Court's emphatic rejection of the notion that NEPA was anything more than a "procedural" statute. Even after *Vermont Yankee*, there was hope among environmental plaintiffs that NEPA might have a substantive, and not just a procedural, impact on agency decision-making by making plain that some courses of action would be arbitrary and capricious by virtue of their environmental consequences. It seemed conceivable that judicial enforcement of NEPA might actually *rule out* federal projects that portended severe environmental impacts.

Yet as time passed, the courts (and particularly the Supreme Court) have tended to "domesticate" NEPA by integrating it into the fabric of administrative law, and declaring it to have only a procedural effect. As we saw in the preceding section, post-*Overton Park* administrative law requires agencies to compile fairly elaborate records and explanations of their actions. The EIS can be conceptualized as merely a specialized application of this general concept.

Still, NEPA has had a significant impact. NEPA heightens the agency's normal duty to consider relevant factors in decision-making. Agencies must advert specifically to environmental factors that they might otherwise ignore. NEPA has had some other, less visible, impacts as well. First, the need to comply with the EIS requirement required agencies to reconsider their missions in light of the environmental impacts those missions caused. *See* DANIEL A. MAZMANIAN & JEANNE NIENABER, CAN ORGANIZATIONS CHANGE? (1979) (tracing history of resistance to NEPA by Army Corps of Engineers in light of commitment to building large water-resource development projects). Second, even if NEPA is "merely procedural"—meaning that once the agency discloses environmental impacts fully it may proceed with its plans—the possibility of challenging a project because the agency failed to do an EIS, or because it produced an insufficient one, provides environmental groups some leverage to insist on mitigation as the price for settling NEPA lawsuits. NEPA thus has a "democratizing" effect on agency decision-making by affording groups that would normally be shut out of these decisions a seat at the bargaining table. Finally, NEPA litigation serves as an information-disclosure and political-rallying mechanism, which can help to generate political opposition to projects with negative environmental impacts. Whereas some developers and agency officials may view this use of NEPA as a form of extortion, environmental organizations tend to be unapologetic. They see this use of NEPA as good legal strategy and a legitimate second-best option: NEPA may be procedural as a legal matter, but it can still be useful as a political matter.

1. THRESHOLD REQUIREMENTS

NEPA requires the filing of an environmental impact statement in connection with "legislation and other major Federal actions significantly affecting the quality of the human environment."[9] Thus, an EIS is needed only when a project is "major," constitutes a "federal action," and has a "significant environmental impact." The following materials cover the scope of these threshold requirements. First, when is an impact "environmental" in nature?

HANLY v. MITCHELL [HANLY I]

United States Court of Appeals, Second Circuit, 1972.
460 F.2d 640, *cert. denied* 409 U.S. 990, 93 S.Ct. 313, 34 L.Ed.2d 256 (1972).

FEINBERG, CIRCUIT JUDGE.

* * * The basic issue before us is whether [NEPA] was complied with in the planning for a nine-story federal jail in back of the United States Court House in Manhattan, just across the street from two large apartment buildings. Plaintiffs, who include some owners of these apartments, allege that defendants violated the Act. [The agency, GSA, had concluded that no impact statement was needed because the project would not have a significant environmental impact.] * * *

There is no doubt that the Act contemplates some agency action that does not require an impact statement because the action is minor and has so little effect on the environment as to be insignificant. * * * There is, however, a further question of statutory construction. Plaintiffs argue that if a federal action is "major," as defendants now concede this one is, it must have a "significant" effect on the environment and call for an impact statement. Defendants claim that the term "major Federal action" refers to the cost of the project, the amount of planning that preceded it, and the time required to complete it, but does not refer to the impact of the project on the environment. We agree with defendants that the two concepts are different and that the responsible federal agency has the authority to make its own threshold determination as to each in deciding whether an impact statement is necessary. * * *

GSA's entire determination regarding the Courthouse Annex—including both office building and jail—is found principally in a memorandum dated February 23, 1971, of George M. Paduano, who was then Regional Director of the Public Buildings Service of GSA, and, according to defendants, the proper official to make such a decision under GSA's regulations. [The court then quotes the document.]

---

9. There are a few explicit exclusions from NEPA, ranging from the important (the Alaska oil pipeline) to the bizarre (the San Antonio Freeway). *See* Frederick R. Anderson, *The National Environmental Policy Act*, *in* FEDERAL ENVIRONMENTAL LAW 273 (Erica L. Dolgin & Thomas G.P. Guilbert, eds. 1974). Note that many EPA actions are also exempt. *See* § 511(c) of the Clean Water Act and 15 U.S.C.A. § 793.

This document is terse, to say the least. Nonetheless, for the purpose of supporting GSA's determination that the proposed office building portion of the Courthouse Annex will have "no adverse effects on the environment," we believe, as did the district judge, that the document is sufficient. True, the memorandum fails to mention aesthetic and architectural considerations, but in a neighborhood such as this with public buildings of wildly varying architecture, we cannot say that failure to mention explicitly such considerations is a vital flaw. Further, as [another] memorandum makes clear, * * * "[t]he building will house 357 people, most of whom are already employed in the same general area." * * *

The proposed jail, however, stands on a different footing. The Paduano memorandum does adequately discuss problems of water, heat, sewage and garbage. But those considerations apply to virtually any building. The memorandum contains no hard look at the peculiar environmental impact of squeezing a jail into a narrow area directly across the street from two large apartment houses. Indeed, there is not even a word about those apartment houses or the others located nearby. If GSA were planning a missile base on that site, a compact discussion of sewage, garbage, water and heat would hardly be adequate. Additional factors would have to be considered, and the same principle holds true here. Plaintiffs claim that the living environment of all the families in this area will be adversely affected by the presence of the jail and by the fears of "riots and disturbances" so generated. In particular, plaintiffs argue that the city prison formerly located at Sixth Avenue and Eighth Street has been vacated because the noise of the inmates, their demonstrations, and the beckoning and signaling between them and their visitors caused disturbances in the neighborhood. The Paduano memorandum contains no hint that such possible disturbances were considered. Nor is there any mention of the potential dangers of housing an out-patient treatment center in this area. * * *

* * * The National Environmental Policy Act contains no exhaustive list of so-called "environmental considerations," but without question its aims extend beyond sewage and garbage and even beyond water and air pollution. The Act must be construed to include protection of the quality of life for city residents. Noise, traffic, overburdened mass transportation systems, crime, congestion and even availability of drugs all affect the urban "environment" and are surely results of the "profound influences of * * * high-density urbanization [and] industrial expansion." Section 101(a). Thus, plaintiffs do raise many "environmental considerations" that should not be ignored. We believe the record in this case indicates that, as to the proposed jail, they were. * * *

We hasten to point out that we do not suggest plaintiffs are correct in claiming that the jail requires a section 102(2)(C) impact statement. The area in back of the Court House may not be a residential area in the usual sense and the entire Courthouse Annex may actually be an improvement in the area—jail and all. Also, GSA is obviously not required to give the same weight to plaintiffs' concerns as plaintiffs do. But the essential point is that GSA must actually consider them.

NOTE

1. Do you agree with the *Hanly* court's expansion of the "environmental impact" concept to include general "quality of life"? Do the general policies established in section 101 of NEPA shed any light on this question? Don't all major government actions have some effect on the quality of someone's life? In this connection, consider *Image of Greater San Antonio v. Brown*, 570 F.2d 517 (5th Cir. 1978). The issue in that case was whether an EIS was required for a managerial decision to eliminate a number of jobs at an Air Force base. The former employees argued, not without justification, that the decision would have an adverse effect on the quality of their lives and those of their families. The court rejected this argument on the ground that:

> Although the language and legislative history of NEPA are somewhat less than clear, we are convinced that Congress did not intend that a managerial decision to discharge a number of employees would require preparation of an EIS. NEPA was enacted in recognition of the effect that man's activities—his technological advances, industrial expansion, resource exploitation, and urban development—have on the "natural environment." The primary concern was with the physical environmental resources of the nation. * * *

> We do not mean to say that socio-economic effects can never be considered under NEPA. When an action will have a primary impact on the natural environment, secondary socio-economic effects may also be considered. But when the threshold requirement of a primary impact on the physical environment is missing, socio-economic effects are insufficient to trigger an agency's obligation to prepare an EIS.

Id. at 522. Do you agree with the court? Is there any basis in the statutory language for this distinction? How much weight should be given to the CEQ's adoption of this distinction in its regulations? *See* 40 C.F.R. section 1508.14.

We now turn to a case that further defines what can count as an "environmental impact" under NEPA. If the residents near a nuclear power plant fear a catastrophic accident, is their fear and any resulting psychological harm something an environmental assessment must take into account?

METROPOLITAN EDISON CO. v. PEOPLE AGAINST NUCLEAR ENERGY

Supreme Court of the United States, 1983.
460 U.S. 766, 103 S.Ct. 1556, 75 L.Ed.2d 534.

JUSTICE REHNQUIST delivered the opinion of the Court.

The issue in these cases is whether petitioner Nuclear Regulatory Commission (NRC) complied with the National Environmental Policy Act, when it considered whether to permit petitioner Metropolitan Edison Co. to resume operation of the Three Mile Island Unit 1 nuclear power plant

(TMI–1). The Court of Appeals for the District of Columbia Circuit held that the NRC improperly failed to consider whether the risk of an accident at TMI–1 might cause harm to the psychological health and community well-being of residents of the surrounding area. We reverse.

Metropolitan owns two nuclear power plants at Three Mile Island near Harrisburg, Pennsylvania. Both of these plants were licensed by the NRC after extensive proceedings, which included preparation of Environmental Impact Statements (EIS). On March 28, 1979, TMI–1 was not operating; it had been shut down for refueling. TMI–2 was operating, and it suffered a serious accident that damaged the reactor * * *.

After the accident, the NRC ordered Metropolitan to keep TMI–1 shut down until it had an opportunity to determine whether the plant could be operated safely. The NRC then published a notice of hearing specifying several safety related issues for consideration. The notice stated that the Commission had not determined whether to consider psychological harm or other indirect effects of the accident or of renewed operation of TMI–1. * * *

All the parties agree that effects on human health can be cognizable under NEPA, and that human health may include psychological health. The Court of Appeals thought these propositions were enough to complete a syllogism that disposes of the case: NEPA requires agencies to consider effects on health. An effect on psychological health is an effect on health. Therefore, NEPA requires agencies to consider the effects on psychological health asserted by PANE. PANE, using similar reasoning, contends that because the psychological health damage to its members would be caused by a change in the environment (renewed operation of TMI–1), NEPA requires the NRC to consider that damage. Although these arguments are appealing at first glance, we believe they skip over an essential step in the analysis. They do not consider the closeness of the relationship between the change in the environment and the "effect" at issue. * * *

To paraphrase the statutory language in light of the facts of this case, where an agency action significantly affects the quality of the human environment, the agency must evaluate the "environmental impact" and any unavoidable adverse environmental effects of its proposal. The theme of § 102 is sounded by the adjective "environmental": NEPA does not require the agency to assess *every* impact or effect of its proposed action, but only the impact or effect on the environment. If we were to seize the word "environmental" out of its context and give it the broadest possible definition, the words "adverse environmental effects" might embrace virtually any consequence of a governmental action that someone thought "adverse." But we think the context of the statute shows that Congress was talking about the physical environment—the world around us, so to speak. NEPA was designed to promote human welfare by alerting governmental actors to the effect of their proposed actions on the physical environment.

To determine whether § 102 requires consideration of a particular effect, we must look at the relationship between that effect and the change in the physical environment caused by the major federal action at issue. For example, if the Department of Health and Human Services were to implement extremely stringent requirements for hospitals and nursing homes receiving federal funds, many perfectly adequate hospitals and homes might be forced out of existence. The remaining facilities might be so limited or so expensive that many ill people would be unable to afford medical care and would suffer severe health damage. Nonetheless, NEPA would not require the Department to prepare an EIS evaluating that health damage because it would not be proximately related to a change in the physical environment.

Some effects that are "caused by" a change in the physical environment in the sense of "but for" causation, will nonetheless not fall within § 102 because the causal chain is too attenuated. For example, residents of the Harrisburg area have relatives in other parts of the country. Renewed operation of TMI–1 may well cause psychological health problems for these people. They may suffer "anxiety, tension and fear, a sense of helplessness," and accompanying physical disorders, because of the risk that their relatives may be harmed in a nuclear accident. However, this harm is simply too remote from the physical environment to justify requiring the NRC to evaluate the psychological health damage to these people that may be caused by renewed operation of TMI–1.

Our understanding of the congressional concerns that led to the enactment of NEPA suggests that the terms "environmental effect" and "environmental impact" in § 102 be read to include a requirement of a reasonably close causal relationship between a change in the physical environment and the effect at issue. This requirement is like the familiar doctrine of proximate cause from tort law.[10] The issue before us then is how to give content to this requirement. This is a question of first impression in this Court.

The federal action that affects the environment in this case is permitting renewed operation of TMI–1. The direct effects on the environment of this action include release of low-level radiation, increased fog in the Harrisburg area (caused by operation of the plant's cooling towers), and the release of warm water into the Susquehanna River. The NRC has considered each of these effects in its EIS, and again in the EIA. Another effect of renewed operation is a risk of a nuclear accident. The NRC has also considered this effect.[11]

---

10. In drawing this analogy, we do not mean to suggest that any cause-effect relation too attenuated to merit damages in a tort suit would also be too attenuated to merit notice in an EIS; nor do we mean to suggest the converse. In the context of both tort law and NEPA, courts must look to the underlying policies or legislative intent in order to draw a manageable line between those causal changes that may make an actor responsible for an effect and those that do not.

11. The NRC concluded that the risk of an accident had not changed significantly since the EIS for TMI–1 was prepared in 1972. We emphasize that in this case we are considering effects caused by the risk of an accident. The situation where an agency is asked to consider effects that will occur if a risk is realized, for example, if an accident occurs at TMI–1, is an entirely different

PANE argues that the psychological health damage it alleges "will flow directly from the risk of [a nuclear] accident." But a *risk* of an accident is not an effect on the physical environment. A risk is, by definition, unrealized in the physical world. In a causal chain from renewed operation of TMI–1 to psychological health damage, the element of risk and its perception by PANE's members are necessary middle links.[12] We believe that the element of risk lengthens the causal chain beyond the reach of NEPA.

Risk is a pervasive element of modern life; to say more would belabor the obvious. Many of the risks we face are generated by modern technology, which brings both the possibility of major accidents and opportunities for tremendous achievements. Medical experts apparently agree that risk can generate stress in human beings, which in turn may rise to the level of serious health damage. For this reason among many others, the question whether the gains from any technological advance are worth its attendant risks may be an important public policy issue. Nonetheless, it is quite different from the question whether the same gains are worth a given level of alteration of our physical environment or depletion of our natural resources. The latter question rather than the former is the central concern of NEPA. * * *

The Court of Appeals thought that PANE's contentions raised an issue of health damage, while those cases presented questions of fear or policy disagreement. We do not believe this line is so easily drawn. Anyone who fears or dislikes a project may find himself suffering from "anxiety, tension, fear, [and] a sense of helplessness." Neither the language nor the history of NEPA suggest that it was intended to give citizens a general opportunity to air their policy objections to proposed federal actions. The political process, and not NEPA, provides the appropriate forum in which to air policy disagreements.[13]

NOTES

1. Does *Metropolitan Edison* overrule *Hanly I, supra,* page 462? After *Metropolitan Edison,* can the term "environmental" ever extend beyond direct effects on the physical environment? *See* WILLIAM H. RODGERS, ENVIRONMENTAL LAW 942–46 (2d ed. 1994). At least one court of appeals has expressed serious doubts about whether socio-economic effects can ever be considered, even if some physical effects are also present. *See* Olmsted Citizens for a

case. The NRC considered, in the original EIS and in the most recent EIA for TMI–1, the possible effects of a number of accidents that might occur at TMI–1.

12. This risk can be perceived differently by different people. Indeed, it appears that the members of PANE perceive a much greater risk of another nuclear accident at Three Mile Island than is perceived by the NRC and its staff.

13. PANE's original contention seems to be addressed as much to the symbolic significance of continued operation of TMI–1 as to the risk of an accident. NEPA does not require consideration of stress caused by the symbolic significance individuals attach to federal actions. Psychological health damage caused by a symbol is even farther removed from the physical environment, and more closely connected with the broader political process, than psychological health damage caused by risk.

Better Community v. United States, 793 F.2d 201, 206 (8th Cir. 1986) (no impact statement required for conversion of a mental hospital into a prison hospital). Also, Judge Posner has argued that aesthetic effects should rarely compel the completion of an impact statement, since they can be adequately described in the environmental assessment. River Rd. Alliance, Inc. v. Corps of Eng'rs of U.S. Army, 764 F.2d 445 (7th Cir. 1985). But other courts continue to require discussion in the EIS of socioeconomic effects that are "interrelated" with physical effects. *See, e.g.*, Tongass Conserv. Soc. v. Cheney, 924 F.2d 1137 (D.C. Cir. 1991) (Ginsburg, J.). For a summary of the post-*PANE* cases, *see* Jacquelyn Smith, *Consideration of Socioeconomic Effects Under NEPA and the EC Directive on Environmental Impact Assessment*, 1992 U. CHI. L. F. 355, 363.

2. Once "environmental effects" are defined, the question still remains how to determine whether such effects are major and significant. The *Hanly* court's distinction between the "major action" and "significant impact" requirements received a mixed reception. It was criticized by other courts[14] and by commentators.[15] If the *Hanly* distinction were valid, then there could be minor federal actions that significantly effect the human environment that would not require an EIS, thus defeating the purpose of NEPA. The CEQ Regulations state that "[m]ajor reinforces but does not have a meaning independent of significantly," so the *Hanly* distinction is out of keeping with the CEQ's own interpretation of NEPA as well. 40 C.F.R. § 1508.18. *See also* Fund for Animals v. Thomas, 127 F.3d 80 (D.C. Cir. 1997) (action with small geographic scope and "negligible" environmental effects is not "major"). Note that even if an action is not "major" and therefore does not require an EIS, § 102(2)(E) of NEPA generally still requires agency consideration of alternatives. The question of significance was the focus of another Second Circuit opinion later in the *Hanly* litigation. As you read the case below, keep in mind the CEQ Regulations defining a significant action, which says " 'significantly' as used in NEPA requires consideration of both context and intensity":

(a) *Context.* This means that the significance of an action must be analyzed in several contexts such as society as a whole (human, national), the affected region, the affected interests, and the locality. Significance varies with the setting of the proposed action. For instance, in the case of a site-specific action, significance would usually depend upon the effects in the locale rather than in the world as a whole. Both short-and long-term effects are relevant.

(b) *Intensity.* This refers to the severity of impact. Responsible officials must bear in mind that more than one agency may make decisions about partial aspects of a major action. The following should be considered in evaluating intensity:

(1) Impacts that may be both beneficial and adverse. A significant effect may exist even if the Federal agency believes that on balance the effect will be beneficial.

---

14. *See, e.g.*, Minnesota Pub. Interest Research Group v. Butz, 498 F.2d 1314, 1321–22 (8th Cir. 1974) (*en banc*); Davis v. Morton, 469 F.2d 593 (10th Cir. 1972).

15. *See* WILLIAM H. RODGERS, ENVIRONMENTAL LAW 873 (2d ed. 1994).

(2) The degree to which the proposed action affects public health or safety.

(3) Unique characteristics of the geographic area such as proximity to historic or cultural resources, park lands, prime farmlands, wetlands, wild and scenic rivers, or ecologically critical areas.

(4) The degree to which the effects on the quality of the human environment are likely to be highly controversial.

(5) The degree to which the possible effects on the human environment are highly uncertain or involve unique or unknown risks.

(6) The degree to which the action may establish a precedent for future actions with significant effects or represents a decision in principle about a future consideration.

(7) Whether the action is related to other actions with individually insignificant but cumulatively significant impacts. Significance exists if it is reasonable to anticipate a cumulatively significant impact on the environment. Significance cannot be avoided by terming an action temporary or by breaking it down into small component parts.

(8) The degree to which the action may adversely affect districts, sites, highways, structures, or objects listed in or eligible for listing in the National Register of Historic Places or may cause loss or destruction of significant scientific, cultural, or historical resources.

(9) The degree to which the action may adversely affect an endangered or threatened species or its habitat that has been determined to be critical under the Endangered Species Act of 1973.

(10) Whether the action threatens a violation of Federal, State, or local law or requirements imposed for the protection of the environment.

40 C.F.R. 1508.27.

HANLY v. KLEINDIENST [HANLY II]

United States Court of Appeals, Second Circuit, 1972.
471 F.2d 823, *cert. denied* 412 U.S. 908, 93 S.Ct. 2290, 36 L.Ed.2d 974 (1973).

Mansfield, Circuit Judge.

Following the remand a new threshold determination in the form of a 25–page "Assessment of the Environmental Impact" ("Assessment" herein) was made by the GSA and submitted to the district court on June 15, 1972. This document * * * reflects a detailed consideration of numerous relevant factors. Among other things, it analyzes the size, exact location, and proposed use of the MCC; its design features, construction, and aesthetic relationship to its surroundings; the extent to which its occupants and activities conducted in it will be visible by the community; the estimated effects of its operation upon traffic, public transit and parking facilities; its approximate population, including detainees and employees; its effect on the level of noise, smoke, dirt, obnoxious odors, sewage and solid waste removal; and its energy demands. It also sets forth possible alternatives, concluding that there is none that is satisfactory. Upon the basis of this Assessment the Acting Commissioner of the Public Building Service Division of the GSA, who is the responsible official in charge, concluded on June 7, 1972, that the MCC was not an action significantly affecting the quality of the human environment. * * *

[The court first considered the proper standard of review and determined that it should apply "arbitrary or capricious" review.]

Notwithstanding the possible availability of the "rational basis" standard, we believe that the appropriate criterion in the present case is the "arbitrary, capricious" standard established by the Administrative Procedure Act, since the meaning of the term "significantly" as used in § 102(2)(C) of NEPA can be isolated as a question of law. This was the course taken by the district court and is in accord with the Supreme Court's decision in [*Overton Park*] * * *

Guidelines issued by the CEQ, which are echoed in rules for implementation published by the Public Buildings Service, the branch of GSA concerned with the construction of the MCC, suggest that a formal impact statement should be prepared with respect to "proposed actions, the environmental impact of which is likely to be highly controversial." However, the term "controversial" apparently refers to cases where a substantial dispute exists as to the size, nature or effect of the major federal action rather than to the existence of opposition to a use, the effect of which is relatively undisputed. This Court in *Hanly I,* for instance, did not require a formal impact statement with respect to the office building portion of the Annex despite the existence of neighborhood opposition to it. The suggestion that "controversial" must be equated with neighborhood opposition has also been rejected by others. *See Citizens for Reid State Park v. Laird,* 336 F. Supp. 783 (D. Me. 1972).

In the absence of any congressional or administrative interpretation of the term, we are persuaded that in deciding whether a major federal action will "significantly" affect the quality of the human environment the agency in charge, although vested with broad discretion, should normally be required to review the proposed action in the light of at least two relevant factors: (1) the extent to which the action will cause adverse environmental effects in excess of those created by existing uses in the area affected by it, and (2) the absolute quantitative adverse environmental effects of the action itself, including the cumulative harm that results from its contribution to existing adverse conditions or uses in the affected area. Where conduct conforms to existing uses, its adverse consequences will usually be less significant than when it represents a radical change. Absent some showing that an entire neighborhood is in the process of redevelopment, its existing environment, though frequently below an ideal standard, represents a norm that cannot be ignored. For instance, one more highway in an area honeycombed with roads usually has less of an adverse impact than if it were constructed through a roadless public park.

Although the existing environment of the area which is the site of a major federal action constitutes one criterion to be considered, it must be recognized that even a slight increase in adverse conditions that form an existing environmental milieu may sometimes threaten harm that is significant. One more factory polluting air and water in an area zoned for industrial use may represent the straw that breaks the back of the environmental camel. Hence the absolute, as well as comparative, effects of a major federal action must be considered.

Chief Judge Friendly's thoughtful dissent, while conceding that we (and governmental agencies) face a difficult problem in determining the meaning of the vague and amorphous term "significantly" as used in § 102(2)(C), offers no solution other than to suggest that an impact statement should be required whenever a major federal action might be "arguably" or "potentially" significant and that such an interpretation would insure the preparation of impact statements except in cases of "true" insignificance. In our view this suggestion merely substitutes one form of semantical vagueness for another. * * *

* * * Now that the GSA has made and submitted its redetermination in the form of a 25–page "Assessment," our task is to determine (1) whether it satisfies the foregoing tests as to environmental significance, and (2) whether GSA, in making its assessment and determination, has observed "procedure required by law" as that term is used in § 10 of the APA, 5 U.S.C.A. § 706(2)(D). * * *

Appellants offer little or no evidence to contradict the detailed facts found by the GSA. For the most part their opposition is based upon a psychological distaste for having a jail located so close to residential apartments, which is understandable enough. It is doubtful whether psychological and sociological effects upon neighbors constitute the type of factors that may be considered in making such a determination since they do not lend themselves to measurement. However we need not decide that issue because these apartments were constructed within two or three blocks of another existing jail, The Manhattan House of Detention for Men, which is much larger than the proposed MCC and houses approximately 1,200 prisoners. Furthermore the area in which the MCC is located has at all times been zoned by the City of New York as a commercial district designed to provide for a wide range of uses, *specifically including* "Prisons."

Despite the GSA's scrupulous efforts the appellants do present one or two factual issues that merit further consideration and findings by the GSA. One bears on the possibility that the MCC will substantially increase the risk of crime in the immediate area, a relevant factor as to which the Assessment fails to make an outright finding despite the direction to do so in *Hanly I.* Appellants urge that the Community Treatment Program and the program for observation and study of nonresident out-patients will endanger the health and safety of the immediate area by exposing neighbors and passersby to drug addicts visiting the MCC for drug maintenance and to drug pushers and hangers-on who would inevitably frequent the vicinity of a drug maintenance center. If the MCC were to be used as a drug treatment center, the potential increase in crime might tip the scales in favor of a mandatory detailed impact statement. * * *

Appellants further contend that they have never been given an opportunity to discuss the MCC with any governmental agency prior to GSA's submission of its Assessment, which raises the question whether the agency acted "without observance of procedure required by law," [citing *Overton Park, supra,* at page 437]. We do not share the Government's view that the procedural mandates of § 102(A), (B), and (D), apply only to actions found by the agency itself to have a significant environmental effect. While these sections are somewhat opaque, they are not expressly limited to "major Federal actions significantly affecting the quality of the human environment." Indeed if they were so limited § 102(D), which requires the agency to develop appropriate alternatives to the recommended course of action, would be duplicative since § 102(C), which does apply to actions "significantly affecting" the environment, specifies that the detailed impact statement must deal with "alternatives to the proposed action." * * *

A more serious question is raised by the GSA's failure to comply with § 102(2)(B), which requires the agency to "identify and develop methods and procedures * * * which will insure that presently unquantified environmental amenities and values may be given appropriate consideration in decisionmaking along with economic and technical considerations." Since an agency, in making a threshold determination as to the "significance" of an action, is called upon to review in a general fashion the same factors that would be studied in depth for preparation of a detailed environmental impact statement, § 102(2)(B) requires that some rudimentary procedures be designed to assure a fair and informed preliminary decision. Otherwise the agency, lacking essential information, might frustrate the purpose of NEPA by a threshold determination that an impact statement is unnecessary. Furthermore, an adequate record serves to preclude later changes in use without consideration of their environmental significance as required by NEPA. * * *

Notwithstanding the absence of statutory or administrative provisions on the subject, this Court has already held in *Hanly I* that federal agencies must "affirmatively develop a reviewable environmental record * * * even for purposes of a threshold section 102(2)(C) determination." We now go further and hold that before a preliminary or threshold determination of significance is made the responsible agency must give notice to the public of the proposed major federal action and an opportunity to submit relevant facts which might bear upon the agency's threshold decision. We do not suggest that a full-fledged formal hearing must be provided before each such determination is made, although it should be apparent that in many cases such a hearing would be advisable for reasons already indicated. The necessity for a hearing will depend greatly upon the circumstances surrounding the particular proposed action and upon the likelihood that a hearing will be more effective than other methods in developing relevant information and an understanding of the proposed action. The precise procedural steps to be adopted are better left to the agency, which should be in a better position than the court to determine whether solution of the problems faced with respect to a specific major federal action can better be achieved through a hearing or by informal acceptance of relevant data.

NOTES

1. Note the court's comment that "[a]bsent some showing that an entire neighborhood is in the process of redevelopment, its existing environment, though frequently below an ideal standard, represents a norm that cannot be ignored." This observation seems innocuous enough, and a similar view is echoed by courts that view compliance with local zoning as evidence against any significant impact. *See* DANIEL R. MANDELKER, NEPA LAW AND LITIGATION section 8.08[3] (2d ed. 1992). But the implications are potentially troubling. Recall the discussion of environmental justice in Chapter 2. Poor and minority neighborhoods are more likely to suffer already from a lack of environmental amenities, and from an excess of environmental harms. Hence, any given project is less likely to be considered significant if it is located in such a neighborhood, rather than in a more affluent area. Is it unfair to suggest that the *Hanly* court would have been less troubled by a proposed jail in a primarily minority neighborhood? Because performing an EIS involves both expense and delay, there is consequently an incentive (other things being equal) to locate environmentally questionable projects in "bad" neighborhoods especially if there is a lack of organized political opposition. Is this "environmental racism" or merely realistic urban planning?

2. Judge Posner has offered another interesting test for whether an impact is significant:

> The statutory concept of "significant" impact has no determinate meaning, and to interpret it sensibly in particular cases requires a comparison that is also a prediction: whether the time and expense of preparing an environmental impact statement are commensurate with the likely benefits from a more searching evaluation than an environmental assessment provides.

River Road Alliance Inc. v. Corps of Engineers, 764 F.2d 445 (7th Cir. 1985). Do you find this test helpful? Principled? The problem of defining a "significant" impact has not proved easy.

3. The *Hanly* court attached little importance to the existence of a public controversy regarding the project. In *Jones v. Gordon,* 792 F.2d 821 (9th Cir. 1986), the court held that public comments arguing that the project would have adverse environmental effects required the agency to prepare an EIS. On the other hand, another court found 120 letters and a petition signed by 558 people insufficient to constitute "a substantial number of persons" opposing the project, which would have required an environmental assessment under agency regulations. West Houston Air Committee v. F.A.A., 784 F.2d 702 (5th Cir. 1986). *See also* Greenpeace Action v. Franklin, 14 F.3d

1324, 1333–34 (9th Cir. 1992). What role should public controversy play in determining the need for an EA or EIS?

4.   Another troublesome problem considered in *Hanly II* is the scope of judicial review on threshold determinations. The lower courts were sharply divided on this issue. *See* E. David Hoskins, *Judicial Review of an Agency's Decision Not to Prepare an Environmental Impact Statement*, 18 ENVTL. L. REP. 10331 (1988). The issue now appears to have been mostly resolved by *Marsh v. Oregon Natural Resources Council* [*infra* page 493], in which the Court adopted the "arbitrary or capricious" standard. *Marsh* involved a somewhat different issue—whether to supplement an existing EIS rather than whether to prepare an EIS at all. Nevertheless, the Court's language in *Marsh* seems quite applicable to review of threshold issues. *See* Daniel R. Mandelker, *NEPA Alive and Well: The Supreme Court Takes Two*, 19 ENVTL. L. REP. 10385, 10386 (1989).

Still, some lack of clarity may still linger regarding the scope of review for threshold requirements. The majority position is that *Marsh* applies. *See* Sierra Club v. Lujan, 949 F.2d 362 (10th Cir. 1991) (citing cases); Greenpeace Action v. Franklin, 14 F.3d 1324, 1331 (9th Cir. 1992). At least one opinion continues to endorse a reasonableness standard. Goos v. Interstate Commerce Comm'n, 911 F.2d 1283, 1292 (8th Cir. 1990) (applying "arbitrary or capricious" test to the significant impact issue, but using a reasonableness test for determining whether there was a major federal action); *see also* Village of Grand View v. Skinner, 947 F.2d 651 (2d Cir. 1991) (asking whether agency took a "hard look" at possible effects of proposed action and then whether agency decision was arbitrary or capricious); National Audubon Soc. v. Hoffman, 132 F.3d 7, 13–14 (2d Cir. 1997) (similar two-step analysis; EIS should be prepared when significance of action is a "close call"). Judicial review can sometimes be very searching under these standards. *See, e.g.*, National Audubon Soc'y v. Department of the Navy, 422 F.3d 174 (4th Cir. 2005) (holding that in conducting the EIS for a landing field to be sited only five miles from a National Wildlife Refuge, the Navy's cursory analysis of the impacts of jets on nearby migratory bird species failed to constitute a sufficient "hard look," and emphasizing that Congress had specifically designated the refuge as an area to be protected).

There are occasions when an agency action fails to pass the threshold because of a problem with causation. Must agencies produce an EIS for environmental effects that they have no ability to prevent? Consider the case below, in which the Supreme Court reviews the Department of Transportation's threshold determination that it did not have to produce an EIS for proposed rules regarding Mexican trucks entering the United States. The rules were part of the Bush administration's effort to comply with the North American Free Trade Agreement.

DEPARTMENT OF TRANSPORTATION
v. PUBLIC CITIZEN

Supreme Court of the United States, 2004.
541 U.S. 752, 124 S.Ct. 2204, 159 L.Ed.2d 60.

JUSTICE THOMAS delivered the opinion of the Court.

* * * FMCSA, an agency within the Department of Transportation (DOT), is responsible for motor carrier safety and registration. *See* 49

U.S.C. § 113(f). FMCSA has a variety of statutory mandates, including "ensur[ing]" safety, establishing minimum levels of financial responsibility for motor carriers, and prescribing federal standards for safety inspections of commercial motor vehicles. * * * FMCSA has no statutory authority to impose or enforce emissions controls or to establish environmental requirements unrelated to motor carrier safety.

B

[In the 1980s, worried about Canadian and Mexican discrimination against U.S. motor carriers, Congress authorized the President to impose a moratorium on the operation of Mexican motor carriers in the United States. As part of the 1994 North American Free Trade Agreement, the United States agreed to lift the moratorium, but because of concerns about the adequacy of Mexican regulation of motor carrier safety, the President would do so only after FMSCA prepared new regulations for the certification of Mexican motor carriers.]

In May 2001, FMCSA published for comment proposed rules concerning safety regulation of Mexican motor carriers. One rule (the Application Rule) addressed the establishment of a new application form for Mexican motor carriers that seek authorization to operate within the United States. Another rule (the Safety Monitoring Rule) addressed the establishment of a safety-inspection regime for all Mexican motor carriers that would receive operating authority under the Application Rule.

In December 2001, Congress enacted the Department of Transportation and Related Agencies Appropriations Act. Section 350 of this Act provided that no funds appropriated under the Act could be obligated or expended to review or to process any application by a Mexican motor carrier for authority to operate in the interior of the United States until FMCSA implemented specific application and safety-monitoring requirements for Mexican carriers. Some of these requirements went beyond those proposed by FMCSA in the Application and Safety Monitoring Rules. Congress extended the § 350 conditions to appropriations for Fiscal Years 2003 and 2004.

In January 2002, acting pursuant to NEPA's mandates, FMCSA issued a programmatic EA for the proposed Application and Safety Monitoring Rules. FMCSA's EA evaluated the environmental impact associated with three separate scenarios: where the President did not lift the moratorium; where the President did but where (contrary to what was legally possible) FMCSA did not issue any new regulations; and the Proposed Action Alternative, where the President would modify the moratorium and where FMCSA would adopt the proposed regulations. The EA considered the environmental impact in the categories of traffic and congestion, public safety and health, air quality, noise, socioeconomic factors, and environmental justice. Vital to the EA's analysis, however, was the assumption that there would be no change in trade volume between the

United States and Mexico due to the issuance of the regulations. FMCSA did note that § 350's restrictions made it impossible for Mexican motor carriers to operate in the interior of the United States before FMCSA's issuance of the regulations. But, FMCSA determined that "this and any other associated effects in trade characteristics would be the result of the modification of the moratorium" by the President, not a result of FMCSA's implementation of the proposed safety regulations. Because FMCSA concluded that the entry of the Mexican trucks was not an "effect" of its regulations, it did not consider any environmental impact that might be caused by the increased presence of Mexican trucks within the United States.

The particular environmental effects on which the EA focused, then, were those likely to arise from the increase in the number of roadside inspections of Mexican trucks and buses due to the proposed regulations. The EA concluded * * * that the issuance of the proposed regulations would have no significant impact on the environment, and hence FMCSA, on the same day as it released the EA, issued a FONSI. * * *

The Court of Appeals concluded that the EA was deficient because it failed to give adequate consideration to the overall environmental impact of lifting the moratorium on the cross-border operation of Mexican motor carriers. According to the Court of Appeals, FMCSA was required to consider the environmental effects of the entry of Mexican trucks because "the President's rescission of the moratorium was 'reasonably foreseeable' at the time the EA was prepared and the decision not to prepare an EIS was made." Due to this perceived deficiency, the Court of Appeals remanded the case for preparation of a full EIS.

The Court of Appeals also directed FMCSA to prepare a full CAA conformity determination for the challenged regulations. It concluded that FMCSA's determination that emissions attributable to the challenged rules would be below the threshold levels was not reliable because the agency's CAA determination reflected the "illusory distinction between the effects of the regulations themselves and the effects of the presidential rescission of the moratorium on Mexican truck entry." * * *

II

An agency's decision not to prepare an EIS can be set aside only upon a showing that it was "arbitrary, capricious, an abuse of discretion, or otherwise not in accordance with law." Here, FMCSA based its FONSI upon the analysis contained within its EA; respondents argue that the issuance of the FONSI was arbitrary and capricious because the EA's analysis was flawed. In particular, respondents criticize the EA's failure to take into account the various environmental effects caused by the increase in cross-border operations of Mexican motor carriers.

Under NEPA, * * * "[e]ffects" is defined to "include: (a) Direct effects, which are caused by the action and occur at the same time and place," and "(b) Indirect effects, which are caused by the action and are later in time or farther removed in distance, but are still reasonably foreseeable." § 1508.8. Thus, the relevant question is whether the increase in cross-border operations of Mexican motor carriers, with the correlative release of emissions by Mexican trucks, is an "effect" of FMCSA's issuance of the Application and Safety Monitoring Rules; if not, FMCSA's failure to address these effects in its EA did not violate NEPA, and so FMCSA's issuance of a FONSI cannot be arbitrary and capricious.

A

[The Court dismissed a challenge to FMCSA's failure to consider alternatives or offer mitigation options, citing opponents' failure to raise the possibility of alternatives in the notice and comment process and FMCSA's lack of statutory authority to impose heightened standards that would keep out the more polluting trucks.]

B

With this point aside, respondents have only one complaint with respect to the EA: It did not take into account the environmental effects of increased cross-border operations of Mexican motor carriers. Respondents' argument that FMCSA was required to consider these effects is simple. Under § 350, FMCSA is barred from expending any funds to process or review any applications by Mexican motor carriers until FMCSA implemented a variety of specific application and safety-monitoring requirements for Mexican carriers. This expenditure bar makes it impossible for any Mexican motor carrier to receive authorization to operate within the United States until FMCSA issued the regulations challenged here. The promulgation of the regulations, the argument goes, would "caus[e]" the entry of Mexican trucks (and hence also cause any emissions such trucks would produce), and the entry of the trucks is "reasonably foreseeable." Thus, the argument concludes, under the relevant CEQ regulations, FMCSA must take these emissions into account in its EA when evaluating whether to produce an EIS.

Respondents' argument, however, overlooks a critical feature of this case: FMCSA has no ability to countermand the President's lifting of the moratorium or otherwise categorically to exclude Mexican motor carriers from operating within the United States.... In particular, FMCSA remains subject to the mandate of 49 U.S.C. § 13902(a)(1), that FMCSA "*shall* register a person to provide transportation ... as a motor carrier if [it] finds that the person is willing and able to comply with" the safety and financial responsibility requirements established by the Department of Transportation. (Emphasis added.) Under FMCSA's entirely reasonable reading of this provision, it must certify *any* motor carrier that can show that it is willing and able to comply with the various substantive requirements for safety and financial responsibility contained in DOT regulations; only the moratorium prevented it from doing so for Mexican motor carriers before 2001. Thus, upon the lifting of the moratorium, if FMCSA refused to authorize a Mexican motor carrier for cross-border services, where the Mexican motor carrier was willing and able to comply with the various substantive safety and financial responsibilities rules, it would violate § 13902(a)(1).

If it were truly impossible for FMCSA to comply with both § 350 and § 13902(a)(1), then we would be presented with an irreconcilable conflict of laws. As the later enacted provision, § 350 would quite possibly win out. But FMCSA can easily satisfy both mandates: It can issue the application and safety inspection rules required by § 350, and start processing applications by Mexican motor carriers and authorize those that satisfy § 13902(a)(1)'s conditions. Without a conflict, then, FMCSA must comply with all of its statutory mandates.

Respondents must rest, then, on a particularly unyielding variation of "but for" causation, where an agency's action is considered a cause of an environmental effect even when the agency has no authority to prevent the effect. However, a "but for" causal relationship is insufficient to make an agency responsible for a particular effect under NEPA and the relevant regulations. As this Court held in *Metropolitan Edison Co. v. People Against Nuclear Energy* [*supra,* at page 464], NEPA requires "a reasonably close causal relationship" between the environmental effect and the alleged cause. The Court analogized this requirement to the "familiar doctrine of proximate cause from tort law." In particular, "courts must look to the underlying policies or legislative intent in order to draw a manageable line between those causal changes that may make an actor responsible for an effect and those that do not."

Also, inherent in NEPA and its implementing regulations is a "rule of reason," which ensures that agencies determine whether and to what extent to prepare an EIS based on the usefulness of any new potential information to the decisionmaking process. Where the preparation of an EIS would serve "no purpose" in light of NEPA's regulatory scheme as a whole, no rule of reason worthy of that title would require an agency to prepare an EIS.

In these circumstances, the underlying policies behind NEPA and Congress' intent, as informed by the "rule of reason," make clear that the causal connection between FMCSA's issuance of the proposed regulations and the entry of the Mexican trucks is insufficient to make FMCSA responsible under NEPA to consider the environmental effects of the entry. The NEPA EIS requirement serves two purposes. First, "[i]t ensures that the agency, in reaching its decision, will have available, and will carefully consider, detailed information concerning significant environmental impacts." *Robertson v. Methow Valley Citizens Council* [*infra,* at page 517 of casebook]. Second, it "guarantees that the relevant information will be made available to the larger audience that may also play a role in both the decisionmaking process and the implementation of that decision." Requiring FMCSA to consider the environmental effects of the entry of Mexican trucks would fulfil neither of these statutory purposes. Since FMCSA has no ability categorically to prevent the cross-border operations of Mexican motor carriers, the environmental impact of the cross-border operations would have no effect on FMCSA's decisionmaking—FMCSA simply lacks the power to act on whatever information might be contained in the EIS.

Similarly, the informational purpose is not served. The "informational role" of an EIS is to "giv[e] the public the assurance that the agency 'has indeed considered environmental concerns in its decisionmaking process,' " *Baltimore Gas & Electric Co.* [*infra*, at page 511] and, perhaps more significantly, provid[e] a springboard for public comment" in the agency decisionmaking process itself. The purpose here is to ensure that the "larger audience," can provide input as necessary to the agency making the relevant decisions. * * * But here, the "larger audience" can have no impact on FMCSA's decisionmaking, since, as just noted, FMCSA simply could not act on whatever input this "larger audience" could provide.[16] * * *

Consideration of the CEQ's "cumulative impact" regulation does not change this analysis. An agency is required to evaluate the "[c]umulative impact" of its action, which is defined as "the impact on the environment which results from the incremental impact of the action when added to other past, present, and reasonably foreseeable future actions regardless of what agency (Federal or non-Federal) or person undertakes such other actions." The "cumulative impact" regulation required FMCSA to consider the "incremental impact" of the safety rules themselves, in the context of the President's lifting of the moratorium and other relevant circumstances. But this is exactly what FMCSA did in its EA. FMCSA appropriately and reasonably examined the incremental impact of its safety rules assuming the President's modification of the moratorium (and, hence, assuming the increase in cross-border operations of Mexican motor carriers). The "cumulative impact" regulation does not require FMCSA to treat the lifting of the moratorium itself, or consequences from the lifting of the moratorium, as an effect of its promulgation of its Application and Safety Monitoring Rules.

C

We hold that where an agency has no ability to prevent a certain effect due to its limited statutory authority over the relevant actions, the agency cannot be considered a legally relevant "cause" of the effect. Hence, under NEPA and the implementing CEQ regulations, the agency need not consider these effects in its EA when determining whether its action is a "major Federal action." Because the President, not FMCSA, could authorize (or not authorize) cross-border operations from Mexican motor carriers, and because FMCSA has no discretion to prevent the entry of Mexican trucks, its EA did not need to consider the environmental effects arising from the entry. * * *

[handwritten margin notes: holding; agency not responsible (b/c pres. has authority here)]

---

16. Respondents are left with arguing that an EIS would be useful for informational purposes entirely outside FMCSA's decisionmaking process. But such an argument overlooks NEPA's core focus on improving agency decisionmaking. *See* 40 CFR §§ 1500.1, 1500.2, 1502.1 (2003).

NOTES

1. Is this a political issue, for which NEPA just isn't the right tool? What other tools might be available to advocate environmental issues that might have little representation in the political process?

2. The Court finds that the FMCSA is not responsible under NEPA for considering the environmental effects of trucks that it has no authority to prevent from entering the United States. But should the capacity to *prevent* the environmental effect from occurring be required before NEPA's EIS requirement is triggered? Wouldn't NEPA's statutory purpose of information disclosure be served by the FMCSA conducting an EIS? Might it not lead to legislative or executive action to mitigate the environmental impact of the trucks?

3. Remember that NEPA has no citizen suit provision, so citizens seeking to enforce the statutory requirements must bring suit under the APA and meet the "zone-of-interest" requirements discussed previously. So citizens must clear this initial procedural hurdle before even arguing the threshold issues discussed above. In *Kanoa Inc. v. Clinton*, 1 F.Supp.2d 1088 (D. Haw. 1998) the plaintiff owner of a whale-watching company brought suit under NEPA and the APA asserting that he had standing because he believed that Naval sonar testing in the area had driven away humpback whales and therefore inflicted a legal wrong on him in the form of reduced business. *Id.* at 1092–93. The court found that the plaintiff did not meet the "zone-of-interest" test since he alleged economic harms and not a "non-pretextual environmental injury." *Id.* Do you agree with the court's ruling in that case? Shouldn't it matter that the alleged economic harm is the result of a non-pretextual environmental harm?

4. Besides the issues considered in the *Hanly* and *Public Citizen* cases, an additional threshold issue sometimes also arises: Is there a *federal* action? The CEQ Regulations provide a good synthesis of the case law:

> "Major Federal action" includes actions with effects that may be major and which are potentially subject to Federal control and responsibility. "Major" reinforces but does not have a meaning independent of significantly (section 1508.27). Actions include the circumstance where the responsible officials fail to act and that failure to act is reviewable by courts or administrative tribunals under the Administrative Procedure Act or other applicable law as agency action.

> (a) Actions include new and continuing activities, including projects and programs entirely or partly financed, assisted, conducted, regulated, or approved by federal agencies; new or revised agency rules, regulations, plans, policies, or procedures; and legislative proposals (sections 1506.8, 1508.17). Actions do not include funding assistance solely in the form of general revenue sharing funds, distributed under the State and Local Fiscal Assistance Act of 1972, 31 U.S.C.A. section 1221 et seq., with no Federal agency control over the subsequent use of such funds. Actions do not include bringing judicial or administrative civil or criminal enforcement actions. 40 C.F.R. § 1508.18.

For a survey of the earlier cases, *see* William B. Ellis & Turner T. Smith, *The Limits of Federal Environmental Responsibility and Control Under the National Environmental Policy Act*, 18 Envtl. L. Rep. 10055 (1988). Under the so-called "small handle" doctrine, if only a minor part of a project is under federal control, only impacts from that portion of the project need be considered. *See, e.g.,* Macht v. Skinner, 916 F.2d 13 (D.C. Cir. 1990).

A closely related problem is posed by attempts to "de-federalize" a project in order to avoid NEPA. Courts have generally been inhospitable to such attempts. *See* San Antonio Conservation Soc'y v. Texas Highway Dep't, 446 F.2d 1013 (5th Cir. 1971); Scottsdale Mall v. Indiana, 549 F.2d 484 (7th Cir. 1977).

Still another related problem arises when the federal government has failed to exercise its power to prevent actions by others. Courts have generally (but not always) held NEPA inapplicable. *See* Defenders of Wildlife v. Andrus, 627 F.2d 1238 (D.C. Cir. 1980); Comment, *Inaction as Action Under NEPA: EIS Not Required for Interior's Failure to Halt Alaskan Wolf Hunt*, 10 Envtl. L. Rep. 10055 (1980). For instance, where a valid contract with a private party did not leave the agency with any discretion to object to a logging road on environmental grounds, neither NEPA nor the ESA applied according to the Ninth Circuit. *See* Sierra Club v. Babbitt, 65 F.3d 1502 (9th Cir. 1995). Likewise, the Forest Service's advice to a logging company on how to avoid violating the ESA was not an agency action requiring an EIS, since the agency was in effect explaining the conditions under which it would decline to take enforcement action. *See* Marbled Murrelet v. Babbitt, 83 F.3d 1068 (9th Cir. 1996).

This issue also arises when state and federal government entities stray from their normal roles—for example, in *Laub v. United States Department of Interior*, 342 F.3d 1080 (9th Cir. 2003), the Ninth Circuit decided that the CALFED Bay–Delta program, a cooperative effort among over a dozen state and federal agencies to manage and regulate the San Francisco Bay Delta together, might intertwine federal with state activity so much that it would have to comply with NEPA as "federal action," and remanded to the district court for further discovery on the matter.

When a project is undertaken by others, but with sufficient federal involvement to trigger NEPA, may an injunction be issued against the nonfederal defendants? In an important case that required an EIS for outdoor genetic engineering experiments, the court upheld an injunction against a university on the ground that "judicial power to enforce NEPA extends to private parties where 'non-federal action cannot lawfully begin or continue without the prior approval of a federal agency.'" Foundation on Econ. Trends v. Heckler, 756 F.2d 143, 155 (D.C. Cir. 1985).

2. SCOPE AND TIMING OF THE EIS

NEPA is supposed to integrate environmental impact analysis into an agency's decision-making process, but at what point in an agency's deliberations should it be required to consider the environmental impacts of the alternatives it is considering? To environmentalists, the sooner the better, since early consideration may prevent the agencies from investing heavily in proposals that agencies may later come to realize impose heavy costs on the environment. Environmental plaintiffs worry that by the time the environmental impacts are assessed, administrative inertia and political momentum may carry the project to fruition despite a clear recognition of its potentially devastating effects on the environment. But to the agencies, the sooner they must prepare environmental assessments and environmental impact statements, the greater the burden on them will be, since they have yet to narrow down their choices. Conceivably, some options will be ruled out early in the decision-making process so it would be a waste of time to study their environmental impacts. And of course, some agencies will wish to wait as late as possible to file an EIS in order to stave off potential opposition as long as possible. Since the statute gives little guidance on the timing issue, courts have attempted to formulate a rule for the timing of environmental impact statements themselves.

An equally difficult question arises as to the true scope of the EIS required for a proposed federal action. To what extent does the agency's own definition of the scope of its proposal determine the scope of the EIS? If an agency defines a proposal as national in scope, but it is bound to have much heavier environmental impacts on a particular region of the country, should the agency be allowed to trade off the environmental impacts of its proposed action on that region by weighing it against the proposal's lesser impacts elsewhere in the nation? Or should the courts closely scrutinize the purported scope of the proposal to see if, in light of its likely impacts, the agency should file a regional impact statement?

So much for the scope being too broad. Another potential problem arises if the responsible agency has no formal proposal for, say, granting oil leases, but is instead reviewing lease applications on a case-by-case basis. Here one worries that the scope of each individual EIS for each individual license is too small in light of the cumulative impact. In this case, must the agency consider the existing leases and their cumulative environmental impact on a locale or region each time it considers a new lease application? Must the agency consider the potential *future* leases it might grant in the same region? Should courts impose a "constructive regional proposal" on an agency that appears to be pursuing an off-the-books regional policy, and allow citizen challenges to force the responsible agency to prepare an EIS for the region?

In the *Kleppe* case excerpted below, both timing and scope were at issue. The agency was found to have contemplated a regional plan at one point in its deliberations (but didn't perform an EIS for that plan), but later adopted a national plan (for which it did perform an EIS). First, then, did the agency delay too long before performing an EIS by waiting until it had adopted a national plan? Second, by adopting a national plan that had profound regional impacts, was the scope of its resulting EIS too broad, or should the agency be allowed to define the scope of an EIS based purely on its own characterization of the reach of its plan?

KLEPPE v. SIERRA CLUB

Supreme Court of the United States, 1976.
427 U.S. 390, 96 S.Ct. 2718, 49 L.Ed.2d 576.

JUSTICE POWELL delivered the opinion of the Court.

Respondents, several organizations concerned with the environment, brought this suit in July 1973 in the United States District Court for the District of Columbia. The defendants in the suit, petitioners here, were the officials of the Department and other federal agencies responsible for issuing coal leases, approving mining plans, granting rights-of-way and taking the other actions necessary to enable private companies and public utilities to develop coal reserves on land owned or controlled by the Federal Government. Citing widespread interest in the reserves of a region identified as the "Northern Great Plains region," and an alleged threat from coal-related operations to their members' enjoyment of the region's environment, respondents claimed that the federal officials could not allow further development without preparing a "comprehensive environmental impact statement" under § 102(2)(C) [of NEPA] on the entire region. They sought declaratory and injunctive relief. * * *

The record and the opinions of the courts below contain extensive facts about coal development and the geographic area involved in this suit. The facts that we consider essential, however, can be stated briefly.

The "Northern Great Plains region" identified in respondents' complaint encompasses portions of four States—northeastern Wyoming, eastern Montana, western North Dakota and western South Dakota. There is no dispute about its richness in coal, nor about the waxing interest in developing that coal, nor about the crucial role the federal petitioners will play due to the significant percentage of the coal to which they control access. The Department has initiated, in this decade, three studies in areas either inclusive of or included within this region. The North Central Power Study was addressed to the potential for coordinated development of electric power in an area encompassing all or part of 15 States in the north central United States. It aborted in 1972 for lack of interest on the part of electric utilities. The Montana–Wyoming Aqueducts Study, intended to recommend the best use of water resources for coal development in southeastern Montana and northeastern Wyoming, was suspended in 1972 with the initiation of the third study, the Northern Great Plains Resources Program (NGPRP).

While the record does not reveal the degree of concern with environmental matters in the first two studies, it is clear that the NGPRP was devoted entirely to the environment. It was carried out by an interagency, federal-state task force with public participation, and was designed "to assess the potential social, economic and environmental impacts" from resource development in five States—Montana, Wyoming, South Dakota, North Dakota, and Nebraska. Its primary objective was "to provide an analytical and informational framework for policy and planning decisions at all levels of government" by formulating several "scenarios" showing the probable consequences for the area's environment and culture from the various possible techniques and levels of resource development. The final interim report of the NGPRP was issued August 1, 1975, shortly after the decision of the Court of Appeals in this case.

In addition, since 1973 the Department has engaged in a complete review of its coal leasing program for the entire Nation. * * * The purpose of the program review was to study the environmental impact of the Department's entire range of coal-related activities and to develop a planning system to guide the national leasing program. The impact statement, known as the "Coal Programmatic EIS," went through several drafts before issuing in final form on September 19, 1975—shortly before the petition for certiorari was filed in this case. * * *

The major issue remains the one with which the suit began: whether NEPA requires petitioners to prepare an environmental impact statement on the entire Northern Great Plains region. Petitioners, arguing the negative, rely squarely upon the facts of the case and the language of § 102(2)(C) of NEPA. We find their reliance well placed.

no proposal

* * * Respondents can prevail only if there has been a report or recommendation on a proposal for major federal action with respect to the Northern Great Plains region. Our statement of the relevant facts shows there has been none; instead, all proposals are for actions of either local or national scope.

The local actions are the decisions by the various petitioners to issue a lease, approve a mining plan, issue a right-of-way permit, or take other action to allow private activity at some point within the region identified by respondents. Several courts of appeals have held that an impact statement must be included in the report or recommendation on a proposal for such action if the private activity to be permitted is one "significantly affecting the quality of the human environment" within the meaning of § 102(2)(C). The petitioners do not dispute this requirement in this case, and indeed have prepared impact statements on several proposed actions of this type in the Northern Great Plains during the course of this litigation. Similarly, the federal petitioners agreed at oral argument that § 102(2)(C) required the Coal Programmatic EIS that was prepared in tandem with the new national coal leasing program and included as part of the final report on the proposal for adoption of that program. Their admission is well made, for the new leasing program is a coherent plan of national scope, and its adoption surely has significant environmental consequences.

But there is no evidence in the record of an action or a proposal for an action of regional scope. The District Court, in fact, expressly found that there was no existing or proposed plan or program on the part of the Federal Government for the regional development of the area described in respondents' complaint. It found also that the three studies initiated by the Department in areas either included within or inclusive of respondents' region—that is, the Montana–Wyoming Aqueducts Study, the North Central Power Study, and the NGPRP—were not parts of any plan or program to develop or encourage development of the Northern Great Plains. That court found no evidence that the individual coal development projects undertaken or proposed by private industry and public utilities in that part of the country are integrated into a plan or otherwise interrelated. These findings were not disturbed by the Court of Appeals, and they remain fully supported by the record in this Court. * * *

The Court of Appeals, in reversing the District Court, did not find that there was a regional plan or program for development of the Northern Great Plains region. It accepted all of the District Court's findings of fact, but concluded nevertheless that the petitioners "contemplated" a regional plan or program. * * *

Even had the record justified a finding that a regional program was contemplated by the petitioners, the legal conclusion drawn by the Court of Appeals cannot be squared with the Act. The court recognized that the mere "contemplation" of certain action is not sufficient to require an impact statement. But it believed the statute nevertheless empowers a court to require the preparation of an impact statement to begin at some point prior to the formal recommendation or report on a proposal. The Court of Appeals accordingly devised its own four-part "balancing" test for determining when, during the contemplation of a plan or other type of federal action, an agency must begin a statement. The factors to be considered were identified as the likelihood and imminence of the program's coming to fruition, the extent to which information is available on the effects of implementing the expected program and on alternatives thereto, the extent to which irretrievable commitments are being made and options precluded "as refinement of the proposal progresses," and the severity of the environmental effects should the action be implemented. * * *

The Court's reasoning and action find no support in the language or legislative history of NEPA. The statute clearly states when an impact statement is required, and mentions nothing about a balancing of factors. Rather, as we noted [in *SCRAP II*] last Term, under the first sentence of § 102(2)(C) the moment at which an agency must have a final statement ready "is the time at which it makes a recommendation or report on a *proposal* for federal action." The procedural duty imposed upon agencies by this section is quite precise, and the role of the courts in enforcing that duty is similarly precise. A court has no authority to depart from the statutory language and, by a balancing of court-devised factors, determine a point during the germination process of a potential proposal at which an impact statement *should be prepared.* Such an assertion of judicial authority would leave the agencies uncertain as to their procedural duties under NEPA, would invite judicial involvement in the day-to-day decision-making process of the agencies, and would invite litigation. As the contemplation of a project and the accompanying study thereof do not necessarily result in a proposal for major federal action, it may be assumed that the balancing process devised by the Court of Appeals also would result in the preparation of a good many unnecessary impact statements. * * *

Our discussion thus far has been addressed primarily to the decision of the Court of Appeals. It remains, however, to consider the contention now urged by respondents. They have not attempted to support the Court of Appeals' decision. Instead, respondents renew an argument they appear to have made to the Court of Appeals, but which that court did not reach. Respondents insist that, even without a comprehensive federal plan for the development of the Northern Great Plains, a "regional" impact statement nevertheless is required on all coal-related projects in the region because they are intimately related.

There are two ways to view this contention. First, it amounts to an attack on the sufficiency of the impact statements already prepared by the petitioners on the coal-related projects that they have approved or stand ready to approve. As such, we cannot consider it in this proceeding, for the case was not brought as a challenge to a particular impact statement and there is no impact statement in the record. It also is possible to view the respondents' argument as an attack upon the decision of the petitioners not to prepare one comprehensive impact statement on all proposed projects in the region. This contention properly is before us, for the petitioners have made it clear they do not intend to prepare such a statement.

We begin by stating our general agreement with respondents' basic premise that § 102(2)(C) may require a comprehensive impact statement in certain situations where several proposed actions are pending at the same time. NEPA announced a national policy of environmental protection and placed a responsibility upon the Federal Government to further specific environmental goals by "all practicable means, consistent with other essential considerations of national policy." NEPA § 101(b). Section 102(2)(C) is one of the "action-forcing" provisions intended as a directive to "all agencies to assure consideration of the environmental impact of their action in decision-making." By requiring an impact statement Congress intended to assure such consideration during the development of a proposal or—as in this case—during the formulation of a position on a proposal submitted by private parties. A comprehensive impact statement may be necessary in some cases for an agency to meet this duty. Thus, when several proposals for coal-related actions that will have cumulative or synergistic environmental impact upon a region are pending concurrently before an agency, their environmental consequences must be considered together.[17] Only through comprehensive consideration of pending proposals can the agency evaluate different courses of action.[18] * * *

---

17. At some points in their brief respondents appear to seek a comprehensive impact statement covering contemplated projects in the region as well as those that already have been proposed. The statute, however, speaks solely in terms of *proposed* actions; it does not require an agency to consider the possible environmental impacts of less imminent actions when preparing the impact statement on proposed actions. Should contemplated actions later reach the stage of actual proposals, impact statements on them will take into account the effect of their approval upon the existing environment; and the condition of that environment presumably will reflect earlier proposed actions and their effects.

18. Neither the statute nor its legislative history contemplates that a court should substitute its judgment for that of the agency as to the environmental consequences of its actions. The only

Respondents conceded at oral argument that to prevail they must show that petitioners have acted arbitrarily in refusing to prepare one comprehensive statement on this entire region, and we agree. The determination of the region, if any, with respect to which a comprehensive statement is necessary requires the weighing of a number of relevant factors, including the extent of the interrelationship among proposed actions and practical considerations of feasibility. Resolving these issues requires a high level of technical expertise and is properly left to the informed discretion of the responsible federal agencies. Absent a showing of arbitrary action, we must assume that the agencies have exercised this discretion appropriately. Respondents have made no showing to the contrary.

Respondents' basic argument is that one comprehensive statement on the Northern Great Plains is required because all coal-related activity in that region is "programmatically, geographically, and environmentally" related. Both the alleged "programmatic" relationship and the alleged "geographic" relationship resolve, ultimately, into an argument that the region is proper for a comprehensive impact statement because the petitioners themselves have approached environmental study in this area on a regional basis. Respondents point primarily to the NGPRP, which they claim—and petitioners deny—focused on the region described in the complaint. The precise region of the NGPRP is unimportant, [because it was only a background study]. As for the alleged "environmental" relationship, respondents contend that the coal-related projects "will produce a wide variety of cumulative environmental impacts" throughout the Northern Great Plains region. They described them as follows: diminished availability of water, air and water pollution, increases in population and industrial densities, and perhaps even climatic changes. Cumulative environmental impacts are, indeed, what require a comprehensive impact statement. But determination of the extent and effect of these factors, and particularly identification of the geographic area within which they may occur, is a task assigned to the special competency of the appropriate agencies. Petitioners dispute respondents' contentions that the interrelationship of environmental impacts is region-wide[19] and, as respondents' own submissions indicate, petitioners appear to have determined that the appropriate scope of comprehensive statements should be based on basins,

---

role for a court is to insure that the agency has taken a "hard look" at environmental consequences; it cannot "interject itself within the area of discretion of the executive as to the choice of the action to be taken." Natural Resources Defense Council v. Morton, 148 U.S. App. D.C. 5, 16, 458 F.2d 827, 838 (1972).

19. For example, respondents assert that coal mines in the region are environmentally interrelated because opening one reduces the supply of water in the region for others. Petitioners contend that the water supply for each aquifer or basin within the region—of which there are many—is independent. Moreover, petitioners state in their reply brief that few active or proposed mines in respondents' region are located within 50 miles of any other mine, and there are only 30 active or proposed mines in the entire 90,000 square miles of the region.

drainage areas, and other factors. We cannot say that petitioners' choices are arbitrary. Even if environmental interrelationships could be shown conclusively to extend across basins and drainage areas, practical considerations of feasibility might well necessitate restricting the scope of comprehensive statements.

holding

In sum, respondents' contention as to the relationships between all proposed coal-related projects in the Northern Great Plains region does not require that petitioners prepare one comprehensive impact statement covering all before proceeding to approve specific pending applications.[20] As we already have determined that there exists no proposal for region-wide action that could require a regional impact statement, the judgment of the Court of Appeals must be reversed, and the judgment of the District Court reinstated and affirmed.

NOTES

1. One fact of interest is that the Sierra Club made a deliberate decision not to challenge the sufficiency of the individual EISs, in part because to do so would require litigation in dozens of cases as additional leases were issued. *See* Richard A. Johnston, Kleppe v. Sierra Club: *An Environmental Planning Catch–22*, 1 HARV. ENVTL. L. REV. 182, 187–88 (1976).

2. *Kleppe* was given a rather critical reception. *See* WILLIAM H. RODGERS, ENVIRONMENTAL LAW 924–28 (2d ed. 1994); A. Koshland, Comment, *The Scope of the Program EIS Requirement: The Need for a Coherent Judicial Approach*, 30 STAN. L. REV. 767 (1978). Two criticisms of *Kleppe* seem most prevalent: First, that the *Kleppe* test is both too mechanical and unhelpful, because it assumes that the presence or absence of a "proposal" is self-evident. Second, that the Court was overly deferential to agency decisions and ignored the overriding policies of NEPA. Do you agree?

3. The CEQ regulations address both the timing and scope issues. On the timing issue, the most important provision is 40 C.F.R. § 1508.23, which defines the term "proposal" as follows:

"Proposal" exists at that stage in the development of an action when an agency subject to the Act has a goal and is actively preparing to make a decision on one or more alternative means of accomplishing that goal and the effects can be meaningfully evaluated. Preparation of an environmental impact statement on a proposal should be timed (section 1502.5) so that the final statement may be completed in time for the statement to be included in any recommendation or report on the proposal. A proposal may exist in fact as well as by agency declaration that one exists.

---

20. Nor is it necessary that petitioners always complete a comprehensive impact statement on all proposed actions in an appropriate region before approving any of the projects. As petitioners have emphasized, and respondents have not disputed, approval of one lease or mining plan does not commit the Secretary to approval of any others; nor, apparently, do single approvals by the other petitioners commit them to subsequent approvals. Thus an agency could approve one pending project that is fully covered by an impact statement, then take into consideration the environmental effects of that existing project when preparing the comprehensive statement on the cumulative impact of the remaining proposals.

Section 1508.23 must be read together with two other sections. Section 1502.5 provides:

> An agency shall commence preparation of an environmental impact statement as close as possible to the time the agency is developing or is presented with a proposal (section 1508.23) so that preparation can be completed in time for the final statement to be included in any recommendation or report on the proposal. The statement shall be prepared early enough so that it can serve practically as an important contribution to the decisionmaking process and will not be used to rationalize or justify decisions already made * * *.

This section is reinforced by § 1501.2, which provides that "[a]gencies shall integrate the NEPA process with other planning at the earliest possible time to insure that planning and decisions reflect environmental values, to avoid delays later in the process, and to head off potential conflicts." These regulations suggest a need to construe the definition of "proposal" in favor of early application. Courts, however, have continued to have difficulty in defining "proposal." For a review of the cases, see DANIEL MANDELKER, NEPA LAW AND LITIGATION section 8.03[4] (2d ed. 1994).

The Regulations also provide explicit criteria on the scope issue:

> Scope consists of the range of actions, alternatives, and impacts to be considered in an environmental impact statement. The scope of an individual statement may depend on its relationships to other statements (sections 1502.20 and 1508.28). To determine the scope of environmental impact statements, agencies shall consider 3 types of actions, 3 types of alternatives, and 3 types of impacts. They include:
>
> (a) Actions (other than unconnected single actions) which may be:
>
> (1) Connected actions, which means that they are closely related and therefore should be discussed in the same impact statement. Actions are connected if they:
>
>> (i) Automatically trigger other actions which may require environmental impact statements.
>>
>> (ii) Cannot or will not proceed unless other actions are taken previously or simultaneously.
>>
>> (iii) Are interdependent parts of a larger action and depend on the larger action for their justification.
>
> (2) Cumulative actions, which when viewed with other proposed actions have cumulatively significant impacts and should therefore be discussed in the same impact statement.
>
> (3) Similar actions, which when viewed with other reasonably foreseeable or proposed agency actions, have similarities that provide a basis for evaluating their environmental consequences together, such as common timing or geography. An agency may wish to analyze these actions in the same impact statement. It should do so when the best way to assess adequately the combined impacts of similar actions or reasonable alternatives to such actions is to treat them in a single impact statement.

(b) Alternatives, which include: (1) No action alternative. (2) Other reasonable courses of actions. (3) Mitigation measures (not in the proposed action).

(c) Impacts, which may be: (1) Direct. (2) Indirect. (3) Cumulative.

40 C.F.R. § 1508.25.

Despite *Kleppe,* the courts of appeals have continued to require agencies to take a "hard look" at cumulative impacts. *See* Resources Ltd. v. Robertson, 35 F.3d 1300, 1305 (9th Cir. 1993). As one court said in a case involving one of a series of dams, the "synergistic impact of the project should be taken into account at some stage, and certainly before the last dam is completed." Oregon Natural Res. Council v. Marsh, 832 F.2d 1489, 1498 (9th Cir. 1987). The lower courts have taken the CEQ regulations seriously. *See* Thomas v. Peterson, 753 F.2d 754 (9th Cir. 1985); LaFlamme v. FERC, 852 F.2d 389, 401 (9th Cir. 1988); Fritiofson v. Alexander, 772 F.2d 1225, 1246–47 (5th Cir. 1985). They have looked to factors like the extent of the current commitment and the specificity of future impacts in determining the need for an impact statement. *See* Sierra Club v. Marsh, 769 F.2d 868, 878 (1st Cir. 1985). *See also* Kern v. United States Bureau of Land Mgmt., 284 F.3d 1062, 1076 (9th Cir. 2002) (ordering the Bureau to consider clearly foreseeable cumulative impacts even at the environmental assessment level; since many more EAs are performed than EISs, cumulative effects must be taken into account in the former to address them fully). On the other hand, a mere allegation that various federal actions have the same general purpose will not suffice as a basis for requiring a programmatic impact statement. *See* Foundation on Econ. Trends v. Lyng, 817 F.2d 882 (D.C. Cir. 1987).

4. Segmentation of projects or proposals to avoid triggering NEPA is another important issue. In considering whether to grant a permit for a river crossing by a 67–mile transmission line, should the Corps of Engineers consider the environmental impact of only the river crossing or the whole line? Does *Kleppe* provide any guidance? Do the CEQ regulations? *See* Winnebago Tribe of Nebraska v. Ray, 621 F.2d 269 (8th Cir. 1980) (holding that only the river crossing need be considered). Similar issues arise in highway construction cases. For example, in *Maryland Conservation Council, Inc. v. Gilchrist,* 808 F.2d 1039, 1042 (4th Cir. 1986), the court required an impact statement for a highway segment because other segments would inevitably cross a state park. The already-proposed segments, the court said, would "stand like gun barrels pointing into the heartland of the park * * *." *See also* Save the Yaak Committee v. Block, 840 F.2d 714, 721 (9th Cir. 1988). Of course, the need to prevent such abuses must be balanced against the importance of allowing planning to remain flexible on long-term projects. *See* Taxpayers Watchdog, Inc. v. Stanley, 819 F.2d 294 (D.C. Cir. 1987) (allowing segmentation of a mass transit project where the record contained no suggestion of any potential environmental abuse).

For a more recent segmentation decision, *see* Preserve Endangered Areas v. United States Army Corps, 87 F.3d 1242 (11th Cir. 1996). The plaintiffs sought to block the construction of a five mile highway which would run through a historic district and impact several acres of wetlands. According to the court, "by far the most important" factor in segmentation decisions is whether the proposed project has independent utility apart from other proposals. Here, the county had shown that the new road would connect residents in the western part of the county to businesses in the east, and some of the other east-west roads in the area were already overloaded. The court seemed impressed with the fact that the county had "support[ed] its position with over fifty exhibits."

As the following case indicates, sometimes the scope and timing issue can merge into the issue of whether any impact statement will *ever* be required.

WEINBERGER v. CATHOLIC ACTION OF HAWAII

Supreme Court of the United States, 1981.
454 U.S. 139, 102 S.Ct. 197, 70 L.Ed.2d 298.

JUSTICE REHNQUIST delivered the opinion of the Court.

The facts relevant to our decision are not seriously controverted. Pursuant to a decision by the Navy to transfer ammunition and weapons stored at various locations on the island of Oahu, Hawaii, to the West Loch branch of the Lualualei Naval Magazine, the Navy prepared an Environmental Impact Assessment (EIA) concerning how the plan would affect the environment. The assessment concluded that the necessary construction of 48 earth-covered magazines and associated structures would have no significant environmental impact, and therefore no Environmental Impact Statement (EIS) was prepared at the construction stage. Construction contracts were let in March 1977 and in April 1978. Construction of the West Loch facilities has been completed and the magazines are now in use. It is stipulated that the magazines are capable of storing nuclear weapons. Because the information is classified for national security reasons, the Navy's regulations forbid it either to admit or deny that nuclear weapons are actually stored at West Loch. * * *

We have previously noted that "[t]he thrust of § 102(2)(C) is * * * that environmental concerns be integrated into the very process of agency decisionmaking. The 'detailed statement' it requires is the outward sign that environmental values and consequences have been considered during the planning stage of agency actions." *Andrus v. Sierra Club*, 442 U.S. 347, 350, 99 S.Ct. 2335, 2337, 60 L.Ed.2d 943 (1979). Section 102(2)(C) thus serves twin aims. The first is to inject environmental considerations into the federal agency's decisionmaking process by requiring the agency to prepare an EIS. The second aim is to inform the public that the agency has considered environmental concerns in its decisionmaking process. Through the disclosure of an EIS, the public is made aware that the agency has taken environmental considerations into account. Public disclosure of the EIS is expressly governed by FOIA. 42 U.S.C. § 4332(2)(C) (1976).

The decisionmaking and public disclosure goals of § 102(2)(C), though certainly compatible, are not necessarily coextensive. Thus, § 102(2)(C) contemplates that in a given situation a federal agency might have to include environmental considerations in its decisionmaking process, yet withhold public disclosure of any NEPA documents, in whole or in part, under the authority of a FOIA exemption. That the decisionmaking and disclosure requirements of NEPA are not coextensive has been recognized by the Department of Defense's regulations, both at the time the West Loch facility was constructed and today.

[One of the exemptions from public disclosure under FOIA relates to classified information, such as that relating to storage of nuclear weapons.]

Since the public disclosure requirements of NEPA are governed by FOIA, it is clear that Congress intended that the public's interest in ensuring that federal agencies comply with NEPA must give way to the Government's need to preserve military secrets. In the instant case, an EIS concerning a proposal to store nuclear weapons at West Loch need not be disclosed. As we indicated earlier, whether or not nuclear weapons are stored at West Loch is classified information exempt from disclosure to the public under Exemption 1.

If the Navy proposes to store nuclear weapons at West Loch, the Department of Defense's regulations can fairly be read to require that an EIS be prepared solely for internal purposes, even though such a document cannot be disclosed to the public. The Navy must consider environmental consequences in its decisionmaking process, even if it is unable to meet NEPA's public disclosure goals by virtue of FOIA Exemption 1.

It does not follow, however, that the Navy is required to prepare an EIS in this case. The Navy is not required to prepare an EIS regarding the hazards of storing nuclear weapons at West Loch simply because the facility is "nuclear capable." As we held in *Kleppe v. Sierra Club*, [*supra,* page 483], an EIS need not be prepared simply because a project is *contemplated,* but only when the project is *proposed.* To say that the West Loch facility is "nuclear capable" is to say little more than that the Navy has contemplated the possibility that nuclear weapons, of whatever variety, may at some time be stored there. It is the proposal to *store* nuclear weapons at West Loch that triggers the Navy's obligation to prepare an EIS. Due to national security reasons, however, the Navy can neither admit nor deny that it proposes to store nuclear weapons at West Loch. In this case, therefore, it has not been and cannot be established that the Navy has proposed the only action that would require the preparation of an EIS dealing with the environmental consequences of nuclear weapons storage at West Loch.

Ultimately, whether or not the Navy has complied with NEPA "to the fullest extent possible" is beyond judicial scrutiny in this case. In other circumstances, we have held that "public policy forbids the maintenance of any suit in a court of justice, the trial of which would inevitably lead to the disclosure of matters which the law itself regards as confidential, and respecting which it will not allow the confidence to be violated." *Totten v. United States,* 92 U.S. 105 (1875). We confront a similar situation in the instant case.

NOTES

1. Note the Court's reasoning: (a) if the Navy proposes to store nuclear weapons it must issue a secret EIS, (b) since the proposal is also secret, the plaintiffs cannot prove whether it exists, therefore (c) the plaintiffs cannot prove the need for an EIS. Thus, the Navy can escape legal scrutiny by making legal non-compliance classified information. *See also* Hudson River Sloop Clearwater v. Department of the Navy, 891 F.2d 414 (2d Cir. 1989) (applying *Catholic Action*).

2. If the government's actions are classified, *Catholic Action* creates a considerable barrier to applying NEPA. Nevertheless, it should not be inferred that there is a "national security" exception to NEPA. Even with respect to important military projects like a major missile program, NEPA still applies. *See* Romer v. Carlucci, 847 F.2d 445 (8th Cir. 1988) (en banc). But it may be difficult or impossible to obtain adequate injunctive relief when the government invokes national security. See Winter v. NRDC, 129 S.Ct. 365 (2008) (holding that a preliminary injunction against a naval sonar training exercise was an abuse of discretion despite evidence of harm to marine mammals and stating in dictum that a permanent injunction would also be an abuse of discretion even if plaintiffs proved a violation of NEPA).

So far, our concerns about timing have been limited to the initial EIS. Because of the long delays often involved in major projects (which are in part fostered by NEPA itself), new information may well appear after the EIS is released. The question then is whether a supplementary EIS is required.

MARSH v. OREGON NATURAL RESOURCES COUNCIL

Supreme Court of the United States, 1989.
490 U.S. 360, 109 S.Ct. 1851, 104 L.Ed.2d 377.

JUSTICE STEVENS delivered the opinion of the Court.

[This case involved the construction of the Elk Creek Dam. The EIS concluded that the dam would have no major effect on fish production, but that its effect on turbidity might occasionally impair fishing. The plaintiffs argued that a supplemental EIS was required because of two new documents: (1) the "Cramer Memorandum," an Oregon Department of Fish & Wildlife (ODFW) document suggesting that the dam would have a greater effect on downstream fishing, and (2) a U.S. Soil Conservation Service (SCS) soil survey that implied greater downstream turbidity than the EIS suggested. Applying a "reasonableness" standard, the Ninth Circuit held that these documents brought significant new information to light and that the Corps had failed to evaluate that information with sufficient care.]

The parties are in essential agreement concerning the standard that governs an agency's decision whether to prepare a supplemental EIS. They agree that an agency should apply a "rule of reason," and the cases they cite in support of this standard explicate this rule in the same basic terms. These cases make clear that an agency need not supplement an EIS

Supp. EIS

every time new information comes to light after the EIS is finalized. To require otherwise would render agency decision making intractable, always awaiting updated information only to find the new information outdated by the time a decision is made. On the other hand, and as the Government concedes, NEPA does require that agencies take a "hard look" at the environmental effects of their planned action, even after a proposal has received initial approval. Application of the "rule of reason" thus turns on the value of the new information to the still pending decisionmaking process. In this respect the decision whether to prepare a supplemental EIS is similar to the decision whether to prepare an EIS in the first instance: If there remains "major Federal actio[n]" to occur, and if the new information is sufficient to show that the remaining action will "affec[t] the quality of the human environment" in a significant manner or to a significant extent not already considered, a supplemental EIS must be prepared.

[The Court stated that as "a classic example of a factual dispute the resolution of which implicates substantial agency expertise," this suit should be decided under an "arbitrary and capricious" standard rather than any less deferential test.] Because analysis of the relevant documents "requires a high level of technical expertise," we must defer to "the informed discretion of the responsible federal agencies." *Kleppe v. Sierra Club,* [*supra,* page 483]. Under these circumstances, we cannot accept respondents' supposition that review is of a legal question and that the Corps' decision "deserves no deference." Accordingly, as long as the Corps' decision not to supplement the FEISS was not "arbitrary or capricious," it should not be set aside.[21]

As we observed in [*Overton Park*] in making the factual inquiry concerning whether an agency decision was "arbitrary or capricious," the reviewing court "must consider whether the decision was based on a consideration of the relevant factors and whether there has been a clear error of judgment." This inquiry must "be searching and careful," but "the ultimate standard of review is a narrow one." *Ibid.* When specialists express conflicting views, an agency must have discretion to rely on the reasonable opinions of its own qualified experts even if, as an original matter, a court might find contrary views more persuasive. On the other hand, in the context of reviewing a decision not to supplement an EIS, courts should not automatically defer to the agency's express reliance on an interest in finality without carefully reviewing the record and satisfying themselves that the agency has made a reasoned decision based on its evaluation of the significance—or lack of significance—of the new information. A contrary approach would not simply render judicial review

---

21. Respondents note that several Courts of Appeals, including the Court of Appeals for the Ninth Circuit as articulated in this and other cases, have adopted a "reasonableness" standard of review, and argue that we should not upset this well-settled doctrine. This standard, however, has not been adopted by all of the Circuits. Moreover, as some of these courts have recognized, the difference between the "arbitrary or capricious" and "reasonableness" standards is not of great pragmatic consequence. Accordingly, our decision today will not require a substantial reworking of long-established NEPA law.

generally meaningless, but would be contrary to the demand that courts ensure that agency decisions are founded on a reasoned evaluation "of the relevant factors." * * *

[The Court went on to discuss the merits of the Cramer Memorandum and the SCS survey. Neither of these documents was brought up pretrial, nor was any concern expressed about the data they provided before litigation commenced, which cut against plaintiffs' insistence on the significance of the information they contained. The Court then reviewed the Corps' response to the information contained in these reports.]

The Court of Appeals attached special significance to two concerns discussed in the Cramer Memorandum: the danger that an increase in water temperature downstream during fall and early winter will cause an early emergence and thus reduce survival of spring chinook fry and the danger that the dam will cause high fish mortality from an epizootic disease. Both concerns were based partly on fact and partly on speculation. * * *

[Justice Stevens stated that the Corps had offered sufficient assurances on the water temperature issue with its explanation that the model used by the OFDW had not been validated and a demonstration that its results were unreliable. The Corps additionally contended that the Cramer Memorandum had not taken into account the full set of variables that would lessen the temperature increase or otherwise mitigate any of its adverse effects on downstream fish reproduction. The Court also accepted the Corps' argument that the hypothesis that the Lost Creek Dam had contributed to the outbreak of an epizootic disease that had killed off many fish in 1979 and 1980 was contradicted by later, inconsistent chinook mortality data, as well as the fact that water testing failed to reveal the diseased organisms thought to cause the epizootic disease in the outflow from the dam.]

In thus concluding that the Cramer Memorandum did not present significant new information requiring supplementation of the [Final Environmental Impact Statement Supplement] (FEISS), the Corps carefully scrutinized the proffered information. Moreover, in disputing the accuracy and significance of this information, the Corps did not simply rely on its own experts. Rather, two independent experts hired by the Corps to evaluate the ODFW study on which the Cramer Memorandum was premised found significant fault in the methodology and conclusions of the study. We also think it relevant that the Cramer Memorandum did not express the official position of ODFW. In preparing the memorandum, the authors noted that the agency had "adopted a neutral stand on Elk Creek Dam" and argued that new information raised the question whether "our agency should continue to remain neutral." The concerns disclosed in the memorandum apparently were not sufficiently serious to persuade ODFW to abandon its neutral position.

The Court of Appeals also expressed concern that the SCS survey, by demonstrating that the soil content in the Elk Creek watershed is different than assumed in the FEISS, suggested a greater turbidity potential than indicated in the FEISS. In addition, the court observed that ODFW scientists believe that logging and road-building in the Elk Creek watershed has caused increased soil disturbance resulting in higher turbidity than forecast by the FEISS. As to this latter point, the SIR simply concluded that although turbidity may have increased in the early 1980's due to logging, "watershed recovery appears to have occurred to reduce the turbidity levels back to those of the 1970's." The implications of the SCS soil survey are of even less concern. As discussed in the FEISS, water quality studies were conducted in 1974 and 1979 using computer simulation models. The 1974 Study indicated that turbidity in the Rogue River would increase by no more than one to three [Jackson Turbity Units] as a result of the Elk Creek Dam, and the 1979 study verified this result. These studies used water samples taken from Elk Creek near the proposed dam site and from near the Lost Creek Dam, and thus did not simply rely on soil composition maps in drawing their conclusions. Although the [Supplemental Information Report] did not expressly comment on the SCS survey, in light of the in-depth 1974 and 1979 studies, its conclusion that "the turbidity effects are not expected to differ from those described in the 1980 FEISS" surely provided a legitimate reason for not preparing a supplemental FEISS to discuss the subject of turbidity.

There is little doubt that if all of the information contained in the Cramer Memorandum and SCS survey was both new and accurate, the Corps would have been required to prepare a second supplemental EIS. It is also clear that, regardless of its eventual assessment of the significance of this information, the Corps had a duty to take a hard look at the proffered evidence. However, having done so and having determined based on careful scientific analysis that the new information was of exaggerated importance, the Corps acted within the dictates of NEPA in concluding that supplementation was unnecessary. Even if another decisionmaker might have reached a contrary result, it was surely not "a clear error of judgment" for the Corps to have found that the new and accurate information contained in the documents was not significant and that the significant information was not new and accurate. As the SIR demonstrates, the Corps conducted a reasoned evaluation of the relevant information and reached a decision that, although perhaps disputable, was not "arbitrary or capricious."

NOTES

1. For conflicting appraisals of *Marsh, see* Antonio Rossman, *NEPA: Not So Well At Twenty*, 20 ENVTL. L. REP. 10174 (1990); Daniel Mandelker, *NEPA Alive and Well: The Supreme Court Takes Two*, 19 ENVTL. L. REP. 10385 (1989). *Marsh* clearly endorses the rule of reason as the standard for agency implementation under NEPA and "arbitrary or capricious" as the test on judicial review. The combination would seem to give the agency a great deal of leeway. And yet, the Court appraised the record very carefully to ensure that

the agency took a "hard look" at the issue. Indeed, lower courts do not appear to have interpreted *Marsh* as a directive for lax judicial review. For instance, in *City of Carmel–By–The–Sea v. United States Department of Transportation*, 123 F.3d 1142 (9th Cir. 1997), the court considered a plan to expand California's beautiful Highway 1. The court found the EIS adequate with respect to the wetlands mitigation plan and that the range of alternatives satisfied NEPA. However, the EIS failed to provide sufficient detail about other possible cumulative impacts to allow the court to evaluate the project. According to the court, the study should have described the area and expected impacts, other actions—"past, proposed, and reasonably foreseeable"—that might impact the same area, and a description of the individual and cumulative impacts.

Similarly, in *Hughes River Watershed Conservancy v. Glickman*, 81 F.3d 437 (4th Cir. 1996), the Court held that the Corps of Engineers violated NEPA by failing to take a sufficiently hard look at the problem of zebra mussel infestation before deciding not to prepare an SEIS. The court also faulted the agency for using distorted economic assumptions to over-inflate the benefits of the project. The agency had used a study that estimated gross rather than net benefits—that is, included benefits from recreational uses that would simply shift from other locations. Because this estimate had played an integral role in the evaluation of the project, the court considered the EIS inadequate:

> Misleading economic assumptions can defeat the first function of an EIS [ensuring a hard look by the agency] by impairing the agency's consideration of the adverse environmental effects of a proposed project. NEPA requires agencies to balance a project's economic benefits against its adverse environmental effects. The use of inflated economic benefits in this balancing process may result in approval of a project that otherwise would not have been approved because of its adverse environmental effects. Similarly, misleading economic assumptions can also defeat the second function of an EIS [public information] by skewing the public's evaluation of a project.

Id. at 446. *But cf.* Norton v. Southern Utah Wilderness Alliance, 542 U.S. 55 (2004) (holding that the Bureau of Land Management did not have to perform an SEIS to analyze an increase in off-road vehicle use in a potential wilderness area where the land use plan for the area had already been approved and there was no longer ongoing "major Federal action").

2.   Climate change is the granddaddy of environmental impacts. Yet no single federal project or regulation can be linked to any specific impact such as an incremental change in sea level. So do increased greenhouse emissions require an EIS (and if so, when)? The Ninth Circuit addressed that issue in the following case.

CENTER FOR BIOLOGICAL DIVERSITY v. NATIONAL HIGHWAY TRAFFIC SAFETY ADMINISTRATION

United States Court of Appeals, Ninth Circuit, 2007.
508 F.3d 508.

BETTY B. FLETCHER, CIRCUIT JUDGE.

Eleven states, the District of Columbia, the City of New York, and four public interest organizations petition for review of a rule issued by the National Highway Traffic Safety Administration (NHTSA) entitled "Average Fuel Economy Standards for Light Trucks, Model Years 2008–2011" * * * Pursuant to the Energy Policy and Conservation Act of 1975 (EPCA)* * *the Final Rule sets corporate average fuel economy (CAFE) standards for light trucks, defined by NHTSA to include many Sport Utility Vehicles (SUVs), minivans, and pickup trucks, for Model Years (MYs) 2008–2011. For MYs 2008–2010, the Final Rule sets new CAFE standards using its traditional method, fleet-wide average (Unreformed CAFE). For MY 2011 and beyond, the Final Rule creates a new CAFE structure that sets varying fuel economy targets depending on vehicle size and requires manufacturers to meet different fuel economy levels depending on their vehicle fleet mix (Reformed CAFE). Petitioners challenge the Final Rule under the EPCA and the National Environmental Policy Act of 1969 (NEPA). * * *

[The argument that the Rule is arbitrary, capricious, and contrary to the EPCA is omitted here. The Court found the Rule to be arbitrary and capricious for among other things, failing "to monetize the value of carbon emissions* * * failure to close the SUV loophole, and failure to set standard for all vehicles in the 8,500 to 10,000 [pounds] gross vehicle weight rating."]

I. FACTUAL AND PROCEDURAL BACKGROUND

A. CAFE Regulation Under the Energy Policy and Conservation Act

In the aftermath of the energy crisis created by the 1973 Mideast oil embargo, Congress enacted the Energy Policy and Conservation Act. * * * Congress observed that "[t]he fundamental reality is that this nation has entered a new era in which energy resources previously abundant, will remain in short supply, retarding our economic growth and necessitating an alteration in our life's habits and expectations." * * * The goals of the EPCA are to "decrease dependence on foreign imports, enhance national security, achieve the efficient utilization of scarce resources, and guarantee the availability of domestic energy supplies at prices consumers can afford." * * * These goals are more pressing today than they were thirty years ago: since 1975, American consumption of oil has risen from 16.3 million barrels per day to over 20 million barrels per day, and the percentage of U.S. oil that is imported has risen from 35.8 to 56 percent. * * *

In furtherance of the goal of energy conservation, Title V of the EPCA establishes automobile fuel economy standards. An "average fuel economy standard" (often referred to as a CAFE standard) is "a performance standard specifying a minimum level of average fuel economy applicable to a manufacturer in a model year." * * * Congress directs the Secretary to set fuel economy standards at "the maximum feasible average fuel economy level that the Secretary decides the manufacturers can achieve in that model year." * * * Under this subsection, the Secretary is authorized to "prescribe separate standards for different classes of automobiles." * * * Congress also provides that "[w]hen deciding maximum feasible average fuel economy under this section, the Secretary of Transportation [which has delegated this authority to NHTSA] shall consider technological feasibility, economic practicability, the effect of other motor vehicle standards of the Government on fuel economy, and the need of the United States to conserve energy." * * *

In response to a request from Congress, the National Academy of Sciences (NAS) published in 2002 a report entitled "Effectiveness and Impact of Corporate Average Fuel Economy (CAFE) Standards." * * * The NAS committee made several findings and recommendations. It found that from 1970 to 1982, CAFE standards helped contribute to a 50 percent increase in fuel economy for new light trucks. In the subsequent decades, however, light trucks became more popular since domestic manufacturers faced less competition in the light truck category and could generate greater profits. The "less stringent CAFE standards for trucks ... provide[d] incentives for manufacturers to invest in minivans and SUVs and to promote them to consumers in place of large cars and station wagons." * * * When the CAFE regulations were originally promulgated in the 1970s, "light truck sales accounted for about 20 percent of the new vehicle market," but now they account for about half. * * * As the market share of light trucks has increased, the overall average fuel economy of the new light duty vehicle fleet (light trucks and passenger automobiles) has declined "from a peak of 25.9 MPG in 1987 to 24.0 MPG in 2000."

The NAS committee found that the CAFE program has increased fuel economy, but that certain aspects of the program "have not functioned as intended," including "[t]he distinction between a car for personal use and a truck for work use/cargo transport," which "has been stretched well beyond the original purpose." * * * The committee also found that technologies exist to "significantly reduce fuel consumption," for cars and light trucks and that raising CAFE standards would reduce fuel consumption. * * * Significantly, the committee found that of the many reasons for improving fuel economy, "[t]he most important * * * is concern about the accumulation in the atmosphere of so-called greenhouse gases, principally carbon dioxide. Continued increases in carbon dioxide emissions are likely to further global warming." * * * In addition, the committee found "externalities of about \$0.30/gal of gasoline associated with the combined impacts of fuel consumption on greenhouse gas emissions and on world oil market conditions." * * *

C. NHTSA's Proposed Rulemaking and Draft Environmental Assessment
* * *

On August 30, 2005, NHTSA issued proposed CAFE standards for light trucks MYs 2008–2011 of 22.5 mpg for MY 2008, 23.1 mpg for MY 2009, and 23.5 mpg for MY 2010. * * * NHTSA determined that these were the "maximum feasible" standards using a marginal cost-benefit analysis. * * * For MY 2011 and beyond, NHTSA proposed to adopt a "Reformed CAFE" system, which would set different CAFE standards for vehicles based on size, measured by the vehicle's footprint (the product of multiplying wheelbase by track width) * * * and it proposed a transition period (MY 2008–2010) to Reformed CAFE, during which manufacturers could choose to comply with either Reformed or Unreformed CAFE. NHTSA also proposed not to change the criteria by which vehicles are classified as passenger automobiles or light trucks. * * *

NHTSA issued a Draft Environmental Assessment in August 2005. The Draft EA analyzed three alternatives to the proposed rule. Alternative A ("No Action") would extend the MY 2007 standard of 22.2 mpg through MY 2011. Alternative B would be Unreformed CAFE in MY 2008–2010 and Reformed CAFE in MY 2011. Alternative C would be Reformed CAFE set at equalized cost with Unreformed CAFE in MY 2008–2010 and Reformed CAFE in MY 2011.

The Draft EA noted that "CO2 ... has started to be viewed as an issue of concern for its global climate change potential." * * * With regard to biological resources, the Draft EA stated, "emissions of criteria pollutants and greenhouse gases could result in ozone layer depletion and promote climate change that could affect species and ecosystems." * * * The projected lifetime fuel savings for MY 2008–2011 light trucks under Alternatives B and C would "rang[e] from 1.3% to 1.7% of their fuel compared to the baseline, corresponding to 4.7–6.0 billion gallons." * * * The estimated lifetime emissions of CO2 ranged from 1,341.4 million metric tons (mmt) under baseline to 1,306.4 and 1,304.0 mmt under Alternatives B and C, respectively. * * * The Draft EA concluded that the proposed standards would "result in reduced emissions of CO2, the predominant greenhouse gas emitted by motor vehicles," "reductions in contamination of water resources," and "minor reductions in impacts to biological resources." * * * In addition, "the cumulative effects estimated to result from both the 2005–2007 and 2008–2011 light truck rulemakings over the lifetimes of the vehicles they would affect are projected to be very small."

NHTSA received over 45,000 comments on the NPRM and Draft EA from states, consumer and environmental organizations, automobile manufacturers and associations, members of Congress, and private individuals. * * * The states and environmental and consumer organizations generally argued that: [among other things, the need to conserve energy and protect national security interests requires more stringent standards, more stringent standards are feasible, NHTSA's use of cost-benefit analysis overemphasizes the costs of technology and is not technology forcing, as it was intended to be, the "maximum feasible" standard cannot be properly determined without considering environmental impacts, NHTSA's draft EA is inadequate and fails to consider the proposed rule's impact on climate change.]

Commenters also submitted to NHTSA numerous scientific reports and studies regarding the relationship between climate change and greenhouse gas emissions and the expected impacts on the environment. * * * Emissions from light trucks make up about eight percent of annual U.S. greenhouse gas emissions. * * * The transportation sectors account for about 31 percent of human-generated CO2 emissions in the U.S. economy. * * * "Overall, U.S. light-duty vehicles [passenger cars and light trucks] produce about 5 percent of the entire world's greenhouse gases." * * * The NAS committee concluded, "Since the United States produces about 25 percent of the world's greenhouse gases, fuel economy improvements could have a significant impact on the rate of CO2 accumulation in the atmosphere." * * *

D. The Final Rule: CAFE Standards for Light Trucks MYs 2008–2011

NHTSA issued the Final Rule on April 6, 2006. NHTSA set the CAFE standards for MY 2008–2010 (Unreformed CAFE) at the same levels as proposed in the NPRM [MY 2008: 22.5 mpg; MY 2009: 23.1 mpg; MY 2010: 23.5 mpg]. * * *

III. DISCUSSION * * *

B. National Environmental Policy Act

1. The EPCA does not Limit NHTSA's NEPA Obligations

NHTSA argues both that it has broad discretion to balance the factors of 49 U.S.C. § 32902(f) in setting fuel economy standards and that the EPCA constrains it from considering more stringent alternatives in the EA. NHTSA can't have it both ways. Its hands are not tied, as demonstrated by its discretionary, substantive decisions to, among other things, value the benefit of carbon emissions reduction at zero, peg its Unreformed CAFE standard to the least capable manufacturer with a substantial share of the market, apply technologies only until marginal cost equals marginal benefit, reject weight reduction as a cost-effective technology for vehicles between 4,000 and 5,000 lbs. curb weight, and not adopt a backstop.

NHTSA relies on *Department of Transportation v. Public Citizen,* 541 U.S. 752 (2004), for its contention that it did not have to consider the effect of its rule on climate change. *Public Citizen* is inapposite.

In *Public Citizen,* the Supreme Court held that the Federal Motor Carrier Safety Administration (FMCSA) did not need to consider the environmental effects of cross-border operations of motor carriers in its EA, since it had no ability to prevent those operations. The "critical feature" of the case was the fact that "FMCSA has no ability to countermand the President's lifting of the moratorium or otherwise categorically to exclude Mexican motor carriers from operating within the United States." * * *

Here, in contrast, NHTSA clearly has a statutory authority to impose or enforce fuel economy standards, 49 U.S.C. § 32902(a), (c), and it could have, in exercising its discretion, set higher standards if an EIS contained evidence that so warranted. * * * Although NEPA does not demand substantive environmental outcomes * * * NHTSA possesses the power to act on whatever information might be contained in an EIS. This court has recognized that "NEPA's legislative history reflects Congress's concern that agencies might attempt to avoid any compliance with NEPA by narrowly construing other statutory directives to create a conflict with NEPA. Section 102(2) of NEPA therefore requires government agencies to comply 'to the fullest extent possible.' " * * *

Moreover, the CAFE standard will affect the level of the nation's greenhouse gas emissions and impact global warming. NHTSA does not dispute that light trucks account for a significant percentage of the U.S. transportation sector, that the U.S. transportation sector accounts for about six percent of the world's greenhouse gases, and that "fuel economy improvements could have a significant impact on the rate of CO_2 accumulation in the atmosphere," which would affect climate change.

In sum, the EPCA does not limit NHTSA's duty under NEPA to assess the environmental impacts, including the impact on climate change, of its rule. EPCA's goal of energy conservation and NEPA's goals of "help[ing] public officials make decisions that are based on understanding of environmental consequences, and take actions that protect, restore, and enhance the environment," 40 C.F.R. § 1500.1(c), and "insur[ing] that environmental information is available to public officials and citizens before decisions are made and before actions are taken," *id.* § 1500.1(b), are complementary. NEPA prohibits uninformed agency action. "The procedures included in § 102 of NEPA are not ends in themselves. They are intended to be 'action forcing.' The unequivocal intent of NEPA is to require agencies to consider and give effect to the environmental goals set forth in the Act, not just to file detailed impact studies which will fill governmental archives."

2. Sufficiency of the Environmental Assessment

We examine the EA with two purposes in mind: to determine whether it has adequately considered and elaborated the possible consequences of the proposed agency action when concluding that it will have no significant impact on the environment, and whether its determination that no EIS is required is a reasonable conclusion. * * *

a. Cumulative impacts of greenhouse gas emissions on climate change and the environment* * *

The EA catalogues the total tonnage of CO_2 emissions for light trucks for MYs 2005–2011. * * * NHTSA estimated that:

together with the previous action raising MY 2005–07 light truck CAFE standards, the various alternatives for the current action will reduce lifetime carbon dioxide (CO_2) emissions from MY 2005–11 light trucks by 122 to 196 million metric tons, or by 2.4 to 3.8 percent *from their level if neither action had been taken.* * * * MY 2008–11 light truck CAFE standards are projected to result in cumulative reductions from the previous and current actions ranging from 0.2 to 0.3 percent of U.S. greenhouse gas emissions over the lifetimes of MY 2005–11 light trucks.

We conclude that the EA's cumulative impacts analysis is inadequate. While the EA quantifies the expected amount of CO_2 emitted from light trucks MYs 2005–2011, it does not evaluate the "incremental impact" that these emissions will have on climate change or on the environment more generally in light of other past, present, and reasonably foreseeable actions such as other light truck and passenger automobile CAFE standards. The EA does not discuss the *actual* environmental effects resulting from those emissions or place those emissions in context of other CAFE rulemakings. * * *

NHTSA does not dispute that the CAFE standard will have an effect on global warming due to an increase in greenhouse gas emissions. The new rule will not actually result in a decrease in carbon emissions, but potentially only a decrease in the rate of growth of carbon emissions. NHTSA concedes that "the new CAFE standards will not entirely offset the projected effect of increases in the number of light trucks." However, NHTSA contends that Congress is "the cause of that shortfall," not the agency, since it "is Congress's decision in EPCA to require that CAFE standards be technologically feasible and economically practicable." NHTSA concludes from this that it has no obligation to assess the cumulative impact of its rule on climate change.

This argument is without merit for the reasons already discussed. NHTSA has the power to change the CAFE standards based on information contained in an EIS. We agree with Petitioners that "[b]y allowing particular fuel economy levels, which NHTSA argues translate directly into particular tailpipe emissions, NHTSA's regulations are the proximate cause of those emissions just as EPA Clean Air Act rules permitting particular smokestack emissions are the proximate cause of those air pollutants and are unquestionably subject to NEPA's cumulative impacts requirements." Thus, the fact that "climate change is largely a global phenomenon that includes actions that are outside of [the agency's] control ... does not release the agency from the duty of assessing the effects of *its* actions on global warming within the context of other actions that also affect global warming." The cumulative impacts regulation specifically provides that the agency must assess the "impact of the action when added to other past, present, and reasonably foreseeable future actions *regardless of what agency (Federal or non-Federal) or person undertakes such other actions.*" 40 C.F.R. § 1508.7. * * *

The impact of greenhouse gas emissions on climate change is precisely the kind of cumulative impacts analysis that NEPA requires agencies to conduct. Any given rule setting a CAFE standard might have an "individually minor" effect on the environment, but these rules are "collectively significant actions taking place over a period of time." 40 C.F.R. § 1508.7. * * * Thus, NHTSA must provide the necessary contextual information about the cumulative and incremental environmental impacts of the Final Rule in light of other CAFE rulemakings and other past, present, and reasonably foreseeable future actions, regardless of what agency or person undertakes such other actions.

b. Reasonable alternatives

NHTSA must "[r]igorously explore and objectively evaluate all reasonable alternatives." 40 C.F.R. § 1502.14(a). The alternatives section is the "heart" of an EIS. * * *

In the EA, NHTSA considered a very narrow range of alternatives. All the alternatives evaluated were derived from NHTSA's cost-benefit analysis. [The Court briefly described the alternatives.]

These alternatives are hardly different from the option that NHTSA ultimately adopted. * * * The entire range of alternatives considered in the EA ranged from "22.2 to 22.7 mpg for MY 2008, 22.2 to 23.3 mpg for MY 2009, and 22.2 to 23.6 mpg for MY 2010." The estimated lifetime fuel and energy use by MY 2008–2011 light trucks under the alternatives ranged from a 1.8 to 2.6 percent decrease from "baseline," and the estimated lifetime emissions of CO_2 ranged from 2,767 to 2,840 mmt, which is extremely small compared to the overall volume of emissions [in 2004 U.S. greenhouse gas emissions were 7,074.4 teragrams of CO_2 equivalents].

* * * [T]he agency justified its choice of range and refusal to consider other alternatives on the ground that "standards more stringent than those represented by the alternatives would not satisfy the statutory requirement to establish standards * * * that are both technologically feasible and economically practicable. * * * NEPA's requirements must be applied in light of the constraints placed on the agency by EPCA." * * * Once again, NHTSA falls back on its contention that it had no discretion to consider setting higher CAFE standards. As before, we conclude that this argument is flawed. * * *

We also disagree with NHTSA that Petitioners' suggested alternatives would not be reasonably related to the project's purpose. The purpose of the Final Rule is to set CAFE standards for light trucks for MYs 2008–2011. NHTSA itself describes the scope of the EA as "analyz[ing] the environmental impacts associated with various alternatives to the existing CAFE program." Since EPCA's overarching goal is energy conservation, consideration of more stringent fuel economy standards that would *conserve more energy* is clearly reasonably related to the purpose of the CAFE standards. Energy conservation and environmental protection are not coextensive, but they often overlap. The Supreme Court has recently recognized as much [citing *Mass v. EPA*].

3.   NHTSA must prepare an Environmental Impact Statement* * *

NHTSA's finding of no significant impact (FONSI) stated that the agency determined that its Final Rule "will not have a significant effect on the human environment." * * * In the Final EA, NHTSA explained that compared to the "baseline" alternative of extending the MY 2007 light truck CAFE standard through MYs 2008–2011, its evaluated alternatives would have a minor beneficial impact on various environmental resources. NHTSA concluded that "the final rule would produce, compared to U.S. emissions of CO2, a small decrease in emissions of CO2, the primary component of greenhouse gas emissions, under the selected alternative. . . ."

Petitioners argue that the evidence raises a substantial question as to whether the Final Rule may have a significant impact on the environment and that NHTSA failed to provide a convincing statement of reasons for why a small decrease (rather than a larger decrease) in the growth of CO 2 emissions would not have a significant impact on the environment. Petitioners note that NHTSA has never evaluated the impacts of carbon emissions from light trucks or other vehicles, much less the effect of any reduction or increase in those emissions on climate change. Petitioners presented evidence that continued increase in greenhouse gas emissions may change the climate in a sudden and non-linear way. Without some analysis, it would be "impossible for NHTSA to know ... whether a change in GHG emissions of 0.2% or 1% or 5% or 10% ... will be a significant step toward averting the 'tipping point'" and irreversible adverse climate change.

We conclude that NHTSA's FONSI is arbitrary and capricious and the agency must prepare an EIS because the evidence raises a substantial question as to whether the Final Rule may have a significant impact on the environment. * * *

Petitioners have raised a "substantial question" as to whether the CAFE standards for light trucks MYs 2008–2011 "may cause significant degradation of some human environmental factor," particularly in light of the compelling scientific evidence concerning "positive feedback mechanisms" in the atmosphere.

Finally, Petitioners have satisfied several of the "intensity" factors listed in 40 C.F.R. § 1508.27(b) for determining "significant effect." For example, the Final Rule clearly may have an "individually insignificant but cumulatively significant" impact with respect to global warming. Evidence that Petitioners submitted in the record also shows that global warming will have an effect on public health and safety. Petitioners do not claim (nor do they have to show) that NHTSA's Final Rule would be the *sole* cause of global warming, and that is NHTSA's only response on this point.

Petitioners have also satisfied the "controversy" factor. * * * NHTSA received over 45,000 individual submissions on its proposal. * * *

In light of the evidence in the record, it is hardly "self-evident" that a 0.2 percent decrease in carbon emissions (as opposed to a greater decrease) is not significant. NHTSA's conclusion that a small reduction (0.2% compared to baseline) in the growth of carbon emissions would not have a significant impact on the environment was unaccompanied by any analysis or supporting data, either in the Final Rule or the EA.

Nowhere does the EA provide a "statement of reasons" for a finding of no significant impact, much less a "convincing statement of reasons." For example, the EA discusses the amount of CO_2 emissions expected from the Rule, but does not discuss the potential impact of such emissions on climate change. * * *

Thus, the FONSI is arbitrary and capricious.

The only reason NHTSA provided for why the environmental impact of the Final Rule would be insignificant is that it results in a decreased rate of growth of GHG emissions compared to the light truck CAFE standard for MY 2007. But simply because the Final Rule may be an improvement over the MY 2007 CAFE standard does not necessarily mean that it will not have a "significant effect" on the environment. NHTSA has not explained why its rule will not have a significant effect. * * *

NOTES

1. Can you anticipate methodological difficulties agencies might face in preparing environmental analyses of climate change impacts? At what point does a proposal have a sufficient climate impact to warrant discussion in an EIS (or to constitute a significant impact requiring an EIS)? Or should the default rule be that every EIS requires a climate impact analysis? It would seem to make sense for CEQ to address these matters on an executive branch-wide basis.

2. The State of California, which has its own environmental assessment statute, the California Environmental Quality Act, (CEQA) is grappling with a number of methodological questions including how to calculate increases in greenhouse gas emissions from projects subject to the statute and whether there is a threshold of emissions that triggers environmental review. See California Governor's Office of Planning and Research, *CEQA Guidelines and Greenhouse Gases*, http://www.opr.ca.gov/index.php?a=ceqa/index.html. On the possible use of CEQA as a model, see Dave Owen, *Climate Change and Environmental Assessment Law*, 33 COLUM. J. ENV. L. 57 (2008).

3. As construed by the Supreme Court, NEPA is essentially a disclosure statute, with little capacity to force long-term planning or structural institutional changes. Are there other steps that should be taken to reorient federal land use planners, energy regulators, and others to integrate climate considerations into their planning? Would it make sense to impose a separate requirement for climate impact statements covering the effect of climate change on federal programs and projects?

3. CONTENT OF THE IMPACT STATEMENT

So far, we have been largely concerned with what documents the agency must produce to satisfy NEPA, and when. We now turn to the question of what the EIS must contain. For instance, must an EIS that considers alternatives to the proposed action include detailed considerations of the environmental impacts of those alternatives? Must an EIS include alternatives that are beyond the power of the responsible agency to effect on its own without the cooperation of other agencies? Must the EIS consider alternatives that are extremely costly? How narrowly may the action agency define the project's purpose?

VERMONT YANKEE NUCLEAR POWER CORP. v. NATURAL RESOURCES DEFENSE COUNCIL, INC.

Supreme Court of the United States, 1978.
435 U.S. 519, 98 S.Ct. 1197, 55 L.Ed.2d 460.

[This is another aspect of the case that appears on page 443, *supra*. This portion of the opinion involves a reactor-license application by Consumers Power Company. A group called Saginaw intervened and submitted 119 environmental contentions, of which 17 related to the general topic of energy conservation. Saginaw participated in none of the hearings in the final stage of the proceedings. The licensing board declined to consider energy conservation issues. At about the time the administrative proceedings ended, the CEQ issued guidelines calling for agency consideration of energy conservation issues. The AEC refused to reopen the case, in part because of Saginaw's procedural default. The court of appeals reversed, holding that the AEC should have explored these issues *sua sponte*.]

JUSTICE REHNQUIST delivered the opinion of the Court.

There is little doubt that under the Atomic Energy Act of 1954 state public utility commissions or similar bodies are empowered to make the initial decision regarding the need for power. The Commission's prime area of concern * * * is public health and safety. * * *

NEPA, of course, has altered slightly the statutory balance, requiring "a detailed statement by the responsible official on * * * alternatives to the proposed action." But as should be obvious even upon a moment's reflection, the term "alternatives" is not self-defining. To make an impact statement something more than an exercise in frivolous boilerplate the concept of alternatives must be bounded by some notion of feasibility. As Court of Appeals for the District of Columbia Circuit has itself recognized:

"There is reason for concluding that NEPA was not meant to require detailed discussion of the environmental effects of 'alternatives' put forward in comments when these effects cannot be readily ascertained and the alternatives are deemed only remote and speculative possibilities, in view of basic changes required in statutes and policies of other agencies—making them available, if at all, only after protracted debate and litigation not meaningfully compatible with the time-frame of the needs to which the underlying proposal is addressed."

Common sense also teaches us that the "detailed statement of alternatives" cannot be found wanting simply because the agency failed to include every alternative device and thought conceivable by the mind of man. Time and resources are simply too limited to hold that an impact statement fails because the agency failed to ferret out every possible alternative, regardless of how uncommon or unknown that alternative may have been at the time the project was approved.

With these principles in mind we now turn to the notion of "energy conservation," an alternative the omission of which was thought by the Court of Appeals to have been "forcefully pointed out by Saginaw in its comments on the draft EIS." Again, as the Commission pointed out, "the phrase 'energy conservation' has a deceptively simple ring in this context. Taken literally, the phrase suggests a virtually limitless range of possible actions and developments that might, in one way or another, ultimately reduce projected demands for electricity from a particular proposed plant." Moreover, as a practical matter, it is hard to dispute the observation that it is largely the events of recent years that have emphasized not only the need but also a large variety of alternatives for energy conservation. Prior to the drastic oil shortages imposed upon the United States in 1973, there was little serious thought in most government circles of energy conservation alternatives. Indeed, the Council on Environmental Quality did not promulgate regulations which even remotely suggested the need to consider energy conservation in impact statements until August 1, 1973. And even then the guidelines were not made applicable to draft and final statements filed with the Council before January 28, 1974. The Federal Power Commission likewise did not require consideration of energy conservation in applications to build hydroelectric facilities until June 19, 1973. And these regulations were not made retroactive either. All this occurred over a year and a half after the draft environmental statement for Midland had been prepared, and over a year after the final environmental statement had been prepared and the hearings completed.

We think these facts amply demonstrate that the concept of "alternatives" is an evolving one, requiring the agency to explore more or fewer alternatives as they become better known and understood. This was well understood by the Commission, which, unlike the Court of Appeals, recognized that the Licensing Board's decision had to be judged by the information then available to it. And judged in that light we have little doubt the Board's actions were well within the proper bounds of its statutory authority. Not only did the record before the agency give every indication that the project was actually needed, but there was nothing before the Board to indicate to the contrary.

We also think the court's criticism of the Commission's "threshold test" displays a lack of understanding of the historical setting within which the agency action took place and of the nature of the test itself. In the first place, while it is true that NEPA places upon an agency the obligation to consider every significant aspect of the environmental impact of a proposed action, it is still incumbent upon intervenors who wish to participate to structure their participation so that it is meaningful, so that it alerts the agency to the intervenors' position and contentions. This is especially true when the intervenors are requesting the agency to embark upon an exploration of uncharted territory, as was the question of energy conservation in the late '60's and early '70's. * * *

We have also made it clear that the role of a court in reviewing the sufficiency of an agency's consideration of environmental factors is a limited one, limited both by the time at which the decision was made and by the statute mandating review.

Neither the statute nor its legislative history contemplates that a court should substitute its judgment for that of an agency as to the environmental consequences of its actions * * * [citing *Kleppe v. Sierra Club, supra,* page 483].

We think the Court of Appeals has forgotten that injunction here and accordingly its judgment in this respect must also be reversed.

NOTES

1.   In *Vermont Yankee,* did the Court go beyond *NRDC v. Morton* in diluting the scope of review of the EIS? Is the agency required only to consider *obvious* alternatives? Under *Marsh,* [*supra,* page 493], could the NRC have been required to prepare a supplemental EIS after energy conservation emerged as an alternative? In applying *Vermont Yankee,* one problem is determining how obvious an alternative must be in order for the agency to have a duty to consider that alternative on its own initiative. One court has indicated that the alternative must be "reasonably apparent." Roosevelt Campobello Int'l Park Comm'n v. EPA, 684 F.2d 1041, 1047 (1st Cir. 1982). Is this a helpful formulation?

2.   When the project in question is proposed by a nonfederal party, the question arises whether that party can control the range of possible alternatives. In *Citizens Against Burlington, Inc. v. Busey,* 938 F.2d 190 (D.C. Cir. 1991), then-Judge Clarence Thomas wrote an opinion giving the project applicant considerable leeway. The case involved a decision by the city of Toledo to expand one of its airports. A NEPA suit was brought against the FAA, challenging the agency's approval of the project. The agency considered only the alternatives of approving the plan and doing nothing, rather than the possibilities of expanding the airport in other ways, changing flight patterns, or expanding other airports. FAA defined the goal for its action as "helping to launch a new cargo hub in Toledo and thereby helping to fuel the Toledo economy." It then eliminated all alternatives that did not promote that goal.

Justice Thomas upheld this very narrow definition of alternatives under NEPA. In dissent, Judge Buckley said:

> By sanctioning the FAA's approach, the majority in effect allows a non-federal party to sort out alternatives based entirely on economic considerations, and then to present its preferred alternative as a take-it-or-leave-it proposition. If allowed to stand, today's decision will undermine the NEPA aim of "inject[ing] environmental considerations into the federal agency's decisionmaking process." The discussion of reasonable alternatives—"the heart of the environmental impact statement"—becomes an empty exercise when the only alternatives addressed are the proposed project and inaction.

For further discussion of this issue, *see* Peter J. Kirsch & Conrad M. Rippy, *Defining the Scope of Alternatives in an EIS After Citizens Against Burlington*, 21 ENVTL. L. REP. 10701 (1991); Michael E. Lackey Jr., *Misdirecting NEPA: Leaving the Definition of Reasonable Alternatives in the EIS to the Applicants*, 60 GEO. WASH. L. REV. 1232 (1992).

3.   The "rule of reason" test does not always operate to the advantage of the agency involved. In *Dubois v. United States Department of Agriculture*, 102 F.3d 1273 (1st Cir. 1996), the court held that the Service had failed to explore all reasonable alternatives for the proposed expansion of a ski facility, including the possibility of using an artificial pond rather than a natural one to store water for snowmaking. The agency had failed to discuss this option in the EIS, even though similar ponds had been used elsewhere in the vicinity. "After a searching and careful review of the record in the instant case," the court concluded, "we are not convinced that the Forest Service's decision was founded on a reasoned evaluation of the relevant factors, or that it articulated a rational connection between the facts found and the choice made." *Id.* at 1289. Hence, the Forest Service's decision was arbitrary and capricious.

At times, courts inquire into the scientific foundations of a decision, usually an arena left to expert agencies, if the science being applied seems especially unreasonable. For example, in *Center for Biological Diversity v. United States Forest Service*, 349 F.3d 1157 (9th Cir. 2003), the Court invalidated an EIS because of a Forest Service assumption in the draft impact statement about the scope of the habitat of a bird species to be affected by its action, criticizing the agency's failure to disclose and analyze the opposing viewpoint.

Another important issue in many NEPA cases is whether the agency has ignored important environmental impacts. A recurring question under NEPA has been how to treat uncertain but highly adverse outcomes. The following two cases are the Supreme Court's response to the problem. The first case is a sequel to *Vermont Yankee*, [*supra,* pages 443 and 507].

BALTIMORE GAS & ELECTRIC CO. v. NATURAL RESOURCES DEFENSE COUNCIL, INC.

Supreme Court of the United States, 1983.
462 U.S. 87, 103 S.Ct. 2246, 76 L.Ed.2d 437.

JUSTICE O'CONNOR delivered the opinion of the Court.

As part of its generic rulemaking proceedings to evaluate the environmental effects of the nuclear fuel cycle for nuclear powerplants, the Nuclear Regulatory Commission (Commission) decided that licensing boards should assume, for purposes of NEPA, that the permanent storage of certain nuclear wastes would have no significant environmental impact and thus should not affect the decision whether to license a particular nuclear powerplant. We conclude that the Commission complied with NEPA and that its decision is not arbitrary or capricious within the meaning of § 10(a) of the Administrative Procedure Act (APA), 5 U.S.C. § 706.

I

The environmental impact of operating a light-water nuclear powerplant[22] includes the effects of offsite activities necessary to provide fuel for the plant ("front end" activities), and of offsite activities necessary to dispose of the highly toxic and long-lived nuclear wastes generated by the plant ("back end" activities). The dispute in these cases concerns the Commission's adoption of a series of generic rules to evaluate the environmental effects of a nuclear powerplant's fuel cycle. At the heart of each rule is Table S–3, a numerical compilation of the estimated resources used and effluents released by fuel cycle activities supporting a year's operation of a typical light-water reactor. The three versions of Table S–3 contained similar numerical values, although the supporting documentation has been amplified during the course of the proceedings.

The Commission first adopted Table S–3 in 1974, after extensive informal rulemaking proceedings. This "original" rule, as it later came to be described, declared that in environmental reports and impact statements for individual licensing proceedings the environmental costs of the fuel cycle "shall be as set forth" in Table S–3 and that "[n]o further discussion of such environmental effects shall be required." The original Table S–3 contained no numerical entry for the long-term environmental effects of storing solidified transuranic and high-level wastes, because the Commission staff believed that technology would be developed to isolate the wastes from the environment. The Commission and the parties have later termed this assumption of complete repository integrity as the "zero-release" assumption: the reasonableness of this assumption is at the core of the present controversy. * * *

---

22. A light-water nuclear powerplant is one that uses ordinary water (H_2O), as opposed to heavy water (D_2O), to remove the heat generated in the nuclear core. The bulk of the reactors in the United States are light-water nuclear reactors.

While *Vermont Yankee* was pending in this Court, the Commission proposed a new "interim" rulemaking proceeding to determine whether to adopt a revised Table S–3. The proposal explicitly acknowledged that the risks from long-term repository failure were uncertain, but suggested that research should resolve most of those uncertainties in the near future. After further proceedings, the Commission promulgated the interim rule in March 1977. Table S–3 now explicitly stated that solidified high-level and transuranic wastes would remain buried in a federal repository and therefore would have no effect on the environment. Like its predecessor, the interim rule stated that "[n]o further discussion of such environmental effects shall be required." The NRDC petitioned for review of the interim rule, challenging the zero-release assumption and faulting the Table S–3 rule for failing to consider the health, cumulative, and socioeconomic effects of the fuel cycle activities. The Court of Appeals stayed proceedings while awaiting this Court's decision in *Vermont Yankee*. In April 1978, the Commission amended the interim rule to clarify that health effects were not covered by Table S–3 and could be litigated in individual licensing proceedings.

In 1979, following further hearings, the Commission adopted the "final" Table S–3 rule. Like the amended interim rule, the final rule expressly stated that Table S–3 should be supplemented in individual proceedings by evidence about the health, socioeconomic, and cumulative aspects of fuel cycle activities. The Commission also continued to adhere to the zero-release assumption that the solidified waste would not escape and harm the environment once the repository was sealed. It acknowledged that this assumption was uncertain because of the remote possibility that water might enter the repository, dissolve the radioactive materials, and transport them to the biosphere. * * *

In its Table S–3 Rule here, the Commission has determined that the probabilities favor the zero-release assumption, because the Nation is likely to develop methods to store the wastes with no leakage to the environment. The NRDC did not challenge and the Court of Appeals did not decide the reasonableness of this determination, and no party seriously challenges it here. The Commission recognized, however, that the geological, chemical, physical and other data it relied on in making this prediction were based, in part, on assumptions which involve substantial uncertainties. Again, no one suggests that the uncertainties are trivial or the potential effects insignificant if time proves the zero-release assumption to have been seriously wrong. After confronting the issue, though, the Commission has determined that the uncertainties concerning the development of nuclear waste storage facilities are not sufficient to affect the outcome of any individual licensing decision.

It is clear that the Commission, in making this determination, has made the careful consideration and disclosure required by NEPA. The sheer volume of proceedings before the Commission is impressive. Of far greater importance, the Commission's Statement of Consideration announcing the final Table S–3 Rule shows that it has digested this mass of material and disclosed all substantial risks. The Statement summarizes the major uncertainty of long-term storage in bedded-salt repositories, which is that water could infiltrate the repository as a result of such diverse factors as geologic faulting, a meteor strike, or accidental or deliberate intrusion by man. The Commission noted that the probability of intrusion was small, and that the plasticity of salt would tend to heal some types of intrusions. The Commission also found the evidence "tentative but favorable" that an appropriate site could be found. Table S–3 refers interested persons to staff studies that discuss the uncertainties in greater detail. Given this record and the Commission's statement, it simply cannot be said that the Commission ignored or failed to disclose the uncertainties surrounding its zero-release assumption.

Congress did not enact NEPA, of course, so that an agency would contemplate the environmental impact of an action as an abstract exercise. Rather, Congress intended that the "hard look" be incorporated as part of the agency's process of deciding whether to pursue a particular federal action. It was on this ground that the Court of Appeals faulted the Commission's action, for failing to allow the uncertainties potentially to "tip the balance" in a particular licensing decision. As a general proposition, we can agree with the Court of Appeals' determination that an agency must allow all significant environmental risks to be factored into the decision whether to undertake a proposed action. We think, however, that the Court of Appeals erred in concluding the Commission had not complied with this standard.

As *Vermont Yankee* made clear, NEPA does not require agencies to adopt any particular internal decisionmaking structure. Here, the agency has chosen to evaluate generically the environmental impact of the fuel cycle and inform individual licensing boards, through the Table S–3 rule, of its evaluation. The generic method chosen by the agency is clearly an appropriate method of conducting the hard look required by NEPA. The environmental effects of much of the fuel cycle are not plant specific, for any plant, regardless of its particular attributes, will create additional wastes that must be stored in a common long-term repository. Administrative efficiency and consistency of decision are both furthered by a generic determination of these effects without needless repetition of the litigation in individual proceedings, which are subject to review by the Commission in any event.

The Court of Appeals recognized that the Commission has discretion to evaluate generically the environmental effects of the fuel cycle and require that these values be "plugged into" individual licensing decisions. The court concluded that the Commission nevertheless violated NEPA by failing to factor the uncertainty surrounding long-term storage into Table S–3 and precluding individual licensing decisionmakers from considering it.

The Commission's decision to affix a zero value to the environmental impact of long-term storage would violate NEPA, however, only if the

Commission acted arbitrarily and capriciously in deciding generically that the uncertainty was insufficient to affect any individual licensing decision. In assessing whether the Commission's decision is arbitrary or capricious, it is crucial to place the zero-release assumption in context. Three factors are particularly important. First is the Commission's repeated emphasis that the zero-risk assumption—and, indeed, all of the Table S–3 rule—was made for a limited purpose. The Commission expressly noted its intention to supplement the rule with an explanatory narrative. It also emphasized that the purpose of the rule was not to evaluate or select the most effective long-term waste disposal technology or develop site selection criteria. A separate and comprehensive series of programs has been undertaken to serve these broader purposes. In the proceedings before us, the Commission's staff did not attempt to evaluate the environmental effects of all possible methods of disposing of waste. Rather, it chose to analyze intensively the most probable long-term waste disposal method— burial in a bedded-salt repository several hundred meters below ground— and then "estimate its impact conservatively, based on the best available information and analysis." The zero-release assumption cannot be evaluated in isolation. Rather, it must be assessed in relation to the limited purpose for which the Commission made the assumption.

Second, the Commission emphasized that the zero-release assumption is but a single figure in an entire Table, which the Commission expressly designed as a risk-averse estimate of the environmental impact of the fuel cycle. It noted that Table S–3 assumed that the fuel storage canisters and the fuel rod cladding would be corroded before a repository is closed and that all volatile materials in the fuel would escape to the environment. Given that assumption, and the improbability that materials would escape after sealing, the Commission determined that the overall Table represented a conservative (i.e., inflated) statement of environmental impacts. It is not unreasonable for the Commission to counteract the uncertainties in post-sealing releases by balancing them with an overestimate of pre-sealing releases. A reviewing court should not magnify a single line item beyond its significance as only part of a larger Table.

Third, a reviewing court must remember that the Commission is making predictions, within its area of special expertise, at the frontiers of science. When examining this kind of scientific determination, as opposed to simple findings of fact, a reviewing court must generally be at its most deferential.

With these three guides in mind, we find the Commission's zero-release assumption to be within the bounds of reasoned decisionmaking required by the APA. * * *

As we have noted, Table S–3 describes effluents and other impacts in technical terms. The Table does not convert that description into tangible effects on human health or other environmental variables. The original and interim rules declared that "the contribution of the environmental effects of * * * fuel cycle activities * * * shall be as set forth in the following Table S–3 [and] no further discussion of such environmental effects shall be required." Since the Table does not specifically mention health effects, socioeconomic impacts, or cumulative impacts, this declaration does not clearly require or preclude their discussion. The Commission later amended the interim rule to clarify that health effects were not covered by Table S–3 and could be litigated in individual licensing proceedings. In the final rule, the Commission expressly required licensing boards to consider the socioeconomic and cumulative effects in addition to the health effects of the releases projected in the Table.

The Court of Appeals held that the original and interim rules violated NEPA by precluding licensing boards from considering the health, socioeconomic, and cumulative effects of the environmental impacts stated in technical terms. As does the Commission, we agree with the Court of Appeals that NEPA requires an EIS to disclose the significant health, socioeconomic and cumulative consequences of the environmental impact of a proposed action. We find no basis, however, for the Court of Appeals' conclusion that the Commission ever precluded a licensing board from considering these effects.

NOTES

1. In another decision relating to the dangers of nuclear power plants, *Carolina Environmental Study Group v. United States*, 510 F.2d 796 (D.C. Cir. 1975), the D.C. Circuit accepted an EIS which declined to discuss the potential impacts of a breach-of-reactor containment accident, or "Class 9 accident," because the probability of its occurrence was so small. There is a certain irony to that decision in light of the later Three Mile Island episode (which was classified as a Class 9 accident). Despite the TMI incident, one court held that the NRC still did not have to consider the possibility of Class 9 accidents:

As we have discussed above, the Commission did not conclude in its Statement of Interim Policy that its original assumption regarding Class Nine accidents was scientifically incorrect. Rather, it recognized the need for renewed study of the issue. The clear import of the Commission's Statement is that, until such time as its research yields a contrary result, the Commission continues to regard Class Nine accidents as highly improbable events.

We do not consider that conclusion unreasonable. Neither the 1978 study by the Risk Assessment Review Group nor the accident at Three Mile Island established that the probability of a Class Nine accident with significant environmental consequences is anything but very small. * * * Because the environmental consequences of Three Mile Island were scientifically and legally inconsequential, the fact that the accident occurred does not establish that accidents with significant environmental impacts will have significant probabilities of occurrence.

NEPA, therefore, does not require the consideration of Class Nine accidents in future EISs, nor does it require that final EISs be supplemented to take account of the Class Nine risk. The approach adopted in the Statement of Interim Policy—to include discussion of such accidents in future EISs—was a discretionary policy choice of the Commission. Because it need not have imposed upon itself the burden it did, the Commission was perfectly free to deny its new policy retroactive effect. We conclude that the Commission did not violate its obligations under NEPA by declining to supplement the Diablo Canyon EIS with a discussion of the environmental impacts of a Class Nine accident.

San Luis Obispo Mothers for Peace v. NRC, 751 F.2d 1287, 1301 (D.C. Cir. 1984), *vacated in part*, 760 F.2d 1320 (D.C. Cir. 1985) (en banc). *But cf.* Limerick Ecology Action, Inc. v. United States Nuclear Regulatory Comm'n, 869 F.2d 719, 739–40 (3d Cir. 1989) (rejecting *San Luis Obispo*). For further discussion, see Daniel A. Farber, *Confronting Uncertainty Under NEPA*, available at http://papers.ssrn.com/sol3/papers.cfm?abstract_id=1403723.

2. The Court in *Baltimore Gas* says that the NRC is entitled to maximum deference here because its finding of no risk was made in a context "at the frontiers of science." It cites in support of this statement a case involving toxic substances. Are the two situations really equivalent? Is the Court saying that under NEPA, the greater the scientific uncertainty, the more the Court should defer to an agency decision to ignore uncertainty?

The prevalence of scientific uncertainties in any environmental decision calls into question the lack of any provision in NEPA for adaptation, experimentation, or even monitoring once an action has been undertaken. One CEQ regulation, 40 C.F.R. section 1505.3, allows agencies to monitor the results of their decisions but does not require them to do so. Numerous scholars have advocated a move toward "adaptive management," which in the context of NEPA might at a minimum entail more flexibility (and obligation) for agencies to respond to the environmental effects of their decisions through mitigation measures. *See* Bradley C. Karkkainen, *Whither NEPA?*, 12 N.Y.U. ENVTL. L.J. 333, 355–58 (2004). However, cases such as *Norton v. Southern Utah Wilderness Alliance*, 542 U.S. 55 (2004) (holding that the Bureau of Land Management's failure to respond to increased off-road vehicle use in a Wilderness Study Area was permissible since the agency had no legal duty to do so under NEPA or any other law), indicate that such a change will not come about without legislative reform.

3. To the extent that NEPA is intended to force agencies to take a hard look at the environmental consequences of their actions, has it achieved this result? Is there *any* way to get an agency like the NRC, which is institutionally structured around a given program, to consider seriously the desirability of terminating the program? If not, how can the government obtain objective expert advice on key policy issues? Would a report from the National Academy of Sciences be more useful than an EIS by the NRC?

4. At one time, a CEQ regulation dealt with the issue of risk by requiring a discussion of the "worst case" scenario. Would that regulation have led to a more useful EIS in *Baltimore Gas*?

This regulation was eventually rescinded, however. In the next case, the plaintiffs ask the Court to require a worst-case analysis despite the rescission.

They also ask the court to require that the agency adopt, rather than just disclose, mitigation measures.

ROBERTSON v. METHOW VALLEY CITIZENS COUNCIL

Supreme Court of the United States, 1989.
490 U.S. 332, 109 S.Ct. 1835, 104 L.Ed.2d 351.

[The plaintiffs challenged the Forest Service's issuance of special-use permits for a ski resort on national forest land. The EIS (entitled the Early Winters Alpine Winter Sports Study and referred to in the Court's opinion as the "Early Winters Study") considered the effect of the resort on wildlife and outlined possible mitigation measures. The Court of Appeals found the EIS inadequate for two reasons. First, the state Game department had predicted a 50% loss in the mule deer herd. The EIS adopted a 15% estimate, but admitted that the off-site effects of the resort were uncertain because they depended on the extent of private development. The EIS relied on mitigation measures to reduce the impact, but those measures had not been fully developed or tested. In light of this uncertainty, the Court of Appeals held that the EIS should have included a worst-case analysis. Second, the Court of Appeals held that the EIS was inadequate because it did not contain a complete mitigation plan to protect wildlife (and it lacked a plan to protect air quality).]

JUSTICE STEVENS delivered the opinion of the Court.

Simply by focusing the agency's attention on the environmental consequences of a proposed project, NEPA ensures that important effects will not be overlooked or underestimated only to be discovered after resources have been committed or the die otherwise cast. Moreover, the strong precatory language of § 101 of the Act and the requirement that agencies prepare detailed impact statements inevitably bring pressure to bear on agencies "to respond to the needs of environmental quality." 115 Cong. Rec. 40425 (1969) (remarks of Sen. Muskie).

Publication of an EIS, both in draft and final form, also serves a larger informational role. It gives the public the assurance that the agency "has indeed considered environmental concerns in its decisionmaking process," [*Baltimore Gas & Electric Co., supra,* page __], and, perhaps more significantly, provides a springboard for public comment. Thus, in this case the final draft of the Early Winters Study reflects not only the work of the Forest Service itself, but also the critical views of the Washington State Department of Game, the Methow Valley Citizens Council, and Friends of the Earth, as well as many others, to whom copies of the draft Study were circulated. Moreover, with respect to a development such as Sandy Butte, where the adverse effects on air quality and the mule deer herd are primarily attributable to predicted off-site development that will be subject to regulation by other governmental bodies, the EIS serves the function of offering those bodies adequate notice of the expected consequences and the opportunity to plan and implement corrective measures in a timely manner.

The sweeping policy goals announced in § 101 of NEPA are thus realized through a set of "action-forcing" procedures that require that agencies take a " 'hard look' at environmental consequences," and that provide for broad dissemination of relevant environmental information. Although these procedures are almost certain to affect the agency's substantive decision, it is now well settled that NEPA itself does not mandate particular results, but simply prescribes the necessary process.
* * *

If the adverse environmental effects of the proposed action are adequately identified and evaluated, the agency is not constrained by NEPA from deciding that other values outweigh the environmental costs. In this case, for example, it would not have violated NEPA if the Forest Service, after complying with the Act's procedural prerequisites, had decided that the benefits to be derived from downhill skiing at Sandy Butte justified the issuance of a special use permit, notwithstanding the loss of 15 percent, 50 percent, or even 100 percent of the mule deer herd. Other statutes may impose substantive environmental obligations on federal agencies, but NEPA merely prohibits uninformed—rather than unwise—agency action.

To be sure, one important ingredient of an EIS is the discussion of steps that can be taken to mitigate adverse environmental consequences.[23] The requirement that an EIS contain a detailed discussion of possible mitigation measures flows from both the language of the Act and, more expressly, from CEQ's implementing regulations. Implicit in NEPA's demand that an agency prepare a detailed statement on "any adverse environmental effects which cannot be avoided should the proposal be implemented," is an understanding that the EIS will discuss the extent to which adverse effects can be avoided. More generally, omission of a reasonably complete discussion of possible mitigation measures would undermine the "action-forcing" function of NEPA. Without such a discussion, neither the agency nor other interested groups and individuals can properly evaluate the severity of the adverse effects. An adverse effect that can be fully remedied by, for example, an inconsequential public expenditure is certainly not as serious as a similar effect that can only be modestly ameliorated through the commitment of vast public and private resources. Recognizing the importance of such a discussion in guaranteeing that the agency has taken a "hard look" at the environmental consequences of proposed federal action, CEQ regulations require that the

---

23.   CEQ regulations define "mitigation" to include:

(a) Avoiding the impact altogether by not taking a certain action or parts of an action.

(b) Minimizing impacts by limiting the degree or magnitude of the action and its implementation.

(c) Rectifying the impact by repairing, rehabilitating, or restoring the affected environment.

(d) Reducing or eliminating the impact over time by preservation and maintenance operations during the life of the action.

(e) Compensating for the impact by replacing or providing substitute resources or environments.

40 CFR § 1508.20 (1987).

agency discuss possible mitigation measures in defining the scope of the EIS, 40 CFR § 1508.25(b) in discussing alternatives to the proposed action, § 1502.14(f), and consequences of that action, § 1502.16(h), and in explaining its ultimate decision, § 1505.2(c).

There is a fundamental distinction, however, between a requirement that mitigation be discussed in sufficient detail to ensure that environmental consequences have been fairly evaluated, on the one hand, and a substantive requirement that a complete mitigation plan be actually formulated and adopted, on the other. In this case, the off-site effects on air quality and on the mule deer herd cannot be mitigated unless nonfederal government agencies take appropriate action. Since it is those state and local governmental bodies that have jurisdiction over the area in which the adverse effects need be addressed and since they have the authority to mitigate them, it would be incongruous to conclude that the Forest Service has no power to act until the local agencies have reached a final conclusion on what mitigating measures they consider necessary. Even more significantly, it would be inconsistent with NEPA's reliance on procedural mechanisms—as opposed to substantive, result-based standards—to demand the presence of a fully developed plan that will mitigate environmental harm before an agency can act. *Cf. Baltimore Gas & Electric Co.,* [*supra,* page 511] ("NEPA does not require agencies to adopt any particular internal decisionmaking structure").

We thus conclude that the Court of Appeals erred, first, in assuming that "NEPA requires that 'action be taken to mitigate the adverse effects of major federal actions,' " and, second, in finding that this substantive requirement entails the further duty to include in every EIS "a detailed explanation of specific measures which *will* be employed to mitigate the adverse impacts of a proposed action."

The Court of Appeals also concluded that the Forest Service had an obligation to make a "worst case analysis" if it could not make a reasoned assessment of the impact of the Early Winters project on the mule deer herd. Such a "worst case analysis" was required at one time by CEQ regulations, but those regulations have since been amended. Moreover, although the prior regulations may well have expressed a permissible application of NEPA, the Act itself does not mandate that uncertainty in predicting environmental harms be addressed exclusively in this manner. Accordingly, we conclude that the Court of Appeals also erred in requiring the "worst case" study.

In 1977, President Carter directed that CEQ promulgate binding regulations implementing the procedural provisions of NEPA. Pursuant to this presidential order, CEQ promulgated implementing regulations. Under § 1502.22 of these regulations—a provision which became known as the "worst case requirement"—CEQ provided that if certain information relevant to the agency's evaluation of the proposed action is either unavailable or too costly to obtain, the agency must include in the EIS a "worst case analysis and an indication of the probability or improbability of its occurrence." 40 CFR § 1502.22 (1985). In 1986, however, CEQ replaced the "worst case" requirement with a requirement that federal agencies, in the face of unavailable information concerning a reasonably foreseeable significant environmental consequence, prepare "a summary of existing credible scientific evidence which is relevant to evaluating the * * * adverse impacts" and prepare an "evaluation of such impacts based upon theoretical approaches or research methods generally accepted in the scientific community." 40 CFR § 1502.22(b) (1987). The amended regulation thus "retains the duty to describe the consequences of a remote, but potentially severe impact, but grounds the duty in evaluation of scientific opinion rather than in the framework of a conjectural 'worst case analysis.' " 50 Fed.Reg. 32237 (1985).

The Court of Appeals recognized that the "worst case analysis" regulation has been superseded, yet held that "[t]his rescission * * * does not nullify the requirement * * * since the regulation was merely a codification of prior NEPA case law." This conclusion, however, is erroneous in a number of respects. Most notably, review of NEPA case law reveals that the regulation, in fact, was not a codification of prior judicial decisions. The cases cited by the Court of Appeals ultimately rely on the Fifth Circuit's decision in *Sierra Club v. Sigler,* 695 F.2d 957 (1983). *Sigler,* however, simply recognized that the "worst case analysis" regulation codified the "judicially created principl[e]" that an EIS must "consider the probabilities of the occurrence of any environmental effects it discusses." *Id.,* at 970–971. As CEQ recognized at the time it superseded the regulation, case law prior to the adoption of the "worst case analysis" provision did require agencies to describe environmental impacts even in the face of substantial uncertainty, but did not require that this obligation necessarily be met through the mechanism of a "worst case analysis." CEQ's abandonment of the "worst case analysis" provision, therefore, is not inconsistent with any previously established judicial interpretation of the statute.

Nor are we convinced that the new CEQ regulation is not controlling simply because it was preceded by a rule that was in some respects more demanding. In *Andrus v. Sierra Club,* 442 U.S., at 358, we held that CEQ regulations are entitled to substantial deference. In that case we recognized that although less deference may be in order in some cases in which the "administrative guidelines" conflict "with earlier pronouncements of the agency," substantial deference is nonetheless appropriate if there appears to have been good reason for the change. Here, the amendment only came after the prior regulation had been subjected to considerable criticism. Moreover, the amendment was designed to better serve the twin functions of an EIS—requiring agencies to take a "hard look" at the consequences of the proposed action and providing important information to other groups and individuals. CEQ explained that by requiring that an EIS focus on reasonably foreseeable impacts, the new regulation "will generate information and discussion on those consequences of greatest concern to the public and of greatest relevance to the agency's decision," rather than distorting the decisionmaking process by overemphasizing highly speculative harms. In light of this well-considered basis for the change, the new regulation is entitled to substantial deference. Accordingly, the Court of Appeals erred in concluding that the Early Winters Study is inadequate because it failed to include a "worst case analysis."

Notes

1. Note that the *Robertson* Court refers to section 101 as "precatory" and says that "NEPA itself does not mandate particular results, but simply prescribes the necessary process." *Robertson* seems to make it clear that NEPA is purely procedural and imposes no substantive restraint on the government. The courts of appeals had divided on the issue of substantive review under NEPA. In *Strycker's Bay Neighborhood Council, Inc. v. Karlen,* 444 U.S. 223 (1980), the Second Circuit had held that an agency's choice of a site for a housing project was unjustifiable under NEPA. The Supreme Court reversed. The opinion contained broad language about the procedural nature of NEPA, such as the following:

> [I]n the present case there is no doubt that [the agency] considered the environmental consequences of its decision to designate the proposed site for low-income housing. NEPA requires no more. 444 U.S. at 228.

A footnote, however, seemed to leave some possible room for substantive judicial review:

> If we could agree with the dissent that the Court of Appeals held [the agency] had acted "arbitrarily" * * * we might also agree that plenary review is warranted. But the District Court expressly concluded that [the agency] had not acted arbitrarily or capriciously and our reading of the opinion of the Court of Appeals satisfies us that it did not overturn that finding. Instead, the Appellate Court required [the agency] to elevate environmental concerns over other, admittedly legitimate considerations. Neither NEPA nor the APA provides any support for such a reordering of priorities by review in court. 444 U.S. at 228 n.2.

2. The *Robertson* Court did not refer to the *Strycker* footnote, but its description of § 101 as "precatory" seems to leave little room for substantive judicial review under NEPA. In adopting this view of NEPA, hasn't the Court overlooked the language of § 102(1)? How can the section 101 policies be completely precatory, when § 102 "directs that, to the fullest extent possible: (1) the policies, regulations, and public laws of the United States shall be interpreted and administered in accordance with the policies set forth in this chapter * * * "?

The Supreme Court's resolution of this issue seems unjustifiable in principle, given the language of § 102(2). *See* Nicholas C. Yost, *NEPA's Promise—Partially Fulfilled*, 20 Envtl. L. 553 (1990). This is particularly ironic, given the emphasis placed by Justice Scalia and others on the need for fidelity to statutory texts. Nevertheless, it may not make much practical difference. Apart from the Second Circuit's ill-fated decision in *Strycker's Bay,* no court of appeals had ever actually reversed an agency decision on the merits under NEPA. One reason may be that NEPA's procedural standard overlaps considerably with the "arbitrary or capricious" standard anyway. Recall that the "arbitrary or capricious" test requires a "reasoned explanation" of the agency's decision. An EIS that fails to meet this "substantive" test can probably be faulted for its discussion of the impact of the action or of alternatives, and thus will be found inadequate. Moreover, most government actions are subject to some restrictions under other statutes, which will usually provide a basis for judicial correction of egregious agency decisions.

4. NEPA'S PAST AND FUTURE

Do you see any overall pattern in the outcomes in the Supreme Court's NEPA decisions? (Hint: Which side always won?) *See* Daniel A. Farber, *Disdain for 17–Year–Old Statute Evident in High Court's Rulings*, NAT'L L.J., May 4, 1987, at 20 (arguing that the Court's consistent rejection of NEPA claims reflects disdain for the statute). For a contrary view, see David C. Shilton, *Is the Supreme Court Hostile to NEPA? Some Possible Explanations for a 12–0 Record*, 20 ENVTL. L. 551 (1990). Two decades after those articles were written, the Supreme Court is *yet* to uphold a NEPA claim. We are not aware of any other federal statute, environmental or otherwise, with a forty-year history of defeat in the Supreme Court.

Despite the Supreme Court's rather narrow reading of the statute, NEPA has remained an important pillar of environmental law. It has been widely imitated—at least fifteen states have adopted their own versions of NEPA, including California (which, unlike NEPA, extends the EIS requirement to private actors and requires mitigation), and EIS-type requirements have now been adopted in over thirty countries. For further details, *see* chapters 13 and 14 of DANIEL MANDELKER, NEPA LAW AND LITIGATION (2d ed. 1994).

How effective in practice has NEPA been? According to the *Robertson* Court, NEPA's procedures are "almost certain to affect the agency's substantive decision." Among those who have studied NEPA, there have been a variety of opinions about the statute's effectiveness. After a review of early airport runway-extension controversies, Professor Sax concluded that NEPA was simply ineffectual. Joseph L. Sax, *The (Unhappy) Truth about NEPA*, 26 OKLA. L. REV. 239 (1973). Other early commentators concluded that NEPA puts useful pressure on agencies to consider environmental issues, but is ultimately incapable of forcing them to do so. Roger C. Cramton & Richard K. Berg, *On Leading a Horse to Water: NEPA and the Federal Bureaucracy*, 71 MICH. L. REV. 511, 536 (1973). *See* Dinah Bear, *Some Modest Suggestions for Improving Implementation of the National Environmental Policy Act,* 43 NAT. RESOURCES J. 931, 935 (2003) for the more recent opinion by a former general counsel of the CEQ that NEPA is not sufficiently incorporated into the decision-making process of many agencies. On the other hand, clear instances exist of agencies substantially changing their actions in light of NEPA. Perhaps the best example is the Corps of Engineers' decision to broaden consideration of whether to issue dredge-and-fill permits to include full consideration of environmental factors, despite substantial opposition. *See* Zabel v. Tabb, 430 F.2d 199 (5th Cir. 1970).

The CEQ attempted in 1978 to determine the effects of NEPA litigation. A survey of 938 NEPA cases indicated the following results: (1) NEPA filings peaked in 1974; (2) a total of 202 cases were delayed by a NEPA injunction, almost half of them for longer than one year; (3) none of the projects were halted by a permanent injunction; (4) 60 of the projects were abandoned after the NEPA action was filed. A later CEQ study found that NEPA has had a highly beneficial effect on EPA's construction grant program for wastewater treatment. *See* CEQ, TWENTI-ETH ANNUAL REPORT 31–37 (1990). For the latest statistics on NEPA litigation trends and outcomes throughout the federal courts, *see* the Council on Environmental Quality's annual NEPA litigation surveys, available at www.nepa.gov.

Some of NEPA's impact may be invisible or hard to measure: agencies may shrink from proposing projects that they would have otherwise proposed absent NEPA requirements. So NEPA may eliminate the most environmentally damaging projects from consideration in the first place. For further discussion of NEPA's effects, *see* SERGE TAYLOR, MAKING BUREAUCRACIES THINK: THE ENVIRONMENTAL IMPACT STATEMENT STRATEGY OF ADMINISTRATIVE REFORM (1984); Dinah Bear, *NEPA at 19*, 19 ENVTL. L. REP. 10062 (1989).

The George W. Bush Administration curtailed NEPA review in several areas in the name of administrative efficiency. Executive Order 13,274 directs federal agencies to "expedite environmental reviews of high-priority transportation infrastructure projects." Exec. Order No. 13,274, 3 C.F.R. § 250 (2003). The Healthy Forests Restoration Act of 2003 "streamlines" the NEPA process by exempting individual Forest Service decisions about "fuel reduction" (*i.e.*, harvesting timber and clearing underbrush, on the theory that this will reduce the likelihood and severity of forest fires) from NEPA for the sake of swift action by the Forest Service in areas threatened by catastrophic wildfires. 16 U.S.C. §§ 6501–6591 (2003). Again citing efficiency concerns, the Forest Service issued a final rule in 2005 allowing a number of its other planning activities to be exempt from NEPA through categorical exclusions. National Forest System Land Management Planning, 70 FED. REG. 1023, 1030–34 (Jan. 5, 2005) (codified at 36 C.F.R. Part 219).

Some more basic changes were suggested for NEPA by a special task force convened by the CEQ in 2002 to find ways to make the statute "more effective, more efficient, and more timely." *See* Memorandum from Horst G. Greczmiel, Director, NEPA Task Force, to James Connaughton, Chairman, Council on Environmental Quality (Sept. 24, 2003), *available at* www.nepa.gov/ntf/20030929memo.pdf. The Task Force's final report suggested several ideas for improving NEPA's operation. Among the most prominent were promoting collaborative agreements; improving regulations for and use of programmatic documents; integrating adaptive management (particularly at the programmatic level); clarifying application of categorical exclusions; and creating more uniform and specific requirements for what to put in EAs, especially with regard to discussion of alternatives (in order to deal with the perceived lack of sufficient deference to EAs by courts). NEPA TASK FORCE, THE NEPA TASK FORCE REPORT TO THE COUNCIL ON ENVIRONMENTAL QUALITY: MODERNIZING NEPA IMPLEMENTATION vii–xvii (2003), *available at*www.nepa.gov/ntf/report/finalreport.pdf. For a critique of the Task Force's recommendations, *see* Bradley C. Karkkainen, *Whither NEPA?*, 12 N.Y.U. ENVTL. L.J. 333 (2004). Much also remains to be done to connect NEPA with modern information technology. See Daniel A. Farber, *Bringing Environmental Assessment into the Digital Age*, available at http://papers.ssrn.com/sol3/papers.cfm?abstract_id =877625.

CHAPTER 6

AIR POLLUTION

■ ■ ■

Introduction

Air pollution comes from many different sources, including stationary sources such as factories, power plants and dry cleaners. Mobile sources such as cars, trucks and buses also contribute significantly to air pollution. Some air pollutants are pervasive whereas others are local; some are harmful in large doses, some in smaller doses; and some are toxic. Air pollution causes adverse health effects, including impaired pulmonary and cardiac function. In some cases, exposure to air pollution can lead to premature death. Air pollution also impairs the health of ecosystems by adversely affecting trees, lakes, streams and other habitats. It can damage crops and animals, as well as buildings. Poor air quality can also have a negative aesthetic impact by reducing visibility in national parks and other wilderness areas, as well as in urban areas.

Why can't the market solve the problem of air pollution without government intervention? Surely people who care about air quality would be willing to pay for it. The problem is that air quality (like national defense) cannot be priced and reserved exclusively for those willing to pay. Clean air is a classic "public good" that will tend to be under-produced by the market. This market failure means that government intervention may be necessary to ensure sufficient production of air quality. Air pollution regulation may also be explained as a cost-internalizing mechanism that forces firms to pay for the real cost of production. In economic terms, air pollution can be understood as an externality of productive economic activity. Since firms do not pay for the air quality they degrade in the course of producing goods (as they would pay for labor and materials), they face an incentive to over-consume this free resource. Firms capture all of the economic benefit of dirtying the air without absorbing the full cost. Instead, most of the cost is borne by the wider community which suffers health and welfare effects caused by air pollution.

A. THE COMMON LAW

1. PRIVATE NUISANCE

The common law of nuisance has historically served as an indirect mechanism for compensating individuals harmed by pollution. As you read the case excerpted below, consider the relative strengths and weaknesses of using the common law to regulate air pollution.

BOOMER v. ATLANTIC CEMENT COMPANY

Court of Appeals of New York, 1970.
26 N.Y.2d 219, 309 N.Y.S.2d 312, 257 N.E.2d 870.

BERGAN, CIRCUIT JUDGE.

Defendant operates a large cement plant near Albany. These are actions for injunction and damages by neighboring land owners alleging injury to property from dirt, smoke and vibration emanating from the plant. A nuisance has been found after trial, temporary damages have been allowed but an injunction has been denied.

The public concern with air pollution arising from many sources in industry and in transportation is currently accorded ever wider recognition accompanied by a growing sense of responsibility in State and Federal Governments to control it. Cement plants are obvious sources of air pollution in the neighborhoods where they operate.

But there is now before the court private litigation in which individual property owners have sought specific relief from a single plant operation. The threshold question raised by the division of view on this appeal is whether the court should resolve the litigation between the parties now before it as equitably as seems possible; or whether, seeking promotion of the general public welfare, it should channel private litigation into broad public objectives.

A court performs its essential function when it decides the rights of parties before it. Its decision of private controversies may sometimes greatly affect public issues. Large questions of law are often resolved by the manner in which private litigation is decided. But this is normally an incident to the court's main function to settle controversy. It is a rare exercise of judicial power to use a decision in private litigation as a purposeful mechanism to achieve direct public objectives greatly beyond the rights and interests before the court.

Effective control of air pollution is a problem presently far from solution even with the full public and financial powers of government. In large measure adequate technical procedures are yet to be developed and some that appear possible may be economically impracticable.

It seems apparent that the amelioration of air pollution will depend on technical research in great depth; on a carefully balanced consideration of the economic impact of close regulation; and of the actual effect on public health. It is likely to require massive public expenditure and to demand more than any local community can accomplish and to depend on regional and interstate controls.

A court should not try to do this on its own as a by-product of private litigation and it seems manifest that the judicial establishment is neither equipped in the limited nature of any judgment it can pronounce nor prepared to lay down and implement an effective policy for the elimination of air pollution. This is an area beyond the circumference of one private lawsuit. It is a direct responsibility for government and should not thus be undertaken as an incident to solving a dispute between property owners and a single cement plant—one of many—in the Hudson River valley.

The cement making operations of defendant have been found by the court at Special Term to have damaged the nearby properties of plaintiffs in these two actions. That court, as it has been noted, accordingly found defendant maintained a nuisance and this has been affirmed at the Appellate Division. The total damage to plaintiffs' properties is, however, relatively small in comparison with the value of defendant's operation and with the consequences of the injunction which plaintiffs seek.

The ground for the denial of injunction, notwithstanding the finding both that there is a nuisance and that plaintiffs have been damaged substantially, is the large disparity in economic consequences of the nuisance and of the injunction. This theory cannot, however, be sustained without overruling a doctrine which has been consistently reaffirmed in several leading cases in this court and which has never been disavowed here, namely that where a nuisance has been found and where there has been any substantial damage shown by the party complaining an injunction will be granted.

The rule in New York has been that such a nuisance will be enjoined although marked disparity be shown in economic consequence between the effect of the injunction and the effect of the nuisance. * * *

* * * [T]o follow the rule literally in these cases would be to close down the plant at once. This court is fully agreed to avoid that immediately drastic remedy; the difference in view is how best to avoid it.

One alternative is to grant the injunction but postpone its effect to a specified future date to give opportunity for technical advances to permit defendant to eliminate the nuisance; another is to grant the injunction conditioned on the payment of permanent damages to plaintiffs which would compensate them for the total economic loss to their property present and future caused by defendant's operations. For reasons which will be developed the court chooses the latter alternative.

If the injunction were to be granted unless within a short period—e.g., 18 months—the nuisance be abated by improved methods, there would be no assurance that any significant technical improvement would occur.

The parties could settle this private litigation at any time if defendant paid enough money and the imminent threat of closing the plant would build up the pressure on defendant. If there were no improved techniques found, there would inevitably be applications to the court at Special Term for extensions of time to perform on showing of good faith efforts to find such techniques.

Moreover, techniques to eliminate dust and other annoying by-products of cement making are unlikely to be developed by any research the defendant can undertake within any short period, but will depend on the total resources of the cement industry nationwide and throughout the world. The problem is universal wherever cement is made.

For obvious reasons the rate of the research is beyond the control of defendant. If at the end of 18 months the whole industry has not found a technical solution a court would be hard put to close down this one cement plant if due regard be given to equitable principles.

On the other hand, to grant the injunction unless defendant pays plaintiffs such permanent damages as may be fixed by the court seems to do justice between the contending parties. All of the attributions of economic loss to the properties on which plaintiffs' complaints are based will have been redressed.

The nuisance complained of by these plaintiffs may have other public or private consequences, but these particular parties are the only ones who have sought remedies and the judgment proposed will fully redress them. The limitation of relief granted is a limitation only within the four corners of these actions and does not foreclose public health or other public agencies from seeking proper relief in a proper court.

It seems reasonable to think that the risk of being required to pay permanent damages to injured property owners by cement plant owners would itself be a reasonably effective spur to research for improved techniques to minimize nuisance.

The power of the court to condition on equitable grounds the continuance of an injunction on the payment of permanent damages seems undoubted. * * *

The judgment, by allowance of permanent damages imposing a servitude on land, which is the basis of the actions, would preclude future recovery by plaintiffs or their grantees * * *.

This should be placed beyond debate by a provision of the judgment that the payment by defendant and the acceptance by plaintiffs of permanent damages found by the court shall be in compensation for a servitude on the land.

JASEN, CIRCUIT JUDGE (dissenting).

It has long been the rule in this State, as the majority acknowledges, that a nuisance which results in substantial continuing damage to neighbors must be enjoined. * * * To now change the rule to permit the cement company to continue polluting the air indefinitely upon the payment of permanent damages is, in my opinion, compounding the magnitude of a very serious problem in our State and Nation today. * * *

I see grave dangers in overruling our long-established rule of granting an injunction where a nuisance results in substantial continuing damage. In permitting the injunction to become inoperative upon the payment of permanent damages, the majority is, in effect, licensing a continuing wrong. It is the same as saying to the cement company, you may continue to do harm to your neighbors so long as you pay a fee for it. Furthermore, once such permanent damages are assessed and paid, the incentive to alleviate the wrong would be eliminated, thereby continuing air pollution of an area without abatement.

It is true that some courts have sanctioned the remedy here proposed by the majority in a number of cases, but none of the authorities relied upon by the majority are analogous to the situation before us. In those cases, the courts, in denying an injunction and awarding money damages, grounded their decision on a showing that the use to which the property was intended to be put was primarily for the public benefit. Here, on the other hand, it is clearly established that the cement company is creating a continuing air pollution nuisance primarily for its own private interest with no public benefit.

This kind of inverse condemnation * * * may not be invoked by a private person or corporation for private gain or advantage. Inverse condemnation should only be permitted when the public is primarily served in the taking or impairment of property. * * * The promotion of the interests of the polluting cement company has, in my opinion, no public use or benefit.

Nor is it constitutionally permissible to impose servitude on land, without consent of the owner, by payment of permanent damages where the continuing impairment of the land is for a private use. * * * This is made clear by the State Constitution which provides that "[p]rivate property shall not be taken for public use without just compensation" (emphasis added). It is, of course, significant that the section makes no mention of taking for a private use. * * *

I would enjoin the defendant cement company from continuing the discharge of dust particles upon its neighbors' properties unless, within 18 months, the cement company abated this nuisance. * * *

I am aware that the trial court found that the most modern dust control devices available have been installed in defendant's plant, but, I submit, this does not mean that *better* and more effective dust control devices could not be developed within the time allowed to abate the pollution.

Moreover, I believe it is incumbent upon the defendant to develop such devices, since the cement company, at the time the plant commenced production (1962), was well aware of the plaintiffs' presence in the area, as well as the probable consequences of its contemplated operation. Yet, it still chose to build and operate the plant at this site.

NOTES

1. Some additional facts about *Boomer* may be helpful in evaluating the case. The court's opinion focuses on air pollution. An examination of the appellate record, however, reveals that *Boomer* did not present simply a conventional pollution problem. Instead, the record suggests a severe but localized impact on neighboring lands, due less to the cement plant than to the operation of the quarry on the same site. In particular, neighbors complained of severe vibrations and heavy dust from blasting operations at the quarry. The main reason the trial judge declined to issue an injunction was not undue hardship to the cement company, but rather the central role of the plant in the local economy. Over half of the assessed value of the township involved the cement company's property—respondent had $45 million invested in the plant and employed more than 300 workers—so closing the plant would have had a devastating effect on the local government, economy, and school system. On remand, the trial judge calculated that the amount of the decline in fair market value for one of the parcels was $140,000 and then added a "kicker" of $35,000 to arrive at the damage award. The cement company's liability, including its settlement of the other pending cases, came to $710,000. For fuller details, *see* Daniel Farber, *Reassessing* Boomer: *Justice, Efficiency, and Nuisance Law*, in ESSAYS ON THE LAW OF PROPERTY AND LEGAL EDUCATION, IN HONOR OF JOHN E. CRIBBET (Michael H. Hoeflich & Peter Hay eds. 1988).

2. Notice that private nuisance cases may only remedy the effects of pollution suffered by a single plaintiff, or a small handful of plaintiffs. What about the effect of air pollutants on communities further away? Or the effect of emissions on trees and streams that have no standing to sue for nuisance? There are other limitations to private nuisance cases as well. Many plaintiffs with meritorious claims may lack the resources to hire a lawyer. In addition, plaintiffs may be at a disadvantage when it comes to the legal test for nuisance. Many courts determine whether interference with use and enjoyment is unreasonable by applying a "gravity of harm" vs. "social utility of the conduct" balancing test. *See* RESTATEMENT OF TORTS (2d) § 826. Using this test, the harm suffered by plaintiffs like Mr. Boomer will likely seem small in comparison to the social utility of an industrial concern like the Atlantic Cement plant, which produces a valuable product, employs hundreds of workers, and pays substantial property taxes. Is there a way to apply this test that is not systematically biased against plaintiffs? Are there other tests for nuisance that do not require such balancing? *See* RESTATEMENT OF TORTS (2d) §§ 826, 829.

By awarding the plaintiff permanent damages instead of injunctive relief the *Boomer* court adapts nuisance law to accommodate the plaintiff's harm without shutting down a socially valuable industry. It may seem obvious that the choice between a damage remedy and an injunctive remedy has enormous practical importance in a case like *Boomer*. Yet this is less clear on further reflection. If Mr. Boomer is entitled to an injunction but has relatively small damages, it might make sense for him to enter into a settlement. Thus, he might choose to forego his injunction in exchange for cash. If so, the pollution will continue. Some economists have suggested, on similar grounds, that the existence or non-existence of liability, quite apart from the remedy, may have no effect on pollution levels. Assuming there are no transaction costs (a large assumption), parties will bargain to the efficient solution: if it is less costly to install pollution abatement controls or to shut down the plant than to compensate plaintiffs like Mr. Boomer, then the pollution will be controlled. Otherwise, it will continue, and Mr. Boomer will be compensated. The article below explains this thesis.

RONALD COASE, THE PROBLEM OF SOCIAL COST[1]

3 J. L. ECON. 1, 1–8, 15–19 (1960).

I propose to start my analysis by examining a case in which most economists would presumably agree that the problem would be solved in a completely satisfactory manner: when the damaging business has to pay for all damage caused *and* the pricing system works smoothly (strictly this means that the operation of a pricing system is without cost).

A good example of the problem under discussion is afforded by the case of straying cattle which destroy crops growing on neighbouring land. Let us suppose that a farmer and a cattle-raiser are operating on neighbouring properties. Let us further suppose that, without any fencing between the properties, an increase in the size of the cattle-raiser's herd increases the total damage to the farmer's crops. * * *

To simplify the argument, I propose to use an arithmetical example. I shall assume that the annual cost of fencing the farmer's property is $9 and that the price of the crop is $1 per ton. Also, I assume that the relation between the number of cattle in the herd and the annual crop loss is as follows:

Number in Herd (Steers)	Annual Crop Loss (Tons)	Additional Crop Loss per Additional Steer (Tons)
1	1	1
2	3	2
3	6	3
4	10	4

Given that the cattle-raiser is liable for the damage caused, the additional annual cost imposed on the cattle-raiser if he increased his herd from, say, 2 to 3 steers is $3 and in deciding on the size of the herd, he will take this into account along with his other costs. That is, he will not increase the size of the herd unless the value of the additional meat produced (assuming that the cattle-raiser slaughters the cattle), is greater than the additional costs that this will entail, including the value of the additional crops destroyed. * * * Given that the annual cost of fencing is

---

$9, the cattle-raiser who wished to have a herd with 4 steers or more would pay for fencing to be erected and maintained, assuming that other means of attaining the same end would not do so more cheaply. * * *

I now turn to the case in which, although the pricing system is assumed to work smoothly (that is, costlessly), the damaging business is not liable for any of the damage which it causes. * * * I propose to show that the allocation of resources will be the same [optimal] as it was when the damaging business was liable for damage caused. * * *

* * * Suppose that the size of the cattle-raiser's herd is 3 steers (and that this is the size of the herd that would be maintained if crop damage was not taken into account). Then the farmer would be willing to pay up to $3 if the cattle-raiser would reduce his herd to 2 steers, up to $5 if the herd were reduced to 1 steer and would pay up to $6 if cattle-raising was abandoned. The cattle-raiser would therefore receive $3 from the farmer if he kept 2 steers instead of 3. This $3 foregone is therefore part of the cost incurred in keeping the third steer. Whether the $3 is a payment which the cattle-raiser has to make if he adds the third steer to his herd (which it would be if the cattle-raiser was liable to the farmer for damage caused to the crop) or whether it is a sum of money which he would have received if he did not keep a third steer (which it would be if the cattle-raiser was not liable to the farmer for damage caused to the crop) does not affect the final result. In both cases $3 is part of the cost of adding a third steer, to be included along with the other costs. If the increase in the value of production in cattle-raising through increasing the size of the herd from 2 to 3 is greater than the additional costs that have to be incurred (including the $3 damage to crops), the size of the herd will be increased. Otherwise, it will not. The size of the herd will be the same whether the cattle-raiser is liable for damage caused to the crop or not. * * *

It is necessary to know whether the damaging business is liable or not for damage caused since without the establishment of this initial delimitation of rights there can be no market transactions to transfer and recombine them. But the ultimate result (which maximizes the value of production) is independent of the legal position if the pricing system is assumed to work without cost. * * *

The argument has proceeded up to this point on the assumption * * * that there were no costs involved in carrying out market transactions. This is, of course, a very unrealistic assumption. In order to carry out a market transaction it is necessary to discover who it is that one wishes to deal with, to inform people that one wishes to deal and on what terms, to conduct negotiations leading up to a bargain, to draw up the contract, to undertake the inspection needed to make sure that the terms of the contract are being observed, and so on. These operations are often extremely costly, sufficiently costly at any rate to prevent many transactions that would be carried out in a world in which the pricing system worked without cost.

* * * Once the costs of carrying out market transactions are taken into account it is clear that such a rearrangement of rights will only be undertaken when the increase in the value of production consequent upon the rearrangement is greater than the costs which would be involved in bringing it about. When it is less, the granting of an injunction (or the knowledge that it would be granted) or the liability to pay damages may result in an activity being discontinued (or may prevent its being started) which would be undertaken if market transactions were costless. In these conditions the initial delimitation of legal rights does have an effect on the efficiency with which the economic system operates. One arrangement of rights may bring about a greater value of production than any other. But unless this is the arrangement of rights established by the legal system, the costs of reaching the same result by altering and combining rights through the market may be so great that this optional arrangement of rights, and the greater value of production which it would bring, may never be achieved. * * *

* * * An alternative solution is direct Government regulation. Instead of instituting a legal system of rights which can be modified by transactions on the market, the government may impose regulations which state what people must or must not do and which have to be obeyed. Thus, the government (by statute or perhaps more likely through an administrative agency) may, to deal with the problem of smoke nuisance, decree that certain methods of production should or should not be used (e.g., that smoke preventing devices should be installed or that coal or oil should not be burned) or may confine certain types of business to certain districts (zoning regulations). * * *

* * * But the governmental administrative machine is not itself costless. It can, in fact, on occasion be extremely costly. Furthermore, there is no reason to suppose that the restrictive and zoning regulations, made by a fallible administration subject to political pressures and operating without any competitive check, will necessarily always be those which increase the efficiency with which the economic system operates. Furthermore, such general regulations, which must apply to a wide variety of cases will be enforced in some cases in which they are clearly inappropriate. From these considerations it follows that direct governmental regulation will not necessarily give better results than leaving the problem to be solved by the market * * *. But equally there is no reason why, on occasion, such governmental administrative regulation should not lead to an improvement in economic efficiency. This would seem particularly likely when, as is normally the case with the smoke nuisance, a large number of people are involved and in which therefore the costs of handling the problem through the market * * * may be high.

NOTES

1. As an exercise, explain how Coase would argue that the result in *Boomer* is irrelevant to the amount of pollution produced, in the absence of transaction costs. Use these two sets of figures:

Case 1: The company's profit from polluting is $3,000,000 per year; the total damage caused is $4,000,000.

Case 2: The company's profit from polluting is $3,000,000 per year; the total damage caused is $2,000,000.

What is the economically efficient result in each case (i.e., the result that would be favored by a cost-benefit analyst)? How might that result be reached if (a) only damage liability exists, (b) injunctions can be obtained, or (c) no liability exists? What effects do the various liability rules have on the distribution of wealth between the company's shareholders and its neighbors?

2. The Coase Theorem has given rise to a considerable literature probing its validity and limitations. Some of the more important works are surveyed in Stewart J. Schwab, *Coase Defends Coase: Why Lawyers Listen and Economists Do Not*, 87 MICH. L. REV. 1171 (1989); Robert Cooter, *The Cost of Coase*, 11 J. LEGAL STUD. 1 (1982). For a more light-hearted look at Coase, *see* Daniel Farber, *The Case Against Brilliance*, 70 MINN. L. REV. 917, 918–20, 923–24 (1986). One particularly interesting (but fairly technical) critique of Coase can be found in Joseph Farrell, *Information and the Coase Theorem*, 1 J. ECON. PERSP. 113 (1987). An important empirical test of Coase was undertaken by John Donahue. He found that the initial assignment of incentive payments between employers and employees had substantial behavioral consequences, contrary to the predictions of the Coase Theorem. John Donahue, *Diverting the Coasean River: Incentive Schemes to Reduce Unemployment Spells*, 99 YALE L.J. 549 (1989). The upshot of all this literature can probably be summarized by saying that people will often (but not always) negotiate their way around legal rules to economically efficient outcomes.

3. Although the "Coase Theorem" is one of the most famous results in law and economics, "The Problem of Social Cost" and Coase's other writings show that Coase regarded the zero-transaction-cost assumption as unrealistic and saw transaction costs as both inevitable and essential to understanding the structure of the economy. As he explained later, his aim in this article was to set up a simple thought experiment to help "make clear the fundamental role which transaction costs do, and should, play in the fashioning of the institutions which make up the economic system." Because of the "very peculiar properties" of a world without transaction costs, Coase concludes, "It would not seem worthwhile to spend much time investigating the properties of such a world." Ronald Coase, *The Firm, The Market, and the Law* 13–15 (1988). Coase observes that the world of zero transaction costs is not "Coasean," but rather the "world of modern economic theory, one which I was hoping to persuade economists to leave." *Id.* at 174. The failure of economists to consider transaction costs is, he believes, the major reason for their inability to account for real-world economic outcomes; consequently, their policy proposals are "the stuff that dreams are made of." *Id.* at 185. Given this widespread misinterpretation of what he intended by his theorem, in certain respects Coase ironically has more in common with some of his critics than with many of his supporters. *See* Daniel Farber, *Parody Lost/Paradigm Regained: The Ironic History of the Coase Theorem*, 83 VA. L. REV. 397 (1997).

4. Because market transactions do have costs, the assignment of liability often affects both ultimate allocation of resources and distribution of income.

Other authors have suggested, like Coase, that the courts might consider the economic efficiency and transaction costs of negotiating changes in established legal rights when selecting liability rules. For example, in the case of a factory whose smoke damages many homeowners, what kinds of transaction costs (informational, organizational, etc.) would be required to alter a legal rule under which: (a) the factory is not liable; (b) the factory is liable only for damage judgments; (c) the factory is liable to injunction at the behest of any injured homeowner? *See* Frank I. Michelman, *Pollution as a Tort: A Non–Accidental Perspective on Calabresi's Costs*, 80 YALE L.J. 647 (1971); Guido Calabresi & A. Douglas Melamed, *Property Rules, Liability Rules, and Inalienability: One View of the Cathedral*, 85 HARV. L. REV. 1089 (1972). Michelman says that in applying a "decentralist or transaction-organizing" version of nuisance law, a court may decide to impose liability on the polluter because it believes the polluter is the "cheapest cost avoider" or because it believes that the polluter is the "best briber." However, if the court acts on the latter ground, it should be wary of "injunctions with their heavy negotiation costs which may prevent the polluter from bribing effectively."

Calabresi and Melamed suggest a fourth legal rule in addition to those mentioned in the preceding paragraph: (d) the factory is liable to injunction, but only if plaintiff homeowners compensate the factory for its costs attributable to the injunction. Is this closer to rule (a) or (c)? For an illustration of rule (d), see the next case. A fifth rule, with seemingly limited practical application, has also been proposed: The factory decides whether or not to stay open, and if it closes, the neighbor pays damages measured by the social cost of the pollution. *See* James E. Krier & Stewart J. Schwab, *Property Rules and Liability Rules: The Cathedral in Another Light*, 70 N.Y.U. L. REV. 440 (1995).

2. PUBLIC NUISANCE

In addition to private nuisance, plaintiffs may bring public nuisance claims to recover for harms suffered as a result of pollution. A public nuisance is an unreasonable interference with a right common to the general public, including public health and safety. Typically, the state brings a public nuisance action on behalf of its citizens and seeks injunctive relief. An example might be a state environmental agency bringing a public nuisance claim against a hazardous waste facility to enjoin operation of a site that, because of leaching chemicals, poses a threat to a community's drinking water supply.

For a private plaintiff to have standing to bring a public nuisance claim, the plaintiff must be able to show "special injury," which requires a difference in kind, and not just extent, of injury. More recently, courts and legislatures have liberalized this test. As a result, it can be fairly easy to satisfy. When reading the case below, consider how effective public nuisance is as a mechanism for air pollution regulation.

SPUR INDUSTRIES, INC. v. DEL E. WEBB DEVELOPMENT CO.

Supreme Court of Arizona, 1972.
108 Ariz. 178, 494 P.2d 700.

[In 1957 Del Webb began construction of a retirement community called Sun City, west of Phoenix. By 1967 the development had moved close to Spur's feedlot, which had been in operation for several years before Webb came into the area.]

CAMERON, VICE CHIEF JUSTICE.

Del Webb's suit complained that the Spur feeding operation was a public nuisance because of the flies and the odor which were drifting or being blown by the prevailing south to north wind over the southern portion of Sun City. At the time of the suit, Spur was feeding between 20,000 and 30,000 head of cattle, and the facts amply support the finding of the trial court that the feed pens had become a nuisance to the people who resided in the southern part of Del Webb's development. The testimony indicated that cattle in a commercial feedlot will produce 35 to 40 pounds of wet manure per day, per head, or over a million pounds of wet manure per day for 30,000 head of cattle, and that despite the admittedly good feedlot management and good housekeeping practices by Spur, the resulting odor and flies produced an annoying if not unhealthy situation as far as the senior citizens of southern Sun City were concerned. There is no doubt that some of the citizens of Sun City were unable to enjoy the outdoor living which Del Webb had advertised and that Del Webb was faced with sales resistance from prospective purchasers as well as strong and persistent complaints from the people who had purchased homes in that area. * * *

The difference between a private nuisance and a public nuisance is generally one of degree. A private nuisance is one affecting a single individual or a definite small number of persons in the enjoyment of private rights not common to the public, while a public nuisance is one affecting the rights enjoyed by citizens as a part of the public. To constitute a public nuisance, the nuisance must affect a considerable number of people or an entire community or neighborhood.

Where the injury is slight, the remedy for minor inconveniences lies in an action for damages rather than in one for an injunction. Moreover, some courts have held, in the "balancing of conveniences" cases, that damages may be the sole remedy. *See Boomer v. Atlantic Cement Co.* [*supra,* page 526].* * *

It is clear that as to the citizens of Sun City, the operation of Spur's feedlot was both a public and a private nuisance. They could have successfully maintained an action to abate the nuisance. Del Webb, having shown a special injury in the loss of sales, had standing to bring suit to enjoin the nuisance. The judgment of the trial court permanently enjoining the operation of the feedlot is affirmed. * * *

In the so-called "coming to the nuisance" cases, the courts have held that the residential landowner may not have relief if he knowingly came into a neighborhood reserved for industrial or agricultural endeavors and has been damaged thereby. * * * Were Webb the only party injured, we would feel justified in holding that the doctrine of "coming to the nuisance" would have been a bar to the relief asked by Webb, and, on the other hand, had Spur located the feedlot near the outskirts of a city and had the city grown toward the feedlot, Spur would have to suffer the cost of abating the nuisance as to those people locating within the growth pattern of the expanding city. * * *

There was no indication in the instant case at the time Spur and its predecessors located in western Maricopa County that a new city would spring up, full-blown, alongside the feeding operation and that the developer of that city would ask the court to order Spur to move because of the new city. Spur is required to move not because of any wrongdoing on the part of Spur, but because of a proper and legitimate regard of the courts for the rights and interests of the public.

Del Webb, on the other hand, is entitled to the relief prayed for (a permanent injunction), not because Webb is blameless, but because of the damage to the people who have been encouraged to purchase homes in Sun City. It does not equitably or legally follow, however, that Webb, being entitled to the injunction, is then free of any liability to Spur if Webb has in fact been the cause of the damage Spur has sustained. It does not seem harsh to require a developer, who has taken advantage of the lesser land values in a rural area as well as the availability of large tracts of land on which to build and develop a new town or city in the area, to indemnify those who are forced to leave as a result.

Having brought people to the nuisance to the foreseeable detriment of Spur, Webb must indemnify Spur for a reasonable amount of the cost of moving or shutting down.

NOTES

1. *Spur* raises some interesting questions of tort law: Should the residents be estopped from seeking relief against Spur because they moved into an area despite conditions of which they should have been aware? About forty states make "coming to the nuisance" an affirmative defense to a private nuisance claim. Does this explain why Del Webb resorted to a public nuisance claim? What would a strict "coming to the nuisance" doctrine do to economic progress and growth?

2. Why doesn't the combination of private nuisance and public nuisance claims deal adequately with the problem of air pollution? Won't successful lawsuits deter industry from polluting? Or if it is cheaper to pay damages and keep polluting than to install pollution-control equipment, then isn't it rational and efficient to do just that, as per the Coase Theorem explored above? Is it problematic that the common law provides remedies after harm has occurred, rather than preventing harm in the first place?

3. Public and private nuisance claims may be argued using either an intentional or a negligence-based theory of liability. Using an intent theory, plaintiff must merely prove that the harm caused by defendant was "substantially foreseeable." Using a negligence theory, plaintiff must show that defendant behaved unreasonably in light of the risk of harm. The difference between the two is especially important in environmental cases. It is much harder to prevail on a nuisance claim using a negligence theory, because the conduct of the defendant and the precautions she has taken become relevant. In most pollution cases, it is easier to prove that intent is satisfied by substantial foreseeability (plaintiff surely knows that emissions or effluent from the daily operation of the factory will have to land somewhere). A negligence-based theory of nuisance might be appropriate in an instance where defendant was careless in maintaining equipment or training workers, causing an accident that results in environmental contamination. In addition, a nuisance claim may be brought based on a strict liability theory of liability. This may be appropriate when defendant is engaging in an abnormally dangerous activity. Many judges are less than precise, however, in distinguishing analytically among the different bases of liability. For an explanation of the different theories of liability on which a nuisance claim can be maintained, *see* State of New York v. Schenectady Chemicals, Inc., 117 Misc.2d 960, 459 N.Y.S.2d 971 (1983).

B. GOVERNMENT REGULATION OF AIR QUALITY

The market failure rationale mentioned in the introduction, together with the limitations of the common law as revealed by cases like *Boomer* and *Spur*, explain why government might seek to regulate pollution by statute. Still, important questions remain. To what extent, and with what mechanisms, should government try to improve air quality? Such choices are inevitably political. Government must determine the socially desirable level of air quality and then design regulatory mechanisms to achieve it. Controlling air pollution may require that we change how we produce goods. For example, we might substitute materials, switch to cleaner burning fuels, or package products differently. Controlling air pollution may require that we reduce our dependence on oil, and develop new technology to power motor vehicles. Ultimately controlling air pollution may require that we reduce consumption—a politically unpopular option in the United States.

The American approach to the problem of air pollution is largely command-and-control, which means that government sets the standards itself, and imposes emission limits directly on sources of pollution. Typical command-and-control measures include mandatory emissions limits, technology and design requirements, and limitations on the use of certain materials or fuels. Permits are a common feature of command-and-control-regulation (although permits are used rather flexibly in practice to accommodate variations among firms and industrial classifications). One might think of permits as a license to pollute subject to certain conditions.

In the typical case, firms subject to a permit requirement must disclose information to regulatory agencies in the application process, agree to emission-control measures, and comply with monitoring and record-keeping requirements. A failure to comply with permit requirements can lead to penalties and, in some cases, permit revocation.

A command-and-control approach can be costly and inefficient if the regulations are insufficiently sensitive to differences among firms. For example, a command-and-control regime that forced all firms to install the same technology, regardless of the age of the plants, would be inefficient. It is often more expensive for older plants to retrofit than for new plants to install state-of-the-art technology. In many cases, however, command-and-control regulation establishes performance standards and leaves it to firms themselves to determine how best to comply. For example, some firms might find it easier to comply with emission limits by switching to cleaner fuels, while others might prefer to curtail hours of production. To illustrate, firms located in or near western states with an abundance of low-sulfur coal might find it relatively cheap to substitute this fuel for comparatively more polluting high-sulfur coal. Firms located further east might find shipping costs prohibitive, and choose to meet emission limits by installing "scrubber" technology or by curtailing their hours of production. An alternative to performance standards is to cap emissions at an overall limit, allocate firms specific amounts of emission credits, and allow them to buy and sell emission credits beneath the cap. This way, older plants can purchase excess increments of pollution from newer firms that are able to reduce their emissions cheaply. If the net amount of pollution produced is lower, why should it matter if some firms pollute more than others?

Critics of command-and-control approaches have argued vigorously that market mechanisms such as these are superior to the "one size fits all" approach that they perceive command-and-control regulation to impose. *See, e.g.,* Bruce A. Ackerman & Richard B. Stewart, *Reforming Environmental Law: The Democratic Case for Market Incentives*, 13 COLUM. J. ENVTL. L. 171 (1988); Robert N. Stavins & Bradley W. Whitehead, *Dealing with Pollution: Market–Based Incentives for Environmental Protection*, 34 ENVIRONMENT 7 (1992) (arguing that market-based incentives, properly managed, likely are the best approach to solving environmental problems). Defenders of command-and-control retort that market schemes may seem theoretically superior, but often fail to deliver their anticipated emissions reductions because of problems designing and monitoring the markets. In practice, some market schemes work quite well whereas others do not. *See* Jody Freeman and Charles D. Kolstad, eds., MOVING TO MARKETS IN ENVIRONMENTAL REGULATION: LESSONS FROM THIRTY YEARS OF EXPERIENCE, forthcoming 2006 (comparing market programs with command-and-control approaches and concluding, based on the empirical evidence, that both approaches can suffer from weaknesses in monitoring and enforcement). Uniform regulation arguably has many advantages over market approaches, including decreased information collection and evaluation costs, greater consistency and predictability of results, greater accessibility of decisions to public scrutiny and participation, increased likelihood that regulations will withstand judicial review, reduced opportunities for manipulative behavior by agencies in response to political or bureaucratic pressures, reduced opportunities for obstructive behavior by regulated parties, and decreased likelihood of social dislocation and "forum shopping" resulting from competitive disadvantages between geographical regions or between firms in regulated industries.

Howard Latin, *Ideal Versus Real Regulatory Efficiency: Implementation of Uniform Standards and "Fine Tuning" Regulatory Reform*, 37 STAN. L. REV. 1267, 1271 (1985).

Of course, choosing the optimal regulatory instruments for purposes of achieving environmental policy goals is not a science. It depends on political feasibility as much as on technological capacity and economic analysis. In fact, there is a wide range of policy options for controlling air pollution: performance standards that leave to firms the decision about how to comply; design constraints; minimum technology requirements; pollution taxes; pollution prevention subsidies; market-trading schemes; restrictions on automobile trips; outright bans of certain fuels; or a combination of these measures. In short, regulation is a matter of design.

1. THE CLEAN AIR ACT

One could teach an entire course in environmental law by studying the Clean Air Act (CAA) alone (though we don't recommend it!). This 800–page statute tells the story of environmental regulation generally: bold legislative aspirations inevitably must be tempered in light of the difficulties of implementation. An underfunded and over-tasked agency subject to congressional, executive and judicial oversight must implement an enormously complicated set of congressional mandates and fill in the gaps left by vague or incomplete statutory language. The regulated community often resists implementation while environmentalists press for more rigorous enforcement, leading to a cacophony of lawsuits. Because of a combination of technical difficulty, complexity, and outright political resistance, compliance is partial, deadlines are missed and new problems, unanticipated by Congress when it originally passed the Act, arise. Periodically, Congress amends the law to extend deadlines and address new problems. Litigation ensues and the cycle continues.

The saga of the Clean Air Act also illustrates the themes we introduced in Chapters 1 and 2. Establishing air quality standards tends to turn on risk-based analyses that are riddled with scientific uncertainty; air pollution regulation in the United States explicitly prohibits cost-benefit analysis for some purposes while embracing it for others; and effective regulation requires a mix of approaches, including both prescriptive regulation and market mechanisms. Air pollution itself crosses physical boundaries, making it necessary—when conceiving of solutions—to cross conceptual boundaries between public and private institutions, or central and local control. And of course air pollution sometimes requires that we make trade-offs between environmental and economic goals. Finally, air pollution regulation is the product of the dynamic institutional environment we described in Chapter 5, one that includes Congress, the Executive branch, the judiciary, and powerful interest groups.

2. HISTORY OF CLEAN AIR LEGISLATION

Congress passed the Air Pollution Control Act, the first federal legislation aimed at curbing air pollution, in 1955. Traditionally, air pollution, like most environmental issues, had been a matter handled by the states. The 1955 legislation sought to assist states in their efforts by providing research support as well as technical and financial aid. This approach was largely ineffective in inducing states to act, however, and Congress finally opted to significantly enhance federal control over air pollution in the Clean Air Act Amendments of 1970. These have become known simply as the Clean Air Act (CAA). While the Act has been further amended since then (notably in 1977 and 1990), the heart of the 1970 legislation remains in place: Congress delegates to the EPA the task of setting National Ambient Air Quality Standards (NAAQS) for pervasive and harmful air pollutants known as "criteria pollutants", and requires states to devise State Implementation Plans (SIPs) to achieve those standards by statutory deadlines. This division of responsibility affords states the flexibility to mete out the pain of emissions reductions in a way that is sensitive to local conditions. These conditions are not just political but also geographical and cultural. Because of the variability among states in terms of their industrial base, geography, climate and tolerance for different kinds of regulation, state governments are thought to be in the best position to determine how to meet federal standards.

The Act stipulates minimum requirements for state plans to achieve federal standards, and the EPA must approve these plans. If the EPA disapproves a SIP, it may substitute a Federal Implementation Plan (FIP) instead. However, the political infeasibility and enormous cost of direct federal implementation means that this provision of the Act is rarely invoked, and leaves states with considerable authority to determine how the CAA plays out on the ground. The federal-state relationship is not, it bears noting, uniformly acrimonious. States frequently invoke the EPA's ultimate authority as the "gorilla in the closet" to provide political cover for state regulatory measures, and to exact concessions from regulated entities. At the same time, regional EPA offices frequently work cooperatively with their state counterparts. The Clean Air Act embodies environmental federalism by dividing authority between the federal and state governments in this way, creating an inter-dependent, though not entirely harmonious, partnership.

The 1970 legislation mandated attainment of NAAQS (with some exceptions) by 1975. It authorized the EPA to establish technology-based performance standards for all new sources of pollution, to regulate hazardous air pollutants at levels providing an "ample margin of safety," and to regulate tailpipe emissions from mobile sources. In the face of widespread non-compliance, Congress amended the Act in 1977 to extend the deadlines for achieving NAAQS to 1982, and provided a further extension to 1987 for "non-attainment" areas—those parts of the country with the most polluted air that were furthest from compliance with NAAQS. The 1977 Amendments also added provisions to prevent significant deterioration of air quality in parts of the country already in compliance with the NAAQS. The 1977 Amendments limited the extent to which air quality can degrade in these areas by establishing annual allowable increases in ambient concentrations.

Even the new deadlines proved too ambitious. While emissions from both stationary and mobile sources had been reduced considerably, many areas of the country still struggled to meet the NAAQS. As of 1989, 96 areas violated the ozone standard and 41 failed to meet the carbon monoxide limit. Env't Rep. (BNA) 815 (Aug, 24, 1990). For a combination of reasons, including the relative lack of scientific data and consensus on toxic exposure, the Act's toxics program had been a failure; the EPA had set standards for only seven toxic air pollutants.

In 1990, Congress significantly amended the Act. For nonattainment areas, it established new deadlines, with graduated requirements keyed to the severity of the nonattainment problem. Areas of the country furthest from compliance received more time to achieve NAAQS, but faced a greater regulatory burden in the interim. This graduated approach is sensitive to the ongoing difficulties that nonattainment areas still face in light of problems such as increasing population densities and the difficulties of controlling pollutants such as ozone (itself the product of a complicated chemical reaction involving more than one pollutant) emanating from a variety of hard-to-control stationary and non-stationary sources. The 1990 Amendments also created a new toxics program in light of the EPA's failure. Congress specifically listed 189 hazardous air pollutants (one has since been de-listed) and required the EPA to establish technology-based standards for all major sources (defined as sources producing 10 tons per year of any single listed hazardous pollutant, or 25 tons per year of any combination of such pollutants).

The 1990 Amendments also enhanced the EPA's enforcement power, affording the agency authority to issue administrative penalties up to $25,000 per day of violation and augmenting many of the Act's criminal sanctions. The Amendments added to the citizen-suit provision as well. Citizens may now bring suits against violators of the Act and against the EPA for failure to perform any non-discretionary duty. The Act provides for penalties and attorney's fees, and awards a $10,000 bounty to anyone providing information leading to a civil or criminal penalty.

Although the harm-based approach to setting national ambient standards, which are then implemented through regulations devised in state plans, remains the core of the Act, this approach has been supplemented by a variety of technology-based emissions standards that are directly imposed on individual sources of pollution, depending on where they are located, what they emit, when they were built, and whether they are considered "major" or not under the Act. These emission limits apply over and above measures states adopt in their SIPs to guarantee compliance with the NAAQS. A single stationary source of pollution may, therefore, be subject to a host of requirements. Until 1990, Congress did not require all major sources of air pollution to obtain permits; the onus was on the sources themselves to scour the statute, as well as the state plans, to determine all the measures they would have to take to comply. With the 1990 amendments, all major stationary sources must obtain a permit, which serves as the umbrella document containing all of the disparate requirements applicable to that source under all of the provisions of the statute. The Clean Air Act's original ambient-air regulatory approach thus has yielded to a permit-based approach like that adopted in the Clean Water Act. (These two laws have converged in various ways, even though they still differ in other respects. We will consider this comparison in more detail in Chapter 7.)

Thus far, the Clean Air Act seems to have produced substantial successes. In order to monitor the achievements and failures of the Act, Congress added a provision as part of the 1990 Amendments requiring that the EPA periodically report on the overall costs and benefits of the legislation. The EPA has issued two such reports thus far, retrospectively assessing the Clean Air Act's performance from 1970 to 1990, and prospectively appraising its costs and benefits from 1990 to 2010. EPA, Benefits and Costs of the Clean Air Act, http://www.epa.gov/oar/sect812 (a third report estimating the costs and benefits through 2020 is currently in preparation). Both of these studies found that the benefits of the Clean Air Act have overwhelmingly outweighed its costs. Environmental Protection Agency, THE BENEFITS AND COSTS OF THE CLEAN AIR ACT, 1970 to 1990 (1997), *available at* http://www.epa.gov/air/sect812/copy.html (benefits quantified at between $6 and $50 trillion; direct compliance costs of only $0.5 trillion); Environmental Protection Agency, THE BENEFITS AND COSTS OF THE CLEAN AIR ACT, 1990 to 2010 (1999), *available at* http://www.epa.gov/air/sect812/copy99.html (net benefit of $510 billion). In terms of absolute emissions, EPA data shows a steady decline in annual emissions of all criteria pollutants. EPA, Air Emissions Trends—Continued Progress Through 2008, http://www.epa.gov/oar/airtrends/agtrends.html comparison. Improvements in air quality are all the more impressive since vehicle miles driven and population have both increased dramatically over the past 35 years. Of course, significant challenges remain. The most easily attained air quality improvements have already been accomplished, mostly through the installation of relatively affordable technological controls. Taking the next steps will likely be more expensive. Many urban areas of the country are out of attainment with some of the NAAQS for a large portion of the year; mobile source emissions remain difficult to control given the political resistance to increased fuel efficiency standards and the prospect of gasoline or carbon taxes; interstate transport of ozone from upwind to downwind states continues to interfere with the ability of the downwind states to achieve compliance with ozone standards; and the rules for "new" and "modified" sources of air pollution are in flux and hotly contested in ongoing litigation. In addition, the emission of greenhouse gases that cause global warming have presented new challenges for air regulators—these emissions appear not to have been contemplated by the Clean Air Act, and may require a separate law, though there is increasing pressure on the federal government to use its authority under the CAA.

3. HELPFUL DISTINCTIONS REGARDING THE CLEAN AIR ACT

It is easy to lose the forest for the trees when studying the CAA. To help organize your thinking as you read the materials in this chapter, keep in mind the following useful distinctions.

a. Harm–Based vs. Technology–Based Regulation

This distinction resurfaces in the next chapter on the Clean Water Act (and also can be useful in thinking through the Resource Conservation and Recovery Act, which we cover in Chapter 8). In the simplest terms, harm-based regulation is aimed at setting standards necessary to protect the public health, whereas technology-based regulation is aimed at setting standards that existing technology is capable of achieving. What is the difference in practice? When air standards are set at a level requisite to protect the public health, the question of whether technology can achieve these standards is secondary. The priority in the harm-based approach is to set concentration levels for pollutants (for example, so many parts per million of ozone in the ambient air) sufficiently low that people exposed to those pollutants will not become sick (setting aside the scientifically and politically contentious question of how to choose the class of people to protect, and how much to protect them). To comply with harm-based standards, industry might need to develop new technologies. In this sense, harm-based regulation can be *technology-forcing*.

Technology-based standards are necessarily derived from the technology that is currently available. Their primary focus is on the available equipment's emissions performance, not public health. As a result, they may be set too low to adequately protect the public health. On the other hand, standards set in this way may be more achievable precisely because the technology to achieve the standards already exists. Industry can be sure that it is in compliance with technology-based standards simply by adopting the same technology that the agency used to set the standards in the first place. The downside of a technology-based approach, according to critics, is that it may lock existing technology in place.

Technology-based standards are typically expressed as emission limits or concentrations (for example, so many parts per million of ozone; so many micrograms per cubic meter of lead; so many pounds per hour of sulfur dioxide). In simple terms, they tell a firm what amount or concentration of a pollutant they can produce, usually measured over some time period. However, these limits can be more or less stringent, depending on the technology used to set the standards. One way to understand the variance among different technology-based standards is to think in terms of the role that cost plays in choosing the technology. If cost plays a relatively large role, then the technology chosen to set the standard will likely be one that is already widely used in the industry. If it is widely used, most firms can adopt it without too much expense. If cost plays a relatively small role in the choice of technology, the agency might set the standard based on the state-of-the-art equipment, used by the industry leader. A standard based on this kind of technology would be expensive for most firms to meet; they might have to purchase new technology or take alternative, and presumably costly, steps to meet this stringent standard. Some firms might go out of business, partly as a result of these costs. There are many technology-based standards in the CAA, including "Lowest Achievable Emission Rate" (LAER), "Best Demonstrated Achievable Technology" (BDAT), and "Maximum Achievable Control Technology" (MACT). Because these acronyms can sound so abstract, think of them in terms of a sliding scale of both stringency and cost. Another tip to keep in mind: frequently, different technology-based standards, like those mentioned above, differ only in theory, and conflate into the same level of control in practice.

b.   Stationary vs. Mobile Sources

Stationary sources include oil refineries, power plants, pulp and paper mills, dry cleaners, and auto repair shops. Mobile sources include automobiles, trucks, and buses. The Act treats mobile sources differently than it does stationary sources. For now, try to imagine what makes it difficult to regulate automobiles versus stationary sources. Keep in mind that regulatory measures that might work well for stationary sources might not work well for mobile sources. Consider the example of an emission trading scheme, under which sources receive an initial allocation of pollution credits which they can then buy or sell. Such an approach may be easy to monitor if the trades occur between a handful of stationary sources, but impossible to monitor if trades occur between millions of cars crossing state lines.

c.   New vs. Existing Sources

Generally speaking, existing sources are treated more leniently than new sources: they are generally grandfathered into the statute by Congress and regulated less stringently. Determining whether a source is "new" is intuitive to some extent. A new source is one built after a given deadline (Congress has established different deadlines for different sections of the Act). For example, a power plant is considered a "new" source under section 111 if it is built *after* the EPA promulgates standards for that category of source (e.g., power plants) under section 111. The date on which the EPA issues the standards is the relevant deadline.

Whether a source is existing or new is not always so clear, however. For example, in a variety of provisions, the Act treats "modified" sources as new sources. In simple terms, a modification is defined as a change that increases, or has the potential to increase, emissions. So when a firm modifies its plant to update its technology (replacing or repairing a boiler for example), it might trigger "new source review" and the application of the more stringent provisions of the Act. In recent years, the question of whether "new" status is triggered has led to an explosion of litigation. Firms have argued that they should not be considered new sources when they are merely conducting "routine maintenance." Indeed, this issue lies at the heart of the Bush Administration's new rules under the Clean Air Act, which are designed to make it easier for firms to update their technology without triggering new source review. As one might imagine, disputes over whether a given change amounts to routine maintenance, or is instead a modification triggering new source review, turn on highly technical questions regarding whether a given change either does or might increase emissions over the baseline emissions that the firm is already producing, or could potentially produce, if the firm were operating at full capacity. (As one might predict, this assessment is made even more complicated by debates about how to calculate baseline emissions.)

This quickly gets complicated. For now, remember this: being considered "new" as opposed to "existing" under the CAA is of monumental importance.

d. Attainment vs. Nonattainment Areas

Areas of the country that are already in compliance with the federal air pollution standards are considered "in attainment." Those areas of the country where the air quality does not yet meet NAAQS are considered nonattainment areas or nonattainment zones (NAZs). Congress added the nonattainment provisions to the Act in 1990, recognizing that its earlier deadlines for compliance with the NAAQS had not been met in every area of the country. The nonattainment provisions allow new stationary sources to be built in nonattainment zones, provided that states still make "reasonable further progress" toward attaining the NAAQS and provided that individual stationary sources comply with a number of stringent requirements. These amendments represent Congress's attempt to balance environmental and economic goals: Theoretically, had Congress not amended the statute to afford nonattainment zones more time to comply with NAAQS, industrial growth in these areas might have come to a standstill. Approving construction of any new industry in areas already badly out of attainment would, by definition, have amounted to a violation of the Act's requirement that states devise plans to meet NAAQS.

The 1990 Amendments require states to classify regions under their jurisdiction as either attainment or nonattainment (or "unclassifiable") areas for the pollutants for which the EPA has established NAAQS. In these Amendments, Congress provided a new set of deadlines for these areas to achieve compliance with NAAQS, and also established interim goals designed to ensure reasonable progress toward compliance over time. In the case of ozone, states must classify areas along a spectrum from "marginally" to "extremely" out of attainment. The more out of attainment an area, the more time Congress allows for that area to achieve compliance with the NAAQS for ozone. For example, a marginal nonattainment zone would have three years to achieve NAAQS, whereas an extreme nonattainment zone (Los Angeles is the only one) has until 2010 before it must comply.

New or modified major sources of air pollution in nonattainment zones are subject to the most stringent regulation under the Act. Among other things, they must obtain a pre-construction permit, meet the most demanding technology-based emissions limits [known as "Lowest Achievable Emission Rate" (LAER)], and obtain offsetting reductions in emissions from other sources to counter-balance any new emissions they introduce into these relatively dirty areas of the country. The amount of offset required depends on the pollutant and the degree of nonattainment. The more polluted the area, the more a proposed new source will have to do to control its emissions. In addition to imposing requirements directly on stationary sources, it is important to stress that the Act's nonattainment provisions constrain the *state's* flexibility to design its implementation plans. Generally, states must do more in nonattainment zones than in other areas to demonstrate that they are making reasonable further progress toward attaining NAAQS.

e. Major vs. Non–Major Sources

Whether a stationary source of air pollution is "major" or not also affects how that source is treated under the Act. Generally, major sources of air pollution are regulated more stringently than non-major or "area" sources. The definition of "major," like the definition of "new," varies throughout the Act. The reason for the variability in this definition is, again, intuitive. In those parts of the country where the air is most polluted (those areas badly out of attainment with the federal ambient standards) it takes fewer emissions to qualify as a major source. For example, in a serious nonattainment zone, producing 50 tons of pollution per year makes a source major, whereas in an extreme nonattainment zone, major status is triggered by only 10 tons per year. Still another definition applies in those areas of the country that are in attainment with federal standards (either 100 tons per year of a listed pollutant or 250 tons per year of any pollutant). Another definition applies to "major" sources of hazardous air pollutants (either 10 tons per year of a single hazardous pollutant or 25 tons per year of any combination of hazardous pollutants). This detail can be overwhelming, but the key is to grasp that the definition of major varies, and that qualifying as a major stationary source matters because it usually means more stringent regulation.

4. OVERVIEW OF THE CLEAN AIR ACT

TITLE I: ATTAINMENT AND MAINTENANCE OF NATIONAL AMBIENT AIR QUALITY STANDARDS

§ 108 Listing: The EPA must list "air pollutants" that, according to scientific evidence, may endanger the public health or welfare. Listing triggers the need to establish national primary and secondary standards.

§ 109 National Ambient Air Quality Standards (NAAQS): The EPA must promulgate health-based primary and secondary national ambient air quality standards for "criteria" pollutants (so named because the EPA prepares a "criteria" document comprised of scientific research for each pollutant). The six criteria pollutants for which the EPA has set standards are: sulfur dioxide, particulate matter, nitrogen dioxide, carbon monoxide, ozone, and lead. Primary standards are set at levels necessary to protect public health; secondary standards are set at standards necessary to protect public welfare, which includes crops, property, visibility and other effects not directly related to human health.

§ 110 State Implementation Plans (SIPs): Each state must establish a plan for the implementation, maintenance, and enforcement of the national standards within its jurisdiction or face sanctions. States must meet minimum statutory requirements in the design of their SIPs but otherwise have flexibility in choosing regulations, measures and methods that will result in the achievement of NAAQS. The EPA must approve or disapprove SIPs by statutory deadlines. If approved, SIPs become binding as a matter of both state and federal law and may be enforced by either state or federal officials. The EPA has the authority to disapprove a SIP if it fails to meet statutory requirements, and impose a federal implementation plan (FIP) instead.

§ 111 New Source Performance Standards (NSPS): The EPA must promulgate technology-based standards for new or modified major stationary sources of pollution. The standard reflects the degree of emission limitation and the percentage reduction achievable through application of the best technological system of continuous emission reduction ("Best Demonstrated Achievable Technology" or BDAT). The EPA establishes these standards on an industrial category basis. Sources built or modified after the EPA promulgates standards for that industrial category are considered new. In addition to whatever measures states adopt in their SIPs, these are the minimum technology-based emission limits imposed on all new stationary sources.

§ 112 National Emission Standards for Hazardous Air Pollutants (NESHAP): The EPA must set technology-based standards for 188[2] hazardous pollutants. The standard requires the maximum degree of reduction in emissions of the hazardous air pollutants, taking into consid-

---

2. Note: One substance was delisted in 1996 on the basis of new scientific evidence, so the list is now 188.

eration the cost of achieving such emission reduction and any non-air quality health and environmental impacts and energy requirements ("Maximum Achievable Control Technology" or MACT). The MACT standards apply to all major sources of hazardous air pollutants.

§ 113 Enforcement: Authorizes the EPA to issue administrative orders against any person not in compliance with the Act, and to issue administrative penalties of up to $25,000 per day of violation. The EPA may bring civil suit against violators. Violators are subject to both civil and criminal penalties. The EPA may also halt construction of any major stationary source in a state that is out of compliance with the rules governing the construction or modification of such sources.

§ 114 Information Disclosure and Inspection: The EPA may require sources to provide reports, maintain records, conduct sampling, and provide information to the EPA. The EPA may inspect any source. Any information obtained under this section is available to the public.

§§ 160–169A Prevention of Significant Deterioration (PSD): In areas that already meet or exceed the NAAQS, SIPs must contain provisions to prevent significant deterioration. The statute divides PSD areas into three classes (national parks and monuments must be Class I or II, for example), each with a separate increment of permissible pollution increases. These increments represent the extent to which the air quality for a given pollutant may be allowed to degrade over the baseline concentration of that pollutant in the air in the PSD area. The purpose of these provisions is to prevent air quality in areas with relatively clean air from falling below the concentration limits set by NAAQS. New or modified major sources in PSD areas must obtain pre-construction permits and comply with emission limits set according to "Best Available Control Technology" (BACT).

§ 171–178 Nonattainment Areas: A region that has not met the NAAQS is deemed a nonattainment area (also called a nonattainment zone or NAZ). New or modified major stationary sources in nonattainment areas must comply with stringent permitting requirements, including a showing that offsetting reductions from other sources will produce a net decrease in total emissions in the area, and achievement of the Lowest Achievable Emission Rate (LAER). Existing sources in nonattainment zones must comply with emission limits set according to Reasonably Available Control Technology (RACT). States must guarantee in their SIPs that they are making "reasonable further progress" toward compliance with NAAQS in nonattainment zones. For ozone, states must classify nonattainment areas according to the severity of the degree of nonattainment, along a spectrum ranging from marginal to extreme nonattainment. The worse the air quality, the longer the area has to achieve compliance with the ozone NAAQS. Nonattainment areas for ozone must implement different control measures depending on their classification. The worse the air quality, the more controls these areas must implement. Similar programs apply to areas that do not meet the NAAQS for carbon monoxide and particulate matter. Depending on the degree to which these areas exceed the carbon monoxide standard, they will be required to implement programs introducing oxygenated fuels and/or enhanced emission inspection programs, among other measures. Depending on their classification, areas exceeding the NAAQS for particulate matter must implement either reasonably available control measures or best available control measures, among other requirements.

TITLE II: MOBILE SOURCES

§§ 201–235 Emission Standards for Mobile Sources: The EPA is authorized to regulate fuels and fuel additives. Congress established stricter emissions standards for motor vehicles in the 1990 Amendments, and added new provisions on alternative fuels and "clean fuel" vehicles. Subject to EPA approval, California may set stricter emission limits than Congress, and other states may adopt California's standards.

TITLE III: GENERAL PROVISIONS

§ 304 Citizen Suits: Any person may file a civil action against any person alleged to have violated an emission standard, limit, or order under the Act, or against the EPA for failure to perform a non-discretionary duty.

§ 307 EPA Procedures and Judicial Review: Provides procedures governing the EPA rulemaking and judicial review. Judicial review is generally available in U.S. Courts of Appeals.

TITLE IV: ACID DEPOSITION

§§ 401–413: To address the problem of acid rain, these sections require rigorous controls on utilities to reduce the production of sulfur dioxide from new and existing plants. Congress created a market-based approach to address acid rain, establishing an overall cap on sulfur dioxide, authorizing the EPA to assign annual allocations of sulfur dioxide to firms based on their past emissions, and allowing firms to buy or sell allocations beneath the cap in a market regime.

TITLE V: PERMITS

§§ 501–507: All major stationary sources, and some others, must obtain an operating permit. Permit requirements include emission limits. The EPA may review state permits and has the authority to veto any permit not in compliance with the Act. Prior to the 1990 Amendments, sources were not obligated to have permits. There was no single document that contained all the control requirements that apply to a particular source. Source obligations were spread throughout the SIP, which made it very difficult for sources to know what compliance required.

The material in the following sections draws heavily on EPA documents available on the web. For more detail, students may wish to consult *The Plain English Guide to the Clean Air Act,* available at http://www.epa. gov/oar/oaqps/peg_caa/pegcaain.html. Other useful sources include MARK S.

SQUILLACE & DAVID WOOLEY, AIR POLLUTION (3d ed. 1999), JOHN-MARK STENSVAAG & CRAIG N. OREN, CLEAN AIR ACT: LAW AND PRACTICE (1991 & Supp. VII 1998), and ROBERT J. MARTINEAU, JR. & DAVID P. NOVELLO, THE CLEAN AIR ACT HANDBOOK (2d ed. 2004).

Technology–Based Control Standards under the CAA
(The Facts about BACTs, MACTs, and RACTs)

CAA Standards (in order of increasing stringency):

Standard:	Applies to:	Statute §:	Impact:
RACT (Reasonably Available Control Technology)	Existing sources in nonattainment areas	§ 172(c)(1)	Requires all such sources to use average existing technology (not cutting-edge "best" technology)
BDAT (Best Demonstrated Available Technology)	Stationary sources under NSPS (New Source Performance Standards)	§ 111(a)(1)	Specifically considers cost, but can require matching reductions of best-controlled similar source
BACT (Best Available Control Technology, sometimes given as BAT)	New major sources in PSD (prevention of significant deterioration) areas	§ 165(a)(4)	Requires maximum feasible pollution reduction, considering cost and other factors on case-by-case basis; must be at least as stringent as NSPS under § 111
MACT (Maximum Achievable Control Technology)	Major sources of hazardous air pollutants	§ 112(d)(2) § 112(d)(3)	Requires existing major sources to match best 12% of industry; new major sources to match best-controlled similar source
LAER (Lowest Achievable Emissions Reduction)	New or modified major stationary sources in nonattainment areas	§ 171(3) § 173(a)(2)	Requires most stringent existing emissions limit, whether achieved in practice or included in any SIP, for the applicable source category

C. THE BASICS OF THE CLEAN AIR ACT

1. AIR QUALITY STANDARDS

The Clean Air Act requires the EPA to list pollutants that are 1) emitted from numerous and diverse sources and 2) emissions of which may endanger public health or welfare. After listing a pollutant, the EPA prepares "criteria documents" which consist of the scientific data indicating the health and welfare effects of the pollutant. The EPA must then establish an ambient standard for the pollutant, based on the health-based criteria documents. The standard is expressed as a maximum concentration limit for that pollutant in the surrounding air. The federal standard applies nationally, meaning that in no area of the country should the concentration of a listed pollutant exceed the federal standard.

These standards are not themselves directly enforceable. Instead they represent the air quality goals that states must achieve when designing SIPs. Subject to limitations provided in the Act, states directly regulate stationary sources and, to a more limited extent, mobile sources of air pollution, imposing the necessary reductions in emissions that will guarantee compliance with the NAAQS. The EPA must set both primary and secondary NAAQS. Primary standards are set at a level "requisite to protect public health," whereas secondary standards are set at a level "requisite to protect the public welfare." The EPA has promulgated primary and secondary NAAQS for only six pollutants: carbon monoxide, lead, nitrogen dioxide, ozone, particulate matter, and sulfur oxides. These six pollutants are known as "criteria pollutants." For all but one criteria pollutant (sulfur dioxide), however, the primary and secondary standards are the same.

a. Criteria Pollutants

According to the EPA, except for nitrogen dioxide and other nitrous oxides, emissions of all criteria pollutants listed below "have decreased significantly since passage of the Clean Air Act in 1970." *See* the EPA's web page on nitrous oxides at http://www.epa.gov/air/urbanair/nox/index. html. The following information regarding criteria pollutants is derived mostly from the EPA's helpful website on air pollutants. *See* http://www. epa.gov/ebtpages/airairpollutants.html.

Carbon Monoxide (CO)

CO is a colorless, odorless, poisonous gas created from the incomplete combustion of fuels. Exhaust from cars produces the majority of CO.

  75 Source: burning of gasoline, natural gas, coal, oil, industrial processes

  75 Health Effects: reduces blood's ability to deliver oxygen to body cells and tissues; may be particularly hazardous to people with heart or circulatory problems and those with damaged lungs or breathing passages; at higher levels, exposure can impair vision, reduce work and learning capacity and affect coordination

Lead (Pb)

  75 Source: Historically leaded gasoline (which has been phased out), paint (houses, cars), smelters (metal refineries), manufacture and disposal of lead storage batteries

  75 Health Effects: accumulates in blood, bones and soft tissue, affecting brain and other nervous system function; high exposure may cause seizure and mental retardation; children are at elevated risk for central nervous system disorder

  75 Welfare Effects: Lead can harm wildlife and sharply reduce property values

Nitrogen Dioxide (NO$_2$)

NO$_2$ is a suffocating brownish gas, part of a family of poisonous and highly reactive gases including nitrous oxides (NO$_x$) that result from burning fuel at high temperatures. It reacts in the atmosphere to form corrosive nitric acid which contributes to acid rain. It plays a major role in the chemical reactions that produce ozone.

  75 Source: car exhaust, electric utilities, industrial boilers

75 Health Effects: lung irritation, respiratory infection, children may be at higher risk of acute respiratory disease when exposed to high concentrations

75 Welfare Effects: contributes to growth of algae and toxic conditions for fish in waterways; as precursor to acid rain, contributes to the acidification of lakes and forests

Ozone (O_3)

Ground level O_3, a poisonous form of pure oxygen, is the principal component of smog. It is the most pervasive and intractable of all the criteria pollutants because it is not directly emitted by sources, but rather results from a chemical reaction to which numerous sources contribute. Ozone is formed when volatile organic compounds (VOCs) like gasoline or other petroleum distillates and nitrous oxides react in sunlight. Ozone concentrations are affected by meteorological conditions as well as trends in VOCs and NO_x emissions.

75 Source: chemical reaction of volatile organic compounds, nitrous oxides and oxygen in sunlight

75 Health Effects: damages lung tissue, decreases lung function, causes respiratory inflammation, asthma, eye irritation and stuffy nose, reduces resistance to colds and other infections, may accelerate aging of lung tissue

75 Welfare Effects: responsible for $1–2 billion in crop damage per year nationally, damages plants making them more susceptible to disease, damages foliage in national parks and recreation areas and impairs habitat for endangered species, as well as reducing visibility.

Particulate Matter (PM)

PM includes solid and liquid particles in the atmosphere, some of which are visible as soot or smoke, others of which are too small to see with the naked eye.

75 Source: burning of wood, diesel and other fuels; industrial plants; agriculture (plowing, burning of fields); unpaved roads

75 Health Effects: impairs breathing and respiratory systems, irritates nose and throat, impairs body's ability to fight disease, aggravates existing pulmonary and cardiac disease, causes damage to lung tissue, carcinogenesis and premature death, and is especially dangerous to the elderly, children and people with chronic lung and heart disease

75 Welfare Effects: particulates are the main source of haze that reduces visibility; ashes, soot, smoke and dust can discolor structures and other property including clothes and furniture

Sulfur Dioxide (SO₂)

75 Source: burning of coal and oil, especially high sulfur coal burned by mid-western power plants; industrial processes (paper, metals)

75 Health Effects: breathing difficulty, respiratory illness, impairs lung defenses, aggravates existing cardiovascular disease

75 Welfare Effects: sulfur dioxide is an ingredient in acid rain, which can damage trees and lakes, corrode buildings and monuments, and reduce visibility

Volatile Organic Compounds (VOCs)

VOCs are not listed under the CAA as a criteria pollutant. However, they are a component of smog and are regulated as an ozone "precursor" under the Act.

75 Source: released from burning of fuel (gasoline, oil, wood, coal, natural gas) or evaporation of solvents, paints, glues and other products used at work or at home. Cars are an important source of VOCs. VOCs include chemicals such as benzene, toluene, methylene chloride and methyl chloroform.

75 Health Effects: In addition to contributing to smog, VOCs can cause serious health problems such as cancer

b. Listing Pollutants

The first step in the process of setting NAAQS is the decision by the EPA to list a pollutant based on scientific "criteria" documents indicating that pollutant's adverse impact on public health. The listing process triggers the need for the EPA to establish primary and secondary air standards, for which states must establish implementation plans. Thus, the decision to list or not list a pollutant is very consequential. In the case below, the EPA had refused to list lead as a pollutant despite overwhelming scientific evidence as to its health impacts. The agency had chosen instead to regulate the lead content of gasoline as its primary strategy of reducing lead emissions. An environmental group sued to force the listing.

NATURAL RESOURCES DEFENSE COUNCIL, INC. v. TRAIN

United States Court of Appeals, Second Circuit, 1976.
545 F.2d 320.

SMITH, CHIEF JUDGE.

The Environmental Protection Agency, ("EPA"), and its Administrator, Russell Train, appeal from an order of the United States District Court for the Southern District of New York, Charles E. Stewart, Jr., Judge, in an action under § 304 of the Clean Air Act, as amended, (a), requiring the Administrator of the EPA, within thirty days, to place lead on a list of air pollutants under § 108(a)(1) of the Clean Air Act ("the Act"). We affirm the order of the district court. * * *

The relevant part of § 108 reads as follows:

(a)(1) For the purpose of establishing national primary and secondary ambient air quality standards, the Administrator shall within 30 days after December 31, 1970, publish, and shall from time to time thereafter revise, a list which includes each air pollutant—

(A) which in his judgment has an adverse effect on public health or welfare;

(B) the presence of which in the ambient air results from numerous or diverse mobile or stationary sources; and

(C) for which air quality criteria had not been issued before December 31, 1970, but for which he plans to issue air quality criteria under this section.

Once a pollutant has been listed under § 108(a)(1), §§ 109 and 110 of the Act are automatically invoked. These sections require that for any pollutant for which air quality criteria are issued under § 108(a)(1)(C) after the date of enactment of the Clean Air Amendments of 1970, the Administrator must simultaneously issue air quality standards. Within nine months of the promulgation of such standards states are required to submit implementation plans to the Administrator. § 110(a)(1). The Administrator must approve or disapprove a state plan within four months. § 110(a)(2). If a state fails to submit an acceptable plan, the Administrator is required to prepare and publish such a plan himself. § 110(c). State implementation plans must provide for the attainment of primary ambient air quality standards no later than three years from the date of approval of a plan. § 110(a)(2)(A)(i). Extension of the three-year period for attaining the primary standard may be granted by the Administrator only in very limited circumstances, and in no case for more than two years. § 110(e).

The EPA concedes that lead meets the conditions of §§ 108(a)(1)(A) and (B)—that it has an adverse effect on public health and welfare, and that the presence of lead in the ambient air results from numerous or diverse mobile or stationary sources. The EPA maintains, however, that under § 108(a)(1)(C) of the Act, the Administrator retains discretion whether to list a pollutant, even though the pollutant meets the criteria of §§ 108(a)(1)(A) and (B). The Agency regards the listing of lead under § 108(a)(1) and the issuance of ambient air quality standards as one of numerous alternative control strategies for lead available to it. Listing of substances is mandatory, the EPA argues, only for those pollutants for which the Administrator "plans to issue air quality criteria." He may, it is contended, choose not to issue, *i.e., not* "plan to issue" such criteria, and decide to control lead solely by regulating emission at the source, regardless of the total concentration of lead in the ambient air. The Administrator argues that if he chooses to control lead (or other pollutants) under § 211, he is not required to list the pollutant under § 108(a)(1) or to set air quality standards. * * *

The issue is one of statutory construction. We agree with the district court and with appellees, National Resources Defense Council, Inc., et al., that the interpretation of the Clean Air Act advanced by the EPA is contrary to the structure of the Act as a whole, and that if accepted, it would vitiate the public policy underlying the enactment of the 1970 Amendments as set forth in the Act and in its legislative history. Recent court decisions are in accord, and have construed § 108(a)(1) to be mandatory if the criteria of subsections A and B are met.

Section 108(a)(1) contains mandatory language. It provides that "the Administrator *shall* ... publish ... a list...." (emphasis added.) If the EPA interpretation were accepted and listing were mandatory only for substances "for which [the Administrator] plans to issue air quality criteria ...", then the mandatory language of § 108(a)(1)(A) would become mere surplusage. The determination to list a pollutant and to issue air quality criteria would remain discretionary with the Administrator, and the rigid deadlines of § 108(a)(2), § 109, and § 110 for attaining air quality standards could be bypassed by him at will. If Congress had enacted § 211 as an alternative to, rather than as a supplement to, §§ 108–110, then one would expect a similar fixed timetable for implementation of the fuel control section. The absence of such a timetable for the enforcement of § 211 lends support to the view that fuel controls were intended by Congress as a means for attaining primary air quality standards rather than as an alternative to the promulgation of such standards.

The EPA Administrator himself initially interpreted § 108(a)(1) as requiring inclusion on the initial list to be issued of those pollutants for which air quality criteria had not been issued but which he had already found in his judgment to have an adverse effect on public health or welfare and to come from sources specified in § 108(a)(1)(B).

We agree with Judge Stewart that it is to the initial list alone that the phrase "but for which he plans to issue air quality criteria" is directed, and that the Administrator must list those pollutants which he has determined meet the requisites set forth in section 108.

When a specific provision of a total statutory scheme may be construed to be in conflict with the congressional purpose expressed in an act, it becomes necessary to examine the act's legislative history to determine whether the specific provision is reconcilable with the intent of Congress. Because state planning and implementation under the Air Quality Act of 1967 had made little progress by 1970, Congress reacted by "taking a stick to the States in the form of the Clean Air Amendments of 1970...." Train v. Natural Resources Defense Council, 421 U.S. 60. It enacted § 108(a)(1) which provides that the Administrator of the Environmental Protection Agency "shall" publish a list which includes each air pollutant which is harmful to health and originates from specified sources. Once a pollutant is listed under § 108(a)(1), §§ 109 and 110 are to be automatically invoked, and promulgation of national air quality standards and implementation thereof by the states within a limited, fixed time schedule becomes mandatory.

The EPA contention that the language of § 108(a)(1)(C) "for which [the Administrator] plans to issue air quality criteria" is a separate and third criterion to be met before § 108 requires listing lead and issuing air quality standards, thereby leaving the decision to list lead within the discretion of the Administrator, finds no support in the legislative history of the 1970 Amendments to the Act. * * *

While the literal language of § 108(a)(1)(C) is somewhat ambiguous, this ambiguity is resolved when this section is placed in the context of the Act as a whole and in its legislative history. The deliberate inclusion of a specific timetable for the attainment of ambient air quality standards incorporated by Congress in §§ 108–110 would become an exercise in futility if the Administrator could avoid listing pollutants simply by choosing not to issue air quality criteria. The discretion given to the Administrator under the Act pertains to the review of state implementation plans under § 110, and to § 211 which authorizes but does not mandate the regulation of fuel or fuel additives. It does not extend to the issuance of air quality standards for substances derived from specified sources which the Administrator had already adjudged injurious to health. * * *

The structure of the Clean Air Act as amended in 1970, its legislative history, and the judicial gloss placed upon the Act leave no room for an interpretation which makes the issuance of air quality standards for lead under § 108 discretionary. The Congress sought to eliminate, not perpetuate, opportunity for administrative foot-dragging. Once the conditions of §§ 108(a)(1)(A) and (B) have been met, the listing of lead and the issuance of air quality standards for lead become mandatory.

The order of the district court is affirmed.

NOTES

1.   The list of criteria pollutants for which national air quality standards have been set remains at six. Why do you think this is the case? The biggest change the EPA has made in recent years is dividing the particulate matter category into fine and course subsets (PM2.5 and PM10) in 1997. This decision was in response to the identification of health problems uniquely caused by fine particles. *See* John H. Cushman, Jr., *Administration Issues Its Proposal for Tightening of Air Standards*, N.Y. TIMES, Nov. 28, 1996, at A1.

2.   By forcing the EPA to list lead as a criteria pollutant, the court is arguably interfering with the EPA's preferred regulatory strategy of addressing lead pollution by regulating fuel content, which the agency is authorized to do. This might be a much more cost-effective, technologically feasible and politically palatable approach. Should courts not defer to the agency when it comes to a policy choice such as this?

3.   The EPA has an obligation under section 109(d) to review and, if necessary, revise the list of air pollutants every five years. The agency has

been sued repeatedly by the American Lung Association for failing to do this. *See, e.g.,* American Lung Association v. Browner, 884 F.Supp. 345 (D. Ariz. 1994). The prevailing view from the courts is that the agency does not have a non-discretionary duty to revise the NAAQS, but it must take *some* action regarding review and revision by the statutory deadline. *See, e.g.,* Environmental Defense Fund v. Thomas, 870 F.2d 892 (2d Cir. 1989). In July 2009, the EPA proposed raising the primary NAAQS for nitrous dioxide. *See* http://www.epa.gov/air/nitrogenoxides/actions.html.

c. Setting Air Standards

The standard-setting process for criteria pollutants is, to say the least, complex. The EPA relies on an independent science advisory panel to advise on the scientific data, but the science itself may lead to no clear conclusions about precisely where to set an ambient air standard. In studying the use of science to update air quality standards in the late nineties, Cary Coglianese and Gary Marchant concluded that the EPA frequently invoked science to cloak the value judgments implicit in the standard-setting process. Cary Coglianese & Gary E. Marchant, *Shifting Sands: The Limits of Science in Setting Risk Standards*, 152 U. PA. L. REV. 1255, 1260–61 (2004). Indeed, science cannot resolve the inherently political task of setting regulatory standards. Frequently, the science points only to a range in which risks due to air pollution increase. But risks to whom? Should we set air standards with children in mind? Asthmatics? The elderly? And how safe is safe? Should we seek to reduce risks to zero, no matter what the cost? Who should decide these things? Congress? Expert agency staff? And what role should courts play in this process?

The case below raises many of these questions. The Court's discussion of lead exposure, its implications for health, and the EPA's rationales for setting lead concentrations is long and technical. But it gives the reader a realistic flavor of the decision-making process that the EPA must go through when setting air standards. It also makes clear how challenging these decisions are for courts to review. Consider that many of the judges now reviewing air pollution regulations, such as these, were appointed to the bench before environmental law was an established field. Few of them ever took a course called "Environmental Law" in law school. As you read the excerpt, imagine yourself as a clerk to a judge having to decide this case.

LEAD INDUSTRIES, INC. v. EPA

United States Court of Appeals, District of Columbia Circuit, 1980.
647 F.2d 1130.

J. SKELLY WRIGHT, CHIEF JUDGE.

[Humans face lead exposure through ingestion or inhalation from food, water, air, dust, and peeling paint. Lead in sufficient concentrations can cause anemia, kidney damage, severe brain damage, or death. Traditionally, breathing atmospheric lead was the third largest source of human body lead. Initially the EPA sought to address this problem informally by reducing but not banning lead additives in gasoline. However, in 1975, the Natural Resources Defense Council and others successfully sued the EPA to force it to list lead as a criteria pollutant under CAA § 108 and promulgate national ambient air quality standards for it under § 109, which the EPA did. The Lead Industry Association, Inc. (LIA), the major nationwide lead industry trade association, and St. Joe Minerals Corporation (St. Joe), then petitioned for review of the EPA's health-based NAAQS for atmospheric lead, questioning whether (1) the EPA Administrator had acted within the scope of statutory authority, (2) the evidence adduced through the rulemaking process supported the NAAQS, and (3) procedural flaws required the EPA to reconsider its final determination on lead.]

II.   THE STATUTORY SCHEME

* * * Section 108 makes it clear that the term "air quality criteria" means something different from the conventional meaning of "criterion"; such "criteria" do not constitute "standards" or "guidelines," but rather refer to a document to be prepared by EPA which is to provide the basis for promulgation of air quality standards for the pollutant. This criteria document must "accurately reflect the latest scientific knowledge useful in indicating the kind and extent of all identifiable effects on public health or welfare which may be expected from the presence of such pollutant in the ambient air, in varying quantities." Section 108(a)(2).

At the same time as he issues air quality criteria for a pollutant, the Administrator must also publish proposed national primary and secondary air quality standards for the pollutant. Section 109(a)(2). National primary ambient air quality standards are standards "the attainment and maintenance of which in the judgment of the Administrator, based on such criteria and allowing an adequate margin of safety, are requisite to protect the public health." Section 109(b)(1). Secondary air quality standards "specify a level of air quality the attainment and maintenance of which in the judgment of the Administrator, based on such criteria, is requisite to protect the public welfare from any known or anticipated adverse effects associated with the presence of such air pollutant in the ambient air." Section 109(b)(2). Effects on "the public welfare" include "effects on soils, water, crops, vegetation, man-made materials, animals, wildlife, weather, visibility, and climate, damage to and deterioration of property, and hazards to transportation, as well as effects on economic values and on personal comfort and well-being." Section 302(h). The Administrator is required to submit the proposed air quality standards for public comment in a rulemaking proceeding, the procedure for which is prescribed by Section 307(d) of the Act.

Within six months of publication of the proposed standards the Administrator must promulgate final primary and secondary ambient air quality standards for the pollutant. Section 307(d)(10). Once EPA has promulgated national ambient air quality standards, responsibility under the Act shifts from the federal government to the states [to achieve the NAAQS].

III. THE LEAD STANDARDS RULEMAKING PROCEEDINGS

As required by statute, EPA's first step toward promulgating air quality standards for lead was to prepare a criteria document. The Lead Criteria Document was the culmination of a process of rigorous scientific and public review, and thus is a comprehensive and thoughtful analysis of the most current scientific information on the subject. * * *

A. *The Lead Criteria Document*

* * * [T]he Criteria Document examined a large number of issues raised by the problem of lead in the environment. One of these was the effects of lead exposure on human health. The Criteria Document concluded that, among the major organ systems, the hematopoietic (blood-forming) and neurological systems are the areas of prime concern. * * *

The Criteria Document identified a variety of effects of lead exposure on the blood-forming system. * * * [It] concluded, after a review of various studies, that in children, a threshold level for anemia is about 40 μg Pb/dl, whereas the corresponding value for adults is about 50 μg Pb/dl. (The concentration of lead in the blood is measured in micrograms of lead per deciliter of blood—μg Pb/dl.)

The Criteria Document also examined other more subtle effects on the blood-forming system, associated with lower levels of lead exposure. The most pertinent of these "subclinical" effects for purposes of these cases is lead-related elevation of erythrocyte protoporphyrin (EP elevation). According to the Criteria Document, this phenomenon must, for a number of reasons, be regarded as an indication of an impairment of human health. * * * The Criteria Document reported that the threshold for EP elevation in children and women is at blood lead levels of 15–20 μg Pb/dl, and 25–30 μg Pb/dl in adult males. * * * The Criteria Document did not identify a particular blood lead level at which regulatory response was appropriate, but it did note with approval the 1975 guidelines issued by the Center For Disease Control, which use elevated EP at blood lead levels of 30 μg Pb/dl as the cut-off point in screening children for lead poisoning.

The Criteria Document also examined the effects of lead exposure on the central nervous system. Among the most deleterious effects of lead poisoning are those associated with severe central nervous system damage at high exposure levels. * * * After a review of various studies, the Criteria Document concluded that the blood lead threshold for these neurological effects of high level exposure is 80–100 μg Pb/dl in children, and 100–200 μg Pb/dl in adults.

The Criteria Document also went on to consider the evidence on whether lower level lead exposures can affect the central nervous system, particularly in children. It acknowledged that the issue is unsettled and somewhat controversial, but it was able to conclude, after a careful review of various studies on the subject, that "a rather consistent pattern of impaired neural and cognitive functions appears to be associated with blood lead levels below those producing the overt symptomatology of lead encephalopathy." The Criteria Document reported that "(t)he blood lead levels at which neurobehavioral deficits occur in otherwise asymptomatic children appear to start at a range of 50 to 60 μg/dl, although some evidence tentatively suggests that such effects may occur at slightly lower levels for some children."

In addition to examining the health effects of lead exposure, the Criteria Document also discussed other issues critical to the task of setting air quality standards for lead. One of these issues is the relationship between air lead exposure and blood lead levels—a relationship commonly referred to as the air lead/blood lead ratio. The Criteria Document acknowledged that derivation of a functional relationship between air lead exposure and blood lead levels is made difficult by the fact that the relationship is not a linear one; rather, the ratio tends to increase as air lead levels are reduced. The Document was nevertheless able to conclude, after a detailed examination of the relevant studies, that air lead/blood lead ratios fall within a range of 1:1 to 1:2 (μg Pb/m^3 air):(μg Pb/dl blood) at the levels of lead exposure generally encountered by the population, i.e., blood lead levels increase by between 1 and 2 g Pb/dl of blood for every 1 μg Pb/m^3 of air. (Air lead content is measured in micrograms of lead per cubic meter of air—μg Pb/m^3.) * * * The Criteria Document looked into the question whether any sub-groups within the population are particularly vulnerable to the effects of lead exposure. It concluded that preschool-age children and pregnant women are particularly sensitive to lead exposure, the latter mainly because of the risk to the unborn child.

B. The Proposed Standards

Simultaneously with the publication of the Lead Criteria Document on December 14, 1977, the Administrator proposed a national primary ambient air quality standard for lead of 1.5 μg Pb/m^3 monthly average. He also proposed that the secondary air quality standard be set at the same level as the primary standard because the welfare effects associated with lead exposure did not warrant imposition of a stricter standard. In the preamble to the proposed standards the Administrator explained the analysis EPA had employed in setting the standards.

The Administrator first pointed out that a number of factors complicate the task of setting air quality standards which will protect the population from the adverse health effects of lead exposure. First, some sub-groups within the population have a greater potential for, or are more susceptible to the effects of, lead exposure. Second, there are a variety of adverse health effects associated with various levels of lead exposure. Third, the variability of individual responses to lead exposure, even within particular sub-groups of the population, would produce a range of blood lead levels at any given air lead level. Fourth, airborne lead is only one of a number of sources of lead exposure and the relative contribution from each source is difficult to quantify. Finally, the relationship between air lead exposure and blood lead levels is a complex one.

In response to the first problem the Administrator began by noting that protection of the most sensitive groups within the population had to be a major consideration in determining the level at which the air quality standards should be set. And he determined that children between the ages of 1 and 5 years are most sensitive to the effects of lead exposure both because the hematologic and neurologic effects associated with lead exposure occur in children at lower threshold levels than in adults, and because the habit of placing hands and other objects in the mouth subjects them to a greater risk of exposure. Next, the Administrator examined the various health effects of lead exposure and proposed that EP elevation should be considered the first adverse health effect of lead exposure because it indicates an impairment of cellular functions, and should be the pivotal health effect on which the lead standards are based. Accordingly, he proposed that the air lead standards be designed to prevent the occurrence of EP elevation in children. In order to accomplish this, and to address the problem of variable responses to lead exposure, the Administrator selected 15 μg Pb/dl, the lowest reported threshold blood lead level for EP elevation in children, as the target mean population blood lead level. He reasoned that setting the target mean population blood lead level at the lowest reported threshold blood lead level for EP elevation would ensure that most of the target population would be kept below blood lead levels at which adverse health effects occur. The Administrator also discussed the alternative approaches of basing the standard on more severe effects such as anemia, or attempting to decide the actual level of EP elevation which represents an adverse effect on health, and then making an adjustment to allow a margin of safety. He specifically invited comments on these alternative approaches. Finally, the Administrator outlined another approach to calculating the target mean population blood lead level involving the use of statistical techniques discussed in the Criteria Document.

[Extrapolating from estimates of the proportion of blood lead attributable to air sources on average across the nation, the Administrator calculated that the ambient air quality lead standard should be 1.5 μg Pb/dl.] * * *

D.   *The Final Air Quality Standards for Lead*

The Administrator promulgated the final air quality standards on October 5, 1978, prescribing national primary and secondary ambient air quality standards for lead of 1.5 μg Pb/m^3, averaged over a calendar quarter. Although the final standards were the same as the proposed standards (with the exception of the change in the averaging period from 30 to 90 days), the Administrator arrived at the final standards through somewhat different analysis. The preamble to the final standards reveals that the comments on the proposed standards had led the Administrator to reconsider his analysis. In particular, he seemed to feel that legitimate questions had been raised concerning the health significance of the early stages of EP elevation and about the threshold blood lead level for this condition. The Administrator's reexamination focused on two key questions: (1) What is the maximum safe individual blood lead level for children? and (2) what proportion of the target population should be kept below this blood lead level? Addressing the first issue required a review of the health effects of lead exposure discussed in the Criteria Document. The Administrator concluded that, although EP elevation beginning at blood lead levels of 15–20 μg Pb/dl is potentially adverse to the health of children, only when blood lead concentration reaches a level of 30 μg Pb/dl is this effect significant enough to be considered adverse to health. Accordingly, he selected 30 μg Pb/dl as the maximum safe individual blood lead level for children. The Administrator based this choice on three mutually supporting grounds. First, it is at this blood lead level that the first adverse health effect of lead exposure impairment of heme synthesis begins to occur in children. Second, a maximum safe individual blood lead level of 30 μg Pb/dl would allow an adequate margin of safety in protecting children against more serious effects of lead exposure anemia, symptoms of which begin to appear in children at blood lead levels of 40 μg Pb/dl, and central nervous system deficits which start to occur in children at blood lead levels of 50 μg Pb/dl. Third, the Administrator reasoned that the maximum safe individual blood lead level should be no higher than the blood lead level used by the Center for Disease Control in screening children for lead poisoning 30 μg Pb/dl.

Having determined the maximum safe individual blood lead level for the target population, the Administrator next focused on the question of what percentage of children between the ages of 1 and 5 years the standard should attempt to keep below this blood lead level. According to the 1970 census, there are approximately 20 million children under the age of 5 years in the United States, 12 million of them in urban areas and 5 million in inner cities where lead exposure may be especially high. The Administrator concluded that in order to provide an adequate margin of safety, and to protect special high risk sub-groups, the standards should aim at keeping 99.5% of the target population below the maximum safe individual blood lead level of 30 μg Pb/dl. . . . Using the lognormal statistical technique he had alluded to in the proposed standards, he calculated that a target mean population blood lead level of 15 μg Pb/dl (the same number as in the proposed standards, but arrived at through different analysis), would accomplish this task. [Once again, this resulted in a recommended] ambient air quality standard of 1.5 μg Pb/m^3, the same as the proposed standard. * * *

V.　STATUTORY AUTHORITY

The petitioners' first claim is that the Administrator exceeded his authority under the statute by promulgating a primary air quality standard for lead which is more stringent than is necessary to protect the public health because it is designed to protect the public against "sub-clinical" effects which are not harmful to health. According to petitioners, Congress only authorized the Administrator to set primary air quality standards that are aimed at protecting the public against health effects which are known to be clearly harmful. They argue that Congress so limited the Administrator's authority because it was concerned that excessively stringent air quality standards could cause massive economic dislocation.

In developing this argument St. Joe contends that EPA erred by refusing to consider the issues of economic and technological feasibility in setting the air quality standards for lead. St. Joe's claim that the Administrator should have considered these issues is based on the statutory provision directing him to allow an "adequate margin of safety" in setting primary air quality standards. In St. Joe's view, the Administrator must consider the economic impact of the proposed standard on industry and the technological feasibility of compliance by emission sources in determining the appropriate allowance for a margin of safety. St. Joe argues that the Administrator abused his discretion by refusing to consider these factors in determining the appropriate margin of safety for the lead standards, and maintains that the lead air quality standards will have a disastrous economic impact on industrial sources of lead emissions.

This argument is totally without merit. St. Joe is unable to point to anything in either the language of the Act or its legislative history that offers any support for its claim that Congress, by specifying that the Administrator is to allow an "adequate margin of safety" in setting primary air quality standards, thereby required the Administrator to consider economic or technological feasibility. To the contrary, the statute and its legislative history make clear that economic considerations play no part in the promulgation of ambient air quality standards under Section 109.

Where Congress intended the Administrator to be concerned about economic and technological feasibility, it expressly so provided. For example, Section 111 of the Act directs the Administrator to consider economic and technological feasibility in establishing standards of performance for new stationary sources of air pollution based on the best available control technology. In contrast, Section 109(b) speaks only of protecting the public health and welfare. Nothing in its language suggests that the Administrator is to consider economic or technological feasibility in setting ambient air quality standards.

The legislative history of the Act also shows the Administrator may not consider economic and technological feasibility in setting air quality standards; the absence of any provision requiring consideration of these factors was no accident; it was the result of a deliberate decision by Congress to subordinate such concerns to the achievement of health goals. * * *

VI.   HEALTH BASIS FOR THE LEAD STANDARDS

* * *

A.   *Maximum Safe Individual Blood Lead Level*

LIA attacks the Administrator's determination that 30 µg Pb/dl should be considered the maximum safe individual blood lead level for children, maintaining that there is no evidence in the record indicating that children suffer any health effects that can be considered adverse at this blood lead level. * * *

First, [LIA] contends that nothing in the record supports the suggestion that EP elevation at 30 µg Pb/dl is harmful to health, arguing that EP elevation is a mere "subclinical effect"—a biological response to lead exposure—which is without health significance, and noting that a number of its experts brought this matter to EPA's attention in their comments on the proposed standards. In LIA's view, the Administrator did not explain precisely how impairment of heme synthesis at blood lead levels of 30 µg Pb/dl adversely affects the health of children. Second, LIA challenges the Administrator's determination that a maximum safe individual blood lead level of 30 µg Pb/dl is justified by the need to allow an adequate margin of safety in protecting children against anemia and central nervous system deficits. It maintains that the evidence in the record does not support the Administrator's conclusion that the blood lead threshold for the symptoms of anemia in children is 40 µg Pb/dl. * * * Third, LIA contends that the preamble to the final regulations does not state the basis for the Administrator's finding that central nervous system deficits occur in children at blood lead levels of 50 µg Pb/dl, thereby precluding this court from being able to test the soundness of this determination. Finally, LIA argues that even if it were to concede that EPA's conclusions about the blood lead thresholds for anemia and central nervous system deficits are correct, there is still no explanation of why the Administrator concluded that a maximum individual safe blood level of 30 µg Pb/dl rather than 35 µg Pb/dl, for example is necessary to provide an adequate margin of safety against these effects.

Our review of the record persuades us that there is adequate support for each of the Administrator's conclusions about the health effects of lead exposure and, consequently, that LIA's challenges to the evidentiary support for these findings must be rejected. Under the statutory scheme enacted by Congress, the Criteria Document prepared with respect to each pollutant is to provide the scientific basis for promulgation of air quality standards for the pollutant. We have already noted that the Lead Criteria Document was the product of a process that allowed the rigorous scientific and public review that are essential to the preparation of a document "accurately reflect(ing) the latest scientific knowledge useful in indicating the kind and extent of all identifiable effects (of lead exposure) on (the) public health." In our view, the Criteria Document provides ample support for the Administrator's findings. * * *

To be sure, the Administrator's conclusions were not unchallenged; both LIA and the Administrator are able to point to an impressive array of experts supporting each of their respective positions. However, disagreement among the experts is inevitable when the issues involved are at the "very frontiers of scientific knowledge," and such disagreement does not preclude us from finding that the Administrator's decisions are adequately supported by the evidence in the record. * * *

disagreemt. doesn't show regulations to be unreasonable

B. Margin of Safety

Both LIA and St. Joe argue that the Administrator erred by including multiple allowances for margins of safety in his calculation of the lead standards. Petitioners note that the statute directs the Administrator to allow an "adequate margin of safety" in setting primary air quality standards, and they maintain that as a matter of statutory construction the Administrator may not interpret "margin" of safety to mean "margins" of safety. In petitioners' view, the Administrator in fact did just this insofar as he made allowances for margins of safety at several points in his analysis. They argue that margin of safety allowances were reflected in the choice of the maximum safe individual blood lead level for children, in the decision to place 99.5 percent of the target population group below that blood lead level, in the selection of an air lead/blood lead ratio at 1:2, and in the Administrator's estimate of the contribution to blood lead levels that should be attributed to non-air sources. The net result of these multiple allowances for margins of safety, petitioners contend, was a standard far more stringent than is necessary to protect the public health. * * *

We agree with the Administrator that nothing in the statutory scheme or the legislative history requires him to adopt the margin of safety approach suggested by St. Joe. Adding the margin of safety at the end of the analysis is one approach, but it is not the only possible method. Indeed, the Administrator considered this approach but decided against it because of complications raised by the multiple sources of lead exposure. The choice between these possible approaches is a policy choice of the type that Congress specifically left to the Administrator's judgment. * * *

XI. CONCLUSION

The national ambient air quality standards for lead were the culmination of a process of rigorous scientific and public review which permitted a thorough ventilation of the complex scientific and technical issues presented by this rulemaking proceeding. Interested parties were allowed a number of opportunities to participate in exploration and resolution of the issues raised by the standard-setting exercise. EPA, and ultimately the public whose health these air quality standards protect, have benefited from their contribution. To be sure, even the experts did not always agree about the answers to the questions that were raised. Indeed, they did not always agree on what the relevant questions were. These disagreements underscore the novelty and complexity of the issues that had to be resolved, and both the EPA and the participants in the rulemaking proceeding deserve to be commended for the diligence with which they approached the task of coming to grips with these difficult issues.

We have accorded these cases the most careful consideration, combining as we must careful scrutiny of the evidence in the record with deference to the Administrator's judgments. We conclude that in this rulemaking proceeding the Administrator complied with the substantive and procedural requirements of the Act, and that his decisions are both adequately explained and amply supported by evidence in the record. Accordingly, we reject petitioners' claims of error. The regulations under review herein are

Affirmed.

NOTES

1. What degree of deference should the court afford an agency in a complicated case such as this, where the agency must make policy decisions in the context of scientific uncertainty? On the applicable standard of review, the court said: "(A)fter our careful study of the record, we must take a step back from the agency's decision. We must look at the decision not as the chemist, biologist or statistician that we are qualified neither by training nor experience to be, but as a reviewing court exercising our narrowly defined duty of holding agencies to certain minimal standards of rationality. * * * We must affirm unless the agency decision is arbitrary or capricious." Do you think this is the appropriate standard of review?

2. When the agency determines the maximum safe blood level for the target population, is it not making policy, rather than scientific judgments? Why choose children—arguably the most sensitive population—as the target population? And why set the maximum blood level where the agency did, if blood levels of lead can rise without manifesting any illness? Aren't reasonable people likely to differ about such judgments? Who should make these decisions, given how politically contentious they are? Congress, courts, or the agency? How should the balance be struck between flexibility to regulate and accountability of the decisionmaker?

3. Basic scientific uncertainty still pervades the process of setting health-based limits. EPA set the lead NAAQS standard based on an assumption that 30 micrograms of lead per deciliter of blood was a conservative estimate of when adverse health effects might occur in children, while industry said the level ought to be at least 35. The CDC now says that blood lead levels in children should not exceed 10 micrograms and many scientists believe that no level of lead in blood is safe. *See* CENTERS FOR DISEASE CONTROL AND PREVENTION, DRAFT TOXICOLOGICAL PROFILE FOR LEAD (2005), *available at* http://www.atsdr.cdc.gov/toxprofiles/tp13.html.

4. Section 109(d) of the Clean Air Act requires the EPA to periodically review and, if necessary, revise existing NAAQS, based on the recommendations of an independent scientific committee. The EPA did update the particulate matter and ozone NAAQS in 1997, dividing the former into fine and

course particulates and amending the latter to be averaged over an eight hour rather than a one hour period. National Ambient Air Quality Standards for Particulate Matter, 62 Fed. Reg. 38,652 (July 18, 1997) (codified at 40 C.F.R. section 50); National Ambient Air Quality Standards for Ozone, 62 Fed. Reg 38,856 (July 18, 1997) (codified at 40 C.F.R. section 50). These were challenged in the case below, *Whitman v. American Trucking Ass'ns*, which upheld the Clean Air Act as a constitutionally permissible delegation of power to the EPA to set these standards; the examination of the standards themselves took place on remand in *American Trucking Ass'ns v. EPA*, 283 F.3d 355 (D.C. Cir. 2002).

5. Note the court's view that cost and technological feasibility should play no role in the setting of air standards under the Act. Before moving on to the next section where we take this up, what do you think of this analysis of § 109? Isn't cost a relevant consideration when establishing the lead standards if emissions reductions will be very burdensome for industry to achieve, perhaps even putting some firms out of business? Why have a public comment period if the agency is free to ignore all the evidence submitted about cost and technological feasibility?

d. The Role of Cost in Standard Setting

In this section, we consider the appropriate role of cost in setting primary standards for air pollution. What did Congress mean when it required in § 109(b)(1) that primary standards be set which, "allowing an adequate margin of safety, are requisite to protect the public health?" In the case excerpted below, a coalition of states and industry groups challenged the EPA's 1997 revisions to the standards for ozone and particulate matter, arguing that the CAA requires the agency to consider cost when setting air standards, which the agency had not done. The agency had revised the standards after a lengthy review process produced evidence that both acute and chronic health impacts could result from exposure to ozone and particulate matter at levels below those allowed by the existing standards.

**WHITMAN v. AMERICAN TRUCKING
ASSOCIATIONS, INC.**

Supreme Court of the United States, 2001.
531 U.S. 457, 121 S.Ct. 903, 149 L.Ed.2d 1.

[The Court's treatment of the non-delegation issue raised in the case appears in Chapter 5 at page 431.]

JUSTICE SCALIA delivered the opinion of the Court.

Section 109(a) of the CAA, as added, 84 Stat. 1679, and amended, 42 U.S.C. § 7409(a), requires the Administrator of the EPA to promulgate NAAQS for each air pollutant for which "air quality criteria" have been issued under § 108, 42 U.S.C. § 7408. Once a NAAQS has been promulgated, the Administrator must review the standard (and the criteria on which it is based) "at five-year intervals" and make "such revisions . . . as may be appropriate." CAA § 109(d)(1), 42 U.S.C. § 7409(d)(1). These cases arose when, on July 18, 1997, the Administrator revised the NAAQS for particulate matter (PM) and ozone. * * *

In *Lead Industries Ass'n, Inc. v. EPA*, the District of Columbia Circuit held that "economic considerations [may] play no part in the promulgation of ambient air quality standards under Section 109" of the CAA. In the present cases, the court adhered to that holding * * * as it had done on many other occasions. * * *

Section 109(b)(1) instructs the EPA to set primary ambient air quality standards "the attainment and maintenance of which . . . are requisite to protect the public health" with "an adequate margin of safety." 42 U.S.C. § 7409(b)(1). Were it not for the hundreds of pages of briefing respondents have submitted on the issue, one would have thought it fairly clear that this text does not permit the EPA to consider costs in setting the standards. The language, as one scholar has noted, "is absolute." The EPA, "based on" the information about health effects contained in the technical "criteria" documents compiled under § 108(a)(2), 42 U.S.C. § 7408(a)(2), is to identify the maximum airborne concentration of a pollutant that the public health can tolerate, decrease the concentration to provide an "adequate" margin of safety, and set the standard at that level. Nowhere are the costs of achieving such a standard made part of that initial calculation.

Against this most natural of readings, respondents make a lengthy, spirited, but ultimately unsuccessful attack. They begin with the object of § 109(b)(1)'s focus, the "public health." When the term first appeared in federal clean air legislation—in the Act of July 14, 1955 (1955 Act), 69 Stat. 322, which expressed "recognition of the dangers to the public health" from air pollution—its ordinary meaning was "[t]he health of the community." Webster's New International Dictionary 2005 (2d ed. 1950). Respondents argue, however, that § 109(b)(1), as added by the Clean Air Amendments of 1970 (1970 Act), 84 Stat. 1676, meant to use the term's secondary meaning: "[t]he ways and means of conserving the health of the members of a community, as by preventive medicine, organized care of the sick, etc." Words that can have more than one meaning are given content, however, by their surroundings, * * * and in the context of § 109(b)(1) this second definition makes no sense. Congress could not have meant to instruct the Administrator to set NAAQS at a level "requisite to protect" "the art and science dealing with the protection and improvement of community health." *Webster's Third New International Dictionary* 1836 (1981). We therefore revert to the primary definition of the term: the health of the public.

Even so, respondents argue, many more factors than air pollution affect public health. In particular, the economic cost of implementing a very stringent standard might produce health losses sufficient to offset the health gains achieved in cleaning the air—for example, by closing down whole industries and thereby impoverishing the workers and consumers dependent upon those industries. That is unquestionably true, and Congress was unquestionably aware of it. * * * Section 110(f)(1) of the CAA permitted the Administrator to waive the compliance deadline for stationary sources if, *inter alia,* sufficient control measures were simply unavailable and "the continued operation of such sources is *essential . . . to the public health* or welfare." 84 Stat. 1683 (emphasis added). Other provisions explicitly permitted or required economic costs to be taken into account in implementing the air quality standards. * * * Subsequent Amendments to the CAA have added many more provisions directing, in explicit language, that the Administrator consider costs in performing various duties. * * * We have therefore refused to find implicit in ambiguous sections of the CAA an authorization to consider costs that has elsewhere, and so often, been expressly granted. * * *

Accordingly, to prevail in their present challenge, respondents must show a textual commitment of authority to the EPA to consider costs in setting NAAQS under § 109(b)(1). And because § 109(b)(1) and the NAAQS for which it provides are the engine that drives nearly all of Title I of the CAA, that textual commitment must be a clear one. Congress, we have held, does not alter the fundamental details of a regulatory scheme in vague terms or ancillary provisions—it does not, one might say, hide elephants in mouseholes. * * * Respondents' textual arguments ultimately founder upon this principle.

Their first claim is that § 109(b)(1)'s terms "adequate margin" and "requisite" leave room to pad health effects with cost concerns. * * * [W]e find it implausible that Congress would give to the EPA through these modest words the power to determine whether implementation costs should moderate national air quality standards. * * *

The same defect inheres in respondents' next two arguments: that while the Administrator's judgment about what is requisite to protect the public health must be "based on [the] criteria" documents developed under § 108(a)(2), *see* § 109(b)(1), it need not be based *solely* on those criteria; and that those criteria themselves, while they must include "effects on public health or welfare which may be expected from the presence of such pollutant in the ambient air," are not necessarily *limited* to those effects. Even if we were to concede those premises, we still would not conclude that one of the unenumerated factors that the agency can consider in developing and applying the criteria is cost of implementation. That factor is *both* so indirectly related to public health *and* so full of potential for canceling the conclusions drawn from direct health effects that it would surely have been expressly mentioned in §§ 108 and 109 had Congress meant it to be considered. Yet while those provisions describe in detail how the health effects of pollutants in the ambient air are to be calculated and given effect, *see* § 108(a)(2), they say not a word about costs.

Respondents point, finally, to a number of provisions in the CAA that *do* require attainment cost data to be generated. Section 108(b)(1), for example, instructs the Administrator to "issue to the States," simultaneously with the criteria documents, "information on air pollution control techniques, which information shall include data relating to the cost of installation and operation." 42 U.S.C. § 7408(b)(*l*). And § 109(d)(2)(C)(iv) requires the Clean Air Scientific Advisory Committee to "advise the Administrator of any adverse public health, welfare, social, economic, or energy effects which may result from various strategies for attainment and maintenance" of NAAQS. 42 U.S.C. § 7409(d)(2)(C)(iv). Respondents argue that these provisions make no sense unless costs are to be considered in setting the NAAQS. That is not so. These provisions enable the Administrator to assist the States in carrying out their statutory role as primary *implementers* of the NAAQS. It is to the States that the Act assigns initial and primary responsibility for deciding what emissions reductions will be required from which sources. * * * It would be impossible to perform that task intelligently without considering which abatement technologies are most efficient, and most economically feasible— which is why we have said that "the most important forum for consideration of claims of economic and technological infeasibility is before the state agency formulating the implementation plan," *Union Elec. Co. v. EPA* [*infra*, page 600]. Thus, federal clean air legislation has, from the very beginning, directed federal agencies to develop and transmit implementation data, including cost data, to the States. * * * That Congress chose to carry forward this research program to assist States in choosing the means through which they would implement the standards is perfectly sensible, and has no bearing upon whether cost considerations are to be taken into account in formulating the standards.

It should be clear from what we have said that the canon requiring texts to be so construed as to avoid serious constitutional problems has no application here. No matter how severe the constitutional doubt, courts may choose only between reasonably available interpretations of a text. * * * The text of § 109(b), interpreted in its statutory and historical context and with appreciation for its importance to the CAA as a whole, unambiguously bars cost considerations from the NAAQS-setting process, and thus ends the matter for us as well as the EPA. We therefore affirm the judgment of the Court of Appeals on this point.

JUSTICE BREYER, concurring in part and concurring in the judgment.

[I agree] that the Clean Air Act does not permit the Environmental Protection Agency to consider the economic costs of implementation when setting national ambient air quality standards under § 109(b)(1) of the Act. But I would not rest this conclusion solely upon § 109's language or upon a presumption, such as the Court's presumption that any authority the Act grants the EPA to consider costs must flow from a "textual commitment" that is "clear." * * * In order better to achieve regulatory goals—for example, to allocate resources so that they save more lives or produce a cleaner environment—regulators must often take account of all of a proposed regulation's adverse effects, at least where those adverse effects clearly threaten serious and disproportionate public harm. Hence, I believe that, other things being equal, we should read silences or ambiguities in the language of regulatory statutes as permitting, not forbidding, this type of rational regulation.

In this case, however, other things are not equal. Here, legislative history, along with the statute's structure, indicates that § 109's language reflects a congressional decision not to delegate to the agency the legal authority to consider economic costs of compliance.

For one thing, the legislative history shows that Congress intended the statute to be "technology forcing." Senator Edmund Muskie, the primary sponsor of the 1970 Amendments to the Act, introduced them by saying that Congress' primary responsibility in drafting the Act was not "to be limited by what is or appears to be technologically or economically feasible," but "to establish what the public interest requires to protect the health of persons," even if that means that *industries will be asked to do what seems to be impossible at the present time.*" * * *

The Senate directly focused upon the technical feasibility and cost of implementing the Act's mandates. And it made clear that it intended the Administrator to develop air quality standards set independently of either. * * *

Indeed, this Court, after reviewing the entire legislative history, concluded that the 1970 Amendments were "expressly designed to force regulated sources to develop pollution control devices that *might at the time appear to be economically or technologically infeasible.*" Union Elec. Co. v. EPA (emphasis added). And the Court added that the 1970 Amendments were intended to be a "drastic remedy to ... a serious and otherwise uncheckable problem." Subsequent legislative history confirms that the technology-forcing goals of the 1970 Amendments are still paramount in today's Act. * * *

To read this legislative history as meaning what it says does not impute to Congress an irrational intent. Technology-forcing hopes can prove realistic. Those persons, for example, who opposed the 1970 Act's insistence on a 90% reduction in auto emission pollutants, on the ground of excessive cost, saw the development of catalytic converter technology that helped achieve substantial reductions without the economic catastrophe that some had feared. * * *

At the same time, the statute's technology-forcing objective makes regulatory efforts to determine the costs of implementation both less important and more difficult. It means that the relevant economic costs are speculative, for they include the cost of unknown future technologies. It also means that efforts to take costs into account can breed time-consuming and potentially unresolvable arguments about the accuracy and significance of cost estimates. Congress could have thought such efforts not worth the delays and uncertainties that would accompany them. In any event, that is what the statute's history seems to say. * * * And the matter is one for Congress to decide.

Moreover, the Act does not, on this reading, wholly ignore cost and feasibility. * * * [T]he Act allows regulators to take those concerns into account when they determine how to implement ambient air quality standards. Thus, States may consider economic costs when they select the particular control devices used to meet the standards, and industries experiencing difficulty in reducing their emissions can seek an exemption or variance from the state implementation plan. * * *

The Act also permits the EPA, within certain limits, to consider costs when it sets deadlines by which areas must attain the ambient air quality standards. * * * And Congress can change those statutory limits if necessary. Given the ambient air quality standards' substantial effects on States, cities, industries, and their suppliers and customers, Congress will hear from those whom compliance deadlines affect adversely, and Congress can consider whether legislative change is warranted. * * *

Finally, contrary to the suggestion of the Court of Appeals and of some parties, this interpretation of § 109 does not require the EPA to eliminate every health risk, however slight, at any economic cost, however great, to the point of "hurtling" industry over "the brink of ruin," or even forcing "deindustrialization." * * * The statute, by its express terms, does not compel the elimination of *all* risk; and it grants the Administrator sufficient flexibility to avoid setting ambient air quality standards ruinous to industry.

Section 109(b)(1) directs the Administrator to set standards that are "requisite to protect the public health" with "an adequate margin of safety." But these words do not describe a world that is free of all risk—an impossible and undesirable objective. * * * Nor are the words "requisite" and "public health" to be understood independent of context. We consider football equipment "safe" even if its use entails a level of risk that would make drinking water "unsafe" for consumption. And what counts as "requisite" to protecting the public health will similarly vary with background circumstances, such as the public's ordinary tolerance of the particular health risk in the particular context at issue. The Administrator can consider such background circumstances when "decid[ing] what risks are acceptable in the world in which we live."

The statute also permits the Administrator to take account of comparative health risks. That is to say, she may consider whether a proposed rule promotes safety overall. A rule likely to cause more harm to health than it prevents is not a rule that is "requisite to protect the public health." * * *

The statute ultimately specifies that the standard set must be "requisite to protect the public health" *"in the judgment of the Administrator,"* § 109(b)(1) (emphasis added), a phrase that grants the Administrator considerable discretionary standard-setting authority.

The statute's words, then, authorize the Administrator to consider the severity of a pollutant's potential adverse health effects, the number of those likely to be affected, the distribution of the adverse effects, and the uncertainties surrounding each estimate. * * * They permit the Administrator to take account of comparative health consequences. They allow her to take account of context when determining the acceptability of small risks to health. And they give her considerable discretion when she does so.

This discretion would seem sufficient to avoid the extreme results that some of the industry parties fear. After all, the EPA, in setting standards that "protect the public health" with "an adequate margin of safety," retains discretionary authority to avoid regulating risks that it reasonably concludes are trivial in context. Nor need regulation lead to deindustrialization. Preindustrial society was not a very healthy society; hence a standard demanding the return of the Stone Age would not prove "requisite to protect the public health."

Although I rely more heavily than does the Court upon legislative history and alternative sources of statutory flexibility, I reach the same ultimate conclusion. Section 109 does not delegate to the EPA authority to base the national ambient air quality standards, in whole or in part, upon the economic costs of compliance.

[handwritten margin note: no concern for economic costs in setting naaqs]

NOTES

1. The Supreme Court's holding that the agency may not consider cost when setting air standards was greeted with a collective sigh of relief by environmentalists. That they were so worried about the possibility of a different outcome, however, signifies the ascendance of cost-benefit analysis in scholarly as well as judicial circles over the last twenty years. On the limitations of cost-benefit analysis, for setting health protective air standards in particular, *see* Lisa Heinzerling, *The Clean Air Act and the Constitution*, 20 ST. LOUIS U. PUB. L. REV. 121 (2001).

2. Prior to *American Trucking*, judges occasionally imposed some form of cost-benefit obligations on the EPA as a requirement of reasoned decision-making, despite statutory silence on the issue. *See* Richard G. Stoll, *Cost–Benefit Analysis Through the Back Door of "Reasoned Decisionmaking,"* 31 Envtl. L. Rep. 10228 (2001). Does this more indirect mechanism for forcing cost consideration seem problematic? Does it matter that judges are requiring cost-benefit analysis where Congress has not clearly required it?

3. The Clean Air Act still allows for consideration of cost in the NAAQS process, as Justice Breyer's concurrence points out, only later, at the implementation stage, when states design their SIPs for meeting the NAAQS. What practical difference does this make? If cost ultimately affects the design of the implementation plans, does cost ultimately constrain the manner and rate at which states comply with national air standards? As practitioners close to the ground know, standards are just numbers: they are arguably meaningless until implemented. If implementation is where the action is, doesn't cost ultimately, if indirectly, control the stringency of air standards?

D. STATUTORY DISCRETION AND MAJOR PROVISIONS OF THE CAA

Though we address the regulation of emissions from mobile sources such as automobiles at greater length in Section E of this chapter, the U.S. Supreme Court recently addressed the extent of discretion accorded the EPA in choosing whether to set mobile source standards for greenhouse gas emissions in *Massachusetts v. EPA,* excerpted below. (The standing portion of the case is included in Chapter 5 on page 403.)

JUSTICE STEVENS delivered the opinion of the Court in which KENNEDY, SOUTER, GINSBURG, and BREYER, JJ., joined.

I

Section 202(a)(1) of the Clean Air Act . . . provides:

"The [EPA] Administrator shall by regulation prescribe (and from time to time revise) in accordance with the provisions of this section, standards applicable to the emission of any air pollutant from any class or classes of new motor vehicles or new motor vehicle engines, which in his judgment cause, or contribute to, air pollution which may reasonably be anticipated to endanger public health or welfare. . . ."

The Act defines "air pollutant" to include "any air pollution agent or combination of such agents, including any physical, chemical, biological, radioactive . . . substance or matter which is emitted into or otherwise enters the ambient air." § 7602(g). "Welfare" is also defined broadly: among other things, it includes "effects on . . . weather . . . and climate." § 7602(h).

When Congress enacted these provisions, the study of climate change was in its infancy. In 1959, shortly after the U. S. Weather Bureau began monitoring atmospheric carbon dioxide levels, an observatory in Mauna Loa, Hawaii, recorded a mean level of 316 parts per million. This was well above the highest carbon dioxide concentration—no more than 300 parts per million—revealed in the 420,000–year–old ice-core record. By the time Congress drafted § 202(a)(1) in 1970, carbon dioxide levels had reached 325 parts per million.

In the late 1970's, the Federal Government began devoting serious attention to the possibility that carbon dioxide emissions associated with human activity could provoke climate change. In 1978, Congress enacted the National Climate Program Act, 92 Stat. 601, which required the President to establish a program to "assist the Nation and the world to understand and respond to natural and man-induced climate processes and their implications," id., § 3. President Carter, in turn, asked the National Research Council, the working arm of the National Academy of Sciences, to investigate the subject. The Council's response was unequivocal: "If carbon dioxide continues to increase, the study group finds no reason to doubt that climate changes will result and no reason to believe that these changes will be negligible.... A wait-and-see policy may mean waiting until it is too late."

Congress next addressed the issue in 1987, when it enacted the Global Climate Protection Act * * *. Finding that "manmade pollution—the release of carbon dioxide, chlorofluorocarbons, methane, and other trace gases into the atmosphere—may be producing a long-term and substantial increase in the average temperature on Earth,"

* * * Congress directed EPA to propose to Congress a "coordinated national policy on global climate change," § 1103(b), and ordered the Secretary of State to work "through the channels of multilateral diplomacy" and coordinate diplomatic efforts to combat global warming, § 1103(c). Congress emphasized that "ongoing pollution and deforestation may be contributing now to an irreversible process" and that "[n]ecessary actions must be identified and implemented in time to protect the climate." § 1102(4).

Meanwhile, the scientific understanding of climate change progressed. In 1990, the Intergovernmental Panel on Climate Change (IPCC), a multinational scientific body organized under the auspices of the United Nations, published its first comprehensive report on the topic. Drawing on expert opinions from across the globe, the IPCC concluded that "emissions resulting from human activities are substantially increasing the atmospheric concentrations of ... greenhouse gases [which] will enhance the greenhouse effect, resulting on average in an additional warming of the Earth's surface."

Responding to the IPCC report, the United Nations convened the "Earth Summit" in 1992 in Rio de Janeiro. The first President Bush attended and signed the United Nations Framework Convention on Climate Change(UNFCCC), a nonbinding agreement among 154 nations to reduce atmospheric concentrations of carbon dioxide and other greenhouse gases for the purpose of "prevent[ing] dangerous anthropogenic [i.e., human-induced] interference with the [Earth's] climate system." * * * The Senate unanimously ratified the treaty.

Some five years later—after the IPCC issued a second comprehensive report in 1995 concluding that "[t]he balance of evidence suggests there is a discernible human influence on global climate"— the UNFCCC signatories met in Kyoto, Japan, and adopted a protocol that assigned mandatory targets for industrialized nations to reduce greenhouse gas emissions. Because those targets did not apply to developing and heavily polluting nations such as China and India, the Senate unanimously passed a resolution expressing its sense that the United States should not enter into the Kyoto Protocol. * * *. President Clinton did not submit the protocol to the Senate for ratification.

* * *

VI

On the merits, the first question is whether § 202(a)(1) of the Clean Air Act authorizes EPA to regulate greenhouse gas emissions from new motor vehicles in the event that it forms a "judgment" that such emissions contribute to climate change. We have little trouble concluding that it does. In relevant part, § 202(a)(1) provides that EPA "shall by regulation prescribe ... standards applicable to the emission of any air pollutant from any class or classes of new motor vehicles or new motor vehicle engines, which in [the Administrator's] judgment cause, or contribute to, air pollution which may reasonably be anticipated to endanger public health or welfare." * * *. Because EPA believes that Congress did not intend it to regulate substances that contribute to climate change, the agency maintains that carbon dioxide is not an "air pollutant" within the meaning of the provision.

The statutory text forecloses EPA's reading. The Clean Air Act's sweeping definition of "air pollutant" includes "any air pollution agent or combination of such agents, including any physical, chemical ... substance or matter which is emitted into or otherwise enters the ambient air...." § 7602(g). On its face, the definition embraces all airborne compounds of whatever stripe, and underscores that intent through the repeated use of the word "any." Carbon dioxide, methane, nitrous oxide, and hydrofluorocarbons are without a doubt "physical [and] chemical ... substance[s] which [are] emitted into ... the ambient air." The statute is unambiguous.[3]

Rather than relying on statutory text, EPA invokes postenactment congressional actions and deliberations it views as tantamount to a congressional command to refrain from regulating greenhouse gas emissions. Even if such post enactment legislative history could shed light on the meaning of an otherwise-unambiguous statute, EPA never identifies any action remotely suggesting that Congress meant to curtail its power to treat greenhouse gases as air pollutants. That subsequent Congresses have eschewed enacting binding emissions limitations to combat global warming tells us nothing about what Congress meant when it amended § 202(a)(1) in 1970 and 1977. And unlike EPA, we have no difficulty reconciling Congress' various efforts to promote interagency collaboration and research to better understand climate change with the agency's pre-existing mandate to

---

3. In dissent, JUSTICE SCALIA maintains that because greenhouse gases permeate the world's atmosphere rather than a limited area near the earth's surface, EPA's exclusion of greenhouse gases from the category of air pollution "agent[s]" is entitled to deference under Chevron * * *EPA's distinction, however, finds no support in the text of the statute, which uses the phrase "the ambient air" without distinguishing between atmospheric layers. Moreover, it is a plainly unreasonable reading of a sweeping statutory provision designed to capture "any physical, chemical ... substance or matter which is emitted into or otherwise enters the ambient air." 42 U. S. C. § 7602(g). JUSTICE SCALIA does not (and cannot) explain why Congress would define "air pollutant" so carefully and so broadly, yet confer on EPA the authority to narrow that definition whenever expedient by asserting that a particular substance is not an "agent." At any rate, no party to this dispute contests that greenhouse gases both "ente[r] the ambient air" and tend to warm the atmosphere. They are therefore unquestionably "agent[s]" of air pollution.

regulate "any air pollutant" that may endanger the public welfare. * * * Collaboration and research do not conflict with any thoughtful regulatory effort; they complement it.

EPA's reliance on Brown & Williamson Tobacco Corp. is similarly misplaced. In holding that tobacco products are not "drugs" or "devices" subject to Food and Drug Administration (FDA) regulation pursuant to the Food, Drug and Cosmetic Act (FDCA) we found critical at least two considerations that have no counterpart in this case.

First, we thought it unlikely that Congress meant to ban tobacco products, which the FDCA would have required had such products been classified as "drugs" or "devices." Here, in contrast, EPA jurisdiction would lead to no such extreme measures. EPA would only regulate emissions, and even then, it would have to delay any action "to permit the development and application of the requisite technology, giving appropriate consideration to the cost of compliance," § 7521(a)(2). However much a ban on tobacco products clashed with the "common sense" intuition that Congress never meant to remove those products from circulation * * * there is nothing counterintuitive to the notion that EPA can curtail the emission of substances that are putting the global climate out of kilter.

Second, in Brown & Williamson we pointed to an unbroken series of congressional enactments that made sense only if adopted "against the backdrop of the FDA's consistent and repeated statements that it lacked authority under the FDCA to regulate tobacco." We can point to no such enactments here: EPA has not identified any congressional action that conflicts in any way with the regulation of greenhouse gases from new motor vehicles. Even if it had, Congress could not have acted against a regulatory "backdrop" of disclaimers of regulatory authority. Prior to the order that provoked this litigation, EPA had never disavowed the authority to regulate greenhouse gases, and in 1998 it in fact affirmed that it had such authority. * * * There is no reason, much less a compelling reason, to accept EPA's invitation to read ambiguity into a clear statute.

EPA finally argues that it cannot regulate carbon dioxide emissions from motor vehicles because doing so would require it to tighten mileage standards, a job (according to EPA) that Congress has assigned to [the Department of Transportation (DOT) under a different statute]. But that DOT sets mileage standards in no way licenses EPA to shirk its environmental responsibilities. EPA has been charged with protecting the public's "health" and "welfare," * * * a statutory obligation wholly independent of DOT's mandate to promote energy efficiency. * * * The two obligations may overlap, but there is no reason to think the two agencies cannot both administer their obligations and yet avoid inconsistency.

While the Congresses that drafted § 202(a)(1) might not have appreciated the possibility that burning fossil fuels could lead to global warming, they did understand that without regulatory flexibility, changing circumstances and scientific developments would soon render the Clean Air Act obsolete. The broad language of § 202(a)(1) reflects an intentional effort to confer the flexibility necessary to forestall such obsolescence. * * * Because greenhouse gases fit well within the Clean Air Act's capacious definition of "air pollutant," we hold that EPA has the statutory authority to regulate the emission of such gases from new motor vehicles.

VII

The alternative basis for EPA's decision—that even if it does have statutory authority to regulate greenhouse gases, it would be unwise to do so at this time—rests on reasoning divorced from the statutory text. While the statute does condition the exercise of EPA's authority on its formation of a "judgment," 42 U. S. C. § 7521(a)(1), that judgment must relate to whether an air pollutant "cause[s], or contribute[s] to, air pollution which may reasonably be anticipated to endanger public health or welfare," ibid. Put another way, the use of the word "judgment" is not a roving license to ignore the statutory text. It is but a direction to exercise discretion within defined statutory limits. If EPA makes a finding of endangerment, the Clean Air Act requires the agency to regulate emissions of the deleterious pollutant from new motor vehicles. Ibid. (stating that "[EPA] shall by regulation prescribe ... standards applicable to the emission of any air pollutant from any class of new motor vehicles"). EPA no doubt has significant latitude as to the manner, timing, content, and coordination of its regulations with those of other agencies. But once EPA has responded to a petition for rulemaking, its reasons for action or inaction must conform to the authorizing statute. Under the clear terms of the Clean Air Act, EPA can avoid taking further action only if it determines that greenhouse gases do not contribute to climate change or if it provides some reasonable explanation as to why it cannot or will not exercise its discretion to determine whether they do. Ibid. To the extent that this constrains agency discretion to pursue other priorities of the Administrator or the President, this is the congressional design.

EPA has refused to comply with this clear statutory command. Instead, it has offered a laundry list of reasons not to regulate. For example, EPA said that a number of voluntary executive branch programs already provide an effective response to the threat of global warming, 68 Fed. Reg. 52932, that regulating greenhouse gases might impair the President's ability to negotiate with "key developing nations" to reduce emissions, id., at 52931, and that curtailing motor-vehicle emissions would reflect "an inefficient, piecemeal approach to address the climate change issue," ibid.

Although we have neither the expertise nor the authority to evaluate these policy judgments, it is evident they have nothing to do with whether greenhouse gas emissions contribute to climate change. Still less do they amount to a reasoned justification for declining to form a scientific judgment. In particular, while the President has broad authority in foreign affairs, that authority does not extend to the refusal to execute domestic laws. In the Global Climate Protection Act of 1987, Congress authorized the State Department—not EPA—to formulate United States foreign policy with reference to environmental matters relating to climate. See § 1103(c), 101 Stat. 1409. EPA has made no showing that it issued the ruling in question here after consultation with the State Department. Congress did direct EPA to consult with other agencies in the formulation of its policies and rules, but the State Department is absent from that list. § 1103(b).

Nor can EPA avoid its statutory obligation by noting the uncertainty surrounding various features of climate change and concluding that it would therefore be better not to regulate at this time. See 68 Fed. Reg. 52930–52931. If the scientific uncertainty is so profound that it precludes EPA from making a reasoned judgment as to whether greenhouse gases contribute to global warming, EPA must say so. That EPA would prefer not to regulate greenhouse gases because of some residual uncertainty—which, contrary to JUSTICE SCALIA's apparent belief [referring to Justice Scalia's dissent] is in fact all that it said, see 68 Fed. Reg. 52929 ("We do not believe . . . that it would be either effective or appropriate for EPA to establish [greenhouse gas] standards for motor vehicles at this time" (emphasis added))—is irrelevant. The statutory question is whether sufficient information exists to make an endangerment finding.

In short, EPA has offered no reasoned explanation for its refusal to decide whether greenhouse gases cause or contribute to climate change. Its action was therefore "arbitrary, capricious, . . . or otherwise not in accordance with law." 42 U. S. C. § 7607(d)(9)(A). We need not and do not reach the question whether on remand EPA must make an endangerment finding, or whether policy concerns can inform EPA's actions in the event that it makes such a finding. We hold only that EPA must ground its reasons for action or inaction in the statute.

VIII

The judgment of the Court of Appeals is reversed, and the case is remanded for further proceedings consistent with this opinion.

JUSTICE SCALIA, with whom THE CHIEF JUSTICE, JUSTICE THOMAS, and JUSTICE ALITO join, dissenting.

I

A

* * * As the Court recognizes, the statute "condition[s] the exercise of EPA's authority on its formation of a 'judgment.' " * * *

There is no dispute that the Administrator has made no such judgment in this case. * * *

The question thus arises: Does anything require the Administrator to make a "judgment" whenever a petition for rulemaking is filed? Without citation of the statute or any other authority, the Court says yes. Why is that so? When Congress wishes to make private action force an agency's hand, it knows how to do so.* * * Where does the CAA say that the EPA Administrator is required to come to a decision on this question whenever a rulemaking petition is filed? The Court points to no such provision because none exists.

Instead, the Court invents a multiple-choice question that the EPA Administrator must answer when a petition for rulemaking is filed. The Administrator must exercise his judgment in one of three ways: (a) by concluding that the pollutant does cause, or contribute to, air pollution that endangers public welfare (in which case EPA is required to regulate); (b) by concluding that the pollutant does not cause, or contribute to, air pollution that endangers public welfare (in which case EPA is not required to regulate); or (c) by "provid[ing] some reasonable explanation as to why it cannot or will not exercise its discretion to determine whether" greenhouse gases endanger public welfare, ante, at 30, (in which case EPA is not required to regulate).

I am willing to assume, for the sake of argument, that the Administrator's discretion in this regard is not entirely unbounded—that if he has no reasonable basis for deferring judgment he must grasp the nettle at once. The Court, however, with no basis in text or precedent, rejects all of EPA's stated "policy judgments" as not "amount[ing] to a reasoned justification," * * * effectively narrowing the universe of potential reasonable bases to a single one: Judgment can be delayed only if the Administrator concludes that "the scientific uncertainty is [too] profound." * * * The Administrator is precluded from concluding for other reasons "that it would . . . be better not to regulate at this time." * * * Such other reasons—perfectly valid reasons—were set forth in the agency's statement.

"We do not believe . . . that it would be either effective or appropriate for EPA to establish [greenhouse gas] standards for motor vehicles at this time. As described in detail below, the President has laid out a comprehensive approach to climate change that calls for near-term voluntary actions and incentives along with programs aimed at reducing scientific uncertainties and encouraging technological development so that the government may effectively and efficiently address the climate change issue over the long term.

. . . . . "[E]stablishing [greenhouse gas] emission standard for U. S. motor vehicles at this time would . . . result in an inefficient, piecemeal approach to addressing the climate change issue. The U. S. motor vehicle fleet is one of many sources of [greenhouse gas] emissions both here and abroad, and different [greenhouse gas] emission sources face different technological and financial challenges in reducing emissions. A sensible regulatory scheme would require that all significant sources and sinks of [greenhouse gas] emissions be considered in deciding how best to achieve any needed emission reductions.

"Unilateral EPA regulation of motor vehicle [greenhouse gas] emissions could also weaken U. S. efforts to persuade developing countries to reduce the [greenhouse gas] intensity of their economies. Considering the large populations and growing economies of some developing countries, increases in their[greenhouse gas] emissions could quickly overwhelm the effects of [greenhouse gas] reduction measures in developed countries. Any potential benefit of EPA regulation could be lost to the extent other nations decided to let their emissions significantly increase in view of U. S. emissions reductions. Unavoidably, climate change raises important foreign policy issues, and it is the President's prerogative to address them." [excerpted from EPA's petition denial]

The Court dismisses this analysis as "rest[ing] on reasoning divorced from the statutory text." "While the statute does condition the exercise of EPA's authority on its formation of a 'judgment,' ... that judgment must relate to whether an air pollutant 'cause[s], o contribute[s] to, air pollution which may reasonably be anticipated to endanger public health or welfare.'" True but irrelevant. When the Administrator makes a judgment whether to regulate greenhouse gases, that judgment must relate to whether they are air pollutants that "cause, or contribute to, air pollution which may reasonably be anticipated to endanger public health or welfare." the statute says nothing at all about the reasons for which the Administrator may defer making a judgment—the permissible reasons for deciding not to grapple with the issue at the present time. Thus, the various "policy" rationales, * * * that the Court criticizes are not "divorced from the statutory text," except in the sense that the statutory text is silent, as texts are often silent about permissible reasons for the exercise of agency discretion. The reasons the EPA gave are surely considerations executive agencies regularly take into account (and ought to take into account) when deciding whether to consider entering a new field: the impact such entry would have on other Executive Branch programs and on foreign policy. There is no basis in law for the Court's imposed limitation.

EPA's interpretation of the discretion conferred by the statutory reference to "its judgment" is not only reasonable, it is the most natural reading of the text. The Court nowhere explains why this interpretation is incorrect, let alone why it is not entitled to deference under Chevron. As the Administrator acted within the law in declining to make a "judgment" for the policy reasons above set forth, I would uphold the decision to deny the rulemaking petition on that ground alone.

B

Even on the Court's own terms, however, the same conclusion follows. As mentioned above, the Court gives EPA the option of determining that the science is too uncertain to allow it to form a "judgment" as to whether greenhouse gases endanger public welfare. Attached to this option (on what basis is unclear) is an essay require- ment: "If," the Court says, "the scientific uncertainty is so profound that it precludes EPA from making a reasoned judgment as to whether greenhouse gases contribute to global warming, EPA must say so." But EPA has said precisely that—and at great length, based on information contained in a 2001 report by the National Research Council (NRC) entitled Climate Change Science: An Analysis of Some Key Questions:

"As the NRC noted in its report, concentrations of [greenhouse gases (GHGs)] are increasing in the atmosphere as a result of human activities (pp. 9–12). It also noted that '[a] diverse array of evidence points to a warming of global surface air temperatures' (p.16). The report goes on to state, however, that '[b]ecause of the large and still uncertain level of natural variability inherent in the climate record and the uncertainties in the time histories of the various forcing agents (and particularly aerosols), a [causal] linkage between the buildup of greenhouse gases in the atmosphere and the observed climate changes during the 20th century cannot be unequivocally established. The fact that the magnitude of the observed warming is large in comparison to natural variability as simulated in climate models is suggestive of such a linkage, but it does not constitute proof of one because the model simulations could be deficient in natural variability on the decadal to century time scale' (p. 17).

"The NRC also observed that 'there is considerable uncertainty in current understanding of how the climate system varies naturally and reacts to emissions of [GHGs] and aerosols' (p. 1). As a result of that uncertainty, the NRC cautioned that 'current estimate of the magnitude of future warming should be regarded as tentative and subject to future adjustments (either upward or downward).' Id. It further advised that '[r]educing the wide range of uncertainty inher- ent in current model predictions of global climate change will require major advances in understanding and modeling of both (1) the factors that determine atmospheric concentrations of [GHGs] and aerosols and (2) the so-called "feedbacks" that determine the sensitivity of the climate system to a prescribed increase in [GHGs].' Id.

"The science of climate change is extraordinarily complex and still evolving. Although there have been substantial advances in climate change science, there continue to be important uncertainties in our understanding of the factors that may affect future climate change and how it should be addressed. As the NRC explained, predicting future climate change necessarily involves a complex web of economic and physical factors including: Our ability to predict future global anthropogenic emissions of GHGs and aerosols; the fate of these emissions once they enter the atmosphere (e.g., what percentage are absorbed by vegetation or are taken up by the oceans); the impact of those emissions that remain in the atmosphere on the radiative properties of the atmosphere; changes in critically important climate feedbacks (e.g., changes in cloud cover and ocean circulation); changes in temperature characteristics (e.g., average temperatures, shifts in daytime and evening temperatures); changes in other climatic parameters (e.g., shifts in precipitation, storms); and ultimately the impact of such changes on human health and welfare (e.g., increases or decreases in agricultural productivity, human health impacts). The NRC noted, in particular, that '[t]he understanding of the relationships between weather/climate and human health is in its infancy and therefore the health consequences of climate change are poorly understood' (p. 20). Substantial scientific uncertainties limit our ability to assess each of these factors and to separate out those changes resulting from natural variability from those that are directly the result of increases in anthropogenic GHGs.

"Reducing the wide range of uncertainty inherent in current model predictions will require major advances in understanding and modeling of the factors that determine atmospheric concentrations of greenhouse gases and aerosols, and the processes that determine the sensitivity of the climate system." [excerpted from EPA's petition denial]

I simply cannot conceive of what else the Court would like EPA to say.

II

A

Even before reaching its discussion of the word "judgment," the Court makes another significant error when it concludes that "§ 202(a)(1) of the Clean Air Act authorizes EPA to regulate greenhouse gas emissions from new motor vehicles in the event that it forms a 'judgment' that such emissions contribute to climate change." Ante, at 25 (emphasis added). For such authorization, the Court relies on what it calls "the Clean Air Act's capacious definition of 'air pollutant.'"

"Air pollutant" is defined by the Act as "any air pollution agent or combination of such agents, including any physical, chemical, . . . substance or matter which is emitted into or otherwise enters the ambient air." 42 U. S. C. § 7602(g). The Court is correct that "[c]arbon dioxide, methane, nitrous oxide, and hydro fluorocarbons," * * * fit within the second half of that definition: They are "physical, chemical, . . . substance[s] or matter which [are] emitted into or otherwise ente[r] the ambient air." But the Court mistakenly believes this to be the end of the analysis. In order to be an "air pollutant" under the Act's definition, the "substance or matter [being] emitted into . . . the ambient air" must also meet the first half of the definition— namely, it must be an "air pollution agent or combination of such agents." The Court simply pretends this half of the definition does not exist.

The Court's analysis faithfully follows the argument advanced by petitioners, which focuses on the word "including" in the statutory definition of "air pollutant." As that argument goes, anything that follows the word "including" must necessarily be a subset of whatever precedes it. Thus, if greenhouse gases qualify under the phrase following the word "including," they must qualify under the phrase preceding it. Since greenhouse gases come within the capacious phrase "any physical, chemical, . . . substance or matter which is emitted into or otherwise enters the ambient air," they must also be "air pollution agent[s] or combination[s] of such agents," and there-fore meet the definition of "air pollutant[s]."

That is certainly one possible interpretation of the statutory definition. The word "including" can indeed indicate that what fol-lows will be an "illustrative" sampling of the general category that precedes the word. Often, however, the examples standing alone are broader than the general category, and must be viewed as limited in light of that category. The Government provides a helpful (and unanswered) example: "The phrase 'any American automobile, in-cluding any truck or minivan,' would not naturally be construed to encompass a foreign-manufactured [truck or] minivan." * * * The general principle enunciated—that the speaker is talking about Amer-ican automobiles—carries forward to the illustrative examples (trucks and minivans), and limits them accordingly, even though in isolation they are broader. Congress often uses the word "including" in this manner.

In short, the word "including" does not require the Court's (or the petitioners') result. It is perfectly reasonable to view the definition of "air pollutant" in its entirety: An air pollutant can be "any physical, chemical, . . . substance or matter which is emitted into or otherwise enters the ambient air," but only if it retains the general characteristic of being an "air pollution agent or combination of such agents." This is precisely the conclusion EPA reached: "[A] substance does not meet the CAA definition of 'air pollutant' simply because it is a 'physical, chemical, . . . substance or matter which is emitted into or otherwise enters the ambient air.' It must also be an 'air pollution agent.' " * * * Once again, in the face of textual ambiguity, the Court's application of Chevron deference to EPA's interpretation of the word "including" is nowhere to be found.[4]

---

4. Not only is EPA's interpretation reasonable, it is far more plausible than the Court's alternative. As the Court correctly points out, "all airborne compounds of whatever stripe," * * *

Evidently, the Court defers only to those reasonable interpretations that it favors.

B

Using (as we ought to) EPA's interpretation of the definition of "air pollutant," we must next determine whether greenhouse gases are "agent[s]" of "air pollution." If so, the statute would authorize regulation; if not, EPA would lack authority.

Unlike "air pollutants," the term "air pollution" is not itself defined by the CAA; thus, once again we must accept EPA's interpretation of that ambiguous term, provided its interpretation is a "permissible construction of the statute." [citing Chevron] In this case, the petition for rulemaking asked EPA for "regulation of [greenhouse gas] emissions from motor vehicles to reduce the risk of global climate change." Thus, in deciding whether it had authority to regulate, EPA had to determine whether the concentration of greenhouse gases assertedly responsible for "global climate change" qualifies as "air pollution." EPA began with the commonsense observation that the "[p]roblems associated with atmospheric concentrations of CO2," * * * bear little resemblance to what would naturally be termed "air pollution" [and that EPA's prior use of the CAA's general regulatory provisions address air pollution problems that occur primarily at ground level or near the surface of the earth].

In other words, regulating the buildup of CO2 and other greenhouse gases in the upper reaches of the atmosphere, which is alleged to be causing global climate change, is no taking to regulating the concentration of some substance that is polluting the air.

We need look no further than the dictionary for confirmation that this interpretation of "air pollution" is eminently reasonable. The definition of "pollute," of course, is "[t]o make or render impure or unclean." Webster's New International Dictionary 1910 (2d ed. 1949). And the first three definitions of "air" are as follows: (1) "[t]he invisible, odorless, and tasteless mixture of gases which surrounds the earth"; (2) "[t]he body of the earth's atmosphere; esp., the part of it near the earth, as distinguished from the upper rarefied part"; (3) "[a] portion of air or of the air considered with respect to physical characteristics or as affecting the senses." EPA's conception of "air pollution"—focusing on impurities in the "ambient air" "at ground level or near the surface of the earth"—is perfectly consistent with the natural meaning of that term.

In the end, EPA concluded that since "CAA authorization to regulate is generally based on a finding that an air pollutant causes or contributes to air pollution," the concentrations of CO2 and other

---

would qualify as "physical, chemical, . . . substance[s] or matter which [are] emitted into or otherwise ente[r] the ambient air," * * *. It follows that everything airborne, from Frisbees to flatulence, qualifies as an "air pollutant." This reading of the statute defies common sense.

greenhouse gases allegedly affecting the global climate are beyond the scope of CAA's authorization to regulate. "[T]he term 'air pollution' as used in the regulatory provisions cannot be interpreted to encompass global climate change." Once again, the Court utterly fails to explain why this interpretation is incorrect, let alone so unreasonable as to be unworthy of Chevron deference.

The Court's alarm over global warming may or may not be justified, but it ought not distort the outcome of this litigation. This is a straightforward administrative-law case, in which Congress has passed a malleable statute giving broad discretion, not to us but to an executive agency. No matter how important the underlying policy issues at stake, this Court has no business substituting its own desired outcome for the reasoned judgment of the responsible agency.

NOTES

1. After a long and protracted battle, the EPA issued an endangerment finding in April, 2009 holding that greenhouse gas emissions in the atmosphere threaten the public health and welfare "of current and future generations." U.S. Environmental Protection Agency, *Overview of EPA's Proposed Endangerment and Cause or Contribute Findings for Greenhouse Gases Under the Clean Air Act*, (April 17, 2009). Does the endangerment finding mean that the EPA will now be required, under *NRDC v. Train*, to list carbon dioxide and other greenhouse gas emissions as a criteria pollutant under Section 108(a)(1)?

2. The EPA's endangerment finding could have enormous implications for the regulation of greenhouse gas emissions. As you read through the remainder of this Chapter we will address some of the ways in which the Act may be used for climate change regulation. Is the Clean Air Act well suited to regulate greenhouse gas emissions? If greenhouse gas emissions are listed as criteria pollutants, what levels should the EPA determine are an appropriate air standard? Does it matter that the U.S. cannot, on its own, reduce greenhouse gas emissions dramatically enough to solve the problem of global climate change?

For an argument that at least parts of the Clean Air Act work well for addressing climate change, *see* Holly Doremus and W. Michael Hanemann, *Of Babies and Bathwater: Why the Clean Air Act's Cooperative Federalism Framework is Useful for Addressing Global Warming*, 50 ARIZONA L. REV. 799 (2008).

3. On the question of whether *MA v. EPA* is a "straightforward administrative law case," as the Chief Justice suggests, see Jody Freeman and Adrian Vermeule, MA v. EPA: *From Politics to Expertise*, 2007 S. CT. Rev. 51 (2008). The authors argue that the decision has significant implications for administrative law, primarily because it makes agency refusals to make threshold findings that would trigger regulation ("decisions not to decide") reviewable on the same terms as affirmative decisions to regulate. The result is that a category of agency decisionmaking that once enjoyed all the benefits of "inaction" is treated as if it were "action" and subjected to review. In this

sense, the authors claim, the case is not *SCRAP*, for a new generation (as the Chief Justice noted in his dissent when decrying the grant of standing and referring to SCRAP as the highwater mark of liberal standing cases); it is instead, *State Farm* for a new generation—*State Farm* being the case in which the Court first decided that even *de*-regulatory decisions by agencies attract "hard look" arbitrary and capricious review, just like affirmative regulatory decisions. *Id.* at 98. This has potentially important implications for environmental law, since many suits involve plaintiff challenges to government failures to act, and these suits have historically been unsuccessful. See e.g. *Norton v. Southern Utah Wilderness Alliance*, 542 U.S. 55 (2004). *See also,* Lisa Bressman, Judicial Review of Agency Inaction: An Arbitrariness Approach, 79 NYU L. Rev. 1657 (2004) (arguing for revision of the Court's nonreviewability doctrine for inaction cases).

4. Is *MA v. EPA* consistent with *FDA v. Brown & Williamson*? In that case, the Food, Drug and Cosmetics Act (FDCA) defined a "drug" as "any article (other than food) intended to affect the structure or any function of the human body." At least facially, nicotine surely met that definition. Yet in interpreting the FDCA, the Court emphasized a canon of construction that statutes should not be construed to give agencies authority over questions of great "economic and political" significance unless Congress has spoken clearly (known as the "major questions" canon). Scholars have referred to this outcome as "democracy-forcing" because it sends the matter back to democratically elected officials for a clear statement. The EPA was arguably in a far stronger position than was the FDA in *Brown & Williamson*: both *Chevron* and the "major questions" canon pulled in the same direction, toward deference to the agency. Yet the Court did not engage in democracy-forcing in *MA v. EPA*. It did not defer to the EPA, which would have required Congress to more clearly authorize GHG regulation if it wanted the EPA to act. How can you reconcile the two cases? Was there a relevant difference in congressional activity in the two fields of tobacco regulation and climate change? Or was *Brown & Williamson* simply an aberrational case, involving an ad hoc doctrinal move that turned out to have no traction? Was *Brown v. Williamson* "democracy forcing" or simply "industry protecting"? After *MA v. EPA*, has *Brown v. Williamson* been limited to its facts (that is, overruled in all but name)?

1. STATE IMPLEMENTATION PLANS

Section 110 of the CAA assigns to states the responsibility for devising implementation plans that will achieve the federal NAAQS. The SIP process is onerous. In developing a SIP, states must first determine the extent to which air quality in the state's air quality regions violates the NAAQS. It must then calculate the emissions reductions necessary to achieve compliance with NAAQS and, finally, it must allocate the reductions among the sources of emissions. This final step requires knowing something about the emissions currently produced by the variety of stationary sources in the state, and predicting what the technological and economic impact of imposing reductions on them would likely be. States must also take into account the contributions that mobile sources make to the failure to meet NAAQS. Though the contribution of mobile sources to air pollution can be substantial, states are severely restricted in their ability to regulate these sources. For example, under the mobile source provisions of the law, emissions standards for automobiles are set by Congress, with a secondary role given to the EPA. Only California may, with an EPA waiver, adopt stricter standards, and other states may adopt California standards.

Even after the 1990 amendments, the SIP process remains central to the Act's structure, but it has been significantly supplemented by a variety of other provisions (including those applicable to PSD and nonattainment areas) that limit the states' discretion and impose additional burdens directly on stationary sources.

Section 110(a)(2) establishes minimum requirements for SIPs. Among other things, SIPs must:

(A) include enforceable emission limitations and other control measures, means or techniques (including economic incentives such as fees, marketable permits, and auctions of emissions rights) * * * as may be necessary or appropriate to meet the applicable requirements of this Act;

(B) provide for the establishment and operation of appropriate devices, methods, systems, and procedures necessary to—

(i) monitor, compile, and analyze data on ambient air quality, and

(ii) upon request, make such data available to the Administrator;

(C) include a program to provide for the enforcement of the measures described in subparagraph A * * * including a permit program as required by parts C and D [the PSD and nonattainment provisions of the Act]

(D) contain adequate provisions—

(i) prohibiting * * * any source or other type of emissions activity within the State from emitting any air pollutant in amounts which will—

(I) contribute significantly to nonattainment in, or interfere with maintenance by, any other State with respect to any such national primary or secondary ambient air quality standard

(E) provide (i) necessary assurances that the State * * * will have adequate personnel, funding, and authority * * * to carry out such implementation plan

Section 110(a) also requires states to revise plans as may be necessary, impose a variety of monitoring and record-keeping requirements on stationary sources, and perform air quality modeling.

Section 110(k) requires the EPA to establish criteria for plan completeness, determine whether those criteria have been met, and approve plans that meet all the applicable requirements. The EPA may call for plan revisions whenever "the Administrator finds that the applicable implementation plan for any area is substantially inadequate to attain or maintain the relevant national ambient air quality standard, to mitigate adequately the interstate pollutant transport * * *, or to otherwise comply with any requirement of this chapter" [§ 110(k)(5)].

If a state fails to submit a plan to the EPA, or if the EPA determines that the plan does not meet the minimum statutory criteria, and the state does not correct the deficiency, the EPA must promulgate a federal implementation plan [§ 110(c)].

The cases below establish the basic principle that the EPA must approve a state plan if it will attain the NAAQS. The agency may not reject a plan because it is weaker than the agency thinks feasible or less rigorous than a previous state plan. Nor may it reject a plan because it is too stringent to be economically or technologically feasible. Thus, so long as the national standards are met, the state may use any mix of controls it wishes, no matter how lax or how strict.

UNION ELECTRIC CO. v. EPA

Supreme Court of the United States, 1976.
427 U.S. 246, 96 S.Ct. 2518, 49 L.Ed.2d 474.

JUSTICE MARSHALL delivered the opinion of the Court.

After the Administrator of the Environmental Protection Agency (EPA) approves a state implementation plan under the Clean Air Act, the plan may be challenged in a court of appeals within 30 days, or after 30 days have run if newly discovered or available information justifies subsequent review. We must decide whether the operator of a regulated emission source, in a petition for review of an EPA-approved state plan filed after the original 30–day appeal period, can raise the claim that it is economically or technologically infeasible to comply with the plan. * * *

Petitioner is an electric utility company servicing the St. Louis metropolitan area, large portions of Missouri, and parts of Illinois and Iowa. Its three coal-fired generating plants in the metropolitan St. Louis area are subject to the sulfur dioxide restrictions in the Missouri implementation plan. Petitioner did not seek review of the Administrator's approval of the plan within 30 days, as it was entitled to do under § 307(b)(1) of the Act, * * * but rather applied to the appropriate state and county agencies for variances from the emission limitations affecting its three plants. Petitioner received one-year variances, which could be extended upon reapplication. The variances on two of petitioner's three plants had expired and petitioner was applying for extensions when, on May 31, 1974, the Administrator notified petitioner that sulfur dioxide emissions from its plants violated the emission limitations contained in the Missouri plan. Shortly thereafter petitioner filed a petition in the

Court of Appeals for the Eighth Circuit for review of the Administrator's 1972 approval of the Missouri implementation plan.

Section 307(b)(1) allows petitions for review to be filed in an appropriate court of appeals more than 30 days after the Administrator's approval of an implementation plan only if the petition is "based solely on grounds arising after such 30th day." Petitioner claimed to meet this requirement by asserting, *inter alia,* that various economic and technological difficulties had arisen more than 30 days after the Administrator's approval and that these difficulties made compliance with the emission limitations impossible. * * *

We reject at the outset petitioner's suggestion that a claim of economic or technological infeasibility may be considered upon a petition for review based on new information and filed more than 30 days after approval of an implementation plan even if such a claim could not be considered by the Administrator in approving a plan or by a court in reviewing a plan challenged within the original 30–day appeal period. * * * Regardless of when a petition for review is filed under § 307(b)(1), the court is limited to reviewing "the Administrator's action in approving * * * [the] implementation plan * * *." Accordingly, if new "grounds" are alleged, they must be such that, had they been known at the time the plan was presented to the Administrator for approval, it would have been an abuse of discretion for the Administrator to approve the plan. To hold otherwise would be to transfer a substantial responsibility in administering the Clean Air Act from the Administrator and the state agencies to the federal courts.

Since a reviewing court—regardless of when the petition for review is filed—may consider claims of economic and technological infeasibility only if the Administrator may consider such claims in approving or rejecting a state implementation plan, we must address ourselves to the scope of the Administrator's responsibility. The Administrator's position is that he has no power whatsoever to reject a state implementation plan on the ground that it is economically or technologically infeasible, and we have previously accorded great deference to the Administrator's construction of the Clean Air Act. After surveying the relevant provisions of the Clean Air Act Amendments of 1970 and their legislative history, we agree that Congress intended claims of economic and technological infeasibility to be wholly foreign to the Administrator's consideration of a state implementation plan.

As we have previously recognized, the 1970 Amendments to the Clean Air Act were a drastic remedy to what was perceived as a serious and otherwise uncheckable problem of air pollution. The Amendments place the primary responsibility for formulating pollution control strategies on the States, but nonetheless subject the States to strict minimum compliance requirements. These requirements are of a "technology-forcing character," * * * and are expressly designed to force regulated sources to develop pollution control devices that might at the time appear to be economically or technologically infeasible.

This approach is apparent on the face of § 110(a)(2). The provision sets out eight criteria that an implementation plan must satisfy, and provides that if these criteria are met and if the plan was adopted after reasonable notice and hearing, the Administrator "shall approve" the proposed state plan. The mandatory "shall" makes it quite clear that the Administrator is not to be concerned with factors other than those specified, and none of the eight factors appears to permit consideration of technological or economic infeasibility. * * *

In sum, we have concluded that claims of economic or technological infeasibility may not be considered by the Administrator in evaluating a state requirement that primary ambient air quality standards be met in the mandatory three years. And, since we further conclude that the States may submit implementation plans more stringent than federal law requires and that the Administrator must approve such plans if they meet the minimum requirements of § 110(a)(2), it follows that the language of § 110(a)(2)(A) provides no basis for the Administrator ever to reject a state implementation plan on the ground that it is economically or technologically infeasible. Accordingly, a court of appeals reviewing an approved plan under § 307(b)(1) cannot set it aside on those grounds, no matter when they are raised.

Some cases where econ./tech. feasibility can be raised

Our conclusion is bolstered by recognition that the Amendments do allow claims of technological and economic infeasibility to be raised in situations where consideration of such claims will not substantially interfere with the primary congressional purpose of prompt attainment of the national air quality standards. Thus, we do not hold that claims of infeasibility are never of relevance in the formulation of an implementation plan or that sources unable to comply with emission limitations must inevitably be shut down.

Perhaps the most important forum for consideration of claims of economic and technological infeasibility is before the state agency formulating the implementation plan. So long as the national standards are met, the State may select whatever mix of control devices it desires, and industries with particular economic or technological problems may seek special treatment in the plan itself. Moreover, if the industry is not exempted from, or accommodated by, the original plan, it may obtain a variance, as petitioner did in this case; and the variance, if granted after notice and a hearing, may be submitted to the EPA as a revision of the plan. Lastly, an industry denied an exemption from the implementation plan, or denied a subsequent variance, may be able to take its claims of economic or technological infeasibility to the state courts. * * *

* * * Congress plainly left with the States, so long as the national standards were met, the power to determine which sources would be burdened by regulation and to what extent. Technology forcing is a concept somewhat new to our national experience and it necessarily

entails certain risks. But Congress considered those risks in passing the 1970 Amendments and decided that the dangers posed by uncontrolled air pollution made them worth taking. Petitioner's theory would render that considered legislative judgment a nullity, and that is a result we refuse to reach.

NOTE

The opinion stresses that there are several points in the SIP regulatory process, at both federal and state levels, where problems of economic and technological infeasibility may properly be considered. Among the most important adjustment mechanisms are variances, exemptions, and enforcement orders. *See, e.g.*, section 118 (exemptions for federal facilities); section 113 (d) (enforcement orders); and section 110(f) and (g) (temporary energy or economic authority). Are there any limits to such exceptions, however? *See* section 110(a)(3)(C). The Supreme Court recently affirmed that a state does not have unlimited discretion in implementing the Clean Air Act, especially if it attempts to exploit flexibility in mechanisms that are traditionally the prerogative of the EPA. *See Alaska Dep't of Envtl. Conservation* v. *EPA*, 540 U.S. 461 (2004) (holding that the EPA has authority to ascertain reasonableness of state agency's determination of Best Achievable Control Technology).

places where feasibility may be considered

Union Electric holds that considerations of feasibility do not justify overturning a SIP as too burdensome. The case below explores the EPA's flexibility to disapprove a SIP that grants variances when the SIP would otherwise meet applicable statutory requirements.

TRAIN v. NATURAL RESOURCES DEFENSE COUNCIL, INC.

Supreme Court of the United States, 1975.
421 U.S. 60, 95 S.Ct. 1470, 43 L.Ed.2d 731.

JUSTICE REHNQUIST delivered the opinion of the Court.

No one can doubt that Congress imposed upon the Agency and States a comprehensive planning task of the first magnitude which was to be accomplished in a relatively short time. In the case of the States, it was soon realized that in order to develop the requisite plans within the statutory nine-month deadline, efforts would have to be focused on determining the stringent emission limitations necessary to comply with national standards. This was true even though compliance with the standards would not be necessary until the attainment date, which normally would be three years after Agency approval of a plan. The issue then arose as to how these stringent limitations, which often could not be satisfied without substantial research and investment, should be applied during the period prior to that date.

One approach was that adopted by Florida, under which the plan's emission limitations would not take effect until the attainment date. Under this approach, no source is subject to enforcement actions during the preattainment period, but all are put on notice of the limitations with which they must eventually comply. * * *

Georgia chose the Agency's preferred approach. Its plan provided for immediately effective categorical emission limitations, but also incorporated a variance procedure whereby particular sources could obtain individually tailored relief from general requirements. This variance provision was one of the bases upon which the Agency's approval of the Georgia plan was successfully challenged by respondents in the Court of Appeals. It is the only aspect of that court's decision as to which the Agency petitioned for certiorari.

The Agency's approval of Georgia's variance provision was based on its interpretation of § 110(a)(3), which provides that the Agency shall approve any revision of an implementation plan which meets the § 110(a)(2) requirements applicable to an original plan. The Agency concluded that § 110(a)(3) permits a State to grant individual variances from generally applicable emission standards, both before and after the attainment date, so long as the variance does not cause the plan to fail to comply with the requirements of § 110(a)(2). * * *

* * * [The position of respondent NRDC and] individual respondents who reside in affected air quality control regions within the State of Georgia, is that variances applicable to individual sources may be approved only if they meet the stringent procedural and substantive standards of § 110(f). This section permits one-year postponements of any requirement of a plan, subject to conditions which will be discussed below. * * *

* * * Since a variance would normally implicate only the § 110(a)(2)(A) requirement that plans provide for attainment and maintenance of national ambient air standards, treatment as revisions would result in variances being readily approved in two situations: first, where the variance does not defer compliance beyond the attainment date; and second, where the national standards have been attained and the variance is not so great that a plan incorporating it could not insure their continued maintenance. Moreover, a § 110(a)(3) revision may be granted on the basis of hearings conducted by the State, whereas a § 110(f) postponement is available only after the Agency itself conducts hearings.

There is thus considerable practical importance attached to the issue of whether variances are to be treated as revisions or as postponements * * *. This practical importance reaches not merely the operator of a particular source who believes that circumstances justify his receiving a variance from categorical limitations. It also reaches the broader issue of whether Congress intended the States to retain any significant degree of control of the manner in which they attain and maintain national standards, at least once their initial plans have been approved * * *. To explain our conclusion as to Congress' intent, it is necessary that we consider the revision and postponement sections in the context of other provisions of the amended Clean Air Act, particularly those which distinguish between national ambient air standards and emission limitations. * * *

The Agency is plainly charged by the Act with the responsibility for setting the national ambient air standards. Just as plainly, however, it is relegated by the Act to a secondary role in the process of determining and enforcing the specific, source-by-source emission limitations which are necessary if the national standards it has set are to be met. Under § 110(a)(2), the agency is *required* to approve a state plan which provides for the timely attainment and subsequent maintenance of ambient air standards, and which also satisfies that section's other general requirements. The Act gives the Agency no authority to question the wisdom of a State's choices of emission limitations if they are part of a plan which satisfies the standards of § 110(a)(2), and the Agency may devise and promulgate a specific plan of its own only if a State fails to submit an implementation plan which satisfies those standards. § 110(c). Thus, so long as the ultimate effect of a State's choice of emission limitations is in compliance with the national standards for ambient air, the State is at liberty to adopt whatever mix of emission limitations it deems best suited to its particular situation.

This analysis of the Act's division of responsibilities is not challenged by respondents insofar as it concerns the process of devising and promulgating an initial implementation plan. Respondents do, however, deny that the States have such latitude once the initial plan is approved. Yet the third paragraph of § 110(a), and the one immediately following the paragraphs which specify that States shall file implementation plans and that the Agency shall approve them if they satisfy certain broad criteria, is the section which *requires* the Agency to "approve any revision of an implementation plan" if it "determines that it meets the requirements" of § 110(a)(2). On its face, this provision applies to *any* revision, without regard either to its breadth of applicability, or to whether it is to be effective before or after the attainment date; rather, Agency approval is subject only to the condition that the revised plan satisfy the general requirements applicable to original implementation plans. Far from evincing congressional intent that the Agency assume control of a State's emission limitations mix once its initial plan is approved, the revision section is to all appearances the mechanism by which the States may obtain approval of their developing policy choices as to the most practicable and desirable methods of restricting total emissions to a level which is consistent with the national ambient air standards.

In order to challenge this characterization of § 110(a)(3), respondents principally rely on the contention that the postponement provision, § 110(f), is the only mechanism by which exceptions to a plan's requirements may be obtained, under any circumstances. Were this an accurate description of § 110(f), we would agree that the revision authority does not have the broad application asserted by the Agency. Like the Ninth Circuit, however, we believe that § 110(f) serves a function different from that of supervising state efforts to modify the initial mix of emission limitations by which they implement national standards.

In our view, § 110(f) is a safety valve by which may be accorded, under certain carefully specified circumstances, exceptions to the national standards themselves. That this is its role is strongly suggested by the process by which it became a part of the Clean Air Act. [The Court analyzed legislative history and other portions of the Act supporting its interpretation.]

* * *

We believe * * * that Congress, consistent with its declaration that, "Each State shall have the primary responsibility for assuring air quality" within its boundaries, § 107(a), left to the States considerable latitude in determining specifically how the standards would be met. This discretion includes the continuing authority to revise choices about the mix of emission limitations. We therefore conclude that the Agency's interpretation of §§ 110(a)(3) and 110(f) was "correct," to the extent that it can be said with complete assurance that any particular interpretation of a complex statute such as this is the "correct" one. * * *

NOTES

1. Section 116 authorizes states, with a few limitations, to regulate air pollution more stringently than required under the CAA. Is it fair to say, therefore, that although Congress has "federalized" environmental law by passing regulatory statutes, states still enjoy considerable flexibility to regulate air pollution?

2. Because *Train* requires that a variance (in the form of a "plan revision") result in NAAQS compliance (or at least a move in that direction), these variances are theoretically unavailable in nonattainment areas. Nevertheless, in response to heavy demand from industry, states continue to issue such "variances" in large numbers, even though they are invalid under federal law. Only occasionally does the EPA exercise its power to enforce the SIP in these circumstances. For a fuller explanation, and two interesting case studies, *see* Marc Melnick & Elizabeth Willes, *Watching the Candy Store: EPA Overfiling in Local Air Pollution Variances*, 20 ECOLOGY L.Q. 207 (1993).

In addition to granting variances to ease the burden on stationary sources that have a difficult time complying with emission limits, states may also resort to creative calculations in order to ease regulatory burdens. Consider Virginia's use of its discretion in the case below, to conclude that new sources of pollution will result in no net increase in pollution.

CITIZENS AGAINST THE REFINERY'S EFFECTS, INC. v. EPA

United States Court of Appeals, Fourth Circuit, 1981.
643 F.2d 183.

HALL, CIRCUIT JUDGE.

Citizens Against the Refinery's Effects (CARE) appeals from a final ruling by the Administrator of the Environmental Protection Agency (EPA) approving the Virginia State Implementation Plan (SIP) for reducing hydrocarbon pollutants. The plan requires the Virginia Highway Department to decrease usage of a certain type of asphalt, thereby reducing hydrocarbon pollution by more than enough to offset expected pollution from the Hampton Roads Energy Company's (HREC) proposed refinery. We affirm the action of the administrator in approving the state plan.

The Clean Air Act establishes National Ambient Air Quality Standards (NAAQS) for five major air pollutants. 42 U.S.C. § 7409. The EPA has divided each state into Air Quality Control Regions (AQCR) and monitors each region to assure that the national standard for each pollutant is met. 42 U.S.C. § 7407. Where the standard has not been attained for a certain pollutant, the state must develop a State Implementation Plan designed to bring the area into attainment within a certain period. 42 U.S.C. § 7410. In addition, no new source of that pollutant may be constructed until the standard is attained. 40 CFR § 51.18 (1973).

The Clean Air Act created a no-growth environment in areas where the clean air requirements had not been attained. EPA recognized the need to develop a program that encouraged attainment of clean air standards without discouraging economic growth. Thus the agency proposed an Interpretive Ruling in 1976 which allowed the states to develop an "offset program" within the State Implementation Plans. The offset program, later codified by Congress in the 1977 Amendments to the Clean Air Act, permits the states to develop plans which allow construction of new pollution sources where accompanied by a corresponding reduction in an existing pollution source. 42 U.S.C. § 7502(b)(6) and § 7503. In effect, a new emitting facility can be built if an existing pollution source decreases its emissions or ceases operations as long as a positive net air quality benefit occurs.

If the proposed factory will emit carbon monoxide, sulfur dioxide, or particulates, the EPA requires that the offsetting pollution source be within the immediate vicinity of the new plant. The other two pollutants, hydrocarbons and nitrogen oxide, are less "site-specific," and thus the ruling permits the offsetting source to locate anywhere within a broad vicinity of the new source.

The offset program has two other important requirements. First, a base time period must be determined in which to calculate how much reduction is needed in existing pollutants to offset the new source. This base period is defined as the first year of the SIP or, where the state has not yet developed a SIP, as the year in which a construction permit application is filed. Second, the offset program requires that the new source adopt the Lowest Achievable Emissions Rate (LAER) using the most modern technology available in the industry.

HREC proposes to build a petroleum refinery and offloading facility in Portsmouth, Virginia. Portsmouth has been unable to reduce air pollution enough to attain the national standard for one pollutant, photochemical oxidants, which is created when hydrocarbons are released into the atmosphere and react with other substances. Since a refinery is a major source of hydrocarbons, the Clean Air Act prevents construction of the HREC plant until the area attains the national standard.

In 1975, HREC applied to the Virginia State Air Pollution Control Board (VSAPCB) for a refinery construction permit. * * * The VSAPCB, in an effort to help HREC meet the clean air requirements, proposed to use the offset ruling to comply with the Clean Air Act.

On November 28, 1977, the VSAPCB submitted a State Implementation Plan to EPA which included the HREC permit. The Virginia Board proposed to offset the new HREC hydrocarbon pollution by reducing the amount of cutback asphalt used for road paving operations in three highway districts by the Virginia Department of Highways. By switching from "cutback" to "emulsified" asphalt, the state can reduce hydrocarbon pollutants by the amount necessary to offset the pollutants from the proposed refinery.

Notices of the proposed plan were published * * *. Numerous comments were received, including several from CARE. The EPA administrator carefully considered the comments and approved the Virginia offset plan on January 31, 1980.

CARE raises four issues regarding the state plan. First, they argue that the geographic area used as the base for the offset was arbitrarily determined and that the area as defined violates the regulations. Second, CARE contends that EPA should have used 1975 instead of 1977 as the base year to compare usage of cutback asphalt. Third, CARE insists that the offset plan should have been disapproved since the state is voluntarily reducing usage of cutback asphalt anyway. Fourth, CARE questions the approval of the plan without definite Lowest Achievable Emissions Rates (LAER) as required by the statute. We reject the CARE challenges to the state plan.

CARE contends that the state plan should not have been approved by EPA since the three highway-district area where cutback usage will be reduced to offset refinery emissions was artificially developed by the state. The ruling permits a broad area (usually within one AQCR) to be used as the offset basis.

The ruling does not specify how to determine the area, nor provide a standard procedure for defining the geographic area. Here the Virginia Board originally proposed to use four highway districts comprising one-half the state as the offset area. When this was found to be much more than necessary to offset pollution expected from the refinery, the state changed it to one highway district plus nine additional counties. Later the proposed plan was again revised to include a geographic area of three highway districts.

The agency action in approving the use of three highway districts was neither arbitrary, capricious, nor outside the statute. First, Congress intended that the states and the EPA be given flexibility in designing and implementing SIPs. Such flexibility allows the states to make reasoned choices as to which areas may be used to offset new pollution and how the plan is to be implemented. Second, the offset program was initiated to encourage economic growth in the state. Thus a state plan designed to reduce highway department pollution in order to attract another industry is a reasonable contribution to economic growth without a corresponding increase in pollution. Third, to be sensibly administered the offset plan had to be divided into districts which could be monitored by the highway department. Use of any areas other than highway districts would be unwieldy and difficult to administer. Fourth, the scientific understanding of ozone pollution is not advanced to the point where exact air transport may be predicted. Designation of the broad area in which hydrocarbons may be transported is well within the discretion and expertise of the agency.

Asphalt consumption varies greatly from year to year, depending upon weather and road conditions. Yet EPA must accurately determine the volume of hydrocarbon emissions from cutback asphalt. Only then can the agency determine whether the reduction in cutback usage will result in an offset great enough to account for the new refinery pollution. To calculate consumption of a material where it constantly varies, a base year must be selected. In this case, EPA's Interpretive Ruling establishes the base year as the year in which the permit application is made. EPA decided that 1977 was an acceptable base year. CARE argues that EPA illegally chose 1977 instead of 1975.

Considering all of the circumstances, including the unusually high asphalt consumption in 1977, the selection by EPA of that as the base year was within the discretion of the agency. Since the EPA Interpretive Ruling allowing the offset was not issued until 1976, 1977 was the first year after the offset ruling and the logical base year in which to calculate the offset. Also, the permit issued by the VSAPCB was reissued in 1977 with extensive additions and revisions after a full hearing. Under these circumstances, 1977 appears to be a logical choice of a base year.

For several years, Virginia has pursued a policy of shifting from cutback asphalt to the less expensive emulsified asphalt in road-paving operations. The policy was initiated in an effort to save money, and was totally unrelated to a State Implementation Plan. Because of this policy, CARE argues that hydrocarbon emissions were decreasing independent of this SIP and therefore are not a proper offset against the refinery. They argue that there is not, in effect, an actual reduction in pollution.

The Virginia voluntary plan is not enforceable and therefore is not in compliance with the 1976 Interpretive Ruling which requires that the offset program be enforceable. The EPA, in approving the state plan, obtained a letter from the Deputy Attorney General of Virginia in which he stated that the requisites had been satisfied for establishing and enforcing the plan with the Department of Highways. Without such authority, no decrease in asphalt-produced pollution is guaranteed. In contrast to the voluntary plan, the offset plan guarantees a reduction in pollution resulting from road-paving operations.

[The Court then deferred to the EPA's calculation of Lowest Achievable Emission Rate.]

CONCLUSION

In approving the state plan, EPA thoroughly examined the data, requested changes in the plan, and approved the plan only after the changes were made. There is no indication that the agency acted in an arbitrary or capricious manner or that it stepped beyond the bounds of the Clean Air Act. We affirm the decision of the administrator in approving the state plan.

NOTES

1. One might get the impression from reading section 110 of the CAA, and from the cases above, that a SIP is a single, coherent document filed on one occasion by the state and reviewed by the EPA in one, or a few, sittings. SIPs are not that simple, however. Like the legendary Loch Ness Monster, SIPs may exist, but people rarely get more than a glimpse of them. One EPA administrator put it this way: "I don't even think I can lift this, but I will try. The box is full. The box is simply the 1979 amendment to the Illinois SIP. We couldn't bring the whole SIP. Nobody could read the whole SIP. Nobody even knows what is in one at this point." When the same administrator was asked how many boxes it would take to carry the SIP from California, he replied, "They would measure it in truckloads." JOHN-MARK STENSVAAG & CRAIG N. OREN, CLEAN AIR ACT: LAW AND PRACTICE 14-4 to 14-5 (1990).

A SIP is best thought of as a collection of regulations, instruments, and measures that a state adopts over time and submits sequentially to the EPA for approval. When considered together as a package, these measures must assure the EPA that the state will make progress toward, and ultimately achieve, compliance with NAAQS by deadlines established in the Act. The SIP process is technically complex, disjointed, and hard to follow, even for experts. Part of the difficulty is that different aspects of a SIP receive approval on a rolling basis. The EPA might approve part of a SIP while sending another part back to the state for revision. It is no exaggeration to say that the SIP approval process is rife with uncertainty and based to a significant extent on both guesswork and hope. Can you imagine a less cumbersome and costly way for states to implement NAAQS?

2. SIPs have been subject to criticism as a less than ideal method for attaining air quality. Arnold W. Reitze, Jr., in a comprehensive review of the Clean Air Act's evolution, highlighted a number of possible reasons for the failure of SIPs to attain air quality standards in many areas: growth in the population and energy use nullifying the progress that has been made in reducing emissions; fear of the costs of the CAA preventing strict application; falling short of reductions goals in the transportation sector, along with a faster-than-projected increase in vehicle miles traveled and a shift towards high-emitting vehicles such as SUVs; suburban sprawl resulting from a disconnect between transportation and land use planning; unreliable and/or expensive models used to demonstrate that SIPs would lead to attainment, at times resting on overly optimistic assumptions; slower than expected phasing out of "grandfathered" emissions sources predating the imposition of control technologies; transport of ozone from "upwind" states in the west to "downwind" states in the east; lack of negative consequences for local officials when air quality targets are not met, leaving no incentives for them to impose costly control measures; inadequacy of EPA sanctions; and the lack of any milestone program to identify and address state missteps. Arnold W. Reitze, Jr., *Air Quality Protection Using State Implementation Plans—Thirty–Seven Years of Increasing Complexity*, 15 VILL. ENVTL. L.J. 209, 358–66 (2004) (noting that "approximately 133 million people in 2001 lived in counties that violated one or more NAAQS"). Reitze points to federally-mandated measures as an increasingly large and important part of SIPs in terms of actually achieving emissions reductions (e.g., mobile source measures such as inspection and maintenance for motor vehicles, reformulated gasoline, and conformity planning; and the acid rain program) and predicts more such federal measures as the major cause of emissions reductions in the future. *See id.* at 366.

2. HAZARDOUS AIR POLLUTANTS

Hazardous air pollutants are those known or suspected to cause cancer and serious illness, such as reproductive effects or birth defects. Large stationary sources like chemical factories, incinerators and coal-burning power plants produce toxic pollutants. So do small sources such as dry cleaners and auto paint shops. When automobiles burn gasoline, they emit toxics, such as formaldehyde and benzene, from their tailpipes. Natural events, such as forest fires, may also release toxics into the air. However, most toxic air pollution is generated by man-made sources.

Once toxic pollution is emitted, wind can carry it far from its original source. Some toxics degrade either slowly or not at all. Metals can remain in the environment forever. Depending on the intensity and duration of exposure, humans exposed to toxics may suffer an increased risk of cancer and other serious health effects, including damage to their neurological, reproductive, respiratory and immune systems. Accidental releases of large quantities of air toxics can kill many people. This was brought home to the American public when, in 1984, a U.S.-owned pesticide manufacturing plant in Bhopal, India released methyl isocyanate, killing approximately 4,000 people and injuring more than 200,000. Toxic pollutants can also cause serious damage to wildlife that may ingest them. The regulation of air toxics not only responds to these kinds of harms, but may also help to reduce concentrations of criteria pollutants such as smog and ozone because some toxics are also volatile organic compounds that contribute to the formation of smog or particulate matter.

In the 1990 Amendments to the CAA, Congress overhauled the toxics program created by the 1970 legislation. The previous version of the Act had required the EPA to set emission limits for air toxics individually, based on their health risks, with an "ample margin of safety." After the 1970 provisions were passed, disagreements erupted over precisely what level of regulation this required, and whether it could include considerations of cost and technological feasibility. The EPA was still relatively inexperienced with risk assessment at this time, and scientists and policy experts could not agree on risk assessment methodologies and assumptions. Nor could they agree on how much data was necessary to support a given level of regulation. As a result of these difficulties, by the late eighties, the EPA had listed only seven air toxics.

In the 1990 Amendments, Congress itself listed 189 hazardous air pollutants (selected on the basis of their potential to be hazardous to health or the environment) and required the EPA to use a technology-based approach to set emissions standards for all major sources. The EPA established standards for each category of source (there are now 175 categories of industrial and commercial sources that emit one or more toxic air pollutants) and classifies sources as major (large) or area (small) sources within each category.

Under the 1990 Amendments, the EPA must set emissions standards for all major toxic sources, using Maximum Available Control Technology (MACT). MACT standards are based on emissions levels that are already being achieved by the better-controlled and lower-emitting sources in each industry. MACT standards come in two varieties: more stringent or less stringent. New major sources must meet the more stringent MACT standard covering their category, defined as the standard of emissions control achieved by the best-controlled similar source through any of the following: clean processes, control devices, work practices, or other methods. Existing sources must meet the less stringent MACT standard, defined as the emissions limit achieved by the best performing 12 percent of sources in that source category. In setting MACT standards, the EPA does not generally require sources to adopt particular technologies. Instead, sources may achieve the required performance level in whatever way is most cost-effective for them. Of course, some sources may find it easiest and most cost-effective to simply adopt the technology that the EPA used to set the standard. The MACT standards are *minimum* standards. The EPA is authorized to impose more stringent standards on individual source categories.

Major sources are defined as sources that emit 10 or more tons per year of any of the listed toxic air pollutants, or 25 or more tons per year of a combination of air toxics. Examples include chemical plants, steel mills, oil refineries and hazardous waste incinerators. Toxics might be emitted through stacks or vents, or they might be "fugitive" emissions that escape from industrial processes without passing through the normal exhaust system. Area sources are smaller sources of air toxics, defined as producing fewer than 10 tons per year of a single air toxic or fewer than 25 tons of any mixture of air toxics. Examples of area sources include dry cleaners and gas stations. Collectively, these emissions can cause serious risks, especially when high numbers of area sources are located in densely populated areas.

MACT standards generally apply to all sources, but the EPA may limit their applicability to major sources and impose on areas sources the separate, and less stringent, requirement of "generally available control technologies or management practices." The EPA need not list all categories of area sources, and it need not establish emission standards for unlisted sources. As of February 2004, the EPA had issued 96 air toxics MACT standards under § 112 of the CAA. These standards affect over 160 categories of industrial sources. Press Release, EPA, Four New Rules Will Reduce Hazardous Air Emissions (Feb. 26, 2004), *available at* http://www.epa.gov/newsroom/newsreleases.htm.

The case below explains the different treatment of major and area sources, and explores the EPA's definition of "major source" for purposes of the NESHAP provisions in § 112 of the Act. The agency had defined the term broadly, leading industry groups to sue.

NATIONAL MINING ASSOCIATION v. EPA

United States Court of Appeals, District of Columbia Circuit, 1995.
59 F.3d 1351.

[Various companies and associations petitioned for review of the EPA order implementing the 1990 Amendments to the CAA requiring identification of "major sources" of hazardous air pollutants. Because major sources are potentially subject to stricter control than area sources, petitioners sought to limit the circumstances under which facilities would be deemed major. Among other things, they challenged the EPA's decision to aggregate all hazardous air emissions within a plant site (instead of counting separately emissions from equipment in similar industrial categories) in determining whether a source was major.]

PER CURIAM:

This is a petition for review of an order of the Environmental Protection Agency implementing the 1990 amendments to § 112 of the Clean Air Act. Petitioners are General Electric Company and four trade associations: (1) National Mining Association, which represents companies that produce metal, coal, and minerals, and that manufacture mining equipment; (2) American Forest and Paper Association, which represents companies that make pulp, paper, paperboard, and solid wood; (3) Chemical Manufacturers Association, which represents companies that manufacture industrial chemicals; and (4) American Petroleum Institute, which represents companies engaged in the petroleum industry. * * *

In 1990, as part of its comprehensive overhaul of the Clean Air Act, Congress revised § 112 of the Act, which regulates emissions of hazardous air pollutants. Dissatisfied with EPA's health-based regulation of hazardous air pollutants under the 1970 program, Congress replaced this approach with a detailed, technology-based regulatory scheme. The 1990 amendments to § 112 establish an initial list, which EPA may periodically revise, of 189 hazardous air pollutants. 42 U.S.C. § 7412(b)(1)–(3). EPA must publish a list of "categories and subcategories" of "major sources" and certain "area sources" that emit these pollutants. 42 U.S.C. § 7412(c). For each listed "category or subcategory of major sources and area sources" of hazardous air pollutants, § 112(d) of the Act directs EPA to promulgate emission standards. 42 U.S.C. § 7412(d)(1).

Under the Act, "major sources" of hazardous air pollutants are potentially subject to stricter regulatory control than are "area sources." For example, major sources must comply with technology-based emission standards requiring the maximum degree of reduction in emissions EPA deems achievable, often referred to as "maximum achievable control technology" or MACT standards. 42 U.S.C. § 7412(d)(1)–(2). In order to obtain an operating permit under title V of the Act, §§ 501–507, major sources must comply with extensive monitoring, reporting and record-keeping requirements. 42 U.S.C. §§ 7661–7661(f). Further, § 112(g) generally conditions the modification, construction or reconstruction of a major source on the source's meeting MACT emission limitations. 42 U.S.C. § 7412(g).

"Area sources" of hazardous air pollutants are not necessarily subject to such stringent regulation. EPA need not list all "categories and subcategories" of area sources, 42 U.S.C. § 7412(c)(3), and it does not have to establish emission standards for unlisted area sources, 42 U.S.C. § 7412(d)(1). For listed area sources, EPA may choose to promulgate emission standards requiring only "generally available control technologies or management practices." 42 U.S.C. § 7412(d)(5). These standards can be less rigorous than those required for major sources under 42 U.S.C. § 7412(d)(1). Area sources are not subject to title V permitting requirements, or to § 112(g)'s restrictions on modification, construction and reconstruction of their facilities. * * *

[The EPA promulgated a rule setting emissions standards for listed source categories as required by § 112(e)].

Among other things, the general provisions rule implements § 112(a)(1)'s definition of "major source." The rule defines "major source" in terms nearly identical to those in § 112(a)(1) of the Clean Air Act:

> Major source means any stationary source or group of stationary sources located within a contiguous area and under common control that emits or has the potential to emit considering controls, in the aggregate, 10 tons per year or more of any hazardous air pollutant or 25 tons per year or more of any combination of hazardous air pollutants, unless the Administrator establishes a lesser quantity, or in the case of radionuclides, different criteria from those specified in this sentence.

A "stationary source" is "any building, structure, facility or installation which emits or may emit any air pollutant." An "area source [is] any stationary source . . . that is not a major source." The preambles to the proposed and final rules, and other definitions adopted in the final rule explain in greater detail how EPA plans to identify major sources.

Petitioners challenge three aspects of EPA's implementation of the definition of "major source." First, National Mining Association and American Forest and Paper Association (collectively referred to as "National Mining Association") and General Electric question EPA's requiring the aggregation of all hazardous air emissions within a plant site— instead of only those emissions from equipment in similar industrial categories—in a § 112 major source determination. * * *

General Electric and National Mining Association have similar arguments against the final rule's implementation of § 112(a)(1). Both maintain that EPA may not, in determining whether a site is a major source, include emissions from all facilities on a contiguous plant site under common control. These petitioners assert that, for purposes of major source determinations, EPA may aggregate emissions from different facilities on a contiguous plant site under common control only when the facilities fall within a similar industrial classification. General Electric says EPA must aggregate emissions on a "source category" basis * * *.

* * * Congress intended, according to EPA, "that all portions of a major source be subject to MACT [emission standards] regardless of the number of source categories into which the facility is divided." "Thus, the EPA will set one or more MACT standards for a major source, and sources within that major source will be covered by the standard(s), regardless of whether, when standing alone, each one those regulated sources would be major." * * *

If § 112(a)(1) is viewed in isolation, EPA's reading of the provision is not simply consistent with the provision; it is nearly compelled by the statutory language. Section 112(a)(1) states that a "group of stationary sources" need meet only three conditions to be termed a "major source": (1) sources within the group must be "located within a contiguous area"; (2) they must be "under common control"; and (3) in the aggregate, they must emit or, considering controls, have the potential to emit 10 or more tons per year of a single hazardous air pollutant or 25 or more tons per year of any combination of hazardous air pollutants. * * *

Petitioners ask us to look beyond the language of § 112(a)(1). In the first of several loosely connected arguments, General Electric recites fragments from § 112's other provisions, including: (1) § 112(c)(1), which directs EPA to publish "a list of all categories and subcategories of major sources and area sources"; (2) § 112(d)(1), which directs EPA to establish emission standards "for each category or subcategory of major sources and area sources"; and (3) § 112(j)(2), which describes what an operator of a "major source in [a] category" must do if EPA does not promulgate an emission standard for that "category of major sources." From these portions of § 112, General Electric leaps to the conclusion that "major source must be defined 'with reference to' (and cannot be broader than) the source category defined by EPA for § 112 regulation."

General Electric's logic is hard to grasp. Rather than supporting General Electric, the provisions the company invokes, read in full and in context, tend to support EPA's implementation of "major source" without reference to source categories. Section § 112 directs EPA to perform certain tasks on a category-wide basis—it is to identify categories of major and area sources of hazardous air pollutants (§ 112(c)(1)), and it must promulgate category-wide emission standards for these sources (§ 112(d)(2)). It by no means follows that because the statute in several provisions uses the terms "major source" and "category" in the same sentence—which is all General Electric's argument amounts to—EPA must read a source category restriction into § 112(a)(1)'s definition of "major source." Nor does § 112(c) somehow prohibit EPA from applying § 112(d)'s MACT emission limitations "to minor sources in a listed category of major sources without complying with the statutory requirements for listing area sources." *See* Brief for General Electric at 18. Section 112(c) simply requires the listing of all major sources and those area sources presenting adverse health or environmental effects. 42 U.S.C. § 7412 (c)(1), (3). Neither § 112(c) nor § 112(d) says anything about EPA's including "minor sources" in a "listed category of major sources." * * *

In sum, EPA's definition of "major source" without respect to source categories * * * is reasonable, as is its requirement that fugitive emissions be included in a source's aggregate emissions in determining whether the source is major. We therefore deny the petition for review with respect to these issues. * * *

[The Court granted review with respect to the agency's decision to calculate a source's potential emissions only by considering federally enforceable emission limits, which, petitioners claimed, would systematically over-estimate potential emissions because facilities are subject to state emissions limits as well.]

NOTES

1. What would the consequences be had the Court agreed with General Electric's interpretation of "major source" in this case?

2. *National Mining Association* illustrates how crucial seemingly techni-cal definitions can be. The agency's regulations interpreting statutory terms like "major" and "new" can determine which sources are regulated and to what extent. Since this is so consequential, why doesn't Congress clarify such things beyond any reasonable doubt, so that the need for these costly lawsuits would disappear? Does Congress just overlook these issues, or is it purposely delegating their resolution to the EPA? What difference would it make if the answer were the former rather than the latter? When considering this question, you may wish to refresh your memory of the Supreme Court's holding and rationale for deferring to the agency interpretation in *Chevron*, *supra*, at page 450.

3. The EPA has faced continuing difficulties in attempting to set stan-dards for hazardous air pollutants. Mossville Envtl. Action Now v. EPA, 370 F.3d 1232, 1235 (D.C. Cir. 2004) (noting the numerous legal challenges to such standards, and holding that the EPA violated the CAA by using the standard for one pollutant, vinyl chloride, as a proxy for all pollutants emitted by polyvinyl chloride and copolymer production facilities).

3. PSD AREAS

The 1970 Clean Air Act did not address areas of the country that were already in compliance with NAAQS or, that exceeded them. This hole in the statutory scheme was first addressed in litigation, when the Sierra Club challenged the EPA's approval of SIPs that allowed power plant emissions to degrade the air in these relatively clean regions. A district judge rejected the EPA's decision, and that outcome was upheld by the D.C. Circuit and then the Supreme Court in 1973. *Sierra Club* v. *Ruckel-shaus*, 344 F.Supp. 253 (D.D.C. 1972), aff'd by an equally divided court, *Fri v. Sierra Club,* 412 U.S. 541 (1973). This meant the EPA could not approve implementation plans that permitted increases in air pollution in these relatively clean areas unless Congress amended the CAA. Congress did just that in the 1977 amendments to the Act, by adding non-degradation, or "prevention of significant deterioration," (PSD) provi-sions. BRUCE A. ACKERMAN & WILLIAM T. HASSLER, CLEAN COAL/DIRTY AIR 28–29 (1981); *see also* Robert L. Glicksman, *The Value of Agency–Forcing Citizen Suits To Enforce Non–Discretionary Duties*, 10 WIDENER L. REV. 353, 358–61 (2004).

Under § 107 of the Act, states must classify areas as in attainment, out of attainment or unclassifiable. For areas that are either in attain-ment or are unclassifiable, SIPs must contain provisions to prevent significant deterioration [§ 110 (a)(2)(j)]. The statute divides PSD areas further into three classes (national parks and monuments must be Class I or II, for example), each with a separate increment of permissible pollu-tion increases. These increments represent the extent to which the air quality for a given pollutant may be allowed to degrade over the baseline concentration of that pollutant in the air in the PSD area. The increments are calculated as a percentage of the NAAQS. For example, the maximum permissible increase annually in the amount of particulate matter in a

Class I PSD area is 2 percent of the NAAQS for particulate matter. Section 163 establishes allowable increments for sulfur dioxide and particulates.

New or modified major sources in PSD areas must meet technology-based emissions limits set using Best Available Control Technology (BACT) and obtain pre-construction permits (§ 165). BACT standards may be no less stringent than New Source Performance Standards (NSPS), which are applicable to all new sources under § 111 and which are set according to BDAT. Sources in PSD areas are subject to NAAQS as a ceiling under § 163 (b)(4). So, even if a source could technically emit more of a pollutant without exceeding the annual allowable increment, it may not do so if those emissions will result in ambient levels that would exceed the NAAQS. In addition, although only new major sources must obtain permits, *all* sources produce emissions that count toward the annual increment. States may need to impose limits on existing sources in PSD areas to avoid falling below the NAAQS, even though these provisions of the CAA do not directly require existing sources to obtain permits or meet technology-based standards.

Now that the EPA has issued an endangerment finding holding that carbon dioxide and other greenhouse gases threaten public health and welfare, should the PSD program to be used to establish BACT standards for new stationary sources such as coal-fired power plants that emit large amounts of carbon dioxide? In Dec., 2008, then-EPA administrator Stephen L. Johnson issued a memorandum interpreting the PSD provisions to avoid BACT requirements for greenhouse gas emissions. *See* U.S. EPA Memorandum, *EPA's Interpretation of Regulations that Determine Pollutants Covered by Federal Prevention of Significant Deterioration Permit Program* (Dec. 18, 2008), available at http://www.epa.gov/nsr/documents/ psd_interpretive_memo_12.18.08.pdf. His memo was issued prior to the EPA's endangerment finding. Environmental groups around the country have targeted the permitting of new coal-fired power plants on a number of grounds, with mixed success. For a listing of such lawsuits and their status *see* Climate Change Litigation in the U.S., http://www.arnoldporter. com/resources/documents/ClimateChangeLitigationChart.pdf#page=1 & view=fit.

4. THE NONATTAINMENT PROBLEM

As we have seen, the 1970 Act afforded states considerable flexibility, through the SIP process, to achieve compliance with the NAAQS as they thought best. Subsequent amendments to deal with the problem of nonattainment have limited that flexibility, however. For example, the 1977 Amendments required all SIPs to provide for the implementation of "reasonably available control measures" (RACM) in nonattainment zones, including the application of "reasonably available control technology" (RACT) at all existing major stationary sources with the potential to emit 100 tons per year of the regulated pollutant or its precursors. Prior to this amendment, states could shelter existing sources from the imposition of such controls. The 1977 Amendments also required states to adopt a permit program for new major stationary sources in nonattainment zones and required states to impose on such sources a stringent technology-based standard known as "lowest achievable emission rate" (LAER). States were forbidden from permitting these new sources unless the new emissions could be offset by a decrease in emissions from existing sources in the same area or another area that contributes to the first area's non-attainment problem and itself has an equal or worse non-attainment problem, and only then if states could ensure "reasonable further progress" toward attainment. The EPA has issued an interpretive rule on its offset policy, which stipulates that only offsets of the same pollutant are acceptable, and that the baseline for determining credit for offsets consists of the SIP limits in effect at the time of the application. Credits may be granted for reductions achieved by a variety of methods, including shutdowns, reduction of hours of operation below baseline levels, and switching to cleaner fuels. All emissions reductions claimed as credits must be federally enforceable. *See* 40 C.F.R. Pt. 51, App. S, §§ IV.A, IV.C.

Between 1977 and 1990, without the benefit of congressional action, the EPA addressed the problem of nonattainment by issuing "SIP calls" to states, demanding SIP revisions for nonattainment areas. States were asked to demonstrate that they were adopting measures that would ensure attainment by the deadlines in the Act, and to guarantee steady progress toward compliance in the interim. The case below illustrates the difficult position the EPA found itself in prior to the 1990 Amendments.

DELANEY v. EPA

United States Court of Appeals, Ninth Circuit, 1990.
898 F.2d 687.

WIGGINS, CIRCUIT JUDGE.

Residents of Maricopa and Pima counties, Arizona, petition this court to vacate as arbitrary or capricious the Environmental Protection Agency's approvals of the counties' Clean Air Act implementation plans. * * *

The Clean Air Act, as amended in 1970, mandated that states as expeditiously as practicable, but not later than December 31, 1975, reduce the levels of certain ambient pollutants to comply with the National Ambient Air Quality Standards set by the EPA. Preliminarily, each state had to develop a state implementation plan to achieve this goal.

After many areas of the country failed to attain some or all of the national ambient air quality standards on time, Congress amended the Act in 1977, providing new deadlines for nonattainment areas. The 1977 amendments required states to submit by January 1, 1979, for each of their nonattainment areas, a revised implementation plan that provided for implementation of all reasonably available control measures to attain the relevant national ambient air quality standards as expeditiously as practicable, but not later than December 31, 1982. If a state did not submit an adequate revised state implementation plan by the 1979 deadline, the EPA had to promulgate its own federal implementation plan. The 1977 amendments provided only one exception: If a state demonstrated in its revised implementation plan that the carbon monoxide or ozone ambient air quality standard could not be attained by the close of 1982 despite implementation of all reasonably available control measures, the state could have until the end of 1987 to attain the relevant air quality standard in that nonattainment area. In that case, the state had to submit a second revised implementation plan to the EPA by July 1, 1982.

In 1978, the EPA designated large areas of both Maricopa and Pima counties as nonattainment areas for carbon monoxide. In 1979, Arizona submitted revised implementation plans for both areas. In 1983, the EPA approved the plans subject to certain conditions. Neither area, however, satisfied the EPA's conditions or attained the carbon monoxide standard by the 1982 deadline. Arizona failed in its attempt to extend both areas' attainment deadlines to 1987, but submitted additional revised plans for the areas to attain by the 1987 deadline anyway. The EPA rejected these additional revised plans and we upheld that decision.

When Arizona thereafter failed to submit adequate plans for Maricopa and Pima counties, petitioners filed suit in the Arizona district court. That court ordered the EPA to promulgate implementation plans for both counties by March 30, 1988 (later extended to August 10, 1988), unless before this date Arizona submitted, and the EPA approved, adequate state plans. *McCarthy v. Thomas*, No. 85–344 (D. Ariz. August 10, 1987). Arizona submitted, and the EPA ultimately approved (with revisions), state implementation plans for both counties on August 10, 1988. Petitioners now challenge these approvals. * * *

Because the Clean Air Act amendments of 1977 made the 1982 compliance deadline absolute (with the one exception noted above), the amendments did not specify an additional deadline for nonattainment areas that failed to obtain revised implementation plan approval and national ambient air quality standard compliance by the 1982 deadline. In this circumstance, the EPA adopted the policy that it should evaluate the adequacy of the Maricopa and Pima county plans based on whether they provide for attainment by three years from the date it approved those plans, August 10, 1991. Petitioners contend that the EPA's policy is arbitrary or capricious. Now that the 1977 amendments' deadline for compliance has passed, petitioners assert, Pima and Maricopa Counties must attain the carbon monoxide ambient air quality standard as soon as possible utilizing every available control measure.

The EPA contends that Congress expressed no clear intent on the attainment deadline that the EPA should apply in evaluating the Maricopa and Pima plans because the 1977 amendments did not specify a deadline for nonattainment areas that failed to obtain revised state implementation plan approval and national ambient air quality standard compliance by the 1982 deadline. The EPA argues that this amounts to a "statutory gap." As a result, the EPA believes, we must uphold its policy of allowing compliance within three years of state implementation plan approval because it is a reasonable construction of the 1977 amendments.

The EPA argues that if Congress had considered that some nonattainment areas would not meet the deadline specified in the 1977 Amendments, Congress would have intended that the EPA administratively establish a new three year attainment period from the date of implementation plan approval deadline, like those provided in the Clean Air Act amendments of 1970. The EPA contends that this result is consistent with the language, history, and overall purposes of the Act. The EPA contends that Congress knew some states would not attain by the 1982 deadline and did not intend that states implement draconian measures. * * *

Although we recognize the EPA's predicament, we cannot accept the EPA's position. As the EPA itself recognizes, Congress explicitly declined to allow extensions of the deadline because it believed an absolute deadline to be necessary. * * *

We, and the EPA, are bound by the statutory scheme until Congress alters that scheme. * * *

When Congress has explicitly set an absolute deadline, congressional intent is clear. It is a semantic game to claim that once a state fails to meet an absolute deadline, a statutory gap is created because Congress has not provided a back-up deadline for its explicitly absolute deadline. If Congress had been more lenient and allowed a one-year fall back extension, the EPA would be bound by that directive. The EPA cannot extract leeway from a statute that Congress explicitly intended to be strict. * * *

CONCLUSION

We grant the petition for review. We vacate the EPA's approvals of Maricopa and Pima counties' Clean Air Act implementation plans. We direct the EPA to disapprove these plans and to promulgate federal implementation plans consistent with this opinion within six months.

NOTES

1. Wasn't the agency's approach here eminently reasonable? What happened to the idea, per *Chevron, supra,* page 450, that a court should defer to an agency's reasonable interpretation of an ambiguous statutory provision? Are the relevant statutory provisions in this case really as clear-cut as the Court suggests?

2. What are the practical consequences of the EPA disapproving a SIP and issuing a FIP? The agency does not seem to be trying hard to avoid this eventuality here. Why?

In the 1990 Amendments, Congress added a new set of nonattainment provisions, further limiting the states' discretion with regard to SIPs and imposing greater burdens on stationary sources in these areas. For ozone, Congress divided areas into categories meant to reflect the severity of the nonattainment problem. Congress then established compliance deadlines on a graduated basis, with more time given to those areas further out of attainment. Control requirements also follow this graduated approach: the further out of attainment, the more controls that area must adopt. For example, an ozone nonattainment area may be classified as marginally, moderately, seriously, severely or extremely out of attainment. The new deadlines are expressed in terms of the number of years after 1990 afforded to the area to comply with NAAQS. Marginal areas have three years beyond 1990 to comply, serious areas have nine years, and extreme areas (currently only Los Angeles) are given twenty years. In addition, every area except marginal nonattainment areas must reduce emissions of volatile organic compounds (which contribute to ozone) by 15% by 1996, with further reductions of 3% to be achieved annually thereafter. Additional restrictions apply as well. For example, in areas classified as serious or worse, gas stations are required to install special hose-and-nozzle controls on gas pumps to capture fuel vapors.

The provisions relating to pollutants other than ozone are generally similar, but the EPA is afforded somewhat more discretion. For example, the carbon monoxide provisions require the use of reformulated gasoline. Reformulated gasoline typically contains additives such as ethanol (made from corn) or Methyl Tertiary–Butyl Ether (MTBE) that increase the amount of oxygen available for combustion, thereby decreasing emissions of carbon monoxide.

Areas out of attainment for a criteria pollutant for which Congress has not specified a deadline must comply with NAAQS within five years of being classified as a nonattainment area. The EPA may extend this deadline, though not indefinitely. States must adopt revisions to their SIPs for nonattainment areas which include the imposition of RACT for existing sources; a permit program for new sources as prescribed by section 173; provisions to ensure reasonable further progress toward attainment; and any other measures that may be necessary to ensure attainment.

Next, we return to the *American Trucking* case, (*supra,* page 568) regarding the role of cost in CAA standard-setting). After the Supreme Court concluded that the EPA could not consider cost in setting NAAQS, the Court reviewed the EPA's determination about how to implement the revised standards in nonattainment zones. Before delving into the complicated excerpt below, refresh your memories about the standard of review courts use to review agency interpretations of law by reviewing the *Chevron,* case *supra,* page 450. This part of the *American Trucking* case is a rare example of the Supreme Court refusing to defer to an agency interpretation of law once it reaches Step Two of the *Chevron* test. Do not confuse step one and two of the *Chevron* test with the issue in the case, which involves "Subpart 1" and "Subpart 2" of Part D of the CAA.

The Court's discussion, below, of whether Subpart 1 or Subpart 2 of Part D of the statute controls the implementation of a revised air standard is confusing for non-experts. Subpart 1 establishes general requirements for nonattainment areas (those areas classified as not meeting applicable air standards) and Subpart 2 contains more specific provisions for attaining primary standards (health based standards, which are involved here) for particular pollutants. Meeting the EPA's revised ozone standard could impose a heavy burden on nonattainment zones already struggling with attaining the old ozone standard. The agency's implementation plan thus had to address what to do about areas that would be classified as "nonattainment" zones for the new standard.

The question is whether the agency has discretion to implement its revised (and more stringent) ozone standard under Subpart 1's general provisions governing nonattainment zones, or whether the more specific timetables in Subpart 2 apply. There are important differences between the two subparts. Subpart 1 requires areas to demonstrate attainment of primary standards within five to ten years following the area's designation as nonattainment. However, areas are exempt from this deadline for pollutants for which specific timetables are established elsewhere in Part D. Some of Subpart 2's provisions thus override the provisions of Subpart 1. Subpart 2 classifies nonattainment areas for ozone into five classes—from Marginal through Extreme—and establishes detailed attainment deadlines for each class.

The EPA had reasoned that Subpart 2's deadlines are tied to the standard for ozone established prior to 1990, when Congress enacted Subpart 2. The agency thus concluded that Subpart 1's attainment deadlines, rather than the specific deadlines for ozone contained in Subpart 2, would apply to its revised standard. As a result, each area classified as a nonattainment zone for the new standard would have to submit a plan demonstrating how it would achieve attainment by Subpart 1's five to ten year deadline. This could pose a hardship for nonattainment areas, by forcing them to attain the new, tougher standard *even before* the specific deadlines in Subpart 2 would require them to reach attainment of the less stringent existing standard. However, this effect can be ameliorated: under Subpart 1, the EPA retains considerable flexibility to extend deadlines, whereas under Subpart 2, the timetables are specific and extensions are more limited. The EPA's strategy in adopting its implementation plan, and this understanding of Part D, were based on the idea that attainment of the new ozone standard would be achieved mostly though adopting a program to reduce emissions of nitrogen oxides that cross state lines. The Supreme Court, in the excerpt below, struggles to discern Congress' intent on the matter, focusing on whether Subpart 2 was meant to cover all areas designated as nonattainment, even those designated as nonattainment in response to a *revised* standard, or whether Subpart 2 is limited to those areas designated as nonattainment only for those standards already in effect when Congress enacted Subpart 2 in 1990. Applying *Chevron*, the Court ultimately concludes that the statute is ambiguous, but that the agency's view of Part D is unreasonable.

[The analysis of Part D above draws heavily on Craig N. Oren, *Run Over by* American Trucking *Part II: Can EPA Implement Revised Air Quality Standards?*, 30 Envtl. L. Rep. 10034 (2000).]

WHITMAN v. AMERICAN TRUCKING
ASSOCIATIONS, INC.

Supreme Court of the United States, 2001.
531 U.S. 457, 121 S.Ct. 903, 149 L.Ed.2d 1.

* * *

Our approach to the merits of the parties' dispute is the familiar one of *Chevron U.S.A. Inc. v. Natural Resources Defense Council, Inc.* If the statute resolves the question whether Subpart 1 or Subpart 2 (or some combination of the two) shall apply to revised ozone NAAQS, then "that is the end of the matter." But if the statute is "silent or ambiguous" with respect to the issue, then we must defer to a "reasonable interpretation made by the administrator of an agency." We cannot agree with the Court of Appeals that Subpart 2 clearly controls the implementation of revised ozone NAAQS, because we find the statute to some extent ambiguous. We conclude, however, that the agency's interpretation goes beyond the limits of what is ambiguous and contradicts what in our view is quite clear. We therefore hold the implementation policy unlawful. * * *

So, does Subpart 2 provide for classifying nonattainment ozone areas under the revised standard? It unquestionably does. The backbone of the subpart is Table 1,* * * which defines five categories of ozone nonattainment areas and prescribes attainment deadlines for each. Section 7511(a)(1) funnels all nonattainment areas into the table for classification, declaring that "[e]ach area designated nonattainment for ozone ... shall be classified at the time of such designation, under table 1, by operation of law." And once an area has been classified, "the primary standard attainment date for ozone shall be as expeditiously as practicable but not later than the date provided in table 1." The EPA argues that this text is not as clear or comprehensive as it seems, because the title of § 7511(a) reads "Classification and attainment dates for 1989 nonattainment areas," which suggests that Subpart 2 applies only to areas that were in nonattainment in 1989, and not to areas later designated nonattainment under a revised ozone standard. The suggestion must be rejected, however, because § 7511(b)(1) specifically provides for the classification of areas that *were* in attainment in 1989 but have subsequently slipped into nonattainment. It thus makes clear that Subpart 2 is *not* limited solely to 1989 nonattainment areas. * * *

* * * [However,] Subpart 2's method for calculating attainment dates * * * make[s] no sense for areas that are first classified under a new standard after November 15, 1990. If, for example, areas were classified in the year 2000, many of the deadlines would already have expired at the time of classification.

These gaps in Subpart 2's scheme prevent us from concluding that Congress clearly intended Subpart 2 to be the exclusive, permanent means of enforcing a revised ozone standard in nonattainment areas. The statute is in our view ambiguous concerning the manner in which Subpart 1 and

Subpart 2 interact with regard to revised ozone standards, and we would defer to the EPA's reasonable resolution of that ambiguity. We cannot defer, however, to the interpretation the EPA has given.

Whatever effect may be accorded the gaps in Subpart 2 as implying some limited applicability of Subpart 1, they cannot be thought to render Subpart 2's carefully designed restrictions on EPA discretion utterly nugatory once a new standard has been promulgated, as the EPA has concluded. The principal distinction between Subpart 1 and Subpart 2 is that the latter eliminates regulatory discretion that the former allowed. While Subpart 1 permits the EPA to establish classifications for nonattainment areas, Subpart 2 classifies areas as a matter of law based on a table. * * * Whereas the EPA has discretion under Subpart 1 to extend attainment dates for as long as 12 years, under Subpart 2 it may grant no more than 2 years' extension. * * * Whereas Subpart 1 gives the EPA considerable discretion to shape nonattainment programs, Subpart 2 prescribes large parts of them by law. * * * To use a few apparent gaps in Subpart 2 to render its textually explicit applicability to nonattainment areas under the new standard utterly inoperative is to go over the edge of reasonable interpretation. The EPA may not construe the statute in a way that completely nullifies textually applicable provisions meant to limit its discretion.

The EPA's interpretation making Subpart 2 abruptly obsolete is all the more astonishing because Subpart 2 was obviously written to govern implementation for some time. Some of the elements required to be included in SIP's under Subpart 2 were not to take effect until many years after the passage of the Act. A plan reaching so far into the future was not enacted to be abandoned the next time the EPA reviewed the ozone standard—which Congress knew could happen at any time, since the technical staff papers had already been completed in late 1989. Yet nothing in the EPA's interpretation would have prevented the agency from aborting Subpart 2 the day after it was enacted. Even now, if the EPA's interpretation were correct, some areas of the country could be required to meet the new, more stringent ozone standard in *at most* the same time that Subpart 2 had allowed them to meet the old standard. Compare § 7502(a)(2) (Subpart 1 attainment dates) with § 7511(a) (Subpart 2 attainment dates). Los Angeles, for instance, "would be required to attain the revised NAAQS under Subpart 1 no later than the same year that marks the outer time limit for attaining Subpart 2's one-hour ozone standard." An interpretation of Subpart 2 so at odds with its structure and manifest purpose cannot be sustained.

We therefore find the EPA's implementation policy to be unlawful, though not in the precise respect determined by the Court of Appeals. After our remand, and the Court of Appeals' final disposition of this case, it is left to the EPA to develop a reasonable interpretation of the nonattainment implementation provisions insofar as they apply to revised ozone NAAQS.

To summarize our holdings in these unusually complex cases: (1) The EPA may not consider implementation costs in setting primary and secondary NAAQS under § 109(b) of the CAA. (2) Section 109(b)(1) does not delegate legislative power to the EPA in contravention of Art. I, § 1, of the Constitution. (3) The Court of Appeals had jurisdiction to review the EPA's interpretation of Part D of Title I of the CAA, relating to the implementation of the revised ozone NAAQS. (4) The EPA's interpretation of that Part is unreasonable.

The judgment of the Court of Appeals is affirmed in part and reversed in part, and the cases are remanded for proceedings consistent with this opinion.

It is so ordered.

NOTES

1.   Given the technical nature of the CAA, the ambiguity left by Congress on how Subparts One and Two interact in the case of revised standards, and the fact that Congress has assigned the implementation of this law to the EPA, shouldn't the Court defer to this agency's expert interpretation? Is the *Chevron* inquiry into legislative intent even sensible in a case like this? The CAA, like other environmental statutes, simply may be "too unwieldy to receive the consideration in Congress that it requires. * * * Given the detail of the statute, it is hard to believe that anyone in Congress made a conscious decision to leave the issue unaddressed. Rather, the intricacy of the statute simply overwhelmed the legislative process." Craig N. Oren, *Run Over by American Trucking Part II,* 30 Envtl. L. Rep. 10034, 10048 (2000).

2.   Remanding the timetable for implementation to the agency is potentially more consequential than it appears on its face. While the case was pending before the Supreme Court, George W. Bush was elected President. As a result, while the original implementation plan was the product of Carol Browner's EPA under President Clinton—the EPA that had developed and promulgated the new standards—the new implementation plan fell to the new Bush Administration, whose first EPA Administrator, Christine Todd Whitman, resigned, partly in frustration with the Administration's policies. Do such personnel changes make a difference to implementation? Should they?

The final version of the 8–hour ozone standard ended up amalgamating Subparts 1 and 2, separating areas by their level of air quality under the 1–hour standard. Areas with ozone levels below the minimum covered by the classifications of Subpart 2 will be subject to the Subpart 1 deadlines, allowing them more flexibility, while those with ozone levels putting them under Subpart 2 will be categorized according to its more prescriptive designations, with corresponding deadlines. 40 C.F.R. sections 51.902–.904; *see also* Final Rule To Implement the 8–Hour Ozone National Ambient Air Quality Standard—Phase 1, Part II, 69 Fed. Reg. 23,951, 23,956–61 (Apr. 30, 2004) (explaining the rationale for choosing that regulatory scheme).

3.   The Supreme Court remanded the case to the D.C. Circuit, leaving open the possibility that the lower court might invalidate the revised stan-

dards under "arbitrary or capricious" review. The appellate court upheld the EPA's new NAAQS for ozone and fine particulate matter on remand, finding ample evidence to justify them. *See American Trucking Ass'ns, Inc.* v. *EPA,* 283 F.3d 355 (D.C. Cir. 2002).

5. NEW SOURCE PERFORMANCE STANDARDS

Section 111 of the CAA authorizes the EPA to establish technology-based standards for new sources, which the EPA promulgates on a category-by-category basis. Examples include petroleum refineries, asphalt and concrete plants, sewage treatment plants, and synthetic organic chemicals manufacturing operations. These standards apply to all new sources, defined as any source built or modified after the EPA promulgates the standard applicable to that type of source. Modification is defined in § 111(a)(4) as any "physical change in, or change in the method of operation of, a stationary source which increases the amount of any air pollutant emitted by such source or which results in the emission of any air pollutant not previously emitted." The technology-based standard the EPA must use is the "degree of emission limitation achievable through the application of the best system of emission reduction which (taking into account the cost * * *) * * * has been adequately demonstrated" [BDAT] [§ 111 (a)(1)]. The emission limits themselves are generally expressed as concentrations or emission rates. These standards are not limited to major facilities. They represent the basic, minimum controls imposed on all new sources, regardless of whether they are major or not, and regardless of where they are located. However, some new source standards might not be terribly stringent because they were set by the EPA years ago, when technology was not as effective at controlling emissions as it is today.

6. NEW SOURCE REVIEW[5]

New Source Review (NSR) refers to pre-construction review and permitting for all new or modified major stationary sources in PSD and nonattainment areas. Section 173 of the Act requires permits for "new or modified major stationary sources" in all nonattainment areas. The EPA has provided detailed rules for implementing this requirement. 40 C.F.R. §§ 51.160–.166 Although NSR is not explicitly required by the Act for PSD areas, the EPA has required it as part of its overall scheme for maintaining air quality. 40 C.F.R. §§ 52.21–.24. Ideally, NSR provides for the installation of pollution controls in new facilities as they are constructed, and also in facilities predating the Act, which were "grandfathered" in without any initial technology requirement, as they modernize their equipment.

---

5. We are grateful to Peter Wyckoff, Counsel, Pillsbury Winthrop Shaw Pittman for generously sharing his insights on the NSR program.

a. What Does NSR Require?

If a source triggers NSR, it must comply with certain technology-based standards—for PSD areas, the best available control technology (BACT), and for nonattainment areas, the lowest achievable emissions rate (LAER). The permitting authority decides on a case-by-case basis what control technology these standards demand. The mandated "top-down" BACT analysis, a fairly rigorous test, requires the permittee to rank available ("demonstrated") technologies and use the most stringent choice unless it can convince the permitting authority that "technical considerations, or energy, environmental, or economic impacts justify a conclusion that the most stringent technology is not 'achievable' in that case." ROBERT J. MARTINEAU, JR. & DAVID P. NOVELLO, THE CLEAN AIR ACT HANDBOOK 157–58 (2d ed. 2004).

Additionally, a PSD source undergoing NSR must perform an "air quality impacts analysis" showing that its new emissions, along with other emissions from the source, will not significantly impact ambient air quality. For criteria pollutants, this requires a demonstration that the emissions will not cause or contribute to violation of any relevant NAAQS or PSD increment. 40 C.F.R. § 51, app. W. The demonstration must utilize dispersion modeling, a computer modeling method that is notoriously poor; yet here, it serves as the basis for important decisions about environmental controls and economic growth.

Other than the different technology required by NSR, and the definition of major source (discussed below), there are only a few differences between NSR in PSD and nonattainment areas. The other pertinent distinctions are the pollutants covered (nonattainment NSR focuses on criteria pollutants) and the increase thresholds for triggering NSR. Rolf R. von Oppenfeld et al., *A Primer on New Source Review and Strategies for Success,* 32 Envtl. L. Rep. 11091 (2002).

b. Triggering NSR

i. *"Major stationary source"*

The default definition of "major stationary sources," in § 302(j), is any source that emits or has the potential to emit 100 tons or more per year of any air pollutant regulated under the Act. A major source for PSD areas is one from a specified list of source categories that has the potential to emit 100 tons per year of a pollutant covered by the Act, any source with the potential to emit 250 tons per year of a regulated pollutant, or an otherwise non-major source undergoing a physical change where the change will by itself increase the potential to emit enough to satisfy the definition of major source (e.g., a plant emitting 90 tons per year of sulfur dioxide that plans to make a change that will increase its potential to emit sulfur dioxide by 260 tons per year). 40 C.F.R. § 51.21(b)(1). In nonattainment zones, the threshold for a major source varies with the severity of nonattainment; and as in PSD areas, a minor source undergoing modification qualifies if the potential to emit from the physical change would itself exceed the emissions limit for a major source. *See* CAA §§ 182, 187, 189.

A source may avoid qualifying as major by accepting enforceable limits on its potential to emit that keep it under the PSD major source threshold. One ongoing debate has been whether those limits must be legally federally enforceable to constitute a valid cap; the regulation states that in calculating a source's potential to emit "under its physical and operational design," an emissions limitation "shall be treated as part of its design if the limitation or the effect it would have on emissions is federally enforceable." 40 C.F.R. §§ 51.165, 52.21. Traditionally, this meant the restriction had to be contained in a permit issued under a federal program, but that requirement was rejected by the D.C. Circuit in 1995. Chemical Mfrs. Ass'n v. EPA, 70 F.3d 637 (D.C. Cir. 1995) (mem.) (vacating the EPA regulations based on National Mining Ass'n v. EPA, 59 F.3d 1351 (D.C. Cir. 1995)). Subsequently, the EPA has interpreted "federally enforceable" to mean only that the limit must be "enforceable as a practical matter," with the permit including provisions for monitoring, record-keeping, and reporting so as to allow the EPA to verify compliance. Prevention of Significant Deterioration (PSD) and Nonattainment New Source Review (NSR), 67 Fed. Reg. 80,186, 80,190–91 (Dec. 31, 2002). Even so, this mechanism requires a certain sacrifice of flexibility by a permittee, and may be less desirable than avoiding the application of NSR altogether.

ii. *"Modified Source"*

Because of the burdensome requirements imposed on a source once it falls under NSR, there has been an extended and heated debate regarding almost every ambiguity in the CAA's dictates. The most contested of these questions has been about what constitutes a "modified source." The Act defines modification as "any physical change in, or change in the method of operation of, a stationary source which increases the amount of any air pollutant emitted by such source or which results in the emission of any air pollutant not previously emitted." § 111(a)(4). The EPA's major task has been to elucidate the meaning of "any physical change ... or change in the method of operation." Since Congress did not intend for every single change in a major source to engage the cumbersome machinery of NSR, the EPA has adopted several exclusions from the domain of changes that would trigger NSR. These exceptions include: Routine Maintenance, Repair, and Replacement (RMRR); an increase in hours of operation or in production rate; and Plantwide Applicability Limits (exempting sources from NSR as long as they stay below a certain cap on facility emissions). 40 C.F.R. § 52.21. In addition, the EPA has determined that a change does not qualify as a modification for the purposes of NSR unless it triggers a "significant" emissions increase, qualifying as a "major modification."

Since firms are understandably eager to take advantage of these exclusions and avoid the onerous emissions limitations that come with

NSR, not to mention the administrative delays and expenses of the process itself, the details of their implementation play a large role in shaping the application of NSR. The most contentious debate has been centered around the definition of the "significant increase" and "routine maintenance, repair, and replacement" provisions.

Significant increase. There are four key issues in calculating a "significant" increase in emissions: (1) the scope across which emissions are calculated (i.e., does one look at emissions across the entire source, or only at the specific increase caused by the change in question); (2) calculation of the baseline from which the increase in emissions is measured; (3) how to determine the post-change emissions for comparison with the baseline; and (4) how much of an increase counts as "significant."

The first of these concerns is covered by the EPA's provision for "netting," which allows an increase from a particular change to be offset by emissions decreases within the same facility. The net emissions are calculated using emissions increases and decreases within a certain time period of the proposed modification, usually five years.

The baseline figure for determining whether a source has "netted out" of NSR or for quantifying its emissions increase can be calculated using historic emissions data. But which data? The first question is what the denominator for calculating emissions should be—per hour or per year. The former option "misses" modifications that allow a facility to operate more hours per year but do not increase its hourly emissions rate. The EPA for the most part uses annual emissions in calculating whether there has been an increase for the purposes of NSR. The NSPS program, on the other hand, bases its determination on hourly emissions, which the Supreme Court upheld in *Environmental Defense v. Duke Energy,* 549 U.S. 561 (2007). In Duke Energy, the company had made 29 extensive changes to its power plants without seeking PSD permits. Although the changes did not change Duke's hourly emissions, the plants operated for more hours and therefore increased overall annual emissions. The EPA sued Duke for violating the NSR provisions and Duke argued that the EPA's use of annual emissions for calculating increases was inconsistent with the NSPS definition and therefore impermissible. The Supreme Court found in favor of the EPA.

However, this still leaves unresolved the issue of which years' emissions to utilize. What constitutes a "typical" year of emissions for a facility? The EPA can give permittees more or less flexibility in this respect by adjusting their discretion in choosing which years are representative of their normal operation (generally, subject to agency approval).

As with the baseline determination, the test for the comparison of "before and after" emissions may be a "worst case scenario," or might offer more flexibility. The two main methodologies for representing post-change emissions are: potential to emit (the source's maximum capacity to emit under its physical and operational design) and "projected actual" (the expected actual emissions from the source in some one or more post-modification years, confirmed by later monitoring).

Once these calculations have been performed, if there is an increase from the baseline it is compared to the numeric thresholds set in agency regulations to determine whether it qualifies the source for NSR. *See* 40 C.F.R. §§ 51.166(b)(23)(iii), 52.21(b)(23)(i).

Routine Maintenance, Repair, and Replacement. As with many legal tests, the RMRR exclusion can take the form of either a rule with general applicability, or a standard more amenable to flexible application to the idiosyncracies of a given situation. The former can provide consistency and clarity in its operation, but may at the same time offer sources unmistakable opportunities to duck the requirements of NSR. On the other hand, while the latter might capture more cases of modification, it also makes application of this exclusion more uncertain (and often more byzantine) for prospective permittees. For more on RMRR as a rule versus a standard, *see* Matthew C. Stephenson, *A Tale of Two Theories: The Legal Basis for EPA's Proposed Revision to the Routine Maintenance, Repair, and Replacement Exception, and the Implications for Administrative Law*, 33 Envtl. L. Rep. (Envtl. L. Inst.) 10789 (2003).

Both of these exclusions have gone through various iterations. The major change came in 2002, when the EPA promulgated a revision of its NSR regulations. *See* Prevention of Significant Deterioration (PSD) and Nonattainment New Source Review (NSR), 67 Fed. Reg. 80,186, 80,190–91 (Dec. 31, 2002). This rule changed, among other things, the baseline determination and the methodology for calculating the emissions increase, in order to "reduce burden, maximize operating flexibility, improve environmental quality, provide additional certainty, and promote administrative efficiency." Originally, for non-utility sources, the baseline was the average annual emissions rate for the two years before the modification; the 2002 rule changed that to allow facilities to use the emissions levels from any consecutive twenty-four month period from the last ten years of operation (a "ten-year lookback"). The 2002 revision also replaced an actual-to-potential test for emissions change with an actual-to-projected measure.

A second rule issued in 2003 altered the definition of RMRR. Previously, whether a proposed change fell within the scope of RMRR was determined on a case-by-case basis. Many stakeholders criticized this approach as fostering uncertainty, increasing the EPA and state environmental agencies' administrative burden, and discouraging owners and operators from modernizing old facilities that would otherwise improve reliability, efficiency, and safety for fear of incurring the costs and risks of new source review. Prevention of Significant Deterioration (PSD) and Non–Attainment New Source Review (NSR): Equipment Replacement Provision of the Routine Maintenance, Repair and Replacement Exclusion, 68 Fed. Reg. 61,248 (Oct. 27, 2003). The new RMRR exclusion, known as the Equipment Replacement Provision, would exempt any proposed modification from NSR if it consists of replacement of an existing portion of a process unit with an identical or functionally equivalent component, the costs of the replacement are less than twenty percent of the replacement value of the whole unit, the replacement does not change the basic design parameters of the process unit, and the replacement does not cause the unit to exceed any emissions limits.

Both of these rules were soon challenged in court, and their applicability, as of this writing, is still unresolved. Most recently, a suit in the D.C. Circuit upheld the newest rule's actual-to-projected test, the use of plantwide applicability limits, and the ten year look-back for baseline determination. However, the court remanded proposed exemptions for plants that already meet strict emissions limitations and for modifications that consist of installation of a pollution control technology that may increase some emissions but on the whole is environmentally beneficial. *New York v. EPA*, 413 F.3d 3 (D.C. Cir. 2005). The most recent developments with respect to the NSR revisions can be found at: EPA, New Source Review: Regulations and Standards, http://www.epa.gov/nsr/actions.html (last visited July 13, 2009). In addition, it has not yet been decided whether, as EPA insists, states that have their own NSR provisions rather than relying on the federal version must either adopt these revisions or some equivalent, or whether they may adopt a more stringent alternative as permitted under current regulations. 40 C.F.R. § 51.166(a)(7)(iv).

The opponents of these changes in the NSR program have accused the EPA of promulgating rules with new loopholes and accounting gimmicks that allow sources to duck NSR even when their emissions are increasing, with the result that older, dirtier firms can keep running longer without installing pollution controls. The EPA responds that, in the long run, allowing firms to modernize without penalizing them through costly pollution control requirements will lead to more efficient and thus cleaner facilities. Part of this dispute stems from disagreement over the basic purpose of the NSR program. Many environmentalists see the program as a mechanism built into the CAA to phase out old facilities that were "grandfathered" in when the Act was first passed, whereas the EPA responds that facilities will not necessarily continue to pollute unabated even if they do not trigger NSR, due to inevitable efficiency improvement. This debate is complicated by the fact that much of the old, polluting equipment at issue has lasted far longer than anyone predicted when clean air regulation began. For a thorough critique of the new rules, *see* Inho Choi, *Is the U.S. Environmental Protection Agency's Revised New Source Review Rule Moving in the Right Direction?: A Deepened New Source Bias, and the Need for Pursuing Sustainable Energy Development in Air Pollution Control Law*, 35 Envtl. L. Rep. 10316 (2005).

Do you think the newest set of regulations (if and when they go into effect) will make enforcement easier or harder? More or less effective? Given the complexity of NSR, isn't there a simpler way to address the problem of grandfathered facilities? Is this really something that the EPA should be managing by rulemaking or by settlements with large emitters? The latter appear to be increasingly popular but they are relatively low-visibility mechanisms for making policy. Should Congress step in to make decisions of this magnitude?

iii.   *The Interaction of NSPS and NSR*

One might reasonably ask what role NSPS standards play, since all "new" sources (whether in PSD areas or non-attainment zones) must go through New Source Review. Why aren't the NSPS standards just superseded by the BACT standards in the PSD program or the LAER standards in the NAZ program?

First, NSPS, like the MACT standards for hazardous air pollutants, are the result of an intensive examination by agency and consultant engineers of particular classes of equipment, focusing on stack and fugitive emissions, available controls, costs, and alternative compliance regimes (which have made quantum leaps in recent years with continuous emissions monitoring). Essentially, these standards are detailed equipment-specific blueprints of "Good Air Pollution Control Management"—what engineers would consider sensible air pollution control measures or "good housekeeping" for particular pieces of equipment. Compared to the approach in setting BACT standards under the PSD provisions, the NSPS approach is very specific and tailored, and it incorporates state-of-the-art monitoring requirements. By contrast, BACT standards are the product of a dialogue between the permit applicant and the (usually state) government; the resources spent on BACT standards are a fraction of those devoted by the EPA to NSPS and MACT standards. And BACT standards tend to focus only on emission limits rather than the most advanced compliance and monitoring regimes. In short, BACT standards piggy-back on the work done in setting NSPS and MACT standards.

Second, the rules for PSD/NSR are different than those for NSPS: they allow more "netting out" of review. NSPS focuses on new or modified "affected facilities" which essentially covers discrete emitting units, and there is no de minimus threshold for calculating what counts as a "modification." By contrast, PSD/NSR is plantwide, offering opportunities to "minor" or "net" out of review, and there are appreciable "significance" thresholds for the determination of what counts as modification. It is possible then, for a new piece of equipment—a mid-sized boiler, say—to escape PSD/NSR and yet still be covered by the NSPS standards. NSPS thus serves as a backstop to PSD/NSR.

7.   TITLE V PERMITS

Prior to the 1990 Amendments, a variety of provisions of the CAA required some stationary sources to obtain a permit. For example, new major stationary sources in both NAZ (§ 173) and PSD areas (§ 165) had to obtain pre-construction permits. Sometimes, sources had to comply with the permit requirements under both of these provisions. This is because no area of the country is out of attainment for all six NAAQS. This means that stationary sources that are in nonattainment zones for one pollutant will by definition be in PSD areas for other pollutants (recall that an area of the country that is *in* attainment for a criteria pollutant is subject to the Act's PSD requirements designed to prevent deterioration of air quality below levels set by NAAQS). Thus, prior to 1990, many sources already had to comply with the permit requirements of *both* the NAZ and the PSD programs. In addition, prior to 1990, some states, such as California, had already adopted a general permit program. For example, California's South Coast Air Quality Management District (SCAQMD) already required operating permits for any equipment that may emit air contaminants (which are defined very broadly). This rule did not establish a threshold of a minimum quantity of emissions.

However, Title V of the 1990 Amendments added an entirely new and more comprehensive permit program to the CAA. The program applies to all major sources [as defined under various provisions of the CAA, including the air toxics provisions (§ 112), and the NAZ provisions (§§ 171–193) and those sources that fit the default definition of major stationary source and major emitting facility in § 302(j)]. Permits also apply to all "affected" sources as defined in Title IV's acid rain provisions; all sources subject to § 111 NSPS; all sources of air toxics regulated under § 112 (including area sources); all sources required to have permits under the PSD and nonattainment provisions of Titles C and D; and any other sources designated by EPA regulations as requiring a permit. Clearly, almost every stationary source regulated under one or another CAA provision will be included in the Title V requirements. Permits contain enforceable emission limits and impose monitoring requirements on permit holders [§§ 504(a) and (b)]. All permitted sources must pay substantial permit fees as well (§ 502). Compliance with the requirements of a Title V permit is deemed to be compliance with the CAA [§ 504(f)].

Title V is administered by the states, which had to amend their SIPs to establish a permit program. The EPA promulgated the rules implementing the Title V permit program in 1992. The rules specify what state permit programs must contain. State-issued permits must incorporate terms and conditions to assure compliance with "applicable requirements under the Act" and impose monitoring and record-keeping requirements on permit-holders, among other things.

Title V has been widely touted as a means of streamlining air quality regulation for individual sources by placing all applicable requirements into a single permit. It was also thought that a general permit requirement would make compliance information more accessible to the public. In theory, the permit requirement is a procedural change, not a substantive one. However, because permits can translate general requirements into detailed and rigid specifications, they may reduce the flexibility of sources to make changes in operations that affect emissions. In addition, for thousands of stationary sources that previously had no obligation to obtain a permit, the permitting process itself can be onerous and costly. Perhaps most significantly, the new monitoring requirements imposed on stationary sources as part of the Title V permit program enable the EPA to press for more stringent monitoring, which, "in effect, cause the underlying emissions control requirements to become more stringent." The new reporting requirements may also make sources more vulnerable to citizen suits. *See* Ivan Tether and Robert S. Nicksin, *New Frontiers for the Push and Pull of Federalism—Implementation of the Clean Air Act's Operating Permit Program in Southern California*, 29 Envtl. L. Rep. 10757, 10763 (1999). That new susceptibility to citizen suits was partially confirmed and partially diluted in *New York Public Interest Research Group v. Johnson*, where the Second Circuit held that the EPA must issue a notice of violation to a plant that the state environmental agency had found to be in violation of Title V, but affirmed the state and federal agencies' previously recognized discretion in using their expertise to decide whether such a violation has in fact occurred. 427 F.3d 172 (2d Cir. 2005) (citing *New York Pub. Interest Research Group v. Whitman*, 321 F.3d 316 (2d Cir. 2003), for the proposition that the agency retains discretion in determining non-compliance).

Electric power companies and industry trade associations scored a victory on this issue, when the D.C. Circuit set aside the EPA's 1998 guidance document directing state permitting authorities to conduct wide-ranging sufficiency reviews and to enhance the monitoring required in individual permits beyond that contained in state or federal emissions standards, where states found existing monitoring requirements inadequate. The Court reasoned that the guidance documents effectively broadened the EPA's underlying rule requiring only periodic monitoring, which the agency could not do without going through the required rulemaking procedure. *See* Appalachian Power Co. v. EPA, 208 F.3d 1015 (D.C. Cir. 2000). The EPA began to promulgate just such a rule in 2002, but then suddenly reversed itself in the final rule, adopting the position that states may not impose requirements beyond the minimum periodic monitoring necessary to confirm a source's compliance with permit requirements. However, the D.C. Circuit found that the EPA's "flip-flop" had not allowed proper notice and opportunity for public comment on this interpretation, and thus vacated the rule. *Environmental Integrity Project v. EPA*, 425 F.3d 992, 997 (D.C. Cir. 2005).

Prior to the adoption of Title V, clean air regulation differed from clean water regulation because under the permit system of water quality, only permitted discharges were allowed, while under clean air regulation, emissions were generally allowed unless specifically prohibited by rules and regulations. Title V thus adopts the "only if permitted" model from the clean water context. See Chapter 7.

E. MOBILE SOURCE, SPILLOVERS AND OTHER SPECIAL PROVISIONS OF THE CLEAN AIR ACT

1. MOBILE SOURCES

Along with stationary sources, mobile sources are the other major cause of air pollution. Motor vehicles are responsible for up to half of the VOCs and nitrogen oxides that form smog, and they produce more than half of all air toxics. In addition, motor vehicles produce up to 90 percent of the carbon monoxide in the urban air. Cars were also the primary source of lead emissions until lead was phased out of gasoline in accordance with § 211(n) of the Act. Motor vehicles pose different problems than do stationary sources because of their vastly greater numbers, and because they cross the borders of states and air regions alike.

The Act regulates mobile sources primarily by requiring standards for tailpipe emissions (which targets the auto industry rather than individual car owners) and by regulating fuels to make them cleaner. As you already know from *Massachusetts v. EPA*, Section 202(a)(1) requires the EPA to promulgate regulations prescribing emission standards "applicable to the emission of any air pollutant from any class or classes of new motor vehicles or new motor vehicle engines which in [the EPA's] judgment cause or contribute to air pollution which may reasonably be anticipated to endanger public health or welfare." These emission standards apply for the "useful life" of the vehicle, which is defined in the 1990 Amendments to be ten years or 100,000 miles, whichever comes first. [§ 202(d)(1)]. The EPA has promulgated separate standards for different classes of vehicles, including passenger vehicles, light duty trucks, heavy duty vehicles and motorcycles. *See* 40 C.F.R. part 86.

Congress has reserved for itself the primary role in setting tailpipe emissions standards, leaving a secondary role to the EPA and pre-empting the states (with the exception of California) from setting more stringent standards. Section 209 of the CAA reserves to the federal government exclusive authority to regulate motor vehicle emissions but specifically allows California to adopt its own standards if California determines that its standards will be no less protective of the public health than the federal standards and if the state applies for a waiver from the EPA. States may adopt these standards under § 177, providing they are "identical" to California's. In addition, SIPs may contain a variety of transportation controls and inspection and maintenance programs, which more directly affect vehicle owners, though Congress has curtailed these measures over the years because they are politically contentious and difficult to implement.

Pollution from cars has improved tremendously in the last 30 years. Today's cars produce 60–80 percent less pollution than cars in the 1960s, and leaded gas has been phased out entirely. The progress is all the more impressive because air pollution has declined even as the number of car miles and car trips per person have gone up dramatically. In 1970, Americans traveled 1 trillion miles in motor vehicles. By 2001 that number had risen to 2.8 trillion miles.

a. History of Mobile Source Provisions

Section 202 of the 1970 Amendments to the Act originally required auto makers to reduce emissions of hydrocarbons and carbon monoxide 90% from average emissions for model year 1970. The new standard was to be effective for model year 1975. Congress also required auto makers to reduce nitrogen oxide emissions in the 1976 models 90% from average emissions in 1971 models. Perhaps surprisingly, these rather dramatic reductions were not calculated based on scientific data. Nor were they based on economic analysis nor on an assessment of technological feasibility. Rather, they were based on the assumption that since air pollution concentrations exceeded NAAQS by five times in the most polluted areas, tailpipe emissions should be reduced by 80% (plus 10% because of increased vehicle use), and this would make air quality sufficiently safe. *See* JAMES E. KRIER & EDMUND URSIN, POLLUTION AND POLICY: A CASE ESSAY ON CALIFORNIA AND FEDERAL EXPERIENCE WITH MOTOR VEHICLE AIR POLLUTION, 1940–1975 at p. 206–7 (1977).

Congress knew when it passed these mandatory emissions reductions that they would be "technology-forcing." Yet although Congress itself set the 90 per cent reduction, it delegated to the EPA the task of translating that mandate into an emissions standard expressed in terms of "grams per mile" for each of the regulated pollutants. To do this, the EPA had to calculate the baseline average emissions of model year 1971, then reduce that figure by 90 percent as required by the Act. For example, the EPA calculated the 1970 baseline for hydrocarbons as 4.1 grams per mile and subsequently required auto makers to reduce it to .41 grams per mile by 1975. Section 202 also provided that the EPA could grant a one-year nonrenewable waiver under certain conditions, including that the manufacturer had made "all good efforts" to achieve the standards. The auto manufacturers sought a waiver in 1972, anticipating that they would not be able to meet the new standards because the technology to do so did not yet exist. The EPA denied the waiver, and the D.C. Circuit reviewed the denial in the case below.

INTERNATIONAL HARVESTER CO. v. RUCKELSHAUS

United States Court of Appeals, District of Columbia Circuit, 1973.
478 F.2d 615.

LEVENTHAL, CIRCUIT JUDGE.

The tension of forces presented by the controversy over automobile emission standards may be focused by two central observations:

(1) The automobile is an essential pillar of the American economy. Some 28 percent of the nonfarm workforce draws its livelihood from the automobile industry and its products.

(2) The automobile has had a devastating impact on the American environment. As of 1970, authoritative voices stated that "[a]utomotive pollution constitutes in excess of 60% of our national air pollution problem" and more than 80 percent of the air pollutants in concentrated urban areas. * * *

On December 31, 1970, Congress grasped the nettle and amended the Clean Air Act to set a statutory standard for required reductions in levels of hydrocarbons (HC) and carbon monoxide (CO) which must be achieved for 1975 models of light duty vehicles. Section 202(b) of the Act added by the Clean Air Amendments of 1970, provides that, beginning with the 1975 model year, exhaust emission of hydrocarbons and carbon monoxide from "light duty vehicles" must be reduced at least 90 percent from the permissible emission levels in the 1970 model year. * * *

Congress was aware that these 1975 standards were "drastic medicine," designed to "force the state of the art." There was, naturally, concern whether the manufacturers would be able to achieve this goal. Therefore, Congress provided, in Senator Baker's phrase, a "realistic escape hatch"; the manufacturers could petition the Administrator of the EPA for a one-year suspension of the 1975 requirements, and Congress took the precaution of directing the National Academy of Sciences to undertake an ongoing study of the feasibility of compliance with the emission standards. * * * Under section 202(b)(5)(D) of the Act, the Administrator is authorized to grant a one-year suspension only if he determines that (i) such suspension is essential to the public interest or the public health and welfare of the United States, (ii) all good faith efforts have been made to meet the standards established by this subsection, (iii) the applicant has established that effective control technology, processes, operating methods, or other alternatives are not available or have not been available for a sufficient period of time to achieve compliance prior to the effective date of such standards, and (iv) the study and investigation of the National Academy of Sciences conducted pursuant to subsection (c) of this section and other information available to him has not indicated that technology, processes, or other alternatives are available to meet such standards. * * *

At the outset of his Decision, the Administrator determined that the most effective system so far developed was the noble metal oxidizing catalyst. * * *

[At that point tests of cars using catalytic converter technology had shown only one model that achieved the necessary standard. The Administrator alleged, however, that the test data did not fully reflect the variables that would determine real-world auto emissions, and that given certain adjustments of the data based on predictions about future real-world conditions such as changes in fuel composition, calculations of the effect of equipment deterioration, regulatory requirements for catalyst replacement, and other variables, 1975 models would in fact be able to achieve the mandated emissions reductions.]

With the data submitted and the above assumptions, the Administrator concluded that no showing had been made that requisite technology was not available. The EPA noted that this did not mean that the variety of vehicles produced in 1975 would be as extensive as before. According to EPA, "Congress clearly intended to require major changes in the kinds of automobiles produced for sale in the United States after 1974" and there "is no basis, therefore, for construing the Act to authorizing suspension of the standards simply because the range of performance of cars with effective emission control may be restricted as compared to present cars." As long as "basic demand" for new light duty motor vehicles was satisfied, the applicants could not establish that technology was not available. * * *

["While the case was on appeal, the National Academy of Sciences (NAS) completed a report on the issue pursuant to its obligation under section 202(b)(5)(D) of the Clean Air Act, and concluded that "the technology necessary to meet the requirements of the Clean Air Act Amendments ... is not available at this time." After the report had been issued, the court remanded the case to allow EPA to comment on it.]

The Administrator apparently relied, however, on the report to bolster his conclusion that the applicants had not established that technology was unavailable. The same NAS Report had stated:

> * * * the status of development and rate of progress made it possible that the larger manufacturers will be able to produce vehicles that will qualify, provided that provisions are made for catalyst replacement and other maintenance, for averaging emissions of production vehicles, and for the general availability of fuel containing suitably low levels of catalyst poisons.

The Administrator pointed out that two of NAS's provisos—catalytic converter replacement and low lead levels—had been accounted for in his analysis of the auto company data, and provision therefore had been insured through regulation. * * *

The most authoritative estimate in the record of the ecological costs of a one-year suspension is that of the NAS Report. Taking into account such "factors as the vehicle-age distribution among all automobiles, the decrease in vehicle miles driven per year, per car as vehicle age increases, the predicted nationwide growth in vehicle miles driven each year" and the effect of emission standards on exhaust control, NAS concluded that:

> * * * the effect on total emissions of a one-year suspension with no additional interim standards appears to be small. The effect is not more significant because the emission reduction now required of model year 1974 vehicles, as compared with uncontrolled vehicles (80 percent for HC and 69 percent for CO), is already so substantial.
> * * *

On balance the record indicates the environmental costs of a one-year suspension are likely to be relatively modest. This must be balanced against the potential economic costs—and ecological costs—if the Administrator's prediction on the availability of effective technology is incorrect. * * *

If in 1974, when model year 1975 cars start to come off the production line, the automobiles of Ford, General Motors and Chrysler cannot meet the 1975 standards and do not qualify for certification, the Administrator of EPA has the theoretical authority, under the Clean Air Act, to shut down the auto industry, as was clearly recognized in congressional debate. We cannot put blinders on the facts before us so as to omit awareness of the reality that this authority would undoubtedly never be exercised. [More realistically, the court said, the standards would be later relaxed if they turned out to be wrong, but this too would cause problems.]

* * * The record before us suggests that there already exists a technological gap between Ford and General Motors, in Ford's favor. General Motors did not make the decision to concentrate on what EPA found to be the most effective system at the time of its decision—the noble metal monolithic catalyst. Instead it relied principally on testing the base metal catalyst as its first choice system. * * *

The case is haunted by the irony that what seems to be Ford's technological lead may operate to its grievous detriment, assuming the relaxation-if-necessary approach * * *. If in 1974, when certification of production vehicles begins, any one of the three major companies cannot meet the 1975 standards, it is a likelihood that standards will be set to permit the higher level of emission control achievable by the laggard. This will be the case whether or not the leader has or has not achieved compliance with the 1975 standards. Even if the relaxation is later made industry-wide, the Government's action, in first imposing a standard not generally achievable and then relaxing it, is likely to be detrimental to the leader who has tooled up to meet a higher standard than will ultimately be required.

In some contexts high achievement bestows the advantage that rightly belongs to the leader of high quality. In this context before us, however, the high achievement in emission control results, under systems presently available, in lessened car performance—an inverse correlation. The competitive disadvantage to the ecological leader presents a forbidding outcome—if the initial assumption of feasibility is not validated, and there is subsequent relaxation—for which we see no remedy. * * *

This case inevitably presents, to the court as to the Administrator, the need for a perspective on the suspension that is informed by an analysis which balances the costs of a "wrong decision" on feasibility against the gains of a correct one. These costs include the risks of grave maladjustments for the technological leader from the eleventh-hour grant of a suspension, and the impact on jobs and the economy from a decision which is only partially accurate, allowing companies to produce cars but at a significantly reduced level of output. Against this must be weighed the environmental savings from denial of suspension. The record indicates that these will be relatively modest. * * *

Another consideration is present, that the real cost to granting a suspension arises from the symbolic compromise with the goal of a clean environment. We emphasize that our view of a one-year suspension, and the intent of Congress as to a one-year suspension, is in no sense to be taken as any support for further suspensions. This would plainly be contrary to the intent of Congress to set an absolute standard in 1976. * * *

We approach the question of the burden of proof on the auto companies with the previous considerations before us.

It is with utmost diffidence that we approach our assignment to review the Administrator's decision on "available technology." The legal issues are intermeshed with technical matters, and as yet judges have no scientific aides. Our diffidence is rooted in the underlying technical complexities, and remains even when we take into account that ours is a judicial review, and not a technical or policy redetermination. * * *

The Act makes suspension dependent on the Administrator's determination that:

> the applicant has established that effective control technology, processes, operating methods, or other alternatives are not available or have not been available for a sufficient period of time to achieve compliance prior to the effective date of such standards * * *.

Clearly this requires that the applicants come forward with data which showed that they could not comply with the contemplated standards. The normal rules place such a burden on the party in control of the relevant information. It was the auto companies who were in possession of the data about emission performance of their cars.

The submission of the auto companies unquestionably showed that no car had actually been driven 50,000 miles and achieved conformity of emissions to the 1975 standards. The Administrator's position is that on the basis of the methodology outlined, he can predict that the auto companies can meet the standards, and that the ability to make a prediction saying the companies can comply means that the petitioners have failed to sustain their burden of proof that they cannot comply. * * *

The number of unexplained assumptions used by the Administrator, the variance in methodology from that of the Report of the National Academy of Sciences, and the absence of an indication of the statistical reliability of the prediction, combine to generate grave doubts as to whether technology is available to meet the 1975 statutory standards. We say this, incidentally, without implying or intending any acceptance of petitioners' substitute assumptions. These grave doubts have a legal consequence. This is customarily couched, by legal convention, in terms of "burden of proof." We visualize the problem in less structured terms although the underlying considerations, relating to risk of error, are related. As we see it the issue must be viewed as one of legislative intent. And since there is neither express wording nor legislative history on the precise issue, the intent must be imputed. The court must seek to discern and reconstruct what the legislature that enacted the statute would have contemplated for the court's action if it could have been able to foresee the precise situation. It is in this perspective that we have not flinched from our discussion of the economic and ecological risks inherent in a "wrong decision" by the Administrator. We think the vehicle manufacturers established by a preponderance of the evidence, in the record before us, that technology was not available, within the meaning of the Act, when they adduced the tests on actual vehicles; that the Administrator's reliance on technological methodology to offset the actual tests raised serious doubts and failed to meet the burden of proof which in our view was properly assignable to him, in the light of accepted legal doctrine and the intent of Congress discerned, in part, by taking into account that the risk of an "erroneous" denial of suspension outweighed the risk of an "erroneous" grant of suspension. We do not use the burden of proof in the conventional sense of civil trials, but the Administrator must sustain the burden of adducing a reasoned presentation supporting the reliability of EPA's methodology. * * *

[T]he parties should have opportunity on remand to address themselves to matters not previously put before them by EPA for comment * * *.

[Meanwhile] the Administrator may consider possible use of interim standards short of complete suspension. The statute permits conditioning of suspension on the adoption, by virtue of the information adduced in the suspension proceeding, of interim standards, higher than those set for 1974.

NOTES

1. For an argument that the court's decision in *International Harvester* flouted the statutory mandate, *see* Daniel Farber, *Statutory Interpretation and Legislative Supremacy*, 78 GEO. L.J. 281, 298–300 (1989).

2. *International Harvester* turned out to be only the first of a series of delays in meeting new car standards. On remand in *International Harvester,* the Administrator granted the suspension and imposed interim emission standards more lenient than the ninety percent reduction, although allowing California to impose a more rigorous standard. In 1974 Congress amended the Act to postpone the final compliance deadlines until 1977, with another "escape hatch" to 1978. In 1975 the Administrator granted another one year suspension. In the 1977 Clean Air Act Amendments, Congress postponed final compliance until 1981, with provision for reductions in the interim and for limited opportunities to obtain additional waivers. *See* James A. Henderson, Jr. & Richard N. Pearson, *Implementing Federal Environmental Policies: The Limits of Aspirational Commands*, 78 COLUM. L. REV. 1429, 1447 (1978). The

1981 standards were also the subject of waivers given to "financially troubled" automakers. *See* 12 Env't Rep. (BNA) 1398 (1981).

3. Suppose the court of appeals had allowed the EPA to deny the suspension; what options would Congress have had if it appeared the industry could not meet the standards on time? What remedial options would Congress have that are not available to a court?

4. Is the following a fair assessment of Judge Leventhal's opinion: The statutory requirement to reduce auto emissions 90 percent, read literally, is a "rule" rather than a "goal." However, when this provision is read as if it were conditioned by the express commitment of Congress to amend the requirements if the manufacturers make a real effort to comply, the section does not constitute a strict rule, but instead a flexible goal. There was no congressional intention to apply the 90 percent requirement in the future; Congress was not about to shut down Detroit and had not concluded that accomplishing the 90 per cent reduction was feasible. For these very reasons, the leading judicial interpretation of the 90 per cent requirement dealt with the requirement primarily as a question of policy rather than one of rule interpretation. *See* David Schoenbrod, *Goals Statutes or Rules Statutes: The Case of the Clean Air Act*, 30 UCLA L. REV. 740, 786 (1983).

5. The 90 percent emission reduction requirement imposed by the 1970 Clean Air Act was an example of "technology forcing" standards, that is, standards which can be met only through development of new technology not in existence at the time the standards are prescribed. Note that the vehicle manufacturers applied for suspensions at almost the earliest possible date (early in 1972), and that the EPA Administrator found against them on all four statutory points except the one concerning "good faith efforts" to meet the standard. In retrospect, wasn't it inevitable, given the language of the statute, that the companies would not meet the 1975 deadline and that either Congress, the Administrator or the court would forgive them? *See* James A. Henderson & Richard N. Pearson, *Implementing Federal Environmental Policies: The Limits of Aspirational Commands*, 78 COLUM. L. REV. 1429, 1445–1453 (1978). What does this say about how realistic Congress tends to be when it passes environmental statutes? Is Congress aware that its laws will be partially implemented, and that, routinely, statutory deadlines will be missed? If Congress is aware of this and continues to set ambitious legislative goals, are members of Congress just not so smart? Or might there be a method to their madness? Why doesn't Congress worry that it will be blamed by the public for passing ineffective laws?

In a more recent attempt at technology-forcing, the EPA, following its duty under CAA section 129(a)(3) to promulgate standards that "reflect the greatest degree of emission reduction achievable" based on the Administrator's projection of what cost-effective technology will be available in the future, issued a rule drastically reducing standards for emissions from diesel engines beginning in 2007. 66 Fed. Reg. 5002 (Jan. 18, 2001). Hearing an industry challenge to the EPA's prediction, the D.C. Circuit upheld all of the standards, finding that the EPA had successfully "identif[ied] the major steps for improvement and give[n] plausible reasons for its belief that the industry will be able to solve those problems in the time remaining," and was not obliged to "provide detailed solutions to every engineering problem." National Petrochemical & Refiners Ass'n v. EPA, 287 F.3d 1130 (D.C. Cir. 2002). Compare the EPA's role here (determining what technology will be available and setting emissions requirements accordingly) versus in *International Harvester* (where Congress had already set the standards, and the agency only decided whether industry would get an extra year to comply). Which method seems best suited to force industry to utilize new emissions-control technology: when Congress puts its foot down and mandates reductions no matter what, or when the agency uses its expert knowledge to judge when technologies are feasible enough to require their implementation? Does either of these mechanisms seem likely to induce the adoption of technology that is expensive but achieves significant emissions reductions? Do you think industry would adopt new technologies as they became available without being required to by the EPA? Would a positive incentive (e.g. research subsidies, tax breaks for environmentally-friendly products) be more efficient in influencing manufacturers' behavior?

The 1990 Amendments to the Clean Air Act added extensive new provisions relating to mobile sources and imposing even stricter standards for new cars: .25 g/m for hydrocarbons; 3.4 g/m of carbon monoxide and .4 g/m of nitrogen dioxide. Manufacturers could phase in the new standards: 40 per cent of the 1994 cars were required to meet this standard; 80 per cent of 1995 cars were required to meet it, and 100 per cent had to comply thereafter. The EPA updated these standards yet again, as required by CAA section 202(g)(1). The agency's "Tier 2" program, among other things, regulates light trucks and SUVs under the same emissions standards as passenger vehicles, reduces ozone and particulate matter standards, and decreases the amount of sulfur in gasoline (sulfur interferes with the operation of catalytic converters). Control of Air Pollution from New Motor Vehicles, 65 Fed. Reg. 6697 (Feb. 10, 2000) (to be codified at 40 C.F.R. pts. 80, 85, 86). This return to mobile source regulation partly stems from the recognition that the transportation sector offers the opportunity for relatively manageable emissions cuts, compared to the economic costs of squeezing more reductions out of already heavily-regulated stationary sources. Henry A. Waxman et al., *Cars, Fuels, and Clean Air: A Review of Title II of the Clean Air Act Amendments of 1990*, 21 ENVTL. L. 1947, 1950 (1991).

b. California's Special Status in Emissions Regulation

The 1990 Amendments left intact California's special status to impose tighter emissions standards. States do sometimes adopt California's standards, and the auto industry regularly launches a legal challenge to try and prevent it. In one instance, a majority of states comprising the "ozone transport commission" (a commission of mid-Atlantic and Northeastern states established under § 184 to address interstate migration of ozone) sought uniform adoption of the California standards regionally. The EPA promulgated a rule mandating that 12 states and the District of Columbia adopt the California standards. *See* 60 Fed. Reg. 4712 (Jan. 24, 1995). In *Virginia v. EPA*, 108 F.3d 1397 (D.C. Cir. 1997), the D.C. Circuit struck down the rule. The Court held that the EPA has no authority under § 110 (the SIP provision of the Act) to *require* adoption of particular control measures such as California's auto emission standards. However, states can still adopt them voluntarily. Complex negotiations followed, involving California, the Northeastern states, and the EPA. The result was an agreement that substantially harmonized the California and national requirements, arguably allowing the EPA to partially leapfrog the pre–2004 statutory freeze on new national standards mandated by the 1990 amendments to the Act. *See* 62 Fed. Reg. 31,192 (June 6, 1997).

California also instituted an ambitious Low Emissions Vehicle (LEV) program that has been plagued by delays and controversy. The program had required 2 per cent of all new vehicles in California to be electric-powered Zero Emission Vehicles (ZEV), with that percentage increasing yearly to 10 per cent by 2003. Auto manufacturers argued that they could not meet these targets because the demand for ZEVs had not yet developed. While the state dropped the sales quotas, it entered private memoranda of agreements (MOAs) with automakers under which automakers agreed to supply a certain number of ZEVs to California markets for the 1998–2000 model years.

As noted earlier, § 177 of the CAA allows other states to adopt California's standards, providing they are "identical." And although the 1990 Amendments prohibit the EPA from adopting new emission standards until model-year 2004, the agency adopted a voluntary national Low Emission Vehicle (LEV) program, under which manufacturers could voluntarily agree to adopt stricter emission standards for new cars sold in the Northeastern states beginning in 1998. In the end, New York adopted California's ZEV-sales requirement anyway, and the Second Circuit upheld it as being in compliance with section 177. *See* Motor Veh. Mfrs. Ass'n v. New York State Dept. of Envtl. Conservation, 17 F.3d 521 (2d Cir. 1994). When California repealed its sales quotas for model years 1998–2000, however, automakers challenged the New York requirements on the ground that they now violated the requirement that they be "identical" to the California program. The Second Circuit agreed, holding that § 209 pre-empted the non-identical program. American Auto. Mfrs. Ass'n v. Cahill, 152 F.3d 196, 200–01 (2d Cir. 1998).

In another instance, Massachusetts, which previously had copied California's LEV program, amended the ZEV portion of its LEV program to duplicate some, but not all, portions of the new MOAs that California had reached with automakers. The Auto Manufacturers' Association sued, arguing that the Massachusetts regulations were preempted by the Act because the California agreements were not a traditional "standard" and the Massachusetts program was not "identical" in any event. After lengthy litigation, in which the First Circuit Court of Appeals took the unusual step of invoking the doctrine of "primary jurisdiction" to refer the matter to the EPA, the Court ultimately held for the auto manufacturers. *See* Association of Int'l. Auto. Mfrs., Inc. v. Commissioner, Massachusetts Dep't. of Envtl. Prot., 208 F.3d 1 (1st Cir. 2000).

In 2002, California's ZEV regulations were temporarily enjoined in *Central Valley Chrysler–Plymouth v. California Air Resources Board*, No. CV–F–02–5017, 2002 WL 34499459 (2002), on the grounds that the regulations were preempted by the federal Energy Policy and Conservation Act, which governs fuel economy standards. The case settled while still on appeal, however, mooting that decision.

Despite the setback to its LEV program, California continues to blaze the trail on automobile emissions regulation generally. On November 5, 1999, the California Air Resources Board voted to impose stricter emission standards for new automobiles sold in California, to be phased in over a three year period starting in 2004. The standards require sport utility vehicles, minivans and pickups to meet the same emission standards as passenger cars. *See In the News: California Emissions Standards*, 29 Envtl. L. Rep. 10055 (1999). Though the EPA's Tier 2 program also regulates these different classes of automobiles evenhandedly, the California standard imposes more stringent emissions limitations. Richard Perez–Pena, *Pataki to Impose Strict New Limits on Auto Emissions*, N.Y. TIMES, Nov. 7, 1999, at 1.

As described in more detail in Chapter 4, *supra*, page 327, in 2000, the South Coast Air Quality Management District (a subdivision of the California government responsible for air quality in the Los Angeles area) adopted the "Fleet Rules," which required local companies with large fleets of vehicles, such as taxicab and street sweeping companies, to purchase certain numbers of low-emissions or alternative-fuel vehicles, essentially phasing out older, dirtier vehicles. The Engine Manufacturers' Association sued the District, asserting that the prohibition in § 209(a) on any state "adopt[ing] or attempt[ing] to enforce any standard relating to the control of emissions from new motor vehicles or new motor vehicle engines" included within its compass this attempt to regulate vehicle purchases based on emissions limitations. The Supreme Court agreed with this view, holding that the purchase restriction qualified as an attempt to enforce an emissions standard, and was thus preempted by federal regulation. Engine Mfrs. Ass'n v. South Coast Air Quality Mgmt. Dist., 541 U.S. 246 (2004). The District subsequently reinstated large portions of the Fleet Rules as they applied to state or local public agencies and private fleets under contract to those agencies, following a 2004 federal district court decision finding that those applications of the rules, as valid procurement requirements, were not preempted by the Clean Air Act. Press Release, S. Coast Air Quality Mgmt. Dist., AQMD Reinstates Major Portions of its Clean Fleet Rules (July 27, 2005), *available at* http:/www.aqmd.gov/news1/2005/FleetRuleAdvisoryPR.html (last visited July 13, 2009).

Most recently, California passed Assembly Bill 1493, authorizing the state's Air Resources Board to establish standards for emissions of carbon dioxide (CO_2), one of the heat trapping gases that contributes to global warming. *See* California Air Resources Board, Climate Change, http://www.arb.ca.gov/cc/cc.htm#Background, for more information about regulations implementing the law, which were to take effect in January 2006 for model years 2009 and thereafter. California could not implement its regulations without a waiver from the federal government. After a long and convoluted battle that included several federal lawsuits and an initial denial of the waiver by the Bush Administration, on June 30, 2009 the EPA finally granted the California waiver. *See* U.S. Environmental Protection Agency, California Greenhouse Gas Waiver Request, available at http://www.epa.gov/OMS/climate/ca-waiver.htm. Moreover President Obama announced in May, 2009 that the California greenhouse gas emissions standards will form the basis for a new federal greenhouse gas emissions standard, combined with a new federal fuel economy standard, that will significantly reduce carbon dioxide and other greenhouse gases from automobiles for model years 2012–2016. *See* U.S. EPA, *Transportation and Climate: Regulations and Standards* http://www.epa.gov/otaq/climate/regulations.htm.

c. Clean Fuels

In addition to these new emission standards, the 1990 amendments contain new provisions for alternative fuels aimed at changing the composition of gasoline in heavily polluted cities. There seem to be two reasons for this program. First, the changed tailpipe standards have only a gradual impact on pollution levels, since they affect only new cars. Second, leaks from the system may defeat even the best exhaust treatment equipment. *See Gasoline: The Unclean Fuel?*, 246 SCIENCE 199 (1989). The new provisions require the nine worst nonattainment areas to sell only reformulated gasoline [§ 211(k)]. These nonattainment areas, collectively, account for about 30 per cent of the gasoline consumed in the United States. The Act also requires states with serious or worse nonattainment classifications to amend their SIPs to implement a clean fuel program [§ 182(c)(4)]. The EPA is also required to adopt a pilot clean-fuel vehicle program in California [§ 249(a)].

The changes in fuel composition are designed to reduce ozone and carbon monoxide levels in the most smog-ridden cities. Reformulated gasoline has certain features that help to ameliorate pollution, including reduced hydrocarbon emissions and sulfur content. Reformulated gasoline need not contain oxygenated fuel additives such as ethanol or MTBE, but these additives help to meet the reformulated fuel requirements by promoting more efficient combustion of fuel. The oxygenates help to convert CO into CO_2, reducing CO emissions as required by the Act. Ironically, it does so at the price of producing CO_2, which contributes to global warming! This is an example of how trying to address one environmental problem can exacerbate others.

Moreover, federal requirements specify that gasoline must contain a minimum weight of oxygenated fuel but leaves the choice of oxygenate to the states. In another example of how environmental regulation can have unanticipated secondary effects, California's choice of MTBE as its oxygenate led to groundwater contamination from leaking underground storage tanks. California chose MTBE because it was readily available, had high octane value, and also reduced toxic emissions from tail pipes. Yet MTBE has leached out of underground storage tanks at gas stations and migrated into the drinking water supply. While MTBE has not been found to be a carcinogen, it has a strong taste and odor, making water undrinkable. As a result, the Governor of California ordered that the oxygenate be phased out. *See* Executive Order D–5–99 (Mar. 25, 1999). California is now faced with the dilemma of how to achieve the mandated oxygen level without using MBTE. (Ethanol could be used as an alternative to MBTE to achieve the proper oxygen content, but that would require almost the entire supply of ethanol produced in the United States, and according to California studies would interfere with achievement of the state's particulate matter and ozone NAAQS.) In 1999, the state sought a waiver of the requirement under CAA § 211(m)(3)(A), which allows it to be set aside if the EPA finds that compliance with the mandated oxygen content will "prevent or interfere with the attainment by the area of a national primary ambient air quality standard." The EPA denied the waiver based on its independent findings that the ramifications for California's ozone attainment were unclear, and never reached the issue of PM attainment. Davis v. EPA, 348 F.3d 772, 777–78 (9th Cir. 2003). That denial was vacated by the Ninth Circuit in 2003 because of the EPA's failure to consider the effect on California's attainment of the particulate matter NAAQS. *Id.* at 784–85. However, on remand the agency once again denied the waiver, claiming that any adverse affect on particulate matter levels would not in fact delay the attainment date. EPA, California Oxygen Waiver Decision (June 2005), *available at* http://www.epa.gov/otaq/regs/fuels/rfg/420s05005.pdf.

The reformulated gasoline requirements have spawned a significant amount of litigation. One important rule was overturned in *American Petroleum Inst. v. EPA*, 52 F.3d 1113 (D.C. Cir. 1995) (striking down a requirement that thirty percent of oxygen in reformulated fuel be derived from renewable sources such as ethanol). Manufacturers complain that some state fuel standards will in effect require stricter emissions standards for cars. *See* Motor Vehicle Mfrs. Ass'n v. New York State Dep't of Envtl. Conservation, 79 F.3d 1298 (2d Cir. 1996) (finding this claim to be unripe). Industry has challenged the authority of states to regulate fuel oxygenation, arguing that the Clean Air Act preempts state authority to require a minimum oxygenate standard greater than 2.7 per cent. Recently, the Ninth Circuit rejected this argument, holding that the statutory preemption provisions focused on the regulation of fuel additives, rather than oxygenate standards, and that states are required under the Act to set minimum oxygen content for fuel in carbon monoxide non-attainment areas in order to meet the NAAQS. *See* Exxon Mobil Corp. v. EPA, 217 F.3d 1246 (9th Cir. 2000).

d. Inspection and Maintenance Programs and Transportation Controls

As long as we drive gasoline-powered motor vehicles, emissions control will be an essential part of air pollution regulation. And no matter how good the controls are when the car is manufactured, they will do little to reduce air pollution unless they remain effective over the life of the car. The EPA has required increasingly strict inspection and maintenance (I & M) programs for this reason, though their implementation has been plagued by delays. *See* Arnold W. Reitze, Jr. & Barry Needleman, *Control of Air Pollution from Mobile Sources Through Inspection and Maintenance Programs*, 30 HARV. J. ON LEG. 409 (1993); GAO, *Delays in Motor Vehicle Inspection Programs Jeopardize Attainment of the Ozone Standard* (GAO/RCED 98–175, June 1998).

I & M programs are unpopular because, unlike direct regulation of stationary sources or emission standards imposed on the auto industry, they tend to inconvenience consumers. For example, states may require "smog checks" before people can register their cars. However I & M programs can be more effective than the alternatives. One study found that repairs to a single high-polluting car would reduce emissions more than fuel alterations in all eighty-four vehicles in the test group combined. Stuart P. Beaton et al., *On–Road Vehicle Emissions: Regulations, Costs, and Benefits*, 268 SCIENCE 991, 992 (1995).

Transportation Control Plans (TCPs), which Congress demanded of the states in the original 1970 Amendments, are also politically unpopular and difficult to implement. In theory, TCPs include things like parking surcharges, limits on driving days and pre-construction review of stationary sources that tend to attract large numbers of cars (e.g., malls, stadiums). Section 110 of the 1970 Amendments originally required SIPs to include "land use and transportation controls" if the Act's other controls would not result in compliance with the NAAQS by mandatory deadlines. The prospect of requirements such as these caused such an outcry from the states that Congress amended § 110 to eliminate or badly weaken the EPA's ability to demand things like parking surcharges in SIPs. The history of both TCPs and the I & M program has been rocky. Congress has eliminated the most controversial aspects of these requirements, only to reinstate them in part later, and to threaten states with sanctions for failing to adopt them. Most recently, Congress has required TCPs in serious, severe and extreme nonattainment areas. *See* § 182(c)(5), § 182(d)(1) and § 182(e).

NOTES

1. Why is it so difficult to control pollution from cars? The technology to produce electric vehicles exists (even if the more advanced fuel cell technology is not yet fully developed). Is the reason really economics? Forced production of fuel-efficient cars is pointless unless the demand for them is there. However, recent events are encouraging on the prospects of developing both a strong supply and demand for cleaner cars including higher gasoline prices and increasing concern about green house gas emissions. Toyota has announced that it intends to eventually produce an all-hybrid fleet, and is increasing their production with the goal of selling at least one million hybrids

in 2010. *Toyota Says It Plans Eventually To Offer an All–Hybrid Fleet*, N.Y. TIMES, Sept. 14, 2005, at C17. That move, accompanied by Toyota's success in marketing hybrids to date, seems to have spurred other automobile manufacturers to rethink their own policies toward hybrid vehicles. James Brooke, *In the Hybrid's Wake, Trying to Catch Up*, N.Y. TIMES, Oct. 20, 2004, at C5. Note that many of these cars are sold in California. Robert Strauss, *Fond of the Ford Escape? Do You Live in Cleveland?*, N.Y. TIMES, Oct. 26, 2005, at G14. What incentives would help to encourage this trend? Why doesn't Congress simply increase gasoline taxes aimed at consumers, or a carbon tax aimed at producers or a mileage tax where mileage is tracked by GPS systems? Wouldn't such measures be the most efficient way to prompt drivers to switch to hybrids, and manufacturers to switch to non-fossil fuels?

2. Why is it so difficult to implement TCPs? What would you think about a proposal to limit drivers to driving on only certain days of the week which has been adopted in Mexico City. Or, congestion taxes and other measures to reduce traffic into urban areas, as London has done? What about increasing parking fees or tolls? How might such a regime work? Instead of punitive measures, what about providing more positive incentives akin to special car-pool lanes, or preferred parking? And what role should public transportation play in controlling both air pollution and greenhouse gases? Note that some of the highest polluting and fastest growing urban centers have weak or non-existent public transportation systems e.g., Phoenix, Atlanta and Los Angeles.

2. INTERSTATE AIR POLLUTION

a. Overview

Air pollution is particularly troublesome because it migrates. As a result, pollution produced by stationary and mobile sources in one state can affect air quality in other states. What are the mechanisms by which the law deals with such "spillovers"? We discuss common law remedies for interstate spillovers in the next chapter, because the leading cases on the matter involve water pollution.

Here we focus on how the CAA, and not the common law, addresses inter-state pollution. The issue has been handled only with great difficulty, because the statutory scheme is largely geared toward a state-by-state approach to achieving air standards. When air pollution fails to respect state lines, institutional innovation is required to deal with the spillover effects. These institutional innovations are particularly troublesome legislatively because it is clear in advance who will be the winners (downwind states) and losers (upwind states). This creates a "zero sum" political situation in which conflict is guaranteed, consensus is difficult, and deadlock is likely. Thus, even in the context of a federal union with strong centralized government, interjurisdictional spillovers are difficult to control.

The principal provisions of the Clean Air Act aimed at interstate pollution are §§ 110(a)(2)(D) and 126. Section 110(a)(2)(D) requires that

SIPs contain adequate provisions prohibiting emissions that will significantly interfere with another's state nonattainment problem. CAA § 126 provides a mechanism whereby downwind states may petition the EPA to directly regulate upwind sources of pollution. Under § 126(b), a downwind state "may petition the Administrator for a finding that any major source or group of stationary sources emits or would emit any air pollutant in violation" of CAA § 110(a)(2)(D).

Notwithstanding these provisions, the EPA largely failed until recently to address the problem of transboundary pollution. Several states invoked these sections of the Act in petitions to, and suits against, the EPA, without tangible results. In *New England Legal Foundation v. Costle,* 475 F.Supp. 425 (D. Conn. 1979), *aff'd* 632 F.2d 936 (2d Cir. 1980) and 666 F.2d 30 (2d Cir. 1981)), Connecticut plaintiffs sued the EPA Administrator and a New York public utility, seeking declaratory and injunctive relief from air pollution allegedly originating in New York and New Jersey. The EPA was claimed to have failed in its statutory duty to insist on revisions to New York and New Jersey SIPs, in order to abate transport of pollutants to Connecticut. The court held that the EPA had no "mandatory duty at this time" and dismissed all causes of action against the Administrator. In another case, *Connecticut v. EPA,* 656 F.2d 902 (2d Cir. 1981), New York had submitted for EPA approval a revision in its air pollution plan allowing a utility company to burn high sulfur oil for one year, and Connecticut and New Jersey had responded by filing protest petitions under section 126(b). With the court's approval, the EPA approved the state plan revision before ruling on the § 126 petitions.

The Sixth Circuit commented on the difficulty of resolving interstate disputes under the 1977 statute:

> In a most practical sense, [the plaintiff's] concerns are understandable. There would appear to be a patent unfairness in an Agency policy which would tolerate so much higher a level of SO_2 emissions in one area than in another, especially given the high costs which [plaintiff] has already incurred to reduce its own pollution. Nevertheless, we believe that the construction placed upon the statute by the EPA appears to be literally correct, even though arguably at odds with the important policy values represented by the 1977 amendments. This conclusion, and our strong preference to achieve an interpretation of the Act which is consistent among the several circuits, compels us to agree with the Agency here.

> It may be that the problem of interstate air pollution abatement requires an effective regional regulative scheme rather than the present unsatisfying reliance upon state boundaries as the basic unit for pollution control. However, we have neither the legislative authority to amend the statute nor the regulatory and technical expertise to set more specific technical standards. As long as the statute mandates that implementation plans be created and reviewed on the basis of state boundaries, there will be differences between the emission

limitations imposed by neighboring states. * * * [W]e conclude that we do not possess the statutory or regulatory expertise to grant any relief.

Air Pollution Control Dist. v. EPA, 739 F.2d 1071, 1088, 1094 (6th Cir. 1984). Consequently, the court held that the emitting state had not been shown to "substantially contribute" to nonattainment in the receiving state. Note that the emitting state placed no emission limit at all on the main pollution source involved. *See* Comment, *Jefferson County's Lament, Clean Air Act Offers No Relief for Interstate Pollution*, 14 Envtl. L. Rep. 10298 (1984).

b. Interstate Ozone and NOx

Nitrogen oxides (NO_x) emissions in other regions results in the creation of ozone, which is transported hundreds of miles into the Northeast. This long-range transport made it impossible for the Northeast states to attain the federally mandated air quality standard for ozone. Under the EPA's own interpretation of the statute, however, ozone transport was no excuse for nonattainment, *see* Southwestern Penn. Growth Alliance v. Browner, 121 F.3d 106 (3d Cir. 1997). As noted above, the EPA avoided the imposition of sanctions against the downwind states, doing nothing to solve the problem. The 1990 amendments established a special mechanism for dealing with such spillovers. Section 176(A)(a) grants the EPA authority to establish "transport regions" when interstate transport of pollutants from one or more states contributes significantly to the failure to meet NAAQS in another state. The EPA must establish an "Interstate Transport Commission" for each transport region, consisting of various representatives designated by the statute. The Commission must evaluate interstate transport of pollutants, assess mitigation strategies and make recommendations to the EPA to ensure all SIPs comply with the requirements of the Act. Congress specifically provided for a Northeast Ozone Transport Region (including Connecticut, Delaware, Maine, Maryland, Massachusetts, New Hampshire, New Jersey, New York, Pennsylvania, Rhode Island, Vermont, and the District of Columbia), since ozone attainment had been a particularly challenging issue in this region. Each state had a representative on the Northeast Ozone Transport Commission, a body with the objective of evaluating possible regional solutions to ozone pollution. In 1994, the Commission reached agreement on the NO_x Budget Program, a proposal to set up a cap-and-trade system among major NO_x sources within its member states in order to achieve the requisite reductions in emissions. James McKinley, Jr., *Agreement Is Reached on Pollution*, N.Y. TIMES, Oct. 2, 1994, at 33. Subsequent evaluations of the program indicate that it has achieved substantial cuts in NO_x emissions. Press Release, EPA, *Report Verifies Deep Reductions in Emissions of Nitrogen Oxide Due to Northeastern Program*, (June 27, 2003) (on file with author); *see generally* EPA, Clean Air Markets—Progress and Results, http://www.epa.gov/airmarkets/cmprpt/index.html (annual compliance reports) (last visited Jan. 24, 2006).

However, it became clear in the 1990s that ozone from upwind states was also significantly hindering eastern states from meeting their air quality standards. Representatives from thirty-seven states and the District of Columbia, along with industry representatives, environmental groups, and EPA officials, formed the Ozone Transport Assessment Group (OTAG) in 1995 to analyze this next obstacle to ozone attainment. Using comprehensive modeling of ozone transport and the effects of various proposed remedies, OTAG was able to determine that the major source of NO_x transported to the eastern states was large fossil fuel fired combustion units, especially electric generating units, in twenty-two southern and Midwestern states. OTAG's analysis, as well as other independent sources, showed that the regional cap-and-trade system would not suffice to meet ozone standards because of ozone coming from upwind sources.

[The above is drawn mainly from Bart E. Cassidy, *Litigation Rages Regarding Interstate Air Pollution*, LEG. INTELLIGENCER, Apr. 12, 1999.]

In response, eight northeastern states petitioned the EPA in 1997 to make a formal finding under § 126 that certain sources (mainly in the Midwest) were significantly contributing to their own nonattainment of ozone standards. John H. Cushman, Jr., *Northeast States Pressuring E.P.A. To Move on Smog*, N.Y. TIMES, Aug. 8, 1997, at A1. In response, the EPA issued a rule in 1998 mandating that 22 states and the District of Columbia revise their SIPs to require sufficient reductions in NO_x emissions to mitigate the interstate transport of ozone (the "NO_x SIP call"); the states had the option to participate in the Northeast's NO_x trading program. This action set off a vociferous debate over whether upwind states should significantly reduce their emissions solely to assist other states in meeting their air quality targets, or whether downwind states should have to further reduce their own emissions, economically disadvantaging them compared to the less stringently controlled Midwest and South, when they might not ever be able to attain air quality standards without reductions by upwind contributors. In the main legal challenge to the rule, the mandated reductions were largely upheld on appeal to the D.C. Circuit, although the Court agreed with certain states that the EPA findings with respect to their contributions of NO_x, and certain of the agency's calculations, were not sufficiently supported. *See* Michigan v. EPA, 213 F.3d 663 (D.C. Cir. 2000). The following case further addressed the issue of interstate transport of NO_x and the EPA's authority under § 126.

APPALACHIAN POWER COMPANY v. EPA

United States Court of Appeals, District of Columbia Circuit, 2001.
249 F.3d 1032.

[Downwind states sought a determination from the EPA under § 126 that upwind states were contributing to their violation of federal air quality standards. The EPA agreed, imposing controls on various upwind sources, who petitioned for judicial review. Based upon its analysis of the cost of emissions controls, the EPA concluded that measures which can reduce NO_x emissions for $2,000 or less per ton are highly cost-effective. The EPA then divided NO_x emission sources into various categories and determined the level of emission reduction that would be highly cost-effective for each category. The EPA also established an emission allowance "cap and trade" program, known as the Federal NO_x Budget Trading Program. Under this program, originally outlined in a May 1999 rule, regulated sources are allocated tradeable NO_x emission allowances and are prohibited from emitting more NO_x than the amount of allowances held. If a facility emits more than its initial allowance allocation, it must purchase additional allowances from another facility, reduce its emissions, or close down. To determine the initial allocations, the EPA established a NO_x emission cap for each upwind state. Each state's cap is based upon expected emission reductions from highly cost-effective controls in that state as of 2007. Ninety-five percent of each state's cap is allocated proportionally among existing sources based upon each facility's heat input. Five percent of the cap is set aside for future sources. These initial allocations will apply for the 2003–07 time period. The EPA will issue revised allocations for the 2008–12 time period, and every five years thereafter.]

PER CURIAM.

In response to petitions from several northeastern states that alleged that nitrogen oxide emitted in neighboring states was harming their local air quality, the Environmental Protection Agency promulgated a rule that requires many NO_x emitting facilities in several midwestern and southeastern states to conform to emission limits set by the EPA and to participate in an emissions trading program. Numerous petitioners challenge the rule as inconsistent with the Clean Air Act, arbitrary or capricious, and technically deficient. We uphold most aspects of the rule but remand several particulars to the Agency for reconsideration.

I. BACKGROUND

On January 18, 2000, the Environmental Protection Agency ("EPA") issued its final rule to control emissions of nitrogen oxide ("NO_x") under § 126 of the Clean Air Act ("CAA"). Under certain conditions, NO_x combines with hydrocarbons in the atmosphere to create ozone, commonly known as "smog." In the January rule, the EPA made final its findings that stationary sources of NO_x emissions in twelve upwind states and the District of Columbia contribute significantly to ozone nonattainment in northeastern states. This finding triggers direct federal regulation of stationary sources of NO_x in the upwind states. The rule further established a "cap and trade" system for NO_x emissions within each upwind jurisdiction. Covered sources must obtain NO_x emission allowances to cover their emissions, adopt additional emission controls, or cease operations. Numerous petitions for review challenge various aspects of the rule.

A. STATUTORY FRAMEWORK

* * *

Much air pollution is a local or regional problem. Some pollution, however, is caused or augmented by emissions from other states. Emissions from "upwind" regions may pollute "downwind" regions. Several provisions of the CAA are designed to address such transboundary air pollution. In particular, § 110(a)(2)(D)(i)(I) of the Act requires states to prohibit emissions within the state in amounts that will "contribute significantly to nonattainment in, or interfere with maintenance by, any other State" of the NAAQS.

CAA § 126 provides a mechanism whereby downwind states may petition the EPA to directly regulate upwind sources of pollution. Under § 126(b), a downwind state "may petition the Administrator for a finding that any major source or group of stationary sources emits or would emit any air pollutant in violation" of CAA § 110(a)(2)(D). Once the EPA makes a § 126(b) finding, § 126(c) provides that:

> it shall be a violation of this section and the applicable implementation plan in such State—
>
> (1) for any major proposed new (or modified) source with respect to which a finding has been made under subsection (b) of this section to be constructed or to operate in violation [of this section or § 110], or
>
> (2) for any major existing source to operate more than three months after such finding has been made with respect to it.

The Administrator may allow the continued operation of existing sources beyond three months provided such sources comply with emission limitations and compliance schedules provided by the Administrator which "bring about compliance . . . as expeditiously as practicable, but in no case later than three years after the date of such finding."

At issue in this case is the extent of the EPA's authority to make findings and directly regulate sources in upwind states under § 126, and whether the EPA's § 126 rule was arbitrary or capricious or contrary to law. * * *

After the EPA published the final section 126 rule in January 2000, numerous groups petitioned this Court for review. Among the petitioners are a group of upwind states from the midwestern and southeastern United States ("MW & SE State Petitioners"); utilities and other operators of electric generating facilities ("Non–State Petitioners"); companies that operate non-electric generating/industrial facilities ("Non–EGU Petitioners"); and several individual companies that have facility-specific concerns ("Facility–Specific Petitioners"). A group of northeastern states ("NE State Petitioners") also petitioned for review alleging that the EPA's rule did not go far enough in controlling upwind NO_x emissions. The northeastern states otherwise intervened in support of the EPA, as did a group of environmental organizations. The various petitions for review were consolidated into this case.

II. COMMON AND GENERAL ISSUES

* * *

C. *Significant Contribution*

* * *

[The EPA had also called on upwind states to issue new SIPs to control NO_x, but these SIP calls became entangled in the *American Trucking* litigation.]

[B]oth the SIP call and the § 126 rulemaking are directly linked to the requirement under § 110(a)(2)(D)(i) that SIPs contain provisions prohibiting "any source or other type of emissions activity within the State from emitting any air pollutant in amounts which will ... contribute significantly to nonattainment...." § 110(a)(2)(D)(1). But the necessary determinations are different in at least two material respects. First, whereas the SIP call exercise yielded a total amount of NO_x cutback for each state, which the state was then free to achieve however it might, here the mandate applies directly to sources. Second, whereas § 110(a)(2)(D)'s broad reference to "any source or other type of emissions activity" supported SIP call findings based on aggregate emissions from within each regulated state, § 126 demands that the significant contribution come from a "major source or group of *stationary* sources." 42 U.S.C. § 7426(b) (emphasis added).

The Non–State Petitioners argue that this latter distinction renders EPA's reliance on the SIP call findings inadequate; the findings based on *all* emissions can't determine whether stationary source emissions are sufficient. Instead of using those findings, petitioners argue, EPA needed first to make the more rigorous finding that the specified stationary sources within a given state *independently* met its threshold test for effect on downwind nonattainment. * * *

EPA defended its approach both as a recognition of the fact that the ozone problem is due to the *accumulation* of emissions and as a sensible reconciliation of § 110(a)(2)(D)(i) and § 126. On the need for some aggregation, of course, there can be no quarrel. Congress's use of the phrase "group of ... sources" plainly reflected a decision to act against sources whose emissions, while harmless individually, could become harmful when combined with others. And, given the relevant statutory provisions, it was reasonable for EPA to link its stationary source findings to the significance of a state's total NO_x emissions. By speaking of stationary sources that emit pollutants "in violation of the prohibition of [§ 110(a)(2)(D)(i)]," Congress clearly hinged the meaning of § 126 on that of § 110(a)(2)(D)(i). EPA reasoned that if it treated any state's entire manmade emissions as the controlling aggregate for both purposes and found a "significant contribution," "then the State's § 126 sources *may be* subject to SIP controls." In other words, a source can be subject to § 126 controls only if it is at least *at risk* of being subject to SIP controls. The effect, of course, is to displace the discretion the state would enjoy in the SIP process under § 110(a)(2)(D)(i). But this displacement of state power seems not materially greater than is inherent in EPA's interpretation of § 126, which we uphold vis-a-vis the objections petitioners raised in their initial briefs. EPA's current reading, to be sure, may not be the only possible or even the most compelling view of § 126. Perhaps the EPA could reasonably read it as petitioners would, and require that stationary sources as a whole independently satisfy some "meaningful contribution" test before they may be subject to § 126 findings. But given § 126's silence on what it means for a stationary source to violate § 110(a)(2)(D)(i), EPA's approach is at least reasonable, and therefore entitled to deference under *Chevron*. * * *

D.   *Emission Limitation Determinations*

In order to allocate NO_x emission allowances to individual sources, the EPA made state-by-state emission projections for 2007. The EPA based each state's NO_x emission budget on projected 2007 heat input (or "utilization") for electric generating units ("EGUs") and projected 2007 emissions for non-electric generating, industrial facilities ("non-EGUs"). The projections were developed with computer models working off of "baseline" emissions and heat input data from 1995 and 1996. Various petitioners challenge the EPA's budget allocations as arbitrary or capricious. While we generally uphold the EPA's authority to make emission projections and set emission limitations accordingly, we do so only where the EPA adequately responded to comments and explained the basis for its decisions. Thus, although we uphold the EPA's use of the Integrated Planning Model ("IPM") as against the specific challenges forwarded by MW & SE Petitioners, we conclude that at least one application of the model is sufficiently unexplained that we must remand the EPA's IPM-derived growth factors for further explanation. * * *

The EPA based its state-specific emission budget limitations on projections of facility utilization for 2007. This projection was calculated by taking a baseline utilization rate and applying a "growth factor" to project the 2007 utilization rate, upon which the emission budget limitation would then be imposed. For the starting baseline utilization rate, the EPA used the actual EGU utilization rate for either 1995 or 1996, whichever was greater. For the growth factors, the EPA relied upon the IPM facility utilization projections for the 2001–2010 period to generate an average annual growth rate that was then applied to the 1996–2007 period.

Petitioners contend that the EPA's resulting projections significantly underestimated growth rates in some states. In Michigan and West Virginia, for example, actual utilization in 1998 already exceeded the EPA's projected levels for 2007. This, on its face, raises questions about the reliability of the EPA's projections. While courts routinely defer to agency modeling of complex phenomena, model assumptions must have a "rational relationship" to the real world. Future growth projections that implicitly assume a baseline of negative growth in electricity generation over the course of a decade appear arbitrary, and the EPA can point to nothing in the record to dispel this appearance.

Despite the apparent disparity between the EPA's growth projections and observed growth rates, the EPA claims its growth factors were reasonable and due deference from this court. Yet even in the face of evidence suggesting the EPA's projections were erroneous, the EPA never explained why it adopted this particular methodology. The EPA claims it made a reasonable choice—and it may be right—but simply to state such a claim does not make it so. There must be an actual reason articulated by the agency at some point in the rulemaking process. There is none here. * * *

The MW & SE State Petitioners have also argued that the permit trading system contravenes CAA § 116, which allows a state to impose a local air quality standard more stringent than the corresponding NAAQS. 42 U.S.C. § 7416. The petitioners' concern is that a source might purchase permits in excess of applicable local limits and then claim the right to pollute in excess of those limits, up to the full amount of its permits. The EPA properly denies that the permit trading program would make such a claim viable. Nothing in the challenged rules exempts from § 116 a source that has acquired permits.

Although they are unable to point to any provision of the rule that allows permit trading to trump a local rule authorized by § 116, the petitioners worry in their reply brief that "other interpretations" might prevail in the future. Perhaps so, but for now, and until such time as it may conduct a new rulemaking, the EPA is committed to the position that it espouses here. The petitioners also suggest that the EPA might decline to approve a SIP that imposes stringent local limits because of its commitment to a market in emissions permits; but non-approval of a SIP is subject to judicial review, and an argument based upon the incompatibility of EPA policy and § 116 may be raised when and if the EPA disapproves a SIP in order to advance the market for emissions permits.

E. Regulation of "Future" Sources

The § 126 rule establishes a NO_x budget for each upwind state found to contribute significantly to nonattainment in the petitioning states. Ninety-five percent of this budget is allocated in the form of NO_x emission allowances to existing sources. Five percent of each state's budget is set aside for future sources. In this fashion, the rule caps emissions on existing and proposed sources, as well as sources to be proposed and built in the future. * * *

Petitioners argue that the EPA's interpretation fails at the first step of *Chevron*, contending that § 126(c) authorizes the EPA to regulate existing and proposed sources but not future sources that are not as yet proposed. In petitioners' view, the enumeration of two classes of sources that may be controlled—"major existing sources" and "proposed new (or modified) sources"—precludes the EPA's authority over a third class of sources—"future as-yet-unproposed" sources. *Expressio unius est exclusio alterius.* Petitioners argue that irrespective of whether the EPA can make findings with regard to future, as-yet-unproposed sources, it is not empowered to prohibit their construction or limit their emissions under § 126(c).

We reject petitioners' contention that the statute unambiguously reflects congressional intent to limit the EPA to the two categories defined by petitioners. Section 126 is at least subject to the interpretation that Congress intended to authorize the regulation of emissions from future sources. Under § 126(b), the EPA may find that "any major source or group of stationary sources emits *or would emit*" pollution in violation of § 110. The inclusion of the future conditional phrase "would emit" arguably contemplates the EPA's intervention to prevent future emissions that would contribute significantly to nonattainment in downwind states. Similarly, as the EPA argues, § 126(c) explicitly bars the construction or operation of "any major new proposed sources." By barring the *construction* of those sources, the statute clearly contemplates the imposition of controls on at least some facilities that do not yet exist. These provisions, taken together, may not compel the regulation of future sources under § 126, but they do not unambiguously forbid it. At the least, they introduce sufficient ambiguity into the statutory scheme to prevent resolution of this issue under *Chevron* step one.

In the absence of an unambiguous expression of congressional intent in the plain language of the statute, we advance to the second step of the *Chevron* analysis to determine whether the EPA's interpretation of § 126 is a reasonable one. We conclude that it is. Prior to 1990, § 126(b) only authorized EPA findings that "a major source emits or would emit any air pollutant" which contributes significantly to nonattainment in a downwind state. The 1990 Clean Air Act Amendments expanded the scope of this provision by allowing EPA findings with regard to "any major source *or group of stationary sources.*" Similarly, the EPA notes that the cross-referenced provision of the act, § 110(a)(2)(D)([i]) prohibits "type[s] of emissions activity" that contribute significantly. Like § 126, § 110 confers authority based upon the kind of activity in question. It does not impose any temporal limit.

The statutory language allows the EPA to regulate facilities in upwind states as a class or category, e.g. all coal-fired power plants in North Carolina. If such facilities, as a class, contribute significantly to nonattainment in northeastern states, this is as true for as-yet-unbuilt plants as it is for existing ones. Therefore, the EPA argues, it is reasonable to include future sources in the "group of stationary sources" found to contribute significantly to downwind nonattainment under § 126(b). Indeed, it would be irrational to enable the EPA to make findings that a group of sources in an upwind state contribute to downwind nonattainment, but then preclude the EPA from regulating new sources that contribute to that same pollution. As the EPA explained in its Response to Comments:

Once EPA has determined that the emissions from the existing sources in an upwind State already make a significant contribution to one or more petitioning downwind States, any additional emissions from a new source in that upwind State would also constitute a portion of that significant contribution, unless the emissions from that new source are limited to the level of highly effective controls.

can regulate new as well

The EPA's construction of § 126 avoids this result.

holding

[The court remanded the rule for reconsideration of how certain electricity co-generators were classified, and also for reconsideration of the modeling of growth in electricity generation, but otherwise upheld the rule.]

NOTES

1. Consider the challenges that the EPA confronted: controversy about its modeling techniques, the untested approach of using tradeable pollution rights under section 126, and difficult problems of how to allocate responsibility for the downwind air quality violations. Is the court's general deference here warranted, given the novelty of the EPA's rule? The Clean Air Act's provisions for controlling interstate pollution are discussed in Karl James Simon, *The Application and Adequacy of the Clean Air Act in Addressing Interstate Ozone Transport*, 5 ENVTL. LAW. 129 (1998).

2. Dealing with ozone transport was urgent for the EPA because attainment deadlines were coming due in many states around this time. To avoid imposing sanctions on downwind states still out of attainment, the EPA initiated a policy in 1998 of extending attainment dates for ozone nonattainment areas that could show that an upwind area in the same state with a later attainment date (or an upwind area in a different state) significantly contributed to the nonattainment problem, as long as the state adopted all required local control measures and demonstrated that it would reach attainment for ozone no later than when the upwind area's controls had to be in place; however, this was disapproved as contrary to congressional intent in 2002. Sierra Club v. EPA, 294 F.3d 155 (D.C. Cir. 2002) (ruling that Congress had addressed when deadlines could be extended in the Act, so no other extensions were authorized, especially since Congress knew about interstate transport issues at the time of the 1990 Amendments). The Fifth, Seventh, and Eleventh Circuits all followed the D.C. Circuit's lead. Ami M. Grace, *The 2005 Clean Air Act Severe Ozone Nonattainment Deadline: A Prime Opportunity to Realize the Goals of the Clean Air Act*, 35 Envtl. L. Rep. 10115 (2005).

3. In 2000, the D.C. Circuit had upheld the NOx Budget Trading Rule against challenges different from those addressed in *Appalachian Power Co. v. EPA*. In *Michigan v. EPA*, 213 F.3d 663 (D.C. Cir. 2000), the court upheld the EPA's methodology for determining which upwind sources were "significant contributors" to downwind air pollution in other states. The court also upheld the EPA's determination that significant contributors "need only reduce their ozone by the amount achievable with 'highly cost-effective controls.'" Highly cost-effective controls were defined as those controls that could be undertaken for less than $2000 per ton.

In 2003, the NOx Budget Trading program began operation with both the original NOx Budget Program participants from the Northeast and many of the states subject to the SIP call requirements. The Bush administration had planned to replace the program with the Clean Air Interstate Rule, but the rule was challenged on a variety of grounds, and invalidated by the D.C. Circuit in the case below. The *Michigan v. EPA* cost-effectiveness definition was contested in the Clean Air Act Interstate Rule case. The ruling may shed light on whether the Clean Air Act has enough flexibility to allow the EPA to create a cap-and-trade scheme for greenhouse gases.

NORTH CAROLINA v. EPA

United States Court of Appeals for the District of Columbia Circuit, 2008.
No. 05–1244.

Before: SENTELLE, CHIEF JUDGE, and ROGERS and BROWN, CIRCUIT JUDGES.

PER CURIAM:

I. Background

[In 1998, EPA relied on section 110(a)(2)(D)(i)(I)[6] of Title I of the CAA to promulgate the NOx SIP Call, which imposed a duty on certain upwind sources to reduce their NOx emissions by a specified amount so that they no longer " 'contribute significantly to nonattainment in, or interfere with maintenance by,' a downwind State." The NOx SIP Call created an optional cap-and-trade program for nitrogen oxides ("NOx"). Like the NOx SIP Call, the Clean Air Interstate Rule (CAIR)—the subject of this case—derives its statutory authority from section 110(a)(2)(D)(i)(I).

Title IV of the CAA aims to reduce acid rain deposition nationwide by creating a cap-and-trade program for sulfur dioxide ("SO_2") emitted by fossil fuel-fired combustion units. Congress capped SO_2 emissions for regulated units, called electric generating units ("EGUs"), at 8.9 million tons nationwide, and distributed "allowances" among those units. One "allowance" authorizes an EGU to emit one ton of SO_2 in a year. Title IV includes detailed provisions for allocating allowances among EGUs based for the most part on their share of total "heat input" of all Title IV EGUs during a 1985–87 baseline period. Whenever an EGU emits one ton of SO_2 in a year, it must surrender one allowance to EPA. Title IV also allows EGUs to transfer unused allowances to other EGUs throughout the nation, or to "bank" excess allowances and use or sell them in future years.]

C. Clean Air Interstate Rule

Pursuant to its Title I authority to ensure that states have plans in place that implement the requirements in section 110(a)(2)(D)(i)(I), EPA

---

6. Section 110(a)(2)(D)(i)(I) requires SIPs to contain adequate provisions—(i) prohibiting, consistent with the provisions of this subchapter, any source or other type of emissions activity within the State from emitting any air pollutant in amounts which will—(I) contribute significantly to nonattainment in, or interfere with maintenance by, any other State with respect to any NAAQS.

promulgated CAIR. CAIR's purpose is to reduce or eliminate the impact of upwind sources on out-of-state downwind nonattainment of NAAQS for fine particulate matter ("PM2.5"), a pollutant associated with respiratory and cardiovascular problems, and eight-hour ozone, a pollutant commonly known as smog. For the most part, EPA defines sources at the state level. EPA determined that 28 states and the District of Columbia ("upwind states") contribute significantly to out-of-state downwind nonattainment of one or both NAAQS. Because SO2 "is a precursor to PM2.5 formation, and NOx is a precursor to both ozone and PM2.5 formation," CAIR requires upwind states "to revise their [SIPs] to include control measures to reduce emissions" of SO2 and NOx. CAIR requires upwind states to reduce their emissions in two phases. NOx reductions are to start in 2009, SO2 reductions are to start in 2010, and the second reduction phase for each air pollutant is to start in 2015. To implement CAIR's emission reductions, the rule also creates optional interstate trading programs for each air pollutant, to which, in the absence of approved SIPs, all upwind sources are now subject. * * * In addition, CAIR revises Title IV's Acid Rain Program regulations governing the SO2 cap-and-trade program and replaces the NOx SIP Call with the CAIR ozone-season NOx trading program.

At issue in much of this litigation is the definition of the term "contribute significantly." In other words, in order to promulgate CAIR, EPA had to determine what amount of emissions constitutes a "significant contribution" to another state's nonattainment problem.

CAIR uses several factors to define "contribute significantly," including one state's impact on another's air quality, the cost of "highly cost-effective" emissions controls, fairness, and equity in the balance between regional and local controls. * * *

States that "contribute significantly" to nonattainment for ozone NAAQS are subject to CAIR's ozone-season limits for NOx and those that "contribute significantly" to nonattainment for PM2.5 NAAQS are subject to CAIR's annual limits for NOx and SO2. The ozone-season NOx limits are a percentage reduction in the annual limits for NOx calculated for PM2.5 contributors. In order to eliminate a state's significant contribution to PM2.5 NAAQS, CAIR sets an annual cap on NOx and SO2 emissions in the region. Each state participating in CAIR's allowance-trading programs receives a budget of allowances, calculated according to a different formula for SO2 and NOx. If a state develops a SIP that opts out of the trading programs to which all its upwind sources are now subject in the absence of an approved SIP, the state must limit its emissions to a cap specified by CAIR.

CAIR sets each state's NOx emissions budget by allocating the region-wide NOx budget among CAIR states according to each state's proportion of oil-, gas-, and coal-fired facilities. The regionwide budget is equal to the upwind states' average annual heat input for EGUs from 1999 to 2002 multiplied by the uniform emissions rate if EGUs were to use "highly cost-effective" emissions controls.

* * * The use of fuel-adjustment factors means states with higher percentages of gas-and oil-fired facilities receive comparably fewer NOx allowances than states with higher percentages of coal-fired facilities. States have discretion to accomplish their NOx emissions caps as they see fit in their SIPs, but if a state takes part in the EPA-administered trading program for NOx, it must follow EPA's rules for that program.

CAIR sets each state's SO2 budget using a process similar to the one used for NOx budgets; it allocates the regionwide SO2 budget among upwind states. However, EPA used a different method to determine the regionwide budget for SO2. Instead of using 1999–2002 data, the agency summed all the Title IV allowances allotted to EGUs in the covered states and reduced them by 50% for 2010 (Phase One) and 65% for 2015 (Phase Two). As stated above, Title IV allocates allowances among EGUs based for the most part on their share of the total heat input of all Title IV EGUs during a 1985–87 baseline period, not the later time period used for NOx allowances in CAIR. States subject to CAIR may opt into the EPA-administered trading program for SO2, but if they do not opt in and at the same time choose to regulate EGUs, their SIPs must include a mechanism for retiring Title IV SO2 allowances in excess of the budget CAIR allocates to each state. A state not participating in CAIR's trading program but regulating other sources of SO2 in addition to EGUs, does not need to surrender quite as many of its Title IV SO2 allowances. Any surrendered allowance may not be used for Title IV compliance purposes and is forever out of circulation. * * *

* * *

II. Analysis

* * *

1. Pollution–Trading Programs

North Carolina challenges the lawfulness of CAIR's tradingprograms for SO2 and NOx. North Carolina contests the lack of reasonable measures in CAIR to assure that upwind states will abate their unlawful emissions as required by section 110(a)(2)(D)(i)(I), but does not submit that any trading is per se unlawful. EPA designed CAIR to eliminate the significant contribution of upwind states, as a whole, to downwind nonattainment. EPA did not purport to measure each state's significant contribution to specific downwind nonattainment areas and eliminate them in an isolated, state-by-state manner. Reasoning that capping emissions in each state would not achieve reductions in the most cost-effective manner,

EPA decided to take a regionwide approach to CAIR and include voluntary emissions trading programs.

* * *

In CAIR's trading system, states are given initial emissions budgets, but sources can choose to sell or purchase emissions credits from sources in other states. As a result, states may emit more or less pollution than their caps would otherwise permit.

Because EPA evaluated whether its proposed emissions reductions were "highly cost effective," at the regionwide level assuming a trading program, it never measured the "significant contribution" from sources within an individual state to downwind nonattainment areas. Using EPA's method, such a regional reduction, although equivalent to the sum of reductions required by all upwind states to meet their budgets, would never equal the aggregate of each state's "significant contribution" for two reasons. State budgets alone, without trading, would not be "highly cost effective." And although EPA has measured the "air quality factor" to include states in CAIR, it has not measured the unlawful amount of pollution for each upwind-downwind linkage. " * * * Thus EPA's apportionment decisions have nothing to do with each state's "significant contribution" because under EPA's method of analysis, state budgets do not matter for significant contribution purposes.

But according to Congress, individual state contributions to downwind nonattainment areas do matter. Section110(a)(2)(D)(i)(I) prohibits sources "within the State" from "contribut[ing] significantly to nonattainment in ... any other State ..." (emphasis added). Yet under CAIR, sources in Alabama, which contribute to nonattainment of PM2.5 NAAQS in Davidson County, North Carolina, would not need to reduce their emissions at all. Theoretically, sources in Alabama could purchase enough NOx and SO2 allowances to cover all their current emissions, resulting in no change in Alabama's contribution to Davidson County, North Carolina's nonattainment. CAIR only assures that the entire region's significant contribution will be eliminated. It is possible that CAIR would achieve section 110(a)(2)(D)(i)(I)'s goals. EPA's modeling shows that sources contributing to North Carolina's nonattainment areas will at least reduce their emissions even after opting into CAIR's trading programs. But EPA is not exercising its section 110(a)(2)(D)(i)(I) duty unless it is promulgating a rule that achieves something measurable toward the goal of prohibiting sources "within the State" from contributing to nonattainment or interfering with maintenance "in any other State."

* * * It is unclear how EPA can assure that the trading programs it has designed in CAIR will achieve section 110(a)(2)(D)(i)(I)'s goals if we do not know what each upwind state's "significant contribution" is to another state. Despite *Michigan's*[7] approval of emissions controls that do not correlate directly with each state's relative contribution to a specific downwind nonattainment area, CAIR must include some assurance that it achieves something measurable towards the goal of prohibiting sources "within the State" from contributing to nonattainment or interfering with maintenance in "any other State."

Because CAIR is designed as a complete remedy to section 110(a)(2)(D)(i)(I) problems, as EPA claims, CAIR must do more than achieve something measurable; it must actually require elimination of emissions from sources that contribute significantly and interfere with maintenance in downwind nonattainment areas. To do so, it must measure each state's "significant contribution" to downwind nonattainment even if that measurement does not directly correlate with each state's individualized air quality impact on downwind nonattainment relative to other upwind states. Otherwise, the rule is not effectuating the statutory mandate of prohibiting emissions moving from one state to another, leaving EPA with no statutory authority for its action. * * *

2.   "Interfere With Maintenance"

* * * North Carolina argues that EPA unlawfully ignored the "interfere with maintenance" language in section 110(a)(2)(D)(i)(I), divesting it of independent effect in CAIR. It contends that instead of limiting the beneficiaries of CAIR to downwind areas that were monitored to be in nonattainment when EPA promulgated CAIR and were modeled to be in nonattainment in 2009 and 2010, when CAIR goes into effect, CAIR, 70 Fed. Reg. at 25,244, EPA should have also included in CAIR upwind states, such as Georgia, that send pollution into downwind areas that are projected to barely meet attainment levels of NAAQS in 2010.

* * *

North Carolina explains that even though all of its counties are projected to attain NAAQS for ozone by 2010, several of its counties are at risk of returning to nonattainment due to interference from upwind sources. * * *

EPA contends that it interpreted "interfere with maintenance" just as it did in the NOx SIP Call, in which it gave the term a meaning "much the same as" the one given to the preceding phrase, "contribute significantly to nonattainment." EPA maintains that "the 'interfere with maintenance' prong may come into play only in circumstances where EPA or the State can reasonably determine or project, based on available data, that an area in a downwind state will achieve attainment, but due to emissions growth or other relevant factors is likely to fall back into nonattainment."

---

7.   [Michigan v. EPA, 213 F.3d 663 (D.C. Cir. 2000)]

* * * Despite using "interfere with maintenance" as a justification for imposing further emissions controls in 2015, CAIR gave no independent significance to the "interfere with maintenance" prong of section 110(a)(2)(D)(i)(I) to separately identify upwind sourcesinterfering with downwind maintenance. Under EPA's reading of the statute, a state can never "interfere with maintenance" unless EPA determines that at one point it "contribute[d] significantly to nonattainment." EPA stated clearly on two occasions "that it would apply the interfere with maintenance provision in section 110(a)(2)(D) in conjunction with the significant contribution to nonattainment provision and so did not use the maintenance prong to separately identify upwind States subject to CAIR." EPA reasoned that this interpretation "avoid[s] giving greater weight to the potentially lesser environmental effect" and strikes "a reasonable balance between controls in upwind states and in-state controls." EPA stated that an interpretation that permitted states that are able to attain NAAQS on their own to benefit from CAIR "could even create a perverse incentive for downwind states to increase local emissions."

All the policy reasons in the world cannot justify reading a substantive provision out of a statute. Areas that find themselves barely meeting attainment in 2010 due in part to upwind sources interfering with that attainment have no recourse under EPA's interpretation of the interference prong of section110(a)(2)(D)(i)(I). 2010 is not insignificant because that is the deadline for downwind areas to attain ozone NAAQS. An outcome that fails to give independent effect to the "interfere with maintenance" prong violates the plain language of section 110(a)(2)(D)(i)(I). The provision at issue is written in the disjunctive.* * * "Canons of construction ordinarily suggest that terms connected by a disjunctive be given separate meanings, unless the context dictates otherwise...." Reiter v. Sonotone Corp., 442 U.S. 330, 339 (1979). There is no context in section 110(a)(2)(D)(i)(I) directing an alternate result; therefore EPA must give effect to both provisions in the statute.

* * *

B. SO2 and NOx Budgets

SO2 Petitioners and petitioner Entergy challenge CAIR's budgets for the SO2 and NOx trading programs. EPA set states' SO2 budgets for 2010 to 50% (35% in 2015) of the allowances the states' EGUs receive under Title IV. SO2 Petitioners argue EPA never explained how these budgets related to section 110(a)(2)(D)(i)(I)'s mandate of prohibiting significant contributions to downwind nonattainment. * * * As for NOx, EPA reduced states' budgets to the extent their EGUs burned oil or gas. Entergy claims EPA made this adjustment purely in the interests of fairness—an improper reason under section 110(a)(2)(D)(i)(I). * * *

1. SO2 Budgets

* * * EPA claims to have based state budgets for SO2 and NOx on the amount of emissions sources can eliminate by applying controls EPA deems "highly cost-effective controls"—an approach EPA says we approved in Michigan v. EPA. * * * EPA's method in setting the SO2 budgets is not what Michigan approved. In that case, the petitioners argued section 110(a)(2)(D)(i)(I) does not permit EPA to consider the cost of reducing ozone. After reconciling petitioners' shifting (and somewhat conflicting) arguments, we answered a well defined question: Could EPA, in selecting the "significant" level of "contribution" under section 110(a)(2)(D)(i)(I), choose a level corresponding to a certain reduction cost? Answering that question in the affirmative, we held EPA may "after [a state's] reduction of all [it] could ... cost-effectively eliminate[ ]," consider "any remaining 'contribution' " insignificant. Michigan also rejected claims that applying a uniform cost criterion across states was irrational because both smaller and larger contributors had to make reductions achievable by the same highly cost-effective controls. This, we said, "flow[ed] ineluctably from the EPA's decision to draw the 'significant contribution' line on a basis of cost." Upholding that decision "logically entail[ed] upholding this consequence." And while EPA's approach did not necessarily ensure "aggregate health benefits" at roughly the lowest cost, EPA researched alternatives, and found none that significantly improved air quality or reduced cost. Since no one offered a "material critique" of this research, we did not upset EPA's judgment.

Here, EPA did not use cost in the manner Michigan approved. Even worse, EPA's choice of SO2 budgets does not track the requirements of section 110(a)(2)(D)(i)(I). That much is evident from EPA's decision to base the budgets on allowances states' EGUs receive under Title IV. Those allowances are not, as EPA asserts, a "logical starting point" for setting CAIR's SO2 emissions caps. Congress designed the Title IV allowance scheme using EGU data from 1985 to 1987 to address the national acid rain problem. Nowhere does EPA explain how reducing Title IV allowances will adequately prohibit states from contributing significantly to downwind nonattainment of the PM2.5 NAAQS. And while "Congress chose a policy of not revisiting and revising these allocations and, apparently, believed that its allocation methodology would be appropriate for future time periods," it is unclear how the quantitative number of allowances created by 1990 legislation to address one substance, acid rain, could be relevant to 2015 levels of an air pollutant, PM2.5.

EPA also explains that it chose Title IV as a starting point "to preserve the viability and emissions reductions of the highly successful title IV program." This goal may be valid, but it is not among the objectives in section 110(a)(2)(D)(i)(I). And if it is somehow compatible with states' obligations to include "adequate provisions" in their SIPs, prohibiting emissions "within the State from ... contribut[ing] significantly" to downwind nonattainment, then EPA should explain how. It has failed to do so. Apart from the arbitrary Title IV baseline, EPA has insufficiently explained how it arrived at the 50% and 65% reduction figures. Though unclear, these numbers appear to represent what EPA thought would be " 'a cost-effective and equitable governmental approach to attainment with the NAAQS for [PM2.5].' " As with the need to "preserve the viability" of the Title IV program, EPA's notions of what is an "equitable governmental approach to attainment" is not among the objectives of section 110(a)(2)(D)(i)(I). Nor does EPA even attempt to reconcile its choice of "equitable" emissions caps with those objectives.

Having chosen these equitable caps for the CAIR region, EPA then "ascertained the costs of these reductions and . . . determine[d] that they should be considered highly cost effective." EPA's use of cost in this manner is not what we approved in Michigan. Whereas Michigan permits EPA to draw the "significant contribution" line based on the cost of reducing that "contribution," here EPA did not draw the line at all. It simply verified sources could meet the SO2 caps with controls EPA dubbed "highly cost-effective." Nor would EPA necessarily cure this problem merely by beginning its analysis with cost. While EPA may require "termination of only a subset of each state's contribution," by having states "cut[ ] back the amount that could be eliminated with 'highly cost-effective controls,' " Michigan, 213 F.3d at 675 (emphasis added), EPA can't just pick a cost for a region, and deem "significant" any emissions that sources can eliminate more cheaply. Such an approach would not necessarily achieve something measurable toward the goal of prohibiting sources "within the State" from contributing significantly to downwind nonattainment.

* * *

2. NOx Budgets

Next, we address EPA's use of "fuel factors" to allocate the regional NOx cap among the CAIR states. EPA determined the cap by multiplying NOx emissions rates (0.15 mmBtu in 2010 and 0.125 mmBtu in 2015) by the heat input of states in the CAIR region. Then, EPA distributed to each state, as its budget of NOx emissions allowances, its proportionate share of the regional cap. But in determining these shares, EPA adjusted each state's heat input for the mix of fuels its power plants used: while a coal-fired EGU contributed its full heat input to the state total, an oil-fired EGU counted for only 60% of its heat input and a gas-fired EGU only 40%. Entergy argues this fuel adjustment was irrational because EPA made it purely for the sake of sharing the burden of emissions reductions fairly. We agree EPA's notion of fairness has nothing to do with states' section 110(a)(2)(D)(i)(I) obligations to prohibit significant contributions to downwind nonattainment.

* * *

* * * Entergy does not challenge the regional NOx emissions rate. It argues that if EPA thinks a certain rate reflects a state's level of "significant contribution" to downwind nonattainment, then section 110(a)(2)(D)(i)(I) requires EPA to assign each state a budget equal to the emissions rate times the state's heat input. The fuel adjustment reduces a state's budget below that level if, say, its power plants use gas instead of coal, without any justification besides fairness. Remarkably, EPA does not deny that fairness is the only reason for the fuel adjustment. According to EPA, "[t]he factors would reflect the inherently higher emissions rate of coal-fired plants, and consequently the greater burden on coal plants to control emissions," thereby creating "a more equitable budget distribution." Instead, EPA criticizes Entergy's preferred method of distributing credits as being equally unjustified. In the EPA's view, assigning credits without the fuel adjustment is just one of "a number of ways that EPA could have distributed the regionwide NOx emissions budget," among which the fuel adjustment is another, equally valid method, and EPA reasonably chose the fuel adjustment as the fairest method.

Not all methods of developing state emission budgets are equally valid, because an agency may not "trespass beyond the bounds of its statutory authority by taking other factors into account" than those to which Congress limited it, nor "substitute new goals in place of the statutory objectives without explaining how [doing so comports with] the statute." Indep. U.S. Tanker Owners Comm. v. Dole, 809 F.2d 847, 854 (D.C. Cir. 1987). Section 110(a)(2)(D)(i)(I) addresses emissions "within the State" that contribute significantly to downwind pollution. Naturally we defer to EPA's interpretation of the Clean Air Act so far as it is reasonable, and we have recognized that significance may include cost. However, EPA's interpretation cannot extend so far as to make one state's significant contribution depend on another state's cost of eliminating emissions.

Yet that is exactly what EPA has done. For example, Louisiana's EGUs use more gas and oil than most states' EGUs. Consequently, instead of the budget of 42,319 tons per year that would be Louisiana's proportional share of the regionwide cap without fuel adjustment, the State only received 29,593 tons per year. The rest of those credits went to states with more coalfired EGUs than average, which necessarily received "larger NOx emissions budgets" than their unadjusted proportional shares. EPA favored coal-fired EGUs in this way because they face a "greater burden . . . to control emissions" than gas-and oil-fired EGUs. In essence, a state having mostly coal-fired EGUs gets more credits because Louisiana can control emissions more cheaply.

EPA responds by suggesting that any allocation of the NOx cap would amount to equitable burden-sharing because EPA did the analysis "on a regionwide basis," and therefore not even the unadjusted shares have any relation to states' significant contributions. If so, that is a weakness of CAIR generally. Having chosen not to evaluate contributing emissions on a state-by-state basis, EPA cannot now rely on the resulting paucity of data to justify its ad hoc approach to spreading the burden of reducing them. When a petitioner complains EPA is requiring a state to eliminate more than its significant contribution, it is inadequate for EPA to respond that it never measured individual states' significant contributions.

* * *

* * * EPA contends the greatest reductions will take place where the greatest emissions are, because that is where most cost-effective reductions are available. Of course, those states with the greatest emissions are those with mainly coal-fired EGUs, which are precisely the states that get extra credits under EPA's fuel-adjustment method. * * * Presumably those EGUs will make their greater reductions and sell them to other EGUs, in states the fuel-adjustment method docked, to recoup their investment in reductions. The net result will be that states with mainly oil-and gas-fired EGUs will subsidize reductions in states with mainly coal-fired EGUs. Again, EPA's approach contravenes section 110(a)(2)(D)(i)(I); the statute requires each state to prohibit emissions "within the State" that contribute significantly to downwind pollution, not to pay for other states to prohibit their own contributions.

EPA's redistributional instinct may be laudatory, but section 110(a)(2)(D)(i)(I) gives EPA no authority to force an upwind state to share the burden of reducing other upwind states' emissions. Each state must eliminate its own significant contribution to downwind pollution. While CAIR should achieve something measurable towards that goal, it may not require some states to exceed the mark. Because the fueladjustment factors shifted the burden of emission reductions solely in pursuit of equity among upwind states—an improper reason—the resulting state budgets were arbitrary and capricious.

C. Title IV Allowances

SO2 Petitioners and a trade association of waste-coal EGUs (together "SO2 Petitioners") also challenge EPA's effort to "harmonize" CAIR's regulation of SO2 with the existing program for trading SO2 emissions allowances under Title IV of the CAA. Since EPA set states' SO2 budgets for 2010 to 50% (35% in 2015) of the allowances the states' EGUs receive under Title IV, EGUs in the region would emit significantly less SO2 under CAIR and could be expected to have substantial numbers of excess Title IV allowances to emit SO2. Concerned about this sudden excess, EPA structured CAIR so that EGUs in states electing to trade give up 2 allowances per ton in 2010, and 2.68 allowances per ton in 2015. (Recall, a Title IV allowance gives the holder the right to emit one ton of SO2 within the Title IV program.) States electing not to trade must have SIP provisions for retiring excess allowances. * * *

SO2 Petitioners argue EPA lacks authority to terminate or limit Title IV allowances, either through a trading program under section 110(a)(2)(D), or by requiring that SIPs have allowance retirement provisions. We agree and grant the petition on this issue. * * *

* * * [E]PA claims section 110(a)(2)(D)(i)(I) gives it authority to set up a program for trading SO2 emissions allowances, and to require EGUs to use Title IV allowances as currency. Once EGUs spend Title IV allowances in the CAIR market, EPA says it can terminate the authorization the allowances provide within the Title IV market. But whatever authority EPA may have to establish such a trading program, we find nothing in section 110(a)(2)(D)(i)(I) granting EPA authority to remove Title IV allowances from circulation in the Title IV market.

Environmental groups, intervening in support of EPA, argue section 301(a) of the CAA also provides EPA authority. That provision authorizes EPA "to prescribe such regulations as are necessary to carry out [its] functions under" the CAA. EPA does not rely on section 301(a), and for good reason: EPA cannot claim retiring excess Title IV allowances is "necessary" for EPA to ensure SIPs comply with section 110(a)(2)(D)(i)(I). Nor does section 301(a) "provide [EPA] Carte blanche authority to promulgate any rules, on any matter relating to the Clean Air Act, in any manner that the [EPA] wishes." Citizens to Save Spencer County v. EPA, 600 F.2d 844, 873 (D.C. Cir. 1979).

Lacking a statutory foundation, EPA appeals to "logic." Logically, says EPA, it was not "required to structure CAIR as a stand-alone program without taking account whatsoever of the effect this might have on the pre-existing" Title IV program. Environmental intervenors add some legal flavoring here, analogizing EPA's action to a court's interpretative obligation to "fit, if possible, all parts" of a statute "into a harmonious whole," FTC v. Mandel Bros., 359 U.S. 385,389 (1959). Although it may be reasonable for EPA, in structuring a program under section 110(a)(2)(D)(i)(I), to consider the impact on the Title IV market, it does not follow that EPA has the authority to remove allowances from that market. Nor can EPA cure its absence of authority by foisting onto SO2 Petitioners the burden of explaining why "two independent programs . . . would produce a better result." Lest EPA forget, it is "a creature of statute," and has "only those authorities conferred upon it by Congress"; "if there is no statute conferring authority, a federal agency has none." Michigan v. EPA. So too here: no statute confers authority on EPA to terminate or limit Title IV allowances, and EPA thus has none.

* * *

We must vacate CAIR because very little will "survive remand in anything approaching recognizable form." * * * EPA's approach—region-wide caps with no state-specific quantitative contribution determinations or emissions requirements—is fundamentally flawed. Moreover, EPA must redo its analysis from the ground up. * * * We note that in the absence of CAIR, the NOx SIP Call trading program will continue, because EPA terminated the program only as part of the CAIR rulemaking. The continuation of the NOx SIP Call should mitigate any disruption that might result from our vacating CAIR at least with regard to NOx. In addition, downwind states retain their statutory right to petition for immediate relief from unlawful interstate pollution under section 126.

NOTES

1. Can you reconcile the reasoning of *Appalachian Power Co v. EPA* and *North Carolina v. EPA*?

2. The court in *North Carolina* allowed the CAIR rule to remain in place pending action by the EPA to replace the rule. See http://www.epa.gov/interstateairquality/.

3. MARKET MECHANISMS TO CONTROL AIR POLLUTION

The NO_x trading scheme described above embodies a market based approach to air pollution—it is a "cap and trade" system under which government establishes the upper limit of pollution (in this case in the form of pollution "budgets"), but then relies on the states to manage the necessary reductions. Although cap-and-trade programs were once thought to be dubious—even immoral—because they essentially allocate "rights" to pollute, they have now become fairly common, as we noted in the Thompson excerpt in Chapter 1, *supra*, page 16. Nevertheless, cap-and-trade systems pose unique problems, and differ from prescriptive regulatory regimes in important ways, which we explore in the material below.

a. Banking, Bubbles, and Offsets

Long before developing the NOx trading program, the EPA first experimented with a variety of smaller-scale market mechanisms in the New Source Review provisions of the Clean Air Act. These techniques include "bubbles," "netting" and "offsets." For example, offsets apply only within a single nonattainment area (or areas with equal or worse nonattainment problems that contribute to the first area's nonattainment), while bubbles cover only a single multi-source plant. The first excerpt below offers a helpful overview of some of these regulatory devices and an early evaluation of them. The second focuses specifically on the bubble rule adopted by the EPA in the famous *Chevron* case, excerpted in Chapter 5, *supra*, page 450.

ROBERT W. HAHN & GORDON L. HESTER, MARKETABLE PERMITS: LESSONS FOR THEORY AND PRACTICE[8]

16 ECOLOGY L. Q. 361 (1989).

Offsets are used by new and modified sources in nonattainment areas and by certain specified sources in attainment areas. The Clean Air Act specifies that no new emission sources would be allowed in areas that did not meet the original 1975 air quality deadlines. Concern that this provision would stifle economic growth prompted EPA to institute the offset rule in 1976. This rule requires new and modified emission sources in these areas to obtain emission credits from sources in the same area to offset their new emissions. The sources are still subject to the most stringent emission limits. Offsets may be obtained through internal or external trades. [O]ffset transactions are controlled at the state level.

Bubbles, first allowed in 1979, are used by existing sources in attainment or nonattainment areas. The name derives from the concept of placing an imaginary bubble over a multi-source plant. The levels of emission controls applied to different sources in a bubble may be adjusted to reduce control costs so long as the aggregate limit is not exceeded. In effect, emission credits are created by some sources within the plant and used by others. Originally, all bubbles had to be submitted by the states to EPA for approval. In 1981 EPA began to approve "generic bubble rules" that enabled states to approve bubbles. Several states now have such rules.

Banking, which was first allowed in 1979, provides a mechanism for firms to save emission credits for future use. EPA has established guidelines for banking programs, but states must set up and administer the rules governing banking. * * *

[L]evels of activity in the three programs have varied widely. * * * An estimated 2,000 offset transactions have taken place, of which only about ten percent have been external. Fewer than 150 bubbles have been approved, only two of which are known to have involved external trades. About twice as many bubbles have been approved by states under generic rules than have been approved at the federal level. In fact, the general pattern seems to be that programs controlled at the state level are much more active than those controlled at the federal level. Banking, however, was not received well by either state regulators or firms. The figures listed for banking are an estimate of the number of times firms have withdrawn banked credits for sale or use. There has been little such activity.

* * * Federally approved bubbles have resulted in savings estimated at $300 million, while state bubbles have resulted in an estimated $135

---

8. Copyright © 1989, Ecology Law Quarterly. Reprinted by permission.

million in cost savings.[9] * * * [O]ffsets result in no direct emission control cost savings because the use of offsets does not allow a firm to avoid any emission limits. However, since a firm using offsets is allowed to locate major new emission sources in nonattainment areas, presumably there is some economic advantage to the firm, or it would locate in an attainment area where offsets are not required. The willingness of firms to go to the expense of obtaining offsets indicates that they derive some net gain from doing so, but the extent of this gain cannot be estimated. Cost savings from banking also cannot be estimated, but are necessarily small given the number of transactions that have occurred.

[T]he effects [of trading] on environmental quality have been, on the whole, insignificant. * * * Offsets, which require trading ratios greater than 1:1, will naturally lead to reduced emissions. For bubbles, the lack of systematic data collection leaves the question of effects on environmental quality unresolved, but early reports indicated that aggregate effects may be slightly positive. Emission credits for a few of these transactions have been created by lowering permitted emission levels, but not making any actual reduction in emissions. Such transactions have an adverse environmental effect in the sense that emission reductions that would otherwise have been required were foregone. However, their aggregate effect on air quality in local areas is thought to be inconsequential. Banking has probably had a very slight positive effect, since banked credits represent emission reductions that have not been used to offset emission increases. However, because there has been little banking activity, this effect is also very small.

The performance evaluation of emissions trading activities reveals a mixed bag of accomplishments and disappointments. The program has clearly afforded many firms flexibility in meeting emission limits. This flexibility has resulted in significant aggregate cost savings—in the billions of dollars—without significantly affecting environmental quality. However, these cost savings have been realized almost entirely from internal trading. They fall far short of the potential savings that could be realized if there were more external trading.

A variety of factors affect the performance of emissions trading. High transaction costs are the single most important determinant of program performance. A large part of these costs result from regulatory restrictions on trading and from administrative requirements that prolong the approval of trades.

---

9. All cost savings figures are for the lives of the different programs, and are not adjusted for inflation. It is interesting to note that although more state bubbles have been approved than federal, the average cost savings for federal bubbles is much higher.

JODY FREEMAN, THE STORY OF CHEVRON: ENVIRONMENTAL LAW AND ADMINISTRATIVE DISCRETION[10]

Environmental Law Stories 171 (Richard Lazarus & Oliver Houck eds. 2005).

* * *

II.   The Debate Over the Bubble Approach

The bubble rule at issue in *Chevron* did not appear overnight. As the EPA began implementing the CAA in the early seventies, the agency began to consider the merits of using the bubble in a variety of CAA programs. This was part of a larger move toward adopting emissions trading, a policy tool that was quickly swept up in the politics of environmental regulation.

In theory, the bubble concept seems completely unobjectionable. It simply treats all the polluting units in a firm as if there were a tent over them, with a single hole for emissions, and allows firms to distribute emissions reductions among the individual units in whichever manner they choose. The bubble concept is a way of affording firms flexibility to make operational decisions about how to reach a given regulatory target in the cheapest way possible, providing they meet the target. Why does this benefit firms? Given the cost of technology, it can be much more expensive to squeeze the last increment of pollution control out of a new piece of equipment than to take other steps—such as shutting down an older and less efficient unit, switching fuels, or finding other practices to change at the facility that will yield improvements in air quality. The bubble allows firms to choose their poison.

To see the potential benefits of such an approach, consider what Mike Levin, Assistant Administrator in EPA's Office of Planning and Management (OPM) at the time, often did in cafeterias around the country to illustrate it.

> Take a salt shaker and a pepper shaker. Assume that command and control regulation typically requires uniform reductions from each emission point within an industrial category. If the shakers each are stacks at (say) a refinery, and each currently is allowed to (and does) emit 250 tons per year (TPY) of volatile organic compounds, a new rule would require each to reduce by 100 TPY. But let's say it will cost 5 times as much to reduce 100 tons at Salt as at Pepper because, for example, there's not enough room to install control equipment there, or because Salt's location is much hotter, so it will have to install condensers & refrigeration to make control equipment work reliably.
>
> Why not allow Pepper (or Pepper plus another unregulated refinery source emitting the same pollutants) to reduce by 200 tons instead? Costs might not only be reduced fivefold in this case, but industry resistance to issuance of the rule in the first place could be reduced.

---

10.   Copyright © 2005. Reprinted by permission with some alterations from original. Footnotes omitted.

So would foot-dragging on compliance, or applications for "variances" on grounds of cost-effectiveness (which if granted, would require little or no reduction at Salt). More important, the rule suddenly seems reasonable, because it allows adjustment for site-specific variations that regulators knew nothing about. Still more important, it encourages regulated sources to come forward with superior and more efficient reduction options than they had previously had reason to seek or disclose. Regulators can use this information to secure further reductions with less friction on a system-wide basis, as long as they do so without directly penalizing the sources that came forward this way. Over time, regulators' jobs get easier, and more real reductions are secured.

Understood in these terms, bubbles seem eminently sensible. Indeed, as an abstract policy idea, the bubble concept garnered praise from everyone: EPA officials, representatives of industry, and even environmentalists. Yet the disagreement lay in details of the *application* of the bubble concept by EPA in nonattainment zones. There is a vast difference between using a bubble to help existing sources achieve compliance under approved state plans, and using it to allow offsets between units in nonattainment zones, as the EPA's bubble rule did.

To appreciate the "dark side" of the bubble consider these objections: as implemented by EPA in nonattainment zones, the bubble allowed firms to retire or modify old units and apply the resulting emission credits to new or modified units. And this would occur without requiring the firm to install pollution control technology that would force an even greater reduction in emission levels over time. Allowing this kind of offsetting essentially enables firms to perpetuate existing emission levels indefinitely. They "bank" the excess pollution from old units, converting existing pollution levels into an entitlement going forward. The public never sees the air quality benefit of retired units with this approach. Over time, the bubble could also result in firms capturing future credits for what are called "anyway" tons—tons of pollution that would have been retired anyway, as firms, in the regular course of business, replace old equipment with new units.

Moreover, when examined closely, the EPA's application of the bubble in fact allowed firms to calculate a net *increase* in pollution as if it were equivalent to no net increase. This was the result of the agency's definition of what constituted a "significant increase" for purposes of triggering NSR. Under the agency's definition, for example, a forty-ton increase in emissions would not be considered significant. So using bubbles in nonattainment zones would actually allow air quality to degrade in areas of the country where health risks were perceived to be greatest.

Perhaps the most fundamental objection to the bubble was that companies were evading controls that were obviously intended to apply when new capital commitments were made, by opportunistically seizing the inevitable "headroom" between the actual operation of existing sources and the regulatory requirements applicable to them. What the regulatory reforms sought to do was to capture that extra "headroom" and give it back to the companies instead of the public. The result for non-attainment zones then, was the exact opposite effect of what Congress seemed to require. Finally, industry's argument that NSR would retard modernization was dubious: pollution control costs, it was argued, are only one factor in a firm's investment decisions.

Leading the opposition to the bubble on these grounds was the Natural Resources Defense Council (NRDC), which had emerged by the mid-seventies as a forceful advocate for the environment (and which, of course, ultimately ended up as the plaintiff in *Chevron*). In the NRDC's view, widespread adoption of the bubble would at worst reduce, and at best delay, the air quality gains that would otherwise have been made under NSR.

Perhaps surprisingly, many states opposed the bubble idea as well. They worried that this new policy idea would provide industry with new opportunities to litigate, potentially interfering with the states' attempts to revise their SIPs, and generally undermining ongoing enforcement efforts. Moreover, a number of states believed they already had the authority to use bubbles, and some were already doing so; they thought they possessed the flexibility that the EPA wanted to bestow upon them.

The divide over bubbles also pervaded the agency itself. Scratch the surface of *Chevron* and one finds not a united EPA seeking policy flexibility and judicial deference, but a struggle within the agency based on two very different views of the law. On one side were regulatory reformers like Mike Levin, who believed that the promise of market mechanisms—in terms of cost savings, ease of administration, and incentives to modernization—outweighed the inflated predictions about what command and control strategies would otherwise achieve. They argued that chasing every small emissions increase was a misallocation of resources that would cost firms dearly for little air quality gain. Command and control regulation was reaching its limits in terms of effectiveness. Bubbles would simply afford states flexibility as they wrote SIPs, and the SIPs could be relied upon to guarantee compliance with NAAQS.

On the other side were many career employees in the agency, both in the Office of Air Quality Planning and Standards (OAQPS) and the enforcement office, who believed that most of the progress on air pollution had been, and would continue to be, the result of forcing firms to apply technology to their sources (as in the New Source Performance Standards Program). * * *

Beyond the matter of whether the bubble policy was a lawful interpretation of the statutory term "stationary source"—the key legal issue in *Chevron*—there remains the question of whether the bubble concept is good policy. At the time, there was little empirical evidence one way or the other; the likely effect of the bubble's widespread adoption was a matter of pure speculation. So the policy debate turned mostly on a normative argument about whether using such a strategy would be, in theory, superior to the alternative of the unit-by-unit approach required by command and control. One's view of this depends heavily on one's beginning assumptions about the appropriate baseline from which to make comparisons. In the debate over whether the EPA's bubble strategy would advance or retard progress toward the federal air quality standards, a key question was, and still is, "What, realistically, would NSR have *otherwise* required?"

This kind of conflict over baselines arises often in environmental regulation, especially in the context of air regulation. Should we assume that a command and control program will be perfectly implemented, and then compare the anticipated results to a market approach? Or is it more realistic to assume incomplete implementation, and to consider the cost and administrative expense associated with the command and control approach, when comparing it to the market alternative? And what are the transaction costs and compliance rates of the market alternative?

Whether trading of this sort, in any of its applications, is good policy, is not a "snapshot" issue. That is, any attempt at a real world answer must take account of how the policy has evolved over time, whether it has been reformed in light of criticism (in the case of the bubble, to eliminate the opportunity for "phony" paper trades). And, most importantly, answering this question requires continually comparing the trading option to the (also evolving and also imperfect) alternatives. Would we have been better off without the bubble? Would cap-and-trade programs—now the preferred policy tool for addressing greenhouse gas regulation—have developed even if *Chevron* had come out the other way? The answer is unclear.

NOTE

Some environmentalists have complained that bubbles and offsets make little contribution to progress on pollution control. For example, Professor Rodgers notes concerns that many offsets are for improvements already required in SIPs, and offsets are rarely available to new sources but are instead used by the owners of existing sources who wish to expand or build new facilities. WILLIAM H. RODGERS, ENVIRONMENTAL LAW 217–18 (2d ed. 1994). Are they still preferable to command-and-control regulation? In which instances would you resort to one over the other?

b. Intra–State Trading Regimes

Congress has sought to encourage states to adopt market mechanisms in their state implementation plans. For example, § 110 specifically authorizes states to adopt economic incentives such as fees, marketable permits, and auctions of emissions rights among the "enforceable emission limits" states must impose in their SIPs. There are also examples of intra-state trading schemes. Yet these measures can be difficult to design. California's South Coast Air Quality Management District adopted Rule

1610, creating the Regional Clean Air Incentives Market (RECLAIM), a "cap and trade" program under which stationary sources like oil refineries were given initial allowances of RECLAIM Trading Credits (or RTCs), which they could either consume or sell to other facilities. RECLAIM was expected to apply initially to about 400 facilities, accounting for between two-thirds and three-quarters of the emissions from stationary sources with permits. The initial allocation was set based on maximum emissions during 1989–1992, with an adjustment to control the total emissions from all sources. The amount of pollution represented by an RTC was to decline steadily each year. For a detailed description of the program, *see* Daniel P. Selmi, *Transforming Economic Incentives from Theory to Reality: The Marketable Permit Program of the South Coast Air Quality Management District*, 24 Envtl. L. Rep. 10695 (1994).

By 1998, more than $42 million in trades had taken place among the 330 facilities in the program. The program has been a disappointment, however. Emission reductions have fallen far short of their targets, and the retrofitting anticipated by the program has been minimal. A November, 2002 EPA report evaluating RECLAIM's performance since its inception, concluded that the program has produced far fewer emission reductions than were projected at time of adoption. The actual rate of reductions has been 19 per cent from 1994–2000, or 3.2 per cent per year, far lower than the 40–60 per cent total reductions projected for the same period (or 6 to 10 per cent reduction per year) that would have applied under the subsumed command and control rules. The report is available at http://www.epa.gov/region09/air/reclaim/report.pdf.

Critics of RECLAIM argue that the initial allocation of credits were so plentiful and cheap that the market could not work effectively to incentivize emission reductions. *See* Gary Polakovic, *Innovative Smog Plan Makes Little Progress*, L.A. TIMES, Apr. 17, 2001, B1. In addition, the scheme has attracted criticism from the environmental justice movement because it proposed to include trades between stationary and mobile sources emissions, potentially creating "hot spots" that concentrate pollution in low-income and minority neighborhoods. *See* Richard T. Drury et al., *Pollution Trading and Environmental Injustice: Los Angeles' Failed Experiment in Air Quality Policy*, 9 DUKE ENVTL. L. & POL'Y F. 231 (1999); Vivien Foster & Robert W. Hahn, *Designing More Efficient Markets: Lessons from Los Angeles Smog Control*, 38 J. L. & ECON. 19 (1995). Another article accused RECLAIM of stifling technological innovation by forcing companies to hurriedly install pollution-control technologies at the outset of the program rather than allowing them to explore developing options. Curtis A. Moore, *RECLAIM: Southern California's Failed Experiment with Air Pollution Trading*, 34 Envtl. L. Rep. 10261 (2004). Moore also criticized the lack of actual emissions reductions under the RECLAIM regime, the lack of any emissions floor to act as a safety net, and the lack of transparency in the program as leading to non-compliance and outright cheating. *Id.*

c. Acid Rain

In addition to using bubbles, banking and offsets, in the late eighties, the EPA successfully phased lead out of gasoline using a program that relied in part on a market based trading approach. *See* Richard Newell & Kristian Rogers, *The Market–Based Lead Phasedown, in* MOVING TO MARKETS IN ENVIRONMENTAL REGULATION: LESSONS FROM THIRTY YEARS OF EXPERIENCE (C. Kolstad & J. Freeman eds. forthcoming 2006). Yet the first wide-scale domestic experiment with a cap and trade system was attempted in the acid rain provisions of the 1990 amendments to the Clean Air Act. The program is widely viewed as a success and as a model for other tradeable permit regimes. Still, it is not without flaws.

Indeed, it was in connection with the problem of acid rain that interstate air pollution spillover effects initially gained widespread public attention. The dimensions of the transport problem were suggested in an article by an EPA official, discussing the clockwise movement of plumes from Ohio Valley power plants through Illinois, Iowa and Minnesota, over the Great Lakes and Canada, down through New England, and out over the Atlantic. *Ruckelshaus Defends Reagan on Acid Rain, Says House, Senate Measures Would Not Work*, 14 Env't Rep. (BNA) 2205 (Apr. 6, 1984). The problem of ozone transport was exacerbated by firms building tall stacks which were designed to disperse pollution more widely in order to meet air pollution standards near the source.

The EPA estimated that sulfur oxides and nitrogen oxides account for 14 per cent (27.4 million metric tons) and 12 per cent, respectively, of total air pollution in the United States. Although other pollutants also are precursors to acid rain, these two oxides are the major contributors. Sulfur oxides are emitted primarily from stationary sources, such as smelters and power plants, which burn coal as a fuel. Nitrogen oxides come from stationary sources using fossil fuels (56 per cent) and from motor vehicles (40 per cent). After being discharged into the atmosphere, the most common sulfur and nitrogen oxides, sulfur dioxide (SO_2) and nitric oxide (NO), can be chemically converted by oxidation into sulfuric and nitric acids, which may return to the earth as components of rain or snow. Early studies of acid rain concluded that the problem was serious:

> Hundreds of lakes in North America and Scandinavia have become so acidic that they can no longer support fish life. More than 90 lakes in the Adirondack mountains in New York State are fishless because acidic conditions have inhibited reproduction. Recent data indicate that other areas of the United States, such as northern Minnesota and Wisconsin, may be vulnerable to similar adverse impacts.

> While many of the aquatic effects of acid precipitation have been well documented, data related to possible terrestrial impacts are just beginning to be developed. Preliminary research indicates that the yield from agricultural crops can be reduced as a result of both the direct effects of acids on foliage, and the indirect effects resulting

from the leaching of minerals from soils. The productivity of forests may be affected in a similar manner.

EPA, *Acid Rain* 2 (Research Summary, 1979). In addition, acid deposition is contributing to the destruction of stone monuments and statuary throughout the world. The 2,500 year old Parthenon and other classical buildings on the Acropolis in Athens, Greece, have shown much more rapid decay in this century as a result of the city's high air pollution levels. Research is underway to clarify the role of acid rain in the destruction.

Under the Reagan Administration, acid rain became a highly controversial, heavily politicized issue. The Administration's position was that no action on the acid rain problem was advisable until a considerable amount of further study. Hence, the Administration opposed congressionally proposed control programs and refused to take action in cooperation with the Canadians on the problem. *Canada Announces New Effort to Cut Acid Rain*, N.Y. TIMES, March 8, 1984. (Note the resemblance to the George W. Bush administration's approach to greenhouse gases and climate change.)

The political deadlock was broken during the first Bush Administration with the passage of the 1990 Amendments. Congress entirely bypassed the existing mechanism for resolving interstate disputes and established a new system to reduce sulfur dioxide emissions nationwide. In Title IV, Congress created a "cap and trade" market system for addressing sulfur dioxide emissions. Congress set the absolute ceiling on emissions by electric utilities nationwide at 8.9 million tons, and authorized the EPA to allocate annual emissions in tons per year to firms. Firms are allowed to transfer (buy and sell) allocations beneath the cap. Each allowance is equal to one ton of emissions. Firms that are able to reduce their emissions can sell unused allocations, which is intended to create incentives to develop better emission-control technology.

The sulfur trading program introduced in the 1990 Amendments was divided into two phases. In Phase I, extending from 1995 to 1999 and covering only a minority of the nation's steam-electric generating units, over one hundred plants (listed in the Act) were required to meet a standard of 2.5 pounds of SO_2 per million British Thermal Units (BTUs). The 111 utility power plants in question were those that in 1990 emitted more than 2.5 pounds of SO_2 per million BTUs. (For example, generator #1 at the Colbert plant in Alabama received a Phase I allowance of 13,570 tons.) This standard had to be attained by 1995, except that plants using scrubbers to meet the standards had until 1997. This provision was intended to encourage the use of scrubbers and thereby continue at least part of the market for eastern high-sulfur coal. The Phase I allowances were expected to reduce SO_2 emissions by about 10 million tons per year.

Phase II, which began in January, 2000 and applies to virtually all steam-electric utility units in the country, requires utilities to reduce emissions by an additional 50 per cent. Large, poorly controlled plants must reduce emissions to 1.2 million lbs/mBTUs. A complex formula applies to smaller plants. While total emissions cannot exceed 8.9 million tons annually, the EPA had a half million extra allowances in reserve for the first ten years. A further forty thousand allowances can be given to high-growth states. The allowances are allocated largely on the basis of past emissions and fuel consumption, but there are extra allowances for a variety of purposes. For example, from 1995 to 1999, an extra 200,000 allowances were allocated to power plants in Illinois, Indiana, and Ohio.

In part, the system of allocations embodies the efficiency concerns of economists. It seems to have been manipulated in the interests of regional equity, however, so that utilities that are required to engage in heavy investments will be able to recoup part of their expenses. The initial allocations are large enough that some of these utilities will find it feasible to control emissions more than required to stay within their initial allowance, thereby allowing them to sell excess allowances. At least some of these excess allowances will have to be purchased by new utility plants in order to operate.

From the outset, the ambitious, innovative sulfur trading program provoked considerable scholarly discussion and controversy as to the program costs, cost savings, and environmental or public health benefits that would result. *See, e.g.,* Paul R. Portney, *Economics and the Clean Air Act*, 4 J. ECON. PERSP. 173, 175–76 (1990). Larry B. Parker, Robert D. Poling, & John L. Moore, *Clean Air Act Allowance Trading*, 21 ENVTL. L. 2021 (1991); Brennan Van Dyke, *Emissions Trading to Reduce Acid Deposition*, 100 YALE L.J. 2707 (1991); Don Munton, *Dispelling the Myths of the Acid Rain Story*, ENVIRONMENT, July/Aug. 1998, at 4; David M. Driesen, *Does Emissions Trading Encourage Innovation?*, 33 Envtl. L. Rep. 10094 (2003); Byron Swift, *How Environmental Laws Work: An Analysis of the Utility Sector's Response to Regulation of Nitrogen Oxides and Sulfur Dioxides Under the Clean Air Act*, 14 TULANE ENVTL. L.J. 309 (2001); Curtis A. Moore, *The 1990 Clean Air Act Amendments: Failing the Acid Test*, 34 Envtl. L. Rep. 10366 (2004).

In the early 1990s, the program suffered from uncertainties as to the future regulatory environment and brought predictions of failure or disappointment. According to a 1993 report:

> So far * * * the market is a non-starter. With the first deadline looming, only a few trades have been announced, and the terms of those have not been made public. As a result, utilities owning more than 15,000 megawatts of coal-fired power stations, nearly 20 percent of the affected total, have decided to build "scrubbers" without a clear idea of how much it would cost to meet their obligations by buying the allowances instead.

Matthew L. Wald, *Risk—Shy Utilities Avoid Trading Emission Credits*, N.Y. TIMES, Jan. 25, 1993, at C2. The report attributed the lack of trading to risk aversion on the part of utility managements, who believed that under state utility regulation, "if a trade saves money, electric rates are cut, but if a trade later turns out to have raised costs, shareholders suffer." In the early years, auction purchases remained limited, partly because of the availability of low-sulfur coal to allow relatively inexpensive compliance with Phase I standards. Trading also was limited by public utility rules and perhaps by flaws in the implementation of the trading programs, though intra-company trades were more common. *See* Dallas Burtraw, *Trading Emissions to Clean the Air: Exchanges Few but Savings Many*, RESOURCES, Winter 1996, at 3.

By the end of the 1990s, however, the EPA and many other observers claimed the trading program was a major success. For several years, the Chicago Board of Trade has conducted an annual auction of sulfur dioxide emission allowances on behalf of the EPA, and during the March 2002 auction, the average purchase price for each of the 125,000 currently usable allowances sold at auction was around $167. *See* Michael Bologna, *Results of Sulfur Dioxide Auction Suggest Companies Anticipate Gentler Enforcement*, 33 Env't Rep. (BNA) 678 (2002). There is general agreement that the sulfur dioxide emissions trading program has substantially reduced total emissions at a fraction of original estimates of control costs. A study by Resources for the Future found "compelling evidence that the program's benefits far exceed its costs." Indeed, the EPA used the sulfur dioxide program as a model for its emission trading system for NO_x, which it implemented in 1999 by rule, pursuant to CAA § 126. *See* Appalachian Power Co. v. EPA, *supra* at page 643.

Recently, the trading program's performance has been uneven. In 2003, there was a four per cent rise in sulfur dioxide emissions. According to environmentalists, the rise was due to lax enforcement of new source review against power plants, whereas the federal government chalked the increase up to greater use of pollution allowances. *EPA Report Shows Uptick in SO_2 in 2003, Amid 38% Decline in Emissions Since 1980*, ELECTRICITY UTIL. WK., Sept. 27, 2004, at 6. But by April 2005, the impending implementation of the Clean Air Interstate Rule, which will cut the emissions cap by halving the value of allowances for vintage years past 2010, along with increased growth in demand for coal-fired generation due to a rise in the price of natural gas, pushed the price of emissions allowances up to $815 per ton by April 2005. This was a quadrupling of the price in a span of only fifteen months, making emissions much more expensive. Matthew Dalton, *Utilities Start to Feel Bite of SO2 Caps*, WALL ST. J., Apr. 13, 2005, at 1. More broadly, for an annual look at the program's successes and failures, *see* EPA, Clean Air Markets—Progress and Results, http://www.epa.gov/airmarkets/cmprpt/index.html (last visited Dec. 7, 2005) (offering annual compliance reports).

The acid rain program has been hailed as a successful example of a market approach to air pollution. Whatever the trading program's relative success at reducing the cost of total cuts in sulfur emissions, the program has drawn criticism for failing to adequately address the problem of interstate pollution transfers and its attendant costs:

At best, the acid-rain provisions of the 1990 amendments are an incomplete mechanism for dealing with interstate externalities. They apply to only two pollutants: sulfur dioxide and nitrogen oxides. Furthermore, they apply to only one type of facility: electric utilities.

Moreover, these provisions are not structured to allocate emissions between upwind and downwind states in a desirable manner. With respect to nitrogen oxides, the provisions set emissions standards for new and existing sources. [E]missions standards are not a well-targeted means for controlling interstate externalities.

Although [the mandated] decreases in the allowable emissions of sulfur dioxide are likely to reduce the amount of acid rain, particularly after the year 2000, they make no attempt to allocate emissions between upwind states and downwind states in an optimal way. The acid-rain problem manifests itself primarily in the Northeast, but is caused primarily by emissions from the Midwest. Because the market is national, Midwestern sources could buy, without restriction, permits from the West and the Northeast. Such trades would have an undesirable impact in the Northeast. In fact, downwind states are attempting to prevent their sources from selling permits to upwind sources, though such measures may well be struck down on constitutional grounds.

Richard Revesz, *Federalism and Interstate Environmental Externalities*, 144 U. Pa. L. Rev. 2341, 2360–61 (1996). Revesz suggests amending marketable permit schemes so that the amount of emissions allowed by each permit would depend on the impact that its emissions would have on air quality at affected locations. However, a New York attempt to prevent state companies from selling their SO_2 emissions credits to ''upwind'' states was struck down in 2003, suggesting that federal action may be necessary to address this aspect of the pollution problem. Clean Air Mkts. Group v. Pataki, 338 F.3d 82 (2d Cir. 2003) (holding that the state statute was preempted by the Clean Air Act sulfur dioxide market scheme).

The political process behind the 1990 Act has also been sharply criticized. To begin with, Congress never really discussed the level of emissions reduction to seek:

Review of the history of the 1990 Amendments reveals that reasoned deliberation did not occur. Indeed, in sharp contrast to the expectations of emissions trading proponents, Congress deliberately refused to debate the emissions limitation as the Amendments made their way through the legislature. The legislation, originally proposed by the Bush administration, called for a reduction in sulfur dioxide emissions of approximately ten million tons from 1980 levels. This directive remained unchanged from the time the 1990 Amendments were first proposed to the time they were enacted into law. The Senate did, however, add the 8.9 million ton cap on emissions, apparently in order to ensure the achievement of the ten million ton reduction.

Lisa Heinzerling, *Selling Pollution, Forcing Democracy*, 14 STAN. ENVTL. L.J. 300, 323–24 (1995). This absence of debate was all the more striking because a key study estimated that reducing emissions by eight million tons would be equally effective and perhaps cost only half as much. *Id.* at 326. What Congress did debate was how to allocate the allowances:

> It is difficult to imagine what lies behind these special bonuses and exemptions [under the Act], other than the kind of special interest deal that proponents of emissions trading had hoped their system would preempt. The criteria for special bonuses and exemptions are, indeed, so disparate as to invite the conclusion that the only master strategy at work in the allocation of allowances under the 1990 Amendments was the satisfaction of powerful interests. As two commentators have observed, "It would appear that the Senators saw little distinction between the Clean Air Act and a fight over which defense installation to close, or an appropriation for public works projects. The pork tastes as good, from whichever barrel it comes." It is easy to see, for example, the hand of the eastern coal industry, which mines mostly high-sulfur coal, in the incentives to install scrubbers and clean-coal technology.

Id. at 330. *But cf.* Paul L. Joskow & Richard Schmalensee, *The Political Economy of Market–Based Environmental Policy: The U.S. Acid Rain Program*, 41 J.L. & ECON. 37 (1998) (statistical study of voting patterns finding only limited influence by "special interests").

Such criticism aside, the widely acknowledged success of the SO_2 Allowance Trading Program has helped to build enthusiasm for more widespread adoption of cap and trade programs. One example is the George W. Bush administration's proposal to create a cap and trade program for pollutants like NOx and mercury. In February 2002, the Bush administration proposed the "Clear Skies" initiative, a plan to build upon the 1990 CAA Amendments by expanding the use of market-based incentives beyond the realm of sulfur dioxide. President Bush called for a "three-pollutant" approach, targeting toxic mercury emissions along with sulfur and nitrogen oxides, specifically with regard to emissions from large stationary sources such as major electric generating stations. Senator Jim Jeffords, then chairman of the Senate committee considering the administration's proposal, offered a "four-pollutant" bill that would similarly harness market incentives to require reductions of carbon dioxide, the principal greenhouse gas, along with steeper cuts in the same three pollutants covered by Clear Skies. Because both bills only would address certain major stationary sources, neither would constitute a full CAA reauthorization as in 1977 or 1990. The president's cap-and-trade plan was to reduce SO_2 emissions by 73 percent and NO_x by 67 percent by 2018. Industry groups feared the potential costs of mercury reductions (Clear Skies called for a 69 percent cut, while absent any new proposal, the CAA would mandate a 90 percent reduction in mercury); they also balked at carbon limits in the Jeffords proposal. Following the November 2002 election, when Republicans took over the leadership of both houses of Congress while the U.S. economy remained sluggish, the prospects for any clean air legislation dimmed considerably. *See generally* http://www.epa.gov/air/clearskies/basic.html; Dallas Burtraw, *Three Pollutants and and Emission: A Playbill for the Multipollutant Legislative Debate*, 20 BROOKINGS REV. 14 (2002), *available at* http://www.brook.edu/press/REVIEW/spring2002/burtraw.htm.

Despite the lack of congressional action on the Clear Skies legislation, the EPA has moved ahead in the interim, issuing the Clean Air Interstate Rule to create an emissions trading system for SO_2 and NOx in the eastern United States, as well as the Clean Air Mercury Rule to do much the same for mercury emissions from coal-fired power plants across the country. These three plans are all modeled on the Acid Rain Program. The Mercury rule would have capped mercury emissions at 38 tons in 2010 and lowered the cap to 15 tons in 2018. The rule sparked controversy because of allegations that the EPA's cost-benefit analysis, which concluded that stricter controls were not warranted by the public health benefits, was flawed. A Harvard University study paid for by the EPA and peer-reviewed by EPA scientists had reached the opposite conclusion, but was not considered by the agency, and an independent review by the non-partisan Government Accountability Office found fault with the EPA's analysis. Mercury regulation has long been the focus of heated debate. Health advocates say mercury pollution (which contaminates waterways and is ingested by fish that humans ultimately consume) is so harmful to pregnant women and fetuses that the government should force sharp emissions reductions from major sources, including coal-fired powerplants. Industry groups have resisted, arguing that overly aggressive measures are excessively costly. EPA's new rule would have removed mercury from the list of "hazardous pollutants" which are strictly regulated under the CAA. The proposed cap and trade approach would have extended the deadlines that normally apply to hazardous air pollutants, and, instead of forcing controls at each power plant, would have allowed plants to buy up emission permits, potentially creating "hot spots" where mercury pollution would be concentrated. The D.C. Circuit struck down the new Mercury Rule on grounds that the EPA had unlawfully removed it from the list of hazardous air pollutants under § 112 of the Act, in order to regulate it under § 111's New Source provisions, without making the specific findings necessary for delisting a hazardous substance. *See* New Jersey v. EPA, 517 F.3d 574 (2008). The Court rejected EPA's explanation for why it skipped the procedures as "the logic of the Queen of Hearts, substituting EPA's desires for the plain text of s.112(c)(9)." *Id.* at 582

d. Addressing Global Warming

Another example of the popularity of cap and trade systems is their proposed use in controlling the greenhouse gases that contribute to global warming. On the international level, the problems of pollution spillover are magnified, particularly when the spillovers involve the global commons as a whole. As noted in Chapter 1, *supra*, global warming poses a classic problem of the commons, and requires an international solution. In 1997, an international conference in Kyoto reached a historic agreement to cooperate in addressing the global greenhouse effect. Forty industrial countries agreed to cut emissions of greenhouse gases (primarily carbon dioxide) by at least five percent below 1990 levels. The agreement contains a commitment to emissions trading among the industrial countries, with the details to be worked out later. The agreement also allows industrialized countries to meet their obligations by purchasing emission reductions from developing countries, which are not themselves subject to the five-percent reduction requirement. *See* James H. Searles, *Analysis of the Kyoto Protocol to the U.N. Framework Convention on Climate Change*, 21 Int'l Env't Rep. (BNA) 131, 133–34 (Feb. 4, 1998). *See also* Laura B. Campbell & Chad W. Carpenter, *From Kyoto to Buenos Aires: Implementing the Kyoto Protocol on Climate Change*, 21 Env't Rep. (BNA) 748 (July 22, 1998).

[handwritten margin note: Kyoto & cap & trade]

As noted earlier, the second Bush Administration withdrew from the Kyoto Protocol to much international consternation. Then EPA Administrator Whitman announced in March 2001 that the administration had no plans to carry out the treaty, after the administration had previously abandoned a campaign pledge to reduce carbon dioxide emissions from power plants. *See U.S. Won't Follow Climate Treaty Provisions, Whitman Says*, N.Y. TIMES, Mar. 28, 2001. Ironically, this occurred just when the scientific consensus about the greenhouse effect was becoming even stronger:

[handwritten margin note: US withdraws]

> Just a few weeks earlier, the Intergovernmental Panel on Climate Change (IPCC) issued its most recent assessment. Not only did the climate science panel reinforce the conclusions about global warming reached in earlier assessments, it raised the upper bound of the estimates for average global temperature rise during this century. And it has also strengthened the theory that the increase experienced during the past hundred years is partially due to emissions from fossil fuel combustion. By now the scientific consensus on global warming is so strong that it leaves little room for the defensive assertions that keep emerging from the cleverly labeled industrial consortium called the Global Climate Coalition and from a shrinking coterie of scientific skeptics. To be sure, the president didn't say he doubted that consensus. He just acted as though he did.

Donald Kennedy, *An Unfortunate U–Turn on Carbon*, 291 SCIENCE 2515 (2001).

Most recently, the European Union began operation of the world's first mandatory carbon dioxide emissions trading scheme in January 2005. Matthew Saltmarsh, *Market for Emissions Picks Up Steam as Kyoto Protocol Takes Hold*, INT'L HERALD TRIB., July 6, 2005, at 19. The program got off to a rocky start, with disputes arising over allocations of emissions among countries and the overall cap on carbon dioxide. David Gow, *UK Victory Rips Hole in EU's Pollution Trading Scheme*, GUARDIAN (London),

[handwritten margin note: EU cap & trade]

Nov. 24, 2005, at 25. The future path for nations to deal with carbon emissions is murky, with little progress made so far towards a plan for after the Kyoto Protocol expires in 2012. *Pricking the Global Conscience; Climate Change*, ECONOMIST, Dec. 17, 2005.

Though the United States at the time we went to press had yet to adopt national climate change legislation the House of Representatives had passed by a slim margin a bill introduced by Congressmen Waxman (D. Ca) and Markey (D. Ma) HR 2454, known as the American Clean Energy and Security Act of 2009. The bill contains a comprehensive cap and trade scheme. President Obama supports the legislation but its fate in the Senate remains uncertain.

e. Design of Cap-and-Trade Systems

Shouldn't the differences between acid rain and these other pollutants or gases give us pause? Is it really appropriate to allow trading in toxic pollutants like mercury, even when there is a risk of creating concentrations or "hot spots" that might affect some sub-populations more than others? And are greenhouse gases like SO_2?

As just noted, recently cap and trade systems have emerged as the preferred policy option for domestic regulation of greenhouse gases. What are the key design questions? Consider the following issues, summarized by a leading Harvard economist:

The first question might be: What should be the scope of coverage? Which sources and industries should be included? This was a major issue of discussion and debate when the European Union's Emissions Trading System was being designed but it is not necessarily the right place to begin. Just posing this question limits the possibilities and omits what may be some of the best options. Instead, we might ask: What should be the point of regulation? The possibilities include downstream sources (i.e., CO_2 emitting sources), which would require issuing CO_2 emission permits. This would be very similar to the SO_2 allowance trading. Alternatively, we might regulate upstream sources (i.e., producers and importers of fossil fuels). In this scenario, carbon rights would be linked with the carbon content of fossil fuels. This approach would be similar to the EPA's lead trading regime, which was part of the lead phase down in the 1980s—a very successful program that removed leaded gasoline from the market in five years with low transaction costs and cost savings of $250 million per year. There are, in addition, various midstream alternatives.

When choosing among the alternative points of regulation we should consider the following criteria: First, breadth of coverage. If the point of regulation were downstream generators, CO_2 emission permits would likely include electricity generators and likely exclude motor vehicles, home furnaces, etc. If the point of regulation were upstream producers, a carbon rights system could provide complete coverage of CO_2 emissions. However, non-combustion uses of fuels would be affected, suggesting a need for compensating credits. And what about carbon management (i.e., the separation and removal of CO_2 from stack gases)? An upstream system provides no incentive for this, again suggesting the need for credits. What about biological carbon sequestration, perhaps through an integrated trading system? This would be much more difficult, but possible and quantitatively important. Second, we should consider the number of regulated entities included in the market. Smaller numbers ease the burden of monitoring and enforcement but could raise competitiveness concerns if the market were very small.

The third relevant criteria is the monitoring regime. Effective monitoring is required for market confidence, but continuous emissions monitoring is very costly. The fourth consideration is the number and type of greenhouse gases to include. This is a design issue itself, and it can affect choice of point of regulation. Should the scheme include only carbon dioxide or others as well? Should the system allow for inter-gas trading?

This brings us to the next design question: What should be the point of allocation? The point of allocation need not be the same as the point of regulation. These are separate design issues. For example, upstream regulation in theory can be combined with mid-stream or downstream allocation of the tradeable permits. Possibilities for point of allocation include downstream sources (e.g., CO_2 emission sources) or sources even further downstream (e.g., electricity users) or upstream producers (e.g., producers and importers of fossil fuels). Note that the point of allocation combined with the nature of the allocation affects the distribution of the cost burden.

The third design question is: What should be the rules for allocation? Should permits or carbon rights be auctioned, given away without charge, or a mix? The political advantages of freely allocating emission rights can lead to efficiency problems. Usually, costs under a tradeable permit regime are independent of initial allocation, so allocation can be left to political process (which is why such systems are so politically attractive). However, the execution of a tradeable permit program—like any such regulatory constraint—can exacerbate distortions & drive up costs. And in contrast to an auctioned permit system—which generates revenues for government—a freely-allocated permit system provides no opportunity for reducing or eliminating the distortions by cutting existing distorting taxes. Further, in the presence of some types of transaction costs, the post-trading outcome is sensitive to the initial allocation. So, a successful attempt to establish a politically viable program through initial (free) allocation can increase costs. There are other issues that arise when choosing the rules for allocation, including the choice of the baseline emissions and baseline year, and the specific allocation cross-sectionally, and over time.

Fourth, what about temporal flexibility? Among the rules that govern trading, those that affect temporal flexibility are exceptionally important. Should the regime allow banking, which entitles the holder to save emission permits for a future time period? Banking has been key in both the lead trading program and the ongoing sulfur dioxide program. But programs that are phased in over time can create emissions leakage from regulated to unregulated sources. There is also the matter of borrowing (using emission permits from a future period). Borrowing can in theory increase cost-effectiveness of a program. The rules for banking and borrowing and for the length of compliance periods (e.g., 1 year in the sulfur dioxide program and five years in the Kyoto Protocol) should depend upon the nature of the environmental problem and the potential solutions. And finally, what kind of enforcement regime is required? Market based instruments such as cap and trade systems are not *deregulation*, but rather can amount to more enlightened regulation. Government enforcement is still required. Stiff penalties provide effective incentives for compliance, but excessive penalties are not credible. For example, in the sulfur dioxide program, the penalty is $2,900 per ton of excess emissions (compared with marginal abatement costs that have been 10% of that); the result is near perfect compliance. The sulfur dioxide program also requires emissions offsets in subsequent years. If this is eliminated, the penalty is a tax on "excess emissions," and we have a "safety valve" on costs. Whether to use such a safety valve is another major design issue. So, reasonable penalties are necessary, but it is wise to avoid prior approval by government for trades because it can drive up transaction costs.

Another worry is whether permits in a cap and trade system might be used as barriers to entry by incumbent firms. In theory, firms with market power in either the permit market or respective product markets can withhold permits from the market, driving up price, and keeping out competition. What to do? The solution in the sulfur dioxide allowance trading program was a zero-revenue annual auction of about 3 per cent of the allowances (i.e., the government is a seller of last resort). While such anti-competitive behavior can be a problem in theory, it has not been a problem to date in either the lead or sulfur dioxide programs. Ultimately the appropriate agency to address this may not be the EPA, but the anti-trust division at the Department of Justice.

Based on material presented by Professor Robert N. Stavins, Director of the Environmental Economics Program, Harvard University, Address at the Harvard Law School Conference on New Prospects for Climate Change Regulation: Learning from Experience: An Overview of Greenhouse Gas Trading Design Issues (Mar. 10, 2006).

Although emissions trading for greenhouse gases has yet to develop into national legislation, several Northeastern states have confronted these design questions and agreed to a carbon cap and trade system among regional power plants known as the Regional Greenhouse Gas Initiative. *See* http://www.rggi.org. This is one of the many state initiatives on greenhouse gas regulation.

Though some criticize state and local initiatives as too limited, or as interfering with the development of a coherent national approach, others praise them. Consider the following appraisal of regional trading systems such as the one created by the Northeastern states:

> This fragmented "bottom-up" approach to carbon trading is not simply a stiff smile to be painted on the wreckage of grander visions for global trading. Rather, it is pragmatic and effective. The architects of global trading were blinded by the theoretical benefits that could arise from trading among diverse economies; a universal system, they thought, would also prevent free riding. However, global institutions are too weak to monitor and enforce what is, in effect, a new monetary system. Global agreements are also vulnerable to exit when commitments become inconvenient (such as when the United States abandoned the Kyoto process). A system that originates from the top takes the speed of its least ambitious nation.
>
> The strength of a bottom-up approach is its ability to tap stronger national and regional institutions for governance.... The EU, although it now has 25 members, initially applied its carbon trading scheme to just the subset of 15 members that have the longest history of cooperation....

David G. Victor, Joshua C. House, & Sarah Joy, *A Madisonian Approach to Climate Policy,* 309 SCIENCE 1820 (2005).

CHAPTER 7

WATER POLLUTION

■ ■ ■

A. BACKGROUND

1. HISTORICAL CONTEXT

Until just after the Second World War, the federal government played a minor role in the regulation of water pollution. Thfe federal Rivers and Harbors Act of 1899 prohibited the discharge of refuse matter into the navigable waters of the United States, but its primary goal was to ensure that dumping did not interfere with navigation and commerce. At this time and well into the twentieth century, water pollution (like air pollution) was viewed as a state and local matter. Private plaintiffs relied on common law nuisance suits and other state-created causes of action to recover for harms related to water contamination. Again, as with air pollution, these remedies were based on property rights, and were limited in their capacity to comprehensively address the contamination of the nation's waterways by widespread industrial and domestic discharge of waste.

In 1948, Congress passed the Federal Water Pollution Control Act (FWPCA). Unlike the Refuse Act, the FWPCA was aimed specifically at reducing pollution in interstate waterways. However, the federal government declined to take the primary regulatory role, instead providing funding to the states for research and for the development of state programs to address pollution control. In the 1965 Amendments to the FWPCA, Congress strengthened its role, requiring states to establish water quality standards subject to federal approval for all water bodies in their jurisdiction, and to develop state implementation plans.

Even as amended, however, the law proved largely ineffective. In the 1965 Act, Congress had adopted an ambient approach to water pollution by requiring states to set water quality standards for receiving bodies. An ambient approach is difficult to administer because it "focuses on the tolerable effects rather than the preventable causes of water pollution." *See* EPA v. California *ex rel.* State Water Resources Control Bd., 426 U.S. 200, 202 (1976). Setting ambient standards requires scientific data to determine the effects of different pollutants under different conditions. Yet the data may not be sufficient to assist in establishing safe levels.

Moreover, even assuming standards can be set, achieving them can be challenging. Regulators must work backwards from water quality standards to controls, identifying dischargers responsible for the failure of the water body to meet standards and then allocating to each a share of the pollutant reductions necessary to ameliorate the problem. And of course each body of water—and there are thousands—requires its own set of standards and controls.

The 1965 legislation contained no regulatory mechanism enabling states to readily identify and individually regulate the multiple sources that might have contributed to the ambient water quality problem. As a result, even assuming states had the political will to regulate water quality (and most did not), enforcement of ambient water quality standards proved nearly impossible. *See generally* Drew Caputo, *A Job Half Finished: The Clean Water Act After 25 Years,* 27 ENVTL. L. REP. 10,574 (1997). Given the difficulty of tracing pollutants from the receiving body back to the responsible source(s), individual sources could, presumably, dispute the findings that they contributed to water quality problems and resist the imposition of cuts. Moreover, federal enforcement capacity was weak. While the federal government was authorized to set water quality standards and file implementation plans where states failed to do so, the Act did not authorize federal officials to impose the implementation plan on states.

In the end, as implemented by the states, the FWPCA's ambient approach did not lead to significant improvement in water quality. Instead, it tended to lock in existing uses and reinforce the status quo. Water bodies that were designated for industrial use were allowed to meet far lower standards than those designated for recreational use. This meant that, typically, waterways were permitted to languish if they had historically been used as a dumping ground for wastewater from industrial facilities.

Indeed, through the late 1960s water pollution continued largely unabated. Cities routinely dumped raw sewage, and industrial plants sent a variety of pollutants including toxics, into the surface waters of the United States. Urban and agricultural runoff choked rivers and streams, as did runoff from resource extraction operations like coal mining and logging. Perhaps the most enduring image of this era is that of Ohio's Cuyohoga River bursting into flames in 1969 because it was so badly polluted with oil and industrial waste. Because of incidents like this, public awareness of the dangers of water pollution began to grow.

It is tempting to over-credit such high profile media events with spurring legislative victories. However, for generalized concerns about environmental issues to crystallize into legislative action a more complicated confluence of events is generally required. Often, a powerful "issue entrepreneur" in Congress helps to position the issue on the national agenda, and the prospect of regulation garners political support from powerful interest groups, including the regulated community itself, which frequently prefers regulation to the alternative—damage suits. In the case of water pollution, an entrepreneurial member of Congress sought to revitalize the long dormant Refuse Act as a tool to sue polluters for discharging waste into navigable waterways. Industry groups, fearing the Supreme Court would extend the Refuse Act to cover ordinary pollution traditionally not covered by the U.S. Army Corps of Engineers' existing permit program, sought a uniform permit system as a shield against citizen suits. *See* ROBERT V. PERCIVAL, ALAN S. MILLER, CHRISTOPHER H. SCHROEDER, & JAMES P. LEAPE, ENVIRONMENTAL REGULATION, at 633–34 (3d ed. 2000) (4th ed. 2003). This, together with the conclusion of the Senate Committee on Public Works that the existing program, "has been inadequate in every vital aspect," and the growing public awareness about environmental problems, helped to push Congress to revisit the FWPCA once more.

2. THE 1972 AMENDMENTS TO THE FEDERAL WATER POLLUTION CONTROL ACT

In the 1972 Amendments to the FWPCA (then renamed the Clean Water Act), Congress acted forcefully, taking the lead in regulating pollution in the nation's waterways. Congress established federal standards to be implemented by states, and backed up the new regime with sanctions. The Amendments relegated the ambient approach of the earlier legislation to secondary status in favor of a new national permit system (the national pollution discharge elimination system, or NPDES) that would impose technology-based effluent limits on all "point sources" of water pollution. The Amendments required the newly created EPA to establish technology-based performance standards for different categories of dischargers and for different types of pollutants. These standards would be set based on technology then available and already in use. Cost was to be taken into consideration to varying degrees when setting these standards, depending on the category of source (existing or new) and the nature of the pollutant.

The NPDES is meant to be comprehensive: section 301 prohibits the discharge of any pollutant into the navigable waterways of the United States by any "point source" without an NPDES permit. A key distinction was drawn in the Amendments between point sources, which could not discharge without a permit, and other producers of water pollution called "nonpoint" sources. Point sources are largely comprised of industrial polluters and municipal treatment works from which effluent flows through a discrete conveyance, such as a pipe. Nonpoint sources consist primarily of facilities or operations from which waste travels via runoff without passing through pipes. Examples include cropland, livestock feedlots, and drainage from waste disposal sites as well as mining and logging operations.

The new Amendments did not wholly abandon water quality standards but used them instead to reinforce the new approach based on "end-of-pipe controls" at the source. States were still required to designate water body uses and to establish water quality standards to support those uses. The Act authorized the EPA to tighten permit requirements where water quality was too low to support designated uses. The Act also required publicly owned treatment works (POTWs), which process sewage, to perform "secondary treatment" before discharging waste into water bodies. The federal government provided generous federal financing to induce states to build more sewage treatment plants, and states readily took the money.

3. COMPARING THE CWA AND THE CAA

The story of water pollution regulation in the United States mirrors, in many ways, the story of air regulation. After years of relying on ineffective state measures, Congress finally assumed the primary role in regulating water quality, just as it had with air quality. Like air pollution, water pollution comes from numerous sources, including large industrial plants (e.g., pulp and paper mills, chemical manufacturers and metal refiners), municipal sewage treatment plants, urban streets, as well as agriculture, mining, and logging operations. The diversity among sources makes water pollution difficult to control. And like air pollution regulation, water pollution regulation relies on the availability of good information about sources of pollution and sound science about the health and environmental effects of different pollutants. Effective regulation also requires the availability of control technology, treatment methods, and management practices capable of reducing the discharge of pollutants or mitigating their harmful effects. These technologies, treatments and practices can be expensive to adopt, especially for older firms, requiring policy makers to make trade-offs between cost and pollution control.

The EPA, created by Executive Order in 1970 and already tasked with implementing the CAA, was charged with implementing the CWA as well. This proved to be an enormous burden. The agency came under considerable pressure from industry groups, states and environmental organizations, which collectively brought hundreds of lawsuits to challenge virtually every regulatory effort the agency undertook, including the agency's first effort to establish effluent standards under the NPDES system. The implementation process of the Clean Water Act (CWA), like the CAA, has been characterized by ambitious targets, missed deadlines, and several rounds of amendments to address lingering problems. In just one example of the many similarities between the two Acts, the EPA's first attempt to regulate toxic pollutants using a health-based approach ended in failure, necessitating instead the control of toxics using technology-based standards.

And yet, Congress's approach to water pollution differs in important ways from its approach to air pollution, as we shall see. One key difference is that the CWA adopted primarily a technology-based approach (relying on "end-of-pipe" controls on point sources), backed up by an ambient strategy that requires maintenance of water quality standards for designated uses where technology-based controls prove insufficient. The Clean Air Act, recall, adopted primarily an ambient approach (the EPA sets national ambient air quality standards to be implemented by states), supplemented by technology-based standards imposed on a variety of sources (new sources, sources of toxics, and those located in PSD and nonattainment areas). In addition, the 1970 Clean Air Act Amendments did not establish a uniform permit system for all stationary sources of air pollutants, relying instead on the sources themselves to comply with applicable regulations. By contrast, a national permit system was at the heart of the 1972 amendments to the CWA.

Many of the differences between the two statutes have narrowed over time, however. By now, both the CWA and the CAA use a mixture of ambient and technology-based controls, to a greater or lesser extent. In addition, both statutes now employ a permit system. As we saw in Chapter 4, Congress adopted the Title V permit system in the 1990 Amendments to the CAA, requiring that most stationary sources of air pollution obtain a federally enforceable permit. At the same time, some differences remain. The CWA continues to exclude non-point sources of water pollution from its permit requirements, leaving a large amount of water pollution uncontrolled, or only minimally controlled. There is no comparable gap in the CAA.

4.　RESULTS

By any measure, the Clean Water Act has been a success. In 1992, The National Academy of Sciences credited the statute with significantly controlling and reducing chemical pollution in rivers, lakes and wetlands, and with reducing loadings of toxic contaminants. *See* National Research Council, RESTORATION OF AQUATIC ECOSYSTEMS: SCIENCE, TECHNOLOGY, AND PUBLIC POLICY 47 (1992). Today, rivers, lakes, and coasts that were once so badly polluted as to be dangerous to human health and aquatic life are thriving. *See* Carol Browner & Dan Glickman, *CLEAN WATER ACTION PLAN: RESTORING AND PROTECTING AMERICA'S WATERS* (1998). THE EXCERPT BELOW PROVIDES AN OVERVIEW OF THE ACT'S ACCOMPLISHMENTS AND IDENTIFIES CHALLENGES FOR THE FUTURE.

WATER POLLUTION CONTROL: 25 YEARS OF PROGRESS AND CHALLENGES FOR THE NEW MILLENNIUM

Office of Wastewater Management, USEPA, 1998.

* * *

Progress

The basic approach in the Clean Water Act (CWA) over the past 25 years has been greater control of "point sources" of water pollution—

primarily factories and city sewers, along with controls on activities that destroy wetlands. In the last decade, federal law and policy has been strengthened several times. These include changes in federal farm policies to substantially improve technical and financial assistance to farmers to protect the environment, new changes in federal land management policies to increase protection of aquatic resources and watersheds, and new authorities to protect coastal waters. As a result of the Clean Water Act, waters that are safe for fishing and swimming have doubled. National clean water standards stop billions of pounds of pollutants from industries from flowing into waters each year. The number of Americans served by sewage treatment facilities has more than doubled. Before 1972, Oregon's Willamette River was off-limits to recreation. The Potomac River near the nation's capital was badly polluted and unfit for swimming and fishing. Today, these and many other water bodies that were once severely polluted are well on the way to recovery and people are increasingly using these waters for fishing, swimming, and other recreation.

* * * In addition to industrial and municipal wastewater treatment facilities, the NPDES permit program includes urban storm water management, control of combined sewer and sanitary sewer overflows, and biosolids (sewage sludge) management. * * * While the program is regulatory, its success is measured in the large number of water quality improvements in the Unites States. Many rivers and streams were off limits to recreational activities which affected economic prosperity; now with these regulations, many of the rivers and streams have been re-opened for public use.

Because of the CWA, thousands of municipalities have received federal funds to construct or expand wastewater treatment facilities to prevent or reduce the discharge of pollutants to the Nation's rivers, lakes and streams. To date, EPA has awarded more than $62 billion in grants to help municipalities with the clean up effort and many water bodies have shown improvement. * * *

Discharges from combined sewer or sanitary sewer overflows caused beach closings, fish and shellfish bans, flooded basements, and a wide range of public health problems. Many of these overflows were the result of deteriorating or antiquated collections systems. To date, more than $6 billion has been awarded to rehabilitate collection systems to reduce these wet weather overflows, thus, improving water quality and making it safe for public use and enjoyment.

Challenges for the New Millennium

Despite impressive progress, many of the nation's rivers, lakes, and coastal waters do not meet water quality goals. Some waters face the threat of degradation from diverse pollution sources which affect citizens' quality of life by reducing recreational opportunities, undermining local economic prosperity, and threatening drinking water supplies and impairing public health. States report that close to 40 percent of the waters they surveyed are too polluted for basic uses like fishing or swimming. The success in cleaning up pollution from point sources (e.g., factories and sewage treatment plants) has not yet been matched by controls over polluted runoff from sources such as farms, urban areas, forestry, ranching, and mining operations. Natural areas that are critical to the health of aquatic systems, such as wetlands, stream corridors, and coastal areas, are not adequately protected. In addition, water pollution poses a continuing threat to public health. The number of fish consumption advisories and beach closings is rising each year and new threats, such as the toxic microorganism *Pfiesteria*, demand effective responses.

It is estimated that $139.5 billion are still needed to construct or improve wastewater treatment facilities to correct current water quality or public health problems. These dollars would be used for replacing or repairing existing sewer collection systems, constructing new sewers or interceptors, treating wastewater overflows from combined sewers, continuing needs for municipal storm water management, and controlling nonpoint sources of pollution.

In addition, there are new technical challenges in addressing control of toxic pollutants and the management of residual biosolids (sewage sludge). Greater concern about toxic pollutants suggests the need for higher levels of wastewater treatment coupled with industrial pretreatment, which in turn will generally lead to the production of greater quantities of biosolids. These higher level processes will be more expensive to build and operate.

Biennial reporting on the nation's waters

Every two years states report to the EPA about the status of water bodies within their borders. *See* THE NATIONAL WATER QUALITY INVENTORY: REPORT TO CONGRESS, 2004 REPORTING CYCLE: FINDINGS (Jan. 2009). In the most recent report for the 2004 reporting cycle (compiled as of January 2009) states report that 44 percent of the streams assessed (states only reported on 16 percent of streams) are impaired for the uses for which they are designated, while 53 percent fully support their designated uses (for a description of the designated use process see pages 759–762). Agriculture is the top source of impairment of rivers and streams.

With respect to the state of the nation's lakes, ponds and reservoirs the story is worse. Of the 39 percent of these water bodies actually assessed, 64 percent are impaired for their designated uses. Mercury contamination is the top cause of impairment in lakes, ponds and reservoirs. Our bays and estuaries appear to be in somewhat better shape, with only 30 percent of them impaired (though only 29 percent have been assessed). By contrast, the Great Lakes shoreline miles experience significant impairment primarily as the result of contaminated sediment, which includes PCBs, pesticides, dioxins and other toxins.

---

5. POLLUTANTS

The following charts convey: 1) the kinds of pollution and the harms they cause to water bodies and 2) the major, human-made sources of pollution respectively:

Major Categories of Pollution	*Resulting Harms*
Siltation (from soil erosion caused by, e.g., agriculture, roadbuilding, urban/suburban construction, mining, logging)	*Alters or destroys habitat, kills aquatic life, complicates treatment for drinking water, diminishes recreational opportunities (e.g., swimming, boating, fishing), obstructs commercial use of waterways*
Oxygen Depletion (biological (BOD): from biodegradable organic wastes, such as food processing wastes, any plant material; chemical (COD): from chemical compounds that react with oxygen when breaking down into byproducts)	*Alters or destroys habitat, kills aquatic life, diminishes recreational opportunities*
Nutrient Overenrichment (from nitrogen and phosphorus from fertilizers, detergents, sewage and manure)	*Causes algal blooms/eutrophication and resulting oxygen depletion, alters or destroys habitat, kills aquatic life, diminishes recreational opportunities*
Pathogenic Bacterial Contamination (from untreated sewage, septic runoff, animal feedlot runoff)	*Complicates treatment for drinking water, diminishes recreational opportunities*
Pesticides (from agriculture, urban/suburban landscaping)	*Kills aquatic life, complicates treatment for drinking water, diminishes recreational opportunities*
Toxic Chemicals/Metals (from industrial point/non-point sources, urban runoff, dump leaching, underground storage tank leakage)	*Kills aquatic life, complicates treatment for drinking water, diminishes recreational opportunities, leads to bioaccumulation and biological magnification (stored in animal tissue at increasing concentrations in animals higher on food chain), increases risk of cancer and genetic mutations*
Toxic-contaminated Sediments	*Acts like toxic chemicals when settled sediments on bottom of a waterway are stirred up*
Oil and Grease (from industrial discharges, restaurants, urban/suburban street/storm sewer runoff, shipping and recreational boating)	*Low-level toxic effect, oxygen-depleting effect, kills or injures aquatic life, diminishes recreational opportunities, biodegrades slowly*
Acidification (from industrial discharges, mine waste runoff/leaching, atmospheric deposition/acid rain)	*Kills aquatic life, alters or destroys habitat*
Salinization (from dumping of oil brine wastes, winter road de-icing, evaporative concentration and coastal salt-water intrusion due to irrigation)	*Kills aquatic life, alters or destroys habitat*
Thermal Pollution/Modification (from industrial/utility boiler coolant water discharges, shade removal due to devegetation of waterway banks)	*Kills aquatic life, alters or destroys habitat*

Major Categories of Pollution	Resulting Harms
Bioinvasion of Non-native Species (from commercial shipping, ballast/bilgewater discharges)	*Kills native aquatic life, alters or destroys habitat*

Pollution Sources and Resulting Problems

Source Categories/Subcategories	Resulting Problems
Agriculture:	
Plowing of fields, erosion	*Siltation*
Pesticide spraying/runoff	*Toxic contamination*
Fertilizer runoff	*Nutrient overenrichment*
Animal feedlot runoff	*Nutrient overenrichment, bacterial contamination*
Dumping agricultural wastes	*Oxygen depletion*
Burning agricultural wastes	*Atmospheric deposition, acidification*
Irrigation	*Salinization*
Hydrologic modifications:	
Damming of waterways	
Filling in of waterways	*Obstruction of waterways, habitat destruction or modification*
Channelization	
Routing through culverts/tunnels	
Dredging of waterways	*Dredging may stir up toxic-contaminated sediments*
Urban/suburban sources:	
Storm sewers/street runoff	*Multiple pollutants, including oil and pesticides*
Dump runoff	*grease, oxygen-depleting substances, toxics, metals*
Backyard/landscaping runoff	*Pesticide and fertilizer pollution, like agriculture*
Septic system runoff	*Bacterial contamination, nutrient overenrichment*
Dumps—underground leaching	*Toxic groundwater contamination, metals*
Sewage/wastewater treatment facilities, if waste is incompletely treated	*Bacterial contamination, multiple pollutants*
Industrial nonpoint sources:	
Construction sites, erosion	*Siltation*
Logging/silviculture, erosion	*Siltation and pesticide runoff, like agriculture*
Mine waste runoff	*Siltation, acidification, toxic contamination, metals*
Oil extraction wastes/brine	*Toxic contamination, salinization*
Dumping excavated earth in waterways	*Obstruction, habitat modification or destruction*
Underground storage tank leakage	*Toxic groundwater contamination*
Commercial shipping	*Oil and grease, bioinvasion of non-native species*
Cruise ships	*Untreated sewage, recreational solid wastes, bacterial contamination*
Industrial point sources:	
Wastewater effluent pipes	*Oxygen depletion, oil and grease, toxic contamination, metals, thermal pollution*
Smokestacks and vents	*Atmospheric deposition, acidification*
Other categories:	
Devegetation of waterway banks and shade removal	*Thermal modification, siltation/erosion*
Recreational boating	*Oil and grease, recreational solid waste*
Winter road de-icing	*Salinization*

B. THE CLEAN WATER ACT AND THE COMMON LAW

Prior to passage of the 1972 Clean Water Act, states sought recourse in the federal courts to resolve disputes over interstate water pollution. In the typical case, a downstream state would complain that its population was suffering adverse health effects because of sewage pumped into a river from the upstream state. The courts grappled with these cases in the absence of congressional action to address the problem. In *Illinois v. Milwaukee,* 406 U.S. 91 (1972) [*Milwaukee I*], the Supreme Court held that interstate pollution violated the federal common law and that nuisance actions could be brought in federal court to redress the violation. Then Congress passed the CWA. This raised obvious questions about how to coordinate the nuisance action with the extensive requirements contained in the new law.

MILWAUKEE v. ILLINOIS [MILWAUKEE II]

Supreme Court of the United States, 1981.
451 U.S. 304, 101 S.Ct. 1784, 68 L.Ed.2d 114.

JUSTICE REHNQUIST delivered the opinion of the Court.

When this litigation was first before us we recognized the existence of a federal "common law" which could give rise to a claim for abatement of a nuisance caused by interstate water pollution. *Illinois v. Milwaukee,* 406 U.S. 91, 92 S. Ct. 1385, 31 L. Ed. 2d 712 (1972). Subsequent to our decision, Congress enacted the Federal Water Pollution Control Act Amendments of 1972. We granted certiorari to consider the effect of this legislation on the previously recognized cause of action. * * *

Federal courts, unlike state courts, are not general common law courts and do not possess a general power to develop and apply their own rules of decision. The enactment of a federal rule in an area of national concern, and the decision whether to displace state law in doing so, is generally made not by the federal judiciary, purposefully insulated from democratic pressures, but by the people through their elected representatives in Congress. * * *

When Congress has not spoken to a particular issue, however, and when there exists a "significant conflict between some federal policy or interest and the use of state law,"[1] the Court has found it necessary, in a "few and restricted" instances, to develop a federal common law. Nothing in this process suggests that courts are better suited to develop national policy in areas governed by federal common law than they are in other areas, or that the usual and important concerns of an appropriate division

---

1. In this regard we note the inconsistency in Illinois' argument and the decision of the District Court that both federal and state nuisance law apply to this case. If state law can be applied, there is no need for federal common law; if federal common law exists, it is because state law cannot be used.

of functions between the Congress and the federal judiciary are inapplicable. * * *

Contrary to the suggestions of respondents, the appropriate analysis in determining if federal statutory law governs a question previously the subject of federal common law is not the same as that employed in deciding if federal law pre-empts state law. In considering the latter question "we start with the assumption that the historic police powers of the States were not to be superseded by the Federal Act unless that was the clear and manifest purpose of Congress." While we have not hesitated to find pre-emption of state law, whether express or implied, when Congress has so indicated, or when enforcement of state regulations would impair "federal superintendence of the field," our analysis has included "due regard for the presuppositions of our embracing federal system, including the principle of diffusion of power not as a matter of doctrinaire localism but as a promoter of democracy." Such concerns are not implicated in the same fashion when the question is whether federal statutory or federal common law governs, and accordingly the same sort of evidence of a clear and manifest purpose is not required. Indeed, as noted, in cases such as the present "we start with the assumption" that it is for Congress, not federal courts, to articulate the appropriate standards to be applied as a matter of federal law.[2]

We conclude that, at least so far as concerns the claims of respondents, Congress has not left the formulation of appropriate federal standards to the courts through application of often vague and indeterminate nuisance concepts and maxims of equity jurisprudence, but rather has occupied the field through the establishment of a comprehensive regulatory program supervised by an expert administrative agency. The 1972 amendments to the Federal Water Pollution Control Act were not merely another law "touching interstate waters" of the sort surveyed in *Illinois v. Milwaukee* and found inadequate to supplant federal common law. Rather, the amendments were viewed by Congress as a "total restructuring" and "complete rewriting" of the existing water pollution legislation considered in that case. Congress' intent in enacting the amendments was clearly to establish an all-encompassing program of water pollution regulation. *Every* point source discharge is prohibited unless covered by a permit, which directly subjects the discharger to the administrative apparatus established by Congress to achieve its goals. The "major purpose" of the amendments was "to establish a *comprehensive* long-range policy for the elimination of water pollution." No Congressman's remarks on the legislation were complete without reference to the "comprehensive" nature of the amendments. * * * The establishment of such a self-consciously comprehensive program by Congress, which certainly did not exist when

---

2. Since the States are represented in Congress but not in the federal courts, the very concerns about displacing state law which counsel against finding pre-emption of *state* law in the absence of clear intent actually suggest a willingness to find congressional displacement of *federal* common law. Simply because the opinion in *Illinois v. Milwaukee* used the term "pre-emption," usually employed in determining if federal law displaces state law, is no reason to assume the analysis used to decide the usual federal-state questions is appropriate here.

Illinois v. Milwaukee was decided, strongly suggests that there is no room for courts to attempt to improve on that program with federal common law.

Turning to the particular claims involved in this case, the action of Congress in supplanting the federal common law is perhaps clearest when the question of effluent limitations for discharges from the two treatment plants is considered. The duly issued permits under which the city commission discharges treated sewage from the Jones Island and South Shore treatment plants incorporate, as required by the Act, *see* § 402(b)(1), the specific effluent limitations established by EPA regulations pursuant to § 301 of the Act. There is thus no question that the problem of effluent limitations has been thoroughly addressed through the administrative scheme established by Congress, as contemplated by Congress. This being so there is no basis for a federal court to impose more stringent limitations than those imposed under the regulatory regime by reference to federal common law, as the District Court did in this case. * * *

Respondents argue that congressional intent to preserve the federal common law remedy recognized in *Illinois v. Milwaukee* is evident in §§ 510 and 505(e) of the statute. Section 510 provides that nothing in the Act shall preclude States from adopting and enforcing limitations on the discharge of pollutants more stringent than those adopted under the Act. It is one thing, however, to say that States may adopt more stringent limitations through state administrative processes, or even that States may establish such limitations through state nuisance law, and apply them to in-state discharges. It is quite another to say that the States may call upon *federal* courts to employ *federal* common law to establish more stringent standards applicable to out-of-state dischargers. Any standards established under federal common law are federal standards, and so the authority of States to impose more stringent standards under § 510 would not seem relevant. Section 510 clearly contemplates state authority to establish more stringent pollution limitations; nothing in it, however, suggests that this was to be done by federal court actions premised on federal common law.

Subsection 505(e) provides:

"Nothing *in this section* shall restrict any right which any person (or class of persons) may have under any statute or common law to seek enforcement of any effluent standard or limitation or to seek any other relief (including relief against the Administrator or a state agency)" (emphasis supplied).

Respondents argue that this evinces an intent to preserve the federal common law of nuisance. We, however, are inclined to view the quoted provision as meaning what it says: that nothing in § 505, the citizen suit provision, should be read as limiting any other remedies which might exist.

Subsection 505(e) is virtually identical to subsections in the citizen suit provisions of several environmental statutes. The subsection is common language accompanying citizen suit provisions and we think that it means only that the provision of such suit does not revoke other remedies. It most assuredly cannot be read to mean that the Act as a whole does not supplant formerly available federal common law actions but only that the particular section authorizing citizen suits does not do so. No one, however, maintains that the citizen-suit provision pre-empts federal common law. * * *

We therefore conclude that no federal common law remedy was available to respondents in this case. The judgment of the Court of Appeals is therefore vacated, and the case remanded for proceedings consistent with this opinion.

JUSTICE BLACKMUN, with whom JUSTICE MARSHALL and JUSTICE STEVENS join, dissenting.

Nine years ago, this Court unanimously determined that Illinois could bring a federal common-law action against the city of Milwaukee, three other Wisconsin cities, and two sewerage commissions. At that time, Illinois alleged that the discharge of raw and untreated sewage by these Wisconsin entities into Lake Michigan created a public nuisance for the citizens of Illinois. The Court remitted the parties to an appropriate federal district court, "whose powers are adequate to resolve the issues."

Illinois promptly initiated the present litigation, and pursued it through more than three years of pretrial discovery, a six-month trial that entailed hundreds of exhibits and scores of witnesses, extensive factual findings by the District Court and an exhaustive review of the evidence by the Court of Appeals. Today, the Court decides that this nine-year judicial exercise has been just a meaningless charade, inasmuch as, it says, the federal common law remedy approved in *Illinois v. Milwaukee* was implicitly extinguished by Congress just six months after the 1972 decision. Because I believe that Congress intended no such extinction, and surely did not contemplate the result reached by the Court today, I respectfully dissent. * * *

[The Clean Water Act] sets forth certain effluent limitations. As did the Court of Appeals, a court applying federal common law in a given instance may well decline to impose effluent limitations more stringent than those required by Congress, because the complainant has failed to show that stricter standards will abate the nuisance or appreciably diminish the threat of injury. But it is a far different proposition to pronounce, as does the Court today, that federal courts "*lack authority* to impose more stringent effluent limitations under federal common law than those imposed" under the statutory scheme. The authority of the federal courts in this area was firmly established by the decision in *Illinois v. Milwaukee*. In delineating the legitimate scope of the federal common law, the Court there expressly noted the relevance of state standards, adding that "a State with high water-quality standards *may well ask that its strict* *standards be honored* and *that it not be compelled to lower itself* to the more degrading standards of a neighbor." (Emphasis added.) The Act attributes comparable respect to the strict effluent limitation levels imposed by individual States. § 510. Since both the Court and Congress fully expected that neighboring States might differ in their approaches to the regulation of the discharge of pollutants into their navigable waters, it is odd, to say the least, that federal courts should now be deprived of the common law power to effect a reconciliation of these differences. * * *

NOTES

1. In *Milwaukee II,* the defendant was in compliance with the requirements of the Clean Water Act. In *Middlesex County Sewerage Authority v. National Sea Clammers Ass'n,* 453 U.S. 1 (1981), the Court extended *Milwaukee II* by holding that even a defendant who is violating the Act is immune from federal nuisance liability. The lower courts have also given *Milwaukee II* an expansive reading. *See, e.g.,* Conner v. Aerovox, Inc., 730 F.2d 835 (1st Cir. 1984) (Clean Water Act preempts federal maritime law).

2. On remand, the Seventh Circuit held that application of Illinois nuisance law to the interstate pollution originating in Wisconsin was also preempted by the Clean Water Act. Illinois v. Milwaukee, 731 F.2d 403 (7th Cir. 1984), *cert. denied* 469 U.S. 1196 (1985). This issue reached the Supreme Court in the next case.

INTERNATIONAL PAPER COMPANY v. OUELLETTE

Supreme Court of the United States, 1987.
479 U.S. 481, 107 S.Ct. 805, 93 L.Ed.2d 883.

[The defendant operated a pulp and paper mill on the New York side of Lake Champlain. Its discharge pipe ran from the mill through the water toward Vermont, ending just before the state line that divides the lake. The plaintiffs owned or rented land on the Vermont shore. They filed suit in state court for compensatory and punitive damages, as well as an injunction requiring the defendant to restructure part of its water treatment system. The action was removed to federal district court. The trial court held that Vermont nuisance law was applicable and was not preempted by the Clean Water Act. The Second Circuit affirmed, relying on the savings clauses in sections 505(e) and 510.]

JUSTICE POWELL delivered the opinion of the court. * * *

To begin with, the plain language of the provisions on which respondents rely by no means compels the result they seek. Section 505(e) merely says that "nothing *in this section,*" i.e., the citizen-suit provisions, shall affect an injured party's right to seek relief under state law; it does not purport to preclude pre-emption of state law by other provisions of the Act. Section 510, moreover, preserves the authority of a State "with respect to the waters (including boundary waters) of such State." This language arguably limits the effect of the clause to discharges flowing *directly* into a State's own waters, i.e., discharges from within the State. The savings clause then, does not preclude pre-emption of the law of an affected State.

Given that the Act itself does not speak directly to the issue, the Court must be guided by the goals and policies of the Act in determining whether it in fact pre-empts an action based on the law of an affected State. After examining the CWA as a whole, its purposes and its history, we are convinced that if affected States were allowed to impose separate discharge standards on a single point source, the inevitable result would be a serious interference with the achievement of the "full purposes and objectives of Congress." Because we do not believe Congress intended to undermine this carefully drawn statute through a general saving clause, we conclude that the CWA precludes a court from applying the law of an affected State against an out-of-state source.

In determining whether Vermont nuisance law "stands as an obstacle" to the full implementation of the CWA, it is not enough to say that the ultimate goal of both federal and state law is to eliminate water pollution. A state law also is pre-empted if it interferes with the methods by which the federal statute was designed to reach this goal. In this case the application of Vermont law against IPC would allow respondents to circumvent the NPDES permit system, thereby upsetting the balance of public and private interests so carefully addressed by the Act.

By establishing a permit system for effluent discharges, Congress implicitly has recognized that the goal of the CWA—elimination of water pollution—cannot be achieved immediately, and that it cannot be realized without incurring costs. The EPA Administrator issues permits according to established effluent standards and water quality standards, that in turn are based upon available technology, and competing public and industrial uses. The Administrator must consider the impact of the discharges on the waterway, the types of effluents, and the schedule for compliance, each of which may vary widely among sources. If a State elects to impose its own standards, it also must consider the technological feasibility of more stringent controls. Given the nature of these complex decisions, it is not surprising that the Act limits the right to administer the permit system to the EPA and the source States.

An interpretation of the saving clause that preserved actions brought under an affected State's law would disrupt this balance of interests. If a New York source were liable for violations of Vermont law, that law could effectively override both the permit requirements and the policy choices made by the source State. The affected State's nuisance laws would subject the point source to the threat of legal and equitable penalties if the permit standards were less stringent than those imposed by the affected State. Such penalties would compel the source to adopt different control standards and a different compliance schedule from those approved by the EPA, even though the affected State had not engaged in the same weighing of the costs and benefits. This case illustrates the problems with such a rule. If the Vermont Court ruled that respondents were entitled to the full amount of damages and injunctive relief sought in the complaint, at a minimum IPC would have to change its methods of doing business and controlling pollution to avoid the threat of ongoing liability. In suits such as this, an affected state court also could require the source to cease operations by ordering immediate abatement. Critically, these liabilities would attach even though the source had complied fully with its state and federal permit obligations. The inevitable result of such suits would be that Vermont and other States could do indirectly what they could not do directly—regulate the conduct of out-of-state sources.

Application of an affected State's law to an out-of-state source also would undermine the important goals of efficiency and predictability in the permit system. The history of the 1972 amendments shows that Congress intended to establish "clear and identifiable" discharge standards. As noted above, under the reading of the saving clause proposed by respondents, a source would be subject to a variety of common-law rules established by the different States along the interstate waterways. These nuisance standards often are "vague" and "indeterminate." The application of numerous States' laws would only exacerbate the vagueness and resulting uncertainty. * * *

Our conclusion that Vermont nuisance law is inapplicable to a New York point source does not leave respondents without a remedy. The CWA precludes only those suits that may require standards of effluent control that are incompatible with those established by the procedures set forth in the Act. The saving clause specifically preserves other state actions, and therefore nothing in the Act bars aggrieved individuals from bringing a nuisance claim pursuant to the law of the *source* State. By its terms the CWA allows States such as New York to impose higher standards on its own point sources, and in *Milwaukee II* we recognized that this authority may include the right to impose higher common-law as well as higher statutory restrictions.

An action brought against IPC under New York nuisance law would not frustrate the goals of the CWA as would a suit governed by Vermont law. First, application of the source State's law does not disturb the balance among federal, source-state, and affected-state interests. Because the Act specifically allows source States to impose stricter standards, the imposition of source-state law does not disrupt the regulatory partnership established by the permit system. Second, the restriction of suits to those brought under source-state nuisance law prevents a source from being subject to an indeterminate number of potential regulations. Although New York nuisance law may impose separate standards and thus create some tension with the permit system, a source only is required to look to a single additional authority, whose rules should be relatively predictable. Moreover, States can be expected to take into account their own nuisance laws in setting permit requirements.

IPC asks the Court to go one step further and hold that all state-law suits also must be brought in source-state *courts*. As petitioner cites little authority or justification for this position, we find no basis for holding that Vermont is an improper forum. Simply because a cause of action is pre-empted does not mean that judicial jurisdiction over the claim is affected as well; the Act pre-empts laws, not courts. In the absence of statutory authority to the contrary, the rule is settled that a district court sitting in diversity is competent to apply the law of a foreign State.

NOTES

1. If the Court had gone the other way regarding application of Vermont law, wouldn't we have come full circle? *Milwaukee I* established federal common law to replace state nuisance law; *Milwaukee II* preempted the federal common law; an affirmance in *Ouellette* would have resurrected the multitude of state laws the Court had buried in *Milwaukee I*. Of course, the answer may be that the mistake was made earlier in the chain—some of the Justices would have argued that the crucial mistake was *Milwaukee II*. But given the *Milwaukee* opinions, a contrary result in the final case of the trilogy would have been decidedly peculiar.

2. Does *Ouellette* apply to air pollution? *See* Her Majesty The Queen In Right of the Province of Ontario v. City of Detroit, 874 F.2d 332 (6th Cir. 1989) (allowing an action by Ontario under the Michigan Environmental Protection Act to enjoin the construction of Detroit's proposed garbage burner). A dissent argued that *Ouellette* allows state law injunctions if a source's pollution causes damage, but not an injunction before the source is constructed. Id. at 346–347 (Boggs, J., dissenting).

3. *Milwaukee II* invokes attractive concepts of judicial competence, legislative supremacy, and federalism. In light of *Ouellette,* has the Court actually furthered any of these goals? For a negative answer, see Daniel Farber & Philip Frickey, *In the Shadow of the Legislature: The Common Law in the Age of the New Public Law*, 89 MICH. L. REV. 875 (1991). Note that *Ouellette* provides a cause of action for violating the *source* state's standards but no forum for complaints based on a *receiving* state's desire to have higher water quality. As we shall see later when we consider *Arkansas v. Oklahoma,* the CWA's provisions regarding state obligations to maintain water quality may provide a mechanism for redressing this problem.

C. MODERN REGULATION OF WATER POLLUTION

1. FEDERAL STATUTES GOVERNING WATER POLLUTION

The CWA is not the only federal statute regulating water pollution. It is supplemented by other statutes targeted at specific problems. The Safe Drinking Water Act, 42 U.S.C. §§ 300f et. seq. (1974) regulates contaminants in drinking water supplied by public water systems and requires the

EPA to set national drinking water regulations that incorporate enforceable maximum contaminant levels or treatment techniques. The Ocean Dumping Act, 33 U.S.C. §§ 1401–1445 (1972) prohibits the unpermitted dumping of wastes in the area seaward of the inner boundary of the U.S. territorial sea. The Oil Pollution Act, 33 U.S.C. §§ 2701–2761 (1990) imposes minimum design standards on vessels operating in U.S. waters and makes owners of vessels discharging oil liable for cleanup costs. The CWA is the most comprehensive federal law regulating water pollution, however, and we take it up in detail below.

2. OVERVIEW OF THE CLEAN WATER ACT

TITLE II: Grants for Construction of Treatment Works

§ 208   Areawide Waste Treatment Management: Requires states to identify areas with substantial water quality control problems and to engage in areawide planning, including identification of both point source and nonpoint source contributions.

TITLE III: Standards and Enforcement

§ 301   Effluent Limitations: Prohibits the discharge of any pollutant by any person, except as permitted by the Act. Sets effluent limits for point sources. Requires that point sources of conventional pollutants apply the best conventional pollutant control technology (BCT) and that point sources of nonconventional pollutants comply with effluent limitations requiring best available technology economically achievable (BAT). Also prohibits the discharge into navigable waters of any radiological, chemical, or biological warfare agent, high-level radioactive waste, or medical waste.

§ 302   Water Quality Related Effluent Limits: Authorizes the Administrator to tighten effluent limitations for point sources when necessary to prevent interference with the attainment or maintenance of water quality standards.

§ 303   Water Quality Standards and Total Maximum Daily Loads (TMDLs): Requires states to adopt water quality standards for intrastate waters subject to EPA approval. Authorizes the EPA to establish water quality standards when states fail to do so or when state standards fail to meet federal requirements. Requires states to identify waters where effluent limits are not stringent enough to implement applicable water quality standards and to establish the total maximum daily load (TMDL) of pollutants for such waters at a level necessary to implement applicable water quality standards.

§ 304   Federal Water Quality Criteria and Guidelines: Requires the EPA to adopt water quality criteria and guidelines for effluent standards, pretreatment programs at publicly owned sewage treatment works (POTWs), and state permit programs. States may depart from EPA criteria.

§ 306 New Source Performance Standards: Requires the EPA to specify technology-based performance standards for industrial categories based on best demonstrated control technology.

§ 307 Toxic and Pretreatment Effluent Standards: Establishes list of toxic pollutants (consisting of 126 "priority" pollutants) and authorizes the EPA to revise list. Requires toxic pollutants to meet effluent limits based on best available technology economically achievable for the applicable category or class of point source. Requires the EPA to establish pretreatment standards for industrial discharges of toxics into POTWs.

§ 309 Enforcement: Authorizes the EPA to issue compliance orders and administrative penalties and to seek civil and criminal penalties for violation of the Act.

§ 319 Nonpoint Source Management Programs: Requires states and tribes to identify waters that do not meet water quality standards due to nonpoint source pollution, to identify nonpoint sources responsible, and to prepare management plans including best management practices and control measures to reduce loadings from nonpoint sources.

TITLE IV: Permits and Licenses

§ 401 Certification: Requires applicants for federal licenses or permits conducting any activity which may result in any discharge into navigable waters to obtain certification from the state in which discharge will originate ensuring that discharge will comply with CWA requirements. Authorizes states to impose conditions, including effluent limits, on applicant for certification.

§ 402 National Pollutant Discharge Elimination System: Establishes the national pollutant discharge elimination system (NPDES) to be administered by the EPA or by states and tribes with EPA-approved programs. The NPDES is the vehicle for imposing § 301–mandated technology-based discharge limits on all point sources. Section 402(p) applies to stormwater pollution.

§ 404 Dredge and Fill Permits: Authorizes U.S. Army Corps of Engineers to issue permits to control the discharge of dredged or fill material into navigable waterways.

TITLE V: General Provisions

§ 505 Citizen Suits: Authorizes citizen suits against violators of effluent standards or compliance orders and against the EPA for failure to perform a non-discretionary duty.

§ 509 Administrative Procedure and Judicial Review: Provides for judicial review of specified EPA actions in the U.S. Courts of Appeals.

§ 510 State Authority: Authorizes states to adopt more stringent standards than those required by the Act.

§ 518 Indian Tribes: Authorizes the EPA to treat Indian tribes as states for purposes of specified portions of the Act, providing tribes have governmental authority and capacity to implement requirements of the Act.

3. EFFLUENT STANDARDS UNDER THE CWA: DISCHARGES, DISTINCTIONS AND DEADLINES

The 1972 Amendments to the FWPCA established a system of standards, permits and enforcement aimed at the ambitious, and in retrospect wildly unrealistic, goal of eliminating all discharges of all pollutants into U.S. waters by 1985, and making all waters safe for swimming and indigenous fish and wildlife by 1983. (Surprisingly, even today, the statute still contains these long-passed deadlines.) This system is complicated, and laden with acronyms for technology-based standards, much like the cornucopia of technology-based controls we studied in Chapter 4. As with the CAA, technology-based standards are effluent limits (for example, numerical concentrations) set by the EPA according to technology that is, typically, currently available and used by at least some members of the industrial category to which it applies. Some simple guiding principles will be helpful as you make your way through the following technology-based standards: Best Practicable Technology (BPT), Best Conventional Technology (BCT), Best Available Technology (BAT), and Best Demonstrated Available Technology (BDAT).

First, at least in theory, the standards vary in terms of stringency. As indicated above, stringency escalates from left to right. Second, and related to stringency, the standards vary with respect to the role cost plays in setting them. For example, the EPA may be obligated to factor cost into its analysis when setting effluent standards for existing point sources under BPT, whereas it might only need to "consider" cost when setting New Source Performance Standards (NSPSs) according to BDAT. These differences seem subtle, and in practice they can shrink to nothing, but they can theoretically result in the EPA choosing (or declining to choose) a particularly expensive and highly effective technology for setting standards. This in turn might make a big difference to the ultimate limits imposed on dischargers in their permits.

Finally, as a general matter, as with the CAA, it is important to remember that new sources are regulated more stringently than existing sources and that less dangerous substances are controlled to a lesser extent than more dangerous ones. For example, toxic water pollutants (e.g., mercury and PCBs) are controlled to a greater extent than "conventional" water pollutants (e.g., oxygen-depleting substances, sediment, nutrients and pH). In between these two categories lies a third group which Congress has labeled "non-conventional" pollutants, including nitrogen and phosphorous. These are more dangerous to public health and aquatic life than conventional pollutants, but not as hazardous as toxic pollutants, and are regulated accordingly.

The final factor to keep in mind is, simply, time. The initial deadlines established by Congress in the 1972 Act expired before the EPA could promulgate effluent standards and incorporate them into the industrial discharge permits required by the NPDES. As a result, in the 1977 Amendments to the Act and again in the 1987 Amendments, Congress extended the deadlines for dischargers to come into compliance, and relaxed or abandoned some requirements. For example, Congress abandoned the health-based approach it had adopted in 1972 to control toxic pollutants in favor of the technology-based approach it had already adopted for other pollutants. Below, we explain how effluent standards developed over time. Figure 1 (infra, page 704) summarizes this story.

Under § 301 of the 1972 Act, all industrial point sources were required to meet BPT by 1977 and BAT (the more stringent level of control) by 1983. At this point, Congress did not distinguish between "conventional" and "non-conventional" pollutants, though it did single out toxic pollutants. The EPA was required in § 307 to list toxic substances and establish separate effluent limitations for them, based on the protection of public health and water quality and providing an "ample margin of safety," including zero discharge where necessary. Under § 306, any new discharger was to meet BDAT standards within a specified time after the EPA set an emissions standard applying to that category of new sources. The EPA was to promulgate the new source standards for 27 specified industrial categories by 1974, with others to follow over time.

The EPA was to set all of these technology-based standards (generally expressed as numerical concentrations of pollutants permissible in a discharger's effluent) on a category-by-category basis, meaning, for example, that the agency would promulgate one set of standards for pulp and paper mills and another for metal finishers.

With § 402, Congress created a permitting mechanism, the National Pollutant Discharge Elimination System (NPDES), through which effluent limits would be binding on dischargers. In § 301, Congress declared unlawful all discharges by point sources, except in compliance with the limitations imposed in an NPDES permit issued under § 402. The EPA was authorized to administer the permit program or to delegate permitting authority to states and tribes with EPA-approved permit programs. Permits had to incorporate applicable effluent limitations established under §§ 301, 302, 306 and 307, including an enforceable schedule of compliance to meet the 1977 and 1983 deadlines.

The 1972 amendments contemplated that enforcement would be primarily by the states. However, the federal government was not constrained, as it had been under the previous FWPCA, from acting to enforce state or federal standards. Provisions allowing for inspection, entry and monitoring, federal enforcement (including emergency action), and citizen suits were all designed to facilitate enforcement of the new standards. Under § 505, citizens could sue to enforce effluent limitations in state or EPA permits and in orders issued by the EPA. Citizens also could sue the EPA for failure to perform nondiscretionary duties. Finally, § 510 left states free to impose more rigorous standards.

The subsequent history of the FWPCA involved a complex series of adjustments to the deadlines established in 1972. Like the Clean Air Act, the FWPCA was substantially amended in 1977 (when it was renamed the Clean Water Act). In these amendments, Congress authorized the EPA to grant case-by-case extensions of the 1977 deadline for BPT if dischargers had attempted in good faith to comply, but all were to achieve BPT by 1979.

1977 amendmt.

Congress also dispensed with the 1983 deadline for industrial dischargers to achieve BAT. Instead, it classified pollutants into three categories and imposed standards and deadlines specific to each: (1) "toxic" pollutants (including a list of 126 specific chemicals called "priority pollutants"); (2) "conventional" pollutants of the kind commonly found in sewage, including BOD, fecal coliform, suspended solids, and pH; and (3) "nonconventional" pollutants, those not classified by the EPA as either toxic or conventional. The deadlines were set as follows:

> *For toxic pollutants,* BAT standards for an initial list of 126 "priority pollutants" were to be achieved by July 1, 1984 (or, for pollutants not on the original list, within three years after EPA adoption of applicable effluent limitations), with no exceptions allowed. § 301(b)(2)(C)–(D).

> *For conventional pollutants,* a new standard, "best conventional pollutant control technology" (BCT), was established. It was to be achieved by July 1, 1984. In establishing effluent limitations for conventional pollutants, the EPA is to consider, among other things, "the reasonableness of the relationship between the costs of attaining a reduction in effluents and the effluent reduction benefits derived." Balancing is not required in formulating BAT limitations for toxic and nonconventional pollutants. §§ 304(a)(4) and (b)(4).

> *For nonconventional pollutants,* effluent limitations based on BAT were to be achieved by July 1, 1987, but the EPA was authorized to modify these standards on a case-by-case basis. §§ 301(b)(2)(F) and 301(g).

types of pollutants

Under the 1977 Amendments, new sources still were required to adopt BDAT subject to the 1972 Amendments' unchanged floating deadline in § 306 based on when the EPA promulgated performance standards for each specific new source.

Conventional Pollutants
Pollutants typical of municipal sewage, and for which municipal secondary treatment plants are typically designed such as BOD, TSS, fecal coliform bacteria, oil and grease, and pH.

Nonconventional Pollutants
All pollutants that are not included in the list of conventional or toxic
pollutants, including pollutants such as chemical oxygen demand
(COD), total organic carbon (TOC), nitrogen, and phosphorus.

Toxic Pollutants
Pollutants or combinations of pollutants, including disease-causing
agents, which after discharge and upon exposure, ingestion, inhalation or assimilation into any organism, either directly from the
environment or indirectly by ingestion through food chains, will, on
the basis of information available to the Administrator of the EPA,
cause death, disease, behavioral abnormalities, cancer, genetic mutations, physiological malfunctions, (including, among others, DDT,
PCBs, dioxins, and other chlorinated hydrocarbons; mercury, cadmium, lead, and other toxic metals).

Figure 1: Legal Categories of Pollutants under the CWA

In 1987, Congress again amended the law to extend the deadline for
achieving both BCT and BAT limits to March 31, 1989. Specifically,
dischargers were to achieve BCT for conventional pollutants by 1989 (an
extension of 5 years), BAT for nonconventional pollutants by 1989 (an
extension of 2 years) and BAT for toxic pollutants by 1989 (an extension
of 5 years). New sources were to achieve BDAT. Such sources are "new"
and subject to NSPS requirements (a) if construction of the source began
after an applicable standard was promulgated, or (b) if construction
commenced after proposal of a standard but before promulgation, where
promulgation occurred within the required 120 days following proposal.
See 40 C.F.R. § 122.2 (2002); NRDC v. EPA, 822 F.2d 104 (D.C. Cir.
1987); *cf.* Pennsylvania Dep't of Envtl. Res. v. EPA, 618 F.2d 991 (3d Cir.
1980).

1972 Amendments

- All Existing Dischargers of non-toxic pollutants: BPT by 1977 and
  BAT by 1983

- Toxics to be listed by the EPA and regulated based on health
  standards

- New Sources to meet BDAT for 27 industry categories established
  by the EPA by 1974, with others to follow

1977 Amendments

- Existing Dischargers of "conventional pollutants," to meet BCT by
  1984 (instead of BAT by 1983)

- Existing Dischargers of "nonconventional pollutants," to meet BAT
  by 1987 (instead of BAT by 1983)

- Dischargers of Toxics to meet BAT by 1984 (abandoning health-
  based approach)

- New Dischargers to meet BDAT

1987 Amendments

- All existing dischargers of conventional pollutants to meet BCT by 1989.

- All existing dischargers of non-conventional and toxic pollutants, to meet BAT as soon as possible within 3 years and no later than 1989 (§ 301(b)(2)(F))

- New Sources to meet BDAT

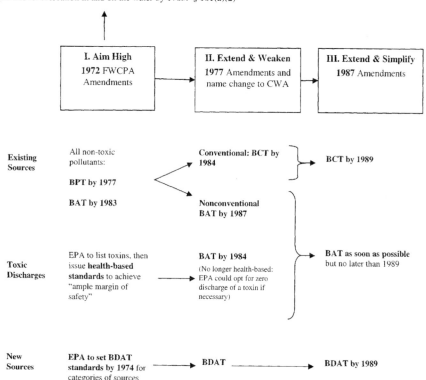

CWA Overall Goals Since 1972:

Goal: Eliminate discharge of pollutants into navigable national waterways by 1985. § 101(a)(1)
Interim Goal: Wherever attainable protect fish, shellfish and wildlife and provide for recreation in and on the water by 1983. § 101(a)(2)

Figure 2: Theoretical Role of Cost in Setting Effluent Limits

The Role of Cost in Setting Technology-based Effluent Standards under the CWA

BPT § 304(b)(1)(B)

The EPA must weigh costs against benefits but need not use "knee of the curve" test (i.e., the point where "incremental costs begin to exceed incremental benefits") nor must EPA measure costs of each additional increment of pollution The EPA has broad discretion to confine weighing costs against benefits to technology it deems available. Weyerhaeuser Co. v. Costle, 590 F.2d 1011, 1048 (D.C. Cir. 1978); Chemical Mfrs. Ass'n v. EPA, 870 F.2d 177, 204 (5th Cir. 1989).

BCT § 304(b)(4)(B)

The EPA must consider the reasonableness of the relationship between the cost to achieve effluent reductions and the benefits in order to ensure standards are cost-effective for an industry. The regulations should not impose costs above the BPT standard that surpass the "knee-of-the-curve." American Paper Inst. v. EPA, 660 F.2d 954, 960 n.14 (4th Cir. 1981). The EPA must also compare the cost for private industry to reduce its effluent levels with that incurred by similar publicly owned treatment works (POTWs).

BAT § 301(b)(2)(A) & (B)

The EPA must consider cost, but need not do a cost-benefit balancing test. Cost is to be given whatever weight the administrator deems appropriate. Weyerhaeuser Co. v. Costle, 590 F.2d 1011, 1045–46 (D.C. Cir. 1978). The EPA must find the technology to be economically achievable using a "cost-reasonableness" analysis, but has broad discretion in weighing cost. Rybachek v. EPA, 904 F.2d 1276, 1290–91 (9th Cir. 1990). The administrator has discretion to set BAT based on the single best performer in an industrial source category, or even based on technology not yet available, so long as there is a reasonable basis for believing it is achievable by the implementation date. Tanners' Council of America, Inc. v. Train, 540 F.2d 1188, 1195 (4th Cir. 1976).

BDAT § 306(a)(1) and (b)(1)(B)

The EPA shall take into consideration the cost to achieve the proposed reduction and other non-water related environmental impacts of the proposed regulation to determine if the costs are reasonable for the regulated facility to bear relative to other sources in the same industry. CPC Int'l, Inc. v. Train, 540 F.2d 1329, 1344 (8th Cir. 1976), *cert. denied*, 430 U.S. 966 (1977). Just as the EPA may determine BAT standards for industrial source categories without balancing costs against benefits, the same holds true of BDAT. It is also permissible for the administrator to force technology.

Figure 4: CWA Technology-based Standards in Order of Increasing Stringency

Standard:	Applies to:	Statute §:	Impact:
BMP (Best Management Practices)	Nonpoint sources	§ 319(a)(1)(C) § 319(b)(2)(A)	Requires states to identify best management practices where state water quality standards are not met due to nonpoint sources; determines state eligibility for federal technical assistance and program planning funds, but creates no directly enforceable standards
BPT (Best Practicable Technology [currently available])	Existing sources	§ 301(b)(1)(A) § 304(b)(1)(A) § 304(b)(1)(B)	Requires sources to meet standards set by average of best performers in source category; EPA must weigh costs v. benefits but deferential standard, no 'knee of curve' test is required

Standard:	Applies to:	Statute §:	Impact:
BCT (Best Conventional [pollutant control] Technology)	Existing sources producing conventional pollutants (e.g., BOD, silt, fecal bacteria) but unable to meet BAT	§ 301(b)(2)(E) § 304(b)(4)(A) § 304(b)(4)(B)	Includes explicit CBA requirement; intended to be more rigorous than BPT while awaiting BAT, but has collapsed into BPT in practice
BAT (Best Available Technology [economically achievable])	Existing Sources	§ 301(b)(2)(A) § 304(b)(2)(A) § 304(b)(2)(B)	The Agency may require such sources to match emissions performance of single best performer in the applicable source category; requires consideration of cost, but not weighing; for toxics, may include zero discharge standard (§ 307(a)(2))
BDAT (Best Demonstrated Available Technology)	New sources (built after promulgation of applicable new source standard by EPA)	§ 306(a)(1)	Requires best control technology demonstrated and available at time of construction; explicitly allows consideration of process changes and zero discharge, cost consideration is mandatory, but as in BAT it does not require a balancing, and the Administrator has broad discretion in factoring in cost.

4. EXCEPTIONS TO THE RULE OF TECHNOLOGY–BASED STANDARDS UNDER CWA: WATER QUALITY STANDARDS AND NONPOINT SOURCE PROVISIONS

Congress retained the ambient water quality standards from the 1965 Act as a backup to the new "end-of-pipe" effluent standards. Under § 303(b), states were required to establish water quality standards (WQS) which consist of two components: designated uses (DUs) for intrastate water bodies and water quality "criteria" (WQC) that will protect those uses. States set WQS subject to EPA approval under § 303(c). The WQS provisions strengthen the technology-based provisions of the Act via § 302(a), which requires that permits issued to point sources contain more stringent effluent limits when necessary to prevent a failure to achieve WQS. In addition, under § 303(d), states must identify waters that fail to meet WQS and establish total maximum daily loads (TMDLs) the receiving water can tolerate without falling below WQS. Indirectly, the TMDL process can lead to controls for nonpoint sources, though there is no mandatory language in § 303(d) to this effect. Finally, § 404 created a permit system for dredge and fill operations to be administered by the U.S. Army Corps of Engineers (ACE), the purpose of which is to ensure protection of marine and freshwater ecology. The applicability of this permit program to developments in wetlands has been controversial, as we shall see later in the chapter.

Congress came to recognize, however, that these water quality provisions were not working as well as envisioned, partly because states were publishing narrative water quality criteria instead of numerical limits. In 1987, Congress amended the Act to require that states adopt numerical criteria for toxic pollutants. In addition, Congress required states to identify controls they would impose on point and nonpoint sources in order to achieve WQS. Section 304(l) requires states to designate toxic "hot spots" where BAT limits are insufficient to satisfy WQS, to identify the responsible sources and pollutants, and then to specify control strategies. Congress also added § 319, which requires states to identify waters that fail to achieve WQS because of nonpoint sources, and to develop management plans subject to EPA approval that include the application of "best management practices." These management plans are not made enforceable against nonpoint sources, however.

The 1987 Amendments also required point sources discharging runoff from construction sites, industrial facilities, and municipal storm sewers to obtain permits by 1992 (later extended to 1994). Permits for effluent from construction and industrial sites were to meet BCT and BAT standards, and discharges from urban storm sewers were to meet standards achievable by best management practices (BMPs). Finally, the 1987 Amendments strengthened federal enforcement power by adding provisions for administrative penalties (up to $10,000 per day of violation) and augmenting civil and criminal penalties (up to $25,000, and $50,000 plus up to 15 years in prison, respectively).

5. FEDERAL AUTHORITY TO REGULATE WATER POLLUTION

a. Waters of the United States

Federal regulatory jurisdiction under the CWA applies to the discharge of a "pollutant" from a "point source" into "waters of the United States." The definition of "discharge of pollutant" includes the addition of any pollutant to the "navigable waters" or to the "waters of the contiguous zone or the ocean from any point source...." § 502(12). The term "navigable waters" means "the waters of the United States, including the territorial seas." § 502(7). This jurisdiction describes both the EPA's authority to impose the NPDES system and the effluent controls under § 301 on dischargers, and it also describes the Army Corps of Engineers' authority to issue dredge and fill permits under § 404.

Not surprisingly, the meaning of "waters of the United States" has been tested repeatedly in the federal courts, with the result that it has come to be very broadly defined, allowing for expansive federal regulatory control. As it turns out, waters subject to federal regulation need not be navigable. The Supreme Court has held that Congress chose to define the waters covered by the Act broadly.

> Although the Act prohibits discharges into 'navigable waters,' the Act's definition of 'navigable waters' as 'the waters of the United States' makes it clear that the term 'navigable' as used in the Act is of limited import. In adopting this definition of 'navigable waters,' Congress evidently intended to repudiate limits that had been placed on federal regulation by earlier water pollution control statutes and to exercise its powers under the Commerce Clause to regulate at least

some waters that would not be deemed 'navigable' under the classical understanding of that term.

United States v. Riverside Bayview Homes, Inc., 474 U.S. 121, 133 (1985). In *Riverside,* the Court held that "waters of the United States" included wetlands adjacent to other bodies of water over which the government has jurisdiction. The Court deferred to the Army Corps' determination that such wetlands fall within the Act's reach because "wetlands adjacent to lakes, rivers, streams, and other bodies of water may function as integral parts of the aquatic environment even when the moisture creating the wetlands does not find its source in the adjacent bodies of water." 474 U.S. at 133. In *Riverside,* respondent's property was part of a wetland that abutted a navigable waterway and respondent was therefore required to obtain a § 404 permit. In SWANCC, however, the court cast doubt on the applicability of the CWA to isolated non-navigable water bodies and will revisit the question of the definition of navigable waters and its application to wetlands during the 2005–06 Supreme Court term. *See* United States v. Rapanos, 376 F.3d 629 (6th Cir. 2004), *cert. granted,* 546 U.S. 932 (2005); Carabell v. United States Army Corps of Engineers, 391 F.3d 704 (6th Cir. 2004), *cert. granted,* 546 U.S. 932 (2005).

The EPA's definition of "waters of the United States" includes but is not limited to all interstate waters used in interstate and/or foreign commerce, tributaries of the above, territorial seas at the cyclical high tide mark, wetlands adjacent to all these, intrastate lakes, rivers, streams (including intermittent streams), mudflats, sand flats, sloughs, prairie potholes, wet meadows, play lakes, or natural ponds. *See* 40 CFR 122.2 for the complete definition. The exact dividing line between "waters of the United States" and other waters, according to the CWA, can be hard to determine, especially with regard to smaller streams, ephemeral waterbodies, and wetlands not adjacent to other "waters of the United States." The limits of the term will be further refined over time through judicial interpretation, EPA rulemaking and legislative amendment.

6.   POINT SOURCES

Because the CWA treats point sources and non-point sources so differently, the determination of what constitutes a point-source is very consequential. Not surprisingly, the definition of the term has been the subject of substantial litigation. In the cases below, the courts grapple with this issue.

a.   Conventional and Non-conventional (non-toxic) Pollutants

NRDC v. COSTLE

United States Court of Appeals, District of Columbia Circuit, 1977.
568 F.2d 1369.

LEVENTHAL, CIRCUIT JUDGE.

Section 402 of the FWPCA provides that under certain circumstances the EPA Administrator "may . . . issue a permit for the discharge of any pollutant" notwithstanding the general proscription of pollutant discharges found in § 301 of the Act. The discharge of a pollutant is defined in the FWPCA as "any addition of any pollutant to navigable waters from any point source" or "any addition of any pollutant to the waters of the contiguous zone or the ocean from any point source other than a vessel or floating craft." 33 U.S.C. § 1362(12). In 1973 the EPA Administrator issued regulations that exempted certain categories of "point sources" of pollution from the permit requirements of § 402. The Administrator's purported authority to make such exemptions turns on the proper interpretation of § 402.

A "point source" is defined in § 502(14) as "any discernible, confined and discrete conveyance, including but not limited to any pipe, ditch, channel, tunnel, conduit, well, discrete fissure, container, rolling stock, concentrated animal feeding operation, or vessel or other floating craft, from which pollutants are or may be discharged."

The 1973 regulations exempted discharges from a number of classes of point sources from the permit requirements of § 402, including all silvicultural point sources; all confined animal feeding operations below a certain size; all irrigation return flows from areas of less than 3,000 contiguous acres or 3,000 noncontiguous acres that use the same drainage system; all nonfeedlot, nonirrigation agricultural point sources; and separate storm sewers containing only storm runoff uncontaminated by any industrial or commercial activity. The EPA's rationale for these exemptions is that in order to conserve the Agency's enforcement resources for more significant point sources of pollution, it is necessary to exclude these smaller sources of pollutant discharges from the permit program.

The National Resources Defense Council, Inc. (NRDC) sought a declaratory judgment that the regulations are unlawful under the FWPCA. Specifically, NRDC contended that the Administrator does not have authority to exempt any class of point source from the permit requirements of § 402. It argued that Congress in enacting §§ 301, 402 of the FWPCA intended to prohibit the discharge of pollutants from *all* point sources unless a permit had been issued to the discharger under § 402 or unless the point source was explicitly exempted from the permit requirements by statute. The District Court granted NRDC's motion for summary judgment. It held that the FWPCA does not authorize the Administrator to exclude any class of point sources from the permit program. The EPA has appealed to this court. * * *

The appellants argue that § 402 not only gives the Administrator the discretion to grant or refuse a permit, but also gives him the authority to exempt classes of point sources from the permit requirements entirely. They argue that this interpretation is supported by the legislative history of § 402 and the fact that unavailability of this exemption power would place unmanageable administrative burdens on the EPA. * * *

Under the EPA's interpretation the Administrator would have broad discretion to exempt large classes of point sources from any or all requirements of the FWPCA. This is a result that the legislators did not intend. Rather they stressed that the FWPCA was a tough law that relied on explicit mandates to a degree uncommon in legislation of this type. * * *

There are innumerable references in the legislative history to the effect that the Act is founded on the "basic premise that a discharge of pollutants without a permit is unlawful and that discharges not in compliance with the limitations and conditions for a permit are unlawful." Even when infeasibility arguments were squarely raised, the legislature declined to abandon the permit requirement. * * *

The wording of the statute, legislative history, and precedents are clear: the EPA Administrator does not have authority to exempt categories of point sources from the permit requirements of § 402. * * *

II. ADMINISTRATIVE INFEASIBILITY

The appellants have stressed in briefs and at oral argument the extraordinary burden on the EPA that will be imposed by the above interpretation of the scope of the NPDES program. The specter of millions of applications for permits is evoked both as part of appellants' legislative history argument—that Congress could not have intended to impose such burdens on the EPA—and as an invitation to this court to uphold the regulations as deviations from the literal terms of the FWPCA necessary to permit the agency to realize the general objectives of that act. * * *

A. Uniform National Effluent Limitations

* * *

EPA contends that certain characteristics of runoff pollution make it difficult to promulgate effluent limitations for most of the point sources exempted by the 1973 regulations:

> The major characteristic of the pollution problem which is generated by runoff ... is that the owner of the discharge point ... has no control over the quantity of the flow or the nature and amounts of the pollutants picked up by the runoff. The amount of flow obviously is unpredictable because it results from the duration and intensity of the rainfall event, the topography, the type of ground cover and the saturation point of the land due to any previous rainfall. Similar factors affect the types of pollutants which will be picked up by that runoff, including the type of farming practices employed, the rate and type of pesticide and fertilizer application, and the conservation practices employed....

> An effluent limitation must be a precise number in order for it to be an effective regulatory tool; both the discharger and the regulatory agency need to have an identifiable standard upon which to determine

whether the facility is in compliance. That was the principal [sic] of the passage of the 1972 Amendments. * * *

As noted in *NRDC v. Train*, the primary purpose of the effluent limitations and guidelines was to provide uniformity among the federal and state jurisdictions enforcing the NPDES program and prevent the "Tragedy of the Commons" that might result if jurisdictions can compete for industry and development by providing more liberal limitations than their neighboring states. The effluent limitations were intended to create floors that had to be respected by state permit programs.

But in *NRDC v. Train* it was also recognized that permits could be issued before national effluent limitations were promulgated and that permits issued subsequent to promulgation of uniform effluent limitations could be modified to take account of special characteristics of subcategories of point sources. * * *

* * * In [*Train*] this court fully appreciated that technological and administrative constraints might prevent the Administrator from developing guidelines and corresponding uniform numeric effluent limitations for certain point sources anytime in the near future. The Administrator was deemed to have the burden of demonstrating that the failure to develop the guidelines on schedule was due to administrative or technological infeasibility. Yet the underlying teaching was that technological or administrative infeasibility was a reason for adjusting court mandates to the minimum extent necessary to realize the general objectives of the Act. It is a number of steps again to suggest that these problems afford the Administrator the authority to exempt categories of point sources from the NPDES program entirely. * * *

In sum, we conclude that the existence of uniform national effluent limitations is not a necessary precondition for incorporating into the NPDES program pollution from agricultural, silvicultural, and storm water runoff point sources. The technological or administrative infeasibility of such limitations may result in adjustments in the permit programs, as will be seen, but it does not authorize the Administrator to exclude the relevant point source from the NPDES program.

B. *Alternative Permit Conditions under § 402(a)*

EPA contends that even if it is possible to issue permits without national effluent limitations, the special characteristics of point sources of runoff pollution make it infeasible to develop restrictions on a case-by-case basis. EPA's implicit premise is that whether limitations are promulgated on a class or individual source basis, it is still necessary to articulate any limitation in terms of a numerical effluent standard. That is not our understanding.

Section 402 provides that a permit may be issued upon condition "that such discharge will meet either all applicable requirements under sections 301, 302, 306, 307, 308 and 403 of this Act, *or prior to taking of necessary implementing actions relating to all such requirements, such conditions as the Administrator determines are necessary to carry out the provisions of this Act."* 33 U.S.C. § 1342(a) (Supp. V 1975) (emphasis added). This provision gives EPA considerable flexibility in framing the permit to achieve a desired reduction in pollutant discharges. The permit may proscribe industry practices that aggravate the problem of point source pollution.

EPA's counsel caricatures the matter by stating that recognition of any such authority would give EPA the power "to instruct each individual farmer on his farming practices." Any limitation on a polluter forces him to modify his conduct and operations. * * * Of course, when alternative techniques are available, Congress intended to give the discharger as much flexibility as possible in choosing his mode of compliance. We only indicate here that when numerical effluent limitations are infeasible, EPA may issue permits with conditions designed to reduce the level of effluent discharges to acceptable levels. This may well mean opting for a gross reduction in pollutant discharge rather than the fine-tuning suggested by numerical limitations. But this ambitious statute is not hospitable to the concept that the appropriate response to a difficult pollution problem is not to try at all.

It may be appropriate in certain circumstances for the EPA to require a permittee simply to monitor and report effluent levels; EPA manifestly has this authority. Such permit conditions might be desirable where the full extent of the pollution problem is not known.

C. *General Permits*

Finally, EPA argues that the number of permits involved in the absence of an exemption authority will simply overwhelm the Agency. Affidavits filed with the District Court indicate, for example, that the number of silviculture point sources may be over 300,000 and that there are approximately 100,000 separate storm sewer point sources. We are and must be sensitive to EPA's concerns of an intolerable permit load. But the District Court and the various parties have suggested devices to mitigate the burden—to accommodate within a practical regulatory scheme Congress's clear mandate that all point sources have permits. All that is required is that EPA make full use of its interpretational authority. The existence of a variety of options belies EPA's infeasibility arguments.

Section 402 does not explicitly describe the necessary scope of a NPDES permit. The most significant requirement is that the permit be in compliance with limitation sections of the Act described above. As a result NRDC and the District Court have suggested the use of area or general permits. The Act allows such techniques. Area-wide regulation is one well-established means of coping with administrative exigency. * * *

There is also a very practical difference between a general permit and an exemption. An exemption tends to become indefinite: the problem drops out of sight, into a pool of inertia, unlikely to be recalled in the absence of crisis or a strong political protagonist. In contrast, the general or area permit approach forces the Agency to focus on the problems of specific regions and requires that the problems of the region be reconsidered at least every five years, the maximum duration of a permit.

NOTES

1. The 1972 FWPCA Amendments undeniably placed a massive administrative burden upon the EPA. Within six months after the new enactment, the EPA had received nearly 33,000 NPDES permit applications, and this number almost doubled by mid–1974. *See* PERCIVAL ET AL., ENVIRONMENTAL REGULATION 680 (4th ed. 2003). Because this task was clearly beyond the resources of the fledgling federal agency, the NPDES permit system was designed to shift much of the burden to the states, which would hold primary responsibility for permitting, monitoring, and enforcement under section 402, while the EPA would only supervise state actions. *See* JACKSON B. BATTLE & MAXINE I. LIPELES, WATER POLLUTION 18–19 (3d ed. 1998). Yet many states were slow to establish NPDES permitting programs. Five states, along with the District of Columbia and U.S. territories such as Guam and Puerto Rico, still had none in 2006, and seven other states only adopted programs between 1990 and 2006. *See* the EPA's website for information on the NPDES program, *available at* http://cfpub.epa.gov/npdes/statestats.cfm.

2. After this case, Congress in 1987 specifically amended the definition of "point source" to exclude "agricultural stormwater discharges and return flows from irrigated agriculture." *See* 33 U.S.C. section 1362(14). Can you justify this exemption?

3. Because of the ambiguity of the term, the Second Circuit has ruled that a human being cannot be a "point source." *See* United States v. Plaza Health Labs., Inc., 3 F.3d 643 (2d Cir. 1993), *cert. denied*, 512 U.S. 1245 (1994) (individual who dropped vials of blood from blood-testing laboratory into Hudson River not criminally liable under CWA). The next case further probes the ambiguity in the definition of "point source."

SIERRA CLUB v. ABSTON CONSTRUCTION COMPANY

United States Court of Appeals, Fifth Circuit, 1980.
620 F.2d 41.

RONEY, CIRCUIT JUDGE.

In this suit to enforce portions of the Federal Water Pollution Control Act Amendments of 1972 against coal strip miners, the issue is whether pollution carried in various ways into a creek from defendant coal miners' strip mines is "point source" pollution controlled by the Act. * * *

Defendants Abston Construction Co., Mitchell & Neely, Inc., Kellerman Mining Co. and The Drummond Co. (hereinafter miners) operate coal mines near Daniel Creek, a tributary of the Black Warrior River, in Tuscaloosa County, Alabama. They each employ the strip mining technique, whereby rock material above the coal—the overburden—is removed, thereby exposing the coal that is close to the land surface. When the overburden is removed, it is pushed aside, and forms "spoil piles." During the mining operations, and thereafter if the land is not reclaimed by replacing the overburden, the spoil piles are highly erodible. Rainwater runoff or water draining from within the mined pit at times carried the material to adjacent streams, causing siltation and acid deposits. In an effort to halt runoff, the miners here occasionally constructed "sediment basins," which were designed to catch the runoff before it reached the creek. Their efforts were not always successful. Rainfall sometimes caused the basins to overflow, again depositing silt and acid materials into Daniel Creek. * * *

The parties do not dispute the ultimate fact that these pollutants appeared in the creek due to excess rainfall. Nor is there any disagreement the activities would be prohibited if the pollutants had been pumped directly into the waterways. The parties differ only on the legal responsibility of the miners for controlling the runoff and the legal effect of their efforts to control the runoff.

Plaintiff may prevail in its citizen suit only if the miners have violated some effluent limitations under the Act. 33 U.S.C.A. § 1365(a)(1)(A). Those limitations, in turn, apply only to "point sources" of pollution, as defined in the Act.

The term "point source" means any discernible, confined and discrete conveyance, including but not limited to any pipe, ditch, channel, tunnel, conduit, well, discrete fissure, container, rolling stock, concentrated animal feeding operation, or vessel or other floating craft, from which pollutants are or may be discharged. 33 U.S.C.A. § 1362(14).

Nonpoint sources, on the other hand, are not due to be controlled.

Thus, the issue is whether defendants' activities amounted to the creation of point sources of pollution. The district court ruled they did not. On the facts before it, the district court found the pollution had not resulted "from any affirmative act of discharge by the defendants." Instead, any water and other materials that were deposited in Daniel Creek were carried by natural forces, mostly erosion caused by rainwater runoff, even though such erosion was "facilitated by the acts of defendants of creating pits and spoil banks in the course of their mining operations."

A preliminary question here is whether the Act may be applied to mining activities at all. The district court, although holding the miners here did not create point sources of pollution, conceded, correctly, we think, that "some strip mine operations may involve the discharge of pollutants in ways which would trigger application of the Act's enforcement provisions." * * *

The district court correctly concluded that mining activities, although embracing at times nonpoint sources of pollution that were intended only to be studied by the EPA, may also implicate point sources of pollution, expressly covered by the Act's effluent limitations.

As to whether the activities here fall under the definition of point sources of pollution, three positions are asserted: plaintiff's, defendants', and a middle ground presented by the Government. We adopt the Government's approach.

Plaintiff would merely require a showing of the original sources of the pollution to find a statutory point source, regardless of how the pollutant found its way from that original source to the waterway. According to this argument, the broad drainage of rainwater carrying oily pollutants from a road paralleling a waterway, or animal pollutants from a grazing field contiguous to the waterway, would violate the Act. * * *

Defendants, on the other hand, would exclude from the point source definition any discharge of pollutants into the waterway through ditches and gullies created by natural erosion and rainfall, even though the pollutant and the base material upon which the erosion could take place to make gullies was created by the mine operation, and even though the miners' efforts may have permitted the rainwater to flow more easily into a natural ditch leading to the waterway. * * *

The United States, which participated in the case as amicus curiae, takes a middle ground: surface runoff collected or channeled by the operator constitutes a point source discharge. Simple erosion over the material surface, resulting in the discharge of water and other materials into navigable waters, does not constitute a point source discharge, absent some effort to change the surface, to direct the waterflow or otherwise impede its progress. Examples of point source pollution in the present case, according to the Government, are the collection, and subsequent percolation, of surface waters in the pits themselves. Sediment basins dug by the miners and designed to collect sediment are likewise point sources under the Government's view even though the materials were carried away from the basins by gravity flow of rainwater.

We agree with the Government's argument. Gravity flow, resulting in a discharge into a navigable body of water, may be part of a point source discharge if the miner at least initially collected or channeled the water and other materials. A point source of pollution may also be present where miners design spoil piles from discarded overburden such that, during periods of precipitation, erosion of spoil pile walls results in discharges into a navigable body of water by means of ditches, gullies and similar conveyances, even if the miners have done nothing beyond the mere collection of rock and other materials. The ultimate question is whether pollutants were discharged from "discernible, confined, and discrete conveyance(s)" either by gravitational or nongravitational means. Nothing in the Act relieves miners from liability simply because the operators did not actually construct those conveyances, so long as they are reasonably likely to be the means by which pollutants are ultimately deposited into a navigable body of water. Conveyances of pollution formed either as a result of natural erosion or by material means, and which constitute a component of a mine drainage system, may fit the statutory definition and thereby subject the operators to liability under the Act. * * *

Under the view of the law adopted here, there remain genuine issues of material fact. * * * Earl Bailey, a Sierra Club vice president and a professor at the University of Alabama, testified by affidavit that he observed,

> gullies and ditches running down the sides of steep spoil piles created by Abston Construction Company. The sedimentation and pollutants are carried through these discernible, confined and discrete conveyances to Daniel Creek.

Bailey's observations of ditches and gullies were confirmed by Philip Abston, president of the Abston Construction Co., who noted that the gullies would carry water and sediment toward the creek.

Dwight Hicks, who served as defendant Drummond Co.'s manager of reclamation and environmental control, testified that in some areas, drainage basins were constructed to catch sediment flowing down the outer edges of the spoil piles. * * *

An affidavit filed by Garry Drummond, president of defendant Drummond Co. in support of its motion for summary judgment, contains starkly contrasting language.

> Neither company has engaged in the operation of any discernible, confined and discrete conveyance, including but not limited to any pipe, ditch, channel, tunnel, conduit, well, discrete fissure, container, rolling stock, concentrated animal feeding operation or vessel or other floating craft from which pollutants are or may be discharged.

> Neither company has discharged any pollutant including surface water runoff into Daniel Creek or the tributaries of the same during the period of operation as noted hereinabove. * * *

Thus, additional findings are necessary to determine the precise nature of spoil basins constructed by defendant Drummond. In light of Hicks's statement that a "standpipe and an emergency spillway" were constructed to guard against spoil basin overflow, we note that a "pipe" from which pollutants are discharged may be a point source of pollution. 33 U.S.C.A. § 1362(14). This design could likewise fit under the *Earth Sciences* finding that "the escape of liquid from [a] confined system is from a point source," [*United States v. Earth Sciences, Inc.*, 599 F.2d 368, 374 (10th Cir. 1979)], since the affidavits and depositions suggest that water and other materials escaped from the mines and sediment basins, eventually finding their way to Daniel Creek. Furthermore, factual findings are lacking insofar as the sediment basins and other devices may be characterized as encompassing "container(s), . . . from which pollutants are or may be discharged." 33 U.S.C.A. § 1362(14).

While defendants have denied taking any direct action resulting in the discharge of pollutants into Daniel Creek, Bailey described "(m)ine spoil pushed into Daniel Creek so as to block the waterway." Even under the district court's requirement that the alleged polluters take some "affirmative act" before a finding of point source pollution is warranted, the activity described by Bailey suggests a discharge of pollutants into the creek. In considering this issue, the district court should deem controlling § 502(12) of the Act, which, as pointed out by the *Earth Sciences* court, defines discharge as "any addition of any pollutant to navigable waters...." 33 U.S.C.A. § 1362(12).

Although the point source definition "excludes unchanneled and uncollected surface waters," *Appalachian Power Co. v. Train*, 545 F.2d 1351, 1373 (4th Cir. 1976), surface runoff from rainfall, when collected or channeled by coal miners in connection with mining activities, constitutes point source pollution. * * *

REVERSED AND REMANDED.

NOTES

1. Does the court's definition of point source pollution create a disincentive to some environmentally beneficial collection and control efforts? Is there anything mine operators like Abston Construction Company can do—or not do—in the future to help prevent a court from characterizing their mine wastes as point sources subject to heightened regulatory requirements? Or does the court's broadened definition of point sources mean that any pile of mine spoil automatically becomes a point source?

2. Where should the line between point and nonpoint sources be drawn? Is it fair to make businesses and individuals responsible for pollution resulting at least in part from circumstances beyond their control? The next case discusses another situation where human conduct and natural weather events interacted to cause pollution, and the court grapples with the relationship between these inputs in deciding where to draw this line.

CONCERNED AREA RESIDENTS FOR THE ENVIRONMENT v. SOUTHVIEW FARM

United States Court of Appeals, Second Circuit, 1994.
34 F.3d 114, *cert. denied*, 514 U.S. 1082, 115 S.Ct. 1793, 131 L.Ed.2d 721 (1995).

OAKES, SENIOR CIRCUIT JUDGE.

This is a citizen's suit under the Clean Water Act of 1977 ("CWA" or the "Act"), with some state law claims for nuisance, negligence and trespass. The suit arises on account of the liquid manure spreading operations of a large dairy farm in western New York. * * *

The appeal by plaintiffs involves only the five CWA violations and raises anew the question what is a "point source" within the meaning of 33 U.S.C. § 1362(14) * * *. The appeal also concerns whether the liquid manure spreading operations fell within the "agricultural stormwater discharges" exception to point source discharges under the Act. 33 U.S.C. § 1362(14).

We now hold that the liquid manure spreading operations are a point source within the meaning of CWA section 1362(14) because the farm itself falls within the definition of a concentrated animal feeding operation ("CAFO") and is not subject to the agricultural exemption.

I. Background

Plaintiffs, who refer to themselves collectively as Concerned Area Residents For the Environment ("CARE"), are a group of land owners who live near Southview Farms, a dairy farm in the town of Castile, in Wyoming County, New York. Defendants are the farm itself, and Richard H. Popp, an individual. Southview Farm is one of the largest dairy farms in the State of New York. It employs twenty-eight full-time and nine part-time employees. As of 1992, it owned 1,100 crop acres and had an animal population of 1,290 head of mature cows with over 900 head of young cattle, heifers and calves, making a total of 2,200 animals.

Unlike old-fashioned dairy farms, Southview's operations do not involve pasturing the cows. Instead, the cows remain in their barns except during the three times per day milking procedure. Also unlike old-fashioned dairy farms where the accumulated manure was spread by a manure spreader, Southview's rather enormous manure operations are largely performed through the use of storage lagoons and liquid cow manure. The storage lagoons number five on the main farm property ("A Farm"). One four-acre manure storage lagoon has a capacity of approximately six-to-eight million gallons of liquid cow manure.

In connection with this particular manure storage lagoon, Southview has installed a separator which pumps the cow manure over a mechanical device which drains off the liquid and passes the solids out through a compressing process. The solids that remain are dropped into bins for transport while the liquid runs by gravity through a pipe to the four-acre manure storage lagoon. This separated liquid was apparently used for the purpose of washing down the barns where the cows are housed.

Insofar as application of the manure as fertilizer to the land is concerned, there is a center pivot irrigation system for spreading liquid manure over the fields. The diameter of the circle of this irrigation system can be modified to conform to the field on which the application is being made. A series of pipes connects the pivot to the liquid manure storage lagoons. The pivot is self-propelled with the height of the arc from the manure spray being somewhere between 12 and 30 feet.

Southview also spreads its manure with a hard hose traveler which is a long piece of plastic tubing on a large reel. The traveler can be unwound and has a nozzle on the end which can send liquid manure 150 feet in either direction making a 300–foot–wide swath for purposes of fertilizing farm fields. The height of the arc from the projected spray is "a couple of feet higher" than that of the center pivot irrigator. Since 1988, a piping system consisting of a six-inch aluminum pipe and running under both the state highway and a town road to a lagoon on at least one Southview Farm other than the "A Farm," has transported liquid manure from the storage lagoon to various locations without the use of vehicles.

Southview also uses conventional manure spreading equipment including spreaders pulled by tractors and self-propelled vehicles which, generally speaking, have a 5,000 gallon capacity for liquid manure. These vehicles were used to spread manure from the smaller lagoons on the "A Farm" which do not receive liquid manure processed through the separation system. Southview's manure spreading record reflects the application of millions of gallons of manure to its fields. * * *

IV. Discussion

The CWA provides that, absent a permit and subject to certain limitations, "the discharge of any pollutant by any person shall be unlawful." 33 U.S.C. § 1311(a); see *Plaza Health*, 3 F.3d at 645. A pollutant includes "solid waste, ... sewage, ... biological materials, ... and agricultural waste discharged into water" and thus includes the manure in this case. 33 U.S.C. § 1362(6). A "discharge" is "any addition of any pollutant to navigable waters from any point source." 33 U.S.C. § 1362(12). The term "point source" includes "any discernible, confined and discrete conveyance, including but not limited to any ... concentrated animal feeding operation.... This term does not include agricultural stormwater discharges and return flows from irrigated agriculture." 33 U.S.C. § 1362(14). Our basic questions on review then are whether the defendants discharged the manure pollutant from any point source into navigable waters and whether the agricultural stormwater exemption or any other limitation applies.

The plaintiff-appellants' contentions relate to [the following] specific CWA violations which the jury found but the district court overturned * * *:

(1) A July 13, 1989, violation on field 104 on the so-called Wyant Farm, located to the east of Middle Reservation Road and bordering on Letchworth State Park through which the Genesee River runs. As to this violation, two of the plaintiffs observed liquid manure flowing into and through a swale on the Wyant Farm and through a drain tile leading directly into a stream which ultimately flows into the Genesee River. * * *

(3) September 26, 1990, and April 15, 1991, violations as to which the appellants claim that the district court erroneously set aside the jury verdicts because no reasonable juror could find that the discharges were not excepted under the Act as agricultural stormwater discharges.

It is at this point that the United States amicus position and the position of the appellants tend to coincide, if not directly meet. It is significant to note, as previously stated, that the cows are not put out to pasture. The fields to which the manure is applied, as above indicated, are used for crops. The United States appears as amicus curiae in support of the appellants on the basis that, because the Southview operations involve more than 700 cattle, it is a facility which is defined in the regulations under the Act as a CAFO, and therefore one type of "point source" under the Act, thereby requiring a permit for discharges which was not obtained in this instance. As we have stated, the Act defines the term "point source" as including "any ... concentrated animal feeding operation." 33 U.S.C. § 1362(14). In this connection, the district court concluded that, as a matter of law, Southview was not a CAFO because crops are grown on a portion of the farm. The United States contends that Southview is a CAFO as a matter of law because crops are not grown in the feed lot in which the milking cows are confined. * * *

A.   July 13, 1989, Violation on Field 104

The July 13 violation, found by the jury but overturned by the district court, as we have said, occurred on field 104 on the Wyant property which shares the boundary line with Letchworth State Park. Field 104 contains a slew or swale which tends to collect liquid manure spread by Southview's tankers and conveys it through a pipe in a stonewall and through the stonewall itself into a ditch which runs for some length on the Southview property before it reaches the boundary of the state park.

On July 13, 1989, appellants Kirk Bly and Philip Karcheski observed the manure collecting in the slew or swale and flowing into the ditch which in turn flowed off of the Southview property into Letchworth State Park property, and, in turn, joined a stream which ultimately flowed into the Genesee River.

The district court held and appellees contend that the July 13 discharge was not a point source discharge because the liquid simply and quite naturally flowed to and through the lowest areas of the field, and that the pollutants reached the stream that flows into the Genesee "in too diffuse a manner to create a point source discharge." The district court also suggested that the pollutants were not "collected" by human activity but in fact the opposite occurred in that the manure was dispersed over the ground.

The appellants argue that, given the testimony and the photographic evidence before the court, even if the liquid manure flowing from field 104 into the swale could be characterized as "diffuse run-off," as the district court characterized it, the manure pollutant was nevertheless thereafter channelled or collected sufficiently to constitute a discharge by a point source. Alternatively, the appellants contend that the appellees' liquid-manure-spreading vehicles themselves may be treated as point sources because 33 U.S.C. § 1362(14) defines a point source to include a "container" or "rolling stock." They point out that a number of district court cases have found vehicles to be within the definition of point sources. See, e.g., *Avoyelles Sportsmen's League, Inc. v. Marsh*, 715 F.2d 897, 922 (5th Cir. 1983) (bulldozers and backhoes constitute point sources under the CWA) * * *. They urge that by pumping the liquid manure from Southview's various lagoons into manure spreading tankers and other vehicles before discharging the liquid manure on to its various fields, Southview has "collected by human effort" the pollutant discharged into the navigable waters.

We agree with the appellants on both counts. We believe that the swale coupled with the pipe under the stonewall leading into the ditch that leads into the stream was in and of itself a point source. As this court has previously noted, the definition of a point source is to be broadly interpreted. [S]ee also *Sierra Club v. Abston Constr. Co.*, 620 F.2d 41, 45–46 (5th Cir.1980) (defendants were engaged in strip mining operations and placed their overburden in highly erodible piles which were then carried away by rain water through naturally created ditches); *United States v. Earth Sciences, Inc.*, 599 F.2d 368, 374 (10th Cir.1979) (discharge from a large capacity reserve sump serving a gold extraction process could be a point source even though "the source of the excess liquid is rainfall or snow melt"). In *Sierra Club*, the Fifth Circuit held that a defendant is not relieved from liability simply because it does not actually construct the conveyances "so long as they are reasonably likely to be the means by which the pollutants are ultimately deposited into a navigable body of water." *Sierra Club*, 620 F.2d at 45; *see also United States v. Oxford Royal Mushroom Prods., Inc.*, 487 F.Supp. 852, 854 (E.D.Pa.1980) (discharge resulting from spraying overabundance of water onto surface of an irrigation field which, in turn, ran off into a nearby stream through a break in a berm around the field may constitute discharge from a point source). Here, the liquid manure was collected and channelized through the ditch or depression in the swale of field 104 and thence into the ditch leading to the stream on the boundary of the Southview property as it adjoins Letchworth State Park. Nothing in *Plaza Health* is to the contrary. There the court simply refused to treat a human being as a "point source" under the criminal provisions of the Act by virtue of the rule of lenity. Plaza Health, 3 F.3d at 649.

Moreover, we agree with the appellants that, alternatively, the manure spreading vehicles themselves were point sources. The collection of liquid manure into tankers and their discharge on fields from which the manure directly flows into navigable waters are point source discharges under the case law. * * *

C.   September 26, 1990, and April 15, 1991, Violations

We believe the district court also erred in setting aside the jury's verdict on the September 26, 1990, and April 15, 1991, violations on the basis that "no reasonable juror could find that these discharges were not excepted under the Act as agricultural stormwater discharges." The district court drew this conclusion even though it had given explicit instructions to the jury on the availability of the "agricultural stormwater" exemption under 33 U.S.C. § 1362(14).

We agree with appellants that, while the statute does include an exception for "agricultural stormwater discharges," there can be no escape from liability for agricultural pollution simply because it occurs on rainy days. * * *

We think the real issue is not whether the discharges occurred during rainfall or were mixed with rain water run-off, but rather, whether the discharges were the result of precipitation. Of course, all discharges eventually mix with precipitation run-off in ditches or streams or navigable waters so the fact that the discharge might have been mixed with run-off cannot be determinative. Accordingly, we must uphold the verdict to the extent that the jury had a reasonable basis to find that the discharges on September 26, 1990, and April 15, 1991, were not the result of rain, but rather simply occurred on days when it rained. * * *

[The Court concluded that the jury could properly find that the run-off was primarily caused by the over-saturation of the fields rather than the rain and that sufficient quantities of manure were present so that the run-off could not be classified as "stormwater."] * * *

2. CAFO Exception To Nonpoint Source Provisions

The New York Farm Bureau, Inc., and American Farm Bureau Federation, as amici curiae, ("Farm Bureau amici"), argue that agricultural activities are regulated as "nonpoint sources" under the Clean Water Act and are not subject to citizens' suits enforcement. * * * The Farm Bureau amici point out that nonpoint sources "were addressed by Congress through the Section 208 planning process * * *." Thus when Congress enacted the 1972 Amendments, it considered and chose to exempt agricultural activities under the Section 208 nonpoint source provisions *"except in the case of [CAFOs]."* Brief of Farm Bureau Amici at 7 (emphasis added).

It is understood that the 1972 framework remains in place and that the revision made in 1977 to the point source definition excluded "return flows from irrigated agriculture," 33 U.S.C. § 1362(14) * * *.

* * * [T]he United States amicus points out that the Clean Water Act by definition includes in the term "point source," "any discernible, confined and discrete conveyance, including but not limited to, any ... concentrated animal feeding operation...." 33 U.S.C. § 1362(14). The regulatory definition of a CAFO is found at 40 C.F.R. 122.23(b) (1994). This provision defines CAFO as an animal feeding operation ("AFO") that meets the criteria of appendix B, which, as pertinent here denotes that the AFO contains more than 700 mature dairy cattle. 40 C.F.R. 122.23(b). The preambles to the regulations indicate that if an AFO exceeds the relevant number of animal units provided in Appendix B Supp. to Part 122 at (a), the AFO is presumably a CAFO, unless "the only time a discharge of pollutants into navigable waters occurs is during a 25 year, 24–hour rainfall event." * * * 41 Fed. Reg. 11458, 11458 (final regulations) * * *. Given that it is undisputed that the feed lot at Southview confines more than 700 mature dairy cattle, and there is no claim that the run-offs in question were caused by a 25–year, 24–hour rainfall event, we face the question whether the fact that crops are grown on the fields, even though the cattle at Southview are not pastured on those fields, prevents Southview from being an AFO.

An AFO is defined in the regulations as "a lot or facility ... where the following conditions are met:

> (i) Animals ... have been, are, or will be stabled or confined and fed or maintained for a total of 45 days or more in any 12–month period, and, (ii) crops, vegetation forage growth, or post-harvest residues are not sustained in the normal growing season over any portion of the lot or facility.

40 C.F.R. 122.23 (b)(1). There appears to be no doubt that Southview's feed lot meets the criteria of sub-paragraph (i). The district court held that Southview was not an AFO because crops are grown on fields adjacent to the feed lot in which the milking cows are penned; therefore, according to the court, Southview does not meet the criteria of sub-paragraph (ii). * * *

V. Conclusion

In short, we conclude with the United States as amicus, that Southview has an animal feeding lot operation with a tremendous number of cattle in a concentrated feeding facility in which no vegetation is grown; that operation in and of itself is a point source within the Clean Water Act and not subject to any agricultural exemption thereto. * * *

NOTES

1. What balance of human and natural inputs should be sufficient to constitute a point source, which is subject to much heavier regulation, enforcement, and possible penalties than a nonpoint source? Is the solution to this line-drawing dilemma just to regulate nonpoint sources more like point sources, notwithstanding the comparative difficulty of controlling nonpoint pollution?

2. To what degree should businesses or individuals be responsible for the weather? The EPA regulations, in presuming a sufficiently large AFO to be a CAFO, and, therefore, a point source, unless discharge only occurs during a 25–year, 24–hour rainfall event, sharply limits polluters' ability to claim an "Act of God" and avoid liability. Rather, AFOs are responsible for predictable outcomes of their activities except under weather conditions so severe as to happen on average only once every 25 years. Is this an appropriate standard?

3. In the modern United States, where the overwhelming majority of the population consists of urban dwellers, most lawyers and law students did not grow up on farms and know little about agriculture. Yet, as noted in the government reports on water quality excerpted at the beginning of this chapter, agricultural operations cumulatively constitute one of the nation's largest and most difficult to control sources of water pollution. Potential pollution problems from agriculture have grown as agricultural operations, like Southview Farms, have expanded to an industrial scale. Is there any good reason to continue to exempt such farms from regulation? If not, what explains Congress' reluctance to regulate them?

4.   In *South Florida Water Mgmt. Dist. v. Miccosukee Tribe of Indians*, 541 U.S. 95 (2004), the U.S. Supreme Court addressed an interesting question about what constituted the "addition" of a pollutant to a water body within the meaning of the Act. The question was whether petitioner's longstanding practice of pumping accumulated water from a water collection canal (which collects ground water and rain water from urban and agricultural development) to a water conservation area (an undeveloped wetland) within the Florida Everglades constitutes an addition of a pollutant from a point source, where the water contains a pollutant but the pumping station source itself adds no pollutants to the water being pumped. (In this case, the pumping moves phosphorous-laden water from the canal to the wetland but does not independently add a pollutant.) The Supreme Court, per Justice O'Connor, held that NPDES permits are required for point sources that do not themselves generate pollutants but that merely convey them. However, the court remanded the case for further proceedings regarding the parties' factual dispute over whether the canal and the water conservation area are meaningfully distinct water bodies. If not, there would be no "addition" of a pollutant from one water body to another within the meaning of the CWA, triggering the need for an NPDES permit.

b.   Stormwater Pollution and Point Sources

Though the CWA focuses extensively on those sources of pollution that are discharged out of discreet pipes, by virtually all accounts, one of the largest sources of water pollution across the country is stormwater pollution. During rain storms, water picks up various contaminants—metals, pesticides, trash, sediments, motor oil, algae-promoting nutrients—and carries those contaminants into streams, rivers, lakes and oceans. *See* Environmental Def. Ctr. v. EPA, 344 F.3d 832, 840–41 (9th Cir. 2003). In many urban areas, stormwater is discharged through storm sewers or drains that carry the contaminants directly into bodies of water. Despite the diffuse nature of stormwater pollution, these storm drains are considered point sources under the Clean Water Act. NRDC v. Costle, 568 F.2d 1369, 1379 (D.C. Cir. 1977) (*supra,* page 709.) Despite the fact that storm drains have long been defined as point sources, for years regulation of the problem was close to non-existent. In 1987, Congress amended the Clean Water Act to add § 402(p) to govern "Municipal and Industrial Stormwater Discharges." Section 402(p) requires NPDES permits for stormwater discharges "associated with industrial activity" and discharges from medium and large municipal separate storm sewer systems. § 402(p)(2)(B)(C)(D). Permits may also be required for stormwater discharges that violate water quality standards or are significant contributors of pollutants. § 402(p)(2)(E). Yet these sources remain extremely difficult to regulate. Virtually every person in a municipal area is a source of stormwater pollution—individuals who use outdoor pesticides, wash their cars, change their oil or leave trash cans uncovered contribute, and countless small businesses, construction sites, parking lots and roadways are sources of stormwater pollution.

These sources are now all theoretically captured by Section 402(p) even though the runoff looks less like a traditional point source with a discreet pipe or other channel because the pollution drains into a storm drain system, which is considered a point source. Many states are regulating municipal storm systems with general statewide stormwater permits and have taken a similar approach with industrial sources. The EPA has recently proposed an updated general industrial permit. *See* EPA NPDES Stormwater Multi–Sector General Permit for Industrial Activites, available at http://cfpub2.epa.gov/npdes/stormwater/msgp.cfm. For examples of municipal permits *see* http://cfpub1.epa.gov/npdes/stormwater/stpermit. cfm. Sources of stormwater pollution that lie outside of municipal stormwater systems can also be regulated as point sources. The case below illustrates the latter point.

ENVIRONMENTAL PROTECTION INFORMATION CENTER v. PACIFIC LUMBER COMPANY

United States District Court for the Northern District of California, 2004.
301 F.Supp.2d 1102.

* * *

At the heart of this litigation is Bear Creek, a brook situated several miles upstream of Scotia, California. A tributary of the Eel River, Bear Creek creates a watershed that covers 5500 acres of land throughout Humboldt County, California. Pacific Lumber Company and its wholly owned subsidiary, defendant Scotia Pacific Lumber Company, own some ninety-five percent of the land in the Bear Creek watershed, much of which PALCO uses for logging.

Both Pacific Lumber and Scotia Pacific Lumber Company are Delaware corporations; both maintain principal places of business in Scotia, California.

According to EPIC, substantial logging activity in the watershed area—primarily that performed by PALCO—has spurred a dramatic increase in the amount of sediment deposited into Bear Creek. Before significant logging began, EPIC claims, Bear Creek's sediment deposit peaked at approximately 8,000 tons per year; after logging practices commenced, sediment deposit climbed to 27,000 tons per year. This sediment increase, EPIC alleges, has a specific source: PALCO's timber harvesting and construction of unpaved roads. According to EPIC, PALCO's logging activity creates a deleterious environmental process. First, EPIC notes, timber harvesting removes vegetation from the ground surface, making soil more susceptible to erosion and landslides; construction of unpaved roads then exposes more soil, which, in turn, further destabilizes slopes. The effect of timber harvesting and road construction, EPIC contends, is to expose far more destabilized soil than is environmentally sustainable. When it rains, EPIC explains, the rain water carries the exposed silts and sediments-as well as other pollutants, like pesticides and diesel fuel-into culverts, ditches, erosion gullies, and other alleged channels. From these various water channels, silts, sediments, and pollutants flow directly into Bear Creek.

According to an April 1998 study conducted by PALCO consultants, sediments and pollutants pile into Bear Creek and its tributaries at no fewer than 179 specific watershed points. Among other channels, pollutant-laden water flows through 156 hillside culverts and 5.5 miles of roadside ditches, all of which drain directly into stream-crossing culverts. The consequences of this system, EPIC contends, are predictable and environmentally adverse: Beneficial uses of Bear Creek are substantially diminished; e.g., fish are significantly less able—if able at all—to use the creek as a nesting and rearing habitat. Worse still, EPIC adds, PALCO's present and future timber harvest plans promise the construction of additional roads and the digging of additional culverts, all of which could increase the amount of sediment, silt, and other pollutants deposited into Bear Creek. PALCO neither holds nor has applied for any relevant permits for these sites, sites EPIC contends should be regulated as "point sources" under the CWA. * * *

Not all pollutants or pollution sources fall under the purview of the NPDES [National Pollution Discharge Elimination System]. Under the CWA, "discharge of pollutant" is defined as "any addition of any pollutant to navigable waters from any *point source.*" 33 U.S.C. § 1362(12)(A) (emphasis added). The CWA's and NPDES's focus, then, trains largely on pollutant discharges from "point sources," a term the Act defines as: any discernible, confined and discrete conveyance, including but not limited to any pipe, ditch, channel, tunnel, conduit, well, discrete fissure, container, rolling stock, concentrated animal feeding operation, or vessel or other floating craft, from which pollutants are or may be discharged. This term does not include agricultural stormwater discharges and return flows from irrigated agriculture. *Id.,* at § 1362(14); *see also id.* at § 1362(6) (defining "pollutant" broadly to include substances ranging from rock and sand to industrial, municipal, and industrial wastes).

The CWA distinguishes "point sources" from "nonpoint sources." The NPDES recognizes-and functions on the basis of-this distinction, requiring permits only for such "point source" emissions. * * * Unlike "point sources," "nonpoint sources" are regulated indirectly: The CWA directs EPA to disseminate information regarding nonpoint pollution sources, *see* 33 U.S.C. § 1314(f), but it is often through state management programs that "nonpoint sources" are monitored and controlled. * * *

1987 Amendments on Municipal and Industrial Stormwater Discharges

In 1987, Congress amended the CWA to include a section on municipal and industrial stormwater discharges. *See* Pub.L. No. 100–4, 101 Stat. 7 (1987) (codified as 33 U.S.C. § 1342(p)). Among other things, this provision—popularly labeled "section 402"—mandates that permits be obtained for stormwater discharges "associated with industrial activity," for stormwater discharges from municipal storm sewer systems, and for stormwater discharges that contribute to water quality violations or are otherwise "significant contributor[s] of pollutants." 33 U.S.C. § 1342(p)(2). In addition, subsection (6) of section 402(p) requires the EPA to designate other sources of stormwater pollution and, in turn, to "establish a comprehensive program to regulate" these discharges. *Id.* at § 1342(p)(6).

For the discharges identified in section 402(p)(2), EPA has issued two batches of regulations. The first set, issued in 1990 and often referred to as the "Phase I" regulations, prompted a number of legal challenges; these "Phase I" regulations were, for the most part, deemed valid by the Ninth Circuit. *See, e.g., American Mining Cong. V. EPA*, 965 F.2d 759, 762 (9th Cir.1992); *NRDC v. EPA*, 966 F.2d 1292, 1295 (9th Cir.1992). The second set, issued in 1999 and generally labeled the "Phase II" regulations, reached the remaining sources in section 402(p)(6). *See* 64 Fed.Reg. 68,722 (Dec. 8, 1999). This second set of regulations also produced a number of legal challenges, and, once again, the regulations largely were upheld by the Ninth Circuit. *See, e.g., Environmental Def. Ctr.*, 344 F.3d at 840, 841. * * *

DISCUSSION

The basic premise of PALCO's motion to dismiss is that, however defined, the pollution sources identified in EPIC's first and second claims do not require NPDES permits. If the sources are "non-point sources," PALCO contends, the sources fall outside the scope of the NPDES by definition; if, by contrast, the sources are "point sources," the sources are nevertheless a type of discharge sources the CWA and EPA have excluded from NPDES permitting mandates. Either way, PALCO concludes, PALCO's decision not to secure permits for Bear Creek discharge sources is legally sustainable. * * *

PALCO's motion seems, at first blush, to depend on a misreading of EPIC's two remaining claims. In pertinent part, EPIC's complaint alleges that PALCO has violated-and continues to violate-various provisions of the CWA through its unlawful discharge of pollutants into Bear Creek. Far from failing to state a facially tenable legal claim under the CWA, EPIC's complaint contends that PALCO, on its Bear Creek site, uses a myriad of unpermitted (and, thus, unlawful) culverts, drainage ditches, and other "point source"—like conduits to discharge stormwater and pollutants. The CWA proscribes precisely this kind of conduct; under the terms of the CWA, then, EPIC's complaint would seem to overcome the Rule 12(b)(6) hurdle without more.

But as PALCO reads the pertinent law, the CWA sections supposedly informing EPIC's complaint actually preclude legal remedy. Section 402(p) of the CWA, PALCO contends, places discharges of the type EPIC targets outside the ambit of the NPDES and exempts such sources from the otherwise applicable CWA permit requirements. No matter how EPIC posits its claims, PALCO concludes, section 402(p) allows precisely the kind of non-permitted discharging PALCO purports to perform; since the discharges are composed of "stormwater," and since the discharges are not "industrial" or "municipal" in nature, the NPDES simply does not, as PALCO understands it, control.

The court is mindful that not all discharges require permits under the CWA. Where a discharge is otherwise in compliance with-or excused by-the CWA, that discharge may not be *de facto* unlawful, even if not shielded by an NPDES permit. According to PALCO, section 402(p) of the CWA provides such an exemption here, absolving PALCO of its NPDES permit obligations for all of the Bear Creek discharge sources. Titled "Municipal and industrial stormwater discharges," section 402(p) provides:

(1) General rule

Prior to October 1, 1994, the Administrator or the State (in the case of a permit program approved under this section) shall not require a permit under this section for discharges composed entirely of stormwater.

(2) Exceptions

Paragraph (1) shall not apply with respect to the following stormwater discharges:

(A) A discharge with respect to which a permit has been issued under this section before February 4, 1987.

(B) A discharge associated with industrial activity.

(C) A discharge from a municipal separate storm sewer system serving a population of 250,000 or more.

As PALCO reads it, section 402(p) requires permits only for particular kinds of stormwater discharge sources-e.g., sources related to "industrial" or particular "municipal" activity-none of which apply here.

Section 402(p) does, as PALCO suggests, assign permitting obligations to a select subset of potential stormwater-discharge sources. *Id.* (targeting a particular type of municipal and industrial sources). But section 402(p) does not, as PALCO implies, apply to all pollution sources in the first instance. As the language of the CWA and Ninth Circuit caselaw make clear, section 402(p) is not the only CWA section imposing duties and obligations on pollution dischargers; both section 301(a) and 402(a), for example, posit pollution-related mandates on putative polluters, including that these polluters obtain NPDES permits for "point source" pollutant discharges. *See, e.g.,*33 U.S.C. § 1342(a); *id.* at § 1311. As the language of the statute and the Ninth Circuit caselaw also make clear, two threshold inquiries govern the applicability of section 402(p): one, whether the relevant discharges are "composed *entirely* of stormwater," *see* 33 U.S.C. § 1342(p) (emphasis added); and, two, whether the relevant discharges are "currently [and properly] unregulated." PALCO's motion elides both of these threshold questions, ignoring the import of related CWA sections and presupposing that section 402(p) applies. Indeed, neither of section 402(p)'s threshold requirements are satisfied here.

To begin, PALCO errs to suggest that EPIC's complaint targets discharges "composed *entirely* of stormwater." 33 U.S.C. § 1342(p) (emphasis added). In relevant part, EPIC's complaint alleges that PALCO's Bear Creek drainage system utilizes a number of "point sources"—whether culverts, drainage ditches, other conduits to discharge—to redirect stormwater *and pollutants* (i.e., something not "composed entirely of stormwater") into Bear Creek. Nowhere does EPIC claim that the discharges consist "entirely" and exclusively of stormwater. On its face, then, EPIC's complaint does not satisfy the "entirely of stormwater" element of section 402(p)'s "general rule."

Nor does EPIC's complaint meet the requirement that the discharges be otherwise "unregulated." In the preamble to the Phase II regulations, the EPA noted that EPA and authorized States continue to exercise the authority to designate remaining *unregulated discharges* composed entirely of stormwater for regulation on a case-by-case basis. . . . In [the Phase II rule], . . . individual instances of stormwater discharge might warrant special regulatory attention, but do not fall neatly into a discrete, predetermined category. 64 Fed.Reg. 68,781 (emphasis added). The Ninth Circuit has adopted this interpretation of the relevant regulations, noting that the Phase II provisions merely "preserve[ ][the] authority for EPA and authorized States to designate *currently unregulated* stormwater discharges." *See Environmental Defense Center*, 344 F.3d at 840. Categorization, treatment, and permitting obligations of *already regulated* sources—like most "point sources" under section 502(14)—remain importantly unaltered; i.e., the Phase II regulations leave wholly unmodified the terms of the CWA—and the NPDES—with regard to regulated sources. Thus, for section 402(p) to apply to PALCO's discharge sources, these sources must have been "unregulated"—both as a matter of time and as a matter of law—at the time of the passage of the 1987 amendments.

They were not necessarily so "unregulated." When understood properly, the "sources" identified in EPIC's complaint were (and are) of an already *regulated* kind. "[P]oint sources" are, in general, an expressly regulated category of pollution dischargers under the CWA, typically governed by the provisions of the NPDES. *See* 33 U.S.C. §§ 1311, 1342. * * * "[P]oint sources" generally "fall neatly into a discrete, predetermined category" under the CWA. They are, as such, subject to the permitting provisions of the CWA; they are not, in short, the kind of previously "unregulated" category at issue in the Phase II regulations.

In its complaint, EPIC alleges that many of the pollution sources in the Bear Creek area are "point sources," discharging both stormwater and pollutants into the creek itself. In so doing, EPIC identifies pollution sources that were not-either before 1987 or after-necessarily "unregulated." Rather, they were (and are) "point sources" like other "point sources," subject to the terms of the CWA and the NPDES. * * *

NOTES

1. Are there wholesale categories of stormwater runoff that remain unregulated?

2. How is the operator of a municipal stormwater system subject to section 402(p) supposed to regulate all of the diffuse sources that drain into the system? Many cities have decried the stormwater provisions for imposing huge, unfunded costs on them. Some states now require, as part of their NPDES permitting systems, municipalities to establish extensive and expensive programs to reduce stormwater pollution from businesses and households within their jurisdictions, to conduct extensive educational outreach, to sample and monitor water bodies into which storm systems drain and to clean their storm drain collection systems. For an overview of the stormwater permitting system in California, *see* John H. Minan, *Municipal Storm Water Permitting in California*, 40 SAN DIEGO L. REV. 245 (2003); Sean Hecht, *Stormwater Regulation*, *in* 2004 S. CAL. ENVTL. REPORT Card 31 (2004).

c. Litigation over the Setting of Technology-based Effluent Limits

The 1972 amendments to the FWPCA were not unequivocal about exactly how the permitting system and technology-based effluent limitations were to be implemented. Would the standards be set nationwide for each industrial category of source, or would the standards be set on a plant-by-plant basis by the issuer of each permit? Certain chemical companies challenged the EPA's authority to issue regulations for classes of existing point sources under § 301 of the FWPCA. They argued that § 301 only provides guidance for any agency (state or federal) *issuing permits* on a plant-by-plant basis under § 402 (NPDES), so the EPA Administrator had overstepped statutory authority in setting effluent limits for entire categories of point source polluters. Moreover, these companies argued that the new source regulations under § 306, which required BDAT standards for seemingly all new plants without exception, must be read as allowing for some variances for individual plants. In the case below, the Supreme Court sided with the Administrator on both challenges and held that the Administrator, not the permit issuing authorities, must set the technology-based limits for classes of facilities under § 301, and that § 306 applies to all new sources without exception and without variances for individual facilities.

E. I. DU PONT DE NEMOURS & CO. v. TRAIN

Supreme Court of the United States, 1977.
430 U.S. 112, 97 S.Ct. 965, 51 L.Ed.2d 204.

MR. JUSTICE STEVENS delivered the opinion of the Court.

Inorganic chemical manufacturing plants operated by the eight petitioners in Nos. 75–978 and 75–1473 discharge various pollutants into the Nation's waters and therefore are "point sources" within the meaning of the Federal Water Pollution Control Act (Act), as added and amended by

§ 2 of the Federal Water Pollution Control Act Amendments of 1972. The Environmental Protection Agency has promulgated industry wide regulations imposing three sets of precise limitations on petitioners' discharges. The first two impose progressively higher levels of pollution control on existing point sources after July 1, 1977 and after July 1, 1983, respectively. The third set imposes limits on "new sources" that may be constructed in the future.

These cases present [the following questions of statutory construction]: whether the EPA has the authority under § 301 of the Act to issue industry wide regulations limiting discharges by existing plants; * * * [and] whether the new-source standards issued under § 306 must allow variances for individual plants. * * *

The Statute

* * *

The first steps required by the Act are described in § 304, which directs the Administrator to develop and publish various kinds of technical data to provide guidance in carrying out responsibilities imposed by other sections of the Act. Thus, within 60 days, 120 days, and 180 days after the date of enactment, the Administrator was to promulgate a series of guidelines to assist the States in developing and carrying out permit programs pursuant to § 402. §§ 304(h), (f), (g). Within 270 days, he was to develop the information to be used in formulating standards for new plants pursuant to § 306. § 304(c). And within one year he was to publish regulations providing guidance for effluent limitations on existing point sources. Section 304(b) goes into great detail concerning the contents of these regulations. They must identify the degree of effluent reduction attainable through use of the best practicable or best available technology for a class of plants. The guidelines must also "specify factors to be taken into account" in determining the control measures applicable to point sources within these classes. A list of factors to be considered then follows. The Administrator was also directed to develop and publish, within one year, elaborate criteria for water quality accurately reflecting the most current scientific knowledge, and also technical information on factors necessary to restore and maintain water quality. § 304(a). The title of § 304 describes it as the "information and guidelines" portion of the statute.

Section 301 is captioned "effluent limitations." Section 301(a) makes the discharge of any pollutant unlawful unless the discharge is in compliance with certain enumerated sections of the Act. The enumerated sections which are relevant to this case are § 301 itself, § 306, and § 402. A brief word about each of these sections is necessary.

Section 402 authorizes the Administrator to issue permits for individual point sources, and also authorizes him to review and approve the plan of any State desiring to administer its own permit program. These permits serve "to transform generally applicable effluent limitations ... into the obligations (including a timetable for compliance) of the individual discharger[s]. . . ." EPA v. California ex rel. State Water Resources Control Board, 426 U.S. 200, 205. Petitioner chemical companies' position in this litigation is that § 402 provides the only statutory authority for the issuance of enforceable limitations on the discharge of pollutants by existing plants. It is noteworthy, however, that although this section authorizes the imposition of limitations in individual permits, the section itself does not mandate either the Administrator or the States to use permits as the method of prescribing effluent limitations.

Section 306 directs the Administrator to publish within 90 days a list of categories of sources discharging pollutants and, within one year thereafter, to publish regulations establishing national standards of performance for new sources within each category. Section 306 contains no provision for exceptions from the standards for individual plants; on the contrary, subsection (e) expressly makes it unlawful to operate a new source in violation of the applicable standard of performance after its effective date. The statute provides that the new-source standards shall reflect the greatest degree of effluent reduction achievable through application of the best available demonstrated control technology.

Section 301(b) defines the effluent limitations that shall be achieved by existing point sources in two stages. By July 1, 1977, the effluent limitations shall require the application of the best practicable control technology currently available; by July 1, 1983, the limitations shall require application of the best available technology economically achievable. The statute expressly provides that the limitations which are to become effective in 1983 are applicable to "categories and classes of point sources"; this phrase is omitted from the description of the 1977 limitations. While § 301 states that these limitations "shall be achieved," it fails to state who will establish the limitations.

Section 301(c) authorizes the Administrator to grant variances from the 1983 limitations. Section 301(e) states that effluent limitations established pursuant to § 301 shall be applied to all point sources.

To summarize, § 301(b) requires the achievement of effluent limitations requiring use of the "best practicable" or "best available" technology. It refers to § 304 for a definition of these terms. Section 304 requires the publication of "regulations, providing guidelines for effluent limitations." Finally, permits issued under § 402 must require compliance with § 301 effluent limitations. Nowhere are we told who sets the § 301 effluent limitations, or precisely how they relate to § 304 guidelines and § 402 permits.

The Regulations

The various deadlines imposed on the Administrator were too ambitious for him to meet. For that reason, the procedure which he followed in adopting the regulations applicable to the inorganic chemical industry and to other classes of point sources is somewhat different from that apparently contemplated by the statute. Specifically, as will appear, he did not adopt guidelines pursuant to § 304 before defining the effluent limitations for existing sources described in § 301(b) or the national standards for new sources described in § 306. This case illustrates the approach the Administrator followed in implementing the Act.

EPA began by engaging a private contractor to prepare a Development Document. This document provided a detailed technical study of pollution control in the industry. The study first divided the industry into categories. For each category, present levels of pollution were measured and plants with exemplary pollution control were investigated. Based on this information, other technical data, and economic studies, a determination was made of the degree of pollution control which could be achieved by the various levels of technology mandated by the statute. The study was made available to the public and circulated to interested persons. It formed the basis of "effluent limitation guideline" regulations issued by EPA after receiving public comment on proposed regulations. These regulations divide the industry into 22 subcategories. Within each subcategory, precise numerical limits are set for various pollutants. The regulations for each subcategory contain a variance clause, applicable only to the 1977 limitations.

Eight chemical companies filed petitions in the United States Court of Appeals for the Fourth Circuit for review of these regulations. The Court of Appeals rejected their challenge to EPA's authority to issue precise, single-number limitations for discharges of pollutants from existing sources. It held, however, that these limitations and the new plant standards were only "presumptively applicable" to individual plants. We granted the chemical companies' petitions for certiorari in order to consider the scope of EPA's authority to issue existing-source regulations. We also granted the Government's cross-petition for review of the ruling that new-source standards are only presumptively applicable. For convenience, we will refer to the chemical companies as the "petitioners."

The Issues

The broad outlines of the parties' respective theories may be stated briefly. EPA contends that § 301 (b) authorizes it to issue regulations establishing effluent limitations for classes of plants. The permits granted under § 402, in EPA's view, simply incorporate these across-the-board limitations, except for the limited variances allowed by the regulations themselves and by § 301(c). The § 304(b) guidelines, according to EPA, were intended to guide it in later establishing § 301 effluent-limitation regulations. Because the process proved more time consuming than Congress assumed when it established this two-stage process, EPA condensed the two stages into a single regulation.

In contrast, petitioners contend that § 301 is not an independent source of authority for setting effluent limitations by regulation. Instead, § 301 is seen as merely a description of the effluent limitations which are set for each plant on an individual basis during the permit-issuance process. Under the industry view, the § 304 guidelines serve the function of guiding the permit issuer in setting the effluent limitations. * * *

We think § 301 itself is the key to the problem. The statutory language concerning the 1983 limitations, in particular, leaves no doubt that these limitations are to be set by regulation. Subsection (b)(2)(A) of § 301 states that by 1983 "effluent limitations for categories and classes of point sources" are to be achieved which will require "application of the best available technology economically achievable for such category or class." These effluent limitations are to require elimination of all discharges if "such elimination is technologically and economically achievable for a category or class of point sources." This is "language difficult to reconcile with the view that individual effluent limitations are to be set when each permit is issued." American Meat Institute v. EPA, 526 F.2d 442, 450 (1975). The statute thus focuses expressly on the characteristics of the "category or class" rather than the characteristics of individual point sources. Normally, such class wide determinations would be made by regulation, not in the course of issuing a permit to one member of the class.

The question of the form of § 301 limitations is tied to the question whether the Act requires the Administrator or the permit issuer to establish the limitations. Section 301 does not itself answer this question, for it speaks only in the passive voice of the achievement and establishment of the limitations. But other parts of the statute leave little doubt on this score. Section 304(b) states that "[f]or the purpose of adopting or revising effluent limitations ... the Administrator shall" issue guideline *admin.* regulations; while the judicial-review section, § 509(b)(1), speaks of "the Administrator's action ... in approving or promulgating any effluent limitation or other limitation under section 301....". And § 101 (d) requires us to resolve any ambiguity on this score in favor of the Administrator. It provides that "[e]xcept as otherwise expressly provided in this Act, the Administrator of the Environmental Protection Agency ... shall administer this Act." In sum, the language of the statute supports the view that § 301 limitations are to be adopted by the Administrator, that they are to be based primarily on classes and categories, and that they are to take the form of regulations. * * *

The remaining issue in this case concerns new plants. Under § 306, EPA is to promulgate "regulations establishing Federal standards of performance for new sources...." § 306(b)(1)(B). A "standard of performance" is a "standard for the control of the discharge of pollutants which reflects the greatest degree of effluent reduction which the Administrator determines to be achievable through application of the best available demonstrated control technology, ... including, where practicable, a standard permitting no discharge of pollutants." § 306(a)(1). In setting the standard, "[t]he Administrator may distinguish among classes, types, and sizes within categories of new sources ... and shall consider the type of process employed (including whether batch or continuous)." § 306(b)(2). * * *

* * * It is clear that Congress intended these regulations to be absolute prohibitions. The use of the word "standards" implies as much. So does the description of the preferred standard as one "permitting no discharge of pollutants." (emphasis added.) It is "unlawful for any owner or operator of any new source to operate such source in violation of any standard of performance applicable to such source." § 306(e) (emphasis added). In striking contrast to § 301(c), there is no statutory provision for variances, and a variance provision would be inappropriate in a standard that was intended to insure national uniformity and "maximum feasible control of new sources." S. Rep. No. 92–414, page 58 (1971), Leg. Hist. 1476.

That portion of the judgment of the Court of Appeals * * * requiring EPA to provide a variance procedure for new sources is reversed. In all other aspects, the judgment of the Court of Appeals are affirmed.

It is so ordered.

NOTES

1. Practically speaking, what would have happened if the Court had agreed with petitioners that the EPA could not set effluent standards by industrial category? Aren't standards tailored to specific facilities always better than standards set by industrial category? Can you imagine why, despite their posture in this case, industry groups might in another circumstance argue against the individualized plant-by-plant approach to setting standards?

2. As illustrated above in Figure 2, *supra,* page 705, the EPA was charged with setting technology-based effluent limits at various levels of stringency to eventually meet the ambitious goal of zero discharge from point sources into the nation's navigable waterways. The EPA had to set and justify each limit for each category of plant or facility it devised, and these limits were vigorously challenged by regulated industries—which argued that the EPA was imposing costs far out of proportion with the intended benefits—*and* by environmentalists, who argued the standards were too lenient to satisfy the statutory mandates. The agency found itself, in this instance, between a rock and a hard place, able to please no one. The Court turned out to be the agency's ally in this case, but this does not always occur. Imagine what it must be like to get up every day and face the overwhelming administrative obstacles that confront agency officials: an unimplementable statute, inadequate funding, an impatient Congress, a meddlesome President, interfering courts, angry interest groups, etc. Does this make you sympathetic to government agencies?

The following case further illustrates the complexity of the standard-setting process and the court's attempt to clarify the role of cost considerations in setting the various standards. Petitioners argued that Congress intended to impose on the EPA's cost considerations for BPT and BCT a "knee-of-the-curve test" (as diagramed below) forbidding the EPA from imposing standards that would limit effluents beyond the knee-of-the-curve. Their theory was that to impose further reductions beyond that limit would be to impose per-unit costs far in excess of potential benefits. The court, however, held that Congress left it to the agency to determine the point of diminishing returns.

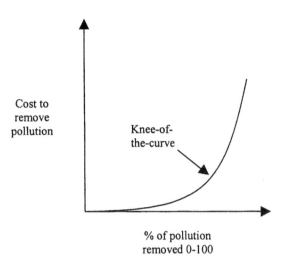

Figure 4: Knee-of-the-curve

CHEMICAL MANUFACTURERS ASSOCIATION v. EPA

United States Court of Appeals, Fifth Circuit, 1989.
870 F.2d 177, *cert. denied,* 495 U.S. 910, 110 S.Ct. 1936, 109 L.Ed.2d 299 (1990).

RUBIN, GARZA and KING, CIRCUIT JUDGES Jointly.

Acting under the mandate of the Clean Water Act (CWA), the Environmental Protection Agency (EPA), has promulgated final regulations limiting the discharge of pollutants into the nation's navigable waters by manufacturing plants in the organic chemicals, plastics, and synthetic fibers (OCPSF) industries. The regulations, which the statute requires to be implemented beginning March 31, 1989, cover both direct discharge and indirect discharge through publicly-owned treatment works (POTWs). The Chemical Manufacturers Association (CMA) and a number of companies affected by the regulations allege both procedural defects in their promulgation and substantive defects in various provisions, as well as defects in the application of specific provisions to particular plants. Intervening in some of the cases consolidated for review and appearing as amicus curiae in the others, the Natural Resources Defense Council (NRDC) also challenges the regulations, but on the different ground that they fail to require a sufficiently high degree of effluent pollution control. Although it contends that the regulations are invalid, the NRDC urges that they be enforced until more stringent standards can be adopted.

The case is of such complexity that the parties have submitted briefs totaling more than 3,000 pages and a joint appendix 9,000 pages long distilled from a 600,000–page administrative record. To enable us to render a decision as promptly as possible, the members of the panel have divided responsibility for preparing portions of this opinion, as the District of Columbia Circuit did in *Alabama Power Co. v. Costle*. Judge Garza prepared sections V, VI, and VII of this opinion, as well as all portions discussing issues raised by the NRDC; Judge Rubin prepared sections I and III; and Judge King prepared sections II and IV, except for those portions discussing issues raised by the NRDC. * * *

The Act requires direct dischargers to comply with technology-based pollutant-effluent limitations that, in time, will become more stringent. First, it orders all direct dischargers of conventional pollutants to comply with effluent limitations achievable by application of the *"best practicable control technology* presently available" (BPT) by July 1, 1977. Second, it orders all direct dischargers of conventional pollutants to comply by March 31, 1989 with effluent limitations based on a more exacting standard, the *"best conventional* pollution control *technology"* (BCT). It mandates in addition that, by the same date, direct dischargers of toxic pollutants must comply with the even more rigorous effluent limitations based on the *"best available technology* economically achievable" (BAT).

The EPA must determine the BPT, BCT, and BAT requirements and announce them in regulations establishing "effluent limitations guidelines" for various classes and categories of dischargers. In establishing each set of standards Congress required the EPA to consider a number of factors including costs, although the cost factor is accorded less weight for facilities not yet constructed and for discharges more harmful to the environment.

New plants constructed after the promulgation of the OCPSF Guidelines that discharge directly into navigable waters are subject to separate standards referred to as "new source performance standards" (NSPS). The new source performance standards are based on the *"best available demonstrated control technology"* (BADCT) as identified by the EPA. * * *

The OCPSF limitations are technology-based and apply to plants grouped into categories based on their industrial characteristics. The EPA, with the concurrence of the state affected, may establish special provisions for a facility that is fundamentally different with respect to one or more of the factors relevant in developing the regulations other than cost. These provisions, which are known as "fundamentally different factor" (FDF) variances, are intended to adjust the general limitations and provide different ones for a plant whose individual characteristics prevent it from performing within the limits set for its industrial category. An FDF variance application may be based on supporting data submitted to the EPA during the rulemaking process or on information that the applicant did not have a reasonable opportunity to submit at that time.

The regulatory process is not static. Various provisions of the Act require the EPA to review the guidelines periodically and to revise them when appropriate.

For the past eleven years the EPA has conducted studies and rule-making proceedings for the purpose of establishing OCPSF pollutant-effluent limitations. The EPA has identified model technologies that in its view satisfy the development criteria for BPT, BAT, NSPS, and PSES. Based on these model technologies, the EPA has determined treatment performances and has established effluent limitations for conventional and toxic pollutants within the range of the performances achieved by the model technologies. The OCPSF limitations provide maximum daily and maximum monthly average limits for the discharge of designated pollutants from each "point source," that is, each discharge pipe. * * *

II. Best Practicable Technology (BPT) Issues

The CWA authorizes the EPA to establish effluent limitations for direct dischargers of conventional pollutants. The Administrator is required to establish effluent limitations for categories or classes of point sources discharging these pollutants based on the "best practicable control technology currently available" (BPT). The CWA does not specifically define BPT, but does identify factors that the EPA should consider in determining it.

Section 304(b) of the CWA, as amended, states that in assessing BPT, the EPA must consider:

> the total cost of application of technology in relation to the effluent reduction benefits to be achieved from such application, and shall also take into account the age of equipment and facilities involved, the process employed, the engineering aspects of the application of various types of control techniques, process changes, non-water quality environmental impact . . . and such other factors as the Administrator deems appropriate. . . .

BPT limitations are intended to represent the average of the best levels of performance by existing plants of various sizes, ages, and unit processes within the category or subcategory for control of conventional pollutants. In promulgating the regulations, the Agency identified a model technology: biological treatment preceded by appropriate process controls and in-plant treatment followed by secondary clarification as necessary to assure adequate control of solids. CMA argues that the EPA's data indicate that its limitations will require the installation of additional treatment equipment at a cost "wholly out of proportion" to the marginal effluent reduction that the equipment would achieve and that the limitations consequently fail to meet the cost-effectiveness test required by Section 304(b)(1)(B) of the Act and the "best conventional technology" (BCT) test enacted in 1977. The EPA asserts that the total cost of the BPT rules is justified by the total amount of pollutant that would be removed.

A. The EPA's Consideration of the Industry's Costs of Complying With the BPT Limitations

CMA maintains that the cost-effectiveness of BPT rulemaking should be measured by a ''knee-of-the-curve'' test to determine the point at which costs rise steeply per pound of pollutant removed and that, under such a test, the BPT rules are not cost-effective.

The CWA contains no specific statutory language establishing a BPT ''knee-of-the-curve'' test or any other quantitative cost-benefit ratio test for BPT. The statute simply requires that the EPA consider ''the total cost of application of technology in relation to the effluent reduction benefits to be achieved from such application.'' The courts of appeal have consistently held that Congress intended Section 304(b) to give the EPA broad discretion in considering the cost of pollution abatement in relation to its benefits and to preclude the EPA from giving the cost of compliance primary importance. * * *

The EPA argues that the Administrator acted well within this broad discretion in concluding that the costs of the OCPSF BPT limitations were justified by the significant quantities of pollutants that would be removed. The EPA notes that the OCPSF industry is currently a national leader in discharging conventional pollutants into our nation's waters. The industry has approximately 300 direct dischargers which annually discharge an estimated 61 million pounds of biochemical oxygen-demanding substances (BODS) and 100 million pounds of total suspended solids (TSS) for a total estimate of approximately 161 million pounds annually. The EPA estimated that the BPT limitations would result annually in the removal of 108 million pounds of conventional pollutants from OCPSF discharges and consequently from our nation's waters at an annualized compliance cost of 76.6 million dollars after a capital investment of 215.8 million dollars. Thus, the EPA concluded that the total cost of BPT is warranted by the total pounds of pollutant removed.

1. CMA's Challenge Based on the ''Knee-of-the-Curve'' Test Cost Effectiveness

CMA argues that Congress was concerned generally that the EPA's regulations not require expenditures that would pass the point at which costs escalate rapidly in relation to benefits—the ''knee-of-the-curve'' on a diagram depicting the cost curve [see Figure 4 above, page 55]. CMA conceives of the knee-of-the-curve test as a generally applicable cost-effectiveness test with the ''knee'' defining the most stringent level of regulation permissible. Thus, CMA asserts, whether the EPA labels its regulations BPT or BCT, the EPA is required to consider whether the marginal costs exceed the marginal benefits of the rule. Applying this test, CMA argues that increasing the removal of conventional pollutants from 96 to 99 percent as required by the limitations would cost the OCPSF industry almost twice as much per pound of pollutant removed as current treatment methods: The annual removal of 108 million pounds would cost 76 million dollars per year—71 cents per pound—whereas industry efforts to date have required an expenditure of only 38 cents per pound. CMA concludes that the cost per pound for removal of pollutants is thus well beyond the knee-of-the-curve and that the regulations are therefore not cost-effective.

The EPA argues, however, that even if the knee-of-the-curve test applies to any of its regulations, the test is applicable only to assess the cost-effectiveness of incremental increases in limitations *beyond* BPT— that is, only to BCT. Representative Roberts, the author of the conference report on the 1977 amendments, emphasized that the additional technology requirements of BCT were to be imposed only to remove additional "cheap pounds" of conventional pollutants beyond BPT. Congress, however, did not specify that initial BPT must be "cheap." In fact, Congress anticipated that initially BPT might cause many plant closures and the loss of 50,000 to 125,000 jobs.

The BCT provisions were intended to establish an intermediate level between BPT and the stricter BAT limitations for conventional pollutants by adding a cost-effectiveness test for incremental technology requirements that exceed BPT technology. Under BCT, additional limitations on conventional pollutants that are more stringent than BPT can be imposed only "to the extent that the increased cost of treatment [would] be reasonable in terms of the degree of environmental benefits."

Thus, Congress intended that cost would occupy a different role in EPA's promulgation of BPT limitations than it would in the promulgation of BCT because of the different aims of the two standards. While Congress did not consider cost to be irrelevant to BPT, it clearly intended it to be a less significant factor than in the promulgation of BCT limitations. The EPA's interpretation of the Act is rational and supported by both the legislative history and the case law insofar as the EPA emphasizes that the BPT limitations are not subject to the type of stringent cost-benefit analysis required for BCT. The relevant inquiry with respect to BPT, as indicated above, is whether the costs are "wholly disproportionate" to the benefits.

To the extent that CMA's claim is that "wholly disproportionate" is to be measured by a knee-of-the-curve test, the EPA responds that CMA misconceives the nature of the test. Rather than displaying the rate at which costs increase relative to pounds of pollutant removed, CMA's curve displays the rate at which the cost-per-pound increases relative to the *percent* of pollutant removed, resulting in a misleadingly steep curve. While both the BPT and BCT tests require a comparison between costs and effluent reduction, neither test requires the comparison of costs to the percentage removed, as implied by CMA's curve. * * *

2. The BCT Cost–Effectiveness Test

CMA also argues that whether or not BPT rules are, as a general matter, subject to a knee-of-the-curve test, the EPA's BPT limitations for conventional pollutants must pass the BCT cost test which Congress enacted in 1977.

In promulgating BCT limitations, the Act directs the EPA to consider:

the reasonableness of the relationship between the costs of attaining a reduction in effluents and the effluent reduction benefits derived, and the comparison of the cost and level of reduction of such pollutants from the discharge from publicly owned treatment works to the cost and level of reduction of such pollutants from a class or category of industrial sources. . . .

CMA contends that this test governs the BPT rules because they represent an increase in regulation over the limitations established on a case-by-case basis by NPDES permits issued before 1977. In other words, CMA contends that the permit limitations established BPT for individual plants and that in enacting the BCT requirements in 1977 Congress intended that any subsequent, more stringent regulations must be evaluated according to the BCT standards.

The EPA responds, however, that its authority to promulgate BPT regulations is not abrogated by the fact that, pursuant to Section 402(a)(1), NPDES permits were issued prior to the promulgation of industry-wide BPT regulations. The EPA notes that, since 1977, it has promulgated BPT regulations limiting conventional pollutants in the iron and steel, metal finishing, coal mining, oil and gas, battery manufacturing, plastics molding and forming, metal molding and casting, coil coating, porcelain enameling, aluminum forming, copper forming, electrical and electronic products, and nonferrous metals forming industries—notwithstanding the fact that most of these facilities had previously been regulated by permits. The oil-and-gas-pollutant effluent limitations were promulgated in 1979 and reviewed by this court in 1981 without any reference to the BCT cost test.

The EPA also maintains that Congress did not intend BCT to displace BPT. The EPA notes that Congress has never repealed the BPT factors as a vital and continuing requirement of the Act and has not stripped the EPA of its explicit authority, under Section 304(b) of the Act, to revise or update BPT periodically. Section 304(b) directs the EPA to "publish . . . regulations, providing guidelines for effluent limitations, and at least annually thereafter, revise, if appropriate, such regulations." Thus, as the EPA interprets the Act, BCT standards, which place cost-effectiveness constraints on incremental technology requirements that exceed BPT technology, do not displace BPT or override the EPA's authority to promulgate BPT for conventional pollutants.

As additional evidence that Congress enacted BCT to supplement, rather than to replace, BPT, the EPA points to the fact that, ten years after the enactment of BCT, Congress enacted a "stricter BPT" provision "requiring a level of control substantially greater or based on fundamentally different control technology" for BPT regulations promulgated after

1981.This applies to all BPT regulations for all pollutants, including conventional pollutants, without limitation.

As evidenced by numerous rulemakings, the EPA has consistently interpreted the Act to allow the promulgation of BPT limitations applicable to facilities operating under NPDES permits despite the enactment of BCT standards in 1977. We must accord "considerable weight" to an agency's construction of a statutory scheme it is entrusted to administer. Finding the EPA's interpretation of the Act to be reasonable, we conclude that CMA's objections do not compel us to remand the limitations.

3. The Cost of Compliance with the BPT Limitations

Finally, having concluded that the EPA construed the statute reasonably in declining to subject the BPT limitations to the BCT cost test, we find that the Administrator did not act arbitrarily and capriciously in determining that the costs of the limitations were justified by the significant amount of pollutants that would be removed.

Although the cost per pound of 71 cents required to meet the BPT limitations is almost double the 38 cents per pound that the OCPSF industry presently spends to remove conventional pollutants, the 71–cents–per–pound figure is not so high as to make the EPA's decision arbitrary or capricious: "The selection of the point of diminishing returns is a matter for agency determination."

B. The EPA's Definition of the BPT Data Base

NRDC challenges the EPA's BPT limitations on BODS and TSS as being too lenient. Specifically, NRDC argues that the BPT limitations are not based on the average of the best dischargers, and that the EPA improperly rejected sequential treatment options. These two arguments will now be more fully examined.

1. The EPA's Determination of the "Average of the Best" Dischargers

The EPA is required to promulgate BPT regulations based on the "average of the best" performers in the industry. We accord some deference to the EPA's interpretation of its controlling statute; therefore, if the statute is capable of more than one reasonable interpretation, we must accept the EPA's interpretation, if reasonable.

NRDC claims that the EPA used data from 71 of 99 plants, approximately 72%, as representing the group of "best dischargers" for purposes of promulgating BPT regulations. How can the group of "best" dischargers encompass 72% of the industry, queries NRDC, leading it to argue that the EPA should have further tightened its editing criteria, which would have led to more stringent regulations.

NRDC's argument is misleading, however. Out of 304 direct dischargers in the industry that will be subject to regulation, the EPA chose a particular technology, namely biological treatment with secondary clarification, which is used by 99 plants. Out of these 99 plants, the EPA then chose data from 71 plants to determine the "average of the best" for the purpose of promulgating its BODS regulations. The EPA defends its decision by noting that its *initial* edit reduced the field from 304 to 99. Thus, the NRDC's complaint that the EPA used 71 of 99 plants is mistaken because the edit in question was the second edit, 205 dischargers having already been weeded out.

We hold, therefore, that the EPA's class of performers for determining the "average of the best" was not unreasonably broad.

Another question is whether the CWA requires the EPA to consider the average of the best performers within an *industrial category*, or the average of the best performers that use a particular chosen technology within an industry. We hold that it is appropriate to extract a group of "best" performers from an industry category; this was done in this case when the EPA selected 99 out of 304 plants in its initial edit. In fact, the EPA went further by narrowing the 99 plants down to 71. The EPA was not required to take the average of the best 99 plants using a particular technology, but merely to take the average of the best 304 plants in the industrial category. The legislative history of the 1972 amendments to the CWA specifies that "the administrator should establish the range of 'best practicable' levels based upon the average of the best performance by plants of various sizes, ages, and unit processes within each industrial category." Therefore, we find that the EPA's methods for setting the BPT standards for BODS were in compliance with the CWA.

Lastly, NRDC argues that the EPA's editing criteria for its representative "best performers," which were 95% biological oxygen demand (BOD) removal and 40 mg/l concentration, are actually below the industry's median. In support of this contention NRDC quotes from the preamble to the final rule, which it interprets as saying that the industry median is 95.8% removal and 29 mg/l concentration. Again, NRDC mischaracterizes the statistics. The median 95.8% removal and 29 mg/l concentration statistics apply to the 99 plants using biological treatment methods, not the 304 plants comprising the industry.

2. The EPA's Rejection of Sequential Treatment Options

NRDC argues that the EPA, in choosing biological treatment plus clarification (Option I) for BPT, improperly rejected other sequential options. Specifically, these options were polishing ponds (Option II) and multimedia filtration (Option III), either of which can be sequentially added to a system already utilizing biological treatment plus clarification. NRDC makes specific arguments with regard to both technologies; these arguments will next be further explored.

NRDC objects on several grounds to the EPA's failure to base BPT on Option II technology, which is biological treatment with clarification followed by polishing ponds. First, NRDC argues that the EPA's conclusion that polishing ponds are not currently used by a representative portion of the industry is incorrect. In support of this, NRDC points out that 64 plants in the industry use polishing ponds, and, of those, 17 meet the EPA's final editing criteria. The EPA defends its conclusion by initially noting that the OCPSF industry is diverse and as a result plants have significantly different wastestream characteristics. Since only 17 plants out of 64 which had installed polishing ponds were able to meet the BPT editing criteria, the EPA in its judgment concluded that polishing ponds are not a sufficiently effective technology upon which to base the BPT limits. Moreover, the question is not merely whether the fact that 17 out of 64 plants using polishing ponds were able to meet the BPT editing criteria proves that polishing ponds are effective, but also whether the experiences of these 17 plants can be applied to the 304 plants subject to regulation. The EPA concluded that this was not possible due to the diverse nature of the industry. The EPA also balanced the questionable feasibility of using polishing ponds against the cost of acquiring the large amounts of land needed for them and concluded that feasibility had not been sufficiently demonstrated to serve as a basis for BPT limitations. We find the EPA's judgment in this regard to be rational and well supported by the record. * * *

[The Court upheld EPA's technology-based standards but remanded for notice-and-comment proceedings as to the best available technology subcategorization.]

NOTES

1.   Long as it might seem, the excerpt above only gives the reader a glimpse into the complexities of standard-setting and judicial review. The full case is over 125 pages long. Industry and environmental groups challenged virtually every aspect of the agency's analytic and statistical methodology for establishing effluent limits. The Court's summary of its many findings itself occupies several pages at the beginning of the case. Can we really expect judges to master the technicalities of BPT, BCT and BAT? Is judicial review the right vehicle for ensuring that the agency is doing its job? What other forms of oversight might be superior?

2.   The cost-benefit calculation required by the EPA when setting BPT is widely construed by courts to "limit the application of technology only where the additional degree of effluent reduction is wholly out of proportion to the costs of achieving such marginal level of reduction." *See* 92 CONG. SENATE DEBATES 33,696 (1972); FWPC 72 LEG. HIST. 12 (statement of Sen. Muskie, chair of the Senate Subcommittee on Air and Water Pollution). The agency may also confine its use of cost-benefit analysis to those technologies that it deems "available." *See* American Iron & Steel Inst. v. EPA, 568 F.2d 284 (3d Cir. 1977).

3.   When establishing BPT, the agency uses an "average of the best performers in the industry" test. To do this, the agency identifies existing facilities in the relevant industrial category that employ exemplary technological controls and then calculates the costs and benefits of the effluent reduction they achieve. Industry has challenged this approach, arguing that the EPA should not limit its analysis to the best performers. The EPA's approach

has been upheld, however. *See* Kennecott Copper Corp. v. EPA, 612 F.2d 1232 (10th Cir. 1979).

4. Section 402(a)(1)(B) authorizes permit writers to use "best practical judgment" (BPJ) to set effluent limits for individual sources, if the EPA has not promulgated effluent standards for that category or class of point sources. The EPA rules instruct permit writers to consider the same factors when exercising BPJ that the EPA considers when setting the national BPT, BCT and BAT standards for categories of sources. *See* 40 C.F.R. section 125.3(c), (d). Permit writers have resorted to BPJ frequently, because of considerable delays in the EPA's standard-setting process. One of the purposes of *categorical* effluent limits is to ensure an even-playing field among competitors in the same industry. Doesn't the possibility that permit writers will use BPJ to write individualized permits undermine this purpose?

ENTERGY CORP. v. RIVERKEEPER, INC., ET AL.

Supreme Court of the United States, 2009.
___ U.S. ___, 129 S.Ct. 1498, 173 L.Ed.2d 369.

Scalia, J., delivered the opinion of the Court.

Justice Scalia delivered the opinion of the Court.

These cases concern a set of regulations adopted by the Environmental Protection Agency (EPA or agency) under § 316(b) of the Clean Water Act, 33 U. S. C. § 1326(b). 69 Fed. Reg. 41576 (2004). Respondents—environmental groups and various States—challenged those regulations, and the Second Circuit set them aside. The issue for our decision is whether, as the Second Circuit held, the EPA is not permitted to use cost-benefit analysis in determining the content of regulations promulgated under § 1326(b).

I

Petitioners operate—or represent those who operate—large power-plants. In the course of generating power, those plants also generate large amounts of heat. To cool their facilities, petitioners employ "cooling water intake structures" that extract water from nearby water sources. These structures pose various threats to the environment, chief among them the squashing against intake screens (elegantly called "impingement") or suction into the cooling system ("entrainment") of aquatic organisms that live in the affected water sources. Accordingly, the facilities are subject to regulation under the Clean Water Act, 33 U. S. C. § 1251 *et seq.*, which mandates:

> "Any standard established pursuant to section 1311 of this title or section 1316 of this title and applicable to a point source shall require that the location, design, construction, and capacity of cooling water intake structures reflect the best technology available for minimizing adverse environmental impact." § 1326(b).

Sections 1311 and 1316, in turn, employ a variety of "best technology" standards to regulate the discharge of effluents into the Nation's waters.

The § 1326(b) regulations at issue here were promulgated by the EPA after nearly three decades in which the determination of the "best technology available for minimizing [cooling water intake structures'] adverse environmental impact" was made by permit-issuing authorities on a case-by-case basis, without benefit of a governing regulation.

In 1995, the EPA entered into a consent decree which, as subsequently amended, set a multiphase timetable for the EPA to promulgate regulations under § 1326(b). In the first phase the EPA adopted regulations governing certain new, large cooling water intake structures. These regulations were upheld in large part by the Second Circuit in *Riverkeeper, Inc. v. EPA*, 358 F. 3d 174 (2004).

The EPA then adopted the so-called "Phase II" rules at issue here. They apply to existing facilities that are point sources, whose primary activity is the generation and transmission (or sale for transmission) of electricity, and whose water-intake flow is more than 50 million gallons of water per day, at least 25 percent of which is used for cooling purposes. Over 500 facilities, accounting for approximately 53 percent of the Nation's electric-power generating capacity, fall within Phase II's ambit.

To address those environmental impacts, the EPA set "national performance standards," requiring Phase II facilities (with some exceptions) to reduce "impingement mortality for all life stages of fish and shellfish by 80 to 95 percent from the calculation baseline"; a subset of facilities must also reduce entrainment of such aquatic organisms by "60 to 90 percent from the calculation baseline." Those targets are based on the environmental improvements achievable through deployment of a mix of remedial technologies, which the EPA determined were "commercially available and economically practicable."

In its Phase II rules, however, the EPA expressly declined to mandate adoption of closed-cycle cooling systems or equivalent reductions in impingement and entrainment, as it had done for new facilities subject to the Phase I rules. It refused to take that step in part because of the "generally high costs" of converting existing facilities to closed-cycle operation, and because "other technologies approach the performance of this option. Thus, while closed-cycle cooling systems could reduce impingement and entrainment mortality by up to 98 percent, (compared to the Phase II targets of 80 to 95 percent impingement reduction), the cost of rendering all Phase II facilities closed-cycle-compliant would be approximately $3.5 billion per year, nine times the estimated cost of compliance with the Phase II performance standards. Moreover, Phase II facilities compelled to convert to closed-cycle cooling systems "would produce 2.4 percent to 4.0 percent less electricity even while burning the same amount of coal," possibly requiring the construction of "20 additional 400–MW plants . . . to replace the generating capacity lost." *Id.,* at 41605. The EPA thus concluded that "[a]lthough not identical, the ranges of impingement and entrainment reduction are similar under both options. . . . [Benefits of compliance with the Phase II rules] can approach those of closed-cycle re-circulating at less cost with fewer implementation problems."

II

In setting the Phase II national performance standards and providing for site-specific cost-benefit variances, the EPA relied on its view that § 1326(b)'s "best technology available" standard permits consideration of the technology's costs, and of the relationship between those costs and the environmental benefits produced. That view governs if it is a reasonable interpretation of the statute—not necessarily the only possible interpretation, nor even the interpretation deemed *most* reasonable by the courts.

As we have described, § 1326(b) instructs the EPA to set standards for cooling water intake structures that reflect "the best technology available for minimizing adverse environmental impact." The Second Circuit took that language to mean the technology that achieves the greatest reduction in adverse environmental impacts at a cost that can reasonably be borne by the industry. That is certainly a plausible interpretation of the statute. The "best" technology—that which is "most advantageous," Webster's New International Dictionary 258 (2d ed. 1953)—may well be the one that produces the most of some good, here a reduction in adverse environmental impact. But "best technology" may also describe the technology that *most efficiently* produces some good. In common parlance one could certainly use the phrase "best technology" to refer to that which produces a good at the lowest per-unit cost, even if it produces a lesser quantity of that good than other available technologies.

Respondents contend that this latter reading is precluded by the statute's use of the phrase "for minimizing adverse environmental impact." Minimizing, they argue, means reducing to the smallest amount possible, and the "best technology available for minimizing adverse environmental impacts," must be the economically feasible technology that achieves the greatest possible reduction in environmental harm. But "minimize" is a term that admits of degree and is not necessarily used to refer exclusively to the "greatest possible reduction." For example, elsewhere in the Clean Water Act, Congress declared that the procedures implementing the Act "shall encourage the drastic minimization of paperwork and interagency decision procedures." 33 U. S. C. § 1251(f). If respondents' definition of the term "minimize" is correct, the statute's use of the modifier "drastic" is superfluous.

Other provisions in the Clean Water Act also suggest the agency's interpretation. When Congress wished to mandate the greatest feasible reduction in water pollution, it did so in plain language: The provision governing the discharge of toxic pollutants into the Nation's waters requires the EPA to set "effluent limitations [which] shall require the *elimination* of discharges of all pollutants if the Administrator finds ... that such elimination is technologically and economically achievable," § 1311(b)(2)(A)(emphasis added). See also § 1316(a)(1) (mandating "where practicable, a standard [for new point sources] permitting *no discharge* of pollutants" (emphasis added)). Section 1326(b)'s use of the less ambitious goal of "minimizing adverse environmental impact" suggests, we think, that the agency retains some discretion to determine the extent of reduction that is warranted under the circumstances. That determination could plausibly involve a consideration of the benefits derived from reductions and the costs of achieving them. It seems to us, therefore, that the phrase "best technology available," even with the added specification "for minimizing adverse environmental impact," does not unambiguously preclude cost-benefit analysis.

Respondents' alternative (and, alas, also more complex) argument rests upon the structure of the Clean Water Act. The Act provided that during its initial implementation period existing "point sources"—discrete conveyances from which pollutants are or may be discharged, 33 U. S. C. § 1362(14)—were subject to "effluent limitations . . . which shall require the application of the *best practicable control technology* currently available." § 1311(b)(1)(A) (emphasis added). (We shall call this the "BPT" test.) Following that transition period, the Act initially mandated adoption, by July 1, 1983 (later extended to March 31, 1989), of stricter effluent limitations requiring "application of the *best available technology economically achievable* for such category or class, which will result in reasonable further progress toward the national goal of eliminating the discharge of all pollutants." § 1311(b)(2)(A) ([T]he "BATEA" test.) Subsequent amendment limited application of this standard to toxic and nonconventional pollutants, and for the remainder established a (presumably laxer) test of "best conventional-pollutant control technology." § 1311(b)(2)(E). (We shall call this "BCT.") Finally, § 1316 subjected certain categories of new point sources to "the greatest degree of effluent reduction which the Administrator determines to be achievable through application of the *best available demonstrated control technology*." § 1316(a)(1); § 1316(b)(1)(B). (We shall call this the "BADT" test.) The provision at issue here, applicable not to effluents but to cooling water intake structures, requires, as we have described, "the *best technology available for minimizing adverse environmental impact*," § 1326(b) (emphasis added). (We shall call this the "BTA" test.)

The first four of these tests are elucidated by statutory factor lists that guide their implementation. To take the standards in (presumed) order of increasing stringency: In applying the BPT test the EPA is instructed to consider, among other factors, "the total cost of application of technology in relation to the effluent reduction benefits to be achieved." § 1314(b)(1)(B). In applying the BCT test it is instructed to consider "the *reasonableness of the relationship* between the costs of attaining a reduction in effluents and the effluent reduction benefits derived." § 1314(b)(4)(B). And in applying the BATEA and BADT tests the EPA is instructed to consider the "cost of achieving such effluent reduction." §§ 1314(b)(2)(B), 1316(b)(1)(B). There is no such elucidating language applicable to the BTA test at issue here.

The Second Circuit, in rejecting the EPA's use of cost-benefit analysis, relied in part on the propositions that (1) cost-benefit analysis is precluded under the BATEA and BADT tests; and (2) that, insofar as the permissibility of cost-benefit analysis is concerned, the BTA test (the one at issue here) is to be treated the same as those two. It is not obvious to us that the first of these propositions is correct, but we need not pursue that point, since we assuredly do not agree with the second. It is certainly reasonable for the agency to conclude that the BTA test need not be interpreted to permit only what those other two tests permit. Its text is not identical to theirs. It has the relatively modest goal of "minimizing adverse environmental impact" as compared with the BATEA's goal of "eliminating the discharge of all pollutants." And it is unencumbered by specified statutory factors of the sort provided for those other two tests, which omission can reasonably be interpreted to suggest that the EPA is accorded greater discretion in determining its precise content.

This extended consideration of the text of § 1326(b), and comparison of that with the text and statutory factors applicable to four parallel provisions of the Clean Water Act, lead us to the conclusion that it was well within the bounds of reasonable interpretation for the EPA to conclude that cost-benefit analysis is not categorically forbidden. Other arguments may be available to preclude such a rigorous form of cost-benefit analysis as that which was prescribed under the statute's former BPT standard, which required weighing "the total cost of application of technology" against "the . . . benefits to be achieved." But that question is not before us.

In the Phase II requirements challenged here the EPA sought only to avoid extreme disparities between costs and benefits. The agency limited variances from the Phase II "national performance standards" to circumstances where the costs are "significantly greater than the benefits" of compliance. In defining the "national performance standards" themselves the EPA assumed the application of technologies whose benefits "approach those estimated" for closed-cycle cooling systems at a fraction of the cost: $389 million per year, as compared with (1) at least $3.5 billion per year to operate compliant closed-cycle cooling systems, (or $1 billion per year to impose similar requirements on a subset of Phase II facilities, (2) significant reduction in the energy output of the altered facilities. And finally, EPA's assessment of the relatively meager financial benefits of the Phase II regulations that it adopted—reduced impingement and entrainment of 1.4 billion aquatic organisms with annualized use benefits of $83 million, and non-use benefits of indeterminate value,—when compared to annual costs of $389 million, demonstrates quite clearly that the agency did not select the Phase II regulatory requirements because their benefits equaled their costs.

In the last analysis, even respondents ultimately recognize that some form of cost-benefit analysis is permissible. They acknowledge that the statute's language is "plainly not so constricted as to require EPA to require industry petitioners to spend billions to save one more fish or plankton." This concedes the principle—the permissibility of at least some cost-benefit analysis—and we see no statutory basis for limiting its use to situations where the benefits are *de minimis* rather than significantly disproportionate.

* * *

We conclude that the EPA permissibly relied on cost-benefit analysis in setting the national performance standards and in providing for cost-benefit variances from those standards as part of the Phase II regulations. The judgment of the Court of Appeals is reversed, and the cases are remanded for further proceedings consistent with this opinion.

JUSTICE STEVENS, with whom JUSTICE SOUTER and JUSTICE GINSBURG join, dissenting.

Section 316(b) of the Clean Water Act (CWA), 33 U. S. C. § 1326(b), which governs industrial powerplant water intake structures, provides that the Environmental Protection Agency (EPA or Agency) "shall require" that such structures "reflect the best technology available for minimizing adverse environmental impact." The EPA has interpreted that mandate to authorize the use of cost-benefit analysis in promulgating regulations under § 316(b). For instance, under the Agency's interpretation, technology that would otherwise qualify as the best available need not be used if its costs are "significantly greater than the benefits" of compliance. 40 CFR § 125.94(a)(5)(ii)(2008).

Like the Court of Appeals, I am convinced that the EPA has misinterpreted the plain text of § 316(b). Unless costs are so high that the best technology is not "available," Congress has decided that they are outweighed by the benefits of minimizing adverse environmental impact. Section 316(b) neither expressly nor implicitly authorizes the EPA to use cost-benefit analysis when setting regulatory standards; fairly read, it prohibits such use.

I

As typically performed by the EPA, cost-benefit analysis requires the Agency to first monetize the costs and benefits of a regulation, balance the results, and then choose the regulation with the greatest net benefits. The process is particularly controversial in the environmental context in which a regulation's financial costs are often more obvious and easier to quantify than its environmental benefits. And cost-benefit analysis often, if not always, yields a result that does not maximize environmental protection.

For instance, although the EPA estimated that water intake structures kill 3.4 billion fish and shellfish each year, the Agency struggled to calculate the value of the aquatic life that would be protected under its § 316(b) regulations, *id*. To compensate, the EPA took a shortcut: Instead of monetizing all aquatic life, the Agency counted only those species that are commercially or recreationally harvested, a tiny slice (1.8 percent to be precise) of all impacted fish and shellfish. This narrow focus in turn skewed the Agency's calculation of benefits. When the EPA attempted to value all aquatic life, the benefits measured $735 million. But when the EPA decided to give zero value to the 98.2 percent of fish not commercially or recreationally harvested, the benefits calculation dropped dramatically—to $83million. *Id.*, at 41666. The Agency acknowledged that its failure to monetize the other 98.2 percent of affected species " 'could result in serious misallocation of resources,' " because its "comparison of complete costs and incomplete benefits does not provide an accurate picture of net benefits to society."

Because benefits can be more accurately monetized in some industries than in others, Congress typically decides whether it is appropriate for an agency to use cost-benefit analysis in crafting regulations. Indeed, this Court has recognized that "[w]hen Congress has intended that an agency engage in cost-benefit analysis, it has clearly indicated such intent on the face of the statute." Accordingly, we should not treat a provision's silence as an implicit source of cost-benefit authority, particularly when such authority is elsewhere expressly granted and it has the potential to fundamentally alter an agency's approach to regulation. Congress, we have noted, "does not alter the fundamental details of a regulatory scheme in vague terms or ancillary provisions—it does not, one might say, hide elephants in mouse holes." [citations omitted].

NOTES

1. Has Justice Scalia, in ruling that the EPA may use cost-benefit analysis, abandoned his commitment to a "texualist" approach to statutory interpretation, under which agencies (and the Court) are to follow literally what a statute says even if the results may be extreme?

2. Are there, paradoxically, positive implications for greenhouse gas emissions reductions in the Court's ruling?

3. Under the Court's ruling, can the EPA on remand adopt new regulations that are more environmentally protective than those challenged in the *Entergy* case?

d. Toxics

In 1972, Congress required the EPA to list toxics (which were broadly defined) and to set health-based standards for their discharge, without regard to cost or technological feasibility. § 307. What followed was primarily delay. The EPA was already reeling under the administrative burdens of both its CWA and CAA obligations, and health-based standard setting proved especially difficult. As Houck puts it,

> EPA simply found itself with more power than it knew how to exercise. The science of toxicity was too rudimentary to allow it to set levels for all but the best documented and most celebrated toxins, e.g., PCBs, DDT, and endrin, for which the levels approached zero. Further, the looming, omnipresent factors of economic and technological feasibility could be neither included nor ignored. The statute appeared

to preclude them and, as a practical matter, if they were included, derivation of the resulting standard would be difficult to distinguish from standards set as best practicable technology and best available technology. On the other hand, the prospects of requiring a technology that did not exist, or forcing an entire industry—pesticide manufacture, steel manufacture—to close, was unthinkable. EPA was paralyzed.

Oliver A. Houck, *The Regulation of Toxic Substances Under the Clean Water Act, 21* ENVTL. L. REP. 10528 (1991).

The NRDC filed suit challenging the EPA's failure to establish effluent standards for toxics as required by the statute. *See* NRDC v. Costle, 561 F.2d 904 (D.C. Cir. 1977) *modified sub nom.* NRDC v. Costle). The suit eventually settled, with the NRDC, the EPA and a variety of industrial intervenors entering a consent decree known as the "Flannery Decree" (so-named for the presiding judge). The Consent Decree established a schedule for EPA promulgation of effluent limits for 65 pollutants (known as "priority pollutants") and 21 industry categories. The Flannery Decree was incorporated into the 1977 Amendments to the Act in § 307(a)(1) with the list of priority pollutants growing to 126 and the number of industry categories expanded to 34. Thus was the initial health-based approach to toxics supplanted by a technology-based approach.

However, the new technology-based approach proved challenging as well. Houck explains:

> The development of technology standards was the most Herculean task ever imposed on an environmental agency. EPA had literally to master the economics, engineering, and technology of every industrial process in the most industrialized and fastest-growing economy in world history. It had to learn state-of-the-art and potential alternative technologies for each process. It had to be able to defend its technology-forcing conclusions against the most experienced engineers, economists and lawyers money could buy. Every draft standard EPA proposed was subject to intense scrutiny, lobbying, and opposition from the affected industry and, within the limits of its resources, at least one organization. Nearly every final standard was immediately taken to court. * * *

> By early 1983, most of EPA's proposals for regulation of the priority pollutants of the consent decree industries had been developed in at least draft form. The transaction costs of the process, however, were already noticeable . . . for several of the high-volume toxic discharges, the Agency was extending compliance deadlines to 1988 but was also retreating from stringent BAT proposals in its earlier draft proposals and adopting, instead, more relaxed requirements equal to no better than BPT. * * *

> By the latter half of the 1980s, EPA's technology standards program was limited to grinding out guidelines for the remaining consent decree categories. No additional categories had been proposed. No

additions to the list of regulated "priority pollutants" were proposed. No revisions were proposed to upgrade standards from those set, in some case, 10 years before.

Houck, *id.*

Congress amended the Act to add a provision requiring the agency a) to develop a plan for scheduling annual review and revision of existing guidelines, b) to identify unregulated industrial source categories, and c) and to issue standards by 1991 (later extended to 1994). However, well into the 1990s, many industrial facilities discharging toxic pollutants remained outside the federal BAT standards and most of the existing BAT standards were fast becoming obsolete.

e. New Source Performance Standards

CHEMICAL MANUFACTURERS ASSOCIATION v. EPA

United States Court of Appeals, Fifth Circuit, 1989.
870 F.2d 177, *cert. denied,* 495 U.S. 910, 110 S.Ct. 1936, 109 L.Ed.2d 299 (1990).

[The facts of the case are excerpted above, at 737. The excerpt below addresses the EPA's methodology for establishing NSPS, and the NRDC's challenge to the EPA's decision to promulgate, for certain chemical manufacturing source categories, NSPS that were identical to the existing source standards.]

RUBIN, GARZA and KING, CIRCUIT JUDGES Jointly.

* * *

V. *New Source Performance Standards (NSPS) Issues*

We now turn to the challenge presented by the NRDC that the EPA violated the Clean Water Act by basing New Source Performance Standards (NSPS) and Pretreatment Standards for New Sources (PSNS) upon BPT for conventional pollutants and upon BAT model technology for toxic discharges.

NRDC argues that effluent limitations for newly constructed dischargers represent the highest level of technology-based treatment under the Clean Water Act. In promulgating the New Source Performance Standards, according to NRDC, Congress intended that new facilities would be required to take advantage of the most current process and treatment innovations, irrespective of whether the cost of the new technologies is justified by any incremental degree of removal achieved by its application. The reason for dropping the cost-benefit analysis from the NSPS, according to NRDC, was the recognition by Congress that new facilities are not limited by cost and engineering constraints inherent in retrofitting existing plants. Congress also recognized that new sources are uniquely situated to push toward the outer envelope of pollution control technology in a way that will further progress toward the national goal of eliminating the discharge of all pollutants.

Instead of establishing effluent guidelines that would tend to achieve these legislative purposes, however, the EPA final rules set out standards for new sources identical to those for existing plants. This, the NRDC urges, violates section 306 of the Clean Water Act. * * *

1.   The EPA's Cost Test in Establishing NSPS

First, NRDC asserts that the EPA used the same cost test for new and existing sources when Congress intended the Agency to use a "stricter cost test" for evaluating the efficacy of treatment technologies for new sources. According to NRDC, the EPA improperly compared "the costs of incremental pollution control technology against water quality benefits," thereby rejecting at least one new treatment technology on the basis of a cost-benefit analysis.

The EPA responds that the Act requires the Agency to "take into consideration the cost of achieving [NSPS] reduction, and any non-water quality environmental impact and energy requirements." This test, the EPA urges, is identical to the cost requirement for establishing BAT. The use of BPT and BAT costing methods to determine the cost of entirely new treatment systems for new sources was, according to EPA, entirely reasonable. The Agency denies that it compared these costs to the benefits accrued from compliance with NSPS.

We are not convinced that the EPA's costing methods for promulgating NSPS violated the Act. With respect to toxic pollutants, we agree that the statutory test for evaluating the costs of NSPS treatment is identical to that required for establishing BAT standards. In both cases, the Administrator must inquire into the initial and annual costs of applying the technology and make an affirmative determination that those costs can be reasonably borne by the industry. Congress may have contemplated that it would cost less to install new technologies in new plants than to retrofit old plants to accommodate new treatment systems. However, the determination whether that contemplation held true, in fact, with respect to any particular technology, was left by statute to the discretion of the Administrator.

For plants that discharge conventional pollutants, the EPA points out that new sources must install secondary clarifiers, biological treatment limits, equalization and other treatment technologies. BPT costing methods, according to the EPA, provide a framework for estimating the capital and operating costs of such systems. Given the legislative grant of discretion vested in the Administrator to determine the economic feasibility of costs under NSPS, we cannot say, on the basis of this record, that the methods used constitute a violation of the Act.

2.   NRDC's Challenge that the EPA Failed to Consider Technology Beyond BPT and BAT

The second reason presented to support NRDC's argument that the NSPS regulations violate the Clean Water Act is the assertion that the

EPA failed to give serious consideration to better control technologies that could be used by new sources. Specifically, NRDC points to indications in the record that 26% of OCPSF plants are "zero or alternative discharge" plants and that 36 plants achieve zero discharge through recycling, a technology the EPA allegedly did not consider in its rulemaking.

The EPA argues that new technologies must be "demonstrated" to achieve more stringent limitations and that they must be "available" in the OCPSF industry before such technologies can form the basis for NSPS. The Agency claims to have considered and rejected technologies other than BPT and BAT. It found, for instance, that requiring filtration in addition to biological treatment for conventional pollutants had not been adequately demonstrated to accomplish better effluent results for the OCPSF industry. As another example, the Agency considered requiring the addition of activated carbon for further control of toxic pollutants but rejected it because of its high cost and because it had not been well-demonstrated to enhance treatment.

Intuitively, there is some force to the observation that Congress would not have devised a completely new statutory scheme for regulation of new sources if it intended that the effluent standards for such plants would be identical to those required for existing sources. This is especially true when one considers that the statute provides an exemption from more stringent standards of performance that the EPA may adopt under NSPS in the future.

The EPA asserts that, at this time, there exist no technologies that have been demonstrated to achieve a greater degree of effluent reduction than existing technologies that meet BPT and BAT standards. The key issue is the meaning attributable to the term "demonstrated." The EPA maintains that "best available demonstrated technology" means "those plant processes and control technology which, at the pilot plant, semi-works, or other level, has [sic] demonstrated both technological performance and economic viability at a level sufficient to reasonably justify the making of investments in such new facilities."

The Third Circuit has concluded, and we agree, that Congress did not intend the term "best available demonstrated control technology" to limit consideration of treatment systems only to those widely in use in the industry. Instead, the present availability of a particular technology may be "demonstrated" if even one plant utilizes the technology in question. NRDC asserts that 36 operating facilities achieve zero discharge by the use of recycling and that the EPA failed to consider this technology when it promulgated effluent limitations for new sources.

The EPA's only response is that NRDC failed to urge consideration of recycling during rulemaking and is therefore precluded from raising the issue on appeal. As to this, as we have previously pointed out, the failure of a petitioner to raise an issue before the Agency may cause us to view the contention less favorably but does not bar our consideration of it.

We frequently defer to the expertise of the EPA. We do this for good reason. Congress entertains the legitimate expectation that the various federal agencies, charged as they are with responsibility for promulgating highly detailed and technical regulations, will be aware of the events and breakthroughs on the technological frontiers that lie within the purview of the agencies' respective fields of expertise.

We do not require, however, that the EPA be fully cognizant of every innovation, wherever employed, that has the potential to achieve greater reductions in the discharge of pollutants into our environment. And we recognize that the purpose of a period of notice and comment during rulemaking is, at least in part, to allow interested parties to bring to the attention of the EPA relevant technologies that may assist the Agency in the discharge of its regulatory duties. Nevertheless, we consider that a treatment system employed by 36 plants in the OCPSF industry is sufficiently common that it is not unreasonable to expect the EPA to know about it. The NSPS statute directs that the "Administrator shall, from time to time, as technology and alternatives change," revise effluent standards for new point sources. We should be able to have confidence that the Administrator will do so, especially since he has chosen at this time to require no more stringent guidelines for new plants than for existing sources.

We know from the record that 36 plants in the industry use recycling and some of them achieve zero discharge. Thus, recycling easily fits the definition of an "available demonstrated technology" under § 306 of the Act. The failure of the EPA even to consider recycling, then, was arbitrary or capricious. We therefore remand these limitations to the EPA for consideration of whether zero discharge limits would be appropriate for new plants in the OCPSF industry because of the existence of recycling.

NOTES

1. Technology-based standards are meant to be dynamic. As technology improves, standards should ratchet up. In practice, however, the Act's elaborate system of phased standards may have virtually collapsed into a single stage of BPT. Commenting on the *CMA* case excerpted above, Houck observed:

> The attempt to set BAT for the organic chemicals, plastics, and synthetic materials category bottomed out, after years of administrative warfare, at a standard no better than BPT. Indeed, EPA concluded by proposing BAT for new sources in this industry, standards intended to be the toughest in the Clean Water Act, without consideration of recycling technologies that had already been adopted by thirty-six plants; twenty-six percent of the industry had already achieved *zero* discharge. These consequences are not unusual; one observer of the process concluded that, while the first-stage BPT inquiry was rigorous, subsequent BAT standards, in general, required little more.

Oliver A. Houck, *Of Bats, Birds, and B–A–T: The Convergent Evolution of Environmental Law*, 63 Miss. L.J. 403, 452 (1994). *See also* Jonathan K.

Baum, *Legislating Cost–Benefit Analysis: The Federal Water Pollution Control Act Experience*, 9 COLUM. J. ENVTL. L. 75, 76 (1983) (arguing that separate cost tests applicable to BPT, BCT, BAT, and BDAT have become indistinguishable, and that this "blurring has resulted in ad hoc evaluations by [EPA] administrators, who treat all steps of the regulatory schedule the same, thus thwarting the goals of predictability and intellectual coherence in the law.").

f. Publicly Owned Treatment Works

Publicly owned treatment works (POTWs) collect wastewater from homes, commercial buildings, and industrial facilities and transport it via a series of pipes, known as a collection system, to the treatment plant. The POTW removes harmful organisms and other contaminants from the sewage so it can be discharged safely into the receiving water body. Generally, POTWs are designed to treat domestic sewage only. However, they also receive wastewater from industrial (non-domestic) users. The Act requires industrial dischargers who send waste to POTWs to meet pretreatment standards to control pollutants which may pass through or interfere with POTW treatment processes, or which may contaminate sewage sludge. These standards are based on BAT.

Section 301 of the 1972 Amendments established standards for POTWs, requiring them to meet secondary treatment standards by 1977 and more stringent standards by 1983. In 1981, Congress amended the POTW provisions to extend the secondary treatment deadline to 1988 and to eliminate the advanced treatment requirement. Industrial dischargers sending waste to POTWs are required by § 307(b) to obtain pretreatment permits to ensure that their discharges (for which they are not required to obtain permits since the waste does not flow directly into surface waters) do not interfere with the POTW.

The 1972 Amendments also created a federal grant program to encourage the construction of POTWs. As a condition of receiving grants-in-aid, § 208 requires states to establish area-wide management agencies with both planning and regulatory functions for waste treatment. The grant program provided nearly $60 billion in federal funding to states, but in the 1987 Amendments, Congress stipulated that all direct federal grants for POTW construction would end as of 1990, and would be replaced by a new revolving loan program to be administered by the states. In 1998, this new fund had $26 billion in assets with approximately $3 billion distributed in new loans annually. "Since its beginning, the SRF [State Revolving Fund] has provided more than 5,700 loans throughout the United States and Puerto Rico. One of the benefits of the SRF is that it gives the states flexibility to provide funding for projects that address their highest priority water quality needs such as urban storm water and nonpoint source management practices, estuarine and groundwater protection programs, and sanitary sewer overflow control projects." OFFICE OF WASTEWATER MANAGEMENT, EPA, WATER POLLUTION CONTROL: 25 YEARS OF PROGRESS AND CHALLENGES FOR THE NEW MILLENNIUM 2 (1998).

g. Water Quality Standards (WQS)

Section 303(a) requires states and tribes to establish water quality standards for all intrastate waters and to review their standards every three years. State WQS are subject to EPA approval. § 303(c). Section 303(d) authorizes the EPA to issue standards for states that fail to submit their own or for state standards that fail to meet the requirements of the Act.

The Water Quality Standards Program consists of three major components: designated uses (DUs), water quality criteria (WQC), and an antidegradation policy. States determine DUs subject to EPA approval. The purpose of designating uses is to identify the activities the state expects the water body to support. Common DUs include the following: drinking water, water-based recreation, fishing/eating, aquatic life, agriculture water supply, and industrial water supply. Although in some cases, the DUs have already been attained, in other cases, the current conditions in a water body do not support all the DUs. In cases like this, DUs might more accurately be thought of as *desired* uses. Generally, states assign different combinations of DUs not only to different water bodies, but to different portions of the same water body. A given segment will almost always be classified for more than one DU.

The second component of WQS is WQC. These are descriptions of the conditions in a water body necessary to support the DUs. WQC can be expressed numerically or in narrative terms. Numeric criteria are scientifically derived ambient concentrations, or other quantitative measures developed by the EPA or states, for various pollutants that adversely affect public health or aquatic life. These pollutants include such things as pH, turbidity units, temperature and toxicity units. WQC can also be narrative statements such as "no unreasonable interference with aquatic life" or "no toxic chemicals in toxic amounts." The EPA has provided states with three different methodologies for translating these criteria into numerical standards for permits. *See* American Paper Inst. v. EPA, 996 F.2d 346 (D.C. Cir. 1993). Economic factors can be considered when setting the DU for a water body but may not be considered when developing the WQC to protect a DU.

Section 304(a) of the Act requires the EPA to develop WQC. These serve as a point of reference for states to consider, though states frequently adopt more lenient standards and the EPA tends to approve them. Water quality standards could theoretically vary from state to state. However, state flexibility is limited by the requirement of EPA approval (even when states decline to follow EPA WQC), and by the EPA's antidegradation policy. This policy is designed to protect "existing uses" which are defined as those uses "actually attained in the water body on or after November 28, 1975, whether or not they are included in WQS." 40 C.F.R. § 131.3(e) (2002). The purpose of the antidegradation policy is to prevent backsliding from higher ambient water quality to lower ambient water quality. (The Prevention of Significant Deterioration provisions of the CAA function to similar effect.)

The respective roles of the federal and state governments in the water quality standards-setting process have not always been clear. In *Mississippi Commission on Natural Resources v. Costle*, 625 F.2d 1269 (5th Cir. 1980), the court attempted to clarify the EPA's relationship with the states. As the court understood the statute, the state's role is primarily to designate the appropriate *use* for a water body, while the EPA sets the criteria appropriate for various levels of use (fishable, swimmable, etc.). This coheres with the EPA's general hesitation to involve itself in the politically contentious question of desirable uses, while being more willing to intervene in the scientifically based process of setting water quality criteria. The court also upheld EPA's contention that economic factors are not relevant to setting the criteria. The *Mississippi Commission* opinion has been sharply criticized, however:

> Only one appellate decision has addressed the extent of EPA's authority to review a state's criteria judgments and use designations. In *Mississippi Commission on Natural Resources v. Costle,* the court found that intensive review by EPA of state use designation would amount to federal exercise of the zoning power Congress explicitly denied it. By contrast, EPA's review of the technical accuracy of state criteria judgments was perfectly proper. The court claimed to be accepting an EPA argument. In fact, however, EPA's regulatory program is approximately the reverse of the court's prescription. EPA's water quality standards rules assert a broad federal power to circumscribe the uses a state may choose for its water. The regulations declare that EPA will not approve state standards that allow water quality in a lake or stream to decline, no matter how compelling an argument might be made concerning local preferences or circumstances. Even if a state simply wants to maintain existing levels of water quality, EPA insists on a showing that improved water quality is unattainable by reasonable control measures.

William F. Pedersen, Jr., *Turning the Tide on Water Quality*, 15 ECOLOGY L.Q. 69, 93 (1988). Pedersen adds that the "legal soundness of these policies is highly debatable," but that Congress under the 1972 CWA effectively denied the EPA the authority and regulatory tools it needed to properly set and implement water quality standards or to ensure attainment of state WQS, such that WQS policy generally is a "muddle." *Id.* at 92–94. He further contends that the current use designations often are arbitrary. *Id.* at 94–95. As time goes on, progress using technology-based standards may slow, because such standards may become more difficult to enforce as they become more burdensome, and because they may be insufficient to assure adequate water quality in some areas. Water quality standards will attain greater significance, however, as it becomes increasingly difficult to make further progress using technology-based standards.

Water quality standards have a number of important consequences. For example, they may result in more stringent regulation of point sources that contribute pollutants to a water body that fails to achieve WQS. Section 301(b)(1)(c) requires the EPA to establish more stringent effluent limitations than § 301 would normally require, if necessary to achieve WQS. EPA regulations also require that permit writers translate state WQS into enforceable effluent controls. This can be challenging however, especially when WQS are expressed as narrative goals such as "no unreasonable interference with aquatic life." (As noted earlier, in order to address this problem, at least in part, Congress has required that states adopt numerical criteria for *toxic* pollutants that could interfere with attaining WQS.) How should this concretely affect the effluent limits imposed on a pulp and paper mill that contributes pollutants to that water body, especially when that mill is already subject to applicable BPT, BCT and BAT standards, which themselves require stringent end-of-pipe controls? What if nonpoint sources also contribute to the failure of a water body to achieve WQS? Should point sources, which alone are subject to NPDES requirements, bear the full burden? Is this fair? To some extent §§ 319 and 303(d) are meant to address this problem. We turn to them in Section D below.

The EPA has been criticized for falling behind in issuance of WQC. *See* GAO, WATER POLLUTION: EPA NEEDS TO SET PRIORITIES FOR WATER QUALITY CRITERIA ISSUES (1994). The plans themselves have also been criticized: "As anyone who has dealt with state water quality plans knows, they are not 'plans' in a dictionary sense of the word; rather . . . they are more of a process composed of criteria/ standards, and abbreviated assessments, some published and some in file drawers, an environment in which site-specific implementation measures can lose their focus, if not simply get lost." Oliver A. Houck, *TMDLs III: A New Framework for the Clean Water Act's Ambient Standards Program*, 28 ENVTL. L. REP.,10415, 10420 (1998).

As with many of the major federal environmental statutes, environmental groups have been pushing—either via traditional lawsuits or agency petitions—to use the statutes to address climate change. The Clean Water Act is no exception. The Center for Biological Diversity has petitioned the EPA to address the problem of ocean acidification and its effect on water quality. Ocean acidification results from the ocean's absorption of carbon dioxide, the most prevalent of the greenhouse gases. Increasing amounts of CO_2 absorption are leading to increases in the acidity of the oceans. Ocean acidification can have profoundly negative consequences for marine animals, including coral reefs, by impairing their ability to manufacturer and maintain their shells and skeletons. In January of 2009 the EPA agreed to review the Center's petition seeking to have the agency establish more stringent PH standards for oceans. If the EPA were to meet the Center's demand and increase the stringency of PH standards, states would presumably need to evaluate and designate water bodies that violate the PH standards as impaired. In turn states would then need to regulate those sources contributing to the increased acidity. Presumably that would mean regulating sources of carbon dioxide emissions under the Clean Water Act. Can you imagine how such regulation might be carried out?

Water quality standards also play an important role in state certification under § 401 of the Act. This provision requires that federal agencies seeking to issue permits or licenses for activities that will discharge pollutants into waterways obtain state certification that the proposed activity will not violate water quality standards.

PUD NO. 1 OF JEFFERSON COUNTY v. WASHINGTON DEPARTMENT OF ECOLOGY

Supreme Court of the United States, 1994.
511 U.S. 700, 114 S.Ct. 1900, 128 L.Ed.2d 716.

JUSTICE O'CONNOR delivered the opinion of the Court.

Petitioners, a city and a local utility district, want to build a hydroelectric project on the Dosewallips River in Washington State. We must decide whether respondent, the state environmental agency, properly conditioned a permit for the project on the maintenance of specific minimum stream flows to protect salmon and steelhead runs.

The principal dispute in this case concerns whether the minimum stream flow requirement that the State imposed on the Elkhorn project [to preserve salmon and trout runs] is a permissible condition of a § 401 certification under the Clean Water Act. To resolve this dispute we must first determine the scope of the State's authority under § 401. We must then determine whether the limitation at issue here, the requirement that petitioners maintain minimum stream flows, falls within the scope of that authority.

There is no dispute that petitioners were required to obtain a certification from the State pursuant to § 401. Petitioners concede that, at a minimum, the project will result in two possible discharges—the release of dredged and fill material during the construction of the project, and the discharge of water at the end of the tailrace after the water has been used to generate electricity. Petitioners contend, however, that the minimum stream flow requirement imposed by the State was unrelated to these specific discharges, and that as a consequence, the State lacked the authority under § 401 to condition its certification on maintenance of stream flows sufficient to protect the Dosewallips fishery.

If § 401 consisted solely of subsection (a), which refers to a state certification that a "discharge" will comply with certain provisions of the Act, petitioners' assessment of the scope of the State's certification authority would have considerable force. Section 401, however, also contains subsection (d), which expands the State's authority to impose conditions on the certification of a project. Section 401(d) provides that any certification shall set forth "any effluent limitations and other limitations * * * necessary to assure that any applicant" will comply with various provisions of the Act and appropriate state law requirements. The language of this subsection contradicts petitioners' claim that the State may only impose water quality limitations specifically tied to a "discharge." The text refers to the compliance of the applicant, not the discharge. Section 401(d) thus allows the State to impose "other limitations" on the project in general to assure compliance with various provisions of the Clean Water Act and with "any other appropriate requirement of State law." Although the dissent asserts that this interpretation of § 401(d) renders § 401(a)(1) superfluous, we see no such anomaly. Section 401(a)(1) identifies the category of activities subject to certification—namely those with discharges. And § 401(d) is most reasonably read as authorizing additional conditions and limitations on the activity as a whole once the threshold condition, the existence of a discharge, is satisfied. * * *

We agree with the State that ensuring compliance with § 303 is a proper function of the § 401 certification. Although § 303 is not one of the statutory provisions listed in § 401(d), the statute allows states to impose limitations to ensure compliance with § 301 of the Act, 33 U.S.C. § 1311. Section 301 in turn incorporates § 303 by reference. As a consequence, state water quality standards adopted pursuant to § 303 are among the "other limitations" with which a State may ensure compliance through the § 401 certification process. This interpretation is consistent with EPA's view of the statute. Moreover, limitations to assure compliance with state water quality standards are also permitted by § 401(d)'s reference to "any other appropriate requirement of State law." We do not speculate on what additional state laws, if any, might be incorporated by this language.[3] But at a minimum, limitations imposed pursuant to state water quality standards adopted pursuant to § 303 are "appropriate" requirements of state law. Indeed, petitioners appear to agree that the State's authority under § 401 includes limitations designed to ensure compliance with state water quality standards.

Having concluded that, pursuant to § 401, States may condition certification upon any limitations necessary to ensure compliance with state water quality standards or any other "appropriate requirement of State law," we consider whether the minimum flow condition is such a limitation. Under § 303, state water quality standards must "consist of the designated uses of the navigable waters involved and the water quality criteria for such waters based upon such uses." In imposing the minimum stream flow requirement, the State determined that construction and operation of the project as planned would be inconsistent with one of the

---

3. The dissent asserts that § 301 is concerned solely with discharges, not broader water quality standards. Although § 301 does make certain discharges unlawful, it also contains a broad enabling provision which requires states to take certain actions, to wit: "In order to carry out the objective of this chapter [viz. the chemical, physical, and biological integrity of the Nation's water] there shall be achieved * * * not later than July 1, 1977, any more stringent limitation, including those necessary to meet water quality standards * * * established pursuant to any State law or regulations." This provision of § 301 expressly refers to state water quality standards, and is not limited to discharges.

designated uses of Class AA water, namely "[s]almonid [and other fish] migration, rearing, spawning, and harvesting." The designated use of the River as a fish habitat directly reflects the Clean Water Act's goal of maintaining the "chemical, physical, and biological integrity of the Nation's waters." Indeed, the Act defines pollution as "the man-made or man induced alteration of the chemical, physical, biological, and radiological integrity of water." Moreover, the Act expressly requires that, in adopting water quality standards, the State must take into consideration the use of waters for "propagation of fish and wildlife."

Petitioners assert, however, that § 303 requires the State to protect designated uses solely through implementation of specific "criteria." According to petitioners, the State may not require them to operate their dam in a manner consistent with a designated "use"; instead, say petitioners, under § 303 the State may only require that the project comply with specific numerical "criteria."

We disagree with petitioners' interpretation of the language of § 303(c)(2)(A). Under the statute, a water quality standard must "consist of the designated uses of the navigable waters involved and the water quality criteria for such waters based upon such uses." The text makes it plain that water quality standards contain two components. We think the language of § 303 is most naturally read to require that a project be consistent with both components, namely the designated use and the water quality criteria. Accordingly, under the literal terms of the statute, a project that does not comply with a designated use of the water does not comply with the applicable water quality standards. * * *

Washington's Class AA water quality standards are typical in that they contain several open-ended criteria which, like the use designation of the River as a fishery, must be translated into specific limitations for individual projects. For example, the standards state that "[t]oxic, radioactive, or deleterious material concentrations shall be less than those which may affect public health, the natural aquatic environment, or the desirability of the water for any use." Similarly, the state standards specify that "[a]esthetic values shall not be impaired by the presence of materials or their effects, excluding those of natural origin, which offend the senses of sight, smell, touch, or taste." We think petitioners' attempt to distinguish between uses and criteria loses much of its force in light of the fact that the Act permits enforcement of broad, narrative criteria based on, for example, "aesthetics." * * *

The State also justified its minimum stream flow as necessary to implement the "antidegradation policy" of § 303. When the Clean Water Act was enacted in 1972, the water quality standards of all 50 States had antidegradation provisions. These provisions were required by federal law. By providing in 1972 that existing state water quality standards would remain in force until revised, the Clean Water Act ensured that the States would continue their antidegradation programs. EPA has consistently required that revised state standards incorporate an antidegradation policy. And, in 1987, Congress explicitly recognized the existence of an "antidegradation policy established under [§ 303]." * * *

Petitioners contend that we should limit the State's authority to impose minimum flow requirements because FERC has comprehensive authority to license hydroelectric projects pursuant to the FPA, 16 U.S.C. § 791a et seq. In petitioners' view, the minimum flow requirement imposed here interferes with FERC's authority under the FPA. * * *

[T]he requirement for a state certification applies not only to applications for licenses from FERC, but to all federal licenses and permits for activities which may result in a discharge into the Nation's navigable waters. For example, a permit from the Army Corps of Engineers is required for the installation of any structure in the navigable waters which may interfere with navigation, including piers, docks, and ramps. Similarly, a permit must be obtained from the Army Corps of Engineers for the discharge of dredged or fill material, and from the Secretary of the Interior or Agriculture for the construction of reservoirs, canals and other water storage systems on federal land. We assume that a § 401 certification would also be required for some licenses obtained pursuant to these statutes. Because § 401's certification requirement applies to other statutes and regulatory schemes, and because any conflict with FERC's authority under the FPA is hypothetical, we are unwilling to read implied limitations into § 401. If FERC issues a license containing a stream flow condition with which petitioners disagree, they may pursue judicial remedies at that time.

In summary, we hold that the State may include minimum stream flow requirements in a certification issued pursuant to § 401 of the Clean Water Act insofar as necessary to enforce a designated use contained in a state water quality standard. The judgment of the Supreme Court of Washington, accordingly, is affirmed.

So ordered.

JUSTICE STEVENS, concurring.

While I agree fully with the thorough analysis in the Court's opinion, I add this comment for emphasis. For judges who find it unnecessary to go behind the statutory text to discern the intent of Congress, this is (or should be) an easy case. Not a single sentence, phrase, or word in the Clean Water Act purports to place any constraint on a State's power to regulate the quality of its own waters more stringently than federal law might require. In fact, the Act explicitly recognizes States' ability to impose stricter standards.

JUSTICE THOMAS, with whom JUSTICE SCALIA joins, dissenting.

The Court today holds that a State, pursuant to § 401 of the Clean Water Act, may condition the certification necessary to obtain a federal license for a proposed hydroelectric project upon the maintenance of a minimum flow rate in the river to be utilized by the project. In my view, the Court makes three fundamental errors. First, it adopts an interpretation that fails adequately to harmonize the subsections of § 401. Second, it places no meaningful limitation on a State's authority under § 401 to impose conditions on certification. Third, it gives little or no consideration to the fact that its interpretation of § 401 will significantly disrupt the carefully crafted federal-state balance embodied in the Federal Power Act. Accordingly, I dissent. * * *

Although the Court notes in passing that "[t]he limitations included in the certification become a condition on any Federal license," it does not acknowledge or discuss the shift of power from FERC to the States that is accomplished by its decision. Indeed, the Court merely notes that "any conflict with FERC's authority under the FPA" in this case is "hypothetical" at this stage, because "FERC has not yet acted on petitioners' license application." We are assured that "it is quite possible * * * that any FERC license would contain the same conditions as the State § 401 certification."

The Court's observations simply miss the point. Even if FERC might have no objection to the stream flow condition established by respondents in this case, such a happy coincidence will likely prove to be the exception, rather than the rule. In issuing licenses, FERC must balance the Nation's power needs together with the need for energy conservation, irrigation, flood control, fish and wildlife protection, and recreation. State environmental agencies, by contrast, need only consider parochial environmental interests. Cf., e.g., Wash.Rev.Code § 90.54.010(2) (1992) (goal of State's water policy is to "insure that waters of the state are protected and fully utilized for the greatest benefit to the people of the state of Washington"). As a result, it is likely that conflicts will arise between a FERC-established stream flow level and a state-imposed level.

NOTES

1. Note Justice Thomas's rather jaundiced view of environmental regulation by the states, which he considers to reflect only parochial local interests, as opposed to the national interests behind increased power generation. It remains to be seen whether this attitude toward the environment will be reflected in his positions on other legal issues.

2. Consider the following assessment of the majority opinion:

After reflecting about the Supreme Court decision in *PUD No. 1*, I recalled my high school chemistry teacher who, after observing my inelegant experimental techniques, stated that the Jesuits used an old Latin expression in such circumstances—*non disputandum resultatem* [sic]. He roughly translated this to mean you don't argue with good results. * * *

In the area of statutory interpretation, unlike high-school chemistry experiments however, good technique is at least as important as good results. A good interpretive approach requires that courts consider more than mere text; they must carefully consider context as well. In the legal dispute at the heart of *PUD No. 1*, that context is defined not only by the

CWA, but also by the FPA, the Court's interpretations of that statute, and how FERC and the state agencies have exercised the powers they believe have been delegated them. In enacting the FPA, Congress gave FERC the power to balance a variety of interests, including aesthetic, wildlife protection, recreation, preservation, and economic interests, against the need for energy. Congress also carved out an exception to FERC's authority and gave states the power to ensure that projects do not violate WQSs. Because, in conducting its balancing, FERC's concerns about the economic, development, and electric power factors have largely overwhelmed all other factors, courts, when they consider the interaction of the CWA and FPA, need to safeguard the single consideration that Congress has identified as beyond FERC's ability to balance out of existence. When interpreting these statutes, courts must also not view the in-state water quality factor so broadly that it alone overwhelms all other factors, at least some of which will have out-of-state impacts unlikely to be considered by the state when identifying its WQSs.

Michael P. Healy, *The Attraction and Limits of Textualism: The Supreme Court Decision in PUD No. 1 of Jefferson County v. Washington Department of Ecology*, 5 N.Y.U. ENVTL. L. J. 382, 441–43 (1996). *See also* Michael P. Healy, *Still Dirty After Twenty–Five Years: Water Quality Standard Enforcement and the Availability of Citizen Suits*, 24 ECOLOGY L.Q. 393 (1997) (considering "whether the Clean Water Act permits citizen suit enforcement of state WQSs and whether allowing such suits constitutes good public policy.").

3.   In *S.D. Warren Co. v. Maine Board of Envt'l Protection*, 547 U.S. 370 (2006), the U.S. Supreme Court held in an unanimous decision that a hydroelectric power company, in applying for renewal of a FERC licence, was required to obtain Section 401 certification from the state of Maine for operating a series of dams on the Presumpscot River. S.D. Warren argued that a discharge of water from the dams did not constitute a discharge subject to Section 401 certification. The Supreme Court disagreed, analyzing the plain language of Section 401 and recognizing that dams alter water quality, can change the movement and flow of a body of water, and can destroy natural habitat for fish and other aquatic life. *Id.*

4.   In an attempt to build on the *PUD* case and address the problem of nonpoint source pollution, a coalition of environmental groups challenged the U.S. Forest Service's issuance of grazing leases without first obtaining certification from the state of Oregon, pursuant to section 401 of the CWA, that the grazing would not cause violations of state water quality standards. On appeal, the court held that water quality certifications under section 401 are not required for nonpoint sources of pollution, apparently closing this avenue for addressing the nonpoint source problem. *See* Oregon Natural Desert Ass'n v. Dombeck, 172 F.3d 1092 (9th Cir. 1998), *cert. denied*, 528 U.S. 964 (1999).

5.   In October, 2000, in the wake of the 9th Circuit's rejection of the section 401 strategy in *Dombeck*, eight federal agencies jointly issued a Unified Federal Policy for a Watershed Approach to Federal Land and Resource Management. *See* 65 Fed. Reg. 62566–601. The policy, which describes how land management will be governed on 800 million acres of federal lands, calls for enhanced collaboration between federal land managers and

state, tribal, and private landowners. The proposed policy may be the one of the most important tools for controlling nonpoint source pollution in the future. We take up the non-point source problem in Section D, below.

h. Water Quality Standards and Interstate Pollution

The EPA has adopted the view that the water quality standards provisions of the Act can be used to regulate interstate water pollution, by requiring the upstream state's permit to be consistent with downstream water quality standards. The Supreme Court reviewed this policy in the following case.

ARKANSAS v. OKLAHOMA

Supreme Court of the United States, 1992.
503 U.S. 91, 112 S.Ct. 1046, 117 L.Ed.2d 239.

JUSTICE STEVENS delivered the opinion of the Court.

[An Arkansas sewage treatment plant received an EPA permit to discharge into a stream that ultimately flows (via some creeks) into the Illinois River 22 miles upstream of the Oklahoma border. The state of Oklahoma challenged the permit before an EPA hearing officer, on the ground that the discharge violated Oklahoma's water quality standards, which allow no degradation of water quality in that portion of the Illinois River. EPA granted the permit after concluding that the discharge would cause no detectable change in water quality. The Court of Appeals ruled, however, that a permit cannot be issued if the proposed discharge would contribute to an existing violation of water quality standards.]

The parties have argued three analytically distinct questions concerning the interpretation of the Clean Water Act. First, does the Act require the EPA, in crafting and issuing a permit to a point source in one State, to apply the water quality standards of downstream States? Second, even if the Act does not require as much, does the Agency have the statutory authority to mandate such compliance? Third, does the Act provide, as the Court of Appeals held, that once a body of water fails to meet water quality standards no discharge that yields effluent that reach the degraded waters will be permitted?

In this case, it is neither necessary nor prudent for us to resolve the first of these questions. In issuing the Fayetteville permit, the EPA assumed it was obligated by both the Act and its own regulations to ensure that the Fayetteville discharge would not violate Oklahoma's standards. As we discuss below, this assumption was permissible and reasonable and therefore there is no need for us to address whether the Act requires as much. Moreover, much of the analysis and argument in the briefs of the parties relies on statutory provisions that govern not only federal permits issued pursuant to §§ 401(a) and 402(a), but also state permits issued under § 402(b). It seems unwise to evaluate those arguments in a case such as this one, which only involves a federal permit.

Our decision not to determine at this time the scope of the Agency's statutory obligations does not affect our resolution of the second question, which concerns the Agency's statutory authority. Even if the Clean Water Act itself does not require the Fayetteville discharge to comply with Oklahoma's water quality standards, the statute clearly does not limit the EPA's authority to mandate such compliance.

Since 1973, EPA regulations have provided that an NPDES permit shall not be issued "[w]hen the imposition of conditions cannot ensure compliance with the applicable water quality requirements of all affected States." Those regulations—relied upon by the EPA in the issuance of the Fayetteville permit—constitute a reasonable exercise of the Agency's statutory authority. * * *

Notwithstanding this apparent reasonableness, Arkansas argues that our description in *Ouellette* [*supra,* page 695] of the role of affected States in the permit process and our characterization of the affected States' position as "subordinate," indicates that the EPA's application of the Oklahoma standards was error. We disagree. Our statement in *Ouellette* concerned only an affected State's input into the permit process; that input is clearly limited by the plain language of § 402(b). Limits on an affected State's direct participation in permitting decisions, however, do not in any way constrain the EPA's authority to require a point source to comply with downstream water quality standards.

Arkansas also argues that regulations requiring compliance with downstream standards are at odds with the legislative history of the Act and with the statutory scheme established by the Act. Although we agree with Arkansas that the Act's legislative history indicates that Congress intended to grant the Administrator discretion in his oversight of the issuance of NPDES permits, we find nothing in that history to indicate that Congress intended to preclude the EPA from establishing a general requirement that such permits be conditioned to ensure compliance with downstream water quality standards.

Similarly, we agree with Arkansas that in the Clean Water Act Congress struck a careful balance among competing policies and interests, but do not find the EPA regulations concerning the application of downstream water quality standards at all incompatible with that balance. Congress, in crafting the Act, protected certain sovereign interests of the States; for example, § 510 allows States to adopt more demanding pollution-control standards than those established under the Act. Arkansas emphasizes that § 510 preserves such state authority only as it is applied to the waters of the regulating State. Even assuming Arkansas's construction of § 510 is correct, that section only concerns state authority and does not constrain the EPA's authority to promulgate reasonable regulations requiring point sources in one State to comply with water quality standards in downstream States.

For these reasons, we find the EPA's requirement that the Fayetteville discharge comply with Oklahoma's water quality standards to be a reasonable exercise of the Agency's substantial statutory discretion.

The Court of Appeals construed the Clean Water Act to prohibit any discharge of effluent that would reach waters already in violation of existing water quality standards. We find nothing in the Act to support this reading.

The interpretation of the statute adopted by the court had not been advanced by any party during the agency or court proceedings. Moreover, the Court of Appeals candidly acknowledged that its theory "has apparently never before been addressed by a federal court." The only statutory provision the court cited to support its legal analysis was § 402(h), which merely authorizes the EPA (or a state permit program) to prohibit a publicly owned treatment plant that is violating a condition of its NPDES permit from accepting any additional pollutants for treatment until the ongoing violation has been corrected. Although the Act contains several provisions directing compliance with state water quality standards, the parties have pointed to nothing that mandates a complete ban on discharges into a waterway that is in violation of those standards. The statute does, however, contain provisions designed to remedy existing water quality violations and to allocate the burden of reducing undesirable discharges between existing sources and new sources. Thus, rather than establishing the categorical ban announced by the Court of Appeals—which might frustrate the construction of new plants that would improve existing conditions—the Clean Water Act vests in the EPA and the States broad authority to develop long-range, area-wide programs to alleviate and eliminate existing pollution. To the extent that the Court of Appeals relied on its interpretation of the Act to reverse the EPA's permitting decision, that reliance was misplaced. * * *

In sum, the Court of Appeals made a policy choice that it was not authorized to make. Arguably, as that court suggested, it might be wise to prohibit any discharge into the Illinois River, even if that discharge would have no adverse impact on water quality. But it was surely not arbitrary for the EPA to conclude—given the benefits to the River from the increased flow of relatively clean water and the benefits achieved in Arkansas by allowing the new plant to operate as designed—that allowing the discharge would be even wiser. It is not our role, or that of the Court of Appeals, to decide which policy choice is the better one, for it is clear that Congress has entrusted such decisions to the Environmental Protection Agency.

NOTES

1. *See also* City of Albuquerque v. Browner, 97 F.3d 415 (10th Cir. 1996) (finding that upstream state must respect water quality standards adopted by downstream Indian tribe acting under authority of section 518).

2. The Court leaves open the question of whether state-issued permits (as opposed to the EPA-approved permit in the case) must comply with the

water quality standards of downstream states. Given the Court's deference to the EPA's regulations, however, there seems to be a strong case for extending the ruling to state permits.

Many states receive more than half of their water pollution from neighboring states, yet major differences exist between permit standards among states. For instance, according to a 1996 GAO Report, Pennsylvania's criterion for arsenic was 2500 times more stringent than New York's. This situation has given rise to increasing concern about disparities, and may result in mounting efforts to take advantage of the *Arkansas* opinion to impose restraints on "underregulated" out-of-state sources. *See* GAO, WATER POLLUTION: DIFFERENCES AMONG THE STATES IN ISSUING PERMITS LIMITING THE DISCHARGE OF POLLUTANTS (1996). For some doubts about the efficacy of the Clean Water Act as construed in *Arkansas v. Oklahoma, see* Robert L. Glicksman, *Watching the River Flow: The Prospects for Improved Interstate Water Pollution Control,* 43 WASH. U. J. URB. & CONTEMP. L. 119 (1993).

D. NONPOINT SOURCE POLLUTION

1. AREA PLANNING

The permits (and related effluent limitations and water quality requirements) that we have considered so far are required only for point sources. Yet most estimates suggest that nonpoint sources contribute a significant percentage of pollutants, including toxic pollutants, to the nation's waterways. And these pollutants are contributing to the failure of water bodies to meet WQS.

* * * The National Water Quality Inventory Report to Congress for 1998 indicates that of the 23 percent of the Nation's rivers and streams that have been assessed, 35 percent do not fully support water quality standards or uses and an additional 10 percent are threatened. Of the 32 percent of estuary waterbodies assessed, 44 percent are not fully supporting water quality standards or uses and an additional 9 percent are threatened. Of the 42 percent of lakes, ponds, and reservoirs assessed (not including the Great Lakes), 45 percent are not fully supporting water quality standards or uses and an additional 9 percent are threatened. The report also indicates that 90 percent of the Great Lakes shoreline miles have been assessed, and that 96 percent of these are not fully supporting water quality standards and an additional 2 percent are threatened.

The report indicates that pollutants in rainwater runoff from urban and agricultural land are a leading source of impairment. Agriculture is the leading source of pollutants in assessed rivers and streams, contributing to 59 percent of the reported water quality problems and affecting about 170,000 river miles. Hydromodification [e.g., dam-building, channelization and streambank erosion] is the second leading source of impairment, and urban runoff/storm sewers is the third major source, contributing respectively 20 percent and 12 percent of reported water quality problems. * * *

65 Fed. Reg. 43,586, 43,587 (July 13, 2000).

As we described above, some of the sources one might consider to be non-point source pollution are now subject to the storm water provisions contained in Section 402 (p). Many other sources, particularly in non-urban areas, are not, however, well regulated. What is to be done about the failure of a substantial number of the nation's water bodies to meet WQS? The most significant remaining gap in the Act is the lack of regulation of runoff from agricultural water pollutants. The Act does provide in § 208 for the adoption of "areawide waste management plans" which may include controls on nonpoint sources, but these plans are unenforceable: the EPA cannot develop and implement a § 208 plan if the state fails to do so, or if the state plan is inadequate. *See* Note, *State and Federal Land Use Regulation: An Application to Groundwater and Non-point Source Pollution Control*, 95 YALE L.J. 1433, 1438–39 (1986). Historically, local governments have been especially resistant to area planning, which was a condition of federal grants for POTW construction:

> * * * Any community that strenuously objected to a section 208 areawide plan could delay POTW construction for years through recourse to judicial review and political lobbying, which would impede the statutory and EPA goal of achieving rapid water pollution control progress. If EPA found areawide or state plans inadequate, its only enforcement sanction was to withhold federal grants, which would delay pollution control progress and would not penalize the communities that resisted construction of large-scale POTWs.

Howard Latin, *Regulatory Failure, Administrative Incentives, and the New Clean Air Act*, 21 ENVTL. L. 1647, 1656 (1991). States are also required to put in place a "continuing planning process" as one requirement for obtaining approval of their permit programs under § 402, but the EPA has been reluctant to enforce regulation of nonpoint sources as a condition of approving state programs.

The 1987 Amendments to the CWA included a new attempt to regulate nonpoint source pollution in § 319, which requires states to identify waters that fail to achieve WQS because of nonpoint sources, and to develop comprehensive management plans, subject to EPA approval. These plans must include a process for identifying "best management practices" and other controls to reduce nonpoint source pollution. The EPA has no authority to prepare and implement nonpoint source controls, however, if the state's program is inadequate, or if the state refuses to produce a plan.

This non-point source provision was part of the motivation for President Reagan's unsuccessful veto attempt on January 30, 1987:

> This new program threatens to become the ultimate whip hand for Federal regulators. For example, in participating States, if farmers

have more run-off from their land than the Environmental Protection Agency decides is right, the Agency will be able to intrude into decisions such as how and where the farmers must plow their fields, what fertilizers they must use, and what kind of cover crops they must plant. To take another example, the Agency will be able to become a major force in local zoning decisions that will determine whether families can do such basic things as build a new home. That is too much power for anyone to have, least of all the Federal Government.

* * * Let me repeat—controlling nonpoint source pollution has the potential to touch, in the most intimate ways, practically all of us as citizens, whether farmers, business people, or homeowners. I do not believe State programs should be subject to Federal control.

Contrary to President Reagan's dire prediction, however, § 319 has been said to have "not enough carrot, not enough stick, and too much of the same planning imperatives that characterized § 208." David Zaring, *Federal Legislative Solutions to Agricultural Nonpoint Source Pollution*, 26 ENVTL. L. REP. 10128, 10132 (1996). Section 319 seems to have "added little in the way of rigor to the Act's nonpoint source controls." Robert W. Adler, *Controlling Nonpoint Source Water Pollution: Is Help on the Way (From the Courts or EPA)?*, 31 ENVTL. L. REP. 10271 (2001). States may provide incentives to nonpoint sources to encourage the adoption of BMPs, but nothing in the statute makes the management plans enforceable against nonpoint sources themselves. The statute authorizes the EPA to provide technical and financial assistance to states to help with the development and implementation of management plans, with federal funds not to exceed 60 per cent of the costs of implementation. § 319(h)(3). Grants are also limited so that no one state can receive more than 15% of the total appropriated for this purpose. § 319(h)(4). Given the massive undertaking any state faces if it chooses to regulate nonpoint sources like agriculture, ranching, mining or forestry, the extent of federal support appears to be vanishingly small. Thus the section's reporting and planning mandate imposed on states by § 319 may prompt states to consider where the nonpoint source problems lie and how to address the nonpoint source problems through BMP plans, but it offers no penalties and very weak financial incentives to motivate meaningful state action. Either the states will undertake to regulate nonpoint sources on their own initiative or they won't, and there appears to be nothing the EPA can do but to cheer on the ambitious and chide the apathetic.

2. TOTAL MAXIMUM DAILY LOADS (TMDLS)

Section 303(d) has emerged as the most promising provision of the Act for addressing the lingering problem of nonpoint source pollution. Under § 303(d), states are required to identify those waters within their boundaries that do not meet water quality standards, to establish TMDLs for those waters capable of achieving those standards, and to incorporate these pollutant loads into a state planning process. This provision of the law remained largely dormant until the EPA was driven by lawsuits to activate it in 1996. *See* Alaska Center for the Environment v. Browner, 20 F.3d 981 (9th Cir. 1994). The TMDL process adopts an ambient approach to regulating water quality, consistent with the use of water quality standards as a back-up to the technology-based thrust of the CWA. The TMDL process requires states to work backwards from effect to cause, in order to ensure that water bodies meet WQS. TMDLs have the potential to turn WQS into enforcement tools. While the TMDL provision does not directly mandate regulation of non-point sources, it does require state *planning* to impose effluent limitations on those sources.

The TMDL process is severely constrained by the difficulties of implementation. Establishing TMDLs requires the states to identify the amounts of pollution that can be tolerated by individual water bodies before WQS will be violated. However, the statute does not dictate the means by which such load targets will be achieved, or by which sources of pollution, nor does it set deadlines by which WQS must be attained. The absence of legal mechanisms for implementing controls on nonpoint sources has created an equity problem because water bodies that do not meet WQS may result in more stringent NPDES permit limits for point sources, even when the failure to meet WQS is substantially the fault of nonpoint sources.

a. Point sources

The following case demonstrates that ambient water quality regulation in the form of WQS and TMDLs can lead the EPA to set effluent limits on point sources (here pulp and paper mills) that are more stringent than would apply under the traditional technology-based limits. As often is the case, however, the EPA was attacked in court by both environmentalists—arguing that the TMDLs were set too low in an arbitrary or capricious manner—and the regulated industry—arguing that the EPA lacked the statutory authority to regulate in line with TMDLs before it had determined if less costly technology-based effluent limits were inadequate to meet the states' WQS. The 9th Circuit rejected both challenges: It held that the EPA acted reasonably in setting the TMDLs at the level it chose, and that the EPA acted within its statutory authority by setting stricter ambient water quality effluent limits for point sources than would have applied under the usual technology-based limits.

DIOXIN/ORGANOCHLORINE CENTER v. EPA

United States Court of Appeals, Ninth Circuit, 1995.
57 F.3d 1517.

LEAVY, CIRCUIT JUDGE.

Appellants, environmental groups and paper and pulp mills, challenge on opposing grounds the district court's grant of summary judgment in favor of the Environmental Protection Agency ("EPA") on appellants' claims that the EPA violated the Clean Water Act ("Act"), by establishing total maximum daily load limits for the discharge of the toxic pollutant dioxin into the Columbia River. We affirm.

FACTS AND PRIOR PROCEEDINGS

In the late 1980's, a series of EPA-sponsored and independent biological studies revealed that high levels of 2,3,7,8—tetrachlorodibenzo-p-dioxin ("TCDD" or for the purposes of this appeal simply "dioxin") were accumulating in the tissue of fish located downstream from pulp and paper mills in the Columbia River Basin. These studies also confirmed that the mills themselves were a significant source of dioxin contamination as a result of their use of chlorine-based chemicals to bleach wood and other raw materials used in the paper production cycle.

Oregon, Washington, and Idaho had already adopted applicable water quality standards under state law for waters in the Columbia Basin including the Columbia, Snake, and Willamette Rivers. The EPA found that these water quality standards limited the permissible ambient concentration of dioxin to 0.013 parts per quadrillion ("ppq") as provided in the EPA's Quality Criteria for Water tables issued in 1986. Due in large part to the mills activity, the dioxin concentration in these waters exceeded the level permitted by the state standards.

Pursuant to 33 U.S.C. § 1314(l), the states listed the mills as particular point sources believed to be impairing the water quality. Section 1314 required the development of individual control strategies ("ICS") expressed as individual National Pollution Discharge Elimination System ("NPDES") permits which would result in the attainment of the applicable water quality standard within three years.

Oregon, Washington, and Idaho also identified the Columbia River as "water quality limited" pursuant to § 1313(d)(1)(A), finding that the levels of dioxin being discharged into the Columbia River violated the applicable state water quality standards. Once the states had made this finding under § 1313(d)(1)(A), the states, pursuant to § 1313(d)(1)(C), or, the EPA, pursuant to § 1313(d)(2), were required to establish a Total Maximum Daily Load ("TMDL") for dioxin.

A TMDL defines the specified maximum amount of a pollutant which can be discharged or "loaded" into the waters at issue from all combined sources. Thus a TMDL represents the cumulative total of all "load allocations" which are in turn best estimates of the discrete loading attributed to nonpoint sources, natural background sources, and individual wasteload allocations ("WLAs"), that is, specific portions of the total load allocated to individual point sources. When a TMDL and specific wasteload allocations for point sources have been established, any NPDES permits issued to a point source must be consistent with the terms of the TMDL and WLA.

The states decided against issuing TMDLs and WLAs on their own authority. Instead, after consultation and involvement in the development of the draft TMDL, the states requested the EPA to issue the proposed and final TMDL as a federal action under the authority of § 1313(d)(2). * * * On February 25, 1991, the EPA established the final TMDL for dioxin discharge into the Columbia River. * * *

[The environmental groups, Dioxin, Organochlorane Center and Columbia River United (DOC)] argues that the TMDL developed by the EPA fails to conform to the water quality standards adopted by the states because it is not stringent enough. DOC asserts that the TMDL was based on arbitrary or capricious decisions by the EPA constituting an abuse of discretion. The Mills, on the other hand, argue that the EPA violated the Clean Water Act by issuing a TMDL prior to establishing less burdensome technology-based limitations which the Mills assert are required by the Act before the EPA can establish TMDLs. * * *

B. Discussion

DOC contends that the TMDL fails to implement state water quality standards because it: 1) inadequately protects aquatic life and wildlife, 2) inadequately protects certain human subpopulations, and 3) fails to consider the cumulative effect of dioxin-related pollutants in the water system.

1. The TMDL: Aquatic Life and Wildlife

DOC's complaints

DOC maintains that the EPA abused its discretion by arbitrarily and capriciously considering only the risk to *human* life and failing to consider the effect of dioxin on *animal* life.

DOC first disputes the evidence relied upon by the district court to support its decision. In order to establish that it appropriately considered the effect of the TMDL on aquatic life and wildlife, the EPA filed in the district court an affidavit of Richard Albright. * * * In his affidavit Albright stated:

> During development of the TMDL, it was determined that an ambient concentration of [dioxin] of .013 ppq was necessary to protect human health. In addition, I concluded during development of the TMDL that an ambient concentration of .013 ppq would be protective of aquatic life and wildlife, and would therefore implement the state narrative water quality standards for aquatic life and wildlife protection.

> In reaching this conclusion, I was aware of the data and analyses regarding the dioxin toxicity to aquatic life and wildlife contained in the following documents. The Fish and Wildlife Service Dioxin Hazard Document, ... EPA's Background Document to the Integrated Risk Assessment for Dioxins and Furans from Chlorine Bleaching in Pulp and Paper Mills, ... and EPA's dioxin criteria guidance document, entitled "Ambient Water Quality Criteria for 2,3,7,8,-tetracholoro-dibenzo-p-diozin," dated 1984.... The TMDL was intended and designed to provide protection to humans aquatic life and wildlife.

DOC discounts the significance of Albright's affidavit and contends that the documents referred to do not support the conclusion that the EPA had adequately considered the effect of the TMDL on aquatic life and wildlife. We consider each of the documents cited by Albright in order to determine whether they provide sufficient evidence to support the EPA's setting of a TMDL at 0.013 ppq to protect aquatic biota and wildlife.

a. EPA, Office of Water Regulations and Standards, *Ambient Water Quality Criteria for 2,3,7,8–Tetrachloro-dibenzo-p-dioxin,* (Feb. 1984).

DOC asserts that this document does not support the conclusion that a dioxin level of 0.013 ppq would protect fish and other wildlife. DOC quotes the study itself:

> The data that are available concerning the effects of [dioxin] on aquatic organisms and their uses do not allow the calculation of an acute or chronic toxicity value for any freshwater animal species.

This report however indicates that the lowest level at which adverse effects on *aquatic life* had been noted was at 0.0001 micrograms per liter or 100 ppq. *Id.* B1–7. The ambient concentration of 0.013 ppq allows for a dioxin exposure only one ten-thousandth of that value.

b. EPA, Office of Pesticides and Toxic Substances, *Background Document to the Integrated Risk Assessment for Dioxins and Furans from Chlorine Bleaching in Pulp and Paper Mills,* (July 1990).

DOC argues that this document fails to establish that the TMDL was protective of aquatic life:

> Currently sufficient data are not available concerning the chronic effect of [dioxin] ... on *aquatic* life to derive national water quality or sediment criteria for these contaminants.

The district court, however, found that this document, while not containing a estimate of the toxicity of dioxin for *aquatic* life, did justify the EPA's decision in regard to *wildlife*. This document indicates that the lowest concentration at which adverse effects had been observed in wildlife feeding upon aquatic life contaminated by dioxin was at dioxin concentrations of 3 parts per trillion ("ppt") in the consumed food items. The EPA estimates that the maximum fish tissue residues in food items expected under the TMDL are 0.07 ppt. This represents a level approximately 1/43rd of the level at which adverse effects had been observed.

c. U.S. Fish and Wildlife Service, *Dioxin Hazards to Fish, Wildlife and Invertebrates: A Synoptic Review,* Contaminant Hazard Reviews Report No. 8 (May 1986).

The Fish and Wildlife Service ("FWS") published this report in 1986. In it the FWS asserted that, "the limited data suggest that [dioxin] concentrations in water should not exceed 0.01 *ppt* to protect aquatic life, or 10 to 12 ppt in food items of birds and other wildlife." DOC argues that since the *Background Document* (b. above) recommended a lower figure of 3 ppt for a safe dioxin concentration in food items, this *Dioxin Hazards* report was "outdated and refuted by all the other more current evidence in the record."

The purpose of this document, however, is to establish that an 0.013 *ppq* ambient concentration of dioxin is protective of *aquatic life* in that the level set by the EPA is one one-thousandth of the 0.01 *ppt* level advocated by the FWS. DOC's focusing on the FWS' high recommendation of the concentration of dioxin which could safely be allowed in wildlife food items, i.e., 10–12 ppt, is irrelevant given the 0.07 ppt residue level estimated to occur in food items under the 0.013 ppq water concentration set by the EPA. * * *

In sum, the EPA was required by § 1313(d)(2) to develop a TMDL for dioxin in the context of inconclusive and diverse scientific data regarding the toxicity of dioxin. * * * We reject DOC's claim that the EPA failed to consider the effect of the TMDL on aquatic life and wildlife, and its claim that the ambient concentration selected fails to protect animal life. We conclude that the EPA's decision is supported by substantial evidence.

2. *The TMDL and Human Life on the Columbia*

Projecting that implementation of the TMDL would result in a 0.013 ppq ambient concentration of dioxin in the Columbia Basin, the EPA calculated that this figure would result in a bioaccumulation of dioxin in the tissue of freshwater fish equal to 65 picograms per kilo, i.e., approximately 0.07 ppt.

In order to calculate the quantity of dioxin that would in turn be consumed by humans, the EPA adopted as one of the relevant variables the national average total consumption rate for all freshwater and estuarine fish of 6.5 grams per day. Assuming a lifetime of consumption of this amount of fish per day, and assuming that all 6.5 grams were contaminated to the highest level possible under the TMDL, the agency determined that the average risk to health would still satisfy the general one-in-a-million risk level provided for by the state water quality standards.

DOC argues, however, that the EPA failed to consider the effect of this dioxin concentration level on certain human subpopulations which consume greater quantities of fish. DOC asserts that these subpopulations would not be protected to the one-in-a-million risk level.

While the EPA acknowledges that continuing scientific studies may indicate that subpopulations are not adequately protected by the TMDL, it states that its conclusion that the TMDL was adequately protective of human health was not at the time arbitrary or capricious. The EPA offers a variety of justifications for its decision:

> First, the EPA notes that the "potency factor" it adopted for dioxin was the most stringent in the world. Potency factors for dioxin used by other agencies or foreign governments would have resulted in numerical values between five and sixteen hundred times less stringent.

Second, the EPA argues that it reasonably concluded that higher consumption of fish among subpopulations did not imply that the total quantity of fish consumed would be maximally contaminated. The EPA notes that no definitive study had established the quantity and variety of *contaminated* fish consumed by these subpopulations. Since much of the fish population in the Columbia Basin consists of anadromous fish, *e.g.,* salmon and steelhead trout, which spend only limited time in contaminated river waters, the EPA argues that it was reasonable to assume that not all the fish tissue consumed by the subpopulations would be contaminated. Further, even if the fish were contaminated, they would not necessarily be contaminated at the highest concentrations possible.

As a result of these uncertainties, the EPA estimated that the total consumption of 150 grams of fish by these subpopulations would lead to no greater dioxin ingestion than would occur by consuming 6.5 grams of fully contaminated fish. On this assumption the subpopulations would be adequately protected.

In addition, the EPA argues that even assuming consumption of 150 grams of fully contaminated fish, as claimed by DOC, the risk level would still be only 23 in a million. This level of risk protection is within levels historically approved by the EPA and upheld by courts. * * *

We hold that the EPA's decision to adopt a 0.013 ppq ambient dioxin concentration cannot be considered arbitrary or capricious with regard to the effect of dioxin on human subpopulations * * *.

3. The TMDL and Dioxin–Related Compounds

DOC argues that limiting the amount of dioxin without consideration of the presence of other chemicals in the water which act in a similar fashion fails to achieve the level of safety mandated by the water quality standards of the states.

Nothing in the Clean Water Act requires TMDLs to be issued for all pollutants at once. In fact, regulations pertaining to TMDL implementation specifically provide that TMDLs may be developed on a specific pollutant basis, and the states bordering the Columbia River had decided to proceed on environmental cleanup according to a chemical-by-chemical priority. * * *

We hold that the EPA's decision to establish the dioxin TMDL at 0.013 ppq was within reasonable limits of its discretionary authority and reflected an adequate consideration of the facts. * * *

None of the bases asserted by the environmental groups provide sufficient grounds for overturning the EPA's decision as arbitrary or capricious. It appears that the EPA consistently took a conservative approach with a reasonably wide margin for safety. * * *

1. The Mills' Argument

The Mills contend that the plain language of 33 U.S.C. § 1313(d)(1)(A) prohibits—prior to the application and proven ineffectiveness of less burdensome technology-based pollution controls—a body of water from being listed as "water quality limited" and from being regulated by TMDLs. The Mills assert that because no effluent limitations were developed for dioxin under § 1311(b)(1)(A) or (B), the states improperly listed, and the EPA improperly approved, such waters as water quality limited. Accordingly, neither could the states or the EPA move to the subsequent step of implementing TMDLs for those waters pursuant to § 1313(d)(1)(C) or (2).

The Mills focus particular attention on the present tense language of § 1313(d)(1)(A), *i.e.,* "the effluent limitations of § 1311 ... *are not stringent enough* to implement any water quality standard applicable to such waters...." The Mills argue that the "plain language" of the provision prohibits the EPA from developing TMDLs prior to the proven failure of technology-based limitations.

The Mills state that the procedure of first developing and applying technology-based limitations is mandated by the legislative history of the Clean Water Act. They claim that Congress intended that technology-based limitations be imposed prior to water-quality-based controls in a manner which "would balance the costs and the benefits of pollution control." * * *

2. The EPA's Interpretation of § 1313(d)

The EPA argues that "we interpret section 1313(d) as requiring TMDLs where existing pollution controls will not lead to attainment of water quality standards." We take this as an assertion that when a state has listed a water as impaired by toxic pollutants, the EPA has authority to implement TMDLs for that toxic pollutant under § 1313(d) even before technological limitations have been developed and implemented pursuant to § 1311(b)(1)(A) or (B). We hold that the EPA's interpretation is reasonable and not contrary to congressional intent.

Section 1313(d)(1)(A) provides that states shall list waters as impaired when any technological limitations required by § 1311(b)(1)(A) and (B) fail to satisfy water quality standards. Section 1311(b)(1)(A) and (B), referred to in § 1313(d)(1)(A), require development of "effluent limitations for point sources ... which shall require the application of the best practicable control technology currently available." Section 1311(b)(1)(A) and (B) therefore require development of technology-based effluent limitations only for those point sources that are discharging pollutants subject by the Act to best practicable technology limitations ("BPT limitations"). The Act is clear, however, that *toxic* pollutants, such as dioxin, are subject, not to BPT limitations, but rather to best *available* technology limitations ("BAT limitations"). Dioxin is not a conventional pollutant but a *toxic* pollutant and is therefore not subject to BPT limitations but BAT limitations. *See* §§ 1311(b)(2), 1317.

The Mills argue:

Given that the Clean Water Act requires EPA to develop *BAT limitations* for toxic pollutants, the Mills acknowledge that a reasonable interpretation of the Act is to permit the establishment of TMDLs if BAT limitations are not stringent enough to achieve water quality standards, rather than interpreting the statute to require EPA to promulgate BPT limitations first in order to determine whether TMDLs are authorized.... Any other interpretation would inevitably lead to the conclusion the TMDLs are not authorized by toxic pollutants because BPT limitations are not established for toxic pollutants.

The Mills contend that the failure of § 1311(d)(1)(A) or (B) to require development of BPT limitations for the discharge of dioxin can only be interpreted to imply either that *BAT* limitations must first be developed and fail prior to listing the water as impaired under § 1313(d), or that TMDLs can never be issued under § 1313(d) for toxic pollutants. We agree with neither argument. * * *

We reject the Mills' claim that, prior to implementing TMDLs, § 1313(d) of the Act requires development and proven failure of BAT limitations for *toxic pollutants*. The Mills offer no authority for this interpretation and it is not supported by the language of the statute. BPT limitations are not required by § 1313(d) for dioxin because the limitations required by the provisions of § 1311 referred to in § 1313(d) are not applicable to toxic pollutants; thus any limitations required by those provisions of § 1311, as a matter of law, "are not stringent enough" to achieve established water quality standards. Nowhere does the Act prohibit the EPA from listing waters as impaired and implementing TMDLs for toxic pollutants pursuant to § 1313(d).

We conclude that § 1313(d) allows the EPA to establish TMDLs for waters contaminated with toxic pollutants without prior development of BAT limitations.* * *

* * * Federal and state governments should not be required to expend time-consuming effort on development and implementation of technology-based limitations when the issue is discharge of toxic pollutants. When only conventional pollutants are at issue, however, there is not the same pressing necessity to impose the burdens created by TMDLs:

Through [technological limitations], large numbers of pollutants and pollutant sources can be regulated, an initial and often preventative level of control can be achieved and economic impacts can be kept within reasonable limits *until such time as toxicity and exposure data are sufficient to justify more stringent control.*

See supra, A Legislative History of the Clean Water Act of 1977 at 1405 (1978) (emphasis added). * * *

We hold that the EPA's establishment of a TMDL for dioxin discharge into the Columbia River Basin is consistent with a reasonable interpretation and application of § 1313(d). * * *

Affirmed.

---

b. Nonpoint sources

Having established that the EPA may skip technology-based effluent limits and regulate point sources of pollution more stringently in order to meet TMDLs set to meet the states' ambient WQS, the next major question concerned the EPA's ability to regulate *nonpoint* sources of pollution, such as sediment run-off from forestry, under the TMDL scheme. In the following case, the EPA not only required California to set TMDLs for the Garcia River over California's objections (thus raising a 10th Amendment issue), but also required private landholders to include costly mitigation measures in their timber-harvesting permits in order to meet the TMDLs. Since there were no point sources of pollution on the stretch of the Garcia River where the logging was set to occur, the landowners argued that the EPA had exceeded its statutory authority because the TMDLs could only limit nonpoint sources of pollution on water bodies that were also polluted by point sources, and for which the existing point source effluent limitations were found to be inadequate to achieve water quality standards. As we shall see below, the 9th Circuit rejected the states' 10th Amendment argument, and held that the EPA's interpretation of the CWA is more reasonable than an interpretation that would exempt any water bodies only impacted by nonpoint sources of pollution from any regulation under the CWA.

PRONSOLINO v. NASTRI

United States Court of Appeals, Ninth Circuit, 2002.
291 F.3d 1123.

BERZON, CIRCUIT JUDGE.

[In 1998 the Pronsolinos and two other private landowners in the Garcia River watershed applied for timber harvesting permits from the California Department of Forestry (Forestry). Although there were no point sources of pollution along the stretch of the Garcia River near the planned logging, the EPA had set a TMDL for sediment that was 60% below historical loadings after entering a consent decree with environmental and fishermen's groups in earlier litigation. As a result, Forestry and the state's Regional Water Quality Control Board required the applicant landowners to incorporate mitigation measures in their logging permits to meet the Garcia River TMDL. The estimated combined loss of profits due to the mitigation measures was $12,314,000. The landowners challenged the EPA's authority under § 309(d) of the CWA to impose TMDLs on bodies of water polluted only by nonpoint sources. The District Court held for the EPA on a motion for summary judgment, and the Pronsolinos appealed.]

The United States Environmental Protection Agency ("EPA") required California to identify the Garcia River as a water body with insufficient pollution controls and, as required for waters so identified, to set so-called "total maximum daily loads" ("TMDLs")—the significance of which we explain later—for pollution entering the river. Appellants challenge the EPA's authority under the Clean Water Act ("CWA" or the "Act") § 303(d), to apply the pertinent identification and TMDL requirements to the Garcia River. The district court rejected this challenge, and we do as well.

CWA 303(d) requires the states to identify and compile a list of waters for which certain effluent limitations are not stringent enough to implement the applicable water quality standards for such waters. § 303(d)(1)(A). Effluent limitations pertain only to point sources of pollution; point sources of pollution are those from a discrete conveyance, such as a pipe or tunnel. Nonpoint sources of pollution are non-discrete sources; sediment run-off from timber harvesting, for example, derives from a nonpoint source. The Garcia River is polluted only by nonpoint sources. Therefore, neither the effluent limitations referenced in § 303(d) nor any other effluent limitations apply to the pollutants entering the Garcia River.

The precise statutory question before us is whether the phrase "are not stringent enough" triggers the identification requirement both for waters as to which effluent limitations apply [because there are point sources polluting them] but do not suffice to attain water quality standards and for waters as to which effluent limitations do not apply at all to the pollution sources impairing the water [because only nonpoint sources are polluting such waters]. We answer this question in the affirmative, a conclusion which triggers the application of the statutory TMDL requirement to waters such as the Garcia River. * * *

A. The Major Goals and Concepts of the CWA

* * *

[The] CWA uses distinctly different methods to control pollution released from point sources and those that are traceable to nonpoint sources. The Act directly mandates technological controls to limit the pollution point sources may discharge into a body of water. On the other hand, the Act "provides no direct mechanism to control nonpoint source pollution but rather uses the 'threat and promise' of federal grants to the states to accomplish this task," (citations omitted), thereby "recognizing, preserving, and protecting the primary responsibilities and rights of States to prevent, reduce, and eliminate pollution, [and] to plan the development and use ... of land and water resources...." § 101(b).

B.   The Structure of CWA 303

1.   *Water Quality Standards*

Section 303 is central to the Act's carrot-and-stick approach to attaining acceptable water quality without direct federal regulation of nonpoint sources of pollution. Entitled Water Quality Standards and Implementation Plans, the provision begins by spelling out the statutory requirements for water quality standards: "Water quality standards" specify a water body's "designated uses" and "water quality criteria," taking into account the water's "use and value for public water supplies, propagation of fish and wildlife, recreational purposes, and agricultural, industrial, and other purposes...." § 303(c)(2). The states are required to set water quality standards for *all* waters within their boundaries regardless of the sources of the pollution entering the waters. If a state does not set water quality standards, or the EPA determines that the state's standards do not meet the requirements of the Act, the EPA promulgates standards for the state. §§ 303(b), (c)(3)–(4).

2.   *Section 303(d): "Identification of Areas with Insufficient Controls; Maximum Daily Load"*

Section 303(d)(1)(A) requires each state to identify as "areas with insufficient controls" "those waters within its boundaries for which the effluent limitations required by section [301(b)(1)(A)] and section [301(b)(1)(B)] of this title are not stringent enough to implement any water quality standard applicable to such waters." *Id.* The CWA defines "effluent limitations" as restrictions on pollutants "discharged from point sources." CWA § 502(11). Section 301(b)(1)(A) mandates application of the "best practicable control technology" effluent limitations for most point source discharges. * * *

For waters identified pursuant to § 303(d)(1)(A) (the § 303(d)(1) list), the states must establish the "total maximum daily load" ("TMDL") for pollutants identified by the EPA as suitable for TMDL calculation. § 303(d)(1)(C). "A TMDL defines the specified maximum amount of a pollutant which can be discharged or 'loaded' into the waters at issue from all combined sources." *Dioxin/Organochlorine Center v. Clarke*, 57 F.3d 1517, 1520 (9th Cir. 1995) The TMDL "shall be established at a level necessary to implement the applicable water quality standards...." § 303(d)(1)(C).

Section 303(d)(2), in turn, requires each state to submit its § 303(d)(1) list and TMDLs to the EPA for its approval or disapproval. If the EPA approves the list and TMDLs, the state must incorporate the list and TMDLs into its continuing process, the requirements for which are set forth in § 303(e). § 303(d)(2). If the EPA disapproves either the § 303(d)(1) list or any TMDLs, the EPA must itself put together the missing document or documents. *Id.* The state then incorporates any EPA-set list or TMDL into the states continuing planning process. *Id.*

Each state must also identify all waters *not* placed on its § 303(d)(1) list (the "§ 303(d)(3) list") and "estimate" TMDLs for pollutants in those waters. § 303(d)(3). There is no requirement that the EPA approve the § 303(d)(3) lists or the TMDLs estimated for those waters. *Id.*

3. Continuing Planning Process

The final pertinent section of § 303, § 303(e), requiring each state to have a continuing planning process, gives some operational force to the prior information-gathering provisions. The EPA may approve a state's continuing planning process only if it "will result in plans for all navigable waters within such State" that include, inter alia, effluent limitations, TMDLs, areawide waste management plans for nonpoint sources of pollution, and plans for "adequate implementation, including schedules of compliance, for revised or new water quality standards." § 303(e)(3).

The upshot of this intricate scheme is that the CWA leaves to the states the responsibility of developing plans to achieve water quality standards if the statutorily-mandated point source controls will not alone suffice, while providing federal funding to aid in the implementation of the state plans. TMDLs are primarily informational tools that allow the states to proceed from the identification of waters requiring additional planning to the required plans. As such, TMDLs serve as a link in an implementation chain that includes federally-regulated point source controls, state or local plans for point and nonpoint source pollution reduction, and assessment of the impact of such measures on water quality, all to the end of attaining water quality goals for the nation's waters.

III. ANALYSIS

* * *

The EPA regulations pertinent to § 303(d)(1) lists and TMDLs focus on the attainment of water quality standards, whatever the source of any pollution. For instance, the EPA's regulations define TMDLs as the "sum of the individual WLAs [wasteload allocations] for point sources and LAs [load allocations] for nonpoint sources and natural background." 40 C.F.R. § 130.2(i). Section 130.2 also defines a "wasteload allocation" as the "portion of a receiving water's loading capacity that is allocated to one of its existing or future point sources of pollution," § 130.2(h), and a "load allocation" as the "portion of a receiving water's loading capacity that is attributed either to one of its existing or future nonpoint sources of pollution or to natural background sources," § 130.2(g). The load allocation regulation also advises that, if possible, "natural and nonpoint source loads should be distinguished." *Id.* No reason appears why, under this TMDL definition, the amount of either point source loads or nonpoint source loads cannot be zero. If the wasteload allocation is zero, then the TMDL would cover only the nonpoint sources and natural background sources. So read, the regulation provides that a TMDL can apply where there is no wasteload allocation for point source pollution.

Section 130.7 evinces the same understanding. That regulation directs states to identify those waters listed pursuant to § 303(d)(1) that still require the establishment of TMDLs if:

(i) Technology-based effluent limitations required by sections 301(b), 306, 307, or other sections of the Act;

(ii) More stringent effluent limitations (including prohibitions) required ... and

(iii) Other pollution control requirements (e.g., best management practices) required by local, States, or Federal authority are not stringent enough to implement any water quality standards ... applicable to such waters.

§ 130.7(b)(1). "Best management practices" pertain to nonpoint sources of pollution. CWA § 208; CWA § 319. So, again, section 130.7 does not distinguish between sources of pollution for purposes of applying the TMDL requirement. Instead, control requirements applicable to either type of pollution receive equal treatment in the quest to achieve water quality standards.

Also consistent with application of the § 303(d)(1) listing and TMDL requirements to waters impaired only by nonpoint sources is the regulation addressing water quality standards. Section 130.3 explains that "such standards serve the dual purposes of establishing the water quality goals for a specific water body and serving as the regulatory basis for establishment of water quality-based treatment controls and strategies beyond the technology-based level of treatment required...." 40 C.F.R. § 130.3. One purpose of water quality standards therefore—and not surprisingly—is to provide federally-approved goals to be achieved *both* by state controls and by federal strategies *other* than point-source technology-based limitations. This purpose pertains to waters impaired by both point and nonpoint source pollution. The regulations addressing states' water quality management plans, intended to attain the promulgated water quality standards, confirm this understanding. Such plans must include, among other things, TMDLs, effluent limitations, and "*nonpoint* source management and control." 40 C.F.R. § 130.6 (emphasis added).

In short, the EPA's regulations concerning § 303(d)(1) lists and TMDLs apply whether a water body receives pollution from point sources only, nonpoint sources only, or a combination of the two. The EPA has issued directives concerning the states' CWA § 303(d) requirements in conformity with this understanding of its regulations. * * * In light of the current regulations and the agency's understanding of those regulations, as well as the delegated authority of the EPA to interpret the CWA, the EPA's interpretation is entitled to *Chevron* deference. * * *

In short, Congress entrusted to the EPA the responsibility of approving or disapproving § 303(d)(1) lists, bestowing upon it the discretion that comes with such responsibility; the EPA has specialized experience regarding the CWA which this court lacks; and the agency has consistently interpreted the provisions at issue.

B. Plain Meaning and Structural Issues

1. The Competing Interpretations

Section 303(d)(1)(A) requires listing and calculation of TMDLs for "those waters within [the states] boundaries for which the effluent limitations required by section [301(b)(1)(A)] and section [301(b)(1)(B)] of this title *are not stringent enough to implement any water quality standard* applicable to such waters." § 303(d) (emphasis added). The precise statutory question before us is whether, as the Pronsolinos maintain, the term "not stringent enough to implement ... water quality standards" as used in § 303(d)(1)(A) must be interpreted to mean *both* that application of effluent limitations will not achieve water quality standards *and* that the waters at issue are subject to effluent limitations. As only waters with point source pollution are subject to effluent limitations, such an interpretation would exclude from the § 303(d) listing and TMDL requirements waters impaired only by nonpoint sources of pollution.

The EPA, as noted, interprets "not stringent enough to implement ... water quality standards" to mean "not adequate" or "not sufficient ... to implement any water quality standard," and does not read the statute as implicitly containing a limitation to waters initially covered by effluent limitations. According to the EPA, if the use of effluent limitations will not implement applicable water quality standards, the water falls within § 303(d)(1)(A) regardless of whether it is point or nonpoint sources, or a combination of the two, that continue to pollute the water.

2. The Language and Structure of § 303(d)

Whether or not the appellants' suggested interpretation is entirely implausible, it is at least considerably weaker than the EPA's competing construction. The Pronsolinos' version necessarily relies upon: (1) understanding "stringent enough" to mean "strict enough" rather than "thoroughgoing enough" or "adequate" or "sufficient"; (2) reading the phrase "not stringent enough" in isolation, rather than with reference to the stated goal of implementing "any water quality standard applicable to such waters." Where the answer to the question "not stringent enough for what?" is "to implement any [applicable] water quality standard," the meaning of "stringent" should be determined by looking forward to the broad goal to be attained, not backwards at the inadequate effluent limitations. * * * Based on the language of the contested phrase alone, then, the more sensible conclusion is that the § 303(d)(1) list must contain any waters for which the particular effluent limitations will not be adequate to attain the statute's water quality goals. * * *

3. The Statutory Scheme as a Whole

The Pronsolinos' objection to this view of § 303(d), and of *Dioxin*, is, in essence, that the CWA as a whole distinguishes between the regulatory schemes applicable to point and nonpoint sources, so we must assume such a distinction in applying §§ 303(d)(1)(A) and (C). We would hesitate in any case to read into a discrete statutory provision something that is not there because it is contained elsewhere in the statute. But here, the premise is wrong: There is no such general division throughout the CWA.

Point sources are treated differently from nonpoint sources for many purposes under the statute, but not all. In particular, there is no such distinction with regard to the basic purpose for which the § 303(d) list and TMDLs are compiled, the eventual attainment of state-defined water quality standards. * * *

True, there are, as the Pronsolinos point out, two sections of the statute as amended, § 208 and § 319, that set requirements exclusively for nonpoint sources of pollution. But the structural inference we are asked to draw from those specialized sections—that no *other* provisions of the Act set requirements for waters polluted by nonpoint sources—simply does not follow. Absent some irreconcilable contradiction between the requirements contained in §§ 208 and 319, on the one hand, and the listing and TMDL requirements of § 303(d), on the other, both apply.

There is no such contradiction. Section 208 provides for federal grants to encourage the development of state areawide waste treatment management plans for areas with substantial water quality problems, §§ 208(a), (f), and requires that those plans include a process for identifying and controlling nonpoint source pollution "to the extent feasible" § 208(b)(2)(F). Section 319, added to the CWA in 1987, directs states to adopt "nonpoint source management programs;" provides grants for nonpoint source pollution reduction; and requires states to submit a report to the EPA that "identifies those navigable waters within the State which, without additional action to control nonpoint sources of pollution, cannot reasonably be expected to attain or maintain applicable water quality standards or the goals and requirements of this chapter." § 319(a)(1)(A). This report must also describe state programs for reducing nonpoint source pollution and the process "to reduce, to the maximum extent practicable, the level of pollution" resulting from particular categories of nonpoint source pollution. §§ 319(a)(1)(C), (D).

The CWA is replete with multiple listing and planning requirements applicable to the same waterways (quite confusingly so, indeed), so no inference can be drawn from the overlap alone. * * *

Essentially § 319 encourages the states to institute an approach to the elimination of nonpoint source pollution similar to the federally-mandated effluent controls contained in the CWA, while § 303 encompasses a water quality based approach applicable to all sources of water pollution. As various sections of the Act encourage different, and complementary, state schemes for cleaning up nonpoint source pollution in the nation's waterways, there is no basis for reading any of those sections—including § 303(d)—out of the statute. * * *

Looking at the statute as a whole, we conclude that the EPA's interpretation of § 303(d) is not only entirely reasonable but considerably more convincing than the one offered by the plaintiffs in this case.

C. Federalism Concerns

The Pronsolinos finally contend that, by establishing TMDLs for waters impaired only by nonpoint source pollution, the EPA has upset the balance of federal-state control established in the CWA by intruding into the state's traditional control over land use. * * * The Garcia River TMDL identifies the maximum load of pollutants that can enter the Garcia River from certain broad categories of nonpoint sources if the river is to attain water quality standards. It does not specify the load of pollutants that may be received from particular parcels of land or describe what measures the state should take to implement the TMDL. Instead, the TMDL expressly recognizes that "implementation and monitoring" "are state responsibilities" and notes that, for this reason, the EPA did not include implementation or monitoring plans within the TMDL. Moreover, § 303(e) requires—separately from the § 303(d)(1) listing and TMDL requirements—that each state include in its continuing planning process "adequate implementation, including schedules of compliance, for revised or new water quality standards" "for all navigable waters within such State." § 303(e)(3). The Garcia River TMDL thus serves as an informational tool for the creation of the state's implementation plan, independently—and explicitly—required by Congress.

California chose both *if* and *how* it would implement the Garcia River TMDL. States must implement TMDLs only to the extent that they seek to avoid losing federal grant money; there is no pertinent statutory provision otherwise requiring implementation of § 303 plans or providing for their enforcement. * * *

We conclude that the Pronsolinos' federalism basis for reading § 303 against its own words and structure is unfounded.

IV. CONCLUSION

* * * We therefore hold that the EPA did not exceed its statutory authority in identifying the Garcia River pursuant to § 303(d)(1)(A) and establishing the Garcia River TMDL, even though the river is polluted only by nonpoint sources of pollution.

The decision of the district court is AFFIRMED.

OLIVER A. HOUCK, THE CLEAN WATER ACT TMDL PROGRAM V: AFTERSHOCK AND PRELUDE[4]

32 ENVTL. L. REP. 10385 (2002).

* * *

I. The Showdown

The year 2000 saw a dramatic showdown between Congress and the executive branch over TMDLs. In retrospect, it was unavoidable. * * *

---

4. Copyright ©, The Environmental Law Institute, 2002. Reprinted by permission. Oliver A. Houck is a Professor of Law at Tulane University.

The showdown concerned EPA's first ever, comprehensive regulations for the TMDL program. The Agency and the states had been operating under skeletal regulations originating in 1978 that repeated requirements of the statute but provided little additional guidance. As written earlier, the stage was set for underperformance, and underperformance happened.

Shocked into motion by citizen suits in the early 1990s, EPA struggled to get ahead of district court mandates with a flurry of TMDL guidance to the states that fleshed out preliminary requirements for impaired water listings and for the contents and schedules for TMDLs themselves. At the same time EPA convened a Federal Advisory Committee Act (FACA) committee with representation from state water agencies, agribusiness, timber, industrial point sources, municipal sources, environmentalists, Native Americans, academics, and, ex officio, EPA and the U.S. Department of Agriculture (USDA). Its mission was to forge a consensus on program regulations.

Consensus was not in the cards. At bottom, the timber and agriculture industries were not going to accept that CWA § 303(d) covered nonpoint sources or that, if it did, it required implementation plans. To these industries, the CWA's only lawful vehicle to abate their discharges was the voluntary, grant-in-aid program under § 319. TMDLs smacked of first ever regulation, a *causa belli*. * * *

EPA, for its part, could not let the issue slide. Environmental lawsuits were setting its agenda, case by case, state by state, with differing and at times highly demanding schedules for impaired waters listings and TMDLs. The Agency and the states were making decisions on the basis of guidance memoranda that had never been subjected to notice-and-comment rulemaking under the Administrative Procedure Act (APA) and that carried no force of law.

In July 1999, EPA proposed draft, comprehensive regulations for the TMDL program and launched a series of meetings, briefing sessions, and telethons in an attempt to calm the waters. This was to no avail. Most states and affected industries remained adamantly opposed. * * * [T]he Agency softened other aspects of its proposal, clarified that TMDL implementation plans could be satisfied through "voluntary means and education," lengthened the deadlines for TMDL submissions, and hoped for the best.

The rulemaking took a year. More than 34,000 comments were received, which, even discounting mass-mailings from industry trade associations, indicated no small controversy. At the same time, with little confidence in the administrative process, states and nonpoint industries turned up the heat and took their case to a very receptive Congress. Congressional committees held field hearings stocked with farmers and small woodlot owners afraid, and told, that EPA was going to require permits for the use of their land. Committees held hearings on Capitol Hill in which their mistrust of EPA was so marked that one took the unprecedented step of insisting that Agency witnesses provide their testimony under oath. Committee members accused EPA of "secret meetings" with environmentalists. Learning that an Undersecretary of Agriculture had cooperated with EPA in developing a timetable for nonpoint source TMDLs, a representative from Arkansas inserted a budget rider in the agriculture appropriations bill removing the Undersecretary from authority in the matter. The legislation passed.

By April 2000, battered by the House and Senate, EPA began adding concessions to its most vocal opponents. It would drop its proposal to include "threatened waters" in TMDLs despite its belief that attending to these waters early would save time and money later on. It would drop a requirement that gave waters used for human consumption and for endangered species priority attention despite its belief that these priorities were required by law. It would drop a process allowing the public to petition for review of TMDL decisions despite its belief that administrative review was preferable to litigation. It would promise flat out that forestry practices would not be subject to national pollutant discharge elimination system (NPDES) permitting "under any circumstances." And at seven congressional hearings, as if the white flag on these issues were not fully visible, the Agency stressed that it was trying to enhance flexibility and leave TMDL implementation to the states.

Too much flexibility, for some parties. Following publication of the proposed rules in 1999 and continuing into the early months of 2000, several environmental groups, including lead TMDL litigating groups, became disenchanted with EPA's concessions. They saw in the proposals a recipe for endless delay, well beyond the deadlines they were establishing through citizen suits. They also saw little assurance in implementation programs based on voluntary measures and education. On another side, however, were environmental groups that, having litigated over lists and TMDL schedules, were now engaged in their states on implementation issues. In their view, without regulations setting implementation standards, the rest of the TMDL process—listings, schedules of submissions etc.—even on accelerated schedules, led to no productive end. The environmental community split, some seeing the doughnut, others the hole.

In May 2000, the split broke open when six national environmental organizations wrote the EPA Administrator calling on her to scrap the regulations and go back to the drawing board. The letter could not have caught the Agency at a more vulnerable moment. Already under attack from the states, industry, and Congress, EPA was left without a single, unified constituency, while its opponents gained the argument that here was a rule that nobody liked.[5] * * *

* * * Congress hosted a competition of bills seeking to derail EPA's regulations. The lead vehicle, Senate Bill 2417, labeled with no apparent irony the "Water Pollution Program Enhancements Act of 2000," characterized the regulations as "hasty," "unscientific," "one-size-fits-all," and "unlikely to improve water quality." It would put the EPA program on hold pending studies on its supporting science and on the effectiveness of alternative, voluntary programs and their costs. Other bills would simply repeal the TMDL rules in full or exempt particular industries, e.g., forestry, from their scope.

Meanwhile, the Administration * * * began a race to beat the clock. Passing whatever bill Congress chose would take time. EPA accelerated its regulations review.

Outraged, now, by what appeared to be a stiff-arm of its concerns and an end-run on its authority, Congress looked for another vehicle to block the Administration. They found it in the Fiscal Year (FY) 2001 Military Constructions/FY 2000 Urgent Supplemental Appropriations Bill, an obscure funding bill that in neither House contained any mention of TMDLs. Overnight and without notice, Congress tacked on a provision that no funds would be used in FY 2000 or 2001 to "make a final determination on or implement any new rule relative" to EPA's regulations. It further mandated a study of the program by the National Academy of Sciences (NAS) to determine the adequacy of the scientific basis for the TMDL program. Among other things, the study would delay the program; even better, the study might derail it.

As appropriations for expenditures that were unavoidable and in some cases already expended, the supplemental appropriations bill was must-sign legislation. It was also, in a decade marked by environmental-legislation-by-appropriations-rider, a high watermark for this political art.[6] President William J. Clinton appeared check-mated; in order to cover, inter alia, monies spent for hurricane relief in Nicaragua, he would have to sign away the TMDL rule. A small window of opportunity remained, however, a gap of several days before which, with or without the president's signature, the bill would become law. The EPA Administrator signed off on the regulations on July 11. The final rule was published on July 13. The same day, the last available, President Clinton signed the appropriations bill prohibiting half of what his Administration had just done.

---

5. Sen. Max Baucus (D–Mont.), for example, vowing to "reverse the [TMDL] decision at the earliest opportunity," characterized the rules as "roundly criticized by states, environmental groups, business organizations, and agricultural interests."

6. For a discussion of the use and abuse of appropriations riders, *see* Sandra A. Zellmer, *Sacrificing Legislative Integrity at the Altar of Appropriations Riders: A Constitutional Crisis*, 21 HARV. L. REV. 457 (1998). In this case, President William J. Clinton complimented Congress for dropping "several anti-environmental riders," without mention of its rider blocking the TMDL rule—which he knew he could finalize before he signed the rider. *See* H.R. 4425. Such is the language of politics. * * *

In the final regulations, EPA acknowledged the appropriations rider by delaying their effect until October 31, 2001, or until the expiration of the rider, whichever came first. As a practical matter, with a ban on funding program implementation, it would be delayed until whichever came second. In the meantime, EPA's skeletal regulations from the 1980s and subsequent guidance would remain in effect. The program would continue under the old rules. Environmentalists left the field bloodied but relieved that the TMDL program had not been repealed. The agriculture and timber industries left triumphant but insecure in their victory. The threat of TMDL-imposed requirements on nonpoint sources had been parried but it had not been eliminated.

II. The Aftermath

On the heels of the TMDL showdown came the national presidential elections, and, when the dust finally settled, a new philosophy toward environmental protection. * * * While TMDL issues continued to play out in the courts and percolated below the surface of a still-suspicious Congress, the lead action, although not all of the action, rebounded to EPA. * * * From EPA's recent initiatives and statements, however, the contours of the new program are evident. * * *

1. State Capacity

* * *

* * * [A]mbient-based water quality management has always been severely challenged by its demands for current, continuous, and definitive data. The information needed to support water quality criteria, to identify polluted waters, to determine the causal pollutants, to identify the sources of these pollutants, to sift out background, natural, atmospheric, and other exogenous sources, to quantify these loadings, and to apportion load reductions among these sources, all in ways that are defensible in a court of law (since any significant restrictions will be challenged), was a primary reason Congress abandoned ambient-based management in 1972 and turned to BAT.

* * * In March 2000, the GAO released its study of the adequacy of the information underlying the evaluation of national water quality and pollution control strategies. * * *

According to the GAO, as of the year 2000, a majority of the nation's waters remain, in practice, unmonitored and unassessed, even by the most primitive of indicators. Assessment levels range from 72% for estuaries, to 40% for lakes, ponds, and reservoirs, to 19% for rivers and streams, and to 6% for oceans shoreline waters. The numbers are worse than they look. Only one-half of the 19% of assessments for rivers and streams was performed by actual monitoring; the other one-half by estimates, extrapolations, and unspecified "other means." Further, the monitoring may be infrequent, e.g., monthly or, for pesticides, annually, for only a few contaminants, e.g., oxygen levels, solids, and bacteria, and not representative of more serious pollution.

The states themselves were equally pessimistic about their data-readiness. Only 6 states reported sufficient information to "fully assess" state waters, and only 18 reported sufficient information even to identify waters as polluted for TMDL listings. Moving on down the TMDL program requirements, while 40 states reported confidence in their ability to identify point sources of pollution (not that hard a trick, given that point source loadings are characterized in each NPDES permit), only 3 reported confidence in their ability to identify nonpoint sources, the sources primarily at issue in the TMDL program. Similarly, while 29 states felt that they had sufficient data to develop point source TMDLs, only 3 had data sufficient to develop nonpoint source TMDLs. In other words, for the type of pollution for which TMDLs are most important—that from crops, cattle, clearcutting, roadbuilding, and suburban and urban construction—only 3 states of 50 have enough data, or will admit to having enough data, to act. * * *

2. Supporting Science

As noted earlier, in July 2000, Congress not only deferred the regulatory program until further notice but mandated a study by the NAS as well. The requested points of study were the sufficiency of knowledge about point and nonpoint sources and the state of monitoring and modeling needed to predict pollution loadings and develop TMDLs. The study began in January 2001, and was due in June—tall orders for a short amount of time. In effect, the report would be written by a few individuals, and, as it happened, ones with strong, preexisting points of view on the TMDL program.

On one level, the NAS report is an affirmation of the TMDL program. The message on the adequacy of the supporting science was blunt: the science is there, its uncertainty can be reduced, and uncertainties that remain should not be used as an excuse for delay or inaction. * * * [The] EPA ... quickly used the National Research Council (NRC) report as a reason to suspend its regulations into the year 2003. * * *

The report cast a * * * shadow over the TMDL program by recommending, repeatedly, that states redetermine their water standards and uses for each impaired water body before TMDLs are performed. It explained:

> [I]t does not follow that a water body lacking integrity [e.g., polluted,] is impaired or that restoring biological integrity is either possible or desirable. A water body that is described as lacking "biological integrity" should not be assumed to be in a less-than-desirable state.

What we have here is an open invitation to lower environmental protection. Were the invitation overlooked, a sidebar in the report entitled, "Six Reasons for Changing Water Quality Standards" provides a recipe for dropping a designation from, say, primary contact recreation to secondary contact recreation when utilities, the sugar industry, or pulp and paper manufacturers dig in their heels. * * *

In the final analysis, reports are written by people. Under normal circumstances, NAS reports are written over several years, by scientists with little financial or political connection to the issues before them, and with a balance of points of view. As the NRC staff director of this report has complained, however, this one was otherwise, a rush job with little time for panel building or, for that matter, report writing. The result was a small group with an attitude. The panel chair, a witness for the Florida Pulp and Paper Association in hearings on the * * * Florida rules who is also reported as having accused EPA of "heavy handed intrusion" in North Carolina TMDLs, has stated that he "jumped at it [the chairmanship], because it was a great opportunity to make some of the arguments I've been making;" he is also quoted as referring to two subsequent TMDL-related consultant contracts as "an opportunity to push my agenda." Florida had its own representative on the committee as well, who happened to write the section endorsing Florida's two-tiered program, a "great job on the committee" according to his state agency supervisors. The report's principal author had, just two months before the committee geared up, published an article through the Cato Institute entitled The Trouble With Implementing TMDL—a title remarkably similar to that of the final chapter of the NRC report—expressing the fear that EPA would turn the TMDL program into a NPDES-like permit system. Such an extension would be "costly, contentious, environmentally suspect, and often inequitable." Warming to a close, he concluded: "Congress should explicitly affirm that the ends of the Act are to secure ambient water quality goals, not to eliminate all discharge." Thus concluded the NRC report as well. Congress, of course, decided otherwise in the CWA of 1972, but the argument lingers on.

At bottom, a small group of industry consultants, state agency representatives, and water quality engineers have affirmed their faith in an ambient-based water quality program. In response to Congress' question, they found that TMDLs are supportable by science—lots more of it. Which leads to the next question: costs.

3. Costs of the TMDL Program

As it put EPA's final TMDL regulations on hold in July 2000, Congress also directed EPA to study the total costs of implementing such a program. * * * While the final version is not available, its basic content, like that of the TMDL program itself, is visible.

The scope of the work was defined by the 1998 state lists of impaired waters under CWA § 303(d), the last of such submissions. About one-third of the nation's waters were polluted * * *. These waters would require an anticipated 36,000 TMDLs.

Turning to the sources of pollution, state data identified less than 5% of impairment from point sources only and about 25% from a combination of point and nonpoint sources. Nonpoint sources were the exclusive sources of pollution for 50% of the listed waters, with the remaining waters polluted by combinations of nonpoint and "other" sources. The leading source of impairment was agriculture at 24.6%, with another 11.4% attributed to unspecified "nonpoint" causes. * * * In overview and subject to regional exceptions, e.g., forestry in the northern Rockies and acid mine drainage in the Appalachians, the task at hand would be more than 20,000 TMDLs for nonpoint sources, primarily for agricultural run-off. * * *

Under EPA's more cost-effective scenario, TMDL implementation was estimated to cost $900 million to $3.2 billion per year. Under the disfavored least flexible scenario, annual costs would range between $1.9 and $4.3 billion per year. Two noteworthy facts appear from the data. The first is that under all scenarios, both point and nonpoint sources took approximately equal cost hits, although nonpoint sources were the overwhelming sources of pollution; i.e., point sources, already regulated, present marginal cost savings compared to agriculture and other sources that have been heretofore requirement-free. The second fact is that even with the most optimistic, cost-minimizing, market-oriented trading imaginable, the high-end projections for the best and worst scenarios were at $3.2 and $4.3 billion, respectively, which is not all that far apart. In other words, you can save money by trading, up to a point, but it is no panacea. * * *

In the final analysis, what is striking about cost estimates for the TMDL program is not the extent to which they differ but rather their common ground. Cost estimates for implementation of the CAA Amendments of 1990 were at odds by a factor of 10. If, all told, TMDL cost estimates come in at somewhere between $25 to $50 billion over 15 years, that is a pretty strong concurrence for a large federal program. Whether Congress is willing to fund such an exercise over the long haul is something very different. * * *

8. The State of the Game

As the year 2001 drew to a close, the states were still using their approved 1998 lists of impaired waters identifying 36,000 water bodies that failed to meet water quality standards for at least one pollutant. Some states, spurred forward by environmental litigation, had begun to make significant investments in TMDL implementation: $5 million in Iowa, $10 million in California. Other states * * * have resorted to a variety of mechanisms to avoid their responsibilities, including revision of antidegradation policies, downgrading, use unattainability, insufficient data, and this author's favorite, "swamp waters," to trim their workload. For the waters remaining, EPA had approved almost 4,000 TMDLs submitted by the states, a pace of action that will only accelerate.

Of course, what matters more than the volume is the content. A review of 55 TMDLs by this author in 1998 found that the early approved submissions met few of the requirements of the statute and Agency guidelines and regulations. Variously, they did not quantify overall loadings, did not quantify loadings from individual sources, neither identified nor quantified nonpoint sources, focused almost exclusively on reductions from point sources, and made little explicit provision either for margins of growth or margins of error; only a few contained implementation plans, and none provided objective assurance that the necessary load reductions would be attained. * * * [A] December 2001 study of TMDLs in West Virginia produced similar findings. The study reviewed 25 TMDLs prepared by EPA and the state for a range of point and nonpoint sources, among them current and abandoned mining operations and agriculture. Not surprisingly, the point sources received specific abatement proposals while the nonpoint sources did not. While new nonpoint source programs had been initiated in four impaired watersheds, "no concrete steps toward implementation had been undertaken in the remaining seven watersheds." No nonpoint source water TMDLs contained implementation plans. Virtually all anticipated nonpoint source abatement was to be paid for through federal funding and supplemented by state funding. * * *

What we have so far from § 303(d) in practice, then, is a process in which TMDLs provide goals with varying levels of specificity. What we also have is a marked dichotomy between the treatment of point and nonpoint sources in the exigence of load reductions and in the question of who pays for them. For the life of water pollution control in this country, while public sewage treatment has been publicly funded, private industry point sources have paid their own abatement costs. Nonpoint source abatement, however, although private and including some of the largest corporations in America, is paid for largely by the government. The state of Wisconsin is in the final stages of adopting rules imposing mandatory controls on nonpoint source runoff but require the state to provide 70% of the costs. The state of New York is providing over $14 million to farmers for runoff abatement, and the city of New York is kicking in another $10 million to protect its drinking water resources. The CWA, by creating a dichotomy between point and nonpoint sources, also created an attitude within the nonpoint industry of an entitlement to pollute akin to a property right. The attitude is that if you, the public, want to abate nonpoint pollution, then you, the public, will foot the bill.

C. Recent TMDL Litigation

* * * Environmental litigation has continued to push the TMDL agenda forward. At the start of 2002, EPA was under court order by decision or consent decree in more than 20 states to establish TMDLs on timetables ranging from 6 to 12 years unless the states stepped forward. Recent decisions and settlements in Hawaii, Iowa, and Tennessee kept this ball rolling despite minimal compliance by EPA and these states to list their waters and develop TMDLs. On the other hand, an increasing number of courts are beginning to show a weariness in overseeing the process and are accepting an any-progress-is-sufficient-progress attitude toward this same low level of performance. Viewed on the "constructive submission" theory, courts in California, Maryland, and Oklahoma have

recently held that the submission of something, anything, sufficed, and that it sufficed under the APA's "arbitrary or capricious" standard as well. In the words of the California court, "California and the EPA have both been doing something about TMDLs, albeit not as rapidly as contemplated by the passage of the [CWA]." The logic of these cases in giving EPA and the states, if they are intent on implementing the program, some leeway in going forward is difficult to gainsay. On the other hand, against a history of noncompliance and a recent, explicit federal policy change from hands-on to hands-off, more rigorous court review may be necessary to keep the program viable. * * *

* * * The nonpoint source pollution that has swamped the nation's waters has many and diverse sources, but the lion's share are agricultural: crops and animals. More than 50% of water impairment nationally comes from agricultural runoff. In some western states dominated by cattle, the number reaches 90%. More than 80% of the eutrophication of the Gulf of Mexico dead zone is attributable to farm loadings over 500 river miles away. * * *

Agriculture is one of the largest industries in the United States, with a total production value of near $200 billion. Its principal field crops are corn, soybeans, hay, and wheat; it also produces on an annual basis 98 million cattle, 366 million egg-laying chickens, 6.75 billion meat chickens, and 61 million hogs. It spends $18 billion on agricultural chemicals a year, more than twice what it spends on gasoline and electricity. Its payroll reaches $16.9 billion in farm and contract employees. Its larger operations are industrial, look industrial, and are managed as any national or multinational corporation. * * *

With even this rudimentary understanding of the industry, the exemption of American agriculture from the CWA is either gross negligence or irresistible politics. Whichever, few of the reasons that have been given for exempting farm sources from the NPDES program obtain today. Far from being trivial, they are mammoth. Far from being site-specific and local, their impacts are multi-state, regional, and even international. Far from being without available control technologies, the control strategies for nonpoint source pollution, e.g., shelterbelts, cover crops, and cattle fences, are orders of magnitude less complex and less costly than other industry controls. To be sure, farms are diverse, but they are no more diverse by crop and production method than the many categories and subcategories of the pulp and paper industry, petrochemicals, metals, rubber, and other industries subject to the NPDES program. Nor is it a persuasive distinction that farm runoff does not emerge from a pipe. Construction, municipal, feedlot, and acid mine drainage do not emerge from pipes either. They all arise from identifiable technologies and practices. They all pollute. They should all share the burden of cleanup and this burden in America begins with adopting BAT. There is something wrong with a picture that regulates the discharges of small Pacific Coast canning factories while Boise Cascade, U.S. Sugar, and Archer Daniels Midland walk free. * * *

NOTES

1.   Houck's article on the future of the proposed TMDL program is, to put it mildly, not optimistic. He notes that the rule's effective date has been postponed several times by a hostile legislature. In 2003, the EPA withdrew the proposed rule. 68 Fed. Reg. 13607–614 (2003). The agency claims that the National Academy of Sciences' National Research Council has suggested numerous improvements to the "new" rules that are not reflected in the July 2000 rules. If these are grounds to abandon regulations, could the EPA *ever* issue new rules? Notwithstanding the withdrawal of the rule, as of early 2006 the EPA had approved more than 18,000 TMDLs for water bodies across the country. EPA, NATIONAL SECTION 303(D) LIST FACT SHEET (2006), available at http://oaspub.epa.gov/waters/national_rept.control. Nevertheless, the agency has provided little recent indication about whether and how the TMDL program will proceed. *See* CONGRESSIONAL RESEARCH SERVICE, CLEAN WATER ACT ISSUES IN THE 109TH CONGRESS (2005), at 11.

2.   Clearly, for the foreseeable future, the TMDL process is going to be where the action is under the CWA. As an exercise, put yourself in the position of: a) a member of Congress from a farm state; b) a state regulator in a state with both farming and heavy industry; c) a member of a national environmental organization and d) President of an agricultural trade association. From each of these perspectives, try to propose a TMDL action plan. Is there any alternative to the TMDL approach if we wish to address the lingering water pollution problems caused by unregulated sources? Specifically regarding the impacts of agriculture on the environment, *see* J.B. Ruhl, *Farms, Their Environmental Harms, and Environmental Law*, 27 ECOLOGY L.Q. 263 (2000). For an account of TMDL litigation, *see* James R. May, *The Rise and Repose of Assimilation–Based Water Quality: Part I: TMDL Litigation*, 34 Envt'l. L. Rep 10247 (2004).

3.   DEVELOPMENT RESTRICTIONS ON PRIVATE WETLANDS

Wetlands were once considered worthless swamps. Today, however, they are understood to have many valuable characteristics:

> Variously dry, wet, or anywhere between, wetlands are by their nature protean. Such constant change makes wetlands ecologically rich; they are often as diverse as rain forests. These shallow water-fed systems are central to the life cycle of many plants and animals, some of them endangered. They provide a habitat as well as spawning grounds for an extraordinary variety of creatures and nesting areas for migratory birds. Some wetlands even perform a global function. The northern peat lands of Canada, Alaska and Eurasia, in particular, may help moderate climatic change by serving as a sink for the greenhouse gas carbon dioxide.

> Wetlands also have commercial and utilitarian functions. They are sources of lucrative harvests of wild rice, fur-bearing animals, fish and

shellfish. Wetlands limit the damaging effects of waves, convey and store floodwaters, trap sediment and reduce pollution—the last attribute has earned them the sobriquet "nature's kidneys."

Jon A. Kusler, et al., *Wetlands,* Sci. Am., Jan. 1994, at 64B. As a result of this shift in awareness, governmental policy has shifted from encouragement of draining and filling wetlands to support for preservation and restricted development. The federal government has taken the lead in protecting wetlands.

The catastrophic hurricane season in Louisiana and Mississippi in 2005 brought renewed attention to the importance of wetlands in protecting areas from flooding. For an interesting account of the history of flood planning and wetlands destruction *see* Oliver Houck, *Can We Save New Orleans?*, 19 TULANE ENVTL. L.J. 1 (2006).

Federal regulation of dredging and filling activities dates back to the Rivers and Harbors Appropriation Act of 1899. Section 13 of the Act prohibits discharge of "any refuse" other than liquid sewage into navigable waters. 33 U.S.C.A. § 407. The Supreme Court later construed this as a ban on water pollution.[7] Section 10 of the Act prohibits the creation of "any obstruction" to navigation, without permission from Congress. 33 U.S.C.A. § 403. At least since the passage of NEPA, issuance of a permit must be based on consideration of a broad range of environmental factors.

The permit program is now part of the Clean Water Act. Section 404 of the Clean Water Act establishes a separate permit system for discharges of dredged or fill materials into navigable waters. (Note that this covers discharges.) Unlike the rest of the Clean Water Act, however, the Army Corps of Engineers is the agency responsible for issuing Section 404 permits with guidance from the EPA. In *Coeur Alaska v. Southeast Alaska Conservation Council*, 129 S.Ct. 2458 (2009), the Supreme Court upheld a decision by the Army Corps and the EPA to classify slurry material from a gold mine as "dredge and fill" rather than as a discharge subject to Section 402 jurisdiction and to new source performance standards. What about draining? *See* United States v. Mango, 997 F.Supp. 264 (N.D.N.Y. 1998) (not covered). Courts have been vigorous in remedying violations of these provisions, even issuing orders for restoration of areas to their natural states. For a detailed overview of federal wetlands regulation, *see* Margaret N. Strand, *Federal Wetlands Law: Part I*, 23 ENVTL. L. REP. 10,185 (1993); Margaret N. Strand, *Federal Wetlands Law: Part II*, 23 ENVTL. L. REP. 10284 (1993).

There has been considerable controversy about the Clean Water Act's coverage of wetlands. Under the Rivers and Harbors Act, wetlands were not covered. Traditionally, the jurisdiction of the Army Corps of Engineers only extended to navigable waters. But the Clean Water Act is much more expansive. United States v. Ashland Oil and Transportation Co., 504 F.2d

---

7. United States v. Standard Oil Co., 384 U.S. 224 (1966); United States v. Pennsylvania Indus. Chem. Corp., 411 U.S. 655 (1973). Section 402(a)(5) of the Clean Water Act terminates the permit program administered by the Army Corps of Engineers in the wake of these decisions.

1317 (6th Cir. 1974), holds that the Clean Water Act extends to any waters flowing into any navigable stream.[8] The court's discussion of the constitutional issue is noteworthy:

> Obviously water pollution is a health threat to the water supply of the nation. It endangers our agriculture by rendering water unfit for irrigation. It can end the public use and enjoyment of our magnificent rivers and lakes for fishing, for boating, and for swimming. These health and welfare concerns are, of course, proper subjects for congressional attention because of their many impacts upon interstate commerce generally. But water pollution is also a direct threat to navigation—the first interstate commerce system in this country's history and still a very important one.

> We also know (and we take judicial notice) that two of the important rivers of this circuit, the Rouge River in Dearborn, Michigan, and the Cuyahoga River in Cleveland, Ohio, reached a point of pollution by flammable materials in the last ten years that they repeatedly caught fire. Such pollution is an obvious hazard to navigation which Congress has every right to seek to abate under its interstate commerce powers.

> It would, of course, make a mockery of those powers if its authority to control pollution was limited to the bed of the navigable stream itself. The tributaries which join to form the river could then be used as open sewers as far as federal regulation was concerned. The navigable part of the river could become a mere conduit for upstream waste.

> Such a situation would have vast impact on interstate commerce. States with cities and industries situated upstream on the nonnavigable tributaries of our great rivers could freely use them for dumping raw sewage and noxious industrial wastes upon their downstream neighboring states. There would be great pressure upon the upstream states to allow such usage. Reduced industrial costs and lower taxes thus resulting would tend to place industries, cities and states located on navigable rivers at a considerable competitive disadvantage in interstate commerce. In such a situation industrial frontage on a creek which flowed ultimately into a navigable stream would become valuable as an access point to an effectively unrestricted sewer.

Given this broad interpretation of the Act's coverage, application of the CWA to at least some wetlands was inevitable. During the Reagan Administration, the Corps' expansive jurisdiction over wetlands became a matter of political controversy, causing the Corps to vacillate in its commitment. *See* Frances L. McChesney, Comment, *Corps Recasts § 404 Permit Program, Braces for Political, Legal Skirmishes*, 13 ENVTL. L. REP.

---

8. The expansion of federal jurisdiction under the Clean Water Act has raised problems concerning the treatment of minor, routine changes in water use. When a farmer digs a ditch which connects to an existing drainage system, must he get a federal permit? The 1977 amendments to the Act exempt a number of "normal farming, silviculture, and ranching activities" from the § 404 permit requirement for dredging and filling, as well as authorizing use of general permits for other activities. Section 404(e)(1), (f)(1). The general permits are not blanket exemptions, but instead contain numerous qualifications and restrictions. *See* United States v. Marathon Dev. Corp., 867 F.2d 96 (1st Cir. 1989). * * *

10 128 (1983). As the next case demonstrates, the controversy spilled over into the courts.

UNITED STATES v. RIVERSIDE BAYVIEW HOMES, INC.

Supreme Court of the United States, 1985.
474 U.S. 121, 106 S.Ct. 455, 88 L.Ed.2d 419.

[A regulation of the Army Corps defines "waters of the United States" to include "freshwater wetlands" that are adjacent to other waters that themselves are subject to the CWA. Wetlands, in turn, are defined to include "those areas that are inundated or saturated by surface or ground water at a frequency and duration sufficient to support, and that under normal circumstances do support, a prevalence of vegetation typically adapted for life in saturated soil conditions." After Riverside Bayview Homes began fill operations on its property near a lake, the Corps filed suit in federal court for an injunction. The Court of Appeals construed the regulation to apply only to wetlands that are flooded by adjacent navigable waters often enough to support aquatic vegetation. The court's rationale was that a broader definition might constitute a taking.]

JUSTICE WHITE delivered the opinion for a unanimous Court.

The question whether the Corps of Engineers may demand that respondent obtain a permit before placing fill material on its property is primarily one of regulatory and statutory interpretation: we must determine whether respondent's property is an "adjacent wetland" within the meaning of the applicable regulation, and, if so, whether the Corps' jurisdiction over "navigable waters" gives it statutory authority to regulate discharges of fill material into such a wetland. In this connection, we first consider the Court of Appeals' position that the Corps' regulatory authority under the statute and its implementing regulations must be narrowly construed to avoid a taking without just compensation in violation of the Fifth Amendment.

We have frequently suggested that governmental land-use regulation may under extreme circumstances amount to a "taking" of the affected property. We have never precisely defined those circumstances, but our general approach [is] that the application of land-use regulations to a particular piece of property is a taking only "if the ordinance does not substantially advance legitimate state interests * * * or denies an owner economically viable use of his land." Moreover, we have made it quite clear that the mere assertion of regulatory jurisdiction by a governmental body does not constitute a regulatory taking. The reasons are obvious. A requirement that a person obtain a permit before engaging in a certain use of his or her property does not itself "take" the property in any sense: after all, the very existence of a permit system implies that permission may be granted, leaving the landowner free to use the property as desired. Moreover, even if the permit is denied, there may be other viable uses available to the owner. Only when a permit is denied and the effect of the denial is to prevent "economically viable" use of the land in question can it be said that a taking has occurred.

If neither the imposition of the permit requirement itself nor the denial of a permit necessarily constitutes a taking, it follows that the Court of Appeals erred in concluding that a narrow reading of the Corps' regulatory jurisdiction over wetlands was "necessary" to avoid "a serious taking problem." We have held that, in general, "[e]quitable relief is not available to enjoin an alleged taking of private property for a public use, duly authorized by law, when a suit for compensation can be brought against the sovereign subsequent to a taking." This maxim rests on the principle that so long as compensation is available for those whose property is in fact taken, the governmental action is not unconstitutional. For precisely the same reason, the possibility that the application of a regulatory program may in some instances result in the taking of individual pieces of property is no justification for the use of narrowing constructions to curtail the program if compensation will in any event be available in those cases where a taking has occurred. * * *

Purged of its spurious constitutional overtones, the question whether the regulation at issue requires respondent to obtain a permit before filling its property is an easy one. The regulation extends the Corps' authority under § 404 to all wetlands adjacent to navigable or interstate waters and their tributaries. Wetlands, in turn, are defined as lands that are "inundated *or saturated* by surface *or ground water* at a frequency and duration sufficient to support, and that under normal circumstances do support, a prevalence of vegetation typically adapted for life in saturated soil conditions." The plain language of the regulation refutes the Court of Appeals' conclusion that inundation or "frequent flooding" by the adjacent body of water is a *sine qua non* of a wetland under the regulation. Indeed, the regulation could hardly state more clearly that saturation by either surface or ground water is sufficient to bring an area within the category of wetlands, provided that the saturation is sufficient to and does support wetland vegetation. * * *

On a purely linguistic level, it may appear unreasonable to classify "lands," wet or otherwise, as "waters." Such a simplistic response, however, does justice neither to the problem faced by the Corps in defining the scope of its authority under § 404(a) nor to the realities of the problem of water pollution that the Clean Water Act was intended to combat. In determining the limits of its power to regulate discharges under the Act, the Corps must necessarily choose some point at which water ends and land begins. Our common experience tells us that this is often no easy task: the transition from water to solid ground is not necessarily or even typically an abrupt one. Rather, between open waters and dry land may lie shallows, marshes, mudflats, swamps, bogs—in short, a huge array of areas that are not wholly aquatic but nevertheless fall far short of being dry land. Where on this continuum to find the limit of "waters" is far from obvious.

Faced with such a problem of defining the bounds of its regulatory authority, an agency may appropriately look to the legislative history and underlying policies of its statutory grants of authority. Neither of these sources provides unambiguous guidance for the Corps in this case, but together they do support the reasonableness of the Corps' approach of defining adjacent wetlands as "waters" within the meaning of § 404(a). Section 404 originated as part of the Federal Water Pollution Control Act Amendments of 1972, which constituted a comprehensive legislative attempt "to restore and maintain the chemical, physical, and biological integrity of the Nation's waters." CWA § 101. This objective incorporated a broad, systemic view of the goal of maintaining and improving water quality: as the House Report on the legislation put it, "the word 'integrity' * * * refers to a condition in which the natural structure and function of ecosystems is maintained." Protection of aquatic ecosystems, Congress recognized, demanded broad federal authority to control pollution, for "[w]ater moves in hydrologic cycles and it is essential that discharge of pollutants be controlled at the source."

In keeping with these views, Congress chose to define the waters covered by the Act broadly. Although the Act prohibits discharges into "navigable waters," the Act's definition of "navigable waters" as "the waters of the United States" makes it clear that the term "navigable" as used in the Act is of limited import. In adopting this definition of "navigable waters," Congress evidently intended to repudiate limits that had been placed on federal regulation by earlier water pollution control statutes and to exercise its powers under the Commerce Clause to regulate at least some waters that would not be deemed "navigable" under the classical understanding of that term.

This holds true even for wetlands that are not the result of flooding or permeation by water having its source in adjacent bodies of open water. The Corps has concluded that wetlands may affect the water quality of adjacent lakes, rivers, and streams even when the waters of those bodies do not actually inundate the wetlands. For example, wetlands that are not flooded by adjacent waters may still tend to drain into those waters. In such circumstances, the Corps has concluded that wetlands may serve to filter and purify water draining into adjacent bodies of water, and to slow the flow of surface runoff into lakes, rivers, and streams and thus prevent flooding and erosion. In addition, adjacent wetlands may "serve significant natural biological functions, including food chain production, general habitat, and nesting, spawning, rearing and resting sites for aquatic * * * species." In short, the Corps has concluded that wetlands adjacent to lakes, rivers, streams, and other bodies of water may function as integral parts of the aquatic environment even when the moisture creating the wetlands does not find its source in the adjacent bodies of water. Again, we cannot say that the Corps' judgment on these matters is unreasonable, and we therefore conclude that a definition of "waters of the United States" encompassing all wetlands adjacent to other bodies of water over which the Corps has jurisdiction is a permissible interpretation of the Act.

Because respondent's property is part of a wetland that actually abuts on a navigable waterway, respondent was required to have a permit in this case.[9]

NOTES

1. For approving commentary on the main case, *see* Kenneth L. Rosenbaum, Comment, *The Supreme Court Endorses A Broad Reading of Corps Wetland Jurisdiction Under FWPCA section 404*, 16 ENVTL. L. REP. 10,008 (1986). *Riverside* led several lower courts to uphold broad claims of jurisdiction on behalf of the Corps. *See* United States v. Banks, 115 F.3d 916 (11th Cir. 1997) (finding that wetlands were "adjacent" despite half-mile gap and debatable hydrological connection); United States v. Pozsgai, 999 F.2d 719 (3d Cir. 1993) (finding that wetlands covered by CWA because adjacent to tributaries of navigable stream).

2. Controversy over the scope of section 404 continues. The National Academy of Sciences issued a report in 1995 suggesting a redefinition in terms of wetland hydrology, exhibiting "constant or recurrent, shallow inundation or saturation at or near the surface of the substrate," with diagnostic features such as hydric soils and hydrophytic vegetation. So far, this proposal has not resulted in any legal changes, although it may have helped block congressional efforts to restrict the definition of wetlands further. *See* Margaret N. Strand, *Recent Developments in Federal Wetlands Law: Part I*, 26 ENVTL. L. REP. 10,283, 10,286–87 (1996); Tina Adler, *Two Views of a Swamp*, SCI. NEWS, July 22, 1995, at 56. Congress has yet to act. In the meantime, however, the Supreme Court revisited the question of federal wetlands jurisdiction in the following case.

SOLID WASTE AGENCY OF NORTHERN COOK COUNTY [SWANCC] v. UNITED STATES ARMY CORPS OF ENGINEERS

Supreme Court of the United States, 2001.
531 U.S. 159, 121 S.Ct. 675, 148 L.Ed.2d 576.

CHIEF JUSTICE REHNQUIST delivered the opinion of the Court.

[SWANCC, a consortium of Chicago suburbs, acquired an abandoned gravel pit, now containing several small ponds. The question before the Court was whether it needed to obtain a permit from the Army Corps of Engineers before filling the site. Section 404(a) of the Clean Water Act (CWA), which is discussed in more detail in Chapter 8, grants the Corps

---

9. Of course, it may well be that not every adjacent wetland is of great importance to the environment of adjoining bodies of water. But the existence of such cases does not seriously undermine the Corps' decision to define all adjacent wetlands as "waters." If it is reasonable for the Corps to conclude that in the majority of cases, adjacent wetlands have significant effects on water quality and the aquatic ecosystem, its definition can stand. That the definition may include some wetlands that are not significantly intertwined with the ecosystem of adjacent waterways is of little moment, for where it appears that a wetland covered by the Corps' definition is in fact lacking in importance to the aquatic environment—or where its importance is outweighed by other values—the Corps may always allow development of the wetland for other uses simply by issuing a permit.

authority to issue permits for the discharge of dredged or fill material into navigable waters. The term "navigable waters" is defined under the Act as "the waters of the United States, including the territorial seas." § 1362(7). The Corps has issued regulations defining the term "waters of the United States" to include "waters such as intrastate lakes, rivers, streams (including intermittent streams), mudflats, sandflats, wetlands, sloughs, prairie potholes, wet meadows, playa lakes, or natural ponds, the use, degradation or destruction of which could affect interstate or foreign commerce ..." In 1986, the Corps stated that § 404(a) extends to intrastate waters which "are or would be used as habitat" by migratory birds that cross state lines. The Corp determined to exercise jurisdiction over the SWANCC site based on this Migratory Bird Rule. Approximately 121 bird species had been observed at the site, including several known to depend upon aquatic environments for a significant portion of their life requirements. SWANCC argued that the CWA did not cover nonnavigable, isolated, intrastate waters based upon the presence of migratory birds and, in the alternative, that Congress lacked the power under the Commerce Clause to grant such regulatory jurisdiction.]

This is not the first time we have been called upon to evaluate the meaning of § 404(a). In *United States v. Riverside Bayview Homes, Inc.* [page 802, *supra*] we held that the Corps had § 404(a) jurisdiction over wetlands that actually abutted on a navigable waterway. In so doing, we noted that the term "navigable" is of "limited import" and that Congress evidenced its intent to "regulate at least some waters that would not be deemed 'navigable' under the classical understanding of that term." But our holding was based in large measure upon Congress' unequivocal acquiescence to, and approval of, the Corps' regulations interpreting the CWA to cover wetlands adjacent to navigable waters. We found that Congress' concern for the protection of water quality and aquatic ecosystems indicated its intent to regulate wetlands "inseparably bound up with the 'waters' of the United States."

It was the significant nexus between the wetlands and "navigable waters" that informed our reading of the CWA in *Riverside Bayview Homes*. Indeed, we did not "express any opinion" on the "question of the authority of the Corps to regulate discharges of fill material into wetlands that are not adjacent to bodies of open water...." In order to rule for respondents here, we would have to hold that the jurisdiction of the Corps extends to ponds that are not adjacent to open water. But we conclude that the text of the statute will not allow this.

[We] decline respondents' invitation to take what they see as the next ineluctable step after *Riverside Bayview Homes*: holding that isolated ponds, some only seasonal, wholly located within two Illinois counties, fall under § 404(a)'s definition of "navigable waters" because they serve as habitat for migratory birds. As counsel for respondents conceded at oral argument, such a ruling would assume that "the use of the word navigable in the statute ... does not have any independent significance." We cannot agree that Congress' separate definitional use of the phrase "waters of the United States" constitutes a basis for reading the term "navigable waters" out of the statute. We said in *Riverside Bayview Homes* that the word "navigable" in the statute was of "limited effect" and went on to hold that § 404(a) extended to nonnavigable wetlands adjacent to open waters. But it is one thing to give a word limited effect and quite another to give it no effect whatever. The term "navigable" has at least the import of showing us what Congress had in mind as its authority for enacting the CWA: its traditional jurisdiction over waters that were or had been navigable in fact or which could reasonably be so made.

Respondents—relying upon all of the arguments addressed above—contend that, at the very least, it must be said that Congress did not address the precise question of § 404(a)'s scope with regard to nonnavigable, isolated, intrastate waters, and that, therefore, we should give deference to the "Migratory Bird Rule". We find § 404(a) to be clear, but even were we to agree with respondents, we would not extend Chevron deference here.

Where an administrative interpretation of a statute invokes the outer limits of Congress' power, we expect a clear indication that Congress intended that result. This requirement stems from our prudential desire not to needlessly reach constitutional issues and our assumption that Congress does not casually authorize administrative agencies to interpret a statute to push the limit of congressional authority. This concern is heightened where the administrative interpretation alters the federal-state framework by permitting federal encroachment upon a traditional state power. Thus, "where an otherwise acceptable construction of a statute would raise serious constitutional problems, the Court will construe the statute to avoid such problems unless such construction is plainly contrary to the intent of Congress."

Twice in the past six years we have reaffirmed the proposition that the grant of authority to Congress under the Commerce Clause, though broad, is not unlimited. *See* United States v. Morrison, 529 U.S. 598 (2000); United States v. Lopez, 514 U.S. 549 (1995). Respondents argue that the "Migratory Bird Rule" falls within Congress' power to regulate intrastate activities that "substantially affect" interstate commerce. They note that the protection of migratory birds is a "national interest of very nearly the first magnitude" [quoting *Missouri v. Holland*, page 287, *supra*], and that, as the Court of Appeals found, millions of people spend over a billion dollars annually on recreational pursuits relating to migratory birds. These arguments raise significant constitutional questions. For example, we would have to evaluate the precise object or activity that, in the aggregate, substantially affects interstate commerce. This is not clear, for although the Corps has claimed jurisdiction over petitioner's land because it contains water areas used as habitat by migratory birds, respondents now, *post litem motam*, focus upon the fact that the regulated activity is petitioner's municipal landfill, which is "plainly of a commercial nature." But this is a far cry, indeed, from the "navigable waters" and "waters of the United States" to which the statute by its terms extends.

These are significant constitutional questions raised by respondents' application of their regulations, and yet we find nothing approaching a clear statement from Congress that it intended § 404(a) to reach an abandoned sand and gravel pit such as we have here. Permitting respondents to claim federal jurisdiction over ponds and mudflats falling within the "Migratory Bird Rule" would result in a significant impingement of the States' traditional and primary power over land and water use. Rather than expressing a desire to readjust the federal-state balance in this manner, Congress chose to "recognize, preserve, and protect the primary responsibilities and rights of States . . . to plan the development and use . . . of land and water resources . . ." 33 U.S.C. § 1251(b). We thus read the statute as written to avoid the significant constitutional and federalism questions raised by respondents' interpretation, and therefore reject the request for administrative deference.

JUSTICE STEVENS, with whom JUSTICE SOUTER, JUSTICE GINSBURG, and JUSTICE BREYER join, dissenting. * * *

Because I am convinced that the Court's miserly construction of the statute is incorrect, I shall comment briefly on petitioner's argument that Congress is without power to prohibit it from filling any part of the 31 acres of ponds on its property in Cook County, Illinois. The Corps' exercise of its § 404 permitting power over "isolated" waters that serve as habitat for migratory birds falls well within the boundaries set by this Court's Commerce Clause jurisprudence.

In *United States v. Lopez*, 514 U.S. 549 (1995), this Court identified "three broad categories of activity that Congress may regulate under its commerce power": (1) channels of interstate commerce; (2) instrumentalities of interstate commerce, or persons and things in interstate commerce; and (3) activities that "substantially affect" interstate commerce. The migratory bird rule at issue here is properly analyzed under the third category. In order to constitute a proper exercise of Congress' power over intrastate activities that "substantially affect" interstate commerce, it is not necessary that each individual instance of the activity substantially affect commerce; it is enough that, taken in the aggregate, the *class of activities* in question has such an effect.

The activity being regulated in this case (and by the Corps' § 404 regulations in general) is the discharge of fill material into water. The Corps did not assert jurisdiction over petitioner's land simply because the waters were "used as habitat by migratory birds." It asserted jurisdiction because petitioner planned to *discharge fill* into waters "used as habitat by migratory birds." Had petitioner intended to engage in some other activity besides discharging fill (*i.e.*, had there been no activity to regulate), or, conversely, had the waters not been habitat for migratory birds (*i.e.*, had there been no basis for federal jurisdiction), the Corps would never have become involved in petitioner's use of its land. There can be no doubt that * * * the discharge of fill material into the Nation's waters is almost always undertaken for economic reasons. Moreover, no one disputes that the discharge of fill into "isolated" waters that serve as migratory bird habitat will, in the aggregate, adversely affect migratory bird populations. Nor does petitioner dispute that the particular waters it seeks to fill are home to many important species of migratory birds, including the second-largest breeding colony of Great Blue Herons in northeastern Illinois, and several species of waterfowl protected by international treaty and Illinois endangered species laws.

In addition to the intrinsic value of migratory birds, it is undisputed that literally millions of people regularly participate in birdwatching and hunting and that those activities generate a host of commercial activities of great value. The causal connection between the filling of wetlands and the decline of commercial activities associated with migratory birds is not "attenuated," it is direct and concrete. Finally, the migratory bird rule does not blur the "distinction between what is truly national and what is truly local." Justice Holmes cogently observed in *Missouri v. Holland* that the protection of migratory birds is a textbook example of a national problem. The destruction of aquatic migratory bird habitat, like so many other environmental problems, is an action in which the benefits (*e.g.*, a new landfill) are disproportionately local, while many of the costs (*e.g.*, fewer migratory birds) are widely dispersed and often borne by citizens living in other States. In such situations, described by economists as involving "externalities," federal regulation is both appropriate and necessary. Identifying the Corps' jurisdiction by reference to waters that serve as habitat for birds that migrate over state lines also satisfies this Court's expressed desire for some "jurisdictional element" that limits federal activity to its proper scope.

The power to regulate commerce among the several States necessarily and properly includes the power to preserve the natural resources that generate such commerce. Migratory birds, and the waters on which they rely, are such resources. Moreover, the protection of migratory birds is a well-established federal responsibility. As Justice Holmes noted in *Missouri v. Holland*, the federal interest in protecting these birds is of "the first magnitude." Because of their transitory nature, they "can be protected only by national action."

Whether it is necessary or appropriate to refuse to allow petitioner to fill those ponds is a question on which we have no voice. Whether the Federal Government has the power to require such permission, however, is a question that is easily answered. If, as it does, the Commerce Clause empowers Congress to regulate particular "activities causing air or water pollution, or other environmental hazards that may have effects in more than one State," there is no merit in petitioner's constitutional argument.

NOTES

1. Notwithstanding *SWANCC*, the Ninth Circuit held that irrigation canals are subject to EPA jurisdiction even at times when they are isolated from navigable waters:

> Because the canals receive water from natural streams and lakes, and divert water to streams and creeks, they are connected as tributaries to other "waters of the United States." TID [the irrigation district] claims that the canals are not tributaries because, during the application of Magnacide H, the canals are a "closed system," isolated from natural streams by a system of closed waste gates ... But even if TID succeeds, at certain times, in preventing the canals from exchanging any water with the local streams and lakes, that does not prevent the canals from being "waters of the United States" for which a permit is necessary. Even tributaries that flow intermittently are "waters of the United States." ... The Clean Water Act is concerned with the pollution of tributaries as well as with the pollution of navigable streams, and "it is incontestable that substantial pollution of one not only may but very probably will affect the other."

Headwaters, Inc. v. Talent Irrigation Dist., 243 F.3d 526, 533–534 (9th Cir. 2001).

2. Following *SWANCC*, EPA and the Corps issued a joint memorandum interpreting it, which reads the decision quite narrowly. The government's view is that the decision negates the "migratory bird" rule but does not eliminate other arguments for covering nonadjacent wetlands (for example, hydrological connections with navigable waters). EPA also decided not to issue any new wetlands rule in the wake of SWANCC. *See* EPA, EPA AND ARMY CORPS ISSUE WETLAND DECISION (2003), *available at*, http://epa.gov/owow/wetlands/guidance/SWANNC.

3. Although isolated wetlands may seem ecologically insignificant, scientists estimate that the *SWANCC* decision may affect almost 30 percent of the nation's wetlands. These wetlands are the source of enormous biodiversity. *See* Nature Serve, *Biodiversity Values of Geographically Isolated Wetlands in the United States* (2005), available at http://www.natureserve.org/library/isolated_wetlands_05/isolated_wetlands.pdf at 41–42. In the wake of SWANCC, however, about two thirds of states have issued no new regulations governing wetlands. *Id.* at 43.

4. Although the jurisdictional issues considered in *Riverside* and *SWANCC* are significant, other important questions involve the operation of the permitting program. The regulations prohibit filling wetlands if "there is a practicable alternative to the proposed discharge which would have less adverse impact on the aquatic ecosystem." There has been considerable controversy over how to determine the applicable alternatives. *See* Fund for Animals Inc. v. Rice, 85 F.3d 535 (11th Cir. 1996); Margaret N. Strand, *Federal Wetlands Law: Part II*, 23 ENVTL. L. REP. 10,284, 10,289–91 (1993).

5. SWANCC was not the last word from the Supreme Court on wetlands jurisdiction under the CWA:

RAPANOS v. UNITED STATES

Supreme Court of the United States, 2006.
547 U.S. 715, 126 S.Ct. 2208, 165 L.Ed.2d 159.

Justice Scalia delivered the judgment of the Court and delivered an opinion in which Chief Justice Roberts, Justice Thomas and Justice Alito join. [Justices Roberts and Kennedy filed separate concurring opinion, excerpted below] * * *

In April 1989, petitioner John A. Rapanos backfilled wetlands on a parcel of land in Michigan that he owned and sought to develop. This parcel included 54 acres of land with sometimes-saturated soil conditions. The nearest body of navigable water was 11 to 20 miles away. Regulators had informed Mr. Rapanos that his saturated fields were "waters of the United States," 33 U. S. C. § 1362(7), that could not be filled without a permit. Twelve years of criminal and civil litigation ensued.

The burden of federal regulation on those who would deposit fill material in locations denominated "waters of the United States" is not trivial. In deciding whether to grant or deny a permit, the U. S. Army Corps of Engineers (Corps) exercises the discretion of an enlightened despot, relying on such factors as "economics," "aesthetics," "recreation," and "in general, the needs and welfare of the people," 33 CFR§ 320.4(a) (2004). The average applicant for an individual permit spends 788 days and $271,596 in completing the process, and the average applicant for a nationwide permit spends 313 days and $28,915—not counting costs of mitigation or design changes.

The enforcement proceedings against Mr. Rapanos are a small part of the immense expansion of federal regulation of land use that has occurred under the Clean Water Act—without any change in the governing statute—during the past five Presidential administrations. In the last three decades, the Corps and the Environmental Protection Agency (EPA) have interpreted their jurisdiction over "the waters of the United States" to cover 270-to-300 million acres of swampy lands in the United States-including half of Alaska and an area the size of California in the lower 48 States. And that was just the beginning. The Corps also asserted jurisdiction over virtually any parcel of land containing a channel or conduit—whether man-made or natural, broad or narrow, permanent or ephemeral—through which rainwater or drainage may occasionally or intermittently flow. On this view, the federally regulated "waters of the United States" include storm drains, roadside ditches, ripples of sand in the desert that may contain water once a year, and lands that are covered by floodwaters once every 100 years. Because they include the land containing storm sewers and desert washes, the statutory "waters of the United States" engulf entire cities and immense arid wastelands. In fact, the entire land area of the United States lies in some drainage basin, and an endless network of visible channels furrows the entire surface, containing water ephemerally wherever the rain falls. Any plot of land containing such a channel may potentially be regulated as a "water of the United States." * * *

* * * Section 1342(a) authorizes the Administrator of the EPA to "issue a permit for the discharge of any pollutant,... notwithstanding section 1311(a) of this title." Section 1344 authorizes the Secretary of the Army, acting through the Corps, to "issue permits ... for the discharge of dredged or fill material into the navigable waters at specified disposal sites." § 1344(a), (d). It is the discharge of "dredged or fill material"—which, unlike traditional water pollutants, are solids that do not readily wash downstream—that we consider today. * * *

The Corps' current regulations interpret "the waters of the United States" to include, in addition to traditional interstate navigable waters, 33 CFR § 328.3(a)(1) (2004), "[a]ll interstate waters including interstate wetlands," § 328.3(a)(2); "[a]ll other waters such as intrastate lakes, rivers, streams (including intermittent streams), mudflats, sandflats, wetlands, sloughs, prairie potholes, wet meadows, playa lakes, or natural ponds, the use, degradation or destruction of which could affect interstate or foreign commerce," § 328.3(a)(3); "[t]ributaries of [such] waters," § 328.3(a)(5); and "[w]etlands adjacent to [such] waters [and tributaries] (other than waters that are themselves wetlands)," § 328.3(a)(7). The regulation defines "adjacent" wetlands as those "bordering, contiguous [to], or neighboring" waters of the United States. § 328.3(c). It specifically provides that "[w]etlands separated from other waters of the United States by man-made dikes or barriers, natural river berms, beach dunes and the like are 'adjacent wetlands.'" *Ibid.* * * *

Following our decision in *Riverside Bayview* (*supra* p. 802), the Corps adopted increasingly broad interpretations of its own regulations under the Act. For example, in 1986, to "clarify" the reach of its jurisdiction, the Corps announced the so-called "Migratory Bird Rule," which purported to extend its jurisdiction to any intrastate waters "[w]hich are or would be used as habitat" by migratory birds. 51 Fed. Reg. 41217; see also *SWANCC* [*supra* p. 805]. In addition, the Corps interpreted its own regulations to include "ephemeral streams" and "drainage ditches" as "tributaries" that are part of the "waters of the United States," see 33 CFR § 328.3(a)(5), provided that they have a perceptible "ordinary high water mark" as defined in § 328.3(e). 65 Fed. Reg. 12823 (2000). This interpretation extended "the waters of the United States" to virtually any land feature over which rainwater or drainage passes and leaves a visible mark-even if only "the presence of litter and debris." 33 CFR § 328.3(e). * * *

In *SWANCC*, * * * we held that "nonnavigable, isolated, intrastate waters,"—which, unlike the wetlands at issue in *Riverside Bayview*, did not "actually abu[t] on a navigable waterway,"—were not included as "waters of the United States."

Following our decision in *SWANCC*, the Corps did not significantly revise its theory of federal jurisdiction under § 1344(a). The Corps provided notice of a proposed rulemaking in light of *SWANCC*, 68 Fed. Reg. 1991 (2003), but ultimately did not amend its published regulations. Because *SWANCC* did not directly address tributaries, the Corps notified its field staff that they "should continue to assert jurisdiction over traditional navigable waters ... and, generally speaking, their tributary systems (and adjacent wetlands)." 68 Fed. Reg. 1998. In addition, because *SWANCC* did not overrule *Riverside Bayview*, the Corps continues to assert jurisdiction over waters " 'neighboring' " traditional navigable waters and their tributaries. 68 Fed. Reg. 1997 (quoting 33 CFR § 328.3(c) (2003)).

Even after *SWANCC*, the lower courts have continued to uphold the Corps' sweeping assertions of jurisdiction over ephemeral channels and drains as "tributaries." * * *

These judicial constructions of "tributaries" are not outliers. Rather, they reflect the breadth of the Corps' determinations in the field. The Corps' enforcement practices vary somewhat from district to district because "the definitions used to make jurisdictional determinations" are deliberately left "vague." But district offices of the Corps have treated, as "waters of the United States," such typically dry land features as "arroyos, coulees, and washes," as well as other "channels that might have little water flow in a given year." They have also applied that definition to such manmade, intermittently flowing features as "drain tiles, storm drains systems, and culverts." * * *

In these consolidated cases, we consider whether four Michigan wetlands, which lie near ditches or man-made drains that eventually empty into traditional navigable waters, constitute "waters of the United States" within the meaning of the Act. [T]he Rapanos and their affiliated businesses deposited fill material without a permit into wetlands on three sites near Midland, Michigan: the "Salzburg site," the "Hines Road site," and the "Pine River site." The wetlands at the Salzburg site are connected to a man-made drain, which drains into Hoppler Creek, which flows into the Kawkawlin River, which empties into Saginaw Bay and Lake Huron. The wetlands at the Hines Road site are connected to something called the "Rose Drain," which has a surface connection to the Tittabawassee River. And the wetlands at the Pine River site have a surface connection to the Pine River, which flows into Lake Huron. It is not clear whether the connections between these wetlands and the nearby drains and ditches are continuous or intermittent, or whether the nearby drains and ditches contain continuous or merely occasional flows of water. * * *

We have twice stated that the meaning of "navigable waters" in the Act is broader than the traditional understanding of that term, *SWANCC* and *Riverside Bayview*. We have also emphasized, however, that the qualifier "navigable" is not devoid of significance.

We need not decide the precise extent to which the qualifiers "navigable" and "of the United States" restrict the coverage of the Act. Whatever the scope of these qualifiers, the CWA authorizes federal jurisdiction only over "waters." The only natural definition of the term "waters," our prior and subsequent judicial constructions of it, clear evidence from other provisions of the statute, and this Court's canons of construction all confirm that "the waters of the United States" in § 1362(7) cannot bear the expansive meaning that the Corps would give it.

The Corps' expansive approach might be arguable if the CSA defined "navigable waters" as "water of the United States." But "the waters of the United States" is something else. The use of the definite article ("the") and the plural number ("waters") show plainly that § 1362(7) does not refer to water in general. In this form, "the waters" refers more narrowly to water "[a]s found in streams and bodies forming geographical features such as oceans, rivers, [and] lakes," or "the flowing or moving masses, as of waves or floods, making up such streams or bodies." Webster's New International Dictionary 2882 (2d ed. 1954) (hereinafter Webster's Second). On this definition, "the waters of the United States" include only relatively permanent, standing or flowing bodies of water.[10] The definition refers to water as found in "streams," "oceans," "rivers," "lakes," and "bodies" of water "forming geographical features." *Ibid.* All of these terms connote continuously present, fixed bodies of water, as opposed to ordinarily dry channels through which water occasionally or intermittently flows. Even the least substantial of the definition's terms, namely "streams," connotes a continuous flow of water in a permanent channel especially when used in company with other terms such as "rivers," "lakes," and "oceans." None of these terms encompasses transitory puddles or ephemeral flows of water.

excludes intermittent

The restriction of "the waters of the United States" to exclude channels containing merely intermittent or ephemeral flow also accords with the commonsense understanding of the term. In applying the definition to "ephemeral streams," "wet meadows," storm sewers and culverts, "directional sheet flow during storm events," drain tiles, man-made drainage ditches, and dry arroyos in the middle of the desert, the Corps has stretched the term "waters of the United States" beyond parody. The plain language of the statute simply does not authorize this "Land Is Waters" approach to federal jurisdiction.

In addition, * * * [a]s we noted in *SWANCC*, the traditional term "navigable waters—even though defined as "the waters of the United States"—carries *some* of its original substance: "[I]t is one thing to give a word limited effect and quite another to give it no effect whatever." That limited effect includes, at bare minimum, the ordinary presence of water.

Our subsequent interpretation of the phrase "the waters of the United States" in the CWA likewise confirms this limitation of its scope.

---

10. By describing "waters" as "relatively permanent," we do not necessarily exclude streams, rivers, or lakes that might dry up in extraordinary circumstances, such as drought. We also do not necessarily exclude *seasonal* rivers, which contain continuous flow during some months of the year but no flow during dry months—such as the 290-day, continuously flowing stream postulated by Justice Stevens' dissent (hereinafter the dissent). Common sense and common usage distinguish between a wash and seasonal river. * * *

* * * [I]n both *Riverside Bayview* and *SWANCC*, we repeatedly described the "navigable waters" covered by the Act as "open water" and "open waters." Under no rational interpretation are typically dry channels described as "*open* waters."

Most significant of all, the CWA itself categorizes the channels and conduits that typically carry intermittent flows of water separately from "navigable waters," by including them in the definition of " 'point source.' " * * * It also defines " 'discharge of a pollutant' " as "any addition of any pollutant *to* navigable waters *from* any point source." § 1362(12)(A) (emphases added). * * *

Moreover, only the foregoing definition of "waters" is consistent with the CWA's stated "policy of Congress to recognize, preserve, and protect the primary responsibilities and rights of the States to prevent, reduce, and eliminate pollution, [and] to plan the development and use (including restoration, preservation, and enhancement) of land and water resources . . . ." § 1251(b). * * *

Even if the phrase "the waters of the United States" were ambiguous as applied to intermittent flows, our own canons of construction would establish that the Corps' interpretation of the statute is impermissible. As we noted in *SWANCC*, the Government's expansive interpretation would "result in a significant impingement of the States' traditional and primary power over land and water use." Regulation of land use, as through the issuance of the development permits sought by petitioners in both of these cases, is a quintessential state and local power. * * *

Likewise, just as we noted in *SWANCC*, the Corps' interpretation stretches the outer limits of Congress's commerce power and raises difficult questions about the ultimate scope of that power. * * *

In sum, on its only plausible interpretation, the phrase "the waters of the United States" includes only those relatively permanent, standing or continuously flowing bodies of water "forming geographic features" that are described in ordinary parlance as "streams[,] . . . oceans, rivers, [and] lakes." See Webster's Second 2882. The phrase does not include channels through which water flows intermittently or ephemerally, or channels that periodically provide drainage for rainfall. The Corps' expansive interpretation of the "the waters of the United States" is thus not "based on a permissible construction of the statute." [citing *Chevron*, casebook p. 450].

* * * We * * * address in this Part whether a wetland may be considered "adjacent to" remote "waters of the United States," because of a mere hydrologic connection to them.

In *Riverside Bayview*, we * * * acknowledged * * * an inherent ambiguity in drawing the boundaries of any "waters": "[T]he Corps must necessarily choose some point at which water ends and land begins. * * * Where on this continuum to find the limit of 'waters' is far from obvious."

Because of this inherent ambiguity, we deferred to the agency's inclusion of wetlands "actually abut[ting]" traditional navigable waters. * * *

* * * [O]nly those wetlands with a continuous surface connection to bodies that are "waters of the United States" in their own right, so that there is no clear demarcation between "waters" and wetlands, are "adjacent to" such waters and covered by the Act. Wetlands with only an intermittent, physically remote hydrologic connection to "waters of the United States" do not implicate the boundary-drawing problem of *Riverside Bayview*, and thus lack the necessary connection to covered waters that we described as a "significant nexus" in *SWANCC*. Thus, establishing that wetlands such as those at the Rapanos and Carabell sites are covered by the Act requires two findings: First, that the adjacent channel contains a "wate[r] of the United States," (*i.e.*, a relatively permanent body of water connected to traditional interstate navigable waters); and second, that the wetland has a continuous surface connection with that water, making it difficult to determine where the "water" ends and the "wetland" begins.* * *

Respondents and their *amici* urge that such restrictions on the scope of "navigable waters" will frustrate enforcement against traditional water polluters under 33 U. S. C. §§ 1311 and 1342. Because the same definition of "navigable waters" applies to the entire statute, respondents contend that water polluters will be able to evade the permitting requirement of § 1342(a) simply by discharging their pollutants into noncovered intermittent watercourses that lie upstream of covered waters.

That is not so. * * * The Act does not forbid the "addition of any pollutant *directly* to navigable waters from any point source," but rather the "addition of any pollutant *to* navigable waters." § 1362(12)(A) (emphasis added); § 1311(a). Thus, from the time of the CWA's enactment, lower courts have held that the discharge into intermittent channels of any pollutant *that naturally washes downstream* likely violates § 1311(a), even if the pollutants discharged from a point source do not emit "directly into" covered waters, but pass "through conveyances" in between.* * *

In fact, many courts have held that such upstream, intermittently flowing channels themselves constitute "point sources" under the Act. We have held that the Act "makes plain that a point source need not be the original source of the pollutant; it need only convey the pollutant to 'navigable waters.' " * * *

In contrast to the pollutants normally covered by the permitting requirement of § 1342(a), "dredged or fill material," which is typically deposited for the sole purpose of staying put, does not normally wash downstream, and thus does not normally constitute an "addition ... to navigable waters" when deposited in upstream isolated wetlands. §§ 1344(a), 1362(12). * * *

Finally, respondents and many *amici* admonish that narrowing the definition of "the waters of the United States" will hamper federal efforts to preserve the Nation's wetlands. It is not clear that the state and local conservation efforts that the CWA explicitly calls for, see 33 U. S. C. § 1251(b), are in any way inadequate for the goal of preservation. In any event, a Comprehensive National Wetlands Protection Act is not before us, and the "wis[dom]" of such a statute is beyond our ken. What is clear, however, is that Congress did not enact one when it granted the Corps jurisdiction over only "the *waters* of the United States." * * *

Absent a plausible ground in our case law for its sweeping position, the dissent relies heavily on "Congress' deliberate acquiescence in the Corps' regulations in 1977." * * * Congress takes no governmental action except by legislation. What the dissent refers to as "Congress' deliberate acquiescence" should more appropriately be called Congress's failure to express any opinion. * * *

Because the Sixth Circuit applied the wrong standard to determine if these wetlands are covered "waters of the United States," and because of the paucity of the record in both of these cases, the lower courts should determine, in the first instance, whether the ditches or drains near each wetland are "waters" in the ordinary sense of containing a relatively permanent flow; and (if they are) whether the wetlands in question are "adjacent" to these "waters" in the sense of possessing a continuous surface connection that creates the boundary-drawing problem we addressed in *Riverside Bayview.* * * *

We vacate the judgments of the Sixth Circuit and remand both cases for further proceedings. * * *

CHIEF JUSTICE ROBERTS, concurring.

Five years ago, this Court rejected the position of the Army Corps of Engineers on the scope of its authority to regulate wetlands under the Clean Water Act, in *SWANCC*. The Corps had taken the view that its authority was essentially limitless; this Court explained that such a boundless view was inconsistent with the limiting terms Congress had used in the Act.

In response to the *SWANCC* decision, the Corps and the Environmental Protection Agency (EPA) initiated a rulemaking to consider "issues associated with the scope of waters that are subject to the Clean Water Act (CWA), in light of the U. S. Supreme Court decision in [*SWANCC*]." 68 Fed. Reg. 1991 (2003). * * *

Agencies delegated rulemaking authority under a statute such as the Clean Water Act are afforded generous leeway by the courts in interpreting the statute they are entrusted to administer. See *Chevron* (*supra* p. 450). Given the broad, somewhat ambiguous, but nonetheless clearly limiting terms Congress employed in the Clean Water Act, the Corps and the EPA would have enjoyed plenty of room to operate in developing *some* notion of an outer bound to the reach of their authority.

The proposed rulemaking went nowhere. Rather than refining its view of its authority in light of our decision in *SWANCC*, and providing

guidance meriting deference under our generous standards, the Corps
chose to adhere to its essentially boundless view of the scope of its power.
The upshot today is another defeat for the agency.* * *

JUSTICE KENNEDY, concurring in the judgment.

* * * In *SWANCC,* the Court held, under the circumstances presented there, that to constitute " 'navigable waters' " under the Act, a water
or wetland must possess a "significant nexus" to waters that are or were
navigable in fact or that could reasonably be so made. *Id.*, at 167, 172. In
the instant cases neither the plurality opinion nor the dissent by Justice
Stevens chooses to apply this test; and though the Court of Appeals
recognized the test's applicability, it did not consider all the factors
necessary to determine whether the lands in question had, or did not
have, the requisite nexus. In my view the cases ought to be remanded to
the Court of Appeals for proper consideration of the nexus requirement.

I

* * *

A

* * *

The statutory term to be interpreted and applied in the two instant
cases is the term "navigable waters." The outcome turns on whether that
phrase reasonably describes certain Michigan wetlands the Corps seeks to
regulate. Under the Act "[t]he term 'navigable waters' means the waters
of the United States, including the territorial seas." § 1362(7). In a
regulation the Corps has construed the term "waters of the United
States" to include * * * tributaries of those waters and, of particular
relevance here, wetlands adjacent to those waters or their tributaries. 33
CFR §§ 328.3(a)(1), (5), (7) (2005). The Corps views tributaries as within
its jurisdiction if they carry a perceptible "ordinary high water mark."
§ 328.4(c); 65 Fed. Reg. 12823 (2000). An ordinary high-water mark is a
"line on the shore established by the fluctuations of water and indicated
by physical characteristics such as clear, natural line impressed on the
bank, shelving, changes in the character of soil, destruction of terrestrial
vegetation, the presence of litter and debris, or other appropriate means
that consider the characteristics of the surrounding areas." 33 CFR
§ 328.3(e).

Contrary to the plurality's description, wetlands are not simply moist
patches of earth. They are defined as "those areas that are inundated or
saturated by surface or ground water at a frequency and duration sufficient to support, and that under normal circumstances do support, a
prevalence of vegetation typically adapted for life in saturated soil conditions. Wetlands generally include swamps, marshes, bogs, and similar
areas." § 328.3(b). The Corps' Wetlands Delineation Manual, including
over 100 pages of technical guidance for Corps officers, interprets this
definition of wetlands to require: (1) prevalence of plant species typically

adapted to saturated soil conditions, determined in accordance with the United States Fish and Wildlife Service's National List of Plant Species that Occur in Wetlands; (2) hydric soil, meaning soil that is saturated, flooded, or ponded for sufficient time during the growing season to become anaerobic, or lacking in oxygen, in the upper part; and (3) wetland hydrology, a term generally requiring continuous inundation or saturation to the surface during at least five percent of the growing season in most years. Under the Corps' regulations, wetlands are adjacent to tributaries, and thus covered by the Act, even if they are "separated from other waters of the United States by man-made dikes or barriers, natural river berms, beach dunes and the like." § 328.3(c). * * *

II

* * *

Riverside Bayview and *SWANCC* establish the framework for the inquiry in the cases now before the Court: Do the Corps' regulations, as applied to the wetlands in [this case], constitute a reasonable interpretation of "navigable waters" as in *Riverside Bayview* or an invalid construction as in *SWANCC?* * * * Absent a significant nexus, jurisdiction under the Act is lacking. * * *

A

* * *

From this reasonable beginning the plurality proceeds to impose two limitations on the Act; but these limitations, it is here submitted, are without support in the language and purposes of the Act or in our cases interpreting it. * * *

The plurality's first requirement—permanent standing water or continuous flow, at least for a period of "some months," and n. 5—makes little practical sense in a statute concerned with downstream water quality. The merest trickle, if continuous, would count as a "water" subject to federal regulation, while torrents thundering at irregular intervals through otherwise dry channels would not. Though the plurality seems to presume that such irregular flows are too insignificant to be of concern in a statute focused on "waters," that may not always be true. Areas in the western parts of the Nation provide some examples. The Los Angeles River, for instance, ordinarily carries only a trickle of water and often looks more like a dry roadway than a river. Yet it periodically releases water-volumes so powerful and destructive that it has been encased in concrete and steel over a length of some 50 miles. Though this particular waterway might satisfy the plurality's test, it is illustrative of what often-dry watercourses can become when rain waters flow. * * *

* * * In fact the *Riverside Bayview* opinion does not cite the dictionary definition on which the plurality relies, and the phrase "hydrographic features" could just as well refer to intermittent streams carrying substantial flow to navigable waters. See Webster's Second 1221 (defining

"hydrography" as "[t]he description and study of seas, lakes, rivers, and other waters; specifically] ... [t]he measurement of flow and investigation of the behavior of streams, esp[ecially] with reference to the control or utilization of their waters"). * * *

The plurality's second limitation—exclusion of wetlands lacking a continuous surface connection to other jurisdictional waters—is also unpersuasive. [T]he plurality is wrong to suggest that wetlands are *"indistinguishable"* from waters to which they bear a surface connection. Even if the precise boundary may be imprecise, a bog or swamp is different from a river. The question is what circumstances permit a bog, swamp, or other nonnavigable wetland to constitute a "navigable water" under the Act—as § 1344(g)(1), if nothing else, indicates is sometimes possible. *Riverside Bayview* addressed that question and its answer is inconsistent with the plurality's theory. There, in upholding the Corps' authority to regulate "wetlands adjacent to other bodies of water over which the Corps has jurisdiction," the Court deemed it irrelevant whether "the moisture creating the wetlands ... find[s] its source in the adjacent bodies of water." The Court further observed that adjacency could serve as a valid basis for regulation even as to "wetlands that are not significantly intertwined with the ecosystem of adjacent waterways." "If it is reasonable," the Court explained, "for the Corps to conclude that in the majority of cases, adjacent wetlands have significant effects on water quality and the aquatic ecosystem, its definition can stand." * * *

As discussed above, the Act's prohibition on the discharge of pollutants into navigable waters, 33 U. S. C. § 1311(a), covers both the discharge of toxic materials such as sewage, chemical waste, biological material, and radioactive material and the discharge of dredged spoil, rock, sand, cellar dirt, and the like. All these substances are defined as pollutants whose discharge into navigable waters violates the Act. §§ 1311(a),1362(6), (12). One reason for the parallel treatment may be that the discharge of fill material can impair downstream water quality. The plurality argues otherwise, asserting that dredged or fill material "does not normally wash downstream." As the dissent points out, this proposition seems questionable as an empirical matter. It seems plausible that new or loose fill, not anchored by grass or roots from other vegetation, could travel downstream through waterways adjacent to a wetland; at the least this is a factual possibility that the Corps' experts can better assess than can the plurality. Silt, whether from natural or human sources, is a major factor in aquatic environments, and it may clog waterways, alter ecosystems, and limit the useful life of dams. * * *

Even granting, however, the plurality's assumption that fill material will stay put, Congress' parallel treatment of fill material and toxic pollution may serve another purpose. As the Court noted in *Riverside Bayview*, "the Corps has concluded that wetlands may serve to filter and purify water draining into adjacent bodies of water, 33 CFR § 320.4(b)(2)(vii) (1985), and to slow the flow of surface runoff into lakes, rivers, and streams and thus prevent flooding and erosion, see

§§ 320.4(b)(2)(iv) and (v)." Where wetlands perform these filtering and runoff control functions, filling them may increase downstream pollution, much as a discharge of toxic pollutants would. Not only will dirty water no longer be stored and filtered but also the act of filling and draining itself may cause the release of nutrients, toxins, and pathogens that were trapped, neutralized, and perhaps amenable to filtering or detoxification in the wetlands. In many cases, moreover, filling in wetlands separated from another water by a berm can mean that flood water, impurities, or runoff that would have been stored or contained in the wetlands will instead flow out to major waterways. With these concerns in mind, the Corps' definition of adjacency is a reasonable one, for it may be the absence of an interchange of waters prior to the dredge and fill activity that makes protection of the wetlands critical to the statutory scheme. * * *

It bears mention also that the plurality's overall tone and approach from the characterization of acres of wetlands destruction as "backfilling ... wet fields," to the rejection of Corps authority over "man-made drainage ditches" and "dry arroyos" without regard to how much water they periodically carry, to the suggestion, seemingly contrary to Congress' judgment, that discharge of fill material is inconsequential for adjacent waterways, seems unduly dismissive of the interests asserted by the United States in these cases. Important public interests are served by the Clean Water Act in general and by the protection of wetlands in particular. To give just one example, *amici* here have noted that nutrient-rich runoff from the Mississippi River has created a hypoxic, or oxygen-depleted, "dead zone" in the Gulf of Mexico that at times approaches the size of Massachusetts and New Jersey. * * *

B

* * *

When the Corps seeks to regulate wetlands adjacent to navigable-in-fact waters, it may rely on adjacency to establish its jurisdiction. Absent more specific regulations, however, the Corps must establish a significant nexus on a case-by-case basis when it seeks to regulate wetlands based on adjacency to nonnavigable tributaries. Given the potential overbreadth of the Corps' regulations, this showing is necessary to avoid unreasonable applications of the statute. Where an adequate nexus is established for a particular wetland, it may be permissible, as a matter of administrative convenience or necessity, to presume covered status for other comparable wetlands in the region. That issue, however, is neither raised by these facts nor addressed by any agency regulation that accommodates the nexus requirement outlined here. * * *

III

In both the consolidated cases before the Court the record contains evidence suggesting the possible existence of a significant nexus according to the principles outlined above. Thus the end result in these cases and many others to be considered by the Corps may be the same as that suggested by the dissent, namely, that the Corps' assertion of jurisdiction is valid. Given, however, that neither the agency nor the reviewing courts properly considered the issue, a remand is appropriate, in my view, for application of the controlling legal standard.

RAPANOS

As the dissent points out, in *Rapanos* an expert whom the District Court found "eminently qualified" and "highly credible," testified that the wetlands were providing "habitat, sediment trapping, nutrient recycling, and flood peak diminution, reduction flow water augmentation." Although the expert had "not studied the upstream drainage of these sites" and thus could not assert that the wetlands were performing important pollutant-trapping functions, he did observe: "we have a situation in which the flood water attenuation in that water is held on the site in the wetland . . . such that it does not add to flood peak. By the same token it would have some additional water flowing into the rivers during the drier periods, thus, increasing the low water flow. . . . By the same token on all of the sites to the extent that they slow the flow of water off of the site they will also accumulate sediment and thus trap sediment and hold nutrients for use in those wetlands systems later in the season as well."

In addition, in assessing the hydrology prong of the three-part wetlands test, the District Court made extensive findings regarding water tables and drainage on the parcels at issue. In applying the Corps' jurisdictional regulations, the District Court found that each of the wetlands bore surface water connections to tributaries of navigable-in-fact waters.

Much the same evidence should permit the establishment of a significant nexus with navigable-in-fact waters, particularly if supplemented by further evidence about the significance of the tributaries to which the wetlands are connected. * * *

In these consolidated cases I would vacate the judgments of the Court of Appeals and remand for consideration whether the specific wetlands at issue possess a significant nexus with navigable waters.

NOTES

1. How are lower courts to determine what legal standard to apply in deciding whether Section 404 jurisdiction exists? The standard established in Justice Scalia's plurality opinion or the standard applied in Justice Kennedy's concurring opinion? *See* Marks v. United States, 430 U.S. 188, 193 (1977) ("When a fragmented Court decides a case and no single rationale explaining the result enjoys the assent of five Justices, the holding of the Court may be viewed as that position taken by those Members who concurred in the judgments on the narrowest grounds.") Courts to date have generally taken three different approaches. The 9th and 11th Circuits, for example, have held

that Justice Kennedy's concurring opinion is controlling. *See Northern California River Watch v. City of Healdsburg*, 496 F.3d 993, 1000 (9th Cir. 2007); *see also United States v. Gerke Excavating*, 464 F.3d 723 (7th Cir. 2006) (same). The First Circuit, by contrast, has held that the U.S. can establish jurisdiction under Section 404 if the government can meet either the Kennedy standard or the standard set forth by the plurality. *United States v. Johnson*, 467 F.3d 56, 60 (1st Cir. 2006). And the 5th and 6th Circuits have refused to decide which test controls, holding that when both the plurality and concurring tests are met, jurisdiction is established. *United States v. Lucas*, 516 F.3d 316, 327 (5th Cir. 2008); *United States v. Cundiff*, 555 F.3d 200, 210–13 (6th Cir. 2009).

2. Can you square Chief Justice Roberts' concurring opinion with Justice Scalia's plurality opinion in which Roberts joined? Put a different way, suppose the Army Corps had in the wake of *SWANNC* issued a rulemaking that resulted in expansively defined jurisdiction that was nonetheless consistent with the ruling in SWANNC. Would Roberts uphold such a rule?

3. The Environmental Protection Agency has issued a guidance memorandum to its EPA regional offices and to the Army Corps to assist staff in implementing the Rapanos decision. http://www.epa.gov/owow/wetlands/guidance/CWAwaters.html The guidance states that the agencies should assert jurisdiction over the following: "traditional navigable waters; wetlands adjacent to traditional navigable waters; non-navigable tributaries of traditional navigable waters that are relatively permanent where the tributaries typically flow year-round or have continuous flow at least seasonally (e.g., typically three months) and wetlands that directly abut such tributaries." The EPA guidance also states that agencies will decide jurisdiction over "the following waters based on a fact-specific analysis to determine whether they have a significant nexus with traditional navigable water: non-navigable tributaries that are not relatively permanent; wetlands adjacent to non-navigable tributaries that are not relatively permanent; and wetlands adjacent to but that do not directly abut a relatively permanent non-navigable tributary."

The guidance makes clear that agencies generally will not assert jurisdiction over "swales or erosional features (e.g., gullies, small washes characterized by low volume, infrequent, or short duration flow); or ditches (including roadside ditches) excavated wholly in and draining only uplands and that do not carry a relatively permanent flow of water."

Finally, the guidance defines the significant nexus standard as follows: A significant nexus analysis will assess the flow characteristics and functions of the tributary itself and the functions performed by all wetlands adjacent to the tributary to determine if they significantly affect the chemical, physical and biological integrity of downstream traditional navigable waters; significant nexus includes consideration of hydrologic and ecologic factors.

Whose opinion do you think the EPA is following in its guidance memorandum? Based on the *Rapanos* decision, does the agency need to use a fact specific analysis to determine the existence of a significant nexus for non-navigable tributaries, as the guidance suggests?

4. A recent internal memorandum at EPA has concluded that a "significant portion" of enforcement efforts had been "adversely affected" by *Rapanos*. The memo says that between July, 2006 and December, 2007 jurisdictional concerns had led to decisions to drop 304 potential enforcement actions and to lower the priority of 147 others. The memo also says that lack of jurisdiction had been asserted in 61 cases as an affirmative defense. See *Internal EDPA Memo Finds Enforcement Decreased Following Rapanos Decision*, 30 ENV. REP. 1392 (July 11, 2008). A recent report by the House Oversight and Transportation Committee, *Decline of Clean Water Act Enforcement Program* (Dec. 16, 2008) found a "drastic deterioration" in post-Rapanos CWA enforcement as "hundreds of violations have not been pursued with enforcement actions and dozens of existing enforcement cases have become informal responses, have had civil penalties reduced, and have experienced significant delays...." The difficulty in complying with *Rapanos* has been compounded by the staff time necessary to demonstrate Justice Kennedy's significant nexus test. Is there a way for the EPA to avoid these enforcement difficulties? Congress? Senator Russell Feingold (D–WI) has introduced the Clean Water Act Restoration Act of 2009 that would adopt an expansive view of jurisdiction under the Act, including the exercise of jurisdiction over isolated waters. If such legislation were enacted would it pass constitutional muster?

5. John Rapanos did not escape liability. He settled the Clean Water Act case against him, paying a $150,000 civil penalty, agreeing to spend $750,000 to restore wetlands he had filled illegally and agreeing to preserve another 134 acres of wetlands on his property. *See* Environment News Service, *Rapanos Will Pay for Clean Water Act Violations* (Dec. 30, 2008), available at http://www.ens-newswire.com/ens/dec2008/2008–12–30–091.asp.

4. TAKINGS CLAIMS AND WETLANDS PROTECTION

Wetlands regulation raises not only Commerce Clause concerns, but can lead to takings claims under the 5th Amendment of the U.S. Constitution. These claims against the federal government must be brought in the Court of Claims, with appellate review in the Federal Circuit. The Federal Circuit has not always followed a consistent path, but on the whole has been sympathetic to landowners' claims. In order to best understand these Federal Circuit cases, a brief explanation of *Lucas v. South Carolina Coastal Council* (excerpted at page 347, *supra)*, is in order.

In *Lucas*, the Court established a new per se rule in takings cases: a taking has occurred "where regulation denies all economically beneficial or productive use of land." 505 U.S. at 1015. The first Federal Circuit case, *Florida Rock Industries, Inc. v. United States,* 18 F.3d 1560 (Fed. Cir. 1994), involved the denial of a permit to mine limestone lying beneath wetlands. The land had originally been acquired in 1972, before the enactment of the Clean Water Act. The court found that all economic value had not been destroyed, so there was no complete diminution in economic value as described in *Lucas*. The court remanded, however, for a determination of the extent to which the actual diminution of value should be considered a partial taking. In considering this issue, the lower court was given broad instructions to consider whether the government had acted in a responsible way.

The second case, *Loveladies Harbor, Inc. v. United States*, 28 F.3d 1171 (Fed. Cir. 1994), involved a permit denial for the final stage of an ongoing real estate development project. The court relied heavily on *Lucas* to conclude that the permit denial was a taking. The court stressed that "nothing in the state's conduct reflected a considered determination that certain defined activities would violate the state's understanding of its nuisance powers. Nor did Loveladies have the opportunity to decide, at the beginning, whether its investment backed expectations could be realized under the regulatory environment the state later attempted to impose."

One difficult issue raised by *Lucas* is the "denominator" problem: where the tract includes some land covered by the permit denial and some that is not, which area is used to determine if there has been a total taking? Should the whole parcel be used to measure whether a total diminution of economic value has occurred or only the portion of the parcel subject to the permit? The Court of Federal Claims has suggested a multi-part test, including "the degree of contiguity, the acquisition dates, the extent to which the protected lands increase the value of the other lands," and especially "how the economic expectations of the claimant, with respect to the parcel at issue, have shaped the owner's actual and projected use of the property." An owner "who treats a series of parcels as one property for the purposes of development, financing, planning and utilization, cannot then segregate the properties for the purpose of establishing a taking claim." Forest Properties, Inc. v. United States, 39 Fed. Cl. 56, 73 (1997). *See also* Mark R. Poirier, *Property, Environment, Community*, 12 J. ENVTL. L. & LITIG. 43, 79 (1997) (test should ask whether developer had separated the sensitive lands from the rest of the tract unreasonably or in bad faith).

A recent federal circuit opinion attempts to clarify this and other related issues of takings law. In *Palm Beach Isles Ass'n v. United States*, 208 F.3d 1374 (Fed. Cir. 2000), a group of investors had bought over three hundred acres of land north of Palm Beach on a long spit of land between the Atlantic and Lake Worth. The investors sold the 261 acres north of a road to a developer in 1968 for almost three times the original purchase price of the whole parcel. The remaining tract consisted of 1.4 acres of shoreline wetlands next to the road and fifty acres of submerged lands, lying in Lake Worth. Lake Worth was originally a freshwater lake but is now a tidal water with direct access to the ocean, which serves as a segment of the Atlantic Intercoastal Waterway. The developers had obtained permits to dredge and fill this area in 1957, but the permit expired in 1963. A new permit application under the CWA was later refused, largely on environmental grounds. The Federal Circuit held that the fifty acres should be considered as a separate tract (for purposes of the denominator) because the company never had planned to develop the parcels as a single unit, and it sold off the rest of the land before the Clean Water Act came into play. Hence, the Court concluded, there was a total taking under *Lucas*, since the land had no other economic value. The navigational servitude counted as a "background principle of property law" limiting the developer's rights, but only if the government's purpose was related to navigation. The court remanded for a determination of whether the government had a navigation-related justification for denying the permit. On petition for rehearing, the court reiterated its view that "reasonable investment-backed expectations" is not a relevant factor in a total taking case. Palm Beach Isles Ass'n v. United States, 231 F.3d 1354 (Fed. Cir. 2000). Thus, it would apparently be irrelevant if the specific land had no development value when acquired, or that the entire initial investment on the larger tract had already been recovered before the suit.

The possibility of a successful takings claim increases the pressure on the government to grant permits. Even in cases where a permit is clearly justified, however, valuable wetlands are lost. The following excerpt describes the government's efforts to reconcile land development and wetlands preservation. Increasingly, these efforts have focused on allowing for mitigation banking, which allows the restoration of one area of wetlands in exchange for the destruction of other wetlands under a § 404 permit.

J.B. RUHL AND R. JUGE GREGG, INTEGRATING ECOSYSTEM SERVICES INTO ENVIRONMENTAL LAW: A CASE STUDY OF WETLANDS MITIGATION BANKING[11]

20 STANFORD ENVT'L L. J. 365 (2001).

The Corps' guidelines for administering wetlands mitigation require it to review 404 permit applications using a preference "sequencing" approach. The first preference is to require the applicant to avoid filling wetland resources; the second preference is to require minimization of adverse impacts that cannot reasonably be avoided; and the least desirable preference is to require the developer to provide compensatory mitigation for those unavoidable adverse impacts that remain after all minimization measures have been exercised. The least desirable option, compensatory mitigation, is the basis for wetlands trading.

Both EPA and the Corps traditionally have preferred on-site to off-site locations for the compensatory mitigation activity and have preferred in-kind mitigation to mitigation that uses a substantially different type of wetland. Regardless of location, EPA and the Corps prefer measures that restore prior wetland areas as the highest form of mitigation, followed by enhancement of low-quality wetlands, then creation of new wetlands, and, least favored of all, preservation of existing wetlands.... * * *

---

11. Copyright © 2001, STANFORD ENVT'L L. J. Reprinted by Permission. * * *

[D]uring the late 1980s the Corps and EPA started shifting compensatory activities increasingly from on-site to off-site mitigation, thus opening the door to the wetlands mitigation banking technique. This approach, its proponents argued, would prove advantageous both in terms of economic efficiency and ecological integrity, aggregating small wetlands threatened by development into larger restored wetlands in a different location. It is defined generally as "a system in which the creation, enhancement, restoration, or preservation of wetlands is recognized by a regulatory agency as generating compensation credits allowing the future development of other wetland sites." In its most basic form, wetlands mitigation banking allows a developer to protect wetlands at one site in advance of development and then draw down the resulting bank of mitigation "credits" as development is implemented and wetlands at another site are filled. Indeed, the concept has progressed beyond this personal bank model. Today, large commercial and public wetlands banks, not tied to a particular development, sell mitigation piecemeal to third-party developers in need of compensatory mitigation.

The Corps and EPA officially endorsed the mitigation banking approach in their 1995 Federal Guidance for the Establishment, Use and Operation of Mitigation Banks, setting out a standard review procedure for establishing and using wetlands banks in the 404 permit process.

In 1995, five United States agencies published the Banking Guidance, as promised in the Mitigation Guidance, in order to detail the use and operation of mitigation banks The document's introduction declares that the "objective of a mitigation bank is to provide for the replacement of the chemical, physical, and biological functions of wetlands and other aquatic resources which are lost as a result of authorized impacts." This perspective is later broadened to acknowledge that "[t]he overall goal of a mitigation bank is to provide economically efficient and flexible mitigation opportunities, while fully compensating for wetland and other aquatic resource losses in a manner that contributes to the long-term ecological functioning of the watershed within which the bank is to be located." The Banking Guidance thus qualifies the goal of replacing ecological functioning by acknowledging economic realities. * * *

Because the crediting and debiting procedure forms the heart of a wetlands mitigation bank, the determination of what will be counted as "currency" is crucial. The Banking Guidance focuses initially on the use of "aquatic functions" as its banking currency—a currency that is easily "exchanged" or translated into service values. But the Banking Guidance then follows the lead of the Mitigation Guidance and allows acreage to be a surrogate measure if functional assessment is impractical. The Banking Guidance then takes one more step back from its vision and allows any "appropriate functional assessment methodology ... acceptable to all signatories" to be used to quantify credits. Once again, therefore, the official guidance provides an opportunity, but not a requirement, to rely on ecosystem indicators as the assessment methodology. * * *

Ecosystem service valuation must be incorporated into wetlands mitigation banking decision making at two critical junctures: the wetlands assessment stage and the wetlands trading stage. The Environmental Law Institute's (ELI) groundbreaking 1993 study of wetlands mitigation banking describes these stages as raising the "credits defined and valued" issues, and recognizes that they are the most complex issues in mitigation banking. To fully capture ecosystem service values, the assessment method must consistently define the services and incorporate measurements of their value both for the wetlands to be lost and for those wetlands used for mitigation. Moreover, the trading ratio between wetlands lost and mitigated should reflect any differences in service population, service delivery type, and efficiency. It should also account for margins of error that may justify deviating from a fixed exchange rate. When function values and service populations are reliably measured and appropriately compared among sites, using a reasonable margin of error, ecosystem service valuation methods can be integrated into the assessment and trading stages of wetland mitigation banking.

In our survey of mitigation banks, however, we found no explicit use of this kind of ecosystem service valuation at either the assessment or trading stages. Wetlands mitigation banking entities seem focused on using the most simple and expedient assessment method the relevant regulatory bodies would approve. Moreover, the regulatory bodies did not appear widely to require or even encourage a more sophisticated approach. These less refined valuation methods may work in situations involving an exchange of wetlands of basically similar attributes in the same watershed, because one can assume that similar wetlands provide similar functions to similar ecosystems. These basic valuation methods also suffice for trades based on gross comparisons between classes of wetlands—e.g., two acres of Type A are worth three acres of Type B. Trades based on wetland classes and fixed ratios thus dominate the wetlands mitigation banking practice. * * *

Given the current state of affairs, there is little promise for the integration of ecosystem service valuation methods into wetlands mitigation banking until methods of wetland assessment are significantly improved. In the absence of widely available, readily applied methods for calculating and comparing ecosystem service values of the wetlands being traded, the Corps will likely put constraints on trading markets to compensate for ecosystem function losses not recognized by acre-based methods. These constraints significantly undercut the market and information advantages ecosystem service valuation would impart to wetlands mitigation banking in general, thus further reducing any incentive to apply such methods.

Hence, unless some way is developed to capture the ecosystem service value of wetlands without costly, time-consuming, and complicated valuation methods—e.g., by measurement of readily determinable indicators of ecosystem service value—wetlands mitigation banking is likely to rely most heavily on acre-based and narrow function-based methods and highly regulated "markets" for trades. Nevertheless, if such assessment methods can be developed, ... the authority to require their use is implicit in the existing legal framework of the section 404 program. By using these new assessment methods, the wetlands mitigation banking program would surely come closer to meeting its environmental protection objectives.

NOTES

1.   Mitigation may allow development to proceed on at least part of a parcel in return for preservation or restoration efforts elsewhere. Thus, a mitigation requirement allows the regulator to avoid a complete, unconditional ban on use of property. This may have constitutional implications. The availability of mitigation banking may convert a complete ban on development, which would likely be found a per se taking under *Lucas*, into a conditional regulatory burden, which will be upheld under other Supreme Court takings cases involving development permits, *Nollan v. California Coastal Com'n*, 483 U.S. 825 (1987) and *Dolan v. City of Tigard*, 512 U.S. 374 (1994), described in more detail at 346, *supra,* given the right factual basis. Presumably, it should not be difficult to show that there is a nexus between the loss of particular wetlands and the need to provide the same ecological services elsewhere, and any reasonably designed program should be able to survive *Dolan*'s rough proportionality test.

2.   What "currency" should be used to measure wetland value? By attempting to quantify wetland services, does the idea of ecosystem service value commodify nature in an inappropriate way?

3.   Would a well-developed market for wetlands mitigation have any significance with respect to Congress's regulatory power? Could Congress indirectly limit development of isolated wetlands by encouraging their use as mitigation for projects that do fall under its jurisdiction? As of 2005 a total of approximately 450 mitgation banks had been approved with another 198 banks proposed. *See* EPA, MITIGATION BANKING (2006), available at http://www.epa.gov/owow/wetlands/facts/fact16.html.

E.   THE FUTURE

Although the Clean Water Act has resulted in significant accomplishments, many of the most straightforward sources of water pollution—municipal sewage treatment plants and traditional industrial point sources—have already been targeted. Urban and agricultural runoff remain significant problems. Many observers believe that a new regulatory direction is necessary, one focused not on individual sources but instead more holistically on an entire watershed. The article below describes a watershed approach to restoring the health of water bodies that remain impaired.

CLEAN WATER ACTION PLAN: RESTORING AND PROTECTING AMERICA'S WATERS

Carole Browner and Dan Glickman, U.S. EPA, U.S. Dep't of Agriculture.
(EPA 840–R–98–001, 1998).

Despite tremendous progress, 40 percent of the nation's waterways assessed by states are still unsafe for fishing and swimming. Pollution from factories and sewage treatment plants, soil erosion, and wetland losses have been dramatically reduced. But runoff from city streets, rural areas, and other sources continues to degrade the environment and puts drinking water at risk. Fish in many waters still contain dangerous levels of mercury, polychlorinated biphenyls (PCBs), and other toxic contaminants. * * *

A. Watershed Approach—The Key to the Future

This Action Plan proposes a new collaborative effort by state, tribal, federal, and local governments, the private sector and the public to restore those watersheds not meeting clean water, natural resource, and public health goals and to sustain healthy conditions in other watersheds.

For the past 25 years, most water pollution control efforts relied on broadly applied national programs that reduced water pollution from individual sources, such as discharges from sewage treatment plants and factories, and from polluted runoff. Today, there is growing recognition that clean water strategies built on this foundation and tailored to specific watershed conditions are the key to the future.

Why Watershed?

Clean water is the product of a healthy watershed—a watershed in which urban, agricultural, rangelands, forest lands, and all other parts of the landscape are well-managed to prevent pollution. Focusing on the whole watershed helps strike the best balance among efforts to control point source pollution and polluted runoff, and protect drinking water sources and sensitive natural resources such as wetlands. A watershed focus also helps identify the most cost-effective pollution control strategies to meet clean water goals.

Working at the watershed level encourages the public to get involved in efforts to restore and protect their water resources and is the foundation for building strong clean water partnerships. The watershed approach is the best way to bring state, tribal, federal, and local programs together to more effectively and efficiently clean up and protect waters. It is also the key to greater accountability and progress toward clean water goals.

Key Elements of the Watershed Approach

This Action Plan proposes a watershed approach built on several key elements.

reduction credits to make further progress towards water quality goals.

EPA, EPA RELEASES INNOVATIVE APPROACH TO CLEANER WATER (2003), *available at* http://www.epa.gov/epahome/headline_011303.htm (last updated Jan. 15, 2003). Copy of the new policy and access to the public comments is available at 68 Fed. Reg. 1608 (2003) and on the EPA's website at http://www.epa.gov/owow/watershed/trading.htm (last updated Jan. 13, 2003).

At this point, however, the EPA makes it clear that the WQTP itself is *guidance* for states to *encourage voluntary* reductions in effluents:

> The purpose of this policy is to encourage states, interstate agencies and tribes to develop and implement water quality trading programs for nutrients, sediments and other pollutants where opportunities exist to achieve water quality improvements at reduced costs. More specifically, the policy is intended to encourage voluntary trading programs that facilitate implementation of TMDLs, reduce the costs of compliance with CWA regulations, establish incentives for voluntary reductions and promote watershed-based initiatives. A number of states are in various stages of developing trading programs. This policy provides guidance for states, interstate agencies and tribes to assist them in developing and implementing such programs.

68 Fed. Reg. 1608, 1609 (2003). Since the January 13, 2003 announcement of the new WQTP and claims that the EPA is giving states $800,000 for 11 pilot projects, it is quite clear that the agency's encouragement of state action is not financial, but more technical and aspirational.

In addition to the WQTP, wetlands mitigation banking offers another relatively new market-based approach to water quality regulation. *See* J. B. Ruhl & R. Juge Gregg, *Integrating Ecosystem Services into Environmental Law: A Case Study of Wetlands Mitigation Banking*, 20 STAN. ENVTL. L.J. 365 (2001).

b. Project XL

Under the Clinton Administration, the EPA adopted Project XL, through which the EPA negotiates alternative compliance plans with individual sources, allowing them greater regulatory relief in exchange for agreements to improve environmental performance beyond what regulatory requirements would demand. In a typical XL project, the EPA might grant pre-approval to process changes that would ordinarily require separate approval, and issue a streamlined permit authorizing cross-pollutant or cross-media trades that might not otherwise be allowed by existing regulations. In exchange, firms must commit, in a quasi-contractual agreement, to make measurable improvements and adopt specific environmentally protective measures that would exceed otherwise applicable compliance requirements. Not surprisingly, this kind of "regulatory reinvention" has proved controversial. Fans argue that it achieves compliance creatively by allowing cross-pollutant and inter-media trades, and that XL is superior because it involves permit holders in a collaborative, quasi-contractual decision making process. *See* Jody Freeman, *Collaborative Governance in the Administrative State*, 45 UCLA L. REV. 1 (1997). Critics charge, however, that XL weakens environmental standards. *See* Rena I. Steinzor, *Regulatory Reinvention and Project XL: Does the Emperor Have Any Clothes?*, 26 ENVTL. L. REP. 10,527 (1996).

Industry reluctance to participate may ultimately wither Project XL. As Richard Stewart sees it:

> Overall, the program's performance to date has been disappointing. Project XL has been plagued with uncertainties and inconsistencies in the establishment of default regulatory baselines, evaluation of proposals' environmental benefits, and the criteria for project approval. This has caused considerable uncertainty and delay and has resulted in companies requesting lengthy lists of exemptions that are unrelated to the promised environmental improvements. These circumstances deter facilities from submitting proposals. Despite the potential benefits available to participating facilities, EPA has not been able to overcome the problem of low industry participation. Only a relatively few agreements have been concluded, and efforts at negotiating others have floundered in stalemate.

> Another problem that hinders wider use of XL is uncertainty about the legality of the alternative requirements that it provides. Questions have arisen regarding EPA's authority to approve requirements that differ from those imposed by otherwise applicable statutes and regulations. Firms are concerned that if they enter into Project XL agreements and fail to comply with otherwise applicable regulatory requirements, they may be vulnerable to enforcement actions brought either by government authorities or in the form of citizen suits. Businesses may also be reluctant to make the capital investments needed to implement alternative requirements, only to find themselves saddled with additional requirements imposed unilaterally by federal or state regulatory authorities pursuant to new regulations that will require further investments in controls that may be inconsistent with the measures already taken to implement the agreement. Such fears may explain low interest in participation in the project. Yet, EPA has not asked Congress to authorize its practice through legislation. Many environmental groups are suspicious of the process, contending that it fails to ensure that the environmental interests at the bargaining table have adequate resources and in other respects fails to ensure the environmental integrity of the projects. Unless resolved soon, the problems noted above may lead to an overall failure of this EPA initiative.

Richard B. Stewart, *A New Generation of Environmental Regulation?* 29 CAP. U. L. REV. 21, 67–68 (2001). The Bush Administration has not pursued Project XL—as of 2003 the agency is no longer accepting XL applications. *See* http://www.epa.gov/ProjectXL.

For more on the debate about this initiative, *see* Bradford C. Mank, *The Environmental Protection Agency's Project XL and Other Regulatory Reform Initiatives: The Need for Legislative Authorization*, 25 ECOLOGY L.Q. 1 (1998); Beth S. Ginsberg & Cynthia Cummis, *EPA's Project XL: A Paradigm for Promising Regulatory Reform*, 26 ENVTL. L. REP. 10,059 (1996). For suggestions on how the XL process might be improved, *see* Lawrence E. Susskind & Joshua Secunda, *The Risks and Advantages of Agency Discretion: Evidence from EPA's Project XL*, 17 UCLA J. ENVTL. L. & POL'Y 67 (1999).

c. SEPs

The EPA has also begun to experiment with innovative remedial approaches, such as Supplemental Environmental Projects (SEPs), which were first pioneered in citizen suits. A SEP is an "environmentally beneficial" project undertaken voluntarily in settlement of an enforcement action in exchange for a decrease in the amount of the penalty. The EPA's SEP policy requires that there be a nexus between the proposed project and the violation subject to settlement. *See* William L. Thomas, Bertram C. Frey, & Fern Fleischer Daves, *Using Auditing, Pollution Prevention, and Management Systems to Craft Superior Environmental Enforcement Solutions*, 30 ENVTL. L. REP. 10299 (2000). Between FY 1996 and FY 1999, the EPA incorporated pollution prevention SEPs in the settlement of 372 enforcement actions. *Id.* at 10307.

While monetary penalties are generally thought to be effective deterrents, there is scant empirical evidence on which enforcement tools work best, and under which conditions. For a survey of the alternatives, not all of them punitive, *see* Mark A. Cohen, *Empirical Research on the Deterrent Effect of Environmental Monitoring and Enforcement*, 30 ENVTL. L. REP. 10245 (2000) (evaluating the relative effectiveness of various monitoring and enforcement mechanisms, including reliance on performance measures, the role of information disclosure, private law enforcement and criminal law enforcement).

d. Audits and Environmental Management Systems

In recent years, environmental auditing has emerged as a potentially effective, though controversial, approach to enforcement. Firms have sought a privilege for voluntary internal environmental audits, arguing that to encourage voluntary self-regulation, any information revealed by such audits should not be used against them in litigation. Many environmentalists oppose such policies because they believe that audits should not immunize companies from enforcement for environmental violations. A variety of states have established an audit privilege, but to date the EPA and the Department of Justice have opposed them. *See* Eric W. Orts & Paula C. Murray, *Environmental Disclosure and Evidentiary Privilege*, 1997 U. ILL. L. REV. 1 (1997). As the debate over audit privilege continues, the empirical evidence is beginning to develop. A National Conference of State Legislatures study found that state environmental audit privilege and immunity laws do not encourage facilities to begin auditing or increase the number of audits they perform or to disclose more violations to legislators. *See* Nancy K. Stoner & Wendy J. Miller, *National Conference of State Legislatures Study Finds That State Environmental Audit Laws Have No Impact on Company Self–Auditing and Disclosure Violations*, 29 ENVTL. L. REP. 10265 (1999).

Despite the EPA's reluctance to provide full protection for firms that self-audit, the agency is increasingly interested in encouraging auditing. For example, the EPA and the National Pork Producers Council agreed to an industry-specific compliance assurance program under which the pork producers can reduce their penalties for violations of the Clean Water Act that they report and correct as part of a comprehensive environmental auditing program. *See* Richard E. Schwartz, Steven P. Quarles, and Ellen B. Steen, *Encouraging Self–Auditing Within the Pork Industry: The Nationwide Clean Water Act Enforcement Agreement for Agriculture's First Industry–Wide Environmental Auditing Program*, 29 ENVTL. L. REP. 10395 (1999).

Environmental audits are only one part of a more comprehensive approach to self-regulation through environmental management. Firms are increasingly adopting environmental management systems (EMSs) to improve environmental performance by "integrating environmental strategies into organizational development." The goal is not merely to reduce violations and limit penalties but to establish "sustainable environmental performance that continuously improves." *See* John Voorhees, *The Changing Environmental Management Scene: Federal Policy Impacts the Private and Public Sectors,* 31 ENVTL. L. REP. 10079 (2001). An EMS typically requires that a firm inventory the environmental aspects of its production process and products, identify "significant" impacts, and adopt a management system that set targets, allocates resources, provides employee training and establishes a system for auditing. Critics argue that while this approach looks good on paper, it does not involve hard, enforceable limits. These must come, they point out, from a regulatory body such as state and federal agencies. For more on self-regulation, *see* Andrew King & Michael Lenox, *Industry Self–Regulation Without Sanctions: The Chemical Industry's Responsible Care Program*, 43 ACAD. MGMT. J. 698 (2000). On information disclosure as a regulatory tool, see, e.g., David W. Case, *The Law and Economics of Environmental Information as Regulation*, 30 ENVTL. L. REP. 10773 (2001); Bradley C. Karkkainen, *Information as Environmental Regulation: TRI and Performance Benchmarking, Precursor to a New Paradigm?*, 89 GEO. L.J. 257, 271 (2001). The Geneva-based Institute for Standards and Organization (ISO), an influential international standard-setting body, has introduced EMS principles into international commerce through publication of its ISO 14000 environmental management standards. Businesses that meet these standards may receive ISO certification, which confers a number of advantages on the certified firm. *See* Paula C. Murray, *The International Environmental Management Standard, ISO 14000: Tariff Barrier of a Step to an Emerging Global Environ-*

mental Policy?, 18 U. PA. J. INT'L ECON. L. 577, 578–82 (1997); Jennifer Nash & John Ehrenfeld, *Codes of Environmental Management Practice: Assessing Their Potential as a Tool for Change*, 22 ANN. REV. ENERGY & ENV'T 487, 507 (1997).

e. Collaboration and Negotiation

State and federal agencies have also experimented in recent years with "collaborative" and "consensus-based" strategies for developing and enforcing environmental regulations. *See* Jody Freeman & Laura I. Langbein, *Regulatory Negotiation and the Legitimacy Benefit*, 9 N.Y.U. ENVTL. L.J. 60 (2000); Charles C. Caldart & Nicholas A. Ashford, *Negotiation as a Means of Developing and Implementing Environmental and Occupational Health and Safety Policy*, 23 HARV. ENVTL. L. REV. 141 (1999). As with Project XL, SEPs and the audit privilege, these initiatives attract both supporters and critics. While proponents view collaborative measures as creative efforts to involve stakeholders in the production of regulations that will affect them and seek to draw on their expertise, opponents fear that negotiation will weaken environmental standards and undermine accountability. For a developed model of collaboration as an alternative to the traditional adversarialism of the regulatory process, *see* Jody Freeman, *Collaborative Governance in the Administrative State*, 45 UCLA L. REV. 1 (1997). On contractual approaches to environmental regulation, *see* Jody Freeman, *The Contracting State*, 28 FLA. ST. U. L. REV. 155 (2000). For an overview of the current competing models of environmental regulation, *see* Daniel A. Farber, *Triangulating the Future of Reinvention: Three Emerging Models of Environmental Protection*, 2000 U. ILL. L. REV. 61 (2000).

CHAPTER 8

HAZARDOUS WASTE

■ ■ ■

A. REGULATING THE TREATMENT, STORAGE AND DISPOSAL OF HAZARDOUS WASTES

As we have seen, in the early 1970s the federal government began its active involvement in the regulation of air and water pollution. In the latter half of the 1970s, Congress turned to a different problem, toxic and hazardous waste disposal. Congress faced the dual problems of dealing with the serious threats posed by many existing waste disposal sites, and regulating future disposal activities so as not to multiply such threats. The result was the enactment of two enormously complex federal statutes, the Resource Conservation and Recovery Act of 1976 (RCRA), which regulates the handling and disposal of hazardous waste (and is hence largely forward-looking), and the Comprehensive Environmental Response, Compensation, and Liability Act of 1980 (CERCLA, also known as the Superfund law) which facilitates the cleanup of leaking sites (and is hence largely backward-looking).

In establishing RCRA, Congress amended the Solid Waste Disposal Act, first passed in 1965 to address the regulation of landfills and dumps. RCRA emerged as Congress gradually became aware that toxics were seeping into groundwater through multiple pathways, including landfills, and posing a threat to human health. Part of this congressional awareness came through the issuance of an EPA report to Congress that had been required by the Solid Waste Disposal Act. The report documented a number of instances of groundwater contamination and human illness as a result of the mishandling of hazardous wastes. *See* Halina Szenjwald Brown, Brian J. Cook, Robert Krueger and Jo Anne Shatkin, *Reassessing the History of U.S. Hazardous Waste Disposal Policy–Problem Definitions, Expert Knowledge and Agenda–Setting*, 8 RISK (1997), http://www.piercelaw.edu/Risk/Vol8/summer/Brown+.htm.

Not long after RCRA's passage, the issue of hazardous waste contamination made national headlines. In August 1978, President Carter declared a state of emergency in the Love Canal area of Niagara Falls, New York. Investigating serious health complaints by residents, the state

838

health department found that toxic chemicals had leaked into the basements of many houses, and into the air, water, and soil. Air pollution levels ranged as high as 5000 times the maximum safe levels. In 1947, Hooker Chemical and Plastics Corporation had purchased an uncompleted waterway and used it as a depository for an estimated 352 million pounds of industrial wastes over the following six years. The land had then been used as a school site and a housing development. As a result, three decades later, over 1000 families were evacuated, $30 million in cleanup costs were required, and over $3 billion in damage claims were filed.[1]

Love Canal was not an isolated incident. In the past, land was regarded as a "safe" repository for wastes that could not be disposed of in the air or water. Decades of uncontrolled dumping have led to contamination of land and of related ground and surface waters. Some of the most serious threats involve disposal or storage of wastes at sites where water contamination may occur, such as sites located in floodplains, over aquifers unprotected by impervious rock or soil, and in filled wetlands. Water filtering through such sites can leach chemicals into ground water, and runoff from rain and snowmelt can carry chemicals to nearby streams and rivers.

Love Canal had a significant effect on Congress and led to the passage of CERCLA. And though Love Canal and other high-profile incidents involved the past handling of hazardous wastes—and thus would become the focus of CERCLA cleanup efforts—they also re-focused congressional attention on the need to regulate the handling and disposal of hazardous waste to avoid the creation of new waste sites and led to significant amendments to RCRA in 1980 and 1984.

1. THE RESOURCE CONSERVATION AND RECOVERY ACT

Although Congress enacted RCRA in 1976, the EPA moved very slowly in promulgating regulations to implement the statute. In part, this was because the task of issuing regulations was highly technical, and because the EPA was a relatively new agency with a number of complicated statutes to implement. Because of the delay, environmental groups sued the EPA, ultimately winning court victories forcing the agency to implement the statute. Yet the EPA continued to move slowly in the early 1980s, largely because of the Reagan Administration's opposition to implementing and enforcing hazardous waste laws. The administration had,

---

1. These facts are drawn from CEQ, ENVTL. QUALITY: TENTH ANN. REP., at 176–77 (1979); Mary Worobec, *An Analysis of the Resource Conservation and Recovery Act*, 11 ENV'T REP. 634–35 (1980).

In 1995, after sixteen years of litigation, the Clinton administration announced that Occidental Chemical Corp. had agreed to pay $129 million to the federal government for its costs of cleaning up the Love Canal neighborhood. $102 million was to go to EPA's Superfund to cover governmental cleanup costs. The other $27 million was to go to the Federal Emergency Management Agency, which undertook the initial evacuation and cleanup. Previously, in 1994, Occidental had entered into a $98 million settlement of claims by the state of New York related to Love Canal. *See* James Gerstenzang, *Firm Agrees to Settle Love Canal Suit*, L.A. TIMES, Dec. 22, 1995, at A43.

after all, campaigned on a de-regulatory agenda, and viewed environmental and health and safety regulation as especially onerous. Eventually, in the face of publicity about Love Canal and other dangerous and highly contaminated sites, the Democratic Congress stepped in and amended RCRA in 1984 (the amendments are known as the Hazardous and Solid Waste Amendments). The 1984 amendments were much more specific and directive, and included provisions to clean up leaking underground storage tanks, expand liability for small generators of hazardous waste and ban land disposal of hazardous waste without treatment. The legislation also included "hammers" that would force industry groups to pressure EPA to meet various statutory deadlines or face much more draconian measures (such as the complete ban on land disposal). The intent of the congressional amendments was to remove much of EPA's discretion by providing detailed statutory provisions and hard deadlines. This example illustrates the institutional dynamic we have noted throughout the casebook: environmental policy is made in the push and pull between the branches. If the executive branch resists implementing environmental statutes, the legislative branch can always amend the law to force agency action. Caught in the middle, of course, are the agencies, which must abide by their statutory mandates and also respond to the legitimate political imperatives of the administration.

RCRA is designed to provide "cradle to grave" coverage for a large percentage of the hazardous waste generated by businesses and government. The statute covers approximately 46 million tons of hazardous wastes generated annually by more than 16,000 generators. *See* EPA, THE NATIONAL BIENNIAL RCRA HAZARDOUS WASTE REPORT (BASED ON 2007 DATA) at 1–17 Chemical manufacturers produce the largest percentage of RCRA hazardous waste, followed by petroleum and coal manufacturing. *Id.* at 1–7. Louisiana leads the country in generating RCRA waste, followed by Texas, Michigan and Mississippi. *Id.* at 1–2.

RCRA's overarching theory is that if we know where the waste is during its life cycle—from the moment of generation through transport to a disposal site, to its ultimate treatment, storage and disposal—then we can avoid the kinds of catastrophes at which CERCLA is aimed. RCRA is a highly prescriptive statute that employs a variety of regulatory strategies, including a permit system, design standards, performance standards, "good character" and capitalization requirements, information disclosure, liability provisions and absolute prohibitions on certain activities. Despite its highly prescriptive nature, RCRA applies only to *hazardous* waste, which means that a great deal of waste that might nevertheless pose public health risks escapes RCRA regulation. RCRA also presents an opportunity to explore the difference between a "health-based" statute like the Clean Air Act, which sets national ambient air quality standards based on public health requirements, and a "technology based" statute that sets levels of pollution control based on what technology can achieve at an acceptable cost. As you read the materials, ask yourself: which kind of statute is RCRA?

RCRA contains ten separate subtitles, three of which contain the primary substantive features of RCRA: Subtitle C is the chapter that regulates hazardous waste; Subtitle D regulates and provides guidelines to states in their management of solid waste; and Subtitle I regulates underground storage tanks (USTs). We will focus most heavily on Subtitle C.

a. An Overview of Subtitle C, the Regulation of Hazardous Waste

Subtitle C is based on the simple premise that hazardous waste should be tracked from the time of its generation to the time of its disposal, and that it should not be disposed of in a manner that may create a danger to human health or to the environment. Naturally, however, the simplicity of the premise is belied by the complexity of the regulatory system. The central components of Subtitle C are as follows:

i. *Definitions of Solid Waste, Hazardous Waste*

Subtitle C covers material that must be both "solid waste" and "hazardous waste." Understandably, these definitional requirements lead to vigorous disputes over which activities and substances fall within the scope of the statute. As we saw in Chapter V with the Clean Water Act (which regulates almost exclusively point sources of water pollution and not non-point source run-off), definitions can function like "on-off" switches: activities that fall within the definitional reach of the statute are fully regulated, but those that fall outside the definitional categories can escape regulation altogether, even when the activities all pose some degree of risk to human health or environment. Falling within RCRA's purview can be very burdensome and highly costly, and escaping coverage can have very significant implications for public health, which explains why the definitional battles over what constitutes solid waste and what constitutes hazardous waste have been so intense.

These definitional questions over what constitutes a hazardous waste have occupied an enormous amount of regulatory energy. EPA has had difficulty identifying those wastes that ought to be considered hazardous, and struggled to define materials that should *not* be regarded as "waste" because they may be reused or recycled in the manufacturing process. In section 3001, Congress requires EPA to promulgate criteria for "identifying the characteristics" of hazardous waste, and for "listing" hazardous waste that should be subject to RCRA regulation. EPA has divided hazardous wastes into two separate categories, those that are "listed" and those that exhibit a particular characteristic—either toxicity, ignitability, corrosivity or reactivity (so called "characteristic" wastes)—that makes the waste hazardous. Generally speaking, listed wastes are subject to more rigorous regulation than characteristic wastes, though both listed and characteristic wastes must be tracked from cradle to grave.

ii. Generators, Transporters and TSD facilities

RCRA applies separate regulatory standards to generators of hazardous wastes, transporters, and treatment, storage and disposal (TSD) facilities. The burden on generators and transporters is relatively lower than on TSDs, and consists primarily of labeling, tracking and reporting requirements. Because TSD requirements are more onerous, generators and transporters tend to take steps to avoid doing anything (such as treating the waste) that might trigger TSD status.

(1). Generators of Hazardous Wastes

Businesses that generate hazardous waste must keep detailed records of the type, quantity and "disposition" of the waste and use a manifest system to ensure that the hazardous waste generated by the source is ultimately processed on-site or at a TSD facility with a § 3005 permit (a manifest is a list or invoice of cargo for a transporter, identifying the cargo and its intended destination.) If the waste is disposed of offsite, the manifest accompanies the waste from the generator's site to the transporter and ultimately to the TSD facility and requires the inclusion of information about the type and quantity of waste being disposed of, along with how it is contained. The generator is responsible for ensuring that the manifest is properly filled out by transporters and TSD facilities. Generators are also subject to limitations on the amount of time they can store hazardous waste prior to shipment; if they store waste for too long they are required to obtain a permit as a TSD facility. Because the regulatory burdens on TSD facilities are so much more onerous, most generators of hazardous waste ship their waste offsite for disposal.

(2). Transporters of Hazardous Waste

Transporters of hazardous waste are also subject to the manifest system and must comply with Department of Transportation regulations concerning the safe transport of hazardous wastes. 49 C.F.R. §§ 171–179 (1999). Transporters can become liable as generators of hazardous wastes if they mix dissimilar wastes; they also have reporting obligations in the event of a spill.

(3). Treatment, Storage and Disposal Facilities

TSD facilities must obtain permits under RCRA § 3005 and are the most extensively regulated parties under the Act. Regulatory obligations include providing appropriate security, emergency planning, adequate employee training, groundwater monitoring, recordkeeping and proving adequate financial security in order to prevent the abandonment of the facility. RCRA also regulates the location, construction and operation of disposal sites. Common methods of disposing of hazardous waste include incinerating the waste; disposing liquid waste in surface impoundments; disposing treated waste on land; and injecting waste into underground storage wells in impermeable rock formations deep beneath the earth's surface.

The permit system established under § 3005 is the key enforcement provision for TSD facilities. EPA is given broad inspection powers (§ 3007) and the authority to issue administrative compliance orders (with violators subject to a civil penalty) or begin civil actions against violators of any requirement (§ 3008). Criminal penalties are also available for violation of the permit requirements or falsification of documents (§ 3008(d)).

iii. Federal Delegation to States for Implementation

As with many federal environmental statutes, RCRA embodies a version of "cooperative federalism." The statute delegates to states the authority to implement RCRA's regulatory requirements, subject to EPA oversight (§ 3006). Most states have been granted the authority to implement at least the basic RCRA programs. For a listing of state delegation under RCRA *see* http://www.ecos.org/section/states/enviro_actlist/rcra. State laws less stringent than federal requirements are preempted. (§ 3009).

Although states play an important role in enforcing RCRA, the EPA sometimes steps in if a state is unable or unwilling to enforce the statute. In a controversial decision, one federal appeals court has held that where EPA had authorized a state to administer and enforce a hazardous waste program, and a state court approved a no-penalty settlement between the state enforcement agency and a serious RCRA violator, § 3006(b) barred EPA from "overfiling," i.e., maintaining a separate action based on the same violations. *Harmon Industries, Inc. v. Browner*, 191 F.3d 894 (8th Cir. 1999). However, two other courts of appeals have rejected *Harmon* and held that EPA's authorization of a state hazardous waste program does not strip the United States of civil or criminal enforcement authority because RCRA contemplates that only the federal regulatory or permitting program is supplanted by authorized state programs. *United States v. Power Eng'g Co.*, 303 F.3d 1232 (10th Cir. 2002); *United States v. Elias*, 269 F.3d 1003 (9th Cir. 2001), *cert. denied*, 537 U.S. 812 (2002).

iv. Land Disposal Standards

RCRA § 3004(*o*) establishes land disposal standards for all landfills, surface impoundments, waste piles, and land treatment units, both new and existing, used to treat, store, or dispose of hazardous waste. They consist of two sets of performance standards. The first is a set of design and operating standards—basically requiring liners and leachate collection systems for certain units—intended to ensure that owners or operators minimize the formation of leachate and the migration of leachate to adjacent subsurface soil and to ground water. The second is a set of ground water monitoring and response requirements applicable to all units—a three-stage program to detect, evaluate, and correct ground water contamination—intended to ensure that owners or operators detect any ground water contamination and perform corrective action when such contamination threatens human health and the environment.

v. Land Disposal Restrictions/Ban

In the 1984 Hazardous and Solid Waste Amendments, Public Law 98–616, 98 Stat. 3221, Congress shifted the focus of hazardous waste management away from safer land disposal to *treatment* alternatives. The amendments ban land disposal of hazardous wastes unless one of two conditions is satisfied: either the waste is treated to comply with standards promulgated by EPA under RCRA § 3004(m), or EPA determines that the hazardous constituents will not "migrate" from the disposal unit. RCRA § 3004(g)(5). These so-called "hammer" provisions were designed by Congress to force a reluctant EPA, which had been slow to implement RCRA, to act. It also created incentives for industry to work together with the agency to develop acceptable treatment standards rather than to fight the EPA's every move, since without them the more draconian ban would apply.

For most toxic as opposed to ignitable, corrosive or reactive characteristic wastes, treatment requires the use of the Best Demonstrated Available Technology (BDAT). More specifically, for many toxics the EPA establishes treatment standards set as concentration levels but the concentration levels are derived from the performance of the BDAT. TSD facilities need not use the particular technology where the standards are set as concentration levels but they must meet the levels. For some other toxics the standard mandates the use of a particular technology when measurement is difficult. *See* EPA, RCRA ORIENTATION MANUAL (2003) at 91 (*available at* http://www.epa.gov/epaoswer/general/orientat/r02016.pdf). The case reprinted at 866, *infra,* involves a challenge to the BDAT requirements.

vi. Corrective Actions/Liability

Section 7003 of RCRA contains liability provisions for facilities that pose an imminent danger to human health or the environment and Section 7002 authorizes citizen suits under the statute. Both provisions are explored on pages 878–882 of this chapter.

b. Subtitle D, State or Regional Solid Waste Plans

Subtitle D of RCRA (§§ 4001 *et. seq)* requires states or regions, where appropriate, to submit solid waste plans to provide for the proper disposal of waste not defined as hazardous by Subtitle C. Subtitle D also provides criteria for sanitary landfills and the upgrading and closing of open dumps, and requires states to provide plans for handling household hazardous waste and small quantity generator waste. For several years in the late 1970s and 1980s RCRA also provided financial assistance to states and localities in developing solid waste plans. It is worth noting the contrast between RCRA's treatement of hazardous waste and all other solid waste. While Subtitle C establishes a detailed, onerous regulatory regime for all aspects of hazardous waste (from cradle to grave), Subtitle D is short and regulates only landfills and dumps.

c. Subtitle I, Underground Storage Tanks

As amended by Public Law 98–616, RCRA for the first time provided for regulation of *underground storage tanks* containing petroleum products and other hazardous liquids such as solvents and pesticides. RCRA §§ 9001–9010. The program is administered by EPA or by states with programs satisfying federal requirements. EPA regulations provide for detection and correction of leaks in existing tanks, and establish performance standards for new tanks. 40 CFR Part 280. The aim is to avoid groundwater pollution. Releases into the air of dangerous chemicals from underground tanks, like that which killed more than 2,000 persons in Bhopal, India in December 1984, are not controlled directly by the 1984 RCRA amendments, which nevertheless may help to prevent such accidents. Section 112(r) of the Clean Air Act, added in 1990, authorizes EPA regulation of accidental releases of hazardous substances into the air.

The 1986 amendments to RCRA established a $500 million Leaking Underground Storage Tank Trust Fund, derived from federal taxes on motor fuels and to be used for the correction of releases of petroleum where EPA cannot identify a solvent owner or operator of the tank who will undertake action properly. The amendments were contained in the Superfund Amendments and Reauthorization Act of 1986, Pub. L. No. 99–499, §§ 521–522, 100 Stat. 1613 (1986).

For an overview of the federal UST program, *see* Laura J. Nagle, *RCRA Subtitle I: The Federal Underground Storage Tank Program*, 24 Envtl. L. Rep. 10057 (1994). Regulations adopted in 1988 gave owners of the nation's three million or so USTs ten years to either remove or upgrade them. The regulations covered tanks capable of holding at least 1,100 gallons. Smaller home heating oil tanks were exempted, though some states regulate them. By March of 2000, EPA reported that about 85 percent of the 750,000 regulated tanks still in the ground were in compliance. Approximately 110,000 other tanks were being operated illegally, including more than 24,000 of the 29,177 active USTs in Ohio. The rate of compliance among private tank owners was much higher than among state and local governmental owners. In 2000, the Trust Fund contained $1.3 billion; but federal law allowed EPA to draw only about $70 million per year (roughly what the fund earned in interest), and that money could be used only to clean up spills, not to find and close leaking tanks or to enforce upgrade regulations. *See* Paul Zielbauer, *States and Cities Flout Law on Underground Fuel Tanks*, N.Y. Times, Aug. 8, 2000, at A1. For an interesting discussion about how UST regulation is managed in California, *see* Bowman Cutter and J.R. Deshazo, *Hazardous Waste,* Southern California Environmental Report Card 32 (2005).

The next section details some of the more contentious issues the EPA has faced in implementing Subtitle C of RCRA. As noted in the introduction, the definition of solid and hazardous waste has proven to be quite difficult.

d. "Solid" and "Hazardous" Waste Defined

Much of the battle over RCRA involves defining who is "in" or "out" of the statute's reach. For example solid waste is covered by RCRA with some exceptions; if a generator or handler of waste can define itself out of the definition of solid waste it can avoid the statute's requirements. And even if waste is defined as solid waste a generator can still avoid RCRA's onerous regulatory requirements if its waste is not considered "hazardous."

RCRA defines "solid waste", in Section 1003(27):

The term "solid waste" means any garbage, refuse, sludge from a waste treatment plant, water supply treatment plant, or air pollution control facility and other discarded material, including solid, liquid, semisolid, or contained gaseous material resulting from industrial, commercial, mining, and agricultural operations, and from community activities, but does not include solid or dissolved material in domestic sewage, or solid or dissolved materials in irrigation return flows or industrial discharges which are point sources subject to permits under [§ 402 of the Clean Water Act], or [certain radioactive wastes regulated under the Atomic Energy Act of 1954].

NOTES

1. Why would Congress include liquid and gaseous wastes in the statutory definition of solid waste? What is the basis for the exclusions from the definition of solid waste?

2. Despite the statutory definition of solid waste, EPA has struggled with which materials are subject to the definition, with particular controversy surrounding whether or not material has been "discarded." The RCRA regulations below provide further definitions:

Section 261.2 Definition of solid waste.

(a)(1) A solid waste is any discarded material that is not excluded by section 261.4(a) or that is not excluded by variance granted under sections 260.30 and 260.31.

(2) A discarded material is any material which is:

(i) Abandoned, as explained in paragraph (b) of this section; or

(ii) Recycled, as explained in paragraph (c) of this section; or

(iii) Considered inherently waste-like, as explained in paragraph (d) of this

section; or

(iv) A military munition identified as a solid waste in 40 CFR 266.202.

(b) Materials are solid waste if they are abandoned by being:

(1) Disposed of; or

(2) Burned or incinerated; or

(3) Accumulated, stored, or treated (but not recycled) before or in lieu of being abandoned by being disposed of, burned, or incinerated.

(c) Materials are solid wastes if they are recycled—or accumulated, stored, or treated before recycling—as specified in paragraphs (c)(1) through (c)(4) of this section. [The regulations then define inherently waste-like materials.] * * *

(e) Materials that are not solid waste when recycled.

(1) Materials are not solid wastes when they can be shown to be recycled by being:

(i) Used or reused as ingredients in an industrial process to make a product, provided the materials are not being reclaimed; or

(ii) Used or reused as effective substitutes for commercial products; or

(iii) Returned to the original process from which they are generated, without first being reclaimed or land disposed. The material must be returned as a substitute for feedstock materials. In cases where the original process to which the material is returned is a secondary process, the materials must be managed such that there is no placement on the land. In cases where the materials are generated and reclaimed within the primary mineral processing industry, the conditions of the exclusion found at section 261.4(a)(17) apply rather than this paragraph.

(2) The following materials are solid wastes, even if the recycling involves use, reuse, or return to the original process (described in paragraphs (e)(1) (i)–(iii) of this section):

(i) Materials used in a manner constituting disposal, or used to produce products that are applied to the land; or

(ii) Materials burned for energy recovery, used to produce a fuel, or contained in fuels; or

(iii) Materials accumulated speculatively; or

(iv) Materials listed in paragraphs (d)(1) and (d)(2) of this section.

(f) Documentation of claims that materials are not solid wastes or are conditionally exempt from regulation. Respondents in actions to enforce regulations implementing Subtitle C of RCRA who raise a claim that a certain material is not a solid waste, or is conditionally exempt from regulation, must demonstrate that there is a known market or disposition for the material, and that they meet the terms of the exclusion or exemption. In doing so, they must provide appropriate documentation (such as contracts showing that a second person uses the material as an ingredient in a production process) to demonstrate that the material is not a waste, or is exempt from regulation. In addition, owners or operators of facilities claiming that they actually are recycling materials must show that they have the necessary equipment to do so.

Prior EPA regulations defining "solid waste" provided that materials were solid waste if they were abandoned by being disposed of, burned, or incinerated; or stored, treated, or accumulated before or in lieu of those activities. 50 Fed. Reg. 614–01 (Jan. 4, 1985). The regulations also provided that certain materials used in recycling might be covered by RCRA, depending on the nature of the material and the recycling activity. The regulations were challenged by the mining and petroleum industries, which argued that materials intended for reuse were not "wastes." The challenge resulted in the following decision.

AMERICAN MINING CONGRESS v. ENVIRONMENTAL PROTECTION AGENCY

United States Court of Appeals, District of Columbia Circuit, 1987.
824 F.2d 1177.

STARR, CIRCUIT JUDGE.

* * * Petitioners, trade associations representing mining and oil refining interests, challenge regulations promulgated by EPA that amend the definition of "solid waste" to establish and define the agency's authority to regulate secondary materials reused within an industry's ongoing production process. In plain English, petitioners maintain that EPA has exceeded its regulatory authority in seeking to bring materials that are not discarded or otherwise disposed of within the compass of "waste."

RCRA is a comprehensive environmental statute under which EPA is granted authority to regulate solid and hazardous wastes. * * *

Congress' "overriding concern" in enacting RCRA was to establish the framework for a national system to insure the safe management of hazardous waste. * * *

RCRA includes two major parts: one deals with nonhazardous solid waste management and the other with hazardous waste management. Under the latter, EPA is directed to promulgate regulations establishing a comprehensive management system. EPA's authority, however, extends only to the regulation of "hazardous waste." Because "hazardous waste" is defined as a subset of "solid waste," § 6903(5), the scope of EPA's jurisdiction is limited to those materials that constitute "solid waste." That pivotal term is defined by RCRA as

> any garbage, refuse, sludge from a waste treatment plant, water supply treatment plant, or air pollution control facility *and other discarded material,* including solid, liquid, semisolid or contained gaseous material, resulting from industrial, commercial, mining, and agricultural operations, and from community activities....

42 U.S.C. § 6903(27) (emphasis added). As will become evident, this case turns on the meaning of the phrase, "and other discarded material," contained in the statute's definitional provisions.

EPA's interpretation of "solid waste" has evolved over time. On May 19, 1980, EPA issued interim regulations defining "solid waste" to include a material that is "a manufacturing or mining by-product and sometimes is discarded." 45 Fed.Reg. 33,119 (1980). This definition contained two terms needing elucidation: "by-product" and "sometimes discarded." In its definition of "a manufacturing or mining by-product," EPA expressly *excluded* "an intermediate manufacturing or mining product which results from one of the steps in a manufacturing or mining process and is typically processed through the next step of the process within a short time."

In 1983, the agency proposed narrowing amendments to the 1980 interim rule. The agency showed especial concern over *recycling* activities. In the preamble to the amendments, the agency observed that, in light of RCRA's legislative history, it was clear that "Congress indeed intended that materials being recycled or held for recycling can be wastes, and if hazardous, hazardous wastes." The agency also asserted that "not only can materials destined for recycling or being recycled be solid and hazardous wastes, but the Agency clearly has the authority to regulate recycling activities as hazardous waste management."

While asserting its interest in recycling activities (and materials being held for recycling), EPA's discussion left unclear whether the agency in fact believed its jurisdiction extended to materials recycled in an industry's on-going production processes, or only to materials disposed of and recycled as part of a waste management program. In its preamble, EPA stated that "the revised definition of solid waste sets out the Agency's view of its jurisdiction over the recycling of hazardous waste.... Proposed section 261.6 then contains exemptions from regulations for those hazardous waste recycling activities that we do not think require regulation." The amended regulatory description of "solid waste" itself, then, did not include materials "used or reused as effective substitutes for raw materials in processes using raw materials as principal feedstocks." EPA explained the exclusion as follows:

> [These] materials are being used essentially as raw materials and so ordinarily are not appropriate candidates for regulatory control. Moreover, when these materials are used to manufacture new products, the processes generally are normal manufacturing operations.... The Agency is reluctant to read the statute as regulating actual manufacturing processes.

This, then, seemed clear: EPA was drawing a line between discarding and ultimate recycling, on the one hand, and a continuous or ongoing manufacturing process with one-site "recycling," on the other. If the activity fell within the latter category, then the materials were not deemed to be "discarded."

After receiving extensive comments, EPA issued its final rule on January 4, 1985. Under the final rule, materials are considered "solid waste" if they are abandoned by being disposed of, burned, or incinerated; or stored, treated, or accumulated before or in lieu of those activities. In addition, certain recycling activities fall within EPA's definition. EPA determines whether a material is a RCRA solid waste when it is recycled by examining both the material or substance itself and the recycling activity involved. The final rule identifies five categories of "secondary materials" (spent materials, sludges, by-products, commercial chemical products, and scrap metal). These "secondary materials" constitute "solid waste" when they are disposed of; burned for energy recovery or used to produce a fuel; reclaimed; or accumulated speculatively. Under the final rule, if a material constitutes "solid waste," it is subject to RCRA regulation *unless* it is directly reused as an ingredient or as an effective substitute for a commercial product, or is returned as a raw material substitute to its original manufacturing process.[2] In the jargon of the trade, the latter category is known as the "closed-loop" exception. In either case, the material must not first be "reclaimed" (processed to recover a usable product or regenerated). EPA exempts these activities "because they are like ordinary usage of commercial products."

Petitioners, American Mining Congress ("AMC") and American Petroleum Institute ("API"), challenge the scope of EPA's final rule. Relying upon the statutory definition of "solid waste," petitioners contend that EPA's authority under RCRA is limited to controlling materials that are *discarded or intended for discard.* They argue that EPA's reuse and recycle rules, as applied to in-process secondary materials, regulate materials that have not been discarded, and therefore exceed EPA's jurisdiction.

[The court then describes how petroleum refineries use a complex retrieval system to recapture escaping hydrocarbons and return them to appropriate parts of the refining process. The court also states that mining facilities reprocess ore and recapture for reuse in the production process metal-and mineral-bearing dusts released during processing. The court notes that the materials recaptured by petroleum refineries and mining facilities are considered "solid waste" under EPA's rule.] * * *

* * * Congress, it will be recalled, granted EPA power to regulate "solid waste." Congress specifically defined "solid waste" as "discarded material." EPA then defined "discarded material" to include materials destined for reuse in an industry's *ongoing* production processes. The challenge to EPA's jurisdictional reach is founded, again, on the proposition that in-process secondary materials are outside the bounds of EPA's lawful authority. Nothing has been *discarded,* the argument goes, and thus RCRA jurisdiction remains untriggered.

The first step in statutory interpretation is, of course, an analysis of the language itself. In pursuit of Congress' intent, we "start with the assumption that the legislative purpose is expressed by the ordinary meaning of the words used." Here, Congress defined "solid waste" as

---

2. Specifically, the final rule excludes materials recycled by being: "(1) [u]sed or reused as ingredients in an industrial process to make a product, *provided the materials are not being reclaimed;* or (2) [u]sed or reused as effective substitutes for commercial products; or (3) [r]eturned to the original process from which they are generated, without first being reclaimed." Id. (emphasis added). In the third category, the material must be returned to the original manufacturing process as a substitute for raw material feedstock, and the process must use raw materials as principal feedstocks.

"discarded material." The ordinary plain-English meaning of the word "discarded" is "disposed of," "thrown away" or "abandoned." Encompassing materials retained for immediate reuse within the scope of "discarded material" strains, to say the least, the everyday usage of that term. * * *

The question we face, then, is whether, in light of the National Legislature's expressly stated objectives and the underlying problems that motivated it to enact RCRA in the first instance, Congress was using the term "discarded" in its ordinary sense—"disposed of" or "abandoned"—or whether Congress was using it in a much more open-ended way, so as to encompass materials no longer useful in their original capacity though destined for immediate reuse in another phase of the industry's ongoing production process.

For the following reasons, we believe the former to be the case. RCRA was enacted, as the congressional objectives and findings make clear, in an effort to help States deal with the ever-increasing problem of solid waste *disposal* by encouraging the search for and use of alternatives to existing methods of disposal (including recycling) and protecting health and the environment by regulating hazardous wastes. To fulfill these purposes, it seems clear that EPA need not regulate "spent" materials that are recycled and reused in an *ongoing* manufacturing or industrial process. These materials have not yet become part of the waste disposal problem; rather, *they are destined for beneficial reuse or recycling in a continuous process by the generating industry itself.* * * *

We are constrained to conclude that, in light of the language and structure of RCRA, the problems animating Congress to enact it, and the relevant portions of the legislative history, Congress clearly and unambiguously expressed its intent that "solid waste" (and therefore EPA's regulatory authority) be limited to materials that are "discarded" by virtue of being disposed of, abandoned, or thrown away. While we do not lightly overturn an agency's reading of its own statute, we are persuaded that by regulating in-process secondary materials, EPA has acted in contravention of Congress' intent. Accordingly, the petition for review is granted.

MIKVA, CIRCUIT JUDGE, dissenting:

* * * In my opinion, the EPA's interpretation of solid waste is completely reasonable in light of the language, policies, and legislative history of RCRA. Congress had broad remedial objectives in mind when it enacted RCRA, most notably to "regulat[e] the treatment, storage, transportation, and disposal of hazardous wastes which have adverse effects on the environment." The disposal problem Congress was combatting encompassed more than just abandoned materials. RCRA makes this clear with its definition of the central statutory term "disposal":

the discharge, deposit, injection, dumping, spilling, leaking, or placing of any solid waste or hazardous waste into or on any land or water so that such solid waste or hazardous waste or any constituent thereof may enter the environment or be emitted into the air or discharged into any waters, including ground waters.

42 U.S.C. § 6903(3). This definition clearly encompasses more than the everyday meaning of disposal, which is a "discarding or throwing away." Webster's Third International Dictionary 654 (2d ed. 1981). The definition is *functional:* waste is disposed under this provision if it is put into contact with land or water in such a way as to pose the risks to health and the environment that animated Congress to pass RCRA. Whether the manufacturer subjectively intends to put the material to additional use is irrelevant to this definition, as indeed it should be, because the manufacturer's state of mind bears no necessary relation to the hazards of the industrial processes he employs.

Faithful to RCRA's functional approach, EPA reasonably concluded that regulation of certain in-process secondary materials was necessary to carry out its mandate. The materials at issue in this case can pose the same risks as abandoned wastes, whether or not the manufacturer intends eventually to put them to further beneficial use. As the agency explained, "[s]imply because a waste is likely to be recycled will not ensure that it will not be spilled or leaked before recycling occurs." The storage, transportation, and even recycling of in-process secondary materials can cause severe environmental harm. Indeed, the EPA documented environmental disasters caused by the handling or storage of such materials. It also pointed out the risk of damage from spills or leaks when certain in-process secondary materials are placed on land or in underground product storage. * * *

* * * [I]n this case the EPA has interpreted solid waste in a manner that seems to expand the everyday usage of the word "discarded." Its conclusion, however, is fully supportable in light of the statutory scheme and legislative history of RCRA. The agency concluded that certain on-site recycled materials constitute an integral part of the waste disposal problem. This judgment is grounded in the EPA's technical expertise and is adequately supported by evidence in the record. The majority nevertheless reverses the agency because it believes that the materials at issue "have not yet become part of the waste disposal problem." This declaration is nothing more than a substitution of the majority's own conclusions for the sound technical judgment of the EPA. The EPA's interpretation is a reasonable construction of an ambiguous statutory provision and should be upheld.

Notes

1.   Should the definition of "solid waste" be based upon whether materials have become a part of the waste disposal problem? Should the definition depend on whether a substance poses a risk warranting regulation? If such considerations are relevant, who—EPA or the courts—should weigh them and make a decision? Under the *Chevron* case, page 450, *supra*, did the majority in *AMC* give sufficient deference to EPA's conclusion?

2. After the *AMC* decision, various industries claimed that numerous substances which EPA had regulated under subtitle C of RCRA were not "solid waste." Thus, the American Mining Congress claimed that EPA could not regulate sludge from wastewater, stored in a surface impoundment, if the sludge was to be reprocessed later for metals recovery. In *American Mining Congress v. EPA (AMC II)*, 907 F.2d 1179, 1186 (D.C. Cir. 1990), the court sided with EPA:

> *AMC*'s holding concerned only materials that are "destined for *immediate reuse* in another phase of the industry's ongoing production process" (emphasis added), and that "have not yet become part of the waste disposal problem." Nothing in *AMC* prevents the agency from treating as "discarded" the wastes at issue in this case, which are managed in land disposal units that *are* part of wastewater treatment systems, which *have* therefore become "part of the waste disposal problem," and which are *not* part of ongoing industrial processes. Indeed, [we have] explicitly rejected the very claim that petitioners assert in this case, * * * namely, that under RCRA, potential reuse of a material prevents the agency from classifying it as "discarded."

3. If materials are in fact recycled, can they be considered wastes at the time of recycling? In reliance upon *AMC*, EPA determined that materials utilized in a metals reclamation process ceased to be solid wastes under RCRA when they arrived at a reclamation facility because they no longer were "discarded material."

Environmentalists challenged this interpretation and prevailed in *American Petroleum Institute v. EPA*, 906 F.2d 729, 741 (D.C. Cir. 1990):

> *AMC* is by no means dispositive of EPA's authority to regulate K061 slag. Unlike the materials in question in *AMC*, K061 is indisputably "discarded" *before* being subject to metals reclamation. Consequently, it *has* "become part of the waste disposal problem"; that is why EPA has the power to require that K061 be subject to mandatory metals reclamation. Nor does anything in *AMC* require EPA to cease treating K061 as "solid waste" once it reaches the metals reclamation facility. K061 is delivered to the facility not as part of an "*ongoing* manufacturing or industrial process" within the generating industry, but as part of a mandatory waste treatment plan prescribed by EPA.

4. In a recent Ninth Circuit case, the court rejected a claim that burnt Kentucky Blue Grass constituted a solid waste under RCRA; it did so by weighing three considerations for determining whether materials had been discarded and hence constitute solid waste: "(1) whether the material is" destined for beneficial reuse or recycling in a continuous process by the generating industry itself, " * * * *; (2) whether the materials are being actively reused, or whether they merely have the *potential* of being reused * * * * [and] (3) whether the materials are being reused by its original owner, as opposed to use by a salvager or reclaimer. . . ." *Safe Air For Everyone v. Meyer*, 373 F.3d 1035 (9th Cir. 2004). Affirmative answers to all three of these questions suggest the materials have not been discarded and hence are not solid waste.

5. Is recycling something the government should encourage by exempting recycled materials from RCRA's requirements? Are there risks in providing such an exemption? * * *

For generators of waste covered by RCRA, the next definitional battle is over whether the solid waste is *hazardous*. Subtitle C of RCRA provides for regulation of *hazardous* solid waste and is significantly more onerous than the regulation of *nonhazardous* solid waste, covered by subtitle D. One very important exemption from the definition of hazardous waste is for *household* waste. 40 C.F.R. section 261.4(b)(1). You should realize, therefore, that a material can be defined as hazardous when used by a business but is subject to no federal regulation when used at home.

RCRA does not indicate precisely how EPA is to determine which solid wastes are hazardous. "Hazardous waste" is defined in section 1004(5):

> The term "hazardous waste" means a solid waste, or combination of solid wastes, which because of its quantity, concentration, or physical, chemical, or infectious characteristics may—

> (A) cause, or significantly contribute to an increase in mortality or an increase in serious irreversible, or incapacitating reversible, illness; or

> (B) pose a substantial present or potential hazard to human health or the environment when improperly treated, stored, transported, or disposed of, or otherwise managed.

Under section 3001, EPA is to promulgate regulations identifying the *characteristics* of hazardous waste and *listing* particular hazardous wastes to be regulated under subtitle C, "taking into account toxicity, persistence, and degradability in nature, potential for accumulation in tissue, and other related factors such as flammability, corrosiveness, and other hazardous characteristics."

EPA regulations provide two principal ways in which solid waste may be deemed "hazardous": by exhibiting one of four hazardous characteristics (*"characteristic wastes"*) or by being identified specifically as a hazardous waste by EPA (*"listed wastes"*). 40 C.F.R. section 261.3. EPA has established four general categories of listed wastes, the "F," "K," "P," and "U" lists. 40 C.F.R. sections 261.31–261.32. On the "P" list are acutely hazardous chemical products. The "U" list includes non-acutely hazardous chemical products. The "F" and "K" lists of waste mixtures and combinations include wastes that meet the criteria for the "P" and "U" lists or one of the four "characteristics" (*toxicity, ignitability, corrosivity, and reactivity*). Listed wastes and wastes that meet the toxicity characteristic are treated differently from the other characteristic wastes in certain respects. Among other differences, listed wastes are considered hazardous regardless of the concentration of hazardous constituents within them, whereas a characteristic waste remains hazardous only as long as it exhibits the characteristic. Thus listed wastes remain hazardous even when mixed with other materials or when their composition is changed. Listed wastes are subject to two special rules, the *"mixture"* rule and the *"derived-from"* rule. The former provides that a mixture of a "listed" hazardous waste with another solid waste is also a hazardous waste. 40 C.F.R. sections 261.3(a)(2)(iii) and (iv). The derived-from rule provides that any solid waste "generated from the treatment, storage, or disposal of a hazardous waste, including any sludge, spill, residue, ash, emission control dust, or leachate (but not including precipitation run-off)," is a hazardous waste. 40 CFR 261.3(c)(2)(i). The derived-from rule includes an exemption for wastes that possess the ignitability, corrosivity and reactivity characteristics. A derived-from by-product from a solid waste exhibiting a characteristic waste remains hazardous if it continues to exhibit the characteristic waste but is not considered hazardous if no longer possessing the characteristic.

The following two cases illustrate the application of these rules for identifying hazardous wastes to be regulated under subtitle C of RCRA. The first case involves "listed" wastes and the "derived-from" and "mixture" rules. The second case involves "characteristic" wastes. In both, note the basic concern about "leachate," which can contaminate underground soil and water supplies.

CHEMICAL WASTE MANAGEMENT, INC.
v. ENVIRONMENTAL PROTECTION
AGENCY

United States Court of Appeals, District of Columbia Circuit, 1989.
869 F.2d 1526.

WALD, CHIEF JUDGE.

* * *

The RCRA was recently modified by the Hazardous Solid Waste Amendments of 1984, which established sweeping restrictions on the land disposal of hazardous wastes. The EPA was required to establish a schedule dividing the hazardous wastes into "thirds," *see* 42 U.S.C. § 6924(g)(4); the agency promulgated the schedule in May of 1986. The division of the schedule into thirds was designed as a means of phasing in the land disposal restrictions. By August 8, 1988, the EPA was required to promulgate treatment standards for each of the first-third scheduled wastes; these wastes may not be land disposed unless they have been treated to meet the applicable standards or the disposal unit is one from which there will be no migration of hazardous constituents for as long as the waste remains hazardous. Similar land disposal restrictions for second-third and third-third wastes are scheduled to take effect on June 8, 1989 and May 8, 1990 * * *.

The present dispute concerns the rule-making in which the EPA established treatment standards for first-third wastes. * * * EPA issued treatment standards for the various wastes; in lengthy preambles to the notices, the agency discussed the interpretive principles which would guide its application of the standards. Three such principles merit discussion here.

One of these principles concerns the treatment standards applicable to leachate produced from hazardous waste. Leachate is produced when liquids, such as rainwater, percolate through wastes stored in a landfill. The resulting fluid will contain suspended components drawn from the original waste. Proper leachate management involves the storage of wastes in lined containers so that leachate may be collected before it seeps into soil or groundwater. The leachate will periodically be pumped out of the container and subsequently treated.

An EPA regulation promulgated in 1980, known as the "derived-from rule," provided that "any solid waste generated from the treatment, storage, or disposal of a hazardous waste, including any sludge, spill residue, ash, emission control dust, or leachate (but not including precipitation run-off) is a hazardous waste." Thus, for some years prior to the 1988 rulemaking, it had been understood that leachate derived from a hazardous waste was itself a hazardous waste. In the 1988 preambles, the agency stated that leachate derived from multiple hazardous wastes would be deemed to contain each of the wastes from which it was generated, and that it must therefore be treated to meet the applicable treatment standards for each of the underlying wastes. This is known as the "waste code carry-through" principle.

The second interpretive principle at issue in this proceeding also involves the treatment requirements for hazardous waste leachate. In its preamble to the August rule, the agency stated that "[h]azardous waste listings are retroactive, so that once a particular waste is listed, all wastes meeting that description are hazardous wastes no matter when disposed." The implications of that statement center around wastes which were not deemed hazardous at the time they were disposed but which are subsequently listed as hazardous wastes. The RCRA does not require that such wastes be cleaned up or moved from the landfill, nor does the agency impose any retroactive penalty on the prior disposal of the waste. Under the August rule, however, the agency announced that leachate which is actively managed after the underlying wastes have been listed as hazardous will itself be deemed a hazardous waste and must be treated to the applicable standards. Under this approach, the fact that the original waste was not deemed hazardous at the time of disposal is simply irrelevant in determining the treatment requirements for the leachate.

Finally, the agency discussed the applicability of the treatment standards to contaminated environmental media such as soil and groundwater. The preamble stated that "[i]n these cases, the mixture is deemed to be the listed waste." Thus, when a listed hazardous waste (or hazardous waste leachate) is mixed with soil or groundwater—as may occur, for example, through spills or leaking—the soil or groundwater is subject to all the treatment standards or restrictions that would be applicable to the original waste.

The Present Litigation

* * *

Petitioners in this case raised a host of substantive and procedural challenges to the August rulemaking. * * *

Shortly before oral argument, * * * the parties filed an Emergency Joint Motion to Defer Oral Argument on Certain Leachate–Related Issues. That motion, which was granted by this court, covered the petitioners' challenge to the waste code carry-through principle—the requirement that derived-from wastes such as leachate would be deemed to contain each of the original wastes from which they were generated. * * * The explanation [was] that a negotiated settlement seemed likely on all issues pertaining to the waste code carry-through principle. Under the terms of the proposed settlement, all multiple-waste leachate would be rescheduled to the third-third, and a leachate treatability study would be undertaken so that appropriate treatment standards could be determined.

The issues argued to the court, and the issues that we decide today, are therefore limited to the following. First, did the agency improperly engage in retroactive rulemaking in ordering that its leachate regulations be made applicable to leachate derived from wastes which were not deemed hazardous at the tie they were disposed? Second, did the agency act in an arbitrary or capricious manner by mandating that environmental media contaminated by hazardous wastes must themselves be treated as hazardous wastes? * * *

* * * Petitioners argue that the EPA lacks the authority to promulgate retroactive regulations, and they correctly observe that such regulations are disfavored. In our view, however, the crucial question is not whether the EPA is authorized to promulgate a retroactive rule. Rather, the crucial question is whether the challenged regulation in fact operates retroactively. We conclude that it does not.

* * * The agency has made no effort to impose a legal penalty on the disposal of waste which was not deemed hazardous at the time it was disposed. Nor, in fact, does this regulation require the cleanup of any newly listed hazardous wastes. The preamble to the final rule expressly provides that "these residues could become subject to the land disposal restrictions for the listed waste from which they derive *if they are managed actively after the effective date of the land disposal prohibition for the underlying waste.*" The rule has prospective effect only: treatment or disposal of leachate will be subject to the regulation only if that treatment or disposal occurs after the promulgation of applicable treatment standards.

As a practical matter, of course, a landfill operator has little choice but to collect and manage its leachate. Active management of leachate is sound environmental practice, and a panoply of regulations require it. * * *

Moreover, we find this aspect of the agency's interpretation of the derived-from rule to be eminently reasonable. The derived-from rule establishes a presumption: leachate generated from hazardous waste will be presumed hazardous unless it is proved nonhazardous or treated to applicable standards. The reasonableness of that presumption does not vary depending upon the time when the underlying waste was disposed. * * *

In reviewing the EPA's application of its 1980 rules to contaminated soil, we are guided by two fundamental principles. The first is that "[a]n agency's interpretation of its own regulations will be accepted unless it is plainly wrong." The second is that on "a highly technical question ... courts necessarily must show considerable deference to an agency's expertise." * * *

The agency's rule, adopted in 1980, provides that "[a] hazardous waste will remain a hazardous waste" until it is delisted. The petitioners argue in essence that an agglomeration of soil and hazardous waste is to be regarded as a new and distinct substance, to which the presumption of hazardousness no longer applies. The agency's position is that hazardous waste cannot be presumed to change character when it is combined with an environmental medium, and that the hazardous waste restrictions therefore continue to apply to waste which is contained in soil or groundwater. * * *

The EPA's approach to contaminated environmental media is * * * consistent with the derived-from and mixture rules established in 1980. These rules provide that a hazardous waste will continue to be presumed hazardous when it is mixed with a solid waste, or when it is contained in a residue from treatment or disposal. The derived-from and mixture rules do not, it is true, apply by their own terms to contaminated soil or groundwater. They nevertheless demonstrate that the agency's rule on contaminated soil is part of a coherent regulatory framework. It is one application of a general principle, consistently adhered to, that a hazardous waste does not lose its hazardous character simply because it changes form or is combined with other substances. In promulgating the mixture rule, the agency did not presume that every mixture of listed wastes and other wastes would in fact present a hazard. Rather, the agency reasoned that "[b]ecause the potential combinations of listed wastes and other wastes are infinite, we have been unable to devise any workable, broadly applicable formula which would distinguish between those waste mixtures which are and are not hazardous." The EPA therefore concluded that it was fair to shift to the individual operator the burden of establishing (through the delisting process) that its own waste mixture is not hazardous. Precisely the same logic applies to combinations of hazardous waste and soil or groundwater. * * *

The EPA's interpretation is also buttressed by one provision of the Hazardous Solid Waste Amendments of 1984, 42 U.S.C. § 6924(e). Congress there provided that certain specified solvents and dioxins would be prohibited from land disposal. The statute further provided that, for a two-year period after the effective date of the ban, the prohibition "shall not apply to any disposal of contaminated soil or debris resulting from a response action taken under section 9604 or 9606 of this title or a corrective action required under this subchapter." This statutory exemption would of course have been superfluous unless contaminated soil would otherwise fall within the terms of the ban * * *.

We need not decide whether any of these factors, or all of them taken together, would *compel* the conclusion that soil or groundwater contaminated with hazardous waste is itself a hazardous waste as defined by EPA regulations. We do believe, however, that, given the agency's broad discretion to interpret its own rules, it was entirely reasonable for the EPA to arrive at that conclusion. We therefore must sustain the agency's position.

NOTES

1. In its long-delayed decision in *Shell Oil Co. v. EPA*, 950 F.2d 741 (D.C. Cir. 1991), the court held that EPA had failed to comply with the Administrative Procedure Act's notice-and-comment requirements when promulgating the mixture and derived-from rules in 1980. The court vacated the rules but suggested that EPA reenact them on an interim basis under the "good cause" exemption of 5 U.S.C.A. section 553(b)(3)(B), pending full notice and opportunity to comment. EPA took the suggestion and reissued the rules in 1992. The reinstated rules were challenged but upheld in *Mobil Oil Corp. v. EPA*, 35 F.3d 579 (D.C. Cir. 1994).

2. In 2001, EPA promulgated a new Hazardous Waste Identification Rule (HWIR), 66 Fed. Reg. 27,266 (Apr. 30, 2001). It replaces the 1992 interim regulations which reinstated the mixture and derived-from rules. The new regulation retains and amends the mixture and derived-from rules, narrowing their scope by (1) granting an expanded exclusion for wastes listed solely for their ignitability, corrosivity, and/or reactivity characteristics, and (2) establishing a new conditional exemption for "mixed" wastes, that is, wastes that are both hazardous and radioactive. The final rule was challenged and upheld in *American Chemistry Council v. EPA*, 337 F.3d 1060 (D.C. Cir. 2003)

3. The next case demonstrates the complexity of formulating and applying rules pertaining to "characteristic" wastes, solid wastes which are not specifically "listed" by EPA as hazardous but which manifest one or more of the four characteristics (toxicity, ignitability, corrosivity, and reactivity) set out in EPA regulations for the purpose of identifying other hazardous wastes.

EDISON ELECTRIC INSTITUTE v. ENVIRONMENTAL PROTECTION AGENCY

United States Court of Appeals, District of Columbia Circuit, 1993.
2 F.3d 438.

Before MIKVA, CHIEF JUDGE, SILBERMAN and D.H. GINSBURG, CIRCUIT JUDGES.

Opinion PER CURIAM.

* * * Congress delegated to the Environmental Protection Agency the duty to "promulgate regulations identifying the characteristics of hazardous waste, and listing particular hazardous wastes ... which shall be

subject to the provisions of [Subtitle C]." 42 U.S.C. § 6921(b)(1). Thus, Congress directed the Agency to identify hazardous wastes in two ways: (1) identify certain characteristics which would render a solid waste hazardous, and (2) list specific solid wastes that are, so to speak, *per se* hazardous.

This appeal concerns only the former category of solid wastes, those deemed hazardous by virtue of possessing certain general characteristics. More specifically, the petitioners [challenge] EPA's final rule revising the Toxicity Characteristic ("TC")—one of the four characteristics (the other three are ignitability, corrosivity, and reactivity) set out in EPA regulations for the purpose of identifying hazardous solid wastes. The TC seeks to "identify waste which, if improperly disposed of, may release toxic materials in sufficient amounts to pose a substantial hazard to human health or the environment."

In 1980, EPA established a "protocol" for determining the TC of solid wastes, which it dubbed the "Extraction Procedure" ("EP"). The EP toxicity test is based on a particular mismanagement scenario—"co-disposal of toxic wastes in an actively decomposing municipal landfill which overlies a groundwater aquifer"—and is intended to simulate the actual leaching of wastes that might occur in a municipal solid waste ("MSW") landfill. The test requires a waste generator to mix a representative sample of its waste with an acidic leaching medium for 24 hours, and then to test the resulting liquid waste to see if it contains unsafe levels of any of 14 toxic contaminants identified in the National Interim Primary Drinking Water Standards ("NIPDWS") promulgated pursuant to 42 U.S.C. § 300g–1.

In order to duplicate the attenuation in concentration expected to occur between the point of leachate generation and the point of human or environmental exposure, the EP applies a dilution and attenuation factor ("DAF") of 100 to the concentration of toxic contaminants observed in the test extract. Thus, a waste would be considered hazardous, and subject to RCRA Subtitle C regulation, if the results of the EP toxicity test revealed the presence of any listed contaminant at a level of at least 100 times the applicable NIPDWS.

The Revised Toxicity Characteristic

* * * The 1986 rulemaking to revise the TC was necessitated by two intervening pieces of legislation. First, in 1980, Congress passed the Bevill Amendment, 42 U.S.C. § 6921(b)(3)(A), as part of the Solid Waste Disposal Act Amendments of 1980. The Bevill Amendment exempted from Subtitle C regulation certain waste produced by fossil fuel combustion and mineral processing and directed EPA to study the environmental effects of such wastes and to determine whether special regulations were necessary to govern their disposal. In litigation to compel EPA to meet the statutory deadlines for implementation, this Court found that Congress intended to exempt "only those wastes from processing ores or minerals that [are] 'high volume, low hazard' wastes." *Environmental Defense Fund v. EPA,*

852 F.2d 1316, 1328–29 (D.C. Cir. 1988) *("EDF II") cert. denied,* 489 U.S. 1011, 109 S.Ct. 1120, 103 L.Ed.2d 183 (1989). In a subsequent rulemaking, EPA decided to exempt only those high volume, low hazard wastes that fell within the top 5% of the largest individual waste streams managed by Subtitle C facilities.

The second piece of intervening legislation was the Hazardous and Solid Waste Amendments of 1984 ("HSWA"), Pub.L. No. 98–616, 98 Stat. 3221. In one provision of HSWA, Congress expressed concern with the TC and the EP toxicity test and directed the Agency to reevaluate * * *. 42 U.S.C. § 6921(g). The legislative history indicates that Congress believed that EPA's test was deficient because it was underinclusive in identifying hazardous wastes.

In response to HSWA, EPA revised its regulations and adopted a new testing procedure in place of the EP, known as the Toxicity Characteristic Leaching Procedure ("TCLP"). * * *

The American Mining Congress ("AMC") and the Edison Electric Institute ("EEI") challenge EPA's application of the TCLP generic mismanagement scenario to mineral processing wastes and manufactured gas plant wastes. The parties agree that EPA treats these wastes similarly, and they are hereinafter referred to collectively as "mineral wastes." They do not fall under Bevill Amendment's exemption from Subtitle C regulation, as implemented in EPA's regulations, because individual waste generators do not produce them in sufficient quantities to qualify for the high volume, low hazard exception. * * *

Statutory Requirement of "Accuracy"

AMC and EEI claim that the application of the TCLP to mineral wastes violates the statutory mandate for a more accurate TCLP, *see* 42 U.S.C. § 6921(g), because the generic mismanagement scenario is based on factual assumptions that do not apply to mineral wastes. They maintain that it is extremely unlikely that mineral wastes will ever be disposed of in municipal solid waste ("MSW") landfills in light of the extremely large volumes of waste that are generated and the relatively small capacity of MSW landfills. * * *

Finally, AMC and EEI assert that the inapplicability of the TCLP generic mismanagement scenario to the mining context renders three specific TCLP elements—the aggressiveness of the leaching medium, the particle size reduction requirement, and the assumed DAF of 100—far too severe in predicting the hazardousness of these types of wastes. * * *

EPA settled on a single mismanagement scenario and rejected a "management-based" approach to identifying hazardous wastes, which would require a separate toxicity test for each category of waste that is typically managed in a particular way. In keeping with the RCRA directive to "promulgate regulations identifying the *characteristics* of hazardous waste," 42 U.S.C. § 6921(b)(1) (emphasis added), EPA decided that "the most effective and appropriate approach [to implementing RCRA] is to . . .

identify[ ] *properties* of wastes that would pose a threat to human health and the environment if improperly managed." The Agency concluded that a management-based approach would raise complex enforcement problems because of the difficulty in determining beforehand how any particular solid waste will eventually be managed. As we have already stated, nothing in the RCRA mandate of a more accurate TC dictates a management-based approach, and the use of a generic mismanagement scenario is a reasonable interpretation of the statutory language.

EPA selected the specific MSW landfill mismanagement scenario because contamination of groundwater through the leaching of land-disposed wastes is a prevalent environmental hazard that is well-documented in EPA damage files and with which Congress was especially concerned in passing RCRA. In response to comments that industrial solid wastes are not often disposed of in MSW landfills, EPA pointed out that states impose few restrictions on the types of non-hazardous wastes accepted at MSW landfills, and that a substantial quantity of the wastes actually received at MSW landfills are industrial wastes. EPA recognized that MSW landfills generate a more aggressive leachate media than other landfills, but chose to adopt a particularly conservative scenario "in view of the statutory mandate to protect human health and the environment, the broad statutory definition of hazardous waste[,] and also because the phenomenon of long term leaching is only incompletely understood." These choices represent a reasonable interpretation of RCRA. * * *

Reasonableness of Applying the TCLP Mismanagement Scenario to Mineral Wastes

The inquiry is not completed by our conclusion that the TCLP mismanagement scenario represents a permissible construction of RCRA under *Chevron*. In addition, to pass muster under the APA, the TCLP must bear some rational relationship to mineral wastes in order for the Agency to justify the application of the toxicity test to those wastes. *See Motor Vehicle Mfrs. Ass'n v. State Farm*, 463 U.S. 29, 43, 103 S.Ct. 2856, 2866, 77 L.Ed.2d 443 (1983). We hold that EPA has failed to demonstrate any such relationship on the record, and therefore remand to the Agency for further proceedings consistent with this opinion. * * *

The record evidence on which EPA relies does not demonstrate that low volume mineral wastes have ever been disposed of in MSW landfills. * * *

Even in the absence of evidence that at least some mineral wastes have actually been disposed in MSW landfills, EPA's application of the TCLP to mineral wastes would nonetheless pass muster if there were evidence on the record that mineral wastes were exposed to conditions similar to those simulated by the TCLP. * * * Again, however, there is no evidence or explanation on the record to justify a conclusion that mineral wastes ever come into contact with any form of acidic leaching medium.

* * * We therefore remand to allow the Agency to provide a fuller and more reasoned explanation for its decision to apply the TCLP to mineral wastes.

NOTES

1. In *Columbia Falls Aluminum Co. v. EPA*, 139 F.3d 914 (D.C. Cir. 1998), the court held that EPA's use of the TCLP to determine compliance with its treatment standard was arbitrary or capricious because the TCLP failed to predict the actual behavior of hazardous constituents in the leachate after a certain type of aluminum waste ("spent potliner") was treated and disposed in a "monofill," a landfill dedicated exclusively to this type of waste. Tests of the actual leachate showed concentrations of the hazardous constituents that were "orders of magnitude" different from the concentrations predicted by the TCLP. EPA attributed this discrepancy to the fact that the extreme alkaline pH soil conditions at the monofill site were "not analogous to" conditions simulated by the TCLP.

In *Association of Battery Recyclers v. EPA*, 208 F.3d 1047 (D.C. Cir. 2000), petitioners challenged EPA's application of the TCLP to 358 different types of mineral processing wastes generated by 41 different sectors of the mineral processing industry. With respect to 357 of the wastes, the court held that EPA had met the *Edison Electric* standard because evidence in the record showed that such wastes probably had been disposed of in municipal landfills. The court rejected application of the TCLP to "MGP waste" because none had been produced in 40 years. EPA argued that prior to the demise of the MGP industry, its waste had been placed in landfills, many of which now are being remediated; but the court found no evidence that any MGP wastes had been sent from remediated sites to municipal landfills. From an institutional perspective, how carefully should courts examine EPA's decisions to apply the TCLP to particular wastes?

2. Because landfill space is scarce, many cities have built incinerators to dispose of municipal waste, often generating electricity in the process. Such incinerators generate millions of tons of ash. Ash residues include fly ash captured by emission control equipment, bottom ash, and the products of incomplete combustion. Heavy metals are present in the residues, especially in the fly ash. When tested using EPA's "toxicity characteristic leaching procedure" (TCLP), described in the *Edison Electric* case, fly ash and bottom ash from municipal incinerators frequently contain lead and cadmium at concentrations greater than the 5 and 1 milligram per liter cutoff levels for the toxicity characteristic.

Regulations adopted by EPA in 1980 provided that "[h]ousehold waste, including household waste that has been collected, transported, stored, treated, disposed, recovered (e.g., refuse-derived fuel) or reused" was not hazardous waste. Moreover, the preamble to the regulations stated that "residues remaining after treatment (e.g., incineration, thermal treatment) are not subject to regulation as a hazardous waste." 45 Fed.Reg. 33,099 (May 19, 1980). The regulations thus provided a "waste stream" exemption for household waste, covering it from generation through treatment to final disposal of residues. The regulations did not, however, exempt municipal incinerator ash from subtitle C coverage if the incinerator burned anything *in addition* to household waste, such as nonhazardous industrial waste. In that case, the facility would qualify as a hazardous waste *generator* if the ash it produced was sufficiently toxic—even though the incinerator still was not considered a subtitle C treatment or disposal facility, since all the waste it took in would be characterized as nonhazardous.

In 1984, as part of the Hazardous and Solid Waste Amendments to RCRA, Congress enacted section 3001(i), "Clarification of Household Waste Exclusion." Section 3001(i) provides that a "resource recovery facility" recovering energy from the burning of municipal solid waste "shall not be deemed to be treating, storing, disposing of, or otherwise managing hazardous wastes" for purposes of regulation under subtitle C, "if [the facility] receives and burns only * * * household waste * * * and solid waste from commercial or industrial sources that does not contain hazardous waste * * *."

City of Chicago v. Environmental Defense Fund, 511 U.S. 328 (1994), was a citizen suit by EDF under RCRA section 7002. Plaintiff alleged that the ash generated by defendant Chicago's incinerator—which burned both household waste and nonhazardous industrial waste—was toxic enough to qualify as "hazardous waste" under EPA's TCLP, and that defendant was not adhering to the requirements of subtitle C in disposing of the ash, which was being sent to landfills licensed to receive only nonhazardous waste. The city and EPA contended that under section 3001(i) the ash was excluded from the category of hazardous waste. (The city also claimed that treating the ash as hazardous waste could increase disposal costs by as much as ten times.) The Supreme Court held that although the *incinerator* was not subject to subtitle C regulation as a facility that treats, stores, disposes of, or manages hazardous waste, section 3001(i) did *not* contain any exclusion for the *ash* itself. The incinerator was a *generator* of hazardous waste; and while section 3001(i) states that the facility "shall not be deemed to be treating, storing, disposing of, or otherwise managing hazardous wastes," it "significantly omits from the catalogue" the word "generating." (Section 1004(7) defines "hazardous waste management" as "the systematic control of the collection, source separation, storage, transportation, processing, treatment, recovery, and disposal of hazardous wastes.") Therefore, Chicago was not entitled to the cost-saving waste stream exemption which it claimed.

3. *Must* a solid waste be "listed" as a hazardous waste if it exhibits the "toxicity characteristic" or any of the other "characteristics" of hazardous waste (ignitability, corrosivity, and reactivity)? EPA regulations provide that the Administrator "*shall* list a solid waste as a hazardous waste *only* upon determining that the solid waste meets one of the following criteria: (1) It exhibits any of the [four] characteristics of hazardous waste * * *. (2) It has been found to be fatal to humans in low doses * * *. (3) It contains any of [certain toxic constituents] and, after considering [eleven enumerated] factors, the Administrator concludes that the waste is capable of posing a substantial present or potential hazard to human health or the environment when improperly treated, stored, transported or disposed of, or otherwise managed * * *. 40 C.F.R. section 261.11(a) (1992) (emphasis added).

In *Natural Resources Defense Council v. EPA,* 25 F.3d 1063 (D.C. Cir. 1994), the court held that nothing in RCRA or the foregoing regulation *required* EPA to list used oils from gasoline engines as a hazardous waste "merely because they exhibit the toxicity characteristic and were thus *eligible* for listing under 40 CFR 261.11(a)(1)" (emphasis added). Instead, the agency "was free * * * to evaluate all used oils under the balancing test set forth in section 261.11(a)(3), [and its evaluation in this case] was reasonable * * *." In other words, wastes exhibiting one or more of the four hazardous "characteristics" need not necessarily be "listed" but may instead be regulated as "characteristic" wastes.

e. The Land Disposal Ban

When it amended RCRA in 1984, Congress sought to discourage land disposal of hazardous waste. Section 1002(b)(7) announced a new national policy that, "to avoid substantial risk to human health and the environment, reliance on land disposal should be minimized or eliminated, and land disposal, particularly landfill and surface impoundment, should be the least favored method for managing hazardous wastes." Section 3004(d)(1) provided a staged prohibition on land disposal of *untreated* hazardous waste unless the EPA Administrator "determines the prohibition of one or more methods of land disposal of such waste is not required in order to protect human health and the environment for so long as the waste remains hazardous." In making these determinations, EPA was directed to take into account the characteristics of the waste, "the long-term uncertainties associated with land disposal," and the importance of encouraging proper management of hazardous waste initially. However, § 3004(d)(1), (e)(1), and (g)(5) limited EPA's discretion by specifying that a method of land disposal may not be determined to be protective of human health and the environment "unless, upon application by an interested person, it has been demonstrated to the Administrator, to a reasonable degree of certainty, that there will be *no migration* of hazardous constituents from the disposal unit or injection zone for as long as the wastes remain hazardous" (emphasis added).

Congress did not entirely ban the land disposal of wastes unable to meet this standard. It provided an exception for wastes treated to "substantially diminish the toxicity of the waste or substantially reduce the likelihood of migration of hazardous constituents from the waste so that short-term and long-term threats to human health and the environment are minimized" § 3004(m). The statute directed EPA to promulgate treatment standards specifying how waste otherwise subject to the "land ban" could satisfy the standard. Thus, the land disposal ban, in effect, applies to *untreated* hazardous wastes and authorizes EPA to require pretreatment of wastes that cannot be shown to be capable of safe disposal on land in untreated form.

To prevent generators of hazardous wastes from frustrating the land ban by simply storing waste indefinitely, § 3004(j) prohibits the *storage* of wastes subject to the land disposal ban "unless such storage is solely for the purpose of the accumulation of such quantities of hazardous wastes as are necessary to facilitate proper recovery, treatment or disposal." In *Edison Electric Institute v. EPA*, 996 F.2d 326 (D.C. Cir. 1993), the court upheld an EPA rule making it unlawful to store hazardous waste indefinitely pending the development of adequate treatment techniques or disposal capacity. While the court expressed its sympathy with generators who had no treatment or disposal alternatives available, it emphasized that RCRA is "a highly prescriptive, technology-forcing statute * * * clearly intended to provide draconian incentives * * * for the rapid development of adequate treatment and storage capacity." If generators of hazardous wastes for which adequate treatment methods have not yet been developed could store those wastes indefinitely, the generators would have an incentive *not* to develop treatment technology—at least if the cost of storage was less than the probable sum of the costs of developing the technology and of treating and then disposing of the wastes. On the other hand, firms other than the generators still would have an economic incentive to devise new treatment methods.

The question of what standards should apply to the pre-treatment of toxic wastes prior to their land disposal was addressed in the following case.

HAZARDOUS WASTE TREATMENT COUNCIL v. EPA

United States Court of Appeals, District of Columbia Circuit, 1989.
886 F.2d 355, *cert. denied by* American Petroleum Institute v. EPA,
498 U.S. 849, 111 S.Ct. 139, 112 L.Ed.2d 106 (1990).

Before WALD, CHIEF JUDGE, SILBERMAN and D.H. GINSBURG, CIRCUIT JUDGES.

Opinion PER CURIAM.

In 1984, Congress amended the Resource Conservation and Recovery Act ("RCRA"), to prohibit land disposal of certain hazardous solvents and wastes containing dioxins except in narrow circumstances to be defined by Environmental Protection Agency ("EPA") regulations. * * * [P]etitioners seek review of EPA's final "solvents and dioxins" rule published pursuant to Congress' 1984 mandate. We conclude that the rule under review is consistent with RCRA, but remand one aspect of the rulemaking to the agency for further explanation.

I.

A. *Statutory Scheme.*

The Hazardous and Solid Waste Amendments of 1984 substantially strengthened EPA's control over the land disposal of hazardous wastes regulated under RCRA's "cradle to grave" statutory scheme. Congress, believing that "land disposal facilities were not capable of assuring long-term containment of certain hazardous wastes," expressed the policy that "reliance on land disposal should be minimized or eliminated." 42 U.S.C. § 6901(b)(7). In order to effectuate this policy, HSWA amended section

3004 of RCRA to prohibit land disposal of hazardous waste unless the waste is "pretreated" in a manner that minimizes "short-term and long-term threats to human health and the environment," § 6924(m), or unless EPA can determine that the waste is to be disposed of in such a fashion as to ensure that "there will be no migration of hazardous constituents from the disposal [facility]...." § 6924(d)(1), (e)(1), & (g)(5).

As amended, RCRA requires EPA to implement the land disposal prohibition in three phases, addressing the most hazardous "listed" wastes first. *See id.* § 6924(g). In accordance with strict statutory deadlines, the Administrator is obligated to specify those methods of land disposal of each listed hazardous waste which "will be protective of human health and the environment." *Id.* In addition, "[s]imultaneously with the promulgation of regulations ... prohibiting .... land disposal of a particular hazardous waste, the Administrator" is required to * * * promulgate regulations specifying those levels or methods of treatment, if any, which substantially diminish the toxicity of the waste or substantially reduce the likelihood of migration of hazardous constituents from the waste so that short-term and long-term threats to human health and the environment are minimized.

Respecting two categories of hazardous wastes, including the solvents and dioxins at issue here Congress, however, declined to wait for phased EPA implementation of the land disposal prohibition. For these wastes, Congress imposed earlier restrictions * * *. These prohibitions, as applied to the solvents and dioxins listed in the HSWA, were to take effect November 8, 1986. * * *

B. *The Rulemaking Under Review.*

In January 1986, EPA issued a notice of proposed rule-making announcing its draft implementation of the land disposal prohibition for solvents and dioxins. Approximately ten months later, after receiving extensive public commentary on the draft blueprint, EPA published a final solvents and dioxins rule differing in some respects from its draft approach. These differences were especially striking in EPA's implementation of section 3004(j) and section 3004(m) of RCRA, governing the storage prohibition and treatment standards, respectively, for solvents and dioxins. * * *

1. *Section 3004(M) Treatment Standards.*

In the Proposed Rule, EPA announced its tentative support for a treatment regime embodying both risk-based and technology-based standards. The technology-based standards would be founded upon what EPA determined to be the Best Demonstrated Available Technology ("BDAT"); parallel risk-based or "screening" levels were to reflect "the maximum concentration [of a hazardous constituent] below which the Agency believes there is no regulatory concern for the land disposal program and which is protective of human health and the environment." The Proposed

Rule provided that these two sets of standards would be melded in the following manner:

First, if BDAT standards were more rigorous than the relevant health-screening levels, the latter would be used to "cap the reductions in toxicity and/or mobility that otherwise would result from the application of BDAT treatment [.]" Thus, "treatment for treatment's sake" would be avoided. Second, if BDAT standards were less rigorous than health-screening levels, BDAT standards would govern and the screening level would be used as "a goal for future changes to the treatment standards as new and more efficient treatment technologies become available." Finally, when EPA determined that the use of BDAT would pose a greater risk to human health and the environment than land disposal, or would provide insufficient safeguards against the threats produced by land disposal, the screening level would actually become the 3004(m) treatment standard.

EPA invited public comment on alternative approaches as well. The first alternative identified in the Proposed Rule (and the one ultimately selected by EPA) was based purely on the capabilities of the "best demonstrated available technology." Capping treatment levels to avoid treatment for treatment's sake, according to EPA, could be accomplished under this technology-based scheme by "the petition process":

Under this approach, if a prescribed level or method of treatment under section 3004(m) resulted in concentration levels that an owner/operator believed to be overly protective, the owner/operator could petition the Agency to allow the use of an alternative treatment level or method or no treatment at all by demonstrating that less treatment would still meet the petition standard of protecting human health and environment. And the function served by health-screening levels of providing a default standard when the application of BDAT technology would itself pose a threat to human health and the environment could likewise be fulfilled by the petition process: "an owner operator could [ ] petition the Agency * * * to allow continued land disposal of the waste upon a demonstration that land disposal of the waste would not result in harm to human health and the environment." *Id.*

The Agency received comments supporting both approaches, but ultimately settled on the pure-technology alternative. Of particular importance to EPA's decision were the comments filed by eleven members of Congress, all of whom served as conferees on the 1984 RCRA amendments. As EPA recorded in the preamble to the Final Rule:

[these] members of Congress argued strongly that [the health screening] approach did not fulfill the intent of the law. They asserted that because of the scientific uncertainty inherent in risk-based decisions, Congress expressly directed the Agency to set treatment standards based on the capabilities of existing technology. The Agency believes that the technology-based approach adopted in [the] final rule, although not the only approach allowable under the law, best responds to the above stated comments.

EPA also relied on passages in the legislative history supporting an approach under which owners and operator of hazardous waste facilities would be required to use "the best [technology] that has been demonstrated to be achievable." And the agency reiterated that the chief advantage offered by the health-screening approach—avoiding "treatment for treatment's sake"—could "be better addressed through changes in other aspects of its regulatory program." * * *

Petitioner CMA challenges this aspect of the rule as an unreasonable construction of section 3004(m)'s mandate to ensure that "short-term and long-term threats to human health and the environment are minimized." In the alternative, CMA argues that EPA has failed to explain the basis-in terms of relevant human health and environmental considerations-for its BDAT regime, which allegedly requires treatment in some circumstances to levels far below the standards for human exposure under other statutes administered by EPA. Thus, CMA claims that EPA's action in promulgating a technology-based rule is arbitrary and capricious. * * *

II. SECTION 3004(M) TREATMENT STANDARDS

CMA challenges EPA's adoption of BDAT treatment standards in preference to the approach it proposed initially primarily on the ground that the regulation is not a reasonable interpretation of the statute. CMA obliquely, and Intervenors Edison Electric and the American Petroleum Institute explicitly, argues in the alternative that the agency did not adequately explain its decision to take the course that it did. We conclude, as to CMA's primary challenge, that EPA's decision to reject the use of screening levels is a reasonable interpretation of the statute. We also find, however, that EPA's justification of its choice is so fatally flawed that we cannot, in conscience, affirm it. We therefore grant the petitions for review to the extent of remanding this issue to the agency for a fuller explanation.

A. *The Consistency of EPA's Interpretation with RCRA.*

* * *

1. **Chevron** *Step I: Is the Statute Clear?*

We repeat the mandate of § 3004(m)(1): the Administrator is required to promulgate "regulations specifying those levels or methods of treatment, if any, which substantially diminish the toxicity of the waste or substantially reduce the likelihood of migration of hazardous constituents from the waste so that short-term and long-term threats to human health and the environment are minimized."

CMA reads the statute as requiring EPA to determine the levels of concentration in waste at which the various solvents here at issue are "safe" and to use those "screening levels" as floors below which treatment would not be required. CMA supports its interpretation with the observation that the statute directs EPA to set standards only to the extent that "threats to human health and the environment are minimized." We are unpersuaded, however, that Congress intended to compel EPA to rely upon screening levels in preference to the levels achievable by BDAT.

The statute directs EPA to set treatment standards based upon either "levels or methods" of treatment. Such a mandate makes clear that the choice whether to use "levels" (screening levels) or "methods" (BDAT) lies within the informed discretion of the agency, as long as the result is "that short-term and long-term threats to human health and the environment are minimized." To "minimize" something is, to quote the Oxford English Dictionary, to "reduce [it] to the smallest possible amount, extent, or degree." But Congress recognized, in the very amendments here at issue, that there are "long-term uncertainties associated with land disposal[.]" In the face of such uncertainties, it cannot be said that a statute that requires that threats be minimized unambiguously requires EPA to set levels at which it is conclusively presumed that no threat to health or the environment exists. * * *

This is not to say that EPA is free, under § 3004(m), to require generators to treat their waste beyond the point at which there is no "threat" to human health or to the environment. That Congress's concern in adopting § 3004(m) was with health and the environment would necessarily make it unreasonable for EPA to promulgate treatment standards wholly without regard to whether there might be a threat to man or nature. That concern is better dealt with, however, at *Chevron*'s second step; for, having concluded that the statute does not unambiguously and in all circumstances foreclose EPA from adopting treatment levels based upon the levels achievable by BDAT, we must now explore whether the particular levels established by the regulations supply a reasonable resolution of the statutory ambiguity.

2. Chevron *Step II: Is EPA's Interpretation Reasonable?*

The screening levels that EPA initially proposed were not those at which the wastes were thought to be entirely safe. Rather, EPA set the levels to reduce risks from the solvents to an "acceptable" level, and it explored, at great length, the manifest (and manifold) uncertainties inherent in any attempt to specify "safe" concentration levels. The agency discussed, for example, the lack of any safe level of exposure to carcinogenic solvents; the extent to which reference dose levels (from which it derived its screening levels) understate the dangers that hazardous solvents pose to particularly sensitive members of the population; the necessarily artificial assumptions that accompany any attempt to model the migration of hazardous wastes from a disposal site; and the lack of dependable data on the effects that solvents have on the liners that bound disposal facilities for the purpose of ensuring that the wastes disposed in a facility stay there. * * *

CMA suggests, despite these uncertainties, that the adoption of a BDAT treatment regime would result in treatment to "below established levels of hazard." * * * [The court then dismissed the basis of CMA's argument as irrelevant.]

In sum, EPA's catalog of the uncertainties inherent in the alternative approach using screening levels supports the reasonableness of its reliance upon BDAT instead. Accordingly, finding no merit in CMA's contention that EPA has required treatment to "below established levels of hazard," we find that EPA's interpretation of § 3004(m) is reasonable. * * *

B. *Was EPA's Explanation Adequate?*

The Supreme Court has made it abundantly clear that a reviewing court is not to supplement an agency's reasons for proceeding as it did, nor to paper over its plainly defective rationale: "The reviewing court should not attempt itself to make up for such deficiencies [in the agency's explanation]; we may not supply a reasoned basis for the agency's action that the agency itself has not given." "We will, however, 'uphold a decision of less than ideal clarity if the agency's path may reasonably be discerned.' " Accordingly, in order to determine whether we can affirm EPA's action here, we must parse the language of the Final Rule to see whether it can be interpreted to make a sensible argument for the approach EPA adopted. We find that it cannot.

As we have said, EPA, in its Proposed Rule, expressed a tentative preference for an approach that combined screening levels and BDAT. It indicated that it thought either that approach or BDAT alone was consistent with the statute, and recognized that there were myriad uncertainties inherent in any attempt to model the health and environmental effects of the land disposal of hazardous wastes. It initially concluded, however, that despite those uncertainties, the better approach was to adopt the combination of screening levels and BDAT. Nevertheless, in the Final Rule, it rejected its earlier approach, and adopted a regime of treatment levels defined by BDAT alone. In order fully to convey the inadequacy of EPA's explanation, we quote the relevant portion of the Final Rule at length:

Although a number of comments on the proposed rule favored the first approach; that is, the use of screening levels to "cap" treatment that can be achieved under BDAT, several commenters, including eleven members of Congress, argued strongly that this approach did not fulfill the intent of the law. They asserted that because of the scientific uncertainty inherent in risk-based decisions, Congress expressly directed the Agency to set treatment standards based on the capabilities of existing technology. The Agency believes that the technology-based approach adopted in today's final rule, although not the only approach allowable under the law, best responds to the above-stated comments. Accordingly, the final rule establishes treatment standards under RCRA section 3004(m) based exclusively on levels achievable by BDAT. The Agency believes that the treatment standards will generally be protective of human health and the environment. Levels less stringent than BDAT may also be protective.
* * *

To summarize: after EPA issued the Proposed Rule, some commenters, including eleven members of Congress, chastised the agency on the ground that the use of screening levels was inconsistent with the intent of the statute. They stated that because of the uncertainties involved, Congress had mandated that BDAT alone be used to set treatment standards. EPA determined that the "best respon[se]" to those comments was to adopt a BDAT standard. It emphasized, however, that either course was consistent with the statute (and that it was therefore not *required* to use BDAT alone). Finally, it asserted, without explanation, that its major purpose in initially proposing screening levels "may be better addressed through changes in other aspects of its regulatory program," and gave an example of one such aspect that might be changed.

This explanation is inadequate. It should go without saying that members of Congress have no power, once a statute has been passed, to alter its interpretation by post-hoc "explanations" of what it means; there may be societies where "history" belongs to those in power, but ours is not among them. In our scheme of things, we consider legislative history because it is just that: *history*. It forms the background against which Congress adopted the relevant statute. Post-enactment statements are a different matter, and they are not to be considered by an agency or by a court as legislative history. An agency has an obligation to consider the comments of legislators, of course, but on the same footing as it would those of other commenters; such comments may have, as Justice Frankfurter said in a different context, "power to persuade, if lacking power to control." * * *

In the entire relevant text of the Final Rule, EPA neither invokes nor discusses the uncertainties inherent in the land disposal process in support of its determination to use BDAT. EPA's only mention of the concept is in its description of the commenters' argument that, because of such uncertainties, Congress mandated BDAT-an argument that EPA rejected. While it may be that EPA intended that reference to act as an incorporation of all the uncertainties it outlined in its Proposed Rule, or all the many challenges to its assumptions that commenters submitted in response to the Proposed Rule, that intent, if indeed it exists, is so shrouded in mist that for this court to say that we could discern its outlines would be as illogical as the agency's explanation in the Final Rule itself. Accordingly, we grant the petitions for review in this respect. * * *

NOTES

1. Does it make more policy sense to mandate the use of BDAT or to require treatment to reduce toxicity to set concentration levels? What are the consequences of a BDAT standard for the development of new technologies to treat toxic wastes? Does BDAT spur innovation or lock certain technologies into place?

2. Chapter 2 describes various approaches to risk analysis and management. Does RCRA's approach strike the right balance between risk and safety?

3.   How is the EPA supposed to respond to congressional pressure to implement a statute in a particular way, especially when the pressure often comes from members of Congress who have budgetary or other oversight powers over the agency? How should the EPA balance corresponding pressure from the executive branch, particularly when the executive branch's goals differ from the goals of influential congressional members?

4.   In the next case, the "NRDC petitioners" challenged EPA's decision not to require the use of "best demonstrated available technologies" (BDATs) in all situations, prior to land disposal. "Industry petitioners," on the other hand, were protesting regulations mandating levels of treatment which in some situations went beyond removal of the characteristic (ignitability, corrosivity, reactivity, or toxicity) which led to the waste's classification as hazardous.

CHEMICAL WASTE MANAGEMENT, INC. v. EPA

United States Court of Appeals, District of Columbia Circuit, 1992.
976 F.2d 2, *cert. denied* 507 U.S. 1057, 113 S.Ct. 1961, 123 L.Ed.2d 664 (1993).

Before Edwards, Buckley, and Henderson, Circuit Judges.

Opinion Per Curiam.

The Hazardous and Solid Waste Amendments of 1984 instituted a ban on the land disposal of classes of hazardous wastes unless certain conditions are met. Those amendments require the Environmental Protection Agency to follow a phased schedule for implementing the ban. In this case we consider various challenges to regulations implementing the final portion of this program, the so-called "third-third" rule, which largely covers the land disposal of wastes deemed hazardous because they possess certain defined characteristics.

Various petitioners raise multi-faceted challenges. A group of industry trade associations and companies (collectively, "industry petitioners") seek review of regulations mandating levels of treatment before land disposal that go beyond the removal of the attribute that led to the waste's classification as hazardous. These petitioners claim that the EPA lacked authority under the statute to require treatment to such levels. * * *

We deny each of these petitions for review. Sections 3004(g)(5) and (m) of [RCRA] give the EPA the statutory authority to mandate the treatment of wastes to levels beyond those at which the wastes present the characteristics that caused them to be deemed hazardous. * * *

Several environmental organizations, as well as the Hazardous Waste Treatment Council, an association representing companies that treat hazardous waste (collectively, "NRDC petitioners") * * * argued that * * * the new rule's "deactivation" treatment standard impermissibly allows the dilution, rather than treatment with specified technologies, of many characteristic wastes prior to land disposal. * * *.

dillution

* * * Under the statute, dilution of characteristic hazardous wastes may constitute treatment, but only if no hazardous constituents are

present following dilution that would endanger human health or the environment. The EPA concedes that dilution will not attain this result for certain characteristic wastes. For others, it has not made clear that dilution will meet the requirements for treatment. The standard is therefore vacated as to those wastes. The dilution of wastes in Clean Water Act facilities is acceptable so long as the toxicity of the waste discharged from the facility is minimized or eliminated consistent with RCRA. Similarly, disposal of wastes in underground injection wells may occur as long as the hazardous characteristics have been eliminated and any health and environmental dangers posed by hazardous constituents of the wastes are minimized. * * *

I. Statutory and Regulatory Background

[Under RCRA, wastes] are deemed hazardous in one of two ways: They possess one of the four hazardous characteristics identified by the EPA ("characteristic wastes"), or have been found to be hazardous as a result of an EPA rulemaking ("listed wastes").

The four characteristics identified as hazardous are ignitability, corrosivity, reactivity, and extraction procedure ("EP") toxicity. * * * Characteristic wastes comprise over fifty percent of all the hazardous wastes generated in the United States each year.

Although the EPA may list a waste if it possesses one of the four characteristics described above, in practice it will only list specific wastes that are either acutely hazardous or possess high levels of toxic constituents. A listed waste loses its hazardous status only after a petition for its "delisting" is approved by the EPA in a notice-and-comment rulemaking.

"Once a waste is listed or identified as hazardous, its subsequent management is regulated" under subtitle C of RCRA. * * * The management of a hazardous waste continues "until such time as it ceases to pose a hazard to the public."

* * * The Hazardous and Solid Waste Amendments of 1984 expressed a general policy preference that "reliance on land disposal should be minimized or eliminated." A prohibition on disposal would apply unless the waste is treated so as to minimize the short-term and long-term threats to human health and the environment posed by toxic and hazardous constituents, or unless the EPA finds that no migration of hazardous constituents from the facility will occur after disposal. * * *

II. Treatment Standards for Characteristic Wastes

* * *

The EPA determined that for most ICR [ignitable, corrosive and reactive] wastes, treatment to characteristic levels would be sufficient. The Agency found upon review that

[t]he environmental concerns from the properties of ignitability, corrosivity, and reactivity are different from the environmental concern

from EP toxic wastes. Toxic constituents can pose a cumulative impact on land disposal even where waste is below the characteristic level. Where wastes pose an ascertainable toxicity concern * * * the Agency has developed treatment standards that address the toxicity concern and (in effect) require treatment below the characteristic level * * *. Otherwise, treatment that removes the properties of ignitability, corrosivity, and reactivity, fully addresses the environmental concern from the properties themselves.

The EPA also retreated from its emphasis on technology-based treatment in the final regulations, altering its position on the use of dilution as a method of treatment:

In all cases, the Agency has determined that for non-toxic hazardous characteristic wastes, it should not matter how the characteristic property is removed so long as it is removed. Thus, dilution is an acceptable treatment method for such wastes.

* * * Only in three subcategories of ICR wastes did the EPA mandate the use of technological treatment * * *.

Industry petitioners contend that RCRA does not provide authority for the EPA to mandate treatment of characteristic wastes after their ignitability, corrosiveness, reactivity, or EP toxicity has been addressed. They make a straightforward argument: Subtitle C regulations attach to a waste only when it is hazardous. The moment a waste ceases to meet the regulatory definition of a hazardous waste, the EPA loses its authority to regulate further. Thus, in industry petitioners' view, RCRA's cradle-to-grave system covers waste only if it remains hazardous throughout its life and at the moment of its burial. * * *

* * * EPA reiterates the rationales stated in its final rule: The key provisions of the land-ban program, sections 3004(g)(5) and (m), can be read as allowing the Agency to apply land disposal restrictions at any time it wishes; those provisions at a minimum contemplate activity that occurs before land disposal; section 3004(m)(1) requires treatment to avoid the prohibition on land disposal; and treatment must take place, by definition, before disposal occurs. * * * The Agency reasons that the subtitle C program can attach at the point of generation, and the broad language of section 3004(m)(1) allows additional treatment to remove risks posed by wastes beyond those inherent in the characteristic.

To succeed in their *Chevron* step one argument, industry petitioners must show that Congress "has directly spoken to the precise question at issue" and has "unambiguously expressed [its] intent." We find little support in the statute or our prior decisions for the notion that Congress mandated the line industry petitioners draw. These petitioners believe that the definition of a hazardous waste acts as a revolving regulatory door, allowing continual entrance and egress from RCRA's requirements. The key provisions of the statute support a contrary view—that hazardous waste becomes subject to the land disposal program as soon as it is generated. * * *

We conclude that, in combination, sections 3004(g)(5) and (m) provide the EPA with authority to bar land disposal of certain wastes unless they have been treated to reduce risks beyond those presented by the characteristics themselves. We also find the Agency's assertion of regulatory authority over the wastes from the moment they are generated to be "based on a permissible construction of the statute." *Chevron.*

NRDC petitioners ask this court to vacate the deactivation treatment standard as applied to ICR wastes because it authorizes the dilution of these wastes to eliminate their ignitability, corrosiveness, or reactivity rather than mandating use of technological treatment. * * * They claim that some form of technology must be used to treat wastes in all instances.

They also contend that dilution fails to satisfy the statutory requirement that treatment minimize short-term and long-term threats to human health and the environment, or to substantially diminish the toxicity of the waste. In their view, the removal of these characteristics through dilution only affects the short-term risk that the waste will manifest that property; it does not address the threats posed by the hazardous organic and inorganic constituents of those wastes. * * *

We believe that dilution can, in principle, constitute an acceptable form of treatment for ICR wastes. We do not read the 1984 Amendments as mandating the use of the best demonstrated available technologies ("BDAT") in all situations. To reiterate, section 3004(m)(1) directs the Administrator to

> specify[ ] those levels or methods of treatment, if any, which substantially diminish the toxicity of the waste or substantially reduce the likelihood of migration of hazardous constituents from the waste so that short-term and long-term threats to human health and the environment are minimized. * * *

We agree that the section imposes an exacting standard: It requires that treatment prior to land disposal "substantially diminish the toxicity of the waste or substantially reduce the likelihood of migration of hazardous constituents from the waste so that short-term and long-term threats to human health and the environment are minimized." But this provision does not bar dilution as a means of treating ICR wastes; instead, it defines the purposes that a method of treatment must achieve. Any treatment that meets those objectives is permissible. When read against RCRA's broad definition of treatment, we cannot say Congress clearly barred dilution as an acceptable methodology. * * *

[The Court also addressed the EPA's the application of the dilution rules to Clean Water Act treatment systems and deep injection wells; its ruling was subsequently overturned by the Land Disposal Flexibility Act of 1996, Public Law 104–119.]

NOTES

1.   Why did EPA decide that "treatment to characteristic levels" would be sufficient for most "ICR wastes" but not for "EP toxic wastes?" How does that degree of treatment differ from treatment involving BDAT? Can the former involve only dilution?

2.   The Hazardous Waste Treatment Council, an association representing companies that treat hazardous waste, joined with environmental organizations in pressing for more stringent treatment standards. Why do you think environmental and industry groups would join forces?

3.   Underground injection is used to dispose of a substantial part of the nation's hazardous wastes. Supposedly such disposal is allowed only where the waste will not mix with groundwater, e.g., because they will be separated by impermeable rock or soil. Can you imagine why this practice remains controversial?

4.   Five federal statutes regulate routine releases of toxic and hazardous pollutants from and within industrial facilities: RCRA, the Clean Water Act, the Clean Air Act, the Occupational Safety and Health Act, and the Emergency Planning and Community Right–To–Know Act (EPCRA, discussed at page 1027, *infra*). Each of these statutes centers on a list that specifies which pollutants are subject to regulation, but there are five different lists, not one. For an analysis of the development of and inconsistencies among the lists, and a proposal to harmonize the five regulatory regimes, *see* John Dernbach, *The Unfocused Regulation of Toxic and Hazardous Pollutants*, 21 HARV. ENVTL. L. REV. 1 (1997).

5.   Section 3008 of RCRA provides that for a violation of any requirement of subchapter III (concerning hazardous waste management), the EPA Administrator may issue a compliance order and assess a penalty that takes into account the seriousness of the violation and any good faith efforts to comply. According to a policy statement by EPA in 1984, such penalties are calculated in part to eliminate the economic benefits of infractions. EPA rates violations according to their seriousness—major, moderate, or minor—based on "extent of deviation" from RCRA requirements and "potential for harm." Enforcement personnel are to calculate any economic gains from noncompliance, factor in the gravity component, and adjust the overall penalty to take into account the violator's past compliance record and good or bad faith. *See* 15 ENV'T REP. 86 (1984).

6.   Enforcement of state hazardous waste laws (usually adopted pursuant to authority in RCRA) against federal facilities has been a problem. *See* Comment, *Lawmaker as Lawbreaker: Assessing Civil Penalties Against Federal Facilities Under RCRA*, 57 U. CHI. L. REV. 845 (1990). *Maine v. Navy Department,* 973 F.2d 1007 (1st Cir. 1992), held that the state of Maine could not recover civil penalties from the Navy Department for past violations of state hazardous waste laws at a Navy shipyard located in the state, because the Supreme Court previously had ruled in *United States Department of Energy v. Ohio,* 503 U.S. 607 (1992), that RCRA did not waive federal agencies' sovereign immunity from imposition of punitive civil penalties. A

few weeks later, Congress approved the Federal Facility Compliance Act, Pub. L. No. 102–386 (1992), amending section 6001 of RCRA to allow state agencies and EPA to enforce hazardous waste laws at federal facilities. The law clarifies that federal sovereign immunity is waived to allow imposition and collection of civil and administrative penalties and fines, even if punitive or coercive, as well as reasonable, nondiscriminatory service charges for permits, review of plans, and inspection and monitoring of facilities.

f.   Liability and Enforcement

Although RCRA is typically viewed as a prospective statute governing the handling of hazardous waste from cradle to grave, the statute also contains provisions for retroactive liability somewhat similar to CERCLA, though with important differences. The following case addresses liability under the "contributor" standard of section 7003.

UNITED STATES v. NORTHEASTERN PHARMACEUTICAL & CHEMICAL CO., INC. [NEPACCO]

United States Court of Appeals for the Eighth Circuit, 1986.
810 F.2d 726, *cert. denied*, 484 U.S. 848, 108 S.Ct. 146, 98 L.Ed.2d 102 (1987).

McMILLIAN, CIRCUIT JUDGE.

I.   Facts

* * * In 1974 [NEPACCO's] corporate assets were liquidated, and the proceeds were used to pay corporate debts and then distributed to the shareholders. Michaels formed NEPACCO, was a major shareholder, and was its president. Lee was NEPACCO's vice-president, the supervisor of its manufacturing plant located in Verona, Missouri, and also a shareholder. Mills was employed as shift supervisor at NEPACCO's Verona plant.

From April 1970 to January 1972 NEPACCO manufactured the disinfectant hexachlorophene at its Verona plant. NEPACCO leased the plant from Hoffman–Taff, Inc.; Syntex Agribusiness, Inc. (Syntex), is the successor to Hoffman–Taff. Michaels and Lee knew that NEPACCO's manufacturing process produced various hazardous and toxic by-products, including 2,4,5–trichlorophenol (TCP), 2,3,7,8–tetrachlorodibenzo-p-dioxin (TCDD or dioxin), and toluene. The waste by-products were pumped into a holding tank which was periodically emptied by waste haulers. Occasionally, however, excess waste by-products were sealed in 55–gallon drums and then stored at the plant.

In July 1971 Mills approached NEPACCO plant manager Bill Ray with a proposal to dispose of the waste-filled 55–gallon drums on a farm owned by James Denney located about seven miles south of Verona. Ray visited the Denney farm and discussed the proposal with Lee; Lee approved the use of Mills' services and the Denney farm as a disposal site. In mid-July 1971 Mills and Gerald Lechner dumped approximately 85 of the 55–gallon drums into a large trench on the Denney farm * * *.

* * * During April 1980 the EPA conducted an on-site investigation, exposed and sampled 13 of the 55–gallon drums, which were found to be badly deteriorated, and took water and soil samples. The samples were found to contain "alarmingly" high concentrations of dioxin, TCP and toluene.

* * * In August 1980 the government filed its initial complaint against NEPACCO, the generator of the hazardous substances; Michaels and Lee, the corporate officers responsible for arranging for the disposal of the hazardous substances; Mills, the transporter of the hazardous substances; and Syntex, the owner and lessor of the Verona plant, seeking injunctive relief and reimbursement of response costs pursuant to RCRA § 7003 * * *.

In the meantime the EPA had been negotiating with Syntex about Syntex's liability for cleanup of the Denney farm site. In September 1980 the government and Syntex entered into a settlement and consent decree. Pursuant to the terms of the settlement, Syntex would pay $100,000 of the government's response costs and handle the removal, storage and permanent disposal of the hazardous substances from the Denney farm site. The EPA approved Syntex's proposed cleanup plan, and in June 1981 Syntex began excavation of the trench. In November 1981 the site was closed. The 55–gallon drums are now stored in a specially constructed concrete bunker on the Denney farm. The drums as stored do not present an imminent and substantial endangerment to health or the environment; however, no plan for permanent disposal has been developed, and the site will continue to require testing and monitoring in the future.

In August 1982 the government filed an amended complaint adding counts for relief pursuant to CERCLA §§ 104, 106, 107 (counts II and III). CERCLA was enacted after the filing of the initial complaint. * * * In September 1983 the district court denied the defense demand for a jury trial, holding the government's request for recovery of its response costs was comparable to restitution and thus an equitable remedy. The trial was conducted during October 1983. * * *

[The portions of the court's opinion dealing with CERCLA appear at page 914, *infra*.] * * *

As alternative basis for recovery of the response costs incurred before December 11, 1980, the government argues on cross-appeal that it can also recover its response costs pursuant to RCRA § 7003(a). The district court did not reach the recovery issue because it held that under RCRA § 7003(a) (prior to 1984 amendments discussed below), proof of fault or negligence was required in order to impose liability upon past off-site generators and transporters. Because the government did not allege or prove negligence, the district court found no liability * * *. The government argues that the standard of liability under RCRA § 7003(a), as initially enacted and as amended in 1984, is strict liability, not negligence, and that liability under RCRA can be imposed even though the acts of disposal occurred before RCRA became effective in 1976. We agree. * * *

The critical issue is the meaning of the phrase "contributing to." Before its amendment in 1984, RCRA § 7003(a), imposed liability upon any person "contributing to" "the handling, storage, treatment, transportation or disposal of any solid or hazardous waste" that "may present an imminent and substantial endangerment to health or the environment." * * *

* * * As amended in 1984, RCRA § 7003(a) (new language underlined; deleted language in brackets), now provides in pertinent part:

> Notwithstanding any other provision of this chapter, upon receipt of evidence that the <u>past or present</u> handling, storage, treatment, transportation or disposal of any solid waste or hazardous waste may present an imminent and substantial endangerment to health or the environment, the Administrator may bring suit on behalf of the United States in the appropriate district court [to immediately restrain any person] <u>against any person (including any past or present generator, past or present transporter, or past or present owner or operator of a treatment, storage, or disposal facility) who has contributed or who is</u> contributing to such handling, storage, treatment, transportation or disposal [to stop] <u>to restrain such person from *such handling, storage, treatment, transportation, or disposal [or to take such other action as may be necessary]*, to order such person to take such other action as may be necessary, or both.</u> * * *

* * * From the legislative history of the 1984 amendments, it is clear that Congress intended RCRA § 7003(a), as initially enacted and as amended, to impose liability without fault or negligence and to apply to the present conditions resulting from past activities. In other words, RCRA § 7003(a), as initially enacted and as amended, applies to past non-negligent off-site generators like NEPACCO and to non-negligent past transporters like Mills.

Appellants argue, however, that the 1984 amendments should not be applied to them because the 1984 amendments are not merely "clarifying" amendments but instead substantively changed the existing law. We disagree. First, Congress itself expressly characterized the 1984 amendments as "clarifying" amendments. Second, as part of the legislative history of the 1984 amendments, Congress expressly stated what its intention had been when it initially passed the RCRA in 1976, even though the 1976 legislative history contained no specific discussion of the standard and scope of liability of § 7003(a). * * * Thus, by passing the 1984 amendments the 98th Congress made clear that the intention of the 94th Congress in enacting the RCRA in 1976 had been to impose liability upon past non-negligent off-site generators and transporters of hazardous waste. * * *

 In summary, we hold that RCRA § 7003(a), as initially enacted and as clarified by the 1984 amendments, imposes strict liability upon past off-site generators of hazardous waste and upon past transporters of hazardous waste. * * *

The government argues * * * that Lee and Michaels can be held individually liable as "contributors" under RCRA § 7003(a). For the reasons discussed below, we agree with the government's liability arguments. * * *

RCRA § 7003(a) imposes strict liability upon "any person" who is contributing or who has contributed to the disposal of hazardous substances that may present an imminent and substantial endangerment to health or the environment. As defined by statute, the term "person" includes both individuals and corporations and does not exclude corporate officers and employees. * * * [I]mposing liability upon only the corporation, but not those corporate officers and employees who actually make corporate decisions, would be inconsistent with Congress' intent to impose liability upon the persons who are involved in the handling and disposal of hazardous substances. * * *

[handwritten margin note: Liability for Corp. Officers]

We hold Lee and Michaels are individually liable as "contributors" under RCRA § 7003(a), 42 U.S.C.A. § 6973(a). Lee actually participated in the conduct that violated RCRA; he personally arranged for the transportation and disposal of hazardous substances that presented an imminent and substantial endangerment to health and the environment. Unlike Lee, Michaels was not personally involved in the actual decision to transport and dispose of the hazardous substances. As NEPACCO's corporate president and as a major NEPACCO shareholder, however, Michaels was the individual in charge of and directly responsible for all of NEPACCO's operations, including those at the Verona plant, and he had the ultimate authority to control the disposal of NEPACCO's hazardous substances. *Cf. New York v. Shore Realty Corp.*, 759 F.2d at 1052–53 (shareholder-manager held liable under CERCLA). * * *

Appellants next argue the district court erred in denying their demand for a jury trial because the government's action for recovery of its response costs under CERCLA and RCRA was essentially a claim for legal damages. We disagree. When the government seeks recovery of its response costs under CERCLA or its abatement costs under RCRA, it is in effect seeking equitable relief in the form of restitution or reimbursement of the costs it expended in order to respond to the health and environmental danger presented by hazardous substances.

NOTES

1. What do you think of the reliance on the legislative history of the 1984 "clarifying" amendments to RCRA for guidance concerning the intended meaning of the original 1976 statute?

2. Is it fair to apply section 7003 to "past [i.e., pre–1976] non-negligent off-site generators and transporters" who acted lawfully at the time they "contributed" to disposal of the hazardous substances? Do you understand the court's rationale for concluding that this does not constitute "retroactive" application of RCRA? Would it be a denial of due process to apply the statute retroactively?

In *Eastern Enterprises v. Apfel*, 524 U.S. 498 (1998), the Supreme Court found a federal law that imposed on a coal mining company a "severe retroactive liability" to pay health benefits for its former employees to be an unconstitutional "taking" of private property. Efforts to extend this reasoning to invalidate "retroactive" liability under RCRA and CERCLA have not been successful. *See, e.g.,* United States v. Dico, Inc., 266 F.3d 864 (8th Cir. 2001), *cert. denied*, 535 U.S. 1095 (2002).

3. How important do you think it is for liability under section 7003 to extend to corporate officers and employees, as well as to the corporation itself?

4. Issues like those in notes 2 and 3 also arise in connection with CERCLA. Although much of the thrust of RCRA is prospective—directed at regulation of future waste treatment and disposal—section 7003 clearly is retrospective also. Thus it overlaps with CERCLA, which is concerned mainly with cleanups of past disposal sites. But there are important differences. Sections 7002 (which authorizes citizen suits brought by private persons) and 7003 of RCRA apply to a different spectrum of substances than do sections 106 and 107 of CERCLA. It is common for public and private plaintiffs in these kinds of cases to rely on both RCRA and CERCLA.

5. Although RCRA provides for liability for retrospective behavior, can a private party bring a RCRA cause of action for the costs of cleanup where a facility does not pose an immediate danger to human health or the environment? Section 7002 of RCRA authorizes citizen suits to be brought against any person alleged to be in violation of a RCRA permit or standard, but also against any person "who has contributed or who is contributing to the past or present handling, storage, treatment, transportation, or disposal of any solid or hazardous wastes which may present an imminent and substantial endangerment to health or the environment." The similarity to section 7003 is evident. However, in *Meghrig v. KFC Western, Inc.*, 516 U.S. 479 (1996) KFC brought suit against the prior owners of a parcel on which KFC operated a restaurant after finding petroleum contamination after KFC had spent more than $200,000 cleaning up the site. The Supreme Court held that RCRA does not authorize such a suit where no imminent threat exists. Because CERCLA exempts petroleum from its reach, *see* 42 U.S.C. section 9601(14), owners of sites contaminated with petroleum are limited to contributions to abate imminent harms, not for clean up reimbursement. Why do you suppose the Court might interpret section 7003 to permit cost recovery after the imminent threat has passed, but not interpret section 7002 to do so?

For a critique of *Meghrig* and an analysis of its practical consequences, *see* Jerome Organ, *Advice for Owners of Contaminated Land after Meghrig v. KFC Western, Inc.,* 26 ENVTL. L. REP. 10582 (1996).

g. Waste Minimization and Pollution Prevention

The concept of waste reduction, or waste minimization, was incorporated into RCRA by the 1984 amendments. Section 1003(b) declares it to be national policy that "wherever feasible, the generation of hazardous waste is to be reduced or eliminated as expeditiously as possible." Section 1003(a)(6) announces the objective of "minimizing the generation of hazardous waste and the land disposal of hazardous waste by encouraging process substitution, materials recovery, properly conducted recycling and reuse, and treatment." Section 3002(a)(6) requires generators to report "efforts undertaken during the year to reduce the volume and toxicity of waste generated;" § 3002(b) requires generators to certify on their waste manifests that they have in place programs "to reduce the volume or quantity and toxicity of such waste to the degree determined by the generator to be economically practicable;" and § 3005(h) requires the same certification in connection with any new permit issued for the "treatment, storage, or disposal of hazardous waste."

In 1993, EPA announced that some 19,000 hazardous waste generators, including many that used incineration, would be asked to make their waste minimization plans public. *See* 24 ENV'T REP. 728 (1993). The agency also said that it planned to publish a list of the targeted generators, those required to certify on their hazardous wastes manifests that they have waste minimization programs in place. The response was that "industry in general will be unalterably opposed to making waste [minimization] plans public." The industry spokesperson denied any statutory authority for EPA to establish such a requirement.

In 1994, EPA released an update of its draft waste minimization guidance. *See* 25 ENV'T REP. 147 (1994). The update said that there should be specific waste reduction targets, short-term and long-term, though it did not specify what the percentage reduction rates should be. EPA sought comments on this matter. The agency said its goal was to achieve a national percentage reduction by 1997 of highly toxic and persistent hazardous wastes that are combusted. By the year 2000, EPA's goal was to achieve an overall reduction of RCRA hazardous waste through source reduction and recycling. However, the goals were not to be applied to individual facilities because EPA said it lacked statutory authority to impose such requirements.

In 2002, EPA established a "National Waste Minimization Partnership Program" to persuade industries to voluntarily reduce the amount of chemicals used in production processes. By 2006, the program—now called the National Partnership for Environmental Priorities, had enrolled 74 companies and federal and state facilities. Participants are asked to establish goals for chemical reduction and are to focus on "priority chemicals PBTs (persistent, bioaccumulative, and toxic chemicals)."

In a related law, the Pollution Prevention Act of 1990, 42 U.S.C.A. §§ 13101–13109 (1990), Congress found that there are "significant opportunities for industry to reduce or prevent pollution at the source through cost-effective changes in production, operation, and raw materials use." Congress further found that opportunities for source reduction are "often not realized because existing regulations, and the industrial resources they require for compliance, focus upon treatment and disposal, rather than source reduction * * *." The Act provided that, as a first step in preventing pollution through source reduction, the EPA should establish a source reduction program which collects and disseminates information and provides financial assistance to states.

Besides providing for EPA matching grants to states for programs to promote the use of source reduction techniques by businesses, the Pollution Prevention Act provides that each owner or operator of a facility required to file an annual toxic chemical release form under the Emergency Planning and Community Right-to-Know Act (*see* page 1027, *infra,*) shall include with each such annual filing a toxic chemical source reduction and recycling report for the preceding calendar year. This report must cover each toxic chemical required to be reported in the annual toxic chemical release form. The toxic chemical source reduction and recycling report must explain, for each toxic chemical, the amount of that chemical which has been recycled; source reduction practices used with respect to that chemical; and the techniques used to identify source reduction opportunities. 42 U.S.C.A. § 13106 (1990). However, in 1994, EPA announced that a final rule detailing how companies should report pollution prevention data on the Toxic Release Inventory (TRI) reporting form was "on hold indefinitely," pending possible changes in the definitions of solid waste and other related terms under RCRA. *See* 25 ENV'T REP. 498 (1994).

In its 1991 Pollution Prevention Strategy, 56 Fed.Reg. 7849 (Feb. 26, 1991), EPA said studies have shown that pollution prevention can be "the most effective way to reduce risks by reducing or eliminating pollution at its source; it also is often the most cost-effective option because it reduces raw material losses, the need for expensive 'end-of-pipe' technologies, and long-term liability." In short, "pollution prevention offers the unique advantage of harmonizing environmental protection with economic efficiency." The strategy included a plan for targeting 15 to 20 high-risk chemicals that offered opportunities for prevention, and set a "voluntary goal of reducing total environmental releases of these chemicals by 33 percent by the end of 1992, and at least 50 percent by the end of 1995." (Hence the name "33/50 Program.") The strategy further provided that when EPA determined that specific regulatory actions were needed, it would investigate "flexible, cost-effective regulatory approaches that avoid prescriptive approaches and that rely on market-based incentives where practical and authorized by law."

A 1992 internal memorandum from the Deputy Administrator to all EPA personnel emphasized that "prevention is our first priority within an environmental management hierarchy that includes: 1) prevention, 2) recycling, 3) treatment, and 4) disposal or release." Memorandum from Henry F. Habicht II, Deputy Administrator, EPA, *Memorandum: EPA Definition of Pollution Prevention* (May 28, 1992), 1 ENV'T REP. (1992). The memorandum stated that pollution prevention means "source reduction," as defined in the Pollution Prevention Act, and other practices that reduce or eliminate the creation of pollutants through increased efficiency in the use of raw materials, energy, water or other resources, or through protection of natural resources by conservation. The Pollution Prevention Act defines "source reduction" to mean any practice which (i) reduces the amount of any hazardous substance, pollutant, or contaminant entering any waste stream or otherwise released into the environment prior to recycling, treatment, or disposal, and (ii) reduces the hazards to public health and the environment associated with the release of such substance, pollutants, or contaminants. Thus, under the Act, recycling, energy recovery, treatment, and disposal are not included within the definition of pollution prevention. However, some practices commonly described as "in-process recycling" may qualify as pollution prevention.

A 1994 study by a private environmental group concluded that EPA's voluntary pollution prevention program was a failure and should be replaced. The study said that many companies had cut their toxic waste at the source, but that for 83 percent of the projects the efforts already were under way before EPA's program was initiated in 1991. The critics said that EPA's industrial toxics project, the "33/50 Program," was "pollution prevention in name only," since "only under 33/50 are waste incineration, treatment, burning for energy recovery, recycling, and production cutbacks considered pollution prevention." *See* 25 ENV'T REP. 280 (1994).

A slightly more positive evaluation of the 33/50 Program is offered by Eric Orts, *Reflexive Environmental Law*, 89 Nw. U. L. REV. 1227, 1284–87 (1995). As of 1994, EPA had invited over 8,000 companies to participate in the program, and 1,200 had agreed to do so. EPA's interim goal of 33% reductions by 1992 was exceeded: a 40% reduction from 1988 levels was achieved, and participating companies claimed to be on target for 50% reductions by 1995. Another author later reported that "the 1,300 participating facilities largely relied on end-of-pipe controls in successfully meeting the fifty percent reduction goal by 1994—one year earlier than planned." Michele Ochsner, *Pollution Prevention: An Overview of Regulatory Incentives and Barriers*, 6 N.Y.U. ENVTL L.J. 586, 592 (1998).

In addition to promoting voluntary pollution prevention actions by businesses, EPA also uses its leverage in enforcement negotiations to encourage such actions. In many cases, pollution prevention programs are required to redress violations and achieve compliance with environmental regulations, often as specific conditions of settlements. With increasing regularity, companies are mitigating cash fines and penalties by undertaking source reduction and similar techniques. *See* William Thomas et al., *Using Auditing, Pollution Prevention, and Management Systems to Craft Superior Environmental Enforcement Solutions*, 30 ENVTL. L. REP. 10299 (2000). "Supplemental Environmental Projects" (SEPs) are discussed further at page 844, *infra*.

States have also instituted various pollution prevention programs, though as the National Pollution Prevention Roundtable suggests, these "efforts, due to poor funding, are still in their infancy." The Roundtable estimates nevertheless that state programs have achieved 167 billion pounds of pollution reduction from air, water and waste programs. *See* National Pollution Prevention Roundtable, An Ounce of Prevention is

Worth Over 167 Billion Pounds of Cure (2003) (*available at* http://www.p2 results/2418_historyfind.pdf.

For further discussion of waste minimization and pollution prevention, see James Salzman, *Sustainable Consumption and the Law*, 27 ENVTL. L. REP. 1243 (1997); Kurt Strasser, *Cleaner Technology, Pollution Prevention and Environmental Regulation*, 9 FORDHAM ENVTL. L.J. 1 (1997); Kurt Strasser, *Preventing Pollution*, 8 FORDHAM ENVTL. L.J. 1 (1996).

2. STATE AND LOCAL SITING OF HAZARDOUS WASTE FACILITIES

As we described in Chapter 2, the concept of environmental justice became prominent in the 1980's and 1990's with a particular focus on the siting of hazardous waste facilities. The article below described the most common process for siting such facilities.

MATA, HAZARDOUS WASTE FACILITIES AND ENVIRONMENTAL EQUITY: A PROPOSED SITING MODEL[3]
13 VA ENVTL. L.J. 375, 377, 401–10 (1994).

Health risks and adverse economic consequences associated with hazardous waste facilities complicate the siting of these facilities. * * * Arguably, local opposition to the siting of a hazardous waste facility is a logical response to the imposition of large risks on a small population for the benefit of a much larger population. * * *

In general, states approach the siting of hazardous waste facilities from one of three approaches: super review, site designation, and local control. Additionally, some states require that developers compensate host communities for accepting facilities. Either way, the statutes assume that facilities are necessary to society and must be sited "with as little social cost (including environmental cost) and disruption as possible."

1. Super Review Model

The super review approach is the most common. It calls for regulatory agencies to await the filing of permit applications before determining whether a particular site is qualified for the intended use. The petition for permit is evaluated according to a set of rules and either satisfied as filed, satisfied with conditions or denied. Under the super review scheme, if a permitting agency denies a permit on grounds that the site is unsuitable, the developer is compelled to give up or propose another site.

Michigan is an example of one state that utilizes the super review siting model,[4] and its statutory scheme contains characteristics typical of

---

3. Copyright © 1994 by Virginia Environmental Law Journal Association. Reprinted with permission.

4. Mich.Comp.Laws Ann. §§ 299.517–.520 (West 1984 & Supp.1993).

the super review approach. The program calls for an initial review of the permit application by the state environmental protection agency. If the application clears this initial hurdle, it is then reviewed for final determination by a specially created site review board. Public participation is expanded during the time the permit application is under review by the board. The program also provides for the reconciliation of state and local interests in instances where concerns are raised by interested parties. * * *

2. Site Designation Model

The selection of preferred sites around the state in advance of project proposals characterizes the site designation approach. In this manner, an inventory of sites is maintained even during periods when no project proposals are submitted by developers. An example of the site designation model is the Minnesota siting program.

Under the Minnesota siting scheme, potential sites are selected in one of two ways. First, a facility operator may propose a candidate site with approval from the owners of the site and the municipal government in which it lies.[5] Second, the state may select potential sites, although it may designate no more than one site per county at a time.

Any county containing a potential site may negotiate a contract with the state's office of waste management once it files a resolution of interest (to host a facility) with the state's waste management board. The county, however, can withdraw the resolution of interest at any time prior to executing a final contract. Contracts are subject to several negotiable terms, as noted in the statute. For example, the state and county can negotiate the procedures pertaining to the evaluation and selection of the site and the construction, operation, and maintenance of a proposed facility. The parties can negotiate guidelines for safe operation of the facility and a compensation package. Finally, the county can negotiate provisions for amending the contract and for resolving disputes. * * *

3. Local Control Model

Under local control siting schemes, state siting programs do not preempt local land use regulations. Thus, a local government can employ tough land use regulations to restrict siting of facilities within its jurisdiction. Colorado is one state with a siting scheme that follows the local control model.[6] * * *

4. Compensation and Incentives Mechanisms

In an effort to eliminate local opposition to hazardous waste facility sitings, some states have incorporated compensation mechanisms into

---

5. Minn.Stat.Ann. § 115A.21(1)(a) (West 1987 & Supp.1994).

6. Colo.Rev.Stat.Ann. §§ 25–15–200.1 to–220 (Bradford 1989 & Supp.1993). Florida also operates a siting program that follows the local control model. Local control, however, is not absolute in Florida because the governor and state cabinet can grant a variance from local ordinances or regulations thereby allowing a facility to be sited. Fla.Stat.Ann. § 403.723 (Harrison 1990 & Supp.1992).

siting laws. Under such schemes, a package of inducements would accompany a proposed facility. The rationale behind the compensation approach is that if incentives to accept the facility outweigh local costs, such as health and environmental risks, a community will be more likely to accept the siting of a facility in its neighborhoods. The provision of compensation and incentives may accompany any of the models previously discussed.

Compensation usually is determined in one of three ways. First, it can be a function of the facility's gross receipts or amount of wastes processed. Alternatively, compensation can be based on a standard tax or fee. Finally, a compensation package can contain a number of inducements agreed upon through negotiations between developers and host communities.

The state of Connecticut, for example, employs a compensation mechanism in which the amount of compensation is based either on a certain monetary value per standard unit of waste,[7] in accordance with predetermined values provided by the statute, or on negotiated incentives. These negotiated incentives may include payment to adjoining landowners for a drop in property values; the purchase of a "green belt buffer" around the proposed facility; provision of open space or recreational facilities for the municipality; purchase of public safety equipment; payment of road repair costs (produced by increased use of local roads); creation of access routes to the proposed facility; or direct financial payments. * * *

Public Participation and State Siting Schemes

In addition to supplementing siting models with compensation and incentive mechanisms, most state siting schemes include devices to promote public participation. Many state siting programs promote active public participation to better inform host community residents of hazardous waste facility proposals and to reduce local opposition and build consensus. These mechanisms are implemented primarily to engage local residents as opposed to the state-wide public. Public participation also is used to "legitimize" the site selection process in the eyes of the public.

One technique that states may use to enhance public participation is to appoint local residents to temporary positions on a state siting board. Such local membership advances the fairness of the siting process and mitigates local opposition by giving local communities a voice on the state siting board. Siting programs also engage the public by holding open administrative hearings. The siting authorities are then able to take into account the comments and objections raised at such meetings when making final decisions. In addition, local siting boards may be created to involve local participants within a more formal review structure. Moreover, local siting boards help reduce difficulties related to regulating from greater distances. Local interests can be heard and addressed with greater efficiency and with more reliability at a local board than if the board were based at a state capital perhaps many miles away and with fewer interests in common with the local community.

---

7. Conn.Gen.Stat.Ann. § 22a–128(b)(1) (West 1985).

Yet another way states promote public participation is by providing technical assistance grants. The purpose of these grants is to eliminate financial and technical barriers that would otherwise keep potential host communities from participating meaningfully in the siting process. These grants supply local site review boards and other public officials and interested parties with adequate resources to study siting proposals. With greater access to technical information and expertise, it is more likely that local communities will be able to make informed decisions about proposals to site a hazardous waste facility in their community.

NOTES

1.   Concerning the form of public participation in siting decisions, one author has suggested that the best procedure—and the one actually used in seeking volunteers for several solid waste facilities—is a referendum of the entire electorate after detailed studies but before the final decision. Michael Gerrard, *Turning NIMBY On Its Head: A Siting Solution Based On Federal Allocation, State Responsibility, and Local Control*, 25 ENV'T REP. 2257 (1995). The author discusses the appropriate geographic extent of the electorate, saying that the referendum should be required to succeed in both the county and the municipality in which the proposed site would be located. If the proposed site were near a border, people in the adjoining jurisdiction also should have a voice. One method to provide this might be to include in the electorate all voters outside the voting jurisdiction but within a certain radius of the facility. An alternative method would be to draw a radius around the facility and allow only people who live within that radius to vote in the referendum, regardless of their political jurisdiction. Gerrard's proposal would link the referendum to a system for compensation of volunteer communities. Do you agree that popular voting on hazardous waste facility siting is a good idea?

2.   Another author has proposed the use of "risk-based compensation committees." A national or state risk assessment process would be used to set (a) maximum allowable levels of risk within a local area, to prevent exploitation of any community, and (b) the minimum amount of compensation that a developer, owner, or operator must provide to the local community. Then a local risk-based siting committee would (1) determine whether to accept a site and (2) negotiate the amount and distribution of compensation. The relative representation that nearby residents, residents elsewhere in the city, and regional neighbors would have on the committee would depend on "the relative amount of risk to which individuals are potentially or actually exposed, as determined by the risk assessment process.... To protect the interests of racial minorities and those exposed to higher risks, special voting systems could be used, such as weighted cumulative voting or proportional voting." Bradford Mank, *Environmental Justice and Discriminatory Siting: Risk–Based Representation and Equitable Compensation*, 56 OHIO ST. L.J. 329, 401 (1995). Should communities be able to exchange risk for compensation?

B. LIABILITY FOR HAZARDOUS WASTE CLEANUP COSTS

1. COMPREHENSIVE ENVIRONMENTAL RESPONSE, COMPENSATION, AND LIABILITY ACT

a. Introduction

As noted earlier, RCRA is primarily a forward-looking statute. Most of its provisions are aimed at creating a regulatory program to control future waste treatment, storage, and disposal activities. However, the statute is also retrospective, imposing civil liability upon past contributors to treatment, storage or disposal facilities which present an "imminent and substantial endangerment" to health or the environment.

CERCLA, by contrast, is primarily backward-looking. Its main thrust is to create broad civil liability for cleanup of leaking waste disposal sites, most of which were contaminated prior to the enactment of RCRA. However, CERCLA also contains some forward-looking elements. Not only does the statute contain some provisions regulating current conduct (one provision, for example, requires that persons in charge of facilities notify EPA of hazardous substance releases) but more importantly, strict liability for cleanup of leaking sites was intended to encourage proper behavior in the future by persons involved in the generation, transportation or disposal of hazardous wastes. Nevertheless, CERCLA is not a prescriptive "command and control" statute like the Clean Air Act or the Clean Water Act. Rather, it is best viewed as a liability and financing regime.

As noted earlier, CERCLA was Congress's response to a number of high profile incidents—including the Love Canal debacle—that increased public awareness about the threat posed by improperly managed hazardous waste. Around the country, in defunct and abandoned plants, factories, mines and refineries, were pits, piles, drums and ditches full of dangerous, toxic substances poised to leach into water supplies, blow into the air and endanger public health and environment. One infamous example is the Stringfellow Acid Pits in Riverside, California, a granite quarry that has served as the county's dumpsite since the 1950s. Over the years, companies big and small dumped millions of gallons and hundreds of different chemicals into huge, uncovered lagoons that the county periodically flushed into the town's open sewers. A century of intensive lead and zinc mining in Northern Oklahoma, to choose another example, has left a landscape littered with mountains of poisonous mine tailings that blow lead, cadmium and other metals onto properties and into heating ducts in the surrounding homes. Add to these stories the innumerable examples of decades of unregulated toxic dumping into the nation's waterways, burial of waste in leaky drums, and midnight dumping on abandoned properties, and you have the ingredients of a public health—and political—disaster.

CERCLA was initially a popular and bipartisan law. It passed at the end of the Carter administration, in a lame duck session of Congress, without significant debate. Yet it quickly became very controversial, as the reality of the costs of cleaning up hazardous waste sites, and the extent of CERCLA's liability regime, came into focus. CERCLA imposes joint, strict, and retroactive liability on a statutorily defined group of persons for the costs of cleaning up hazardous waste that may be "released" into the environment. Unlike the traditional tort system, imposition of this liability does not require that causation be proved under either the "but-for" or "substantial factor" test, and the waste released, or at risk of release into the environment, need not be "fingerprinted" or linked directly back to a particular party for that party to be responsible for cleanup costs.

According to one view, CERCLA is a necessary response to the serious threat posed by abandoned hazardous waste dumps. It is a law that largely affects those companies and persons who most profited from unregulated disposal practices in the past. According to another view, CERCLA is a draconian and overly broad effort to recover costs from "deep pocket" defendants for hazardous waste handling practices that were in many cases legal at the time they were used, and often encouraged, directly or indirectly, by government. As you read the materials below, ask yourself whether as a policymaker you might reform the statute and if so, how.

The following excerpt provides an early overview of CERCLA's main purposes.

U.S. COUNCIL ON ENVIRONMENTAL QUALITY, ENVIRONMENTAL QUALITY 1981: 12TH ANNUAL REPORT
99–101 (1981).

In December of 1980, the Comprehensive Environmental Response, Compensation, and Liability Act of 1980 (CERCLA), was signed into law. The goals of the legislation are to eliminate the threats from uncontrolled hazardous waste sites and to remove hazardous substance threats to public health and the environment in a cost-effective manner.

The act has four basic elements. First, it establishes an information-gathering and analysis system which will enable federal and state governments to characterize chemical dump site problems more accurately and to develop priorities for their investigation and response. Owners of hazardous waste sites were required to notify EPA by June 9, 1981, of the nature of the wastes buried at their sites. This notification data will help form the basis for a national list of uncontrolled sites to be used in planning appropriate responses.

Second, the act establishes federal authority to respond to hazardous substance emergencies and to clean up leaking chemical dump sites. Federal response actions are limited to cases in which the responsible party either cannot be found or does not take the required actions. The legislation mandates the revision of the National Contingency Plan currently published under Section 311 of the Clean Water Act to serve as a framework for such response actions.

Third, the act creates a hazardous substance response trust fund to pay for the removal, remedy, and cleanup of released hazardous substances and hazardous waste sites. * * * Most of the total * * * will be raised by an industry-based tax on manufacturers of petrochemical feedstocks and toxic organic chemicals, and importers of crude oil. The remaining portion * * * will come from general revenues.

Fourth, the act makes those persons responsible for hazardous substance release liable for cleanup and restitution costs. Thus, it creates a strong incentive both for prevention of releases and voluntary cleanup of releases by responsible parties. Furthermore, it replenishes the fund to assure that adequate response capability is available to mitigate environmental emergencies in the future.

CERCLA identifies two categories of federal response to releases of hazardous substances: removal activities (emergency response) and remedial activities (long-term solution). For a site or spill releasing hazardous substances into the environment, a preliminary assessment is made to determine the source and nature of the problem, the existence of an identifiable responsible party, and the appropriate type of response.

During the 1981 fiscal year, EPA responded to 33 emergency removal situations * * *.

In the remedial action category, EPA has compiled a list of 115 top priority sites that are targeted for Superfund action, i.e., enforcement action and/or federally financed cleanup. These sites will also be candidates for inclusion on the list of * * * national priority "response targets" that the Superfund law requires EPA to identify. * * *

The guiding policy behind these efforts is derived from CERCLA itself; private party cleanup, either voluntary or through enforcement action, is the preferred approach, but federally financed cleanup will be implemented when states and the federal government determine it is appropriate. * * *

A cornerstone of the CERCLA implementation program is the negotiation of cooperative agreements with the states under which they will take the lead responsibility for cleaning up hazardous waste sites. * * *

Where a responsible party is involved in the release of a hazardous substance, EPA works closely and expeditiously with the states to effect an adequate cleanup by that party. Where the responsible party cannot initially be found or is unable to provide cleanup measures, the Fund can be used to clean up and later recover the costs from the responsible party. In other cases the states, or EPA in consultation with the Department of Justice, will negotiate agreements on the level of cleanup appropriate at a site.

b. Definitions

Which "hazardous substances" does CERCLA cover? Section 101(14), which defines the term, incorporates by reference the substances designated as hazardous under section 112 of the Clean Air Act, sections 311(b)(2)(A) and 307(a) of the Clean Water Act, section 3001 of RCRA, and section 7 of TSCA. The term does *not* include petroleum; thus CERCLA is not applicable to oil spills, though it may apply to spills of oil contaminated with other hazardous substances. United States v. Mexico Feed & Seed Co., 980 F.2d 478 (8th Cir. 1992). (Statutes that create liability for oil spills include the Outer Continental Shelf Lands Act amendments of 1978, 43 U.S.C. §§ 1841–1847, and the Oil Pollution Act of 1990, 33 U.S.C. §§ 2701–2761.)

What does "liability" mean under CERCLA? Section 101 (32) defines liability somewhat obscurely, by reference to the the Federal Water Pollution Control Act, which would become the Clean Water Act. Courts had interpreted liability under this provision to be "joint and several." Thus, although Congress did not specify that liability under CERCLA would be joint and several, it authorized courts to so find.

i. Basis and Scope of Liability

The heart of CERCLA is section 107, which establishes four categories of potentially liable parties and describes what they are liable for. Much of CERCLA litigation concerns the scope of this section.

§ 107 (a) * * * Notwithstanding any other provision or rule of law, and subject only to the defenses set forth in subsection (b) of this section—

(1) the owner and operator of a vessel or a facility,

(2) any person who at the time of disposal of any hazardous substance owned or operated any facility at which such hazardous substances were disposed of,

(3) any person who by contract, agreement, or otherwise arranged for disposal or treatment, or arranged with a transporter for transport for disposal or treatment, of hazardous substances owned or possessed by such person, by any other party or entity, at any facility or incineration vessel owned or operated by another party or entity and containing such hazardous substances, and

(4) any person who accepts or accepted any hazardous substances for transport to disposal or treatment facilities, incineration vessels or sites selected by such person, from which there is a release, or a threatened release which causes the incurrence of response costs, of a hazardous substance, shall be liable for—

(A) all costs of removal or remedial action incurred by the United States Government or a State or an Indian tribe not inconsistent with the national contingency plan;

(B) any other necessary costs of response incurred by any other person consistent with the national contingency plan;

(C) damages for injury to, destruction of, or loss of natural resources, including the reasonable costs of assessing such injury, destruction, or loss resulting from such a release; and

(D) the costs of any health assessment or health effects study carried out under section 104(i).

42 U.S.C. § 9607(a) (2000).

The following case explains CERCLA's strict liability scheme, and, among other things, establishes that non-negligent off-site generators of hazardous waste can be held liable for cleanup costs even when the waste found at the site is not theirs.

UNITED STATES v. MONSANTO CO.

United States Court of Appeals for the Fourth Circuit, 1988.
858 F.2d 160, *cert. denied*, 490 U.S. 1106, 109 S.Ct. 3156, 104 L.Ed.2d 1019 (1989).

SPROUSE, CIRCUIT JUDGE.

Oscar Seidenberg and Harvey Hutchinson (the site-owners) and Allied Corporation, Monsanto Company, and EM Industries, Inc. (the generator defendants), appeal from the district court's entry of summary judgment holding them liable to the United States and the State of South Carolina (the governments) under section 107(a) of [CERCLA]. The court determined that the defendants were liable jointly and severally for $1,813,624 in response costs accrued from the partial removal of hazardous waste from a disposal facility located near Columbia, South Carolina. * * * We affirm the district court's liability holdings * * *.

[The site-owners had leased rural land to COCC and SCRDI, which between 1976 and 1980 accepted for disposal there 7,000 drums of chemical waste generated by third parties. The governments entered into settlement agreements under which twelve of the generators (but not defendants who were also third party generators) paid 75% of the cost of a surface cleanup at the site. The governments paid the other 25% and brought this action for reimbursement.]

II

The site-owners and the generator defendants first contest the imposition of CERCLA liability *vel non,* and they challenge the propriety of summary judgment in light of the evidence presented to the trial court. The site-owners also reassert the "innocent landowner" defense that the district court rejected, and claim that the court erroneously precluded them from presenting evidence of a valid affirmative defense under section 107(b)(3). The generator defendants likewise repeat their arguments based on the governments' failure to establish a nexus between their specific waste and the harm at the site. They also claim that the trial court ignored material factual issues relevant to affirmative defenses to liability. * * *

[The Court reviewed section 107.] In our view, the plain language of section 107(a) clearly defines the scope of intended liability under the statute and the elements of proof necessary to establish it. We agree with the overwhelming body of precedent that has interpreted section 107(a) as establishing a strict liability scheme. Further, in light of the evidence presented here, we are persuaded that the district court correctly held that the governments satisfied all the elements of section 107(a) liability as to both the site-owners and the generator defendants.

A. *Site–Owners' Liability*

In light of the strict liability imposed by section 107(a), we cannot agree with the site-owners contention that they are not within the class of owners Congress intended to hold liable. The traditional elements of tort culpability on which the site-owners rely simply are absent from the statute. The plain language of section 107(a)(2) extends liability to owners of waste facilities regardless of their degree of participation in the subsequent disposal of hazardous waste.

Under section 107(a)(2), *any* person who owned a facility at a time when hazardous substances were deposited there may be held liable for all costs of removal or remedial action if a release or threatened release[8] of a hazardous substance occurs. The site-owners do not dispute their ownership of the Bluff Road facility, or the fact that releases occurred there during their period of ownership. Under these circumstances, all the prerequisites to section 107(a) liability have been satisfied.[9] *See* [State of New York v. Shore Realty Corp., 759 F.2d 1032 (2d Cir. 1985)] (site-owner held liable under CERCLA section 107(a)(1) even though he did not

---

8. The statute defines "release" to include "any spilling, leaking, pumping, pouring, emitting, emptying, discharging, injecting, escaping, leaching, dumping, or disposing into the environment (including the abandonment or discarding of barrels, containers, and other closed receptacles containing any hazardous substance or pollutant or contaminant)." 42 U.S.C. § 9601(22) (West Supp. 1987).

9. The site-owners' relative degree of fault would, of course, be relevant in any subsequent action for contribution brought pursuant to 42 U.S.C.A. § 9613(f) (West Supp. 1987). Congress, in the Superfund Amendments and Reauthorization Act of 1986, Pub.L. 99–499, § 113, 100 Stat. 1613, 1647 (1986) [hereafter SARA], established a right of contribution in favor of defendants sued under CERCLA section 107(a). Section 113(f)(1) provides:

Any person may seek contribution from any other person who is liable or potentially liable under section 9607(a) of this title, during or following any civil action under section 9606 of this title or under section 9607(a) of this title. Such claims shall be brought in accordance with this section and the Federal Rules of Civil Procedure, and shall be governed by Federal law. In resolving contribution claims, the court may allocate response costs among liable parties using such equitable factors as the court determines are appropriate. Nothing in this subsection shall diminish the right of any person to bring an action for contribution in the absence of a civil action under section 9606 or section 9607 of this title. 42 U.S.C.A. § 9613(f) (West Supp. 1987).

The legislative history of this amendment suggests that in arriving at an equitable allocation of costs, a court may consider, among other things, the degree of involvement by parties in the generation, transportation, treatment, storage, or disposal of hazardous substances. H.R. Rep. No. 253(III), 99th Cong., 1st Sess. 19 (1985), *reprinted in* 1986 U.S. Code Cong. & Admin. News 2835, 3038, 3042.

contribute to the presence or cause the release of hazardous substances at the facility).[10]

The site-owners nonetheless contend that the district court's grant of summary judgment improperly denied them the opportunity to present an affirmative defense under section 107(b)(3). Section 107(b)(3) sets forth a limited affirmative defense based on the complete absence of causation. *See Shore Realty,* 759 F.2d at 1044. It requires proof that the release or threatened release of hazardous substances and resulting damages were caused solely by "a third party other than ... one whose act or omission occurs in connection with a contractual relationship, existing directly or indirectly, with the defendant...." A second element of the defense requires proof that the defendant "took precautions against foreseeable acts or omissions of any such third party and the consequences that could foreseeably result from such acts or omissions." We agree with the district court that under no view of the evidence could the site-owners satisfy either of these proof requirements.

First, the site-owners could not establish the absence of a direct or indirect contractual relationship necessary to maintain the affirmative defense. They concede they entered into a lease agreement with COCC. They accepted rent from COCC, and after SCRDI was incorporated, they accepted rent from SCRDI. Second, the site-owners presented no evidence that they took precautionary action against the foreseeable conduct of COCC or SCRDI. They argued to the trial court that, although they were aware COCC was a chemical manufacturing company, they were completely ignorant of all waste disposal activities at Bluff Road before 1977. They maintained that they never inspected the site prior to that time. In our view, the statute does not sanction such willful or negligent blindness on the part of absentee owners. The district court committed no error in entering summary judgment against the site-owners.

B.   Generator Defendants' Liability

The generator defendants first contend that the district court misinterpreted section 107(a)(3) because it failed to read into the statute a requirement that the governments prove a nexus between the waste they sent to the site and the resulting environmental harm. They maintain that the statutory phrase "containing such hazardous substances" requires proof that the specific substances they generated and sent to the site were present at the facility at the time of release. The district court held, however, that the statute was satisfied by proof that hazardous substances "like" those contained in the generator defendants' waste were found at the site. We agree with the district court's interpretation.

---

10. Congress, in section 101(35) of SARA, acknowledged that landowners may affirmatively avoid liability if they can prove they did not know and had no reason to know that hazardous substances were disposed of on their land *at the time they acquired title or possession.* 42 U.S.C. § 9601(35) (West Supp. 1987). This explicitly drafted exception further signals Congress' intent to impose liability on landowners who cannot satisfy its express requirements.

Reduced of surplus language, sections 107(a)(3) and (4) impose liability on off-site waste generators who:

> "arranged for disposal ... of hazardous substances ... at any facility ... *containing such hazardous substances* ... from which there is a release ... of a hazardous substance."

In our view, the plain meaning of the adjective "such" in the phrase "containing such hazardous substances" is "[a]like, similar, of the like kind." BLACK'S LAW DICTIONARY 1284 (5th ed. 1979). As used in the statute, the phrase "such hazardous substances" denotes hazardous substances alike, similar, or of a like kind to those that were present in a generator defendant's waste or that could have been produced by the mixture of the defendant's waste with other waste present at the site. It does not mean that the plaintiff must trace the ownership of each generic chemical compound found at a site. Absent proof that a generator defendant's specific waste remained at a facility at the time of release, a showing of chemical similarity between hazardous substances is sufficient.[11]

The overall structure of CERCLA's liability provisions also militates against the generator defendants' "proof of ownership" argument. In *Shore Realty,* the Second Circuit held with respect to site-owners that requiring proof of ownership at any time later than the time of disposal would go far toward rendering the section 107(b) defenses superfluous. *Shore Realty,* 759 F.2d at 1044. We agree with the court's reading of the statute and conclude that its reasoning applies equally to the generator defendants' contentions. As the statute provides—"[n]otwithstanding any other provision or rule of law"—liability under section 107(a) is "subject *only* to the defenses set forth" in section 107(b). Each of the three defenses[12] established in section 107(b) "carves out from liability an exception based on causation." *Shore Realty,* 759 F.2d at 1044. Congress has, therefore, allocated the burden of disproving causation to the defendant who profited from the generation and inexpensive disposal of hazardous waste. We decline to interpret the statute in a way that would neutralize the force of Congress' intent.[13]

---

11. CERCLA plaintiffs need not perform exhaustive chemical analyses of hazardous substances found at a disposal site. *See* SCRDI, 653 F.Supp. at 993 n. 6. They must, however, present evidence that a generator defendant's waste was shipped to a site and that hazardous substances similar to those contained in the defendant's waste remained present at the time of release. The defendant, of course, may in turn present evidence of an affirmative defense to liability.

12. In addition to the limited third-party defense discussed above, sections 107(b)(1) and (2) respectively allow defendants to avoid liability by proving that the release and resulting damages were "caused solely" by an act of God or an act of war. 42 U.S.C. § 9607(b)(1), (2).

13. In fact, Congress specifically declined to include a similar nexus requirement in CERCLA. As the Second Circuit in *Shore Realty* observed, an early House version of what ultimately became section 107(a) limited liability to "any person who caused or contributed to the release or threatened release." 759 F.2d at 1044 (quoting H.R. Rep. 7020, 96th Cong., 2d Sess. § 307(a) (1980), *reprinted in* 2 A LEGISLATIVE HISTORY OF THE COMPREHENSIVE ENVIRONMENTAL RESPONSE, COMPENSATION AND LIABILITY ACT OF 1980 at 438. As ultimately enacted after House and Senate compromise, however, CERCLA "imposed liability on classes of persons without reference to whether they caused or contributed to the release or threat of release." *Shore Realty,* 759 F.2d at 1044. The legislature thus eliminated the element of causation from the plaintiff's liability case.

Finally, the purpose underlying CERCLA's liability provisions counsels against the generator defendants' argument. Throughout the statute's legislative history, there appears the recurring theme of facilitating prompt action to remedy the environmental blight of unscrupulous waste disposal.[14] In deleting causation language from section 107(a), we assume as have many other courts, that Congress knew of the synergistic and migratory capacities of leaking chemical waste, and the technological infeasibility of tracing improperly disposed waste to its source. In view of this, we will not frustrate the statute's salutary goals by engrafting a "proof of ownership" requirement, which in practice, would be as onerous as the language Congress saw fit to delete. * * *

III

The appellants next challenge the district court's imposition of joint and several liability for the governments' response costs.[15] The court concluded that joint and several liability was appropriate because the environmental harm at Bluff Road was "indivisible" and the appellants had "failed to meet their burden of proving otherwise." We agree with its conclusion.

While CERCLA does not mandate the imposition of joint and several liability, it permits it in cases of indivisible harm. *See Shore Realty,* 759 F.2d at 1042 n. 13; *United States v. Chem–Dyne,* 572 F.Supp. 802, 810–11 (S.D. Ohio 1983). In each case, the court must consider traditional and evolving principles of federal common law,[16] which Congress has left to the courts to supply interstitially.

Under common law rules, when two or more persons act independently to cause a single harm for which there is a reasonable basis of apportionment according to the contribution of each, each is held liable only for the portion of harm that he causes. *Edmonds v. Compagnie Generale Transatlantique,* 443 U.S. 256, 260 n.8, 99 S. Ct. 2753, 2756 n.8, 61 L. Ed. 2d 521 (1979). When such persons cause a single and indivisible harm, however, they are held liable jointly and severally for the entire harm. *Id.* (citing Restatement (Second) of Torts § 433A (1965)). We think

---

14. The legislative history underlying the Superfund Amendments and Reauthorization Act of 1986 echoed this theme with even greater force than that underlying CERCLA's original enactment in 1980.

15. The site-owners limit their joint and several liability argument to the contention that it is inequitable under the circumstances of this case, *i.e.,* their limited degree of participation in waste disposal activities at Bluff Road. As we have stated, however, such equitable factors are relevant in subsequent actions for contribution. They are not pertinent to the question of joint and several liability, which focuses principally on the divisibility among responsible parties of the harm to the environment.

16. As many courts have noted, a proposed requirement that joint and several liability be imposed in all CERCLA cases was deleted from the final version of the bill. *See, e.g.,* Chem–Dyne, 572 F.Supp. at 806. "The deletion," however, "was not intended as a rejection of joint and several liability," but rather "to have the scope of liability determined under common law principles." *Id.* at 808. We adopt the *Chem–Dyne* court's thorough discussion of CERCLA's legislative history with respect to joint and several liability. We note that the approach taken in *Chem–Dyne* was subsequently confirmed as correct by Congress in its consideration of SARA's contribution provisions. *See* H.R. Rep. No. 253(I), 99th Cong. 2d Sess., 79–80 (1985), *reprinted in* 1986 U.S. Code Cong. & Admin. News at 2835, 2861–62.

these principles, as reflected in the Restatement (Second) of Torts, represent the correct and uniform federal rules applicable to CERCLA cases.

Section 433A of the Restatement provides:

> (1) Damages for harm are to be apportioned among two or more causes where
>
>> (a) there are distinct harms, or
>>
>> (b) there is a reasonable basis for determining the contribution of each cause to a single harm.
>
> (2) Damages for any other harm cannot be apportioned among two or more causes.

RESTATEMENT (SECOND) OF TORTS § 433A (1965).

Placing their argument into the Restatement framework, the generator defendants concede that the environmental damage at Bluff Road constituted a "single harm," but contend that there was a reasonable basis for apportioning the harm. They observe that each of the off-site generators with whom SCRDI contracted sent a potentially identifiable volume of waste to the Bluff Road site, and they maintain that liability should have been apportioned according to the volume they deposited as compared to the total volume disposed of there by all parties. In light of the conditions at Bluff Road, we cannot accept this method as a basis for apportionment.

The generator defendants bore the burden of establishing a reasonable basis for apportioning liability among responsible parties. *Chem–Dyne,* 572 F. Supp. at 810; RESTATEMENT (SECOND) OF TORTS § 433B (1965).[17] To meet this burden, the generator defendants had to establish that the environmental harm at Bluff Road was divisible among responsible parties. They presented no evidence, however, showing a relationship between waste volume, the release of hazardous substances, and the harm at the site.[18] Further, in light of the commingling of hazardous substances, the district court could not have reasonably apportioned liability without some evidence disclosing the individual and interactive qualities of the substances deposited there. Common sense counsels that a million gallons of certain substances could be mixed together without significant conse-

---

17. Section 433(B)(2) of the Restatement provides:

Where the tortious conduct of two or more actors has combined to bring about harm to the plaintiff, and one or more of the actors seeks to limit his liability on the ground that the harm is capable of apportionment among them, the burden of proof as to the apportionment is upon each such actor.

RESTATEMENT (SECOND) OF TORTS § 433(B)(2) (1965).

18. At minimum, such evidence was crucial to demonstrate that a volumetric apportionment scheme was reasonable. The governments presented considerable evidence identifying numerous hazardous substances found at Bluff Road. An EPA investigator reported, for example, that in the first cleanup phase RAD Services encountered substances "in every hazard class, including explosives such as crystalized dynamite and nitroglycerine. Numerous examples were found of oxidizers, flammable and non-flammable liquids, poisons, corrosives, containerized gases, and even a small amount of radioactive material." Under these circumstances, volumetric apportionment based on the overall quantity of waste, as opposed to the quantity and quality of hazardous substances contained in the waste would have made little sense.

quences, whereas a few pints of others improperly mixed could result in disastrous consequences.[19] Under other circumstances proportionate volumes of hazardous substances may well be probative of contributory harm.[20] In this case, however, volume could not establish the effective contribution of each waste generator to the harm at the Bluff Road site.

Although we find no error in the trial court's imposition of joint and several liability, we share the appellants' concern that they not be ultimately responsible for reimbursing more than their just portion of the governments' response costs.[21] In its refusal to apportion liability, the district court likewise recognized the validity of their demand that they not be required to shoulder a disproportionate amount of the costs. It ruled, however, that making the governments whole for response costs was the primary consideration and that cost allocation was a matter "more appropriately considered in an action for contribution between responsible parties after plaintiff has been made whole." Had we sat in place of the district court, we would have ruled as it did on the apportionment issue, but may well have retained the action to dispose of the contribution questions. *See* [CERCLA § 113(f)]. That procedural course, however, was committed to the trial court's discretion and we find no abuse of it. As we have stated, the defendants still have the right to sue responsible parties for contribution, and in that action they may assert both legal and equitable theories of cost allocation.

IV

The generator defendants raise numerous constitutional challenges to the district court's interpretation and application of CERCLA. * * *

Many courts have concluded that Congress intended CERCLA's liability provisions to apply retroactively to pre-enactment disposal activities of off-site waste generators. They have held uniformly that retroactive operation survives the Supreme Court's tests for due process validity. We agree with their analyses. * * *

* * * While the generator defendants profited from inexpensive waste disposal methods that may have been technically "legal" prior to CERC-

---

19. We agree with the district court that evidence disclosing the relative toxicity, migratory potential, and synergistic capacity of the hazardous substances at the site would be relevant to establishing divisibility of harm.

20. Volumetric contributions provide a reasonable basis for apportioning liability only if it can be reasonably assumed, or it has been demonstrated, that independent factors had no substantial effect on the harm to the environment. *Cf.* RESTATEMENT (SECOND) OF TORTS § 433(A) comment d, illustrations 4, 5 (1965).

21. The final judgment holds the defendants liable for slightly less than half of the total costs incurred in the cleanup, while it appears that the generator defendants collectively produced approximately 22% of the waste that SCRDI handled. Other evidence indicates that agencies of the federal government produced more waste than did generator defendant Monsanto, and suggests that the amounts contributed by the settling parties do not bear a strictly proportionate relationship to the total costs of cleaning the facility. We note, however, that a substantial portion of the final judgment is attributable to litigation costs. We also observe that the EPA has contributed upwards of $50,000 to the Bluff Road cleanup, and that any further claims against the EPA and other responsible government instrumentalities may be resolved in a contribution action pursuant to CERCLA section 113(f).

LA's enactment, it was certainly foreseeable at the time that improper disposal could cause enormous damage to the environment. CERCLA operates remedially to spread the costs of responding to improper waste disposal among all parties that played a role in creating the hazardous conditions. * * *

In view of the above, the judgment of the district court as to the CERCLA liability of the site-owners and generator defendants is affirmed. * * *

WIDENER, CIRCUIT JUDGE, concurring and dissenting:

I concur in the majority opinion in all respects save its decision not to require the district court to treat the issue of allocation of costs of cleanup among the various defendants, and, as to that, I respectfully dissent. While it may be true that a subsequent suit for contribution may adequately apportion the damages among the defendants, I am of opinion that the district court, as a court of equity, is required to retain jurisdiction and answer that question now. * * *

I see great danger in postponing the ultimate apportioning of the damages to a later day. As an example, a small generator which deposited a few gallons of relatively innocuous waste liquid at a site is jointly and severally liable for the entire cost of cleanup under this decision. And with that I agree. If that generator were readily available and solvent, however, the government might well, and probably would, proceed against him first in collecting its judgment. The vagaries of and delays in his subsequent suit for contribution might result in needless financial disaster. I do not see this as a desired or even permissible result.

The statute involved, 42 U.S.C. 9613(f)(1), provides that "*[a]ny person* may seek contribution from any other person who is liable or potentially liable under section 9607(a) of this title during or following any civil action under section 9606 of this title or under section 9607(a) of this title." (Italics added.) Thus, the statute plainly provides that discretion with respect to contribution is not in the district court to consider relief or not as the majority opinion holds; rather, it is in the generator to seek relief, for "any person" certainly includes the generators of the waste. So, since the matter was brought before the district court, that court had no discretion but to decide the question. To repeat, the discretion is in the party to make the claim, not in the district court to defer decision. While I agree that the claims may be asserted in a separate action, if they are asserted in the main case they must be decided.

NOTES

1. Compare the approach to causation in *Monsanto* to what would be required in a common law negligence suit. What is the rationale for creating such a different scheme here? Does it matter that the plaintiff in a section 107 action is pursuing cost recovery for clean up and not personal injury damages? Note that CERCLA does not preclude such a common law action. *See, e.g.*,

Anderson v. Cryovac, Inc., 862 F.2d 910 (1st Cir. 1988), *remanded to* Anderson v. Beatrice Foods Co., 127 F.R.D. 1 (D. Mass. 1989).

2. Notice how the *Monsanto* court reads the word "such" to refer to "chemically similar" waste. The Court refers to dictionary definitions as well as legislative history. Is this convincing? Isn't the more plausible reading that "such" refers specifically to the waste the defendant generator actually sent to the site? What would be the effect of this alternate reading?

3. The U.S. Supreme Court recently tackled the question of how to determine apportionment in the case excerpted below.

BURLINGTON NORTHERN & SANTA FE RAILWAY CO. v. UNITED STATES

Supreme Court of the United States, 2009.
129 S.Ct. 1870.

[the facts of the case and the portion addressing Potentially Responsible Party liability are excerpted at page 916, *infra*.]

We must ... determine whether the Railroads were properly held jointly and severally liable for the full cost of the Governments' response efforts. Apportionment is proper when "there is a reasonable basis for determining the contribution of each cause to a single harm." Restatement (Second) of Torts§ 433A(1)(b), p. 434 (1963–1964).

Not all harms are capable of apportionment, however, and CERCLA defendants seeking to avoid joint and several liability bear the burden of proving that a reasonable basis for apportionment exists. When two or more causes produce a single, indivisible harm, "courts have refused to make an arbitrary apportionment for its own sake, and each of the causes is charged with responsibility for the entire harm."

The District Court calculated the Railroads' liability based on three figures. First, the court noted that the Railroad parcel constituted only 19% of the surface area of the Arvin site. Second, the court observed that the Railroads had leased their parcel to B & B for 13 years, which was only 45% of the time B & B operated the Arvin facility. Finally, the court found that the volume of hazardous substance-releasing activities on the B & B property was at least 10 times greater than the releases that occurred onthe Railroad parcel, and it concluded that only spills of two chemicals, Nemagon and dinoseb (not D–D), substantially contributed to the contamination that had originated on the Railroad parcel and that those two chemicals had contributed to two-thirds of the overall site contamination requiring remediation. The court then multiplied .19 by .45 by .66 (two-thirds) and rounded up to determine that the Railroads were responsible for approximately 6% of the remediation costs. "Allowing for calculation errors up to 50%," the court concluded that the Railroads could be held responsible for 9% of the total CERCLA response cost for the Arvin site.

We conclude that the facts contained in the record reasonably supported the apportionment of liability. The District Court's detailed findings make it abundantly clear that the primary pollution at the Arvin facility was contained in an unlined sump and an unlined pond in the southeastern portion of the facility most distant from the Railroads' parcel and that the spills of hazardous chemicals that occurred on the Railroad parcel contributed to no more than 10% of the total site contamination, some of which did not require remediation. With those background facts in mind, we are persuaded that it was reasonable for the court to use the size of the leased parcel and the duration of the lease as the starting point for its analysis.

The Court of Appeals criticized the District Court's assumption that spills of Nemagon and dinoseb were responsible for only two-thirds of the chemical spills requiring remediation, observing that each PRP's share of the total harm was not necessarily equal to the quantity of pollutants that were deposited on its portion of the total facility. Although the evidence adduced by the parties did not allow the court to calculate precisely the amount of hazardous chemicals contributed by the Railroad parcel to the total site contamination or the exact percentage of harm caused by each chemical, the evidence did show that fewer spills occurred on the Railroad parcel and that of those spills that occurred, not all were carried across the Railroad parcel to the B & B sump and pond from which most of the contamination originated. The fact that no D–D spills on the Railroad parcel required remediation lends strength to the District Court's conclusion that the Railroad parcel contributed only Nemagon and dinoseb in quantities requiring remediation.

The District Court's conclusion that those two chemicals accounted for only two-thirds of the contamination requiring remediation finds less support in the record; however, any miscalculation on that point is harmless in light of the District Court's ultimate allocation of liability, which included a 50% margin of error equal to the 3% reduction in liability the District Court provided based on its assessment of the effect of the Nemagon and dinoseb spills. Had the District Court limited its apportionment calculations to the amount of time the Railroad parcel was in use and the percentage of the facility located on that parcel, it would have assigned the Railroads 9% of the response cost. By including a two-thirds reduction in liability for the Nemagon and dinoseb with a 50% "margin of error," the District Court reached the same result. Because the District Court's ultimate allocation of liability is supported by the evidence and comports with the apportionment principles outlined above, we reverse the Court of Appeals' conclusion that the Railroads are subject to joint and several liability for all response costs arising out of the contamination of the Arvin facility.

1.   Should it matter to the Court's determination that Shell knew that chemicals were leaking upon transfer from Shell's tankers to B & B's storage tanks every time a delivery was made over a twenty year time-frame? See Justice Ginsberg's dissent, 129 S.Ct. at 1884.

ii. *Responsible Parties*

As noted in section 107(a), *supra*, there are three main categories of responsible parties under CERCLA: (1) owners and operators, (2) arrangers, and (3) transporters. Who is covered within each category?

(1) Owners and Operators

a. Officer and Shareholder Liability

Section 107(a)(1) and (2) of CERCLA imposes liability on the *current* "owner and operator" of a disposal or treatment facility from which there is a release or threatened release, and on "any person who *at the time of disposal* * * * owned or operated" the facility (emphasis added).

In *State of New York v. Shore Realty Corp.*, 759 F.2d 1032 (2d Cir. 1985), the state brought suit against Shore and its officer and shareholder, LeoGrande, who had incorporated Shore solely for the purpose of purchasing and developing the Shore Road property. At the time of acquisition, LeoGrande—who directed and controlled all corporate decisions and actions—knew that hazardous waste was stored there, though neither Shore nor LeoGrande had participated in its generation or transportation. The court held that Shore and LeoGrande were jointly and severally liable under CERCLA for the state's response costs.

> We hold LeoGrande liable as an "operator" under CERCLA, 42 U.S.C. § 9607, for the State's response costs. Under CERCLA "owner or operator" is defined to mean "any person owning or operating" an onshore facility, id. § 9601(20)(A), and "person" includes individuals as well as corporations, id. § 9601(21). More important, the definition of "owner or operator" excludes "a person, who, without participating in the management of a * * * facility, holds indicia of ownership primarily to protect his security interest in the facility." *Id.* § 9601(20)(A). The use of this exception implies that an owning stockholder who manages the corporation, such as LeoGrande, is liable under CERCLA as an "owner or operator." That conclusion is consistent with that of other courts that have addressed the issue. In any event, LeoGrande is in charge of the operation of the facility in question, and as such is an "operator" within the meaning of CERCLA.

On the other hand, a "consultant" who also was the corporate secretary and chairman of the board, and who owned 85 percent of the company's stock, was held not to be an owner or operator under section 107 in *Riverside Market Development Corp. v. International Building Products, Inc.*, 931 F.2d 327 (5th Cir. 1991). The court of appeals found that plaintiffs had failed to produce any evidence showing that the individual personally participated in any conduct that violated CERCLA. He lived in New York and visited the New Orleans plant only two to four times a year, and his participation in plant operations was limited to reviewing financial statements and attending meetings of the officers. *See generally* Kathryn R. Heidt, *Liability of Shareholders Under the Compre-*

hensive Environmental Response, Compensation and Liability Act (CERC-LA), 52 OHIO ST. L.J. 133 (1991); Michael P. Healy, *Direct Liability for Hazardous Substance Cleanups Under CERCLA: A Comprehensive Approach,* 42 CASE W. RES. L. REV. 65 (1992).

United States v. Gurley, 43 F.3d 1188 (8th Cir. 1994), imposed "operator" liability not only upon the principal shareholder and president of the corporate owner of a disposal site, but also upon his son who was an employee of the corporation. Citing trial court findings that the son "personally participated in the disposal of the hazardous substances" and that he "had extensive authority ... to implement the policies and practices of the corporate entity, which included the disposal of these hazardous substances," the court of appeals concluded that the evidence clearly established that the son "had *authority* to determine [the corporation's] hazardous waste disposal activities and that he actually *exercised* that authority" (emphasis added). (Query: Would the son also be liable as an "arranger"?)

Even an "environmental contractor employed to investigate and assist in constructing a facility for remedying contamination already in the soils" could be held liable as an "operator" if he had control over monitoring wells that served to disperse the contamination. Geraghty & Miller, Inc. v. Conoco, Inc., 234 F.3d 917 (5th Cir. 2000), *cert. denied,* 533 U.S. 950 (2001).

b.   Corporate and Parent Liability

Is a parent corporation necessarily the "owner or operator" of a hazardous waste facility owned by its wholly owned subsidiary? In *United States v. Bestfoods,* 524 U.S. 51 (1998), the Supreme Court said that the issue was "whether a parent corporation that actively participated in, and exercised control over, the operations of a subsidiary may, without more, be held liable as an operator of a polluting facility owned or operated by the subsidiary." The Court then said, "We answer no, unless the corporate veil may be pierced. But a corporate parent that actively participated in, and exercised control over, the operations of the *facility itself* may be held directly liable in its own right [under CERCLA] as an operator of the facility" (emphasis added.) Under general corporate law, the corporate veil may be pierced and the parent held liable for the subsidiary's conduct when, e.g., the corporate form would otherwise be misused to accomplish wrongful purposes, most notably fraud, on the parent's behalf; or when stock ownership has been resorted to for the purpose of controlling a subsidiary company so that it may be used as a mere agency or instrumentality of the parent company. But under section 107(a) of CERCLA, according to the Court, an "operator" is one who "directs the workings of, manages, or conducts the affairs of a facility." The operator—e.g., a parent corporation acting through an agent who is not an officer of the subsidiary—"must manage, direct, or conduct operations specifically related to pollution, that is, operations having to do with the leakage or disposal of hazardous waste, or decisions about compliance with environmental regulations." The critical question under section 107(a) is "whether, in degree and detail, actions directed to the facility by an agent of the parent alone are eccentric under accepted norms of parental oversight of a subsidiary's facility." Would a parent that satisfied this test also be liable as an "arranger"?

Carter–Jones Lumber Co. v. LTV Steel Co., 237 F.3d 745 (6th Cir. 2001), held that state, rather than federal, common law should apply in CERCLA "veil piercing" claims under *Bestfoods*. For further discussion of this issue, and of the definition of "operator" for purposes of assessing direct liability, *see* Lucia Silecchia, *Pinning the Blame & Piercing the Veil in the Mists of Metaphor: The Supreme Court's New Standards for the CERCLA Liability of Parent Companies and a Proposal for Legislative Reform*, 67 FORDHAM L. REV. 115 (1998).

c. Lessee Liability

Does owner liability extend to lessees? Under which circumstances? The Second Circuit confronted this issue in the case below.

COMMANDER OIL CORP. v. BARLO EQUIPMENT CORP.

United States Court of Appeals for the Second Circuit, 2000.
215 F.3d 321, *cert. denied*, 531 U.S. 979, 121 S.Ct. 427, 148 L.Ed.2d 436 (2000).

WALKER, CIRCUIT JUDGE.

BACKGROUND

In 1963, Commander Oil became the owner of two lots in Nassau County, lots 7A and 7B * * *. Lot 7A contained office and warehouse space; 7B, the parcel at issue in this case, housed twelve above-ground petroleum storage tanks * * *. In 1964, Commander Oil leased the office and warehouse space on lot 7A to Barlo, which was in the business of buying, manufacturing, and distributing petroleum-handling equipment. In 1969, Commander Oil leased lot 7B to Pasley Solvents & Chemicals, Inc. ("Pasley"), which used the site to repackage solvents purchased in bulk and to reclaim and revitalize used solvents. Under Pasley's lease, Commander Oil retained the use of three oil storage tanks on lot 7B.

The arrangement at the heart of the present dispute arose in 1972 when Commander Oil consolidated its leases. Under a single new lease, Commander Oil rented both lots 7A and 7B to Barlo, which in turn subleased 7B to Pasley. This arrangement simplified Commander Oil's bookkeeping and also delegated responsibility to Barlo for basic maintenance and payment of taxes on both lots. The nature of the sublease from Barlo to Pasley is fiercely contested. Barlo characterizes itself simply as a rent conduit and the lease and sublease of 7B as a bookkeeping measure implemented entirely at Commander Oil's behest. Barlo claims that the new arrangement did not change the actual relationship between the three parties and that Pasley continued to treat Commander Oil as its lessor. Commander Oil paints a substantially different picture, referring to instances of Barlo's alleged involvement with Pasley's activities on 7B, and to the fact that Barlo derived a profit, albeit a small one, from the sublease arrangement. We need not resolve this dispute, however, because it does not affect the legal result.

In 1981, an investigation by the Nassau County Department of Health ("DOH") led to the discovery of contamination on lot 7B. * * *

In 1988, the EPA sought reimbursement from Commander Oil and other defendants for response costs incurred by the federal government in remediating the site. On January 26, 1996, Commander Oil and other defendants entered into a consent decree in which "Commander agreed to design and implement response actions at the site and to reimburse the United States for past and future response costs incurred in connection with the Site." * * *

In 1990, Commander Oil filed this action, demanding contribution or indemnification for additional costs from Barlo and Pasley. Commander Oil's complaint seeks, *inter alia*, indemnification or contribution under CERCLA, [among other claims].

On June 12, 1997, * * * [t]he district court held that Barlo was an owner within the meaning of § 9607(a)(1) by virtue of its "authority and control" over lot 7B. In so holding, the district court implicitly rejected Barlo's argument that "owner" in § 9607(a)(1) means "record owner" and instead ruled that "a lessee who has control over and responsibility for the use of the property is the owner of the property" for CERCLA purposes. * * *

Barlo appeals from that judgment, arguing that its status as a lessee/sublessor did not make it an "owner" within the meaning of CERCLA and that the district court's apportionment of liability was clearly erroneous. * * *

DISCUSSION

We are called upon in this case to resolve yet another ambiguity within CERCLA's miasmatic provisions. * * *

* * * Whether, and under what circumstances, a lessee/sublessor may be held liable as an owner for CERCLA purposes is a question of first impression in this circuit and we review the district court's legal conclusions de novo.

I.

CERCLA's text offers no helpful guidance for interpreting the extent of owner liability. According to the statute: "The term 'owner or operator' means . . . any person owning or operating [a] facility." 42 U.S.C. § 9601(20)(A). We are thus required to give content to a statutory tautology, a position to which we have become increasingly accustomed in the environmental context. * * *

A

* * *

We therefore begin our analysis of the term "owner" in § 9607(a) by doing "the best we can to give the term its ordinary or natural meaning." *Bestfoods*, 524 U.S. at 66 (internal quotation marks omitted). * * * Barlo urges that CERCLA's owner liability is restricted to record owners. Commander Oil argues for a more expansive definition that relies primarily on the right to control property * * *. Neither position is obviously implausible. According to Webster's dictionary, an owner is "[O]ne that has the legal or rightful title whether the possessor or not." Webster's Third New International Dictionary of the English Language Unabridged 1612 (1981). Black's Law Dictionary, however, equivocates between titular and possessory owner, defining an owner variously as "[o]ne who has the right to possess, use, and convey something," and as "[o]ne who has the primary or residuary title to property." Black's Law Dictionary 1130 (7th ed. 1999). This definition's ambiguity comes as no surprise. Long-standing scholarship has informed us that ownership—and its attendant concept "property"—has limited inherent content. * * *

Most of the district courts that have considered this question have held that site control is a sufficient indicator of ownership to impose liability on lessees or sublessors. * * * The reasoning of these district courts is not without its appeal; if the lessee is the active user and polluter of the property, imposition of CERCLA liability seems particularly appropriate. But, while the imposition of liability in such a situation is surely correct, imposing owner liability instead of operator liability threatens to conflate two statutorily distinct categories of potentially responsible parties.

It is settled in this circuit that owner and operator liability should be treated separately. * * * Imposing owner liability on the basis of site control threatens to make owners of all operators and surplusage of most of operator liability. * * * Because we strive to avoid redundancy in our interpretation of statutes, * * * we believe that site control alone is an improper basis for the imposition of owner liability. Lessees may frequently be liable as operators but most lessees are not owners within the meaning of § 9607(a).

B

While the typical lessee should not be held liable as an owner, there may be circumstances when owner liability for a lessee would be appropriate. Some district courts, for example, have treated lessees as owners for CERCLA purposes when they sublet the premises to other entities. * * * These courts have reasoned that a sublessor, by virtue of its relationship to the sublessee, will often be in the best position—or at least in a better position than the record owner—to prevent pollution at a facility. However, this reasoning improperly emphasizes the relationship between the lessee/sublessor and the sublessee, instead of the relationship between the owner and the lessee/sublessor.

[W]e find no basis in CERCLA for supposing that the relationship between the sublessor and sublessee is the critical relationship for identifying owner liability * * *. In fact, there are good reasons why this relationship cannot be dispositive for purposes of establishing strict owner liability.

Strict liability is a narrowly tailored tool, capturing a specific kind of responsibility. [The court then discussed the reference in CERCLA's legislative history to *Rylands v. Fletcher*, the English case that enunciated the principle that, when a party derives benefit from a business or activity that is harmful to others, the party should bear responsibility for that harm.] CERCLA's strict owner liability, therefore, can be justified in part on the grounds that owners—even as lessors—derive benefit from the activities conducted on their property.

The same justification for strict liability does not necessarily or automatically apply to lessees/sublessors, as the facts of the present case make clear. The arrangement that led to Pasley's contamination of the site was between Commander Oil and Pasley, not between Pasley and Barlo. The terms of the original lease between Pasley and Commander Oil were set before Barlo was interposed as a sublessor. Commander was a sophisticated lessor and fully capable of including in the price of the lease the risk of Pasley contaminating the site. As we explain in part II of this opinion, *infra*, owner liability might attach to a sophisticated lessee/sublessor who exploits unanticipated risks on the property of an unsophisticated owner. But here, and in the normal course of events, such liability will not attach to lessees/sublessors.

There is an additional policy reason supporting our conclusion that owner liability should not automatically apply to lessees/sublessors. * * * CERCLA has raised the costs of owning polluted land, and owners and potential owners are on notice of their liability and are wise to ensure that a potential acquisition is not encumbered by massive environmental liability. So far as we are able to discern, the same is not true of lessees/sublessors. * * * We are reluctant to surprise Barlo with new and unexpected liability, and to undermine the security of lessees/sublessors throughout the circuit who have entered into subleases before this decision.

II

We do not foreclose the possibility that in some circumstances lessees/sublessors may be liable as owners under CERCLA. * * * While we need not define with specificity those factors that might transform a lessee into an owner, we note several that we think could be important, specifically: (1) whether the lease is for an extensive term and admits of no rights in the owner/lessor to determine how the property is used; (2) whether the lease cannot be terminated by the owner before it expires by its terms; (3) whether the lessee has the right to sublet all or some of the property without notifying the owner; (4) whether the lessee is responsible for payment of all taxes, assessments, insurance, and operation and maintenance costs; and (5) whether the lessee is responsible for making all structural and other repairs. This non-exclusive list is meant to reinforce the point that the critical question is whether the lessee's status is that of a de facto owner and not whether it exercises control over the facility. * * * Moreover, the critical relationship is that between the lessee/sublessor and the owner/lessor, not that between the lessee/sublessor and the sublessee. * * *

Applying these principles to the case at hand, we conclude that the district court erred in holding Barlo strictly liable as an owner pursuant to 42 U.S.C. § 9607(a)(1). Whether or not Barlo was simply a rent conduit between Commander Oil and Pasley—as Barlo claims—it did not possess sufficient attributes of ownership over lot 7B. By the terms of the lease between Barlo and Commander Oil, Barlo was, *inter alia*, (1) limited to using lot 7A, and only "for that business presently conducted by tenant on a portion of the same premises leased hereunder"; (2) required to obtain written consent from Commander Oil before making "any additions, alterations or improvements" on the land * * *; (3) required to obtain written approval from Commander Oil to sublet the property, and prohibited from subletting to any entity that had "any connection with the fuel, fuel oil or oil business"; (4) required to obtain written permission from Commander Oil to display any "sign, advertisement, notice or other lettering" on the building; (5) required to keep the property "clean and in order to the satisfaction of" Commander Oil, and responsible for any damage Barlo itself caused to the premises * * *; and (6) prohibited from doing anything that would "in any way increase the rate of fire insurance" on the property, and from bringing or keeping upon the premises "any inflammable, combustible or explosive fluid, chemical or substance." In addition, the lease was limited to a five-year term with one option for renewal. * * *

To be sure, Barlo possessed some attributes of ownership with respect to lot 7B. For instance, Barlo was obligated to secure insurance for the property, was liable to Commander Oil for all assessments on the property and any increases (but only increases) in taxes, and assumed responsibility for all nonstructural repairs * * *. Notwithstanding these attributes, however, Barlo lacked most of the bundle of rights that comes with ownership of property. Accordingly, it may not be held liable under CERCLA as an owner, and the judgment of the district court is reversed to the extent that it imposed liability against Barlo for the contamination on lot 7B.

NOTES

1. Would an indemnification agreement between the lessor and lessee help in such cases? *See* Colleen E. Healy and Mark S. Hacker, Comment, *The Importance of Identifying and Allocating Environmental Liabilities in the Sale or Purchase of Assets,* 10 Vill. Envtl. L.J. 91, 112 (1999). Note that such agreements allocate liability among potentially responsible parties but do not bar government cost recovery actions.

2. The Court here seems to be concerned about the unfairness of finding Barlo liable in a strict liability regime. The court uses dictionary definitions of "owner" and appeals to policy considerations in its decision. But doesn't such an approach deviate from Congress' intent? Aren't there policy arguments on the other side as well? CERCLA liability is meant to be far-reaching in order to allow for site cleanup and cost recovery.

Because section 107(a) extends liability for cleanup costs to all "owners" of contaminated properties, regardless of the circumstances of their ownership, parties who *involuntarily or innocently* acquired former disposal sites have been required to pay for cleanup, even when the cost exceeded the value of the land. Prompted by the perceived unfairness of such results, Congress in 1986 added a new defense to protect "innocent landowners." *See* Superfund Amendments and Reauthorization Act of 1986 (SARA), Pub. L. 99–499, 99th Cong., 2d Sess. (1986). (The defense will be discussed in greater detail in the defenses section, *infra.*) This new provision, and the adoption of a new contribution provision enabling PRPs to sue each other for contribution, and immunizing settling parties from contribution actions, were intended to soften the perceived unfairness in CERCLA's strict joint and several regime.

The Small Business Liability Relief and Brownfields Revitalization Act of 2002, Pub. L. No. 107–118, 115 Stat. 2356 altered the liability under section 107(a) not only of certain owners and operators but also of certain arrangers and transporters, as discussed in section (*ii*), *infra.* (The Act also added new provisions for settlements under section 122(g), discussed in the settlements section, *infra*, and new brownfields provisions, discussed in the brownfields section, *infra.*) The Act created two additional exclusions for owner/operator liability. New section 107(q) provides protection for the owner of property "contiguous" to land from which there is a hazardous substance release, and new section 107(r) exempts "bona fide prospective purchasers" (BFPPs) so long as they do not impede response actions or natural resource restoration.

Under section 107(q), an owner of land contaminated by a "contiguous property" is not considered to be an owner or operator under section 107(a) if that person (1) did not cause or contribute to the release of hazardous substances; (2) is not potentially liable or affiliated with any other person potentially liable for the release; (3) takes reasonable steps to stop or prevent any continuing or future release and to prevent or limit exposure to hazardous substances released on his own property; (4) provides full cooperation and access to persons authorized to undertake response action and natural resource restoration; (5) complies with all land use restrictions related to the response action; (6) does not impede any institutional controls related to the response action; (7) complies with all lawful information requests; (8) provides all legally required notices concerning discovery of the release; and (9) conducted "all appropriate inquiry" within the meaning of section 101(35) concerning "innocent landowners." If a person does not qualify for liability relief as a contiguous landowner because he knew of the contamination at the time of purchase, and therefore cannot satisfy item (9), he nevertheless may qualify for liability relief as a "bona fide prospective purchaser" under section 107(r).

Section 107(r) exempts "bona fide prospective purchasers" from owner or operator liability under section 107(a) so long as they do not impede a response action or natural resource restoration. The purpose of section 107(r) is to facilitate the acquisition, cleanup, and redevelopment of brownfields. Section 101(40) defines "bona fide prospective purchaser" as one who establishes that (1) all disposal on her land occurred before she purchased it; (2) she made "all appropriate inquiry" within the meaning of section 101(35); (3) she exercises appropriate care to stop or prevent any continuing or future release and prevent or limit exposure; (4) she provides full cooperation and access to persons authorized to undertake response actions or natural resource restoration; (5) she complies with land use restrictions, and does not impede institutional controls, related to the response action; and (6) she is not potentially liable or affiliated with any other person that is potentially liable for response costs through any familial, contractual, corporate, or financial relationship (other than the relationship created by the instruments by which title to the facility is conveyed or financed). The BFPP exemption is qualified by section 107(r)(2), which gives the United States a "windfall lien" on the property if EPA has incurred unrecovered response costs there and the response action increases the fair market value of the property.

d.   Passive Intervening Landowners

What about landowners who know the contaminated condition of a site when they acquire ownership, who may or may not claim to be BFPPs, who do nothing affirmative to aggravate the situation, and who then transfer it to another person after disclosing the condition? Are such "passive intervening landowners" liable under § 107(a)(2) if the contamination spreads within or beyond the site? The answer can depend on the definition of "disposal" in § 107(a)(2) and in § 101(40)(A) related to BFPPs. Section 101(29) states that "disposal" shall have the meaning provided in § 1004(3) of the Solid Waste Disposal Act, which defines it to include "discharge, deposit, injection, dumping, *spilling*, *leaking*, or placing of ... hazardous waste into or on any land or water ..." (emphasis added). *United States v. Waste Industries, Inc.*, 734 F.2d 159, 164–65 (4th Cir. 1984) discusses that definition:

> The inclusion of "leaking" as one of the diverse definitional components of "disposal" demonstrates that Congress intended "disposal" to have a range of meanings, including conduct, a physical state, and an occurrence. Discharging, dumping, and injection (conduct), hazardous waste reposing (a physical state) and movement of the waste after it has been placed in a state of repose (an occurrence) are all

encompassed in the broad definition of disposal. "Leaking" ordinarily occurs when landfills are not constructed soundly or when drums and tank trucks filled with waste materials corrode, rust, or rot. Thus "leaking" is an occurrence included in the meaning of "disposal."

The district court's statutory analysis relied heavily upon the present-tense definition of "disposal" as indicative of an intent to restrain only ongoing human conduct. The Act, however, permits a court to order a responsible party to "stop" activities "*or to take such other action as may be necessary*" (emphasis added) to abate the endangerment. Such grammatical niceties as tense may be useful in arriving at a narrowly-sculpted meaning, but they are of little help in interpreting remedial statutes in which actions such as "may be necessary" are contemplated in order to abate gross dangers to a community. Since the term "disposal" is used throughout the Act, its definition in section 6903(3) must necessarily be broad and general to encompass both routine regulatory and the less common emergency situations. Thus it includes such diverse characteristics as "deposit, injection, dumping, spilling, leaking, or placing" wastes. We must assume that Congress included "leaking" as a definitional component of "disposal" for a purpose. We conclude that Congress made "leaking" a part of the definition of "disposal" to meet the need to respond to the possibility of endangerment, among other reasons.

Courts have differed somewhat on the question of CERCLA liability of passive intervening landowners. In *Nurad, Inc. v. William E. Hooper & Sons Co.*, 966 F.2d 837 (4th Cir. 1992), the current owner of contaminated property brought an action against previous owners and previous tenants, seeking reimbursement of costs incurred in removing from the property underground storage tanks and their hazardous contents. The court held that § 107(a)(2) imposes liability not only for active involvement in the "dumping" or "placing" of hazardous wastes at the facility, but for ownership of the facility at a time that hazardous waste was "spilling" or "leaking." The previous owners were held liable to the plaintiff, but the claims against the tenants were dismissed on the ground that they lacked authority to control the storage tanks and therefore did not "operate" a facility under § 107(a). However, in *United States v. CDMG Realty Co.*, 96 F.3d 706 (3d Cir. 1996), the court rejected the view taken in *Waste Industries* and *Nurad* and held that, "while 'leaking' and 'spilling' may not require affirmative human conduct, neither word denotes the gradual spreading of contamination." The court said that it is especially unjustified to stretch the meaning of "leaking" and "spilling" to encompass the passive migration that generally occurs in landfills in view of the fact that another word used in CERCLA, "release," shows that Congress "knew precisely how to refer to this spreading of waste." (A prior owner who owned a waste site at the time of "disposal" is liable under § 107(a) only in the event of a "release" or "threatened release." Section 101(22) defines "release" as "any spilling, leaking, ... escaping, leaching....") The court said that "[l]eaching of contaminants from rain and groundwater movement is a principal cause of contaminant movement in landfills," and that "leaching" is the word commonly used in the environmental context to describe the passive migration of contaminants. The court also said that because CERCLA conditions the innocent landowner defense on the defendant's having purchased the property "after the disposal" of hazardous waste there, "disposal" cannot consist of the constant spreading of contaminants. "Otherwise, the defense would almost never apply, as there would generally be no point 'after disposal'." *See* Michael Caplan, *Escaping CERCLA Liability: The Interim Owner Passive Migration Defense Gains Circuit Recognition*, 28 ENVTL. L. REP. 10121 (1998). The most recent appellate decision, *Carson Harbor Village, Ltd. v. Unocal Corp.*, 270 F.3d 863 (9th Cir. 2001) (en banc), held that "disposal" does "not include passive soil migration but ... may include other passive migration [including leaking of contaminants out of underground barrels or storage tanks] that fits within the plain meaning of the terms used to define 'disposal'." For summaries of other authorities see the *Carson* opinion and James Periconi & Robert Roesener, *"Passive" Disposal Through Migration: Theory Still Alive and Kicking*, 32 ENV'T REP. 461 (2001).

(2) Arrangers

Arranger liability (also known as generator liability, since the arrangers are typically those who generated the hazardous waste) arises under CERCLA § 107(a)(3), which imposes strict liability upon "any person" who "arranged for" disposal or treatment, or transport for disposal or treatment, of hazardous substances "owned or possessed" by such person. CERCLA defines person in section 101(21) as "an individual, firm, corporation, association, partnership, consortium, joint venture, commercial entity, United States Government, State, municipality, commission, political subdivision of a State, or any interstate body." The case below explains the breadth of the arranger category, and explores its application in conjunction with owner and operator liability.

UNITED STATES v. NORTHEASTERN PHARMACEUTICAL & CHEMICAL CO., INC. [NEPACCO]

United States Court of Appeals for the Eighth Circuit, 1986.
810 F.2d 726, *cert. denied*, 484 U.S. 848, 108 S.Ct. 146, 98 L.Ed.2d 102 (1987).

[The portions of the court's opinion discussing the facts and the applicability of RCRA appear at page 878, *supra*.]

A.   Liability Under CERCLA § 107(a)(1)

First, appellants argue the district court erred in finding them liable under CERCLA § 107(a)(1) as the "owners and operators" of a "facility" where hazardous substances are located. Appellants argue that, regardless of their relationship to the NEPACCO plant, they neither owned nor operated the Denney farm site, and that it is the Denney farm site, not the NEPACCO plant, that is a "facility" for purposes of "owner and operator" liability under CERCLA § 107(a)(1). We agree.

CERCLA defines the term "facility" in part as "any site or area where a hazardous substance has been deposited, stored, disposed of, or placed, or otherwise come to be located." CERCLA § 101(9)(B); *see New York v. Shore Realty Corp.,* 759 F.2d 1032, 1043 n. 15 (2d Cir. 1985). The term "facility" should be construed very broadly to include "virtually any place at which hazardous wastes have been dumped, or otherwise disposed of." *United States v. Ward,* 618 F.Supp. at 895 (definition of "facility" includes roadsides where hazardous waste was dumped) * * *. In the present case, however, the place where the hazardous substances were disposed of and where the government has concentrated its clean-up efforts is the Denney farm site, not the NEPACCO plant. The Denney farm site is the "facility." Because NEPACCO, Lee and Michaels did not own or operate the Denney farm site, they cannot be held liable as the "owners or operators" of a "facility" where hazardous substances are located under CERCLA § 107(a)(1).

B.   Individual Liability under CERCLA § 107(a)(3)

CERCLA § 107(a)(3) imposes strict liability upon "any person" who arranged for the disposal or transportation for disposal of hazardous substances. As defined by statute, the term "person" includes both individuals and corporations and does not exclude corporate officers or employees. *See* CERCLA § 101(21). Congress could have limited the statutory definition of "person" but chose not to do so. Moreover, construction of CERCLA to impose liability upon only the corporation and not the individual corporate officers and employees who are responsible for making corporate decisions about the handling and disposal of hazardous substances would open an enormous, and clearly unintended, loophole in the statutory scheme.

First, Lee argues he cannot be held individually liable for having arranged for the transportation and disposal of hazardous substances under CERCLA § 107(a)(3) because he did not personally own or possess the hazardous substances. Lee argues NEPACCO owned or possessed the hazardous substances.

The government argues Lee "possessed" the hazardous substances within the meaning of CERCLA § 107(a)(3) because, as NEPACCO's plant supervisor, Lee had actual "control" over the NEPACCO plant's hazardous substances. We agree. It is the authority to control the handling and disposal of hazardous substances that is critical under the statutory scheme. The district court found that Lee, as plant supervisor, actually knew about, had immediate supervision over, and was directly responsible for arranging for the transportation and disposal of the NEPACCO plant's hazardous substances at the Denney farm site. * * *

The government argues Lee can be held individually liable, without "piercing the corporate veil," because Lee personally arranged for the disposal of hazardous substances in violation of CERCLA § 107(a)(3). We agree. As discussed below, Lee can be held individually liable because he personally participated in conduct that violated CERCLA; this personal liability is distinct from the derivative liability that results from "piercing the corporate veil." * * *

We now turn to Lee's basic argument. Lee argues that he cannot be held individually liable for NEPACCO's wrongful conduct because he acted solely as a corporate officer or employee on behalf of NEPACCO. The liability imposed upon Lee, however, was not derivative but personal. Liability was not premised solely upon Lee's status as a corporate officer or employee. Rather, Lee is individually liable under CERCLA § 107(a)(3) because he personally arranged for the transportation and disposal of hazardous substances on behalf of NEPACCO and thus actually participated in NEPACCO's CERCLA violations. * * *

The question of what constitutes arranger liability when one company supplies chemicals not for disposal but that it knows or reasonably should know will be disposed of improperly has proven vexing to courts. The U.S. Supreme Court weighed in on the question in the case excerpted below:

BURLINGTON NORTHERN & SANTA FE RAILWAY CO. v. UNITED STATES

Supreme Court of the United States, 2009.
129 S.Ct. 1870.

JUSTICE STEVENS delivered the opinion of the Court.

In 1980, Congress enacted the Comprehensive Environmental Response, Compensation, and Liability Act (CERCLA), in response to the serious environmental and health risks posed by industrial pollution. The Act was designed to promote the " 'timely cleanup of hazardous waste sites' " and to ensure that the costs of such cleanup efforts were borne by those responsible for the contamination. These cases raise the questions whether and to what extent a party associated with a contaminated site may be held responsible for the full costs of remediation.

I

In 1960, Brown & Bryant, Inc. (B & B), began operating an agricultural chemical distribution business, purchasing pesticides and other chemical products from suppliers such as Shell Oil Company (Shell). Using its own equipment, B & B applied its products to customers' farms. B & B opened its business on a 3.8 acre parcel of former farmland in Arvin, California, and in 1975, expanded operations onto an adjacent .9 acre parcel of land owned jointly by what is now known as the Burlington Northern and Santa Fe Railway Company and Union Pacific Railroad Company (Railroads). Both parcels of the Arvin facility were graded toward a sump and drainage pond located on the southeast corner of the primary parcel. Neither the sump nor the drainage pond was lined until 1979, allowing waste water and chemical runoff from the facility to seep into the ground water below.

During its years of operation, B & B stored and distributed various hazardous chemicals on its property. Among these were the herbicide dinoseb, sold by Dow Chemicals, and the pesticides D–D and Nemagon, both sold by Shell. Dinoseb was stored in 55–gallon drums and 5–gallon containers on a concrete slab outside B & B's warehouse. Nemagon was stored in 30–gallon drums and 5–gallon containers inside the warehouse. Originally, B & B purchased D–D in 55–gallon drums; beginning in the mid1960's, however, Shell began requiring its distributors to maintain bulk storage facilities for D–D. From that time onward, B & B purchased D–D in bulk.[22]

When B & B purchased D–D, Shell would arrange for delivery by common carrier, f.o.b. destination.[23] When the product arrived, it was *Carrier* transferred from tanker trucks to a bulk storage tank located on B & B's primary parcel. From there, the chemical was transferred to bobtail trucks, nurse tanks, and pull rigs. During each of these transfers leaks and spills could—and often did—occur. Although the common carrier and B & B used buckets to catch spills from hoses and gaskets connecting the tanker trucks to its bulk storage tank, the buckets sometimes overflowed or were knocked over, causing D–D to spill onto the ground during the transfer process.

Aware that spills of D–D were commonplace among its distributors, in the late 1970's Shell took several steps to encourage the safe handling of its products. Shell provided distributors with detailed safety manuals and instituted a voluntary discount program for distributors that made improvements in their bulk handling and safety facilities. Later, Shell revised its program to require distributors to obtain an inspection by a qualified engineer and provide self-certification of compliance with applicable laws and regulations. B & B's Arvin facility was inspected twice, and in 1981, B & B certified to Shell that it had made a number of recommended improvements to its facilities.

Despite these improvements, B & B remained a " '[s]loppy' [o]operator." Over the course of B & B's 28 years of operation, delivery spills, equipment failures, and the rinsing of tanks and trucks allowed Nemagon, D–D and dinoseb to seep into the soil and upper levels of ground water of the Arvin facility. In 1983, the California Department of Toxic Substances Control (DTSC) began investigating B & B's violation of hazardous waste laws, and the United States Environmental Protection Agency (EPA) soon followed suit, discovering significant contamination of soil and ground water. Of particular concern was a plume of contaminated ground water located under the facility that threatened to leach into an adjacent supply of potential drinking water.

Although B & B undertook some efforts at remediation, by 1989 it had become insolvent and ceased all operations. That same year, the Arvin facility was added to the National Priority List, see 54 Fed. Reg. 41027,

---

22. Because D–D is corrosive, bulk storage of the chemical led to numerous tank failures and spills as the chemical rusted tanks and eroded valves.

23. F.o.b. destination means "the seller must at his own expense and risk transport the goods to [the destination] and there tender delivery of them . . .

and subsequently, DTSC and EPA (Governments) exercised their authority under 42 U. S. C. § 9604 to undertake cleanup efforts at the site. By 1998, the Governments had spent more than $8 million responding to the site contamination; their costs have continued to accrue.

In 1991, EPA issued an administrative order to the Railroads directing them, as owners of a portion of the property on which the Arvin facility was located, to perform certain remedial tasks in connection with the site. The Railroads did so, incurring expenses of more than $3 million in the process. Seeking to recover at least a portion of their response costs, in 1992 the Railroads brought suit against B & B.

II

CERCLA liability

CERCLA imposes strict liability for environmental contamination upon [Potentially Responsible Parties (PRP) as defined in] 42 U. S. C. § 9607(a).

Once an entity is identified as a PRP, it may be compelled to clean up a contaminated area or reimburse the Government for its past and future response costs.

RRs qualify

In these cases, it is undisputed that the Railroads qualify as PRPs under both §§ 9607(a)(1) and 9607(a)(2) because they owned the land leased by B & B at the time of the contamination and continue to own it now. The more difficult question is whether Shell also qualifies as a PRP under § 9607(a)(3) by virtue of the circumstances surrounding its sales to B & B.

harder Q: is Shell an arranger

To determine whether Shell may be held liable as an arranger, we begin with the language of the statute. As relevant here, § 9607(a)(3) applies to an entity that "arrange[s] for disposal ... of hazardous substances." It is plain from the language of the statute that CERCLA liability would attach under § 9607(a)(3) if an entity were to enter into a transaction for the sole purpose of discarding a used and no longer useful hazardous substance. It is similarly clear that an entity could not be held liable as an arranger merely for selling a new and useful product if the purchaser of that product later, and unbeknownst to the seller, disposed of the product in a way that led to contamination. Less clear is the liability attaching to the many permutations of "arrangements" that fall between these two extremes—cases in which the seller has some knowledge of the buyers' planned disposal or whose motives for the "sale" of a hazardous substance are less than clear. In such cases, courts have concluded that the determination whether an entity is an arranger requires a fact-intensive inquiry that looks beyond the parties' characterization of the transaction as a "disposal" or a "sale" and seeks to discern whether the arrangement was one Congress intended to fall within the scope of CERCLA's strict-liability provisions.

Although we agree that the question whether § 9607(a)(3) liability attaches is fact intensive and case specific, such liability may not extend beyond the limits of the statute itself. Because CERCLA does not specifically define what it means to "arrang[e] for" disposal of a hazardous substance, we give the phrase its ordinary meaning. In common parlance, the word "arrange" implies action directed to a specific purpose. See Merriam–Webster's Collegiate Dictionary 64 (10th ed. 1993) (defining "arrange" as "to make preparations for: plan[;] ... to bring about an agreement or understanding concerning"). Consequently, under the plain language of the statute, an entity may qualify as an arranger under § 9607(a)(3) when it takes intentional steps to dispose of a hazardous substance.

The Governments do not deny that the statute requires an entity to "arrang[e] for" disposal; however, they interpret that phrase by reference to the statutory term "disposal," which the Act broadly defines as "the discharge, deposit, injection, dumping, spilling, leaking, or placing of any solid waste or hazardous waste into or on any land or water." The Governments assert that by including unintentional acts such as "spilling" and "leaking" in the definition of disposal, Congress intended to impose liability on entities not only when they directly dispose of waste products but also when they engage in legitimate sales of hazardous substances knowing that some disposal may occur as a collateral consequence of the sale itself. Applying that reading of the statute, the Governments contend that Shell arranged for the disposal of D–D within the meaning of § 9607(a)(3) by shipping D–D to B & B under conditions it knew would result in the spilling of a portion of the hazardous substance by the purchaser or common carrier. Because these spills resulted in wasted D–D, a result Shell anticipated, the Governments insist that Shell was properly found to have arranged for the disposal of D–D.

While it is true that in some instances an entity's knowledge that its product will be leaked, spilled, dumped, or otherwise discarded may provide evidence of the entity's intent to dispose of its hazardous wastes, knowledge alone is insufficient to prove that an entity "planned for" the disposal, particularly when the disposal occurs as a peripheral result of the legitimate sale of an unused, useful product. In order to qualify as an arranger, Shell must have entered into the sale of D–D with the intention that at least a portion of the product be disposed of during the transfer process by one or more of the methods described in § 6903(3). Here, the facts found by the District Court do not support such a conclusion.

Although the evidence adduced at trial showed that Shell was aware that minor, accidental spills occurred during the transfer of D–D from the common carrier to B & B's bulk storage tanks after the product had arrived at the Arvin facility and had come under B & B's stewardship, the evidence does not support an inference that Shell intended such spills to occur. To the contrary, the evidence revealed that Shell took numerous steps to encourage its distributors to reduce the likelihood of such spills, providing them with detailed safety manuals, requiring them to maintain adequate storage facilities, and providing discounts for those that took safety precautions. Although Shell's efforts were less than wholly successful, given these facts, Shell's mere knowledge that spills and leaks continued to occur is insufficient grounds for concluding that Shell "arranged for" the disposal of D–D within the meaning of § 9607(a)(3). Accordingly, we conclude that Shell was not liable as an arranger for the contamination that occurred at B & B's Arvin facility.

JUSTICE GINSBURG, dissenting.

Although the question is close, I would uphold the de-terminations of the courts below that Shell qualifies as an arranger within the compass of (CERCLA).

In the 1950's and early 1960's, Shell shipped most of its products to Brown and Bryant (B & B) in 55–gallon drums, thereby ensuring against spillage or leakage during delivery and transfer. Later, Shell found it economically advantageous, in lieu of shipping in drums, to require B & B to maintain bulk storage facilities for receipt of the chemicals B & B purchased from Shell. By the mid–1960's, Shell was delivering its chemical to B & B in bulk tank truckloads. As the Court recognizes, "bulk storage of the chemical led to numerous tank failures and spills as the chemical rusted tanks and eroded valves."

Shell furthermore specified the equipment to be used in transferring the chemicals from the delivery truck to B & B's storage tanks. In the process, spills and leaks were inevitable, indeed spills occurred every time deliveries were made.

The deliveries, Shell was well aware, directly and routinely resulted in disposals of hazardous substances (through spills and leaks) for more than 20 years. "[M]ere knowledge" may not be enough, but Shell did not simply know of the spills and leaks without contributing to them. Given the control rein held by Shell over the mode of delivery and transfer, the lower courts held and I agree, Shell was properly ranked an arranger.

I would return these cases to the District Court to give all parties a fair opportunity to address that court's endeavor to allocate costs. Because the Court's disposition precludes that opportunity, I dissent from the Court's judgment.

NOTES

1. Several cases on arranger liability involve arrangements between different companies to handle hazardous substances. In *United States v. Aceto Agric. Chem. Corp.*, 872 F.2d 1373 (8th Cir. 1989), plaintiffs alleged that defendant pesticide manufacturers contracted with Aidex Corp. (a bankrupt company at the time of litigation) for the "formulation" of their technical grade pesticides into commercial grade pesticides; that inherent in the formulation process (involving mixture of the manufacturers' active ingredients with inert materials according to the manufacturers' specifications) was the generation and disposal of wastes containing defendants' hazardous substances; and that defendants retained ownership of their hazardous substances throughout the formulation process. The court held that these allegations were sufficient to establish—for purposes of defeating defendants'

motion to dismiss—that defendants "arranged for" disposal of the hazardous waste under CERCLA section 107(a)(3). Defendants unsuccessfully sought to analogize the case to previous ones in which district courts had refused to impose liability where a "useful" substance was sold to another party who then incorporated it into a product which was later disposed of. *See also United States v. Hercules, Inc.*, 247 F.3d 706 (8th Cir. 2001).

2. In 1999, Congress enacted the Superfund Recycling Equity Act, CERCLA section 127. The Act grants relief from liability under section 107(a)(3) and (4) to persons who "arranged for recycling of recyclable material." The term "recyclable material" means "scrap" paper, plastic, glass, textiles, rubber (other than whole tires) and metal, and "spent batteries." To qualify for relief, arrangers must prove that various requirements were met at the time of the transaction, e.g., that the arranger exercised "reasonable care" to determine that the recycling facility was in compliance with "substantive" federal, state and local environmental laws and regulations. Although several criteria for determining "reasonable care" are set forth in section 127(c)(6), scrap metal dealers and battery recyclers have asked EPA to issue guidance or a rule further clarifying what they must do to comply with the standard. 31 ENV'T REP. 1512 (2000). For examples of judicial application of the requirements and exemptions of section 127(c)(6), see Gould, Inc. v. A & M Battery and Tire Service, 176 F.Supp.2d 324 (M.D. Pa. 2001); United States v. Mountain Metal Co., 137 F.Supp.2d 1267 (N.D. Ala. 2001).

3. Arranger liability also may be used to reach corporate officers and parent corporations. In *United States v. TIC Investment Corp.*, 68 F.3d 1082 (8th Cir. 1995), the questions were whether an officer and the corporate parents of a subsidiary corporation were liable as arrangers for disposal of hazardous wastes. With respect to the corporate officer, the court held that the proper standard would impose direct arranger liability on him if he had the authority to control and did in fact exercise actual or substantial control, directly or indirectly, over the arrangement for disposal or the off-site disposal of hazardous substances. The court found that the officer did not delegate authority and left no room for others to exercise any decisionmaking authority or judgment in any area of the business, including hazardous waste disposal. Thus, as a matter of law, he was liable as an arranger. With respect to the parent corporations, the court said that in order for them to incur direct arranger liability for a subsidiary's off-site disposal practices, "[T]here must be some causal connection or nexus between the parent corporation's conduct and the subsidiary's arrangement for disposal, or the off-site disposal itself." The court of appeals reversed the summary judgment against the parent corporations, saying that there were genuine issues of material fact concerning whether they not only had the authority to control but also "exercised actual or substantial control, directly or indirectly, over [the subsidiary's] waste disposal arrangement." (Compare to the test for "owner and operator" liability, discussed above.)

4. The Small Business Liability Relief and Brownfields Revitalization Act of 2002 created new exclusions for the liability of arrangers and transporters as well as owners and operators. New section 107(*o*), the "de micromis exemption," protects a PRP from liability under section 107(a)(3) or (4) if he can demonstrate that (1) the total amount of the materials containing

hazardous substances which he contributed was less than 110 gallons of liquid materials or 200 pounds of solid materials (or such greater or lesser amounts as the EPA may determine by regulation), and (2) all or part of the disposal, treatment, or transport occurred before April 1, 2001. Several exceptions to the de micromis exemption are set forth in section 107(o)(2). The exemption does not apply where (a) the materials in question contribute significantly to the cost of the response action or natural resource restoration, (b) the person fails to comply with an information request or impedes the response action or restoration, or (c) the person has been convicted of a criminal violation for conduct to which the exemption would apply.

Another new section, 107(p), creates an exemption from "arranger" liability for a person who is (1) an owner, operator, or lessee of residential property from which any "municipal solid waste" (MSW) (defined as waste generated by a household, or by a business or institutional entity to the extent that the waste is essentially the same as that normally generated by a household) is generated; (2) a business that employed on average not more than 100 full-time individuals (or equivalent) in the three tax years before notification of its potential liability, and is a "small business concern" (within the meaning of the Small Business Act, 15 U.S.C. section 631 et. seq.); or (3) a "501(c)(3)" nonprofit organization that employed not more than 100 paid individuals during the preceding year at the location from which the MSW was generated. The exceptions to the MSW exemption are identical to exceptions (a) and (b) above, for the de micromis exemption.

(3) Transporters

The principal contested issue with respect to *transporter* liability has been the meaning of section 107(a)(4)'s requirement that the disposal or treatment facility be "selected by" the transporter. In *Tippins, Inc. v. USX Corp.*, 37 F.3d 87 (3d Cir. 1994), the court concluded that a person is liable as a transporter not only if it "ultimately selects" the disposal facility but also when it "actively participates in the disposal decision to the extent of having had substantial input" in the choice of disposal facility. Similarly, *United States v. Davis*, 261 F.3d 1 (1st Cir. 2001), held that transporter liability requires "substantial input" into the choice of the disposal facility.

United States v. USX Corp., 68 F.3d 811 (3d Cir. 1995), involved a claim against the principal shareholders and officers of a closely held corporation that transported hazardous substances. The United States argued that section 107(a)(4) was intended to impose liability on those who control the affairs of a responsible corporation, irrespective of whether those in control actually participated in the liability-creating conduct. The court rejected that argument, saying that liability may not be imposed solely on the basis of an officer's or shareholder's active involvement in the corporation's day-to-day affairs: "Instead, there must be a showing that the person sought to be held liable actually participated in the liability-creating conduct." However, liability is not limited to those who personally participate in the transportation of hazardous wastes, nor is it necessary that the officer participate in the selection of the disposal facility. "Liability may be imposed where the officer is aware of the acceptance of materials for transport and of his company's substantial participation in the selection of the disposal facility. An officer who has authority to control disposal decisions should not escape liability under section 107(a)(4) when he or she has actual knowledge that a subordinate has selected a disposal site and, effectively, acquiesces in the subordinate's actions."

In *American Cyanamid v. Capuano*, 381 F.3d 6 (1st Cir. 2004), the court held that the district court's finding that defendants were transporters was not clearly erroneous, on the basis of three factors. First, defendants had substantial input in the decision of where to dispose of the waste, often making the final determination of whether to allow the waste to be dumped at their own landfill or to send it to the disposal site. Second, the trucks carrying the hazardous waste would arrive at defendants' place of business only to be redirected by defendants to the disposal site. Third, although payments by defendants to the transportation drivers did not prove, in and of themselves, that defendants transported the waste, the court found that the payments did support the inference that defendants were involved with transportation of waste to the site.

(4) Other Parties: Successors, Lenders, and Government Entities

a. Successors

Based on the terms of CERCLA section 107(a), which allow for liability to be placed on any "person" who fits within the four categories of potentially responsible parties, federal courts have held that CERCLA allows for the imposition of liability on successor corporations. *See* B.F. Goodrich v. Betkoski, 99 F.3d 505, 518 (2d Cir. 1996). Beyond this general proposition, however, the decisions of which common law—federal or state—to apply and which factors to consider in setting liability have been somewhat less clear. In *Louisiana–Pacific Corp. v. Asarco, Inc.*, 909 F.2d 1260 (9th Cir. 1990), applying federal common law, the court held that CERCLA liability may be imposed upon "successors"—companies that purchase the stock or assets of hazardous waste disposers—under the narrow liability rules applied in most states. Under those rules an asset purchaser may be liable only if (1) it expressly or impliedly agreed to assume the predecessor's liabilities, (2) the transaction amounted to a "de facto" merger, (3) the successor is "merely a continuation" of the predecessor, or (4) the transaction involved fraud in an attempt to escape liability. The court left open the possible application of two more expansive successor liability rules, the "product line" rule and the "continuing business enterprise" rule. *See* Ronald R. Janke & Matthew L. Kuryla, *Environmental Liability Risks for Asset Purchasers*, 24 ENV'T REP. 2237 (1994); Alfred R. Light, *'Product Line' and 'Continuity of Enterprise' Theories of Corporation Successor Liability Under CERCLA*, 11 MISS. C. L. REV. 63 (1990).

Applying "evolving principles of federal common law" the court in *United States v. Carolina Transformer Co.*, 978 F.2d 832 (4th Cir. 1992), applied the continuing business enterprise rule (which it called the "continuity of enterprise" or "substantial continuity" rule) in a case that did not come within the "mere continuation" rule because there was no overlap of stock ownership between the seller and the buyer of a transformer construction business. The factors which the court considered in holding the purchaser liable under CERCLA were (1) retention of the same employees, (2) retention of the same supervisory personnel, (3) retention of the same production facilities in the same location, (4) production of the same product, (5) retention of the same name, (6) continuity of assets, (7) continuity of general business operations, and (8) successor's holding itself out as the continuation of the previous enterprise.

In *Atchison, Topeka & Santa Fe Railway Co. v. Brown & Bryant, Inc.*, 159 F.3d 358 (9th Cir. 1997), the Ninth Circuit expressed doubt about the correctness of its earlier view in *Louisiana-Pacific, supra*, that federal rather than state common law should govern successor liability under CERCLA. Citing intervening decisions by the Supreme Court in *O'Melveny & Myers v. FDIC*, 512 U.S. 79 (1994), and *Atherton v. FDIC*, 519 U.S. 213 (1997), neither of which involved CERCLA, the Ninth Circuit said that the Supreme Court had "rejected many of the very arguments that *Louisiana-Pacific* accepted in deciding CERCLA necessitated a set of uniform federal rules for successor liability." The court read *O'Melveny* to mean that when dealing with a "comprehensive and detailed" federal statutory regulation, a court should "presume that matters left unaddressed in such a scheme are subject to state law."

More recently, in *United States v. Davis*, 261 F.3d 1 (1st Cir. 2001), the First Circuit followed the reasoning of the Ninth Circuit in *Atchison, Topeka* and concluded that state rather than federal common law should govern successor liability under CERCLA. The court chose to apply Connecticut's "mere continuation" test rather than the federal "substantial continuation" test, and consequently imposed successor liability on successor corporation Black & Decker.

The most important recent development concerning successor liability is *United States v. General Battery Corp.*, 423 F.3d 294 (3d Cir. 2005), in which the court disagreed with *Davis*, holding that, based on the precedent of *Bestfoods* (discussed in the owner and operator liability section, *supra*), a uniform *federal* standard should apply in determining successor liability. According to the court, although successor liability rests at "the intersection of tort and corporate law," both of which tend to rely on state law, applying a uniform federal standard—rather than the varying state standards—of successor liability better serves CERCLA's objectives of predictability, uniformity, encouraging settlements, and facilitating a market in brownfield assets.

Turning to the case at hand—in which defendant General Battery Corporation had acquired a defunct generator corporation and then merged with an existing corporation—the court applied the "fundamental" common-law principles of successor liability, as recommended by *Bestfoods*. Under these principles, a successor is not liable unless it meets one of four exceptions: (1) it assumes liability; (2) the transaction amounts to a consolidation or merger; (3) the transaction is fraudulent and intended to provide an escape from liability; or (4) the purchasing corporation is a mere continuation of the selling company. Noting that the case involved the "de facto merger" exception, the court then found that the transaction met all four elements of a de facto merger under the majority standard: (1) continuity of enterprise; (2) continuity of shareholders; (3) seller corporation ceased operation, liquidated, and dissolved as soon as possible; and (4) buyer assumed obligations ordinarily necessary for the uninterrupted continuation of normal business operations.

Both federal and state rules concerning the liability of successors may be modified by contract. Indemnification agreements are often used in transactions involving the acquisition of property to address environmental and other liabilities related to the assets and business transferred. Two key issues raised by CERCLA's language and judicial decisions concerning the enforceability of indemnification agreements are (1) whether indemnification agreements are barred by section 107(e), and, if not, (2) whether they nevertheless should be construed narrowly. Section 107(e)(1) provides:

> No indemnification, hold harmless, or similar agreement or conveyance shall be effective to transfer from the owner or operator of any vessel or facility or from any person who may be liable for a release or threat of release under this section, to any other person the liability imposed under this section. Nothing in this subsection shall bar any agreement to insure, hold harmless, or indemnify a party to such agreement for any liability under this section.

A majority of federal courts interpret section 107(e) as allowing indemnity agreements. As a result, indemnity agreements have become an integral part of real estate transactions. For example, in *Mardan Corp. v. C.G.C. Music, Ltd.*, 804 F.2d 1454 (9th Cir. 1986), a seller sold land on which it had manufactured musical instruments and deposited waste. As part of the sale, the purchaser agreed to release the seller from undisclosed environmental liabilities. After the EPA brought an enforcement action against the purchaser (which also had deposited waste upon the property), the purchaser sued the seller under section 107 for recovery of its cleanup costs. The court affirmed a summary judgment for the seller, stating that, while it is true that indemnification agreements cannot alter or excuse the underlying liability, they *can* change who ultimately pays for that liability. Similarly, in *AM International v. International Forging Equipment Corp.*, 982 F.2d 989 (6th Cir. 1993), the court agreed that section 107(e) does not bar indemnification agreements, holding that the second sentence of section 107(e)(1) permits the shifting or allocation of the cost of liability between parties, so long as CERCLA liability for the cleanup itself is not diluted.

Concerning the construction of indemnification agreements, most courts have applied, either explicitly or implicitly, a rule that such arrangements can bar CERCLA liability between the parties only if there is clear language in the agreement anticipating and requiring such a result. *See* Mobay Corp. v. Allied–Signal, Inc., 761 F.Supp. 345 (D.N.J. 1991); Southland Corp. v. Ashland Oil, Inc., 696 F.Supp. 994 (D.N.J. 1988).

b. Lenders and Trustees

Section 101(20)(A) of CERCLA excludes from the definition of "owner or operator" any "person, who, without participating in the management of a * * * facility, holds indicia of ownership primarily to protect his security interest in the * * * facility." Financial institutions and other secured creditors were shocked by the decision in *United States v. Fleet Factors Corp.*, 901 F.2d 1550 (11th Cir. 1990), which held that it was not necessary to the imposition of liability that the creditor actually involve itself in day-to-day operations of the facility; it was enough if the involvement with management was "sufficiently broad to support the inference that it could affect hazardous waste decisions if it so chose." Prior district court decisions had permitted lenders to participate in the financial affairs of the borrowers without risking CERCLA liability, so long as the lenders did not become too involved in the borrowers' day-to-day operations.

Responding to the ensuing clamor from the banking community and to the federal government's increasing role as a secured creditor after taking over failed savings and loans, the EPA issued in 1992 a regulation that employed a framework of specific tests to provide clearer articulation of a lender's CERCLA liability. Lender Liability Under CERCLA, 57 Fed. Reg. 18,344, 18,382 (Apr. 29, 1992) (codified at 40 C.F.R. section 300.1100). The rule was vacated on procedural grounds in *Kelley v. Environmental Protection Agency*, 15 F.3d 1100 (D.C. Cir. 1994). But in 1996, Congress amended the lender liability provisions, essentially adopting the EPA's rule. The phrase "participate in management" is now defined in section 101(20)(E) to mean "actually participating in the management or operational affairs" of a facility, and "does not include merely having the capacity to influence, or the unexercised right to control," facility operations. *See* Public Law 104–208 (1996). Subsequently, *Monarch Tile, Inc. v. City of Florence*, 212 F.3d 1219 (11th Cir. 2000) held that a city that purchased land to foster private economic development thereon, leasing it to a private company and retaining title to secure payment of the development bonds that financed the property's acquisition, qualified for CERCLA's "secured creditor" liability exception.

Prior to 1996 there was uncertainty and litigation concerning the possible CERCLA liability of trustees when trust property is contaminated. Could a trustee be personally liable, beyond the extent of the trust assets, for cleanup costs? CERCLA was silent on the matter. The leading case was *City of Phoenix v. Garbage Services Co.*, 816 F.Supp. 564 (D. Ariz. 1993), in which the court held that the defendant trustee, a bank, would be liable under section 107(a)(2), without regard to the amount of trust assets available to indemnify it, if the plaintiff could prove at trial that hazardous substances were disposed of at the site when the bank held title.

In 1996, Congress enacted the Asset Conservation Act, amending section 107 of CERCLA to limit fiduciaries' personal liability. Under new section 107(n), the general rule is that a fiduciary's liability for the release or threatened release of a hazardous substance at a facility held in a fiduciary capacity shall not exceed the assets so held. The general rule does not apply, however, to the extent that a person is liable independently of his position or actions as a fiduciary, nor does it limit liability if the negligence of a fiduciary causes or contributes to the release or threatened release. Applying the negligence exception, the court in *Canadyne–Georgia Corp. v. NationsBank, N.A. (South)*, 183 F.3d 1269 (11th Cir. 1999), sustained a complaint against a bank that acted as a trustee for trusts whose assets included partnership interests in a company at the time the company allegedly contaminated certain property. The court looked to state law in determining that the bank could be deemed an "owner" for purposes of CERCLA liability. On remand, the trial court granted the trustee-bank's motion for summary judgment because plaintiff had presented no evidence that the bank "took particular negligent actions that caused or contributed to the release of hazardous substances." *Canadyne–Georgia Corp. v. Bank of America*, 174 F.Supp.2d 1360 (M.D. Ga. 2001).

c. Governmental Entities

Prior to the 1986 SARA amendments to CERCLA, the Third Circuit held in *United States v. Union Gas Co.*, 792 F.2d 372 (3d Cir. 1986), *vacated and remanded*, 479 U.S. 1025 (1987), that the Eleventh Amendment to the Constitution barred the imposition of cleanup liability against states because section 107 did not specifically identify states as liable parties. The court stated that, in order to overcome the Eleventh Amendment, the statute had to make clear that Congress consciously and directly focused on the issue of state sovereign immunity and chose to abrogate it. Subsequently, in 1986, Congress amended section 101(20), defining "owner or operator," to provide for state and local governmental liability under section 107. The Supreme Court then concluded that Congress did intend to subject states to suits for response costs if states caused or contributed to hazardous substance releases. Pennsylvania v. Union Gas Co., 491 U.S. 1 (1989). In *Seminole Tribe of Florida v. Florida*, 517 U.S. 44 (1996), however, the Supreme Court overruled its decision in *Union Gas*. The Court held that the Commerce Clause does not authorize Congress to abrogate a state's Eleventh Amendment immunity to suit without its consent.

There has been much controversy about the CERCLA liability of municipal governments, many of which own or operate disposal or treatment facilities, transport wastes to such facilities, or arrange for disposal, treatment or transport. Municipalities, which are not protected by the Eleventh Amendment, hoped that the courts would interpret CERCLA narrowly to exclude them from section 107(a)'s list of "covered persons." However, federal courts consistently have interpreted the law broadly, holding that municipalities may be liable as owners and operators of hazardous waste sites as well as transporters and generators of hazardous waste. *See* Joseph M. Manko & Madeleine H. Cozine, *The Battle Over Municipal Liability Under CERCLA Heats Up: An Analysis of Proposed Congressional Amendments to Superfund*, 5 Vill. Envtl. L.J. 23 (1994).

The most important case on this subject is *B.F. Goodrich Co. v. Murtha,* 958 F.2d 1192 (2d Cir. 1992). In holding that municipalities which send their residents' household waste to landfills can be liable under CERCLA, the court rejected the following arguments by the municipal defendants: (1) that a municipality cannot be liable under CERCLA for the disposal of hazardous substances since it is acting in its sovereign capacity; (2) that CERCLA's silence regarding municipal solid waste is evidence that Congress intended to exclude it from the definition of hazardous substances; (3) that the exemption for household hazardous waste under RCRA is incorporated into CERCLA's definition of hazardous substances; (4) that CERCLA's legislative history evinces an intent to exclude municipalities from liability for the disposal of municipal solid waste; and (5) that the EPA interpreted CERCLA as imposing no liability on municipalities for the disposal of municipal waste.

Under its 1989 "Interim Policy on CERCLA Settlements Involving Municipalities and Municipal Wastes," 54 Fed. Reg. 51,071 (Dec. 12, 1989). EPA has attempted to ameliorate the perceived harshness of CERCLA as applied to municipalities. EPA supplemented this policy in 1998 with its "Policy for Municipality and Municipal Solid Waste; CERCLA Settlements at NPL Co–Disposal Sites," 63 Fed. Reg. 8,197 (Feb. 18, 1998). Under this policy, EPA generally does not pursue municipalities under CERCLA as generators or transporters of MSW unless the waste contains hazardous substances derived from commercial, institutional or industrial activity. For municipal owners/operators of NPL sites that wish to resolve their potential CERCLA liability and obtain contribution protection pursuant to section 113(f), the policy establishes 20% of total estimated response costs for the site as a presumptive baseline settlement amount for an individual municipality. EPA may offer settlements varying upward or downward from this presumption, generally not to exceed 35%, based on site-specific factors.

With respect to hazardous waste facilities owned or operated by the federal government, section 120 of CERCLA provides that "[e]ach department, agency and instrumentality of the United States * * * shall be subject to * * * this chapter * * * to the same extent * * * as any nongovernmental entity, including liability under section [107]." Federal facilities are included on the NPL, but funds for cleanup must come from the budget of the responsible department or agency, not from the Superfund.

The greatest potential U.S. liability under section 120 appears to stem from contaminated military bases and nuclear weapons facilities. *See Cleaning Up Federal Facilities: Controversy Over an Environmental Peace Dividend*, 23 ENV'T REP. 2659 (1993). The facilities need not be owned by the federal government. In *FMC Corp. v. Department of Commerce*, 29 F.3d 833 (3d Cir. 1994) (en banc), a contribution suit by a private PRP, the court held that section 120 waives the federal government's immunity from CERCLA liability when the government engages in activities that would subject private parties to liability. The government was, therefore, liable under section 107 as "operator" of a private manufacturing facility over which the government "exerted considerable day-to-day control" during World War II to meet production goals for high-tenacity rayon. Rejecting the government's argument for a *"per se* rule that regulatory activities cannot constitute the basis for CERCLA liability," the court stated that "the government can be liable when it engages in regulatory activities extensive enough to make it an operator of a facility or an arranger of the disposal of hazardous wastes."

d.   Defenses

Section 107 (b) Defenses. There shall be no liability under subsection (a) of this section for a person otherwise liable who can establish by a preponderance of the evidence that the release or threat of release of a hazardous substance and the damages resulting therefrom were caused solely by—

(1) an act of God;

(2) an act of war;

(3) an act or omission of a third party other than an employee or agent of the defendant, or than one whose act or omission occurs in connection with a contractual relationship, existing directly or indirectly, with the defendant (except where the sole contractual arrangement arises from a published tariff and acceptance for carriage by a common carrier by rail), if the defendant establishes by a preponderance of the evidence that (a) he exercised due care with respect to the hazardous substance concerned, taking into consideration the characteristics of such hazardous substance, in light of all relevant facts and circumstances, and (b) he took precautions against foreseeable acts or omissions of any such third party and the consequences that could foreseeably result from such acts or omissions; or

(4) any combination of the foregoing paragraphs.

42 U.S.C. section 9607 (2000).

The defenses available to PRPs under Section 107(b) are narrow. In *Blasland, Bouck & Lee v. City of North Miami*, 283 F.3d 1286, 1302–05 (11th Cir. 2002), the court expressly affirmed this narrowness, noting that, while it would appear that CERCLA sets out other defenses in parts of the statute other than section 107(b), there are only three potential defenses for PRPs.

The most prominent of the three defenses is section 107(b)(3), regarding acts or omissions by a third party. As mentioned in the discussion of owners and operators, *supra*, Congress attempted to address the perceived unfairness of section 107(a) in the SARA amendments of 1986 by adding a new defense for innocent landowners. While section 107(a)'s general liability standard for "owners and operators" was maintained, Congress expanded section 107(b)(3)'s third-party exception by redefining the term "contractual relationship" in section 101(35):

> Section 101 (35) (A). The term "contractual relationship", for the purpose of section 9607(b)(3) of this title, includes, but is not limited to, land contracts, deeds, easements, leases, or other instruments transferring title or possession, unless the real property on which the facility concerned is located was acquired by the defendant after the disposal or placement of the hazardous substance on, in, or at the facility, and one of more of the circumstances described in clause (i), (ii), or (iii) is also established by the defendant by a preponderance of the evidence:

> (i) At the time the defendant acquired the facility the defendant did not know and had no reason to know that any hazardous substance which is the subject of the release or threatened release was disposed of on, in, or at the facility.

> (ii) The defendant is a government entity which acquired the facility by escheat, or through any other involuntary transfer or acquisition, or through the exercise of eminent domain authority by purchase or condemnation.

> (iii) The defendant acquired the facility by inheritance of bequest.

42 U.S.C. section 9601(35)(A) (2000).

With respect to the "reason to know" limitation, section 101(35)(B)(i), after being further amended in 2002 by the Small Business Liability Relief and Brownfields Revitalization Act, provides in part:

> (B)(i) * * * To establish that the defendant had no reason to know * * *, the defendant must demonstrate to a court that—

> (I) * * * before [acquiring] the facility, the defendant carried out all appropriate inquiries [due diligence, pursuant to "standards and practices" to be established by EPA] into the previous ownership and uses of the facility in accordance with generally accepted good commercial and customary standards and practices; and

> (II) the defendant took reasonable steps to—

>> (aa) stop any continuing release;

>> (bb) prevent any threatened future release; and

(cc) prevent or limit any human, environmental, or natural resource exposure to any previously released hazardous substance.

42 U.S.C. section 9601(35)(B).

All "innocent landowners," whether they acquired the land voluntarily or involuntarily, also must establish that they have cooperated fully with persons conducting any response actions and have complied with any land use restrictions or institutional controls related to the response actions.

The 2002 amendments also require that, within two years of the amendments' passage, EPA establish standards and practices for the purpose of fulfilling the 'all appropriate inquiries' requirement. On May 9, 2003, EPA promulgated these standards and practices, currently located at 40 C.F.R. Pt. 312. The text of the regulations is brief, stating simply that the procedures of the American Society for Testing and Materials ("ASTM") entitled "Standard Practice for Environmental Site Assessment: Phase 1 Environmental Site Assessment Process" shall satisfy the requirements for conducting all appropriate inquiry.

In *Franklin County Convention Facilities Authority v. American Premier Underwriters, Inc.*, 240 F.3d 534 (6th Cir. 2001), the court reversed the district court's holding that a PRP was entitled to the innocent landowner defense. Though the PRP played no role in placing the hazardous substance at the site—in this case, a buried box of creosote that the PRP's contractor accidentally split open while excavating—and the PRP could not be held liable for the "accidental and unavoidable" splitting open of the box, the PRP did not exercise due care after discovering the spill. Upon discovery, the PRP immediately ceased work and contacted an environmental contractor, but nevertheless allowed the spill to migrate forty-five feet through a sewer trench. Accordingly, the court held the PRP did not act with due care and, therefore, was not entitled to the innocent landowner defense.

More recently, in *Western Properties Service Corp. v. Shell Oil Co.*, 358 F.3d 678 (9th Cir. 2004), the Ninth Circuit rejected a claim requesting a broadening of the innocent landowner defense. The court's holding suggests that, though there is no legal basis for the broadening of the three section 107(b) defenses, the limits on what the court may consider in contribution actions under section 113(f) (discussed *infra*) are much less strict:

> There is some attraction, in certain circumstances, to a broad innocent-landowner rule for non-polluting landowners who are not statutorily innocent under section 101(35). The attractiveness is equitable, not textual, and the contribution statute already allows for equity to be taken into account. Suppose a person bought a lot on which to build a home, not knowing that some years ago a truck had overturned and spilled hazardous substances into the ground, which had seeped down into the water table. Suppose further that by due

diligence he could have found out and is deemed to have had reason to know, so he is not a statutory innocent owner. In such a case, the district court would be able to consider the equities, as between the almost-innocent PRP landowner and the company whose truck had overturned, using its section 113(f)(1) authority to "allocate response costs among liable parties using such equitable factors as the court determines are appropriate."

Id. at 690. The court also discussed the proposition, noted also in *Blasland*, *supra*, and other circuits, that equitable defenses are barred under section 107(a) and therefore may not be admitted in a section 107 action. On the other hand, such equitable defenses may be considered in a contribution action under section 113(f).

Though section 107(b)(3) tends to be the most litigated of the three defenses, in *United States v. Shell Oil Co.*, 294 F.3d 1045 (9th Cir. 2002), defendant oil companies claimed a defense under section 107(b)(2), the "act of war" exception. In a suit under section 107(a), the United States and the State of California attempted to recover cleanup costs from oil companies that had produced aviation fuel for the federal government during World War II. Through the War Powers Clause of the Constitution, President Roosevelt had entered the U.S. into contractual agreements with the oil companies for their continued production of aviation fuel. While the U.S. provided low-cost loans for the production of facilities to increase production of the fuel, the companies ultimately retained ownership of the facilities. After the war, the federal government paid for the cleanup of "acid sludge" waste at the sites and subsequently brought a section 107 suit against the companies, who then claimed the act of war defense under section 107(b)(2). In rejecting the companies' claim, the court noted the dearth of case law and legislative history on the act of war defense. Based on the definition of "act of war" under international law and "dictum" from the Supreme Court, the court focused on the narrowness of the term and the logical division between unilateral acts and acts of mutual contract in wartime. The court held that the companies' "argument that any governmental act taken by authority of the War Powers Clause is an 'act of war' [swept] too broadly," and accordingly rejected the companies' defense.

Discussion Problem #1 on CERCLA Liability

In 1970, Chemco, a new and wholly owned subsidiary of Padre Corp., purchased Blackacre (a warehouse on five acres of land) and began manufacturing specialized industrial chemicals there. Smith, an officer of Padre, was president of Chemco, and Jones was vice-president and plant manager.

Initially, toxic wastes generated by Chemco were kept in 55–gallon drums at Blackacre. In 1971, Jones told Smith that the drums were "piling up," and Smith suggested that Jones "find another solution" to the problem. Jones ordered the excavation of a "holding pond" at the rear of Blackacre, into which were placed the contents of the drums and most of the wastes subsequently generated by Chemco until it ceased operations in 1975. By 1979 the contents of the holding pond had seeped into the ground. In anticipation of selling Blackacre, Chemco filled in the former pond, planted grass there, and removed and sold all equipment from the building.

In 1980, Able purchased Blackacre from Chemco without knowledge of the waste disposal that had occurred there, though Able was aware that Chemco had manufactured chemicals at the site. (At that point Chemco was dissolved, and its only assets—the monies received from Able—were given to Padre.) Able used the building as a warehouse without any problem until 1990, when she sold Blackacre to Baker. Baker did not know that Blackacre previously had been owned by Chemco or that the building ever had been used for anything other than a warehouse. Baker has continued to use it for that purpose.

Now chemicals from Chemco's prior operations have appeared in the soil and well water of Whiteacre, neighboring land owned by White. White has spent thousands of dollars for soil and water tests and for an alternative water supply. On the basis of the *(NEPACCO)* case and the text following it, how would you answer the following questions regarding various parties' possible liability to White under section 107 of CERCLA?

1. May Padre be liable as an "owner or operator" under § 107(a)(2)? As a "successor" to Chemco? What kinds of additional facts would be helpful in answering either of these questions?

2. Is either Smith or Jones liable under § 107(a)(2) as an "operator," or under § 107(a)(3) as a person who "arranged for disposal"?

3. Is Able liable under § 107(a)(2) as a person who "at the time of disposal" owned Blackacre?

4. Is Baker liable under § 107(a)(1), or does he have a defense as an "innocent landowner" under §§ 107(b)(3) and 101(35)(A)?

5. May White's recovery rights be limited because of the specific ways in which she has responded to the contamination?

e. Cost Recovery: Private Versus Government Actions

[Persons covered by section 107(a)] shall be liable for—

(A) all costs of removal or remedial action incurred by the United States Government or a State or an Indian tribe not inconsistent with the national contingency plan;

(B) any other necessary costs of response incurred by any other person consistent with the national contingency plan.

42 U.S.C. 9607(a) (2000).

As can be seen from the language above, there is a difference in the standard applied to cost recovery under section 107(a) by a government entity versus cost recovery by a private party. In *Monsanto, supra,* the court described the two standards in these terms:

Appellants argue the district court erred in requiring them to prove the response costs were inconsistent with the NCP, not cost-effective or unnecessary. Appellants further argue the district court erred in assuming all costs that are consistent with the NCP are conclusively presumed to be reasonable. Appellants note that the information and facts necessary to establish consistency with the NCP are matters within the possession of the government.

We believe the district court's analysis is correct. * * * The statutory language itself establishes an exception for costs that are inconsistent with the NCP, but appellants, as the parties claiming the benefit of the exception, have the burden of proving that certain costs are inconsistent with the NCP and, therefore, not recoverable. Contrary to appellants' argument, "not inconsistent" is not, at least for purposes of statutory construction and not syntax, the same as "consistent."

The statutory scheme also supports allocation of the burden of proof of inconsistency with the NCP upon the defendants when the *government* seeks recovery of its response costs. As noted above, CERCLA § 107(a)(4)(A) provides that the federal government or a state can recover "all costs of removal or remedial action * * * not inconsistent with the [NCP]." In comparison, CERCLA § 107(a)(4)(B) provides that "any other person," referring to any "person" other than the federal government or a state, can recover "any other necessary costs of response * * * consistent with the [NCP]." That statutory language indicates that *non*-governmental entities must prove that their response costs are consistent with the NCP in order to recover them. The statutory scheme thus differentiates between governmental and non-governmental entities in allocating the burden of proof of whether response costs are consistent with the NCP.

The statutory language also supports the district court's reasoning that under CERCLA § 107(a)(4)(A) "all costs" incurred by the government that are not inconsistent with the NCP are conclusively presumed to be reasonable. CERCLA does not refer to "all *reasonable* costs" but simply to "all costs." * * *

The key difference then between the government's burden and the burden for private parties is that the costs claimed by a private party must affirmatively be shown to be consistent with the National Contingency Plan, whereas costs incurred by the government will be presumed consistent unless shown to be inconsistent with the NCP.

But which private parties may recover response costs under section 107(a)? Local governments that conduct cleanups? The private owner of land adjacent to a leaking disposal site? The owner of the leaking disposal site? In *Jones v. Inmont Corp.*, 584 F.Supp. 1425 (S.D. Ohio 1984), the court held that under section 107(a)(4)(B) private parties owning land adjoining an illegal dump site were included within the phrase "any other person" and could recover their response costs from a past generator of hazardous waste deposited there. *See also* Pinole Point Properties, Inc. v. Bethlehem Steel Corp., 596 F.Supp. 283 (N.D. Cal. 1984). In *City of Philadelphia v. Stepan Chemical Co.*, 544 F.Supp. 1135 (E.D. Pa. 1982), the court held that the city, which owned land on which hazardous industrial wastes were dumped illegally without its permission, was not precluded from recovering its actual cleanup costs from defendant generators, even though the city itself, as site owner, might be liable for any response costs later incurred by the state or federal government. The court said that Philadelphia qualified as "any other person" under § 107(a)(4)(B).

Costs recoverable by private plaintiffs do not include compensation for lost property value, income, or medical monitoring. *See* Piccolini v. Simon's Wrecking, 686 F.Supp. 1063 (M.D. Pa. 1988); Lutz v. Chromatex, Inc., 718 F.Supp. 413 (M.D. Pa. 1989). Plaintiffs in *Daigle v. Shell Oil Co.*, 972 F.2d 1527 (10th Cir. 1992), were neighbors of the Rocky Mountain Arsenal, a federal chemical weapons facility generally regarded as one of the worst hazardous waste sites in the United States. Plaintiffs pointed out that CERCLA's definitions of "removal" and "remedial" actions both refer to "monitoring" necessary to protect "public health and welfare." Section 101(23)–(24). Plaintiffs argued that this language supported their claims for the costs of long term "medical monitoring" or "medical surveillance" designed to detect the onset of any latent disease that might be caused by exposure to toxic fumes released during cleanup of the arsenal. The court rejected the argument, saying that the definitions of removal and remedial actions are directed at containing and cleaning up hazardous substance releases. The court held that the monitoring contemplated by the statute is intended to prevent contact between contaminants and the public, and does not include long term health monitoring of the sort requested by plaintiffs. For a similar result, *see Price v. United States Navy*, 39 F.3d 1011 (9th Cir. 1994).

In *Key Tronic Corp. v. United States*, 511 U.S. 809 (1994), one of several parties responsible for contaminating a landfill settled a lawsuit filed by EPA and then brought an action against the Air Force and other responsible parties to recover a share of its cleanup costs, including *attorneys' fees* for legal services in connection with (1) the identification of other PRPs, (2) the preparation and negotiation of the consent decree with EPA, and (3) the prosecution of its action against the Air Force. Since CERCLA §§ 107 and 113(f) do not expressly mention attorneys' fees, in contrast to §§ 310(f) (citizen suits) and 106(b)(2)(E) (persons erroneously ordered to pay response costs), the issue was whether attorneys' fees may constitute "necessary costs of response" recoverable under § 107(a)(4)(B). The Court held that under the "American Rule", Key Tronic could not recover attorneys' fees for prosecuting its action against the Air Force. Neither was plaintiff allowed to recover for legal services in connection with the negotiations culminating in the consent decree with EPA. The Court viewed those services as "primarily protecting Key Tronic's interests as a defendant in the proceedings that established the extent of its

liability," not as "necessary costs of response." However, "lawyers' work
that is closely tied to the actual cleanup may constitute a necessary cost of
response in and of itself," and the component of plaintiff's claim that
covered work performed in identifying other PRPs was held to fall into
this category. "Unlike the litigation services at issue in *Alyeska,* these
efforts might well be performed by engineers, chemists, private investiga-
tors or other professionals who are not lawyers." (A court of appeals
subsequently has held, in *United States v. Chapman,* 146 F.3d 1166 (9th
Cir. 1998), that response costs recoverable under § 107 by the EPA, in
contrast to a private plaintiff, may include attorneys' fees for litigation
and negotiations.)

Discussion Problem #2 on CERCLA Liability

Suppose that during the early 1970s each of five industrial firms sent
between 100 and 500 drums containing various hazardous wastes to a
rural site owned by farmer Fred and leased for $200 per month to Walt,
who was doing business as Walt's Waste Handlers. After collecting $10 per
drum, Walt simply buried the drums in trenches or left them standing in
an open field. Now, more than 30 years later, the drums are leaking and
have contaminated the soil and groundwater on Fred's farm. Having
learned of this situation and of the federal Superfund, neighboring landowners have demanded that the U.S. EPA take action to clean up the
disposal site and prevent the contamination from spreading.

On the basis of the CERCLA materials you have read, and §§ 104,
106 and 107, how would you answer the following questions?

1. What types of action are EPA authorized to take? Does it matter
    that the contamination has not spread beyond the boundaries of
    Fred's farm? What are the controlling statutory provisions?

2. Assuming that they all can be located and have some assets,
    which of the firms and individuals mentioned above are potential-
    ly responsible parties (PRPs) under CERCLA? Is it important to
    determining anyone's liability whether, at the time of disposal,
    Walt was (a) complying with state and local regulatory require-
    ments applicable to disposal sites or (b) acting reasonably, i.e.,
    non-negligently? Is it relevant that all of the disposal activities
    occurred prior to enactment of RCRA and CERCLA? Why or why
    not? What are the relevant policy considerations?

3. For what portion of a total site cleanup might each party be
    legally responsible? Could the extent of liability differ depending
    on the identity of the claimant (EPA or other), or on the type of
    proceeding? What evidentiary rules, including presumptions and
    burdens of proof, would apply?

4. Under CERCLA, can the neighboring landowners take action
    directly against any of the PRPs? Can the neighbors recover for
    losses in the value of their property, or for the costs of medical

monitoring (periodic checkups) to determine whether they are becoming ill from exposure to the contamination?

f. Administrative Orders

In addition to authorizing the President to clean up hazardous waste sites (section 104) and recover the government's costs (section 107), Congress authorized the President to compel PRPs to clean up contaminated sites. (These powers are delegated by the President to the EPA.) Thus, under section 106, when the EPA determines that a facility poses an "imminent and substantial endangerment to the public health or welfare or the environment because of an actual or threatened release of a hazardous substance," the agency may issue administrative orders directing PRPs to take response actions. The EPA may also seek injunctive or other equitable relief from a federal district court under § 106(a). For example, EPA could seek an injunction compelling one or more PRPs to take "removal" or "remedial" action, or to fence the site so as to prevent human exposure to the hazardous substance. The relevant statutory provisions appears below.

> Section 106 (a) * * * In addition to any other action taken by a State or local government, when the President determines that there may be an imminent and substantial endangerment to the public health or welfare or the environment because of an actual or threatened release of a hazardous substance from a facility, he may require the Attorney General of the United States to secure such relief as may be necessary to abate such danger or threat, and the district court of the United States in the district in which the threat occurs shall have jurisdiction to grant such relief as the public interest and the equities of the case may require. The President may also, after notice to the affected State, take other action under this section including, but not limited to, issuing such orders as may be necessary to protect public health and welfare and the environment.
>
> (b)(1) Any person who, without sufficient cause, willfully violates, or fails or refuses to comply with, any order of the President under subsection (a) may * * * be fined not more than $25,000 for each day in which such violation occurs or such failure to comply continues.

42 U.S.C. § 9606 (2000).

> Section 107 (c) (3) If any person who is liable for a release or threat of release of a hazardous substance fails without sufficient cause to properly provide removal or remedial action upon order of the President * * *, such person may be liable to the United States in an amount at least equal to, and not more than three times, the amount of any costs incurred by the Fund * * *. 42 U.S.C. § 9607(c)(3) (2000).

Failure to comply with a section 106 administrative order "without sufficient cause" can result in a fine of up to $25,000 per day under § 106 and, under § 107(c)(3), in liability for "punitive damages in an amount at least equal to, and not more than three times, the amount of any costs incurred by the Fund as a result of such failure to take proper action." *See* J. Wylie Donald, *Defending Against Daily Fines and Punitive Damages under CERCLA: The Meaning of "Without Sufficient Cause,"* 19 COLUM. J. ENVTL. L. 185 (1994). *Solid State Circuits, Inc. v. Environmental Protection Agency*, 812 F.2d 383 (8th Cir. 1987), upheld the constitutionality of section 107(c)(3). *United States v. Parsons*, 936 F.2d 526 (11th Cir. 1991), held that the federal government could recover *four times* the amount that EPA spent to clean up a site after defendants failed to comply with an administrative order by EPA to perform the cleanup. The government recovered its full response costs under section 107(a) and treble that amount under § 107(c)(3). Clearly, these provisions are very government-friendly—they encourage compliance with section 106 orders and allow for challenge after the fact. This is consistent with CERCLA's priority on making sure that sites are cleaned up, and that legal disputes do not delay response and remediation. Not surprisingly, however, the EPA's section 106 authority has been subject to challenge.

In *General Electric Co. v. Johnson*, 362 F.Supp.2d 327 (D.D.C. 2005), plaintiffs brought several constitutional challenges against CERCLA section 106, alleging, among other things, that section 106 violates the Due Process Clause of the Fifth Amendment because section 106 orders deprive PRPs of property without a meaningful hearing. The court granted EPA summary judgment, holding that PRPs are not deprived of meaningful hearings, as they can choose not to comply with a section 106 order or to challenge the order under the Administrative Procedure Act, thereby guaranteeing a judicial hearing.

Note the similarity of the "imminent and substantial endangerment" liability standard to that found in RCRA sections 7002(a)(1)(B) and 7003(a). Are different remedies available? Why might EPA prefer issuing a section 106 administrative order in lieu of cleaning up the site itself and pursuing cost recovery under section 107? Why might PRPs themselves prefer the administrative order? What would you advise a client PRP faced with a section 106 administrative order?

g. Allocation, Contribution, and Settlements

(i) Apportionment and Allocation

As a general matter, while CERCLA does not dictate the imposition of joint and several liability, federal courts have held that the statute does allow for it. Indeed, most courts now impose some form of joint and several liability when dealing with multiple PRPs and indivisible harm. *United States v. Monsanto*, excerpted page 894, *supra*, is an instructive example of such a strict imposition. While joint and several liability is the norm for cases of indivisible harm, controversies and differences among courts begin to arise as to "the timing of the resolution of the divisibility question, whether equitable factors should be considered, and whether a defendant can avoid liability at all, or for only some portion, of the damages." *See* In re Bell Petroleum Services, Inc., page 940, *infra*. Because of the frequent commingling of wastes at dump sites, along with their potential to migrate and the fact that even small amounts of waste can be extremely dangerous, courts traditionally have rejected the notion that volume of waste alone should be a basis for apportionment. In general, courts resist considering equitable factors at the liability stage, refusing to apportion damages and instead leaving cost allocation for parties to sort out in the (inevitable) contribution action. Still, some courts have allowed the introduction of equitable factors as a consideration in the apportionment stage.

For example, in *United States v. A & F Materials Co.*, 578 F.Supp. 1249, 1256 (S.D. Ill. 1984), the court concluded that "a rigid application of the Restatement approach to joint and several liability is inappropriate" because such extensive liability would be unfair to a defendant who contributed only a small amount of waste to a site. The court preferred a "moderate approach" under which the court (a) had the power to impose joint and several liability whenever a defendant could not prove his contribution to an injury but (b) still could apportion damages according to the following factors contained in an unsuccessful amendment to CERCLA proposed by then Representative (later Vice President) Al Gore which became known as the "Gore factors":

(i) the ability of the parties to demonstrate that their contribution to a discharge, release or disposal of a hazardous waste can be distinguished;

(ii) the amount of the hazardous waste involved;

(iii) the degree of toxicity of the hazardous waste involved;

(iv) the degree of involvement by the parties in the generation, transportation, treatment, storage, or disposal of the hazardous waste;

(v) the degree of care exercised by the parties with respect to the hazardous waste concerned, taking into account the characteristics of such hazardous waste; and

(vi) the degree of cooperation by the parties with Federal, State, or local officials to prevent any harm to the public health or the environment.

Similarly, in *United States v. Alcan Aluminum Corp.*, 964 F.2d 252 (3d Cir. 1992), the court allowed the defendant to introduce evidence of apportionment. The government had argued that Alcan was jointly and severally liable for cleanup costs even though Alcan claimed that the only waste it had taken to the site was a non-hazardous, non-toxic emulsion with heavy metal fragments "orders of magnitude below ambient or naturally occurring background levels." The court of appeals vacated the judgment of the district court and remanded the case for "further factual development concerning the scope of Alcan's liability." Because of the "intensely factual nature of the 'divisibility' issue," the appeals court held that the district court erred in granting the United States summary judgment for its full claim against Alcan without benefit of a hearing.

Alcan recognizes that proving divisibility will require "an assessment of the relative toxicity, migratory potential and synergistic capacity of the hazardous waste at issue."[24]

Some critics have argued that EPA often settles early with large defendants for amounts far below the actual costs incurred in cleaning up the wastes for which those defendants are responsible. Under joint and several liability, defendants that settle late or litigate bear the brunt of the EPA's failure to exact reasonable settlement amounts from the early settlors. *Alcan* is viewed as a vehicle for ameliorating inequitable results in such situations. *See* Daniel P. Harris & David M. Milan, *Avoiding Joint and Several Liability under CERCLA*, 23 ENV'T REP. 1726 (1992).

The dominant approach to apportionment and allocation is summed up in *In re Bell Petroleum Services, Inc.*, 3 F.3d 889 (5th Cir. 1993), which reversed a district court's judgment imposing joint and several liability upon each of three successive owners of a chrome-plating shop. Each owner had discharged rinse water onto the ground, causing the underlying aquifer to become contaminated with chromium. The court of appeals reviewed the *Chem–Dyne*-Restatement approach to joint and several liability adopted in *Monsanto, supra,* the "moderate approach" of *A & F Materials,* and the *Alcan* approach:

> The Fourth Circuit [in *Monsanto* rejected] the *A & F* moderate approach, stating that, while equitable factors are relevant in an action for contribution, "[t]hey are not pertinent to the question of joint and several liability, which focuses principally on the divisibility among responsible parties of the harm to the environment." 858 F.2d at 171 n.22. Other courts have similarly concluded that equitable factors, such as those listed in the Gore amendment, have no place in making the decision whether to impose joint and several liability, but are appropriate in an action for contribution among jointly and severally liable defendants. *See* Alcan, 964 F.2d at 270 n. 29. * * *
>
> * * * Under the *Restatement,* the plaintiff must first prove that the defendant's conduct was a substantial factor in causing the harm; the defendant may limit its liability by proving its contribution to the harm. In contrast, the *Alcan* approach suggests that a defendant may escape liability altogether if it can prove that its waste, even when mixed with other wastes at the site, did not cause the incurrence of response costs. * * *

---

24. In a similar case also involving Alcan, the Second Circuit largely adopted the Third Circuit's reasoning. United States v. Alcan Aluminum Corp., 990 F.2d 711 (2d Cir. 1993). "Alcan may escape liability for response costs if it either succeeds in proving that its oil emulsion, when mixed with other hazardous wastes, did not contribute to the release and the clean-up costs that followed, or contributed at most to only a divisible portion of the harm. Alcan as the polluter bears the ultimate burden of establishing a reasonable basis for apportioning liability." The court acknowledged that Alcan was being allowed to bring the issue of causation back into the case, "through the backdoor, after being denied entry at the frontdoor," but only to escape payment "where its pollutants did not contribute more than background contamination and also cannot concentrate."

Although these approaches are not entirely uniform, certain basic principles emerge. First, joint and several liability is not mandated under CERCLA; Congress intended that the federal courts impose joint and several liability only in appropriate cases, applying common-law principles. Second, all of the cases rely on the *Restatement* in resolving the issues of joint and several liability. The major differences among the cases concern the timing of the resolution of the divisibility question, whether equitable factors should be considered, and whether a defendant can avoid liability for all, or only some portion, of the damages. Third, even where commingled wastes of unknown toxicity, migratory potential, and synergistic effect are present, defendants are allowed an opportunity to attempt to prove that there is a reasonable basis for apportionment (although they rarely succeed); where such factors are not present, volume may be a reasonable means of apportioning liability.

With respect to the timing of the "divisibility" inquiry, we believe that an early resolution is preferable. We agree with the Second Circuit, however, that this is a matter best left to the sound discretion of the district court. We also agree with the majority view that equitable factors, such as those listed in the Gore amendment, are more appropriately considered in actions for contribution among jointly and severally liable parties, than in making the initial determination of whether to impose joint and several liability. We therefore conclude that the *Chem–Dyne* approach is an appropriate framework for resolving issues of joint and several liability in CERCLA cases. Although we express no opinion with respect to the *Alcan* approach, because it is not necessary with respect to the issues we are faced with in this case, we nevertheless recognize that the *Restatement* principles must be adapted, where necessary, to implement congressional intent with respect to liability under the unique statutory scheme of CERCLA.

In *United States v. Hercules, Inc.*, 247 F.3d 706 (8th Cir. 2001), the court clarified the difference between "distinct harms" and "divisibility of harm":

"Distinct harms" are those that may properly be regarded as separate injuries. Defendants may be able to demonstrate that harms are distinct based on geographical considerations, such as where a site consists of "non-contiguous" areas of soil contamination, or separate and distinct subterranean "plumes" of groundwater contamination.

Other cases, by contrast, involve a "single harm" that is nonetheless divisible because it is possible to discern the degree to which different parties contributed to the damage. The basis for division in such situations is that "it is clear that each [defendant] has caused a separate amount of harm, limited in time, and that neither has any responsibility for the harm caused by the other," such as where "two defendants, independently operating the same plant, pollute a stream *over successive periods of time."* Bell, 3 F.3d at 895. Single harms may also be "treated as divisible in terms of degree," based, for example, on the relative quantities of waste discharged into the stream. Divisibility of this type may be provable even where wastes have become cross-contaminated and commingled.... *Alcan II,* 990 F.2d at 772; *see also* Bell, 3 F.3d at 903.

Evidence supporting divisibility must be concrete and specific. The preliminary issue of whether the harm to the environment is capable of apportionment among two or more causes is a question of law. *Bell,* 3 F.3d at 902. Then, "[o]nce it has been determined that the harm is capable of being apportioned among the various causes of it, the actual apportionment of damages is a question of fact."

We also observe that the divisibility doctrine is conceptually distinct from contribution or allocation of damages. At the allocation phase, the only question is the extent to which a defendant's liability may be offset by the liability of another; the inquiry at this state is an equitable one and courts generally take into account the so-called "Gore factors." The divisibility of harm inquiry, by contrast, is guided not by equity—specifically, not by the Gore factors—but by principles of causation alone. Thus, where causation is unclear, divisibility is not an opportunity for courts to "split the difference" in an attempt to achieve equity.

The *Alcan* and *Bell* cases are discussed in Lynda Oswald, *New Directions in Joint and Several Liability under CERCLA?,* 28 U.C. DAVIS L. REV. 299 (1995). *See also* Richard White & John Butler, *Applying Cost Causation Principles in Superfund Allocation Cases,* 28 ENVTL. L. REP. 10067 (1998).

What is the practical difference between apportionment in a section 107 action and allocation at the contribution stage? Is it the difference between several *versus* joint liability? Certainty and uncertainty? If courts generally allowed apportionment based on volume alone, wouldn't it defeat the strict, joint, and several scheme of section 107, and undermine its incentives?

(ii) Contribution

Section 113(f) of CERCLA, concerning contribution, provides in part as follows:

> Any person may seek contribution from any other person who is liable or potentially liable under [§ 107(a)], during or following any civil action under [§ 106 or 107(a)]. Such claims * * * shall be governed by Federal law. In resolving contribution claims, the court may allocate response costs among liable parties using such equitable factors as the court determines are appropriate.

42 U.S.C. § 9613(f) (2000).

Section 113(f) was among the additions to CERCLA in 1986 as part of the SARA amendments. Who can seek contribution under the section? Must a party have been party to an action under sections 106 or 107 in order to bring a contribution action, or may a party who has voluntarily cleaned a site seek contribution, too? The circuits were split on the resolution of this question until 2004, when the Supreme Court decided the next case.

COOPER INDUSTRIES, INC. v. AVIALL SERVICES, INC.

Supreme Court of the United States, 2004.
543 U.S. 157, 125 S.Ct. 577, 160 L.Ed.2d 548.

Justice Thomas delivered the opinion of the Court.

Section 113(f)(1) of the Comprehensive Environmental Response, Compensation, and Liability Act of 1980 (CERCLA) allows persons who have undertaken efforts to clean up properties contaminated by hazardous substances to seek contribution from other parties liable under CERCLA. Section 113(f)(1) specifies that a party may obtain contribution "during or following any civil action" under CERCLA § 106 or § 107(a). The issue we must decide is whether a private party who has not been sued under § 106 or § 107(a) may nevertheless obtain contribution under § 113(f)(1) from other liable parties. We hold that it may not.

I

Under CERCLA, 94 Stat. 2767, the Federal Government may clean up a contaminated area itself, see § 104, or it may compel responsible parties to perform the cleanup, see § 106(a). *See* Key Tronic Corp. v. United States, 511 U.S. 809, 814 (1994). In either case, the Government may recover its response costs under § 107, 42 U.S.C. § 9607 (2000 ed. and Supp. I), the "cost recovery" section of CERCLA. Section 107(a) lists four classes of potentially responsible persons (PRPs) and provides that they "shall be liable" for, among other things, "all costs of removal or remedial action incurred by the United States Government . . . not inconsistent with the national contingency plan." § 107(a)(4)(A). Section 107(a) further provides that PRPs shall be liable for "any other necessary costs of response incurred by any other person consistent with the national contingency plan." § 107(a)(4)(B).

After CERCLA's enactment in 1980, litigation arose over whether § 107, in addition to allowing the Government and certain private parties to recover costs from PRPs, also allowed a PRP that had incurred response costs to recover costs from other PRPs. More specifically, the question was whether a private party that had incurred response costs, but that had done so voluntarily and was not itself subject to suit, had a cause of action for cost recovery against other PRPs. Various courts held that § 107(a)(4)(B) and its predecessors authorized such a cause of action. *See, e.g.*, Wickland Oil Terminals v. Asarco, Inc., 792 F.2d 887, 890–92 (9th Cir. 1986); Walls v. Waste Resource Corp., 761 F.2d 311, 317–18 (6th

Cir. 1985); Philadelphia v. Stepan Chemical Co., 544 F.Supp. 1135, 1140–43 (E.D. Pa. 1982).

After CERCLA's passage, litigation also ensued over the separate question whether a private entity that had been sued in a cost recovery action (by the Government or by another PRP) could obtain contribution from other PRPs. As originally enacted in 1980, CERCLA contained no provision expressly providing for a right of action for contribution. A number of District Courts nonetheless held that, although CERCLA did not mention the word "contribution," such a right arose either impliedly from provisions of the statute, or as a matter of federal common law. *See, e.g.*, United States v. New Castle County, 642 F.Supp. 1258, 1263–69 (Del. 1986) (contribution right arises under federal common law); Colorado v. ASARCO, Inc., 608 F.Supp. 1484, 1486–93 (Colo. 1985) (same); Wehner v. Syntex Agribusiness, Inc., 616 F.Supp. 27, 31 (E.D. Mo. 1985) (contribution right is implied from § 107(e)(2)). That conclusion was debatable in light of two decisions of this Court that refused to recognize implied or common-law rights to contribution in other federal statutes. *See* Texas Industries, Inc. v. Radcliff Materials, Inc., 451 U.S. 630, 638–47 (1981) (refusing to recognize implied or common-law right to contribution in the Sherman Act or the Clayton Act); Northwest Airlines, Inc. v. Transport Workers Union, 451 U.S. 77, 90–99 (1981) (refusing to recognize implied or common-law right to contribution in the Equal Pay Act of 1963 or Title VII of the Civil Rights Act of 1964).

Congress subsequently amended CERCLA in the Superfund Amendments and Reauthorization Act of 1986 (SARA), 100 Stat. 1613, to provide an express cause of action for contribution, codified as CERCLA § 113(f)(1):

> "Any person may seek contribution from any other person who is liable or potentially liable under section 9607(a) of this title, during or following any civil action under section 9606 of this title or under section 9607(a) of this title. Such claims shall be brought in accordance with this section and the Federal Rules of Civil Procedure, and shall be governed by Federal law. In resolving contribution claims, the court may allocate response costs among liable parties using such equitable factors as the court determines are appropriate. Nothing in this subsection shall diminish the right of any person to bring an action for contribution in the absence of a civil action under section 9606 of this title or section 9607 of this title." *Id.*, at 1647, as codified in 42 U.S.C. § 9613(f)(1).

SARA also created a separate express right of contribution, § 113(f)(3)(B), for "[a] person who has resolved its liability to the United States or a State for some or all of a response action or for some or all of the costs of such action in an administrative or judicially approved settlement." In short, after SARA, CERCLA provided for a right to cost recovery in certain circumstances, § 107(a), and separate rights to contribution in other circumstances, §§ 113(f)(1), 113(f)(3)(B).

II

This case concerns four contaminated aircraft engine maintenance sites in Texas. Cooper Industries, Inc., owned and operated those sites until 1981, when it sold them to Aviall Services, Inc. Aviall operated the four sites for a number of years. Ultimately, Aviall discovered that both it and Cooper had contaminated the facilities when petroleum and other hazardous substances leaked into the ground and ground water through underground storage tanks and spills. * * *

Aviall cleaned up the properties under the State's supervision, beginning in 1984. Aviall sold the properties to a third party in 1995 and 1996, but remains contractually responsible for the cleanup. Aviall has incurred approximately $5 million in cleanup costs; the total costs may be even greater. In August 1997, Aviall filed this action against Cooper in the United States District Court for the Northern District of Texas, seeking to recover cleanup costs. The original complaint asserted a claim for cost recovery under CERCLA § 107(a), a separate claim for contribution under CERCLA § 113(f)(1), and state-law claims. Aviall later amended the complaint, combining its two CERCLA claims into a single, joint CERCLA claim. That claim alleged that, pursuant to § 113(f)(1), Aviall was entitled to seek contribution from Cooper, as a PRP under § 107(a), for response costs and other liability Aviall incurred in connection with the Texas facilities. * * *

Both parties moved for summary judgment, and the District Court granted Cooper's motion. The court held that Aviall, having abandoned its § 107 claim, sought contribution only under § 113(f)(1). The court held that § 113(f)(1) relief was unavailable to Aviall because it had not been sued under CERCLA § 106 or § 107.

A divided panel of the Court of Appeals for the Fifth Circuit affirmed. 263 F.3d 134 (2001). The majority, relying principally on the "during or following" language in the first sentence of § 113(f)(1), held that "a PRP seeking contribution from other PRPs under § 113(f)(1) must have a pending or adjudged § 106 administrative order or § 107(a) cost recovery action against it." *Id.*, at 145. The dissent reasoned that the final sentence of § 113(f)(1), the saving clause, clarified that the federal common-law right to contribution survived the enactment of § 113(f)(1), even absent a § 106 or § 107(a) civil action. *Id.*, at 148–150 (opinion of Wiener, J.).

On rehearing en banc, the Fifth Circuit reversed by a divided vote, holding that § 113(f)(1) allows a PRP to obtain contribution from other PRPs regardless of whether the PRP has been sued under § 106 or § 107. 312 F.3d 677 (2002). The court held that "[s]ection 113(f)(1) authorizes suits against PRPs in both its first and last sentence[,] which states without qualification that 'nothing' in the section shall 'diminish' any person's right to bring a contribution action in the absence of a section 106 or section 107(a) action." *Id.*, at 681. The court reasoned in part that "may" in § 113(f)(1) did not mean "may only." *Id.*, at 686–87. Three members of the en banc court dissented for essentially the reasons given by the panel majority. *Id.*, at 691–93 (opinion of Garza, J.). We granted certiorari, * * *, and now reverse.

III

A

Section 113(f)(1) does not authorize Aviall's suit. The first sentence, the enabling clause that establishes the right of contribution, provides: "Any person *may* seek contribution ... *during or following* any civil action under section 9606 of this title or under section 9607(a) of this title," 42 USC § 9613(f)(1) (emphasis added). The natural meaning of this sentence is that contribution may only be sought subject to the specified conditions, namely, "during or following" a specified civil action. * * *

The last sentence of § 113(f)(1), the saving clause, does not change our conclusion. That sentence provides: "Nothing in this subsection shall diminish the right of any person to bring an action for contribution in the absence of a civil action under section 9606 of this title or section 9607 of this title." 42 U.S.C. § 9613(f)(1). The sole function of the sentence is to clarify that § 113(f)(1) does nothing to "diminish" any cause(s) of action for contribution that may exist independently of § 113(f)(1). In other words, the sentence rebuts any presumption that the express right of contribution provided by the enabling clause is the exclusive cause of action for contribution available to a PRP. The sentence, however, does not itself establish a cause of action; nor does it expand § 113(f)(1) to authorize contribution actions not brought "during or following" a § 106 or § 107(a) civil action; nor does it specify what causes of action for contribution, if any, exist outside § 113(f)(1). * * *

Our conclusion follows not simply from § 113(f)(1) itself, but also from the whole of § 113. As noted above, § 113 provides two express avenues for contribution: § 113(f)(1) ("during or following" specified civil actions) and § 113(f)(3)(B) (after an administrative or judicially approved settlement that resolves liability to the United States or a State). Section 113(g)(3) then provides two corresponding 3–year limitations periods for contribution actions, one beginning at the date of judgment, § 113(g)(3)(A), and one beginning at the date of settlement, § 113(g)(3)(B). Notably absent from § 113(g)(3) is any provision for starting the limitations period if a judgment or settlement never occurs, as is the case with a purely voluntary cleanup. The lack of such a provision supports the conclusion that, to assert a contribution claim under § 113(f), a party must satisfy the conditions of either § 113(f)(1) or § 113(f)(3)(B). * * *

* * * Section 113(f)(1), 100 Stat. 1647, authorizes contribution claims only "during or following" a civil action under § 106 or § 107(a), and it is undisputed that Aviall has never been subject to such an action. Aviall therefore has no § 113(f)(1) claim.

B

Aviall and *amicus* Lockheed Martin contend that, in the alternative to an action for contribution under § 113(f)(1), Aviall may recover costs under § 107(a)(4)(B) even though it is a PRP. The dissent would have us so hold. We decline to address the issue. Neither the District Court, nor the Fifth Circuit panel, nor the Fifth Circuit sitting en banc considered Aviall's § 107 claim. * * *

* * * Both the question whether Aviall has waived this claim and the underlying § 107 question (if it is not waived) may depend in part on the relationship between §§ 107 and 113. That relationship is a significant issue in its own right. It is also well beyond the scope of the briefing and, indeed, the question presented, which asks simply whether a private party "may bring an action seeking contribution pursuant to CERCLA Section 113(f)(1)." Pet. for Cert. i. The § 107 claim and the preliminary waiver question merit full consideration by the courts below. * * *

In view of the importance of the § 107 issue and the absence of briefing and decisions by the courts below, we are not prepared—as the dissent would have it—to resolve the § 107 question solely on the basis of dictum in *Key Tronic*. * * *

C

In addition to leaving open whether Aviall may seek cost recovery under § 107, Part III–B, *supra*, we decline to decide whether Aviall has an implied right to contribution under § 107. Portions of the Fifth Circuit's opinion below might be taken to endorse the latter cause of action, 312 F.3d, at 687; others appear to reserve the question whether such a cause of action exists, *id.*, at 685, n. 15. To the extent that Aviall chooses to frame its § 107 claim on remand as an implied right of contribution (as opposed to a right of cost recovery), we note that this Court has visited the subject of implied rights of contribution before. * * *

We hold only that § 113(f)(1) does not support Aviall's suit. We therefore reverse the judgment of the Fifth Circuit and remand the case for further proceedings consistent with this opinion.

It is so ordered.

JUSTICE GINSBURG, with whom JUSTICE STEVENS joins, dissenting.

* * * In my view, the Court unnecessarily defers decision on Aviall's entitlement to recover cleanup costs from Cooper.

In *Key Tronic Corp. v. United States*, * * * all Members of this Court agreed that § 107 of the Comprehensive Environmental Response, Compensation, and Liability Act of 1980 (CERCLA), 42 U.S.C. § 9607, "unquestionably provides a cause of action for [potentially responsible persons (PRPs)] to seek recovery of cleanup costs." The Court rested that determination squarely and solely on § 107(a)(4)(B), which allows any person who has incurred costs for cleaning up a hazardous waste site to recover all or a portion of those costs from any other person liable under CERCLA.

The *Key Tronic* Court divided, however, on the question whether the right to contribution is implicit in § 107(a)'s text, as the majority determined, or whether § 107(a) expressly confers the right, as the dissenters urged. The majority stated: Section 107 "*implies*—but does not expressly *command*—that [a PRP] may have a claim for contribution against those treated as joint tortfeasors." 511 U.S., at 818, and n. 11 (emphasis added). The dissent maintained: "Section 107(a)(4)(B) states, as clearly as can be, that '[c]overed persons ... shall be liable for ... necessary costs of response incurred by any other person.' Surely to say that A shall be liable to B is the express creation of a right of action." *Id.*, at 822. But no Justice expressed the slightest doubt that § 107 indeed did enable a PRP to sue other covered persons for reimbursement, in whole or part, of cleanup costs the PRP legitimately incurred.

In its original complaint, Aviall identified § 107 as the federal-law basis for an independent cost-recovery claim against Cooper, and § 113 as the basis for a contribution claim. * * * In amended pleadings, Aviall alleged both §§ 107 and 113 as the federal underpinning for its contribution claim. * * * Aviall's use of §§ 113 and 107 in tandem to assert a contribution claim conformed its pleading to then-governing Fifth Circuit precedent, which held that a CERCLA contribution action arises through the joint operation of § 107(a) and § 113(f)(1). *See* Geraghty and Miller, Inc. v. Conoco, Inc., 234 F.3d 917, 924 (2000) ("[W]hile section 113(f) is the vehicle for bringing a contribution action, it does not create a new cause of action or create any new liabilities. Rather, it is a mechanism for apportioning costs that are recoverable under section 107." (footnote omitted)). A party obliged by circuit precedent to plead in a certain way can hardly be deemed to have waived a plea the party could have maintained had the law of the Circuit permitted him to do so. * * *

In the Fifth Circuit's view, § 107 supplied the right of action for Aviall's claim, and § 113(f)(1) prescribed the procedural framework. * * *

I see no cause for protracting this litigation by requiring the Fifth Circuit to revisit a determination it has essentially made already: Federal courts, prior to the enactment of § 113(f)(1), had correctly held that PRPs could "recover [under § 107] a proportionate share of their costs in actions for contribution against other PRPs," 312 F.3d, at 687; nothing in § 113 retracts that right, *ibid.* (noting that § 113(f)'s saving clause preserves all preexisting state and federal rights of action for contribution, including the § 107 implied right this Court recognized in *Key Tronic*, 511 U.S., at 816). Accordingly, I would not defer a definitive ruling by this Court on the question whether Aviall may pursue a § 107 claim for relief against Cooper. * * *

NOTES

1. In *U.S. v. Atlantic Research Corp.*, a unanimous Court cleared up the lingering uncertainty created by *Cooper v. Aviall*. The Court held, per Justice Thomas, that § 113(f) does not provide the exclusive remedy for recovering

cleanup costs and that § 107(a)(4)(B) provides a cause of action to any person other than those permitted to sue under § 107(a)(4)(A). Respondent Atlantic Research had cleaned up a government site it leased and contaminated while doing government work, and had sued the government to recover some of its costs under § 107(a). The Court reasoned that § 107(a)(4)(B)'s phrase "other necessary costs" refers to and differentiates the relevant costs from those listed in subparagraph (A). To hold, as the government argued, that "any other person" refers only to a person not identified as a PRP in §§ 107(a)(1)–(4), would destroy the symmetry of subparagraphs (A) and (B), and render subparagraph (B) internally confusing. Because the statute defines PRPs so broadly as to sweep in virtually all persons likely to incur cleanup costs, that interpretation would reduce the number of potential plaintiffs to almost zero, rendering subparagraph (B) a dead letter. This interpretation would not create friction between § 107(a) and § 113(f), said the Court, because their two clearly distinct remedies complement each other: § 113(f)(1) authorizes a contribution action to PRPs with common liability stemming from an action instituted under § 106 or § 107(a), while § 107(a) permits cost recovery (as distinct from contribution) by a private party that has itself incurred cleanup costs.

2.   In addition to the threshold issue decided in *Aviall*, other questions remain about the operation of section 113(f). For example, what factors may be taken into account in contribution suits—the Gore factors alone? What is the plaintiff's burden of proof—is it the same as the government's burden in a section 107 cost recovery action? And what sort of liability can courts impose on parties to contribution suits? In *Environmental Transportation Systems, Inc. v. ENSCO, Inc.,* 969 F.2d 503 (7th Cir. 1992), defendant Northern States Power Co. had generated PCB-contaminated waste and hired defendant ENSCO to arrange for disposal. ENSCO hired plaintiff Environmental Transportation Systems (ETS) to transport the waste to a disposal facility. En route, the ETS truck overturned because it was driven at an excessive speed while the driver attempted to negotiate a highway access ramp. ETS paid for the cost of cleanup of the spill and sought contribution from ENSCO and Northern States under section 113(f) of CERCLA. Defendants moved for summary judgment. After concluding that ETS was responsible for all costs of cleanup because the accident was entirely ETS's fault, the district court granted defendants' motion. The district court held that, although ENSCO and Northern States would have been liable if sued under section 107, such liability does not necessarily lead to mandatory contribution for cleanup costs. The court of appeals affirmed the judgment of the district court, on the ground that Congress' intent in enacting section 113(f) was that the court should "equitably allocate costs of cleanup according to the relative culpability of the parties rather than an automatic equal shares rule." The court of appeals specifically mentioned that the legislative history of section 113(f) cites the *A & F Materials* criteria (the "Gore factors"), *supra*, as factors that a court may consider in deciding whether to grant apportionment in a contribution action.

In *Control Data Corp. v. S.C.S.C. Corp.,* 53 F.3d 930 (8th Cir. 1995), plaintiff sought contribution under section 113(f) after having cleaned up contamination caused by both plaintiff and defendant. Citing the "Gore factors," the court allocated one-third of the total cleanup costs to defendant because the chemical released by it—constituting only ten percent of the total contamination by volume—was much more toxic and difficult to remove than was the chemical released by plaintiff.

3. Several cases have held that a defendant's potential liability under section 107(a) does not preclude a zero allocation of response costs to that defendant in a contribution suit under section 113(f). Thus, in *Kalamazoo River Study Group v. Rockwell International Corp.*, 274 F.3d 1043 (6th Cir. 2001), where the trial court found that defendant had released less than 20 pounds of PCBs into the river (in contrast to the hundreds of thousands of pounds released by plaintiffs), the appellate court affirmed the lower court's decision, made after a full trial, not to allocate any response costs to defendant. The court of appeals said that "a defendant's release of what, standing alone, would be a significant amount of such material might have no impact on the total cost of cleaning up a contaminated site." For further discussion of zero allocations of response costs, and additional citations, *see* Douglas McWilliams, *District Courts Can Inject Some Fairness Into CERCLA Liability Scheme*, 33 Env't Rep. 663 (2002).

A few cases have considered specifically plaintiff's burden of proof in a contribution suit. In *Acushnet Co. v. Coaters, Inc.*, 937 F.Supp. 988 (D. Mass. 1996), the court granted a defendant's motion for summary judgment because plaintiff failed to prove that defendant's wastes had caused the incurrence of any response costs. In a later decision in the same case, 948 F.Supp. 128, 134–38 (1996), the court established a "threshold-of-significance standard," stating that "plaintiffs must proffer sufficient evidence as to a particular defendant to satisfy a minimum standard of significance of that defendant's responsibility as a source of one or more hazardous substances deposited at the site." However, the appellate court, though affirming the trial court's summary judgment for defendant, rejected the lower court's rationale:

> As we understand it, the district court ruled principally that the defendants deposited so little waste at the site that it could not reasonably be said that they caused plaintiffs to incur response costs. To the extent that the court's ruling may be interpreted to incorporate into CERCLA a causation standard that would require a polluter's waste to meet a minimum quantitative threshold, we disagree. Nevertheless, we conclude that the record was insufficient to permit a meaningful equitable allocation of remediation costs against any of the defendants under [section 113(f)].

Acushnet Co. v. Mohasco Corp., 191 F.3d 69, 72 (1st Cir. 1999).

One view of the appropriate standard in such a case is that the defendant in a contribution action ought to be entitled to summary judgment if it can demonstrate that, on the undisputed facts, (i) defendant is not liable under section 107(a) or is entitled to a defense under section 107(b), or (ii) it would not be equitable to require defendant to reimburse plaintiff for a portion of plaintiff's response costs. John Hyson, *The Plaintiff's Burden in CERCLA Contribution Actions: Unscrambling the First Circuit's Acushnet Decision*, 31 Envtl. L. Rep. 10180 (2001). For example, under (ii), even if defendant were shown to have been responsible for a small amount of hazardous substances which may have caused a small amount of plaintiff's response costs, a court might find that it would be inequitable to deny defendant summary judgment if it appeared that the public and private costs of conducting a full allocation hearing would exceed the amount of any likely reimbursement order.

In *New Jersey Turnpike Authority v. PPG Industries, Inc.*, 197 F.3d 96 (3d Cir. 1999), the court refused to apply a theory that would shift the burden of proof to defendants in a contribution suit. Relying on *Sindell v. Abbott Laboratories*, 26 Cal.3d 588, 607 P.2d 924 (1980), plaintiff argued that defendant chromium processors should bear the burden of proving that their wastes did not contaminate the New Jersey Turnpike. Contractors which built the highway had used chromate ore processing residue as fill material but maintained no records concerning the sources of the material. Defendants were the only chromium ore processors in New Jersey.

Discussion Problem #3 on CERCLA Liability

Consider the hypothetical case discussed in William Araiza, *Text, Purpose and Facts: The Relationship Between CERCLA Sections 107 and 113*, 72 NOTRE DAME L. REV. 193 (1996). The EPA determines that GM sent large quantities of waste oil, paint, and solvents to a now abandoned landfill. EPA negotiates a consent decree in which GM, while denying that it is liable under CERCLA, nevertheless agrees to undertake a multi-million dollar cleanup. GM then discovers that Ford and Chrysler disposed of similar materials at the site. GM also discovers that significant contamination was caused by Eastern Airlines, Smith–Corona and Studebaker, all of which subsequently have gone bankrupt, as well as by several other corporations that cannot be identified. GM sues Ford and Chrysler under CERCLA, seeking 100 percent reimbursement of the cleanup costs incurred by GM.

A claim by one PRP against other PRPs can involve three complex and often interrelated issues:

1. May one PRP, as suggested by the district court in the *ENSCO* case and briefly discussed but not decided by the *Aviall* Court, *supra*, seek reimbursement from other PRPs by suing them under section 107 rather than under § 113(f)? Section 107 is more favorable in several respects, including the statute of limitations.

2. In a suit under § 113(f) is the court authorized to find defendants both jointly and severally liable (as under § 107), or only severally liable for their specific shares of the total cleanup costs?

3. May courts under § 113(f) allocate "orphan shares" of CERCLA response costs among the PRP defendants, or is the liability of each such defendant limited to the proportion of the cleanup costs attributable to its own releases?

With respect to issue #1, most courts of appeals that have confronted the issue have concluded that a § 107 action for recovery of costs may be brought only by *innocent* parties that have undertaken cleanups. Generally, therefore, an action by a PRP must be a § 113 action for contribution (though bear in mind, of course, that, per the Court's holding in *Aviall*, a PRP bringing a section 113 action must be the subject of a suit under section 106 or 107). *See* Axel Johnson, Inc. v. Carroll Carolina Oil Co., 191 F.3d 409 (4th Cir. 1999); Centerior Serv. Co. v. Acme Scrap Iron & Metal Corp., 153 F.3d 344 (6th Cir. 1998) (leaving open the question whether volunteers and innocent parties could sue for joint and several cost recovery under § 107); Pinal Creek Group v. Newmont Mining Corp., 118 F.3d 1298 (9th Cir. 1997); Rumpke of Ind., Inc. v. Cummins Engine Co., 107 F.3d 1235 (7th Cir. 1997); Akzo Coatings, Inc. v. Aigner Corp., 30 F.3d 761 (7th Cir. 1994). However, under the so-called *Akzo* exception, a landowner that is technically a PRP may bring a § 107 action to recover for its direct injuries "if the party seeking relief is itself not responsible for having caused any of the hazardous materials to be spilled onto the property."

In *Rumpke*, plaintiff's suit was based on both the cost recovery theory of § 107(a) and the contribution theory of § 113(f). The court stated:

> The question is whether our *Akzo* exception applies to Rumpke: may a landowner PRP bring a direct liability suit for cost recovery under § 107(a) against other PRPs (in this case "arrangers"), if it contributed nothing to the hazardous conditions at the site; or is the *Akzo* exception available only to a narrower group of parties, such as the landowner who discovers someone surreptitiously dumping wastes on its land?

The court concluded, "If one were to read § 107(a) as implicitly denying standing to sue even to landowners like Rumpke who did not create the hazardous conditions, this would come perilously close to reading § 107(a) itself out of the statute." On the other hand, "If it turns out that Rumpke is not the innocent party it portrays itself to be, then Rumpke will not qualify for the *Akzo* exception. It would still be entitled to seek contribution for its expenses from the other PRPs" under § 113(f).

Morrison Enterprises v. McShares, Inc., 302 F.3d 1127 (10th Cir. 2002), flatly rejected the *Akzo* position that an "innocent" owner of a contaminated site who did not qualify for any of the express defenses to liability in § 107(b) should be permitted to pursue recovery under § 107(a). In *Morrison*, the spill by defendant, while delivering a chemical at plaintiff's property, occurred "in connection with a contractual relationship" between the parties, so that "[a]s a matter of law, [plaintiff] does not qualify for the third party defense under" § 107(b)(3).

Of course, in the aftermath of *Aviall*, the above question and decisions are much more important, since, as noted by Aronovsky, *supra*, the denial of recovery under section 107(a) by PRPs could result in the absence of any CERCLA cost recovery remedy whatsoever for some, if not most PRPs (since most PRPs neither have been sued under sections 106 or 107(a) nor qualify for the *Akzo* exception). *Dico, Inc. v. Chevron Chemical Co.*, 340 F.3d 525 (8th Cir. 2003), provides a good discussion of case law of the various circuits on this issue.

With respect to issue #2, contribution liability under CERCLA usually is held to be several, rather than joint and several. *Pinal Creek, supra*, is an example. Thus, a party suing in contribution may only be able to shift to the contribution defendant the share of the joint liability (under § 107) fairly allocable to that defendant. Professor Araiza proposes that courts employ their equitable apportionment powers under § 113 to impose a modified joint and several liability regime, under which the liability of defendants could be joint and several if equitable factors called for such a result. *Browning–Ferris Industries of Illinois, Inc. v. Ter Maat*, 195 F.3d 953 (7th Cir. 1999), held that liability in a contribution suit may be joint rather than only several, it being "up to the district judge, guided only by equitable considerations." *See also* Western Props. Serv. Corp. v. Shell Oil Co., 358 F.3d 678 (9th Cir. 2004) (discussing the issue of joint and several liability, as applied to section 113(f) claims).

Issue #3 can be closely related to issue #2. In Araiza's hypothetical, an urgent question is who must pay for the "orphan shares" of the bankrupt and unidentified contributors to the hazardous waste site. If GM is indeed innocent, as it claims, should it nevertheless—rather than Ford and Chrysler—have to pay for the orphan shares? Suppose that Ford and Chrysler acknowledge that each is responsible for twenty percent of the contamination or cleanup costs. If Ford and Chrysler are jointly as well as severally liable, they would be responsible for the orphan shares. Even without joint liability, a court may have the authority to allocate to Ford and Chrysler, perhaps along with GM, at least some of part of the orphan shares. If not, GM, an allegedly innocent party, would be stuck with all of the orphan shares. The Ninth Circuit, in *Pinal Creek, supra*, said, "Under § 113(f)(1), the cost of orphan shares is distributed equitably among all PRPs, just as cleanup costs are." On these matters, in addition to the Araiza article, *see* Robert Redemann & Michael Smith, *The Evolution of PRP Standing under the Comprehensive Environmental Response, Compensation, and Liability Act of 1980*, 21 WM. & MARY ENVTL. L. & POL'Y REV. 300 (1997); William Evans, *The Phantom PRP in CERCLA Contribution Litigation: EPA to the Rescue?*, 26 ENV'T REP. 2109 (1996).

(iii) Settlements

Section 122 (a) * * * The President, in his discretion, may enter into an agreement with any person (including the owner or operator of the facility from which a release or substantial threat of release emanates, or any other potentially responsible person), to perform any response action (including any action described in section 104(b) if the President determines that such action will be done properly by such person. Whenever practicable and in the public interest, as determined by the President, the President shall act to facilitate agreements under this section that are in the public interest and consistent with the National Contingency Plan in order to expedite effective remedial actions and minimize litigation. * * *

(d) Enforcement.

(A) * * * Whenever the President enters into an agreement under this section with any potentially responsible party with respect to remedial action under section 106, following approval of the agreement by the Attorney General, except as otherwise provided in the case of certain administrative settlements referred to in subsection (g), the agreement shall be entered in the appropriate United States district court as a consent decree. The President need not make any finding regarding an imminent and substantial endangerment to the public health or the environment in connection with any such agreement or consent decree. * * *

(g) De minimis settlements.

(1) * * * Whenever practicable and in the public interest, as determined by the President, the President shall as promptly as possible reach a final settlement with a potentially responsible party in an administrative or civil action under section 106 or 107 if such settlement involves only a minor portion of the response costs at the facility concerned and, in the judgment of the President, the conditions in either of the following subparagraph (A) or (B) are met:

(A) Both of the following are minimal in comparison to other hazardous substances at the facility:

(i) The amount of the hazardous substances contributed by that party to the facility.

(ii) The toxic or other hazardous effects of the substances contributed by that party to the facility.

(B) The potentially responsible party—

(i) is the owner of the real property on or in which the facility is located;

(ii) did not conduct or permit the generation, transportation, storage, treatment, or disposal of any hazardous substance at the facility; and

(iii) did not contribute to the release or threat of release of a hazardous substance at the facility through any action or omission.

This subparagraph (B) does not apply if the potentially responsible party purchased the real property with actual or constructive knowledge that the property was used for the generation, transportation, storage, treatment, or disposal of any hazardous substance.

(2) Covenant not to sue. The President may provide a covenant not to sue with respect to the facility concerned to any party who has entered into a settlement under this subsection unless such a covenant would be inconsistent with the public interest as determined under subsection (f). * * *

(5) Effect of agreement. A party who has resolved its liability to the United States under this subsection shall not be liable for

claims for contribution regarding matters addressed in the settlement. Such settlement does not discharge any of the other potentially responsible parties unless its terms so provide, but it reduces the potential liability of the others by the amount of the settlement.

U.S.C. § 9622 (2000).

Among the tools authorized by section 122 to facilitate cost allocations, reduce transaction costs, and otherwise promote settlements, are (1) de minimis settlements—expedited settlements for small-volume waste contributors; (2) nonbinding preliminary allocations of responsibility ("NBARs") for cleanup costs—developed by EPA for PRPs; (3) mixed-funding agreements to share cleanup costs—permitting use of a combination of federal, state, and PRP funds; (4) covenants not to sue—protecting PRPs who settle from future liability to the United States related to the hazardous substance release addressed by a remedial action; and (5) alternative dispute resolution—the use of neutral third parties to help resolve liability and cost-allocation problems.

Section 122(g), concerning de minimis settlements, was amended in 2002 by the Small Business Liability Relief and Brownfields Revitalization Act. New subsection (7) provides for conditional expedited settlements between the United States and de minimis PRPs who demonstrate an "inability or a limited ability to pay response costs." In determining ability to pay, EPA shall consider whether the PRP can "pay response costs and still maintain its basic business operations."

Settling has significant benefits. In addition to securing some relative certainty about liability to the government, settlement also provides the benefit of immunity from contribution for matters "addressed in the settlement." The relevant provision is below:

> § 113(f)(2) A person who has resolved its liability to the United States or a State in an administrative or judicially approved settlement shall not be liable for claims for contribution regarding matters addressed in the settlement. Such settlement does not discharge any of the other potentially liable persons unless its terms so provide, but it reduces the potential liability of the others by the amount of the settlement.

Note that the last part of section 113(f)(2) ensures that the government cannot "double dip" by recovering from more than one party for the same costs.

The following case illustrates EPA's management of the settlement process. The court considered objections to a proposed consent decree made by seven non-settling PRP defendants. The objectors, who feared that they would be left with a disproportionate share of the total liability for cleanup costs, were seeking to protect their rights of contribution against the settling defendants. Note the court's deferential posture to the agency. Thinking back to the administrative law principles in Chapter 5, consider why, in this instance, a court might be so deferential.

UNITED STATES v. CANNONS ENGINEERING CORP.

United States Court of Appeals for the First Circuit, 1990.
899 F.2d 79.

SELYA, CIRCUIT JUDGE.

Superfund sites are those which require priority remedial attention because of the presence, or suspected presence, of a dangerous accumulation of hazardous wastes. Expenditures to clean up such sites are specially authorized pursuant to [CERCLA § 111]. After the federal government, through the United States Environmental Protection Agency (EPA), identified four such sites in Bridgewater, Massachusetts, Plymouth, Massachusetts, Londonderry, New Hampshire, and Nashua, New Hampshire (collectively, the Sites), the EPA undertook an intensive investigation to locate potentially responsible parties (PRPs). In the course of this investigation, the agency created a de minimis classification (DMC), putting in this category persons or firms whose discerned contribution to pollution of the Sites was minimal both in the amount and toxicity of the hazardous wastes involved. The agency staked out the DMC on the basis of volumetric shares, grouping within it entities identifiable as generators of less than one percent of the waste sent to the Sites. To arrive at a PRP's volumetric share, the agency, using estimates, constituted a ratio between the volume of wastes that the PRP sent to the Sites and the total amount of wastes sent there.

The EPA sent notices of possible liability to some 671 PRPs, including generators and nongenerators. Administrative settlements were thereafter achieved with 300 generators (all de minimis PRPs). In short order, the United States and the two host states, Massachusetts and New Hampshire, brought suits in the United States District Court for the District of Massachusetts against 84 of the PRPs who had rejected, or were ineligible for, the administrative settlement. The suits sought recovery of previously incurred cleanup costs and declarations of liability for future remediation under [CERCLA]. The actions were consolidated.

With its complaint, the United States filed two proposed consent decrees. The first (the MP decree) embodied a contemplated settlement with 47 major PRPs, that is, responsible parties who were ineligible for membership in the DMC. This assemblage included certain generators whose volumetric shares exceeded the 1% cutoff point and certain nongenerators (like the owners of the Sites and hazardous waste transporters). The second consent decree (the DMC decree) embodied a contemplated settlement with 12 de minimis PRPs who had eschewed participation in the administrative settlement. As required by statute, notice of the decrees' proposed entry was published in the Federal Register. No comments were received.

The government thereupon moved to enter the decrees. Seven non-settling defendants [de minimis PRPs] objected. After considering written submissions and hearing arguments of counsel, the district court approved both consent decrees and dismissed all cross-claims against the settling defendants. The court proceeded to certify the decrees as final under Fed.R.Civ.P. 54(b). These appeals followed.

I

We approach our task mindful that, on appeal, a district court's approval of a consent decree in CERCLA litigation is encased in a double layer of swaddling. In the first place, it is the policy of the law to encourage settlements. That policy has particular force where, as here, a government actor committed to the protection of the public interest has pulled the laboring oar in constructing the proposed settlement. While "the true measure of the deference due depends on the persuasive power of the agency's proposal and rationale, given whatever practical considerations may impinge and the full panoply of the attendant circumstances," the district court must refrain from second-guessing the Executive Branch.

Respect for the agency's role is heightened in a situation where the cards have been dealt face up and a crew of sophisticated players, with sharply conflicting interests, sit at the table. That so many affected parties, themselves knowledgeable and represented by experienced lawyers, have hammered out an agreement at arm's length and advocate its embodiment in a judicial decree, itself deserves weight in the ensuing balance. The relevant standard, after all, is not whether the settlement is one which the court itself might have fashioned, or considers as ideal, but whether the proposed decree is fair, reasonable, and faithful to the objectives of the governing statute. * * *

The second layer of swaddling derives from the nature of appellate review. Because approval of a consent decree is committed to the trial court's informed discretion, the court of appeals should be reluctant to disturb a reasoned exercise of that discretion. In this context, the test for abuse of discretion is itself a fairly deferential one. * * *

II

* * *

Originally, the EPA extended an open offer to all de minimis PRPs, including five of the six appellants,[25] proposing an administrative settlement based on 160% of each PRP's volumetric share of the total projected response cost, that is, the price of remedial actions, past and anticipated. The settlement figure included a 60% premium to cover unexpected costs and/or unforeseen conditions. Settling PRPs paid their shares in cash and

---

25. Crown was ineligible to receive the initial offer because of its failure to respond to information requests.

were released outright from all liability. They were also exempted from suits for contribution.

Following consummation of the administrative settlement, plaintiffs entered into negotiations with the remaining PRPs. These negotiations resulted in the proposed MP decree (accepted by 47 "major" defendants) and the DMC decree. The latter was modelled upon the administrative settlement, but featured an increased premium: rather than allowing de minimis PRPs to cash out at a 160% level, an eligible generator could resolve its liability only by agreeing to pay 260% of its volumetric share of the total projected response cost. The EPA justified the incremental 100% premium as being in the nature of delay damages. * * *

III

* * *

Our starting point is well defined. [SARA] authorized a variety of types of settlements which the EPA may utilize in CERCLA actions, including consent decrees providing for PRPs to contribute to cleanup costs and/or to undertake response activities themselves. SARA's legislative history makes pellucid that, when such consent decrees are forged, the trial court's review function is only to "satisfy itself that the settlement is reasonable, fair, and consistent with the purposes that CERCLA is intended to serve." Reasonableness, fairness, and fidelity to the statute are, therefore, the horses which district judges must ride. * * *

A. Procedural Fairness.

We agree with the district court that fairness in the CERCLA settlement context has both procedural and substantive components. To measure procedural fairness, a court should ordinarily look to the negotiation process and attempt to gauge its candor, openness, and bargaining balance.

In this instance, the district court found the proposed decrees to possess the requisite procedural integrity, and appellants have produced no persuasive reason to alter this finding.

* * * But their flagship argument—that the procedural integrity of the settlement was ruptured because appellants were neither allowed to join the MP decree nor informed in advance that they would be excluded—requires comment.

Appellants claim that they were relatively close to the 1% cutoff point, and were thus arbitrarily excluded from the major party settlement, avails them naught. Congress intended to give the EPA broad discretion to structure classes of PRPs for settlement purposes. We cannot say that the government acted beyond the scope of that discretion in separating minor and major players in this instance, that is, in determining that generators who had sent less than 1% of the volume of hazardous waste to the Sites would comprise the DMC and those generators who were responsible for a greater percentage would be treated as major PRPs. While the dividing line was only one of many which the agency could have selected, it was well within the universe of plausibility. * * *

Nor can we say that appellants were entitled to more advance warning of the EPA's negotiating strategy than they received. At the time de minimis PRPs were initially invited to participate in the administrative settlement, the EPA, by letter, informed all of them, including appellants, that:

The government is anxious to achieve a high degree of participation in this *de minimis* settlement. Accordingly, the terms contained in this settlement offer are the most favorable terms that the government intends to make available to parties eligible for *de minimis* settlement in this case.

Appellants knew, early on, that they were within the DMC and could spurn the EPA's proposal only at the risk of paying more at a later time. Although appellants may have assumed that they could ride on the coattails of the major parties and join whatever MP decree emerged—the government had, on other occasions, allowed such cafeteria-style settlements—the agency was neither asked for, nor did it give, any such assurance in this instance. * * *

B. Substantive Fairness.

Substantive fairness introduces into the equation concepts of corrective justice and accountability: a party should bear the cost of the harm for which it is legally responsible. *See generally Developments in the Law—Toxic Waste Litigation*, 99 HARV. L. REV. 1458, 1477 (1986). The logic behind these concepts dictates that settlement terms must be based upon, and roughly correlated with, some acceptable measure of comparative fault, apportioning liability among the settling parties according to rational (if necessarily imprecise) estimates of how much harm each PRP has done.

Even accepting substantive fairness as linked to comparative fault, an important issue still remains as to how comparative fault is to be measured. There is no universally correct approach. It appears very clear to us that what constitutes the best measure of comparative fault at a particular Superfund site under particular factual circumstances should be left largely to the EPA's expertise. Whatever formula or scheme EPA advances for measuring comparative fault and allocating liability should be upheld so long as the agency supplies a plausible explanation for it, welding some reasonable linkage between the factors it includes in its formula or scheme and the proportionate shares of the settling PRPs. Put in slightly different terms, the chosen measure of comparative fault should be upheld unless it is arbitrary, capricious, and devoid of a rational basis.

Not only must the EPA be given leeway to construct the barometer of comparative fault, but the agency must also be accorded flexibility to diverge from an apportionment formula in order to address special factors not conducive to regimented treatment. While the list of possible variables is virtually limitless, two frequently encountered reasons warranting departure from strict formulaic comparability are the uncertainty of future events and the timing of particular settlement decisions. Common sense suggests that a PRP's assumption of open-ended risks may merit a discount on comparative fault, while obtaining a complete release from uncertain future liability may call for a premium. By the same token, the need to encourage (and suitably reward) early, cost-effective settlements, and to account *inter alia* for anticipated savings in transaction costs inuring from celeritous settlement, can affect the construct. Because we are confident that Congress intended EPA to have considerable flexibility in negotiating and structuring settlements, we think reviewing courts should permit the agency to depart from rigid adherence to formulae wherever the agency proffers a reasonable good-faith justification for departure.

We also believe that a district court should give the EPA's expertise the benefit of the doubt when weighing substantive fairness—particularly when the agency, and hence the court, has been confronted by ambiguous, incomplete, or inscrutable information. * * *

In this instance, we agree with the court below that the consent decrees pass muster from a standpoint of substantive fairness. They adhere generally to principles of comparative fault according to a volumetric standard, determining the liability of each PRP according to volumetric contribution. And, to the extent they deviate from this formulaic approach, they do so on the basis of adequate justification. In particular, the premiums charged to de minimis PRPs in the administrative settlement, and the increased premium charged in the DMC decree, seem well warranted.

The argument that the EPA should have used relative toxicity as a determinant of proportionate liability for response costs, instead of a strictly volumetric ranking, is a stalking horse. Having selected a reasonable method of weighing comparative fault, the agency need not show that it is the best, or even the fairest, of all conceivable methods. The choice of the yardstick to be used for allocating liability must be left primarily to the expert discretion of the EPA, particularly when the PRPs involved are numerous and the situation is complex. We cannot reverse the court below for refusing to second-guess the agency on this score. * * *

The last point which merits discussion under this rubric involves the fact that the agency upped the ante as the game continued, that is, the premium assessed as part of the administrative settlement was increased substantially for purposes of the later DMC decree. Like the district court, we see no unfairness in this approach. For one thing, litigation is expensive—and having called the tune by their refusal to subscribe to the administrative settlement, we think it not unfair that appellants, thereafter, would have to pay the piper. For another thing, rewarding PRPs who settle sooner rather than later is completely consonant with CERCLA's makeup. * * *

D. *Fidelity to the Statute.*

* * *

We have recently described the two major policy concerns underlying CERCLA:

> First, Congress intended that the federal government be immediately given the tools necessary for a prompt and effective response to the problems of national magnitude resulting from hazardous waste disposal. Second, Congress intended that those responsible for problems caused by the disposal of chemical poisons bear the costs and responsibility for remedying the harmful conditions they created.

The district court thought that these concerns were addressed, and assuaged, by the proposed settlements. So do we. * * *

In the SARA Amendments, Congress explicitly created a statutory framework that left nonsettlors at risk of bearing a disproportionate amount of liability. The statute immunizes settling parties from liability for contribution and provides that only the amount of the settlement—not the pro rata share attributable to the settling party—shall be subtracted from the liability of the nonsettlors. This can prove to be a substantial benefit to settling PRPs—and a corresponding detriment to their more recalcitrant counterparts.

Although such immunity creates a palpable risk of disproportionate liability, that is not to say that the device is forbidden. To the exact contrary, Congress has made its will explicit and the courts must defer. Disproportionate liability, a technique which promotes early settlements and deters litigation for litigation's sake, is an integral part of the statutory plan. * * *

The CERCLA statutes do not require the agency to open all settlement offers to all PRPs; and we refuse to insert such a requirement into the law by judicial fiat. Under the SARA Amendments, the right to draw fine lines, and to structure the order and pace of settlement negotiations to suit, is an agency prerogative. After all, "divide and conquer" has been a recognized negotiating tactic since the days of the Roman Empire, and in the absence of a congressional directive, we cannot deny the EPA use of so conventional a tool. So long as it operates in good faith, the EPA is at liberty to negotiate and settle with whomever it chooses. * * *

NOTES

1. As mentioned in the text preceding *Cannons,* section 113(f)(2) provides that a settling PRP shall not be liable for claims for contribution "regarding matters addressed in the settlement." The meaning of this phrase was at issue in *Akzo Coatings, Inc. v. Aigner Corp.,* 30 F.3d 761 (7th Cir. 1994). In response to a section 106 administrative order by EPA, Akzo conducted certain "emergency removal activities" at the "Two–Line Road" facility, incurring costs of more than $1.2 million. Meanwhile, more than 200

other PRPs (including Aigner, but not Akzo) entered into a court-approved settlement with EPA concerning subsequent "remedial" activities to be performed by the settlors at the "Fisher–Calo site," of which the Two–Line Road facility was a part. Akzo then brought suit against Aigner, seeking contribution under section 113(f)(1) for the initial cleanup work which Akzo had performed at the behest of EPA as well as voluntary costs incurred in studying the long-term cleanup of the site with other PRPs. The trial court gave summary judgment for Aigner, finding that Akzo sought contribution for a "matter addressed" in the consent decree. In a split decision the Seventh Circuit reversed because Akzo's work "stands apart in kind, context, and time from the work envisioned by the consent decree." Akzo had engaged in "removal" work, while the settlement provided for the kind of "remedial" work needed to accomplish a complete cleanup of the site. The majority of the court perceived "no unfairness to Aigner" because Akzo's work was "over and done with by the time Aigner signed the consent decree." Thus, acknowledging a right to contribution did "not subject a settling PRP like Aigner to open-ended liability for contribution claims based on future, unanticipated remedial work." In a vigorous dissent, Judge Easterbrook said that the majority "plucks some language ["equitable factors"] from section 113(f)(1) and uses this language as a warrant to disregard the scope of the settlement." Judge Easterbrook expressed concern that the "[r]isk that in the name of equity a court will disregard the actual language of the parties' [settlement] bargain will lead potentially responsible parties to fight harder to avoid liability (and to pay less in settlements, reserving the residue to meet contribution claims), undermining the function of section 113(f)(2)."

The government and settling parties frequently enter into consent decrees that explicitly define the "matters addressed" therein in such a way as to attempt to bar all third-party contribution claims, even for voluntary private party cleanups not addressed in the decrees. James Brusslan, *Truth In Superfund Settlements: The Courts Strike Back on "Matters Addressed" Contribution Protection*, 27 ENV'T REP. 2522 (1997). For discussion of practical aspects of representing PRPs in the negotiation of CERCLA settlement agreements, *see* Peter E. Hapke & Andrew N. Davis, *Negotiating EPA Consent Orders and Consent Decrees: Steering Your Client Through the Shoals*, 24 ENVTL. L. REP. 10116 (1994).

2.   In *Dravo Corp. v. Zuber*, 13 F.3d 1222 (8th Cir. 1994), a contribution suit, defendant PRPs had entered into a de minimis settlement agreement with EPA under CERCLA section 122(g). Paragraph (5) of that subsection provides that a party who "has resolved its liability to the United States under this subsection" shall not be liable for claims of contribution regarding matters addressed in the settlement. Plaintiff, which had incurred response costs, contended that defendants were not protected from contribution claims until after they fulfilled the obligations which they assumed by entering into the settlement agreement. The court held against plaintiffs on this contention. In the court's words, "[b]ecause Congress clearly * * * expressed its desire to minimize litigation by granting de minimis PRPs protection from contribution actions as soon as possible, and because this agreement expressly incorporates that mandate," defendants "are protected from contribution actions upon signing the agreement and will be protected so long as they

comply with the agreement." Further, since section 122(a) says that "a decision of the President to use or not use the procedures in this section is not subject to judicial review," the court denied plaintiff's requests for discovery by which plaintiff wanted to determine whether—contrary to the EPA's conclusion—defendants had contributed to contamination of the site in more than a de minimis way. Because the settlement agreement was embodied in an administrative order under section 122(g)(4), rather than being entered as a consent decree, plaintiff's sole opportunity to block the de minimis agreement had been by filing comments with the EPA under section 122(i)(2) within 30 days after notice of the proposed settlement was published in the Federal Register.

3. Another important aspect of EPA settlement policy is the use of "supplemental environmental projects" (SEPs) as elements of some settlement agreements. A SEP is an "environmentally beneficial project" undertaken voluntarily in settlement of an enforcement action, in exchange for a decrease in the amount of the penalty. Approved SEPs have included environmental assessments and compliance audits as well as waste minimization and pollution prevention measures. *See also* William Thomas et al., *Using Auditing, Pollution Prevention, and Management Systems to Craft Superior Environmental Enforcement Solutions*, 30 ENVTL. L. REP. 10299, 10304–08 (2000).

EPA set forth the "Policy on the Use of Supplemental Environmental Projects in EPA Settlements" initially in 1991, and updated the policy effective May 1, 1998. The 1998 SEP policy requires that there be a nexus, or relationship, between the violation and the project. *See* Memorandum from Steven A. Herman, Assistant Administrator, to Regional Administrators (Apr. 10, 1998). In 2002, EPA reiterated the constraints of the 1998 policy (e.g., consistency with the statutory provisions, adequate nexus with the objectives of the environmental statutes) in order to ensure compliance by parties undertaking the SEPs. EPA was careful to note that the "constraints are intended to ensure compliance with statutory requirements and cannot be waived by Agency officials." On June 11, 2003, EPA issued a memorandum noting that it hoped to expand the use of SEPs in the settlement of enforcement action. As the expansion must still be constrained by the statutory nexus requirement, EPA announced plans to simplify its policy guidance and to initiate public dialogue. Subsequently, EPA has issued several new guidance documents for different areas of SEPs, including community involvement, the use of third parties, and green building. *See* Memorandum from Sylvia K. Lowrance, Acting Assistant Administrator, to Regional Administrators (Mar. 2, 2002); Memorandum from John Peter Suarez, Assistant Administrator, to Administrators and Enforcement Staff (Jun. 11, 2003). For EPA's current documents and policies, *see* EPA, SEPs Policy and Guidance, http://cfpub.epa.gov/compliance/resources/policies/civil/seps/ (last visited Feb. 11, 2006).

4. In the *Cannons* case, the objectors to the consent decrees were "nonsettling [PRP] defendants." That is, they were named defendants in the cost recovery action brought by the United States. However, if they had not been named as defendants, as PRPs they still would have had an interest in the outcome of the settlement because of (a) its effect on the amount of their

liability for the remaining cleanup costs and (b) the statutory restriction on their right of contribution against other settling PRPs.

United States v. Union Electric Co., 64 F.3d 1152 (8th Cir. 1995), raised the procedural question whether non-settling, non-defendant PRPs should be allowed to intervene, in an action by the United States against other PRPs, to oppose a consent decree that the government had reached with settling PRPs. The court held that because CERCLA protects settling PRPs from contribution claims of non-settling PRPs, the latter have a legally protectable interest sufficient to support their intervention of right, under section 113(i), to challenge the consent decree. Section 113(i) provides that in any action commenced under CERCLA in a federal court, "any person may intervene as a matter of right when such person claims an interest relating to the subject of the action and is so situated that the disposition of the action may, as a practical matter, impair or impede the person's ability to protect that interest."

A subsequent decision in the same case, *United States v. Union Electric Co.*, 132 F.3d 422 (8th Cir. 1997), held that the non-settling intervenor-PRPs would not be bound by a cost-allocation formula set forth in the consent decree and therefore could not block approval of the decree by objecting to the formula. The formula apportioned the liability of settling PRPs who had sent transformer oil to the site, on the basis of the volume of oil sent, unless a PRP could prove its oil could not have contained more than two parts per billion PCBs.

h.   Site Remediation, Brownfields, and the Superfund

(i) Site Remediation

Although we have focused thus far on the liability provisions of the statute, CERCLA also establishes a set of rules that govern the cleanup of hazardous waste sites. The remediation process can be lengthy and expensive, consuming many years and hundreds of millions of dollars.

Section 105 of CERCLA establishes the basic process by which the EPA ranks and then lists sites on the "National Priorities List."[26] The

---

26. The original NPL listed 406 sites. *See* Amendment to National Oil and Hazardous Substance Contingency Plan; National Priorities List, 48 Fed. Reg. 40,658, 40,660 (Sept. 8, 1983) (to be codified at 40 C.F.R. pt. 300). This number was chosen because CERCLA originally required that, to the extent practicable, at least 400 sites be listed individually. *Id.* at 40,658. In order to reach that number of sites, EPA chose to list any site with a Hazard Ranking System ("HRS") score of above 28.50, along with all sites listed as states' top priorities. *Id.* at 40,659. As of January 6, 2006, there are 1,238 sites on the National Priorities List (NPL) of hazardous waste sites eligible for long-term remedial action. Of these sites, 1,086 are non-federal and 158 are federal. *See* Environmental Protection Agency, NPL Site Totals by Status and Milestone, http://www.epa.gov/superfund/sites/query/queryhtm/npltotal.htm (last visited Jan. 21, 2006). New Jersey has the most of any state, at 113 final sites, followed by Pennsylvania (ninety-four sites), California (ninety-four), and New York (eighty-six). *See* Environmental Protection Agency, National Priorities List Sites in the U.S., http://www.epa.gov/superfund/sites/npl/npl.htm (last visited Apr. 27, 2006).

There has been controversy over the standards to be applied by EPA in determining whether to include a particular site on the NPL. In several cases, the D.C. Circuit has vacated EPA decisions to add sites to the NPL and remanded to the agency in light of its failure to explain adequately the scientific bases for its decisions and its failure to offer substantial evidence in support of those decisions. *See* Tex Tin Corp. v. EPA, 992 F.2d 353 (D.C. Cir. 1993); National Gypsum Co. v. EPA, 968 F.2d 40 (D.C. Cir. 1992) (citing three similar decisions of that court in 1991 and 1992).

statute establishes a "Hazard Ranking System" which the agency uses to establish priorities for clean up based on risks posed to human health. Section 105 of CERCLA also requires the EPA to produce the National Contingency Plan—essentially a blueprint document containing the standards, guidelines, and procedures that governs cleanups. 42 U.S.C. section 9605(a) (2000). EPA published its original section 105 National Contingency Plan (NCP) under court order in 1982. 47 Fed. Reg. 31,180 (July 16, 1982). The plan governs the use of Superfund monies in responding to hazardous substance spills and waste sites; it provides for determination of appropriate levels of response in individual situations, and for the establishment of priorities among spills and sites. The most recent major revisions to the plan were promulgated by the EPA in 1994. 59 Fed. Reg. 47,384, 47,440 (Sept. 15, 1994). The plan appears at 40 C.F.R. Pt. 300.

CERCLA defines two general types of responses to releases or threats of releases of hazardous substances. *"Removal"* means the short-term cleanup of released substances, usually from the surface of the ground, or necessary actions in cases of threats of releases. *"Remedial action"* means long-term actions "consistent with permanent remedy taken instead of or in addition to removal actions * * *." 42 U.S.C. § 9601(23)–(24). Section 104 authorizes the President to order such responses—consistent with the National Contingency Plan, and subject to certain conditions—when a release or threatened release "may present an imminent and substantial danger to the public health or welfare." 42 U.S.C. § 9604.

Selection of an appropriate remedy for cleaning up a contaminated disposal site often is a difficult process involving strong differences of opinion among federal, state and local officials, private PRPs, and neighboring landowners: The PRPs do not want to pay for excessively elaborate and expensive responses ("cadillac cleanups"); neighbors may be concerned that the cleanup will be inadequate, or that it will exacerbate the situation by releasing contaminants that pose little current danger, or that it will be too disruptive of their lives for too long a time; state officials may want enforcement of state regulatory standards which are stricter than federal standards but which EPA believes should be waived; and local officials may be concerned about when and whether the site can be redeveloped and again be a source of jobs and tax revenues. As with the Hazard Ranking System, risk assessment is used for establishing a baseline for site cleanup, for determining the appropriate range of acceptable risk, and for choosing a response. *See* John S. Applegate, *The Perils of Unreasonable Risk: Information, Regulatory Policy, and Toxic Substances Control*, 91 COLUM. L. REV. 261, 284 n.119, 293 n.174 (1991).

Under the SARA amendments of 1986, Congress established schedules for response actions and preferences among types of responses. Section 121 establishes a preference (in remedial actions under section 104 or 106) for treatment which permanently and significantly reduces the

---

However, *Barmet Aluminum Corp. v. Reilly*, 927 F.2d 289 (6th Cir. 1991), held that section 113(h) of CERCLA precluded federal courts from reviewing pre-enforcement challenges to proposed placements of waste sites on the NPL.

volume, toxicity or mobility of the hazardous substances. Offsite transport and disposal of the hazardous substances or contaminated materials are least favored if "practical [onsite] treatment technologies" are available. Remedial actions are to be "cost-effective," considering total short-term and long-term costs. The actions taken are to attain a degree of cleanup and control of further releases which, at a minimum, "assures protection" of human health and the environment.

The following article analyzes the legal framework for remedy selection at CERCLA sites.

CASEY SCOTT PADGETT, SELECTING REMEDIES AT SUPERFUND SITES: HOW SHOULD 'CLEAN' BE DETERMINED?[27]

18 VT. L. REV. 361, 367–70, 381–87, 391–405 (1994).

The original Superfund statute failed to answer the following two questions: how clean is "clean" and how should "clean" be accomplished? Section 121 [enacted in 1986] was the congressional response to its earlier virtual silence on these issues. * * * While filling this void * * *, Congress embedded a fundamental conflict into the foundation of CERCLA's remedy selection process. Remedies selected in accordance with section 121 were required to protect human health and the environment, attain compliance with ARARs, and be both "cost effective" and "permanent" through the use of treatment technologies to the "maximum extent practicable." The conflict inherent in these directives lies in the fact that, at nearly every Superfund site, a remedy that permanently eliminates the risks posed by the hazardous substances through the use of treatment technology will be far more costly than a remedy that reduces risks by containing or limiting human exposure to the hazardous substances. * * *

Section 121 established four basic objectives to guide the selection of remedial actions at Superfund sites. Remedial actions must:

> protect human health and the environment, attain applicable or relevant and appropriate requirements [ARARs], be cost effective, and utilize permanent solutions, and alternative treatment or resource recovery technologies, to the maximum extent practicable.

Specifically, section 121(b), which identifies "[g]eneral rules" for selecting remedies, provides that "[t]he President shall select a remedial action that is protective of human health and the environment, that is cost effective, and that utilizes permanent solutions and alternative treatment technologies or resource recovery technologies to the maximum extent practicable."

Subsection (d) of section 121, which establishes the "[d]egree of cleanup" required of remedial actions, reiterates the idea that remedial actions "shall attain a degree of cleanup of hazardous substances . . . and of control of further release at a minimum which assures protection of

---

27. Copyright © 1994 by the Vermont Law Review. Reprinted with permission.

human health and the environment." In circumstances where any hazardous substance, pollutant, or contaminant will remain onsite, subsection (d) further specifies that remedial actions also must comply with any ARAR. Specifically, such remedial action must require "a level or standard of control for such hazardous substance or pollutant or contaminant which at least attains such legally applicable or relevant and appropriate standard, requirement, criteria, or limitation."

Although section 121 specifies that the use of treatment to reduce the volume, toxicity, or mobility of hazardous substances is a "preference," remedies which do not utilize such treatment may be selected if the President "publish[es] an explanation as to why a remedial action involving such reductions was not selected." In addition, the requirement that any particular ARAR be attained by a remedy may be waived by EPA under enumerated circumstances. * * *

Section 300.430 of the NCP establishes the regulatory parameters for identifying, developing, evaluating, and selecting a proposed remedy for cleaning up a CERCLA site. Section 300.430(e) identifies the requirement of a feasibility study ("FS") for developing and evaluating a range of remedial action alternatives. Section 300.430(f) defines the factors to be used in selecting a preferred remedy from among the range of alternatives developed in the FS. Together, these two subsections establish the heart of EPA's regulatory approach to implementing the remedy selection provisions of section 121 * * *.

* * * EPA translated the statutory requirements and preferences of section 121 into nine criteria for use in evaluating alternative remedies. Remedial alternatives that survive an initial screening are subject to a detailed comparative and objective assessment. Remedies are evaluated based on the following nine criteria:

1. Overall protection of human health and the environment;
2. Compliance with ARARs;
3. Long-term effectiveness and permanence;
4. Reduction of toxicity, mobility, or volume through treatment;
5. Short-term effectiveness;
6. Implementability;
7. Cost;
8. State acceptance; and
9. Community acceptance.

EPA organized these criteria into three categories. The first two criteria, protectiveness and compliance with ARARs, are "[t]hreshold criteria," which an alternative must satisfy to be eligible for selection. The next five criteria are "[p]rimary balancing criteria." The final two criteria, state and community acceptance, are "[m]odifying criteria." * * *

To determine whether a remedy is cost effective, the NCP instructs:

Cost-effectiveness is determined by evaluating the following three of the five balancing criteria . . . to determine *overall effectiveness:* long-term effectiveness and permanence, reduction of toxicity, mobility, or volume through treatment, and short-term effectiveness. *Overall effectiveness is then compared to cost* to ensure that the remedy is cost-effective. A remedy shall be cost-effective if its *costs are proportional to its overall effectiveness.*

In essence, the NCP offers a tautology to define cost effectiveness. A remedy is effective if, overall, it is effective, based on its long-and short-term effectiveness and the reduction of hazards posed by the hazardous substances. Further, the remedy is cost effective if its costs and effectiveness are "proportional."

The NCP defines a process for determining the maximum extent to which permanent treatment technologies are practicable that is similarly circular and ambiguous. The remedy will be found to utilize such treatment technologies to the maximum extent practicable if it

provides the *best balance of trade-offs among alternatives* in terms of the five primary balancing criteria. . . . The balancing shall *emphasize* long-term effectiveness and reduction of toxicity, mobility, or volume through treatment. The balancing shall also *consider* the preference for treatment as a principal element and the bias against off-site land disposal of untreated waste.

Thus, pursuant to the NCP, a treatment technology, or remedy which employs such a technology, may be found *impracticable* if the "trade-offs" that arise from a consideration of the five balancing criteria are "worse" than those that arise from another remedy. Conversely, if the trade offs seem "better" than those trade offs posed by other remedial alternatives, a remedy that utilizes a permanent treatment technology may be determined to be practicable. Since the NCP requires that two of the balancing criteria be weighed in the balance initially, as well as given additional emphasis and consideration, remedies that incorporate treatment technologies may be more likely to be considered practicable. * * *

For the CERCLA remedy selection process to produce results that are better understood and that achieve greater acceptance among stakeholders, EPA or another lead agency should not be expected to balance the many ambiguous and subjective criteria inherent to remedy selection. Instead, a different approach should be developed that more effectively allows those whose interests are at stake to weigh the trade offs and strike the balance among competing objectives.

NOTES

1. After the foregoing discussion, the author proposed changes in the EPA's remedy-selection process. The first question he would ask in each case is, "Why do we want to clean up the site?" That is, he believes that site-specific cleanup objectives must be based more explicitly on achieving defined

future uses for that site, taking into account the uses and values of surrounding properties and natural resources which have been impacted by the release of hazardous substances at the site. In 1994, when the article was published, the EPA's remedy-selection process, in contrast, assumed that the future use of, and access to, the site would be unrestricted. Padgett urged that for the process to be more effective, all the "stakeholders"—the site owner, neighboring property owners, community residents, state and local government representatives, and other parties with a legitimate interest in the cleanup and future use of the site—"must become players in the process, not merely watchdogs over it."

2.   In 1995, EPA announced a comprehensive program of 20 administrative reforms related to CERCLA and centered on the promise of smarter and more cost-effective cleanups. U.S. EPA, "Superfund Administrative Reforms: Reform Initiatives" (Oct. 2, 1995), discussed in Michael Steinberg & Joshua Swift, *EPA's New National Remedy Review Board Aims to Improve Superfund Decisions*, 26 Env't Rep. 2353 (1996), and at 27 Env't Rep. 2641 (1997). One of the most important reforms was creation of a new National Remedy Review Board to help control remedy costs by providing a cross-Regional, management-level review of high cost decisions on a site-specific basis.

Another important reform was a policy of updating previous remedy decisions at individual sites. This encouraged EPA Regional offices to examine and modify past remedy decisions when significant new factual, scientific, or technological information suggests that the same level of protectiveness of human health and the environment can be achieved at a lower cost. The importance of this reform was emphasized by a district court decision holding that cleanup cost overruns incurred because of EPA's failure to reconsider its selected site remedy, when changed circumstances fundamentally altered the estimated scope and cost of the remedy, were costs "inconsistent with the national contingency plan" for which PRPs were not liable under CERCLA section 107(a). United States v. Broderick Inv. Co., 955 F.Supp. 1268 (D. Colo. 1997). *See* Timothy Malloy, *Second–Look Remedies: Strategies for Re–Evaluating Superfund Cleanups*, 26 Env't Rep. 1420 (1995).

3.   *Ohio v. EPA*, 997 F.2d 1520 (D.C. Cir. 1993), upheld several provisions of the NCP that had been challenged by various states and private parties as inconsistent with CERCLA. Among the provisions sustained were the definition of applicable or relevant and appropriate requirements (ARARs), various remedy selection provisions, and provisions concerning both the role of states in CERCLA cleanups and cost allocations between state and federal governments.

The court approved the NCP's restriction of state ARARs to "standards [that] are of general applicability and are legally enforceable." Although the Safe Drinking Water Act is cited in CERCLA section 121(d)(2)(A) as one of the federal laws containing ARARs for Superfund cleanups, the court upheld EPA's decision that Maximum Contaminant Level Goals ("MCLGs") established under the SDWA do not have to be attained for contaminants whose MCLG has been set at a level of zero. Under the SDWA, MCLGs are generally unenforceable goals that reflect the level for each contaminant at which "no known or anticipated adverse effects on the health of persons occur and which allows an adequate margin of safety." Many MCLGs for carcinogens are set at zero. The second type of standards, Maximum Contaminant Levels ("MCLs")—the actual maximum permissible concentration levels under the SWDA—must be set as close as "feasible" to their corresponding MCLGs, taking into account available technology and cost. While MCLGs are unenforceable under the SWDA, section 121(d)(2)(A) of CERCLA converts them into enforceable limits (ARARs) where they are "relevant and appropriate under the circumstances of the release or threatened release." In essence, the EPA made a categorical determination in the NCP that MCLGs set at a level of zero are *never* relevant and appropriate under the circumstances of a release because "it is impossible to detect whether 'true' zero has actually been attained."

Remedy-selection issues in *Ohio v. EPA* concerned the role of cost-benefit analysis in choosing remedies; the NCP's failure to require the selection of "permanent" remedies to the maximum extent practicable; the use of a cancer risk range between 1 in 10,000 and 1 in 1,000,000 (rather than a minimum risk of 1 in 1,000,000); and the requirement of five-year review of certain remedial actions. CERCLA section 121(b)(1) requires the President to select a remedial action "that is protective of human health and the environment, that is cost effective, and that utilizes permanent solutions * * * to the maximum extent practicable." The court upheld the NCP's classification of permanence as one of several "balancing criteria" rather than as "an overarching statutory principle."

4. *United States v. Akzo Coatings of America, Inc.,* 949 F.2d 1409 (6th Cir. 1991), was an appeal by the state of Michigan from the entry of a consent decree between EPA and twelve PRPs, requiring the defendants to engage in remedial work at a contaminated site. The proposed remedial plan called for the excavation and incineration of surface soils contaminated with PCBs, lead, arsenic and other toxic materials, and the flushing of the subsurface soils contaminated with various volatile and semi-volatile organic compounds. The state challenged the effectiveness of soil flushing at the site in question, and the PRPs cross-appealed the district court's determination that the decree must comply with Michigan's groundwater antidegradation law. The court held that the record supported EPA's conclusion that the site was conducive to soil flushing; and that Michigan's antidegradation law was an ARAR because it was "of general applicability" and not too vague or lacking in a quantifiable standard to be "legally enforceable," as required by the NCP, and was "more stringent than any Federal standard, requirement, criteria or limitation," as required by CERCLA section 121(d)(2)(A)(ii).

5. Suppose that the EPA, unable to reach a settlement with the PRPs, proposes to implement on its own, under CERCLA section 104, a more elaborate and expensive cleanup program than the PRPs believe is necessary. Knowing that EPA will come after them later for reimbursement under section 107, could the PRPs obtain judicial review of EPA's program before it is implemented, as a means of trying to limit their ultimate liability under CERCLA? Before the 1986 amendments to CERCLA, *Lone Pine Steering Committee v. EPA,* 777 F.2d 882 (3d Cir. 1985), held that the federal district court lacked jurisdiction to review plaintiff's challenge to the EPA's method of cleanup until the Agency brings suit to recover its cleanup costs. The court

was concerned that such suits would frustrate Congress' intention that EPA act quickly to remedy problems posed by hazardous waste sites.

In 1986, Congress codified in section 113(h) the general denial of access to the courts to obtain pre-enforcement review of remedial action. Congress remained troubled, however, by the effect the rule might have on citizen groups wishing to challenge the adequacy of remedial action before cleanup was completed. Therefore, Congress created an exception authorizing the filing of citizen suits after a removal or remedial action has been taken under section 104 or secured under section 106. Congress encouraged liberal construction of the exception by explaining that such suits can be filed after the completion of "distinct and separate phases" of a remedial action, thus indicating that it is not necessary to wait until the entire action has been completed. The intent was to permit judicial review early enough so that the direction of a multi-stage cleanup could be modified, if necessary, prior to completion. *See* discussion of the conference report and other legislative history in *Superfund II: A New Mandate*, 17 ENV'T REP. 70–71 (1987).

In *McClellan Ecological Seepage Situation v. Perry*, 47 F.3d 325 (9th Cir. 1995), *cert. denied*, 516 U.S. 807 the court held that private citizens cannot circumvent the bar to judicial review of ongoing cleanups under CERCLA by suing under other federal and state environmental statutes. Hence, a federal district court lacked jurisdiction to hear a citizen suit claiming that the Defense Department's cleanup of an Air Force base violated state and federal environmental statutes, including RCRA and the Clean Water Act.[28] The case is discussed in Marianne Dugan, *Are Citizen Suits CERCLA section 113(h)'s Unintended Victims?*, 27 ENVTL. L. REP. 10003 (1997). Concerning section 113(h) generally, *see* Michael P. Healy, *Judicial Review and CERCLA Response Actions: Interpretive Strategies In the Face of Plain Meaning*, 17 HARV. ENVTL. L. REV. 1 (1993).

A novel approach to the application of section 113(h) to cleanups at federal facilities was taken in *Fort Ord Toxics Project, Inc. v. California Environ. Protect. Agency*, 189 F.3d 828 (9th Cir. 1999). The court held that section 113(h) did not bar private persons' suit challenging ongoing "remedial" action at a military base which was on EPA's National Priorities List. The court concluded that section 113(h) applies to both removal and remedial actions under § section 104 and 106, but that "remedial" (though not "removal") actions at federal facilities are governed solely by section 120, which is not mentioned in section 113(h). *See* Ingrid Wuerth, *Challenges to Federal Facility Cleanups and CERCLA Section 113(h)*, 8 TUL. ENVTL. L.J. 353, 370 (1995).

(ii) Brownfields

Brownfields may be defined as vacant, contaminated, former industrial sites, often in the inner cities. The EPA has estimated that there are more than 450,000 brownfield sites nationwide. *See* Environmental Pro-

---

28. Similarly, in *Boarhead Corp. v. Erickson,* 923 F.2d 1011 (3d Cir. 1991), the court held that section 113(h) prevented a federal district court from reviewing a claim that CERCLA-related activities which EPA planned to conduct on a Pennsylvania farm would violate the National Historic Preservation Act. Even though the lack of review might harm Native–American artifacts on the farm, the court said that it must follow Congress' will that cleanups not be delayed by pre-enforcement challenges.

tection Agency, About Brownfields, http://www.epa.gov/swerosps/bf/about.htm (last visited Feb. 12, 2006). Many of these sites are well located in relation to highways, rail facilities, public utilities, and workers in need of employment. However, because of potential CERCLA liabilities, businesses which could use these sites were reluctant to acquire and develop them. As a result, opportunities to create jobs and increase property tax revenues in the central cities were lost. City governments demanded a solution to this problem, and many states enacted voluntary cleanup laws or programs to address the brownfields problem. *See* the state-by-state summaries at 28 ENV'T REP. 2086, 2488 (1998).

The EPA developed a Brownfields Program in 1995, and Congress finally responded legislatively in 2002 with the Small Business Liability Relief and Brownfields Revitalization Act. With the passage of the Act, Congress hoped to incentivize cleanup and redevelopment of brownfields in three main ways: (1) increased federal funding for brownfields programs, (2) elimination of CERCLA liability for brownfields cleanups, and (3) a reduction of the federal government's role in administering brownfields sites. *See* Kelly J. Shira, Comment and Legislative Review, *Returning Common Sense to Cleanup? The Small Business Liability Relief and Brownfields Revitalization Act*, 34 ARIZ. ST. L.J. 991 (2002).

The Act defines brownfield sites to include "real property, the expansion, redevelopment, or reuse of which may be complicated by the presence or potential presence of a hazardous substance, pollutant, or contaminant." 42 U.S.C. section 9601(39). As discussed in greater detail, *supra*, the Act's liability provisions provide exemptions for owners of "contiguous properties" and for "bona fide prospective purchasers" (subsections 107(q) and (r)) a "de micromis" exemption for arrangers and transporters (subsection 107(*o*)), and expedited settlements for parties with an inability or a limited ability to pay response costs (subsection 122(g)(7)). With regard to funding, new subsection 104(k) provides substantial federal funding for brownfields redevelopment—an increase in funds from $98 million to $200 million annually for site assessment and cleanup. Entities eligible to receive brownfields funding include states, Indian tribes, local governments, land clearance authorities, regional councils, redevelopment agencies, other quasi-governmental entities created by states or local governments, and in limited circumstances private non-profit groups. In addition, new section 128 of CERCLA authorizes $50 million per year for grants to assist states and Indian tribes in the development of response programs. Addressing the reduced federal role in brownfields cleanup, subsection 128(b) restricts the EPA's authority, with limited exceptions, to take enforcement action under section 106(a), or to seek cost recovery under section 107(a), at eligible sites cleaned up in compliance with a state response program. The exceptions to this restriction include that the EPA will take response action if a state requests so or if the site contamination has migrated across state lines. Additionally, the EPA may act if new information about the site comes to light. *See* Flannary P. Collins, Note,

The Small Business Liability Relief and Brownfields Revitalization Act: A Critique, 13 DUKE ENVTL. L. & POL'Y F. 303 (2003).

In the aftermath of *Cooper Industries, Inc. v. Aviall Services, Inc.*, excerpted and discussed, *supra*, questions have arisen as to the case's impact on the cleanup of brownfields. As the cleanup of brownfields is often voluntary and not compelled by suit under sections 106 or 107, there are concerns that *Aviall* will chill participation in such cleanups. If a party is unable to recover the costs of its brownfield cleanup efforts unless sued by the EPA, it may choose not to clean and instead to wait for the EPA to sue it under sections 106 or 107. In cases where the migration of waste is occurring on the contaminated site, this delay in remediation may result in greater environmental danger and more difficult cleanups later. Indeed, some have alleged that this disincentive to clean the site runs counter to CERCLA's goals of promptly cleaning hazardous waste.

(iii) The Trust Fund

In the original 1980 statute, Congress authorized a Trust Fund of $1.6 billion to fund cleanups of "orphan" sites on the NPL, emergencies, and longer-term cleanups. The 1986 SARA amendments increased this amount to $8.5 billion. This "Superfund," as the fund (and CERCLA) has come to be called, may pay for both cleanup costs and enforcement actions by EPA. The Superfund is also available to pay for certain natural resource damages, reimbursement of local governments, and claims by private parties.

The most important benefit of the Superfund is that it allows for the EPA to address a hazardous substance released before a court determination of liability or a settlement. Later, when the liability is determined, the EPA can recovers its response costs and the Superfund will be reimbursed. This ability clean up first and collect later is one of the CERCLA's most important innovations. *See* ENVIRONMENTAL PROTECTION AGENCY, SUPERFUND 20TH ANNIVERSARY REPORT 9 (2000), (*available at* http://www.epa.gov/superfund/action/20years/20yrpt1.pdf).

The actual funding of the Superfund comes from a combination of general tax revenues, taxes of crude oil received at U.S. refineries, environmental taxes on corporations, recovery of response costs from responsible parties, taxes on imported petroleum products, and taxes on certain chemicals. The two main sources of the Fund were originally the taxes on crude oil and certain chemicals. ENVIRONMENTAL PROTECTION AGENCY, FISCAL YEAR 2004 SUPERFUND ANNUAL REPORT (2005), *available at* http://www.epa.gov/superfund/action/process/fy2004.htm. With the enactment of the SARA amendments in 1986, a third source of funding was added: the corporate environmental income tax. *See* SUPERFUND SUBCOMMITTEE OF THE NATIONAL ADVISORY COUNCIL FOR ENVIRONMENTAL POLICY AND TECHNOLOGY, FINAL REPORT 8 (2004), *available at* http://www.epa.gov/oswer/docs/naceptdocs/NACEPTsuperfund–Final–Report.pdf.

These special taxes—excise taxes payable by petroleum and chemical industries, and an environmental income tax payable by corporations with annual profits of more than $2 million—which provided $4 million per day for the trust fund, expired in December 1995. As of this writing, Congress and the second Bush administration have refused to reinstate the taxes. In the absence of funding by the taxes, the Superfund continues to receive revenue from other sources, including cost recoveries, interest from investments, fines, and penalties. Recently, the Program has been increasingly funded through appropriations from general revenues.

The fund has remained stable over the past decade in current year dollars, with a brief drop of around $100 million per year from fiscal year 2000 to fiscal year 2002. Looking to the same figures in constant year 2004 dollars, the funding has dropped by approximately $200 million between fiscal year 1993 and fiscal year 2005. *See* GOVERNMENT ACCOUNTABILITY OFFICE, HAZARDOUS WASTE PROGRAMS: INFORMATION ON APPROPRIATIONS AND EXPENDITURES FOR SUPERFUND, BROWNFIELDS, AND RELATED PROGRAMS 4 (2005), *available at* www.gao.gov/new.items/d05746r.pdf.

i. The Future of CERCLA

Is CERCLA effectively meeting its goals? How might it be improved? In 1992, on the eve of Congress' reauthorization debate over CERCLA, two members of the social science research organization Resources for the Future produced a report on the program's future. Though now nearly fifteen years old, the Report's framing of the unresolved issues is still apt.

Katherine N. Probst & Paul R. Portney, *Assigning Liability for Superfund Cleanups: An Analysis of Policy Options* vii, 43, 45–47 (1992) * * *

We now have more than 11 years of experience under Superfund, and high hopes for a quick and effective solution to the problem of site cleanup have gradually given way to frustration and cynicism. Opinion polls suggest that the public is still extremely concerned about hazardous waste sites. But those who follow Superfund closely have come increasingly to recognize that cleanups take a very long time to be completed, that resources which contribute nothing to reduced risks to human health and the environment are consumed in the process, and that the program Congress put in place more than a decade ago creates several inequities. Less obvious to all, perhaps, are the salutary effects Superfund may be having on the actions of all those who deal with hazardous substances, not to mention the risk reductions arising from the emergency removals and remedial actions themselves, in other words, Superfund—and particularly its liability provisions—have both positive and negative effects. Similarly, the alternatives to Superfund and its liability standards—including the options described in the preceding chapters—have their own strengths and weaknesses, the most prominent of which we hope have been identified here. * * *

The Site Cleanup Process Could be Expedited by Changing Superfund's Liability Standards. It Could Also be Expedited Under the Current System.

All would agree that the remedial process takes too long. The U.S. Environmental Protection Agency's own data suggest that it takes nearly 11 years, on average, between the initiation of a site study and the implementation of the remedy at a site on the National Priorities List. While such delays are due in part to the nature of the site study, remedy design, and cleanup processes—features that would be a part of any Superfund program—they are also the result of time-consuming negotiation and litigation between EPA and potentially responsible parties. Releasing PRPs from some or all liability at a subset of NPL sites (as in Options 2 through 5) should reduce these latter sorts of delays.

Just as clearly, however, the remedial process could be accelerated under the existing liability standards. One of the ways this might be accomplished would be for EPA to go back to a "clean up first/recover costs later" strategy that would be roughly consistent with the "polluter pays" principle so long as cost recovery is aggressively pursued. This strategy would require increased revenues for the Trust Fund, but so would all of the alternative liability approaches considered in this report. Second, the current law provides EPA with tools that could speed settlements at sites—such as *de minimis* buyouts, mixed funding, and nonbinding allocations of responsibility—although the promise of these tools is uncertain because they have been little used. Finally, many opportunities exist for EPA to streamline the site evaluation and remedy selection process (as the agency recently proposed), which now takes years.

Transactions Costs Could be Reduced Through Modification of Superfund Liability.

Eliminating the need for EPA to reach agreement on cleanups with PRPs at some sites by releasing them from liability (under Options 3 through 5) would reduce transactions costs. About this we are confident. There is, however, far too little information available on the current magnitude of transactions costs to know just how large the savings would be under each option. We speculate in chapter 3 that the savings would range from $2 billion to $8 billion, albeit spread out over a number of years. Better data are needed on the magnitude of transactions costs at different kinds of sites as well as on the distribution of these sites among all those on the NPL before one could have much confidence in this "guesstimate" of the savings from revising the current liability standards.

Relaxing Superfund's Liability Standards Would Have Some Adverse Effects.

The most vexing and controversial issue addressed in this report is whether relaxation of Superfund liability (in one form or another) would blunt the incentives many believe the law provides for PRPs both to clean up sites not yet on the NPL and also to manage hazardous substances more carefully. It is important to reiterate that we can provide no convincing statistical evidence that Superfund is having these salutary effects, although recent studies and anecdotal evidence suggest that the effect is a real one. These reports accord well with our own intuition: it simply makes sense to us that PRPs will take measures to keep sites not yet on the NPL off the list. By doing so, they can avoid the sometimes very high costs, protracted delays, and negative publicity that can result from an NPL listing. Any alternative that eliminates liability for a subset of sites could greatly diminish—if not eliminate—this incentive.

It is much more difficult to determine how a change in liability would affect incentives for the careful management of hazardous substances. There is broad agreement that *prospective* liability provides such an incentive. A more difficult question is the effect that retroactive liability under Superfund may have. Some preliminary data support the contention that Superfund does affect firms' waste management practices, especially with respect to substances not currently regulated under the Resource Conservation and Recovery Act (RCRA). Retroactive liability certainly may not be the best way to achieve this objective; indeed, we would be surprised if it was. Nevertheless, one cannot overlook the positive incentive it provides for the careful management of hazardous substances.

On the subject of incentives, another important consideration should not go unmentioned. Those PRPs who have already stepped forward and begun to pay for cleanups at sites like those to be released from liability under Options 2 through 5 would be unfairly treated if, as we suspect is likely, they are not reimbursed for the costs they have incurred. This potential inequity would carry with it a very important incentive effect: the message that it may not be wise to comply immediately with environmental laws because, if one hangs back and waits, the law may be changed. In principle, we find this a very disturbing possibility; it may not be a serious problem in practice given other incentives for compliance and given the relatively small expenditures PRPs have made to date on cleanups.

Any of the Modifications to the Present Liability Standards Will Create at Least Some New Inequities, even as They Ameliorate Others.

We have identified three definitions of fairness that could reasonably be used to evaluate the Superfund program—first, that polluters should pay for the problems they create; second, that PRPs who handled hazardous substances in a similar fashion should be treated equally; and third, that changes in rules should not be made retroactively.

To the extent that the existing liability rules in Superfund require some "polluters"—that is, solvent PRPs—to pay for problems created by others (insolvent PRPs), they do not comport well with the polluter-pays notion. On the other hand, recently collected data show that at many sites on the NPL, contamination was caused solely by a single owner/operator. Thus, liability at these sites will attach to the party (or parties) which most observers would view as being responsible for the contamination— whether willful or not. So long as it is possible to ascertain PRPs' "fair shares" at NPL sites, aggressive mixed funding of orphan shares * * * would be the best approach from the standpoint of the polluter-pays principle. Correspondingly, abolishing liability for all NPL sites at the time of reauthorization would probably move farthest from adherence to this principle. Treating similarly situated PRPs equitably is difficult. * * *

The current program clearly flunks against a standard that holds that any changes in the law be forward-looking only. That is, under Superfund, responsible parties are being held liable retroactively in cases where they followed all the rules in effect at the time (and in some cases where they made special efforts to find safe places to dispose of hazardous substances). If redressing such inequities was deemed to be of paramount importance, then eliminating PRP liability at sites that closed before Superfund was enacted * * * would be especially attractive.

Much Better Data are Needed to Assess the Financial Implications of the Present Liability Standards as Well as Any Proposed Alternatives to Them.

Considering that the Superfund program apparently costs the country several billion dollars per year in direct cleanup costs and an unknown amount in legal fees and other transactions costs, we do a very poor job of keeping track of any expenditures related to Superfund other than those made by EPA. This might be acceptable if PRPs and insurers were content with the status quo. But they are not, and one of their complaints is the cost burden associated with the present liability standards. Until and unless PRPs and insurers compile data on Superfund-related expenditures and make this information available to the public, such complaints will be difficult if not impossible to evaluate.

Each of the alternative approaches that we consider * * * would require major increases in the corporate environmental tax—from a 70 percent increase for one to an 800 percent hike for another. Yet, as we have noted, there is a great deal of uncertainty about each of the building blocks on which our estimates are based: the average cost of a cleanup, the number of sites likely to be affected by each of the options, and the time horizon over which cleanup would take place. Without better information on all these questions, it is virtually impossible to come up with a realistic estimate of the cost of the current program, much less the alternatives to it. Any serious consideration of liability alternatives by Congress will, we hope, be based on more sophisticated analysis of the costs of the current program and the financial impacts of any change in liability.

CHAPTER 9

REGULATION OF TOXIC SUBSTANCES AND GENETICALLY MODIFIED ORGANISMS

■ ■ ■

Toxic chemicals and genetically modified organisms provoke significant controversy and fears over the widespread ecological and health damage they could wreak. But both also provide benefits: pesticides kill pests that can destroy agricultural crops, therefore increasing food supply (and hence have been called "economic poison"); genetically modified organisms can, according to proponents, help feed an ever-increasing world population with healthier food but, critics fear, could cause major ecological disturbances by, for example, destroying native plants. How to weigh the costs and benefits of toxic chemicals and genetically modified organisms is the central question we examine in this chapter. Perhaps more than any other area of environmental law, this chapter faces head on the question of risk examined extensively in Chapter 2. Section A provides an overview of the Federal Insecticide, Fungicide and Rodenticide Act (FIFRA) and the Toxic Substances Control Act (TSCA), which were intended to prevent commercial distribution of chemicals whose use would pose unreasonable risks to health or the environment while allowing the use of chemicals that provide significant benefits with lower risks. Section B describes and evaluates the federal program for the regulation of genetically modified organisms. Section C examines statutes that use information disclosure as a tool to regulate the use of chemicals, including the the Emergency Planning and Community Right-to-Know Act (EPCRA) and the federal securities laws.

A. REGULATING THE SALE OF TOXIC SUBSTANCES

1. PESTICIDE CONTROL

In 1962, Rachel Carson published SILENT SPRING, a book that, through its focus on the environmental harms of the pesticide DDT, brought the hazards of agricultural pesticide use to public attention and galvanized public opinion. As Carson dramatically described, "For the first time in the history of the world, every human being I know is subjected to contact with dangerous chemicals, from the moment of conception until death."[1] Carson's words are well-illustrated by a recently published study that tested streams and groundwater across the country for the presence of pesticides. Every stream tested contained the residue of at least one pesticide. Unites States Geological Survey, *Pesticides in the Nation's Streams and Ground Water, 1992–2001 A Summary* (released March, 2006), available at http://pubs.usgs./gov/fs/2006/3028. Many streams have concentrations unlikely to affect humans but that may affect fish and wildlife. *Id.* No one can, of course, deny that pesticides are toxic—their intent, after all, is to kill pests. But of course pesticides also confer widespread benefits by dramatically increasing crop yield. These benefits can be of special importance in developing countries, with their acute need to feed their populace. Pesticide usage remains widespread: in the United States in 2001, agriculture, industry and households used 1.2 billion pounds of pesticides, about 20 percent of the worldwide total of just over 5 billion pounds. *See* EPA, *Pesticides Industry Sales and Usage, 2000 and 2001, Market Estimates* at 8. How to balance the benefits of pesticide usage against the very real harms these economic poisons can cause is the central quandary of pesticide regulation.

In 1972, Congress amended FIFRA, which had previously required the registration and listing of pesticides, to enact a much more comprehensive regulatory scheme.

FIFRA, 7 U.S.C.A § 136, provides a framework for regulating the sale and distribution of pesticides within the United States. Under the statute, EPA may not approve a pesticide's introduction into commerce unless the Administrator finds that the pesticide "will not generally cause unreasonable adverse effects on the environment" when used in accordance with any EPA-imposed restrictions and "with widespread and commonly recognized practice." 7 U.S.C.A. § 136a(5)(D). "Unreasonable adverse effects on the environment" are defined to include "any unreasonable risk to man or the environment, taking into account the economic, social, and environmental costs and benefits of the use of any pesticide." § 136(bb). With few exceptions, FIFRA prohibits the sale, distribution, and professional use of unregistered pesticides. §§ 136a(a) & 136j(a)(1).

Because of the explicit requirement of a cost/benefit analysis, FIFRA's "unreasonable adverse effects" standard is unusual among federal environmental statutes: most others (except the Toxic Substances Control Act) employ risk-based standards softened only by the availability of control technologies. By disregarding the benefits of the regulated substances, these risk-based statutes provide more protection to health and the environment and less protection to industry than do FIFRA and TSCA.

As part of a registration, EPA must classify the pesticide for either "general" or "restricted" use. § 136a(d). Restrictions relate to such factors as methods of application, qualifications of applicators, amounts to be used, geographic areas of use, and species of targeted pests. EPA may

---

1. Rachel Carson, SILENT SPRING, 15 (1962).

"conditionally" register a pesticide if the pesticide and its proposed use are identical or substantially similar to any currently registered pesticide and use thereof, or differ only in ways that would not significantly increase the risk of unreasonable adverse effects on the environment. A pesticide containing an active ingredient not contained in any currently registered pesticide also may be conditionally registered for a period reasonably sufficient for the generation of required data. EPA may determine that use of the pesticide during such period will not cause any unreasonable adverse effects on the environment, and that use of the pesticide is in the public interest. § 136a(c)(7).

Once registered, pesticides are still subject to continuing scrutiny by EPA. § 136d. Indeed, section 6 of FIFRA requires EPA to cancel a pesticide's registration after the first five years in which the registration has been effective (and at the conclusion of subsequent five year periods if the registration is renewed) "unless the registrant, or other interested person with the concurrence of the registrant, ... requests ... that the registration be continued in effect." § 136d(a). And at any time, EPA may propose cancellation of a registration and initiate elaborate cancellation proceedings if "it appears to the Administrator that a pesticide ... does not comply with [FIFRA] or ... generally causes unreasonable adverse effects on the environment...." § 136d(b).

During the pendency of cancellation proceedings, the registration remains in effect unless the Administrator "suspend[s] the registration of the pesticide immediately." § 136d(c). But before suspending, the Administrator must determine that an "imminent hazard" exists. Even then, FIFRA guarantees registrants the right to an expedited administrative hearing on that issue, and the pesticide's registration remains effective during this latter proceeding. § 136d(c)(2). Only if "the Administrator determines that an emergency exists that does not permit the Administrator to hold a hearing before suspending" may she prohibit commerce in the pesticide in advance of notification to the registrant. § 136d(c)(3).

While commerce in unregistered pesticides is generally prohibited, the Administrator may permit continued sale and use of existing stocks of pesticides whose registrations have been cancelled provided "he determines that such sale or use is not inconsistent with the purposes of this subchapter and will not have unreasonable adverse effects on the environment." § 136d(a)(1).

The following case, from 1972, discusses some of the statutory scheme (7 U.S.C.A. § 135) in effect *prior* to a major revision of FIFRA in 1972. In that revision, new § 136 essentially replaced § 135 with respect to pesticides. However, the court's treatment of the process of *suspension* of a previous registration remains valid and important today.

ENVIRONMENTAL DEFENSE FUND, INC.
v. ENVIRONMENTAL PROTECTION
AGENCY [ALDRIN AND DIELDRIN]

United States Court of Appeals, District of Columbia Circuit, 1972.
465 F.2d 528.

LEVENTHAL, CIRCUIT JUDGE.

On December 3, 1970, petitioner Environmental Defense Fund (EDF), a non-profit New York corporation, petitioned the Environmental Protection Agency (EPA) under the Federal Insecticide, Fungicide and Rodenticide Act (FIFRA), 7 U.S.C.A. §§ 135–135k, for the immediate suspension and ultimate cancellation of all registered uses of aldrin and dieldrin, two chemically similar chlorinated hydrocarbon pesticides. On March 18, 1971, the Administrator of the EPA announced the issuance of "notices of cancellation" for aldrin and dieldrin because of "a substantial question as to the safety of the registered products which has not been effectively countered by the registrant." He declined to order the interim remedy of suspension, pending final decision on cancellation after completion of the pertinent administrative procedure, in light of his decision that "present uses [of aldrin and dieldrin] do not pose an imminent threat to the public such as to require immediate action." EDF filed this petition to review the EPA's failure to suspend the registration.

I. Significance of EPA's Decision on Immediate
Suspension of FIFRA Registration

We begin by reviewing the significance of an EPA decision to issue or withhold an order of immediate suspension of a pesticide registration, pending final administrative consideration.

A. *The Statutory Framework of FIFRA*

Since 1970 the Administrator of the EPA has been charged with administering the two systems provided by Congress to regulate the introduction of potentially harmful pesticides into the environment: the establishment of registration and labeling requirements for "economic poisons" under FIFRA, formerly assigned to the Secretary of Agriculture; and the establishment of tolerance limits for shipment in interstate commerce of crops "adulterated" by pesticide residues, under the Food, Drug and Cosmetic Act, 21 U.S.C.A. 301 et seq., formerly assigned to the Department of Health, Education & Welfare.

Aldrin and dieldrin are "economic poisons" under the definition in § 2 of FIFRA, and hence are required to be registered with EPA before they may be distributed in interstate commerce. An economic poison may lawfully be registered only if it is properly labeled—not "misbranded." Section 2(z) of FIFRA, insofar relevant here, provides that an economic poison is "misbranded"—

(c) if the labeling accompanying it does not contain directions for use which are necessary and if complied with adequate for the protection of the public;

(d) if the label does not contain a warning or caution statement which may be necessary and if complied with adequate to prevent injury to living man and other vertebrate animals, vegetation, and useful invertebrate animals; * * *

(g) if in the case of an insecticide, nematocide, fungicide, or herbicide when used as directed or in accordance with commonly recognized practice it shall be injurious to living man or other vertebrate animals, or vegetation, except weeds, to which it is applied, or to the person applying such economic poison.

If an economic poison is such that a label with adequate safeguards cannot be written, it may not be registered or sold in interstate commerce.

The burden of establishing the safety of a product requisite for compliance with the labeling requirements, remains at all times on the applicant and registrant. Whenever it appears that a registered economic poison may be or has become "misbranded," the Administrator is required to issue a notice of cancellation.

In § 4 of FIFRA, Congress has provided extensive safeguards for those whose FIFRA registrations are challenged. * * *

The elaborate procedural protection against improvident cancellations emphasizes the importance of the immediate suspension provision available under § 4 of FIFRA, for use when appropriate:

Notwithstanding any other provision of this section, the Administrator may, when he finds that such action is necessary to prevent an imminent hazard to the public, by order, suspend the registration of an economic poison immediately. In such case, he shall give the registrant prompt notice of such action and afford the registrant the opportunity to have the matter submitted to an advisory committee and for an expedited hearing under this section.

Because of the potential for delay, and consequent possibility of serious and irreparable environmental damage from an erroneous decision on suspension, a refusal to suspend is a final order reviewable immediately. * * *

II.   EPA's Reasons for Declining to Order Immediate Suspension of Aldrin and Dieldrin Registrations

1.   The Decisions Taken by the EPA Administrator

The EPA initiated an administrative investigation into registrations for aldrin and dieldrin that resulted in cancellation of registrations for certain uses. On December 2, 1970, the EDF addressed a petition to the Administrator requesting the suspension and eventual cancellation of registrations for all products containing aldrin and dieldrin. In order to expedite the administrative process, and in light of our January 1971 decisions in *EDF v. Ruckelshaus* and *Wellford v. Ruckelshaus,* relating to DDT, and 2, 4, 5–T, the Administrator consolidated the consideration of registrations of DDT; 2, 4, 5–T; aldrin and dieldrin. On March 18, 1971, he issued his Statement of Reasons Underlying the Registration Decisions concerning these products, the decision to issue notices of cancellation for all registrations for those substances, and also the decision not to order interim suspension of registrations pending administrative decision. * * *

2. *General Approach of EPA Statement of Reasons*

This suffices for an introduction to the Statement of Reasons. We now examine it with greater care, and begin with the considerations voiced by the Administrator as defining EPA's general approach.

Statutory Tests

* * *

The EPA points out that the final decision on registration depends on a balance struck between benefits and dangers to the public health and welfare from the product's use, and comments that the concept of safety of the product is under evolution and refinement in the light of increasing knowledge.

Suspension

[EPA's general criteria for suspension were as follows.]

* * * An "imminent hazard" may be declared at any point in a chain of events which may ultimately result in harm to the public. It is not necessary that the final anticipated injury actually have occurred prior to a determination that an "imminent hazard" exists. In this connection, significant injury or potential injury to plants or animals alone could justify a finding of imminent hazard to the public from the use of an economic poison. The type, extent, probability and duration of potential or actual injury to man, plants and animals will be measured in light of the positive benefits accruing from, for example, use of the responsible economic poison in human or animal disease control or food production.

General Standards

* * *

* * * EPA cites "dramatic steps in disease control" and the gradual amelioration of "the chronic problem of world hunger" as examples of the kind of beneficial effect to be looked for in balancing benefits against harm for specific substances. But it cautions that "triumphs of public health achieved in the past" will not be permitted to justify future registrations, recognizing that fundamentally different considerations are at work in evaluating use of a dangerous pesticide in a developed country such as the United States rather than in a developing non-industrial nation.

The immense difficulties of achieving a comprehensive solution to pesticide control are manifest from the Administrator's Statement of Reasons. It records that there are nearly 45,000 presently outstanding pesticide registrations for "hundreds" of substances in use over approximately five percent of the total land area of the United States. Available data show wide variety among individual substances both as to effectiveness against target species and as to potential harm to non-target species. Laboratory tests with some substances have raised serious questions regarding carcinogenicity that "deserve particular searching" because carcinogenic effects are generally cumulative and irreversible when discovered. Threats presented by individual substances vary not only as to observed persistence in the environment but also as to environmental mobility—which in turn depends in part on how a particular pesticide is introduced into the environment, either by ground insertion or by dispersal directly into the ambient air or water.

Based on the discussion of these general considerations, the EPA concludes that individual decisions on initial or continued registration must depend on a complex administrative calculus, in which the "nature and magnitude of the foreseeable hazards associated with use of a particular product" is weighed against the "nature of the benefit conferred" by its use.

3. Discussion of Aldrin and Dieldrin

The EPA's general analysis for suspension, set forth above, is supplemented in the Statement of Reasons by discussions concerning the particular products. Part IV, Dieldrin and Aldrin, comprises slightly more than two pages of the Statement. * * *

The Administrator's reasons for denial of suspension, as to aldrin and dieldrin, appear in the following paragraphs of the Statement:

[B]ecause the vast majority of the present use of these products is restricted to ground insertion, which presents little foreseeable damage from general environmental mobility, because of the pattern of declining gross use, and because of the lower historic introduction of these products into the environmental residue burden to be faced by man and the other biota, the delay inherent in the administrative process does not present an imminent hazard. Thus the substantial question of the safety of these registrations is primarily raised by theoretical data, while review of the evidence from the ambient environment indicates that such potential hazards are not imminent in light of the present registrations.

It is significant to note that no residues of either aldrin or dieldrin are now permitted on corn, eggs, milk, poultry, or animal fats shipped in interstate commerce. Because of the use patterns of aldrin and dieldrin, these products constitute the major sources whereby these substances would find their way into human food chains. During the pendency of the administrative process hereby initiated, this Agency will take no action to grant any residue tolerances for these foodstuffs pursuant to the Food, Drug and Cosmetic Act, although initial tolerances have been requested by the manufacturer.

III. The EDF's Contentions of Invalidity of Non-suspension Decisions

* * *

Judicial doctrine teaches that a court must consider possibility of success on the merits, the nature and extent of the damage to each of the parties from the granting or denial of the injunction, and where the public interest lies. It was not inappropriate for the Administrator to have chosen a general approach to suspension that permits analysis of similar factors. By definition, a substantial question of safety exists when notices of cancellation issue. If there is no offsetting claim of any benefit to the public, then the EPA has the burden of showing that the substantial safety question does not pose an "imminent hazard" to the public.

Lack of Discussion of Benefits of Aldrin–Dieldrin

EDF is on sound ground in noting that while the EPA's general approach contemplates a decision as to suspension based on a balance of benefit and harm, the later discussion of aldrin and dieldrin relates only to harm.

The Administrator's mere mention of these products' major uses, emphasized by the EPA, cannot suffice as a discussion of benefits, even though

> the data before him * * * reflected the view that aldrin-dieldrin pesticides are the only control presently available for some twenty insects which attack corn and for one pest which poses a real danger to citrus orchards * * *.

Brief for EPA, page 19. The interests at stake here are too important to permit the decision to be sustained on the basis of speculative inference as to what the Administrator's findings and conclusions might have been regarding benefits. * * *

Our conclusion that a mere recitation of a pesticide's uses does not suffice as an analysis of benefits is fortified where, as here, there was a submission, by EDF, that alternative pest control mechanisms are available for such use. The analysis of benefit requires some consideration of whether such proposed alternatives are available or feasible, or whether such availability is in doubt. * * *

Flexibility as to Limits

Our concern over EPA's failure to discuss benefits reflects our concern that what is done tacitly or by implication may mean that the agency has not taken into account the possibility of orders falling short of complete suspension. EPA has flexibility not only to confine suspensions to certain uses, but also to order conditional suspensions for uses, available only if certain volumes or limits are not exceeded. EPA apparently assumed certain limits of use would prevail. But if there are dangers, and if the benefits of use may be satisfied within certain limits of use, the EPA should consider whether to exercise its authority to determine that the extent of use permitted pending final determination must be held within announced limits.

Analysis of Limited Short–Run Harm

We do not say there is an absolute need for analysis of benefits. It might have been possible for EPA to say that although there were no significant benefits from aldrin-dieldrin the possibility of harm—though substantial enough to present a long-run danger to the public warranting cancellation proceedings—did not present a serious short-run danger that constituted an imminent hazard. EPA's counsel offers this as a justification for its action.

If this is to be said, it must be said clearly, so that it may be reviewed carefully. Logically, there is room for the concept. But we must caution against any approach to the term "imminent hazard," used in the statute, that restricts it to a concept of crisis. It is enough if there is substantial likelihood that serious harm will be experienced during the year or two required in any realistic projection of the administrative process. It is not good practice for an agency to defend an order on the hypothesis that it is valid even assuming there are no benefits, when the reality is that some conclusion of benefits was visualized by the agency. This kind of abstraction pushes argument—and judicial review—to the wall of extremes, when realism calls for an awareness of middle ground.

NOTES

1. As construed by the court, to what extent does the statute permit use of a pesticide which is found to present a substantial health risk?

2. The court places the burden of proof on the EPA to show the lack of an imminent hazard when there is no offsetting claim of a benefit. What is the source of this allocation of the burden of proof?

3. The following events occurred on remand:

* * * After considering the Report [of an advisory committee] and further public comments, the EPA issued an order on December 7, 1972, which affirmed its previous decisions to issue a notice of intent to cancel, without interim suspension.

Cancellation hearings began before Chief Administrative Law Judge (ALJ) Perlman on August 7, 1973. Twelve months into the hearings, on August 2, 1974, the Administrator issued a notice of intent to suspend on the ground that evidence developed since December 1972 indicated that the continued use of aldrin/dieldrin presented an "imminent hazard" to the public. Shell and USDA requested a public hearing on the suspension question. The hearing began before ALJ Perlman on August 14, 1974, and was concluded on September 12, 1974. ALJ Perlman recommended suspension, and, on October 1, 1974, the Administrator suspended the registrations.

EDF, Inc. v. EPA, 510 F.2d 1292, 1297 (D.C. Cir. 1975). The Court of Appeals affirmed, in another opinion by Judge Leventhal. Burden of proof was again a significant part of the decision:

> Shell, FCM and the USDA further challenge the Administrator's finding that the benefits derived from the suspended uses of aldrin/dieldrin do not outweigh the harms done.

> The responsibility to demonstrate that the benefits outweigh the risks is upon the proponents of continued registration. The statute places a heavy burden on any administrative officer to explain the basis for his decision to permit the continued use of a chemical known to produce cancer in experimental animals.

> In our 1972 opinion, Environmental Defense Fund, Inc. v. EPA, *supra*, we said that "a mere recitation of a pesticide's uses does not suffice as an analysis of benefits" where the EPA has refused to initiate suspension proceedings despite evidence of carcinogenicity and a submission that alternative pest control mechanisms exist. We sought a further "elucidation of basis" from the agency to ensure that the evidence of harm was indeed outweighed by benefits flowing from the continued use of the pesticide. Where, as in that case, the agency declines to act in the face of evidence of carcinogenicity it bears the burden of justifying its lack of action:

>> By definition, a substantial question of safety exists when notices of cancellation issue. If there is no offsetting claim of any benefit to the public, then the EPA has the burden of showing that the substantial safety question does not pose an "imminent hazard" to the public.

> 150 U.S.App.D.C. at 359, 465 F.2d at 539. In the present case, in contrast, the agency has decided to act, and the burden is on the registrant to establish that continued registration poses no safety threat.

Id. at 1302. Thus, the EPA decision shifted the burden of proof to the registrant. Has Judge Leventhal created ad hoc burden of proof rules for each case? [Cf. his opinion in *International Harvester,* page 627, *supra.*] Or is there a coherent underlying rationale? Is it significant that in each case the burden was placed on the party advocating continued registration?

4. Unlike the preceding case, the next one below was decided after the major amendments of 1972 that resulted in the "new" FIFRA, which, though subsequently further amended in some respects, remains in effect today.

ENVIRONMENTAL DEFENSE FUND, INC. v. ENVIRONMENTAL PROTECTION AGENCY [HEPTACHLOR AND CHLORDANE]

United States Court of Appeals, District of Columbia Circuit, 1976.
548 F.2d 998.

LEVENTHAL, CIRCUIT JUDGE.

This case involves the pesticides heptachlor and chlordane. Consolidated petitions seek review of an order of the Environmental Protection

Agency (EPA) suspending the registration of those pesticides under the Federal Insecticide, Fungicide and Rodenticide Act (FIFRA) for certain uses. The Administrator of EPA issued an order on December 24, 1975. The order prohibited further production of these pesticides for the suspended uses, but permitted the pesticides' continued production and sale for limited minor uses. Even as to the suspended uses, the Order tempered its impact in certain respects: It delayed until August 1, 1976, the effective date of the prohibition of production for use on corn pests; and it permitted the continued sale and use of existing stocks of registered products formulated prior to July 29, 1975.

One petition to review was filed by Earl L. Butz, Secretary of Agriculture of the United States (U.S.D.A.). Secretary Butz and intervenor Velsicol Chemical Corporation, the sole manufacturer of heptachlor and chlordane, urge that the EPA order as to chlordane be set aside on both substantive and procedural grounds. They contend that substantial evidence does not support the Administrator's conclusion that continued use of chlordane poses an "imminent hazard" to human health, and that the Administrator made critical errors in assessing the burden of proof. * * *

Velsicol and USDA contend that the laboratory tests on mice and rats do not "conclusively" demonstrate that chlordane is carcinogenic to those animals; that mice are too prone to tumors to be used in carcinogenicity testing in any case; and that human exposure to chlordane is insufficient to create a cancer risk. * * *

[The Court's discussion of the animal tests is omitted.]

Human epidemiology studies so far attempted on chlordane and heptachlor gave no basis for concluding that the two pesticides are safe with respect to the issue of cancer. To conclude that they pose a carcinogenic risk to humans on the basis of such a finding of risk to laboratory animals, the Administrator must show a causal connection between the uses of the pesticides challenged and resultant exposure of humans to those pesticides. He made that link by showing that widespread residues of heptachlor and chlordane are present in the human diet and in human tissues. Their widespread occurrence in the environment and accumulation in the food chain is explained by their chemical properties of persistence, mobility and high solubility in lipids (the fats contained in all organic substances.) Residues of chlordane and heptachlor remain in soils and in air and aquatic ecosystems for long periods of time. They are readily transported by means of vaporization, aerial drift, and runoff of eroding soil particles. The residues have been consistently found in meat, fish, poultry and dairy products monitored in the FDA Market Basket Survey and are also frequent in components of animal feeds. This evidence supports a finding that a major route of human exposure is ingestion of contaminated foodstuffs. EPA's National Human Monitoring Survey data shows that heptachlor epoxide and oxychlordane, the principal metabolites of heptachlor and chlordane respectively, are present in the adipose tissue of over 90% of the U.S. population.

The population's exposure to these pesticides, in large part involuntary, can be divided into agricultural and nonagricultural related routes. Seven million pounds of heptachlor and chlordane were used as corn soil insecticide in 1975, producing residues which persist in the soil for several years after application. These residues are taken up by such food, feed, and forage crops as soybeans, barley, oats, and hays typically rotated with corn. By volatilization the pesticides contaminate corn and other plant leaves. And root crops like potatoes, carrots and beets directly absorb the pesticides from the soil. Other sources of agricultural-related residues include exposure to contaminated dust particles and agricultural runoff containing eroded soil particles.

Velsicol urges that the dietary exposure resulting from agricultural uses of the pesticides is insignificant, and that current exposure is well below "safe" dose levels as calculated by the Mantel–Bryan formula, or by the World Health Organization's Acceptable Daily Intake figures. Mantel himself criticized the use of the formula for a persistent pesticide, and the Administrator rejected the concept of a "safe" dose level defined by mathematical modeling because of "the incomplete assumptions made by the registrant's witnesses about the sources of human exposure in the environment, the natural variation in human susceptibility to cancer, the lack of any evidence relating the level of human susceptibility to cancer from heptachlor and chlordane as opposed to that of the mouse, and the absence of precise knowledge as to the minimum exposure to a carcinogen necessary to cause cancer." That explanation is within the reasonable bounds of the agency's expertise in evaluating evidence. And it is confirmed by the common sense recognition that reliance on average "safe" dietary levels fail to protect people with dietary patterns based on high proportional consumption of residue-contaminated foods (e.g., children who ingest greater quantities of milk than the general population).

There are several non-agricultural uses which involve a large volume of heptachlor and chlordane as well as significant human exposures. For example, the record shows that approximately six million pounds of chlordane are used annually on home lawns and gardens. The Administrator found that these uses involve high risks of human intake "due to the many avenues which exist for direct exposure, through improper handling and misuse, inhalation, and absorption through the skin from direct contact." Velsicol asserts that the mice studies showing carcinogenic effects after ingestion of chlordane do not warrant an inference about the carcinogenic effects of inhaling it or absorbing it through the skin, and that consequently nonagricultural routes of exposure cannot be considered to present a cancer risk. * * * [T]he FIFRA statutory scheme mandates explicit relief—the suspension of registration—when an unreasonable risk to health is made out. We have previously held that it is not necessary to have evidence on a specific use to be able to conclude that the use of a pesticide in general is hazardous. Once the initial showing of hazard is made for one mode of exposure in a suspension proceeding, and the pesticide is shown to be present in human tissues, the burden shifts to the registrant to rebut the inference that other modes of exposure may also pose a carcinogenic hazard for humans. Velsicol has totally failed to meet that burden here. Although it was put on notice in the Notice to Suspend of EPA's intent to rely on direct inhalation and dermal exposure as reasons to suspend household lawn and turf uses of chlordane, it failed to offer even a medical theory as to why the significant inhalation or dermal exposure associated with such uses would not pose a carcinogenic threat. In view of the general failure to understand the mechanics of carcinogenicity, the lack of hypothetical explanation may be based on Velsicol's own data that exposure to vapors of chlordane and heptachlor in the work place, leads (as dietary exposure leads) to storage of oxychlordane, heptachlor epoxide, and other components in the fat tissue, and to circulation of these compounds in the blood, with consequent exposure to other organs in the body. Nor did Velsicol focus on the individual user's intense inhalation exposure associated with lawn and turf uses in its response to the point made in the EPA Staff's exceptions to the ALJ recommended decision, that the evidence showed that an individual using these chemicals for lawn and turf applications is subjected to a marked intensity of inhalation. Instead Velsicol attacked as inconsistent with the minimal amounts of chlordane and heptachlor normally found in ambient air, the EPA Staff's proposed reliance on inhalation as a major route of human exposure for the general population. However, the Administrator did not proceed on this basis. And if Velsicol hypothesized that chlordane residues are safe so long as they reach the tissue only through inhalation (even intense inhalation) it should have presented witnesses expressing that hypothesis. Instead they argue, in general and procedural terms, that the evidence presented by the Administrator was not sufficient to meet his full burden, and this in our view seeks to impose a broader burden on the Administrator than is appropriate in a suspension proceeding.

[The suspension order was therefore affirmed.]

NOTES

1. Note the appearance of another burden of proof rule, this time relating to carcinogens. Is the presumption created by the court reasonable? Suppose the agency rejected the inference that a substance which causes cancer under one mode of exposure probably causes cancer under other modes. Should a court reverse based on its own view as to what presumption should apply?

In a law review article, Judge Leventhal maintained he had used "burden of proof" concepts in a different sense than the conventional usage in civil procedure. Instead, he said, burden of proof was used to refer to the burden of "adducing a reasoned presentation supporting [EPA's conclusions]." Leventhal, *Environmental Decisionmaking and the Role of the Courts*, 122 U. PA. L. REV. 509, 535–36 (1974). He also stated that burden of proof concepts are "nothing more or less than devices for controlling risks of error." *Id.* Do you find this to be a persuasive explanation of the pesticide cases? For further discussion, see Rodgers, *Benefits, Costs, and Risks: Oversight of Health and Environmental Decisionmaking*, 4 HARV. ENV. L. REV. 191, 219–24 (1980).

Which is preferable: Judge Leventhal's approach to burden of proof, or that of the plurality in the *Benzene* case?

2. On denial of the petition for rehearing, the court issued a lengthy supplemental opinion rejecting the contention that the Administrative Procedure Act placed the burden of proof on the EPA throughout the proceeding. *EDF, Inc. v. EPA*, 548 F.2d 998, 1012–18 (D.C. Cir. 1976).

3. Subsequent federal pesticide litigation has focused largely on deviations from the normal suspension/cancellation process discussed in the preceding cases. *See* Love v. Thomas, 858 F.2d 1347 (9th Cir. 1988), *cert. denied,* 490 U.S. 1035 (1989) (right of pesticide users to judicial review of emergency suspension order when no registrant requests a hearing); National Coalition Against the Misuse of Pesticides v. EPA, 867 F.2d 636 (D.C. Cir. 1989) (authority of EPA to enter into agreement providing for voluntary cancellation of registration but allowing continued sale and use of existing stocks of cancelled pesticide).

4. Stricter state and local regulation of pesticide use is permitted. In *People v. County of Mendocino*, 36 Cal.3d 476, 204 Cal.Rptr. 897, 683 P.2d 1150 (1984), the Supreme Court of California held that a county initiative ordinance prohibiting aerial application of phenoxy herbicides, including 2, 4, 5–T, Silvex, 2, 4–D and any matter containing dioxin, was not preempted by either state law or FIFRA. The court said that Congress, by providing in section 24(a) for further "State" regulation of federally registered pesticides, did not intend to preclude local regulation authorized under state law.

In *Wisconsin Public Intervenor v. Mortier,* 501 U.S. 597 (1991), the Supreme Court held that FIFRA does not preempt local pesticide-regulation ordinances.

5. Section 136v(b) of FIFRA provides that a state "shall not impose or continue in effect any requirements for labeling or packaging in addition to or different from those required under this subchapter." In *Bates v. Dow Agrosciences*, 544 U.S. 431 (2005), the Supreme Court authorized a lawsuit brought under Texas law by Texas peanut farmers who alleged that their crops were damaged by a pesticide called "Strongarm." Dow moved to dismiss the case on the grounds that FIFRA preempted the state law claims. The Court found that as long as a state labeling law "is equivalent to, and fully consistent with, FIFRA's ... provisions," the state cause of action can proceed. FIFRA requires that a pesticide label cannot contain "false or misleading statements;" as long as a state law contains a similar prohibition it can proceed. 125 S.Ct. at 1800. The Court effectively overruled a series of cases that had found state claims preempted, including *Etcheverry v. Tri–Ag Service, Inc.,* 993 P.2d 366 (Cal.2000) and *Arkansas–Platte & Gulf Partnership v. Van Waters & Rogers, Inc.,* 981 F.2d 1177 (10th Cir. 1993).

The California Safe Drinking Water and Toxic Enforcement Act of 1986 ("Proposition 65") requires California to *list* substances that it determines to be carcinogenic or reproductively toxic. Twelve months after a substance has been listed by the state, the manufacturers of products containing the listed substances must provide adequate *warnings* to the consuming public that their products pose a health risk. In *Chemical Specialties Manufacturers Ass'n v. Allenby,* 958 F.2d 941 (9th Cir. 1992), *cert. denied,* 506 U.S. 825 (1992), CSMA, a trade association of insecticide, disinfectant, and antimicrobial product manufacturers, contended that the adequate warning requirements of Proposition 65 were preempted as applied to products regulated under FIFRA. Proposition 65 provides that the required "warning" need not be provided separately to each exposed individual and may be provided by general methods "such as labels on consumer products, inclusion of notices in mailings to water customers, posting of notices, placing notices in the public news media, and the like, provided that the warning accomplished is clear and reasonable." CAL. HEALTH & SAFETY CODE section 25249.11(f). Relying on FIFRA's definitions of "label" and "labeling," the court rejected CSMA's position and found that point-of-sale warnings satisfying the requirements of Proposition 65 did not constitute additional labeling.

6. *Safe Alternatives for Fruit Fly Eradication v. Berryhill,* 1984 WL 178937 (C.D.Cal.1984), held that citizens living or working in the area of aerial spraying of the pesticide Malathion by a *state* agency to control the Mexican fruit fly lacked standing to seek an injunction against the spraying program because (a) FIFRA provided no private right of action, and (b) plaintiffs were foreclosed by *Middlesex County Sewerage Authority v. National Sea Clammers Ass'n,* 453 U.S. 1 (1981), from enforcing FIFRA rights under the Civil Rights Act of 1866, 42 U.S.C.A. section 1983.

7. *Headwaters, Inc. v. Talent Irrigation District,* 243 F.3d 526 (9th Cir. 2001), held that an irrigation district was liable under the Clean Water Act for discharging an aquatic herbicide into irrigation canals without an NPDES permit. The district contended that it did not require a CWA permit because the label approved for the herbicide by EPA under FIFRA did not mention a need for a CWA permit. The court of appeals rejected this contention, saying that the CWA and FIFRA serve different purposes. "FIFRA's labels are the same nationwide, and so the statute does not and cannot consider local environmental conditions. By contrast, the NPDES program under the CWA does just that." The spraying of herbicide on canals constituted a discharge of pollutants from a point source, and the canals were "waters of the United States" to which discharge permit requirements applied.

8. Pesticides in and on raw agricultural commodities are regulated under the Federal Food, Drug and Cosmetic Act, 21 U.S.C.A. section 301 et seq. EPA sets *tolerance* levels of pesticide concentrations in or on commodities consumed in the United States; the Food and Drug Administration monitors actual pesticide *content* of commodities and has the authority to confiscate foods containing either excessive concentrations of registered pesticides or unsafe residues of unregistered pesticides. 21 U.S.C.A. sections 342, 346a. Under section 346a, the EPA Administrator is to consider, when establishing tolerances, "the necessity for the production of an adequate, wholesome, and economical food supply" as well as health effects.

Some foods imported into the United States may contain unsafe pesticide residues, including residues of pesticides not registered here.

The following case considered allowable tolerance levels for pesticides in foods and led to a 1996 amendment to the FFDCA exempting pesticide chemical residues from the "Delaney clause."

LES v. REILLY

United States Court of Appeals, Ninth Circuit, 1992.
968 F.2d 985, *cert. denied,* 507 U.S. 950, 113 S.Ct. 1361, 122 L.Ed.2d 740 (1993).

SCHROEDER, CIRCUIT JUDGE.

Petitioners seek review of a final order of the Environmental Protection Agency permitting the use of four pesticides as food additives although they have been found to induce cancer. Petitioners challenge the final order on the ground that it violates the provisions of the Delaney clause, 21 U.S.C. § 348(c)(3), which prohibits the use of any food additive that is found to induce cancer. * * *

The Federal Food, Drug, and Cosmetic Act (FFDCA), 21 U.S.C. §§ 301–394 (West 1972 & Supp.1992), is designed to ensure the safety of the food we eat by prohibiting the sale of food that is "adulterated." 21 U.S.C. § 331(a). Adulterated food is in turn defined as food containing any unsafe food "additive." 21 U.S.C. § 342(a)(2)(C). A food "additive" is defined broadly as "any substance the intended use of which results or may reasonably be expected to result ... in its becoming a component ... of any food." 21 U.S.C. § 321(s). A food additive is considered unsafe unless there is a specific exemption for the substance or a regulation prescribing the conditions under which it may be used safely. 21 U.S.C. § 348(a). * * *

The FFDCA also contains special provisions which regulate the occurrence of pesticide residues on raw agricultural commodities. Section 402 of the FFDCA, 21 U.S.C. § 342(a)(2)(B), provides that a raw food containing a pesticide residue is deemed adulterated unless the residue is authorized under section 408 of the FFDCA, 21 U.S.C. § 346a, which allows tolerance regulations setting maximum permissible levels and also provides for exemption from tolerances under certain circumstances. When a tolerance or an exemption has been established for use of a pesticide on a raw agricultural commodity, then the FFDCA allows for the "flow-through" of such pesticide residue to processed foods, even when the pesticide may be a carcinogen. This flow-through is allowed, however, only to the extent that the concentration of the pesticide in the processed food does not exceed the concentration allowed in the raw food.... 21 U.S.C. § 342(a)(2)(C). It is undisputed that the EPA regulations at issue in this case allow for the concentration of cancer-causing pesticides during processing to levels in excess of those permitted in the raw foods. * * *

The issue before us is whether the EPA has violated section 409 of the FFDCA, the Delaney clause, by permitting the use of carcinogenic food additives which it finds to present only a de minimis or negligible risk of causing cancer. The Agency acknowledges that its interpretation of the law is a new and changed one. From the initial enactment of the Delaney clause in 1958 to the time of the rulings here in issue, the statute had been strictly and literally enforced. The EPA also acknowledges that the language of the statute itself appears, at first glance, to be clear on its face. ("[S]ection 409 mandates a zero risk standard for carcinogenic pesticides in processed foods in those instances where the pesticide concentrates during processing or is applied during or after processing.")

The language is clear and mandatory. The Delaney clause provides that no additive shall be deemed safe if it induces cancer. 21 U.S.C. § 348(c)(3). The EPA states in its final order that appropriate tests have established that the pesticides at issue here induce cancer in humans or animals. The statute provides that once the finding of carcinogenicity is made, the EPA has no discretion.... * * *

The Agency asks us to look behind the language of the Delaney clause to the overall statutory scheme governing pesticides, which permits the use of carcinogenic pesticides on raw food without regard to the Delaney clause. Yet section 402 of the FFDCA, 21 U.S.C. § 342(a)(2)(C), expressly harmonizes that scheme with the Delaney clause by providing that residues on processed foods may not exceed the tolerance level established for the raw food. The statute unambiguously provides that pesticides which concentrate in processed food are to be treated as food additives, and these are governed by the Delaney food additive provision contained in section 409. If pesticides which concentrate in processed foods induce cancer in humans or animals, they render the food adulterated and must be prohibited. * * *

The EPA's refusal to revoke regulations permitting the use of benomyl, mancozeb, phosmet and trifluralin as food additives on the ground the cancer risk they pose is de minimis is contrary to the provisions of the Delaney clause prohibiting food additives that induce cancer. The EPA's final order is set aside.

NOTES

1. In 1996 Congress amended the Federal Food, Drug and Cosmetic Act to exempt pesticide chemical residues from the Delaney clause. Food Quality Protection Act of 1996, P. L. 104–170, section 405 (Aug. 3, 1996), amending FFDCA section 408, 21 U.S.C. section 346a. For such residues, the Delaney distinction between "carcinogen" and "noncarcinogen" was replaced with a new distinction between "threshold" and "nonthreshold" toxicants. The *"general rule,"* for *threshold* toxicants, is that the EPA Administrator may establish a tolerance for a residue in or on a food if she determines that the tolerance is "safe," i.e., "that there is a reasonable certainty that no harm will result from aggregate exposure to the pesticide chemical residue, including all anticipated dietary exposures and all other exposures for which there is reliable information." 21 U.S.C. section 346a(b)(2)(A). For *nonthreshold* ("eligible") toxicants, a tolerance must meet at least *one* of the two conditions described in clause (iii), below, and *both* of the conditions described in clause (iv), 21 U.S.C. section 346a(b)(2)(B):

(iii) Conditions regarding use

(I) Use of the pesticide chemical that produces the residue protects consumers from adverse effects on health that would pose a greater risk than the dietary risk from the residue.

(II) Use of the pesticide chemical that produces the residue is necessary to avoid a significant disruption in domestic production of an adequate, wholesome, and economical food supply.

(iv) Conditions regarding risk

(I) The yearly risk associated with the nonthreshold effect from aggregate exposure to the residue does not exceed 10 times the yearly risk that would be allowed under [the "general rule"] for such effect.

(II) The tolerance is limited so as to ensure that the risk over a lifetime associated with the nonthreshold effect from aggregate exposure to the residue is not greater than twice the lifetime risk that would be allowed under [the "general rule"] for such effect.

The amendments also require that, in establishing a tolerance for a pesticide chemical residue, the Administrator (i) shall assess the risk of the residue based on available information about consumption patterns (exposure) among infants and children, and about their special susceptibility to the residue, and (ii) shall ensure that there is a reasonable certainty that no harm will result to infants and children from aggregate exposure to the residue. "In the case of threshold effects, for purposes of clause (ii)(I) an additional tenfold margin of safety for the pesticide chemical residue and other sources of exposure shall be applied for infants and children to take into account potential pre-and post-natal toxicity and completeness of the data with respect to exposure and toxicity to infants and children." 21 U.S.C. section 346a(b)(2)(C).

For a discussion of the continuing effects of the Delaney clause in the FFDCA after the 1996 amendments, *see* James Turner, *Delaney Lives! Reports of Delaney's Death Are Greatly Exaggerated*, 28 ENVTL L. REP. 10003 (1998).

For a more general discussion of the 1996 amendments, *see* Kenneth Weinstein et al., *The Food Quality Protection Act: A New Way of Looking at Pesticides*, 28 ENVTL L. REP. 10559 (1998).

2. As discussed in Chapter 3, GATT trade rules may affect domestic environmental regulations, as applied to imports. Section 346a(b)(2)(B)(iii) makes one of the conditions for a tolerance a finding that use is "necessary to avoid a significant disruption in domestic production." This provision may discriminate against foreign producers claiming a tolerance in order to avoid disruption in their production. Because of this discriminatory feature, the provision may be a prima facie violation of Article III of GATT. Other aspects of the provision, though facially neutral, might be found to have a disparate impact on foreign producers, also causing a potential GATT problem.

3. The following article was published after the decision in *Les v. Reilly* but before enactment of the Food Quality Protection Act of 1996, discussed in note 1 above. Although that act also included some amendments to FIFRA,

they did not incorporate the aggressive "alternative framework of environmental law reform" advocated by Professor Hornstein. As he feared, the opportunity for real change was squandered because congressional debate was framed in terms of "risk" rather than "alternative agriculture."

DONALD HORNSTEIN, LESSONS FROM FEDERAL PESTICIDE REGULATION ON THE PARADIGMS AND POLITICS OF ENVIRONMENTAL LAW REFORM[2]

10 YALE J. ON REG. 369, 371–72, 380, 392–405, 436–46 (1993).

[O]ne of the first environmental problems to come before the Clinton Administration and the 103rd Congress [is] the reform of federal pesticide policy. The policy debate is now framed as a choice between evaluating pesticide residues on processed foods with modern risk assessment techniques or continuing the blanket prohibition of such residues now found in the so-called "Delaney Clause." Although described as a referendum on "science" versus "politics," the Delaney debate in fact avoids much of the important science governing pest management, ignores virtually all of the economics of pesticide use, and marginalizes many of the public health and environmental values implicated by agricultural chemicals. To avoid being misunderstood, this criticism does not reflect a conviction that Delaney is necessarily good policy. There is plausible evidence that a blanket prohibition on all detectible carcinogenic residues can be counterproductive. But there is also plausible evidence that risk assessments frequently sit atop both suspect data and contentious methodological assumptions. More to the point, the use of risk assessments to discern "reasonable risk" under the Federal Insecticide Fungicide and Rodenticide Act (FIFRA) has arguably led to one of the most colossal regulatory failures in Washington. Yet despite these well-known criticisms, the Delaney debate continues as if the only policy options for sound pesticide policy—and environmental regulation in general—were the status quo or a new regime dominated by scientific risk assessments. * * *

This Article argues for an alternative framework of environmental law reform, one more aggressive in identifying and addressing the causes of environmental problems than either existing regulatory programs or reform proposals that emphasize risk-based priority-setting. This alternative framework would focus especially on the role played by existing economic incentives in causing environmental problems and the role that better-designed incentives can play in solving them. * * *

As a general matter, cause-oriented reforms focus on reducing human pressures on natural resources, often by encouraging "clean" technologies or changes in consumption and use patterns. Roughly speaking, this approach contrasts with the focus of risk-based reforms on managing environmental effects to some level of acceptable risk. * * *

---

2. Copyright © 1993 by the Yale Journal on Regulation. Reprinted with permission.

For all its complexity, * * * it is important to underscore what pesticide regulation is not: it is not a body of law that addresses in any strategic way the underlying prevalence of pesticides in American agriculture, nor is it a body of law designed to minimize pesticide use. On reflection, this characteristic is especially striking because the impetus for modern pesticide regulation, if not for the modern environmental movement in general, was the argument made in 1962 by Rachel Carson in *Silent Spring* for developing just such a strategic environmental law. * * *

At the core of any alternative legal framework must be an appreciation of the strengths and limitations of what is typically described as "alternative" agriculture. [T]here are basically four types of alternative measures most commonly in use, and about which a scientific literature has developed or is developing. First, there are "cultural" methods to control insects, weeds, and diseases, such as crop rotations, altered planting dates, cultivation, and the planting of border crops. Second, there are "biological control" methods such as the release of predatory or parasitic insects. Third, there is the deployment of "biorational" pest control measures such as pheromone-baited traps, the release of microbiological pathogens of insects or weeds, and the use of genetically engineered pest control products. Fourth, and probably most importantly, there is the use of "integrated pest management" (IPM), a decisionmaking system designed to use all "suitable" pest control techniques, including chemical pesticides, to keep pest populations below economically injurious levels while satisfying environmental and production objectives.

It is fairly plain that alternative pest controls can impose on farmers two types of costs that are generally not imposed to the same extent by chemical pesticides. First, there are often significant information costs involved with more finely-tailored alternative forms of crop protection— such as the need to "scout" a crop to discern the optimal timing of pesticide applications (perhaps the most common IPM technique) or the need to familiarize oneself with the relative effectiveness of a wide assortment of nonchemical measures or products—that clearly transcend the information costs involved in the more routine spraying of a chemical pesticide that may be "automatically" effective against a broad range of pests. Second, to the extent that pest-specific products are used, they will by definition cost more than products that work against a broader range of pests because the pest-specific user market will be smaller and the producer must charge proportionately higher prices to recoup her investments in research and development.

Alternative pest control can also pose free rider and collective action problems. For example, the release of predatory insects will rarely be in an individual farmer's economic self-interest because they cannot be confined to the farmer's property and thus will become to that extent a public good whose full value cannot be recouped. Conversely, if farmers seek to join in an areawide organization for the purposes of cooperative pest control, they may face "hold-outs" who attempt to free-ride on the cooperating farmers' efforts—or, worse, hold-outs whose recalcitrant activities actually undermine the cooperative efforts (say, by maintaining fields which serve as "reservoirs" for common pests or by continuing the use of chemical pesticides that kill predatory insects released by the alternative farmers). * * *

There are, currently, dozens of policy options to encourage low-input agriculture, ranging from mandated reductions in pesticide use by target dates to pesticide risk taxes to expedited registration of "alternative" pest control products. I endorse none of these specific options here. Rather, I want only to underscore two criteria that should guide the merits of the long-overdue development of a true environmental policy for pesticides.

First, Congress should encourage governmental intervention that addresses the underlying reasons for pesticide overuse. Fitting this criteria would be consideration of two obvious problems for any system of low-input agriculture: risk averse farmers may overuse pesticides as a minimax strategy to avoid catastrophic crop losses, and farmers may overuse pesticides because of their relatively low informational costs. Although the issues have their complexities, the arguments appear strong at least in the near term for public subsidization of "IPM" crop insurance premiums and of significant enhancements for existing "extension" programs that have already been developed to train farmers in the new techniques. * * *

Second, Congress should bypass the risk-dominated structures in EPA's pesticide office and legislate direct disincentives to pesticide use. Such an approach would have the benefit of "locking in" structural incentives for low-input agriculture and avoiding the implementation slippage that has inevitably occurred in pesticide regulation. * * *

Third, risk analysis offers the conceptual umbrella of "science" under which numerous non-scientific values can take shelter from public scrutiny and yet prolong the longevity of pesticides that may be neither desirable nor needed. Consider, for example, the decidedly nonscientific question of deciding how risk averse to be when evaluating uncertain data. * * *

Reform of pesticide regulation is in theory, and will probably soon prove to be in practice, a logical starting point for self-conscious attention to cause-oriented reform. FIFRA reform legislation was reported from most of the relevant congressional committees near the close of the 102nd Congress, and has been reintroduced early in the 103rd. Congressional attention to pesticides will be driven by the often-noted implications of the proposed North American Free Trade Agreement for acceptable levels of pesticide residues and the Ninth Circuit's recent holding in *Les v. Reilly,* which will require EPA to revoke tolerances and cancel registrations for some twenty-five or more pesticides unless affected by congressional action. A recently released major study by the National Academy of Sciences has focused attention on the EPA's inadequate attention to the tolerance of children to pesticide residues. * * *

Unfortunately, the expected upsurge in public attention to pesticides will be largely squandered if the congressional debate is framed, as it is likely to be, solely in terms of "risk." By all indications, FIFRA reform will focus on administrative improvements to expedite risk-based decisional processes for reregistration and cancellation. And the debate over food safety legislation may well be dominated by the "Delaney paradox" (claiming that the Delaney Clause increases aggregate carcinogenic risk by prohibiting the registration of new pesticides with safer carcinogenic profiles than older, existing ones that are awaiting reregistration or are otherwise permissible under FFDCA). The Delaney debate can be expected to focus on an esoteric battle between those who prefer a specified one-in-one-million standard of acceptable risk and those who prefer the unspecified requirement of "reasonable risk." Although some discussion of risk methodologies is unavoidable and probably beneficial, there is every reason to hope that the debate can be supplemented by formulation of a concrete, long-overdue framework for reducing inefficient pesticide use.

NOTES

1. The Food Quality Protection Act of 1996, discussed in the notes preceding the Hornstein article, did give a nod to adoption of Integrated Pest Management (IPM). The act added to FIFRA this provision, 7 U.S.C. section 136r–1:

The Secretary of Agriculture, in cooperation with the [EPA] Administrator, shall implement research, demonstration, and education programs to support adoption of Integrated Pest Management. [IPM] is a sustainable approach to managing pests by combining biological, cultural, physical, and chemical tools in a way that minimizes economic, health, and environmental risks. The Secretary ... and the Administrator shall make information on [IPM] widely available to pesticide users.... Federal agencies shall use [IPM] techniques in carrying out pest management activities and shall promote [IPM] through procurement and regulatory policies, and other activities.

2. Another major risk of the threatening aspect of the improvident use of pesticides is widespread contamination of underground water sources, aquifers which are or may be tapped by wells to supply drinking water to individual homes and entire cities. For example, before it was banned in 1977 for causing sterility in humans and cancer in laboratory animals, the soil fumigant "DBCP" was used widely in California vineyards and orchards to combat root worms. Now, up and down the San Joaquin Valley, more than 100 municipal wells have been shut down because of unsafe levels of DBCP. In 18 California counties, including Los Angeles, Riverside, San Bernardino, Orange, and San Diego, more than 1,700 public and private wells serving 200,000 people now exceed federal standards for exposure to DBCP. Cities are faced with retiring more wells or equipping them with elaborate carbon filtration systems. Between 1980 and 1995, the city of Fresno had to close 29 wells and install five carbon filtration systems at a cost of $800,000 each. *See* Mark Arax, *Banned DBCP Still Haunts San Joaquin Valley Water*, LOS ANGELES TIMES, June 12, 1995, at A1.

3.   Another major risk of the improvident use of pesticides is the health harms pesticides may cause to farm workers who apply the chemicals or work in affected fields. Since many of the workers are poor immigrants, these risks raise environmental justice issues.

For extreme cases of thousands of farm workers in Latin America becoming sterile from unprotected exposure to pesticides manufactured in the United States and used on plantations owned by subsidiaries of U.S. corporations, *see Dow Chemical Co. v. Castro Alfaro*, 786 S.W.2d 674 (Tex.1990), *cert. denied*, 498 U.S. 1024 (1991); Diana Schemo, *Pesticide From U.S. Kills the Hopes of Fruit Pickers in the Third World*, N. Y. TIMES, Dec. 6, 1995, at A8, col. 4.

2.   THE TOXIC SUBSTANCES CONTROL ACT

Congress enacted the Toxic Substances Control Act[3] (TSCA) in 1976 to prevent "unreasonable risks of injury to health or the environment" associated with the manufacture, processing, distribution, use or disposal of chemical substances other than drugs and pesticides. TSCA's emphasis is on regulating products—principally industrial chemicals—rather than wastes.[4]

The Act as a whole must be read in light of the policy section (§ 2(b)). Three policies are set forth. First, data should be developed on the environmental effects of chemicals; primary responsibility for the development of these data is placed on industry. Second, the government should have adequate authority to prevent unreasonable risks of injury to health or the environment, particularly imminent hazards. Finally, this authority should be exercised so as "not to impede unduly or create unnecessary economic barriers to technological innovation while fulfilling the primary purpose of this Act to assure that * * * such chemical substances * * * do not present an unreasonable risk of injury * * *." (§ 2(b)(3)). Obviously, much depends on the relative weights given to these conflicting goals of protecting technological development and assuring environmental safety.[5]

The most important substantive provisions of the Act are found in sections 4, 5, and 6. These sections concern testing, premanufacturing clearance, and regulation of manufacturing and distribution of chemical substances. We will consider only the main outlines of these provisions, without too much attention to the innumerable exemptions, exceptions, qualifications and procedural details. It is important to note the difference in treatment by TOSCA of *new* v. *existing* chemicals. With the exception of Section 6 of the act, those chemicals that were already in commerce at the time TOSCA was enacted are largely exempted from the act's provisions (researchers estimate that about 62,000 chemicals are largely outside the

---

3.   90 Stat. 2003 (1976), 15 U.S.C.A. section 2601, et seq.

4.   For an extended discussion of TSCA and its implementation, *see* Hathaway, Hayes and Rawson, *A Practitioner's Guide to the Toxic Substances Control Act*, parts I–III, 24 ENVTL. L. REP. 10207, 10285, 10357 (1994).

5.   For a general discussion, *see* Comment, *Risk–Benefit Analysis and Technology Forcing Under the Toxic Substances Control Act*, 62 IOWA L. REV. 942, 945–57 (1977).

statute's regulatory reach). *See* UC CENTERS FOR OCCUPATIONAL AND ENVIRONMENTAL HEALTH, GREEN CHEMISTRY: CORNERSTONE TO A SUSTAINABLE CALIFORNIA (2008) at 6.

Section 4 relates to testing. It empowers the EPA to adopt rules requiring manufacturers to test substances. Such rules must be based on a finding that insufficient data are currently available concerning the substance, and that the substance may "present an unreasonable risk" (§ 4(a)(1)(A)(i)), "enter the environment in substantial quantities" (§ 4(a)(1)(B)(i)(I)), *or* present a likelihood of "substantial human exposure" (§ 4(a)(1)(B)(i)(II)). There are, naturally, a variety of complicated procedural devices set out in exhaustive detail in the remainder of the section. In addition to section 4, the statute contains several other provisions aimed at collection of information.[6]

Section 5 requires a manufacturer to give notice to the EPA before manufacturing a *new* chemical substance.[7] If the substance is covered by a § 4 rule, the § 4 test results must be submitted along with the § 5 notice (§ 5(b)(1)(A)).[8] For substances not covered by § 4, but listed by EPA as possibly hazardous, the manufacturer is to submit data it believes show the absence of any unreasonable risk of injury (§ 5(b)(2)(A), (B)). Normally, the next step would be a § 6 proceeding (Section 6 is described in the next paragraph). But if EPA finds that an unreasonable risk may be presented before a § 6 rule can be promulgated, it can issue a "proposed § 6 rule" which will be immediately effective, issue an administrative order, or seek an injunction (§ 5(f)). Often, EPA will not have sufficient information to make a definite finding about safety. EPA can then make risk or prevalence findings similar to those triggering the § 4 testing rules and issue an administrative order. (If a timely objection to the order is filed, however, EPA must seek injunctive relief (§ 5(e)).

Section 6, unlike § 5, applies to all chemicals, not just to new chemicals or new uses. The finding necessary to trigger § 6 is that "there is a reasonable basis to conclude" that the substance "presents or will present an unreasonable risk of injury to health or the environment * * *." Having made such a finding, EPA may by rule apply any of a number of restrictions "to the extent necessary to protect adequately against such risk using the least burdensome requirements" (§ 6(a)). EPA can, for example, ban the chemical all together or limit production or require warnings for its use. §§ 6(a),(b). Obviously, much will depend on whether more weight is given to "protect adequately" or to "least burdensome." In general, EPA is directed to use its regulatory powers under other statutes in preference to § 6 (§ 6(c)). The effective date of a proposed rule may be accelerated if the EPA finds a likelihood of "an

---

6. Section 8 gives EPA far-reaching powers to obtain reports and records. This section was given a broad reading in *Dow Chemical v. EPA,* 605 F.2d 673 (3d Cir. 1979), which upheld extension of the statute to research and development projects. Section 11 gives EPA inspection and subpoena powers.

7. Or an old substance for a "significant new use" § 5(a)(1)(B).

8. There is a special provision, § 5(b)(1)(B), for persons exempted from § 4.

unreasonable risk of serious or widespread injury to health or the environment" before the effective date of the final rule. The requirements for acceleration under § 6(d), it should be noted, are somewhat different from those applicable to new chemicals under § 5(f). Finally, § 6 contains a special provision for the phasing out of polychlorinated biphenyls (PCBs).

One other provision which deserves mention is § 7, which allows EPA to obtain emergency judicial relief in case of "imminent hazards." *See* Walker and Eisenfeld, *How to Handle Difficult Chemicals: The Unused Tool in EPA's Chemical Toolbox—Section 7 of the Toxic Substances Control Act*, 24 ENVTL. L. REP. 10015 (1994). The Act also contains the usual panoply of provisions on civil and criminal penalties, judicial enforcement, judicial review, hybrid rule-making, and preemption. The following case challenged the EPA's delay in failing to initiate rule making procedures after designating the chemicals as highly risky.

NATURAL RESOURCES DEFENSE COUNCIL, INC. v. ENVIRONMENTAL PROTECTION AGENCY

United States District Court, Southern District of New York, 1984.
595 F.Supp. 1255.

DUFFY, DISTRICT JUDGE

[Section 4 of TSCA] provides for EPA issuance of rules requiring testing of chemicals which may present unreasonable risks of injury to human health or the environment. The testing required by such rules is to be carried out and financed by the manufacturers and/or processors of the chemical substances. *See* TSCA, 15 U.S.C. § 2603(b)(3). In section 2603(e) of the Act, Congress established an expert panel of government scientists, known as the "Interagency Testing Committee" ("ITC"). ITC is directed to select and recommend to EPA a list of those chemicals whose potential risks to health and the environment are determined to warrant "priority consideration by the agency for the promulgation of a rule. * * * "Thereafter the EPA is required within twelve months of the date on which the substances are first designated to "either initiate a rulemaking proceeding under subsection (a) * * * or if such a proceeding is not initiated within such period, publish in the Federal Register the [EPA] Administrator's reason for not initiating such a proceeding."

A test rule "shall" be promulgated if EPA finds that [the conditions described in section 2603(a) exist].

The final test rule must identify, *inter alia,* the chemical(s) to be tested, the specific effects for which testing must be done, the test standards or protocols, and the deadlines for test completion and submission of data. See id. § 2603(b)(1). To formulate a final rule, EPA is required first to publish proposed rules with these characteristics, soliciting public commentary. * * *

In late 1981 and early 1982, EPA announced in the *Federal Register* that it would consider accepting voluntary testing programs in certain circumstances. These programs would be negotiated and conducted by manufacturers or processors of ITC designated chemical substances in lieu of initiating a rulemaking proceeding. EPA asserts that it adopted this new policy based upon the belief that such agreements would provide the required health and environmental effect test data in an expeditious manner. * * *

Plaintiff's first four claims are based on ITC's designation, between November 1980 and May 1982, of four chemicals warranting priority rulemaking consideration and review by EPA. In the two to four years since their designations, EPA has not initiated rulemaking proceedings; rather, within twelve months of each of the designations EPA accepted or tentatively accepted voluntary testing programs negotiated with industry. * * *

Plaintiffs brought this action pursuant to 15 U.S.C. § 2619(a)(2) which provides that "any person may commence a civil action * * * against the [EPA] Administrator to compel the Administrator to perform any duty under this Act which is not discretionary." EPA contends that it has no mandatory duty to issue test rules and therefore its discretionary acts are not subject to review by a citizen-suit civil action.

... Section 2603(e)(1)(B) provides the agency with a choice of either initiating a rulemaking proceeding or publishing its reasons for not doing so. It is evident, however, that the Administrator's duty to choose either to initiate rulemaking proceedings or to publish its reasons for not doing so is a mandatory choice that it must make. Thus, plaintiffs may invoke section 2619(a)(2) to review whether EPA carried out this nondiscretionary act. * * *

Both in the legislative history of TSCA and on the face of the statute, Congress has evinced its intention that chemicals on which there is insufficient data will be tested pursuant to formal rulemaking. * * *

* * * Section 2603 was promulgated to mandate the testing of potentially dangerous chemicals on which there was insufficient data existing at the present time. EPA's negotiation and acceptance of voluntary testing agreements by the manufacturers obviously reflects EPA's belief that additional data concerning the chemicals in question needs to be developed. The absence of a formal finding of testing necessity cannot hide EPA's evident *de facto* findings of such a necessity. * * *

Furthermore, I can find no support for EPA's decision to utilize negotiated testing agreements instead of the statutorily-prescribed initiation of rulemaking proceedings either on the face of the statute or based on some vague assertion of agency discretion. * * *

The chemicals * * * were recommended for testing by ITC nearly seven years ago * * *. They were among the first chemicals so designated by ITC. No rulemaking activity concerning these chemicals, however, took place until after NRDC brought a successful action to compel EPA's compliance with TSCA in 1979. Thereafter, pursuant to a stipulated timetable, EPA proposed rules for the * * * chemicals * * *. Since then, there have been three and four years without any formal rulemaking accomplished. In effect, EPA has accepted *de facto* voluntary testing programs in place of rulemaking. Voluntary testing programs, I already have held, are inadequate to fulfill the statutory mandate. * * * Accordingly, I find that defendants have unreasonably delayed agency action * * *.

* * * Plaintiffs' motion for partial summary judgment on the [foregoing issues] is granted * * *.

NOTES

1. Is there any argument that voluntary testing programs have benefits that formal rule making lacks? The foregoing decision resulted in a complete revamping of EPA's procedures for negotiating test rules under section 4 of TSCA. The agency now seeks to make consent agreements enforceable on the same basis as test rules. 40 C.F.R. 790. *See* W. Rodgers, 3 ENVIRONMENTAL LAW: PESTICIDES AND TOXIC SUBSTANCES 426–29 (1988) concerning EPA procedures related to consent agreements and test rules.

The requirement that EPA issue a rule before requiring testing distinguishes TSCA from food, drug, and pesticide statutes, which mandate production of safety data prior to marketing. It seems that TSCA essentially establishes a presumption of safety, which EPA must overcome before it may require further testing of a chemical. *See* Lyndon, *Information Economics and Chemical Toxicity: Designing Laws to Produce and Use Data*, 87 MICH. L. REV. 1795, 1824 (1989). Because of the elaborate procedural barriers, EPA has promulgated relatively few test rules under TSCA. *See* Applegate, *The Perils of Unreasonable Risk: Information, Regulatory Policy, and Toxic Substances Control*, 91 COLUM. L. REV. 261, 318–19 (1991).

Manufacturers sometimes challenge EPA test rules judicially, and the courts review in detail the agency's findings and reasons for demanding tests. *See Chemical Manufacturers Ass'n v. EPA*, 899 F.2d 344 (5th Cir. 1990) (rule requiring manufacturers and processors of chemical cumene to perform toxicological testing, remanded for EPA to articulate the standards or criteria on the basis of which it found the quantities of cumene entering the environment from the facilities in question to be "substantial," and the human exposure potentially resulting to be "substantial," under TSCA section 4(a)(1)(B)(i)); *Chemical Manufacturers Ass'n v. EPA*, 919 F.2d 158 (D.C. Cir. 1990) (upholding EPA's interpretation of section 4(a)(1)(A)(i) as authorizing issuance of a test rule where there is a "more than theoretical basis" to suspect the presence of unreasonable risk of injury to health, and finding that EPA had presented "substantial evidence" of exposure and toxicity so as to justify a test rule).

2. Section 6(a) of TSCA provides that if the Administrator finds that there is "a reasonable basis to conclude" that the manufacture, processing, distribution in commerce, use, or disposal of a chemical substance or mixture "presents or will present an unreasonable risk of injury to health or the environment," he "shall by rule apply one or more of [seven specific]

requirements * * * to the extent necessary to protect adequately against such risk *using the least burdensome requirements*" (emphasis added). The listed requirements include, among others, the prohibition of, or limitations on (e.g., total amount, maximum concentration, permissible uses) the manufacture, processing or distribution of such substance; regulation of the manner or method of use or disposal; and mandatory testing, record-keeping, and issuance of instructions, notices and warnings by manufacturers and processors. Section 6(c) prescribes criteria and procedures for promulgation of "subsection (a) rules." The case below involves a challenge to a rule promulgated under Section 6.

CORROSION PROOF FITTINGS v. ENVIRONMENTAL PROTECTION AGENCY

United States Court of Appeals, Fifth Circuit, 1991.
947 F.2d 1201.

JERRY E. SMITH, CIRCUIT JUDGE.

The Environmental Protection Agency (EPA) issued a final rule under section 6 of the Toxic Substances Control Act (TSCA) to prohibit the future manufacture, importation, processing, and distribution of asbestos in almost all products. Petitioners claim that the EPA's rulemaking procedure was flawed and that the rule was not promulgated on the basis of substantial evidence. * * *

Asbestos is a naturally occurring fibrous material that resists fire and most solvents. Its major uses include heat-resistant insulators, cements, building materials, fireproof gloves and clothing, and motor vehicle brake linings. Asbestos is a toxic material, and occupational exposure to asbestos dust can result in mesothelioma, asbestosis, and lung cancer. * * *

* * * Finding that asbestos constituted an unreasonable risk to health and the environment, the EPA promulgated a staged ban of most commercial uses of asbestos. The EPA estimates that this rule will save either 202 or 148 lives, depending upon whether the benefits are discounted, at a cost of approximately \$450–800 million, depending upon the price of substitutes.

The rule is to take effect in three stages, depending upon the EPA's assessment of how toxic each substance is and how soon adequate substitutes will be available. The rule allows affected persons one more year at each stage to sell existing stocks of prohibited products. The rule also imposes labeling requirements on stage 2 or stage 3 products and allows for exemptions from the rule in certain cases. * * *

Our inquiry into the legitimacy of the EPA rulemaking begins with a discussion of the standard of review governing this case. EPA's phase-out ban of most commercial uses of asbestos is a TSCA section 6(a) rulemaking. TSCA provides that a reviewing court "shall hold unlawful and set aside" a final rule promulgated under § 6(a) "if the court finds that the rule is not supported by substantial evidence in the rulemaking record ... taken as a whole." * * *

"Under the substantial evidence standard, a reviewing court must give careful scrutiny to agency findings and, at the same time, accord appropriate deference to administrative decisions that are based on agency experience and expertise." As with consumer product legislation, "Congress put the substantial evidence test in the statute because it wanted the courts to scrutinize the Commission's actions more closely than an 'arbitrary or capricious' standard would allow."

The recent case of *Chemical Mfrs. Ass'n v. EPA,* 899 F.2d 344 (5th Cir. 1990), provides our basic framework for reviewing the EPA's actions. In evaluating whether the EPA has presented substantial evidence, we examine (1) whether the quantities of the regulated chemical entering into the environment are "substantial" and (2) whether human exposure to the chemical is "substantial" or "significant." An agency may exercise its judgment without strictly relying upon quantifiable risks, costs, and benefits, but it must "cogently explain why it has exercised its discretion in a given manner" and "must offer a 'rational connection between the facts found and the choice made.'"

We note that in undertaking our review, we give all agency rules a presumption of validity, and it is up to the challenger to any rule to show that the agency action is invalid. The burden remains on the EPA, however, to justify that the products it bans present an unreasonable risk, no matter how regulated. *See Industrial Union Dep't v. American Petroleum Inst.,* 448 U.S. 607, 662, 100 S.Ct. 2844, 2874, 65 L.Ed.2d 1010 (1980). Finally, as we discuss in detail *infra,* because TSCA instructs the EPA to undertake the least burdensome regulation sufficient to regulate the substance at issue, the agency bears a heavier burden when it seeks a partial or total ban of a substance than when it merely seeks to regulate that product. *See* 15 U.S.C. § 2605(a).

TSCA provides, in pertinent part, as follows:

> (a) Scope of regulation.—If the Administrator finds that there is a *reasonable basis* to conclude that the manufacture, processing, distribution in commerce, use, or disposal of a chemical substance or mixture, or that any combination of such activities, presents or will present an *unreasonable risk of injury* to health or the environment, the Administrator shall by rule apply one or more of the following requirements to such substance or mixture to the extent necessary *to protect adequately* against such risk using the *least burdensome* requirements.

As the highlighted language shows, Congress did not enact TSCA as a zero-risk statute. The EPA, rather, was required to consider both alternatives to a ban and the costs of any proposed actions and to "carry out this chapter in a reasonable and prudent manner [after considering] the environmental, economic, and social impact of any action." 15 U.S.C. § 2601(c).

We conclude that the EPA has presented insufficient evidence to justify its asbestos ban. We base this conclusion upon two grounds: the failure of the EPA to consider all necessary evidence and its failure to give adequate weight to statutory language requiring it to promulgate the least burdensome, reasonable regulation required to protect the environment adequately. Because the EPA failed to address these concerns, and because the EPA is required to articulate a "reasoned basis" for its rules, we are compelled to return the regulation to the agency for reconsideration.

TSCA requires that the EPA use the least burdensome regulation to achieve its goal of minimum reasonable risk. This statutory requirement can create problems in evaluating just what is a "reasonable risk." Congress's rejection of a no-risk policy, however, also means that in certain cases, the least burdensome yet still adequate solution may entail somewhat more risk than would other, known regulations that are far more burdensome on the industry and the economy. The very language of TSCA requires that the EPA, once it has determined what an acceptable level of non-zero risk is, choose the least burdensome method of reaching that level.

In this case, the EPA banned, for all practical purposes, all present and future uses of asbestos—a position the petitioners characterize as the "death penalty alternative," as this is the *most* burdensome of all possible alternatives listed as open to the EPA under TSCA. TSCA not only provides the EPA with a list of alternative actions, but also provides those alternatives in order of how burdensome they are. The regulations [sic] thus provide for EPA regulation ranging from labeling the least toxic chemicals to limiting the total amount of chemicals an industry may use. Total bans head the list as the most burdensome regulatory option.

By choosing the harshest remedy given to it under TSCA, the EPA assigned to itself the toughest burden in satisfying TSCA's requirement that its alternative be the least burdensome of all those offered to it. Since, both by definition and by the terms of TSCA, the complete ban of manufacturing is the most burdensome alternative—for even stringent regulation at least allows a manufacturer the chance to invest and meet the new, higher standard—the EPA's regulation cannot stand if there is any other regulation that would achieve an acceptable level of risk as mandated by TSCA. * * *

The EPA considered, and rejected, such options as labeling asbestos products, thereby warning users and workers involved in the manufacture of asbestos-containing products of the chemical's dangers, and stricter workplace rules. EPA also rejected controlled use of asbestos in the workplace and deferral to other government agencies charged with worker and consumer exposure to industrial and product hazards, such as OSHA, the CPSC, and the MSHA. The EPA determined that deferral to these other agencies was inappropriate because no one other authority could address all the risks posed "throughout the life cycle" by asbestos, and any action by one or more of the other agencies still would leave an unacceptable residual risk.

Much of the EPA's analysis is correct, and the EPA's basic decision to use TSCA as a comprehensive statute designed to fight a multi-industry problem was a proper one that we uphold today on review. What concerns us, however, is the manner in which the EPA conducted some of its analysis. TSCA requires the EPA to consider, along with the effects of toxic substances on human health and the environment, "the benefits of such substance[s] or mixture[s] for various uses and the availability of substitutes for such uses," as well as "the reasonably ascertainable economic consequences of the rule, after consideration for the effect on the national economy, small business, technological innovation, the environment, and public health." *Id.* § 2605(c)(1)(C–D).

The EPA presented two comparisons in the record: a world with no further regulation under TSCA, and a world in which no manufacture of asbestos takes place. The EPA rejected calculating how many lives a less burdensome regulation would save, and at what cost. Furthermore the EPA, when calculating the benefits of its ban, explicitly refused to compare it to an improved workplace in which currently available control technology is utilized. This decision artificially inflated the purported benefits of the rule by using a baseline comparison substantially lower than what currently available technology could yield.

Under TSCA, the EPA was required to evaluate, rather than ignore, less burdensome regulatory alternatives. TSCA imposes a least-to-most-burdensome hierarchy. In order to impose a regulation at the top of the hierarchy—a total ban of asbestos—the EPA must show not only that its proposed action reduces the risk of the product to an adequate level, but also that the actions Congress identified as less burdensome also would not do the job. The failure of the EPA to do this constitutes a failure to meet its burden of showing that its actions not only reduce the risk but do so in the *least burdensome* fashion.

Thus it was not enough for the EPA to show, as it did in this case, that banning some asbestos products might reduce the harm that could occur from the use of these products. If that were the standard, it would be no standard at all, for few indeed are the products that are so safe that a complete ban of them would not make the world still safer.

This comparison of two static worlds is insufficient to satisfy the dictates of TSCA. While the EPA may have shown that a world with a complete ban of asbestos might be preferable to one in which there is only the current amount of regulation, the EPA has failed to show that there is not some intermediate state of regulation that would be superior to both the currently-regulated and the completely-banned world. Without showing that asbestos regulation would be ineffective, the EPA cannot discharge its TSCA burden of showing that its regulation is the least burdensome available to it.

Upon an initial showing of product danger, the proper course for the EPA to follow is to consider each regulatory option, beginning with the least burdensome, and the costs and benefits of regulation under each option. The EPA cannot simply skip several rungs, as it did in this case, for in doing so, it may skip a less-burdensome alternative mandated by TSCA. Here, although the EPA mentions the problems posed by intermediate levels of regulation, it takes no steps to calculate the costs and benefits of these intermediate levels. Without doing this it is impossible, both for the EPA and for this court on review, to know that none of these alternatives was less burdensome than the ban in fact chosen by the agency.

The EPA's offhand rejection of these intermediate regulatory steps is "not the stuff of which substantial evidence is made." While it is true that the EPA considered five different ban options, these differed solely with respect to their effective dates. The EPA did not calculate the risk levels for intermediate levels of regulation, as it believed that there was no asbestos exposure level for which the risk of injury or death was zero. Reducing risk to zero, however, was not the task that Congress set for the EPA in enacting TSCA. The EPA thus has failed "cogently [to] explain why it has exercised its discretion in a given manner," by failing to explore in more than a cursory way the less burdensome alternatives to a total ban. * * *

In addition to showing that its regulation is the least burdensome one necessary to protect the environment adequately, the EPA also must show that it has a reasonable basis for the regulation. To some extent, our inquiry in this area mirrors that used above, for many of the methodological problems we have noted also indicate that the EPA did not have a reasonable basis. We here take the opportunity to highlight some areas of additional concern.

Most problematical to us is the EPA's ban of products for which no substitutes presently are available. In these cases, the EPA bears a tough burden indeed to show that under TSCA a ban is the least burdensome alternative, as TSCA explicitly instructs the EPA to consider "the benefits of such substance or mixture for various uses and the availability of substitutes for such uses." These words are particularly appropriate where the EPA actually has decided to ban a product, rather than simply restrict its use, for it is in these cases that the lack of an adequate substitute is most troubling under TSCA. * * *

We also are concerned with the EPA's evaluation of substitutes even in those instances in which the record shows that they are available. The EPA explicitly rejects considering the harm that may flow from the increased use of products designed to substitute for asbestos, even where the probable substitutes themselves are known carcinogens. The EPA justifies this by stating that it has "more concern about the continued use and exposure to asbestos than it has for the future replacement of asbestos in the products subject to this rule with other fibrous substitutes." The agency thus concludes that any "[r]egulatory decisions about asbestos which poses well-recognized, serious risks should not be delayed until the risks of all replacement materials are fully quantified."

This presents two problems. First, TSCA instructs the EPA to consider the relative merits of its ban, as compared to the economic effects of its actions. The EPA cannot make this calculation if it fails to consider the effects that alternative substitutes will pose after a ban.

Second, the EPA cannot say with any assurance that its regulation will increase workplace safety when it refuses to evaluate the harm that will result from the increased use of substitute products. While the EPA may be correct in its conclusion that the alternate materials pose less risk than asbestos, we cannot say with any more assurance than that flowing from an educated guess that this conclusion is true.

Considering that many of the substitutes that the EPA itself concedes will be used in the place of asbestos have known carcinogenic effects, the EPA not only cannot assure this court that it has taken the least burdensome alternative, but cannot even prove that its regulations will increase workplace safety. Eager to douse the dangers of asbestos, the agency inadvertently actually may increase the risk of injury Americans face. The EPA's explicit failure to consider the toxicity of likely substitutes thus deprives its order of a reasonable basis.

Our opinion should not be construed to state that the EPA has an affirmative duty to seek out and test every workplace substitute for any product it seeks to regulate. TSCA does not place such a burden upon the agency. We do not think it unreasonable, however, once interested parties introduce credible studies and evidence showing the toxicity of workplace substitutes, or the decreased effectiveness of safety alternatives such as non-asbestos brakes, that the EPA then consider whether its regulations are even increasing workplace safety, and whether the increased risk occasioned by dangerous substitutes makes the proposed regulation no longer reasonable. . . .

The final requirement the EPA must satisfy before engaging in any TSCA rulemaking is that it only takes steps designed to prevent "unreasonable" risks. In evaluating what is "unreasonable," the EPA is required to consider the costs of any proposed actions and to "carry out this chapter in a reasonable and prudent manner [after considering] the environmental, economic, and social impact of any action." 15 U.S.C. § 2601(c). * * *

That the EPA must balance the costs of its regulations against their benefits further is reinforced by the requirement that it seek the least burdensome regulation. While Congress did not dictate that the EPA engage in an exhaustive, full-scale cost-benefit analysis, it did require the EPA to consider both sides of the regulatory equation, and it rejected the notion that the EPA should pursue the reduction of workplace risk at any cost. See *American Textile Mfrs. Inst.,* 452 U.S. at 510 n. 30, 101 S.Ct. at 2491 n. 30 ("unreasonable risk" statutes require "a generalized balancing of costs and benefits"). . . .

Even taking all of the EPA's figures as true, and evaluating them in the light most favorable to the agency's decision (non-discounted benefits, discounted costs, analogous exposure estimates included), the agency's analysis results in figures as high as $74 million per life saved. For example, the EPA states that its ban of asbestos pipe will save three lives over the next thirteen years, at a cost of $128–227 million ($43–76 million per life saved), depending upon the price of substitutes; that its ban of asbestos shingles will cost $23–34 million to save 0.32 statistical lives ($72–106 million per life saved); that its ban of asbestos coatings will cost $46–181 million to save 3.33 lives ($14–54 million per life saved); and that its ban of asbestos paper products will save 0.60 lives at a cost of $4–5 million ($7–8 million per life saved). Were the analogous exposure estimates not included, the cancer risks from substitutes such as ductile iron pipe factored in, and the benefits of the ban appropriately discounted from the time of the manifestation of an injury rather than the time of exposure, the costs would shift even more sharply against the EPA's position.

While we do not sit as a regulatory agency that must make the difficult decision as to what an appropriate expenditure is to prevent someone from incurring the risk of an asbestos-related death, we do note that the EPA, in its zeal to ban any and all asbestos products, basically ignored the cost side of the TSCA equation. The EPA would have this court believe that Congress, when it enacted its requirement that the EPA consider the economic impacts of its regulations, thought that spending $200–300 million to save approximately seven lives (approximately $30–40 million per life) over thirteen years is reasonable.

As we stated in the OSHA context, until an agency "can provide substantial evidence that the benefits to be achieved by [a regulation] bear a reasonable relationship to the costs imposed by the reduction, it cannot show that the standard is reasonably necessary to provide safe or healthful workplaces."

NOTES

1. Environmentalists condemned the foregoing decision as a "death knell" for TSCA. One said that "if the agency can't use TSCA to ban asbestos, then it can't use Section 6 [to regulate any chemical] because the data base on adverse health effects of asbestos is one of the best." Another said, "The largely unworkable Section 6, which was unwieldly before, is now even more useless." *See* 22 ENV'T. REP. 1607 (1991).

Professor Thomas McGarity went to the legal heart of the matter, observing acidly that the Fifth Circuit's opinion

> is so lacking in deference to the agency's exercise of expertise and policy judgment, and so full of attempts to impose on the agency the judges' own views of the proper role of regulation in society, that it is virtually indistinguishable from the documents that OMB prepares in connection with its oversight of EPA rulemaking.

Thomas O. McGarity, *Some Thoughts on 'Deossifying' the Rulemaking Process,* 41 DUKE L.J. 1385, 1423 (1992).

2. Is the regulatory standard prescribed by FIFRA and applied in the cases at pages 981–990, *supra,* different from the TSCA standard applied in *Corrosion Proof Fittings*? *See* Rosenthal, Gray and Graham, *Legislating Acceptable Cancer Risk from Exposure to Toxic Chemicals,* 19 ECOLOGY L.Q. 269, 306–07 (1992) ("The narrative ['unreasonable risk'] standard in [TSCA] was modeled after the one in FIFRA, so it is not surprising that EPA decisions to limit production or use of a specific chemical under TSCA involve a similar balancing process. As under FIFRA, [EPA] must consider the economic implications of regulation."). *See also* Applegate, *The Perils of Unreasonable Risk: Information, Regulatory Policy, and Toxic Substances Control,* 91 COLUMBIA L. REV. 261, 267–68 (1991) ("EPA is empowered to regulate the 'life cycle' of toxic chemicals through four major statutes: FIFRA, TSCA, [RCRA and CERCLA].... Although the statutes are phrased in different ways and use different regulatory structures, all adopt a standard that can generically be called unreasonable risk. 'Unreasonable' describes an undefined, nonzero level of risk determined on an ad hoc basis by balancing both health considerations and nonhealth concerns such as technology, feasibility, and cost.").

3. Are the estimated costs per life saved under EPA's asbestos regulations blatantly unreasonable, as the court seems to suggest at the end of the *Corrosion Proof Fittings* opinion? A study by Resources for the Future reviewed economic data used by EPA in support of its asbestos, pesticide, and carcinogenic air pollutant regulations. The study concluded that EPA implicitly had attached a value of $15 million to $45 million to the prevention of one case of cancer, much more than individuals appeared to be willing to spend to reduce their own risks of death. *See* Van Houtven and Cropper, *When Is a Life Too Costly to Save? The Evidence from Environmental Regulations,* RESOURCES, Winter 1994, at 6.

A more recent study of regulatory costs of lives saved casts considerable doubt upon the validity of high estimates like those in *Corrosion Proof Fittings* and in the *Resources* article just cited. *See* Lisa Heinzerling, *Regulatory Costs of Mythic Proportions,* 107 YALE L.J. 1981 (1998). The author suggests that the same data relied upon in most prior studies indicate "a cost per life saved of less than $5 million" in most cases. "This means that ... the costs per life saved ... are below the range of current estimates of the monetary value of a human life based on studies of wage premiums for risky jobs. A figure of about $9 million is commonly reported today to be the preference-based value of life for nonmanual labor; for manual laborers, it is much lower, around $2.5 million. Another frequently cited range for the value of a human life is $3 million to $7 million." *Id.* at 2038–40.

4. The court in *Corrosion Proof Fittings* also held that EPA must *discount* future benefits and that EPA's benefit-cost analysis gave too much weight to future deaths. For an exploration of the complexities of the choice of discount rates, with particular emphasis on the issue of discounting lives, *see* Farber and Hemmersbaugh, *The Shadow of the Future: Discount Rates, Later Generations, and the Environment,* 46 VAND. L. REV. 267 (1993). *See also* Richard Revesz, *Environmental Regulation, Cost–Benefit Analysis, and the Discounting of Human Lives,* 99 COL. L. REV. 941 (1999).

Professor Heinzerling, in her article cited in note 3 *supra*, challenges the propriety of "discounting lives," i.e., lives saved in the future, in estimating the benefits of environmental regulation. She points out that the economic study most cited by persons claiming that regulatory costs are excessive in relation to benefits applied an annual discount rate of 10 percent in reducing lives saved in the future to present terms. Thus, 10 lives saved one year in the future are equivalent to 9 lives saved today, 10 lives saved two years in the future equal 8.3 lives saved today, and 10 lives saved 10 years in the future equal 3.9 lives saved today. *Id*. at 2018, 2043. Heinzerling argues that while discounting lives may be appropriate "as long as the value of a human life is measured in dollars" (though the proper discount *rate* may not be 10 percent), the case for discounting the future benefits of health regulation is "less straightforward" if one does not assign a monetary value to human life. She states the various arguments in support of such nonmonetary discounting and presents interesting counterarguments. *Id*. at 2044–56. Her case against discounting is presented more fully, and expanded to include not only fatal illnesses but also non-fatal mental and physical ailments during the "latency" period following toxic exposure, in Lisa Heinzerling, The *Temporal Dimension in Environmental Law*, 31 ENVTL L. REP. 11055 (2001).

5.   Does the principal case indicate that the authority of *Reserve Mining*, page 81, *supra*, and of the other appellate court decisions cited in note 3 at pages 88–89, now is in serious doubt? Does the principal case suggest that the Supreme Court's views in the OSHA cases, pages 89 and 105, will be applied in most non-OSHA toxics cases?

6.   U.S. chemical policy has increasingly been subject to criticism and to regulatory reform proposals. The central criticisms are that the policies suffer from various regulatory "gaps": a data gap because most chemicals can be sold without any disclosure of information about their risks; a safety gap because regulatory activity cannot take place given the absence of data; and a technology gap because of a lack of investment in alternative "green" chemistry. *See See* UC CENTERS FOR OCCUPATIONAL AND ENVIRONMENTAL HEALTH, GREEN CHEMISTRY: CORNERSTONE TO A SUSTAINABLE CALIFORNIA (2008) at 8–9.

7.   The European Union has taken a new and much different tack in addressing the production and use of chemicals, particularly with respect to the distinction between chemicals already in commerce versus new chemicals. In 2007 the EU passed a regulation known as Registration, Evaluation, Authorisation and Restriction of Chemicals (REACH). The law is extraordinarily complex (it is more than 800 pages in length) but at its core is a requirement that any companies that manufacture or import chemical substances of one ton per year or more must register the substances with an EU agency and provide the agency with information about the properties of the substances. In addition, REACH requires information about downstream users of chemical substances. For a description of REACH's major provisions, *see* EUROPEAN COMMISSION, ENVIRONMENT DIRECTORATE GENERAL, REACH IN BRIEF (OCT. 2007).

B. EFFECTS OF BIOTECHNOLOGY

1. REGULATING THE ENVIRONMENTAL EFFECTS OF BIOTECHNOLOGY

FIFRA and TSCA were enacted before the widespread advances in biotechnology, though FIFRA in particular now plays a role in regulating certain aspects of biotechnology. The article below provides background about biotechnology regulation.

GREGORY N. MANDEL, GAPS, INEXPERIENCE, INCONSISTENCIES, AND OVERLAPS: CRISIS IN THE REGULATION OF GENETICALLY MODIFIED PLANTS AND ANIMALS[9]

45 WM. & MARY L. REV. 2167 (2004).

INTRODUCTION

Biotechnology may help ameliorate some of the greatest crises currently facing the United States and the world, including hunger and malnutrition, environmental degradation, and widespread disease. Genetically modifying crops through the use of biotechnology potentially allows for greater agricultural efficiency, increased nutritional content of food, and reduced environmental impacts. Genetically engineering animals may create cheaper food, reduce pressures on wild animal populations, and provide organs or tissues for human transplant. Modifying plants and animals to produce pharmaceuticals could provide for widespread, inexpensive dissemination of critical pharmaceuticals and vaccines throughout the United States and the world.

On the other hand, biotechnology could have harmful consequences. Potential problems include human health impacts resulting from the introduction of new allergens or toxins, widespread environmental and ecological damage resulting from the introduction of invasive species or loss of biodiversity, and unforeseen injury arising from the unintentional release of pharmaceuticals or industrial compounds into the food supply. * * *

CURRENT REGULATION OF GENETICALLY MODIFIED PLANTS AND ANIMALS

A. The Coordinated Framework

As the biotechnology industry developed in the early 1980s, it was recognized that regulation was necessary to protect human health and the environment from the potential deleterious effects of transgenic products. This recognition culminated in the promulgation of the federal government's Coordinated Framework for Regulation of Biotechnology by the

---

9. Copyright © 2004. Reprinted by permission.

White House Office of Science and Technology Policy in 1986. The Coordinated Framework instituted a "comprehensive federal regulatory policy for ... biotechnology research and products." It specified that bioengineered products generally would be regulated under the then-existing statutory and regulatory structure. The foundation for this decision was a determination that the process of biotechnology was not inherently risky, and therefore, that only the products of biotechnology, not the process itself, required oversight. On this basis, the Coordinated Framework established that existing laws and regulations were sufficient to handle the products of biotechnology. This decision was based in part on a desire not to impose regulatory restrictions that could hamper the development of a promising and fledgling industry.

As a result of the Coordinated Framework, three administrative agencies are involved in the regulation of the genetically modified products discussed in this Article: The FDA is responsible for food safety issues for transgenic crop and food-animal varieties, and for drug safety issues for modified pharmaceutical-producing plants or animals; the EPA handles health and environmental effects of pest-protected plants; and the USDA regulates the effect of genetically modified plants on other plants and animals in both agricultural and nonagricultural environments. Because the Coordinated Framework would result in multiple agencies acting in closely related areas, two basic principles were delineated to guide regulatory policy. First, "[a]gencies should seek to adopt consistent definitions of those genetically engineered organisms subject to review to the extent permitted by their respective statutory authorities." Second, the "agencies should utilize scientific reviews of comparable rigor."

Implicit in the decision to regulate genetically modified products under preexisting statutes was the belief that bioengineered plants and animals were not significantly different from their conventional counterparts. This view was explicitly reiterated in a 1987 National Academy of Sciences report that reached three conclusions:

[1]   There is no evidence that unique hazards exist either in the use of rDNA techniques or in the movement of genes between unrelated organisms.

[2]   The risks associated with the introduction of rDNA-engineered organisms are the same in kind as those associated with the introduction of unmodified organisms and organisms modified by other methods.

[3]   Assessment of the risks of introducing rDNA-engineered organisms into the environment should be based on the nature of the organism and the environment into which it is introduced, not on the method by which it was produced.

With the Coordinated Framework in place, the regulation of biotechnology was left to the administrative agencies.

B.   The Food and Drug Administration

The FDA is responsible for insuring that all food products on the market in the United States, other than meat and poultry, are safe. In furtherance of this goal, the FDA provides voluntary premarket consultations with food companies, seed companies, and plant developers regarding the safety of transgenic foods.

* * * No statutory provisions or FDA regulations expressly cover genetically modified foods. Pursuant to FDA regulations, plants modified through modern rDNA techniques are not treated any differently from conventionally modified plants.

Section 402(a)(1) of the FFDCA authorizes the FDA to regulate "adulterated foods," defined as food that "bears or contains any poisonous or deleterious substance which may render it injurious to health." In addition, section 409 of the FFDCA provides for the regulation of "food additives," which are substances that are intended for use in food, that may reasonably be expected to become a component of food, or that otherwise may affect the characteristics of food. A food additive must be approved by the FDA prior to being used in food. Manufacturers, however, do not need approval for a food additive if such substance is generally recognized as safe (GRAS) by experts. Thus, both the inserted gene of a transgenic plant and the product that it expresses are food additives, unless they are GRAS. With respect to genetically modified foods, the FDA has determined that "[i]n most cases, the substances expected to become components of food as a result of genetic modification of a plant will be the same as or substantially similar to substances commonly found in food, such as proteins, fats and oils, and carbohydrates," and therefore will be GRAS.

The food additive manufacturer determines whether a food additive is GRAS, not the FDA. A manufacturer does not need to report to the FDA that it has made a GRAS determination, but it may do so and may receive from the FDA an affirmation that the particular substance is GRAS. Thus, the FDA's regulatory requirements with respect to genetically modified food are primarily voluntary. This decision was explicitly made by the FDA based on its determination that "[a]ny genetic modification technique has the potential to alter the composition of food in a manner relevant to food safety, although, based on experience, the likelihood of a safety hazard is typically very low."

In 1995, the FDA conducted a safety review of the first genetically modified food product to be commercialized, the Flavr Savr tomato. This review was conducted at the request of the manufacturer, who was attempting to build public confidence. Since that time, the FDA has not conducted a safety review of any of the scores of other genetically modified food products that have been commercialized; however, the FDA believes that manufacturers have voluntarily consulted with it regarding each of these products.

The FDA does not require that genetically modified foods be labeled as such. The basis for this determination is the FDA's conclusion that genetically modified products do not differ materially from, or create greater safety concerns than, their conventional counterparts. To the extent that there are significant safety concerns or usage issues, such as substantial changes in composition or nutritive value, the FDA requires labeling.

The FDA explicitly has waived its regulatory authority over genetically modified pest-protected plants, so long as the plants have not also been modified to express other, nonpesticidal proteins. These plants are regulated by the EPA as pesticides, and are discussed below.

* * * The FDA asserts regulatory authority over genetically modified fish and other animals pursuant to the "new animal drug" provisions of the FFDCA. These provisions allow the FDA to evaluate the new animal drug's safety with "reference to the health of man or animal," which the FDA interprets to include environmental effects that directly or indirectly affect the health of humans or animals other than those intended to receive the new drug.

The FDA has regulatory authority over pharmaceuticals grown in genetically modified plants that are intended for use in humans pursuant to the Public Health Service Act and the FFDCA. * * * FDA regulations are similar to those governing transgenic plants used for food. In both cases, the FDA regulates the use of plants that might express an allergenic or toxic compound in the pharmaceutical, and protects against the introduction of nonfood material into food or feed. The FDA regulations governing human drugs and biologics and animal drugs do not specifically address biotechnology. The USDA shares regulatory authority over the growth of the genetically engineered pharmaceutical-producing plants, as discussed below.

C.   The Environmental Protection Agency

The EPA regulates genetically modified products through its authority to regulate pesticide use and pesticide residue in food products. All pesticides must be registered with the EPA prior to their distribution, sale, or use, pursuant to the Federal Insecticide, Fungicide, and Rodenticide Act (FIFRA). * * *

FIFRA was enacted to regulate chemical substances, not biotechnological products (it was enacted prior to Watson and Crick's discovery of the DNA molecule). Based on FIFRA's statutory definition of "pesticide," however, the EPA regulates the genetic material inserted into transgenic plants to express pesticidal products, as well as the expression products themselves, as pesticides. Thus, manufacturers of transgenic pest-protected plants must receive registration of the plants from the EPA prior to commercialization. * * *

In 1988, just prior to the widespread development of genetically engineered pest-protected plants, the EPA exempted plants and microorganisms with pesticidal properties from the requirements of FIFRA. This exemption was intended for plants, such as chrysanthemums, that are naturally pest-protected. Due to these regulations, the EPA does not regulate any plants themselves, including genetically modified ones. As discussed above, the EPA does regulate the inserted genetic material and the products it expresses.

The EPA is responsible for regulating both the environmental and human health impacts of plants genetically modified to produce their own pesticides, as the FDA has ceded regulatory authority over pest-protected plants to the EPA. Where use of a pesticide will result in any residue being left on food, the pesticide is subject to regulation by the EPA pursuant to the FFDCA. In these instances, the EPA establishes "tolerance" levels for the allowable amount of pesticide residue that can be left on food products. Currently, all FIFRA-registered, pest-protected plants are exempt from tolerance level requirements because tests of these transgenic plants have not revealed a human health risk.

The EPA does not regulate genetically engineered plants other than those modified to contain pesticides, and it does not regulate the environmental impacts or potential impacts of genetically engineered animals.

D.   The U.S. Department of Agriculture

The USDA is responsible for protecting and promoting American agriculture. On the principle that genetically modified plants could pose a risk to agricultural crops, the USDA oversees the agricultural safety of the movement, importation, and field testing of transgenic plants.

In order to grow transgenic plants outside of a laboratory, approval must be obtained from the Animal and Plant Health Inspection Service (APHIS) of the USDA. APHIS' authority to regulate genetically modified plants stems from the Plant Protection Act (PPA). The PPA was enacted in 2000, and thus, at first glance, appears to deviate from the trend of regulating biotechnology under ancient statutes. The PPA, however, essentially consolidated authority from two previous statutes that APHIS had used to regulate genetically modified organisms: the Federal Plant Pest Act (FPPA), enacted in 1957, and the Federal Plant Quarantine Act (PQA), enacted in 1912. Both the FPPA and PQA were originally enacted to regulate the introduction of nonindigenous plant species. APHIS regulations governing genetically modified plants under the PPA are simply those established pursuant to the FPPA and the PQA. No modification to APHIS' regulation of biotechnology products has been made pursuant to the PPA.

Pursuant to the PPA, APHIS has primary regulatory authority for all genetically modified plants except pest-protected ones. As APHIS is supposed to carry out its mandate while not impeding the growth of the biotechnology industry, critics have contended that an agency charged with promoting agriculture (including the biotechnology industry), "may not be able to objectively assess the safety of new products of agricultural biotechnology."

Under the PPA, anyone seeking to introduce (i.e., import, transport interstate, or release into the environment) a regulated article must receive authorization from APHIS. "Regulated article" includes [a]ny organism which has been altered or produced through genetic engineering, * * *

Prior to conducting a field trial of a new transgenic plant, a developer must perform a risk evaluation on the plant to determine whether the plant may be a plant pest. No consideration of any other risks, such as other human health or environmental risks, must be evaluated prior to the field test.

Authorization from APHIS can come via a notification or permitting process, each of which is aimed at ensuring that the transgenic organisms are grown and handled in a manner to prevent their escape into the environment. For most genetically modified plants, under certain conditions, simple notification of APHIS prior to release (without the requirement of receiving a permit) is sufficient. Nearly 99% of all field tests, importations, and interstate movement of genetically engineered plants take place under the notification system.

Permits are required for the movement, importation, and field testing of transgenic plants that do not qualify for notification, such as pharmaceutical-producing plants, and for plants denied notification. APHIS uses the permitting process to evaluate potential plant pest risk and to require prevention measures to reduce risk. The primary emphasis of the permitting process is confinement. * * *

APHIS regulates transgenic pharmaceutical-producing plants pursuant to the same authority under which it regulates other transgenic plants, such as "regulated articles" under the PPA. Thus, applicants must acquire a permit prior to the field test of transgenic pharmaceutical-producing plants, as such plants are specifically excluded from the notification process. Various measures must then be taken to confine the transgenic plants to the field site during the period of release, and to prevent the plants or their offspring from persisting in the environment subsequently.

With respect to biotechnology developments beyond plants, the Food Safety and Inspection Service (FSIS) of the USDA is responsible for the safety of food products prepared from domestic livestock and poultry. The Federal Meat Inspection Act (FMIA) and the Poultry Products Inspection Act (PPIA) require FSIS to inspect cattle, sheep, swine, goats, equines, poultry, and food products prepared from them, which are intended for use as human food. Pursuant to these acts, the FSIS has regulatory authority over genetically modified domestic livestock and poultry.

APHIS also has regulatory authority over the release of insects for pest management, and presumably would regulate the release of transgenic insects in the same manner. No agency regulates research and commercialization of transgenic insects other than for their intentional release, and no guidelines exist that govern their containment or the potential ecological risks posed by their release. * * *

2. TRANSGENIC PLANTS

* * *

In a report released in February 2002, a committee of the National Academies' National Research Council recommended that the public should be more involved in the review process of transgenic plants; that before making precedent-setting decisions regarding field-testing or deregulation, APHIS should solicit broad external scientific and public review well beyond use of the *Federal Register*; that the agency should convene a scientific advisory group before any changes in regulatory policy are made; and that ecological testing and monitoring should continue after commercial production of a transgenic plant has been approved. Excerpts from this report appear below.

While the report identifies some desirable regulatory changes, it does not condemn the 1986 Coordinated Framework for Regulation of Biotechnology as basically flawed and inadequate. For a more vigorous critique of the piecemeal approach of using mostly pre–1986 laws to regulate the environmental effects of biotechnology, *see* John Kunich, *Mother Frankenstein, Doctor Nature, and the Environmental Law of Genetic Engineering,* 74 S. Cal. L. Rev. 807 (2001) (advocating enactment of a new, comprehensive "Transgenic Release Act").

NATIONAL RESEARCH COUNCIL, COMMITTEE ON ENVIRONMENTAL IMPACTS ASSOCIATED WITH COMMERCIALIZATION OF TRANSGENIC PLANTS, ENVIRONMENTAL EFFECTS OF TRANSGENIC PLANTS: THE SCOPE AND ADEQUACY OF REGULATION[10]

9, 76, 176–77, 223–24, 229, 237, 246–49 (2002).

... Plants that cannot be grown in the field, based on notification, include those that produce substances intended for use as pharmaceuticals and those that could affect non-target organisms....

Non-target Hazards

* * *

Non-target organisms are any species that is not the direct target of the transgenic crop. To date, the vast majority of the published studies that examine non-target hazards have focused on *Bt* [from the bacterium *Bacillus thuringiensis*] crops. For example, *Bt* corn is presently targeted to

---

10. Copyright © 2002 by the National Academy of Sciences. Reprinted with permission.

control the key pests, European corn borer ... and southwestern corn borer ..., and *Bt* rice is targeted against striped stem borer ... and yellow stem borer.... Any other species affected by *Bt* corn or *Bt* rice is a non-target species; consequently, the list of potential non-target species is very long. These organisms can be grouped conveniently into five categories that are not mutually exclusive: (1) beneficial species, including natural enemies of pests (lacewings, ladybird beetles, parasitic wasps, and microbial parasites) and pollinators (bees, flies, beetles, butterflies and moths, birds and bats); (2) non-target pests; (3) soil organisms, which usually are difficult to study and identify to species; (4) species of conservation concern, including endangered species and popular, charismatic species (monarch butterfly); and (5) biodiversity, which may include the species richness in an area. * * *

Hazard of Resistance Evolution

Resistance evolution can occur in pests that are targeted for control by or associated with a transgenic crop. This is a potential environmental hazard because if the pest becomes resistant to control, alternative, more environmentally damaging controls may be used. In addition, new control tactics may be rushed into use before their environmental risks are completely assessed. Insects, weeds, and microbial pathogens all have the potential to overcome most control tactics used against them.... * * *

GENERAL COMMENTS AND CONCERNS

Geopolitical Scale

The scope of APHIS oversight is limited to whether and how transgenic plants are moved and released in the United States. Although APHIS determinations sometimes include consideration of environmental impacts of deregulated genetically modified organisms outside the confines of the United States, the agency is under no obligation to do so. Indeed, relevant scientific data may be unavailable for many countries that are centers of diversity for wild relatives of a transgenic crop. Yet these locations might be the very places where environmental impacts might occur due to transgene flow into those populations. Also, once a transgenic plant is deregulated, descendants of that plant may find themselves intentionally or unintentionally transported far beyond the borders of the United States, to radically different environments. A transgenic crop variety developed to fit into U.S. systems of agriculture may cause changes in the agricultural systems of other countries that would cause environmental degradation.

One can imagine an argument being made by certain stakeholders, that if the U.S. government found a plant to be safe, that judgment should be good enough for a country without the resources to conduct its own environmental analysis. That would be wrong. Just because APHIS finds a transgenic plant to have no significant impact in the United States is not a guarantee that it will not have an impact elsewhere. To its credit, APHIS has held biosafety meetings in a number of developing countries to inform policymakers of the potential environmental effects of transgenic plants.

CBI in APHIS Decision Documents

Many people, including those generally supportive of biotechnology, decry the apparently large amount of data and information in submissions marked "CBI" (confidential business information). Under this CBI stamp, all manner of data are hidden from public view and even from independent scientific scrutiny.... This committee sometimes found that it could not provide an independent scientific assessment of APHIS rulings because of the broad use of CBI.... Without a transparent mechanism to evaluate and judge confidential data from applicants, APHIS appears to accept without question an applicant's assertion of what is CBI. Public credibility is eroded when the same information marked CBI in APHIS documents is not considered CBI and is open to public inspection in other jurisdictions, such as Canada or Europe. It must be understood that U.S. standards for what constitutes CBI are very broad. A company can claim that certain information is CBI as long as it can show there is any possibility that disclosure of the information could directly or indirectly harm its business.... * * *

THE NEXT TRANSGENIC CROPS

* * *

Improved Postharvest Processing

... The global demand for wood and wood products is growing along with the human population. To reduce pressure on existing forests, forest plantations that grow transgenic trees are expected to play an increasingly important role in meeting the demand for tree products.... [T]he first traits being genetically engineered into trees are herbicide tolerance and insect resistance, which are useful for establishing and maintaining young trees. Several traits are under development to better adapt trees to postharvest processing, and these may become commercially available in the near future. For example, there is research under way to modify the lignin content of certain tree species, in order to improve pulping, the process by which wood fibers are separated to make paper. Reduced lignin may improve the efficiency of paper production and may reduce environmental pollution from the paper production process. * * *

There is also interest in using genetic engineering technology to turn annual crop plants into factories that produce valuable chemicals. Plants have the capacity to synthesize a variety of complex molecules, given the simple inputs of a few minerals, carbon dioxide, water, and sunshine. It is widely thought that plants could provide a "green" renewable source of chemicals to replace those currently obtained from petroleum.... * * *

Mitigation of Environmental Pollution

In the future, transgenic plants may be grown for reasons other than commercialization. For example, it has been proposed that transgenic plants could contribute to removing or detoxifying heavy metal pollutants in contaminated soils ("phytoremediation"). A particular problem in some locations is mercury. Plants have already been created that can accumulate mercury. Thus, growing such plants is a potential solution for cleaning up mercury pollution at despoiled sites. * * *

FUTURE POLICY ISSUES

* * *

Agricultural Structure

Issues related to changing agricultural structure might have indirect environmental consequences. The socioeconomic considerations for evaluating transgenic crops have proven to be more volatile than was predicted only a few years ago. The desire of some consumers, both foreign and domestic, to avoid consumption of foods containing transgenes has led to the segmentation of markets for "genetically modified" ("GM") and "GM-free" crops. In the United States the creation of marketing standards for certified organic crops that do not contain transgenes or transgene products has established a market niche for producers. These forms of market segmentation create an opportunity for U.S. farmers to capture a price premium for nontransgenic crops. At the same time, the existence of a market for nontransgenic crops creates a new kind of environmental risk from transgenics: If they cannot be environmentally isolated, pollen and residues from transgenic crops can affect/influence the economic value of nontransgenic crop production. The development of market standards and international trade rules for nontransgenic crops will have economic implications for U.S. agriculture. In the worst-case scenario, U.S. producers may effectively be excluded from these emerging world markets.... * * *

Regulatory Issues

* * *

U.S. and Global Capacity for Environmental Regulation

* * *

As noted above, some of the coming applications of biotechnology may involve the use of plants to produce pharmaceutical products, biologics, fuels, and other substances not intended for human food use. The introduction of such transgenes poses the potential for environmentally associated risks of a wholly different order than those associated with existing transgenic crops. If such a transgene moves into food crops, either through pollen transfer or physical contamination, there could be serious human safety risks. If such a transgene moves into a wild relative, there could be widespread environmental dissemination of the pharmaceutical substance or other nonfood substances that could have impacts on wildlife as well as microbial populations. * * *

The Precautionary Principle

At the same time that new products and applications of gene transfer are being applied in crop production, there has been discussion of new regulatory approaches. One important component of this discussion has been the "precautionary principle." . . . Language endorsing a precautionary principle and taking a precautionary approach in regulatory decision making is in the European Union's (EU) Directive 90/220 on biotechnology and its revision in 2001, the Cartagena Protocol on Biosafety, which was finalized in Montreal during 2000, under the Convention on Biological Diversity (CBD). The CBD has been ratified by many countries but not the United States. It is an international agreement to conserve and use sustainably biological diversity for the benefit of present and future generations. * * *

The European discussion of the precautionary principle has occurred in the context of attempts to harmonize grades, standards, and regulatory approaches among member states. These discussions have occurred during a spate of food scares and failings in government oversight, most notably associated with transmissible bovine spongiform encephalopathy (Mad Cow Disease), that have rocked public confidence in government regulation of the food system. Although debate over the food safety and environmental risks of transgenic crops has figured prominently in Europe, European pronouncements on the precautionary principle neither offer a specific evaluation of transgenic crops nor provide language that would give regulators specific instructions on how to take a precautionary approach with respect to transgenic crops. The March 12, 2001, revision to EU Directive 90/220 states that the requirements of the Biosafety Protocol, including the precautionary principle, should be respected. The 2001 directive indicates that the precautionary principle was taken into account in the drafting of the directive and must be taken into account when implementing it. Consequently, the directive does not provide a statement of the precautionary principle but identifies regulatory processes that are precautionary. It is beyond the scope of this report to provide a detailed analysis of this new directive, but suffice it to say that the precautionary principle has been incorporated into at least the labeling and traceability standards, the monitoring standards, and the EU approval process. Much the same as in the Biosafety Protocol, the precautionary principle will be defined in Europe through its application to specific cases.

NOTES

1. Plants which are genetically engineered to produce their own pesticides are regulated not only by APHIS but also by EPA under FIFRA. *See* John Kunich, *Mother Frankenstein, Doctor Nature, and the Environmental Law of Genetic Engineering*, 74 S. CAL. L. REV. 807, 831–837 (2001).

2. Directive 90/220 of the European Union, referred to in the final section of the foregoing article, was repealed as of October 2002 and replaced by Directive 2001/18/EC of March 12, 2001, on the deliberate release into the

environment of genetically modified organisms. It requires that member states of the EU adopt and enforce national laws and regulations consistent with the detailed framework set forth in the Directive. Its requirements are more comprehensive and demanding than U.S. regulatory requirements. Article 4 puts the precautionary principle at the heart of the EU approach to GMOs. Each notification of intent to undertake a deliberate release of a GMO must include a plan for monitoring its effects on human health or the environment (Article 6). Governmental consents for releases may be conditional and may not exceed 10 years in duration, and products must be labeled "contains genetically modified organisms" (Articles 13, 19, 20, 21, 26).

3.   A coalition of consumer and environmental groups has asked APHIS to halt outdoor cultivation of crops engineered to produce pharmaceutical or industrial chemicals. Field trials of hundreds of "biopharm" crops have been conducted in at least 12 states, and several firms claim to be close to production of crop-based chemicals. Supporters of biopharming say that genetically engineered plants, especially corn, could be efficient producers of products such as industrial chemicals, antibodies for herpes and influenza, growth hormones, and blood-clotting agents. Critics claim that the risks outweigh potential benefits. *See* Mike Toner, *Coalition Wants to Ban Engineered Drug Crops*, BEND, OREGON BULLETIN (Cox News Service), July 12, 2002, at A2, col. 5. The NRC report excerpted above acknowledged that crops transformed to produce pharmaceutical or industrial compounds might mate with plants grown for human consumption and introduce novel chemicals into the food supply. In March 2003, APHIS proposed changes in field test permit conditions for pharmaceutical corn, aimed at insulating food crops from the biopharm crops to prevent cross-fertilization. 68 FED. REG. 11337 (Mar. 10, 2003).

4.   Biotech companies also are developing genetically modified *animals* for human consumption. They include pigs that produce leaner pork chops and less harmful manure, meatier chickens, disease-resistant shrimp, and fast-growing salmon and catfish. It is not clear how, and by whom, releases of such creatures will be regulated. With respect to the salmon, which are expected to be the first such modified animals to be marketed commercially, only the Food and Drug Administration seems to have asserted regulatory authority, which FDA claimed by designating the fish's foreign genes and the growth hormone they produce as a drug for animals. EPA and the Department of Agriculture bowed out, leaving critics concerned that while FDA may be rigorous in examining food safety, it is not qualified to evaluate the ecological risks posed by releases of transgenic salmon into oceans. Farmed salmon typically are grown in enclosures in the sea, known as net pens, which frequently are torn by waves or hungry wild animals. If the transgenic fish are grown in such pens and slip out, wild salmon could be devastated. According to one study, if wild females preferred to mate with genetically engineered males, and if those matings produced offspring that did not survive well, wild populations could be wiped out—a result known as the "Trojan gene effect." In many species of fish, females prefer larger males as mates, setting the scene for an advantage for growth-enhanced fish. *See* Carol Yoon, *Altered Salmon Leading Way to Dinner Plates, but Rules Lag*, N. Y.

TIMES, May 1, 2000, page A1, col. 1; Aaron Zitner, *Gene–Altered Catfish Raise Environmental, Legal Issues*, LOS ANGELES TIMES, Jan. 2, 2001, at A1, col. 1.

In 2001, FDA's Center for Veterinary Medicine asked the National Research Council's Committee on Agricultural Biotechnology, Health, and the Environment to convene an ad hoc committee of experts to identify and evaluate the science-based risks associated with animal biotechnology, prior to any regulatory review by FDA of the food and environmental safety of products resulting from such technology. A prepublication internet version of the ensuing report by the special Committee on Defining Science–Based Concerns Associated with Products of Animal Biotechnology, *Animal Biotechnology: Science–Based Concerns*, was released in August, 2002. Among the various topics considered, the effects on the environment were believed to have the greatest potential for long-term impact. The taxonomic groups presenting the greatest environmental concerns were found to be aquatic organisms and insects because their mobility poses serious containment problems and because, unlike domestic farm birds and mammals, they can easily become feral and compete with indigenous populations. Of immediate concern, the report said, is the release of transgenic fish and shellfish. The executive summary concluded as follows:

> The current regulatory framework might not be adequate to address unique problems and characteristics associated with animal biotechnologies. The responsibilities of federal agencies for regulating animal biotechnology are unclear. How each agency will deal with scientific uncertainty remains to be seen. The committee notes a particular concern about the lack of any established regulatory framework for the oversight of scientific research and commercial application of biotechnology to arthropods. In addition to the potential lack of clarity about regulatory responsibilities and data collection requirements, the committee also notes a concern about the legal and technical capacity of the agencies to address potential hazards, particularly in the environmental area.

C. MANDATORY DISCLOSURE OF INFORMATION CONCERNING CHEMICAL HAZARDS AND RELATED LIABILITIES

Parts A and B of this chapter, as well as much of Chapters 6 and 7, have dealt with traditional "command and control" regulation. However, we also have explored, and will explore, alternate regulatory approaches. Chapter 2 contains important materials on economic incentive systems, such as effluent charges and marketable discharge permits, used increasingly as complements to traditional pollution regulation. Chapter 8 has examined the extensive civil liabilities—another type of economic incentive—created by RCRA, CERCLA, and the common law of "toxic torts." And the NEPA materials in Chapter 5 involve the most prominent example of mandating disclosure of information as a means of influencing both the behavior of the disclosers and the responses of the public and the political system.

This part of Chapter 9 discusses two other important examples of disclosure requirements. The first, arising from enactment in 1986 of the federal Emergency Planning and Community Right-to-Know Act (EP-CRA), involves disclosure of the existence of physical conditions which pose potential chemical hazards. The second, stemming from reporting requirements under the federal securities laws, involves disclosure of potential corporate liabilities, especially liabilities of the types discussed in Chapter 8.

BLOMQUIST, THE LOGIC AND LIMITS OF PUBLIC INFORMATION MANDATES UNDER FEDERAL HAZARDOUS WASTE LAW: A POLICY ANALYSIS[11]

14 Vt. L. Rev. 559, 571–78 (1990).

The Emergency Planning and Community Right-to-Know Act was passed by Congress as Title III to SARA.[12] The two general objectives of Title III are to encourage and support emergency planning efforts by local governments with regard to chemical hazards, and to provide citizens and local governments with information concerning potential community-based chemical hazards. Congress included three provisions within Title III to effectuate these objectives. The first concerns government emergency response planning. The second provision addresses emergency release notification by private industry. The third requires the compilation and reporting of information concerning chemical properties, manufacturing, usage, properties, and release.

The first provision of Title III requires the governors of the various states to have established a state emergency response commission by April 17, 1987. State commissions are also required to have established emergency planning districts no later than July 17, 1987, and to have appointed local emergency planning committees for each district by August 17, 1987.

Each local committee is required to have completed preparation of an emergency response plan, no later than October 17, 1988, containing the following information:

1) facilities within the district at which any one of numerous statutorily designated "extremely hazardous substances" at "threshold planning quantities" are present;

2) methods and procedures for reporting a release of an extremely hazardous substance;

3) names of community and facility coordinators;

4) public notification procedures;

---

11. Copyright 1990 by Vermont Law Review. Reprinted by permission.

12. Superfund Amendment and Reauthorization Act of 1986 (SARA), Pub.L. No. 99–499, §§ 301–330, 100 Stat. 1613, 1729 (1986) (codified at 42 U.S.C. §§ 11001–11050 (Supp. V 1987)).

5) methods for determining the occurrence of a release and the geographic area or population likely to be impacted;

6) the available emergency equipment and facilities within the community;

7) training programs; and

8) evacuation plans.

"Congress intended the local planning process to be a truly community-based activity, and not simply an exercise carried out by a few representatives of industry and the government bureaucracy in a back room at city hall."

The second component of Title III—the emergency release notification provisions—requires the owner or operator of a "facility" to provide notification of a hazardous substance release within any affected area to the community emergency coordinator of the local committee and to the affected state's commission.[13] The statute mandates that the notification contain specific information. This information must include data about the chemical released, the estimated quantity of the hazardous substance, "the time and duration of the release," "[a]ny known or anticipated acute or chronic health risks associated with the emergency and, where appropriate, advice regarding medical attention necessary for exposed individuals," precautions to be taken in response to the release, and pertinent details regarding the contact person who can provide further information.

The final provision is perhaps the most important public environmental information mandate under Title III. This provision contains reporting requirements for chemical usage, chemical properties, manufacturing, and environmental releases. "In order to inform citizens about chemicals located in their communities, Title III requires the owners and operators of certain facilities to submit three types of information concerning such chemicals to state and local authorities." This information entails: (a) material safety data sheets (MSDS) and hazardous chemical lists; (b) hazardous chemical inventory information; and (c) toxic chemical usage, manufacture, and release information.

All three components of Title III—government emergency response planning, emergency release notification procedures, and chemical inventory and usage reporting—are accessible to the public. Three specific public environmental information policies promote this accessibility: first, public participation requirements for local emergency response committees' formulation of emergency response plans; second, liberal public availability of local facility records (emergency response plans, follow-up emergency release notification, MSDS's, inventory forms, lists of hazardous chemicals, toxic chemical release forms); and, third, the EPA's development of a national computerized toxic chemical inventory database.[14]

---

13. SARA § 304(b)(1), 42 U.S.C. § 11004(b)(1) (Supp. V 1987); 40 C.F.R. § 355.40(b)(1) (1988).

14. SARA § 313(j), 42 U.S.C. § 11023(j) (Supp. V 1987). *See also* 53 Fed.Reg. 6567 (Mar. 9, 1988) (notice of public meeting to discuss options for making information available).

Moreover, citizen suit provisions create "the possibility of community self-help enforcement of SARA Title III by allowing suits against the facility owners or operators, state and local governments, or the EPA."[15] * * *

SARA's public information programs, particularly the Title III component, will promote six different policy goals. First, Title III will produce a baseline of

> data [that] can be used to characterize exposure levels, evaluate existing regulatory strategies and develop new ones, focus on specific locations of concern, identify important chemical releases and the types of operations they come from, compare permitted releases to reported releases, and aid in the development of waste minimization strategies.

Second, Title III holds promise for acting as "a valuable mechanism for effective emergency management, protecting environmental concerns, offering local citizens the opportunity to have a significant impact on the safety of their community, and for providing a structured forum in which industry, government, and citizens can work collectively on these issues."

Third, Title III should be applauded as "Congress' most significant experiment to involve the private sector and decentralize environmental problem solving. . . . [C]itizens [must] be informed about hazardous materials being stored, handled, or manufactured in their community, and local communities [must] have a coordinated emergency response plan to respond to chemical emergencies."

Fourth, while the information gathered in the Title III process should be viewed as preliminary, and subject to refinement, this public environmental information law will "provide Americans with at least two powerful pictures of the industries that put them at risk. Total annual discharges from the [*Toxic Release Inventory*, or "TRI"] data will be one picture. Another is the 'plume maps' or 'footprints' of potential chemical gas releases as they travel downwind or downstream." In a related way, the Toxic Release Inventory data generated by the imprimatur of section 313 will promote the better understanding of two major risk management problems: (a) identifying and specifying the "[m]any U.S. chemical plants [that] do not [currently] use the Best Achievable Control Technology (BACT) to minimize chemical discharges"; and (b) developing some rudimentary information "regarding chemical discharges once they have left the plant."

Fifth, the emergence of information regarding toxic chemical releases and mass balance inventories will, no doubt, serve as "strong public educational and motivational tools toward the improvement of chemical safety." Finally, Title III will facilitate the development of comparative emissions statistics of hazardous substances that will spur some industrial firms to take a leadership role by "openly communicating about risks" with the public in meetings that may reflect a "new era, and a new

---

15. Title III follows the "citizen as prosecutor" model by permitting citizen suits for civil penalties as well as injunctive relief. SARA § 326(c), 42 U.S.C. § 11046(c) (Supp. V 1987).

partnership." This industrial leadership has the potential of providing exemplary corporate models that will inspire other companies to respond to the competitive need to match the leaders' efforts.

NOTES

1. EPA regulations concerning annual Toxic Release Inventory (TRI) reports by various industries are found at 40 C.F.R. Part 372. There are now more than 650 toxic chemicals and toxic chemical categories on the list of chemicals that must be reported to EPA and the states under the EPCRA/TRI Program. A facility must report to TRI if it meets the following three criteria:

  a. Conducts manufacturing operations within Standard Industrial Classification (SIC) codes 20 through 39; or, beginning in 1998, is in one of the following industry categories: metal mining, coal mining, electric utilities that burn coal or oil, chemical wholesale distributors, petroleum terminals and bulk storage facilities, RCRA hazardous waste TSD facilities, solvent recovery services, and federal facilities regardless of SIC codes.

  b. Has ten or more full-time employee equivalents.

  c. For all but certain persistent bioaccumulative toxic (PBT) chemicals, manufactures or processes more than 25,000 pounds or otherwise uses more than 10,000 pounds of any listed chemical during the calendar year. The reporting threshold for PBT chemicals is 100 pounds manufactured, processed, or used, except that for "highly persistent and highly bioaccumulative" chemicals it is 10 pounds.

2. The data disclosed by industries' annual TRI reports, and the reductions in releases seemingly attributable to EPCRA's disclosure requirements, have been remarkable. In 1988, the first reporting year, 18,500 companies disclosed that they had released 10.4 billion pounds of toxic chemicals in 1987: 3.9 billion into landfills, 3.3 billion to treatment and disposal facilities, 2.7 billion into the air, and 550 million into surface waters. These figures were far beyond EPA's expectations. *See* Weisskopf, *EPA Finds Pollution 'Unacceptably High'*, WASHINGTON POST, April 13, 1989, at A33. EPA subsequently revised the total of 10.4 billion pounds downward to 7 billion pounds because some mining companies which had reported were not required (prior to 1998) to do so. * * *

For 2007, 22,000 facilities reported 4.1 billion pounds of on-site and off-site disposal or other releases of almost 650 toxic chemicals. Persistent bioaccumulative toxic (PBT) chemicals accounted for about ten percent of that total, and lead represented more than 90 percent of all PBT chemicals released. Total disposal of all chemicals has been declining steadily, from the initial 10.4 billion pounds in 1987 to 7.3 billion pounds in 1998 to the 4.1 billion pounds in 2007. The metal mining and primary metals sectors accounted for the largest amount of total disposal or other releases in 2007. Of course not all chemicals released into the environment are reported in the TRI; emissions from individuals, principally through driving, make up a large percentage of overall chemical releases. *See* Michael P. Vandenbergh, From

Smokestack to SUV: The Individual as Regulated Entity in the New Era of Environmental Law, 57 VAND. L. REV. 515, 518 (2004)

The most complete and current TRI data and data release reports may be accessed through EPA's TRI homepage http://www.epa.gov/TRI/tridata/tri07/ pdr/key_findings_v12a.pdf, which includes the 2007 Toxics Release Inventory (TRI) Public Data Release Report, released by EPA in January, 2008.

For further discussion of EPCRA, see Abell, Note, *Emergency Planning and Community Right to Know: The Toxics Release Inventory*, 47 SMU L. REV. 581 (1994); Abrams and Ward, *Prospects for Safer Communities: Emergency Response, Community Right to Know, and Prevention of Chemical Accidents*, 14 HARV. ENVTL. L. REV. 135 (1990). For overviews not only of EPCRA but of other federal statutes requiring reports of releases of pollutants or contaminants, see Cleary, Gottlieb, Steen & Hamilton, *Release Reporting Requirements Under CERCLA and EPCRA*, and *Release Reporting Requirements Under TSCA, FIFRA, OSHA, RCRA, CWA, and CAA*, 27 ENV'T REP. 1171 and 1250 (1996); Arnold Reitze and Steven Schell, *Reporting Requirements for Nonroutine Hazardous Pollutant Releases Under Federal Environmental Laws*, 5 ENVTL. LAW. 1 (1998).

3. In *Atlantic States Legal Foundation v. Whiting Roll–Up Door Mfg. Corp.,* 1994 WL 236473 (W.D.N.Y.1994), plaintiffs brought a citizen's enforcement action under section 326 of EPCRA, alleging that defendant had failed to file timely hazardous chemical information with state and federal authorities under sections 311–313. Among other forms of relief, plaintiffs sought civil penalties, a permanent injunction prohibiting further EPCRA violations, and attorneys' fees and costs. Under a settlement agreement, plaintiffs were "prevailing parties" within the meaning of section 326(f), and the court therefore awarded them more than $32,000 in attorneys' fees and costs.

However, in *Steel Co. v. Citizens for a Better Environment, supra,* page 394, the Supreme Court held that an environmental group *lacked standing* to bring a citizen suit under EPCRA for "purely past violations." In 1995, plaintiff sent a notice to defendant, to the EPA, and to Illinois authorities, alleging (accurately) that defendant had failed since 1988 (the first year of EPCRA's filing deadlines) to complete and to submit the requisite hazardous-chemical inventory and toxic-chemical release forms. Upon receiving the notice, defendant filed all of the overdue forms with the relevant agencies. EPA chose not to bring suit, e.g., to recover civil penalties; and when the 60–day, post-notice waiting period expired, plaintiff filed suit in the federal district court. The complaint asked for a declaratory judgment that defendant had violated EPCRA, an order requiring defendant to pay civil penalties of $25,000 per day for each EPCRA violation, and an award of plaintiff's attorney and expert witness fees. The Supreme Court held that the constitutional requirement of "redressability—a likelihood that the requested relief will redress the alleged injury"—was not satisfied because none of the items of relief sought "would serve to reimburse [plaintiff] for losses caused by the late reporting, or to eliminate any effects of that late reporting upon [plaintiff]." The penalties would be payable to the government, not to plaintiff, and "plaintiff cannot achieve standing to litigate a substantive issue by bringing suit for the cost of bringing suit."

Subsequently, in the *Laidlaw* decision, page 394, *supra*, the Court allowed a citizen suit for civil penalties where defendant's violations of the Clean Water Act continued until after the filing of plaintiff's complaint but ended prior to judgment by the district court.

MARK COHEN, INFORMATION AS A POLICY INSTRUMENT IN PROTECTING THE ENVIRONMENT: WHAT HAVE WE LEARNED?[16]

31 ENVTL. L. REP. 10425, 10425–27 (2001).

Since the introduction of the toxic release inventory (TRI) in 1988, there has been considerable interest in environmental information disclosure as a possible complement or substitute for traditional forms of regulation. Among the most important reasons for this growing interest are the following: (1) the TRI program led to a significant voluntary decrease in the total amount of TRI chemicals released in the United States, beyond any mandated levels; (2) information disclosure programs serve another very important social function—they satisfy the belief that the public has a "right to know" that they might be affected by third-party pollution; (3) new information technologies (both hardware and software) that facilitate the dissemination of environmental information in a meaningful way; (4) the fact that these programs are generally thought to cost the government far less than drafting and implementing industry-wide regulations; and (5) these approaches are often politically more feasible to adopt since they are generally framed as "right to know" laws and thus not easily characterized as coercive new regulations. * * *

Information Disclosure Programs Affect Firm Behavior

Empirically, it has been shown that mandatory disclosure programs such as TRI can have a significant effect on the environmental performance of firms. What is not fully understood, however, is the mechanism by which these programs induce firms to voluntarily reduce emissions beyond any legal requirement. For example, when the first such disclosure of TRI was made, there was a significant reduction in the market value for some publicly traded firms while other firms saw an increase in market value. Subsequently, firms dramatically reduced their emissions. However, the emissions reductions were not uniformly distributed across firms. One study found that firms with the largest negative stock price returns upon the initial announcement of TRI data were the firms that reduced emissions the most.

Thus, the important question remains as to why information disclosure may affect both stock prices of publicly traded companies and, ultimately, emissions of all firms subject to disclosure. Information about a firm's environmental performance—whether good or bad—may be of interest to shareholders or lenders for a variety of reasons. To the extent that the information concerns monetary sanctions or an announcement of

---

16.   Copyright © 2001 by the Environmental Law Institute. Reprinted with permission.

an agreement to spend money on new pollution control equipment, we might expect these monetary outlays to reduce the expected value of the firm, thus reducing the share price and/or bond rating of the firm. It may also give lenders pause about risking more capital on that particular firm. Other costs of "bad information" might include future debarment from government contracts, targeted enforcement by environmental agencies, and lost sales to "green consumers." Some socially conscious investors might even shun the firm's stock, thereby depressing its value. Finally, it is possible that investors will update their assessment of the quality of management in the firm and view this information as a signal that the firm is not as well managed as they thought.

Aside from the stock market, there are other mechanisms through which information disclosure programs might ultimately result in improved environmental performance. In particular, there is empirical evidence that informal community pressure and social norms may play an important role in emissions and/or compliance. Not surprisingly, the ability of communities to play this role is an increasing function of income and education level as well as the degree of environmental activism by the local residents. * * *

Information Disclosure Programs Empower Local Communities and Other Stakeholders

The increasing availability of environmental information has permitted stakeholder involvement to take on new, expanded roles. At the facility level, information can help empower a local community to take actions such as opposing a new permit or zoning application or beginning a meaningful dialogue on issues of concern with nearby industrial facilities. A recent study comparing TRI emissions across states found that states with higher membership levels of environmental organizations had larger TRI emission reductions, consistent with the theory that environmental group pressure can reduce emissions. * * *

Information Disclosure Programs Can Increase Cooperation Between EPA and Regulated Industries

Many of these environmental information disclosure programs involve new channels of communication and cooperation between industry and the U.S. Environmental Protection Agency that can lead to both improved environmental performance and less costly methods of achieving these results. Instead of focusing the dialogue on technology standards, the health risks of varying regulatory standards, and other contentious issues, EPA and the regulated industry often find themselves in a new role of having common interests—how to find cost-effective methods of reducing emissions. The classic example of this was EPA's 33/50 Program, in which EPA invited firms to participate in a voluntary effort to reduce toxic emissions. Another example is EPA Region I's Environmental Leadership Program (known as StarTrack), which (among other things) rewards firms that regularly audit and disclose their environmental performance results with preferential treatment on compliance issues.

Benchmarking and Incentives to Go Beyond Compliance

The wide availability of environmental information due to current programs provides significant benchmarking opportunities, as firms are able to identify industry leaders in environmental performance. Numerous corporate environmental managers have told me that they closely watch the disclosures of their competitors to determine who the leaders and laggards are and how their company ranks. This information is useful in setting priorities and looking for areas where a company might be able to improve its environmental performance.

Coupled with the apparent desire of firms to be looked upon as environmental leaders (or at least not to be looked upon as among the worst environmental performers), information disclosure can take on many of the positive attributes of market-based regulatory mechanisms such as emission fees or marketable permits. Firms now have an incentive to go beyond compliance as long as the cost of doing so is less than the perceived benefit to the firm. Moreover, society is likely to benefit as these emission reductions are concentrated in companies that can do so at least cost.

In one very important way, information disclosure programs are more akin to emissions fees than to marketable permits. In a marketable permit regime, the government can set the level of emissions and knows in advance that it will be achieved (subject to adequate compliance). However, emissions fees and information disclosure programs have no such guarantee. Although they have the added feature of encouraging beyond compliance behavior, they might not achieve any reduction at all. This has important implications when thinking about information disclosure as a *substitute* for regulation (as opposed to a complementary program)....
* * *

Disclosure Programs Must Take Into Account
Needs and Knowledge of Stakeholders

Current environmental information disclosure programs are generally designed to provide information to environmentally knowledgeable people rather than to the average citizen attempting to learn about the environment. Emissions information is generally disclosed without related hazard or risk content to place the information in a more meaningful context. This has the potential of misdirecting the attention of stakeholders toward lesser hazards or by focusing their attention on the wrong facilities. It also has the potential for confusing stakeholders about the extent to which they would support or oppose the existence of a polluting facility in their neighborhoods.

Although there is no easy solution to the potential misinformation on the part of the public, two programs could help alleviate this problem: (1)

research on the information needs of stakeholders, and (2) expanded investment in educating the public (including children) about the meaning of the information being disseminated.

Although admittedly more knowledgeable than the average public, securities analysts and others in the financial markets currently have little use for environmental information disclosure programs. This is partly due to the fact that current programs do not provide information in a format that financial markets can use to accurately and effectively evaluate the environmental performance of firms. Once again, working with the financial community to assess their needs would potentially increase the value of these programs. One possibility is to ultimately standardize disclosure along the lines of financial statements monitored by the U.S. Securities and Exchange Commission.

MICHELLE CHAN–FISHEL, AFTER ENRON: HOW ACCOUNTING AND SEC REFORM CAN PROMOTE CORPORATE ACCOUNTABILITY WHILE RESTORING PUBLIC CONFIDENCE[17]

32 ENVTL. L. REP. 10965, 10968–73 (2002).

The SEC and Corporate Disclosure

Although the TRI is the best-known disclosure law in the environmental community, many publicly traded companies perceive the disclosure duties imposed by the SEC as their most rigorous and important reporting obligation. The SEC was created with the authority to require corporations to disclose any information that would benefit the interests of investors and/or the general public. * * *

Since 1998, the Corporate Sunshine Working Group (CSWG), an alliance of investors and public interest organizations, has worked to reform a key gatekeeper, the SEC, in an effort to broaden and deepen corporate nonfinancial disclosure rules to benefit investors, as well as the larger public interest. Members of this alliance include investors, asset managers, and public interest organizations who have submitted public comments to the SEC, produced case studies illustrating company noncompliance with existing SEC disclosure requirements, and advocated for broader, deeper, and more specific disclosure on nonfinancial matters, such as environmental performance, labor relations, and good governance. * * *

Current SEC Environmental Disclosure Regulations

Current SEC disclosure rules require publicly traded companies to disclose actual or potential environmental liabilities under Regulation S–K,[18] Items 101,[19] 103,[20] and 303.[21]

---

17. Copyright © 2002 by the Environmental Law Institute. Reprinted with permission.

18. 17 C.F.R. pt. 229.

19. Id. § 229.101.

20. Id. § 229.103.

21. Id. § 229.303.

Item 101, governing the company's general description of business operations, requires disclosure of the material effects that complying with federal, state, and local environmental provisions may have upon the capital expenditures, earnings and competitive position of the registrant and its subsidiaries. The company is required to disclose any "material estimated capital expenditures for environmental control facilities for the remainder of its current fiscal year and its succeeding fiscal year and for such further periods as the registrant may deem material."

Item 103, governing the disclosure of legal proceedings, requires a company to disclose material environmentally related administrative or judicial proceedings. The SEC provides two specific materiality thresholds which require disclosure if the proceeding involves a claim, sanction or expenditure that exceeds 10% of current assets, or if the proceeding involves a governmental authority seeking potential sanctions over $100,000.

Item 303, governing disclosure in the Management Discussion and Analysis section of a financial report, requires a registrant to disclose "where a trend, demand, commitment, event or uncertainty is both presently known to management and reasonably likely to have material effects on the registrant's financial condition or results of operation." Such trends can include environmental issues such as impending environmental regulation.

Companies' environmental disclosures are also subject to the anti-fraud provisions of SEC Rule 10b–5,[22] which prohibits a company from making false or misleading statements in SEC filings. The rule also prohibits a company from underreporting or omitting information that a reasonable investor would likely consider material given the total amount of information available to the investor.

The body of Generally Accepted Accounting Principles (GAAP) governing environmental and other types of accounting and disclosure are established through the SEC, the American Institute for Certified Public Accountants (AICPA), and the Financial Accounting Standards Board (FASB). GAAP is codified by the SEC through SEC Staff Accounting Bulletins (SAB), which reiterate and often provide interpretive guidance on SEC, AICPA, and FASB reporting and disclosure guidelines. * * *

Materiality

Disclosure of nonfinancial information, whether it be related to environmental liabilities, legal proceedings, or future trends, is triggered by the "materiality," or significance, of the data. Materiality has been defined with various levels of specificity by companies, private auditors, the SEC, and the accounting profession through the establishment of GAAP and through case law.

---

22. 52 Id. § 240.10b–5.

Many registrants and auditors use a general and quantitative definition of materiality that defines material disclosures as those data with financial impact exceeding 5%–10% of net income. Although the 5% threshold is widely used, the SEC points out that that materiality definition has no basis in accounting literature or law.[23]

On the contrary, the SEC's most recent (1999) pronouncement on materiality, SAB 99 clarifies that qualitative information can be material, and that "exclusive reliance on certain quantitative benchmarks to assess materiality in preparing financial statements and performing audits of those financial statements is inappropriate; misstatements are not immaterial simply because they fall beneath a numerical threshold." The bulletin provides several cases in which disclosures that fall beneath the 5% threshold can in fact be material, such as when the disclosure refers to a company's regulatory compliance, or if it relates to an important portion of the registrant's business operations.

The FASB provided another definition of materiality in its Statement of Financial Accounting Concepts No. 2 (FAS 2), which takes a relatively expansive view. FAS 2 states that a disclosure should be made if its omission or correction would probably change or influence "the judgment of a reasonable person relying upon the report."

Case law is consistent with FASB's expansive definition of materiality. In 1976, the Supreme Court, in *TSC Industries, Inc. v. Northway, Inc.*[24] mirrored FAS 2's definition by concluding that a disclosure is material if there is "a substantial likelihood that the disclosure of the omitted fact would have been viewed by the reasonable investor as having significantly altered the total mix' of information available." In addition, the Court maintained that a disclosure it material if "there is a substantial likelihood that a reasonable shareholder would consider it important in deciding how to vote." * * *

A Pattern of Inadequate Nonfinancial Disclosure

Since 1997, individual members of the CSWG have monitored companies' disclosure of nonfinancial data, and notified the SEC of alleged misstatements or omissions of material environmental and social information. The complaints have been varied, with allegations of material misstatements of environmental, labor, and legal issues in several types of public filings, including annual reports, quarterly statements and registration documents. The group maintains that noncompliance with SEC environmental and social reporting requirements is a systemic problem, and that better enforcement is needed. * * *

Investor Lawsuits Alleging Inadequate Disclosure of Labor and Environmental Matters

In addition to the complaints filed with the SEC, shareholders have also recently filed lawsuits against companies for providing allegedly false

---

23. SEC, SAB–99–Materiality (Aug. 12, 1999).

24. 426 U.S. 438 (1976).

or misleading information to investors, again illustrating a systemic problem of underreporting of environmental and social matters. * * *

In 1999, the shareholders of U.S. Liquids, Inc. filed a class action suit against the company for allegedly misleading shareholders about material environmental issues while raising capital through a public offering. In 1998, the company had claimed that its liquid waste management services would generate 20% earnings per share growth in 1999. This claim allowed U.S. Liquids to raise $30 million through share offerings in 1998 and 1999, and inflated its stock to a Class Period high in early 1999. Several months later, the public learned that EPA and the Federal Bureau of Investigation were investigating illegal dumping activities at one of the company's most profitable sites. Share price dropped by 50%, and trading of the stock was halted after the company announced that earnings would be substantially lower than originally projected. The plaintiffs allege that the company deliberately misled the investing public by representing that it was in environmental compliance when the company either knew or was reckless in not knowing that illegal disposal of PCBs into the Detroit sewer system had occurred. The company has, in turn, sued its contractor. The lawsuit is still ongoing.

The SEC Responds to the Systemic Problem of Inadequate Disclosure

In 2001, EPA stepped up its efforts to educate companies of their SEC obligations regarding disclosure of environmental liabilities and enforcement actions. In 2001, the Agency publicly released a 1997 study which found that 74% of companies failed to report cases in which a national, state, or municipal agency is contemplating or has initiated an environmentally related legal proceeding that could result in monetary sanctions of over $100,000 (for which disclosure is required under Regulation S–K, Item 103). In fall 2001, the Agency issued an Enforcement Alert newsletter that notified companies of their SEC-mandated environmental disclosure duties. EPA is also preparing a guide to assist investors and the public on how to access environmental information on companies using EPA databases, some of which provide information on a facility rather than corporate basis.

INDEX

References are to Pages